HANDBOOK OF

ENVIRONMENTAL

PSYCHOLOGY

HANDBOOK OF ENVIRONMENTAL PSYCHOLOGY

Edited by

ROBERT B. BECHTEL and ARZA CHURCHMAN

John Wiley & Sons, Inc.

Library of Congress Cataloging-in-Publication Data:

Bechtel, Robert B.
  Handbook of environmental psychology / Robert Bechtel, Arza Churchman.
    p. cm.
  Includes bibliographical references and index.
    ISBN 0-471-40594-9 (hardcover : alk. paper)
    1. Environmental psychology. I. Ts'erts'man, Arzah. II. Title.
  BF353 .B425 2001
  155.9—dc21

                                                      2001026449

Printed in the United States of America.

10 9 8 7 6 5 4 3 2 1

Contributors

Irwin Altman, PhD
Department of Psychology
University of Utah
Salt Lake City, Utah

Kathryn H. Anthony, PhD
Department of Landscape Architecture and
    Women's Studies Program
University of Illinois at Urbana-Champaign
Champaign, Illinois

Robert B. Bechtel
Department of Psychology
University of Arizona
Tucson, Arizona

Anders Biel, PhD
Department of Psychology
Göteborg University
Göteborg, Sweden

Stephen C. Bitgood, PhD
Psychology Institute
Jacksonville State University
Jacksonville, Alabama

Marino Bonaiuto
Department of Developmental and Social
    Psychology
University of Rome 'La Sapienza'
Rome, Italy

Mirilia Bonnes
Department of Developmental and Social
    Psychology
University of Rome 'La Sapienza'
Rome, Italy

Arline L. Bronzaft, PhD
Lehman College, City University of New York
Bronx, New York

Barbara B. Brown, PhD
Department of Psychology
University of Utah
Salt Lake City, Utah

Margaret P. Calkins, PhD
Innovative Designs in Environments for
    an Aging Society
Kirtland, Ohio

Janet R. Carpman, PhD
Carpman Grant Associates
Wayfinding Consultants
Ann Arbor, Michigan

Arza Churchman, PhD
Faculty of Architecture and Town Planning
Technion-Israel Institute of Technology
Haifa, Israel

Ellen G. Cohn, PhD
Department of Criminal Justice
Florida International University
Miami, Florida

Victor Corral-Verdugo, PhD
Department of Psychology
University of Sonora
Hermosillo, Sonora, Mexico

Mihaly Csikszentmihalyi, PhD
Department of Psychology
Claremont Graduate University
Claremont, California

Kristen Day, PhD
Department of Urban and Regional Planning
University of California, Irvine
Irvine, California

Jack Demick, PhD
Center for Adoption Research
University of Massachusetts Medical School
Worcester, Massachusetts

Tamra Pearson d'Estrée, PhD
Institute for Conflict Analysis and Resolution
George Mason University
Fairfax, Virginia

E. Franklin Dukes, PhD
Institute for Environmental Negotiation
University of Virginia
Charlottesville, Virginia

Riley E. Dunlap
Department of Sociology and
Department of Rural Sociology
Washington State University
Pullman, Washington

Angela Ebreo, PhD
Center for Race and Public Policy
University of Illinois at Chicago
Chicago, Illinois

Michael R. Edelstein, PhD
School of Social Science and Human Services
Ramapo College of New Jersey
Mahwah, New Jersey

Karen A. Franck, PhD
School of Architecture and Department of Social
    Science and Humanities
New Jersey Institute of Technology
Newark, New Jersey

Tommy Gärling, PhD
Department of Psychology
Göteborg University
Göteborg, Sweden

E. Scott Geller, PhD
Department of Psychology
Virginia Polytechnic Institute and State University
Blacksburg, Virginia

Robert Gifford
Department of Psychology
University of Victoria
Victoria, BC, Canada

Reginald G. Golledge, BA (Hons), MA, PhD, LLD
University of California, Santa Barbara
Santa Barbara, California

Myron A. Grant, MLA
Carpman Grant Associates
Wayfinding Consultants
Ann Arbor, Michigan

Carl F. Graumann
Psychologisches Institut
der Universität Heidelberg
Heidelberg, Germany

Mathias Gustafsson, PhD
Department of Psychology
Göteborg University
Göteborg, Sweden

Joel M. Hektner, PhD
Department of Child Development and
    Family Science
North Dakota State University
Fargo, North Dakota

Robert Hershberger, PhD, FAIA
Tucson, Arizona

Liisa Horelli, PhD
Helsinki University of Technology
Helsinki, Finland

Kalevi Korpela, PhD
Department of Psychology
University of Tampere
Finland

Frances E. Kuo
Human-Environment Research Laboratory
University of Illinois, Urbana-Champaign
Champaign, Illinois

Roderick J. Lawrence, B.Arch (hons), MA, DSc
Center for Human Ecology and
    Environmental Sciences
University of Geneva
Geneva, Switzerland

Edward B. Liebow, PhD
Environmental Health and Social Policy Center
Seattle, Washington

Janetta Mitchell McCoy, BLS, MS, PhD
College of Architecture and Environmental Design
Arizona State University
Tempe, Arizona

Dennis S. Mileti, PhD, MA, BA
Department of Sociology and Natural Hazards
  Research and Applications Information Center
University of Colorado
Boulder, Colorado

Maria Montero, PhD
Department of Psychology
Autonomous University of Mexico
Mexico City, DF, Mexico

Jessica Navarrete-Romero
Institute for Conflict Analysis and Resolution
George Mason University
Fairfax, Virginia

Russ Parsons
Department of Landscape Architecture
University of Illinois at Urbana-Champaign
Champaign, Illinois

Lori A. Peek, MEd
Department of Sociology and Natural Hazards
  Research and Applications Information Center
University of Colorado
Boulder, Colorado

John Peponis
Georgia Institute of Technology
Atlanta, Georgia

Enric Pol, PhD
Departament de Psicologia Social
Formació Continuada Les Heures
Barcelona, Spain

Leanne G. Rivlin, PhD
Graduate School–CUNY
New York, New York

James Rotton, PhD
Department of Psychology
Florida International University
Miami, Florida

Euclides Sánchez, PhD
Institute of Psychology
Central University of Venezuela
Czazcas, Venezuela

Robert Sommer, PhD
University of California
Davis, California

Arthur E. Stamps III, PhD
Institute of Environmental Quality
San Francisco, California

Daniel Stokols, PhD
Department of Urban and Regional Planning
School of Social Ecology
University of California, Irvine
Irvine, California

Louis G. Tassinary
Department of Architecture
Texas A&M University
College Station, Texas

Ralph B. Taylor
Department of Criminal Justice and Environmental
  Studies Program
Temple University
Philadelphia, Pennsylvania

Joanne Vining, PhD
Department of Natural Resources and
  Environmental Sciences
University of Illinois at Urbana-Champaign
Urbana, Illinois

Seymour Wapner, PhD
HeinzWerner Institute for Developmental Analysis
Clark University
Worcester, Massachusetts

Nicholas J. Watkins, BA
School of Architecture
University of Illinois at Urbana-Champaign
Champaign, Illinois

Carol M. Werner, PhD
Department of Psychology
University of Utah
Salt Lake City, Utah

Allan W. Wicker, PhD
Claremont Graduate University
Claremont, California

Esther Wesenfeld, PhD
Institute of Psychology
Central University of Venezuela

Jean Wineman
The University of Michigan
Ann Arbor, Michigan

Craig Zimring
College of Architecture
Georgia Institute of Technology
Atlanta, Georgia

Preface

IN HIS BOOK, *The Lexus and The Olive Tree,* Thomas Friedman (1999) claims that the world we live in is only 10 years old, referring to the globalization that is ostensibly taking over our cultures. Globalization is assisted by the Internet, which provides instant access to persons having the necessary equipment no matter where they are located. Friedman argues that this has made us more of a global village than ever before. It is a unique time in history. Although globalization is seen by some as threatening local cultures and local identities, local and microlevel processes have distinct strengths.

This handbook serves as an example of how global and local approaches can coexist and contribute to each other. We (the environmental psychologists) are cognizant of the nested nature of contexts: The immediate environment is imbedded in an ever-widening one, with each level interdependent. The authors in this handbook come from different countries and different disciplines, representing different theoretical and methodological approaches. And yet, there are many common aspects shared by all. All of the contributing authors reject physical determinism. All recognize that our approach must be contextual in nature and that one cannot talk about "universal" phenomena. Thus, we learn from each other without denying the specific nature of any given situation or space.

The structure of the handbook represents our pluralistic approach to the field—not one but many voices. Our approach in this handbook is to see Environmental Psychology, not merely as a specialized area of psychology, but as an interdisciplinary effort with links to other disciplines, some stronger and some weaker, as the chapters illustrate.

The issue that has dogged Environmental Psychology from its beginning is the appropriate balance between theoretical and applied work. This handbook presents both but we have not tried to represent each view equally on this or any other issue. However, because the purpose of this handbook is to show how things are being done at the forefront, we have selected authors and topics that best represent the field as it exists at the time of this printing. We have tried to be representative of the literature as it exists, rather than take a stance on how it should be. We have also left it up to each author to reflect on the future. Ten years from now, we will undoubtedly have another handbook that will carry the field into its next phase.

We hope you, the reader, will share some of the excitement we experienced in putting this handbook together. Representing the international nature of the field, the authors come from ten countries and four continents. Thirty-nine percent of the chapters have multiple authors and thirty-eight percent of the authors are women.

We started from the premise that Environmental Psychology *does* make a difference. The chapters illustrate what a difference has been made in the world, not just in the field of psychology. Accordingly, this handbook has been divided into five sections: Section I deals with sharpening theories, Section II with links to other disciplines, Section III with methods, Section IV with applications, and Section V with the future.

However, categorizing the chapters in other ways enables the reader to find other connections. Those interested in the history of the field will find various aspects in Chapters 3, 6, 7, 10, 14, 19, 20, 22, 23, 25, 29, 32, 33, 36, 38, 39 across all parts. Theoretical expositions appear in all of the parts, not just the one devoted to theory (see Chapters 8–11, 13, 16, 18, 23, 24, 26, 27, 31, 33–40). Methodological issues and descriptions also appear in many chapters (Chapters 2, 4–8, 26, 27, 30, 31, 35–40). While ideas for research will be stimulated by all of the chapters, some directly propose research directions (see Chapters 7, 15, 16, 22, 25, 27, 28, 39, 40). If we look at the environmental scales addressed in the various chapters, we find that as we increase in scale, the number of chapters decreases from 16 chapters specifically addressing building scale to 12 addressing neighborhood scale, 7 addressing city scale, and 8 relating to country or more global scale issues. In terms of an individual versus group dichotomy, the focus within psychology on the individual is evident from the fact that 27 chapters focus on the individual while 16 address group or societal issues with many chapters discussing both. Another type of dichotomy finds 24 chapters focusing on processes within the individual, group, system, or research process. Only 11 chapters discuss the "product"—the environment itself.

The sea change that has occurred in the past decade or so is indicated by the number of chapters relating to the ecological aspects of the environment. Some of these chapters were defined initially as relating to these issues, but not all of them (Chapters 3–5, 9, 10, 12, 13, 17, 21, 26, 31–38).

To many people, the term *environment* relates only to ecological aspects. We use the term in a much broader and more inclusive sense. When we interact with others, each one of us should strive to make this difference clear.

Another area of increasing interest is citizen-public-resident participation. While two chapters are directly devoted to this topic (Chapters 33 and 37) it appears in five others (Chapters 5, 12, 23, 29, 36).

This new *Handbook of Environmental Psychology* takes us further into the proliferating directions of environmental psychology, striving to solve the problem of our survival on this planet. No longer is environmental psychology an academic exercise for publication in esoteric academic journals; it is aimed directly at the attitudes, beliefs, and behaviors that are destroying our environment and putting our lives in jeopardy.

Contents

SECTION I. SHARPENING THEORIES

CHAPTER 1   The Increasing *Contexts* of *Context* in the Study of Environment Behavior Relations   3
             Seymour Wapner and Jack Demick

CHAPTER 2   The Ethical Imperative   15
             Leanne G. Rivlin

CHAPTER 3   Environmental Psychology: From Spatial-Physical Environment to
             Sustainable Development   28
             Mirilia Bonnes and Marino Bonaiuto

CHAPTER 4   Environmental Management: A Perspective from Environmental Psychology   55
             Enric Pol

CHAPTER 5   The New Environmental Psychology: The Human Interdependence Paradigm   85
             Tommy Gärling, Anders Biel, and Mathias Gustafsson

CHAPTER 6   The Phenomenological Approach to People-Environment Studies   95
             Carl F. Graumann

CHAPTER 7   Ecological Psychology: Historical Contexts, Current Conception,
             Prospective Directions   114
             Allan W. Wicker

SECTION II. SHARPENING LINKS TO OTHER DISCIPLINES

CHAPTER 8   Exploring Pathology: Relationships between Clinical and
             Environmental Psychology   129
             Kathryn H. Anthony and Nicholas J. Watkins

CHAPTER 9   Environmental Anthropology   147
             Edward B. Liebow

CHAPTER 10   Environmental Sociology   160
             Riley E. Dunlap

CHAPTER 11   Environmental Psychophysiology   172
             Russ Parsons and Louis G. Tassinary

CHAPTER 12   Environmental Psychology and Urban Planning: Where Can the Twain Meet?   191
             Arza Churchman

SECTION III. SHARPENING METHODS

CHAPTER 13   Transactionally Oriented Research: Examples and Strategies   203
             Carol M. Werner, Barbara B. Brown, and Irwin Altman

CHAPTER 14   Meta-Analysis   222
Arthur E. Stamps III

CHAPTER 15   The Experience Sampling Method: Measuring the Context and Content of Lives   233
Joel M. Hektner and Mihaly Csikszentmihalyi

CHAPTER 16   The Open Door of GIS   244
Reginald G. Golledge

CHAPTER 17   Structural Equation Modeling   256
Victor Corral-Verdugo

CHAPTER 18   Spatial Structure of Environment and Behavior   271
John Peponis and Jean Wineman

CHAPTER 19   Behavioral-Based Architectural Programming   292
Robert Hershberger

CHAPTER 20   Postoccupancy Evaluation: Issues and Implementation   306
Craig Zimring

SECTION IV. SHARPENING APPLICATION

CHAPTER 21   Making a Difference: Some Ways Environmental Psychology Has Improved the World   323
Robert Gifford

CHAPTER 22   Bridging the Gap: How Scientists Can Make a Difference   335
Frances E. Kuo

CHAPTER 23   Women and Environment   347
Karen A. Franck

CHAPTER 24   Children's Environment   363
Kalevi Korpela

CHAPTER 25   Design and Dementia   374
Kristen Day and Margaret P. Calkins

CHAPTER 26   Healthy Residential Environments   394
Roderick J. Lawrence

CHAPTER 27   Crime Prevention through Environmental Design (CPTED): Yes, No, Maybe, Unknowable, and All of the Above   413
Ralph B. Taylor

CHAPTER 28   Wayfinding: A Broad View   427
Janet R. Carpman and Myron A. Grant

CHAPTER 29   Work Environments   443
Janetta Mitchell McCoy

CHAPTER 30   Environmental Psychology in Museums, Zoos, and Other Exhibition Centers   461
Stephen C. Bitgood

CHAPTER 31   Climate, Weather, and Crime   481
James Rotton and Ellen G. Cohn

CHAPTER 32   Noise Pollution: A Hazard to Physical and Mental Well-Being   499
Arline L. Bronzaft

CHAPTER 33   The History and Future of Disaster Research   511
             Lori A. Peek and Dennis S. Mileti

CHAPTER 34   The Challenge of Increasing Proenvironment Behavior   525
             E. Scott Geller

CHAPTER 35   Emerging Theoretical and Methodological Perspectives on Conservation Behavior   541
             Joanne Vining and Angela Ebreo

CHAPTER 36   Contamination: The Invisible Built Environment   559
             Michael R. Edelstein

CHAPTER 37   Environmental Conflict and Its Resolution   589
             Tamra Pearson d'Estrée, E. Franklin Dukes, and Jessica Navarrete-Romero

CHAPTER 38   A Methodology of Participatory Planning   607
             Liisa Horelli

CHAPTER 39   Sustained Participation: A Community Based Approach to Addressing
             Environmental Problems   629
             Esther Wiesenfeld and Euclides Sánchez

SECTION V. THE FUTURE

CHAPTER 40   Personal Space in a Digital Age   647
             Robert Sommer

CHAPTER 41   Toward an Environmental Psychology of the Internet   661
             Daniel Stokols and Maria Montero

CHAPTER 42   On to Mars!   676
             Robert B. Bechtel

AUTHOR INDEX   687

SUBJECT INDEX   709

SHARPENING THEORIES

The Increasing *Contexts* of *Context* in the Study of Environment Behavior Relations

SEYMOUR WAPNER and JACK DEMICK

RESEARCHERS IN A WIDE VARIETY of fields—including those interested in the study of environment behavior relations—have increasingly emphasized the role of context in human functioning. It may be worthwhile for those of us interested in environment behavior research to review some systematic approaches to context as a means for identifying new research problems and for advancing our theoretical perspectives, which may have practical implications for improving the functioning of human beings in their everyday life environments. Accordingly, we shall examine the notion of "context" as treated in the literature; then we shall examine its use in our holistic, developmental, systems-oriented perspective; and finally we shall consider the application of our contextual notions to environment behavior research problems.

REFLECTIONS ON CONTEXT

Although often used interchangeably with *environment* or *system*, *context* implies different things for those in different disciplines and subfields within a discipline. For example, *context* in clinical psychology has most often referred to the family (e.g., the pathology of the individual is a function of his or her familial relationships and interactions; see Minuchin, 1978) and, only more recently, to culture (e.g., the need to match characteristics of counselors and clients on the basis of race, ethnicity, and gender; see

Sue, Sue, & Sue, 1997). In developmental psychology, those who adhere to *contextualist* developmental models of human functioning (e.g., Baltes, 1979; Bronfenbrenner, 1986; Dixon & Nesselroade, 1983; Lerner, 1986; Lerner & von Eye, 1998; Wachs & Shpancer, 1998) seem to equate context with various behavior settings (e.g., home, school, recreational). More recently within developmental psychology, there has been renewed interest (e.g., Valsiner, 1994) in similarities and differences in psychological functioning in different cultural contexts (e.g., Japan, United States). In cognitive psychology, Duranti and Goodwin (1992), for example, have comprehensively reviewed language as a phenomenon primarily involving the interpersonal context. In social-personality psychology, researchers (e.g., Brown, 1965) have traditionally focused on the interpersonal context, while in architecture researchers (e.g., Lang, 1987; Takahashi, 2000) have conceptualized context basically as the built environment.

With a few notable exceptions (e.g., Stokols, 1987), there exist relatively few theoretical discussions of the precise meaning of the term *context. Merriam-Webster's Collegiate Dictionary* (10th ed., 1995) provides two separate definitions. The first concerns "the parts of a discourse that surround a word or passage and [that] can throw light on its meaning" (p. 250). The second treats "the interrelated conditions in which something exists or occurs: environment" (p. 250). Although, for us, the first and second

3

definitions are interrelated (e.g., sentences are contexts for individual words), we do not see either of them as synonymous with our concept of context. Toward this end, we will review Stokols's (1987) extensive consideration of context in environmental psychological theories. We will then demonstrate the ways in which our own notion of context is similar to and different from Stokols and others (cf. Moore, 2000; Stringer, 1980).

STOKOLS'S TREATMENT OF CONTEXT

In his comprehensive overview, Stokols (1987) has seen within environment behavior research the emergence of a focus on context in the holistic emphases of Schwartz (1982), Magnusson and Allen (1983), and Wapner and Kaplan (1983). He has also cited additional examples in developmental psychology (e.g., Bronfenbrenner, 1979; Scarr, 1979) and in various aspects of cognitive, personality, and social psychology as evident in the work of such researchers as Gergen (1992), Neisser (1982), Kelly (1985), Little (1983), Altman (1982), and others.

Specifically Stokols (1987) has defined "contexts" as "everyday environmental settings" (p. 42) and then as ". . . the situational boundaries of psychological phenomena . . ." (p. 43). From there, he has gone on to distinguish *contextual* versus *noncontextual* research as follows:

> Whereas [n]on-contextual research deals with target predictor and outcome variables, contextual research includes supplementary predictor and outcome variables (e.g., the immediate situations and the person's life situations that impact the relationships among target variables). Moreover, whereas non-contextual analysis does not address relations among target variables, contextual analysis is directed toward assessing relations between situational and target variables.

To exemplify, he has stated that

> non-contextual research focuses entirely on the relationships between target predictor and outcome variables (e.g., commuting distance and blood pressure levels) [the former pertaining to the target independent/predictor variable and the latter to the dependent/outcome variable]. Contextual research, on the other hand incorporates supplementary predictor variables drawn from the immediate situation (e.g., levels of traffic congestion encountered along the route, size and amenities of one's vehicle)

or from other areas of a person's life situation (e.g., levels of residential and job satisfaction) that presumably qualify the relationship between the target variables. (p. 44)

Whereas Stokols has made strong inroads into the general problem of context by identifying "the full range of important contextual *moderators* [italics added] of the target variables" (p. 47), our holistic, developmental, systems-oriented perspective (e.g., Wapner, 1987; Wapner & Demick, 1998, 1999, 2000a, 2000b) has characteristically adopted an even broader view of context than that implied by the notion of moderator variables. Similar to Stokols, we have used the term *context* to connote the specific situation (overt and covert events and processes) in which the individual finds himself or herself (cf. Lewin, 1935, 1946, and Murray, 1938, on contextual or situational factors). However, for us, context alternatively refers to variation within each of six aspects of person and environment as well as the relations among these aspects.

For example, given assessment of variations of the person, for the physical aspect, there may be contextual variation with respect to a large variety of health conditions (e.g., heart condition, arthritis, etc.); for the psychological aspect, there may be contextual variation (e.g., loss of self-esteem, anxiety); and for the sociocultural aspect, there may be contextual variation (e.g., role as biological or adoptive parent, as professor). Given assessment of variation of the environment: for the physical aspect, there may be a variety of contexts (e.g., focus on the natural environment or the built environment); for the interpersonal environment, contexts will vary (e.g., falling in or out of love, loss of a loved one, crowding); and for the sociocultural environmental context, there will also be variation (e.g., laws of use of automobile safety belts, regulations concerning education). Similarly, for relations between person and environmental aspects, there may be different contexts (e.g., physical illness of a relative, relation between physical environment and illness). Thus, such conceptualization—which has suggested six general contexts (physical, psychological/intrapersonal, and sociocultural aspects of person and physical, interpersonal, and sociocultural aspects of environment) and an infinite number of specific situations or contexts at each of these levels of organization—provides a more systematic means for conceptualizing and studying the wide range of possible contextual variation inherent in environment behavior relations.

In line with our underlying assumptions, there are a number of other differences between Stokols's and our approach to context, including the conditions to which it is applicable, the treatment of spatial and temporal features, the range of research problems uncovered by holistic conceptualization, and so forth. Thus, these and other features of our approach that go beyond what is usually considered in more traditional notions of context (e.g., Stokols, 1987) are elaborated below.

THE HOLISTIC, DEVELOPMENTAL, SYSTEMS-ORIENTED APPROACH

HOLISTIC ASSUMPTIONS

Person-in-Environment System as Unit of Analysis

A basic assumption in keeping with holism is that the person-in-environment system* is the unit of analysis that involves transactions (experience and action) of the person with the environment. This unit of analysis has the advantage of corresponding to and representing the complexity of human functioning in the real-life situation. It further implies analysis of the person's experience and action in a variety of contexts. That is, the person context and the environmental context as well as the interrelations between them are, as noted previously, built into and are an essential part of our unit of analysis.

Concept of Person and of Environment

Central to the person-in-environment system with respect to levels of integration is the assumption that the person is comprised of mutually defining *physical/biological* (e.g., health), *psychological* (e.g., self-esteem), and *sociocultural* (e.g., role as worker) aspects; and the environment is comprised of mutually defining aspects, including *physical* (natural and built), *interpersonal* (e.g. friend, spouse), and *sociocultural* (rules of home, community, and culture) aspects. Thus, unlike Stokols (1987) who appears to have equated context with situational moderator variables, our approach assumes that context systematically encompasses all aspects of the person-in-environment system, that is, all aspects of the person as well as all aspects of the environment and their interrelations within the person-in-environment system.

Structural and Dynamic Analyses

Also in keeping with holism, our approach espouses the use of both structural and dynamic analyses. Viewing the person and the environment as structural components, structural analyses address whether the parts of subsystems are more or less differentiated and/or integrated with one another in specifiable ways. Dynamic analyses entail a determination of the means by which a characteristic structure or goal is achieved or maintained. Here, like Werner (1937), we assume that the final solution to a problem (end) may be arrived at through diverse processes (means) reflecting different activities of various structures in the central nervous system (process-achievement distinction). Both types of analyses are viewed as complementary aspects of a formal description of the variety of contexts of the person-in-environment system (exemplified in our empirical work discussed next).

Constructivism

Also relevant to holism, we assume that the person-in-environment system constructs objects of perception and thought and thereby actively contributes to the cognitive process. Such an approach rejects all "copy" theories of perception and instead asserts that reality is relative to the person's interpretation (cf. Lavine, 1950a, 1950b). This constructivist assumption also leads us to consider the distinction between the experienced and the physical environment; the former has also been referred to as the behavioral environment (Koffka, 1935), *umwelt*, phenomenal world, or self-world (von Uexkull, 1957), and psychological environment (Lewin, 1935). Thus, for methodology our approach is wedded to the complementarity of explication (description) and causal explanation (conditions under which cause-effect relations occur) rather than being restricted to one or the other.

Our holistic emphasis has also indicated the need to consider the context in both objective and experiential terms. Useful here is Werner's (1940/1957) distinction between geometric technical (objective) and physiognomic (psychological—cognitive-affective or expressive) perception, which may or may not exhibit a one-to-one correspondence. Such

---

*Here, we will discuss only human beings. It should be noted, however, that our approach is also relevant to all organism-in-environment systems.

holistic underpinnings have led us to study the inter-relations between and among levels of functioning (e.g., adaptation to the nursing home as related to the possession of cherished objects; see Wapner, Demick, & Redondo, 1990) as well as between experience and action (e.g., doing what one wants to or should do). Necessarily complex to reflect the character of every-day life, such research has suggested that the notion of context may indeed be a multifaceted one.

Spatiotemporal Nature of Experience

We also assume that the person-in-environment system is always undergoing change. For example, within our culture, we typically get up, leave the bedroom, go into the kitchen, eat breakfast, get dressed, get in the car, drive to work, and so forth. We also assume that, although this ongoing flow of events is continuous, it is usually structured into a series of discrete units (e.g., eating breakfast) that are separated from preceding and subsequent units by temporal boundaries (Wapner & Lebensfeld-Schwartz, 1976).

Against this backdrop, there are several major differences between our conceptualization of con-text and that of Stokols. First, for us context includes spatial as well as temporal features relevant to the three aspects of person, the three aspects of environ-ment, and the interrelations among them. Second, while Stokols (1987) has pointed to the importance of the spatial and temporal milieu as well as to the need for considering the temporal dimensions of context, spatiality and temporality are treated as in-dependent entities. In contrast, we have recognized that human functioning involves ongoing spatiotem-poral experience and action and that, although the flow of events is continuous, they may be structured in a series of discrete spatial units independent of temporality or in a series of discrete temporal units independent of spatiality. That is, the human has the constructivist capacity of emphasizing one aspect (e.g., time) and subordinating the other (e.g., space) or vice versa.

DEVELOPMENTAL ASSUMPTIONS

In our perspective, developmental changes in the person-in-environment system are not restricted to child growth, ontogenesis, but are seen as a mode of analysis with applicability to diverse aspects of person-in-environment functioning. In addition to ontogenesis, developmental changes apply as well to microgenesis (e.g., development of a spatial orga-nization of an environment), pathogenesis (e.g., development of neuro- and psychopathology), phy-logenesis (e.g., development of a species), and ethno-genesis (e.g., development of a culture). Again, such conceptualization has typically pointed to the need to consider wider contextual variation within all as-pects of the person-in-environment system (e.g., de-velopment of the psychological aspect of person as embodied in microgenesis, pathogenesis, etc.).

Further, components of the person-in-environment system are assumed to be developmentally orderable in terms of the orthogenetic principle, which defines development in terms of the degree to which the sys-tem is organized. The orthogenetic principle (e.g., Werner & Kaplan, 1956, 1963) states that develop-ment of the person-in-environment system proceeds from a relative lack of differentiation toward the goal of differentiation and hierarchic integration of or-ganismic functioning. The more differentiated and hierarchically integrated the system is in its parts, its means, and its ends, the more highly developed it is said to be. This presentation in formal terms makes it applicable to a multiplicity of content areas, including contextual features of the variety of as-pects of person and of environment and their rela-tion to each other; again, this encompasses what Stokols (1987) has referred to as target features.

Polarities

The applicability of the orthogenetic principle is more readily evident when one considers its specifi-cation with respect to a number of polarities, which at one extreme represent developmentally less ad-vanced and at the other developmentally more advanced functioning (cf. Kaplan, 1959; Werner 1940/1957; Werner & Kaplan, 1956). These polarities (the first less developmentally advanced than the second), illustrated with examples relevant to con-textual aspects of environment behavior relations, are as follows.

1. *Interfused to subordinated.* In the former, ends or goals are not sharply differentiated; in the latter, functions are differentiated and hierar-chized with drives and momentary states sub-ordinated to long-term goals. For example, for the less developmentally advanced person, comfort is not differentiated from the need to

be safe by using the automobile safety belt in the context of driving (physical, interpersonal, and sociocultural contexts of the environment); in contrast, the more developmentally advanced person subordinates the short-term goal of comfort for the long-term goal, safety achieved by wearing a seat belt.

2. *Syncretic to discrete. Syncretic* refers to the merging of several mental phenomena, whereas *discrete* refers to functions, acts, and meanings that represent something specific and unambiguous. Syncretic thinking is represented, for example, by the individual in the context of retirement (sociocultural context of person) who exhibits lack of differentiation between inner and outer experience (i.e., lack of separation of one's own feelings from that of others out there, e.g., one's spouse). In contrast, discrete thinking is exemplified by the retiree's capacity for accurately distinguishing between her or his own feelings and those of others out there.

3. *Diffuse to articulate. Diffuse* represents a relatively uniform, homogeneous structure with little differentiation of parts, whereas *articulate* refers to a structure where differentiated parts make up the whole. For example, diffuse is represented by the law of *pars pro toto,* where a part (living in the physical context of a bad neighborhood) is not distinguished from one's judgment and affective experience of the physical context (city) as a whole (see Demick, Hoffman, & Wapner, 1985). *Articulate* is represented by experience where distinguishable parts make up the whole, each contributing to and yet being distinguishable from the whole.

4. *Rigid to flexible. Rigid* refers to behavior that is fixed and not readily changeable; *flexible* refers to behavior that is readily changeable or plastic. *Rigid* is exemplified by unchangeability in routine behavior such as living in the context of fellow migrants as opposed to the capacity to change living arrangements when of value to the goal of becoming enculturated within the larger society.

5. *Labile to stable.* Finally, *labile* refers to the fluidity and inconsistency that go along with changeability; *stable* refers to the consistency or nonambiguity that occurs with fixed properties. For example, lability is evident in a person exhibiting inconsistent behavior, such as

ambivalently shifting from liking to not liking (and vice versa) the construction of the building in which he or she lives (physical context of environment) versus stability in feelings, positive or negative, about an architectural structure (see Wapner & Demick, 1998, for an elaborated discussion).

Individual Differences

The examples in the above characterization of developmental polarities speaks clearly to individual differences with respect to environment behavior relations. However, the orthogenetic principle, for example, can be used more directly to characterize individual differences in modes of coping—a problem with significant relevance for those concerned with contextual aspects of environment behavior relations. Let us illustrate such individual differences with respect to the contexts of undergraduate seniors planning what they would do after graduation (Apter, 1976); the individual living in a contemporaneous high-speed environment (Wapner, 1980a, 1980b); and the impact of a hurricane on island inhabitants (Chea & Wapner, 1995).

Apter (1976) has examined college seniors' means for handling conflict. Specifically, she has interviewed seniors in the context of those with and without articulated plans for their future (psychological context of person). She found that there were four types of conflict resolution or modes of coping that ranged from less developmentally advanced (i.e., for those without articulated plans) to more developmentally advanced (i.e., articulated plans) as follows:

1. A *de-differentiated* mode of coping involved accommodation, that is, going along with or accepting the status quo, conforming outwardly to fit in with the general context of the environment;

2. A *de-differentiated and isolated* mode of coping that involved the distancing of self from a painful situation by laughing, becoming cynical, withdrawing from the general context of the environment, and so forth;

3. A *de-differentiated and in-conflict* mode of coping that involved nonconstructive ventilation, that is, exhibiting an aggressive act toward a source of conflict, becoming angry and/or disappointed, and not suggesting constructive ways

of remedying the specific context of the situation; and

4. A *differentiated and hierarchically integrated* mode of coping, which involved constructive assertion—that is, recommending planned action and different creative alternatives for achieving a goal and being less dominated by emotions (psychological context of person).

Individual differences in a high-speed society (Wapner, 1980a, 1980b) have been studied as follows. Suppose there is a mismatch between an individual's natural tempo (contextual aspect of person) and her or his experienced high-speed environment (contextual aspect of environment). According to the orthogenetic principle, the individual differences in modes of coping (and corresponding self-world relationships) are as follows:

1. *De-differentiated* self-world relationship: The person changes in keeping with the general context of the high speed environment, where, for example, the auto worker increases his or her tempo beyond the usual pace to keep up with the more specific context of the assembly line.

2. *Differentiated and isolated* self-world relationship: The person continues to operate at her or his own personal tempo by withdrawing from or becoming isolated from the general context of the experienced high-speed environment.

3. *Differentiated and in-conflict* self-world relationship: The person continues to operate at his or her personal tempo in the general context of the high-speed environment and is in open conflict with it.

4. *Differentiated and hierarchically integrated* self-world relationship: The person might control her or his relationship with the general context of the environment by participating or by withdrawing depending on her or his current goals, long-term values, likes, and dislikes. There may be integration insofar as the person might introduce into city living some features of nature (e.g., pets, gardening) and/or other humanistic activities characteristic of a pre-high-tech world and indulge in those activities while limiting involvement in high-speed external temporal demands.

Modes of coping were also studied with respect to the impact of a hurricane (i.e., contextual aspect of physical environment) on island inhabitants by Chea and Wapner (1995). Here, these researchers have again found striking individual differences utilizing the categories of the orthogenetic principle.

1. With warning of the disaster, the *de-differentiated* person-in-environment system state was in evidence insofar as there was wishful thinking in denial of danger, greater dependence on authority figures, and egocentricity (psychological context of person). There was also evidence of a *differentiated and isolated* person-in-environment system state, illustrated by those who indicated that they could do nothing about the storm or withdrew by locking themselves in rooms or the church (physical context of environment). Still others represented the *differentiated and in-conflict* system state with their blaming authorities for not warning them properly.

2. With the impact of the hurricane, the more regressed mode of coping was reported frequently, and soon after the impact there was evidence of the differentiated and in-conflict mode of coping (e.g., annoyed at the relief efforts, some residents nonetheless began to start repairs in the specific context of their homes).

3. The *differentiated and hierarchically integrated* mode of coping most frequently occurred a year after impact, which, for example, involved the development of committees concerned with rebuilding and planning for coping with future disasters (interpersonal context of environment).

In summation, our concept of context—which now may be defined as the range of specific situations at all levels of organization—appears broader than that of many current environment behavior researchers (e.g., Moore, 2000; Stokols, 1987; Stringer, 1980). Thus, our approach assumes that context encompasses all aspects of the person, all aspects of the environment, and their interrelations within the person-in-environment system (general context) as well as the range of situations (specific contexts) in each of the six general contexts. Further, the concept becomes even broader when one acknowledges that context additionally includes aspects of human evolutionary history, the culture in which the individual resides, the particular historical period in which he or she lives, the communities of which he or she is a part, the surrounding economic climate, his or her multiple worlds, and so forth. Thus, the implications of these general and specific notions of context for empirical research (in each of the three general contexts of person and of the three general contexts of environment) are delineated below for a variety of specific situations or contexts.

RESEARCH FROM OUR APPROACH

To exemplify the ways in which our perspective shapes problems of relevance for contextual aspects of environment behavior research, we now complement previous mention of our studies with a more comprehensive description of our work on six problems. These six problems (three treating the general contexts of the person and three of the environment) are as follows: onset of diabetes (physical context of person); changes in experience and action related to psychiatric hospitalization (psychological context of person); transition to parenthood (sociocultural context of person); urban contexts for children (physical context of environment); protection against AIDS in sexual situations (interpersonal context of environment); and experience and action in the context of automobile driving before and after mandatory legislation (sociocultural context of environment).

ONSET OF DIABETES (PHYSICAL CONTEXT OF PERSON)

Relevant here is a study by Collazo (1985) that examined the transition from health to illness as exemplified in the onset of diabetes (specific physical context within the general physical context of the person). His focus was on analyzing a number of relations between the focal person and other parts of her or his person-in-environment system. Most relevant here, Collazo has identified: (1) relations between one's biological and psychological contexts as influenced by changes in the metabolism of sugar; (2) transactions with physical contexts of the environment (e.g., unwillingness to move beyond the physical context of the home community because of concern for the availability of insulin supplies); (3) relations with the interpersonal contexts of the environment (e.g., fear of getting married, dependence on others); and (4) relations to the sociocultural context (e.g., changes in values and behavior of the individual related to culturally defined attitudes toward the sick).

CHANGES ASSOCIATED WITH PSYCHIATRIC HOSPITALIZATION (PSYCHOLOGICAL CONTEXT OF PERSON)

An example relevant to the general psychological context of the person may be found in our study (Demick, Peicott, & Wapner, 1985) of patients on an addictions treatment unit of a psychiatric hospital in Massachusetts. A variety of tests (e.g., covering rules and regulations, mental illness attitudes, expectations concerning length of stay) were administered on six test occasions: 1 to 2 days after admission; 1, 2, 3, 4, and 5 weeks later, immediately prior to discharge. Changes in many contextual aspects of self-world relations occurred: specifically during the stressful transition periods of entering and leaving the hospital setting (with the most potent changes occurring with the more immediate changes in the physical context, i.e., immediately following admission and immediately preceding discharge) and, more generally, over the course of hospitalization within the psychological context of the person (in the direction of less denial and thus less rigid differentiation between person and environmental, or self and world, contexts).

TRANSITION TO PARENTHOOD (SOCIOCULTURAL CONTEXT OF PERSON)

Extensive consideration of the sociocultural context of the person with respect to role is readily illustrated in our work on family transitions, for example, the transition to parenthood. Wapner (1993) has presented an analysis of parental development, giving consideration to why people become parents, stages of parenthood (e.g., Demick, in press; Galinsky, 1981), and specific issues such as divorce, stepparenthood, adoption, and child abuse.

For example, the question of why people want to become parents may be readily answered by considering our elaborated concept of context. That is, potential reasons may include factors related to the physical context of the person (e.g., age, physical maturity), the psychological context of the person (e.g., expansion and enhancement of one's self-concept), the sociocultural context of the person (e.g., fulfilling and/or validating one's social role), the physical context of the environment (e.g., adding positively to the human population); the interpersonal context of the environment (e.g., creating a family, power and/or influence); and the sociocultural context of the environment (e.g., fulfilling the values of one's society).

URBAN CONTEXTS FOR CHILDREN
(PHYSICAL CONTEXT OF ENVIRONMENT)

Wapner (1998) has identified several features of our approach with particular relevance for the design of urban contexts for children. These include: (1) the child as an active organism who constructs a psychological context that is distinguished from the physical, geographic context; (2) the child as capable of multiple intentionality, that is, the capacity in his or her experience to shift back and forth among different contexts (person, environment); (3) the child as an inhabitant of multiple physical contexts or worlds; and (4) the child as an organism with a variety of means or instrumentalities such as conceptual systems, tools, and/or body parts (psychological context of person) to accomplish ends.

Based on these assumptions, Wapner has recommended that the design of urban contexts for children include the following goals: (1) to provide optimal environmental contexts (physical, interpersonal, sociocultural) matched to the contexts of the child for promoting her or his physical, mental, and social development; and (2) to optimize the transactions (experience and action) of the child with the physical, interpersonal, and sociocultural contexts of the environment. This latter goal might involve providing both general and specific (person and environmental) contexts that foster development of the ideal differentiated and hierarchically integrated person-in-environment system state. This state is conceptualized as involving control over self-world relations, greater salience of positive affective states, diminution of isolation, anonymity, helplessness, and depersonalization, coordination of short- and long-term goals and planning processes, and movement toward a unity of overt and covert actions.

Demick, Hoffman, and Wapner (1985) have supported such conceptualization through their work on the ways in which one's immediate physical context or neighborhood (part) varying in quality impacts one's experience of a larger physical context (city as a whole) with implications for urban renewal. In a related manner, Demick (in press) has more recently applied such conceptualization to the person-in-environment experience of those children who were adopted (psychological context of person). That is, those who experience an open adoption (communication between birth and adoptive parents) may exhibit a heightened awareness of the physical context of the environment (fearing intrusion, etc.). These and other relationships are currently under investigation.

PROTECTION AGAINST AIDS (INTERPERSONAL CONTEXT OF ENVIRONMENT)

Drawing from our work on the relations between experience and action, two studies are relevant here. First, Ferguson, Wapner, and Quirk (1993) asked college students to report on specific sexual situations (interpersonal context of environment) in which they "did not do what they wanted to do" and situations in which they "did do what they wanted to do" with respect to protection against the sexual transmission of HIV. Responses were categorized in our developmental terms as follows: (1) de-differentiated (e.g., "I was so aroused at that point that I didn't worry about HIV"); (2) differentiated and isolated (e.g., "I do everything except that because it decreases my chances of contracting HIV"); (3) differentiated and in conflict (e.g., "She insisted that I not use a condom, so I didn't against my will"); and (4) differentiated and hierarchically integrated (e.g., "I use protection because I am aware of the consequences of unprotected sex . . . protected sex is of utmost importance"). Findings indicated that, when individuals reported specific contexts in which they "did what they wanted to," differentiated and hierarchically integrated responses were most frequent; when they reported specific contexts in which they "did not do what they wanted to do," their responses were characteristically less advanced (i.e., de-differentiated, differentiated, and in conflict).

On the basis of these data, Clark (1995) introduced three interventions to change unsafe behavior in such sexual contexts: (1) providing information about the HIV/AIDS disease and how the virus is transmitted; (2) providing information on how HIV/AIDS is transmitted as well as accounts from Ferguson et al. (1993) of actions when "they did what they wanted to do" and when they "did not do what they wanted to do"; and (3) providing information about how HIV/AIDS is transmitted and a tailored imagery exercise (in which they were asked to imagine the consequences of one of the accounts of reported unsafe behavior from which they were to assume that they had contracted HIV). Results indicated that, relative to those in the first two contexts, those in the third context (personalized treatment to decrease the psychological distance between the participant and the threat of

HIV/AIDS) reported a significantly greater frequency of practicing safe sex.

CULTURE AND AUTOMOBILE DRIVING (SOCIOCULTURAL CONTEXT OF ENVIRONMENT)

Relations between experience and action in the specific physical context of automobile driving were assessed in a series of studies. First, Rioux and Wapner (1986) conducted an experiential description and process analysis of individuals' experience in the context of automobile safety-belt usage in the United States (Massachusetts). The analysis led to the identification of individual differences in usage—namely, committed safety belt users (who, e.g., had relatives injured in accidents), nonusers (who, e.g., perceived automobiles as objects that could be fixed after accidents), and variable users (who used safety belts depending on the context, e.g., in rain and snow only).

Wapner, Demick, Inoue, Ishii, and Yamamoto (1986) then studied automobile safety belt experience and action prior to mandatory legislation in the context of two cultures, namely, Japan and the United States. Questionnaires to the three user groups in both cultures revealed differences in (1) factors preparing individuals for using safety belts (e.g., the Japanese placed higher value on safety belts than Americans); (2) specific triggers for using belts (e.g., feelings of preoccupation lead Americans, but not the Japanese, to forget to use belts); (3) action (e.g., the Japanese wore safety belts more often than Americans in the context of highway driving); and (4) experience of the action (e.g., relative to Americans, the Japanese felt "virtuous" but not "confident" when wearing safety belts).

Demick et al. (1992) assessed individuals' experience and action of safety belt usage prior to and following the initiation of mandatory safety belt legislation (sociocultural context of environment) in two cultural contexts: Japan (Hiroshima) and the United States (Massachusetts). These observations were complemented by Bertini and Wapner (1992) in a third cultural context, Italy (Rome). All three cultures exhibited the three user groups and increased usage with the introduction of a law. However, differential patterns of usage were obtained across the three cultures. In Japan, there was strong adherence to the law (immediately following legislation). In the United States, usage increased significantly immediately following the law; however, over time,

Massachusetts residents first voted to repeal the law because it interfered with individual freedom. Following this, even lower usage rates than before the law were observed (subsequently, the law was again put in force). In Italy, the degree of adherence to the mandatory safety belt law was almost negligible.

In a related program on age differences (21–94 years) in the physical context of automobile driving, Demick and Harkins (1999) have found that, of the numerous variables implicated in driving behavior (age, cognitive style, selective attention, personality), cognitive disembedding ability (cognitive style) was a better predictor of overall driving ability than was age. Such holistic research has attempted to tease apart factors affecting the person-in-environment system in the specific context of driving.

CONCLUSIONS

To complement our elaborated conceptions of persons, of environments, and of person-in-environment systems, we now offer an elaborated version of context. On the general level, our approach has suggested six contexts, namely, the physical, psychological (intrapersonal), and sociocultural contexts of the person and, analogously, the physical, interpersonal, and sociocultural contexts of the environment. On the specific level, our view has proposed that there are an infinite number of specific situations or contexts within each of the previous six more general contexts, which include aspects of both the person *and* the environment. This conceptualization—standing in marked contrast to many approaches that have equated context with situational moderator variables (supplementary predictor variables drawn only from the immediate situation)—has the potential to provide a more systematic means for attacking open research problems on the wide range of contextual variation inherent in environment behavior relations.

Further, in addition to helping those concerned with environment behavior relations to conceptualize problems more in line with the complex character of everyday life (since contextual aspects of person, of environment, and of their relations are interrelated), such reframing may also help psychology both to see itself and to be seen by others as a unified (differentiated and integrated) science, one concerned not only with the study of human functioning in isolated contexts, but also with the study of problems that cut across the various aspects of persons, environments, systems, and their multifaceted contexts (cf. Wapner & Demick, 1988, 1998, 1999, 2000a, 2000b).

REFERENCES

Altman, L. (1982). *Problems and prospects of environmental psychology.* Presidential address to the Division of Population and Environmental Psychology, American Psychological Association annual meeting, Washington, DC.

Apter, D. (1976). *Modes of coping with conflict in the presently inhabited environment as a function of plans to move to a new environment.* Unpublished master's thesis, Clark University, Worcester, MA.

Baltes, P. B. (1979). Life-span developmental psychology: Some converging observations on history and theory. In P. B. Baltes & O. G. Brim (Eds.), *Life-span development and behavior* (Vol. 2, pp. 256–279). New York: Academic Press.

Bertini, G., & Wapner, S. (1992). *Automobile seat belt use in Italy prior to and following legislation.* Unpublished study, Clark University, Worcester, MA.

Bronfenbrenner, U. (1979). *The ecology of human development.* Cambridge, MA: Harvard University Press.

Bronfenbrenner, U. (1986). Ecology of the family as a context for human development: Research perspectives. *Developmental Psychology, 22,* 723–742.

Brown, R. (1965). *Social psychology.* New York: Free Press.

Chea, W. E., & Wapner, S. (1995). Retrospections of Bahamians concerning the impact of hurricane Andrew. In J. L. Nasar, P. Granis, & K. Hanyu (Eds.), *Proceedings of the twenty-sixth annual conference of the Environmental Design Research Association* (pp. 87–92). Oklahoma City, OK: Environmental Design Research Association.

Clark, E. F. (1995). *Women's self-reported experience and action in relation to protection against sexual transmission of HIV: A randomized comparison study of those interventions.* Doctoral dissertation, Clark University, Worcester, MA.

Collazo, J. (1985). *Transition from health to illness: Experiential changes following the onset of diabetes.* Presented as part of a symposium on Environmental Psychology: In Search of a Theory. Annual meetings of the Eastern Psychological Association, Boston.

Demick, J. (2001). Stages of parental development. In M. Bornstein (Ed.), *Handbook of parenting* (2nd ed.). Mahwah, NJ: Erlbaum.

Demick, J. (in press). "Roots that clutch": What adoption and foster care can tell us about adult development. In J. Demick & C. Andreoletti (Eds.), *Handbook of adult development.* New York: Kluwer Academic/Plenum.

Demick, J., & Harkins, D. (1999). Cognitive style and driving skills in adulthood: Implications for licensing of older adults. *International Association of Traffic Science and Safety (IATSS) Research, 23*(1), 1–16.

Demick, J., Hoffman, A., & Wapner, S. (1985). Residential context and environmental change as determinants of urban experience. *Children's Environments Quarterly, 2*(3), 44–54.

Demick, J., Inoue, W., Wapner, S., Ishii, S., Minami, H., Nishiyama, S., & Yamamoto, T. (1992). Cultural differences in impact of governmental legislation: Automobile safety belt usage. *Journal of Cross-Cultural Psychology, 23*(4), 468–487.

Demick, J., Peicott, J., & Wapner, S. (1985). *Temporal changes in hospitalized alcoholics' self-world relationships.* Paper presented at the annual meeting of the American Psychological Association, Los Angeles.

Dixon, R. A., & Nesselroade, J. R. (1983). Rumors of historiography. In R. M. Lerner (Ed.), *Developmental psychology: Historical and philosophical perspectives* (pp. 241–256). New York: Wiley.

Duranti, A., & Goodwin, C. (1992). *Rethinking context: Language as an interactive phenomenon.* Cambridge, England: Cambridge University Press.

Ferguson, E., Wapner, S., & Quirk, M. (1993, April). *Sexual behavior in relation to protection against transmission of HIV in college students.* Paper presented at the annual meeting of the Eastern Psychological Association. Arlington, VA.

Galinsky, E. (1981). *Between generations: The six stages of parenthood.* New York: Berkley Books.

Gergen, K. J. (1992). Toward a postmodern psychology. In S. Kvale (Ed.), *Psychology and postmodernism* (pp. 17–30). London: Sage.

Kaplan, B. (1959). The study of language in psychiatry. In S. Arieti (Ed.), *American handbook of psychiatry* (Vol. 3, pp. 659–668). New York: Basic Books.

Kelly, J. G. (1985). *Context and process: An ecological view of the interdependence of practice and research.* Paper presented at the American Psychological Association annual meeting, Los Angeles.

Koffka, K. (1935). *Principles of gestalt psychology.* New York: Harcourt Brace.

Lang, J. T. (1987). *Creating architectural theory.* New York: Van Nostrand-Reinhold.

Lavine, T. (1950a). Knowledge as interpretation: An historical survey. *Philosophy and Phenomenological Research, 10,* 526–540.

Lavine, T. (1950b). Knowledge as interpretation: An historical survey. *Philosophy and Phenomenological Research, 11,* 80–103.

Lerner, R. M. (1986). *Concepts and theories of human development* (2nd ed.). New York: Random House.

Lerner, R. M., & von Eye, A. (1998). Integrating youth- and context-focused research and outreach: A developmental model. In D. Gorlitz, H. J. Harloff, G. Mey, & J. Valsiner (Eds.), *Children, cities and psychological theories: Developing relationships* (pp. 573–597). Berlin, Germany: Walter de Gruyter.

Lewin, K. (1935). *A dynamic theory of personality.* New York: McGraw-Hill.

Lewin, K. (1946). Action research and minority problems. *Journal of Social Issues, 26,* 3–13.

Little, B. R. (1983). Personal projects: A rationale and method for investigation. *Environment and Behavior, 15,* 273–309.

Magnusson, D., & Allen, V. L. (Eds.). (1983). *Human development: An interactional perspective.* New York: Academic Press.

Merriam-Webster's Collegiate Dictionary. (1995). Springfield, MA: Merriam-Webster.

Minuchin, S. (1978). *Families and family therapy.* Cambridge, MA: Harvard University Press.

Moore, J. (2000). Placing home in context. *Journal of Environmental Psychology, 20,* 207–217.

Murray, H. A. (1938). *Explorations in personality.* New York: Oxford University Press.

Neisser, U. (1982). *Memory observed: Remembering in natural contexts.* New York: Freeman.

Rioux, S., & Wapner, S. (1986). Commitment to use of automobile seat belts: An experimental analysis. *Journal of Environmental Psychology, 6,* 189–204.

Scarr, S. (1979). Psychology and children: Current research and practice. *American Psychologist, 34,* 809–811.

Schwartz, G. E. (1982). Testing the biopsychosocial model: The ultimate challenge facing behavioral medicine? *Journal of Consulting and Clinical Psychology, 50,* 1040–1053.

Stokols, D. (1987). Conceptual strategies of environmental psychology. In D. Stokols & I. Altman (Eds.), *Handbook of environmental psychology* (pp. 41–70). New York: Wiley.

Stringer, P. (1980). The meaning of alternative future environments for individuals. In G. Broadbent, R. Bunt, & T. Llorens (Eds.), *Meaning and behavior in the built environment* (pp. 93–120). New York: Wiley.

Sue, D., Sue, D., & Sue, S. (1997). *Understanding abnormal behavior* (5th ed.). Boston: Houghton-Mifflin.

Takahashi, T. (2000). Sympathetic methods in environmental design and education. In S. Wapner, J. Demick, T. Yamamoto, & H. Minami (Eds.), *Theoretical perspectives in environment-behavior research: Underlying assumptions, research problems, and methodologies* (pp. 229–236). New York: Kluwer Academic/Plenum.

Valsiner, J. (1994). Culture and human development: A co-constructionist perspective. In P. van Geert, L. P. Mos, & W. J. Baker (Eds.), *Annals of theoretical psychology* (Vol. 10, pp. 247–298). New York: Plenum Press.

von Uexkull, J. (1957). A stroll through the world of animals and men. In C. H. Schiller & K. S. Lashley (Eds. and Trans.), *Instinctive behavior: The development of a modern concept.* New York: International Universities Press.

Wachs, T. D., & Shpancer, N. (1998). A contextualist perspective on child-environment relations. In D. Gorlitz,

H. J. Harloff, G. Mey, & J. Valsiner (Eds.), *Children, cities and psychological theories: Developing relationships* (pp. 164–192). Berlin, Germany: Walter de Gruyter.

Wapner, S. (1980a). Notes on a trip to Japan—1980. *Design Research News, 11,* 1–3.

Wapner, S. (1980b). Toward an analysis of transactions of persons-in-a-high-speed society. *Reports on man and a high speed society: The IATSS Symposium on Traffic Science* (pp. 35–43). Tokyo: IATSS.

Wapner, S. (1987). A holistic, developmental, systems-oriented environmental psychology: Some beginnings. In D. Stokols & I. Altman (Eds.), *Handbook of environmental psychology* (pp. 1433–1465). New York: Wiley.

Wapner, S. (1993). Parental development: A holistic, developmental, systems-oriented perspective. In J. Demick, K. Bursik, & R. DiBiase (Eds.), *Parental development* (pp. 3–37). Hillsdale, NJ: Erlbaum.

Wapner, S. (1998). A holistic, developmental, systems-oriented perspective: Child-environment relations. In D. Gorlitz, H. J. Harloff, G. Mey, & J. Valsiner (Eds.), *Children, cities, and psychological theories: Developing relationships* (pp. 278–300). Berlin, Germany: Walter de Gruyter.

Wapner, S., & Demick, J. (1998). Developmental analysis: A holistic, developmental, systems-oriented perspective. In W. Damon (Series Ed.) & R. M. Lerner (Vol. Ed.), *Handbook of child psychology: Vol. 1. Theoretical models of human development* (5th ed., pp. 761–805). New York: Wiley.

Wapner, S., & Demick, J. (1999). Developmental theory and clinical practice: A holistic, developmental, systems-oriented approach. In W. K. Silverman & T. H. Ollendick (Eds.), *Developmental issues in the clinical treatment of children* (pp. 3–30). Boston: Allyn & Bacon.

Wapner, S., & Demick, J. (2000a). Assumptions, methods, and research problems of the holistic, developmental, systems-oriented perspective. In S. Wapner, J. Demick, T. Yamamoto, & H. Minami (Eds.), *Theoretical perspectives in environment-behavior research: Underlying assumptions, research problems, and methodologies* (pp. 7–19). New York: Kluwer Academic/Plenum.

Wapner, S., & Demick, J. (2000b). Person-in-environment psychology: A holistic, developmental, systems-oriented perspective. In W. B. Walsh, K. H. Craik, & R. H. Price (Eds.), *Person-environment psychology: New directions and perspectives* (2nd ed., pp. 25–60). Hillsdale, NJ: Erlbaum.

Wapner, S., Demick, J., Inoue, W., Ishii, S., & Yamamoto, T. (1986). Relations between experience and action: Automobile seat belt usage in Japan and the United States. In W. H. Ittelson, M. Asai, & M. Carr (Eds.), *Proceedings of the 2nd Japan-USA Seminar on Environment-Behavior Research.* Tucson, AZ: University of Arizona Press.

Wapner, S., Demick, J., & Redondo, J. P. (1990). Cherished possessions and adaptation of older people to nursing homes. *International Journal on Aging and Human Development, 31*(3), 299–315.

Wapner, S., & Kaplan, B. (Eds.). (1983). *Heinz Werner: 1890–1964.* Worcester, MA: Clark University Press.

Wapner, S., & Lebensfeld-Schwartz, P. (1976). Toward a structural analysis of event experience. *Acta Psychologica, 41,* 308–401.

Werner, H. (1937). Process and achievement: A basic problem of education and developmental psychology. *Harvard Educational Review, 7,* 353–368.

Werner, H. (1957). *Comparative psychology of mental development.* New York: International Universities Press. (Original work published 1940)

Werner, H., & Kaplan, B. (1956). The developmental approach to cognition: Its relevance to the psychological interpretation of anthropological and ethnolinguistic data. *American Anthropologist, 58,* 866–880.

Werner, H., & Kaplan, B. (1963). *Symbol formation.* New York: Wiley.

CHAPTER 2

The Ethical Imperative

LEANNE G. RIVLIN

IN IMMANUEL KANT'S VIEW (cited in Johnson, 1965), "imperatives are only formulas expressing the relation of objective laws of volition in general to the imperfection of the will of this or that rational being, e.g., the human will" (p. 190). This chapter will offer my perspectives on ethical imperatives in environmental psychology, a field to which I feel deeply connected. It therefore is a personal view, offering my own "laws of volition," and although it suffers from my "imperfections" it is driven by the research in which I have been involved as well as the work of students and other colleagues.

For many years, the rights of human beings and animals participating in scientific research received little if any consideration. In recent years, researchers have become more concerned with the ethical issues that underlie their work. Some are driven by the formal ethical principles outlined by their professions and the requirements set by the U.S. government for acceptable research. This has included increasingly elaborated rules for the proper treatment of animals in laboratories as well as for the involvement of human beings in research.

Environmental psychology shares with other social sciences a number of ethical and moral concerns related to informed consent, participants' confidentiality, anonymity, privacy, deception, and risks. However, there are some other issues particular to our field, issues that grow out of the topics that are studied, the type of methods used, and the implications, applications, and publication of the results. Our research strategies and project involvements have raised additional questions that require attention.

Sieber's 1992 book on ethical research outlines the principles that underlie research involving human beings, drawing on the "ethical principles and scientific norms" of the U.S. National Commission for the Protection of Human Subjects in Biomedical and Behavioral Research. These are useful as a beginning examination of the complex decisions that a researcher must make. Three basic ethical principles and six norms that are derived from the principles are first steps in the journey toward appropriate strategies.

The principles begin with "Beneficence—maximizing good outcomes for science, humanity, and the individual research participants while avoiding unnecessary risk, harm, or wrong" (Sieber, 1992, p. 18). It is useful to recognize that we follow on the coattails of generations of researchers who exploited participants, then called "subjects," in their medical or social science research, in some cases using approaches that we look upon with horror today. We must examine ethical principles before undertaking studies in order to sensitize ourselves to the possible consequences of what we are doing and to make changes in the design of the research if abuses are identified.

The second principle is "Respect—protecting the autonomy of (autonomous) persons with courtesy and respect for individuals as persons, including those who are not autonomous (e.g., infants, the mentally retarded, senile persons)" (p. 18). This principle suggests that we must go beyond merely avoiding risk and cover the total treatment of participants in our research, considering their dignity and rights whatever their physical condition or developmental stage.

The final principle is "Justice—ensuring reasonable, nonexploitative, and carefully considered procedures and their fair administration; fair distribution of costs and benefits among persons and groups (i.e., those who bear the risks of research should be those who benefit from it)" (p. 18). This is a complicated goal to achieve, one that we will return to later. Although research in environmental psychology does not involve the physical risks such as those in biomedical research, there are other threats created by our work that require consideration.

The norms that Sieber describes involve "Valid research design," "Competence of the researcher," "Identification of consequences," "Selection of subjects," "Voluntary informed consent," and "Compensation for injury" (Sieber, 1992, p. 19). These concerns are important to environmental research and need attention.

Very few articles in the environment and behavior field have given sufficient attention to these issues. Textbooks on environmental psychology have been notoriously devoid of ethical concerns. An exception is Bell, Greene, Fisher, and Baum's introductory book (2001) that includes a short section on "Ethical Considerations" in research (pp. 19–20) as well as a somewhat more detailed consideration of "Values and Attitudes" (pp. 26–34). Bechtel's book (1997) also addresses "Environmental Ethics" (pp. 116–118), and other sections deal with a range of environmental issues that are based on values and attitudes. Values concerning environmental preservation and the quality of the environment, including the impacts of changes on the natural ecology of the earth and the universe, draw together many contemporary problems and highlight the urgent need to think beyond the present in developing policies about the environment.

Research evidence on the topics of ethics and values of environmental professionals is also limited. However, the study by Chapin, Choriki, and Wolfe (1990) offers some useful empirical findings from the researchers and practitioners who were asked in a survey to provide examples of ethical concerns in their work. Among their results was the fact that a number of their respondents raised ethical and value-related issues that were not included in the codes of their professional organizations.

The development of Geographic Information Systems (GIS), especially in the geography and planning fields, has generated many ethical problems. This technique has been widely used to analyze complex environmental statistical bases, and "the geographic analysis process is replete with normative, value-based decisions that drive particular results" (Schmidt, 1999, p. 6). Various questions have been raised regarding responsible use, the interpretation of findings from GIS studies, and the uneven access to people, especially to those who are disadvantaged (Schmidt, 1999). Although not unique to the GIS methodology, these issues underline the extent to which new methods can raise ethical problems as they provide useful data.

Professional conferences rarely include ethics and values in their offerings, a reflection of the failure of those attending to submit papers or symposia that address these concerns. The Chapin, Choriki, and Wolfe, research is an exception since it was presented at the 1990 meeting of the International Association for the Study of People and their Physical Surroundings (IAPS).

ETHICAL CONSIDERATIONS IN ENVIRONMENTAL PSYCHOLOGY

Research in environmental psychology is filled with ethical issues that demand the attention of students, scholars, and practitioners. This chapter will address some but certainly not all of them. For example, the quality of the environment and ethical management of the environment are of deep concern, but the focus in this chapter will be on environmental research. Much of the analysis is based on a combination of common sense and desired civil behavior, qualities that can be lost in the conduct of research.

Every empirical study, design project, and change process undertaken, whether a project or paper done by members of a class or professionals engaged in design or research, requires a careful consideration of ethics and values. This reflection needs to go beyond what is required for the Institutional Review Boards of universities and other institutions and the professional codes of individual professions. A number of questions must be addressed.

IS THE RESEARCH WORTH DOING?

Consideration of whether the work is worth doing at all is needed well before the research begins. Worth is part of an equation that requires balancing the physical, social, emotional, and temporal costs to the staff and the participants involved against the benefits for each party and for society as a whole. All of this needs to be considered in light of the presumed outcomes. If a study is solely to advance the professionals' careers with no redeeming features or assets for the persons tested, observed, surveyed, or questioned, the value that accrues is not fairly distributed. If the work places members of the research team—the persons hired to collect the data, often students—in danger or under extreme stress, there is a serious concern as to whether the work should be undertaken.

Proshansky (1987) described Kurt Lewin's view that "social research could be theoretically meaningful as well as socially useful" (p. 1469). If no attempts will be made to extract either the contributions toward theory development or the implications that can be applied toward ameliorating the lives of people, in my view, the work is of dubious value.

There is a distance between the professionals and others who are associated with the study or project that needs careful reflection. Rarely is there parity between researchers and participants, including instances when people are financially compensated for their time. It is the professional who is gaining most from these efforts. Some consideration of the short-term and long-term impacts on the lives of respondents should enter the determination as to whether the research should proceed. Although participatory research and action research (Lewin, 1948) include the persons involved in defining the research questions, selection of methods, and conduct of the work, the presence of so-called experts in the area often leads to unequal distribution of decision-making power.

DO THE TOPICS ADDRESSED RAISE ETHICAL CONCERNS?

The very nature of work in environmental psychology and the topics that are subjected to study are filled with issues that have complex ethical, moral, and political considerations. Environmental psychology deals with the everyday lives of people in their homes, workplaces, schools, public spaces, play and recreational places, hospitals and other institutions, as well as wilderness areas and "natural" environments. These settings resound with issues that are value based and culturally grounded and require attention to ethical concerns.

In my studies of homelessness, people welcomed members of the research teams with whom I worked into their living spaces—their newly acquired apartments or temporary shelters, or the huts that squatters had built on empty lots. They not only opened their doors to us but they opened up their feelings, sharing what their homeless life was like. Walking through these experiences was difficult for them and for us. However, it was an essential part of our study, which centered on understanding how the homelessness occurred, what they did to deal with it, what their past residential experiences were like, the nature of their relationships with family members and friends, and their plans for the near and distant future.

They often expressed gratitude for the opportunity to tell their stories, despite the stress they created. The descriptions were very powerful and painful ones that made it very clear that the equations of costs and benefits were not equal. The costs (the pain of sharing their trying experiences) may have far exceeded the benefits (the relief of having someone listening to them).

Their comments also were filled with political issues, for example, the housing and welfare policies in New York and the treatment of people facing poverty. They exposed shortcomings in the social services provided, but we had little power to address them in ways that would assure changes.

DOES THE SELECTION OF PARTICIPANTS RAISE ETHICAL CONCERNS?

For many years the participants in social science research were students in classes and in the subject pools maintained by universities. The requirement to participate in research was explained (or perhaps rationalized) as a useful training experience, an introduction to engaging in research. Subject pools still exist, servicing the needs of faculty members in conducting their research. Although students in introductory psychology classes in U.S. universities often are given the choice of becoming part of a subject pool or writing a paper, one can question the equity and morality of these options. There also is the added concern of whether research with student samples can be generalized beyond a similar U.S. university student population.

There are other concerns regarding persons selected as research participants. If a special group is needed, for example, victims of domestic violence or elderly persons, how do we get them to volunteer? Is the system for attracting them coercive, making promises that cannot be fulfilled, offering money that people desperately need?

The word "volunteer" indicates that the action is voluntary, "proceeding from the will or from one's own choice or consent" (*Merriam-Webster's Collegiate Dictionary*, 1996, p. 1324). This suggests that the offer gives the person the freedom to accept or refuse. In the sciences and social sciences we use the term "informed consent" so that the choices made by participants in our research follow a briefing on what is involved and a signed statement that they are willing to participate. However, there are restrictions on what can be considered a voluntary act—the decision as to whether to get involved in a study. The researcher must try to determine whether someone is pressuring the person to agree to participate—a parent, a work supervisor, or service provider.

Setting up the conditions of voluntary participation is a vital stage in the planning of research. It needs to follow criteria required by Institutional Review Boards and professional organizations as well as the values of the individual researcher.

Do the Methods Used Raise Ethical Concerns?

It is not the setting alone that can raise ethical concerns, but the ways we go about studying them that introduce problems. Qualitative approaches to uncovering life histories and experiences in places are methods that open up domains rather than offer choices of answers. They enable respondents to go into details that clarify issues and move into areas important to the explanations of their lives. The open-ended quality of our methods can lead to painful memories and to deeply felt reactions that an environmental researcher may not be equipped to handle.

Within institutions such as schools, hospitals, and facilities for elderly persons, our questions to and observations of the people within them (some of them defined as at-risk persons by U.S. federal regulations) can expose issues that were not anticipated. This may lead to recognition that our methods had identified some serious problems. These are issues that we could address by bringing them to the attention of responsible authorities, or in some cases, by offering information to the persons involved. There is the realization of the limits of our power to implement change since we are neither clinicians nor official agents for change.

Environmental psychologists are not the only professionals who have faced the reality that their methods can uncover problems but not fix them. In my work involving the residents of shelters for homeless families, we found examples of misplacement of families, locating them at great distances from their relatives and friends (Rivlin, 1990). In addition, there were serious interruptions in their children's schooling and imposed school changes, sometimes multiple relocations. Residents also described complex bureaucratic steps and elaborate rule systems for acquiring shelter space. In some cases the regulations required that their teenage children be placed in foster care, in separate institutions, or with relatives. Parents complained that shelters dictated the way they had to deal with their children. They had to share the living environment with families who were strangers, and there was limited assistance in locating the affordable housing they desperately needed.

Their environmental autobiographies, past residential histories, elicited painful memories of important places that contrasted with their present living conditions. There was little that we could do to avoid this discomfort, other than omit these questions. What we gained from the reports was the recognition that these families had connections to people and places, facts that contradicted the prevailing stereotypes of homeless persons as disaffiliated and placeless.

We did point out these findings to the persons in charge of the shelter system as well as in a policy statement prepared for the mayor of New York City. Little was done to address these difficulties or change the conditions.

The open-ended nature of our studies, offering opportunities for respondents to address many issues, although enriching the findings, also contributed to the pain of telling their stories. This was true not only of my own research but also of the research of many students and colleagues. Research on elderly people identified lack of nearby public transportation, constraints on their ability to move out into the public domain, what Maldonado-Lugo

(1996) identified as limited "environmental extension." Cooper Marcus (1992) used environmental autobiographies with architecture and landscape architecture students and found that "these earliest childhood places are powerful images, resonating into adulthood via memories, dreams, even the creative work of some adult designers" (p. 89). Her research, documented in *House as a Mirror of the Self* (1996), considered the ways these memories have long-term effects on people's feelings and were reflected in the rich descriptions and drawings of houses, evoking the pain of nostalgia as well as some frightening memories, including those of domestic abuse.

In field studies, case studies, ethnographic research, and unobtrusive measures, which are frequently used in environmental studies, it is difficult to know, in advance, where conversations and observations are likely to go. Qualitative research is a means for opening up themes (see Denzin & Lincoln, 1994). This suggests the necessity to prepare, well in advance, how to handle such difficulties and to determine whether there is any information that the researcher can offer respondents.

For example, in a dissertation study on the quality of life of residents of a small city that had the reputation of being an affluent community, Gornitsky (1982) found a number of people who had questions concerning their health, low-income problems, and day-to-day needs. At the suggestion of her dissertation committee, she located material from the local city hall that covered many of these concerns. Before leaving she would point out to her interviewees the agencies that could assist them and the agencies' telephone numbers—a small effort that paid some attention to the problems.

This has become a frequent recommendation made to students entering research situations that may open up requests for help that go beyond their ability to provide information. Researchers should go into the field equipped with material on resources that could be useful to their respondents so that any serious difficulties that arise during interviews can be addressed. Where necessary, interviewers may need to move on to other questions or carefully terminate the interview.

Although the specific details of what may arise cannot be predicted, it is possible to anticipate some categories of problems that could be generated by the study, especially if there are pilot data that can offer some clues. There may be deep emotional reactions to questions or "secrets" divulged that could get respondents or others into difficulties, issues of sexual abuse, violation of rights, and the consequences of poverty (hunger, illness, loss of housing). All of these possibilities point out the need to properly train researchers and to accompany and monitor novices before they enter the field.

Observations unlock another Pandora's box. It is impossible to anticipate everything that is likely to occur in a setting, but as in the case of open-ended questioning, some preparation can be made. Consideration should be given to the distinction between being a researcher and a human. If a child under observation is about to get into a dangerous situation—for example, running in front of moving swings or falling into water—the role of concerned adult should take priority over that of researcher, even if this compromises the "scientific" quality of the research.

These precautions reflect respect for the dignity and humanity of people that takes priority over the demands for distance and neutrality that are common criteria for research. In field research there always is the possibility of triggering more than we intended to address. This requires careful planning, skill in handling the unexpected, and an open view of the role of researcher, qualities that are not always included in textbooks on methods and are rarely given attention in training students.

Another methodological issue that researchers in the field of environmental psychology have faced, over the years, relates to the variety of visual techniques used for both gathering research data and illustrating findings. With the use of photographs, slides, videotapes, and other filming techniques, including computer-based forms, rich image banks have been collected, raising a number of questions about accuracy and privacy.

In the same way that filming can be an essential component of research it also is subject to "distortion and manipulation" (Langford, 1997). Sensitivity to these possibilities is a prerequisite to their use. Although the image creates a powerful message, one that mimics "reality," it is not always an accurate descriptor of what occurred. The framing of films, which cuts off part of the context, is only one aspect of this problem. There is no way of knowing whether a situation has been "composed" by the researcher with people posed to create the image. We know this to be an issue in photojournalism (Langford, 1997), but it can also affect research.

There also is the consideration of informed permission. Filming of all sorts is a commonplace activity both in public and private spaces. Although we may ask people in their homes or workplaces, as a common courtesy, whether they mind being photographed, rarely are people in public asked for this permission. In fact, there is a view that anything in public is open for filming and that, if filming does not call attention to itself, it will be more effective in capturing "reality" (see Collier, in Harper, 1994, p. 405).

However, in research there are considerations that go beyond these simplistic distinctions. At the very least, there is the issue of the "unequal relationships" in using photography, the inequity between the persons or groups filmed and those who are doing the filming (Harper, 1994). The gender, class, and age differences that can separate photographer or video or movie specialist from the persons being filmed create an imbalance in both the images that are captured and the interpretations of them. All aspects of what is filmed may be subject to criticism by persons who appear in the images if they have the opportunity to review the material.

Under other conditions these material images may be open to future legal subpoenas. In reflecting on this possibility, whether addressing the public or private domain, the decision may be not to film. In some cases, the filming may be used for a political agenda of the researcher, who decides to run the risk of a lawsuit in the interests of larger issues. But there also are risks of having the images co-opted, misinterpreted, and used for other persons' political goals with or without the researcher's knowledge. These are part of the politics of research, which require careful consideration when methods are being selected.

All kinds of records can be subject to subpoena in court cases, but filmed records have particular risks for the researcher. This concern is raised not to discourage the use of any procedure but to urge reflection on whether the images are essential and how to deal with the storage and disposition of research materials both during a study and after its completion.

In his 1967 book on the use of photography in research, John Collier Jr. offered some cogent reasons why informed use of filming is essential. For many persons, having their photograph taken is not a threat and is something that can help a researcher gain "a foothold in a community" (Collier, 1967, p. 42). However for others, creating this image may violate a basic religious principle, a religious ceremony, or the Biblical injunction against the creation of "graven images." What is ordinary in many cultures may not be permissible in others. Researchers, as well as those doing documentaries, need to be sensitive to these possibilities.

There are precautions that can be followed to respect the people and places that are being filmed. First, is determining whether filming is a violation of the cultural values or religious practices of the people who are being studied. If filming is not permitted, the filming should not be done. In other cases, where privacy and anonymity are concerns, the researcher can avoid filming faces, focusing instead on what is happening. By capturing the overall activities, the group as a whole, some level of the privacy of individuals can be provided. Keeping at a distance from the participants and using the proper angle for making a filmed record can avoid many problems associated with privacy and anonymity. This does not mean that the filming should be hidden. Much like observations of people, entering the situation with an understanding of the religious and social values of a group, acclimating the participants to the researcher's presence, and assuring them that faces will not appear in filming, may be sufficient to create a sense of comfort with the experience.

The use of computers in research introduces another dimension of ethical concerns. Although many of the associated issues also apply to other methods, for example, informed consent, privacy, and anonymity, in the case of computer-based research, the physical distance between researcher and participant offers means for deception on both ends. The use of surveys administered on computers and detailed, qualitative interviews may give the respondent a false sense of anonymity and confidentiality. This is particularly the case for at-risk populations (e.g., minors, elderly people, and persons who are mentally or physically ill).

Studies underway by doctoral students at the City University of New York, one relating to the Web pages of elderly people (Heather Larson) and another concerning computer-based distance learning (Carol Oliver), are just two examples of the increasing use of computers to access data and involve participants. Sieber (1992) offers examples of the violation of confidentiality, "agreements with persons about what may be done with their data" (p. 52). One included an incident in which a computer hacker entered the researcher's files and accessed information that was used to blackmail some informants. "When storing data on computers to which others have access," Sieber suggests, "identifiers must be stored elsewhere, such as in a safe deposit box" (p. 53). Again, these issues go beyond the Institutional Review Board considerations and represent another category requiring special attention.

These concerns regarding the topics studied and methods used suggest the need for backup groups for all researchers, a committee of colleagues, perhaps including an ethicist, who can offer help in dealing with research dilemmas and crises. When the questions involve specialized knowledge, an appropriate additional member may be required. Students also need a place for bringing up these difficulties, a setting of trust and empathy—a dissertation seminar, a research crisis team, or an ombuds office—an in-place mechanism that enables an open discussion of the issues. In the university with which I am affiliated, among the responsibilities of the Ombuds Officer are ethical concerns, offering students, faculty, and staff a confidential setting in which to address issues related to work, conflicts with other persons, and problems in the conduct of research.

Researchers need to recognize that they cannot resolve all the problems by themselves. Where possible it is useful to set up studies in a team model with collaborators who understand the research and can provide the grounds for informed discussions. At times it may be important to invite an outsider to the meetings to offer the views of someone who is not directly involved in the research. But some means of discussing problems, even multiple ways, are essential to ethically appropriate studies.

TRUST, CONFIDENTIALITY, AND ANONYMITY

There are other risks in engaging in environmental research, indeed, in many forms of research. The conduct of ethically driven research requires that students be trained to deal with risks, and all members of a research team need to be made aware of them and how they can be addressed.

HOW DO WE CREATE AND RESPECT A SENSE OF TRUST?

Issues of trust constitute one area. We frequently speak of the establishment of empathy and rapport between the researcher and participants in the

research. In fact, it is a quality emphasized in training interviewers. Yet the creation of a sense of trust implies that the person can say things to the interviewer that will remain confidential, secret, private, and not to be disclosed, exactly the opposite of what is possible in doing research. This is a perplexing research dilemma that researchers need to recognize.

HOW DO WE KEEP PROMISES OF CONFIDENTIALITY AND ANONYMITY?

We can promise anonymity—that names and other identifying information will not be used in publications—without too many difficulties. But even when writing up a group story, specific quotes or examples run the risk of identifying individuals, groups of individuals, or their contexts. Confidentiality, withholding private or personal information revealed to the researcher, is more difficult, if not impossible, to fulfill since presenting results is a component of the research process. Whether in print or in presentations, communication of findings may compromise the agreement between the researcher and respondent.

This was a continuing concern for me in studies in shelters for homeless families (Rivlin, 1990). Among other research objectives, we were interested in the qualities of the places that residents liked and disliked, the conditions that made their lives comfortable or uncomfortable. We also interviewed members of the staff for their views on the setting. In writing up the reactions, we had to be extremely careful that the comments chosen to illustrate points, which are major substantiating data in qualitative research, would not jeopardize the status of respondents. This was a critical factor since part of our agreement with the cooperating shelter organizers and administrators was feedback on our findings. In describing interview results, we presented overall responses, and if individuals were quoted we provided a simple cover for them—omitting the borough in which they were located and any revealing information special to the individuals. By having the research group meet and review this material, we had some assurance that anonymity and confidentiality were respected. Although we wanted the nonprofit groups that were running the shelters to receive information that they could use in the creation and management of shelters, we had told them, prior to undertaking the research, that the anonymity and confidentiality of residents were primary responsibilities.

A study of the temporary and permanent moves of the university with which I am affiliated (Rivlin, Steinmayer, & Chapin, 2000) raised similar issues, in some ways even more pressing in this case because the research team members continued to be part of that school. We had to be extremely careful about presenting the interview results and the often revealing responses made to the open-ended questions in the surveys. We also had to be discreet about the off-handed comments people continued to make to us after distributing the forms—comments often preceded by "I'm telling you this because I know I can trust you." As members of the institution, we were seen in the elevators, hallways, and cafeteria. Knowing that we were concerned about issues related to the physical spaces and the impacts of the move, people persisted in offering their ideas and opinions, which included criticisms of the designers and specific members of the administration. In writing up the study and presenting our findings, we had to pay close attention to privacy and confidentiality and make every effort to prevent the disclosure of the identities and affiliations of people.

These privacy-related issues of confidentiality and anonymity are common in studies of institutions and workplaces where a "loose lip" can threaten the status of a participant or group of participants. This concern is not unique to environmental research. However, it is of particular importance when a respondent's views are not lost in a large group database and when feedback to the organization that could benefit from the information enters as an additional risk factor.

INFORMED CONSENT

The issue of informed consent is another complex concern, one that also is a U.S. government requirement for research. Even when researchers follow the guidelines and prepare explanations that are clear and free of jargon, it is impossible to know whether people are fully informed and whether they understand the ramifications of their participation. Few people can anticipate what it will be like to see their thoughts, their words, in publications. There is a question as to whether people agreeing to participate in research can judge the level of protection offered in promises of anonymity and confidentiality.

Researchers are obligated to use the signing of the consent form as an opportunity to address potential participants' questions and to clarify any points raised in the discussion of the research. It also is important for researchers to be sensitive to people's worries and identify their hesitations and doubts so that the "informed" component of the agreement is fully addressed.

PAYMENT TO RESPONDENTS

In many cases researchers offer payment to those participating in their research, something that must be carefully considered well before the consent form is presented. If the persons being recruited are poor, and in difficult circumstances, they may find the offer too good to turn down, even though they are otherwise reluctant to participate. There also is the concern of determining an appropriate payment for the pain, stress, and embarrassment that questioning on personal matters may generate. The economic "compensation" to the respondent, although perhaps relieving some of the guilt of the researcher, certainly does not cover the aftereffects of our questioning, which may stretch far into the future.

Whether to pay people is a very personal decision researchers must make in recruiting potential interviewees. Researchers are not likely to be helped by the rules laid out by professional organizations or the government. However, as long as the choice is made in a reflective manner, after consideration of the issues on both sides, and after consultation with other researchers, the decision must be left to the individual researcher. This is one of many issues that would benefit from discussion with a community of scholars/researchers. It also may be useful to review the situation with an ethicist in order to expose the underlying arguments.

The issue of payment has been a concern of mine for many years. My decision has been to treat the entry into people's living spaces to do interviews much as a visit to any person's home. In the case of homeless families in shelters, the research team members and I determined the ages of the children before the visit so that appropriate toys could be purchased as gifts. We also brought something for the adult, usually an item useful for their living space. These steps clearly helped to assuage the discomfort of intruding into their lives, but somewhere in my thinking, it was perceived as a courtesy that would be offered by any visitor. The issue of payment continues to be problematic throughout the conduct of any research.

TERMINATING THE EXPERIENCE

The institutional and shelter research in which I have been involved opened up another issue, especially in longitudinal and over-time studies that may not have a clear or limited ending point. It is perhaps best reflected in the study of a children's psychiatric hospital that Maxine Wolfe and I undertook over a six-and-a-half-year period (Rivlin & Wolfe, 1985). We began the research before the hospital opened, and followed the hiring and training of staff and the admission of patients, children, and adolescents. Along with members of our research team we then initiated a series of observation and interview studies in which we documented the patterns over time of space use by patients and staff, the different treatment policies, and the experiences of the people in the setting.

We were called the "space people" by the patients, and we moved about without being challenged. When there was a gap in our visits, we were welcomed on our return. Although we tried to be "invisible," clearly we were noticed on some level. Terminating this study was a difficult experience because the years of going there had led to a sense of connection to the place and people and concern for the patients. For residents, we had been an outlet to the outside, and their trust in us was reflected in what they told us in their interviews. We have no way of knowing whether we were missed in any way, but for some time after the study ended, the spaces that had been created in a participatory design project with members of the children's unit and the adolescent unit continued to function. Perhaps these rooms were tangible reminders of the "space people" and their presence in the hospital.

In a follow-up study of families in shelters who moved into apartments (Rivlin & Johnson, 1990), we found that some of the women looked forward to the regular visits. It was very difficult to end the research, and some participants continued to call us well after termination of the work. This was a powerful lesson on how a research experience can impact the different persons involved. It raised ethical issues of friendship and equity that influenced later studies that we undertook.

In the same ways that entering a setting and conducting the early phases of a study need to be planned, the termination of research requires advance attention. If the work continues over a period of time, there may be a need for some form of a departure ceremony, a means of thanking people who were involved in the work and defining an end to the research. It is a way of moving out of the researcher role and into a mode of seeing participants as human beings who assisted an effort in which they do not directly benefit. At the very least, a farewell letter could be used to communicate a similar message.

IMPLIED PROMISES

Associated with concerns about terminating a study are implied promises as well—an issue arising in longitudinal research but common to other studies. The eagerness to recruit participants in research can lead to emphasizing the value of the work and may carry with it expectations, albeit silent ones, that something will be done with respect to the problems that are identified. Researchers often are viewed as authority figures or "experts" in an area and are expected to have answers to troubling concerns. In fact, we are collectors of data that may raise important issues. Participatory research can offer something in exchange for cooperation.

Implied promises can be managed, to some degree, in the preparatory stages of the work. Most Institutional Review Boards are concerned about promising more than what can be accomplished, but the agencies and respondents cooperating with the researcher may continue to expect help. Although we have been careful in our research with homeless persons to make it clear that their willingness to participate in our research would not change their housing status (and the decision not to participate would not threaten their status), they requested ideas on how to find apartments or how to change their shelter locations. We had to emphasize that we did not have this information and that they should see the housing person in their shelter. But a common refrain was that they had tried this many times and had been placed on very long waiting lists. As researchers we were left with a distinct sense of our lack of power in dealing with the conditions that we were studying. It raised yet another issue to consider in preparing for a study and something that needed to be repeated to participants over the course of the work.

HANDLING RESEARCH PROTOCOLS

What should be done with the mass of research materials, some of them with identifying information about participants? In the use of computers, cited earlier, great care is required to thwart efforts to compromise privacy, anonymity, and confidentiality. Again, this issue is not unique to environmental research. However, in addition to piles of observation records, survey forms, and interview protocols, including oral and transcribed tapes, the visual tradition in the field has led to extensive photographic, slide, film, and videotape collections dealing with both the participants and places involved in research.

Institutional Review Boards require that the researcher detail how these materials will be handled to respect the rights of participants. It is easy to say, "they will be stored in locked files," but the long-term disposition is much more complex. It requires anticipating what may happen in the years to come. More than that, it requires an honest consideration of what must be kept and what can be destroyed, a delicate decision that many researchers are loathe to make. A five-year rule is useful to follow. What is stored beyond this period is unlikely to be needed in the future and can be safely put to rest, unless, of course, a follow-up study is planned.

Many environmental researchers maintain a permanent file of photographs, slides, videos, and movies documenting places and people. This may not be a problem if the images do not distinguish faces. This is best judged by a research team or a panel of colleagues who are mindful of the need to respect the privacy and anonymity of the persons involved. Requesting permission of people to be filmed or interviewed is not always sufficient protection because they may not be able to anticipate the future applications of the research and give an "informed consent." They may not understand the consequences of sharing their images or words with a wide audience, whether in print or in presentations.

Researchers need to become skilled communicators in the description of their work and to explain carefully to the persons to be interviewed all of the ways that the research protocols will be used.

This is a complex task that could benefit from studies of the ways the needed information can be described.

CONCERN FOR RESEARCH ASSISTANTS AND EMPLOYEES

There are a number of issues that arise when looking at the conduct of research from the perspective of research assistants and other people hired to help in the work. One aspect relates to the training of the staff—whether they are prepared sufficiently to assume the responsibilities of a researcher. It is useful to recognize that the training of researchers is an ongoing process in which careful supervision and regular discussion of problems is an integral component of the work.

It also is important to assign work in a reasonable manner. There are many research supervisors who set out work schedules that ignore the physical and emotional drain on the observers and interviewers. Punch (1986) describes "the stress, the deep personal involvement, the role-conflicts, the physical and mental effort, the drudgery and discomfort (and even danger), and the time-consuming nature of observational studies for the researcher" (p. 16). Research assistants may be sent to areas that the principal investigators would be loath to go to themselves. This can be particularly threatening when people are sent alone rather than in groups or pairs.

Punch (1986) also criticizes the tendency of researchers to eliminate descriptions of difficulties they had in doing the research when preparing articles, presentations, or books. It is as though everything went along smoothly with no problems—a false description of the way most studies proceed. As a result, new researchers cannot learn from the problems faced by others, and they may interpret the difficulties they find as unique to their own studies, blaming themselves for the obstacles.

Another violation of the rights of research assistants is the failure of the principal investigator to give them credit in presenting or writing up the study. This was an ethical issue cited by respondents to the Chapin, Choriki, and Wolfe (1990), questionnaires mentioned earlier. In addition, people reported having sections of their papers used by faculty as their own writing or having research ideas taken by mentors. Plagiarism and appropriation of ideas is a continuing problem in academia, as well as in other areas.

There are some venues for dealing with these issues—for example through ombudspersons—but the inequality in power between principal investigator and worker may constrain the use of this means of protest. There also is the reality of whether the research assistants know of this misuse of their work.

In the same way that Institutional Review Boards supervise adherence to the government rules for the treatment of "human subjects," they also could have a broader mandate, that of addressing the ethical and value-laden dimensions of research. This function would not be in the interests of a single code or a narrow moral monitor. Rather, it would require the formation of a group that reminds its constituents of the qualities of good research and practice and how it can be compromised by abuses of people's rights, including the rights of those engaged in gathering the data.

POLITICS AND PERSONAL ORIENTATIONS IN RESEARCH AND PRACTICE

From discussions at the meetings of environmental organizations, it is clear that there are some professionals within the environmental psychology/ environment and behavior fields who are strongly opposed to using research to make political statements. They believe that scholars and researchers should produce scientifically verifiable data and have no business in generating political tracts or emphasizing political concerns. While respecting their rights to these positions, I find this stance to be impossible to follow; in some ways it is a misconception for persons who believe they can carry it off.

All research has some political dimensions, from the selection of the topics for study to the research approach, analysis of data, and preparation of reports, presentations, and publications. This is especially true in environmental psychology, where the topics studied resound with people's lives. Although we can question having a single political agenda guide all the research in a field, at the very least there should be some recognition of the political issues embedded in the work. In dealing with the implications of the work, the researcher should extract the information that is useful to those dealing with the problems. Even the most theoretical and structured work in environmental psychology can yield ideas of value to practice. By acknowledging that research is laden with values and political

positions, we can strengthen the work and open it up to discussion. Denying or ignoring this can only lead to false impressions and narrow interpretations of the findings.

A question was raised by one of the editors of this volume, Arza Churchman, concerning the interpretation or misinterpretation of our findings by politicians and policy makers. If researchers, hoping to influence policy, communicate their findings to policy makers, "are we responsible for the way in which our research is used?" (A. Churchman, personal communication, January 23, 2001). This is an important issue, one that many have faced.

There is no way that a researcher can guarantee that a study will be used in an accurate manner, however clearly the study is written. In the case of findings that will be used by political and social agencies, it is useful to present the report in person, explaining the results and answering questions about the work. But a research report or published paper has its own momentum, and it is impossible to control how people, policy makers included, will interpret publications and use them for their own political purposes.

When asked to prepare a policy statement on homelessness for an incoming mayor of New York City I worked out a detailed set of strategies that were needed, drawing on the implications of my own research and that of others. Based on this mayor's previous history, I had expected that the city agencies would make some constructive changes in dealing with this serious urban problem. Little or nothing was done during this administration. The report was ignored.

Others have had their work misinterpreted or reinterpreted to meet the agendas of politicians and policy makers. Can we be held responsible? If the writing or presentations are vague and subject to misinterpretation we can take some blame. But if efforts are made toward sharpness and clarity in presenting findings, there is little that we can do other than meet and discuss these realities and work directly with groups or agencies in order to communicate our messages accurately.

A FINAL VIEW: WHAT ARE THE ETHICAL IMPERATIVES?

A range of problems have emerged from this voyage through the ethical imperatives of environmental psychology—the issues that need attention, as much as any other step, in the preparation of research. In fact, consideration of ethical concerns is a continuing task throughout the research process and includes the presentation and publication stage.

Beneath the topics that have been addressed lie some principles of the treatment of people: their right to dignity; the obligation to give them clear descriptions about their participation in research, including the emotional and physical risks they may face in the present and future; and information about services that could help with problems that surface during questioning. We need to make sure that persons involved in our work, especially students, receive mentoring and support when facing the realities of the research experiences. But there are other forms of assistance that are needed.

Recently, I chaired a workshop on ethics at a conference devoted to qualitative research. After a brief presentation of some of the issues, the session was opened up for discussion. I suggested that people draw on their own experiences and offer examples that we could address. An impressive array of topics emerged, many of them included in this paper. Most critical was the expression that there had been no place to bring these concerns; they lacked an arena that would not jeopardize their situations.

This serious gap emphasizes the need for some kind of structure for dealing with ethical concerns. The issues people confront are extremely difficult to resolve as individuals and demand a forum for discussion. If I learned anything from that workshop, it was the prevalence of these problems across researchers and their desire to have some assistance in addressing them. Along with the sophisticated technological equipment available today, we also need some down-to-earth contacts and sharing. Not all of our concerns can be addressed by lists of ethical rules and principles, especially in the case of field research and qualitative methods. Professional organizations, workplaces, and universities can truly move into a new age of research by offering a context for safe, open discussion of these troubling and persisting issues.

REFERENCES

Bechtel, R. B. (1997). *Environment & behavior: An introduction.* Thousand Oaks, CA: Sage.

Bell, P. A., Greene, T. C., Fisher, J. D., & Baum, A. (2001). *Environmental psychology* (5th ed.). Fort Worth, TX: Harcourt College Publishers.

Chapin, D., Choriki, D., & Wolfe, M. (1990, July). Ought to do and what to do? A comparison of personal ethical statements with professional ethical codes [Abstract]. Proceedings of the 11th *biennial conference of the International Association for the Study of People and Their Physical Surroundings* (Vol. 1, pp. 54–55), Ankara, Turkey.

Collier, J., Jr. (1967). *Visual anthropology: Photography as a research method.* New York: Holt, Rinehart and Winston.

Cooper Marcus, C. (1992). Environmental memories. In I. Altman & S. M. Low (Eds.), *Place attachment* (pp. 87–112). New York: Plenum Press.

Cooper Marcus, C. (1996). *House as mirror of the self: Exploring the deeper meaning of home.* Berkeley, CA: Conari Press.

Denzin, N. K., & Lincoln, Y. S. (1994). *Handbook of qualitative research.* Thousand Oaks, CA: Sage.

Gornitsky, L. B. (1982). *Quality of life.* Unpublished doctoral dissertation, City University of New York Graduate School.

Harper, D. (1994). On the authority of the image: Visual methods at the crossroads. In N. K. Denzin & Y. S. Lincoln (Eds.), *Handbook of qualitative research* (pp. 403–412). Thousand Oaks, CA: Sage.

Kant, I. (1965). Foundations of the metaphysics of morals. In O. A. Johnson (Ed.), *Ethics: Selections from classical and contemporary writers* (pp. 181–201). New York: Holt, Rinehart and Winston.

Langford, M. (1997). *Story of photography* (2nd ed.). Oxford, England: Focal Press.

Lewin, K. (1948). *Resolving social conflicts.* New York: Harper & Row.

Maldonado-Lugo, R. (1996). *Environmental extension: A concept emerging from the importance of mass transportation in the lives of elderly New Yorkers.* Unpublished doctoral dissertation, City University of New York.

Merriam-Webster's collegiate dictionary. (10th ed.). (1996). Springfield, MA: Merriam-Webster.

Proshansky, H. M. (1987). The field of environmental psychology: Securing its future. In D. Stokols & I. Altman (Eds.), *Handbook of environmental psychology* (Vol. 2, pp. 1467–1488). New York: Wiley.

Punch, M. (1986). *The politics and ethics of fieldwork.* Sage University Paper Series on Qualitative Research Methods (Vol. 3). Beverly Hills, CA: Sage.

Rivlin, L. G. (1990). The significance of home and homelessness. *Marriage and Family Review, 15*(1/2), 39–56.

Rivlin, L. G., & Johnson, L. (1990, August). *The ecology of homelessness.* Paper presented at the annual convention of the American Psychological Association, Miniconvention on the struggle for housing: Continuities among the housed and homeless people, Boston.

Rivlin, L. G., Steinmayer, K. M., & Chapin, D. (2000, August). *Moving places: Analysis of research on an urban university's relocation.* Poster session presented at the annual meeting of the American Psychological Association, Washington, DC.

Rivlin, L. G., & Wolfe, M. (1985). *Institutional settings in children's lives.* New York: Wiley.

Schmidt, J. (1999). *The normative/ethical aspects of GIS in planning.* Unpublished manuscript, Princeton University, Princeton, NJ.

Sieber, J. E. (1992). *Planning ethically responsible research.* Newbury Park, CA: Sage.

CHAPTER 3

Environmental Psychology:
From Spatial-Physical Environment
to Sustainable Development

MIRILIA BONNES and MARINO BONAIUTO

THE EMERGING ENVIRONMENTAL PSYCHOLOGY AS A PSYCHOLOGY OF THE SPATIAL-PHYSICAL ENVIRONMENT

"ENVIRONMENTAL PSYCHOLOGY CAN only be understood and defined in the context of the environmental sciences in general: the large body of study concerned with the consequences of man's manipulation of his environment, [it] deals with the man-ordered and defined environment; [environmental sciences] grow out of pressing social problems; they are multidisciplinary in nature and include the study of man as an integral part of every problem. In short, the environmental sciences are concerned with human problems in relation to an environment of which man is both victim and conqueror" (p. 5). With these words Proshansky, Ittelson, and Rivlin (1970) presented the emerging field of environmental psychology in their first published volume, titled *Environmental Psychology: Man and His Physical Setting*. In the same year and with the same aim of introducing the new field of environmental psychology, other authors made their first systematic presentations of this new emerging discipline (see Craik, 1970; Wohlwill, 1970).

The environmental psychology that was formed during the 1950s and 1960s focused research attention on the physical features of the environment where human behavior occurs. The aim was to gain a better understanding of the relationship between human behavior and the physical environment. This was considered as primary, directly perceptible through the sensory organs and defined and considered in spatial and physical terms, whether built or natural, on a small or large scale (Craik, 1970).

In considering the relationship between behavior and the physical environment, two main directions were also pointed out at that time (Craik, 1970; Stokols, 1978; Wohlwill, 1970). On the one hand, when the built (architectural, technological, and engineering) physical environment was considered, human behavior was mainly conceived as the "result" of the physical environment; thus, the more "reactive forms" of psychological processes were studied such as, according to Stokols (1978), the "evaluative" and "responsive" ones. On the other hand, when the natural environment was considered, human behavior was mainly conceived as a "cause" of this physical environment; thus, the more "active forms" of psychological processes were studied, such as the "interpretative" and "operative" ones. At the same time the distinction between cognitive and behavioral emphases of these studies was also pointed out (Holahan, 1986; Stokols, 1978).

Various converging factors originating inside, around, and outside the psychological field contributed to the emergence and development of environmental psychology. The origin and the past and present development of this new area of psychological inquiry can only be understood by looking at all these factors to outline a disciplinary identity extending beyond the generic label of "applied psychology" (see Bonnes & Secchiaroli, 1995; A. Rapoport, 2000; Sommer, 1987).

Interests within and around Psychology

Psychology as a science has been traditionally interested in environment behavior interactions in a very general way. However, the basic interest of this new field of psychological inquiry rested on psychology's concomitant discovery of the importance of the spatial-physical dimension of the environment as constituting part of human actions and experience at the intrapersonal, interpersonal, group, intergroup, and societal levels (see Stokols & Altman, 1987a, 1987b). Thus, attention was first given to the spatial-physical property of the surroundings where human behavior takes place. At the same time the importance was often stressed of considering it not in a "molecular" but in a "molar" sense (Craik, 1970; Ittelson, 1973). However, not by chance, Hall (1966) defined this spatial-physical property as "the hidden dimension" since its influence and relevance for human psychological processes often tends to remain outside individual and collective awareness.

As Proshansky and Fabian (1986) observed,

> The objective physical world and its properties has consequences on the behaviour and experience of the person quite often without his "awareness.". . . Under these circumstances, the individual can neither identify nor verbalise these influences, and indeed it is only by objective analysis of the "external observer" that this influence of the physical environment on the person's behaviour and experience can be determined. . . . However, the influence of the physical settings on the behaviour and experience of the person that "bypass" awareness and interpretation by the individual cannot and should not be ignored. (p. 25)

It is important to note that this discovery in the field of psychology was due to some pioneering studies. They were characterized by an incidental interest in those aspects mainly developed as part of other research aims. These include the human factors in work performance (Mayo, 1933), the development of social influence networks (Festinger, Shachter, &

Back, 1950) and the analysis of the "stream" of human behavior in natural settings (Barker, 1960). All of these studies were guided by a common general methodological interest in studying human behavior in its natural setting by using the methodology of the field experiment (Festinger et al., 1950; Mayo, 1933) or of nonobtrusive observation in natural settings, as in the ecological psychology of Barker (1960, 1968) and others. In all of these cases the crucial importance of the specific features of the physical surrounding was at the core of the research findings, although typically as part of other unexpected results.

However, other pioneering psychologists also played a crucial role since they were open to receive and develop ideas coming from disciplinary areas that bordered on psychology and were traditionally interested in studying behavior in natural contexts. These areas included cultural anthropology about human and animal proxemics (Hall, 1966), animal ethology (e.g., Ardrey, 1966), and microsociology (e.g., Goffman, 1959). Also, they were generally opposed to the main experimental and laboratory-based method used for psychological research and consequently were more willing to use other methodologies such as field experiments and observations, both natural or systematic. Barker's (1968) early studies on behavior settings in the area of ecological psychology and Sommer's (1959, 1969) and Altman's (1975) studies on personal space and social behavior remain as cornerstones of the early environmental psychology.

As noted by Canter (1986), in order to be concerned with the spatial-physical environment, psychology had to get out from its habitual place, that is, the research laboratory, which was the traditional domain of psychological research but, by definition, a nonenvironment.

In general, enthusiasm over the emergence of this new field of inquiry was the result of psychologists' uncertainty over or dissatisfaction with the *social relevance* of their research and the *ecological validity* of results obtained in the laboratory and with the consequent search for a "real world psychology" (e.g., Proshansky, 1976). This frequent dissatisfaction can be traced to the various forms of ecological demand specifically raised since the 1940s and 1950s by various authors and psychological schools (i.e., from Lewin and Brunswick onwards; see Bonnes & Secchiaroli, 1995). This trend later developed into what has been called "contextualism" or the "contextual revolution" (Altman & Rogoff, 1987; Little, 1987;

Sarbin, 1977; Stokols, 1987), which arose in most fields of psychology during the 1970s and 1980s and which in many ways is still active today. This revolution is certainly at the core of the development of environmental psychology, particularly in its transactional-contextual approach, which has been progressively accepted since the beginning (Altman & Rogoff, 1987; Ittelson, 1973; Saegert & Winkel, 1990; Stokols, 1978, 1987; Wapner, 1987; Wapner & Demick, 2000).

Initially, two main theoretical psychological traditions promoted this new awareness of the crucial effect physical features of the everyday environment have on human behavior and experience (see Bonnes & Secchiaroli, 1995). The first theoretical tradition refers to the psychology of perception as developed in the more ecologically oriented perspectives of the *new look* school, Brunswik's (1943, 1957) "lens model," the transactional school of the Princeton group (Ittelson, 1973; Kilpatrick, 1961), and Gibson's (1950, 1966) "ecological approach" to perception. The second tradition is based on the social psychology approach evolved through the pioneering work of authors such as Lewin (1944, 1951), Tolman (1948), Barker (1968), and Bronfenbrenner (1979).

The first tradition is more associated with a "molecular" approach to the spatial-physical environment. It places specific attention on the discrete sensory-perceptual features of the environment, considered to have a direct correspondence at the sensory-perceptual level.

The second tradition pursues a more "holistic" or "molar" perspective (e.g., Altman, 1975; Ittelson, 1973), which developed in the "transactional-contextual" approach to the person environment relationship as systematically outlined by many authors in the first handbook devoted to the field (e.g., Altman & Rogoff, 1987; Stokols, 1987; Wapner, 1987). This approach is still considered the main founding theoretical perspective for environmental psychology (e.g., Saegert & Winkel, 1990; Wapner & Demick, 2000; Werner & Altman, 2000). The main characteristics of this approach can be synthesized as follows (e.g., Saegert & Winkel, 1990, among others):

1. The person-in-environment provides the unit of analysis.
2. Both person and environment dynamically define and transform each other over time as aspects of a unitary whole.

3. Stability and change coexist continuously.
4. The direction of change is emergent, not pre-established.
5. The changes that occur at one level affect the other levels, creating new person environment configurations.

Basically, such a view goes beyond the previous distinction between reactive versus active and cognitive versus behavioral forms of psychological processes, moving toward a more unified vision of them. However, this transactional-contextual approach often remained an ideal program, being difficult to be realized in the common research praxis.

Following this tension between wide theoretical intentions on one side and empirical and methodological practices on the other, the physical environment or *physical setting* has been increasingly considered as a sociophysical environment with a growing emphasis on the social aspects of both the physical environment considered and the psychological processes involved (Bonaiuto & Bonnes, 2000; Bonnes & Secchiaroli, 1995; Evans & Saegert, 2000; Stokols, 1978; Stokols & Altman, 1987b; Wicker, 1987).

In this perspective, the *place* construct, with related environmental-psychological processes, became a central sociophysical unit of analysis, used to complement the original physical setting. It was conceived as an experiential unit of the geographical environment (Russell & Ward, 1982) with both an individual and a collective dimension consisting of (1) spatial-physical properties, (2) activities, and (3) cognitive and evaluative experiences or "meanings" (e.g., Relph, 1976; A. Rapoport, 1982) related to both these activities and physical properties (Bonnes & Secchiaroli, 1995; Canter, 1977, 1986; Russell & Ward, 1982). Thus, "behaviour that occurs in one place, would be out of place elsewhere. This place specificity of behaviour is the fundamental fact of environmental psychology" (Russell & Ward, 1982, p. 652); "the central postulate is that people always situate their actions in a specific place and that the nature of the place, so specified, is an important ingredient in understanding human action and experience" (Canter, 1986, p. 8).

However, through this sociophysical unit of analysis, the environment is often viewed as mainly: (1) spatially and temporally limited and thus very localized, (2) tending to be primarily static except for human interventions such as the actions of various planners or users of the environment, and (3) able to influence (and also be influenced by) individual behavior and experience outside of personal awareness.

This place-specific perspective also developed into other more systemic conceptions, such as the "system of settings" or the "multi-place" or "inter-place" perspective (Bonnes, Mannetti, Secchiaroli, & Tanucci, 1990; A. Rapoport, 1990, 2000). The aim was to overcome the often too narrow intrasetting or intraplace perspective and to move toward a more system-oriented perspective. Emphasis was placed on the prevalent multiplace nature of any individual environmental or place experience and thus on the importance of looking at the interplace system of activities in order to fully understand one place's activities, evaluations, and characteristics (Bonaiuto & Bonnes, 1996, 2001; Bonaiuto, Bonnes, & Continisio, in press; Bonnes et al., 1990).

THE IMPORTANCE OF EXTERNAL FACTORS

The major disciplinary areas outside of psychology involved in these early stages of environmental psychology were architecture and engineering for the built or technological environment and geography for the natural environment. The influence of the bioecological field of the natural sciences was also present, although indirectly through the mediation of the field of human geography (see Bonnes & Secchiaroli, 1995; Sommer, 1987; Whyte, 1984).

In architecture, those who were dissatisfied with an egocentric approach to design desired to move toward a user-centered design and from design and planning of "product" to that of "processes" (e.g., Moore, 1987; Zeisel, 1981). In engineering, technology, and ergonomics, the growing concern with the human use dimension of design technologies moved in the same direction (e.g., Norman, 1988). For both fields the contribution of environmental psychology was seen as necessary in all three main design phases, namely, ideation, specification, and appraisal/evaluation (Canter & Lee, 1974).

Because of the influence of all of these factors, environmental psychology has developed greatly during the last 30 years, mainly along the following lines:

1. Attention to the spatial-physical characteristics of the environment where behavior take place
2. Variety of research methods adopted

3. Orientation toward problems with clear social relevance
4. Interdisciplinary orientation of research (see Bonnes & Secchiaroli, 1995, p. 59–60)

CHANGES IN THE HUMAN PHYSICAL ENVIRONMENT AND THE ECOLOGICAL REVOLUTION

During the past 30 years, parallel to the initial development of environmental psychology, important scientific, technological, and cultural changes took place in the human physical environment. Two main revolutionary changes should be noted: (1) the "ecological revolution" originating in the natural sciences and (2) the "telecommunication revolution" associated with the development of new information and communications technology and the advent of the information society (e.g., Castells, 1996; di Castri, 1998). Both imposed great changes on today's physical environment and consequently on the nature of environment behavior problems. For brevity's sake, we will focus only on the impact of the first change here. The impact of the second one will be treated in some of the other chapters of this handbook.

FROM *NATURAL ECOLOGY* TO *FULL ECOLOGY*

As Bechtel (1997) pointed out, during the last century a pervasive cultural and scientific revolution has taken place primarily in the natural sciences through the new science of ecology, defined as "the science that studies life in its environment" (Giacomini, 1983). In particular, in the second half of the twentieth century, the biological sciences started to impose an ecological revolution on all of the other environmental sciences. This not only included the other natural sciences, such as physics and chemistry, but also the human, social, and behavioral sciences (di Castri, 1981, 2000; di Castri, Barker, & Hadley, 1984; Giacomini, 1983; Odum, 1953). This revolution led to great advances during the last 30 years, thanks also to various United Nations and international initiatives and programs concerning the human environment. Among these, the United Nations Rio de Janeiro Conference on Environment and Development (1992) is considered the cornerstone.

This ecological revolution is based on the *ecosystem* as the unit of analysis. It claims a holistic, systemic, and dynamically integrated perspective in conceiving the relations of any living being—from the most elementary to the most complex living organisms—with its physical environment, both biotic and abiotic. The same perspective claims the need to expand the spatial and the temporal scale of any phenomenon according to a process perspective, which goes from the most elementary, specific, and local to the most complex, general, and spatially and temporally broad processes, such as global or biosphere processes. At the same time it stresses the necessary interdependence of these local and global processes.

However, two major perspectives should be distinguished in this ecological revolution since they have different ways of viewing the relationship between the natural and the human environment in general and thus environment-human behavior problems in particular. These perspectives can be called "natural ecology" or "partial ecology" on the one hand and "full ecology" on the other (Bonnes, 1998).

Natural or partial ecology is relevant primarily in the natural sciences. It requires collaboration and integration of knowledge among the different natural sciences. It fosters collaboration/integration in the biological sciences (for the biotic aspects) and the physical and chemical sciences (for the abiotic aspects) at various levels of life complexity, from the most elementary plants to the most complex animals. According to this natural or partial ecology, human beings and particularly their behaviors/actions, activities, and experiences affecting the biotic and abiotic processes/aspects of the considered ecosystems tend to remain apart from bioecological processes, considered exclusively as natural processes. Human activities and behaviors are identified in a very generic sense as "human factor" or "human impact." In this sense, they are only considered as a source of physical-chemical transformations of the biotic and abiotic components of ecosystems. Thus, they are mainly seen as altering, perturbing, and destroying the nature-based equilibrium of any natural ecosystem.

The full ecology perspective at the core of the early developments of the ecological revolution contrasts with the previous one (di Castri, 1981, 2000; Giacomini, 1983). In fact, this perspective considers human beings not only as a component, as the human factor, of existing ecosystems but as the major force or organizing principle of the physical-biological features of every ecosystem or of every

"human use system" (di Castri, Hadley, & Dalmanian, 1981; di Castri et al., 1984). Therefore, this view advocates always considering the human dimension—in its psychological, social, cultural, economic, and historical aspects—as a central aspect of every ecosystem (Bonnes, 1984, 1987, 1991, 1993; di Castri et al., 1984). In particular, to emphasize this important change in perspective, at the end of the 1970s the human use-system construct was proposed as a new unit of analysis for the ecological sciences, conceived as a development of the traditional concept of the ecosystem (di Castri et al., 1981). It was specified that this new unit of analysis should be considered to have three major dimensions. Besides the two traditional dimensions typical of the natural sciences, that is, the space and time dimensions, a third dimension was proposed, environmental perception. This was considered just as important as the first two and typically representative of the human dimension of each physical-biological or environmental system.

THE FULL ECOLOGY ENVIRONMENT: NATURAL PROCESSES, RESOURCES, BIODIVERSITY, AND SUSTAINABILITY

The growing importance of this full ecology perspective in the environmental sciences gave impetus to multidisciplinary collaboration in the ecological natural sciences specifically in the direction of the social and human sciences, which also include environmental psychology. At the same time, it brought about important conceptual and methodological changes in environment-human behavior studies and in environmental psychology by focusing research attention on the physical environment as considered by the full ecology perspective.

In this case, the environment primarily consists of biophysical components of *natural processes* (i.e., bioecological processes) and thus is typically characterized more in a dynamic than in a static sense. Thus, any kind of environment is primarily defined and considered through its bioecological processes of exchange and interdependence of its various parts or elements. These processes have spatial and temporal continuity with all levels of the ecosystems considered, from the most local, circumscribed, and short-term to the most general and long-term levels, such as the global ecosystem, involving the entire biosphere.

Further, the physical characteristics of this environment with particular reference to their physical and biological processes are considered primarily as *resources* for the life forms, from the most circumscribed to the most comprehensive, present in the various ecosystems. Therefore, the physical characteristics of this environment, as life resources of ecosystems, are both "natural" and "common," or collective resources for all life forms existing there; thus, they are a common good. The extent to which these common natural resources are able to maintain or renew themselves to support the life forms of specific ecosystems over time creates *sustainability* in the use of these resources and in the entire ecosystem.

However, these common natural resources tend to be characterized by a circular process of existence, use, and availability. On one side, these resources are available for the needs of the various living beings belonging to the same ecosystem. On the other, they are accessible and utilizable depending on the specific modalities of use adopted by other individuals or categories of living beings—nonhuman and human—also interested in them. The more these resources are limited or scarce, or in any case hardly or not at all renewable, the more this process becomes evident (e.g., G. Hardin, 1968; Meadows, Meadows, Randers, & Behrens, 1972). Therefore, under the full ecology perspective, every use activity of the environmental resources inevitably assumes a social dimension because the use activity of each individual influences the possibilities of use allowed to other life forms equally dependent on the same resources.

At the same time, the ecological perspective shows the existence and importance of *biodiversity*, that is, having a variety of life forms, in every ecosystem to ensure its vitality and sustainability over time (e.g., Barbarbault, 1995). Therefore, on one side there are needs regarding use of resources in correspondence with the diversity of life forms existing in a particular ecosystem (also including the human species). On the other side, there is a tendency toward conflict created by the mutual use of the same resources by different species present in the ecosystem or by members of the same species.

Natural ecology studies the conflicts among the various nonhuman living species (animals and plants) and simply assumes and emphasizes, in a very generic sense, the conflict existing between these nonhuman species and humanity as a whole. Full ecology is more concerned with the interspecies conflicts that take place between humans and various nonhuman species (animals and plants) and tries to gain an articulated vision of them.

Social and human sciences traditionally investigate intrahuman conflicts. Greater attention is given to the level of the conflicts between groups and human collectivities in the social sciences and to the intragroup level and the intraindividual level in the psychological sciences. Social psychology in particular—defined as an interface disciplinary area between the individual and the collective or social level—is primarily interested in exploring the dynamics and the conflicts between the individual and the collective level (Bonnes, 1999; Moscovici, 1984; Moscovici & Doise, 1992).

In every ecosystem, when these various conflicts are considered in the perspective of natural or partial ecology, that is, only as a function of physical-chemical-biological processes, they are resolved or integrated according to physical-biological laws. Following these laws, the necessary interdependencies are established between the various uses to guarantee the sustainability, or integrated functioning over time, of the entire ecosystem, the so-called harmony of nature.

The composition of these inevitable conflicts appears more problematic within the full ecology perspective because of the role played by human use systems in ecosystems. In this case, given the centrality attributed to human activities and to related environmental perceptions about common natural resources, a peculiarity can be recognized in the human use of natural resources compared to that of all other life forms of the same ecosystems.

In the case of human uses, natural resources tend to lose their simple connotation of physical-biological resource, typical of partial or natural ecology, and take on specific social-perceptual connotations. Not by chance, these social-perceptual or environmental-perceptual aspects were defined by some schools of human ecology as "the intangibles" of ecosystems (Boyden, Millar, Newcomb, & O'Neill, 1981), that is, physically and sensorially intangible aspects but crucial components of every ecosystem.

Psychology considers these social-perceptual and symbolic systems of representations or meanings as basic processes, both at the individual level in a social-psychological sense and at the collective-shared level in a sociocultural sense (Bonnes, 1999; Bruner, 1990; Moscovici, 1984). Within a full ecology perspective, the mediation of these social-perceptual systems is responsible for constructing the interdependencies or integration necessary for reconciling the often incompatible needs and expectations of use of the various life forms existing in each ecosystem.

THE UNITED NATIONS MANDATE FOR SUSTAINABLE DEVELOPMENT

During the 1960s, increasing preoccupation was also expressed by full ecology concerning the progressive and excessive voracity of the needs of human uses/activities compared to those of other living species and the physical and biological limits of every ecosystem including the global biosphere (e.g., Carson, 1962; Meadows et al., 1972). This led to the emergence of the environmental movement. At first it was associated with natural ecology and tended to dramatize the changes induced in ecosystems by human activities, emphasizing the aforementioned conflict between the needs of the nonhuman species on one hand and those of human activities on the other (di Castri, 2000). With increasing preoccupation, attention was called to several transformation processes taking place throughout the entire biosphere that were posing a potential threat for the survival of life on the planet. These processes, identified as "global changes," include the greenhouse effect with its various related climactic changes, the loss of biodiversity, the depletion of the ozone layer, the scarcity and pollution of fresh water, and so forth (Malone & Roederer, 1985).

Because of this increasing environmental awareness, the United Nations launched various initiatives to promote and support the full ecology approach rather than the partial or natural ecology approach. In 1972, the first United Nations Conference on the Human Environment was organized in Stockholm. Then, specific international programs and collaborations were promoted such as the United Nations Environmental Program (UNEP), Man and Biosphere (MAB) program, and Habitat program, with the support of various United Nations organizations. These included the United Nations Educational, Scientific, and Cultural Organization (UNESCO), World Health Organization (WHO), Food and Agriculture Organization (FAO), and others. Important stages in this effort should be noted: (1) the launching of the MAB Program in 1971 by the UNESCO Division of Ecological Sciences as a "progamme of applied research on the interactions between man and his environment, with the aim of providing scientific knowledge and trained personnel to manage natural resources in a rational and sustained manner"

(di Castri et al., 1984, Vol. 1, p. 3; this program is still very active today; UNESCO, 2001) and (2) the publication of the Brundtland World Commission on Environment and Development—with the significant title of "Our common future"—systematizing the concept of sustainable development and formally proposing it as "development that meets the needs of the present without compromising the ability of future generations to meet their own needs" (World Commission on Environment and Development, 1987, p. 43). The dynamic perspective of the sustainable development concept was also stressed. It was defined as "not a fixed state of harmony, but rather processes of change in which the exploitation of resources, the direction of investments, the orientation of technological development and institutional changes are made consistent with future as well as present needs" (p. 9).

At the Rio de Janeiro conference of 1992, this concept/program was then confirmed and assumed by the United Nations as a general program on the human environment for the next millennium through the related Plan of Action of Agenda 21; its continuity was subsequently confirmed over the years by various organizations and initiatives of the United Nations.

The concept of sustainable development has been widely discussed and also specifically criticized as being fuzzy or too vague (e.g., di Castri, 1995; Oldeman, 1995). However, it should be considered as specifically proposed by the United Nations to move toward the full ecology perspective. It is a typical contradictory or internally conflicting concept/program. In fact, sustainable development primarily proposes the integration or conciliation of the various conflicts of both the world of nature and the human world by trying to find new forms of interdependence between them. It includes the awareness of the state of continuous change that always characterizes these worlds within the local-global dimension and along the dyachronic (i.e., intergenerational) as well as the synchronic (i.e., intragenerational) perspectives (di Castri, 1995).

According to both classical and more recent definitions of sustainable development, requests for human activity are seen as primarily pushed by the continuous desire for better conditions of life or for development in an economic, social, and cultural sense (e.g., di Castri, 1995). Therefore, attention is placed, on the one hand, on human requests to satisfy economic activities and to increase the quantity of economic resources available for human development and other activities such as social and cultural ones—not typically economic and even contrasting with them. But, on the other hand, these human requests should be compatible with the need for maintenance and development over time of both natural resources and other life forms depending on the same resources. The general intention is to achieve and to renew over time the integration or interdependence of human and nonhuman production and use of these various natural, economic, social, and cultural resources. The final goal is to maintain and develop the overall individual and collective vitality of various ecosystems, including the global biosphere, to ensure sustainability and development of both natural and human systems (di Castri, 2000).

Over the past 20 years, also stimulated by the sustainable development program, various new disciplinary developments have emerged in the social and human sciences in the direction of full ecology or sustainability: in economics, ecological economy (e.g., Costanza, 1991); in law and legal sciences, environmental law or green justice (e.g., Nash, 1989; Opotow & Clayton, 1994); in philosophy, environmental philosophy (e.g., Katz, 1997; Taylor, 1986), in environmental psychology, various new developments within the sustainable development perspective, also defined as "sustainability" (Bonnes, 1998; Kruse, 1997; Winter, 2000).

THE ENVIRONMENTAL PSYCHOLOGY OF SUSTAINABLE DEVELOPMENT

In the past 15 years, through the growing influence of the full ecology perspective, the ecologically considered environment has become increasingly central to environmental psychology. This typically dynamic environment, articulated on local and global levels as well as in physical and social aspects, appears in many ways different from the spatial-physical environment or surroundings considered by the previous mainstream environmental psychology.

As a consequence, several changes can be noted in environmental psychology over the past 10 to 15 years. First, increasing attention has been given to the physical-biological aspects or processes of the natural physical environment, in addition to the built, architectural and technological ones. This tendency can be noted also in the numerous proposals for new names or subnames in environmental psychology to mark the presence of these specific interests. Some examples are "green psychology" (Pol, 1993), "natural psychology" (Gifford, 1995), "psychology of global environmental change" (Pawlik, 1991; Stern, 1992), "eco-psychology" and "ecological psychology" (Howard, 1997; Kruse & Graumann, 1987; Roszak, 1992; Winter, 1996), "psychology of sustainability" (Bonnes, 1998; Kruse, 1996; Winter, 2000).

A second important change is the growing sociophysical complexity with which environmental spatial-physical characteristics, directly perceptible at the sensory level, become part of the psychological processes considered. In various ways it is underlined that the fully ecologically considered environment has a problematic correspondence with direct sensory perception. Thus, in general it is characterized by uncertainty at the sensory-perceptual and cognitive level (e.g., Gärling, Biel, & Gustafsson, 1998; Graumann & Kruse, 1990). In particular, its unusual "sensory a-modality" and "temporal graduality" have been stressed (Graumann & Kruse, 1990). In the first case, the sense organs are unable to perceive environmental conditions such as nuclear pollution or ozone pollution. In the second case, the slowness of environmental changes, such as climactic ones that may take place over very long periods of time, make their direct sensory perception impossible. This has led to the decreased importance of the more reactive and individualistic approaches originating in the psychology of perception and to the increasing importance of the more constructivist, molar, and social psychological approaches (Bonaiuto & Bonnes, 2000; Bonnes & Secchiaroli, 1995; Stokols & Altman, 1987b). In general, more attention is given to the sociocultural or collective level of the environmental psychological processes considered (Proshansky & Fabian, 1986; Saegert & Winkel, 1990; Wapner & Demick, 2000).

Finally and most importantly, special attention is given to manifest behaviors and actions in everyday environments that affect related natural processes or resources of the ecologically considered environment at the local and global level. These behaviors/actions are defined as "environmentally relevant behaviours" (e.g., Stern, 2000) or "ecological behaviours" (e.g., Kaiser, 1998) and refer to either repeated or occasional concrete behavioral choices made in everyday environments. They concern specific natural and common resources of these daily environments such as choices of use/maintenance of specific resources, including water, air, land, sources of energy (electricity, oil, gas, etc.) and other more or less recyclable materials (refuse in general, paper, glass, etc.) as well as of life forms (plants and animals) present in the environment. All behavioral choices leading to the deterioration of these natural common resources at the local and global level are considered. For example, these behaviors include the emission/dissemination of various types of polluting refuse materials on the ground (littering and pollution by solid and other types of refuse), in the water (pollution of waterways and water sources of lakes and seas), in the air (emission of gas, noise, and radiation dangerous for important natural processes of the environment, for example, the greenhouse effect and climactic changes, acid rain, the hole in the ozone layer), or whatever is dangerous for the well-being and health of living beings. In general, when all these environmentally relevant behaviors are oriented toward the optimal maintenance of these natural resources, they are defined as proenvironmental behaviors.

It can be noted that the progressive influence of the full ecology, or sustainability, perspective led environmental psychology to shift its main perspective of observation. Different from its initial attention to the spatial-physical environment and to related place-specific behaviors, present-day environmental psychology gives increasing attention to environmentally relevant behaviors in general. Specific attention is often given to the sociophysical actions practiced in the ecologically considered environment, viewed both as "object" and "product" of the behaviors considered.

Therefore, in accordance with Lewin's (1944) first "psychological ecology," one of the primary tasks of this expanding area of environmental psychology is to understand how this ecologically considered environment becomes psychologically relevant in and through the actions and experiences of the persons living and acting in it (Wapner & Demick, 2000). Thus, all constructs and processes assumed to underlie individual environmentally relevant behaviors are receiving increasing attention. In particular, all psychological processes aimed at preparing, guiding, and establishing environmentally aware behavioral choices in a more or less proenvironmental direction are of particular interest.

It can also be noted that, in this perspective, individual actions and experiences in and about the ecologically considered environment tend to lose the

lack of environmental awareness which often characterized place-specific human actions and experiences according to the early environmental psychology. On the contrary, constructs such as *environmental awareness* (e.g., Bechtel, 1997; Takala, 1991); *environmental concern* (e.g., Fransson & Gärling, 1999; Hine & Gifford, 1991; Schan & Holzer, 1990; Stern, Dietz, & Kalof, 1993) and the related constructs of *environmental* (or *ecological*) *responsibility* (e.g., Blamey, 1998; Hines, Hungerford, & Tomera, 1987; Winter, 2000) and *environmental commitment* (e.g., Montada & Kales, 2000) are becoming increasingly central to the environmental psychology of sustainable development.

On the one hand, these constructs are assumed to connect individual, locally practiced, environmentally relevant behaviors/actions with the possible social-perceptual systems of personal orientation toward the same environment, such as environmental attitudes, beliefs, knowledge, feelings, values, world views, and so forth. On the other hand, they are assumed to give intra-individual and intersituational stability to the related environmental behaviors/actions considered and thus to allow the prevision of them.

During the 1990s, also because of the impetus provided by the international mandate on sustainable development, the pressing nature of environmental problems caused by human activities and behaviors received greater attention in psychology (e.g., Bechtel, 1997; Pawlik, 1991; Stern, 1992; Vlek, 2000; Zube, 1992). Throughout this decade psychologists were requested to make specific efforts to cope with these problems by developing ways to orient human behavior toward sustainability. Recently, for example, five coordinated articles were published in the *American Psychologist* along these lines (Howard, 2000; McKenzie-Mohr, 2000; Oskamp, 2000; Stern, 2000; Winter, 2000):

> Human actions are producing many harmful and possibly irreversible changes to environmental conditions that support life on Earth. . . . Urgent changes in human lifestyles and cultural practices are required for the world to escape ecological disaster and psychologists should lead the way in helping people adopt sustainable patterns of living. (Oskamp, 2000, p. 496, introducing the previously mentioned articles)

Many of the research perspectives developed in environmental psychology in the past 10 to 15 years under the influence of full ecology had already started during the 1970s and 1980s (e.g., Fischhoff, Svenson, & Slovic, 1987; Pitt & Zube, 1987; Stern & Oskamp, 1987).

During the 1990s, also thanks to the international mandate on sustainable development, these interests underwent extraordinary development, extending environmental psychology in various directions of inquiry and toward wider interdisciplinary collaboration with other environmental sciences, in particular with environmental economics, politics, management, and legislation.

Because of the multidimensional nature of the ecologically considered environment, with local and global dimensions as well as physical and social ones, the environmental psychology of sustainable development has to deal with multiform and multilevel environmental actions and experiences.

On the one hand, environmental actions related to people's life environments are individually performed. Thus, they are characterized as individual and as local—or localized—with the typical place specificity assumed by environmental psychology for human behaviors (Bonnes & Secchiaroli, 1995; Canter, 1986; Russell & Ward, 1982; Stokols, 1987). On the other hand, these same individual and localized actions tend to become much more important environmentally the more they are directly implicated in the macroprocesses of the global changes of the biosphere and the more they are collectively diffused and shared among persons in the same ecosystem. Also, the same specific and localized actions can involve different physical or social local levels; for example, they can refer to home, neighborhood, city, region, nation, biosphere, or to the inhabitant, citizen, European, human being, living being, and so forth.

In this perspective, the field of environmental psychology of sustainable development has expanded in many directions. Various consolidated research traditions of psychology have been stimulated to enlarge their range of study and application as a function of the many new complexities deriving from the consideration of sociophysical actions and experiences in the ecologically considered environment. The great variety of research perspectives developed along these lines over the years cannot be examined here in detail. However, by outlining some of the main trends, their degree of continuity or discontinuity with the first environmental psychology of the spatial-physical environment and of place-specific behavior and experience can be considered.

Following the central distinction between the global and the local level in ecology, it also seems possible to find differences in the variety of environmental psychology studies of sustainable development. First of all, we can distinguish those studies that are more globally oriented (i.e., regarding aspects that render the ecologically considered environment psychologically relevant) from those that are more centered on specific behaviors (i.e., more circumscribed and focused on a local level of analysis).

In the first case, the environmental psychology of sustainable development seems to be more directly influenced by natural ecology. In emphasizing the danger of the global transformations occurring at the biosphere level and the related globalization of the physical-biological processes involved, natural ecology tends to assume the need for equally global changes at the human level, thus also at the psychological level.

In the second case, the environmental psychology of sustainable development seems to follow the perspective of full ecology. Through the sustainable development program, it aims at encouraging the most articulated approach toward ecologically relevant human factors. In particular, the focus is on a wide variety of personal and collective actions and experiences involved in human uses of the ecologically considered environment.

ECOLOGICAL WORLD VIEWS, GLOBAL VALUES, ECOLOGICAL SELF

The environmental psychology of sustainable development primarily affected the psychology concerned with beliefs and world views about the self in the world and about social and personal values. Specifically, it assumed that to have a global perspective or to believe in global values at the personal level is the major guide for orienting individual behavior in a proenvironmental direction.

In the 1970s, various studies appeared that were aimed at identifying the salient aspects of these general systems of reference, more or less oriented in the direction of full ecology (Dunlap & Van Liere, 1978; Maloney & Ward, 1973; Weigel & Weigel, 1978). In particular, Dunlap and Van Liere (1978) defined these belief systems as "world views" or "primitive belief systems" and proposed to identify them with the name "New Environmental Paradigm" (NEP). This was to counter the antiecological "Dominant Social Paradigm" (DSP), also defined as the

"Human Exemptionalism Paradigm" (HEP) since it is based on the idea that humans, unlike other living species, are exempt from the constraints of nature. As the authors also observed recently: "We are in the midst of a fundamental re-evaluation of the underlying world view that has guided our relationship to the physical environment. . . . In particular, suggestions that a more ecologically sound world view is emerging have gained credibility in the past decades" (Dunlap, Van Liere, Mertig, & Jones, 2000, p. 426).

The NEP Scale, a specific psychometric instrument proposed by these authors for differentiating persons, became very popular and was used by various researchers in different countries, and now, in the updated version (Dunlap et al., 2000), it includes the most recent orientations of the sustainable development proposal. In the NEP Scale, this new ecologically sound vision of the world, or ecological world view, seems mostly based on the "new awareness" of the following aspects: (1) the existence of limits in the Earth environment in the availability and use of resources by humans; (2) the fragility of the so-called natural balances and the risk incurred by human activities, which can be dangerously disturbing when they are not sufficiently concerned with the environment; and (3) the resulting need for human activities to be directed toward the natural world with a proper awareness of it, that is, respecting natural resources rather than exclusively dominating and dedicating them for the exclusive satisfaction of human needs.

During the 1990s many lines of research were aimed at further investigating the different world views able to establish proenvironmental behaviors. Various sociopsychological perspectives were identified in this regard, such as "nonanthropocentrism" (Chandler & Dreger, 1993) or "ecocentrism versus anthropocentrism" (Thompson & Burton, 1994) or "biocentrism versus anthropocentrism" (McFarlane & Boxall, 2000). In this same perspective, other studies were focused on identifying the most general values underlying environmental concern at the personal level. The importance of "universal values" in general and of "altruistic" ones in particular, compared to "individual" and "egoistic" ones, was often shown (e.g., Schwartz, 1994, 1996; Stern & Dietz, 1994; Stern, Dietz, Abel, Guagnano, & Kalof, 1999; Stern et al., 1993), as well as the importance of so-called "postmaterialist" values (Inglehart, 1997).

By using contributions from other disciplinary areas such as environmental philosophy (Dower, 1989; Katz, 1997), other studies emphasize the most general ethical implications connected with the assumption of environmental values. In this sense, they are also defined as "global values" or "global ethics" (R. Rapoport, 1993), similar to the global orientation of the full ecology perspective. Their salient aspects can be identified in relation to the following three main dimensions: (1) orientation toward "humanity as a whole" through the extension of humanistic values to all human beings everywhere in the world; (2) orientation toward "all life," or all the various life forms of the entire biosphere; and (3) orientation toward "the future," or "sustainability" and long-term planning (R. Rapoport, 1993, p. 180). Recent developments of environmental psychology, such as eco-psychology (Roszak, 1992) or ecological psychology (Howard, 1997; Winter, 1996), are moving along similar lines. All these contributions are characterized by their emphasis on the conflicting use of natural resources by human beings on one side and by nonhuman beings on the other. At the same time, the importance and urgency for psychology to promote personal global, ecologically oriented changes is stressed to improve not only the environment's current conditions but also individual psychological well-being. The acquisition of an "ecological self" (Bragg, 1996) or an "ecological ego" (Roszak, 1992) or a "sustainable mind" (Gladwing, Newburry, & Reiskin, 1997) is claimed since "more self change is necessary to chart a sustainable course for the world," as affirmed by Howard (2000, p. 513).

Overall, these lines of development of the environmental psychology of sustainable development tend to approach the problem of the psychological relevance of environmental actions and experiences and, thus, of environmental concern in a very general or global sense without sufficient attention to adopting a more local perspective toward them. In general, they seem to bring the environmental psychology of sustainable development to problems very distant from the place-specific perspective of the early environmental psychology; thus, they tend to drive the new developments of environmental psychology more toward discontinuity than continuity with the previous ones (as noted also by Bonaiuto, Carrus, Martorella, & Bonnes, in press; Bonnes, Carrus, & Bonaiuto, 2000; R. Rapoport, 1993).

SPECIFIC ENVIRONMENTALLY RELEVANT BEHAVIORS

Perspectives vary greatly when the environmental psychology of sustainable development concentrates primarily on the analysis of specific behaviors carried out concretely with respect to particular, more or less local, natural resources of life environments to promote a change in these environmental behaviors in a more eco-compatible or sustainable direction. In particular, various social psychological theories have been used to hypothesize how these environmental behaviors are connected, on the one hand, with the other social-perceptual systems of global personal orientation such as perceptions, evaluations, attitudes, values, and so forth and, on the other hand, with the various specific aspects of the local contexts considered. Psychology has always been concerned with the correspondence among behaviors, actions, and decision making and related social attitudes (e.g., Manstead, 1996; Wicker, 1969). This is even truer since the environmental psychology of sustainable development began to work on the associations among attitudes, values, beliefs, proenvironment world views and related behaviors/actions actually carried out in specific daily-life environments or places (for a review, see McKenzie-Mohr, 2000; Staats, in press).

As already noted, in the sustainability perspective, which considers both the local and global components of every environmental issue, the problem of locally practiced and environmentally relevant individual behaviors is initially posed at the psychological level. Specifically, the confrontation and possible conflict becomes salient between implications in local terms (spatially, temporally, and socially circumscribed) or in global terms (spatially, temporally, and socially enlarged) of the possible benefits and costs of these behaviors. This concerns the distinction and the conflict arising from the confrontation, as stated by Vlek (2000, p. 159), between "the benefits and costs of the 'here and now,' as opposed to the benefits and costs or risk of 'yonder and later.'"

On a more empirical level, various studies demonstrate the importance of favoring the contextual or place-centered perspective in order to understand and predict environmentally relevant behaviors (Levy-Leboyer, Bonnes, Chase, Ferreira-Marques, & Pawlik, 1996). In general, they underline the need for a multicomponential place perspective to understand environmentally relevant individual behaviors

(e.g., Bonaiuto, Aiello, Perugini, Bonnes, & Ercolani, 1999; Stern, 2000; Vlek, 2000) and the importance of the place-centered perspective also in studying general environmental concern (Bonaiuto & Bonnes, 2000; Bonaiuto et al., in press; Bonnes et al., 2000).

In the environmental psychology of sustainable development, a first perspective in the 1970s and 1980s that focused on the local level belongs to the tradition of "applied behavioral analysis" (Geller, 1987, 1995; Katzev & Wang, 1994; McKenzie-Mohr, 2000; Oskamp, 2000). Among other things, this perspective emphasizes that behavioral change interventions aimed at improving proenvironmental human uses of places should be established at the level of the local community of reference and entrusted to the typical social psychological processes of community psychology, in particular those of belongingness and empowerment (Geller, 1995). This environmental behaviorism approach is also criticized for its limits (Porter, Leeming, & Dwyer, 1995; Stern & Oskamp, 1987; Thøgersen, 1996). Primarily, it is considered too "reactive" as a function of typically contingent costs and benefits; but it is also considered too locally circumscribed physically and socially since it primarily refers to a community view (see Chavis & Newbrough, 1986; Heller, 1989).

In the following three sections, we will briefly review other major psychological approaches to specific, environmentally relevant behaviors.

Environmentally Relevant Behaviors and Attitudes

Various specific social-psychological theoretical perspectives are used by the environmental psychology of sustainable development to focus on understanding proenvironmental behaviors/actions in relation to environmental attitudes and situational and local contexts. In this sense, the most widely used theories are the "theory of planned behavior" (TPB; Ajzen, 1991), developed from the previous "theory of reasoned action" (TRA; Ajzen & Fishbein, 1980; Fishbein & Ajzen, 1975), and the theories on normative conducts, such as Schwartz's (1977) "norm activation theory" and its more contextual development in the "focus theory of normative conduct" (Cialdini, Kallgren, & Reno, 1991). According to the theory of planned behavior, various types of relevant environmental behaviors are investigated as outcomes of behavioral intentions rationally constructed at the personal level through the combination of three main components of personal attitudes and evaluations.

These are represented by the following elements: "attitude toward behavior," "subjective norm," and "perceived behavioral control." The variations related to conditions of high or low, or "automatic," control in the activation of the attitude in question do not seem to involve differences in the degree of behavioral intention prediction obtained starting from those elements (e.g., Ajzen & Fishbein, 2000).

This theory is also widely used in the psychology of economic choices and consumption (Bagozzi, 1992). It is also considered by various authors as particularly useful for explaining environmentally relevant behaviors (e.g., Staats, in press). There are numerous examples of studies that use this theory to explain the adoption of various specific, environmentally relevant behaviors (e.g., Allen, Davis, & Soskin, 1993; Bagozzi & Dabholkar, 1994; Goldenhar & Connell, 1992–1993). This theory can also be used to consider the use of systems of incentives and disincentives, primarily of an economic nature, in local programs of environmental politics (e.g., Lynne, Franklin-Casey, Hodges, & Rahmani, 1995).

However, often the limits of the use of this theory are also pointed out. In particular, the theory is seen as outlining a prevalently individualist and too rationally guided human paradigm regarding behavioral choices in general and proenvironmental behavioral choices in particular (e.g., Thøgersen, 1996). It has also been shown that the explanatory capacity of this theoretical model regarding the adoption of specific proenvironmental behaviors in relation to related proenvironmental attitudes increases when the external local conditions make it easier to perform the considered behavior (e.g., Corraliza & Berenguer, 2000; Derksen & Gartrell, 1993; Guagnano, Stern, & Dietz, 1995; Kaiser, Wölfing, & Fuhrer, 1999). This shows the importance of structural-contextual features (both social and physical) in codetermining individual behavior, over and above individual differences.

In fact, studies that consider environmentally relevant behaviors as specific normative conducts have a clearer contextual orientation. Most of them are based on the "norm activation theory" developed by Schwartz (1970, 1977) and Schwartz and Howard (1981) to explain prosocial helping behavior. Thus, proenvironmental behaviors are assimilated in altruistic or social-help or prosocial behaviors. "Awareness of need," "awareness of consequences," and "awareness of responsibility" are the three main components of this theoretical model for explaining the activation of related normative conduct.

The numerous contributions of environmental psychology in this direction date from the 1970s (Van Liere & Dunlap, 1978). They concern a large variety of local, environmentally relevant behaviors such as recycling (e.g., Guagnano et al., 1995; Hopper & Nielsen, 1991; Lee, De Young, & Marans, 1995; Thøgersen, 1996; Vining & Ebreo, 1992), the use of energy (Black, Stern, & Elworth, 1985), "yard burning" and support for environmental protection in general (Stern, Dietz, & Black, 1986).

However, studies revealing the limits of this theoretical model for explaining proenvironmental behaviors and advancing proposals for extending it in various ways are increasingly numerous (Blamey, 1998; Montada & Kales, 2000; Stern et al., 1999). In fact, proenvironmental choices appear rather different from behaviors normatively oriented toward the altruistic helping behavior at the base of this model. In particular, the already enhanced collective characteristics of the common good of environmental resources (e.g., Edney, 1980; G. Hardin, 1968) tend to present proenvironment normative conducts as more socially oriented, rather than interindividually oriented as assumed by Schwartz's theory's core idea of helping behavior. In this sense, since proenvironmental normative conduct is involved in the acquisition of collective goods or common goods, it seems more similar to the collective actions at the core of the social sciences of economics, law, and political science (e.g., G. Hardin & Baden, 1977; Olson, 1965; Ostrom, 1998) than to the more individualistic action of the intra- and interindividual psychology of helping behavior.

In fact, proenvironmental behavioral choices concern not only the problem of the intraindividual intention and related individual behavioral choice typical of altruistic helping behavior but mostly the problem of convergence versus divergence between individual choice and collective choices regarding the same perceived environmental need. Thus, prior to the individual decision to act in a proenvironmental way, that is, assuming environmental responsibility, there is the problem of the perceived effectiveness of the outcome of the individual choice. Since this effectiveness is more a collective than an individual result (e.g., Olson, 1965), the well-known uncertainty characterizing individual environmental choices increases because the person ignores others' environmental choices and behaviors (e.g., Gärling et al., 1998).

In fact, in the case of individual proenvironmental behavioral choices, it seems necessary to focus on the problem of the inevitable interdependence between individual and collective choices related to the same type of environmentally relevant behavior. This is typically approached in the so-called commons dilemmas paradigm (see the next section). In this perspective, individual proenvironmental behavior tends to become more or less socially cooperative behavior since it is typically aimed at reaching joint outcomes and thus becomes better framed within the paradigm of "socially interdependent behavior" (Messick, 2000b; Van Lange, 2000). The possibility of acting to acquire or save a collective resource considered a common good involves the problem of cooperating and therefore of establishing interdependence between individual and collective cooperative behaviors for the effectiveness of individual proenvironmental behavior (see Van Vugt, Biel, Snyder, & Tyler, 2000).

Along these theoretical lines, which treat environmentally relevant behaviors as specific normative conduct and thus as morally relevant actions (e.g., Thøgersen, 1996), the recent developments of environmental psychology tend to further enlarge its interdisciplinary dialogue, in this case with particular reference to the psychology of law, the social psychology of social justice (e.g., Montada & Kales, 2000; Opotow & Clayton, 1994), and the legal sciences. In particular, various new environmental psychological constructs are proposed and used in this area, such as those of "ecological justice" or "ecological equity" (e.g., Montada & Kales, 2000), and "green justice" (e.g., Opotow & Clayton, 1994). In relation to these new constructs and to other already consolidated ones in the area of the psychology of "social justice," such as those of "perceived fairness," "distributive justice," and "procedural justice" (Mikula & Wenzel, 2000; Tyler, 2000), the possibility of developing "proenvironmental commitment," "environmental responsibility," and related proenvironmental choices is also becoming an interesting option (e.g., Blamey, 1998; Montada & Kales, 2000).

Commons Dilemmas, Collective Decisions, and the Social Psychology of Interdependence

Other theoretical perspectives that take into consideration specific environmentally relevant behaviors by focusing attention on other problematic aspects of the social and local contexts of action are "social dilemmas" or "commons dilemmas," also specifically defined as "environmental dilemmas" (Dawes, 1980; Dawes & Messick, 2000; Van Vugt et al., 2000; Vlek, 2000), on one side, and the processes of "collective decisions" or "deliberations and collective consultation" (Dietz, 1994; Dietz & Stern, 1998; Moscovici & Doise, 1992) on the other.

In recent years, both of these perspectives have gained increasing attention from the environmental psychology of sustainability. Both approaches are based on the previously mentioned characteristic of common good of the natural resources of the environment and on the resulting eminently conflictual nature of environmental choices found at the intraindividual and collective level, both in an intra- and intergroup sense (e.g., Brown, 2000; Tajfel & Turner, 1986).

In connection with the characteristic of common good and related local and global dimensions of environmental resources stressed by the full ecology perspective, it should be noted that proenvironment choices almost always appear as choices for limitation of personal or group benefits, circumscribed to specific groups or categories of users. These limitations are more or less localized, favoring more extended benefits in a collective sense for the various possible levels of extension of that collectivity in a spatial and temporal way. They include group, community, region, humanity, and so forth. In particular, the sustainable development perspective stretches this extension to future generations.

Already during the 1960s, exponents in various disciplinary fields outside of psychology began to focus on problems of conflict in the use/management or acquisition of common resources or collective goods (e.g., G. Hardin, 1968; Olson, 1965). In his famous article entitled "The Tragedy of the Commons," biologist Garrett Hardin (1968) pointed out that there are no technical solutions for many environmental problems (such as overpopulation, pollution), which appear to be problems of misuse of resources or common goods, but only human-social solutions. "A technical solution may be defined as one that requires a change only in the techniques of the natural sciences, demanding little or nothing in the way of change in human values or ideas of morality" (p. 1243). In fact, he states that, "We are locked into a system of 'fouling our own nest,' so long as we behave only as independent, rational, free enterprises" (p. 1245). "Each man is locked into a system that compels him to increase his herd without limit in a world that is limited. Ruin is the destination toward which all men rush, each pursuing his own best interest in a society that believes in the freedom of the commons. Freedom in a commons brings ruin to all" (p. 1244). The only solution he sees for this possible tragedy is for human beings to develop systems of "mutual coercion mutually agreed upon" (p. 1247) at the social level, that is, of shared normative systems of self-coercion, or ethics, aimed at the "fundamental extension in morality" considered necessary by Hardin. He believes that this is the only way for humans to regain their freedom with regard to pressing environmental problems. "Individuals locked into the logic of the commons are free only to bring on universal ruin: once they see the necessity of mutual coercion, they become free to pursue other goals" (p. 1248).

On the other side, economist Mancur Olson, in his famous book *The Logic of Collective Actions* (1965), tried to show, even through a mathematical formula, how it is very probable that, if possible, people will not orient their action in the expected direction to acquire a collective good. However, this probability depends on the logical structure of the group in question, with particular reference to the size and to the capacity of the group as a whole to show sensitivity toward the action of the individual. Therefore, it is easier for people to adopt so-called "free-riding" behaviors the more the collective good refers to a large group where the contribution of the individual tends to remain invisible: "In a large group in which no single individual's contribution makes a perceptible difference to the group as a whole . . . it is certain that a collective good will not be provided unless there is coercion or some outside inducement" (p. 44).

These types of problems, which generally hold a central position in political science and economics, have received increasing attention in psychology and, in particular, in the environmental psychology of sustainability, through important developments of the research perspective of commons dilemmas derived from the initial paradigm of the "prisoner's dilemma" game (Stern & Oskamp, 1987; Van Vugt et al., 2000; Vlek, 2000). R. Hardin (1971) demonstrated, also through the use of mathematical models, the similarity of the strategic structure of the classical prisoner's dilemma game with the problem of collective action outlined by Olson (1965).

"Social dilemmas are situations that contain a conflict of interest between the private interests of individuals and the broader public interest of society at large" (Van Vugt et al., 2000, p. 3). "In a social dilemma situation, each individual always receives a higher payoff for defecting than for co-operating, but all are better off if all co-operate than if all defect" (Dawes, 2000). In this perspective, environmentally relevant behaviors can be investigated as a particular type of collective action, bringing the problems of conflict and interdependence between individual and collective interest choices to the front line with the emergence of more or less socially cooperative behaviors or, alternately, of social defection or free-riding behaviors. These problems are receiving increasing attention from the social psychology of common dilemmas, organizational behaviors, and interdependence, as well as from economics and political science (Dawes & Messick, 2000; Messick & Brewer, 1983; Van Vugt et al., 2000). Following this theoretical perspective, it can be noted that the psychology of sustainable development is further enlarging its interdisciplinary dialogue with economics and political science and also with organizational and management sciences.

Although the commons dilemma paradigm was initially developed in experimental laboratory psychology through the use of experimental games, it has recently been successfully used in field studies on natural and locally situated groups (e.g., Dawes & Messick, 2000; Van Vugt, in press; Van Vugt, Meertens, & Van Lange, 1995). Overall, the knowledge this type of theoretical approach has acquired over the years demonstrates the situational complexity, in terms of conflict, presented by environmental choices at the individual psychological level and related contexts of action (e.g., Van Vugt et al., 2000; Vlek, 2000). These various conflicting perspectives have not received enough attention by most of the other approaches of the environmental psychology of sustainability, although they received some attention by the first environmental psychology of the spatial physical environment (e.g., Churchman, 1993; Churchman & Altman, 1994).

Also, results from studies based on the paradigm of conflict between the individual and the collective show the crucial role of all of those social-psychological processes involved in creating intermediate shared contexts, between the two extreme poles of individual/local and collective/global, for the emergence of cooperative and proenvironmental choices. In particular, these include all the possible and multilevel group processes, from the communication and sharing of social values (Dawes & Messick, 2000; De Cremer & Van Vugt, 1999; Gärling, 1999; Messick, 1999; Van Lange, 2000) to social identity processes (Kramer & Brewer, 1986; Van Vugt, in press). The importance of focusing on these types of social psychological processes has already been shown for various types of environmentally relevant behaviors. These include the perception of environmental pollution (Bonaiuto, Breakwell, & Cano, 1996) and support for or opposition to the institution of new natural protected areas (Bonaiuto et al., in press; Bonnes et al., 2000). In this view, also with reference to collective decision-making processes, the intra- and intergroup environmental communications processes, also referred to as "environmental discourse," are of central interest (e.g., Bonaiuto & Bonnes, 2000; Bonnes, Bonaiuto, Metastasio, Aiello, & Sensales, 1997; Graumann & Kruse, 1990) (see next section). This relevance can also be linked to the general relevance of communication processes for cooperation, which in turn is claimed to be crucial for the solution of commons dilemmas.

As a matter of fact, as Van Vugt et al. (2000) noted, modern history is full of examples of critical situations which have been overcome thanks to the cooperation of the community. Conflicts and dilemmas are problems which are solved through citizens' cooperation in the form of restraint to preserve scarce natural resources ("common resource problems" such as saving the environment and energy and water conservation) or contributions to create communal goods ("common good problems" such as financing public services and donating time and money). In this view, environmental dilemmas are conceived as dependent not on altruistic choices but on cooperation choices, that is, on a mixture between altruistic and selfish motives based on a prolonged period of time rather than on a single moment or event (i.e., common interdependence across time). In this view, environmental behavior cannot be reduced to helping behavior and to the merely interpersonal perspectives adopted to explain it. However, traditional perspectives on social dilemmas are often quite pessimistic and envisage coercion and punishment as the only way to induce short term-centered and self-centered individuals to act for the social group and the community long-term interests.

On the contrary, recent perspectives emphasize the importance of people's norms, values, and social identities as crucial motives underlying cooperation. For example, people seem more willing to cooperate when they can consider themselves part of a group rather than when they see themselves as distinct individuals. "According to social identity theory (Tajfel & Turner, 1986), in highly cohesive groups people define their self-concept primarily at a collective level rather than at a personal level. This suggests that solutions to collective problems in society might be found in stressing the common fate or identity between individual group members (Brewer & Kramer, 1986)" (Van Vugt et al., 2000, p. 12). Or, at least in present day democracies, people seem to cooperate more when the society emphasizes participation, collaboration, and empowerment rather than coercion, punishment, and control (pp. 13–14). This opens the way for a democratization of decision-making processes about spaces and environments as common resources, stressing the need for a communicative or interpretative or argumentative model in planning theory (see Healey, 1997).

In any case, the point is to link the fate of the individual with that of other people, to tie members of a community together, to attach them to it, to have them establish positive social connections where all relational needs are not necessarily altruistic but rather a mix of altruistic and selfish concerns (going from ideological motives to group-belonging to self-presentation to self-esteem motives). Such elements would also be necessary to legitimize and facilitate acceptance of authority structures that others claim are needed in order to regulate citizens' behavior. Thus, authorities should aim to improve relations with the public, for example, via community involvement procedures. On the whole, it is important to stress that such a view underlines the need to manage environmental issues at different levels: "the macro-level, the functioning of authorities; the meso-level, the functioning of communities; and the micro-level, the functioning of the individual self" (Van Vugt et al., 2000, p. 17).

This sensitivity—not simply toward the way the situation is structured by the authority but also toward the way it is interpreted by the individuals acting in it—is crucial for the efficacy of structural solutions (Messick, 2000a). According to Messick (2000a; see also Messick & Brewer, 1983), to promote cooperation in collective action or in overcoming common dilemmas, there can be two solutions: (1) individual solutions, based on voluntary choice of single individuals (e.g., their individual differences in terms of social value orientation) or (2) structural solutions, based on the design of social arrangements in societies (e.g., changing payoffs, altering institutions, adding or deleting alternative choices). If not "mutually agreed upon" (G. Hardin, 1968, p. 1247), structural solutions, although attractive for eradicating the problem at its origin, tend to transform a commonly shared collective problem into an individual problem, with possible side effects undermining their efficacy. On the whole, structural solutions—whether provided by a state, an organization, or an authority figure—seem to work by increasing people's cooperation when they "see themselves as part of a group and when they see the problem as a group problem that needs a collective solution" (Messick, 2000a, p. 236). Therefore, the main point is to foster people's perception of a situation as a collective problem rather than as a personal one. This should have a number of useful consequences for solving the social dilemma, namely, "Others' interests will be considered, others will be treated with respect, [and] self-restraint will be seen as appropriate" (Messick, 2000a, p. 237).

Generally, this way of considering decisions about environmentally relevant behaviors/actions dilemmas claims the relevance of the "theory of interdependence" (Gärling et al., 1998; Kelly & Thibaut, 1978; Van Lange, 2000). This theory was developed to study behavioral choices in situations of social interdependence, that is, in which two or more parties determine the outcome (Messick, 2000b). In this sense, it seems particularly apt for developing the environmental psychology of sustainable development and in particular for approaching the various multilevel interdependencies existing between circumscribed local levels and broader collective levels, including the global one. Moreover, in order to understand environmentally relevant behavioral choices, this theory seems to propose the same relational and interdependent approach typical of full ecology.

Furthermore, there is not always a clear opposition among structural and individual solutions. In fact, an organizing structure facilitating cooperation among people can either be imposed upon people from a formal authority, that is, from "the top down," or emerge from informal social interactions among people, that is, from "the bottom up." Thus—by analogy with pairs of opposite concepts such as prescriptive/descriptive norms (Cialdini et al., 1991) or formal/informal cultures and norms coexisting within any organization—a difference could exist between "informal" or "formal" structures.

The commons dilemma approach often seems to have forgotten those seminal social-psychological studies that show the positive effects on cooperation from the advent of a superordinate goal within a scenario characterized by intergroup conflict and competition (the so-called "Robbers Cave experiment" by Sherif, Harvey, White, Hood, & Sherif, 1961; Sherif & Sherif, 1953; Sherif, White, & Harvey, 1955). Specifically, those experiments offer empirical evidence about how people and groups that are competing with each other succeed in overcoming the conflict through their awareness of having a common fate which needs a joint effort. What is important is the contribution of all persons and groups within the given situation to reach a superordinate goal that would otherwise be unattainable by the single individual or by the single group.

In a more general sense, this kind of evidence stresses the importance of restoring a concrete character to ethics, that is, linking desired behaviors (included proenvironmental ones) to the achievement of concrete superordinate goals that are useful and interesting for the people and the groups rather than to abstract values, norms, and concerns.

Moreover, the way a structural solution can develop and effectively work, decreasing the risk of side effects, is through adequate communication-shaping frames, rules, and norms among the different levels involved (authorities, communities, individuals)—that is, in the creation of those contextual or "situational details" (Messick, 2000a, p. 232) that help single individuals to orient their action within a collective action project. In this sense communication can be conceived as an instrument that contributes to promoting different frames and norms, from an individual-costs-and-benefits view promoting free-riding choices to group identification and shared collective understanding of rules of cooperation.

Environmental Communication: Discursive Construction and Use of Environmental Categories

Increasing research interest in the cognitive or discursive dynamics governing the definition and categorization of environmental questions corresponds to the increasing importance of processes of consultation and collective deliberation in environmental management. In fact, the idea has been affirmed that linguistic uses and communicative practices have a decisive constructive role in the environment. This idea has multidisciplinary roots in philosophy, geography, anthropology, and sociology (e.g., Douglas,

1966; Douglas & Wildavsky, 1982; Tuan, 1980), even before environmental psychology (e.g., Graumann & Kruse, 1990).

These theoretical considerations can be considered part of a broader linguistic, discursive, or rhetorical turn that progressively affected the human and social sciences in the second half of the twentieth century and that consequently affected environmental psychology in the 1980s and 1990s (e.g., Aiello & Bonaiuto, in press; Bonaiuto & Bonnes, 2000; Dixon & Durrheim, 2000). Here, research increasingly focused on two complementary levels: The study of communicative strategies and practices through which environmental representations are concretely realized and differently framed and the study of people's reactions to different discursive constructions and the framing of the environment.

Concerning the first level, research has investigated how environmental issues are communicated by the mass media (e.g., Bell, 1994) and by people involved in a public dispute (e.g., Macnaghten, 1993). More specifically, this concerns which environmental features are selected for attention; how they are framed in terms of causes, consequences, and remedies at different temporal, spatial, and social levels; which environmental categories are made salient; how different definitions of an environmental category (say, *nature*) are defined; and how they are reciprocally contrasted. In sum, at this level the focus is on discursive strategies that are used to concretely realize different representations of an environmental issue. They implicitly or explicitly favor different interpretations and different meanings of the environmental issue. The main assumption is that the environment, or at least its meaning, is socially constructed within an argumentative context where each counterpart is engaged in justifying one position and criticizing the opposing one (i.e., according to the same basic pervasive rhetorical principle that inspires social life in general in such an approach; Billig, 1987/1996). This assumption tends to be demonstrated by descriptive studies using qualitative or quantitative methodologies showing how the same environmental issue, change, or category is differently constructed in a discursive sense by different agents/agencies (from single individuals involved in a group discussion to mass media communications). For example, Macnaghten (1993) pointed out that in a public dispute about a dump proposal, participants (from designers to public officers to environmentalists, etc.) offered discursive

constructions of four different versions of the *nature* category. Each category appears to be coherently developed according to the different positions and counterpositions involved in the debate (e.g., being more or less favorable to the specific environmental proposal). These different discursive constructions are also strategically deployed by the discussants during their verbal battles, according to a flexible-social, not prepackaged, logic (for similar results, see, for example, Dixon & Durrheim, 2000; Michael, 1991; Ranyard, 1991; Rydin & Myerson, 1989). These studies show that, just like categories in general (e.g., Edwards, 1991), environmental categories (from *nature* to *radiation, noise* to *water pollution*, etc.) are also continuously redefined, reshaped, reconceptualized—that is, negotiated by people engaged in group processes aimed at local environmental management. Moreover, no discursive constructions are randomly produced. They function to explicitly or implicitly support a certain version of events, facts, or reality (and to oppose different ones) and are intertwined with cultural, social, economic, political, and ideological stances and interests (Potter, 1996). Finally, a certain discursive construction (e.g., a specific version of what should be intended by *natural*) can be considered as a concrete action that has practical effects (Edwards & Potter, 1992). It also affects other collective actions (e.g., via laws, campaigns) that have an impact on environmental features by creating, maintaining, or modifying them (as shown in Dixon, Reicher, & Foster, 1997; Macnaghten, 1993).

Some other studies specifically focused on mass media communications show that the active discursive selection and framing adopted in reporting environmental issues can have agenda-setting effects (e.g., Bell, 1994; Bonnes et al., 1997; Burgess & Harrison, 1993; Metastasio, Bonaiuto, Sensales, Aiello, & Bonnes, 1998). This highlights both the "perspective" character of social constructions of environmental problems and the fact that, as a rule, one political group regards the way others view and evaluate the "same" problem (i.e., the opposite or alternative perspective) as biased (Graumann & Kruse, 1990; see also Edwards & Potter, 1992). Some of the phenomena highlighted in this research parallel Billig's (e.g., 1987/1996, 1991) more general theoretical position. The latter stresses that common sense and common places offer discursive resources that the speaker or writer can draw upon rhetorically and flexibly to justify her or his own position and criticize that of her or his counterpart. Expressing an attitude about the environment also means taking a position in a public debate. It is a rhetorical move that must take into account the specific situation and the contingent argumentative context.

On another level, research has been aimed at understanding whether different discursive constructions affect audiences psychologically. Generally, these studies converge in pointing out how different framing of an environmental issue can lead to different opinions, evaluations, and decisions by people, similar to the well-known framing effects studied by Kahneman and Tversky (1984). Typically, researchers manipulated the linguistic frame through which a specific environmental issue was presented to measure variability in subjects' judgments, choices, and decisions. For example, they showed that environmental changes, phenomena, and consequences (e.g., radioactivity) are more accepted or preferred when they are presented as "natural" rather than "man-made" (e.g., Kaplan, Kaplan, & Wendt, 1972; Reicher, Podpadec, Macnaghten, Brown, & Eiser, 1993; Wohlwill, 1983). But they also showed that people's acceptance of specific environmental changes in landscapes can depend on different alternative definitions of the very same category of *nature* (Eiser, Reicher, & Podpadec, 1993; Macnaghten, Brown, & Reicher, 1992).

CONCLUDING REMARKS

In general, the various research perspectives of the environmental psychology of sustainability show the importance of paying attention to conflicting or interdependent aspects involved in individual specific environmental actions and to the multilevel character of these interdependencies, ranging from the most individual, local, and very circumscribed level up to the most collective, wide, and general one (e.g., Bonnes, 1998; Gärling et al., 1998; Messick, 1999; Van Vugt, in press; Vlek, 2000). Specifically, in this perspective several studies showed the importance of all social-psychological processes aimed at creating intermediate shared contexts of reference among the individual and the collective levels in view of possible multilevel contextual interdependencies such as, for example, processes of social and place identity as well as of environmental communications practices (Bonaiuto & Bonnes, 2000; Bonnes et al., 2000; Van Vugt, in press).

The consideration of all these processes seems particularly important in view of problems of management and solution of local conflicts between groups and categories of local stakeholders that tend to underlie every decision of environmental politics (e.g., Eisto, Hokkanem, Öhman, & Repola, 1999). This can be seen in recent years by the growing attention devoted to these problems by environmental psychology, specifically by its increasing involvement in the decision-making problems of environmental politics (e.g., Dietz & Stern, 1998; Vlek, 2000), and by the specific stimulus of the UN Agenda 21 mandate of sustainable development. With the political dimension, we refer to the interest in studying environmental issues to better understand ways to manage them. This political dimension is evident in the fact that most of the aforementioned approaches share an interest in modifying the status quo in the management of the environmental changes. Those approaches' common ground, over and above their different theoretical assumptions and methodological praxis, is the idea that environmental psychology, as well as all other sciences, should contribute to the general effort toward a more aware and better management of places, studying and giving suggestions for intervention at a local level but always bearing in mind a broader, that is, global, framework. Specifically they all share the idea that true, politically meaningful understanding of environmental issues necessarily merges different levels and avoids considering the environment in a unilateral way favoring only one level of analysis. Briefly, these approaches stress the reciprocal interdependence among the two elements of all the following pairs: the individual and the collective, the local and the global, the physical and the social, the present and future time. Such shared ground can be considered an expression of their common roots in the full ecology perspective reviewed in the second part of this chapter. Obviously, in environmental psychology there have always been political implications of some kind. However, in the past they at least partially focused on how to intervene in specific spatial-physical aspects in order to affect the single individual or community. More recent approaches tend to shift the balance in favor of a focus on complex social and collective processes that are at the basis of local and global environmental management.

A social-psychological view based on the reciprocal interdependence among people and among people and places is coherent with the full ecology perspective. In fact, as previously shown, it incorporates both the tendency toward conflict and the need for integration or interdependence between diverse life forms of every ecosystem. At the same time, through the approach of the psychology of interdependence, the environmental psychology of sustainable development also seems better able to retrieve the contextual dimension, in a place-specific sense, of environmental actions and experiences that is often neglected by the environmental psychology of global environmental concern and global values. Thus, within this perspective environmental psychology also seems better able to further develop the transactional and contextual approach in person environment research that has always been a basic feature of environmental psychology (e.g., Stokols & Altman, 1987a, 1987b; Wapner & Demick, 2000).

Overall, through the perspective of sustainable development, present-day environmental psychology contributes not only as a highly socially relevant field of applied psychology but also as an opportunity for developing psychology in a more contextual and social direction, thus toward the real-world psychology continuously envisaged in environmental psychology from its beginning to the present (e.g., Altman, 1975; Bechtel, 1997; Bonnes & Secchiaroli 1995; Proshansky, 1976; Stern, 2000; Wapner, Demick, Yamamoto, & Minami, 2000).

In this sense, the new development of environmental psychology seems able to embody the spirit of the sustainable development slogan "think globally, act locally."

In fact, on one hand it tries to focus on concrete and specific behaviors rather than on generic attitudes, views, orientations, and so forth. It aims to study and understand people's environmental actions as localized and place-specific activities, that is, carried out within certain contexts, with a theoretical orientation focusing on the interplay between people and their contexts (conceived both as codeterminants and codetermined). However, such actions are not considered in reductionist terms (e.g., as mere behaviorism). They are always considered as parts of a network of meanings based on people's belonging to territories and groups, which mold one's individual identity in terms of both place and social identity (Bonaiuto & Bonnes, 2000; Twigger-Ross,

Bonaiuto, & Breakwell, 2001). Thus, on the one hand, environmental actions cannot be simply conceived as individual behavior (although it includes this level too), because they are nested in a broader social dynamic where even a single individual act seems to follow principles different from the logic of mere rational short-term self-interest.

On the other hand, it is this subtle and pervasive weaving among the individual, local, specific dimension and the social, global, general dimension that theoretically allows for exploiting these links in order to orient people's actions toward the global interest of humankind (including future generations) rather than individual interests. This optimism is counterbalanced by empirical evidence showing how group interest is often the agent of self-interest. In this sense, it has to be accepted that managing environmental issues and orienting environmental actions necessarily includes dealing with conflict. This is essentially a social conflict among groups and among territories. Thus, perhaps the challenge is to exploit people's orientation to act in terms of interterritory and intergroup logic in order to benefit as large a territory and group as possible.

REFERENCES

Aiello, A., & Bonaiuto, M. (in press). Rhetorical approach and discursive psychology: The study of environmental discourses. In M. Bonnes, T. Lee, & M. Bonaiuto (Eds.), *Psychological theories to address environmental issues*. Aldershot, England: Ashgate.

Ajzen, I. (1991). The theory of planned behavior. *Organizational behavior and human decision processes, 50*, 179–211.

Ajzen, I., & Fishbein, M. (1980). *Understanding attitudes and predicting social behavior*. Englewood Cliffs, NJ: Prentice-Hall.

Ajzen, I., & Fishbein, M. (2000). Attitudes and attitude-behavior relation: reasons and automatic processes. In W. Stoebe & M. Hewstoe (Eds.), *European review of social psychology* (Vol. 11, pp. 1–33). New York: Wiley.

Allen, J., Davis, D., & Soskin, M. (1993). Using coupon incentives in recycling aluminum: A market approach to energy conservation policy. *Journal of Consumer Affairs, 27*(2), 300–318.

Altman, I. (1975). *The environment and social behavior: Privacy, personal space, territoriality and crowding*. Monterey, CA: Brooks/Cole.

Altman, I., & Rogoff, B. (1987). World views in psychology: Trait, interactional, organismic and transactional perspectives. In D. Stokols & I. Altman (Eds.), *Handbook of environmental psychology* (Vol. 1, pp. 7–40). New York: Wiley.

Ardrey, R. (1966). *The territorial imperative.* New York: Atheneum.

Bagozzi, R. P. (1992). The self-regulation of attitudes, intentions, and behavior. *Social Psychology Quarterly, 55*(2), 178–204.

Bagozzi, R. P., & Dabholkar, P. A. (1994). Consumer recycling goals and their effect on decisions to recycle: A means-end chain analysis. *Psychology & Marketing, 11*(5), 313–340.

Barbarbault, R. (1995). Biodiversity: Stakes and opportunities. *Nature & Resources, 31,* 19–26.

Barker, R. G. (1960). Ecology of motivation. In M. R. Jones (Ed.), *Nebraska Symposium on Motivation* (pp. 1–49). Lincoln: University of Nebraska Press.

Barker, R. G. (1968). *Ecological psychology: Concepts and methods for studying the environment of human behavior.* Stanford, CA: Stanford University Press.

Bechtel, R. (1997). *Environment and behavior: An introduction.* London: Sage.

Bell, A. (1994). Climate of opinion: Public and media discourse on the global environment. *Discourse & Society, 5,* 33–64.

Billig, M. (1991). *Ideology and opinions: Studies in rhetorical psychology.* London: Sage.

Billig, M. (1996). *Arguing and thinking. A rhetorical approach to social psychology.* Cambridge: Cambridge University Press. (Original work published 1987)

Black, J. S., Stern, P. C., & Elworth, J. T. (1985). Personal and contextual influences on household energy adaptations. *Journal of Applied Psychology, 70,* 3–21.

Blamey, R. (1998). The activation of environmental norms: Extending Schwartz's model. *Environment and Behavior, 30*(5), 676–708.

Bonaiuto, M., Aiello, A., Perugini, M., & Ercolani, A. P. (1999). Multidimensional perception of residential environment quality and neighbourhood attachment in the urban environment. *Journal of Environmental Psychology, 19,* 331–352.

Bonaiuto, M., & Bonnes, M. (1996). Multi-place analysis of the urban environment: A comparison between a large and a small Italian city. *Environment and Behaviour, 28*(6), 699–747.

Bonaiuto, M., & Bonnes, M. (2000). Social psychological approaches in environment-behaviours studies: Identity theories and the discursive approach. In S. Wapner, J. Demick, T. Yamamoto, & H. Minami (Eds.), *Theoretical perspectives in environment-behavior research: Underlying assumptions, research problems, and methodologies* (pp. 67–78). New York: Kluwer Academic/Plenum Press.

Bonaiuto, M., & Bonnes, M. (2001). Residential satisfaction in the urban environment within the UNESCO-MAB Rome Project. In J. I. Aragonés, G. Francescato,

T. Gärling (Eds.), *Residential environments: Choice, satisfaction, and behavior* (pp. 101–133). Westport, CT: Greenwood Press.

Bonaiuto, M., Bonnes, M., & Continisio, M. (in press). Neighborhood evaluation within a multi-place perspective on urban activities. *Environment and Behavior.*

Bonaiuto, M., Breakwell, G., & Cano, I. (1996). Identity processes and environmental threat: The effect of nationalism and local identity upon perception of beach pollution. *Journal of Community and Applied Social Psychology, 6,* 157–175.

Bonaiuto, M., Carrus, G., Martorella, H., & Bonnes, M. (in press). Local identity processes and environmental attitudes in land use changes: The case of natural protected areas. *Journal of Economic Psychology.*

Bonnes, M. (1984). Mobilizing scientists, planners, and local community in a large scale urban situation: The Rome case study. In F. di Castri, F. W. Baker, & M. Hadley (Eds.), *Ecology in practice* (pp. 57–62). Dublin: Tycooly.

Bonnes, M. (Ed.). (1987). *Urban ecology applied to the city of Rome* UNESCO-MAB Project No. 11, Progress Rep. No. 3. Rome: Instituto di Psicologia del Consiolio Nazionale Ricerche [C.N.R.].

Bonnes, M. (Ed.). (1991). *Urban ecology applied to the city of Rome.* UNESCO-MAB Project No. 11, Progress Rep. No. 4. Rome: Instituto di Psicologia del Consiolio Nazionale Ricerche [C.N.R.].

Bonnes, M. (1993). The MAB-UNESCO Program and environmental perception studies. In M. Bonnes (Ed.), *Perception and evaluation of urban environment quality: A pluridisciplinary approach in the European context* (pp. 9–13). Rome: Ente Nazionale Energia Elettrica [E.N.E.L.].

Bonnes, M. (1998). The ecological-global shift, environmental sustainability and the "shifting balances." In J. Teklenburg, J. van Andel, J. Smeets, & A. Seidel (Eds.), *Shifting balances, changing roles in policy, research and design* (pp. 165–174). Eindhoven, The Netherlands: European Institute of Retailing and Services Studies [EIRASS].

Bonnes, M. (1999). Serge Moscovici. Un innovatore e rifondatore della psicologia sociale [Serge Moscovici: An innovator and re-founder of social psychology]. In M. Bonnes (Ed.), *Moscovici. La vita, il percorso intellettuale, i temi, le opere* [Moscovici: Life, intellectual course, themes, works] (pp. 16–36). Milan: Franco Angeli.

Bonnes, M., Bonaiuto, M., Metastasio, M., Aiello, A., & Sensales, G. (1997). Environmental discourse and ecological responsibility in media communication in Italy. In R. Garcia-Mira, C. Arce, & J. M. Sabucedo (Eds.), *Responsabilidad ecologica y gestiòn de los recursos ambientales* [Ecological responsibility and environmental resources management] (pp. 99–135). La Coruña, Spain: Diputacion Provincial de La Coruña.

Bonnes, M., Carrus, G., & Bonaiuto, M. (2000). *Environmental concern in a "place specific" context: The case of natural protected areas.* Paper presented at Social Psychology and Economics in Environmental Research (SPEER) workshop, Cambridge, England.

Bonnes, M., Mannetti, I., Secchiaroli, G., & Tanucci, G. (1990). The city as a multi-place system: An analysis of people-urban environment transactions. *Journal of Environmental Psychology, 10,* 37–65.

Bonnes, M., & Secchiaroli, G. (1995). *Environmental psychology: A psycho-social introduction* (C. Montagna, Trans.). London: Sage. (Original work published 1992)

Boyden, S., Millar, S., Newcomb, K., & O'Neill, B. (1981). *The ecology of a city and its people.* Camberra: Australian National University Press.

Bragg, E. A. (1996). Towards ecological self: Deep ecology meets contructionist self theory. *Journal of Environmental Psychology, 16,* 93–108.

Brewer, M. B., & Kramer, R. M. (1986). Choice behavior in social dilemmas: Effects of social identity, group size and decision framing. *Journal of Personality and Social Psychology, 50,* 543–549.

Bronfenbrenner, H. (1979). *The ecology of human development.* Cambridge, MA: Harvard University Press.

Brown, R. (2000). *Group processes: Dynamics within and between groups* (2nd ed.). Oxford: Blackwell.

Bruner, J. (1990). *Acts of meaning.* Cambridge, MA: Harvard University Press.

Brunswik, E. (1943). Organismic achievement and environmental probability. *Psychological Review, 50,* 255–272.

Brunswik, E. (1957). Scope and aspects of cognitive problems. In J. Bruner, E. Brunswik, L. Festinger, F. Heider, K. Muenzinger, C. Osgood, & D. Rapaport (Eds.), *Contemporary approaches to cognition* (pp. 5–31). Cambridge, MA: Harvard University Press.

Burgess, J., & Harrison, C. M. (1993). The circulation of claims in the cultural politics of environmental change. In A. Hansen (Ed.), *The mass media and environmental issues.* Leicester, England: Leicester University Press.

Canter, D. (1977). *The psychology of place.* London: Architectural Press.

Canter, D. (1986). Putting situations in their place: Foundations for a bridge between social and environmental psychology. In A. Furnham (Ed.), *Social behaviour in context* (pp. 208–239). London: Allyn & Bacon.

Canter, D., & Lee, T. (Eds.). (1974). *Psychology and the built environment.* London: Architectural Press.

Carson, R. L. (1962). *Silent spring.* Boston: Houghton Mifflin.

Castells, M. (1996). *The rise of network society.* Oxford: Blackwell.

Chandler, E. F., & Dreger, R. M. (1993). Anthropocentrism: Construct validity and measurement. *Journal of Social Behavior and Personality, 8,* 169–188.

Chavis, D. M., & Newbrough, J. R. (1986). The meaning of "community" in community psychology. *American Journal of Community Psychology, 14,* 7–23.

Churchman, A. (1993). A differentiated perspective on urban quality of life: Women, children and the elderly. In M. Bonnes (Ed.), *Perception and evaluation of urban environment quality: A pluridisciplinary approach in the European context* (pp. 165–178). Rome: Ente Nazionale Energia Elettrica [E.N.E.L.].

Churchman, A., & Altman, I. (1994). Women and environment: A perspective on research, design and policy. In I. Altman & A. Churchman (Eds.), *Women and environment* (pp. 1–15). New York: Plenum Press.

Cialdini, R. B., Kallgren, C. A., & Reno, R. R. (1991). A focus theory of normative conduct. In L. Berkowitz (Ed.), *Advances in experimental social psychology* (Vol. 24, pp. 201–234). New York: Academic Press.

Corraliza, J. A., & Berenguer, J. (2000). Environmental values, beliefs, and action: A situational approach. *Environment and Behavior, 32*(6), 832–847.

Costanza, R. (Ed.). (1991). *Ecological economics: The science and management of sustainability.* New York: Columbia University Press.

Craik, K. H. (1970). Environmental psychology. In K. H. Craik, R. Kleinmuntz, R. Rosnow, R. Rosental, J. A. Cheyne, & R. H. Walters (Eds.), *New directions in psychology* (Vol. 4, pp. 1–122). New York: Holt, Rinehart and Winston.

Dawes, R. M. (1980). Social dilemmas. *Annual Review of Psychology, 31,* 169–193.

Dawes, R. M. (2000). *Human cooperation: The critical role of group identity and commitment.* Paper presented at Diplomacy and Psychology Dag HammarskJöld Memorial Seminar. Twenty-Seventh International Congress of Psychology, Stockholm.

Dawes, R. M., & Messick, D. M. (2000). Social dilemmas. *International Journal of Psychology, 35*(2), 111–116.

De Cremer, D., & Van Vugt, M. (1999). Social identification effects in social dilemmas: A transformation of motives. *European Journal of Social Psychology, 29,* 871–893.

Derksen, L., & Gartrell, J. (1993). The social context of recycling. *American Sociological Review, 58,* 434–442.

di Castri, F. (1981, April). Ecology: The genesis of a science of man and nature. *UNESCO Courier,* 6–11.

di Castri, F. (1995). The chair of sustainable development. *Nature and Resources, 13*(3), 2–7.

di Castri, F. (1998). Environment in a global information society. *Nature & Resources, 13*(3), 4–7.

di Castri, F. (2000). Ecology in context of economic globalization. *BioScience, 50*(4), 321–332.

di Castri, F., Barker, F. W., & Hadley, M. (Eds.). (1984). *Ecology in practice.* Dublin: Tycooly.

di Castri, F., Hadley, M., & Dalmanian, J. (1981). MAB: The Man and Biosphere Program as an evolving system. *Ambio, 10*(2–3), 52–57.

Dietz, T. (1994). "What should we do?" Human ecology and collective decision making. *Human Ecology Review, 1,* 301–309.

Dietz, T., & Stern, P. C. (1998). Science, values, and biodiversity. *BioScience, 48*(6), 441–444.

Dixon, J., & Durrheim, K. (2000). Displacing place-identity: A discursive approach to locating self and other. *British Journal of Social Psychology, 39,* 27–44.

Dixon, J. A., Reicher, S., & Foster, D. H. (1997). Ideology, geography and racial exclusion: The spatter camp as "blot on the landscape." *Text, 17,* 317–348.

Douglas, M. (1966). *Purity and danger: An analysis of the concepts of pollution and taboo.* London: Routledge & Kegan Paul.

Douglas, M., & Wildavsky, A. (1982). *Risk and culture. An essay on the selection of technological and environmental dangers.* Berkeley: University of California Press.

Dower, N. (Ed.). (1989). *Ethics and environmental responsibility.* Aldershot, England: Avebury.

Dunlap, R. E., & Van Liere, K. D. (1978). The "New Environmental Paradigm": A proposed measuring instrument and preliminary results. *Journal of Environmental Education, 9,* 10–19.

Dunlap, R. E., Van Liere, K. D., Mertig, A. G., & Jones, R. E. (2000). Measuring endorsement of the new ecological paradigm: A revised NEP scale. *Journal of Social Issues, 56*(3), 425–442.

Edney, J. J. (1980). The common problem: Alternative perspectives. *American Psychologist, 35,* 131–150.

Edwards, D. (1991). Categories are for talking: On the cognitive and discursive bases of categorization. *Theory and Psychology, 1,* 515–542.

Edwards, D., & Potter, J. (1992). *Discursive psychology.* London: Sage.

Eiser, J. R., Reicher, S. D., & Podpadec, T. J. (1993). What's the beach like? Context effects in judgements of environmental quality. *Journal of Environmental Psychology, 13,* 343–352.

Eisto, I., Hokkanem, T. J., Öhman, M., & Repola, A. (Eds.). (1999). *Local involvement and economic dimensions in biosphere reserve activities.* Helsinki: Academy of Finland.

Evans, G. W., & Saegert, S. (2000). Residential crowding in the context of inner city poverty. In S. Wapner, J. Demick, T. Yamamoto, & H. Minami (Eds.), *Theoretical perspectives in environment-behavior research: Underlying assumptions, research problems, and methodologies* (pp. 247–268). New York: Kluwer Academic/Plenum Press.

Festinger, L., Shachter, S., & Back, K. (1950). *Social pressure in informal groups.* Stanford, CA: Stanford University Press.

Fischhoff, B., Svenson, O., & Slovic, P. (1987). Active response to environmental hazards: Perceptions and decision making. In D. Stokol & I. Altman (Eds.), *Handbook of environmental psychology* (pp. 1089–1133). New York: Wiley.

Fishbein, M., & Ajzen, I. (1975). *Belief, attitude, intention, and behavior.* Reading, MA: Addison-Wesley.

Fransson, N., & Gärling, T. (1999). Environmental concern: Conceptual definitions, measurement methods and research. *Journal of Environmental Psychology, 19,* 369–382.

Gärling, T. (1999). Value priorities, social value orientation and cooperation in social dilemmas. *British Journal of Social Psychology, 38,* 397–408.

Gärling, T., Biel, A., & Gustafsson, M. (1998). Different kinds and roles of environmental uncertainty. *Journal of Environmental Psychology, 18,* 75–83.

Geller, E. S. (1987). Applied behavioral analysis and environmental psychology: From strange bedfellows to a productive marriage. In D. Stokols & I. Altman (Eds.), *Handbook of environmental psychology* (pp. 361–388). New York: Wiley.

Geller, E. S. (1995). Integrating behaviorism and humanism for environmental protection. *Journal of Social Issues, 51*(4), 179–195.

Giacomini, V. (1983). *La rivoluzione tolemaica* [The Ptolemaic revolution]. Brescia, Italy: Editrice La Scuola.

Gibson, J. J. (1950). *The perception of the visual world.* Boston: Houghton Mifflin.

Gibson, J. J. (1966). *The senses considered as perceptual systems.* Boston: Houghton Mifflin.

Gifford, D. (1995). Natural psychology: An introduction. *Journal of Environmental Psychology, 15,* 167–168.

Gladwing, T. N., Newburry, W. E., & Reiskin, E. D. (1997). Why is northern elite mind biased against community, the environment and a sustainable future? In M. H. Bazerman, D. M. Messick, A. E. Tenbrunsel, & K. A. Wade-Benzioni (Eds.), *Environment, ethicism and behavior: The psychology of environmental valuation and degradation* (pp. 234–274). San Francisco: New Lexington Press.

Goffman, E. (1959). *The presentation of self in everyday life.* New York: Doubleday.

Goldenhar, L. M., & Connell, C. M. (1992–1993). Understanding and predicting recycling behavior: An application of the theory of reasoned action. *Journal of Environmental Systems, 22*(1), 91–103.

Graumann, K., & Kruse, L. (1990). The environment: Social construction and psychological problems. In H. T. Himmelveit & G. Garkell (Eds.), *Societal psychology* (pp. 212–229). London: Sage.

Guagnano, G. A., Stern, P. C., & Dietz, T. (1995). Influences on attitude-behavior relationships: A natural experiment with curb-side recycling. *Environment and Behavior, 27,* 699–718.

Hall, E. T. (1966). *The hidden dimension.* New York: Doubleday.

Hardin, G. J. (1968). The tragedy of the commons. *Sciences, 162,* 1243–1248.

Hardin, G. J., & Baden, J. (Eds.). (1977). *Managing the commons.* San Francisco: Freeman.

Hardin, R. (1971). Collective action as an agreeable prisoners' dilemma. *Behavioral Science, 16,* 472–481.

Healey, P. (1997). *Collaborative planning: Shaping places in fragmented societies.* London: Macmillan.

Heller, K. (1989). The return to community. *American Journal of Community Psychology, 17*(1), 1–15.

Hine, D. W., & Gifford, R. (1991). Fear appeals, individual differences, and environmental concern. *Journal of Environmental Education, 23,* 36–41.

Hines, J. M., Hungerford, H. R., & Tomera, A. N. (1987). Analysis and synthesis of research on responsible environmental behavior: A meta-analysis. *Journal of Environmental Education, 18,* 1–18.

Holahan, C. H. (1986). Environmental psychology. *Annual Review of Psychology, 37,* 381–407.

Hopper, J. R., & Nielsen, J. Mc. C. (1991). Recycling as altruistic behavior: Normative and behavioral strategies to expand participation in a community recycling program. *Environment and Behavior, 23,* 195–220.

Howard, G. S. (1997). *Ecological psychology: Creating a more earth-friendly human nature.* Notre Dame, IN: University of Notre Dame Press.

Howard, G. S. (2000). Adapting human lifestyles for the 21st century. *American Psychologist, 55,* 509–515.

Inglehart, R. (1997). *Modernization and postmodernization: Cultural economic and political change in 43 societies.* Princeton, NJ: Princeton University Press.

Ittelson, W. H. (1973). Environmental perception and contemporary perceptual theory. In W. H. Ittelson (Ed.), *Environment and cognition* (pp. 1–19). New York: Academic Press.

Kahneman, D., & Tversky, A. (1984). Choices, values, and frames. *American Psychologist, 39,* 341–350.

Kaiser, F. G. (1998). A general measure of ecological behavior. *Journal of Applied Social Psychology, 28,* 395–422.

Kaiser, F. G., Wölfing, S., & Fuhrer, U. (1999). Environmental attitude and ecological behaviour. *Journal of Environmental Psychology, 19,* 1–19.

Kaplan, S., Kaplan, R., & Wendt, J. S. (1972). Rated preference and complexity for natural and urban visual material. *Perception & Psychophysics, 12,* 354–356.

Katz, E. (1997). *Nature as subject: Human obligation and natural community.* London: Rowman & Littlefield.

Katzev, R., & Wang, T. (1994). Can commitment change behavior? A case study of environmental actions. *Journal of Social Behavior and Personality, 9,* 13–26.

Kelley, H. H., & Thibaut, J. W. (1978). *Interpersonal relations: A theory of interdependence.* New York: Wiley.

Kilpatrick, F. P. (1961). Introduction. In F. P. Kilpatrick (Ed.), *Explorations in transactional psychology* (pp. 1–5). New York: New York University Press.

Kramer, R. M., & Brewer, M. B. (1986). Social group identity and the emergence of cooperation in resource conservation dilemmas. In H. Wilke, D. Messick, & C. Rutte (Eds.), *Experimental social dilemmas* (pp. 177–203). Frankfurt am Main, Germany: Verlag Peter Lang.

Kruse, L. (1997). Evolving the concept of sustainability. In M. Gray (Ed.), *Evolving environmental ideals: Proceedings of 14th International Association People Environment Studies conference* (pp. 10–13). Stockholm: IAPS.

Kruse, L., & Graumann, K. (1987). Environmental psychology in Germany. In D. Stokol & I. Altman (Eds.), *Handbook of environmental psychology* (pp. 1195–1225). New York: Wiley.

Lee, Y.-J., De Young, R. D., & Marans, R. W. (1995). Factors influencing individual recycling behavior in office settings: A study of office workers in Taiwan. *Environment and Behavior, 27*(3), 380–403.

Levy-Leboyer, C., Bonnes, M., Chase, J., Ferreira-Marques, J., & Pawlik, K. (1996). Determinants of proenvironmental behavior: A five countries comparison. *European Psychologist, 1,* 123–129.

Lewin, K. (1944). Constructs in psychology and psychological ecology. *University of Iowa Studies in Child Welfare, 20,* 17–21.

Lewin, K. (1951). *Field theory in social science.* New York: Harper.

Little, B. R. (1987). Personality and environment. In D. Stokols & I. Altman (Eds.), *Handbook of environmental psychology* (pp. 205–244). New York: Wiley.

Lynne, G. D., Franklin-Casey, C., Hodges, A., & Rahmani, M. (1995). Conservation technology adoption decision and the theory of planned behavior. *Journal of Economic Psychology, 16,* 581–598.

Macnaghten, P. (1993). Discourses of nature: Argumentation and power. In E. Burman & I. Parker (Eds.), *Discourse analytic research: Repertoires and readings of texts in action* (pp. 52–72). London: Routledge & Kegan Paul.

Macnaghten, P., Brown, R., & Reicher, S. (1992). On the nature of the nature: Experimental studies in the power of rhetoric. *Journal of Community and Applied Social Psychology, 2,* 5–28.

Malone, T. F., & Roederer, J. G. (Eds.). (1985). *Global change.* Cambridge: Cambridge University Press.

Maloney, M. P., & Ward, M. P. (1973). Ecology: Let's hear from people. *American Psychologist, 28,* 583–586.

Manstead, A. S. R. (1996). Attitudes and behaviour. In G. R. Semin & K. Fiedler (Eds.), *Applied social psychology* (pp. 2–29). London: Sage.

Mayo, E. (1933). *The human problems of an industrial civilization.* New York: Macmillan.

McFarlane, B. L., & Boxall, P. C. (2000). Factors influencing forest values and attitudes of two stake holder groups: The case of the Foothills Model Forest, Alberta, Canada. *Society and Natural Research, 13,* 649–661.

McKenzie-Mohr, D. (2000). Fostering sustainable behavior through community-based social marketing. *American Psychologists, 55,* 531–537.

Meadows, D. H., Meadows, D. L., Randers, J., & Behrens, W. W. (1972). *The limits of growth: A report for the Club of*

Rome's project on the predicament of mankind. New York: Potomac Associates.

Messick, D. M. (1999). Alternative logics for decision making in social situations. *Journal of Economic Behavior and Organization, 39,* 11–28.

Messick, D. M. (2000a). Context, norms, and cooperation in modern society: A postscript. In M. Van Vugt, M. Snyder, T. R. Tyler, & A. Biel (Eds.), *Cooperation in modern society: Promoting the welfare of communities, states, and organizations* (pp. 231–240). London: Routledge.

Messick, D. M. (2000b). *Decision making and interdependence.* Paper presented at Diplomacy and Psychology Dag Hammarskjöld Memorial Seminar. Twenty-Seventh International Congress of Psychology, Stockholm, Sweden.

Messick, D. M., & Brewer, M. B. (1983). Solving social dilemmas: A review. In L. Wheeler & P. Shaver (Eds.), *Review of Personality and Social Psychology* (Vol. 4, pp. 11–44). Beverly Hills, CA: Sage.

Metastasio, R., Bonaiuto, M., Sensales, G., Aiello, A., & Bonnes, M. (1998). La comunicazione di eventi ambientali nella stampa quotidiana. Esame di tre principali testate italiane [Environmental issues communication in newspapers: Examination of three main Italian headings]. *Rassegna di Psicologia, 15,* 111–135.

Michael, M. (1991). Discourses of danger and dangerous discourses: Patrolling the borders of science, nature and society. *Discourse & Society, 2,* 5–28.

Mikula, G., & Wenzel, M. (2000). Justice and social conflict. *International Journal of Psychology, 35*(2), 126–135.

Montada, L., & Kales, E. (2000). Political implications of psychological research on ecological justice and pro-environmental behaviour. *International Journal of Psychology, 35*(2), 168–176.

Moore, G. (1987). Environment and behavior research in North America: History, developments, and unresolved issues. In D. Stokol & I. Altman (Eds.), *Handbook of environmental psychology* (pp. 1371–1410). New York: Wiley.

Moscovici, S. (1984). Introduction. In S. Moscovici (Ed.), *Psychologie sociale* (pp. 5–22). Paris: Puf.

Moscovici, S. (1992). The question of the nature in Europe. In B. Bremer (Ed.), *Europe by nature: Starting-point for sustainable development* (pp. 176–203). Paris: Conspectus Europae.

Moscovici, S., & Doise, W. (1992). *Dissensions et consensus.* Paris: Puf.

Nash, R. F. (1989). *The rights of nature: A history of environmental ethics.* Madison, WI: University of Wisconsin Press.

Norman, D. A. (1988). *The psychology of everyday things.* New York: Basic Books.

Odum, E. P. (1953). *Fundamentals of ecology.* Philadelphia: Saunders.

Oldeman, R. A. A. (1995). Sustainable development is a fuzzy development. *Nature & Resources, 13*(3), 1.

Olson, M., Jr. (1965). *The logic of collective action.* New York: Schocken.

Opotow, S., & Clayton, S. (1994). Green justice: Conceptions of fairness and the natural world. *Journal of Social Issues, 50*(3), 1–11.

Oskamp, S. (2000). A sustainable future for humanity? How can psychology help? *American Psychologist, 55,* 496–508.

Ostrom, E. (1998). A behavioral approach to the rational choice theory of collective action. *American Political Science Review, 92*(1), 1–22.

Pawlik, K. (1991). The psychology of global environmental change: Some basic data and agenda for cooperative international research. *International Journal of Psychology, 26,* 547–563.

Pitt, D., & Zube, E. (1987). Management of natural environments. In D. Stokol & I. Altman (Eds.), *Handbook of environmental psychology* (pp. 1009–1042). New York: Wiley.

Pol, E. (1993). *Environmental psychology in Europe: From architectural psychology to green psychology.* Aldershot, England: Avebury.

Porter, B. E., Leeming, F. C., & Dwyer, W. O. (1995). Solid waste recovery: A review of behavioral programs to increase recycling. *Environment and Behavior, 27,* 122–152.

Potter, J. (1996). *Representing reality: Discourse, rhetoric and social construction.* London: Sage.

Proshansky, H., & Fabian, A. (1986). Psychological aspects of the quality of urban life. In D. Frick (Ed.), *The quality of urban life* (pp. 19–29). Berlin: Walter de Gruyter.

Proshansky, H. M. (1976). Environmental psychology and the real world. *American Psychologist, 4,* 303–310.

Proshansky, H. M., Ittelson, W., & Rivlin, L. G. (Eds.). (1970). *Environmental psychology: Man and his physical setting.* New York: Holt, Rinehart and Winston.

Ranyard, R. (1991). Structure and strategy in justifying environmental decision. *Journal of Environmental Psychology, 11,* 43–57.

Rapoport, A. (1982). *The meaning of the built environment: A non-verbal communication approach.* Beverly Hills, CA: Sage.

Rapoport, A. (1990). Systems of activities and systems of settings. In S. Kent (Ed.), *Domestic architecture and the use of space* (pp. 9–19). Cambridge: Cambridge University Press.

Rapoport, A. (2000). Science, explanatory theory, and environment behavior studies. In S. Wapner, J. Demick, T. Yamamoto, & H. Minami (Eds.), *Theoretical perspectives in environment-behavior research: Underlying assumptions, research problems, and methodologies* (pp. 107–140). New York: Kluwer Academic/Plenum Press.

Rapoport, R. (1993). Environmental values and the search for a global ethic. *Journal of Environmental Psychology, 13,* 173–182.

Reicher, S. D., Podpadec, T. J., Macnaghten, P., Brown, R., & Eiser, J. R. (1993). Taking the dread out of radiation? Consequences of and arguments over the inclusion of radiation from nuclear power production in the category of the natural. *Journal of Environmental Psychology, 13,* 93–109.

Relph, E. (1976). *Place and placelessness.* London: Pion.

Roszak, T. (1992). *The voice of the Earth: An exploration of ecopsychology.* New York: Simon & Schuster.

Russell, J. A., & Ward, L. M. (1982). Environmental psychology. *Annual Review of Psychology, 33,* 651–688.

Rydin, Y., & Myerson, G. (1989). Explaining and interpreting ideological effects: A rhetorical approach to green belts. *Environment and Planning D: Society and Space, 7,* 463–479.

Saegert, S., & Winkel, G. (1990). Environmental psychology. *Annual Review of Psychology, 41,* 441–477.

Sarbin, T. R. (1977). Contextualism: A world view for modern psychology. In A. W. Landfield (Ed.), *Nebraska Symposium on Motivation* (Vol. 24, pp. 1–41). Lincoln: University of Nebraska Press.

Schan, J., & Holzer, E. (1990). Studies of individual environmental concern: The role of knowledge, gender and background variables. *Environment and Behavior, 22,* 767–786.

Schwartz, S. H. (1970). Moral decision making and behavior. In M. Macauley & L. Berkowitz (Eds.), *Altruism and helping behavior* (pp. 127–141). New York: Academic Press.

Schwartz, S. H. (1977). Normative influence on altruism. In L. Berkowitz (Ed.), *Advances in experimental social psychology* (Vol. 10, pp. 221–279). New York: Academic Press.

Schwartz, S. H. (1994). Are there universal aspects in the structure and contents of human values? *Journal of Social Issues, 50*(4), 19–46.

Schwartz, S. H. (1996). Values priorities and behavior: Applying a theory of integrated value system. In S. Seligman, J. M. Olson, & M. P. Zanna (Eds.), *The psychology of values: The Ontario Symposium* (Vol. 8, pp. 52–74). Hillsdale, NJ: Erlbaum.

Schwartz, S. H., & Howard, J. A. (1981). A normative decision making model of altruism. In J. P. Rushton & R. M. Sorrentino (Eds.), *Altruism and helping behavior* (pp. 189–211). Hillsdale, NJ: Erlbaum.

Sherif, M., Harvey, O. J., White, B. J., Hood, W. R., & Sherif, C. W. (1961). *Intergroup conflict and cooperation. The Robbers Cave experiment.* Norman: University of Oklahoma.

Sherif, M., & Sherif, C. W. (1953). *Groups in harmony and tension: An integration of studies on intergroup relations.* New York: Octagon Books.

Sherif, M., White, B. J., & Harvey, O. J. (1955). Status in experimentally produced groups. *American Journal of Sociology, 60,* 370–379.

Sommer, R. (1959). Studies in personal space. *Sociometry, 22,* 247–260.

Sommer, R. (1969). *Personal space: The behavioral basis of design.* Englewood Cliffs, NJ: Prentice-Hall.

Sommer, R. (1987). Dream reality and the future of environmental psychology. In D. Stokols & I. Altman (Eds.), *Handbook of environmental psychology* (pp. 1489–1512). New York: Wiley.

Staats, H. (in press). Understanding pro-environmental attitudes and behavior: An analysis and review of research based on the theory of planned behavior. In M. Bonnes, T. Lee, & M. Bonaiuto (Eds.), *Psychological theories to address environmental issues.* Aldershot: Ashgate.

Stern, P. C. (1992). Psychological dimensions of global environmental change. *Annual Review of Psychology, 43,* 269–302.

Stern, P. C. (2000). Psychology and the science of human-environment interactions. *American Psychologists, 55,* 523–530.

Stern, P. C., & Dietz, T. (1994). The value basis of environmental concern. *Journal of Social Issues, 50*(3), 65–84.

Stern, P. C., Dietz, T., Abel, T., Guagnano, G. A., & Kalof, L. (1999). A value-belief-norm theory of support for social movements: The case of environmentalism. *Research in Human Ecology, 6*(2), 81–97.

Stern, P. C., Dietz, T., & Black, J. S. (1986). Support for environmental protection: The role of moral norms. *Population and Environment, 8,* 204–222.

Stern, P. C., Dietz, T., & Kalof, L. (1993). Value orientations, gender, and environmental concern. *Environment and Behavior, 25,* 322–348.

Stern, P. C., & Oskamp, S. (1987). Managing scarce environmental resources. In D. Stokols & I. Altman (Eds.), *Handbook of environmental psychology* (pp. 1043–1088). New York: Wiley.

Stokols, D. (1978). Environmental psychology. *Annual Review of Psychology, 29,* 253–295.

Stokols, D. (1987). Conceptual strategies of environmental psychology. In D. Stokols & I. Altman (Eds.), *Handbook of environmental psychology* (pp. 41–70). New York: Wiley.

Stokols, D., & Altman, I. (Eds.). (1987a). *Handbook of environmental psychology.* New York: Wiley.

Stokols, D., & Altman, I. (1987b). Introduction. In D. Stokols & I. Altman (Eds.), *Handbook of environmental psychology* (pp. 1–4). New York: Wiley.

Tajfel, H., & Turner, J. C. (1986). The social identity theory of intergroup behavior. In S. Worchel & W. Austin (Eds.), *Psychology of intergroup relations* (pp. 7–24). Chicago: Nelson-Hall.

Takala, M. (1991). Environmental awareness and human activity. *International Journal of Psychology, 26,* 565–597.

Taylor, P. W. (1986). *Respect for nature: A theory of environmental ethics.* Princeton, NJ: Princeton University Press.

Thøgersen, J. (1996). Recycling and morality: A critical review of the literature. *Environment and Behavior, 28*(4), 536–558.

Thompson, S. C. G., & Burton, M. A. (1994). Ecocentric and anthropocentric attitudes towards the environment. *Journal of Environmental Psychology, 14,* 149–158.

Tolman, E. C. (1948). Cognitive maps in rats and men. *Psychological Review, 55,* 189–208.

Tuan, Y. F. (1980). Rootedness versus sense of place. *Landscape, 24,* 3–8.

Twigger-Ross, C., Bonaiuto, M., & Breakwell, G. M. (2001). Identity theories and environmental psychology. In M. Bonnes, T. Lee, & M. Bonaiuto (Eds.), *Psychological theories to address environmental issues.* Aldershot: Ashgate.

Tyler, T. R. (2000). Social justice: Outcome and procedure. *International Journal of Psychology, 35*(2), 117–125.

United Nations Educational, Scientific, & Cultural Organization (UNESCO). (2001). *International Co-ordinating Council of the Programme Man and Biosphere (MAB). Sixteenth Session, Final Report* (Series No. 68). Paris: Author.

Van Lange, P. A. M. (2000). Beyond self-interest: A set of propositions relevant to interpersonal orientations. In W. Stroebe & M. Hewstone (Eds.), *European review of social psychology* (Vol. 11, pp. 298–330). New York: Wiley.

Van Liere, K. D., & Dunlap, R. E. (1978). Moral norms and environmental behavior: An application of Schwartz's norm activation model to yard burning. *Journal of Applied Social Psychology, 8,* 174–188.

Van Vugt, M. (in press). Community identification moderating the impact of financial incentives in a natural social dilemma: Water conservation. *Personality and Social Psychology Bulletin.*

Van Vugt, M., Biel, A., Snyder, M., & Tyler, T. (2000). Perspective on cooperation in modern society: Helping the self, the community, and society. In M. Van Vugt, M. Snyder, T. R. Tyler, & A. Biel (Eds.), *Cooperation in modern society: Promoting the welfare of communities, states, and organizations* (pp. 3–24). London: Routledge.

Van Vugt, M., Meertens, R. M., & Van Lange, P. A. M. (1995). Car versus public transportation? The role of social value orientation in a real-life social dilemma. *Journal of Applied Social Psychology, 25,* 258–278.

Vining, J., & Ebreo, A. (1992). Predicting recycling behavior from global and specific environmental attitudes and changes in recycling opportunities. *Journal of Applied Social Psychology, 22,* 1580–1607.

Vlek, C. (2000). Essential psychology for environmental policy making. *International Journal of Psychology, 35*(2), 153–167.

Wapner, S. (1987). A holistic, developmental, system-oriented environmental psychology: Some beginnings. In D. Stokol & I. Altman (Eds.), *Handbook of environmental psychology* (pp. 1433–1466). New York: Wiley.

Wapner, S., & Demick, J. (2000). Assumptions, methods and research problems of the holistic, developmental, system-oriented perspective. In S. Wapner, J. Demick, T. Yamamoto, & H. Minami (Eds.), *Theoretical perspectives in environment-behavior research: Underlying assumptions, research problems, and methodologies* (pp. 7–19). New York: Kluwer Academic/Plenum Press.

Wapner, S., Demick, J., Yamamoto, T., & Minami, H. (2000). *Theoretical perspectives in environment-behavior research: Underlying assumptions, research problems, and methodologies.* New York: Kluwer Academic/Plenum Press.

Weigel, R. H., & Weigel, J. (1978). Environmental concern: The development of a measure. *Environment and Behavior, 10,* 3–15.

Werner, C., & Altman, I. (2000). Humans and nature: Insights from a transactional view. In S. Wapner, J. Demick, T. Yamamoto, & H. Minami (Eds.), *Theoretical perspectives in environment-behavior research: Underlying assumptions, research problems, and methodologies* (pp. 21–37). New York: Kluwer Academic/Plenum Press.

Whyte, A. (1984). Integration of nature and social sciences in environmental research: A case study of the MAB Program. In F. di Castri, F. W. Barker, & M. Hadley (Eds.), *Ecology in practice* (Vol. 2, pp. 298–323). Dublin: Tycooly.

Wicker, A. W. (1969). Attitudes vs. actions: The relationship of verbal and overt behavioral responses to attitude objects. *Journal of Social Issues, 25,* 41–78.

Wicker, A. W. (1987). Behavioral settings reconsidered: Temporal stages, resources, internal dynamics, context. In D. Stokol & I. Altman (Eds.), *Handbook of environmental psychology* (pp. 613–653). New York: Wiley.

Winter, D. D. (1996). *Ecological psychology: Healing the split between planet and self.* New York: HarperCollins.

Winter, D. D. (2000). Some big ideas for some big problems. *American Psychologist, 55*(5), 516–522.

Wohlwill, J. F. (1970). The emerging discipline of environmental psychology. *American Psychologist, 25,* 303–312.

Wohlwill, J. F. (1983). The concept of nature. In I. Altman & J. K. Wohlwill (Eds.), *Human behavior and the environment: Behavior and the natural environment.* New York: Plenum Press.

World Commission on Environment and Development [WCED]. (1987). *Our common future.* Oxford: Oxford University Press.

Zeisel, J. (1981). *Inquiry by design.* Monterey, CA: Brooks/Cole.

Zube, W. H. (1992). Environmental psychology, global issues and local landscape research. *Journal of Environmental Psychology, 11,* 321–334.

CHAPTER 4

Environmental Management: A Perspective from Environmental Psychology

ENRIC POL

ENVIRONMENTAL MANAGEMENT (EM): A DEFINITION

THE CREATION, ESTABLISHMENT, OR modification of any industrial project, urban development, or service provision leads to changes in its setting—an environmental impact (*environment* understood in its widest sense) that can extend well beyond the immediate site. These changes can be managed positively in an attempt to mitigate this impact, or they can be ignored, allowing the transformed environment (in its physical and social aspects) to continue along its path of change, often in an increasingly rapid process of degradation. The impact of such interventions could be positive, though negative effects are more frequent. Environmental management (EM) is today understood to include preventive and palliative actions aimed at minimizing the environmental impact of human activity.

In recent decades, EM has slowly taken shape so that by the 1990s it could stake a claim to being a discipline in its own right, with its own training courses, specialized conferences, reports, books, and journals. EM was born within what might be called the "technocratic paradigm," the belief that the solution to environmental problems is above all technological, based on the development of more technology to optimize resources. However, groups working with a conservationist approach are also increasingly taking up the concept of EM. Sustainable development underpins the present conception of EM, as we shall see throughout this chapter.

I am sure by now you will have asked yourself the question: What place does EM have in a handbook about environmental psychology? There are two fundamental reasons for its inclusion. First of all, if environmental issues constitute a problem then this is because of human and social behavior, the organization of the habitat, social structures, the technologies of production, and their effects on the environment. Second, EM is above all concerned with management of human behavior (in both a direct and indirect way), with decision making based on socially constructed values and with the goal of modifying habits and behavior both within and outside organizations. The question that should be posed therefore is whether environmental psychology has sufficient experience—or whether it is willing to develop the experience—to face the challenge and take on the responsibilities of being present within EM.

In a 1987 handbook on environmental psychology (Stokols & Altman), EM is present but never dealt with head on. Many of the concerns, concepts, and tools that shape EM today are mentioned in the handbook but in a variety of subordinate guises. The subject is given basically an academic approach rather than one designed for the use of managers—that is, oriented more toward theory than practice.

However, in the chapter written by Pitt and Zube (1987), "Management of Natural Environments," and in that written by Stern and Oskamp (1987), "Managing Scarce Environmental Resources," an integrated perspective is constructed of the human dimension of environmental problems that form part of EM today from a psychological perspective. Stern and Oskamp (1987) stress the point that psychology has restricted itself to residential energy efficiency and waste reduction, adopting a perspective more closely attuned to individual behavior than to institutional management.

On the one hand, in a review of environmental psychology in Europe (Pol, 1993) an emerging trend was detected toward what we would now call environmental psychology for sustainability, with a clear purpose to be useful for management. Thus, Levy-Leboyer and Duron (1991), Stern (1992), and Kruse (1994) take up the challenge of global change, and McKenzie-Mohr and Oskamp (1995) provide a detailed summary of the environmental problems that must be faced. On the other hand, Oskamp (1995a, 1995b), Gardner and Stern (1996), McKenzie-Mohr (1994), and Winter (1996) offer solutions from within "classical" environmental psychology. Castro, Aragonés, and Corraliza (1990) as well as García-Mira, Arce, and Sabucedo (1997) describe intervention programs for the conservation of the environment. Pol and Vidal (1996) and Pol and Moreno (1998) outline a professional field in environmental management, defining the specific areas and roles that the psychologist might develop. Moreno and Pol (1999) propose a framework based on theories of social and environmental psychology for environmental intervention and management and its tools.

A number of studies have focused on the psychosocial construction of sustainability (Bonnes, 1998; Corraliza, 1998; McKenzie-Mohr & Oskamp, 1995; Pol, 1998a, 1998b). Additionally, conferences in environmental psychology have taken sustainability as their theme, including the Sixteenth International Association for People—Environment Studies Conference (Moser et al., 2000). Moreover, in the most recent textbooks, subjects linked to the preservation of the environment and to natural resources, contamination, and global change have gained an importance and presence which they did not previously enjoy (Bechtel, 1997b), including in certain cases chapters explicitly dealing with environmental management (Aragonés and Amérigo, 1998).

Bonnes and Secchiaroli (1995) emphasize a psychosocial perspective. For Sime (1999), when the psychosocial dimension is emphasized, it leads to losing the physical world, which has been the most characteristic feature of environmental psychology. Veitch and Arkkelin (1995) emphasize *environmental-ambient* effects on people and the environmental preservation for human survival. Bell, Greene, Fisher, and Baum (1996) included a new chapter (contrasting with the three last editions) on nature and human nature and concluded with a chapter on changing human behavior to save the environment but not explicitly on environmental management. Cassidy (1997) argues that social and physical factors are inextricably linked. His book is focused on human impact upon the environment, emphasizing stress effects rather than management. He proposes an integration of theory and practice. Gifford (1997) gives certain space to workplace, natural environmental psychology, and management of limited resources. He discusses the relationship between the academic researcher and the practicing environmental psychologist as a consultant engaged in intervention. He includes the concept of social management.

Within the context of global environmental concern, Bechtel (1997b) reviews a large number of studies on environmental factors that influence human behavior and discusses planet survival. More specifically, Stern and Easterling (1999) outline the human dimension of climate variability.

As Sime affirms (1999), as one moves from physical detail to local molar units of analysis to global concerns, there is a tendency in environmental psychology to increasing emphasis of the social context. This implies the risk to "lose" the physical environment. However, Sime shapes the environmental psychologist's role (cf. Saegert, 1987) as a mediating agent in change processes that will need to be considered more explicitly in the future.

Yet despite the growing amount of literature, Stokols claim (1995, 1997) remains true that this is one of the least developed areas within environmental psychology. This is due to, perhaps, the reason that Bechtel (1997a) identifies when commenting on postoccupancy evaluations: Many professional reports are written, but they do not cross over into high-profile journals or other publications. This situation makes it difficult to determine the real size of this professional field. The same idea is developed by Philip (1996) in his article "The Practical Failure of Architectural Psychology." Philip advocates measuring the success of environmental psychology more in terms of practical results than in published papers never read.

In this chapter we shall examine how the current understanding of EM emerges from the definition of *sustainability*. We shall examine the implications of this concept in relation to human and social behavior, which should enable us to draft an agenda of professional work for environmental psychology in EM.

SUSTAINABILITY AS A FRAMEWORK

The growth in interest in EM during the 1990s needs to be seen within the context of the generalized concern for our planet and its resources in earlier decades (see the World Watch Foundation [WWF] reports undertaken by Brown and his team; see also Corraliza, 1997; Meadows, Meadows, & Randers, 1992; Meadows, Meadows, Randers, & Behrens, 1972; G. Miller, 1994; Postel, 1994; Reppeto, 1986; among others), and the development of the concept of sustainability. Sustainable development, as defined in the Brundtland Report (1987), is development that meets the needs of today's generations without jeopardizing the ability of future generations to meet their own. Sustainable development is presented as a global concept that seeks the integration of environmental management and economic development. The concept was devised because of the impossibility of extending the Western model of development to the rest of the world. This is due to the high levels of consumption of nonrenewable resources that this model entailed and the danger that the planet's "carrying capacity" would be exceeded (Brown, Flavin, & Kane 1992; Brown, Flavin, & Postel, 1991; McKenzie-Mohr, Nemiroff, Beers, & Desmarais, 1995; Meadows et al., 1992; Milbrath, 1989).

SUSTAINABILITY, SOLIDARITY, AND QUALITY OF LIFE

Following the Brundtland Report (1987), the Rio Summit Declaration (United Nations, 1992) lies at the heart of the implementation of the concept of sustainability. The summit set down the guidelines for regulating individual and collective rights and obligations in the field of the environment and development. Agenda 21 (see United Nations, 1999) was the main consensus plan of action agreed on at the summit.

Both in the Brundtland Report and the documents produced at Rio 1992, the concept of sustainability incorporates an unequivocal component of equity and solidarity in its definition (Gardner & Stern, 1996; G. Miller, 1994; Reppeto, 1986). Sustainable development implies both *intragenerational solidarity*, which seeks to meet the needs of the present generation, and *intergenerational solidarity*, which also undertakes to protect the resources of future generations (Pol, 1998a, 1998b). Moreover, according to the definition from another well-known document, the report *Caring for the Earth: A Strategy for Sustainable Living* (International Union for Conservation of Nature [IUCN], United Nations Environmental Program [UNEP], and World Watch Foundation [WWF], 1991), sustainable development aims to improve the quality of human life without exceeding the carrying capacity of the ecosystems that sustain it. This joint commitment to solidarity and to improvement in the quality of life calls into question the standards associated with the actual levels of well-being reached in the Western world. It calls for a rethinking of the traditional notion of quality of life as a concept associated with progress (Corraliza, 1999; McKenzie-Mohr & Oskamp, 1995; Pol, 1998a), since in the West it has become common practice to associate the defense of quality of life with the defense of the situation of privilege that has been reached. Sustainable development, as defined in Rio 1992 and by the IUCN, the UNEP, and the WWF in 1991, does not imply so much raising living standards (in the economic sense) as attaining a level of social, ecological, and technological equilibrium that guarantees the possibilities of the planet and humankind's future (an interpretation concordant with the concept of quality of life defined by Levi and Anderson (1975) in a report for the 1974 World Population Conference, United Nations).

SUSTAINABILITY AS A POINT OF CONVERGENCE

It has been claimed that within the worlds of politics (Sureda, 1992; Sureda & Canals, 2000) and environmental psychology (Pol, 1998a, 1998b, 2001) the concept of sustainable development acts as a point of convergence (though not necessarily as a point of agreement) between sections of society that are traditionally diametrically opposed in their way of thinking. On the one hand, there are those who from a position of power (economic or political) consider that development should continue. Nevertheless, they also admit that, if they wish to continue growing economically, the need for moderation or certain modifications to "their" model is required (for example, this is the case of the World Business Council for Sustainable Development; see Fussler and James, 1996). On the other hand, there are those groups who hold radical environmental ideas, who, arguing from a position based on the concept of sustainability, admit the need for a certain degree of development, but who place more emphasis on *sustainable* than on *development.* The vagueness of the definition allows it to function as an umbrella term, thereby allowing us to advance toward sustainability, converting it into a new positive social value. A more precise definition would not have allowed the same to occur.

Sustainability as a New Positive Social Value

Sustainability is becoming—if it is not already—a positive social value, which takes a stage further what in their day Dunlap and Van Liere (1978) coined the new environmental paradigm (NEP) as opposed to the dominant social paradigm (DSP). This move toward the NEP has been evaluated in a range of contexts and countries with different instruments and varying results (Arcury & Christianson, 1990; Bechtel, Corral, & Pinheiro, 1997; Dunlap, Van Liere, Mertig, & Jones, 2000; Hernández, Suárez, & Martínez-Torvisco, 1997; Noe & Snow, 1990; Stern & Dietz, 1994; Stern, Dietz, & Kalof, 1993; Van Liere & Dunlap, 1980, 1981).

Gardner and Stern (1996) demonstrate the importance of values and beliefs in proenvironmental behavior. They point out that these values can affect proenvironmental action directly and indirectly, through the beliefs concerning their consequences. The ideological debate helps to build new socially shared values. This debate combined with the objective environmental information has converted sustainability into a new social value. This raises the ideological debate to a significant level, insofar as it helps build a scale of values that are widely shared—hence, the importance of sustainability as a new social value. But as Gardner and Stern conclude, a change in values, beliefs, and worldview is not in itself sufficient to bring about the revolution of sustainability. Such change would require actions that would raise awareness and the provision of necessary resources to create the opportunities for such behavior and the development of necessary skills (Castro, 2000; Corraliza & Berenguer, 2000;

Costanzo, Archer, Aronson, & Pettigrew, 1986; Finger, 1994; Hines, Hungerford, & Tomera, 1987; Oskamp, 1995b; Oskamp et al., 1991; Stern & Oskamp, 1987). It is on the foundation of these shared social values (Jodelet, 1996; Moscovici, 1984) that efficient programs of behavioral change can be constructed (Íñiguez, 1994, 1996). This is clearly what lies at the heart of EM.

Sustainability and Social Cohesion

The classical literature focused on changes in individual behavior. It does not assign great importance to processes of social influence as a factor in the adoption of sustainable behaviors (Cialdini, 1993; Costanzo et al., 1986; Fishbein & Ajzen, 1975; Manzo & Weinstein, 1987; McKenzie-Mohr et al., 1995). The groups of reference, the structural relations within these groups, and the shared values (as salient and prototypical categories), which give the group and its components their identity (applying the terms of Tajfel, 1981; Tajfel & Turner, 1986; and Turner, 1987), play an active role in the adoption of sustainable behaviors. This needs to be kept in mind when putting EM into practice. However, sustainability is often called into question in developing countries, where greater importance is attached to the basic requisites that will guarantee survival. Yet as Gardner and Stern (1996) show, environmental concern and the opportunities for sustainability do not depend solely on the level of economic development. They claim that the increased concern for the environment in developing countries shows that it is not necessary to be able to meet first what in the developed countries are considered basic necessities. Others claim that the concern for the environment is more dependent on the quality of social relations in the community than the level of wealth. A number of recent research papers (Aguilar, in press; Buchecker, 2000; Guàrdia & Pol, in press; Jiménez & López, in press; Moser, Ratiu, & Bahi-Fleury, in press; Pol, in press; Pol, Moreno, Guàrdia, & Íñiguez, in press; Uzzell, Pol, & Baddenes, in press; Valera & Guàrdia, in press; Wiesenfeld & Giuliani, in press) show that sustainability is more viable when a consolidated network of social relations is in place (Pol, 1998b) and there is a well-established social identity of place (Hunter, 1987; Lalli, 1988, 1992; Proshansky, Fabian, & Kaminoff, 1983; Valera, 1993, 1997) than when individual survival strategies are dominant (to use Castells's expression, 1987, 1996). Therefore, the EM that is required to advance towards sustainability needs to start (or at least it should not neglect this aspect) by establishing the conditions needed to strengthen the mechanisms of community cohesion (in the sense described by Rappaport, 1981, 1987; Wiesenfeld, 1994; Wiesenfeld & Giuliani, in press) and identification with its environment (Valera & Guàrdia, in press) (see Chapter 39 by Wiesenfeld and Sánchez in this volume).

Yet in our society there are more forces of disintegration than integration currently operating. Among these, as far as environmental management and sustainability are concerned, two should be highlighted (Pol, 1998b). First, urban planning can have a negative effect when it fails to respect the consolidated social network and breaks networks of informal social support (Freudenburg, 1986), which in the best of cases will have to be reinvented or substituted by the social services (Palmorani & Zani, 1980; Zani, 1992). Second, the effects of uniformity associated with the processes of globalization as they affect culture, consumption, and standardization of lifestyles, can have a negative effect on an ecosystem and its carrying capacity and associated effects on biodiversity (Margalef, 1957), which is one of the requisites of sustainability highlighted in Rio 1992.

GLOBALIZATION OR GLOBALIZATIONS?

Sustainability is usually linked to *global change* and by extension to *globalization* as a generic phenomenon, even in critical revisions of the concept (see for example Bauman, 1998). Globalization is plural and diverse and responds to different, even contradictory, dynamics and interests (Pol, 2000; Quintana & Vela, 2001).

When *global (environmental) change* was first spoken about, it was with the intention of highlighting the fact that the environmental impact of local activities has global effects on the planet (Jacobson & Price, 1990; Kruse, 1994; Malone & Roederer, 1985; Stern, Young, & Druckman, 1992). *Economic globalization* was introduced to describe a phenomenon of the free circulation of capital and the unification of markets that requires the large-scale reorganization of society (Omahe, 1990). There is a major ideological debate concerning the virtues and the problems of the global economic system, whether it will redistribute wealth or widen even further the gap between rich and poor, the haves and have-nots (Cobb, 1995; Fussler & James, 1996; Martínez-Alier, 1992).

If we focus on the dynamics of demography and migrations, we can speak of *population globalization.*

The geographical distribution of the population on the planet, the availability of resources that ensure survival, the different birth rates, and similar factors give rise to population "excesses" in some places and population "shortages" in others (Bierbawer & Pedersen, 1996). This phenomenon increases the migration movements looking for survival opportunities, migrations that are systematically halted, controlled, or impeded (Massey & Jess, 1995).

Information globalization (what Castells calls the "network society," 1996) reduces distances, facilitates communication, opens up new creative and interactive possibilities, and so forth (for sustainability implications see Ahmed & Hardaker, 1999) at the same time as it gives rise to new sectors that are being excluded from society (Mattelart, 1996; Young, 1996).

Other areas with their own globalizing tendencies, yet different from those above, could be described, but it is not necessary. Our concern here is to highlight the plurality of the process and the contradiction of interests that prevents us from speaking of globalization as a single phenomenon. However, the effects of different globalizations are similar: an increasing homogenization of a society that consumes the same products, standardizes behavior patterns and lifestyles, holds increasingly similar aesthetic values, is forced to use the same code (more than the same language) in order to communicate, and so forth. The adoption of universal patterns of behavior carries with it a great propensity towards overexploitation or inadequate use of the resources of the local ecosystems. This leads to an increase in the number of environmental impacts (ecological and social degradation) (Gardner & Stern, 1996; Ostrom, 1990), with global consequences, as well as cultural impoverishment and loss of local control (Martínez-Alier, 1992). A form of environmental management that seeks sustainable development requires, therefore, a global vision of social, economic, informational, and environmental questions that is adapted to the possibilities and characteristics of the local community, both its ecology and its social organization.

A REVOLUTION FROM THE TOP

According to a study conducted by Inglehart and Abramson (1992), 47% of the population in 1990 in 12 European countries expressed their willingness to vote for one of the ecology parties, a result in stark contrast to the political reality of Europe in the nineties. A possible explanation for this might lie in the fact that most European political parties have adopted an environmentalist stance, at least nominally. This has come about for two reasons: potential social pressure and institutional pressure applied via environmental legislation that has become increasingly more strict and restrictive.

On one hand, social pressure is generated through mechanisms of "minority influence" (Moscovici, 1994) by conservationist groups as well as through the effect on public opinion of information concerning environmental problems. For example, the use of technical reports may show environmental information either in an apocalyptic context or in a positive one—for example, the information published about the Rio Summit (see studies on press and environmental issues: Bonnes, Bonaiuto, Metastasio, Aiello, & Sensales 1997; Castrechini, 2000; Keating, 1993; LaMay & Dennis, 1991).

On the other hand, institutional pressure, generated through the introduction of legislation that regulates actions and management of the environment, places us before what might be called a *revolution from the top* (Meadows et al., 1992, speak of a revolution of sustainability). Meeting the requisites of the law has become, at least nominally, an agent of social change and promotion of environmental values (Ballard, 2000; Moreno, 1999; Pol, 1998a). The population is subjected to institutional pressure aimed at changing environmental values coinciding in the main (though not entirely) with the pressure from conservationist groups, a situation that has never before been recorded in history. All this is taking specific shape in environmental management and education, although environmental education does not always achieve the desired results (Uzzell, 1996, 2001) and might even lead to "eco-fatigue."

ENVIRONMENTAL EDUCATION VERSUS ENVIRONMENTAL MANAGEMENT

The relationship between environmental education and management presents a dilemma. The dilemma is whether greater emphasis should be placed globally on environmental education (information, the raising of awareness of these issues) or on environmental management (regulating practices, providing the resources to meet objectives, and ensuring norms are respected). At the heart lies the problem of attributing responsibilities: Responsibility lies either with the people, the residents as individuals, or with society as a facilitating or impeding structure of behaviors and the authorities as establishers of norms and controllers. However, the dilemma is false since both levels share the responsibilities, and, therefore, both are necessary and complementary. Furthermore, as Corraliza (1998) points out, an environmental management that adequately considers the psychological processes involved in the changes of attitude and behavior required of the residents is in itself a tool for education to advance toward sustainability.

CRITICISMS MADE OF SUSTAINABLE DEVELOPMENT

The concept of sustainable development is not exempt from criticism. One criticism can be summarized in the fact that the Brundtland Report (1987) offers only technocratic solutions (Allende, 1995) that in the medium term are not sustainable (Olson, 1995), whereas the best solutions would preserve the self-sufficiency of the world's regions (Cobb, 1995). The solution is not provided by growing more but rather by redistributing resources and technology more equitably, respecting the local forms of production adapted to the capacity of the ecosystem (Martínez-Alier, 1992). Milbrath (1986, 1995) identifies the problem as lying within the current system of beliefs of the "dominant social paradigm." Corson (1995) recommends that environmental awareness programs be intensified while social and political injustices should be reduced.

ENVIRONMENTAL MANAGEMENT AND THE ROLE OF THE PSYCHOLOGIST

Environmental intervention can be defined as any change in the physical structures of a place that, directly or indirectly, causes an alteration in the ecosystem, the social structure, or the social interaction of the population—in other words, an environmental impact (including the natural and built environments). It may be a spontaneous or a planned action (Pol, 1996). This change might be the result of direct action on the environment and population—whether by strengthening, inhibiting, or altering forms of social relations—that in the final instance will change the forms of interaction with the ecosystem. Every intervention is managed, by action or omission. Thus, management can be conducted with awareness of the environment or by giving priority to other interests and values.

Environmental management can be defined as the management process that incorporates the values of sustainable development in the corporate aims of the firm or mission of the government agency. EM integrates programs and practices that respect the environment in a process that seeks to constantly improve its management. Environmental management entails educating, teaching, and motivating both the employees and the community to adopt the values of environmentalism and sustainability. It seeks the development of products and services with the smallest possible impact on the environment. Moreover, it seeks the highest degree of eco-efficiency and applies the best and cleanest technologies available. It also seeks the reduction of energy consumption and use of raw materials and nonrenewable resources, that is, an improvement in efficiency. It places a premium on minimizing waste, recycling, reusing, and eventually disposing unavoidable waste in a way that poses no threat to the environment. EM seeks transparency at all times in its undertakings, with an emphasis on dialogue, participation, and control by the social groups that are directly or indirectly affected and residents in general (Pol & Moreno, 1998).

EM requires frameworks and information concerning the initial situation with which it has to deal and the acceptable range of possibilities. Concerning the physical environment, the parameters are usually fixed by specific legislation or by the carrying capacity of an ecosystem that provide guidelines such as those for acceptable levels of carbon dioxide or nitrogen oxide. (Moreno, 1997). The social frameworks are typically much more fuzzy, varied, and determined by the history and the specific context of the place of intervention. Frequently, it is argued that the only valid frame of reference for evaluating a social impact is the community potentially involved (Freudenburg, 1986; Interorganizational Committee on Guidelines and Principles for Social Impact Assessment [ICGPSIA], 1995; Íñiguez & Vivas, 1997; Moreno & Pol, 2001b; Oskamp, 1995a, 1995b; Pol, 2000; Torgerson, 1980).

THE ROLE OF THE ENVIRONMENTAL PSYCHOLOGIST IN EM

No environmental problem, nor any social problem, has just one solution. Such problems have several feasible solutions (Munné, 1991; Shimmin, 1981).

The solution chosen depends on the effects sought and the framework that has been established. In this context, the role of the environmental psychologist, in common with that of any other technical expert in environmental intervention or management, is not to make decisions on his or her own (Pol, 1997). Rather his or her role is to make available to the client (policy maker, industrialist, manager, consultant, trade union, nongovernmental organization [NGO], etc.) his or her expertise in analyzing the reality and proposing actions aimed at meeting the objective proposed (whether intervention for no change or conservation). The final decision lies with the policy maker, who must draw on the proposals of the technical expert and act in line with a previously established policy and explicit or implicit values and with a thorough technical understanding of the problem that includes a transdisciplinary analysis and construction of proposed solutions (see Sime, 2000).

The environmental psychologist in her or his role as a citizen can act as an environmental activist and apply her or his knowledge within this framework. However, the most typical intervention of the psychologist in EM arises when an environmental policy has already been explicitly established (for example, the National Environmental Protection Act [NEPA] in the United States and the Environmental Action Programs in the European Union and the legislation derived from these). This context defines various opportunities for professional action that we may classify as four types of organizations working within the field of environmental protection (Pol, 1996).

1. *NGOs, green parties, residents associations, and the like.* Environmental psychologists working within EM might collaborate as experts through organizations that seek environmental change. They might apply their professional expertise in seeking a change in the environmental values, attitudes, and behaviors of residents. Also, environmental psychologists might supervise or place pressure on firms or public institutions to change their environmental policies and even the laws and regulations governing the environment.

2. *Environmental consultancy.* In this framework, the psychologist (based on social and psychological background) assesses, evaluates, and proposes environmental actions and strategies linked in most cases with the prototypical tools of environmental

management, including environmental impact assessments, environmental auditing, environmental certificates, and so forth. In this context, the psychologist also analyzes, proposes, and assesses processes of communication and environmental participation that are always present in EM.

3. *A company's environmental department.* In this case the psychologist usually forms part of the human resources management team and is concerned

with environmental behavior, internal processes of communication, community relations, environmental training, organizational culture, management of organizational change in the introduction of environmental management systems, and so forth.

4. *Government agencies.* The work of the environmental psychologist is determined by the three roles played by public administration: (a) The government agency is the *responsible body* for the control of firms'

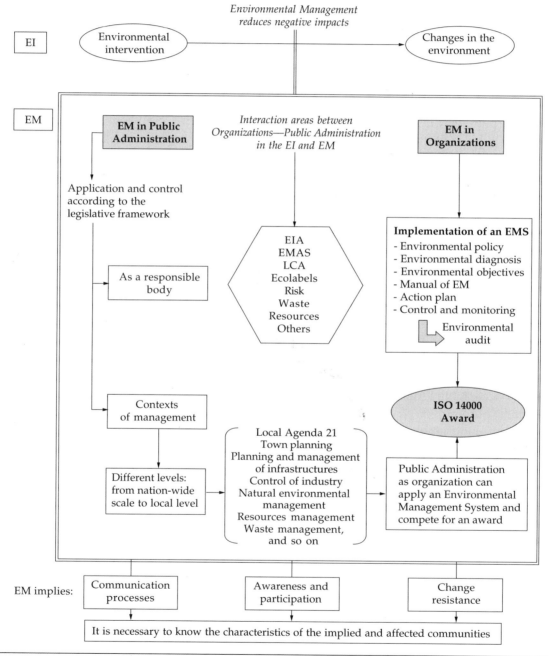

Figure 4.1 Environmental Management (EM) in organizations and in public administration. Contexts, interactions, and responsibilities. *Source:* E. Moreno and E. Pol (1999). Nociones psicosociales para la intervención y la gestión ambiental [Psychosocial notions for environmental intervention and management]. [Monografies]. *Socio/Ambientals, 14.* Barcelona: Publicacions Universitat de Barcelona (p. 12). Notes: EI: Environmental intervention; EIA: Environmental inpact assessment; EM: Environmental management; LCA: Life cycle assessment.

environmental action (industrial permits, environmental impact assessment, environmental certificates to companies or their products, etc.). (b) The governmental body applies *its own environmental management* in those areas over which it has jurisdiction (establishment of environmental policies at the national, regional, and local levels; regional planning; management of natural spaces; energy policy and management of waste; transport; application of a local Agenda 21, etc.). (c) Yet at the same time, the government agencies are also *organizations* and as such can (or should) possess their own environmental management system that has the right to be recognized or accredited (via International Organization for Standardization [ISO] 14000, for example).

Figure 4.1 outlines the interactions between the different levels of responsibility in the processes of intervention and management and between organizations and government agencies (this is discussed in the following section). Private firms applying systems of environmental management and the most common tools interact with government agencies insofar as the latter are the relevant bodies exercising control. Yet this interaction, which takes place at the same time as the carrying out of the duties that are specific to each firm or government agency, always depends on the characteristics and specific nature of the place and the culture of the community. This gives special importance to the individual and social dimensions, areas in which environmental psychology has developed its own background. In any case, as Oskamp (1995a) warns in referring to R. Miller (1991), social scientists have to be careful not to promise too much or to make hasty recommendations for public policies that oversimplify the problem. Each intervention, each policy, interacts with countless other variables. It is the context of each intervention that allows us to assess success or failure based on the other variables and synergies that are operational.

MAIN TOOLS OF ENVIRONMENTAL MANAGEMENT: PSYCHOLOGICAL IMPLICATIONS AND SOME EXPERIENCES FROM THE PROFESSIONAL FIELD

In previous sections, the concept of sustainable development was considered as the context for the development of environmental management and

professional opportunities for psychologists. In this section, the first focus will be on the legal context as the defining device of competent spaces in which environmental psychology is and can be active and necessary. The second focus will be on the psychological dimensions of some tools that are prototypical for environmental management.

THE LEGAL CONTEXT AS A DEFINING ELEMENT OF EM

Legislation defines a large portion of the opportunities for intervention of the environmental psychologist working in EM, based on the delimitation of the problems and the specification of the tools for their treatment and resolution. Arguably the best known legal norms are the NEPA in the United States, passed in 1969 and operational since 1970 (see United States Environmental Protection Agency, 1969). The European Union (EU) passed its first Environmental Action Program in 1972, although the one to have the greatest impact was the Fifth Program, *Towards Sustainable Development*, passed in 1992 (see European Commission [EC], 1993a). The European programs do not strictly have the authority of laws. They are declarations of principles that should serve as the inspiration for and be respected by *directives* (the name given to main laws in the EU) and should be incorporated by all member states (see also European Union Network for the Implementation and Enforcement of Environmental Law [IMPEL], 1998; European Commission, 1997b). Each country as well as each state (in the United States), *Länder, Comunidad Autónoma,* and *canton* in Europe (readers must excuse the somewhat Eurocentric view given here) has the power to make these directives more stringent but never less than the levels demanded by national or community laws. The rest of the world also has its specific body of legislation, though it is impossible to discuss this here in any detail (for more detail see Wathern, 1992). However, for our interests here, fairly common traits and general processes characterize the main laws that regulate the environment.

Another source of regulations that should not be overlooked is that of private agreements or, rather, those emanating from the civil society. In the field of EM the main source is the International Standardization Organization (ISO). Its proposals are not laws but rather recommendations that the interested organization can voluntarily adopt and by so doing be awarded with a "certification" or "accreditation." Norms such as the International Organization for Standardization (ISO) 14000 (1996) usually have wide-ranging repercussions in business sectors (and also in government agencies) around the world.

Environmental laws, in general and with very few exceptions, do not refer to specific professions or scientific disciplines and therefore scarcely demand the work of "experts" in the field. They focus on problems and pinpoint aspects and dimensions that need to be taken into consideration (Moreno, 1997). Thus, when impacts, alterations, or effects on the environment are mentioned, usually they refer to land, fauna, flora, cultural or architectural heritage, and human beings and their well-being. Thus a strict reading of the legislation shows that what is required is the participation of social and behavioral scientists in the role of expert.

Environmental legislation has ushered in a new legal typology: the rules as an incentive device. Historically, until now the law has always been punitive. In contrast, these incentives (based on reinforcement psychology) reward those who achieve better results than the minimum environmental performances required by law and those who open themselves to voluntary reviews to verify this improvement (Geller, 1995, discusses the effectiveness of this strategy). This is the case of eco-labels, and the Environmental Management and Auditing Scheme (EMAS) in Europe (see European Commission, 1993b). A system of incentives also lies at the heart of the ISO 14000. Yet this has a perverse effect: It places the person, and his or her behavior as consumer, in the position of having ultimate responsibility for the environmental performance of the firms. However, at the same time, it creates a certain sense of the relinquishing of control that the authorities should be exerting over industries that act in an aggressive manner to the environment. This fact overassigns responsibility to residents and can lead to eco-fatigue.

Whatever the case, the most prototypical set of laws and regulations of environmental legislation outlines contexts in which human behavior is the key to the desired change or improvement. Therefore, these are the challenges for environmental psychology as a science and as a profession. In the next section we shall examine the most typical tools being employed. These include environmental management systems, environmental auditing of organizations (public and private) and regions, environmental impact assessments, life cycle assessments, and the Local Agenda 21. Table 4.1 provides a comparison of these tools in summary form.

MANAGEMENT AND ENVIRONMENTAL MANAGEMENT SYSTEMS (EMS): THE ISO 14000

An EMS, according to the definition provided by ISO 14000 (1996), is that part of the general management system of an organization comprising the organizational structure, responsibilities, practices, procedures, processes, and resources that determine and dictate the implementation of its environmental policy. The introduction of an EMS within an organization represents a significant change. Optimizing the technological, productive, and management processes frequently requires the restructuring of the organization chart, changes in the places of work, a change of habits, establishment of "best practices," and, therefore, the education and training of the personnel (see Table 4.2). There are many studies that, for example, following an analysis of environmental management in the chemical industries (Baas & Boons, 2000) or the management of forests (Carr, Selin, & Schuett, 1998), conclude that the adoption of environmental management systems should always be based on basic changes in the organizational culture. Furthermore, EMS needs to pay particular attention to strategies of communication and the dissemination of information (Schaefer & Harvey, 2000, in a study of six UK water and electricity utilities).

EMS requires that all members of the organization (firm or government agency) adopt and identify with the values of sustainability, explicit in the establishment of the Environmental Policy, in a public declaration. However, given the nature of these principles, this is not something that can be attained with information alone (what was called "management by instruction"); neither can it be an objective in itself, which can be attained simply by "management of objectives." In criticizing the ISO 14000 system, Moxen and Strachan (2000) highlight the need to convert it into a system based on wider participation and geared better to establish the objectives. The model of "management by values" (Blanchard & O'Connor, 1997; Dolan & García, 2000; García & Dolan, 1997) would appear to be more closely in line with the proposals of EMS. Management by values is centered more on the development of principles and values than on changes of the organization chart or on the transmission of technological knowledge.

Table 4.1

Environmental Management System. Different Tools

Environmental Management System (EMS)

Object: Part of the general system of management that consists of organizational structure, practices, and procedures to develop an environmental policy

Objective: To improve the environmental performance of the organization

Application: Industries, services, and public administration as organizations

Implied psychological aspects: Organization and management of human resources; Culture and organizational values; Management of the change in the organization; People concern and participation

Regulations: EMAS (EU): 1836/93/CE; ISO 14000

	Environmental Impact Assessment (EIA)	Environmental Audit (EA)	Life Cycle Assessments (LCA)	Local Agenda 21 (LA21)
Object	Industries, infrastructures, and services projects before being built	Organizations in operation, industries, services, public administration, regions, and so on	Product (or service) in design phase (sometimes it is applied also to evaluate products or services in operation)	Specific areas (municipality, district, region, etc.)
Objective	To detect and evaluate potential impacts in order to correct them and/or to compensate for their impact. Environmental statement: authorization/no authorization of construction and activity	To evaluate environmental performance. Adjust to the policies and objectives set down by the organization. Adjust to the legal requirements of the activity. Requirement for *Environmental Accreditation*	To evaluate the environmental performance in order to minimize the environmental effects in the production, use and final disposal. To show environmental quality in order to obtain the *Ecological Labels*	To know the environmental performance. Diagnosis. Action plan. People concern, participation, joint responsibility, and awareness
Application	Public and private projects	Industries and services, public administration as an organization, specific areas (it takes the name of "Municipal" or "Regional" Audit)	Products. Services	Society in general, including public administration, organizations, and residents of the place
Implied psychological aspects	Change in perceived well-being. Objective and perceived changes in the landscape and environmental conditions. Symbolism of the place. Social Participation processes: acceptance or rejection of the project by the population	Individual and social environmental behavior. Culture and values of the organization. Environmental education and awareness. Social representation of the resources	Human behavior in the extraction of natural resources and in the production process. Behavior in the use and appropriate/inadequate disposal of the product	Social participation. Awareness and environmental education. Perception of the risk. Transport habits. Uses and social representation of the resources (water, air, energy, waste). Consumption habits. Residential preference
Regulations	European Union: 85/337/CEE; 91/11/CE. United States: NEPA (1970). International: according to the specific country laws	European Union: 1836/93/CE and EMAS. United States: OSHA (1970) and EAPS (1986). ISO 14010: International: according to the country	European Union: 1836/93/CE. ISO 14040: International: according to the country	Earth Summit recommendations (Rio 1992) and following conferences. European Union: Aalborg Declaration and following conferences

Table 4.2

Process of Implementing an Environmental Management System (EMS)

In the implementation of an EMS there are usually five stages:

1. Awareness: involvement of top managers
2. Commitment: formulation of environmental policy
3. Organization: initial diagnosis, flowchart, programs, and manuals of functions
4. Implementation of the EMS: operations monitoring, management, and control of registrations
5. Verification and revision: environmental audits, information, communication, reports, marketing, and so on

EMS requires the involvement of those responsible for different areas of the organization as well as of all of the personnel who develop activities with environmental effects. As many of the policies of the EMS must be registered in the *Manual of EM*, they must define the *Environmental Objectives* that should include a commitment to continuous improvement. Of these objectives, some environmental goals must be defined as detailed performance requirements that must be quantifiable and reachable.

The *Environmental Program* must specify the means to achieve the objectives and the environmental goals. It must include the schedule, the assignment of responsibilities inside the organization, and the adopted means foreseen to reach the fixed objectives. Finally, the *Program of Environmental Audits* will settle down to evaluate, in a systematic way, the concordance of the EMS with the environmental policy of the company.

Once proved and the effectiveness of the system and the fulfillment of the requirements have settled down in the norm, the next step is to apply for an *Accreditation System*. Obtaining an accreditation implies the recognition of the EMS goodness. In other words, it means the successful implementation of the organizational structure, operative procedures, monitoring systems to assure the success of the environmental policy and its program. There are two ways to obtain the accreditation, which have differences between them: the ISO 14000 (international context) and the EMAS (Environmental Management and Audit Scheme, Regulation 1836/93, in the European context). United States law has been in discussion since 2000.

In implementing and certifying an EMS, the ISO 14000 norms are the most widely adopted because of their international, rather than regional, nature. However, certain criticisms have been raised and various limitations identified. There is a significant gap between EMS theory and practice (Kirkland & Thompson, 1999). The main obstacles to introduce an EMS are to be encountered within the organization itself (Hillary, 1999; Moxen & Strachan, 2000), because it requires internal changes, in addition to the relationships with external partners (Jørgensen, 2000). Moreover, the typical practice in the introduction of ISO 14000, because of the dominant organizational culture, encourages risk avoidance, places a premium on tradition and precedent, and discourages originality and creativity (Moxen & Strachan, 2000). ISO 14000 should be revised to incorporate a real participatory and more flexible system of management. In this sense, Klaver and Jonker (2000) say that organizations lag behind society.

The shortage of trained personnel and errors in the management of human resources, the high financial costs of the certification systems and the uncertainty of the market profits are some of the main problems that act as obstacles to the introduction of an EMS (Hillary, 1999). Moreover, positive attitudes toward the environment are not always appropriately transferred to management. Firms have the perception that they do not cause any major environmental impacts, and they believe that customers are indifferent to environmental performance. Customers are the key driver for the adoption of an EMS, but legislation and the regulators are more important drivers for general environmental improvements (Hillary, 1999). A more far-reaching criticism considers that the private nature of some regulatory programs (such as ISO 14000) generates problems for equity, laws, and democracy because of its significant reshaping of domestic and international policy institutions (Meidinger, 2000).

Despite the obstacles and criticisms, the introduction of an EMS is a step forward compared with the previous situation. An example of this is that the EMS, designed originally for contaminating industries and those with a high environmental risk, is being extended to other productive sectors and services, including universities (Ali Khan, 1995, 1996; Capdevila, 1999; Peris & Martin, 1998). In particular, universities have an amplifying effect since the future technical experts and managers are being trained there. More and more frequently, however, we hear about *integrated management* as a new approach that has put together environmental management systems, quality management, and the management of health and risk prevention at work (Bessa, 2000; Harrison, 1995). This already constitutes a common practice in some leading multinational firms.

SOME PROTOTYPICAL TOOLS: ENVIRONMENTAL
AUDITS, ENVIRONMENTAL IMPACT ASSESSMENTS, LIFE
CYCLE ASSESSMENTS, AND ECO-LABELS

Environmental Audits (EA)

As we summarize in Table 4.1, an environmental
audit [EA] can be defined as a tool that allows for a
systematic and documented evaluation, conducted
periodically and in an objective manner, of the efficiency of the organization, the EMS, and the procedures designed to protect the environment. It aims
to enable the management of the organization (firm
or government agency) to monitor the work that
might cause effects on the environment and to evaluate its performance in terms of the established environmental policy (Roca, Serena, & Pol, 1996). This
definition is quite similar in American (Environmental Auditing Policy Statement [EAPS]; see
United States Environmental Protection Agency,
1986) and European law (Environmental Management and Auditing Scheme, EC Regulation 1836/
93, 1993b) as well as in International Organization of
Standardization 14010 (1996). There is a growing
tendency in Europe to include within the EA aspects related to working conditions and workplace
health and safety. In the United States the evaluation of risk in the EAs of the chemical industries is
mandatory (Occupational Safety and Health Administration [OSHA]; see United States Environmental Protection Agency, 1970).

The professional manuals for conducting environmental audits in organizations provide questionnaires, checklists, observation tables, and so forth
(Harrison, 1995). Yet they frequently focus from the
outset solely on technological aspects and do not
take into consideration as possible causes of problems in the environmental performance, as we saw
in various studies mentioned above, an inadequate
organization chart or people's behavior in the organization. However, it is here where the psychologist
can contribute to the EA. A number of cases show
the importance of considering personnel behavior,
the behavior of the organization, and its processes
(González, Aronson, & Costanzo, 1988; McKenzie-
Mohr & Oskamp, 1995). Cheremisinoff and Cheremisinoff (1993), the authors of a well-known
professional manual for conducting EA, present considerations similar to those just made, and yet, having done so, they do not include them among the
items of their protocols except as regards training.

Paulesich and Reiger (1997) consider the standardized checklist insufficient, at least for the EAs
conducted within the European system, EMAS.
Table 4.3 presents a sample of items that consider
the human aspects of an organization, integrated
within the method used in conducting EAs by a private firm of environmental consultants in Barcelona
that, since 1991, has employed environmental psychologists as a matter of course on their staff.

EA has been extended also to the regional and
municipal levels (municipal or regional environmental audit, MEA). The MEA seeks to identify the environmental effects of industries and services within a
specific region; the effects on the environment of the
habits, lifestyles, and behaviors of its residents; and
its adherence to previously established environmental policy and objectives. Usually this is linked to
the application of Local Agenda 21 (which I discuss
in a later section). In this context, Pearson and
Barnes (1999) report the case of Cheshire where,
through the MEA, not only public administration
but also private organizations document the environmental impacts caused by their activities and operations and are kept informed of the benefits of a
move to formal environmental management.

Environmental Impact Assessment (EIA)

The EIA is the oldest tool for the preventive management of the environment. An EIA is performed on an
industry, infrastructure, or service project before the
authorization is given for its construction. An EIA
seeks to assess the effects that an industrial plant
or service project might have on the environment,
human welfare, and the cultural heritage and, where
they are deemed necessary, to recommend corrective
or preventive measures or compensation. An EIA is
an administrative procedure with a prescriptive nature for the authorization of any intervention. EIAs
are regulated by NEPA (1970; see United States Environmental Protection Agency, 1969) in the United
States and by Directives 85/337/EEC and 97/11/EC
in the European Union (see European Commission,
1985, 1997a). In Wathern (1992) acts from all regions
and their enforcement are reviewed.

A distinction should be drawn between the environmental impact study (EIS) and the environmental impact assessment (EIA). An EIS is the report
produced following the analysis, detection, and
description of the foreseeable effects linked or

Table 4.3
Organizational, Behavioral, and Social Aspects to Be Considered in an Environmental Audit

Recommended audit team. At least one expert in each of the following areas: engineering aspects; legal disciplines; economic and financial field; and organizational, behavioral, and social aspects

Protocol for Organizational Aspects

1a *The organizational structure*
Sector and activity; Company size; Shares and shareholders; Organizational chart; System of inter- and intradepartmental relations; Company's concern for environmental issues; Management style; Degree of employee participation in decision making; Recent changes in the company's management; Employees' characterization; Internal promotion system; Adjustment level between official organizational chart and actual organization structure

1b *Leadership and decision making process*
Level where the decisions are made; Dissemination of decision throughout whole organization

1c *Organizational climate*
Communication methods of decision-making process; Control process; Main mechanism of coordination; Contingency factors

1d *Organizational change*
Motivation toward change; Strategies adopted to reduce resistance to change (education, communication, participation, facilitation and support, negotiation, manipulation and cooptation, coercion); Agents of change

2 *The environmental policy (EP)*
Has the firm written the EP?; Factors which contribute to the creation of an EP; Who has decided to create an EP?; Is there a Manual of E. Management?; Who is responsible for reviewing it?; Objectives, strategies, and priorities; Check whether each worker is aware of environmental objectives and knows the manual of environmental operations

3 *The Environment Department (ED)*
If not ED, who is responsible for environmental performance?; Duties; Difficulties faced from: internal, other departments, the general management

4 *Human resources related to the EP*
Job descriptions and responsibilities; Employee training; Working conditions

5 *Motivation*
System of employee recognition and appraisal in relation to environmental issues; Internal promotion system; Evaluate whether working conditions of the firm are the minimum necessary to enable its employees to correctly perform their task

6 *Communication*

6a *Internal communication*

From the firm to employees and from employees to the firm, to correctly perform his/her task, and to be aware of the environmental performance of the firm; Methods of internal communication: hierarchic, participative, encourage feedback; Methods to develop the culture of the firm

6b *External communication*

Environmental reports are available to the public?; Environmental reports which have not been published (reasons); Products with eco-labels; Whether firm publishes its environmental policy; Communication with public authorities, involved groups or local communities concerning environmental issues; System used to review and answer the complaints received; Site visits and open days

Source: Summarized from E. Moreno, 1995, "Organization Protocol." In J. M. Serena, E. Moreno, J. Pallisé, D. Brugada, J. Ester, G. Herranz, et al. (Eds.), *Environmental Audit Manual.* Barcelona, AUMA Environmental Consultancy Co.

potentially linked to the installation or service project and should include proposals to minimize these effects. The study should accompany the project that is to undergo the assessment. The EIA is the global decision process that the official agencies must apply in examining the project and the study of the environmental impact. The corresponding agency will undertake to make an environmental impact statement, will grant or refuse to grant its authorization for the construction of the project, and if necessary will increase the preventive or compensatory measures.

There are many methods for conducting an environmental impact study, but relatively few are sensitive enough to detect and assess social impacts. In a review of 110 studies subjected to EIAs in the United Kingdom, Glasson and Heaney (1993) found that social and economic impacts were considered in less than half of the projects, and this despite the fact that legislation usually considers, in an explicit manner, the effects on people and communities.

The main problem impeding the integration of human and social aspects in the studies of environmental impact is that the techniques employed for so doing have been found to be lacking in efficiency for social aspects (Bond, 1996). However, many methods have been proposed to do just this. Moreno and Pol (2001a) briefly outline more than 40 different methods for social impact studies.

One of the main difficulties affecting the techniques and methods employed is the definition of the aspects that should be taken into consideration. The Interorganizational Committee on Guidelines and Principles for Social Impact Assessment (ICGP-SIA) (1995) in the United States lays down the guidelines as to what the social component of an EIA should contain. It defines *social impact* as the consequences for human populations of any action, either public or private, that alters the way in which people live, work, behave, relate to each other, and organize themselves to satisfy their needs and in general how they behave as members of society. It presents a series of items for inclusion as well as the steps to take in drawing up an environmental impact study. Thus, a social impact study (SIS) should be concerned with: land use and the resources available to the community, the provision of essential services and how they might be affected, the impact on employment opportunities, the distribution of costs and profits, social relations, the quality of life, the subjective meanings that spaces might have, resources, and the effects that intervention might have.

SISs have used *network systems and matrices* (Hepner, 1981; Leopold, Clark, Hanshaw, & Balsley, 1971; Sorensen, 1971); methods of *numerical orientation* (to use the expression coined by Carley, 1983) (Battelle-Columbus Laboratories, 1972; Dee et al., 1973); *methods based on indicators and indices* (Canter, Atkinson, & Leistritz, 1985; Fitzsimmons, Stuart, & Wolff, 1975); *checklists and questionnaires* (Canter, 1996; United States Department of Agriculture [USDA],

1990; World Bank, 1979); and *methods of qualitative and participative orientation* (Freudenburg, 1986, 1989; Freudenburg & Pastor, 1992; Furia & Wallace-Jones, 1998; Taylor & Bryan, 1990; Torgerson, 1980). Another methodological revision and contribution on SIS may be found in the work of Finsterbusch and his team (1980, 1981, 1983).

Useful tools, although complementary (because they cannot capture all the shades of an assessment of social interaction), are the cartographic systems and computerized geographical information system (GIS) that allow simulation models to be devised. Some local and national government agencies allow databases to be consulted in GIS format. For example, the Miramon project (available at www.gencat.es/mediamb/sig) offers a large quantity of geographical information as well as data about human land uses of a small region, Catalonia, in Europe. On a larger scale, the Environmental Information Management System (EIMS) of the U.S. Environmental Protection Agency (2000) offers descriptive information, databases, projects, and spatial data (see www.epa.gov/eims/eimshome.html). Environmental psychology has recorded significant experiences in its history such as the development of the environmental simulator at the University of California, Berkeley, directed at the beginning of the 1970s by Appleyard and Craik (1978).

Table 4.4 summarizes Social Impact Detection/Barcelona (DIS/BCN), a multimethod approach combining various forms of recording and processing data. Flexible in its nature and adaptable to each social reality and project, it uses checklists, qualitative methods, indicators, and indexes in a format that is compatible with the technological and ecological dimensions of the EIA. The DIS/BCN includes a manual for conducting an initial social inventory and a protocol for detecting, assessing, and systematizing social, cultural, and economic aspects susceptible to the effects of an intervention. It also includes a theoretical framework for the analysis and interpretation of its parameters and categories (see Moreno and Pol, 2001a, 2001b).

Life Cycle Assessments (LCA) and Eco-Labels

A life cycle assessment (LCA) is a management tool for evaluating specific products rather than the overall activity of an organization. Its purpose is to evaluate and reduce the environmental impacts associated actually and potentially with the product

Table 4.4

Detection and Valuation of Social Impacts in Environmental Impact Assessment (EIA) and the DIS/BCN Tool

---

Detection and Valuation of Social Impacts in the Environmental Impact Study (EIS)

According to the legal regulation, the EIA, besides the physical and ecological changes, has to detect and evaluate the reach of changes that will take place in the living conditions and in the well-being of people and social communities potentially involved in an intervention.

Summarized index of an EIS:

1. Introduction
2. Description of the project
3. Inventory of the physical environment
4. Inventory of the social environment
5. Interactions project-environment and detection of physical and social impacts (including community acceptance or rejection)
6. Explanation of the detected impacts
7. Proposal and explanation of corrective and compensatory measures

The DIS/BCN is a tool for detection and valuation of social impacts. It includes:

1. Script of parameters and descriptors for the elaboration of a social inventory
2. Check list and protocols for identification and valuation of impacts
3. Protocol for the presentation and valuation of relevant impacts and corrective measures
4. Model for a summary table of impacts and corrective measures

The DIS/BCN defines 14 social parameters, each one of which includes a variable number of categories that guide the construction of a social inventory and which forms the protocol of impact detection:

1. *Limits:* administrative, geographical, sociological, perceived or psychological limits
2. *Temporal dimension:* consistency with the past and prospective
3. *Perception and evaluation of the landscape:* texture, color, vegetation, fauna, scents and contamination, light, climate, presence of infrastructures, intimacy/privacy
4. *Population description:* social-demographic variables, migration, social class, cultural groups, and social deviations
5. *Economical and productive structures:* distribution and balance between sectors, services, transport, unemployment index, distribution of the property and of the wealth
6. *System of population nuclei and infrastructures:* nuclei, interdependencies, road network; rail, marine and air infrastructures; services, urban morphology
7. *Change of resources:* commercial, sport, ludic, educational, cultural, sanitation, housing, and social services
8. *Social and cultural vertebration:* values, norms and characteristic beliefs, cultural signs, family and informal social support structures, social balance, lifestyles, symbolic elements of the quality of life, symbolic places, places of social interest, places of cultural interest, historical and architectural heritage
9. *Town planning, consistency with:* urban, economic and sector aspects, infrastructures, protection and restoration of environments
10. *Effects on well-being and health:* well-being, noise, gases, water, waste, contamination, dirt, odors, light, perceived security, density
11. *Current uses of the place:* activity, function, maintenance, occupation; ecological, cultural, historical value; and attitudes toward the place
12. *Expectations:* adjust to future expectations that population has of the place
13. *External perception:* idem but by external people
14. *Level of acceptance of the project by the population:* information that they have, acceptance or rejection; knowledge on offered compensations

---

Source: Moreno and Pol, 2001a, 2001b.

while it is still in the design phase. It seeks to reduce consumption of raw materials and the impacts associated with their extraction and transport, substituting them (where possible) with the subproducts of other industrial processes or recycling used products. It seeks to reduce and optimize the consumption of energy in the phases of industrial production and use of the product. It aims to reduce the volume and toxicity of the wastes produced. Like the various national regulations, LCAs are standardized by ISO 14040 (2000b).

The human and social dimension of the LCA is linked in particular to the uses (those that are foreseen in the design stage as well as those that are not) to which the consumer puts the product and the adequate and inadequate forms of disposal and/or elimination that is made of it. It should be borne in mind that there is a certain tendency toward the reuse of products (often out of a simple economic necessity and sometimes as a result of environmental awareness). The use of the product for secondary purposes not originally foreseen in its design is not always desirable and can have major environmental impacts (Rieradevall, Moreno, Serena, & Pol, 1996; Weidema, 2000). It is necessary to draw up a catalogue of possible secondary functions and uses and of eventual ways of disposal that should be avoided. The role of the environmental psychologist in this case is to analyze, explain, and predict the uses and processes that intervene between the person and the product (Rieradevall et al., 1996).

The practical application of the LCA that follows the standards of ISO 14042 has been criticized for being biased toward the natural sciences, promoting corporate secrecy about emissions, and inhibiting or distorting innovation in LCA methods (Hertwich & Pease, 1998). Weidema (2000) argues for the need to understand the public's perception of a product's environmental impact and points out the uncertainties related with the product, the type of substitutions to which it will give rise in the market, and the habits that will undergo a change with the substitution of one product for another, and so forth—none of which is not easily obtained from quantitative data. The debate is very much on-going and can be followed at the Global LCA Village at www.ecomed .de/journals/lca/village/aboutLCAvillage.htm.

Among other aims linked to eco-efficiency, the LCA is associated with the granting of eco-labels to identify those products that are environmentally friendly. The eco-labels are regulated by ISO 14020 (2000a) and the specific laws of each country.

Local Agenda 21 (LA21)

Local Agenda 21 (LA21), an initiative taken at Rio 1992, with working proposals being drafted in subsequent meetings (European Conference on Sustainable Cities and Towns in Aalborg, 1994; Lisbon, 1996; the UN Conference Habitat II in Istanbul, 1996; Hannover, 2000; see International Conference for Local Environmental Initiatives [ICLEI], 1994, 2000a, 2000b) encourages local governments to adopt a local action plan, as a key element in attaining sustainable development. In chapter 28 of the LA21, governments are urged to exercise their

responsibility and engage in processes of dialogue with the residents, organizations, and associations in an open and participative process. LA21 is an inclusive, participatory, comprehensive agenda for action (International Conference for Local Environmental Initiatives, 2000a) that more than 2,000 local governments are now instituting. Figure 4.2 shows the processes to be followed in establishing a Local Agenda 21.

As all the ICLEI (International Council for Local Environmental Initiatives) documents highlight, the genuine involvement of all social groups and broad public participation in decision making are fundamental prerequisites. To promote LA21 and test models for its development, the ICLEI (2000a) launched an international action research program in 1994 called Local Agenda 21 Model Communities Program (MCP). This was a four-year partnership with 14 municipalities in 12 countries around the world. The recommendations arising from this research are organized according to several guiding principles for sustainable development: partnerships, participation and transparency, systemic approach, concern for the future, accountability, equity and justice, and ecological limits (learning to live within the Earth's carrying capacity).

However, the focus of each LA21 is quite different. Using examples we shall describe three quite distinct cases. First, in Hanover, Germany, the focus was placed on local problems—specifically on individual behavior related to global environmental change (renewable energy, heating power systems, waste management, transportation, freshwater management, rainwater absorption, and exploitation, etc.) with strong social marketing campaigns (International Conference for Local Environmental Initiatives, 2000b). Second, the city of Santos, Brazil, tried to reverse the process of environmental degradation that was affecting the economic and social conditions of the municipality and to improve the quality of life for both the local population and tourists. The emphasis was placed on communication with established organizations and community participation in environmental initiatives and issues analysis, with special attention to the participation of low-income earners constrained by their living and working conditions (International Conference for Local Environmental Initiatives, 2000c). Finally, Jinja, the second largest urban center in Uganda, faces problems of widespread poverty, unemployment, insufficient low-cost housing, malnutrition, unaffordable electric service, and inadequate health

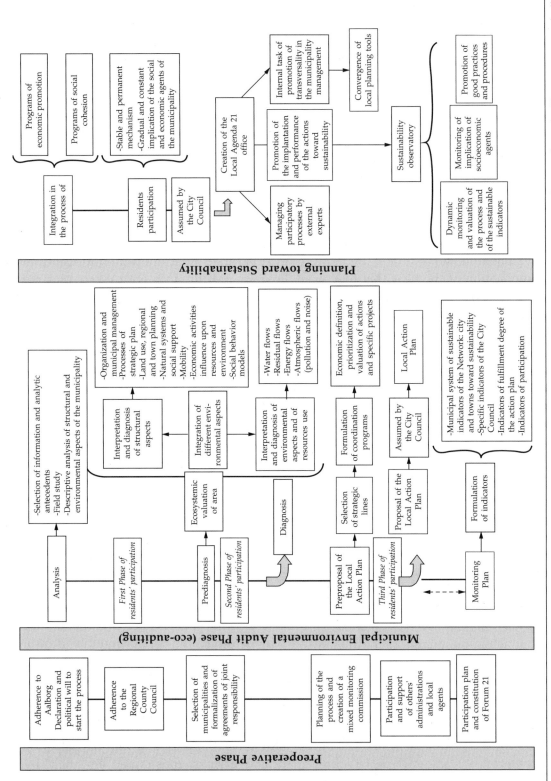

Figure 4.2 Local Agenda 21 process promoted by the Barcelona County Council. *Source:* V. Sureda and R. M. Canals (2000). *Els processos de l'Agenda 21 Local en els Municipis de Barcelona. Metodologia per a l'elaboració d'auditories ambientals municipals* [The local Agenda 21 processes in Barcelona counties. Methodology for the elaboration of environmental county audits]. Col·lecció Manuals, Vol. 10(1), 36. Barcelona: Diputació de Barcelona. Area de Medi Ambient.

and educational facilities. The objective of the LA21 planning process was to improve services to residents while protecting and improving the natural environment. Undertaking the planning with people from different social groups, particularly the very poor sector of the community, was not easy. It showed that it is necessary to identify common interests. Identifying a local leader as a contact person is useful in mobilizing the community. Regardless of the lack of technical orientation, people have a clear sense of environmental concern and the capacity to identify issues and set priorities (International Conference for Local Environmental Initiatives, 2000d).

So far we have seen the major application of LA21 in cities. However, its usage is not limited to this scale. It has begun to be used as a point of reference in the construction of buildings and housing estates, with some positive results in Sweden (Svane, 1997).

INDICATORS OF SUSTAINABILITY

One of the requirements of the LA21 is the establishment of a system of indicators of sustainability that allows local developments to be monitored and comparisons to be drawn with other settlements. A good system of indicators can be useful also for the other EM tools discussed here. Agenda 21 emphasizes the need to incorporate residents as users of the resources at the time of evaluating physical and ecological aspects. In doing so, it is not sufficient to measure consumption or waste production. However, it is more than common to find a number of merely social indicators (neither socioenvironmental nor psychoenvironmental) added to typical indicators of natural resources, energy supplies, and waste. We need to know how the residents conceptualize and assess them to obtain the social representation of the resource. This representation underlies the residents' behavior (Íñiguez, 1994, 1996), as has been demonstrated in the conduct of various municipal environmental audits within LA21s (Audhispana Media Ambiente [AUMA], 1999).

The ICLEI (2000a) proposes various aspects which can be used in developing sustainability indicators based on basic needs, education, and information, decentralization and participation, climatic change, energy supply and renewable resources, infrastructure and urban form, protection of human health, transportation, waste and resources management, and freshwater resources management. The European Commission at the Conference of Hanover (2000) proposed a number of common European indicators, which aim to express the interactions between "strictly environmental" questions and those that are more of a social and economic nature (Punsola, 2000). Independently of considerations as to whether sufficient attention is paid to the psycho/socioenvironmental dimension that we mentioned, Table 4.5 provides a summary of this system of indicators.

SOME APPLIED FIELDS AS CONCLUSIONS

In this chapter we have reviewed concepts, tools, and applications of EM as they have been developed during the 1990s. Main intersection issues with environmental psychology have been mentioned based on some real experiences.

Environmental psychology, as discussed earlier, has been concerned more for a scientific analysis of individual and social behavior than for the same behavior seen from the management sector (private firms or public administrations). However, EM always has a relationship with human behavior, and that is very important for policy makers, as some of them recognize (Torres, 1997, 1999).

An aspect common to all areas of EM (which requires a complete chapter by itself) is the management of communication and participation of community (Hockings, Leverington, & Carter, 1998; Pol & Vidal, 2000). These specific aspects are part of the agenda of classic environmental psychology. On the one hand, some experiences that frequently happen in the application area do not always generate scientific literature nor become an academic reference, even though these experiences are important to developing the professional field and stimulating academic research. These examples deserve to be mentioned. Thus, for example, communication and civic participation are present in preventing climate change effects (Linneweber, 1995, 1997; Stern & Easterling, 1999); creating a sustainable city (Blowers, 1993; Centre de Cultura Contemporánia de Barcelona [CCCB], 1998; Rueda, 1999); or developing and operationalizing the concept of "sociodiversity" through modeling a measure of variety of formal activities per unity of urban space (Rueda, 2000a).

On the other hand, there are some experiences on ecological restoration projects in urban contexts (Remesar & Pol, 1999, 2000) or for urban projects of a very social nature (Davidovitch-Marton, Cohen, &

Table 4.5

Toward a Local Sustainability Profile: Common European Indicators

Main Indicators		Principles					
Number	Indicator	1	2	3	4	5	6
1	Resident satisfaction with the local community	X	X		X	X	X
2	Local contribution to global climatic change	X		X	X	X	
3	Local mobility and passengers' transport	X		X	X	X	X
4	Availability of public green areas and local services	X		X		X	X
5	Quality of the local air	X				X	X

Additional Indicators		Principles					
Number	Indicator	1	2	3	4	5	6
6	Children's way to school	X		X	X	X	
7	Sustainable management by authorities and local companies			X	X	X	
8	Noise pollution	X				X	X
9	Sustainable use of the earth	X		X		X	X
10	Products that promote sustainability	X		X	X	X	

Principles that serve as a basis for the indicators:

1. *Equality and social inclusion* (accessibility to appropriate basic services: education, work, energy, health, housing, transport, and so on)
2. *Local administration* (democracy, taking of power, participation of all sectors in decision making)
3. *Local/global relationship* (confronting local necessities locally—from the production to the consumption including the residuals—solving the necessities that cannot be satisfied locally in the most sustainable way)
4. *Local economy* (taking advantage of the local capacities with availability of work places so that it is a minimum threat for the environment and the natural resources)
5. *Environmental protection* (adopting an ecosystem focus; minimizing the use of natural resources and earth; and minimizing the generation of waste and residuals and pollution emission and improving the biodiversity)
6. *Cultural heritage/quality of the built environment* (protection, preservation and rehabilitation of the historical, cultural and architectural values, including the monuments, buildings; and improving the attractiveness and functionality of spaces and buildings)

Source: A. Punsola, 2000. La mesura comuna per l' Agenda 21 Local (The common measure for the Local Agenda 21). *Sostenible, 8,* p. 10.

Amoyal, 2000; Sanoff, 2000) that reach a "design for all" (Aragall, 1998; Norway Ministry of the Environment [NME], 1999). Other examples include managing natural resources by a government agency (Bellamy & Johnson, 2000; Carr et al., 1998; Castro, 1998), writing technical reports for policy makers concerning the management and evaluation of children's playgrounds, parks, and gardens (Brower, 1998; Moore, Goltsman, & Iacofano, 1992; Morales & Bonet, 2000), and writing recommendations that have changed the policy of creating urban green areas (Pol, 1999).

Similarly, the day-to-day management of waste is an area in which psychologists can play—and are in fact playing—an active professional role. It includes drafting and implementing plans and strategies for the selective collection of urban waste (Ebreo & Vining, 2000; Matheau, in press; Moser & Matheau, in press; Oskamp, 1995b; Rueda, 2000b). Psychologists also participate in facilitating the reduction of the *NIMBY* (not in my backyard) effect by easing social management of installing an industrial waste treatment plant that nobody wants but that is necessary (AUMA, 1994; Moreno, 1996). Finally, they may also intervene in discouraging the construction of an industrial waste tip because of its potential social effects (Grup d'Estudis Psico/Socio/Ambientals [GEPSA], 1997).

The NIMBY effect influences directly the perception of risk more than objective risk (Cutter, 1993; Puy, 1995; Slovic, Fischhoff, & Lichtenstein, 1980; Uzzell and Jones, 1996; Valera, 2000). Transparency in information and communication and social participation are key aspects in the management of the NIMBY effect (Moreno & Pol, 1999; Pol, 2000; Recchia, 1999). However, social participation is not free of critics; for some experts it generates confusion, as Dickinson (1996) and Rossi (1996) affirm.

In all these cases, communication, participation, and environmental marketing are particularly important (Meffert, Brubçhn, Schubert, & Walther, 1986; Pol & Vidal, 2000; Remesar & Morales, 1996). However, a full analysis of these issues would require a further chapter.

Many of these cases—as well as many others that could be reported—occurring with an essential participation of the environmental psychologist (as was the case of the postoccupancy evaluation mentioned at the beginning of this chapter, referring to Bechtel, 1997a) are not cited in an academic context since, being professional tasks, they have not been reported in any scientific journal. However, they add much to our knowledge and experience and point to the possibilities and opportunities that are being opened to the environmental psychologist in the field of EM.

REFERENCES

Aguilar, M. A. (in press). Identity and daily space in two municipalities in Mexico City. *Environment and Behavior.*

Ahmed, P. K., & Hardaker, G. (1999). The role of on-line communities on the Internet for sustainable development. *Business Strategy and the Environment, 8*(1), 75–81.

Ali Khan, S. (1995). *Taking responsibility: promoting sustainable practice through higher education curricula: Overview.* London: Pluto Press.

Ali Khan, S. (1996). *Environmental responsibility: a review of the 1993 Toyne report.* London: Her Majesty's Stationery Office.

Allende, J. (1995). Desarrollo Sostenible. De lo global a lo local (Sustainable development. From global to local). *Ciudad y Territorio, 3*(104), 267–281.

Appleyard, D., & Craik, K. H. (1978). The Berkeley environmental simulation laboratory and its research program. *International Review of Applied Psychology, 27*(1), 53–55.

Aragall, F. (1998). *Design for all: Toolkit.* Barcelona: Centre de Recursos Informació per disminuits.

Aragonés, J. I., & Amérigo, M. (Comp.). (1998). *Psicología Ambiental* (Environmental Psychology). Madrid: Pirámide.

Arcury, T., & Christianson, E. H. (1990). Environmental worldview in response to environmental problems. *Environment and Behavior, 22,* 387–407.

AUMA. (1994). Estudio de impacto ambiental de la planta incineradora de residuos industriales de Constantí [Environmental impact study of the Constantí plant of industrial waste incinerator]. Barcelona. Technical report for Catalonian government.

AUMA. (1999). Auditoría ambiental municipal de Sant Andreu de la Barca [Municipal environmental audit of Sant Andreu de la Barca]. Barcelona. Technical report for Sant Andreu City Council (Barcelona County).

Baas, L., & Boons, F. (2000). Inventing the intervention: How organizations deal with alternative approaches to eco-management. *Eco-Management and Auditing, 7*(2), 67–73.

Ballard, D. (2000). The cultural aspects of changes for sustainable development. *Eco-management and Auditing, 7*(2), 53–59.

Battelle-Columbus Laboratories. (1972). *Environmental evaluation system.* Springfield, MA: Author.

Bauman, Z. (1998). *Globalization: The human consequences.* Cambridge: Blackwell.

Bechtel, R. B. (1997a). Some concerns about the future of environmental psychology. *Population and Environmental Psychology Bulletin, 23,* 13–15.

Bechtel, R. B. (1997b). *Environment and behavior: An introduction.* Thousand Oaks, CA: Sage.

Bechtel, R. B., Corral, V., & Pinheiro, J. (1997). *The structure of environmental belief systems in students from three American countries: U.S.A., Mexico and Brazil.* Twenty-Sixth Inter-American Congress of Psychology. Sao Paulo, Brazil.

Bell, P. A., Greene, T. C., Fisher, J. D., & Baum, A. (1996). *Environmental psychology.* (4th ed.). Fort Worth, TX: Harcourt Brace.

Bellamy, J. A., & Johnson, A. K. (2000). Integrated resource management: Moving from rhetoric to practice in Australian agriculture. *Environmental Management, 25,* 265–280.

Bessa, J. (2000). Hacia la integración de los sistemas de calidad, medio ambiente y prevención de riesgos

[Toward the integration of quality systems, environment, and risk prevention]. *Mercado Ambiental, 48,* 52–56.

Bierbawer, G., & Pedersen, P. (1996). Culture and migration. In G. R. Semin & K. Fiedler (Eds.) *Applied social psychology* (pp. 399–422). London: Sage.

Blanchard, K., & O'Connor, M. (1997). *Managing by values.* San Francisco: Berrett-Coehler.

Blowers, A. (Ed.). (1993). *Planning for a sustainable environment.* London: Earthscan Publication, Town and Country Planning Association.

Bond, A. (1995). Integrating socioeconomic impact assessment into EIA. *Environmental Assessment, 3*(4), 125–127.

Bonnes, M. (1998). *The ecological shift, environmental sustainability and the "shifting balances."* Fifteenth International Association People-Environment Studies Congress (pp. 165–176). Eindhoven: European Institute of Retailing and Services Studies.

Bonnes, M., Bonaiuto, M., Metastasio, R., Aiello, A., & Sensales, G. (1997). Environmental discourse and ecological responsibility in media communication. In R. García-Mira, C. Arce, & J. M. Sabucedo (Eds.), *Responsabilidad ecológica y gestión de los recursos ambientales* [Ecological responsibility and environmental resources management](pp. 99–135). La Coruña, Spain: Diputación Provincial.

Bonnes, M., & Secchiaroli, G. (1995). *Environmental psychology: A psychosocial introduction.* London: Sage.

Brower, S. (1998). *Compartiendo la responsabilidad: La participación de la comunidad en la planificación y la gestión de parques urbanos* [Sharing responsibility: Community participation in planning and management of urban parks]. Keynote address at VI Congreso de Psicología Ambiental. La Coruña, Spain.

Brown, L. R., Abramovitz, J., Bright, C., Flavin, C., Gardner, G., Kane, H., Platt, A., Roodman, D., Sachs, A., & Starke, L. (Eds.). (1996). *State of the world: A World Watch Institute report on progress toward a sustainable society.* New York: Norton.

Brown, L. R., Denniston, D., Flavin, C., French, H., Kane, H., Lenssen, N., Renner, M., Roodman, D., Ryan, M., Sachs, A., Weber, P., & Young, J. (Eds.). (1995). *State of the world: A World Watch Institute report on progress toward a sustainable society.* New York: Norton.

Brown, L. R., Flavin, C., Dunn, S., Mattoon, A., Sampat, S., & Starke, L. (Eds.). (2001). *State of the world: A World Watch Institute report on progress toward a sustainable society.* New York: Norton.

Brown, L. R., Flavin, C., French, H. F., Abramovitz, J., Bright, C., Dunn, S., Gardner, G., Mattoon, A., Platt, A., Mitchell, J., O'Meara, M., Renner, M., Roodman, D., Sampat, P., Tuxill, J., & Starke, L. (Eds.). (1999). *State of the world: A World Watch Institute report on progress toward a sustainable society.* New York: Norton.

Brown, L. R., Flavin, C., French, H. F., Abramovitz, J., Bright, C., Dunn, S., Gardner, G., Mattoon, A., Platt, A., O'Meara, M., Renner, M., Bright, C., Postel, S., Halweil, B., & Starke, L. (Eds.). (2000). *State of the world: A World Watch Institute report on progress toward a sustainable society.* New York: Norton.

Brown, L. R., Flavin, C., French, H. F., Abramovitz, J., Bright, C., Dunn, S., Gardner, G., Platt, A., Mitchell, J., Renner, M., Roodman, D., Tuxill, J., & Starke, L. (Eds.). (1998). *State of the world: A World Watch Institute report on progress toward a sustainable society.* New York: Norton.

Brown, L. R., Flavin, C., French, H. F., Abramovitz, J., Bright, C., Gardner, G., Platt, A., Renner, M., Roodman, D., & Starke, L. (Eds.). (1997). *State of the world: A World Watch Institute report on progress toward a sustainable society.* New York: Norton.

Brown, L. R., Flavin, C., & Kane, H. (1992). *Vital signs 1992: The trends that are shaping our future.* New York: Norton.

Brown, L. R., Flavin, C., & Postel, S. (1991). *Saving the planet: How to shape an environmentally sustainable global economy.* New York: Norton.

Brundtland, G. H. (1987). *Our common future.* Oxford: Oxford University Press.

Buchecker, M. (2000). Finding a balance between individual and collective identification as a key factor for sustainable development of the everyday landscape. (CD-ROM). *16 IAPS proceedings: Metropolis 2000. Socio/Environmental Monographs,* 16. Barcelona: PUB. (Symposia 3).

Canter, L. W. (1996). *Environmental impact assessment.* New York: McGraw-Hill.

Canter, L. W., Atkinson, S. F., & Leistritz, F. L. (1985). *Impact of growth.* Chelsea, MI: Lewis.

Capdevila, I. (1999). *L'ambientalització de la universitat* [Environmental management at the university]. Mallorca: Di7/Societat Balear i Societat Catalana d'Educació Ambiental.

Carley, M. J. (1983). A review of selected methods. In K. Finsterbusch, L. G. Llewellyn, & C. P. Wolf (Eds.), *Social impact assessment methods.* Beverly Hills, CA: Sage.

Carr, D. S., Selin, S. W., & Schuett, M. A. (1998). Managing public forests: Understanding the role of collaborative planning. *Environmental Management, 22,* 767–776.

Cassidy, T. (1997). *Environmental psychology: Behavior and experience in context.* Hove, East Sussex, U.K.: Psychology Press.

Castells, M. (1987). Reestructuración Económica, revolución tecnológica y nueva organización del Territorio [Economic restructuring, technologic revolution and new organization of regions]. *Documentación Social, 67,* 43–68.

Castells, M. (1996). *The power of identity: The information age: Economy, society, & culture* (Vol. 3). Cambridge, MA: Blackwell.

Castrechini, A. (2000). *The media coverage of environmental issues in Barcelona.* (CD-ROM). Sixteenth International Association People-Environment Studies proceedings: Metropolis 2000. Socio/Environmental Monographs, 16 (Paper 177). Barcelona: Publicacions Universitat de Barcelona.

Castro, R. de (1998). Gestión de conflictos en espacios naturales protegidos: Intervención preventiva e intervención en crisis [Management of conflict in protected natural spaces: Preventive and crisis intervention]. In J. Gómez-Limón (Ed.). *Cooperación y resolución de conflictos en espacios naturales protegidos* [Cooperation and conflicts resolution in protected natural spaces]. Madrid: Europarc.

Castro, R. de (2000). *Voluntariado ambiental: Claves para la acción proambiental de la comunidad* [Environmental volunteering: Keys for community environmental action]. Illes Ballears, Spain: Di7 edicions.

Castro, R. de, Aragonés, J. I., & Corraliza, J. A. (Eds.). (1990). *La conservación del entorno: Programas de intervención en psicología ambiental* [Environmental conservation: Intervention programs in environmental psychology]. Seville, Spain: Junta de Andalucía. Agencia de Medio Ambiente.

Centre de Cultura Contemporánia de Barcelona (CCCB). (1998). *The sustainable city.* Barcelona: Author.

Cheremisinoff, P. N., & Cheremisinoff, N. P. (1993). *Professional environmental auditor's guidebook.* Park Ridge, NJ: Noyes.

Cialdini, R. B. (1993). *Influence: Science and practice* (3rd ed.). New York: HarperCollins.

Cobb, J. B. (1995). Toward a just and sustainable economic order. *Journal of Social Issues, 51*(4), 83–100.

Corraliza, J. A. (1997). La psicología ambiental y los problemas medioambientales [Environmental psychology and environmental problems]. *Papeles del Psicólogo, 3*(67), 26–30.

Corraliza, J. A. (1998). Human behavior and ecological crisis: Social and psychological dimensions. *IAPS Bulletin of People-Environment Studies, 11,* 36–40.

Corraliza, J. A. (1999). Exclusión social y calidad ambiental [Social exclusion and environmental quality]. In *Ciudades para vivir: II Concurso de Naciones Unidas de buenas prácticas para una ciudad sostenible* [Cities for living: II. Competition of United Nations of good practices for a sustainable city] (pp. 27–37). Madrid: Centro de Publicaciones del Ministerio de Fomento.

Corraliza, J. A., & Berenguer, J. (2000). Environmental values, beliefs and actions: A situational approach. *Environment and Behavior, 32,* 832–848.

Corson, W. (1995). Priorities for a sustainable future: The role of education, the media and tax reform. *Journal of Social Issues, 51*(4), 37–61.

Costanzo, M., Archer, D., Aronson, E., & Pettigrew, T. (1986). Energy conservation behavior: The difficult path from information to action. *American Psychologist, 41,* 521–528.

Cutter, S. L. (1993). *Living with risk.* London: Edward Arnold.

Davidovitch-Marton, R., Cohen, I., & Amoyal, R. (2000). *Senior citizens—from a "receiving" group to a development and empowerment challenge* [CD-ROM]. Sixteenth IAPS proceedings: Metropolis 2000. Socio/Environmental Monographs, 16 (Paper 208). Barcelona: Publicacions Universitat de Barcelona.

Dee, N., Baker, J. K., Drobny, N. L., Duke, K. M., Whitman, I., & Fahringer, D. C. (1973). Environmental evaluation system for water resource planning. *Water Resources Research, 9,* 523–535.

Dickinson, J. (1996). Public involvement in environmental assessment. *European Environment, 6*(1), 14–20.

Dolan, S., & García, S. (2000). *Managing by values in the next millennium: Cultural redesign for strategic organizational change* [Online]. Economics and Business Working Paper Series (June). Barcelona: Universitat Pompeu Fabra. Available: www.econ.upf.es

Dunlap, R. E., & Van Liere, K. D. (1978). The new environmental paradigm. *Journal of Environmental Education, 9,* 10–19.

Dunlap, R. E., Van Liere, K. D., Mertig, A. G., & Jones, R. E. (2000). Measuring endorsement of the new ecological paradigm: A revised NEP scale. *Journal of Social Issues, 56,* 425–442.

Ebreo, A., & Vining, J. (2000). Motives as predictors of the public's attitudes toward solid waste issues. *Environmental Management, 25,* 153–168.

European Commission. (1985). Council directive of 27 June 1985 on the assessment of the effects of certain public and private projects on the environment. 85/337/EEC. *Official Journal No. L 175, 05/07/1985;* pp. 0040–0048. (Online). Available: europa.eu.int/comm/environment/eia/full-legal-text/85337.htm

European Commission. (1993a). *"Towards sustainability": The European Community program of policy and action in relation to the environment and sustainable development* [better known as *The Fifth EC Environmental Action Program;* online]. Available: europa.eu.int/comm/environment/actionpr.htm

European Commission. (1993b). *EMAS: Environmental management and auditing scheme. Council Regulation 1836/93* [Online]. Available: europa.eu.int/comm/environment/emas/emas_reg_en.htm

European Commission. (1997a). Council Directive 97/11/EC of 3 March 1997 amending Directive 85/337/EEC on the assessment of the effects of certain public and private projects on the environment. *Official Journal No. L073, 14/03/1997,* p. 5 [Online]. Available: europa.eu.int/comm/environment/eia/full-legal-text/9711.htm

European Commission. (1997b). *Guide to the approximation of European Union environmental legislation* [Online].

Available: europa.eu.int/comm/environment/guide /contents.htm

European Union Network for the Implementation and Enforcement of Environmental Law. (1998). *Interrelationship between IPPC, EIA, SEVESO, directives and EMAS regulation* [Online]. Available: europa.eu.int /comm/environment/eia/eia-studies-and-reports /impel.htm

Finger, M. (1994). From knowledge to action? Exploring the relationships between environmental experiences, learning and behavior. *Journal of Social Issues, 50*(3), 141–160.

Finsterbusch, K. (1980). *Understanding social impacts: Assessing the effects of public projects.* Beverly Hills, CA: Sage.

Finsterbusch, K., Llwellyn, L., & Wolf, C. P. (1983). *Social impact assessment methods.* Beverly Hills, CA: Sage.

Finsterbusch, K., & Wolf, C. P. (Eds.). (1981). *Methodology of social impact assessment.* Stroudsburg, PA: Hutchinson Ross.

Fishbein, M., & Ajzen, I. (1975). *Belief, attitude, intention and behavior: An introduction to theory and research.* New York: Addison Wesley.

Fitzsimmons, S. J., Stuart, L. I., & Wolff, P. C. (1975). *A guide to the preparation of the social well-being account: Social assessment manual.* Cambridge, MA: Abt Associates.

Freudenburg, W. R. (1986). Social impact assessment. *Annual Review of Sociology, 12,* 451–478.

Freudenburg, W. R. (1989). Social scientists' contributions to environmental management. *Journal of Social Issues, 45*(1), 133–152.

Freudenburg, W. R., & Pastor, S. K. (1992). NIMBYs and LULUs: Stalking the syndromes. *Journal of Social Issues, 48*(4), 39–61.

Furia, L. del, & Wallace-Jones, J. (1998, November). The effectiveness of provisions and quality of practices concerning public participation in the EIA procedures in Italy and the UK [Online]. *SSRN Journal.* Abstract at: papers.ssrn.com/paper.taf?ABSTRACT_ID=135648

Fussler, C., & James, P. (1996). *Driving eco-innovation.* London: Pearson Professional Limited/Financial Times Management.

García, S., & Dolan, S. L. (1997). *La dirección por valores* [Management by values]. Madrid: McGraw-Hill.

García-Mira, R., Arce, C., & Sabucedo, J. M. (Eds.). (1997). *Responsabilidad ecológica y gestión de los recursos ambientales* [Ecological responsibility and environmental resources management]. La Coruña, Spain: Diputación Provincial.

Gardner, G. T., & Stern, P. C. (1996). *Environmental problems and human behavior.* Boston: Allyn & Bacon.

Geller, E. S. (1995). Integrating behaviorism and humanism for environmental protection. *Journal of Social Issues, 51*(4), 179–196.

Gifford, R. (1997). *Environmental psychology: Principles and practice* (2nd ed.). Boston: Allyn & Bacon.

Glasson, J., & Heaney, D. (1993). Socioeconomic impacts: The poor relations in British environmental impact statements. *Journal of Environmental Planning and Management, 36,* 335–343.

Global Life Cycle Assessment Village. (2000). [Online]. Available: www.ecomed.de/journals/lca/village /about-LCAvillage.htm

González, M. H., Aronson, E., & Costanzo, M. A. (1988). Using social cognition and persuasion to promote energy conservation: A quasi-experiment. *Journal of Applied Social Psychology, 18*(12), 1049–1066.

Grup d'Estudis Psico/Socio/Ambientals. (1997). *Efectes socials de la proposta de dipòsit controlat de residus industrials especials a les mines de Cardona.* (Social effects of the proposal on controlled industrial waste deposit at Cardona mine). Universitat de Barcelona/Fundació Bosch i Gimpera. Technical report for the Catalonian government, Department of Environment.

Guàrdia, J., & Pol, E. (in press). A critical study of theoretical models of sustainability through structural equation systems. *Environment and Behavior.*

Harrison, L. (Ed.). (1995). *Environmental, health and safety auditing handbook* (2nd ed.). New York: McGraw-Hill.

Hepner, G. F. (1981). A directed graph approach to locational analysis of fringe residential development. *Geographical Analysis, 13*(3), 276–283.

Hernández, B., Suárez, E., & Martínez-Torvisco, J. (1997). La participación ambiental: Influencia del sentido de comunidad, la motivación para participar y el riesgo percibido [Environmental participation: Community sense, motivation and perceived participation influence]. *Revista Mexicana de Psicología, 14*(2), 161–171.

Hertwich, E. G., & Pease, W. S. (1998). ISO 14042: Restricts use and development of impact assessment. *International Journal of Life Cycle Assessment, 3*(4), 180–181. (Letters to the Editor). [Online]. Available: www.ecomed.de/journals/lca/welcome.htm

Hillary, R. (1999). *Evaluation of study reports on the barriers, opportunities and drivers for SMEs in the adoption of environmental management systems* [Online]. Available: www.inem.org/htdocs/iso/hillary.html#Anchor-49575

Hines, J. M., Hungerford, H. R., & Tomera, A. N. (1987). Analysis and synthesis of research on responsible environmental behavior: A meta-analysis. *Journal of Environmental Education, 18,* 1–8.

Hockings, M., Leverington, F., & Carter, B. (1998). An integrated model of public contact planning for conservation management. *Environmental Management, 22*(5), 643–654.

Hunter, A. (1987). The symbolic ecology of suburbia. In I. Altman & A. Wandersman (Eds.), *Neighborhood and community environments. Human behavior and environment* (Vol. 9, pp. 191–219). New York: Plenum Press.

Inglehart, R., & Abramson, P. (1992). Generational replacement and value change in eight West European societies. *British Journal of Political Science, 22*(2), 183–228.

Íñiguez, L. (1994). Estrategias psico-sociales para la gestión del agua: del enfoque individualista al enfoque social [Psychosocial strategies for water management: From individual to social approach]. In B. Hernández, J. Martínez, & E. Suárez (Comps.), *Psicología ambiental y responsabilidad ecológica* (pp. 162–190). Las Palmas de Gran Canaria, Spain: Universidad de Las Palmas de Gran Canaria.

Íñiguez, L. (1996). Estrategias psico-sociales para la gestión de los recursos naturales: del enfoque individualista al enfoque social [Psychosocial strategies for natural resources management: From individual to social approach]. In L. Íñiguez & E. Pol (Comps.), *Cognición, representación y apropiación del espacio*. Monografías Psico/Socio/Ambientales, 9. Barcelona: Publicacions Universitat de Barcelona.

Íñiguez, L., & Vivas, J. (1997). Reflexiones teórico-metodológicas sobre la intervención medioambiental [Theoretical and methodological thoughts about environmental intervention]. *Papeles del Psicólogo, 67,* 19–25.

International Council for Local Environmental Initiatives. (1994). *Charter of European cities and towns towards sustainability: The Aalborg Charter* [Online]. Available: www.iclei.org/europe/echarter.htm

International Council for Local Environmental Initiatives. (2000a). *Local Agenda 21. Model communities program* [Online]. Available: www.iclei.org/la21/la21updt.htm

International Council for Local Environmental Initiatives. (2000b). *City of Hannover, Germany In Local Agenda 21: Model communities program* [Online]. Available: www.iclei.org/cities21/hannover.htm

International Council for Local Environmental Initiatives. (2000c). *Santos, Brasil. In Local Agenda 21: Model communities program* [Online]. Available: www.iclei.org/la21/cities/santos.htm

International Council for Local Environmental Initiatives. (2000d). *Jinja, Uganda. In Local Agenda 21: Model communities program* [Online]. Available: www.iclei.org/la21/cities/jinja.htm

International Organization for Standardization. (1996). *ISO 14000: Environmental management systems* [Online]. Available: www.isogroup.iserv.net/iso14000.html

International Organization for Standardization. (1996). *ISO 14010: Guidelines for environmental auditing—General principles* [Online]. Available: www.scc.ca/iso14000/thestnds.html

International Organization for Standardization. (2000a). *ISO 14020: Environmental labels and declarations—General principles* [Online]. Available: www.scc.ca/iso14000/thestnds.html

International Organization for Standardization. (2000b). *ISO 14040: Life cycle assessment—Principles and guidelines* [Online]. Available: www.scc.ca/iso14000/thestnds.html

International Union for Conservation of Nature, United Nations Environmental Program, & World Watch Foundation. (1991). *Caring for the Earth. A strategy for sustainable living.* Gland, Switzerland: Authors.

Interorganizational Committee on Guidelines and Principles for Social Impact Assessment. (1995). Guidelines and principles for social impact assessment. *Environmental Impact Assessment Review, 15,* 11–43.

Jacobson, H., & Price, M. (1990). *A framework for research on the human dimensions of global environment change.* Paris: International Social Science Council, Human Dimensions of Global Environmental Change Program.

Jiménez, B., & López, R. (in press). Identity and sustainability in two neighborhoods of Guadalajara (Mexico). *Environment and Behavior.*

Jodelet, D. (1996). Las representaciones sociales del medio ambiente [Social representations of environment]. In L. Íñiguez & E. Pol (Eds.), *Cognición, representación y apropiación del espacio* [Cognition, representation and space appropriation] (pp. 29–44). Monografías Psico/Socio/Ambientales, 9. Barcelona: Publicacions Universitat de Barcelona.

Jørgensen, T. (2000). Environmental management systems and organizational change. *Eco-Management and Auditing, 7*(2), 60–66.

Keating, M. (1993). *A handbook on environmental journalism.* Ontario: University of Western Ontario.

Kirkland, L. H., & Thompson, D. (1999). Challenges in designing, implementing and operating an environmental management system. *Business Strategy and the Environment, 8*(2), 128–143.

Klaver, J., & Jonker, J. (2000). Changing corporate environmental management: Development of new management systems. *Eco-Management and Auditing, 7*(2), 91–97.

Kruse, L. (1994). Psychology and global environmental change. In B. Hernández, J. Martínez-Torbisco, & E. Suárez (Comps.), *Psicología ambiental y responsabilidad ecológica* [Environmental psychology and ecological responsibility] (pp. 62–199). Las Palmas de Gran Canaria: Universidad de Las Palmas de Gran Canaria.

Lalli, M. (1988). Urban identity. In D. Canter (Ed.), *Environmental social psychology.* NATO ASI series. Series D, Behavioral and social sciences, No. 45 (pp. 303–311). Dordrecht, The Netherlands: Kluwer Academic Publishers.

Lalli, M. (1992). Urban-related identity: Theory, measurement and empirical findings. *Journal of Environmental Psychology, 12*(4), 285–303.

LaMay, C., & Dennis, E. E. (1991). *Media and the environment.* Washington, DC: Island Press.

Leopold, L. B., Clark, F. E., Hanshaw, B. B., & Balsley, J. R. (1971). *A procedure for evaluating environmental impact.* United States Geological Survey Circular, 645. Washington, DC: U.S. Department of Interior.

Levi, L., & Anderson, L. (1975). *Psychosocial stress: Population, environment and quality of life.* Holliswood, NY: Spectrum.

Levy-Leboyer, C., & Duron, Y. (1991). Global change: New challenges for psychology. *International Journal of Psychology, 26*(5), 575–584.

Linneweber, V. (1995). Evaluating the use of global commons: Lessons form research on social judgment. In A. Katama (Ed.), *Equity and social considerations related to climate change* (pp. 75–83). Nairobi: ICIPE Science Press.

Linneweber, V. (1997). Psychologische und gesellschaftliche Dimensionen globaler Klimaänderungen [Psychological and social dimensions of global environmental changes]. In K. H. Erdmann (Hrsg.), *Internationaler naturschutz* (pp. 117–143). Berlin, Heidelberg: Springer.

Malone, T., & Roederer, J. (Eds.). (1985). *International Council of Scientific Unions (ICSU)*. Cambridge: Cambridge University Press.

Manzo, L. C., & Weinstein, M. D. (1987). Behavioral commitment to environmental protection: A study of active and non-active members of the Sierra Club. *Environment and Behavior, 19*(6), 673–694.

Margalef, R. (1957). La teoría de la información en ecología. *Memorias de la Real Academia de las Ciencias de Barcelona, 32,* 373–447. [English version: Margalef, R. (1958). Information theory in ecology]. *General Systems, 3,* 36–71.

Martínez-Alier, J. (1992). *De la economía ecológica al ecologismo popular* [From ecological economy to popular environmentalism]. Barcelona: Icaria.

Massey, O., & Jess, P. (1995). *A place in the world?* Oxford: Oxford University Press (The Open University).

Matheau, A. (in press). Individual and situational variables influencing the sorting of household waste: The effects of perceived constraint. *Journal of Environmental Psychology.*

Mattelart, A. (1996). *La mondialisation de la communication* [Globalization of communication]. Paris: Presses Universitaires de France.

McKenzie-Mohr, D. (1994). *Psychological determinants of energy efficiency investments: Analysis and recommendations.* Burnaby: British Columbia Hydro.

McKenzie-Mohr, D., Nemiroff, L. S., Beers, L., & Desmarais, S. (1995). Determinants of responsible environmental behavior. *Journal of Social Issues, 51*(4), 139–156.

McKenzie-Mohr, D., & Oskamp, S. (1995). Psychology and sustainability: An introduction. *Journal of Social Issues, 51*(4), 1–14.

Meadows, D. H., Meadows, D. L., & Randers, J. (1992). *Beyond the limits: Confronting global collapse, envisioning a sustainable future.* Toronto: McClelland & Steward.

Meadows, D. H., Meadows, D. L., Randers, J., & Behrens, W. (1972). *The limits to growth.* New York: New American Library.

Meffert, H., Brubçhn, M., Schubert, F., & Walther, T. (1986). *Marketing und Ökologie: Chancen und risiken unweltorientierter abastzsstrategien der unternehmungen* [Marketing and ecology: Opportunities and risks of ecological market strategies of firms]. DB, 2. *Die Betriebswirtschaft, 46*(2), 140–159. Cited by W. Hopfenbeck (1993). *Dirección y márketing ecológicos.* Bilbao: Deusto. [Ecological management and marketing].

Meidinger, E. (2000). "Private" Environmental Regulation, Human Rights, and Community [Online]. *SSRN Journal* (Mayo). Available: papers.ssrn.com/paper.taf?ABSTRACT_ID=209548

Milbrath, L. W. (1986). Environmental beliefs and values. In M. G. Hermann (Ed.), *Political psychology: Contemporary problems and issues* (pp. 97–138). San Francisco: Jossey-Bass.

Milbrath, L. W. (1989). *Envisioning a sustainable society: Learning our way out.* Albany, NY: State University of New York Press.

Milbrath, L. W. (1995). Psychological, cultural, and informational barriers to sustainability. *Journal of Social Issues, 51*(4), 101–120.

Miller, G. T., Jr. (1994). *Living in the environment.* Belmont, CA: Wadsworth.

Miller, R. B. (1991). Social science and the challenge of global environmental change. *International Social Science Journal, 43,* 609–617.

Moore, R. C., Goltsman, S. M., & Iacofano, D. S. (1992). *Play for all guidelines: Planning, design and management of outdoors play settings for all children.* Berkeley, CA: Mig Communications.

Morales, M., & Bonet, M. R. (2000). *Modele pour la reflexion et l'evaluation des espaces de jeu* [Models to evaluate children's playgrounds] [CD-ROM]. 16 IAPS proceedings: Metropolis 2000. Socioenvironmental Monographs, 16 (Paper 63). Barcelona: Publicacions Universitat de Barcelona.

Moreno, E. (1995). Organization protocol. In J. M. Serena, E. Moreno, J. Pallisé, D. Brugada, J. Ester, G. Herranz, & F. Miret (Eds.), *Environmental audit manual.* Barcelona: Auma Environmental Consultancy.

Moreno, E. (1996). Efectos ambientales y rechazo social de una planta de reciclaje de basuras: Propuestas para su minimización [Environmental effects and social rejection of a waste recycling plant]. *Monografías Psico/Socio/Ambientales,* 3. Barcelona: Publicacions Universitat de Barcelona.

Moreno, E. (1997). La cobertura legal del psicólogo ambiental [The legal cover of environmental psychology]. *Papeles del Psicólogo, 3*(67), 31–38.

Moreno, E. (1999). *Impacto social e impacto ambiental* [Social and environmental impact]. Doctoral dissertation, University of Barcelona, Spain.

Moreno, E., & Pol, E. (1999). *Nociones psicosociales para la intervención y la gestión ambiental* [Psychosocial notions for environmental intervention and management]. *Monografies Socio/Ambientals,* 14. Barcelona: Publicacions Universitat de Barcelona.

Moreno, E., & Pol, E. (2001a). *Metodologies per a la detecció dels impactes sobre el medi social/humà en les avaluacions d'impacte ambiental* [Methodologies for impact detection upon social/human environment in environmental impact assessment]. *Colecció Quaderns de Medi Ambiente*, 8. Direcció General de Patrimoni Natural i del Medi Físic, Dep. Medi Ambient, Generalitat de Catalunya, Spain.

Moreno, E., & Pol, E. (2001b). *DIS/BCN: Social Impact Detection* [CD-ROM]. *Monografies Socio/Ambientals*, 20. Barcelona: Publicacions Universitat de Barcelona.

Moscovici, S. (1984). The phenomenon of social representations. In R. Farr & S. Moscovici (Eds.), *Social representations* (pp. 3–70). Cambridge: Cambridge University Press.

Moscovici, S. (1994). Three concepts: Minority, conflict, and behavioral style. In S. Moscovici, A. Mucchi-Faina, & A. Maass (Eds.), *Minority influence* (pp. 233–251). Chicago: Nelson-Hall.

Moser, G., & Matheau, A. (in press). Promote the selective littering: The effect of the feeling of personal responsibility and the awareness of consequences. In A. Kantas (Ed.), *Applied Psychology in Europe*. Athens, Greece.

Moser, G., Pol, E., Bernard, Y., Bonnes, M., Corraliza, J., & Giuliani, M. V. (Eds.). (2000). *Metropolis 2000: Which perspectives? cities, social life and sustainable development* [CD-ROM]. Sixteenth IAPS. *Socio/Environmental Monographs*, 16. Barcelona: Publicacions Universitat de Barcelona.

Moser, G., Ratiu, E., & Bahi-Fleury, G. (in press). Appropriation and interpersonal relationships: From dwelling to city through the neighborhood. *Environment and Behavior*.

Moxen, J., & Strachan, P. A. (2000). ISO 14001: A case of cultural myopia. *Eco-Management and Auditing*, 7(2), 82–90.

Munné, F. (1991). La intervención psicosocial en las organizaciones: Mito y realidad [Psychosocial intervention in organizations: Myth and reality]. *Revista de Psicología Social Aplicada*, 1(1), 51–70.

Noe, F. P., & Snow, R. (1990). The new environmental paradigm and further scale analysis. *Journal of Environmental Education*, 21, 20–26.

Norway Ministry of the Environment. (1999). *Planning for all: Introduction to priority area*. Oslo: Ministry of the Environment and Ministry of Health and Social Affairs.

Olson, R. (1995). Sustainability as a social vision. *Journal of Social Issues*, 51(4), 15–35.

Omahe, K. (1990). *The borderless world: Power and strategy in the interlinked economy*. New York: Harper & Row.

Oskamp, S. (1995a). Applying social psychology to avoid ecological disaster. *Journal of Social Issues*, 51(4), 217–239.

Oskamp, S. (1995b). Resource conservation and recycling: Behavior and policy. *Journal of Social Issues*, 51(4), 157–177.

Oskamp, S., Harrington, M. J., Edwards, T. C., Sherwood, D. L., Okuda, S. M., & Swanson, D. C. (1991). Factors influencing household recycling behavior. *Environment & Behavior*, 23, 494–519.

Ostrom, E. (1990). *Governing the commons: The evolution of institutions for collective action*. Cambridge: Cambridge University Press.

Palmorani, A., & Zani, B. (1980). *Psicologia sociale di comunità* [Community social psychology]. Bologna: Il Mulino.

Paulesich, R., & Reiger, H. (1997). Methods of eco-auditing and verifying environmental statements derived from qualitative methods of social research. *Eco-Management and Auditing*, 4(2), 44–56.

Pearson, J., & Barnes, T. (1999). Improving environmental performance through community action. *Eco-Management and Auditing*, 6(2), 76–79.

Peris, M. E., & Martin, J. E. (1998). Environmental management systems within the university. *Eco-Management and Auditing*, 5(3), 136–145.

Philip, D. (1996). The practical failure of architectural psychology. *Journal of Environmental Psychology*, 16(3), 277–284.

Pitt, D. G., & Zube, E. H. (1987). Management of natural environments. In D. Stokols & I. Altman (Eds.), *Handbook of Environmental Psychology* (Vol. 2). New York: Wiley.

Pol, E. (1993). *Environmental psychology in Europe: From architectural psychology to green psychology*. London: Avebury.

Pol, E. (1996). *El problema, l'objecte i l'objectiu: Ciències socials, qüestió ambiental i canvi global* [The problem, the object and the objective: Social sciences, environmental issue and global change]. In E. Pol & T. Vidal (Comp.), *Perfils socials en la intervenció ambiental: Una perspectiva professional* [Social profiles in environmental intervention: A professional perspective]. Monografías Psico/Socio/Ambientales, 1 (pp. 5–28). Barcelona: Publicacions Universitat de Barcelona.

Pol, E. (1997). El desarrollo profesional de la psicología ambiental: Ambitos y estrategias [Professional development of environmental psychology: Areas and strategies]. *Papeles del Psicólogo*, 3(67), 62–69.

Pol, E. (1998a). Sostenibilitat, valors socials i comportament humà: Estratègies i contradiccions [Sustainability, social values and human behavior: Strategies and contradictions]. In R. Folch, T. Franquesa, E. Pol, E. Ferreres, L. Chacón, R. Díez Hochleitner, & R. Margalef. *Desenvolupament sostenible. Els llindars en la construcció de les relacions humanes i el medi ambient* [Sustainable development: Limits in the construction of human relationships and environment]. Col. Pensaments, 7. Lleida, Spain: Universitat de Lleida.

Pol, E. (1998b). Evoluciones de la Psicología Ambiental hacia la sostenibilidad: Tres propuestas teóricas y orientaciones para la gestión [Environmental psychology evolution toward sustainability: Three theoretical approaches and guidelines for management]. In D. Páez & S. Ayestarán (Eds.), *Los desarrollos de la psicología social en España* (pp. 105–120). Madrid: Infancia y Aprendizaje.

Pol, E. (1999). Simbolisme, usos i funcions socials del parc urbà [Symbolism, uses and social functions of the urban park]. *Barcelona verda, 64*, 28–29.

Pol, E. (2000). *Impacte social, comunicació ambiental i participació* [Social impact, environmental communication and participation]. Monografies Universitaries. Barcelona: Dept. Medi Ambient, Generalitat de Catalunya.

Pol, E. (in press). The theoretical background to the city-identity-sustainability (CIS) network. *Environment and behavior.*

Pol, E., & Moreno, E. (1998). Gestión ambiental en la empresa y en la administración pública: Aportaciones desde la psicología [Environmental management in organizations and public administration]. In J. I. Aragonés & M. Amérigo (Eds.), *Psicología Ambiental* (pp. 375–399). Madrid: Pirámide.

Pol, E., Moreno, E., Guàrdia, J., & Íñiguez, L. (in press). Identity, quality of life and sustainability in an urban suburb of Barcelona: Adjustment to the CIS (City-Identity-Sustainability) network structural model. *Environment and behavior.*

Pol, E., & Vidal, T. (Eds.). (1996). *Perfils socials en la intervenció ambiental: Una perspectiva professional* [Social profiles in environmental intervention: A professional perspective]. Monografías Psico/Socio/Ambientales, 1. Barcelona: Publicacions Universitat de Barcelona.

Pol, E., & Vidal, T. (2000). *La publicitat ambiental i el màrqueting ecològic* [Environmental publicity and ecological marketing]. Barcelona: Editorial Universitat Oberta de Catalunya.

Postel, S. (1994). Carrying capacity: Earth's bottom line. In L. R. Brown (Ed.), *State of the world* (pp. 3–21). New York: Norton.

Proshansky, H. M., Fabian, A. K., & Kaminoff, R. (1983). Place identity: Physical world socialization of the self. *Journal of Environmental Psychology, 3*(1), 57–83.

Punsola, A. (2000). La mesura comuna per l'Agenda 21 Local [The common measure for Local Agenda 21]. *Sostenible, 8*, p. 10.

Puy, A. (1995). *Percepción social de los riesgos* [Social perception of risks]. Madrid: Fundación Mapfre.

Quintana, F., & Vela, C. (2001). Asalto a la fábrica: Luchas autónomas y reestructuración capitalista, 1970–1990 [Assault to the industry: Autonomous fights and capitalist restructuring, 1970–1990]. Barcelona: Alikornio.

Rappaport, J. (1981). In praise of paradox: A social policy of empowerment over prevention. *American Journal of Community Psychology, 9*(1), 1–25.

Rappaport, J. (1987). Terms of empowerment/exemplars of prevention: Toward a theory for community psychology. *American Journal of Community Psychology, 15*(2), 121–148.

Recchia, V. (1999). Risk communication and public perception of technological hazards [Online]. Available: papers.ssrn.com/paper.taf?ABSTRACT_ID=200573

Remesar, A., & Morales, M. (1996). Màrqueting, promoció i educació ambiental [Environmental marketing, promotion and education]. In E. Pol & T. Vidal (Comps.), *Perfils socials en la intervenció ambiental: Una perspectiva professional* [Social profiles in environmental intervention: A professional perspective]. *Monografías Psico/Socio/Ambientales, 1* (pp. 131–141). Barcelona: Publicacions Universitat de Barcelona.

Remesar, A., & Pol, E. (Eds.). (1999). *Taller de participación ciudadana: Usos sociales del rio Besòs: Repensar el río.* [Citizen participation workshop: social uses of Besòs river: Re-thinking the river] [CD-ROM]. Barcelona: Publicacions Universitat de Barcelona.

Remesar, A., & Pol, E. (2000). *Workshops of participatory intervention (TIP): Designing a social and ecological regeneration of a river in Sant Adrià de Besós, Barcelona* [CD-ROM]. Sixteenth IAPS proceedings: Metropolis 2000. Socio/Environmental Monographs, 16 (Paper 181). Barcelona: Publicacions Universitat de Barcelona.

Reppeto, R. C. (1986). *World enough and time: Successful strategies for resource management.* New Haven, CT: Yale University Press.

Rieradevall, J., Moreno, E., Serena, J. M., & Pol, E. (1996). Anàlisi del cicle de vida de productes: Millora ambiental de la producció i el consum [Life cycle assessment of products: Environmental improvement of production and consumption]. In E. Pol & T. Vidal (Comps.), *Perfils Socials en la Intervenció Ambiental. Una perspectiva professional* [Social profiles in environmental intervention: A professional perspective]. *Monografías Psico/Socio/Ambientales, 1* (pp. 87–101). Barcelona: Publicacions Universitat de Barcelona.

Roca, M., Serena, J. M., & Pol, E. (1996). Auditories ambientals a la indústria i al territori [Environmental audit in industries and territory]. In E. Pol & T. Vidal (Comps.), *Perfils Sociales en la Intervenció Ambiental: Una perspectiva professional* [Social profiles in environmental intervention: A professional perspective]. *Monografías Psico/Socio/Ambientales, 1* (pp. 73–86). Barcelona: Publicacions Universitat de Barcelona.

Rossi, J. (1996). *Participation run amok: The costs of mass participation for deliberative agency decision making* [Online]. Available: papers.ssrn.com/paper.taf?ABSTRACT_ID=10254

Rueda, S. (1999). *Modelos e indicadores de huella y calidad ambiental urbana* [Models and indicators of environmental trace and urban quality]. Barcelona: Fundació Fòrum Ambiental, Generalitat de Cataluña (Dpt. Medi Ambient) & Agencia Europea de Medio Ambiente.

Rueda, S. (2000a). *Sistema d'informació i modelització urbana* [Information system and urban modeling] [Online]. Barcelona: Agencia d'Ecologia Urbana. Available: www.bcnecologia.net

Rueda, S. (2000b). *Una recollida selectiva eficient* [An efficient selective waste collection]. I Jornada Técnica sobre gestió de residus municipals. Barcelona. Area Metropolitana. Entitat del Medi Ambient.

Saegert, S. (1987). Environmental psychology and social change. In D. Stokols and I. Altman (Eds.), *Handbook of environmental psychology* (Vol. 1, pp. 99–128). New York: Wiley.

Sanoff, H. (2000). *Participatory action research.* [CD-ROM]. Sixteenth IAPS proceedings: Metropolis 2000. Socio/Environmental Monographs, 16 (Paper 106). Barcelona: Publicacions Universitat de Barcelona.

Schaefer, A., & Harvey, B. (2000). Environmental knowledge and the adoption of ready-made environmental management solutions. *Eco-Management and Auditing, 7*(2), 74–81.

Shimmin, S. (1981). Applying psychology in organizations. *International Review of Applied Psychology, 30,* 377–386.

Sime, J. (1999). What is environmental psychology? Texts, content and context. *Journal of Environmental Psychology, 19,* 191–206.

Sime, J. (2000). *Where is the environment in environmental psychology? Transdisciplinary considerations* [CD-ROM]. Sixteenth IAPS proceedings: Metropolis 2000. Socio/Environmental Monographs, 16. Symposia 3. Barcelona: Publicacions Universitat de Barcelona.

Slovic, P., Fischhoff, B., & Lichtenstein, S. (1980). Facts and fears: Understanding perceived risk. In R. C. Schwing & W. A. Albers (Eds.), *Societal risk assessment: How safe is safe enough.* London: Plenum.

Sorensen, J. (1971). *A framework for identification and control of resource degradation and conflict in the multiple use of the coastal zone.* Unpublished master's thesis. University of California, Berkeley. Cited by L. Canter (1996).

Stern, P. C. (1992). Psychological dimensions of global environmental change. *Annual Review of Psychology, 43,* 269–302.

Stern, P. C., & Dietz, T. (1994). The value basis of environmental concern. *Journal of Social Issues, 50,* 65–84.

Stern, P. C., Dietz, T., & Kalof, L. (1993). Value orientations, gender, and environmental concern. *Environmental and Behavior, 25,* 322–348.

Stern, P. C., & Easterling, W. E. (1999). *Human dimensions of climate variability.* Washington, DC: National Academic Press and World Scientific Publishing.

Stern, P. C., & Oskamp, S. (1987). Managing scarce environmental resources. In D. Stokols & I. Altman (Eds.), *Handbook of environmental psychology* (Vol. 2; pp. 1043–1088). New York: Wiley.

Stern, P. C., Young, O. R., & Druckman, D. (Eds.). (1992). *Global environmental change: Understanding the human dimensions.* Washington, DC: National Academy Press.

Stokols, D. (1995). The paradox of environmental psychology. *American Psychologist, 50,* 821–837.

Stokols, D. (1997). Directions of environmental psychology in the twenty-first century. In S. Wapner, J. Demick, T. Yamamoto, & T. Takahashi (Eds.), *Handbook of Japan-United States environment-behavior research: Toward a transactional approach* (pp. 333–353). New York: Plenum.

Stokols, D., & Altman, I. (Eds.). (1987). *Handbook of environmental psychology.* New York: Wiley.

Sureda, V. (1992). *La cònferencia mundial sobre medi ambient i desenvolupament de Rio de Janeiro (Rio 1992)* [The world congress on environment and development of Rio de Janeiro (Rio 92)]. Barcelona: Diputación de Barcelona. Area d'Agricultura i Medi Natural.

Sureda, V., & Canals, R. M. (2000). *Els processos de l'Agenda 21 Local en els Municipis de Barcelona: Metodologia per a l'elaboració d'auditories ambientals municipals* [The Local Agenda 21 processes in Barcelona Counties: Methodology for the elaboration of environmental county audits]. *Collecció Manuals, 10*(1). Barcelona: Diputació de Barcelona. Area de Medi Ambient (English version, 2001; available from the same publisher).

Svane, O. (1997). Agenda 21 practiced in Swedish housing management: Results from a multi-case study. *Eco-Management and Auditing, 4*(2), 73–80.

Tajfel, H. (1981). *Human groups and social categories.* Cambridge: Cambridge University Press.

Tajfel, H., & Turner, J. (1986). The social identity theory of intergroup behavior. In S. Worchel & W. G. Austin (Eds.), *The social psychology of intergroup relations.* (pp. 7–24). Chicago: Nelson-Hall.

Taylor, N. C., & Bryan, H. (1990). A New Zealand issues-oriented approach to social impact assessment. In K. Finsterbusch, J. Indersoll, & L. G. Llewellyn (Eds.). *Methods for social analysis in developing countries.* Boulder, CO: Westview Press.

Third European Conference on Sustainable Cities and Towns. Hannover, Germany. (2000). [Online]. Available: www.hannover.de/deutsch/download/shortrep.doc

Torgerson, D. (1980). *Industrialization and assessment: Social impact assessment as a social phenomenon.* Toronto: York University Press.

Torres, P. (1997). La percepció social de l'estat del medi ambient [The social perception of the environment state]. In J. Vilà-Valentí (Coord.), *Recerques i reflexions sobre el medi ambient a Catalunya* [Investigations and reflections on the environment in Catalunya] (pp. 143–158). Barcelona: Fundació Catalana per a la Recerca.

Torres, P. (1999). *Residus industrials: Blocs de comunicació ambiental* [Industrial waste: Environmental communication pieces]. Barcelona: Institut Català de Tecnologia.

Turner, J. C. (1987). *Rediscovering the social group. A self-categorization theory.* Oxford: Blackwell.

United Nations. (1972). *Declaration of the United Nations Conference on the Human Environment.* Stockholm: Author.

United Nations. (1992). *Rio declaration on environment and development*. The United Nations Conference on Environment and Development. Rio de Janeiro [Online]. Available: www.earthcharter.org/resources/riodeclar_en.htm

United Nations. Division for Sustainable Development (1999). *Agenda 21* [Online]. Available www.un.org/esa/sustdev/agenda21text.htm

United States Department for Agriculture. (1990). *Checklist for summarizing the environmental impacts of proposed projects*. Cooperative State Research Service. Stillwater, OK: Author.

United States Environmental Protection Agency. (1969). *National Environmental Policy Act (NEPA)* [Online]. Available: www.epa.gov/region5/defs/html/nepa.htm

United States Environmental Protection Agency. (1970). *Occupational Safety and Health Act (OSHA)* [Online]. Available: www.epa.gov/region5/defs/html/osha.htm

United States Environmental Protection Agency. (1986, July 9). *Environmental Auditing Policy Statement*, 51 *Fed. Reg.* 25,004.

United States Environmental Protection Agency. (2000). *Environmental Information Management System (EIMS)* [Online]. Available: www.epa.gov/eims/eimshome.html

Uzzell, D. (1996). *Environmental hyperopia and global environmental problems*. V Congreso de Psicología Ambiental. Barcelona, Spain.

Uzzell, D. L. (in press). The psycho-spatial dimension to global environmental problems. Journal of Environmental Psychology.

Uzzell, D., & Jones, E. M. (1996). *Meeting the expectations of visitor groups: Safety management in theme parks*. Monografías Psico/Socio/Ambientales, 8. Barcelona: Publicacions Universitat de Barcelona.

Uzzell, D., Pol, E., & Baddenes, D. (in press). A transactional perspective on the relationship between place identity, social cohesion and environmental sustainability. *Environment and behavior*.

Valera, S. (1993). El símbolisme en la ciutat: Funcions de l'espai simbólic urba [Symbolism in the city: Functions of the urban symbolic space]. Doctoral dissertation, University of Barcelona, Spain.

Valera, S. (1997). Estudio de la relación entre el espacio simbólico urbano y los procesos de identidad social [Study of the relationship between urban symbolic space and social identity processes]. *Revista de Psicología Social, 12*(1), 17–30.

Valera, S. (2000). La percepción de riesgo en la población (Social perception of risk). In Diputació de Tarragona, *Fòrum de la Seguretat: La Directiva Seveso II* (pp. 240–243). Barcelona: Beta.

Valera, S., & Guàrdia, J. (in press). Urban sustainability and social identity: Barcelona's Olympic Village. *Environment and Behavior*.

Van Liere, K. D., & Dunlap, R. E. (1980). The social bases of environmental concern: A review of hypothesis, explanations and empirical evidence. *Public Opinion Quarterly, 44*, 43–59.

Van Liere, K. D., & Dunlap, R. E. (1981). Environmental concern: Does it make a difference how it is measured? *Environment and Behavior, 13*, 651–676.

Veitch, R. & Arkkelin, D. (1995). *Environmental psychology: An interdisciplinary perspective*. Upper Saddle River, NJ: Prentice-Hall.

Wathern, P. (Ed.). (1992). *Environmental impact assessment. Theory and practice*. London and New York: Routledge.

Weidema, B. (2000). Increasing credibility of LCA. *International Journal of Life Cycle Assessment, 5*(2), 63–64 [Online]. Available: www.ecomed.de/journals/lca/welcome.htm

Wiesenfeld, E. (1994). La psicología ambiental en el contexto de la comunidad: Hacia una psicología ambiental comunitaria [Environmental psychology in the community context: Toward a community environmental psychology]. *Psicología Contemporánea, 1*(2), 40–49.

Wiesenfeld, E., & Giuliani, F. (in press). Sustainable development, identity and community: The Venezuelan case. *Environment and Behavior*.

Winter, D. (1996) *Ecological psychology: Healing the split between planet and self*. New York: HarperCollins.

World Bank. (1979). *Environment and development*. Washington, DC: Author.

Young, J. (1996). *Red global: Los ordenadores en una sociedad sostenible* [Global network: Computers in a sustainable city]. Bilbao: Bakeaz.

Zani, B. (1992). Psicología de la intervención social: Tendencias actuales y perspectivas futuras [Psychology of the social intervention: Current trends and future perspectives]. *Revista de Psicología Social Aplicada, 2*, 15–31.

CHAPTER 5

The New Environmental Psychology: The Human Interdependence Paradigm

TOMMY GÄRLING, ANDERS BIEL, and MATHIAS GUSTAFSSON

HOW PEOPLE INTERACT with the built environment at a micro level has traditionally been a dominant focus of environmental psychology (Proshansky, Ittelson, & Rivlin, 1976). However, in the past few decades its scope has been widened to include people's impact on the natural environment. In the 1987 *Handbook of Environmental Psychology*, Stern and Oskamp reviewed this research, targeting recycling. Everett and Watson reviewed related research on transportation. Attesting to the sustained interest in the topic, the 2001 handbook features a chapter on proenvironmental behavior (Vining & Ebreo). We will not duplicate this chapter but describe a new research paradigm labeled *human interdependence* that is being employed in environmental psychological research on sustainability. Some noteworthy precursors include the research by Edney (Edney & Harper, 1978) and Platt (1973). The new research paradigm acknowledges that environmentally damaging behavior is essentially the negative outcomes at an aggregate level of choices that individuals and groups make in self-interest (e.g., Hardin, 1968; Samuelson, 1990; Van Vugt & Samuelson, 1999). The research paradigm is basically a tool for analyzing these choices.

After a section in which the human interdependence research paradigm is described, we provide two examples from our own research of its application. The first example focuses on decision making by citizens to act environmentally responsible when facing conflicts between self-interest and societal interests in preserving the environment, whereas the other example focuses on decision making by municipal politicians facing differences between governmental goals to improve the environment and the conflicting interests of their constituencies. Choosing examples at both an individual and organizational level has two purposes. One is to illustrate the generality of the paradigm. More importantly, the choice reflects a common opinion that sustainability cannot be attained through changes in citizen behavior alone, at least not unless preceded by political change. However, the barriers to solving the problems at a political-organizational level do not seem to be less than at the individual level. Thus, research is also needed to address problems at this level.

THE HUMAN INTERDEPENDENCE RESEARCH PARADIGM

A basic tenet of the human interdependence research paradigm is that people make decisions resulting in choices between alternatives that have outcomes in the future. A ubiquitous feature of the real world mimicked by this research paradigm is that it is not known with certainty how good or bad the outcomes will be and when in the future they will occur.

In many accounts of human decision making (e.g., Hogarth, 1987), three tasks are identified. One task is to evaluate the outcomes of alternative choices, another task is to predict the occurrence of these outcomes, and a third task is to form an overall evaluation or preference for the alternatives by modifying the evaluations of outcomes by taking the predictive judgements into account. Utility theory (Edwards, 1954; Savage, 1954; von Neumann & Morgernstern, 1944) is the cornerstone of theories of how decisions are made. In this theory, observed evaluations or preferences are assumed to reflect an underlying stable utility.* Thus, any two outcomes can be compared. Based on this comparison, a preference for one over the other is formed. Today many generalized utility theories exist (Barberà, Hammond, & Seidl, 1998a, 1998b). Some of these theories (e.g., prospect theory; Kahneman & Tversky, 1979; Tversky & Fox, 1995) are reasonably successful in accounting for empirical observations (Camerer, 1989).

Another feature of the human interdependence research paradigm is that the outcomes of decisions made by different people are interdependent. This is formalized in different games that have been analyzed by applied mathematics (e.g., Colman, 1999). Two fundamental types of outcome dependencies are competition and fixed-sum games. One of two "players" of a competition game gains an amount that equals the other player's loss. In contrast, in cooperation or fixed-difference games, both players obtain the same outcome. This is illustrated in Figure 5.1, where A and B both face a binary choice of C (cooperation) or D (defection). The points indicated in the table represent (are proportional to) the benefits of the outcomes for each of the players. As may be seen, the players' interests show a perfect negative correlation in the upper payoff matrix, whereas they show a perfect positive correlation in the lower payoff matrix.

Competition (fixed-sum game)

A \ B	C	D
C	I A: 5 B: –5	II A: –8 B: 8
D	III A: 8 B: –8	IV A: –2 B: 2

Cooperation (fixed-difference game)

A \ B	C	D
C	I A: 5 B: 5	II A: 8 B: 8
D	III A: –8 B: –8	IV A: –2 B: –2

Figure 5.1 Fundamental types of outcome dependencies.

In the *prisoner's dilemma game* (PDG), which has attracted much research interest (Luce & Raifa, 1957; Pruitt & Kimmel, 1977; Rapoport & Chammah, 1965), both players face a choice of cooperation or competition (Figure 5.2). If both either cooperate or compete, they will receive the same outcome. If one competes and the other cooperates, the former will receive a higher outcome than the latter. A necessary feature is that the outcome is always better for each player if he or she chooses to compete. However, the dilemma is that if both compete they will receive a worse outcome than if they both cooperate. The joint interest, that is, group or collective interest, is served if both cooperate.

One drawback with the PDG as a research paradigm for analyzing real-world conflicts between self-interest and collective interest is that it assumes that there are only two interdependent individuals. Thus, it may apply to relationships within dyads but not necessarily to the relationships between individuals in larger groups. An extension of the PDG (the *N*-person game; Komorita, 1976) has therefore been proposed. For this and related extensions Dawes (1980) coined the generic term *social dilemma*

A \ B	C	D
C	I A: 5 B: 5	II A: –8 B: 8
D	III A: 8 B: –8	IV A: –2 B: –2

Figure 5.2 The payoff in the prisoners' dilemma game.

*By *underlying stable utility* is meant an invariant scale for assessing any type of benefits.

to identify the following defining features: (1) The payoff to each individual acting in her or his own interest (called *defection*) is higher than the payoff for acting in the interest of the group (called *cooperation*), regardless of what other group members do, but (2) all individuals receive a lower payoff if all defect than if all cooperate.

The left graphs in Figure 5.3 show how in a social dilemma the payoff to an individual increases with the number of others who cooperate. The payoff is continuous in the upper graph. An example would be that air pollution decreases with the number of car owners who use public transport instead of driving to work. The payoff follows a step function in the lower graph. An example is that investment in infrastructure for public transport requires tax contributions from a specified number of people. If this critical number, called the *provision threshold*, is not attained, no investment can be made. The PDG payoff structure is preserved in that the individual will always benefit more from choosing not to cooperate. In contrast, in a *trust game* the payoff is worse for the noncooperator when the number who cooperate increases (the right graphs). In general the payoff in this game may more adequately describe environmental problems, where the long-term consequences (of a deteriorating environment) are more negative for the individual than belonging to the minority who cooperate. For instance, comfort is likely to be sacrificed when the alternative outcome is a deterio-rating environment causing serious health risks or problems.

In social dilemmas, people make choices with uncertain outcomes. Furthermore, decisions in social dilemmas are sometimes made in groups that activate different social-decision heuristics investigated in research on group decision making (Davis, 1992). There are two different forms of uncertainty, *social uncertainty* and *environmental uncertainty*. Reducing these two forms of uncertainty is believed to be particularly important for the solution of large-scale social dilemmas with environmental consequences. Each of the forms of uncertainty will be discussed.

Outcome interdependence implies that the outcome depends on how others decide. This is referred to as *social* or *strategic uncertainty* (Suleiman & Rapoport, 1988). An important motive for defection in social dilemmas is that others are not trusted to cooperate. Since communication may reduce social uncertainty, its role for cooperation has been extensively studied. Type of outcome dependence (pure competition or a choice between competition and cooperation) and presence or absence of communication distinguish between, on the one hand, the *ultimatum* and PDG games and, on the other hand, *distributive* (or fixed-sum) negotiations and *integrative* (or variable-sum) negotiations. In the simplest, one-period ultimatum game (Güth, Schmittberger, & Schwarze, 1982), a participant is asked to split a resource between himself or herself and an unknown person. If the other person accepts the offer, both will receive what is proposed; otherwise she or he will receive nothing. The ultimatum game may be seen as the last offer (ultimatum) in a distributive negotiation (Bazerman, Curhan, Moore, & Valley, 2000; Carnevale & Pruitt, 1992) preceded by offers and counteroffers, for instance, in a negotiation between a seller and buyer about the price of a nonstandardized product or service (Kristensen & Gärling, 2000). In contrast, an integrative negotiation entails several outcome dimensions so that trade-offs can be made between them. For instance, communication may lead to recognizing that some outcomes are more important to one of the opponents, other outcomes more important to the other opponent.

Research has tried to disentangle what makes communication effective. Face-to-face contact may in itself increase cooperation (Sally, 1995). Yet, it appears to be essential that the communication entail a discussion focusing on the solution of the dilemma. In addition to giving group members an opportunity to

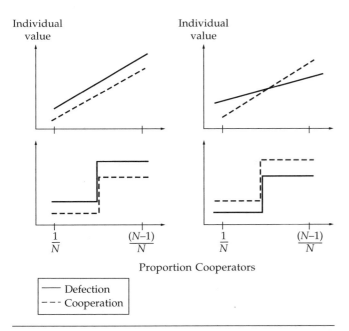

Figure 5.3 The payoffs in social dilemmas.

understand the dilemma they face so that they can make joint decisions about solution strategies to follow (Edney, 1980), communication appears to lead to the formation of mutual commitments or contracts (Dawes, van de Kragt, & Orbell, 1988). This may, however, not be possible unless communication promotes a *group identity*, with a substitution of group interest or self-interest (Caporael, Dawes, Orbell, & van de Kragt, 1989). As witnessed in research in the minimal group paradigm (Tajfel & Turner, 1986), a group identity may in fact easily develop. An example is a study by Kramer and Brewer (1984) showing that cooperation in a social dilemma increased when participants were told that they belonged to the same category of students. The reason was that they acquired a group identity. Furthermore, social pressure in a group facilitates the implementation of social norms, such as keeping promises, being fair, and reciprocating (Kerr & Kaufman-Gilliland, 1994).

It has been argued that cooperation is difficult if not impossible to evoke in large groups (Olson, 1965) because of social loafing. In large groups people are anonymous, their responsibility is diluted, and they feel that their actions make little difference. All these factors are known to decrease cooperation (Komorita & Parks, 1995). However, it is noteworthy that increased group size per se is not what decreases cooperation. In contemporary democratic societies with all their available communication means, issues of the provision of public goods or the deterioration of the environment are regularly discussed among people and in the mass media. This may create increased feelings of group identity, willingness to act, and knowledge of how to act in the collective interest. Legislation is an example of how such awareness results in contracts formed at the societal level with the aim of increasing cooperation and decreasing defection or free riding. A drawback is that forming strong bonds within groups to enhance cooperation appears to have negative effects on cooperation between groups (Bornstein, 1992). In competing-group social dilemmas each participant faces a social dilemma within his or her own group, while there is a simultaneous social dilemma that exists between groups. This is created experimentally by constructing a group competition between two groups in which the one with more self-sacrificing individuals receives greater benefit than the one with fewer. Almost invariably, group members benefit only their own group.

A ubiquitous feature of real-life resource dilemmas, exemplified by many environmental problems,

is that uncertainty exists about the resource (Biel & Gärling, 1995; Suleiman & Rapoport, 1988), such as its current degree of depletion or devastation. This uncertainty may primarily originate from a lack of knowledge. For instance, people do not know how much waste they may dump in a lake before it deteriorates, how many trees can be felled before the land turns into a desert, or for how long there will be sufficient gasoline to make driving possible. Everyday observations appear to confirm the "big pool" illusion in such instances (Messick & McClelland, 1983), that is, that a resource pool is perceived to be large, perhaps infinite, when its size is unknown. Overharvesting may then be expected. A limited number of studies have been carried out with the aim of investigating if such is the case. As noted by Gärling, Gustafsson, and Biel (1999) in their review, the available scant evidence consistently supports the existence of the big-pool illusion.

In a series of laboratory experiments by Rapoport and colleagues (Budescu, Rapoport, & Suleiman, 1990; Rapoport, Budescu, Suleiman, & Weg, 1992), participants in small groups were told that they could request as much as they wanted from a hypothetical common-pool resource. However, if the requested total amount exceeded the resource, none would receive what they requested. In one condition participants always knew the size of the resource, whereas in other conditions different degrees of uncertainty about its size were introduced. The results showed that participants in the uncertainty conditions requested too much. This is a recurrent finding that also occurs under somewhat different conditions. As an example proving this point, Hine and Gifford (1996) found a similar effect of uncertainty about replenishment rate.

Gustafsson, Biel, and Gärling (1999a, 1999b) have shown that overharvesting due to environmental uncertainty is an individual outcome-desirability bias (Budescu & Bruderman, 1995; Zakay, 1983). Thus, although some research initially seemed to show that social uncertainty augmented the individual bias (Wit & Wilke, 1998), it is now clear that outcome interdependence is not a necessary condition for the bias to occur. In other words, individuals overestimate the size of the resource and request too much irrespective of whether they act alone or in a social context.

By analogy to reduction of social uncertainty, it may be asked whether environmental uncertainty is similarly reduced by communication. If members of a group or society at large inform each other, the interdependence that exists may tempt some people to take advantage of this information. However, a study by Gustafsson, Biel, and Gärling (2000) instead yielded a debiasing effect, in particular if the debiasing information (pessimistic estimates of resource size) was presented before any optimistically biased information. Thus, one may be optimistic about the possibility that communication will also reduce or eliminate effects of environmental uncertainty. The problem is, however, that unambiguous information almost never exists. How then can uncertainty be communicated in a way that is not misinterpreted?

APPLICATIONS OF THE HUMAN INTERDEPENDENCE RESEARCH PARADIGM

The preceding section described the human interdependence research paradigm. It highlighted that people make decisions about future courses of action that have outcomes that are uncertain, because of lack of knowledge of the future (environmental uncertainty) or because the outcomes depend on others' decisions (social uncertainty). In the following we will illustrate how the research paradigm has been applied.

INTERDEPENDENCE IN CITIZEN DECISION MAKING

An important difference to laboratory research is that in real life many decisions are made routinely, presumably without much deliberation (Bargh, 1997). Thus, defection in a real-life social dilemma may become "habitual" (Fujii, Gärling, & Kitamura, 2001).

If the same choice is made over and over again in a stable context, a habit of making the choice develops (Ronis, Yates, & Kirscht, 1989). Verplanken and Aarts (1999, p. 104) define such habits as "learned sequences of acts that have become automatic responses to specific cues, and are functional in obtaining certain goals or end-states." Such a definition implies that habits have once been deliberate. When a new behavior is acquired, it may in fact be consciously and deliberately determined. This accounts for why the behavior is still functional. Nevertheless, once established, the behavior may be performed automatically. Several behaviors with environmental consequences qualify: for instance, travel mode choice (Verplanken, Aarts, & van Knippenberg, 1997), many purchases of consumer goods

(Dahlstrand & Biel, 1997; Grankvist & Biel, 2001), and recycling (Thøgersen, 1996).

Let us assume that a behavior is practiced to the point that it becomes automatic. At the time the habit was established, environmental consequences were perhaps not salient. Later, people are requested to perform environmentally friendly behaviors, such as commuting by public transport, buying organic food products, or recycling into five different categories rather than two. New intentions must first be formed. However, those who have developed a strong habit are not likely to attend to information targeted at the well-practiced behavior (Verplanken & Aarts, 1999). Furthermore, not only should a new behavior be acquired; people must also disengage in the old behavior. This implies that the new intention will be in conflict with the habit. Still another problem is that a value that was not part of the original goal must now be made to influence the choice. Environmental considerations need to be taken into account when behavioral alternatives are evaluated.

A theory of the process of changing an old habit into a new one has been described elsewhere (Dahlstrand & Biel, 1997). In this process environmental values and norms play significant roles. Once people are asked to take not only individual consequences—for instance, personal costs—into account but also environmental consequences, the behavior is performed in a *social* context. This is at the heart of the human interdependence research paradigm: What a person does has consequences not only for himself or herself but also for others. At the same time, this is also valid for others. In social dilemmas the negative effects or costs of one individual's behavior are negligible. Thus, personal benefits often outweigh the interest of the group. This highlights the need to establish *standards* for environmentally friendly behaviors. In social contexts, norms serve the function of specifying what is proper behavior. The social context also prescribes sanctions for departures from the norms.

According to Schwartz (1977, p. 227), a norm is defined as "the self-expectations for specific action in particular situations that are constructed by the individual." This conception of norm parallels what Cialdini, Reno, and Kallgren (1990) refer to as an *injunctive* or *prescriptive* norm. This is the "ought" meaning of social norms. Cialdini (1988) has recognized that social norms also have a descriptive meaning. A *descriptive* norm alludes to what most others are doing in a particular situation. It serves as a heuristic rule specifying how to behave. In this form the norm functions as a social convention.

Prescriptive norms are frequently associated with sanctions for improper behavior (or rewards for appropriate behavior). Such sanctions can be enforced by the collective or by the individual himself or herself if the norm is internalized. Hence, there may be both situational and individual variation in norm strength. The former has been emphasized by Schwartz in his norm-activation theory (1973, 1977), where altruistic concerns about other people are assumed to activate feelings of moral obligation to act. In their value-belief-norm (VBN) theory, Stern, Dietz, Abel, Guagnano, and Kalof (1999) generalized this hypothesis to include other valued objects. Hence, exactly as people value other human beings, they may value other species or tropical forests—and act to protect them. This extension of Schwartz's norm concept highlights the role of *personal norms* for proenvironmental behavior.

Turning to the social aspect of prescriptive norms, why are some social dilemmas characterized by a strong imperative to behave in an environmentally friendly manner while others are not? No definite answer to this question can be given. A suggestion in line with Schwartz (1977) is that important factors include a high level of ascribed responsibility and a belief that particular conditions pose threats to others. Support for the first factor was obtained in a study where perceptions of norm strength were investigated in four environmental social dilemmas (Biel, von Borgstede, & Dahlstrand, 1999). The level of ascribed responsibility significantly contributed to norm strength. However, awareness of adverse consequences was not related. This indicates that awareness of serious environmental problems in a particular situation is not a sufficient condition for the influence of social norms. As an example, the public may recognize that there are adverse environmental consequences from car traffic without perceiving that they ought to change their behavior (Biel et al., 1999). Why not? People may fail to acknowledge that changing their present behavior is important for themselves and others. Alternatively, changing their present behavior may not be seen as feasible. If changing a behavior is seen as not feasible, the moral obligation to change would result in what Festinger (1957) called *cognitive dissonance.* This is a motivational conflict that people avoid.

We conclude that social norms frequently guide behavior in social dilemmas. However, as has been argued by Cialdini et al. (1990), such norms are not uniformly in force. Norms need to be activated in situations where they have a potential to affect behavior. To take but one example, Cialdini et al. found that people littered more in a clean parking garage than they did when a single piece of litter was placed on the ground beforehand. In the latter condition the injunctive norm that one should not litter was made salient.

Furthermore, the effect of social norms is also affected by the degree of support they achieve. This idea was tested in an experiment where false feedback was provided about the proportion of the population that in social dilemmas supported the injunctive norm (von Borgstede, Biel, & Dahlstrand, 1999). As an example, people were asked to recycle and told that the proportion of the population that morally supported recycling varied between 18% and 82%. When the support was strong, they were more prepared to cooperate than when support was weak. Information about support served the function of reducing social uncertainty. If the moral imperative is perceived as strong, others are expected to act accordingly. If it is perceived as weak, there is less reason to believe that they will cooperate.

People seek to simplify their decision making. In an individual context, habits serve this role. In a human interdependence context, social norms play the same role. Furthermore, once social norms are established, less control by authorities is needed. Since coercion is costly, social norms also have a positive effect from a societal point of view. It should be kept in mind, though, that social norms are not likely to emerge in all social dilemmas. Conditions for when a common perception of "what we ought to do" emerges in social dilemmas is an important topic for future research.

INTERDEPENDENCE IN POLITICAL DECISION MAKING

The need to implement efficient measures to combat environmental degradation is urgent. Would it be possible to implement structural solutions (Samuelson & Messick, 1986), for instance, different types of sanctioning systems? In experimental studies on social dilemmas, it has been found that people are willing to accept and support sanctions for noncooperation if they perceive that failure to solve the social dilemma is harmful (Yamagishi, 1986, 1988).

Different types of road-pricing schemes aimed at reducing air pollution and congestion from car traffic are on the political agenda in many European cities. A high enough fee level may force a sufficient number of car users to choose other, more environmentally friendly travel modes (e.g., public transport). In this section we are, however, interested not in the effects of road-pricing schemes that decision makers may implement in, for instance, municipalities but in the conflicts that appear to shape political decision making in such cases. We will explore this in some depth with the aim of exemplifying the usefulness of the human interdependence research paradigm.

A complementary perspective on interest conflicts between different actors is the principal-agent theory (Arrow, 1970; Eisenhardt, 1989; Wilson, 1968). The theory deals with situations in which one party (the principal) wants to ensure that another party (the agent) will act in the interest of the principal. It is assumed that the agent will only do so if it is in his or her interest. Thus, the principal must offer the agent incentives for acting in the interest of the principal or disincentives for acting against the interests of the principal. Stated in another way, the utility for the agent acting in the interest of the principal must at least be as high as the utility the agent can derive from alternative options. A principal-agent problem is similar to the ultimatum game described earlier in that the decision task requires finding the agent's reservation level (i.e., the least offered amount that is acceptable). The relationship between municipal decision makers who decide on fee levels and citizens who must pay the fees may be framed as a principal-agent problem. Given that the aim of the decision maker is, for instance, to reduce car use, he or she must find the car users' reservation level. This may be the level at which travel modes other than the car will become preferred.

Local municipalities also stand in a principal-agent relationship to the federal or regional government. In this relationship the government is the principal, while the municipality is the agent. The government can, for instance, authorize the municipality to make its own decisions about road pricing. The government-principal then acts on the belief that the municipality-agent will use this measure to abate environmental degradation from car use, that is, to act in the government's interest. However, municipal decision makers may not do that, since they face a conflict between the governmental goal and the interests of their citizens.

If actors are faced with conflicting goals, pursuing one goal will lead to other goals being downplayed. Political decision making (e.g., Matheson, 1998) is an area where mixed-motive conflicts are particularly salient. Politicians who make decisions must weigh the interests of different groups with different goals. In the political arena, federal politicians can often be assumed to adopt a national perspective, while regional or local politicians are more inclined to emphasize local interests. However, environmental problems have no regional or national boundaries. It is easy to see then that an actor can pursue self-interest goals (e.g., financial), while negative consequences stemming from this pursuit (e.g., environmental) are diffused over several other actors (e.g., other municipalities). Besides the environmental and financial goals, one can also distinguish a third goal, fairness. When structural solutions such as pricing environmentally unfriendly behaviors are implemented, different groups will be affected differently. Assuming that the fee is equal for all, lower-income citizens will be hit harder than higher-income citizens. From the perspective of a municipality, the situation can thus be viewed as a social dilemma where financial goals directly relevant to the local municipality are given more weight than environmental considerations. Also fairness may be given more weight than environmental goals. Wilke (1991) proposed the greed-efficiency-fairness (GEF) hypothesis, stating that in social dilemmas these three motives are in conflict. The hypothesis assumes that greed is the strongest motive. However, greed or self-interest is held back if the motives of fairness and efficiency (e.g., preserving the environment) are made salient. Still, conflicts also arise between efficiency and fairness. This will be the case if pricing has an asymmetric effect that is considered unfair due to wealth/income differences. Thus, if fairness considerations are salient, these may prevent an efficient solution.

Is there any evidence for the existence of goal conflicts in municipal decision making, and if there is, how will these conflicts affect structural solutions such as road pricing? In structured interviews and survey questionnaires (Gustafsson, Falkemark, Gärling, Johansson-Stenman, & Johansson, 2001; Johansson, Gustafsson, Falkemark, Gärling, & Johansson-Stenman, 2001), municipal politicians were asked to indicate their preference for a number of principles (e.g., reducing car use, affordability for a majority of car users, financing new road infrastructure) for how to set the level of a road-pricing fee given that the government had authorized the municipality to implement road pricing. The principles corresponded to greed, efficiency, and fairness. Although there were some clear political party differences, for the political majority the hypothesized goal conflicts existed in that the governmental goal of a clean environment was not optimized. Instead, greed and especially fairness were found to be in conflict with the governmental goal.

An important question that needs to be addressed is what measures can be chosen to reduce or eliminate the types of conflicts that, if they remain, will lead to environmentally unfriendly political decisions. If we return to the principal-agent relationship between the government and the municipality, the government's task is to implement incentives or disincentives that are effective in forcing the municipalities to pursue the environmental goal. Greed could of course be counteracted if the government confiscates any revenues. However, given that fairness is another, perhaps even larger obstacle, this will not altogether solve the conflict. Instead, disincentives in the form of reduction of governmental subsidies if municipalities fail to reach specified environmental goals may be effective. Of course, whether these measures would work needs to be empirically addressed. Although this is difficult to study in field settings, the human interdependence paradigm has in the past been successfully applied in experimental research. Findings from experiments may in fact prove to be very useful as guides for what measures should be applied in order to solve interest conflicts in municipal political decision making.

SUMMARY AND CONCLUSIONS

This chapter has described and exemplified the application of the human interdependence research paradigm. By highlighting the interdependent nature of people's behavior in a human society, the paradigm makes salient the fact that environmental problems are frequently caused by people acting in self-interest rather than in the collective interest. Importing the paradigm to environmental psychology changes the traditional research focus from the individual's response to the environment to the role of the social context. Analyses of the interaction between the social and physical environment have certainly not been lacking in environmental

psychology. In fact, some critics (e.g., Gärling, 1988) have argued that this has resulted in an unfortunate neglect of the physical environment. Yet, such analyses have often used an approach not different from that used to study individual behavior. In contrast, the human interdependence paradigm places at center stage the role of exchanges of environmental resources as a primary motive for human behavior. Therefore, it does not ignore the physical environment. Furthermore, although not explicitly discussed in this chapter, it provides mathematical-statistical tools to analyze conflicts over scarce resources. Furthermore, as the chapter has alluded to, a solid body of research findings has accumulated. There are also interesting ways in which this body of knowledge of facts and research tools can be extended to questions that should be of concern to a new environmental psychology.

REFERENCES

Arrow, K. J. (1970). *Essays in the theory of risk bearing.* Chicago: Chicago University Press.

Barberà, S., Hammond, P., & Seidl, C. (Eds.). (1998a). *Handbook of utility theory: Vol. 1. Principles.* Dordrecht, The Netherlands: Kluwer Press.

Barberà, S., Hammond, P., & Seidl, C. (Eds.). (1998b). *Handbook of utility theory: Vol. 2. Extensions.* Dordrecht, The Netherlands: Kluwer Press.

Bargh, J. A. (1997). The automaticity of everyday life. In R. S. Wyer Jr. (Ed.), *The automaticity of everyday life: Advances in social cognition* (Vol. 10, pp. 1–61). Mahwah, NJ: Erlbaum.

Bazerman, M. H., Curhan, J. R., Moore, D. A., & Valley, K. L. (2000). Negotiation. *Annual Review of Psychology, 51,* 279–314.

Biel, A., & Gärling, T. (1995). The role of uncertainty in resource dilemmas. *Journal of Environmental Psychology, 15,* 222–233.

Biel, A., von Borgstede, C., & Dahlstrand, U. (1999). Norm perception and cooperation in large-scale social dilemmas. In M. Foddy, M. Smithson, S. Schneider, & M. Hogg (Eds.), *Resolving social dilemmas: Dynamic, structural, and intergroup aspects.* Philadelphia: Psychology Press.

Bornstein, G. (1992). The free-rider problem in intergroup conflicts over step-level and continuous public goods. *Journal of Personality and Social Psychology, 62,* 597–606.

Budescu, D., & Bruderman, M. (1995). The relationship between the illusion of control and the desirability bias. *Journal of Behavioral Decision Making, 8,* 109–125.

Budescu, D. V., Rapoport, A., & Suleiman, R. (1990). Resource dilemmas with environmental uncertainty and asymmetric players. *European Journal of Social Psychology, 20,* 475–487.

Camerer, C. F. (1989). An experimental test of several generalized utility theories. *Journal of Risk and Uncertainty, 2,* 61–104.

Caporael, L. R., Dawes, R. M., Orbell, J. M., & van de Kragt, A. J. (1989). Selfishness examined: Cooperation in the absence of egoistic incentives. *Behavioral and Brain Sciences, 12,* 683–739.

Carnevale, P. J. D., & Pruitt, D. G. (1992). Negotiation and mediation. *Annual Review of Psychology, 43,* 511–582.

Cialdini, R. B. (1988). *Influence: Science and practice* (2nd ed.). Glenview, IL: Scott, Foresman.

Cialdini, R. B., Reno, R. R., & Kallgren, C. A. (1990). A focus theory of normative conduct: Recycling the concept of norms to reduce littering in public places. *Journal of Personality and Social Psychology, 58,* 1015–1026.

Colman, A. W. (1999). *Game theory and its applications in the social and behavioral sciences.* London: Routledge.

Dahlstrand, U., & Biel, A. (1997). Proenvironmental habits: Propensity levels in behavioural change. *Journal of Applied Social Psychology, 27,* 588–601.

Davis, J. H. (1992). Some compelling intuitions about group consensus decisions, theoretical and empirical research, and interpersonal aggregation phenomena: Selected examples, 1950–1990. *Organizational Behavior and Human Decision Processes, 52,* 3–38.

Dawes, R. M. (1980). Social dilemmas. *Annual Review of Psychology, 31,* 169–193.

Dawes, R. M., van de Kragt, A. J. C., & Orbell, J. (1988). Not or thee but we: The importance of group identity in eliciting cooperation in dilemma situations. *Acta Psychologica, 68,* 83–97.

Edney, J. J. (1980). The commons problem: Alternative perspectives. *American Psychologist, 35,* 131–150.

Edney, J. J., & Harper, C. S. (1978). The commons dilemma: Review of contributions from psychology. *Environmental Management, 2,* 491–507.

Edwards, W. (1954). The theory of decision making. *Psychological Bulletin, 51,* 380–417.

Eisenhardt, K. M. (1989). Agency theory: An assesment and review. *Academy of Management Review, 14,* 57–74.

Everett, B. P., & Watson, G. B. (1987). Psychological contributions to transportation. In D. Stokols & I. Altman (Eds.), *Handbook of environmental psychology* (Vol. 2, pp. 987–1007). New York: Wiley.

Festinger, L. (1957). *A theory of cognitive dissonance.* Palo Alto, CA: Stanford University Press.

Fujii, S., Gärling, T., & Kitamura, R. (2001). Changes in drivers' perceptions and use of public transport during a freeway closure. *Environment and Behavior.*

Gärling, T. (1988). What is environmental about environmental psychology? *Journal of Environmental Psychology, 2,* 161–162.

Gärling, T., Gustafsson, M., & Biel, A. (1999). Managing uncertain common resources. In M. Foddy, M. Smithson, M. Hogg, & S. Schneider (Eds.), *Resolving social dilemmas* (pp. 219–225). Philadelphia: Psychology Press.

Grankvist, G., & Biel A. (2001). *The importance of beliefs, purchase criteria and habits for the choice of environmentally friendly food products.* Manuscript submitted for publication.

Gustafsson, M., Biel, A., & Gärling, T. (1999a). Outcome-desirability bias in resource management problems. *Thinking and Reasoning, 4,* 327–338.

Gustafsson, M., Biel, A., & Gärling, T. (1999b). Overharvesting of resources of unknown size. *Acta Psychologica, 103,* 47–64.

Gustafsson, M., Biel, A., & Gärling, T. (2000). Egoism bias in social dilemmas with resource uncertainty. *Group Processes and Intergroup Relations, 3,* 351–365.

Gustafsson, M., Falkemark, G., Gärling, T., Johansson-Stenman, O., & Johansson, L.-O. (2001). *Goal conflicts in municipality decision making.* Manuscript submitted for publication.

Güth, W., Schmittberger, R., & Schwarze, B. (1982). An experimental analysis of ultimatum bargaining. *Journal of Economic Behavior, 3,* 367–388.

Hardin, G. (1968). The tragedy of the commons. *Science, 162,* 1243–1248.

Hine, D. V., & Gifford, R. (1996). Individual restraint and group efficiency in common dilemmas: The effects of uncertainty and risk-seeking. *Journal of Applied Social Psychology, 26,* 993–1009.

Hogarth, R. M. (1987). *Judgement and choice* (2nd ed.). Chichester, England: Wiley.

Johansson, L.-O., Gustafsson, M., Falkemark, G., Gärling, T., & Johansson-Stenman, O. (2001). *Goal conflicts in political decision making about road pricing: A survey of municipality politicians.* Manuscript submitted for publication.

Kahneman, D., & Tversky, A. (1979). Prospect theory: An analysis of decision under risk. *Econometrika, 47,* 263–291.

Kerr, N. L., & Kaufman-Gilliland, C. M. (1994). Communication, commitment and cooperation in social dilemmas. *Journal of Personality and Social Psychology, 66,* 513–529.

Komorita, S. S. (1976). A model of the *N*-person dilemma-type game. *Journal of Experimental Social Psychology, 12,* 357–373.

Komorita, S. S., & Parks, C. D. (1995). Interpersonal relations: Mixed-motive interaction. *Annual Review of Psychology, 46,* 183–207.

Kramer, R. M., & Brewer, M. B. (1984). Effects of group identity on resource use in a simulated commons dilemma. *Journal of Personality and Social Psychology, 46,* 1044–1057.

Kristensen, H., & Gärling, T. (2000). Anchor points, reference points, and counteroffers in negotiations. *Group Decision and Negotiation, 9,* 493–505.

Luce, R. D., & Raifa, H. (1957). *Games and decisions.* New York: Wiley.

Matheson, C. (1998). Rationality and decision-making in Australian federal government. *Australian Journal of Political Science, 33,* 57–72.

Messick, D. M., & McClelland, C. L. (1983). Social traps and temporal traps. *Personality and Social Psychology Bulletin, 9,* 105–110.

Olson, M. (1965). *The logic of collective action.* Cambridge, MA: Harvard University Press.

Platt, J. (1973). Social traps. *American Psychologist, 28,* 641–651.

Proshansky, H. M., Ittelson, W. H., & Rivlin, L. G. (1976). *Environmental psychology.* New York: Holt, Rinehart and Winston.

Pruitt, D. G., & Kimmel, M. J. (1977). Twenty years of experimental gaming: Critique, synthesis, and suggestions for the future. *Annual Review of Psychology, 28,* 363–392.

Rapoport, A., Budescu, D. V., Suleiman, R., & Weg, E. (1992). Social dilemmas with uniformly distributed resources. In W. Liebrand, D. M. Messick, & H. Wilke (Eds.), *Social dilemmas: Theoretical issues and research findings* (pp. 43–57). Oxford, England: Pergamon Press.

Rapoport, A., & Chammah, A. M. (1969). *Prisoner's dilemma.* Ann Arbour: University of Michigan Press.

Ronis, D. L., Yates, J. F., & Kirscht, J. P. (1989). Attitudes, decisions, and habits as determinants of repeated behavior. In A. R. Pratkanis & S. J Breckler (Eds.), *Attitude structure and function: The third Ohio State University volume on attitudes and persuasion* (pp. 213–239). Hillsdale, NJ: Erlbaum.

Sally, D. (1995). Conversation and cooperation in social dilemmas: A meta-analysis of experiments from 1958 to 1992. *Rationality and Society, 7,* 58–92.

Samuelson, C. D. (1990) Energy conservation: A social dilemma approach. *Social Behavior, 5,* 207–230.

Samuelson, C. D., & Messick, D. M. (1986). Alternative structural solutions to resource dilemmas. *Organizational Behavior and Decision Processes, 37,* 139–155.

Savage, L. J. (1954). *The foundations of statistics.* New York: Wiley.

Schwartz, S. H. (1973). Normative explanations of helping behavior: A critique, proposal, and empirical test. *Journal of Experimental Social Psychology, 9,* 349–364.

Schwartz, S. H. (1977). Normative influence on altruism. In L. Berkowitz (Ed.), *Advances in experimental social psychology* (Vol. 10, pp. 221–279). San Diego, CA: Academic Press.

Stern, P. C., Dietz, T., Abel, T., Guagnano, A., & Kalof, L. (1999). A value-belief-norm theory of support for social movements: The case of environmentalism. *Human Ecology Review, 6,* 81–97.

Stern, P. C., & Oskamp, S. (1987). Managing scarce environmental resources. In D. Stokols & I. Altman (Eds.), *Handbook of environmental psychology* (Vol. 2, pp. 1043–1088). New York: Wiley.

Suleiman, R., & Rapoport, A. (1988). Environmental and social uncertainty in single-trial resource dilemmas. *Acta Psychologica, 68,* 99–112.

Tajfel, H., & Turner, J. C. (1986). The social identity theory of intergroup behavior. In S. Worchel & W. G. Austin (Eds.), *Psychology of integroup relations* (pp. 7–24). Chicago: Nelson-Hall.

Thøgersen, J. (1996). Recycling and morality: A critical review of the literature. *Environment and Behavior, 28,* 536–558.

Tversky, A., & Fox, C. R. (1995). Weighing risk and uncertainty. *Psychological Review, 102,* 269–283.

Van Vugt, M., & Samuelson, C. D. (1999). The impact of metering in a natural resource crisis: A social dilemma analysis. *Personality and Social Psychology Bulletin, 25,* 731–745.

Verplanken, B., & Aarts, H. (1999). Habit, attitude, and planned behaviour: Is habit an empty construct or an interesting case of goal-directed automaticity? In W. Stroebe & M. Hewstone (Eds.), *European review of social psychology* (Vol. 10, pp. 101–134). Chichester, England: Wiley.

Verplanken, B., Aarts, H., & van Knippenberg, A. (1997). Habit, information acquisition, and the process of making travel mode choices. *European Journal of Social Psychology, 27,* 539–560.

von Borgstede, C., Biel, A., & Dahlstrand, U. (1999). *From ought to is: Moral norms in large-scale social dilemmas* (Göteborg Psychological Reports, 29, No. 5). Göteborg, Sweden: Göteborg University, Department of Psychology.

von Neumann, J., & Morgenstern, O. (1944). *Theory of games and economic behavior.* Princeton, NJ: Princeton University Press.

Wilke, H. A. M. (1991). Greed, efficiency and fairness in resource management situations. In W. Stroebe & M. Hewstone (Eds.), *European review of social psychology* (Vol. 2, pp. 165–187). London: Wiley.

Wilson, R. B. (1968). On the theory of Syndicates. *Econometrica, 36,* 119–132.

Wit, A., & Wilke, H. (1998). Public good provision under environmental and social uncertainty. *European Journal of Social Psychology, 28,* 249–256.

Yamagishi, T. (1986). The provision of a sanctioning system as a public good. *Journal of Personality and Social Psychology, 51,* 110–116.

Yamagishi, T. (1988). Seriousness of a social dilemma and the provision of a sanctioning system. *Social Psychology Quarterly, 51,* 32–42.

Zakay, D. (1983). The relationship between the probability assessor and the outcomes of an event as a determiner of subjective probability. *Acta Psychologica, 53,* 271–280.

CHAPTER 6

The Phenomenological Approach to People-Environment Studies

CARL F. GRAUMANN

FOR A CHAPTER on the phenomenological approach to people-environment studies within a handbook of environmental psychology, an introductory comment with respect to both parts of its title may be helpful since both terms, *phenomenological approach* and *people-environment studies,* need interpreting. At least, my phenomenological preference for *approach* rather than *method* or *methodology* and for *people-environment studies* rather than *environmental psychology* should be made clear, and also why these two parts of the title and topic are seen as mutually related. They are increasingly related in research, which is the proper justification for this chapter.

PHENOMENOLOGICAL APPROACH

What is meant by *phenomenology* in people-environment studies will be the subject of the first major part of this chapter. Here the argument is only for the choice of *approach* rather than *method.* If we understand *approach* as both the way of gaining access to a goal, such as the solution of a problem, and the process of getting closer to a destination, then *approach* may involve a whole set of techniques and methods plus the rules of how to use them. That is why, from a phenomenological perspective, *approach,* which always includes the approaching agent, that is, the researcher (cf. Giorgi, 1970), may be taken as a more comprehensive term than *method.* It covers the

whole rule-guided process of getting close to the solution of a problem, from the definition of the point of departure and viewpoint (perspective), to the proper way of asking meaningful questions, through the consideration of the relevant context, to the (experientially) faithful description of the phenomenon under study.

Though essentials of the phenomenological approach to environmental problems will be given below, for purposes of introduction it will do to outline its main ground rule as it has been explicated by the late Gestalt psychologist W. Metzger (1975, p. 12) for a phenomenological orientation in psychology:

> First, take the phenomenon simply as it is given, even if it appears unusual, unexpected, illogical, absurd, or contrary to unquestioned assumptions and familiar trains of thought. Let the things speak for themselves, without side glances at the well-known, at what has been learned earlier, at knowledge taken for granted, at claims of logic, linguistic biases, and deficits of the vocabulary. Face the phenomenon with respect and sympathy, but question and distrust the presuppositions and conceptions with which the phenomenon in question has hitherto been grasped.

Although this ground rule may be understood as a paraphrase of what Husserl repeatedly formulated as an essential of phenomenological methodology, Metzger, who explicitly acknowledged the Husserlian heritage, also claimed Goethe as an exemplary forebear. Goethe was not only a great poet; as a natural scientist who had published a theory of color in 1812 he had pleaded for a "gentle empiricism" (*sanfte Empirie*).

This lineage is mentioned here for two reasons. First and principally, Goethe's method of an open-minded and unprejudiced description and explanation of phenomena, which has had many followers in modern descriptive science, is part of what is meant by the term *phenomenological approach* in this chapter. Although Goethe himself did not use the term, his method could rightfully be claimed as a "phenomenological method" as early as 1934 (Heinemann, 1934).

Second, recently (though circa 50 years after Metzger's claim) Goethe's "phenomenology of nature" was retrieved and rediscovered by representatives of an "environmental phenomenology" (Seamon & Zajonc, 1998).

Although Metzger's ground rule was published in a textbook of psychology and meant for psychological research, it is not restricted to this field: Goethe's phenomenology was of nature in general; it served the observation and description of plants and animals. Historically and metatheoretically, Spiegelberg (1972, p. xliv), assessed it as part of the "countermovement to the wave of abstractive science initiated by Galileo with his suppression of the mathematically unmanageable world of the qualitative and the 'subjective.'" According to Spiegelberg, Goethe's theory of color was the "first highlight in the larger countermovement, which wanted to 'save the phenomena' and recover the full breadth and depth of qualitative experience" (p. xliv).

Not only in this highly descriptive standard but also in the critical stance regarding a dominating theory, namely, Newton's, Goethe's "way of science" (Seamon & Zajonc, 1998) became a model for later phenomenological approaches for which the combination of critical and descriptive efforts is a significant feature.

One final note concerning the phenomenology of approach: As stated in the chapter's opening, *approach* emphasizes the process of bringing us closer to an envisioned goal or destination; it does not put a stress on reaching the goal or on getting hold of whatever has been aspired to. It is this open-endedness of proceeding that makes *approach* the most suitable term for doing phenomenology.

PEOPLE-ENVIRONMENT STUDIES

Since one criterion, many would say the most essential feature, of any phenomenological approach, however broadly conceived, is its *focus on meaning*, the context in which its meaning, its constitution, maintenance, and transformation is to be studied should be people-environment relations. The reasons for this terminological choice are, briefly stated, the following.

Subject to a practicable definition of *meaning*, it can be stated right from the outset that meaning is neither an individual's "subjective" state (of mind), nor an intrapersonal process, nor an "objective" attribute of something in the (extrapersonal) environment. The meaning of an environmental object, as, for example, a toy or weapon, home or pub, garden or wilderness, is not restricted to a person environment relation, but for all practical purposes is an *intersubjective* matter of people-environment relations. Members of a culture group invest places and buildings with meaning and significance. Not individuals but people agree on what is a forest or a jungle, what is downtown or suburb. It is essentially the *language* that people, that is, the members of a language or cultural community, share (with, of course, individual, sometimes idiosyncratic, variations) that communicates meaning.

For a phenomenological study of the environment, for example, of nature, individual persons are primarily of interest as members of social (cultural, linguistic) groups and only in a secondary (and highly generalized) sense as isolated individuals. On the one hand, since psychology is commonly taken to be the scientific study of "psychological," such as mental or cognitive, processes and states which are assumed to occur or take place *within* individuals or individuals' minds, the prototypical preoccupation with inner processes is inappropriate, or at least "suboptimal," for the study of meaning-centered people-environment relations. On the other hand, we know from the history of environmental psychology that, from its beginnings, psychologists have acted as a kind of "main contractor" for an otherwise interdisciplinary enterprise rather than as dominating and "psychologizing" agents.

Finally, the choice of people-environment studies instead of environmental psychology is, at least for a phenomenological approach, justified by the growth and diversification of this approach in disciplines other than psychology, mainly in human and social geography, environmental sociology, and design and architectural studies. In the recent past there have been more phenomenological initiatives in sociology and geography than in psychology (cf. Graumann, 2001; Seamon, 1982, 1997; Werlen, 1993, 1997).

THE PHENOMENOLOGICAL APPROACH TO PEOPLE-ENVIRONMENT (P-E) STUDIES AS A CONVERGENCE OF TWO DEVELOPMENTS

The phenomenological approach, as it exists at the beginning of the twenty-first century, is the outcome of two interacting and converging developments. The first is the history of phenomenology itself as it has developed from an analysis of pure consciousness to a comprehensive study of the lifeworld—that is, the world as it is lived and experienced, in which humans perceive and act and of which they are constitutive parts. It is the increasing emphasis on the lifeworld that has made phenomenology interested in and relevant for environmental studies. As this article will exemplify, the analysis of the lifeworld, while initiated by Husserl himself, owes much to phenomenologists like Gurwitsch and Merleau-Ponty, who were also students of Gestalt psychology, or like Schütz, whose major concern was the social world. Moreover, it was a phenomenologically oriented psychology that explicated the spatially and temporally articulated situation of the body subject and that emphasized the experiential meaning of places, distances, times, and relations.

In a complementary sense, in some of the natural sciences we observe an increasing awareness that natural phenomena must not be (mis)taken as primarily or even exclusively physical facts and processes. *Nature is human nature* if it is perceived, categorized, and treated by humans is the second development. Mainly in geography there has been a growing awareness that this discipline not only is a physical science of the earth's surface, forms, climates, and so forth but also has to account for the elementary fact that the earth is the habitat of human beings and, hence, an ensemble of meanings. In the analysis of such meanings we recognize the convergence of developments in phenomenology and in sciences that, even if natural, are human sciences.

Both developments will be exemplified before the present state of the art is presented and the heuristic, conceptual, and methodological relevance of the phenomenological approach in the "human sciences" is discussed.

PHENOMENOLOGY: THE RECOVERY OF THE LIFEWORLD

The development of phenomenology is a broad and complex affair. In this chapter it will be referred to only in a very selective manner. The criteria for this selectivity must be the relevance for P-E studies and especially for the thesis presented here that there has been a convergence of two trends: The development in phenomenology will be highlighted as a recovery of the lifeworld, whereas for the corresponding trend in P-E studies an emphasis will be given to the "discovery" of the lifespace. Both highlights are accentuations and should be taken with a grain of salt.

Phenomenology exists in many forms and ramifications. Hence, a unitary and consensual definition is difficult. After all, phenomenology has been a movement rather than a school, more precisely a "century-old, international, and multidisciplinary movement" according to Embree and Mohanty (in Embree et al., 1997, p. 2). Whoever is interested in the vicissitudes of its history should consult Spiegelberg's two volumes covering the history of the movement until the midtwentieth century (Spiegelberg, 1960) and the companion volume on phenomenology in psychology and psychiatry (Spiegelberg, 1972). The present state is, however, better reflected and documented in the *Encyclopedia of Phenomenology* edited by Embree et al.

In this comprehensive encyclopedia two of its senior editors identify four major varieties and phases in phenomenology: an early realistic, a constitutive, a (subsequent) existential, followed by a hermeneutical phenomenology (Embree et al., 1997, p. 2). Since the evolution of the phenomenological movement is closely connected with the political history of the twentieth century, it is also possible to differentiate between periods when phenomenology had its major centers in Germany and when, due to forced migration, it found footholds in France, northwestern Europe, the United States, and, generally, in countries where phenomenologists fleeing Nazism found permanent refuge. As a consequence, existential phenomenology, although essentially shaped by Heidegger, became prominent in France, while hermeneutic phenomenology, also originally in Heidegger's and Gadamer's philosophy, has now its widest and most diversified following in the United States. More important, however, than this geographical spread of phenomenology is its dissemination in all human and some natural sciences.

This dissemination has never been a unilateral influence but has originated and resulted in various forms of interaction. Historically documented best is the interaction with psychology, as in Husserl's initial endeavours toward a descriptive psychology and in the fruitful adoption and development of Gestalt theoretical conceptions by influential phenomenologists like Gurwitsch (1964, 1966, 1979) and Merleau-Ponty (1962, 1963). Furthermore, there has been a lively interaction with sociology, initiated and mediated by Alfred Schütz and his disciples (Schütz, 1962–1966; Schütz & Luckmann, 1974, 1983; Berger & Luckmann, 1966).

Further relationships and interactions with most human and a few natural sciences will be discussed below. As far as true interaction was involved, these relationships are historically important since the changing focus of phenomenologists on psychological, social, historical, or linguistic problems has more than marginally affected the development of philosophical phenomenology.

For the purpose of this chapter, this development will briefly be sketched. The phenomenology that Husserl developed from Brentano's lectures on descriptive psychology in the 1880s focused on the fundamental function of human consciousness: to represent. The term *intentionality* was to signify that every consciousness is consciousness of something (which it is not). With this basic notion, an *indissoluble correlation* between the experiencing person and the experienced world was posited, an essential relationship which was to overcome the Cartesian dualism that after all had given birth to modern psychology. Speaking of this essential correlation implies that persons are to be understood as intending, that is, sensing or meaning-giving, agents and their environment is, in principle, experienced (e.g., perceived, felt, judged, remembered) as meaningful. (That is why occasionally phenomenology has been simplified as the "science of meaning.")

Intrinsically connected with the fundamental intentional relationship is the idea that the person pole has to be considered as a *bodily* center of orientation. Again in contrast with Cartesian conceptions, the subject of intentionality is bodily, which means that it occupies a place, or *viewpoint*, from which "standpoint" environmental objects are perceived (even remembered and imagined) *in perspective* in aspects or "profiles." Being perceived in one of its aspects that corresponds to a person's viewpoint implies that each aspect of an object (e.g., by "adumbration") refers to further aspects and further views of the same object that all together make up the inner *horizon* of what is perceived. And since a perspectively given object refers the perceiver to further objects ("co-objects") in its immediate context, which Husserl (1973) named the "outer horizon," each perceptual (and, ultimately, cognitive experience) is, phenomenologically speaking, not only perspectival, that is, viewpoint related, but also horizonal, that is, intrinsically context related. As, moreover, each horizon refers the perceiver to wider horizons, each experience is ultimately embedded in the *Welthorizont* (Husserl) as the horizon of all horizons. It is from here that the phenomenological key concept of *lifeworld* can be understood best. The world as it is lived, that is, experienced and acted upon, and that, in turn, acts upon the experiencing subject, is horizonal. Taking *horizon* in its full phenomenological sense (Husserl, 1973; van Peursen, 1954), it means openness and constraint, actuality and potentiality, from-whichness and toward-whichness, past, present, and future experience. These horizonal dimensions are essential for a phenomenologically informed conception of person- or people-environment relationships. It is necessary to emphasize the intentional, that is, perspectival-horizonal, character of the indissoluble person environment relationship. The mere assumption that people and their environment are an inseparable unit and must not be defined separately is also shared by representatives of the "transactional view" (cf. Altman & Rogoff, 1987; Ittelson, 1973).

An essential implication of this conception, of the strictly correlative character of each person environment relationship, is a shift of focus on the two terms of the relation.

Although within the Cartesian tradition it is almost a truism to locate physical (material) characteristics on the environmental side in objects and objective states of affairs but to preserve the "subjective" for the person side, the correlation, if taken seriously, does not only make the phenomenologist look for "personal" or human qualities in environmental objects. Of equal interest are environment-related attributes and functions in the person. Hence, while objects are primarily conceived as human things, spaces as places, buildings as homes, and so forth, conversely, human activity or behavior is analysed in terms of its spatiality. Heidegger (1962, 1971), in his study of equipment, that is, things encountered in the lifeworld as "ready-to-hand," illustrates the predominance of the prereflective practical value and human use of objects. In a complementary way, Heidegger argues that our awareness of space is grounded in human activities toward the world of things, such as distancing. Briefly summarized, the spatiality of experience precedes and makes possible the experience of space.

There is one other (fully compatible) meaning of *lifeworld* that is also relevant for the potential contribution of phenomenology to the study of P-E relationships: the world as it is experienced "naively," that is, unreflectedly in our everyday lives. It was mainly Schütz and his students (Schütz, 1962–1966; Schütz & Luckmann, 1974, 1983) who emphasized the character of our everyday lifeworld taken-for-grantedness. If we want to know how people act in their environment, objective (physical and geographical) definitions of the environment are not helpful at all. Humans do not react to what is objectively the case. They act and react with respect to what they perceive or think or feel to be the case. It is misleading to call this kind of behavior "naive"; it may be quite sophisticated if, for instance, people make use of a vulgarized and hence simplified version of psychoanalytic theory. But whether influenced by lay theories or by stereotypes and prejudices, for instance, about the determination of human behavior by natural or human-made environmental states and events, it is to a large degree rather what people believe is the truth than the objective (e.g., scientifically founded) reality as such that motivates people to act. That is why for ecological purposes and policies it is important to account for and try to change what people take for granted.

THE HUMAN SCIENCES: APPROXIMATIONS TO CONCEPTIONS OF LIVED SPACE

If one may interpret the evolution of the concept of *lifeworld* as an important way in which philosophy overcame Cartesian dualism, it is also possible to identify related developments in the "human sciences." These developments are less fundamental and coherent, but looking back from today's studies of P-E relationships, these diverse approaches have consistently contributed to the conception that persons or people and their environment have basically to be taken and studied in their interrelationship, so that, ultimately, speaking of space or environment means speaking of lived space or of lived environment and, conversely, our study of human experience and behavior has to account for its spatiality or, to make use of the more comprehensive phenomenological term, its *situatedness*.

The introduction of the important concept of *Umwelt* in the "subjective biology" of J. von Uexküll and the differentiation of *Umwelt* into a sensible world (corresponding to an organism's sense organs) and an effective world (corresponding to the same organism's motor organs) was a lasting achievement, as was the spread of this concept of a species-specific environment to a subject-specific world in Uexküll's later theoretical biology. The adoption of *Umwelt* in the sociology and social psychology of Ervin Goffman and Rom Harré has, although briefly, been referred to in Kruse & Graumann (1987, p. 1196). These authors also discussed the relationship of environmental with Gestalt notions in Koffka and Tolman. Therefore, the following paragraph will concentrate on what may be considered the phenomenological content of these notions.

For von Uexküll the phenomenologically relevant feature is the subject-centeredness and specificity of the *Umwelt* and, hence, the strict correlation between the sensory and motor makeups of the (animal or human) subject and the qualities of the subject's environment *(Umwelt)*. Furthermore—and von Uexküll explicated this in his later "theory of meaning" (von Uexküll, 1956)—it is the significance for the subject that turns indifferent and unnoticed (objective) attributes of environmental objects into qualities that attract a subject's attention. This significance originates in the interaction between subject and environment (p. 106).

Hence, it is no exaggeration to state that von Uexküll, with his introduction of the concept and theory of *Umwelt* and in his "theory of meaning," became a precursor, although not more than a precursor, of a phenomenological approach to people-environment studies.

The emphasis on the range of meanings that a subject is aware of and acts on has made it possible and legitimate to transfer the *Umwelt* notion of the environment into phenomenological psychology and the social sciences. Goffman's (1972) observation that, at least in large American cities, there are some environments in which "wariness is particularly important, constant monitoring and scanning must be sustained, and any untoward event calls forth a quick and full reaction" (p. 242) has prompted him to adopt von Uexküll's term *Umwelten* for the immediate surrounds of people that normally can be taken for granted but sometimes are potential sources of alarm (p. 252). In Goffman's microstudy we find two further topics that are central for phenomenological studies of P-E relations. One is that a crucial concern of the person moving in an unsafe *Umwelt* is his or her *body* or rather its vulnerability. This keeps persons away from places and areas outside their field of vision and what may be "lurking" there. "Lurk lines" (p. 293) structure the immediate *Umwelt*, mainly, of individuals who are not familiar with such areas. The other phenomenologically relevant observation is that as people move their surrounds change too. But, "what is changing is not the position of events but their *at-handedness*" (p. 285, emphasis added). At-handedness (which is distantly related to Heidegger's "ready-to-hand" equipment) is to be interpreted in two directions: (1) to the persons and objects of an individual's environment as far as they are at hand (or, in Schütz's terms, within reach) and (2) to the individual as far as she or he is bodily and with all personal belongings within other people's reach, either facilitated or inhibited, favored or endangered, by others. Evidently, with regard to the social being of humans, it would be highly artificial and "Cartesian" again to separate the social from the material or physical environment.

Consequently, for Harré's concept of *Umwelt* as the environment of social action (Harré, 1979, p. 194) the proper (formulaic) definition is

Umwelt = Physical environment × Social meanings

practically a Boolean product. Harré, who derives the original idea of a social texture of space and time from Kurt Lewin's (1936) topological psychology, cites (but does not quote) an untranslated early essay on the "war landscape" (Lewin, 1917/1982). This first publication of Lewin's is his only paper that is explicitly introduced as phenomenological, namely, as "a chapter in the 'phenomenology of landscape.'" For Lewin, phenomenology involves the identification of the viewpoint, that is, the position from which a landscape is experienced and described. At least, he underlines right at the outset that his encounter with the war landscape is that of an artilleryman, well knowing that a landscape is different for an infantryman. We then learn how in trench warfare, a landscape changes when approaching the front line from the rear area, namely, in its extension, its limitation, its directedness, and in its differentiation into danger and battle zones, positions, and objects as compared with "peace" objects and zones. One and the same object, such as a "battle object," is experienced, valued, and treated differently from its experience as a "peace object." The similarity with Goffman's threatening *Umwelten* is evident. The characteristics of parts of the environment, such as giving protection, cover, or subsistence or exposing a soldier to enemy action, for which Lewin later introduced the term of *valence*, make any lived environment a context of significations.

As will be shown below, Lewin's field theory has not promoted phenomenological thinking, but the field concept has. So have other Gestalt conceptions. Two of them have a special relevance for people-environment studies.

One is Koffka's (1935) basic distinction between the "geographic" (physical) and the "behavioral [psychological] environment." Of this famous distinction it is worth remembering that, although behavior takes place in the behavioral environment, we must account for an ultimately reciprocal relation between the geographical and the behavioral environment since behavior changes the geographic environment, which in turn acts back on behavior.

Theoretically more important is that, owing to the Gestalt theoretical refusal of the constancy hypothesis, which had assumed a one-to-one correspondence between physical stimuli and sensations, there is a relative autonomy of the behavioral environment. For a phenomenology of the environment this means that human activity must be accounted for in terms of what is experienced as real, whatever its geographical counterpart. Based on Koffka's distinction, Charles Taylor (1964, p. 62) introduced his (slightly more phenomenological) distinction between geography and *intentional* environment.

Phenomenologically informed and helpful, if properly interpreted, is also Tolman's conception of *sign-gestalten* (Tolman, 1958). As a "molar behaviorist," he had confessed to being "tremendously influenced" by Lewin and other Gestalt psychologists. He tried to "rewrite . . . what gestalt psychologists had called a phenomenology in operational behavioristic terms," which effort made Wolfgang Köhler name Tolman a "cryptophenomenologist" (Tolman, 1959, p. 94).

In this effort of defining and describing environmental objects strictly in terms of observable behavioral operations with respect to such objects, we see the interesting and, in its radicality, unique attempt at reducing all attributes of an environment to what an organism or subject *does* with respect to them.

Three types of behavioral operations are to be distinguished: (1) Environmental objects have different or discriminable properties by means of which living beings (organisms) accomplish their orientation: the *discriminanda.* They refer not only to (sensory) qualities of objects (e.g., color, shape, weight) by means of which we discriminate between them and orient ourselves. They also refer to the specific structured sense organ permitting discrimination. (2) Other attributes are definable by an organism's manipulations. A chair, for example, is behaviorally defined by its *manipulanda,* its sit-upon-ableness, its stand-upon-ableness, its moveability but also its throw-about-ableness (for an enraged drunkard). Again, the correlation between the object's and the organism's properties is close: "One and the same environmental object will afford quite different manipulanda to an animal which possesses hands from what it can and will to an animal which possesses only a mouth, or only a bill, or only claws" (Tolman, 1958, p. 82). (3) Animals and humans do not discriminate and manipulate per se; they do these for a purpose. Discriminanda and manipulanda are used as means to ends. In this relationship they become what Tolman and Brunswik (1935) aptly called *utilitanda,* if, for example, the manipulanda of an environmental object will "lead on" to others. Also this means-end relationship is defined strictly in behavioral terms, for instance, as persistence-until.

The reason why this behavioristic piece is inserted in this chapter is not historical but systematic. Since for a phenomenological approach to P-E relationships the indissolubility of P and corresponding E attributes is a criterion, a psychological model joining an environment that is exclusively defined in behavioral terms and environmental behavior deserves closer attention, even if the context is described not as intentional but as a causal texture.

LIFESPACE

If the indissoluble mutual relationship between living beings and their environment is one necessary though not sufficient criterion of the phenomenological approach to environmental problems, then the construct of *lifespace,* in all its ambiguities, is an exemplary case for the diffusion of phenomenological and protophenomenological conceptions in the twentieth century. But in order to recognize what is phenomenological in the concept of lifespace and what is not, it is necessary to disentangle its ambiguity (Graumann & Kruse, 1995).

Historically, we are confronted with two typical but significantly different constructions of space for living beings. One may be specified as a *biogeographical* construct; the other has developed within the *phenomenological-anthropological* universe of discourse. Since the original German term *Lebensraum* is used in both contexts, a first aid in unravelling the prevailing equivocation is the recourse to the English usage: *living space* for the biological, geographical, and (geo)political(!) construct and *lifespace* for the phenomenological, anthropological, and psychological equivalent of Lebensraum. *Living space* has found acceptance in everyday vocabulary and in nontechnical dictionaries, where it figures as the closest correspondence of the German Lebensraum as the term for a territory for political and economic expansion or, more specifically, "a territory which the Germans believed was needed for their natural development" (*Concise Oxford English Dictionary,* 1964). Although Lebensraum, originally constructed for usage in political geography as a term for the ground that facilitates or inhibits the growth of nations, has, after its extended and popularized use and misuse in imperialist ideologies and geopolitics and after the demise of Nazi and fascist imperialism, been tentatively reduced to a neutral core, the term is still burdened with two different kinds of ideological baggage: (1) the old connotation that goes with the mere use of the word Lebensraum or *living space* and (2) its occasional usage in the ongoing and unsettled controversy between advocates and critics of a *geographical, mainly climate, determinism.*

The theoretical relevance of climate determinism for a potentially scientific usage of a living space, favorable or detrimental to the health and wellness of people, may be taken from the central hypothesis of the leading and best known representative of climate determinism, Ellsworth Huntington (1924, p. 313): "Climatic conditions constitute a distinct optimum (and conversely a downside) and with it varies the advance of civilization and the quality of people."

Since climate is considered to be relatively constant, there is a coincidence of optimal climate conditions and geographical areas in which alone the *quality of people* may reach an optimum—a statement that in its affinity with (other) ethnocentric and racist doctrines has provoked the most severe criticism.

In sharp contrast with this biogeographical construction of the living space, the phenomenological (anthropological, psychological) construct of *lifespace* was developed in the 1920s and 1930s. Psychologists who have made the most intensive use of it did not coin the term but took it from everyday usage and adapted it for their special purpose. Martha Muchow, a student of William Stern's but also influenced by von Uexküll, acknowledged that *lifespace* in ordinary language use refers to the space "in which one lives." But with its adaptation as a developmental psychological term, she saw the necessity to differentiate between "the space in which the child lives," the "space that the child experiences," and the "space that the child lives" (Muchow & Muchow, 1935/1980; cf. Wohlwill, 1985). Of these three perspectives on urban space (Muchow's research interest was children in the city), only the second and the third are phenomenologically relevant. While the "space in which the child lives" is the objective space for everybody, as exemplified by a map or a street register, the other two are subject related, that is, conceived and described from the perspective of an urban child. The city as far as it is experienced by the child is any modality of *experiential space,* such as perceived (visual, auditory, tactual, kinesthetically perceived) space, emotionally tinged or tuned space. Also the related terms *oriented* and *personal* space refer to space as experienced by a centered subject (cf. Kruse, 1974; Ströker, 1987).

While experiential space in one of the above modalities presupposes that subjects are consciously aware of their immediate environment, the space as lived is Muchow's "behavioral" complement *(avant la lettre)* to a phenomenologically comprehensive conception of the person environment relation. It is only in the combination of being experienced and acted upon that the spatial environment is intrinsically related to human (and animal) subjects as agents. It must be added, however, that acting or behaving with respect to spatial objects and relations does not presuppose (full) consciousness of what one is doing. The repeated climbing of stairs or sitting in an easy chair will leave traces and signs of wear of which the user is not aware until they become so salient as to make him or her consciously adapt. Hence, the space that we live in (in Muchow's terminology) is not only the space and spatial objects that we act upon but inevitably the lifespace as acting and reacting on us. Methodologically, the distinction between space-as-experienced and space-as-lived will lead to different demands and procedures. Since lived space is not necessarily cognitively represented and perceived space does not necessarily imply action, self-reports and the whole gamut of (preferably unobtrusive) observational methods will have to go together in order to make the lifespace of a person or a group of persons psychologically meaningful.

Muchow's favorite research topic, children at play, brings in two further phenomenologically relevant dimensions of the lifespace: (1) intersubjectivity and (2) age specificity.

Intersubjectivity

At play, children, as well as interacting individuals in general, generate, invent, construct, and deconstruct, "define" and "redefine" elements, features, and whole scenarios of their common lifespace. Between two or more kids strolling along, a tin can will become a "ball" to be kicked around and toward a door that has become a "goal" in a street transformed into a "football field," and so forth. The "definition" of the various elements is achieved implicitly, by *doing*, not by verbal communication. In other words, it is the shared performance that makes things "mean" something, that makes lived space into an environment that can be experienced as a special lifespace.

Age Specificity

As Muchow demonstrated, the intersubjectively agreed-upon lifespace will mean different things to different people. The squares and lines of the pavement that will make a child hop on one leg avoiding the lines will not make an adult do this. Following

Muchow's train of thought, Kruse and Graumann (1998) have demonstrated how environments undergo *metamorphoses* in the life cycle, offering different lifespaces to different ages. If we contrast childhood with old age, changes of the lifespace may be drastic: What for a junior may be a tempting object to climb upon, jump over, or even do acrobatic exercises on, will for a senior became a stumbling block or other obstacle to be avoided. Such differences with respect to one and the same object or surrounding are not merely matters of evaluation. They are—in Muchow's terminology—differences of the "space in which" a person lives or—in Gibson's terminology—differences in the *affordances* of environmental objects.

To round off Muchow's contribution to the conception of lifespace it should be added that lifespaces vary not only with age but also with *gender.* For girls in the Muchow samples, the big department store held more and other attractions and facilities than for boys, a finding that regularly should be reviewed given the historicity of both gender and lifespace. That boys' and girls' lifespaces differ was only one of the many data of Muchow's pioneer study. But it may be deepened and reinforced by the recently developed concept of *gendered environment.* The clarification of this concept suggests that to be *gendered* may apply to all three varieties of Muchow's lifespace: the space women and men live in, the space they experience, and the space they live differently according to gender.

An additional remark about the historicity of lifespace: Although it was not controlled in Muchow's study it is far from trivial that, mainly in developmental studies, not only persons but also environmental objects and settings grow old and show their age and (sometimes) their origin. This holds for natural as well as for built environments, for individual objects (like trees and houses) as well as for whole settings (like landscapes or towns).

If in contemporary psychology lifespace has become a current term, this is less due to Martha Muchow than to Kurt Lewin (Martha Muchow's professional life was brief, ended by suicide in 1933 after the Nazis had driven her Jewish teacher, William Stern, out of his own department). In spite of its prominence, Lewin's construct of lifespace can be dealt with rather briefly in the context of the present topic. The reason is that Lewin's lifespace (Lewin, 1936) is not a phenomenological concept. As a key construct of Lewin's field theory it refers to "the manifold of co-existing facts which determine the behavior of an individual at a given moment" (Deutsch, 1968, p. 423). "Psychological fields" and "total situation" are presented as synonyms of the lifespace, which in turn is considered to be a product of interactions between a person (P) and her or his environment (E). Unfortunately, the usage of these constituents, P and E, is nonuniform. Hence, the popular formula according to which behavior may be defined as a function of the interaction between person and environment [B = f − (P, E)] is of little help in disambiguating the quasi-mathematical quantities. Phenomenologically meaningful, however, is the theoretical notion behind this formula, namely, that person and environment are intrinsically connected, literally, interdependent. But to refer to the lifespace as a "product" of the interaction between person and environment presupposes P and E as independent factors—a contradiction with the postulate of interdependence.

Since Lewin repeatedly proclaimed his field theory as the paragon of the new *Galileian* mode of thought (Lewin, 1935) with its emphasis on the concurrence of interacting forces, reason demands that the postulate of interdependence be upheld. Yet this adoption from force-field physics, according to which P in his or her *locomotion* is impelled or drawn by *forces* along power *vectors,* is far from a phenomenological mode of thought and discourse. The physicalist terminology is hardly descriptive of lifespaces as experienced or lived.

The phenomenologically appropriate term for regions of the lifespace that either attract or repel persons was originally *Aufforderungscharakter,* an *invitational* or *demand character* if and when the things themselves are experienced as inviting or demanding us to do something with or about them. (Demand characters are related but not to be mixed up with the *demand characteristics* of the experimental situation.) In Lewin's theory each such character corresponds to a need or an intention in the person. The person environment correspondence is considered to be a case of interdependence. When the water kettle whistles, we are called to take it off the stove if we have the intention to make coffee; a delicious dish gives an appetite only to the hungry; the same food is not appetizing to one who already has had enough; and so forth. When the attractive and repulsive qualities of environmental objects and regions were named (positive or negative) *valences,* the dynamic meaning of the original term was replaced by a focus on the (subjective) value character of environmental objects, regions, and relations. It is subjective since it is always correlated with a need or intention (for Lewin a "quasi-need") of the person.

While the major dynamic features of the lifespace are the valences of and the forces in the field, Lewin also considered nonpsychological data (strangely named the "foreign hull") making up the boundary conditions that determine the lifespace. This special study of the psychological environment came under the name *psychological ecology* (in Lewin, 1951), a field marginal to the psychology of those days but full of hopes for future cooperation between and synthesis of ecology and psychology. But whatever became of the synthesis, certainly Morton Deutsch was right when he predicted that after the introduction of the concept of lifespace it would be pointless to speak of behavior without relating it to both person and environment.

FROM LIFESPACE TO LIFE WORLDS

Since the verb *to live* is usually not used transitively, the use of the term *lived space* implies the (semantic) temptation to underrate its active component. If, however, we envisage that right from birth we have to appropriate our environment, the active and, above all, interactive character of the person environment relationship is evident.

The Appropriation of Space

Appropriation (Aneignung), as the term was introduced into environmental psychology in Europe (Graumann, 1996; Korosec-Serfaty, 1976) in its originally Hegelian-Marxian conception, is the term for the *dialectical* nature of the P-E relationship. On the one hand, it is only by means of human (mental and bodily) activities that the world has become a truly human habitat, that objects and occurrences become human things and affairs. Also, appropriation, which literally means making (something) one's own and taking for one's own use, presupposes that it is features of the spatiotemporal environment that arouse, foment, afford, and sustain environment-related intentionality.

Within the context of the so-called cultural-historical school of Vygotsky, Leont'ev, and Luria, the sociocultural and interpersonal context of all appropriation was emphasized. What a person knows things to be; what they are called; how they are to be dealt with; which areas or regions are home or foreign, safe or unsafe to move in, accessible or inaccessible; and so forth—all these are learned from others either by instruction or, more often, by doing as others do. Those others have, in turn, appropriated the world in interaction with others who have acquired their environmental and social knowledge from predecessors and contemporaries (cf. Schütz, 1962–1966; Schütz & Luckmann, 1974, 1983). It is therefore appropriate to speak of a dual sociality of appropriation; it is societally as well as interpersonally situated. "How to use a spoon, a ladder, an oar, must be learned by each individual through trial and error, but the resulting sensorimotor coordination (of eating, climbing, rowing) need not be invented anew; it is handed down to each person by others who instruct, correct, and reinforce the learner" (Graumann & Kruse, 1998, p. 365).

On the other hand, it is important to realize that persons, while appropriating their environment, change themselves by the acquisition of new cognitive and motor schemata, of new patterns of behavior, and ultimately of skills that enable them to deal with new and untoward environmental features and events (Graumann, 1996). To summarize the dialectics of appropriation: Persons change by changing their environment (cf. also Werner, Altman, & Oxley, 1985, p. 5).

On a global scale, Graumann and Kruse (1976; Graumann, 1996) presented an overview of the major *modes of appropriation of space,* from two perspectives. From an *anthropological/historical* perspective, they addressed the many and varied modes of marking, naming, defining, categorizing, and evaluating space as appropriate or inappropriate, owned or free, by signs, words, rules, regulations, and laws; but also by regular locomotion resulting in paths and roads; by the cultivation of nature as subsistence or supply of resources; by the domestication of animals; by the conquest of foreign land and the subjugation of other people(s); by building, constructing, and settling; but also by the artistic and scientific representation of space; and, finally, by the overcoming of distance by developing means of communication.

The *psychological* perspective on appropriation was exemplified by the development of (sensory, motor, cognitive, and communicative) exploratory and destructive behavior, by the many ways of taking possession of environmental objects and spaces, and by the various forms of personalizing space and making it more habitable.

In any case, the results of collective as well as individual, of constructive as well as destructive, appropriative behavior are, taken together, what we call our environment—our steadily changing since continuously appropriated environment.

Without having the term, Martha Muchow described how boys and girls, children of different ages, appropriate, that is, experience and live, the urban environment differently. Although since then times, customs, and children's games have changed considerably, this finding has been replicated several times. More than 70 years after Muchow's study it still seems to be true that public space is used much more and extensively by boys than by girls, that the spatial range of boys' activities is wider than that of girls; that playgrounds for rough ball games are preferred by boys (Harloff, Lehnert, & Eibisch, 1998).

But what about adult women and men? Do they live in different lifeworlds? The fact that the concept of *gendered environments* could be firmly established in recent environmental psychology and sociology and in the feminist literature is merely an indication that the problem of gender specificity has become part of P-E research. It informs us that there are, on the one hand, gender-specific preferences for certain environments and, on the other hand, spaces and places that, by their structure, location, or history, encourage or discourage a given gender to visit and appropriate them. But studies of either kind of gender specificity have so far, for unclear reasons, not been informed by phenomenology. This may be due to the fact that, at least in our culture and our time, men and women spend some of their time in gendered environments but inhabit a common world, which inference, however, will remain a mere hypothesis until further (empirical) evidence is collected.

The Landscape in Phenomenological Psychology

Whenever psychologists adopted the phenomenological attitude, mainly informed and inspired by Husserl, Heidegger, Merleau-Ponty, and Schütz, a major feature of their reorientation was a shift of focus away from the individual per se and his or her inner (mental or conscious) life toward the *situated person*, that is, the embodied individual in her or his lived context of a spatial, social-communicative, and temporal-historical environment (Graumann, 1988; Kockelmans, 1987; van den Berg & Linschoten, 1953). To study human intentionality in its embodiment, spatiality, sociality, and historicity transforms each phenomenologically informed psychological investigation into an analysis of situations as lifeworlds. Its relevance for P-E studies can briefly be outlined.

Each situation is centered in the person, the body-subject of all intentional acts. Phenomenology focuses on the person's *bodily* nature because persons do not only occupy a *place* from which and according to which they perceive and act upon their environment. Also the meaning of environmental objects and events is contingent upon a subject's bodily condition. It will be different for the fit and healthy, the sick and bedridden, the small, the overweight, the intoxicated, and so forth. The correlate of such bodily states and traits is to be found in the materiality and spatiality of a person's "intentional environment," which must be qualified (Taylor, 1964) in terms of what Heidegger has called the readiness-to-hand of objects of our everyday concern. In our daily, often routine activities we encounter environmental objects as near or far, manageable or intractable, and reachable by hand, on foot, or by car, or out of reach, objects that appear as edible or inedible, useful or useless, delicious or revolting, beautiful or ugly, as means or ends, and so forth. All these are human qualities and valences of the world of things through which both the kind and measure of our appropriation, but also our alienation, manifest themselves.

In order to emphasize this human quality of the intentional environment and (like Straus, 1963) to contrast it with the scientifically constructed world of geography, Linschoten (1953) preferred the terms *world* and *landscape.* In each situation the whole world is implied but perspectively structured by a specific intentionality (e.g., of thinking, of perceiving, of imagining) in its own "landscape" (van den Berg & Linschoten, 1953, p. 249). Each human activity in whichever intentional modality is embedded in and interpretable by its landscape. The intentional description of such (horizontal) landscapes is, for Linschoten and other phenomenologists, the methodological approach to the person-world relationship: "Phenomenological psychology begins as descriptive cosmology" (p. 249). It is in the perspectival conception that *landscape* later was adopted by phenomenologically oriented geographers.

The structural analysis of a lifeworldly situation requires the observance of two further heuristic rules: One draws attention to the *temporality,* or, more generally, the *historicity*, of both experience and what is experienced. In learning and memory, environmental objects often remind us of what we—as individuals or collectives—have planned to do or not to do. Not only special devices like alarm clocks, memo books, beepers, and knots in the handkerchief do the job of reminding us. Remembering as such would hardly be possible without the help of environmentally marked "loci" and props (E. S. Casey, 1987) and the mnemonic assistance of our fellow humans.

But in a much more fundamental sense, other persons as well as things have a history of their own that sometimes is conspicuous, sometimes a matter of inference. For Wilhelm Schapp, an early student of Husserl's, contemporaries of mine become part of my history while I become "entangled" in their histories (Schapp, 1976). For Schapp, everybody and everything is comprehensible only in stories and, since humans and the history in which they are "entangled" coincide, nobody can go beyond the historicity of the world nor jump the shadow of language. With the historicity of the human environment, its dependence on language is a topic that recently was also discovered by environmentalists and phenomenologically informed architects like Mugerauer (in Mugerauer, 1994; Seamon & Mugerauer, 1985).

To the historicity of human situatedness and, consequently, the P-E relations belong, right from the beginning, not only the others with whom we *communicate*. The horizon of our experience and our expectations is enlarged or restricted by that of our fellow humans. From our birth, we live not only in a world of things but in a world of fellow humans (*Mitmenschheit*) with the "human horizon" constituted and interpreted by the language we speak. Everything and everybody is encountered in the "we-horizon" of a language community.

With the bodily nature of the intentional subject, the landscape, with historicity and intersubjectivity, the major components of the human situation are indicated. But, mainly with respect to a phenomenological conception of the environment, it is essential to recognize the interdependence of these features.

We experience the bodily nature of intentional subjects—in others or through others in us. We live the intentional environment with others and have learned to appropriate it through work, language, and art. What Merleau-Ponty (1963) in his phenomenological

structural analysis of behavior calls the "dialectics" of the "human order" is characterized through this interplay of the mutually determining structural elements. For a phenomenological conception of lifeworld situations, this perspectival-horizonal structure is the distinctive feature.

THE PHENOMENOLOGICAL-HERMENEUTIC APPROACH IN ENVIRONMENTAL DISCIPLINES

As with several other sections, the title of this final one will be interpreted.

If *the* phenomenological approaches are replaced by a "phenomenological-hermeneutical approach," this is in accordance with the thesis of this chapter, that there has been a convergence of developments in phenomenology and phenomenologically oriented human science with history and intersubjectivity by communication. For this convergence some evidence has been presented.

What must be added and emphasized is that phenomenology became hermeneutical. If, as it mainly was presented by Heidegger (1962) in *Being and Time* and related works, phenomenology is seen as focusing on something that, at least partly, is concealed and not open to an intuitive access and therefore has to be *interpreted*, phenomenology becomes hermeneutic. Practically, this means that human consciousness, experience as well as behavior, whose intentionality was uncovered by Husserl, is to be treated, that is, interpreted, like a text or even as a text.

Since many researchers in the environmental disciplines as well as architects are conversant with the works of Heidegger (1962, 1971) and of Gadamer (1975), they prefer to call their own method hermeneutical.

The other comment concerns the phrase *environmental disciplines:* The study of people-environment relationships is not the monopoly of any individual science, nor is the phenomenological approach. There was a time when it was mainly anchored in psychology and psychopathology. In the recent past, however, it has shifted to other human sciences and to the theory of architecture. Since the disciplinary identity of fields where this approach is cultivated is secondary if not arbitrary, this chapter mainly follows the interdisciplinary tradition of Altman and his coeditors' series "Human Behavior and Environment," whose contributors hail from a variety of disciplines.

Because essentials of the phenomenological approach have been outlined in the first part of this chapter and research in the behavior-and-environment field is sufficiently publicized, a few exemplifications should be sufficient to illustrate what is considered to be phenomenologically and hermeneutically informed in people-environment studies. Favorite topics relate to spatiality, space and place attachment, home, dwelling, and building and living in cities. What these environmental themes have in common is that they refer to foci of an intensive and existentially relevant interaction and interrelationship between people and their environment.

Whoever is interested in the relationship between phenomenology and the sciences cannot help noticing that, for the greater part of the twentieth century, the list of such sciences was restricted to psychology, the social sciences (sociology, anthropology, history, political science, economics, legal studies, linguistics), and psychiatry. In the recent past, however, this situation has changed toward a stronger influence of phenomenology on the environmental sciences, with human geography at the head (cf. Seamon, 1997; Werlen, 1997) and on architecture and design (cf. T. Casey, 1997; Norberg-Schulz, 1971, 1980, 1985; and the periodical *Environmental & Architectural Newsletter,* edited by David Seamon).

The relationship between phenomenology and the sciences is not without reservations, only one of which shall be addressed here. One of the inveterate prejudices positivistic scientists hold against the phenomenological approach is rooted in the misconception that (1) its qualitative methodology is restricted to intuition (or even introspection) and that (2) the pronounced emphasis on a subject's experience remains "subjective," that is, idiosyncratic, and therefore cannot be generalized. Both biases miss the truth.

The phenomenological interest in the lifeworld requires that it be studied as it is experienced by its inhabitants. Phenomenology is, as Natanson (1973, Vol. 1, p. 22) summarizes, "the conceptual conscience of the quotidian." An essential feature of this quotidian world is its recurrent typicality. Everyday experience is largely typification (Schütz, 1962–1966); the lifeworld is a preinterpreted world. Therefore it is phenomenologically imperative to try to capture the lifeworld in its inhabitants' views and interpretations. Their views or constructions remain, properly understood, "subjective," but they

yield "the world as it is experienced *from the perspective of the other one*" (Graumann, 1994, p. 285).

It is the original actors', not the researcher's, reality that is of phenomenological interest. That is why for a phenomenologically informed human scientist, things are real, if they are perceived or believed to be real. Neither a child's fear of a bogeyman lurking in a sinister place nor the belief of a group of adults in extraterrestrial beings threatening humankind from outer space must be rationally explained away as not really there. Both fears have to be taken as real and interpreted as to their subjective or collective meaning. "The basic methodological rule of a phenomenological approach is to accept and to describe things and events as they present themselves to individuals or to groups, but *only within the limits in which they present themselves*" (Graumann, 1994, p. 285; emphasis added), that is, in other people's experience, language, and behavior without any special recourse to "introspection" or to the researcher's "intuition."

Spatiality, Space, and Place

While space—in its major forms of land, water, and air and their distribution over the surface of the earth, and as the foundation and means for the life of plants, animals, and humans—has been a traditional topic of geography, the intrinsic mutual relations between humans and space became issues of research only when and where human geography was phenomenologically informed, as it has happened since the 1970s in behavioral and social geography. The quasi-paradigmatic shift was the transition from a predominantly physical geography to a human science of the earth as a *human habitat*.

Mainly under the influence of Heidegger's (1962) and Merleau-Ponty's (1962, 1963) philosophies, the spatiality of human existence as a bodily being-in-the world became a central topic of interest. Instead of a juxtaposition of space and organisms (which live in space as in a container) the *generation of space* by living in the world has become the foundation of reflecting and studying space. If we take behavior in its phenomenological sense as intentional activity, there is no behavior that does not, literally, "take place" (including, but leaving undiscussed, behavior in cognitive space). Taking place implies the notion of *making place* (Dovey, 1985b), that is, creating place for human existence in motion and rest: getting up and walking, reaching out and grasping, aiming and hitting—the long list of modalities of human appropriation of space (Graumann, 1996; Graumann & Kruse, 1976). As bodily or mental locomotions they are also space-making, space-changing, space-defining, or space-annihilating activities prior to and constitutive for the perception and cognition of space. It is in the human comportment toward fellow humans and things that space as we know and categorize it originates.

This generation of space and of spatial qualities has been implicit in the conception of "lived space" that is usually ascribed to Bollnow (1967) but dates back to William Stern's, Dürckheim's, and Minkowki's work in the 1930s (as discussed in Kruse, 1974; Ströker, 1987). It has also remained largely unexplicated since the phenomenological conceptions of the lifeworld and being-in-the-world were adopted in behavioral geography in the 1970s (Buttimer, 1993; Relph, 1976; Seamon, 1979; Tuan, 1977), a notable exception being Pickles's (1985) chapter on "man's spatiality." But, as could be exemplified by Martha Muchow's study of 1935 (Muchow & Muchow, 1980) the distinction (originally Stern's) between *gelebt* (lived) and *erlebt* (experienced) was meant to differentiate between a *prereflexive* ("automatic," quasi-instinctual, or habitual) behavior without awareness of one's whereabouts and a more conscious orientation in which the lifeworld is cognitively represented as is typical for what we call conduct.

Related to this differentiation is the distinction that has become significant for contemporary P-E studies, namely, between space and *place*. Although there is no unanimous definition, *space* (without further qualification) is the term for abstract geometrical extension indifferent with respect to any human activities. Or, if human activity, experience, or behavior is necessary to characterize space, an appropriate attribute is called for, as in *personal space, pragmatic space, perceptual space, existential space.* Even *geographical space* is "a reflection of man's basic awareness of the world" (Relph, 1976, p. 16).

Place, in contrast, has in itself a strongly experiential connotation. Places "are constructed in our memories and affections through repeated encounters and complex associations . . . place is an origin, it is where one knows others and is known to others, it is one's own," summarizes Relph (1985, p. 27), following Heidegger (1971) and Dardel (1952).

The attachment of poets to places as embodiments of affect, passions, sentiments, and sentimental (romantic) memories is dealt with in Bachelard's

(1969) *Poetics of Space,* while the most systematic and comprehensive phenomenological investigation of place was presented by E. S. Casey (1993), who earlier had studied major aspects of (body and) place memory (E. S. Casey, 1987; for a place-related ecology of memory, cf. Graumann, 1986).

Since places are centers of human action and interaction, they are favorite areas of psychological as well as phenomenologically informed geographic research. Concepts like place making (Dovey, 1985b), place attachment (Altman & Low, 1992), place identity (Proshansky, Fabian, & Kaminoff, 1983), and sense of place, or "topophilia" (Tuan, 1974, 1977), are familiar to environmental psychologists. They indicate a wide range of research foci only part of which is phenomenologically informed. Canter (1997), who in 1977 presented one of the first research monographs on the psychology of place, which had little in common with phenomenology, 20 years later saw a kind of rapprochement between the two traditions—however, from the psychologist's point of view, with the well-known reservation. Since, phenomenologically, places are locations of our departure and return with which we entertain emotional bonds and where we are known and know others, it is understandable that places will be encountered on various levels of space appropriation: my place at the table, my house, my neighborhood, my country, and, moving up to the globe as seen by an astronaut on the moon, my planet. Whatever we rightfully call "place" (with the obligatory possessive pronoun) is a condensed form or focus of lifeworld.

That, regardless of space, not everybody has found his or her place or everybody is at least uncertain about it is one important feature of the situation of socially or economically underprivileged fellow humans. Mazey and Lee's (1983) *Her Space, Her Place* is an early study in the new "geography of women," which since 1983 has broadened and become radicalized in the writings and actions of *ecofeminism* (Mies & Shiva, 1993). There is more about spaces and places for children, ever since Muchow a favorite topic of developmental and environmental psychology, less of phenomenology (cf. Altman & Wohlwill, 1978; Graumann & Kruse, 1998; Harloff et al., 1998).

Dwelling, Home, and Building

To give the topic of dwelling and building a paragraph of its own is, on the one hand, quite arbitrary because the better part of a phenomenology of place has to do with dwelling and building, and what people call home is the paradigm of a place. It is a fact that in the recent literature the unity of dwelling and building has become a paradigm of Heidegger's (1971) hermeneutical phenomenology that almost exclusively has influenced Seamon and Mugerauer's (1985) "phenomenology of person and world" (cf. Seamon, 1993) and Norberg-Schultz's (1971, 1980, 1985) "phenomenology of architecture" (cf. Dovey, 1993; Mugerauer, 1994).

On the other hand, home is not only a paradigm of place. Home and being-at-home (Dovey, 1985b; Graumann, 1989) also models perfectly what phenomenologists mean when they emphasize that our lifeworld is primarily our *habitat*, and that the human way of living on this earth (or maybe elsewhere) is *inhabiting* or *dwelling*. Heidegger has presented an explicit hermeneutic interpretation of dwelling and of the dwelling in which we make our home. This interpretation has been taken up and reinterpreted by geographers and architects (e.g., Dovey, Mugerauer, Pickles, Relph, and Seamon). The reinterpretation, usually in Heideggerian language, will not be repeated here since it would be a further reinterpretation. The message, however, of hermeneutic phenomenology is worth summing up as follows.

The P-E relationship, in all its modalities of active engagement and comportment and of active or passive experience is interpretive, that is, intentionally directed toward meaningful persons, objects, and events. These meanings that in their totality make up the lifeworld originate in the reciprocal interaction (or transaction) between people and their environment. This constitution of meaning is achieved intersubjectively. Interpretive experiences take place in perspectively structured (horizonal) situations. By means of intentional (individual as well as collective) experiences, humans appropriate their environment, by which dialectical process and procedure the environment incessantly, for better or for worse, becomes a human environment, while human subjects are continuously constituted as environmental beings.

Identity of and Identification with Cities

A related but more empirical approach was chosen by Graumann and Schneider in their comprehensive study of cities and city quarters as urban habitants (Graumann & Kruse, 1993; Schneider, 1986). This investigation (of five German and three French cities plus some typical city quarters) was phenomenologically informed for two theoretical and methodological reasons.

1. The question we asked was how the *identity of* a city or a city quarter was related with the inhabitants' degree and kind of their *identification with* their city. The identity, for example, of Paris or of the inner city *(Altstadt)* of Heidelberg was defined exclusively in terms of what their respective inhabitants had to say or express about their identification with the place in question. Hence, the identity of a place was closely tied to its inhabitants' experience.

2. Also, as phenomenologically required, we let our respondents speak for themselves and present their city, quarter, or neighborhood in their own words. Here we took advice from Ledrut (1977) that the "image" of a city is not so much a pictorial representation but the manner in which people, inhabitants as well as visitors, talk about a place. To tap the full experience of a place we first of all practiced *epoché*, that is, abstention from current theories and ideas, and did not concentrate on the inhabitants' cognitive representations but tried to include people's feelings, motives, and intentions. To get, for instance, at the affective component of identification, we explicitly asked our respondents whether there is anything in their environment they are proud or ashamed of or, generally, what is highly valued. This could be physical features (rivers, bridges, monuments) by which to identify a city. Primary objects of identification are one's own house or street, but equally important, mainly at the neighborhood level, are social relationships and memberships. One of the criteria of high valuation was the (confessed) readiness to defend a physical or social structure against changes or, generally, to become involved in communal activities.

Urban experience as we came to know it from our research refers us to "a considerable range of phenomena and above all, meanings: from the physical structures symbolizing history and culture, power and beauty, and, last but not least, epochs and anecdotes of our own biography, through the social climate of belonging or non-belonging, of being an insider or staying outside, of being 'somebody' or 'nobody,' of communal responsibility or indifference, down to the little pleasures and annoyances of everyday life: in commuting, shopping, childcare, petcare and leisure activities" (Graumann & Kruse,

1993, p. 161). A phenomenologically informed study of the interrelationship and the interaction between a human habitat and the human's inhabiting it supplies "the double perspective which is inherent in the interaction between the identity of and the identification with a city: to understand the city from the cognitions, feelings, motives, intentions, and activities of its inhabitants, but, equally, to understand the city dweller from the constraints and the facilities afforded in the physical and social structure of the urban environment" (p. 162).

POSTSCRIPT: SIMILARITIES AND DIFFERENCES

Since the attribute *phenomenological* is occasionally (and mostly in American texts) used rather broadly, a brief final word about similarities and differences with related currents of thought may be appropriate.

The crucial difference is with positivist positions which still abound in many social and behavioral sciences. The significant distinctive feature is that in positivist positions, experience, the common denominator of all empirical sciences, tends to be reduced to the "verifying" methods of observation and measurement of facts—a procedure that ultimately equates any empirical approach with that of the natural sciences. In contrast, a phenomenological-hermeneutic approach does not focus on objects (facts and events) per se but on objects (factual or fictive) as they are encountered in human situations.

As outlined above, such encountering is characterized by its sense-giving (interpreting) intentionality, which in itself is perspectival; that is, the structure of the intentional environment is horizonal. Phenomenologically seen, human experience is a meaning-centered reciprocal interaction between body-subjects and their environment. Hence, this conception emphasizes whole unitary situations, it respects the phenomena, and it does involve the ever changing give-and-take character of P-E transactions. However, by its significant features, it is richer and therefore methodologically more demanding, and sufficiently different from mere contextualism, situationism, phenomenalism, interactionism, and transactionalism in P-E studies (cf. Altman & Rogoff, 1987).

REFERENCES

Altman, I., & Low, S. M. (Eds.). (1992). *Place attachment.* New York: Plenum Press.

Altman, I., & Rogoff, B. (1987). World views in psychology: Trait, interactional, organismic, and transactional perspectives. In D. Stokols & I. Altman (Eds.), *Handbook of environmental psychology* (pp. 7–40). New York: Wiley.

Altman, I., & Wohlwill, J. F. (Eds.). (1978). *Children and the environment.* New York: Plenum Press.

Bachelard, G. (1969). *The poetics of space.* Boston: Beacon Press.

Berger, P. L., & Luckmann, T. (1966). *The social construction of reality: A treatise in the sociology of knowledge.* Garden City, NY: Doubleday.

Bollnow, O. (1967). Lived space. In N. Lawrence & D. O'-Connor (Eds.), *Readings in existential phenomenology* (pp. 178–186). Englewood Cliffs, NJ: Prentice-Hall.

Buttimer, A. (1993). *Geography and the human spirit.* Baltimore: Johns Hopkins University Press.

Canter, D. (1977). *The psychology of place.* London: Architectural Press.

Canter, D. (1997). The facets of place. In G. T. Moore & R. W. Marans (Eds.), *Advances in environment, behavior, and design: Vol. 4. Toward the integration of theory, methods, research, and utilization* (pp. 109–147). New York: Plenum Press.

Casey, E. S. (1987). *Remembering: A phenomenological study.* Bloomington: Indiana University Press.

Casey, E. S. (1993). *Getting back into place: Toward a renewed understanding of the place world.* Bloomington: Indiana University Press.

Casey, T. (1997). Architecture. In L. Embree, E. A. Behnke, D. Carr, J. C. Evans, J. Huertas-Jourda, J. J. Kockelmans, W. R. McKenna, A. Mickunas, J. N. Mohanty, T. M. Seebohm, & R. M. Zaner (Eds.), *Encyclopedia of phenomenology* (pp. 25–29). Dordrecht, The Netherlands: Kluwer Press.

Concise Oxford dictionary of current English (5th ed.). (1964). Oxford, England: Clarendon Press.

Dardel, E. (1952). *L'homme et la terre: Nature de la réalité géographique.* Paris: Presses Universitaires de France.

Deutsch, M. (1968). Field theory in social psychology. In C. Lindzey & E. Aronson (Eds.), *The handbook of social psychology* (2nd ed., Vol. 1, pp. 412–487). Reading, MA: Addison-Wesley.

Dovey, K. (1985a). Home and homelessness. In I. Altman & C. Werner (Eds.), *Home environments: Vol. 8. Human behavior and environment: Advances in theory and research* (pp. 33–64). New York: Plenum Press.

Dovey, K. (1985b). The ecology of place and place-making. In K. Dovey, P. Downton & G. Missingham (Eds.), *Place and place-making* (pp. 93–109). Melbourne, Australia: Faculty of Architecture and Building.

Dovey, K. (1985c). The quest for authenticity and the replication of environmental meaning. In D. Seamon & R. Mugerauer (Eds.), *Dwelling, place, and environment* (pp. 33–49). Dordrecht, The Netherlands: Martinus Nijhoff.

Dovey, K. (1993). Putting geometry in its place: Toward a phenomenology of the design process. In D. Seamon (Ed.), *Dwelling, seeing, and designing* (pp. 247–269). Albany, NY: State University of New York Press.

Embree, L., Behnke, E. A., Carr, D., Evans, J. C., Huertas-Jourda, J., Kockelmans, J. J., McKenna, W. R., Mickunas, A., Mohanty, J. N., Seebohm, T. M., & Zaner, R. M. (Eds.). (1997). *Encyclopedia of phenomenology* (pp. 477–480). Dordrecht, The Netherlands: Kluwer Press.

Gadamer, H.-G. (1975). *Truth and method* (G. Borden & J. Cumming, Trans.). New York: Seabury Press.

Goffman, E. (1972). *Relations in public—Microstudies of the public order.* New York: Harper & Row.

Giorgi, A. (1970). *Psychology as a human science—A phenomenologically based approach.* New York: Harper & Row.

Graumann, C. F. (1976). The concept of appropriation (Aneignung) and the modes of appropriation of space. In P. Korosec-Serfaty (Ed.), *Appropriation of space* (pp. 113–125). (Proceedings of the Strasbourg conference.) Strasbourg, France: Université Louis Pasteur.

Graumann, C. F. (1986). Memorabilia, mementos, memoranda: Toward an ecology of memory. In F. Klix & W. Hagendorf (Eds.), *Human memory and cognition* (pp. 63–69). Amsterdam: Elsevier.

Graumann, C. F. (1988). Phenomenological analysis and experimental method in psychology: The problem of their compatibility. *Journal of the Theory of Social Behaviour, 18,* 33–50.

Graumann, C. F. (1989). Towards a phenomenology of being at home. *Architecture & Comportment/Architecture and Behaviour, 5,* 117–126.

Graumann, C. F. (1994). A phenomenological approach to social research: The perception of the other. In I. Borg & P. P. Mohler (Eds.), *Trends and perspectives in empirical social research* (pp. 283–293). Berlin, Germany: de Gruyter.

Graumann, C. F. (1996). Aneignung [Appropriation]. In L. Kruse, C. F. Graumann, & E. O. Lantermann (Eds.), *Ökologische Psychologie: Ein Handbuch in Schlüsselbegriffen* (pp. 124–130). Weinheim, Germany: Psychologie Verlags Union.

Graumann, C. F. (2001). Phenomenology in human science. In N. J. Smelser & P. B. Baltes (Eds.), *International encyclopedia of the social and behavioral sciences.* Amsterdam: Elsevier.

Graumann, C. F., & Kruse, L. (1976). The concept of appropriation *(Aneignung)* and modes of appropriation of space. In P. Korosec-Serfaty (Ed.), *Appropriation of space* (pp. 113–125). Strasbourg, France: Université Louis Pasteur.

Graumann, C. F., & Kruse, L. (1995). Der Lebensraum—Die Mehrdeutigkeit seiner wissenschaftlichen Konstruktion [Lifespace—The ambiguity of its scientific construction]. In A. Kruse & R. Schmitz-Scherzer (Eds.), *Psychologie der Lebensalter* [Psychology of the life periods] (pp. 45–52). Darmstadt, Germany: Steinkopff.

Graumann, C. F., & Kruse, L. (1998). Children's environments: The phenomenological approach. In D. Görlitz, H. U. Harloff, G. Mey, & J. Valsiner (Eds.), *Children, cities, and psychological theories* (pp. 357–369). Berlin: de Gruyter.

Gurwitsch, A. (1964). *The field of consciousness.* Pittsburgh, PA: Duquesne University Press.

Gurwitsch, A. (1966). *Studies in phenomenology and psychology.* Evanston, IL: Northwestern University Press.

Gurwitsch, A. (1979). *Human encounters in the social world* (Fred Kersten, Trans.). Pittsburgh, PA: Duquesne University Press.

Harré, R. (1979). *Social being: A theory for social psychology.* Oxford, England: Blackwell.

Harloff, H. J., Lehnert, S., & Eibisch, C. (1998). Children's life worlds in urban environments. In D. Görlitz, H. J. Harloff, G. Mey, & J. Valsiner (Eds.), *Children, cities, and psychological theories* (pp. 55–84). Berlin: de Gruyter.

Heidegger, M. (1962). *Being and time* (J. Macquarrie & E. Robinson, Trans.). New York: Harper & Row.

Heidegger, M. (1971). Building, dwelling, thinking. In A. Hofstadter (Trans.), *Poetry, language, and thought* (pp. 143–161). New York: Harper & Row.

Heinemann, F. (1934). Goethe's phenomenological method. *Philosophy, 8,* 67–81.

Huntington, E. (1924). *Civilization and climate* (3rd ed.). New Haven, CT: Yale University Press.

Husserl, E. (1973). *Experience and judgment* (J. S. Churchill & K. Ameriks, Trans.). Evanston, IL: Northwestern University Press.

Ittelson, W. H. (1973). Environment perception and contemporary conceptual theory. In W. H. Ittelson (Ed.), *Environment and cognition* (pp. 1–19). New York: Seminar Press.

Kockelmans, J. J. (Ed.). (1987). *Phenomenological psychology: The Dutch School.* Dordrecht, The Netherlands: Martinus Nijhoff.

Koffka, K. (1935). *Principles of Gestalt psychology.* New York: Harcourt, Brace & World.

Korosec-Serfaty, P. (Ed.). (1976). Appropriation of space (Proceedings of the Strasbourg conference). Strasbourg, France: Université Louis Pasteur.

Kruse, L. (1974). *Räumliche Umwelt: Die Phänomenologie des Verhaltens als Beitrag zu einer psychologischen Umwelttheorie* [Spatial environment: The phenomenology of spatial behavior as a contribution to a psychological theory of the environment]. Berlin: de Gruyter.

Kruse, L., & Graumann, C. F. (1987). Environmental psychology in Germany. In D. Stokols & I. Altman (Eds.), *Handbook of environmental psychology* (pp. 1195–1225). New York: Wiley.

Kruse, L., & Graumann, C. F. (1998). Metamorphosen der Umwelt im Lebenslauf [Environmental metamorphoses during the life cycle]. In A. Kruse (Ed.), *Psychosoziale Gerontologie* [Psychosocial gerontology] (Vol. 1, pp. 51–64). Göttingen, Germany: Hogrefe.

Lewin, K. (1982). Kriegslandschaft [War landscape]. In K. Lewin (Ed.), *Werkausgabe: Vol. 4. Feldtheorie* (pp. 315–325). Bern, Switzerland/Stuttgart: Huber/Klett-Cotta. (Reprinted from *Zeitschrift für angewandte Psychologie, 12,* 1917, 440–447)

Lewin, K. (1935). The conflict between Aristotelian and Galileian modes of thought in contemporary psychology. In *A dynamic theory of personality* (pp. 1–42). New York: McGraw-Hill.

Lewin, K. (1936). *Principles of topological psychology.* New York: McGraw-Hill.

Lewin, K. (1951). *Field theory in social science.* New York: McGraw-Hill.

Linschoten, J. (1953). Naaword (Postscript). In J. H. van den Berg & J. Linschoten (Eds.), *Persoon en wereld* [Person and world]. Utrecht, The Netherlands: Bijleveld.

Mazey, M. E., & Lee, D. R. (1983). *Her space, her place: A geography of women.* Washington, DC: Association of American Geography.

Merleau-Ponty, M. (1962). *The phenomenology of perception.* (Colin Smith, Trans.). New York: Humanities Press.

Merleau-Ponty, M (1963). *The structure of behavior.* (A. L. Fisher, Trans.). Boston: Beacon Press.

Metzger, W. (1975). *Psychologie* [Psychology]. Darmstadt, Germany: Steinkopff.

Mies, M., & Shiva, V. (1993). *Ecofeminism.* London:

Muchow, M., & Muchow, H. (1980). *Der Lebensraum des Großstadtkindes* [The lifespace of the urban child]. Bensheim, Germany: Riegel. (Original work published 1935)

Mugerauer, R. (1994). *Interpretation on behalf of place: Environmental displacements and alternative responses.* Albany, NY: State University of New York Press.

Natanson, M. (Ed.). (1973). *Phenomenology and the social sciences* (Vols. 1–2). Evanston, IL: Northwestern University Press.

Norberg-Schulz, C. (1971). *Existence, space, and architecture.* New York: Praeger.

Norberg-Schulz, C. (1980). *Genius loci: Towards a phenomenology of architecture.* New York: Rizzoli.

Norberg-Schulz, C. (1985). *The concept of dwelling: On the way to a figurative architecture.* New York, Rizzoli.

Pickles, J. (1985). *Phenomenology, science, and geography: Spatiality and the human sciences.* Cambridge, England: Cambridge University Press.

Proshansky, H. M., Fabian, A. K., & Kaminoff, R. (1983). Place identity: Physical world socialization of the self. *Journal of Environmental Psychology, 3,* 57–83.

Relph, E. C. (1976). *Place and Placelessness.* London: Pion.

Relph, E. C. (1985). Geographical experiences and being-in-the-world. In D. Seamon & R. Mugerauer (Eds.), *Dwelling, place, and environment* (pp. 15–31). Dordrecht, The Netherlands: Martinus Nijhoff.

Schapp, W. (1976). *In Geschichten verstrickt* [Entangled in stories] (2nd ed.). Wiesbaden, Germany: Heymann.

Schütz, A. (1962–1966). *Collected Papers* (Vols. 1–3). The Hague: Martinus Nijhoff.

Schütz, A., & Luckmann, T. (1974). *The structures of the life world* (Vol. 1) (R. M. Zaner & H. T. Engelhardt Jr., Trans.). London: Heinemann.

Schütz, A., & Luckmann, T. (1983). *The structures of the life-world* (Vol. 2) (R. M. Zaner & D. J. Parent, Trans.). Evanston, IL: Northwestern University Press.

Seamon, D. (1979). *A Geography of the life world.* New York: St. Martin's Press.

Seamon, D. (1982). A phenomenological contribution to environmental psychology. *Journal of Environmental Psychology, 2,* 119–140.

Seamon, D. (Ed.). (1993). *Dwelling, seeing and designing: Toward a phenomenological ecology.* Albany, NY: State University of New York Press.

Seamon, D. (1997). Behavioral geography. In L. Embree, E. A. Behnke, D. Carr, J. C. Evans, J. Huertas-Jourda, J. J. Kockelmans, W. R. McKenna, A. Mickunas, J. N. Mohanty, T. M. Seebohm, & R. M. Zaner (Eds.), *Encyclopedia of phenomenology* (pp. 53–56). Dordrecht, The Netherlands: Kluwer.

Seamon, D., & Mugerauer, R. (Eds.). (1985). *Dwelling, place and environment: Toward a phenomenology of person and world.* New York: Columbia University Press.

Seamon, D., & Zajonc, A. (Eds.). (1998). *Goethe's way of science: A phenomenology of nature* (pp. 15–30). Albany, NY: State University of New York Press.

Spiegelberg, H. (1960). *The phenomenological movement: A historical introduction* (Vols. 1–2). The Hague: Martinus Nijhoff.

Spiegelberg, H. (1972). *Phenomenology in psychology and psychiatry.* Evanston, IL: Northwestern University Press.

Straus, E. (1963). *The primary world of the senses: An indication of sensory experience.* (J. Needleman, Trans.). New York: Free Press of Glenere.

Ströker, E. (1987). *Investigations in philosophy of space.* Athens, OH: Ohio University Press.

Taylor, C. (1964). *The explanation of behaviour.* London: Routledge & Kegan Press.

Tolman, E. C. (1958). *Behavior and psychological man.* Berkeley: University of California Press.

Tolman, E. C., & Brunswik, E. (1935). The organism and the causal texture of the environment. *Psychological Review, 42,* 43–77.

Tuan, Y.-F. (1974). *Topophilia: A study of environmental perception, attitudes, and values.* Englewood Cliffs, NJ: Prentice-Hall.

Tuan, Y.-F. (1977). *Space and place: The perspective of experience.* Minneapolis, MN: University of Minneapolis Press.

Tuan, Y.-F. (1982). *Segmented worlds and self: Group life and individual consciousness.* Minneapolis, MN: University of Minneapolis Press.

van den Berg, J. H., & Linschoten, J. (Eds.). (1953). *Persoon an wereld: Bijdragen tot de phaenomenologische psychologie.* Utrecht, The Netherlands: Bijleveld.

van Peursen, C. A. (1954). L'horizon, *Situation, 1,* 204–234.

von Uexküll, J. (1909). *Umwelt und Innenwelt der Tiere.*[Environment and the inner worlds of animals]. Berlin: Springer.

von Uexküll, J. (1957). A stroll through the world of animals and men. In C. H. Schiller (Ed.), *Instinctive behavior.* New York: International University Press.

von Uexküll, J., & Kriszat, G. (1956). *Streifzüge durch die Umwelten von Tieren und Menschen: Bedeutungslehre* [Strolls through the environments of animals and men: Theory of meaning]. Hamburg, Germany: Rowohlt.

Werlen, B. (1993). *Society, action, and space: An Alternative Human Geography.* London: Routledge.

Werlen, B. (1997). Social geography. In L. Embree, E. A. Behnke, D. Carr, J. C. Evans, J. Huertas-Jourda, J. J. Kockelmans, W. R. McKenna, A. Mickunas, J. N. Mohanty, T. M. Seebohm, & R. M. Zaner (Eds.), *Encyclopedia of phenomenology* (pp. 646–650). Dordrecht, The Netherlands: Kluwer Press.

Werner, C. M., Altman, I., & Oxley, D. (1985). Temporal aspects of home: A transactional perspective. In I. Altman & C. M. Werner (Eds.), *Home environment: Human behavior and environment* (Vol. 8, pp. 1–32). New York: Plenum Press.

Wohlwill, J. F. (1985). Martha Muchow and the life-space of the urban child, *Human Development, 28,* 200–209.

CHAPTER 7

Ecological Psychology: Historical Contexts, Current Conception, Prospective Directions

ALLAN W. WICKER

ECOLOGICAL PSYCHOLOGY EMERGED as a divergent development within North American psychology in the middle decades of the last century. Over the years, the concepts and methods developed by its founders, Roger Barker and Herbert Wright, have been refined and expanded by their associates and other researchers. Although research of the type conducted by the founders is now rare, the influence of their work is evident in several specialties of psychology and related disciplines. Further broadening and revitalizing is anticipated as new intellectual developments present opportunities and challenges for the field. In this chapter I first situate ecological psychology within the psychological discipline and within American society. I then sketch a current conception of the field, noting some ways that the original work has been modified and expanded. In the final section, I suggest that the best way to increase the vitality of ecological psychology is further engagement with compatible specialties in psychology and other social sciences.

SOCIETAL AND DISCIPLINARY CONTEXTS IN THE DEVELOPMENT OF ECOLOGICAL PSYCHOLOGY

Half a century ago, Roger G. Barker and Herbert F. Wright (1949) first proposed an ecological perspective for psychology. Both men spent the remainder of their professional lives demonstrating the feasibility and value of their vision. Working at first together and then independently, R. G. Barker, Wright, and their associates documented and analyzed the everyday lives of children in several small towns. They also catalogued and analyzed the publicly available environments of the towns. These efforts contributed new methods, concepts, and theories to psychology and related disciplines. Perhaps the most important contributions to environmental psychology were the identification of a natural environmental unit, the behavior setting, and the formulation of a theory of behavior setting functioning.

Portions of this chapter were presented in an invited address at the meeting of the German Congress for Environmental Psychology, Magdeburg, Germany, September 1999.

I am grateful to the following colleagues for comments on a previous version of this chapter: Irwin Altman, Daniel Fishman, Gerhard Kaminski, M. Brewster Smith, Daniel Stokols, Norman Sundberg, and Gunnela Westlander.

Behavior settings are systems of happenings on the scale of retail shops, offices, court sessions, church worship services, and academic classes. They are characterized by specific place and time boundaries, and human and nonhuman components organized in such a way that regularly occurring activities can be carried out relatively smoothly. To illustrate, an elementary school class meets in a particular room at specified times. Its components include a teacher, pupils, desks, books, and other objects that are arranged so that teaching and learning can occur. For example, the pupils' desks all face in the same direction so they can see the teacher. According to the theory, behavior settings are self-regulating. They act in ways that counteract threats to their programs, whether the threats arise from outside or within the setting. If a child is disruptive in the classroom, or if there is no chalk for the teacher to write with, or if there is intrusive noise coming from outside, corrective actions will be taken to deal with these threats to the program. (Summaries of the work by R. G. Barker and his associates, and their retrospective commentaries on the work, are available from several sources. For example, see R. G. Barker & Associates, 1978; R. G. Barker, 1987; Bechtel, 1990; Schoggen, 1989; Wicker, 1983.)

DIVERGING FROM THE MAINSTREAM IN A PERIOD OF CONSOLIDATION

Ecological psychology has never been in the mainstream of North American psychology. However, it has been subject to the same societal, institutional, and intellectual forces as the rest of the discipline. Some of these forces have been described by Altman (1987), who argued that United States psychology in the twentieth century can be characterized as having two contrasting periods. In the first period, from 1900 to about 1960, psychology was consolidating into a relatively unified discipline. Behaviorism was dominant. Laboratory experiments were the benchmark research strategy. Logical positivism provided the philosophical base. Psychologists who embraced these ideals were considered to be scientists. During this same period, Altman argues, U.S. society was also consolidating and unifying, even as it coped with three wars and a great depression.

Ecological psychology emerged during the last decade of this consolidating period as a divergent perspective. R. G. Barker and Wright (1949) pointed

out the limits of laboratory experimentation and standardized testing. As naturalists, they advocated unobtrusive collection of descriptive data documenting everyday life. Their proposals drew selectively upon biology and on a few seminal thinkers in psychology, most notably Kurt Lewin and Fritz Heider. For the most part, however, ecological psychology grew out of the interpretations of the researchers who explored everyday life in the small American town of Oskaloosa, Kansas.

In these formative years, R. G. Barker and Wright did not openly attack the dominant view. Rather they pointed out benefits that an alternative perspective could provide. Although their proposals departed significantly from the mainstream thinking of that time (R. G. Barker, 1987, p. 1415), the divergence was not complete. Importantly, they focused on *behavior.* Cognitive and emotional processes were considered only when manifested in overt behaviors; subjective reports were largely excluded. The key environmental concept was called *behavior setting.*

Although *ecology* is a biological term, Barker repeatedly used metaphors and concepts from the physical sciences, most notably the machine, to communicate his ideas. Behavior settings were said to maintain their relative stability due to the operation of a variety of regulatory *mechanisms* that operated via *circuits* (R. G. Barker, 1968, pp. 171–182). Undermanned settings were characterized in terms of *centripetal forces,* and optimally manned settings in terms of *centrifugal forces.* The towns studied were represented as "behavior-generating *machines"* (R. G. Barker & Schoggen, 1973, pp. 140–445). Naturalistic researchers were to act as *transducers* (R. G. Barker, 1968, pp. 140–145).

Barker did not conduct laboratory or field experiments within the framework of ecological psychology. However, the empirical research he oversaw was compatible in important ways with the positivist view of how one should conduct psychological research. Operational definitions were carefully developed and applied. Boundaries of the key units, such as the episode and behavior setting, were systematically defined. Researchers followed explicit guidelines for attaching descriptive scale values to the units. The resulting quantitative data were analyzed using standard statistical procedures. The daily lives and environments of people were portrayed largely in quantitative terms; only limited supplemental information was provided (e.g., R. G. Barker & Wright, 1955).

STAYING ON COURSE IN A
PERIOD OF DIVERSIFICATION

The significant societal changes in the United States in the 1960s fostered greater diversity in thought and action that significantly affected the discipline of psychology (Altman, 1987). Contributing to this diversification were the civil rights movement, the Vietnam War and protests against it, and changing norms about sexual practices, marriage, and family structure. Life in higher education became more turbulent. Universities and their faculties became more entrepreneurial. Graduate training became more specialized and more vocational. Psychologists increasingly found employment outside psychology departments and outside academia. Contact with other fields and disciplines increased. Although some observers might view this splintering as harmful to psychology, Altman (1987) contended that emerging new ideas contribute vitality to the field. He stated that academic psychologists should encourage their students to "view the field as receptive to new directions of theory, methods and philosophy of science" (p. 1069).

Altman did not name the new directions presented to psychology in the 1960s and beyond, but Fishman (1999) has suggested that they include the following: humanistic perspectives, the "cognitive revolution," general systems theory, hermeneutics, social constructivism, qualitative methods, narrative modes of thought, feminist research methods, and postmodernism.

During the 1960s and 1970s, when psychology was becoming more diversified, R. G. Barker and his associates followed the course they had set earlier, even though it embraced behaviorist and positivist tenets that were increasingly being challenged. As they explored and developed their ecological orientation, the Barker group concentrated on the research problems they had identified and did not make serious attempts to engage the emerging new perspectives. One observer (Price, 1990) has speculated that these choices may have limited the appeal of ecological psychology in subsequent decades.

However, the chosen path seems understandable. The concepts and methods that Barker and his associates developed in the 1950s represented a coherent set of ideas not yet fully exploited. Tinkering with or deviating from them might shake the foundations of hard-won achievements. The emphasis on behavior and the use of the mechanistic metaphor were part of ecological psychology's conceptual underpinnings.

The focus on behavior was not exclusive, however. Perhaps the most important departure was Barker's theory of undermanning, later known as *staffing theory*. It considered both behavioral and psychological consequences of insufficient staffing of behavior settings. The psychological consequences were described as tertiary, following primary effects on the setting itself and secondary effects on the behaviors of setting occupants (R. G. Barker, 1968). A study of the actions and experiences of students in large and small high schools provided the initial support for the theory (R. G. Barker & Gump, 1964). Other psychological conceptions in the early work were evident in the "episode" unit used in analyzing children's actions and the descriptions of behavior settings in terms of "action patterns," both of which are related to action theory. Barker also drew upon early cybernetic theory, notably the TOTE unit (G. Miller, 1960).

Once the newly developed methods were shown to be feasible and to yield important new data, they became a procedural standard. Moreover, with longitudinal research on community behavior settings underway, changing behavior-setting survey methods in any major way probably did not seem an option. Some refinements were made, however, most notably the development of the *urb* concept for measuring the extent of community settings (R. G. Barker & Schoggen, 1973).

Ecological psychology enjoyed substantial grant support and professional recognition in the 1960s and 1970s. The Midwest Field Station in Oskaloosa flourished. During this period Barker received several prestigious awards for his contributions to psychology.[1] Broader intellectual and social developments provided a supportive context for ecological psychology during

---

[1] Most notably, Barker received the Kurt Lewin Award from the Society for the Psychological Study of Social Issues, the Research Contribution Award from the American Psychological Association, and the G. Stanley Hall Award from the Division of Developmental Psychology of the American Psychological Association. In spite of these accolades, however, by the late sixties Barker had concluded that human environments could not be properly studied within the discipline of psychology. He called for a new, "eco-behavioral" science that would permit the study of intact natural units of the environment and that would create archives documenting environments and behaviors in situ. However, in the ensuing years the entire body of work that Barker and Wright initiated continued to be known to most outsiders as *ecological psychology*.

this period. General systems theory, whose metatheoretical perspective is compatible with Barker's (cf. R. G. Barker, 1968, chap. 2), gained acceptance in several psychological specialties, notably in organizational psychology (cf. Katz & Kahn, 1966). Greater environmental awareness and concern among university students and the larger public made ecological concerns in psychology seem relevant and timely. Environmental psychology was spawned and rapidly became a popular course on many college and university campuses.[2] As an older, more developed specialty, ecological psychology may have helped legitimize this new field even as it was carried along by it. Ecological psychology did participate in some aspects of the diversification of psychology as its influence spread to other disciplines and to other continents. A research group led by economist Karl Fox began to use and extrapolate behavior-setting survey data (e.g., Fox & Ghosh, 1981). And in the late 1970s, German psychologists launched a program of research that drew upon ecological psychology concepts (cf. Kaminski, 1986, 1989, 1996).

Despite these developments, ecological psychology did not become a major force in the diversification of psychology in North America. It did achieve recognition and varying degrees of influence in several psychological specialties, notably environmental, community, and developmental psychology. The impact on other relevant specialties, however, including social and organizational psychology, was very limited. Commentators have offered explanations why the work of the Barker group has not had a greater influence. They have mentioned its neglect of the individual system, including cognition, motives, personality, and emotion (Price, 1990); its laborious methods; and its disregard of relevant literature in psychology, sociology, and anthropology (Altman, 1990; Smith, 1974). A group of German social scientists point to limitations of ecological psychology's concepts and methods for capturing the complexity of everyday reality, including the social and cultural contexts beyond the behavior setting. They have called for clearer and more detailed accounts of how behavior settings are linked to the personal goals of setting occupants and how behavior setting programs function (Kaminski, 1983).

---

[2] See Sommer (1987) for an account of the origins of environmental psychology.

RECENT DEVELOPMENTS IN ECOLOGICAL PSYCHOLOGY

The first edition of this handbook included a retrospective chapter by R. G. Barker (1987) and a forward-looking chapter by Wicker (1987) that addressed some concerns of ecological psychology's critics. Barker's chapter provided one of his clearest and most succinct statements of key aspects of his ecological perspective. Human experience and behavior (the "psychological system"), he said, are significantly influenced by events that are outside of the individual (the ecological environment) as well as by events and qualities within the person (the psychological environment). Data he cited indicated that the ecological environment is, in fact, a significant source of the inputs that initiate and terminate the actions of children. He suggested that these findings were problematic for environmental psychology because ecologically based inputs cannot be accounted for by psychological processes. The ecological environment, notably behavior settings, has its own structure and follows nonpsychological principles. Yet environmental psychology aspires to use scientific psychology to study the nonpsychological environment, such as conditions in behavior settings and features of the built environment (J. Barker, 1987).

Barker did not believe it was possible to solve this problem conceptually. Researchers should, he said, recognize the interdependence of individuals and the behavior settings they occupy. Barker indicated several related issues worthy of study. One was the degree to which the pressures arising from the ecological environment converge with the desires of people who experience those pressures. For example, how do people respond to legitimate demands to support setting programs when the demands are incompatible with what they personally want to do? He recognized that tensions can arise from the divergence of such demands and people's desires. He suggested that people use their recognition of the power of settings in order to create, modify, and choose settings that are compatible with their desires. Such efforts should be undertaken by outsiders, not by setting participants, who are subject to local forces, he said. Providing such expertise "is an important task for psychology" (R. G. Barker, 1987, p. 1427).

It is worth noting that, although Barker asserted that the environment of human behavior is structured or ordered and therefore knowable, this claim was primarily made about the "immediate ecological environment," that is, the surroundings represented by the behavior setting. The "remote ecological environment," in contrast, "often extends without limit into the spatial-temporal surround" (R. G. Barker, 1987, p. 1418).

In the previous *Handbook*, I described an alternative to the traditional conception of the behavior setting (Wicker, 1987). In the revised conception, behavior settings have developmental cycles, including a beginning and an ending. They are social structures that result from interactions of the occupants and thus are influenced by particular persons, notably their founders. Behavior settings are linked not only to the people and behavior within them but also to other settings and to conditions in their larger social-physical environment. I suggested that a wide range of investigative strategies is appropriate for expanding this revised concept. This revision drew selectively on theoretical analyses of organizations by sociologists, social psychologists, and general systems theorists (particularly Katz & Kahn, 1966; J. Miller, 1971, 1972; Strauss, 1978; Weick, 1979). In addition to presenting the revised conception of behavior settings, the chapter summarized recent research on staffing theory and suggested several directions for future investigation (Wicker, 1987, p. 647).

A CURRENT CONCEPTION

Further modifications and elaborations have been suggested since the publication of the last *Handbook*. A brief characterization of the main aspects of my current conception of some key issues in ecological psychology follows. I then describe potentially fruitful directions for the future.

With regard to the problem of the incommensurability of the ecological and the psychological environments noted previously, I have suggested that the operation of behavior settings can be explained in terms of some general psychological processes. Rather than characterizing the self-regulation of behavior settings as extrapersonal setting circuits and mechanisms, as Barker did, I suggest representing the internal dynamics of settings in terms of the sense-making processes of setting occupants (see Wicker, 1992, for details; also see Fuhrer, 1990, 1993, for another approach to the problem). This revision is based on Weick's (1979) model of organizational sense making.

The Weick model employs as a central construct, the *cause map*, a complex cognitive structure that in some ways resembles Lewinian lifespace. It is a schema that incorporates what people have retained from previous transactions with their environments. Various perceived entities, including objects and abstract ideas, may be among the cognitive content of a person's cause map. According to the model, the cognitive field is dynamic. It changes with mental processing of the events that impinge upon a person's consciousness.

This revision incorporates the phenomenal world of particular persons. An individual's current perspectives and interpretations are significantly conditioned by the beliefs that he or she has retained from his or her previous transactions with the environment. That is, the person's past experience considerably constrains what she or he perceives in the present. As occupants of settings interpret, attend to, and act on events in settings, their cause maps will change.

The individuality of behavior setting occupants is both a problem and an opportunity for the setting. On the one hand, individuality is a problem in that the cognitions of different people must somehow converge in order for them to coordinate their actions and thus to carry out the setting program. Such coordination requires time and effort. On the other hand, individuality is an opportunity in that the diverse perspectives of setting occupants afford variations within the setting. Some of these variations can be used to make the setting more satisfying to participants and more adaptive to its environment.

According to this way of thinking, change is always underway in behavior settings. They are continually constructed and reconstructed by participants on a moment-to-moment, hour-to-hour, day-to-day basis. This does not mean, of course, that settings are chaotic. The opposite is generally true, since many of the reconstructions of settings are very close to previous ones, resulting in continuity and apparent stability. But whenever inputs from outside a setting or actions within it cannot be readily interpreted and routinely processed by the setting occupants, the possibility of substantial change exists.

The time scale is important when considering change. When we focus on a longer time span—analogous to taking time-lapse photographs—it is evident that behavior settings can and do change, often in significant ways. The following example is more an extension than a revision of Barker's work, which generally assumed behavior settings to be mature, fully functional systems.

All behavior settings have at least two temporal anchoring points: a beginning, or what I call *convergence*, and an ending (perhaps not yet reached, but inevitable), which I call *divergence*. Before the setting emerges, there is a *preconvergence* stage. After it emerges, there is a variable-term intermediate state, *continued existence*, on which R. G. Barker and his associates concentrated. These stages constitute the life cycles of behavior settings.

I have described some transactions that are likely to occur during each stage. For example when a setting is being created, the founder and staff must assemble and configure necessary setting resources (spaces, objects, people, information, reserves). They must also come to terms concerning who will do what and when to carry out the setting program. These negotiating and organizing processes help us see the essential role of particular persons in settings. The founder's plans, knowledge, skills, and abilities greatly influence the configuration of the new setting. However, founders do not fully define a setting. The ultimate configuration emerges through the interactions of the founder with staff members and others and with many facets of the environment. Every new setting is unique because of these processes (Wicker, 1987).

These conceptual developments in ecological psychology have methodological implications. They indicate that investigators should concentrate on a limited number of behavior settings, closely monitor setting transactions as they unfold (over time), and obtain accounts of how people make sense of and respond to the settings they occupy. More generally, researchers should get close to the settings, groups, or persons they want to learn about. They should conduct "grounded" research and peruse their data in an effort to refine, elaborate, and modify their working theories. I have called this activity *substantive theorizing* (Wicker, 1989).

My associates and I have used two strategies to generate the kind of data appropriate for such analyses. One is the intensive, longitudinal case study, which we applied to the founding of a single behavior setting, a coffee shop. We held frequent interviews with the founder for more than two years, starting months before the establishment opened. We also made numerous visits to the coffee shop site to follow progress of the construction and, subsequently, to study the setting in operation (Wicker, 1992).

This investigation was part of a program of research on life cycles of small retail and service businesses in Southern California (cf. Wicker & King, 1988). Other studies, employing analysis of archival data, interviews, and surveys, provided useful background information for interpreting the case we studied intensively.

The second method shares several characteristics with R. G. Barker and Wright's (1951) *specimen record technique*, in which observers record a child's activities for an entire day. It is person centered, focusing on particular, but often rather unexceptional individuals who are allowed considerable latitude of expression. In a program of research extending over several years, we asked workers in Ghana, West Africa, to tell us what they did in their jobs, what relations they had with other people at work, what work meant to them, and how it affected their personal and family life. Their accounts have been summarized in *work narratives*. The narrative method contrasts with the specimen record technique in several ways. The latter is a continuous account of goal-directed activity by an observer, while the former is a retrospective self-description that integrates and summarizes different aspects of a person's life obtained by an interviewer. The full texts of more than 50 work narratives are available on the Internet (Wicker, 1996). In dissertation research, my former student Rachel August used similar methods to explore the work lives of late-career women teachers, nurses, and therapists (August, 1997).

Our close examination of individual cases (whether behavior settings or persons) has yielded multiple benefits. Subjectively, the most compelling gain is a heightened sense of understanding and appreciation of the targets of the research and their situations. The full potential of the data in these studies has yet to be realized. Further processing and reporting are needed. I will mention a few conceptual developments that have emerged from these preliminary efforts at substantive theorizing.

These ways of studying persons and environments led us to some conceptual formulations that transcend the focal behavior setting. In trying to understand the actions of the coffee shop founder, we found it helpful to think of her activities as a *pursuit of a major life goal* (Wicker, 1992). Creating the coffee shop was for her the realization of a long-standing dream. In pursuing this goal, she participated in a number of different behavior settings including government offices and restaurant supply firms. She also enacted a wide range of behaviors that were guided by, and at the same time shaped, her incomplete and ever-changing cause map of how one creates a coffee shop. We came to the view that the notions of hierarchy and sequencing of subgoals can usefully be incorporated into the conception of cause maps. However, the process appeared to be somewhat more fluid and haphazard than the systematic procedures that action theory (e.g., Hacker, 1985), for example, seems to assume. This case also made us more aware of the range of factors and forces in the larger environment that bear on behavior settings, including governmental, economic, and geographic influences. And the unfolding of events over the course of the study convinced us that the information gains from longitudinal case studies are worth the additional time and effort they require.

Our analysis of people's accounts of their work lives (the work narratives) led us to a position that is, in a way, parallel to the discovery of the importance of behavior settings from analyses of specimen records (R. G. Barker, 1968). Our reading of the accounts confirmed that workplaces (work behavior settings) are very important in people's work lives. But we could also see the influence of other, extrasetting environmental systems that have not been emphasized in ecological psychology. For example, workers' family situations were linked to their work lives in various ways. Several other normative systems, in addition to work setting and family, are also important. They include the worker's trade or occupation, the employing organization, informal social groups, locality or region, and the larger society (Wicker & August, 2000).

PROSPECTIVE DIRECTIONS FOR ECOLOGICAL PSYCHOLOGY

The foregoing account has portrayed ecological psychology as gaining vitality and momentum by selectively assimilating ideas from the larger intellectual environment rather than closely adhering to the independent paths taken by its founders. I believe that this will continue to be the case in the future. In the remainder of the chapter I consider several specific developments that hold promise for further development of the field.

M. Brewster Smith (1999) has speculated about the future of "the humane core of psychology," which he identified as personality, developmental, and social psychology. He states that in spite of recent developments that might imply a unification of psychology in biological or evolutionary terms, these fields hold considerable promise for the future. They should thrive, he believes, because they are needed to contribute to "human self-understanding" and to guide public policy and professional practice in such human services as mental health, education, and corrections. Ecological and environmental psychology can be included in this humane core because their content overlaps those of the specialties Smith mentions and because they can make similar kinds of contributions.

Like Altman, Smith (1999) values diversification in psychology. He attributes his optimism to a number of recent developments that recognize and deal with greater complexity in their subject matter than do traditional approaches. These developments, he says, grapple with "the distinctively human aspects of meaning, values, intentionality, history and culture" (p. 9). Furthermore, they are compatible with the fading of our "Euro-American culture boundedness . . . and our heritage of sexism" (p. 11). One of the developments that gives Smith hope is the narrative approach to personality and identity, in which people relate their own life stories. Another source of hope is cultural psychology, exemplified by the work of Cole (1996) and others, which greatly enriches our conceptions of context. The third is pragmatic psychology, whose philosophical base is not new but which is undergoing a revival stimulated by a recent book by Fishman (1999).

Each of the perspectives Smith identifies is a potential or actual impetus for the further development of ecological psychology. For example, as noted earlier, Wicker and August (2000) used narratives to identify significant contexts of workers and to gain insider perspectives of their situations. Cultural psychology has already provided significant inputs to ecological psychology, best exemplified by Fuhrer's (1998, 2001) research linking acculturation processes, child development, and behavior settings. Fuhrer joins Simmel's (1908) theory of culture and R. G. Barker's (1968) behavior setting theory to portray acculturation and personal development as a dynamic, grounded, contextualized process. Fuhrer's conceptual contributions are supported and strengthened by empirical studies of children in community behavior settings (1998).

Pragmatic Psychology

Pragmatic psychology also provides clear, direct, promising paths to continued development of ecological psychology. Because these connections have not been made explicit elsewhere, I discuss them next.

Fishman (1999) has proposed a radical reorientation of the discipline of psychology. The core argument follows. For most psychologists, improving the human condition is a central value. But the prevailing psychological system based on the positivist paradigm limits the contributions that psychologists can make. To improve the lives of individuals, groups, and organizations, psychologists must directly engage the problems they study. They should design programs of change based on their theoretical and philosophical orientations, their past professional experience, and relevant research literature. These change programs should be implemented, and the results carefully monitored and evaluated. The interventions will generally be small-scale, localized programs in specific, real-life settings. The conception, intervention, and evaluation of programs are then written up as case studies that provide numerous details, including information on several levels of context. In this process, psychologists draw upon both positivist and hermeneutic (qualitative) approaches and methods. Over time, a body of literature composed of case studies will become available to assist psychologists in addressing future problems[3] (Fishman, 1999).

Problems should be situated in multiple interconnected systems and considered in several dimensions, including "historical, psychological, social, [and] organizational" aspects (Fishman, 1999, p. 168). Contexts are not presumed to have an objective reality but are subject to varied interpretations by people having different interests. Drawing boundaries around problems is a task that pragmatic psychologists must grapple with and resolve for each case. For example, "should a high school case involve an individual English class teacher working with one specific class or with all the five classes . . . she sees over the course of a day? Or should the case involve a broader unit, such as the whole English department, or the whole school, or the whole school district? And what should be the time span of the case—a semester? a year? or multiple years, such as the four years a particular [cohort of students] might spend in the high school before graduation?" (p. 168). Fishman says psychologists should try to identify "natural units" that can be justified "in

terms of [their] potential for practical application" (p. 168).

For many applied problems, such advice could lead to the selection of behavior settings either as the focal units (e.g., an English class), as subunits (of a school), or as contexts (of problem behaviors in a class). Ecological psychology represents a useful template for conceptualizing a wide range of the problems that human service practitioners face. This includes physical features and arrangements in settings as well as what initially appear to be personal, group, and organizational problems. Behavior setting theory should be among the "alternative conceptual tools" (Fishman, 1999, p. 167) that practitioners consider when they identify problems and formulate programs to solve them.

When the ecological psychology framework is brought to bear on applied problems, it should provide new ways of thinking for theorists and practitioners. Taylor (1998) has made this argument in the study of urban crime. Criminal justice researchers have recently begun to map the locations of crimes in order to identify "hot-spots," or places where crimes are frequently committed. Maps of crimes provide a kind of institutional memory, which is used for assigning patrols of police officers to reduce crime. These procedures appear to have been successful for some kinds of crime, such as burglaries. However, Taylor expresses conceptual and methodological concerns about the hot-spot metaphor and how it is used. Based on the geological term for hot magma rising to the earth's surface, the metaphor conveys the notion of "bubbling up" of individual or group problems to the surface, resulting in crime. Taylor argues that a more appropriate conception would include features of the crime scenes and of the surrounding areas. He proposes that street blocks, that is, both sides of a street between two cross streets, be studied as behavior settings. Crime locations should be viewed in terms of routine activities that occur in the vicinity, the physical structures and arrangements present, regular rhythms of activity, and links to nearby settings, such as traffic ways. All of these are recognized to change over time. Such units are more appropriate, Taylor argues, than the circles and ellipses drawn on maps by computer programs that process data on crimes.

A similar point has been made by Latkin and Knowlton (2000), whose concern is prevention of AIDS among drug users. They argue that person-centered prevention programs are inadequate because such programs ignore significant social and

---

[3] Weisman (1998) has outlined a model for architectural research and design based on a "neo-pragmatic" approach that somewhat resembles Fishman's proposals for psychology.

contextual factors. Their multifactored approach considers the behavior settings drug users frequent, including places where the users inject drugs, the norms among users, and network analysis of the settings visited by various users.

Although most ecological psychologists have not emphasized applications, their empirical research can be useful to pragmatic psychologists. Studies have examined local political organizations in several cultures (J. Barker, 1999), illegal drug injection sites (Latkin, Mandell, Vlahov, & Oziemkowska, 1994), street blocks (Perkins, Wandersman, Rich, & Taylor, 1993), retail and service establishments (Wicker & King, 1988), communities, neighborhoods, housing complexes, government agencies, churches, hospitals, clinics, schools, workplaces, retail and service firms, and parks (see Schoggen, 1989; Wicker, 1983, 1987). The literature on understaffing (see Schoggen, 1989; Wicker, 1983) also has potentially wide applicability. Interventions to improve settings following a strategy called *behavior setting technology* have also been described (Wicker, 1983, 1987).

Ecological psychology could develop renewed vigor by embracing pragmatic psychology's basic agenda, especially if researchers concentrated on systematically extracting knowledge and building grounded theories (cf. Wicker, 1989). The "problem-centered, contextualized pragmatic understanding" (Fishman, 1999, p. 195) gained from thoughtful practical applications could and should be brought to bear on the more formal theoretical and philosophical frameworks that are part of many practitioners' thinking.

Here is one way it might happen. In their case reports, pragmatic psychologists would not only report on what seems to work under specified conditions (and thus fulfill the pragmatic agenda) but also indicate what aspects of their orienting theories or assumptions were most and least helpful in the case, and why. Practitioners might speculate about the range of applicability or limiting conditions of their orienting conceptions, based on what they observed in the present concrete case. Of course, these commentaries would not be "tests" of the theories but rather informed judgments of their applicability to particular situations.

If practitioners routinely included such commentaries, theoretically oriented psychologists could draw upon that feedback to reexamine, revise, and expand their theories. For example, theorists might

become aware of specific difficulties in applying the behavior setting concept or the sense-making model to concrete problems and make appropriate clarifications and adjustments in subsequent publications. Such a process might well lead to the development of more locally relevant and more useful concepts and theories applicable to particular kinds of settings, such as school classrooms, court sessions, or even gasoline stations (cf. Sommer & Wicker, 1991). Eventually, these theoretical modifications could find their way into the literature used to train professional psychologists, affording them better conceptual tools for diagnosing problems and devising intervention strategies.

OTHER PROMISING DIRECTIONS

Several additional developments based on ecological psychology bear mention here.[4] R. G. Barker and Wright's descriptive studies of children as they went about their normal activities in a typical day (e.g., *One Boy's Day*, R. G. Barker & Wright, 1951) have inspired two recent investigations that could provide important new directions for ecological psychology.

Craik (2000) proposes analyzing in detail the "lived days" of individual persons as a means of examining person-environment transactions. His approach is notable for bringing three powerful concepts to bear on a single unit of analysis, the *act episode*. Such episodes might include preparing breakfast, offering assistance to a colleague, making a request for service at a bank, or completing a report. Episodes are examined in terms of the behavior settings a person enters, the goals or pursuits of the person, and the traits that the person's actions reveal. In the initial exposition of this approach, Craik draws upon lived days documented via Barker and Wright's specimen record technique, literary work, and video recordings supplemented by personal accounts. Noting the limited temporal nature of this approach, Craik proposes tracking the impact of selected episodes on personality and on social systems, such as behavior settings and organizations. He further notes the need to depict multiple points

---

[4] An additional development, economist Karl Fox's application of behavior setting theory and data to social accounts of rural communities, was described in my chapter in the previous *Handbook* (Wicker, 1987). Two notable publications of this research program have appeared since then (Fox, 1989, 1990).

of view, including the (inside) view of the person under study and views of outsiders.

A German study (Kaminski & Rapp, 1999) conducted a constructive replication of *One Boy's Day.* A young man recorded in fine-grained detail his activities and thoughts for the duration of two full days. He also noted the various situations in which these events occurred. The episodes in the record thus obtained were analyzed and characterized in several ways: Comparisons were made with the specimen record of R. G. Barker and Wright (1951), psychological processes such as decision making and orienting were noted, and the contexts in which episodes occurred were described and categorized. An illustrative finding was that behavior settings as traditionally defined did not capture all of the situations recorded: Other kinds and levels of "happening systems" with varying degrees of coherence were noted. The record is being further analyzed in an attempt to link the natural flow of behavior and experience with basic psychological processes, such as thinking, remembering, and deciding, that are most often studied in the laboratory.

Another potential direction for ecological psychology is adaptation of its concepts and methods to accommodate new social arrangements that have been stimulated by technological change. For example, the traditional conception of the behavior setting does not precisely fit this increasingly common situation: social interactions that are mediated through computer communications such as electronic mail. Although a number of features of behavior settings are found in electronically linked groups, the spatial and temporal requirements of settings often are not met. Blanchard (1997) applied the behavior setting framework to stable groups that are linked electronically and that have a sense of community or place. Within such groups, e-mailed communications are the basis for negotiations and sense making about the nature of the *virtual behavior setting.* Blanchard's analysis considers analogs of various behavior setting features in the virtual setting, such as synomorphy, program, and self-regulation. In a subsequent empirical investigation, she used participant observation and telephone interviews to explore sense of community and sense of place among members of two virtual communities (Blanchard, 2000).

The fact that the participants of virtual behavior settings simultaneously occupy face-to-face settings is a complication worthy of exploration as well.

Stokols (1999) notes that when requirements or goals of the two systems are not compatible, psychological and interpersonal tensions may result. He describes various methodological challenges of exploring such complexities.

Although the theory of staffing has not attracted many researchers over the last decade, its wide applicability and strong empirical base justify further investigations and theory development. Wicker and August (1995) have recently demonstrated the utility of the theory for studying people's workloads in a wide variety of settings. Because the theory links psychological outcomes with particular conditions in behavior settings, it represents a possible meeting ground for what Barker called ecobehavioral science (the study of behavior settings as units) and the psychological study of mental and emotional processes in individuals.

The final illustration of new directions for ecological psychology is a recent book by political scientist Jonathan Barker, the son of Roger and Louise Barker (J. Barker, 1999). J. Barker makes a case for studying political activities at the local level by examining *political activity settings,* that is, public behavior settings in which people discuss, decide, and act on matters of community concern. His political focus directs attention to some processes discussed previously, notably the origins, modification, and dissolution of settings, and the relations of settings to larger normative systems. His analysis goes further by listing theoretical bases for social regulation in settings, calling attention to traditional cultural practices, presenting elaborated ways of conceiving of authority systems, and offering a new conception, *political space,* which overlaps with but is distinct from governmental settings. These and other contributions provide a framework for considering the impacts of globalization on people and communities. The utility of the political settings approach is documented in six chapters devoted to case studies of local political activities on several continents. All but one of the chapters were written by J. Barker's doctoral students; the exception is his reexamination of behavior setting survey data from Oskaloosa, Kansas, and Leyburn, Yorkshire, England, originally reported by R. G. Barker and Schoggen (1973).

CONCLUSION

The ecological perspective that emerged from the work of a few dedicated researchers in an obscure

Kansas town more than 50 years ago has shown amazing survivability. Its relevance to current societal trends, such as new paradigms of work, the electronic revolution, and globalization has been demonstrated. Other evidence of the currency of ecological psychology is the recent publication of an introductory text in Swedish (Westlander, 1999) and the fact that journal citations to Barker's publications have occurred with nearly the same frequency in recent years as when the Midwest Field Station was operating. Roughly half of the citations appeared in a diverse set of nonpsychological journals (Kaminski, 2000). Perhaps we should not be surprised that ecological psychology's long life as a divergent perspective has become the subject of historical analysis by a psychologist (Scott, 2000) and by a historian of science (Pandora, 1996, 2000, 2001).

I am optimistic that subsequent editions of this handbook will describe other, presently unimaginable developments that can be traced to the conceptual and methodological formulations of R. G. Barker and Wright and their associates. Possibly the early methods will be revived and applied to the same or similar targets to provide comparative studies of children's lives or of communities. But if the past 50 years are any guide, we can expect that future contributions will result from selective adaptations of ecological psychology's core ideas—and their revisions—to accommodate new intellectual, societal, and practical challenges.

REFERENCES

Altman, I. (1987). Centripetal and centrifugal trends in psychology. *American Psychologist, 42,* 1058–1069.

Altman, I. (1990). [Review of the book *Behavior Settings*]. *Environment and Behavior, 22,* 538–541.

August, R. A. (1997). Career retrospectives: Late career women's reflections on the experiences and meanings of work and retirement. (Doctoral dissertation, Claremont Graduate University, 1997). *Dissertation Abstracts International, 58*(03B), 1574.

Barker, J. (1999). *Street-level democracy: Political settings at the margins of global power.* West Hartford, CT: Kumarian Press.

Barker, R. G. (1968). *Ecological psychology: Concepts and methods for studying the environment of human behavior.* Stanford, CA: Stanford University Press.

Barker, R. G. (1987). Prospecting in environmental psychology. In D. Stokols & I. Altman (Eds.), *Handbook of environmental psychology* (Vol. 2, pp. 1413–1432). New York: Wiley.

Barker, R. G., & Associates (1978). *Habitats, environments, and human behavior: Studies in ecological psychology and eco-behavioral science from the Midwest Psychological Field Station, 1947–1972.* San Francisco: Jossey-Bass.

Barker, R. G., & Gump, P. V. (1964). *Big school, small school: High school size and student behavior.* Stanford, CA: Stanford University Press.

Barker, R. G., & Schoggen, P. (1973). *Qualities of community life: Methods of measuring environment and behavior applied to an American and an English town.* San Francisco: Jossey-Bass.

Barker, R. G., & Wright, H. F. (1949). Psychological ecology and the problem of psycho-social development. *Child Development, 20,* 131–143.

Barker, R. G., & Wright, H. F. (1951). *One boy's day.* New York: Harper & Row.

Barker, R. G., & Wright, H. F. (1955). *Midwest and its children.* Evanston, IL: Row, Peterson.

Bechtel, R. B. (Ed.). (1990). The Midwest Psychological Field Station: A celebration of its founding [Special issue]. *Environment and Behavior, 22*(4), 435–552.

Blanchard, A. (1997). *Virtual behavior settings: An application of behavior setting theories to virtual communities.* Unpublished manuscript, Claremont Graduate University.

Blanchard, A. (2000). *Virtual behavior settings: A framework for understanding virtual communities.* (Doctoral dissertation, Claremont Graduate University, 2000). *Dissertation Abstracts International, 61*(05B), 2814.

Cole, M. (1996). *Cultural psychology: A once and future discipline.* Cambridge, MA: Harvard University Press.

Craik, K. H. (2000). The lived day of an individual: A person-environment perspective. In W. B. Walsh, K. H. Craik, & R. H. Price (Eds.), *New directions in person-environment psychology* (2nd ed., pp. 233–266). Hillsdale, NJ: Lawrence Erlbaum.

Fishman, D. B. (1999). *The case for pragmatic psychology.* New York: New York University Press.

Fox, K. A. (1989). Behavior settings and social system accounting. In P. Schoggen (Ed.), *Behavior settings: A revision and extension of Roger G. Barker's Ecological Psychology.* Stanford, CA: Stanford University Press.

Fox, K. A. (1990). *The eco-behavioral approach to surveys and social accounts for rural communities: Exploratory analyses and interpretations of Roger G. Barker's microdata from the behavior setting survey of Midwest Kansas in 1963–1964.* Ames, IA: Iowa State University, North Central Center for Rural Development.

Fox, K. A., & Ghosh, S. K. (1981). A behavior setting approach to social accounts, combining concepts and data from ecological psychology, economics, and studies of time use. In F. T. Juster & K. C. Land (Eds.), *Social accounting systems: Essays on the state of the art* (pp. 131–217). New York: Academic Press.

Fuhrer, U. (1990). Bridging the ecological-psychological gap: Behavior settings as interfaces. *Environment and Behavior, 22,* 518–537.

Fuhrer, U. (1993). Behavior setting analysis of situated learning: The case of newcomers. In S. Chaiklin & J. Lave (Eds.), *Understanding practice: Perspectives on activity and context* (pp. 179–211). New York: Cambridge University Press.

Fuhrer, U. (1998). Behavior settings as vehicles of children's cultivation. In D. Gorlitz, H. J. Harloff, G. Mey, & J. Valsiner (Eds.), *Children, cities, and psychological theories* (pp. 411–434). Berlin: de Gruyter.

Fuhrer, U. (2001). *Cultivating minds.* Manuscript in preparation.

Hacker, W. (1985). On some fundamentals of action regulation. In G. P. Ginsburg, M. Brenner, & M. von Cranach (Eds.), *Discovery strategies in the psychology of action* (pp. 63–84). San Diego: Academic Press.

Kaminski, G. (1983). The enigma of ecological psychology. *Journal of Environmental Psychology, 3,* 85–94.

Kaminski, G. (1986). *Ordnung und Variabilität im Alltagsgeschehen: Das Behavior Setting-Konzept in den Verhaltenso- und Socialwissenschaften* [Regularity and variability in everyday happenings: The behavior setting concept in the behavioral and social sciences]. Göttingen, Germany: Hogrefe.

Kaminski, G. (1989). The relevance of ecologically oriented conceptualizations for theory building in environment and behavior research. In E. H. Zube & G. T. Moore (Eds.), *Advances in environment, behavior, and design* (Vol. 2, pp. 3–36). New York: Plenum.

Kaminski, G. (1996, November). *Describing and understanding the development of ecopsychology in Germany and some reflections on its future.* Paper presented at the meeting of the Congreso de Psicologia Ambiental, Barcelona, Spain.

Kaminski, G. (2000). Roger G. Barker and associates: Habitats, environments, and human behavior. Studies in ecological psychology and eco-behavioral science from the Midwest Psychological Field Station, 1947–1972 (1978). In H. E. Lück, R. Miller, & G. Sewz-Vosshenrich (Hrsg.), *Klassiker der Psychologie.* (S. 236–240). Stuttgart: Kohlhammer.

Kaminski, G., & Rapp, H. (1999, September). *One student's (two) days. Versuch einer modernisierten Replikation* [An attempt at a modern replication]. Paper presented at the meeting of the German Congress for Environmental Psychology, Magdeburg, Germany.

Katz, D., & Kahn, R. L. (1966). *The social psychology of organizations.* New York: Wiley.

Latkin, C. A., & Knowlton, A. R. (2000). New directions in HIV prevention among drug users: Settings, norms, and network approaches to AIDS prevention (SNNAAP), A social influence approach. In J. A. Levy, R. C. Stephens, & D. C. McBride (Eds.), *Advances in medical sociology* (Vol. 7, pp. 261–287). New York: JAI Press.

Latkin, C. A., Mandell, W., Vlahov, D., & Oziemkowska, M. (1994). My place, your place, and no place: Behavior settings as a risk factor for HIV-related injection practices of drug users in Baltimore, Maryland. *American Journal of Community Psychology, 22,* 415–430.

Miller, G. A. (1960). *Plans and the structure of behavior.* New York: Holt, Rinehart and Winston.

Miller, J. G. (1971). Living systems: The group. *Behavioral Science, 16,* 302–398.

Miller, J. G. (1972). Living systems: The organization. *Behavioral Science, 17,* 1–182.

Pandora, K. (1996, November). *Natural history and psychological habitats: Roger G. Barker and the emergency of ecological psychology in post-World War II America.* Paper presented at the History of Science Society, Atlanta, GA.

Pandora, K. (2000, August). *Historical conventions, psychological innovations, and the politics of memory: Reflections on the early careers of Lois Barclay Murphy and Roger Barker.* Paper presented at the meeting of the American Psychological Association, Washington, DC.

Pandora, K. (2001). *Science in the American vernacular: Improvisations in natural history across the 20th century.* Manuscript in preparation.

Perkins, D. D., Wandersman, A. H., Rich, R. C., & Taylor, R. B. (1993). The physical environment of street crime: Defensible space, territoriality and incivilities. *Journal of Environmental Psychology, 13,* 29–49.

Price, R. H. (1990). [Review of the book *Behavior Settings*]. *Environment and Behavior, 22,* 541–544.

Schoggen, P. (1989). *Behavior settings: A revision and extension of Roger G. Barker's Ecological Psychology.* Stanford, CA: Stanford University Press.

Scott, M. M. (2000, August). *Lewin's other legacy: Oral histories of ecological psychologists.* Paper presented at the meeting of the American Psychological Association, Washington, DC.

Simmel, G. (1908). *Soziologie: Untersuchungen über die Formen der Vergesellschaftung* [Sociology: Studies on the forms of socialization]. Leipzig, Germany: Duncker & Humblot.

Smith, M. B. (1974). Psychology in two small towns. *Science, 184,* 671–673.

Smith, M. B. (1999, July). *Hope for the humane core of psychology.* Paper presented at the meeting of the Interamerican Society of Psychology, Caracas, Venezuela.

Sommer, R. (1987). Dreams, reality, and the future of environmental psychology. In D. Stokols & I. Altman (Eds.), *Handbook of environmental psychology* (Vol. 2, pp. 1489–1511). New York: Wiley.

Sommer, R., & Wicker, A. W. (1991). Gas station psychology: The case for specialization in ecological psychology. *Environment & Behavior, 23,* 131–149.

Stokols, D. (1999). Human development in the age of the Internet: Conceptual and methodological horizons. In S. L. Friedman & T. D. Wachs (Eds.), *Measuring environment across the lifespan* (pp. 327–356). Washington, DC: American Psychological Association.

Strauss, A. (1978). *Negotiations: Varieties, contexts, processes, and social order.* San Francisco: Jossey-Bass.

Taylor, R. B. (1998). Crime and small-scale places: What we know, what we can prevent, and what else we need to know. In *Crime and place: Plenary papers of the 1997 Conference on Criminal Justice Research and Evaluation* [Online]. Available: www.ncjrs.org/txtfiles/168618.txt

Weick, K. E. (1979). *The social psychology of organizing* (2nd ed.). Reading, MA: Addison-Wesley.

Weisman, G. D. (1998, May). *Toward a model for architectural research and design: Pragmatism, place and patterns.* Paper presented to the AIJ Sub-Committee of Environmental-Behavior Studies and the Working Group for Person-Environment Models, Architectural Institute of Japan, Osaka, Japan.

Westlander, G. (1999). *Ekologisk psykologi och behavior setting-teorin* [Ecological psychology and behavior setting theory]. Lund, Sweden: Studentlitteratur.

Wicker, A. W. (1983). *An introduction to ecological psychology.* New York: Cambridge University Press.

Wicker, A. W. (1987). Behavior settings reconsidered: Temporal stages, resources, internal dynamics, context. In D. Stokols & I. Altman (Eds.), *Handbook of environmental psychology* (Vol. 2, pp. 613–653). New York: Wiley.

Wicker, A. W. (1989). Substantive theorizing. *American Journal of Community Psychology, 17,* 531–547.

Wicker, A. W. (1992). Making sense of environments. In W. B. Walsh, K. H. Craik, & R. H. Price (Eds.), *Person environment psychology: Models and perspectives* (pp. 157–192). Hillsdale, NJ: Erlbaum.

Wicker, A. W. (1996). *The "working in Ghana" project* [Online]. Available: fac.cgu.edu/~wickera/working.htm

Wicker, A. W., & August, R. A. (1995). How far should we generalize? The case of a workload model. *Psychological science, 6,* 39–44.

Wicker, A. W., & August, R. A. (2000). Working lives in context: Engaging the views of participants and analysts. In W. B. Walsh, K. H. Craik, & R. H. Price (Eds.), *New directions in person-environment psychology* (2nd ed., pp. 197–232). Hillsdale, NJ: Erlbaum.

Wicker, A. W., & King, J. C. (1988). Life cycles of behavior settings. In J. E. McGrath (Ed.), *The social psychology of time: New perspectives* (pp. 182–200). Newbury Park, CA: Sage.

SECTION II

SHARPENING LINKS
TO OTHER DISCIPLINES

Exploring Pathology: Relationships between Clinical and Environmental Psychology

KATHRYN H. ANTHONY and NICHOLAS J. WATKINS

WHAT ARE THE RELATIONSHIPS between clinical and environmental psychology? What have these relationships been in the past, and what potential do they have for the future? How have clinicians drawn upon the physical environment in their practice? And how have scholars in the environment behavior field relied upon clinical psychology in their research? Has the relationship between clinical and environmental psychology made an impact on actual environments? What behavior has changed as a result of new research or discoveries? This chapter addresses these issues.

We begin by describing some theoretical and conceptual frameworks that help explain the relationship between these two fields, focusing on how a systems or socioecological approach can link the two. We next examine *environmental approaches to clinical psychology.* Our sources are drawn primarily from the clinical literature in psychology and psychiatry, and they include at least some reference—often not obvious to the casual reader—to the physical environment. For example, what places or spaces trigger obsessive-compulsive disorders? What role does the physical environment play in post-traumatic stress disorder? We next examine treatment approaches in which the physical environment has begun to play a role in altering problematic behavior. Following this is a section analyzing the environmental psychology of treatment settings, that is, issues concerning the design and arrangement of psychotherapists' offices.

Later we examine *clinical approaches to environmental psychology.* This section discusses sources drawn primarily from the environment behavior literature that address issues of interest to clinicians. For example, what are the psychological impacts of moving or visiting a favorite home in which you no longer live? What kinds of design features can elevate an individual's psychological state? Finally, we draw our conclusions about the links between these two disciplines.

THEORETICAL AND CONCEPTUAL FRAMEWORKS

Some theoretical and conceptual frameworks shed light on the relationships between clinical and environmental psychology.

"Clinical psychology can most broadly be seen as a field involving problems, theories, and methods that cut across a range of activities (e.g., psychotherapy, testing, supervision, consultation, research, teaching) and populations (e.g., patients, trainers, trainees, organizations) with potential applicability to a range of environmental psychological phenomena" (Demick & Andreoletti, 1995, p. 58). Clinical psychologists tend to focus on some form of pathology. For example, a child may have difficulty adjusting to parental divorce or an adult may be experiencing chronic signs of depression and even suicidal tendencies. Environmental psychologists tend to be less exclusively problem focused in their approach. Also, environmental psychologists are more concerned with the larger picture. Individuals are conceptualized as members of social groups and cultures. In turn, these conglomerates of social groups and cultures affect the individual throughout a system composed of differing levels of analysis. Intrapsychic relationships within the individual are de-emphasized.

Clinicians are primarily concerned with the diagnosis and treatment of emotional, biological, psychological, social, and behavioral maladjustment, disability, and discomfort (Sayette, Mayne, & Norcross, 1992, p. 1). Diagnosis often involves the use of sophisticated tests to measure the incidence of a particular condition. Neither diagnosis nor treatment is typically the goal of environmental psychologists. Often the aims of researchers in environment and behavior are simply to gain a deeper understanding of how the physical environment facilitates or hinders a particular set of attitudes and behaviors. Issues of mutual interest include assessment of the effects of physical relocation, natural disasters, environmental stressors, social support networks, and role transitions in the psychological functioning of patients, students, faculty, and organizations (Demick & Andreoletti, 1995, p. 59).

Clinical psychologists generally focus on the individual as the unit of analysis. Most of their theoretical approaches are person centered. By contrast, environmental psychologists focus on the person-in-environment system as the primary unit of analysis. Yet some of these concerns can overlap.

One can conceptualize an individual's socioecological environment along different levels, from the micro- to the meso-, exo-, and macrosystems (Bronfenbrenner, 1979). The *microsystem* is a "pattern of activities, roles, and interpersonal relations experienced by the developing person in a given setting with particular physical and material characteristics" (p. 22). An example of the microsystem is the immediate home environment. *Mesosystems* involve settings in which individuals engage for a significant amount of time, such as school or work environments. *Exosystems* include systems outside of individuals that affect them, for example, the local police. Finally, *macrosystems* entail social and cultural values that exert a strong influence on attitudes and behavior. We argue for the necessity of a systems or socioecological approach in the conception of a field of work that embraces both clinical psychology and environmental psychology.

As an example, an analogy can be drawn between the relationships of clinical and environmental psychology and an ecological analysis of health promotion. Stokols (1992) discusses how an ecological perspective is emerging in the field of health promotion, with an emphasis on linking individually focused, small-group, organizational, and community approaches. Along these lines, he stresses the importance of examining *situations,* sequences of individual or group activities occurring at a particular time and place; *settings,* geographical locations where personal or interpersonal situations occur regularly; *life domains,* different spheres of a person's life such as family, education, spiritual activities, recreation, employment, and commuting; and *overall life situations,* the major domains in which a person is involved during a particular period of life. Stokols argues that researchers still need to delineate specific environmental leverage points that can help promote better health in society at large.

Clinical psychology could also benefit from a systems or socioecological approach. Clinical researchers need to identify environmental features that can exacerbate or minimize both psychological wellness as well as mental illness on a variety of levels. From the perspective of environment behavior researchers, the type of problems that clinicians address can not be fully understood without taking into account the environment in which they are embedded. A systems approach would allow a clinical researcher to examine how mental disorders operate on a variety of levels of human-environment interactions. Specific mental disorders may operate along a variety of scales. For example, a teenage girl who suffers from bulimia is preoccupied with her self image, which is influenced by her family interactions and role models, her peers and teachers at school, and social and cultural influences that she sees on television and film.

Systems or socioecological theory also benefits from a transactionalist perspective. A transactionalist approach views several aspects of persons and environment as mutually defining (Wapner, 1987). A person is comprised of physical and biological traits such as age and sex, intrapersonal and psychological traits such as self-esteem, and sociocultural traits such as roles. The environment is comprised of physical (e.g., natural and built), interpersonal, and sociocultural (e.g., mores, rules) characteristics.

Important to note are traditional theories of psychology integrating both environment and intrapsychic processes in the etiology of mental disorders.

For example, attachment theory is one useful framework with which to view the relationships between the two fields of clinical and environmental psychology when considering a socioecological or systems approach. Developmental psychologists have conducted decades of research about how infants and toddlers form attachments with their parent figures. John Bowlby and Mary Salter Ainsworth made major contributions to the understanding of attachment theory (Bowlby, 1969, 1973, 1980; Bretherton, 1992). The nature of these attachments can be extremely significant when clinicians diagnose and treat adults later in therapy. Attachment theory is also systemic. Infants become attached to a secure base, usually their mother. From that base they gradually venture out to explore the hierarchical levels of the environment: home, neighborhood, community, region, then wider geographies. In close conjunction with attachment theory is an abundance of literature in phenomenological environmental psychology. Rather than mainly focusing on how individuals become attached to other people, environmental psychologists have examined how people form attachments to places; one of the most notable examples is Tuan's (1974) *Topophilia*.

Certain pathological concepts merit discussion here as well. Dissociation is another key concept in understanding how the two fields of clinical and environmental psychology connect. It often occurs while an individual experiences a traumatic event (Bremner & Marmar, 1998). It can manifest itself in a variety of ways, from feeling disconnected from one's body to believing that one is watching oneself in a movie or a play so that it seems as if the trauma is happening to someone else. Trauma victims may experience alternate states of consciousness and compartmentalize what actually occurred. Some individuals repress unpleasant parts of the past, allowing only fragments of memory to surface. Clinical psychologists who handle traumatic events, such as child abuse, must uncover their client's dissociation before they can begin to make headway in

therapy. And while it is rarely the primary focus of clinicians, these dissociative patterns often include an environmental component. A particular object, place, or space may later serve as an unpleasant stimulus or trigger that unleashes the memory of the trauma—what one has tried to bury in the subconscious—all over again. For example, a young girl who had been molested by her father in an attic may have tried to mentally divorce herself from what was happening at the time, yet later in life she may develop a phobia of attics, steps, or heights. A woman who was raped in a parking lot may later be terrorized simply getting in and out of a car. As Rubinstein (1993a, 1993b) argues, traumatic events may weaken the person-place bond. Trauma survivors may become emotionally, cognitively, or behaviorally detached from the aspect of lifespace associated with the trauma.

Natural disasters pose a different kind of trauma that may cause one to dissociate as well. A young boy who survived a tornado roaring through his neighborhood may tremble every time he hears not only a tornado siren but also an alarm clock or a telephone ringing. A camper who survived a devastating forest fire may become anxious simply smelling the smoke of a harmless barbecue. Here learning theory comes into play: The physical environment assumes the role of a conditioned stimulus that elicits a conditioned response. Just the sight, sound, or smell of a traumatic environmental experience may trigger a negative reaction. Suedfeld (1987) refers to these precipitating events as extreme experiences, and he notes the proliferation of terms such as *concentration camp syndrome, disaster syndrome,* and *shell shock.*

Table 8.1 illustrates how the systems or socioecological approach relates to the pathologies of dissociation, agoraphobia, and anorexia nervosa. In each disorder, notice how the different levels of micro, meso, exo, and macro have a bearing on each other. For example, dissociation may operate at the microsystem, where an individual's conception of self is

Table 8.1

A Socioecological or Systems Approach to Mental Disorders

Mental Disorder	Body/Self	Micro	Meso	Exo	Macro
			Level of Analysis		
Dissociation	Trauma	Family	Community	Police	Laws
Agoraphobia	Bodily sensations	Home	Public spaces	Avoided environment	Catastrophes
Anorexia Nervosa	Image	Family	School	Neighborhood	Cultural ideals

deeply affected; at the mesosystem, where family dynamics play a role; at the exosystem, where child sexual abuse (the trauma) may be detected by a school official or by the local police; and at the macrosystem, where the perpetrator is punishable under the law.

Turning to agoraphobia, at the individual level agoraphobics react negatively to endogenous (internal) or exogenous (external) stimuli. Because of their intense fears, agoraphobics are usually confined to their homes. Public spaces such as supermarkets or crowded environments often provoke panic attacks, and as a result, persons with agoraphobia avoid them. Agoraphobics often generalize from their experiences with past panic attacks. They imagine that panic attacks will be repeated elsewhere in the future, even in places where they have never had any. The outside world itself, or the macroenvironmental level, becomes a source of phobia. Agoraphobics tend to associate personal catastrophes with the macrolevel. Victims of panic attacks often feel they are at the point of no return, fearing that they are going to die. They view the outside world holistically, and specific contexts become irrelevant compared to the overwhelming experience of being threatened by a hostile environment.

In the case of anorexia nervosa, a young woman's body image may be shaped by her family, classmates at school, neighborhood norms, and social and cultural ideals of beauty that she sees in advertisements on television and in magazines. In order for therapists to understand and treat anorexia nervosa disorder, they must disentangle a woman's relationship with each part of this socioecological system.

Note that Table 8.1 represents a gross simplification of processes that shift constantly from one level to another. For example, cases of dissociation popularized by the media might propel this disorder into national prominence, albeit for a short time. Changes in policies or laws may result from widespread exposure and political awareness of this disorder. We may also see a trickle-down or bubbling-up effect from one level to another.

In sum, from a theoretical perspective, the physical environment can deepen psychologists' understanding of the development, diagnosis, and treatment of various mental disorders. Socioecological, systems, and transactionalist approaches to environment and behavior help explain the multiple levels on which the physical environment operates. Attachment theory offers insights about how people become attached

to places and objects, an attachment that, if tampered with, can play a role in precipitating certain mental disorders. The concept of dissociation often includes an environmental link whereby a space or place serves as a trigger of traumatic memories. With this framework in mind, we turn to an examination of how the physical environment is presented in the clinical literature.

ENVIRONMENTAL APPROACHES IN CLINICAL PSYCHOLOGY

Despite over 30 years of environment behavior research, the role of the physical environment in clinical psychology remains somewhat minimal. A review of recent clinical literature reveals that the physical environment is rarely mentioned. Clinicians and researchers tend to use the word *environment* to denote situational rather than physical surroundings. For instance, clinicians analyzing children's home environments are likely to focus primarily on the relationships among children, their parents, and their peers—but rarely on the physical dwelling. Similarly those addressing children's school environments usually examine the relationships among children, their teachers, counselors and other staff members, and peers—while ignoring the physical condition of the classroom or school building. Diagnostic and treatment measures rarely stress the physical environment.

Our examination of the *Diagnostic and Statistical Manual of Mental Disorders, Fourth Edition* (1994), or *DSM-IV*, reveals that the physical environment is mentioned only in a peripheral manner. *DSM-IV* is the primary source used by psychiatrists, physicians, psychologists, social workers, nurses, occupational and rehabilitation therapists, counselors, and other health and mental health professionals to diagnose mental disorders. One section of the *DSM-IV* addresses multiaxial assessment, that is, different domains of information that can assist clinicians in planning and predicting outcomes. Five axes are included: Axis I, Clinical Disorders, Other Conditions That May Be a Focus of Clinical Attention; Axis II, Personality Disorders, Mental Retardation; Axis III, General Medical Conditions; Axis IV, Psychosocial and Environmental Problems; and Axis V, Global Assessment of Functioning.

Axis IV is most relevant to environment and behavior. "Axis IV is for reporting psychosocial and environmental problems that may affect the diagnosis, treatment, and prognosis of mental disorders (Axes I and II). A psychosocial or environmental problem may be a negative life event, an environmental difficulty or deficiency, a familial or other interpersonal stress, an inadequacy of social support or personal resources, or other problem relating to the context in which a person's difficulties have developed" (*DSM-IV*, 1994, p. 29). The manual suggests that clinicians should note only those psychosocial or environmental problems present during the year preceding the current evaluation and that clinicians may opt to note such problems that occurred prior to the previous year if they clearly contribute to the mental disorder or have become a focus of treatment. In practice, most psychosocial or environmental problems are indicated on Axis IV; however, if such a problem is the primary focus of clinical attention, it would also be recorded on Axis I with a code derived from the section on "Other Conditions That May Be a Focus of Clinical Attention."

Psychosocial and environmental problems are grouped under the following categories: *problems with primary support group, problems related to the social environment, educational problems, occupational problems, housing problems, economic problems, problems with access to health care services, problems related to interaction with the legal system/crime, and other psychosocial and environmental problems. Problems related to the social environment* include the death or loss of a friend, inadequate social support, living alone, and difficulty with acculturation, discrimination, and adjustment to life-cycle transition, such as retirement. Note that these reflect situational rather than physical issues. *Housing problems* include homelessness, inadequate housing, unsafe neighborhood, and discord with neighbors or landlord. *Other psychosocial and environmental problems* include exposure to disasters, war, or other hostilities; discord with nonfamily caregivers such as a counselor, social worker, or physician; and unavailability of social service agencies. The categories of *housing problems* and *other psychosocial and environmental problems* reveal at least some attention paid to the physical environment, but mainly in the form of extreme problems such as homelessness or disasters. For example, an individual troubled by an inadequate physical work environment, rather than home environment, is not included here.

Along with situational factors, however, the physical environment cannot be ignored. Although clinicians rarely pay the environment the attention it deserves, we argue that it can often play a significant role in deepening our understanding of psychopathology such as anxiety disorders (panic disorders, agoraphobia, specific phobias, obsessive-compulsive disorders, and post-traumatic stress disorder [PTSD]), eating disorders (anorexia nervosa, bulimia nervosa), and substance-related disorders (alcohol use disorders, drug use or drug-induced disorders, and nicotine-related disorders). The environment may well play a role in promoting and in reducing other unhealthy behavior patterns such as overeating and smoking.

Panic disorder falls under the rubric of anxiety disorders in the *DSM-IV*. It can occur with or without agoraphobia. Conversely, persons with agoraphobia often have a history of panic disorders, but some do not. Panic attacks usually come on suddenly, lasting on average from 30 to 90 minutes. Sometimes they can be only a few minutes in length. Panic attacks occur frequently in nonclinical populations as well as in those with a variety of psychiatric and physical disorders. The initial attack most frequently occurs away from home, often in a setting where individuals feel trapped or liable to draw attention to themselves (Swinson & Kuch, 1990). Situational precipitants or environmental contingencies of the first panic attacks experienced are often described in terms of the external context; clients recall where they were and what they were doing. In Great Britain, Burns and Thorpe (1977) investigated the fears of agoraphobics who responded to a questionnaire by mail in a large survey of 963 subjects. Results showed that the most frequently feared situations were joining a line in a store, having to keep a definite appointment, feeling trapped at the hairdressers, and increasing the distance from home. In large cities, agoraphobics tend to avoid confining situations like the subway, driving on an elevated highway, taking an elevator beyond the first few floors, or using an underground parking garage. Swinson and Kuch (1990) found it striking that few agoraphobics were aware of the full range of their avoidance until they were asked specific questions about their mobility. "Similarly," they also state, "it is striking how few therapists, who are not engaged in behavioral assessment and treatment, determine the extent of their patients' disability from avoidance behavior" (Swinson & Kuch, 1990, p. 18). Research in the 1990s began to examine how panic attacks and panic disorders vary cross-culturally (Katschnig &

Amering, 1990); the epidemiology of panic disorder and agoraphobia (Weissman, 1990); coping styles that agoraphobia sufferers adopt when attempting to cope with symptoms of anxiety and panic (Hughes, Budd, & Greenaway, 1999); and mechanisms involved in the observational conditioning of fear (Mineka & Cook, 1993). Hughes et al. (1999) describe several cognitive strategies for coping with agoraphobic and panic-induced anxiety relating to four possible directions of attention: to the self, away from the self, to the environment, and away from the environment. In addition, the researchers cite the use of positive self-talk and relaxation as coping strategies.

Research on specific phobias also has an environmental component. Psychologists have long been investigating fear of heights, fear of flying, and, more recently, fear of driving. Findings reveal that nonphobics have had a safe exposure to a stimulus that invokes a phobia in other individuals. Menzies and Clarke (1993) discovered that only 18% of height-fearful subjects attributed their fear to a direct conditioning experience. In a subsequent study using only clinical subjects, they found that only 11% of acrophobic cases studied could be directly attributed to direct traumatic experiences involving heights (Menzies & Clarke, 1995). As a result, the etiology of height phobia differs sharply from that of other phobias, such as dog phobia and dental phobia, where high levels of direct conditioning experiences play a major role. Davey, Menzies, and Gallardo (1997) suggest that the frequently found comorbidity between agoraphobia and acrophobia may be explained by cognitive biases in the discrimination and interpretation that agoraphobia and acrophobia have in common. According to cognitive-behavioral theory, anxiety disorders arise when situations are perceived as more dangerous than they actually are. Once a threat is perceived—or more accurately, misperceived—at least three mechanisms may help maintain persistent high levels of anxiety: selective attention to threat-relevant stimuli, physiological arousal, and safety-seeking behaviors. People then engage in coping responses to control anxiety and in avoidance responses to prevent perceived danger (Salkovskis, Clark, Hackmann, Wells, & Gelder, 1999).

Van Gerwen, Spinhoven, Diekstra, and Van Dyck (1997) investigated the association of flight anxiety with different types of phobia among 419 people who sought help for fear of flying. They identified four foci of fear: fear of an aircraft accident and the need to be in control of the situation; fear of loss of self-control or social anxiety; fear of water or claustrophobia, agoraphobia, or both with panic attacks; and acrophobia. Taylor, Deane, and Podd (2000) examined fear of driving. Taylor's research team cites that previous studies of driving phobia found a mixture of cognitions associated with different anxiety disorders, such as fear of accidents (specific phobia), fear of anxiety and its symptoms (panic disorder), and fear of embarrassment (social phobia). Their own study sampled 190 volunteers recruited through media advertisements asking for respondents who had a fear of driving; 85 of these participated in a follow-up study. Findings revealed that subjects had high expectations of negative events and that there were no significant differences in terms of fear severity between those who had had and had not had a motor vehicle accident.

Research on obsessive-compulsive disorder (OCD) has revealed that environmental cues may have an impact on the waxing and waning of this disorder (Ristvedt, Mackenzie, & Christenson, 1993). Eighty-one subjects with OCD completed a 339-item cues checklist (CCL) developed by Mackenzie, Ristvedt, Christenson, Lebow, and Mitchell (1992) of rationally derived cues and circumstances that might be expected to elicit or worsen symptoms. Analyses of principal components identified four components: *household order and organization, contamination and cleaning, negative affect,* and *prevention of harm and checking. Household order and organization* cues included housework and daily activities around the home: cleaning the kitchen, organizing things, vacuum cleaning, arranging things, house cleaning, washing dishes, making beds, washing clothes, packing suitcases, cooking, returning home, sorting through bureau drawers, and preparing for bed. *Contamination and cleaning* included: the touch of others, germs, blood, public restrooms, dirt, trash, AIDS, garbage cans, an illness, a doctor's visit, hospitals, money, hand washing, and door knobs. The *negative affect* component contained several cues involving depression, anxiety, and anger and situations that would evoke negative affect, but only three environmental items: one's workplace, shopping, and shopping malls. Finally, *prevention of harm and checking* cues included objects and activities that normally require some level of care and attention to prevent harm to oneself or to others: locking doors, turning off appliances, oven, locks, leaving your home, light switches, writing checks, stoves, being uncertain, and driving a car. This body of research suggests a link between *DSM-IV* Axis II pathology and OCD symptoms, so that negative affect serves as a precipitant of symptoms. Depressive affect may heighten an OCD patient's reactions to affect-laden stimuli, which later impedes habituation to these stimuli. The researchers also note that the format of the CCL does not allow individuals to comment on the potency of individual cues or the extent to which each cue may result in pathological behavior on any one occasion. They argue that a single cue may prove equally troublesome as several other minor cues combined. The use of the CCL requires still further refinement.

Other scholars have been investigating the extent to which the family accommodates patients with OCD. For example, one study examined the experiences of spouses or parents for 34 patients with OCD and found that 88% of these caregivers reported accommodating the patient. Among the more extreme findings: "The mother of one patient regularly used a neighbor's bathroom because hers was constantly occupied by her son; one wife was unable to cook or clean because her home was entirely cluttered with hoarded newspapers" (Calvocoressi et al., 1995, p. 442).

In fact, hoarding behavior is one form of OCD that has only recently been the subject of empirical research. Until the mid-1990s, most research in this area focused on food hoarding among rodents, small animals, and birds—with hardly any on humans. Yet of all the disorders examined, hoarding reflects one of the strongest ties to the physical environment. When people hoard, they hoard things, and this in turn affects their primary territory and those of others around them. Frost and Gross (1993) and Frost, Krause, and Steketee (1996) conducted one of the first series of empirical studies examining the association of hoarding and obsessive-compulsive symptomatology, for which they developed a 21-item Hoarding Scale (referred to in the subjects' materials as the "Questionnaire on Saving Things"). Two groups of subjects comprised their study. The first group responded to a newspaper advertisement soliciting volunteers who were "pack rats or chronic savers" to participate in a study. The subjects qualified for inclusion in the study if they saved a large number of items that were not part of collections, and if a large percent of what they saved went unused. The second inclusion criterion was a cutoff score of 70 on the Hoarding Scale (Frost & Gross, 1993). The second group comprised staff members at a small liberal arts college, randomly selected from the telephone directory, who scored below the

median (60) on the Hoarding Scale. The final subject pool included 11 hoarders and 16 nonhoarders. Results showed that hoarders had significantly and substantially scored higher on the Yale-Brown Obsessive-Compulsive Scale (Goodman et al., 1989). Among a community sample, hoarding was strongly associated with obsessive and compulsive symptoms in general and with several related characteristics including indecisiveness and pathological responsibility, as well as with general psychopathology symptoms and distress. The findings suggest that hoarding behavior is widespread, even in nonclinical populations, and that more research is needed to identify the extent to which hoarding poses a problem that requires intervention.

Frost and Gross (1993, p. 374) confirmed the presence of hoarding behavior by visiting several of their subjects' homes. They found that the degree of clutter varied; it could be highly visible in the major living areas of the home or hidden completely in selected spaces. According to the researchers, "One subject's house was a series of maze-like paths through rooms piled to the ceiling with miscellaneous objects. Another subject had virtually no clutter in her house; however, her basement and attic had hundreds of boxes neatly labeled and stacked in rows from floor to ceiling—like the stacks of a library." Hoarders tend to buy extras of certain things so that they are not caught without them. They also tend to carry more possessions with them in their purses or cars "just in case. . . ." Self-reported hoarders reported higher levels of emotional attachment to their possessions. Hoarders had more first degree relatives who engaged in excessive saving than nonhoarders, and hoarders were less likely to be married. Throwing things away upsets hoarders emotionally and physically such that hoarders engage in the behavior to prevent some future harm—being without something they need. Surprisingly, hoarding was not related to material deprivation. The researchers suggest a model that conceptualizes hoarding as an avoidance behavior tied to indecision and perfectionism. Saving allows hoarders to avoid the decision required to throw something away and the fear or worry that they have made a mistake in tossing something out. It also allows hoarders to avoid emotional reactions that accompany parting with cherished possessions, resulting in a greater perceived sense of control over their environment.

Sexual abuse, whether it occurs in childhood or adulthood, has been a major source of post-traumatic stress disorder and has been the focus of an extensive body of research. Dissociation occurs both peritraumatically—at the time of the traumatic event—and posttraumatically—as a long-term consequence of traumatic exposure. Dissociative symptoms deriving from childhood abuse frequently include depersonalization, derealization, dissociative amnesia, fragmentation of identity, and posttraumatic reexperiencing phenomena such as flashbacks of traumatic events (Chu, 1998). When a trauma occurs, whether it be abuse or another form of traumatic stress, people begin to dissociate what is happening through an altered sense of time, either much slower or accelerated than it actually is; profound feelings of unreality, that the event is not actually happening to them; confusion and disorientation; feelings of being disconnected from their bodies (Marmar, Weiss, & Metzler, 1998).

Holman and Stokols (1994) analyzed child sexual abuse, drawing upon theoretical constructs from clinical, social, developmental, and environmental psychology. They examined contextual influences on the etiology and psychosocial outcomes of child sexual abuse and suggest clinical and environmental design strategies to reduce the prevalence and disruptive impacts of this pressing social problem. They speculate that microlevel sociospatial factors may increase opportunities or motivations for perpetrators to molest children. Conversely the degree to which the layout of a home includes a sense of defensible space may influence patterns of territorial and self-protective behavior. A home that offers a strong sense of control over personal space without extreme physical, visual, or auditory isolation may reduce opportunities for abuse.

The study of PTSD has mushroomed in recent decades. In the United States this was in part precipitated by thousands of Vietnam War veterans who had experienced gruesome traumas on the battlefield that continued to plague them long after they returned home. Many returning soldiers watched in shock as bullets struck their buddies only inches away. Others witnessed the enemy exploding in a wall of fire. Still others were tortured and beaten themselves. Scenes like these resurfaced in flashbacks or tormented them in dreams years after the war had ended.

More recently, hundreds of those who have witnessed terrorist attacks, such as the 1993 bombing of the World Trade Center in New York City or the 1995 bombing of the Alfred P. Murrah Federal Building in Oklahoma City, have suffered from PTSD. Buildings that had been safe workplaces for years became death traps in a matter of seconds.

Even before terrorism became relatively widespread, building failures have occasionally precipitated PTSD. For example, the 1981 collapse of a walkway in the Hyatt Regency Hotel in Kansas City, Missouri, left 114 people dead and over 200 injured. The disaster occurred during an atrium tea dance when the lobby was packed. Thousands of lives were adversely affected by this catastrophic event. One researcher studied the psychological effects of this structural failure on those who survived (Wilkinson, 1983).

Environmental disasters such as the 1989 Loma Prieta earthquake, which rocked the San Francisco Bay Area; the 1991 firestorm in Oakland, California; and the 1993 devastating wildfires in Orange County, California, also left thousands of PTSD victims in their wakes. The 1989 earthquake caused the collapse of the Nimitz Freeway near downtown Oakland. Some fascinating research involved interviews of 367 emergency services personnel who responded to the Bay Area disaster, 154 of whom were involved in the freeway collapse (Marmar, Weiss, & Metzler, 1996; Weiss, Marmar, & Metzler, 1995). These included emergency medical technicians, paramedics, firefighters, police, and California Department of Transportation workers. Several predictors of current symptomatic distress were measured, including level of critical incident exposure, psychological traits, locus of control, social support, general dissociative tendencies, and peritraumatic dissociation. Results lent further support to a growing body of literature linking dissociative tendencies and experiences to distress resulting from exposure to traumatic stressors. The same research team investigated the relationship between peritraumatic dissociation and post-traumatic stress response in greater Los Angeles area residents who survived the 1994 Northridge earthquake (Marmar et al., 1998). Researchers evaluated 60 men and women working for a large private insurance company who lived close to the epicenter of the quake. Again, reports of dissociation during the traumatic event predicted current post-traumatic stress response symptoms.

In sum, upon close examination, it appears that a wide variety of mental disorders have at least some relationship to the physical environment. In some of these, such as agoraphobia, specific phobias, and certain forms of obsessive-compulsive disorder (such as hoarding behavior) the environmental link is strong, holding promise for both diagnosis and treatment. With that in mind, let us now examine ways in which the physical environment has been used in treatment of mental disorders.

TREATMENT

Because the physical environment is mentioned only tangentially in the clinical literature, it has been a challenge to find examples of how clinicians have used the physical environment in treatment. Nonetheless, we were able to locate a few examples. Undoubtedly, there must be others as well.

Frueh, Turner, and Beidel (1995) examined the role of exposure therapy for combat-related PTSD, an issue that they argue remains underdeveloped. The researchers studied *exposure therapy,* a general term for the category of treatments, and distinguish between *intensive exposure* (sometimes referred to as flooding) and *graduated exposure* (systematic desensitization). They reviewed single case studies, group outcome studies, and studies based on other exposure-based strategies. Their research provides considerable evidence that intensive exposure to trauma-related cues benefits patients suffering from combat-related PTSD, especially in alleviating symptoms of intrusion and physiological reactivity to stimuli associated with traumatic events. Nonetheless, data fail to indicate that exposure therapy has a significant effect upon the negative symptoms of PTSD, such as avoidance, social withdrawal, and emotional numbing, nor on certain aspects of managing emotions, such as anger control.

A technique called *attention fixation training* (AFT) has proven effective in helping agoraphobics habituate to phobic settings (Kallai, Kosztolanyi, Osvath, & Jacobs, 1999). AFT has three components. First is *directed attention* to the physical environment. Clients are taught to pay attention to their surrounding environments as they experience them. Second is *topographical synthesis,* whereby clients are encouraged to experience the environment in the here and now as opposed to using preconceptions. Topographical synthesis is used to update stunted cognitive maps that clients carry around with them internally. Third is *directed orientation* in space-time. In this procedure, clients are encouraged to explore objects in the space of the present while also recalling their past memories. Thus clients advance spatially and temporally in their thought process as related to the environment. The "goal object" under exploration successfully

integrates present experiences with the past and the future to create an ongoing spatiotemporal context. Researchers used AFT to examine nine individuals diagnosed with panic disorder with agoraphobia and how they handled five panic-inducing situations while walking a standard 2.5 kilometer route: walking along near a busy street with the examiner following close behind; walking alone near a busy street with the examiner out of client's visual field; shopping with the examiner present; traveling on a bus alone; and shopping alone. Heart rate activity was monitored during each of these situations as an indicator of the effects of individual external stimuli, triggers, and the stimulus complex. Researchers discovered that, with the exception of using public transportation, AFT resulted in considerably decreased heart rate activity as well as in decreased panic anxiety. They suggest that longitudinal studies are needed to test the long-term effects of AFT.

In addition to the many disorders described earlier, clinicians diagnose and treat eating disorders such as binge eating, anorexia nervosa, and bulimia nervosa. Eating disorders become problematic when they interfere with how a person functions in everyday life, and at their worst, they can even be fatal. Certain environmental stimuli may function as triggers for promoting and reducing eating disorders. Organizations such as Overeaters Anonymous and Weight Watchers address the needs of the nonclinical population, that is, individuals who do not necessarily seek out formal clinical treatment but who nonetheless desire an informal support group in order to help control their problematic eating habits. Such organizations counsel their members to beware of settings where they tend to engage in overeating. For example, in an effort to prevent weight gain over the 2000 holiday season, a public service announcement from the American Dietetics Association cautioned party goers to stay away from the food table. They are urged to take only a small plate of food and eat only what is on it instead of munching away continuously without knowing how much food they consume. Avoiding a specific environment—in this case, a buffet table filled with an array of tempting appetizers—can affect a specific behavior, overeating.

The treatment of substance-related disorders, such as alcohol use disorders, drug use or drug-induced disorders, and nicotine-related disorders, may have environmental components as well. Here too those who do not seek out formal clinical expertise often benefit from support groups such as Alcoholics

Anonymous or smoking cessation groups to curb their habits. Such organizations often alert their members to avoid environmental settings that may trigger the addictive behavior. For example, people prone to alcoholism and smoking are less likely to continue their harmful addictions if they avoid hanging around bars filled with cigarette smoke.

THE ENVIRONMENTAL PSYCHOLOGY OF TREATMENT SETTINGS

One of the most intriguing areas where environmental and clinical psychology overlap is the study of treatment settings. From a historical perspective, Natalija Subotincic (1999a, 1999b) provides a fascinating analysis of Sigmund Freud's office and its relationship with his theories and practices. She investigated how Freud arranged the rooms in which he lived and worked during several periods of his professional life, including the famous 19 Berggasse in Vienna, Austria, his home and offices from 1891 to 1938. In addition to constructing measured drawings of the consulting room where Freud met with his patients, she also studied how he organized furniture as well his large collection of antiquities. As Subotincic (1999b) argued, "he carefully and self consciously assembled the contents of his work spaces in a manner that reflected the organization of his thoughts and beliefs." Around 1890, a grateful patient, Madame Benevisti, gave him a memorable present, what later became his world-famous psychoanalytic couch. While at first he collected copies, photographs, prints, and plaster casts of Florentine statues, when he became more financially secure, he decided to collect original statues and vases from Egyptian, Greek, Roman, and later Chinese periods.

Subotincic's research revealed that major shifts in the development of Freud's theories of psychoanalysis were either directly preceded or followed by physical and spatial alterations that he made to his office. Freud often referred to his antiquities, especially the statuettes which decorated his writing table and which he greeted each morning, as his "audience." He was so attached to his collection that he took a substantial part of it with him during his summer holidays. By 1938, he had placed at least six statues of Eros, the God of love, in a glass display cabinet at the foot of the couch. His patients were staring straight at them—rather than at Freud himself—during analysis. His consulting room addresses themes of dreams, sexuality, and life. By contrast, behind his desk in his study was an assemblage of antiques based on the theme of death; all these themes were central to Freud's intellectual development. These included an Egyptian funerary barge and two mummy masks. A Greek vase given to him by his pupil and friend, Marie Bonaparte, sat on a round glass tabletop behind Freud's chair; after his death his ashes were placed in it.

From a contemporary perspective, Division 34 of the American Psychological Association, Population and Environmental Psychology, sponsored a symposium at the 1998 annual convention on "Environments for Psychotherapy—Problems in Office Design." The session was one of the first to explore the links between clinical and environmental psychology and the first to examine this topic. The discussion drew about 60 attendees. In preparing for the symposium, organizer James Richards (1998) conducted an intriguing pilot study. He selected a number of therapists' offices from the Yellow Pages of the Tucson, Arizona, phone book. He then drove around the city to see what these offices looked like from the outside. Results of his study revealed that all the sites he visited had an institutional feel. Most were part of a medical complex, and they created a visual impression of a doctor's office. All were designed for occupancy during daylight hours, and he speculated that night lighting could potentially be a problem. Security for both clients and therapists is a significant issue. Accessibility, too, may be another problem area. It appeared that most met only the minimum standards for accommodating wheelchairs. Richards also noted that the vast majority of therapists' offices were located in a more affluent area of Tucson. Therapists may have selected the location of their offices on purely economic grounds without giving much thought to other issues that may be relevant to clients.

At the same APA symposium, Richards delivered a paper on behalf of Penny McClellan (1998), a practitioner employed by the American Indian Health Center in San Diego, California. Her presentation addressed how therapists select an office and what they failed to learn about this process in graduate school. She stressed that the quality of the neighborhood in which the therapist's office is located is especially important. It should be accessible from the freeway and from public transportation and ideally should have parking nearby. Therapists must be attentive to such issues as air quality, freeway noise, and airplane flight paths, all of which influence the environment in which they practice. Concurring with Richards's findings, McClellan argued that safety at night is another important concern. Therapists will also find it useful to have some type of signal system in place, for example, to announce when clients arrive or to contact someone in case of an emergency. Accommodating children in a waiting area may also be an issue for clients who cannot afford babysitting or child care arrangements.

As a final part of the APA symposium, Anthony (1998) presented an analysis of environment behavior issues in the design of psychotherapists' offices. She began by reviewing images of therapists' offices in American film, such as *Ordinary People* (1980), *Prince of Tides* (1991), and *Good Will Hunting* (1997). She also noted that director Woody Allen has featured therapists' offices in several of his films, for example, *Husbands and Wives* (1992) and *Deconstructing Harry* (1997). What kinds of stereotypes about the field do these films promote or reflect? What roles do therapists' offices play in film: backdrop or center stage? How do these mass-produced images help or hinder the psychological profession?

Two examples of how therapists' offices are portrayed in film are analyzed here: *Good Will Hunting* and *Husbands and Wives*. In the former, the main character, Will Hunting (Matt Damon) visits several therapists in an attempt to address his psychological problems. The first office reflects a formal academic setting with Gothic architecture, dark woodwork, and high bookshelves. At the second office Will Hunting reclines on a couch while a therapist performs hypnosis. Lights are dimmed and curtains are shut. A decorative screen is positioned behind the therapist, perhaps symbolizing the hidden self. The third office is that of Dr. Sean McGuire (Robin Williams), the only therapist with whom Hunting eventually connects and opens up to psychologically. In contrast to the previous two office environments, McGuire's office appears much more lived in, personalized by a coatrack, plants, and pictures, even a paint-by-numbers painting of the sea. Opaque glass windows shield his office from view. Furthermore, McGuire's physical appearance contrasts with those of his two predecessors. While the first two dressed formally, McGuire dressed more casually. In all three cases, the therapists' clothing reflected the overall ambience of their offices.

In *Husbands and Wives*, the psychologist is merely a voice offscreen, and the main characters often change therapeutic settings. Office settings tended to be shown for sessions with individuals, while more domesticlike settings were backdrops for sessions with couples. During one individual counseling session, Judy (Mia Farrow) is shown in front of a backdrop of venetian blinds, and at another she is positioned in front of a semicircular window. In this film, one gets the impression that therapeutic settings are used as props to amplify the trite angst of New York yuppies.

Surprisingly, an extensive search of several databases covering thousands of scholarly journals, newspapers, and popular magazines, revealed virtually no information at all about the office designs of psychotherapists, therapists, or counselors. A request to the e-mail bulletin board of Division 12 of the American Psychological Association yielded only one response. Nonetheless, informal interviews with therapists combined with the author's personal reflections revealed several issues to be important in the design of therapists' offices:

- *Location.* How convenient is the location of the office for clients? If the office is right off a busy freeway intersection, for example, the stress of traffic can predispose one to an even more stressful session with the psychotherapist.
- *Image.* Does the building where the office is located have a homelike or an institutional image?
- *Degree of visibility.* Do some clients want to hide? Do they fear running into people they know? Or, at the other extreme, do some wish to advertise they are seeing a therapist?
- *Proximity to rest room.* How far away is the rest room? Having one nearby gives clients a place to escape. A long hike down a hallway can make clients anxious.
- *Privacy.* This is one of the most important concerns. Can clients be seen or heard by others outside the therapist's office? Can clients see or hear other clients in adjoining therapy rooms?
- *Easy-to-read clocks.* Are clients surprised when their appointment time has ended? Have therapists paced themselves adequately throughout the therapy session?
- *Entrances and exits.* Are the number and placement of entrances and exits helpful or harmful? One therapist said that in seeking out new office space she was concerned that the client could leave her office without walking through the waiting room, thus minimizing the need

to interact or be seen in a state of emotional fragility.

- *Furniture.* Is the therapist face-to-face with clients or side by side? Which seating arrangement is most/least intimidating? How much choice is available? Might certain types of furniture make clients more or less likely to lose emotional control? Or do some types of furniture actually help clients feel better?
- *Lighting.* How bright or dim is the therapist's office? Bright lights may seem cheerful to some clients, but glaring or overwhelming to others. Conversely, dim lights can seem soothing to some but spooky or depressing to others. Who controls the lighting? How much control does a client have or need? Are lights overhead or on side walls or tables? Glare may affect how patients view their therapists and vice versa.
- *Views.* What role does an outside view play? A view of nature could have a healing effect, as has been demonstrated in medical settings (Ulrich, 1984).
- *Plants.* In what condition are plants kept? Dead plants can send a signal to clients: If therapists can't even take care of their plants, how well can they take care of their clients?
- *Artwork.* Color, texture, intensity, degree of abstraction, and subject matter may all play a role in how clients respond.

In sum, the physical environment of therapists' offices may well significantly influence the attitudes and behavior of clients, and the success or failure of the therapeutic process itself. It may exacerbate clients' preexisting conditions—for better or for worse. Environment behavior researchers, architects, interior designers, and psychotherapists must collaborate to further investigate these important issues.

CLINICAL APPROACHES IN ENVIRONMENTAL PSYCHOLOGY

In addition to the work just described examining the role of the physical environment in therapeutic settings, other distinct areas of work have emerged where clinical approaches have been used to examine issues in environmental psychology. One body of research has addressed the experience of moving. Another body of work has examined the role of the home in family conflict and its role in precipitating

and adjusting to a divorce. Another area of concentration has addressed the house as a symbol of self and the environment as an autobiography of self. No doubt there may be others as well.

The process of moving is one area where clinical and environmental psychology intersect. Individuals who have recently experienced a move may present themselves to clinicians with a variety of psychological problems. In their classic Social Readjustment Rating Scale, T. H. Holmes and R. H. Rahe (1967) and T. S. Holmes and T. H. Holmes (1970) cite a change in residence and change in living conditions as events likely to increase life stress. One of the earliest pieces to examine the phenomenon of losing one's home was done by Fried (1963). Several researchers have compared the process of moving to the grief reaction of losing a loved one (Bronfenbrenner, 1967; Marris, 1974; McCollum, 1990; Weissman & Paykel, 1972). Anthony (1984a) explored memories of favorite homes, the experience of moving away and later returning to visit them. Interviews with 97 Southern California residents revealed that most feelings about moving out of the favorite home were negative (57%), as were return visits to the home after moving out (88%).

In an early study, Anthony analyzed the role of the home environment in family conflict (1984b). Forty therapists in the Los Angeles area involved in marriage, family, and child counseling were interviewed as part of an exploratory study. Counselors were asked to describe their clients' problems about territoriality and privacy in the home. Most therapists failed to focus on the physical environment as a key concern in their practice yet, after having been questioned about it, recognized its importance. The physical environment often served as a significant backdrop to problems reported by their clients. Results showed that the bedroom was most prone to territorial and privacy conflicts. Closely following the bedroom were the kitchen, bathroom, and living room. Pieces of furniture that sparked the greatest conflict were televisions, stereos, and desks. Today computers, cellular telephones, and other electronic equipment might provoke domestic controversy as well.

Subsequent work by Anthony (1997) examined parents' and children's perceptions of their housing environments before and after a separation or divorce, as well as the role that the home may play during a marriage. Two phases of research were involved: first, an exploratory study at the Center for the Family in Transition in Corte Madera, California;

and second, a study of 58 individuals in two support organizations for children and parents of divorce in St. Louis, Missouri. Survey and interview findings revealed that while the home is rarely the direct cause of divorce, it often exacerbates preexisting conditions in a marriage. Subsequent to a divorce, some parents and children still maintain a strong emotional attachment to the home they inhabited while the marriage was intact. Moving out of that home can take a serious toll on family members and, for some, cause severe grief much like the loss of a loved one. Respondents' perceptions of their post-divorce housing arrangements were also discussed. Based on her research, the author concluded that the physical housing environment, typically viewed as a backdrop to everyday life, may well merit center stage.

Clare Cooper Marcus (1974, 1995) has studied individuals' relationships with their home environments for decades, beginning with her seminal paper "The House as a Symbol of Self" and culminating in the publication of her book *The House as Mirror of Self.* She draws upon the theories of Carl Jung, particularly his notion of archetypes, to understand how people relate to their houses. The book attracted widespread publicity including an appearance on the popular *Oprah Winfrey Show,* an event that caused the book to go into a second printing almost overnight.

The methodological tool of environmental autobiography (Cooper Marcus, 1978; Hester, 1979) has been widely used among environment behavior researchers, and it holds great promise for clinicians as well. One of the most significant findings from this method has been that adults often look upon their childhood home as "haven," a standard upon which to base their ideal home environment. Yet the opposite can also be true. For those who experienced an unhappy childhood or, even worse, who were the victims of trauma, the home can serve as a trap, one that triggers unpleasant memories. In fact, for this reason some students who are asked to write an environmental autobiography as part of a course requirement have been unable to complete the assignment. Although the tool can be an excellent means of uncovering one's environmental biases and values, for some vulnerable individuals the technique raises a host of ethical problems (Rubinstein, 1993a, 1993b). Yet when used by a clinician with the appropriate psychological training, the technique can elicit insights that no other assessment measure can offer.

Peled and Schwartz (1999) published two case studies exploring the role of the ideal home in psychotherapy. As part of their therapeutic approach, they used the method of *eco-analysis* in the analysis of homes. Eco-analysis involves a comparison of the client's concept of an ideal home with his or her present home. This comparison is then used as a projective measure in therapy. Similarly, Peled and Ayalon (1988) published a case study examining the role of the spatial organization of the home in family therapy. The experience of a couple in therapy who underwent eco-analysis revealed similar dimensions of conflict in their relationship and in the spatial configurations of their respective ideal homes.

Rowles (1983, 1984) examined place and personal identity in old age as manifested in a small Appalachian community. He argues that, for many elderly, the environment is an autobiography of the self and refers to this phenomenon as *autobiographical insidedness.* Inside versus outside represents the dichotomy between what the elderly view as their community and as the outside world. This concept has strong implications for therapeutic approaches. Autobiographical recollections of significant spaces and places may reveal internalized geographies that influence how clients cope with PTSD and other mental disorders and changes in the physical environment.

Israel (1998, 1999) has been using environmental autobiography methods to understand the roots underlying the work of well-known designers. She conducted in-depth interviews with architect Michael Graves and architecture critic Charles Jencks, based on a series of exercises derived from topoanalysis (see Bachelard, 1969). Her tools included an environmental genealogy exercise. Israel's research uncovered how both Graves and Jencks had unconsciously reworked their history of places to create their own homes as well as their well-known public buildings.

In their firm, Forrest Painter Design, Constance Forrest (1999a, 1999b) and Susan Painter (1999) routinely rely upon clients' unique relationships with their physical environments as part of their design and clinical practice. Forrest, a clinical psychologist, and Painter, an interior designer who is also a developmental psychologist, have branded their approach "design psychology." Design psychology relies upon interviews and assessment tools from clinical psychology. The information derived from these tools is used as the basis for design. Their objectives are to create spaces that function as therapeutic environments. This is achieved in part through a design prescription the goal of which is to create environments that support and enhance both privacy and social affiliation, positive beliefs about the self and self-esteem, sense of control, optimism about the future, and reminders about the meaning of life.

Forrest has developed three assessment tools to determine the environmental factors that evoke such positive psychological states for individual clients: *developmental history of place, five objects,* and *favorite place.* The first, *developmental history of place,* asks clients to recall where they have lived, when they lived there, and what important events occurred. The second is a projective assessment technique whereby clients are asked to select *five objects* about which they feel so positively that the feeling could be characterized as love. Forrest then asks her clients to describe what about each object drew them to it and what emotions and associations the object evokes. The third tool asks clients to describe a *favorite place,* the place in which they have felt the best of all places they have ever been, not necessarily a place where they have lived. With this image of the place in their minds, Forrest uses a relaxation technique to guide clients to enhance their memories and recreate the experience of each of their senses, focusing on sound, color, texture, visual image, temperature, and spatial relationships. Her objective as a design psychologist is not to try to recreate the favorite place but rather to bring elements into the design that will recreate the experience that clients feel in this place. She weaves together information from all three assessment tools to produce a design for each individual client.

Painter (1999) has extended the principles of design psychology to design for groups of people rather than for individuals. She draws upon three principles from developmental psychology. *Security-exploration balance* is the notion that emotional well-being is fostered by the proper balance between familiarity and novelty in the environment. *Environment-as-mirror* is the principle that people experience the environment as a reflection of themselves and their intrinsic worth. The *caregiving for the caregiver* principle asserts that in order to do their job effectively, those who care for others must meet their own psychological and physical needs as well. All three psychological principles are used as the basis for a needs assessment, a series of needs statements about the clients and the environment, which becomes the basis for subsequent design work.

Other works involving clinical approaches to environmental psychology have included ethnographies, interviews, and surveys examining the relationships between institutions and the large-scale communities in which persons with mental disorders reside. They exemplify the aforementioned systems approach as they involve different levels of analysis from macro- to microsystems. For example, Roosens (1979) analyzed Geel, Belgium, Europe's first therapeutic community. The city soon became a pilgrimage site for those with mental disorders, in response to the cult of St. Dymphna. St. Dymphna was the daughter of a seventh-century Irish king. After refusing to commit incest with her father, she fled to Flanders. Her father later discovered her there and murdered her. By refusing her father's desires, legend has it that she defeated his madness. Since the mid-thirteenth century, persons suffering from mental illness have entered the Church of St. Dymphna to partake in a series of exorcisms. Many patients moved permanently to Geel, and the city benefited economically from its fame.

Shoultz (1988) addressed the needs of individuals with mental disabilities and disorders at a microsystem level with macrosystem implications. She argues that placing these individuals on a continuum with institutional care at one end of the scale and community living on the other can be problematic. Committing most troubled persons to institutions isolates them from normality. Clients are assumed to progress along the continuum from institutional to community living. By contrast, Shoultz proposed what she called "permanency planning," a concept whereby individuals remain within the confines of their own homes and communities. They are encouraged to become active and normalized members of their communities, and any treatment they receive is given at home. In fact, permanency planning reflects principles similar to those seen at the therapeutic community of Geel.

At the institutional level, Colarelli and Siegel (1966) explored the effects of changing social roles in Ward H, a psychiatric ward in Topeka State Hospital in Topeka, Kansas. Aides assumed management positions formerly held by psychiatrists, nurses, social workers, and other staff members. No longer were the aides passive recipients of their superiors' orders. Instead they had the authority to make pivotal decisions about the ward. In order to help schizophrenic patients better distinguish between fantasy and reality and between themselves and the surrounding environment, the aides initiated exercise routines and focusing activities for them. They also improved the ward's appearance, which had previously been stripped of sharp objects, picture frames, and other potentially dangerous items. A four-year longitudinal study revealed that patients became more sociable and better oriented, strong indicators of normalization.

Fairweather, Sanders, Maynard, Cressler, and Bleck (1969) demonstrated the important relationships between psychiatric patients and their physical surroundings. They supervised an experiment in which patients from a mental hospital were relocated to a lodge in the community. At the lodge, patients felt a sense of autonomy that led to leadership roles and empowerment. The mental health of the patients improved at half the cost of institutionalization. Furthermore, living in the lodge had an even greater positive effect on patients who had been hospitalized for the longest time.

In sum, with the exception of the body of work cited here, clinical approaches to environmental psychology are relatively few and far between. Nonetheless they offer many possibilities for future research.

CONCLUSIONS

Has the relationship between clinical and environmental psychology made an impact on actual environments? For the most part, not yet. Because the links between these two disciplines have only emerged in the last decades of the twentieth century, not much has changed since then. A handful of enlightened designers are using clinical techniques in their practice, and the insights they have gained through these approaches have been significant. Some enlightened psychologists have begun paying attention to the role that the physical environment can play in diagnosing and treating mental disorders. The research that we uncovered holds tremendous promise for the future.

What behavior has changed as a result of new research or discoveries? Intensive exposure to trauma-related cues appears to benefit patients suffering from certain forms of PTSD, such as combat-related PTSD, especially in alleviating symptoms of intrusion and physiological reactivity to stimuli associated with traumatic events. Attention fixation training can help reduce the symptoms of agoraphobia. And the few clinical psychologists who have participated in environment behavior research have become more aware of the role of the physical environment.

Much more rigorous research is needed to link the two disciplines of clinical and environmental psychology. More clinical case studies and more studies of group outcomes are required. More sophisticated assessment techniques that incorporate environmental issues need to be developed. A handful were identified here, but many more are needed. Assessment tools that focus on the physical environment need to be made widely available to clinical psychologists. Eventually, studies with larger sample sizes are needed. Ultimately, future versions of the *DSM* need to better incorporate the physical environment in their descriptions of mental disorders. This could have a major impact on all those involved in diagnosing and treating mental disorders. Finally, research needs to be published concurrently in both clinical and environmental literature, so that each may learn about the other.

Just as design practitioners and design educators need to be better informed about the role that psychology can play in spaces and places, clinicians and clinical psychology faculty must be better informed about the role that spaces and places may play in the etiology, diagnosis, and treatment of mental disorders. It may well take a new generation of clinical psychologists in the twenty-first century to pay even greater attention to the built environment and give it the recognition that it rightly deserves.

REFERENCES

American Psychiatric Association. (1994). *Diagnostic and statistical manual of mental disorders* (4th ed.). Washington, DC: Author.

Anthony, K. H. (1984a). Moving experiences: Memories of favorite homes. In D. Duerk & D. Campbell (Eds.), *The challenge of diversity: Proceedings of the fifteenth annual Environmental Design Research Association (EDRA) conference* (pp. 141–149). Washington, DC: EDRA.

Anthony, K. H. (1984b). The role of the home in family conflict. In D. Duerk and D. Campbell (Eds.), *The challenge of diversity: Proceedings of the fifteenth annual Environmental Design Research Association (EDRA) conference* (pp. 219–226). Washington, DC: EDRA.

Anthony, K. H. (1997). Bitter homes and gardens: The role of the home in families of divorce. *Journal of Architectural and Planning Research, 14*(1), 1–19.

Anthony, K. H. (1998). *Designing psychotherapists' offices: Reflections of an environment-behavior researcher.* Paper presented at the American Psychological Association Convention, San Francisco.

Bachelard, G. (1969). *The poetics of space.* Boston: Beacon Press.

Bowlby, J. (1969). *Attachment and loss: Vol. 1. Attachment.* New York: Basic Books.

Bowlby, J. (1973). *Attachment and loss: Vol. 2. Separation.* New York: Basic Books.

Bowlby, J. (1980). *Attachment and loss: Vol. 3. Loss, sadness and depression.* New York: Basic Books.

Bremner, J. D., & Marmar, C. R. (Eds.). (1998). *Trauma, memory, and dissociation.* Washington, DC: American Psychiatric Press.

Bretherton, I. (1992). The origins of attachment theory: John Bowlby and Mary Ainsworth. *Developmental Psychology, 28*(5), 759–775.

Bronfenbrenner, U. (1979). *The ecology of human development.* Cambridge, MA: Harvard University Press.

Burns, L. E., & Thorpe, G. L. (1977). The epidemiology of fears and phobias with particular reference to the national survey of agoraphobics. *Journal of International Medical Research, 5* (Supplement 5), 1–7.

Calvocoressi, L., Lewis, B., Harris, M., Trufan, S. J., Goodman, W. K., McDougle, C. J., & Price, L. H. (1995). Family accommodation in obsessive-compulsive disorder. *American Journal of Psychiatry, 152*(3), 441–443.

Chu, J. A. (1998). Dissociative symptomatology in adult patients with histories of childhood physical and sexual abuse. In J. D. Bremmer and C. R. Marmar (Eds.), *Trauma, memory, and dissociation* (pp. 179–203). Washington, DC: American Psychiatric Press.

Colarelli, C. J., & Siegel, S. (1966). *Ward H: An adventure in innovation.* Princeton, NJ: D. Van Nostrand.

Cooper Marcus, C. (1974). The house as symbol of self. In J. Lang, C. Burnette, W. Moleski, & D. Vachon (Eds.), *Designing for human behavior* (pp. 130–146). Stroudsburg, PA: Dowden, Hutchinson and Ross.

Cooper Marcus, C. (1978). Remembrances of landscapes past. *Landscape, 22*(3), 34–43.

Cooper Marcus, C. (1995). *House as a mirror of self: Exploring the deeper meaning of home.* Berkeley, CA: Conari Press.

Davey, G. C. L., Menzies, R., & Gallardo, B. (1997). Height phobia and biases in the interpretation of bodily sensations: Some links between acrophobia and agoraphobia. *Behaviour Research and Therapy, 35*(11), 997–1001.

Demick, J., & Andreoletti, C. (1995). Some relations between clinical and environmental psychology. *Environment and Behavior, 27*(1), 56–72.

Fairweather, G. W., Sanders, D. H., Maynard, H., Cressler, D. L., & Bleck, D. S. (1969). *Community life for the mentally ill: An alternative to institutional care.* Chicago: Aldine Publishing.

Forrest, C. (1999a). *Design psychology.* Unpublished manuscript.

Forrest, C. (1999b). Using design psychology to foster psychological growth and change: A case study in the design of a psychotherapist's office. In T. Mann (Ed.), *The power of imagination: Proceedings of the thirtieth annual Environmental Design Research Association (EDRA) conference* (pp. 278). Edmond, OK: EDRA.

Fried, M. (1963). Grieving for a lost home. In L. Duhl (Ed.), *The urban condition* (pp. 151–171). New York: Basic Books.

Frost, R. O., & Gross, R. C. (1993). The hoarding of possessions. *Behaviour Research and Therapy, 31*(4), 367–381.

Frost, R. O., Krause, M. S., & Steketee, G. (1996). Hoarding and obsessive-compulsive symptoms. *Behavior Modification, 20*(1), 116–132.

Frueh, B. C., Turner, S. M., & Beidel, D. C. (1995). Exposure therapy for combat-related PTSD: A critical review. *Clinical Psychology Review, 15*(8), 799–817.

Goodman, W. K., Price, L. H., Rasmussen, S. A., Mazure, C., Fleischmann, R. L., Hill, C. L., Heninger, G. R., & Charney, D. S. (1989). The Yale-Brown obsessive compulsive scale I: Development, use, and reliability. *Archives of General Psychiatry, 46,* 1006–1011.

Hester, R. (1979, September). A womb with a view: How spatial nostalgia affects the designer. *Landscape Architecture, 69,* 475–481.

Holman, E. A., & Stokols, D. (1994). The environmental psychology of child sexual abuse. *Journal of Environmental Psychology, 14,* 237–252.

Holmes, T. S., & Holmes, T. H. (1970). Short-term intrusions into the life-style routine. *Journal of Psychosomatic Research, 14*(2), 121–132.

Holmes, T. H., & Rahe, R. H. (1967). The social readjustment rating scale. *Journal of Psychosomatic Research, 11,* 213–218.

Hughes, I., Budd, R., & Greenaway, S. (1999). Coping with anxiety and panic: A factor analytic study. *British Journal of Clinical Psychology, 38,* 295–304.

Israel, T. (1998, July/August). Some place like home: Matching people and place through topoanalysis. *Holistic Living,* 52–57.

Israel, T. (1999). Using design psychology to explore the relationship between person and place: A case study of Michael Graves and Charles Jencks. In T. Mann (Ed.), *The power of imagination: Proceedings of the thirtieth annual Environmental Design Research Association (EDRA) conference* (p. 278). Edmond, OK: EDRA.

Kallai, J., Kosztolanyi, P., Osvath, A., & Jacobs, W. J. (1999). Attention fixation training: Training people to form cognitive maps to help control symptoms of panic disorder with agoraphobia. *Journal of Behavior Therapy and Experimental Psychiatry, 30,* 273–288.

Katschnig, H., & Amering, M. (1990). Panic attacks and panic disorder in cross-cultural perspective. In J. Ballenger (Ed.), *Clinical aspects of panic disorder* (pp. 67–80). New York: Wiley-Liss.

Mackenzie, T. B., Ristvedt, S. L., Christenson, G. A., Lebow, A. S., & Mitchell, J. E. (1992). *Identification of cues associated with compulsive, bulimic, and hair-pulling symptoms.* Unpublished manuscript. (cited in Ristvedt et al., 1993, p. 729)

Marmar, C. R., Weiss, D. S., & Metzler, T. J. (1996). Stress response of emergency services personnel to the Loma Prieta earthquake Interstate-880 freeway collapse and control traumatic incidents. *Journal of Traumatic Stress, 9,* 68–85.

Marmar, C. R., Weiss, D. S., & Metzler, T. J. (1998). Peritraumatic dissociation and posttraumatic stress disorder. In J. D. Bremner and C. R. Marmar (Eds.), *Trauma, memory, and dissociation* (pp. 229–247). Washington, DC: American Psychiatric Press.

Marris, P. (1974). *Loss and change.* London: Routledge and Kegan Paul.

McClellan, P. J. (1998). Finding an office: Reflections of a practitioner. Paper presented at the American Psychological Association Convention, San Francisco.

McCollum, A. T. (1990). *The trauma of moving: Psychological issues for women.* Newbury Park, CA: Sage.

Menzies, R. G., & Clarke, J. C. (1993). The etiology of fear of heights and its relationship to severity and individual response patterns. *Behaviour Research and Therapy, 31,* 350–365.

Menzies, R. G., & Clarke, J. C. (1995). The aetiology of phobias: A non-associative account. *Clinical Psychology Review, 15,* 23–48.

Mineka, S., & Cook, M. (1993). Mechanisms involved in the observational conditioning of fear. *Journal of Experimental Psychology, 122*(1), 23–38.

Painter, S. L. (1999). Using design psychology as an educational tool: A case study in the teaching of human factors at UCLA. In T. Mann (Ed.), *The power of imagination: Proceedings of the thirtieth annual Environmental Design Research Association (EDRA) conference* (pp. 278–279). Edmond, OK: EDRA.

Peled, A., & Ayalon, O. (1988). The role of the spatial organization of the home in family therapy: A case study. *Journal of Environmental Psychology, 8,* 87–106.

Peled, A., & Schwartz, H. (1999). Exploring the ideal home in psychotherapy: Two case studies. *Journal of Environmental Psychology, 19,* 87–94.

Richards, J. (1998). *Characteristics of psychotherapy offices: Reflections on some exploratory data.* Paper presented at the American Psychological Association Convention, San Francisco.

Ristvedt, S. L., Mackenzie, T. B., & Christenson, G. A. (1993). Cues to obsessive-compulsive symptoms: Relationships with other patient characteristics. *Behaviour Research and Therapy, 31*(8), 721–729.

Roosens, E. (1979). *Mental Patients in Town Life: Geel—Europe's First Therapeutic Community.* Beverly Hills, CA: Sage.

Rowles, G. (1983). Place and personal identity in old age: Observations from Appalachia. *Journal of Environmental Psychology, 3,* 299–313.

Rowles, G. (1984). Aging in rural environments. In I. Altman, M. P. Lawton, & J. F. Wohlwill (Eds.), *Elderly people and the environment* (pp. 129–157). New York: Plenum Press.

Rubinstein, N. J. (1993a). Environmental autobiography and places of "trauma": Lessons of the unspoken. In R. M. Feldman, G. Hardie, and D. Saile (Eds.), *Power by design: Proceedings of the twenty-fourth annual Environmental Design Research Association (EDRA) conference* (pp. 262–267). Oklahoma City, OK: EDRA.

Rubinstein, N. J. (1993b). There's *NO* place like "home." Home as "trauma": The lessons of the unspoken. In R. M. Feldman, G. Hardie, & D. Saile (Eds.), *Power by Design: Proceedings of the twenty-fourth annual Environmental Design Research Association (EDRA) conference* (pp. 267–273). Oklahoma City, OK: EDRA.

Salkovskis, P. M., Clark, D. M., Hackmann, A., Wells, A., & Gelder, M. G. (1999). An experimental investigation of the role of safety-seeking behaviours in the maintenance of panic disorder with agoraphobia. *Behaviour Research and Therapy, 37,* 559–574.

Sayette, M. A., Mayne, T. J., & Norcross, J. C. (1992). *Insider's guide to graduate programs in clinical psychology* (1992/1993 ed.). New York: Guilford.

Shoultz, B. (1988). My home, not theirs: Promising approaches to mental health and developmental disabilities. In S. Friedman & K. G. Terkelson (Eds.), *Issues in community mental health* (pp. 23–42). Canton, MA: Prodist.

Stokols, D. (1992). Establishing and maintaining healthy environments: Toward a social ecology of health promotion. *American Psychologist, 47*(1), 6–22.

Subotincic, N. (1999a). Interior thoughts: A spatial analysis of the relationship between Sigmund Freud's offices and his theories and practice. In T. Mann (Ed.), *The power of imagination: Proceedings of the thirtieth annual Environmental Design Research Association (EDRA) conference,* pp. 266–267. Edmond, OK: EDRA.

Subotincic, N. (1999b). *Interior thoughts: Sigmund Freud's spatial wanderings.* Unpublished manuscript.

Suedfeld, P. (1987). Extreme and unusual environments. In D. Stokols & I. Altman (Eds.), *Handbook of environmental psychology* (Vol. 1, pp. 863–887). New York: Wiley.

Swinson, R. P., & Kuch, K. (1990). Clinical features of panic and related disorders. In J. Ballenger (Ed.), *Clinical aspects of panic disorder* (pp. 13–30). New York: Wiley-Liss.

Taylor, J. E., Deane, F. P., & Podd, J. V. (2000). Determining the focus of driving fears. *Journal of Anxiety Disorders, 14*(5), 453–470.

Tuan, Y. R. (1974). *Topophilia: A study of environmental perception, attitudes, and values.* Englewood Cliffs, NJ: Prentice-Hall.

Ulrich, R. (1984, May). View through a window may influence recovery from surgery. *Science, 224,* 420–421.

Van Gerwen, L. J., Spinhoven, P., Diekstra, R. F. W., & Van Dyck, R. (1997). People who seek help for fear of flying: Typology of flying phobics. *Behavior Therapy, 28,* 237–251.

Wapner, S. (1987). A holistic, developmental, systems-oriented environmental psychology: Some beginnings. In D. Stokols and I. Altman (Eds.), *Handbook of environmental psychology* (Vol. 2, pp. 1433–1465). New York: Wiley.

Weiss, D. S., Marmar, C. R., & Metzler, T. J. (1995). Predicting symptomatic distress in emergency services personnel. *Journal of Consulting and Clinical Psychology, 63,* 361–368.

Weissman, M. M. (1990). Epidemiology of panic disorder and agoraphobia. In J. Ballenger (Ed.), *Clinical aspects of panic disorder* (pp. 57–65). New York: Wiley-Liss.

Weissman, M., & Paykel, E. S. (1972). Moving and depression in women. *Society, 9*(9), 24–28.

Wilkinson, C. R. (1983). Aftermath of a disaster: The collapse of the Hyatt Regency Hotel skywalks. *American Journal of Psychiatry, 140,* 1134–1139.

ced
CHAPTER 9

Environmental Anthropology

EDWARD B. LIEBOW

FROM THE 1987 HANDBOOK, we learned that context matters (Stokols, 1987) and that individuals are active participants in their environment rather than simply being buffeted about by biophysical forces of nature (Fischhoff, Svenson, & Slovic, 1987). Environmental anthropology focuses on context and individuals' actions in groups, suggesting that work with such a focus would engage social scientists from a variety of disciplinary backgrounds, including environmental psychology.

Environmental anthropology is not strikingly different from anthropology's other content area specialties. In practice, it depends mainly on participant-observation for collecting data, often amplified by measurements of environmental indicators using a repertory of quantitative techniques. It relies on local language to reveal the experiences that anthropologists observe in their indigenous context and the meanings that local people ascribe to their experiences. At its best, linguistic and biophysical evidence are integrated with historical and archeological data to situate contemporary circumstances in a more encompassing regional and temporal context. The same epistemological tensions that have gripped the discipline as a whole—the struggle to define the "metanarratives" we reinforce about the relationship between anthropologists and the communities with whom we work—challenge us as environmental anthropologists to render our analysis recognizable to our community-based collaborators.

The notion of an environmental anthropology is about as old as the institutionalized discipline itself,

that is, dating to the mid-nineteenth century. Social Darwinists from that formative era, like Edward Tylor and Herbert Spencer in Britain and Louis Henry Morgan in the United States, were impressed by a seemingly inexorable pattern of development from simple to complex forms of political organization over the sweep of human history. They believed territorial expansion and the need to govern over varied terrain and multiple environmental settings encouraged the elaboration of regional alliances and governmental institutions, resulting in the unilinear evolution of cultural groups from primitive hordes to highly structured states. Franz Boas, who in 1899 founded the first American university anthropology department at Columbia University, formulated a critical response to the racist implications of this view of cultural evolution, arguing on the basis of exhaustive evidence that, even among the most "primitive"-seeming cultural groups like the Arctic Inuit, one could see a remarkably complex and highly developed body of local knowledge that resulted from the historical particularities of place. Boas, a Polish Jew who had emigrated to the United States, was especially intent on advancing the antiracist notion of "cultural relativism"—no culture should be judged to be intrinsically "better" or "worse" than any other. Rather, each culture is best understood on its own terms and situated in its own local place-based history.

An intellectual response to world events continued to mark anthropological scholarship as the twentieth century unfolded, with *the environment* often used as an explanatory counterpoint to essentialist identities. In 1957, for example, Austrian émigré Karl Wittfogel first published his "hydraulic hypothesis" about the origins of the city-state in human history. Wittfogel had been imprisoned by the Nazis, and his classic study on "Oriental despotism" was a direct response to Hitlerian assertions about Aryan supremacy, arguing that, instead of some essential entitlement, the city-state first emerged in arid settings where institutions were needed to coordinate the work of constructing and maintaining agricultural irrigation works.

Since the 1987 environmental psychology handbook's publication, a number of surveys have appeared highlighting this history of scholarship and policy applications in environmental anthropology. For the nonspecialist, Townsend (2000) provides an overview of more recent work in the domain, beginning with the concept of "cultural ecology" (as embodied in Julian Steward's work from the 1940s and 1950s) and continuing with the pursuit of "ethnobiology," which came into favor in the early 1960s and relied heavily on language to characterize traditional ecological knowledge about plants, animals, and other aspects of the environment. As Townsend observes, work that gained currency in the 1960s and 1970s brought concepts and methods into anthropology from other disciplines, especially the biology of ecosystems. Application of ecosystem concepts is exemplified in the writings of Roy Rappaport in New Guinea (1968/2000) and several researchers (e.g., Robert Carneiro, 1970; Phillipe Descola, 1994; Anna Roosevelt, 1989; Eric Ross, 1978), all of whom examined hunting and gathering and horticultural practices in the Amazon; and works by Frederik Barth in Pakistan (1958); Clifford Geertz in Indonesia (1963); Robert Netting (1981), and Eric Wolf (1982) in Switzerland, all of which involved larger agricultural populations in more complex societies.

During the 1980s, there also emerged a number of works examining linkages between local environmental conditions and the more encompassing institutions whose impacts reach to far-flung places. The concept of environmental risk was introduced (e.g., Douglas, 1985; Douglas & Wildavsky, 1982), and several subsequent works (see for example, Wolfe & Liebow, 1993) have illustrated how ethnographic analysis often helps deflect "blaming the victim" style arguments by situating risk and hazard in their social context rather than assuming that threats of environmental degradation are the result of individual decision making.

The work of biologists, chemists, geologists, and mathematicians has transformed the ecological sciences over the past decade, particularly on issues of scale and systemic equilibrium. This conceptual transformation has also been reflected in changes in environmental anthropology. Little (1999) shows how matters of scale (linking the local to the global) have been accommodated in the emerging conceptual approach of political ecology and how anthropologists are trying to make room in their models for temporal and spatial variability. Little also points to the other recent thrust in environmental anthropology, a growing interest in the ethnographic analysis of environmentalist social movements (e.g., Guha, 2000; Kempton, Boster, & Hartley, 1995). Scoones (1999) deals explicitly with new developments in ecological thinking, especially the focus on nonequilibrium dynamics that informs emerging policy perspectives that call into question past assumptions about the efficacy of natural resource prediction, management, and control.

Rocheleau and her colleagues (1996) have compiled an extensive array of feminist scholarship in political ecology that, collectively, treat gender as a critical variable in shaping resource access and control, interacting with class, caste, race, culture, and ethnicity to shape processes of ecological change, the struggle of men and women to sustain ecologically viable livelihoods, and the prospects of any community for "sustainable development." This scholarship focuses on the gendered knowledge used in the creation and maintenance of healthy environments; gendered environmental rights and responsibilities, including property, resources, space, and legal and customary rights; and gendered environmental politics and grassroots activism.

Oliver-Smith (1996) argues that an important contribution is made to our understanding of sustainable human-environment adaptations by considering environmental hazards and disasters. In particular, he reviews recent work by environmental anthropologists that generally can be placed into one of three areas of emphasis: (1) individual behavioral and organizational responses to hazards, (2) the social construction of vulnerability to hazards, and (3) the social consequences of hazards and disasters.

And finally, Low (1996) describes recent anthropological scholarship on cities and urban environments, extracting from this work the city's treatment as the locus of transnational political economy as well as the product of everyday lives and social practices. She further argues that some areas of research have been particularly influential within urban policy circles. "The anthropological twist on globalization has focused attention on transnational aspects of migration, culture-making and identity management, and on the shifting cultural environments and meanings that contextualize (and decontextualize) behavior" (Low, 1996, p. 402).

That recent works in the field of environmental anthropology can be organized according to such a range of categorizing schemes is perhaps due in part to the eclectic legacy of the discipline, seeking patterns in the stitched-together patchwork of local cases developed from extended participant observation. But several common themes are evident and have direct relevance to the current discussion about constructing an environmental psychology that makes a difference. Among these common themes, the remaining sections of this chapter will address four, acknowledging along the way several specific domains of practical application (e.g., bioconservation and pharmaceutical prospecting, disaster preparedness and response, and environmental health interventions). The four key themes include:

1. *Agency.* To what extent and under what circumstances do environmental conditions influence, shape, or determine the way we organize ourselves into settlements and political groups?
2. *Traditional Ecological Knowledge.* Did the "original affluent societies," to borrow Marshall Sahlins's term (1972), contain in their traditional ecological wisdom the ingredients for harmonious, sustainable living, or is this just a romantic notion to which we cling, without substantial supporting historical evidence?
3. *Risk.* How do we select from among the ongoing stream of possible environmental, health, and safety hazards the ones that we consider significant? If there is not universal agreement on what constitute the most important sources of hazard, how does this judgment vary from culture to culture?
4. *Growth and Scarcity.* Are there finite limits to human population growth, or are we such creative, resourceful, adaptive creatures that, as we approach what appear to be such limits, we inevitably are capable of overcoming them?

AGENCY

The earlier *Handbook* discussion in which Stokols (1987) suggested strategies for conceptualizing the contextual variables that can be said to influence the "target" phenomenon or behavioral pattern has as its premise a specific notion of natural agency. That is, the configuration and actions of the biophysical world are thought to impinge upon, set limits to, or otherwise influence in predictable fashion the range of variability in human behavior. Embedded in this view of natural agency is the notion of *adaptation,* which is a central concept to the cultural ecologists who have Julian Steward as their main intellectual creditor.

Steward conducted extensive fieldwork among the indigenous groups of the high, arid Great Basin region of Utah and Nevada. In addition to providing valuable documentation about a rapidly changing way of life among these local settlements, his work led to a more general observation about how economic and social organization resulted from the use of a particular subsistence technology in a given biophysical setting (1955). In Steward's view, the economic system of allocating scarce goods and services is associated with the social organization of work, which in turn is associated with other patterned behavioral aspects of culture such as kinship, politics, and religious activities. A more recent formulation along the same lines argues that "the functional structure of ecosystems, insofar as they determine the productivity of natural resources, affects the conditions of production of value and surplus value" (Leff, 1995, p. 21).

To avoid the trivial extreme that every behavior pattern we observe must somehow be "adaptive"—or, as Kottak put it, "the natives did a reasonable job of managing their resources and preserving their ecosystems" (1999, p. 24)—most anthropologists using this analytical strategy emphasize the *process* of adapting to changing environmental circumstances rather than assessing the efficiency, effectiveness, or sustainability of adaptive *outcomes.* For example, Guyer and Lambin (1993) characterize the process of West African agricultural intensification (changes in cropping, land use, and labor intensity) in the face of population pressure. McGuire (1997) describes the depletion of the North Atlantic cod fishery in terms of technology change (finer mesh traps, fish finders), which in turn have altered economic markets and led to an unvirtuous cycle of degradation.

The logical inversion of natural agency in environmental anthropology would hold that nature is socially constructed, a position that was voiced frequently enough in the 1980s and 1990s (cf. Soulé & Lease, 1995). Now, this constructivist perspective, even in its most elaborated forms, does not deny the presence of biophysical forces (e.g., Gottdiener, 1995; Ricoeur, 1980; Said, 1983). However, arguments from this perspective attempt to demonstrate that any attempt to explain behavior in terms of "objective circumstances" and "material needs" must also see behavior as "rooted in the collective imagination and the projects it spawns, [with] desire as much as need motivat[ing] human-nature relations" (Biersack, 1999, p. 11). Extremist claims on behalf of *either* natural or cultural causal exclusivity can productively be abandoned by adhering to a combined notion of agency that presumes the contingent and complex interaction of biophysical and social forces (Latour, 1993; Vayda & Walters 1999).

If nature as an agent of cultural change has engaged critical scholarship, humans as agents of environmental change have also received a good deal of attention in the past decade at local, regional, and global levels. At the local level, for example, recent scholarship has called into question the ecological consequences of Native Americans' traditional practices (Krech, 1999) or, if not their practices, then their motivations (Martin, 1978, 1992). At the regional level, Stonich (1993) draws attention to the agency of rural peasants in undermining the environmental quality in large areas of southern Honduras in the name of survival. She also indicates, however, how these peasants have been backed into a corner, left with little strategic choice in the larger context of development schemes imposed by outsiders. And at the global level, anthropologists such as Gunn (1994), Rayner and Malone (1998), and Moran (1993) have long been involved in examining human dimensions of global climate change, including appropriate points of intervention aimed at reducing the pace of change.

What looks like individual agency in environmental change at one level of analysis looks altogether different when viewed on a more encompassing scale. The distinction drawn between different levels or scales of analysis has received considerable attention from environmental anthropologists in recent years, along with articulations, or linkages between these different levels. When shrimp harvesters bring their catch into port on Mississippi's Gulf Coast,

they will receive a "world price," a price that reflects global, not local, conditions of supply and demand, the same as their counterparts in Honduras and the Philippines. So it is with loggers in the deciduous forests of Alberta and with wool growers in Australia. Thus, at the local level of analysis, a traditional ethnographic project might examine the internal logic of decision-making strategies (e.g., Barlett, 1982) among a well-bounded local population. But stopping with the acknowledgment that these local strategies have a bounded rationality falls short of examining the regional consequences of local choice making (DeWalt & DeWalt, 1992; Durham, 1995), the justifying discourse about national interests served at the expense of local environmental burdens (Liebow, 2000), or the unequal distribution of power and differing degrees of articulation of transnational, national, regional, and local levels of agency (Ribeiro, 1994). Methodological issues associated with linking levels of analysis are certainly formidable, and considerable attention has been directed toward delimiting boundaries, defining populations, and establishing clear criteria for asserting the presence of a linkage (DeWalt & Pelto, 1985; Kottak & Colson, 1994).

While explanatory model development in environmental anthropology has tried to anticipate the interaction of social and biophysical forces at individual, group, and intergroup levels, natural and physical scientists are transforming their thinking about ecosystems. A static view of biophysical forces arrayed into ecosystems, with its emphasis on equilibrium, limits, and carrying capacity, has been transformed into a view that features a contingent and dynamic theory of environmental change as nonlinear and fraught with uncertainty. As Scoones (1999) puts it, "new ecological thinking suggests that there is no straightforward relationship between people and environment in processes of environmental change. Environments are dynamically and recursively created in a nonlinear, nondeterministic, and contingent fashion" (p. 492).

If there is some chance that this nonequilibrium view of nature is accurate, its implications for environmental management policy are significant. As I have noted elsewhere, the inherent uncertainty of the phenomena under investigation requires a healthy admixture of "fact" and "value" in determining the proper policy course of action (Liebow, 1993). In the realm of "values," environmental scientists are just as far out of their depth as they allege nonspecialists to be in dealing with matters of scientific "fact." To come up with an appropriate response to changing environmental conditions, a variety of viewpoints must be heard, from credentialed specialists to local graduates of the school of hard knocks who must live with the consequences of environmental policy choices. If nature's predictability is in fact illusory, our current repertory of environmental management tools, such as carrying capacity, maximum sustained yield, effective dose commitments, and so forth, should give way to incremental responses with close monitoring and iterative learning built into the process so that thresholds and surprises can be responded to (Folke, Berkes, & Colding, 1998). Environmental anthropologists are especially interested in how people from different backgrounds (e.g., specialist vs. generalist, "scientific" vs. "lay," outsider vs. indigenous) come to construct problems, decide on the appropriate information needed to support a resolution of such problems, and interpret evidence about whether purported solutions are taking hold (Agrawal, 1995; Wynne, 1996).

TRADITIONAL ECOLOGICAL KNOWLEDGE

The second main theme receiving considerable recent attention in environmental anthropology has to do with traditional ecological knowledge and whether nonindustrial peoples contain in their traditional ecological wisdom the ingredients for harmonious, sustainable living. The 1992 International Symposium on Indigenous Knowledge and Sustainable Development agreed on the following working definition of indigenous knowledge, proposed by D. Michael Warren (1993):

> The term "indigenous knowledge" (IK) is used synonymously with "traditional" and "local knowledge" to differentiate the knowledge developed by a given community from the international knowledge system, sometimes also called "Western" system, generated through universities, government research centres and private industry. IK refers to the knowledge of indigenous peoples as well as any other defined community.

Further, indigenous knowledge systems relate to the way members of a given community define and classify phenomena in the physical/natural, social, and ideational environments. Examples include local classifications of soils, knowledge of which local crop varieties grow in difficult environments and of migratory patterns for game animal herds and anadromous fishes, and traditional ways of treating human and animal diseases. Indigenous knowledge systems provide the basis for local decision making. This frequently occurs through formal and informal community associations and organizations. Communities often identify problems and seek solutions to them in such local forums, capitalizing on information exchanges among knowledgeable persons and encouraging experimentation and innovations. In this way, technological innovations with the promise of success can be added to the indigenous knowledge system. Indigenous (in contrast with superimposed) forms of communication used in these local forums are vital to the preservation, development, and spread of indigenous knowledge.

For several decades, anthropologists have maintained a continuing interest in characterizing traditional ecological knowledge systems, usually with an encompassing view of ecosystem processes (e.g., Berlin 1992; Collier, 1975; Conklin, 1980; Hunn & Selam, 1990; Posey & Balée, 1989), but sometimes focusing more narrowly on ethnobotany (e.g., Balée, 1999; Nazarea, 1998). Some of these more narrowly focused works have emphasized the pharmacological properties of plants (even the first Carlos Castañeda book, *The Teachings of Don Juan*, 1968, contains an ethnobotanical taxonomy that was the object of his master's thesis in anthropology).

The aim of identifying and classifying traditional ecological knowledge is quite practical: preserving biodiversity while producing equitable, ecologically sustainable economic development. Many of the out-of-the-way places around the world where traditional ecological knowledge still flourishes are vulnerable to degradation as resources become more accessible and disappear. Without romanticizing the potential of such places—ranging from tropical rainforests to arid highland steppe regions—they remain repositories of considerable biological and financial significance. If alternative commercially viable uses can be found, the pressure to realize short-term gains from natural resource exploitation (e.g., hard currency revenues to improve debtor nations' balance of trade, return on corporate investors' shares) may be reduced and biodiversity conserved for future generations. "Bioprospecting" for medicinal plants is one such alternative use. Protecting the intellectual property rights for indigenous peoples' traditional knowledge is fraught with problems, however, and has been the object of considerable attention by anthropologists (Greaves, 1994). Moreover, the economic development dimensions of such efforts undertaken to date—in the sense of enhancements in employment, investment, savings, and infrastructure expansion—have yet to be demonstrated (Green, Goodman, & Hare, 1999).

Anthropologists have been interested in folk classification schemes for plants, animals, and landscapes for other practical reasons, as well. For example, Stoffle and his colleagues (1990) have attempted to quantify the cultural significance of threatened plants, with a specific eye towards prioritizing habitat protection efforts in the face of large-scale development projects like a permanent nuclear waste storage facility in the American desert Southwest. Also in the desert Southwest, Nabhan's extensive body of work (e.g., 1982, 1985, 1997) points to appropriate strategies for land restoration, conservation, and even nutrition contained in traditional ecological knowledge of native peoples.

For as long as anthropologists have been interested in traditional ecological knowledge, they have also been at odds with one another over the methods for inferring what actually constitutes this traditional knowledge and how appropriate it is to assume that this knowledge directs people to live in harmony with nature. As Townsend points out (2000, pp. 22–23), a noteworthy accomplishment of anthropologists working to characterize traditional ecological knowledge is to:

bring recognition to the traditional environmental knowledge of indigenous peoples, who are often ethnic minorities held in contempt by racists among the majority populations in their country. Their subsistence systems are often criticized too, by outsiders who see them as backward and who covet their land for raising cash crops or more intensive farming. Following ethnoecological studies, it is clear that traditional environmental knowledge is a body of knowledge that is extensive, observationally grounded, and complementary to scientific knowledge.

However, while calling attention to the insights to be gained from traditional ecological knowledge, anthropologists have also unwittingly made it possible for environmental movements to use romanticized stereotypes for their own aims, often without consulting the traditional peoples whose interests they purport to serve (Headland, 1997). Krech (1999) is among several recent observers (others include Edgerton, 1992; Martin, 1978, 1992; Redford, 1990) who argue that the image of indigenous peoples as keepers of the environment may well be fashioned by mythmakers, some naïve and others manipulative. If conservation entails intentionality, Krech argues, a closer look at the historical record suggests that only under conditions of scarcity and territorial pressure are local settlements likely to act in a "conservationist" manner.

RISK

The third main theme receiving considerable recent attention in environmental anthropology has to do with environmental risk and hazard. In perhaps the most important contribution by an anthropologist to this discussion, Mary Douglas and her political scientist colleague, Aaron Wildavsky (1982), argue that people everywhere are beset by an ongoing stream of possible environmental health and safety hazards and that the process of selecting from this whole set of possibilities the ones that are considered more significant is embedded in more encompassing processes of social organization. In the Douglas and Wildavsky formulation, the "risk problem" may not appear as an explicit matter of choice making. Instead, the selection of risks to worry about is entrained within a more complex set of local value orientations concerning equity, consent, liability, and trust and how far out in the future contemporary events are felt to have salient consequences (Rayner & Cantor, 1987).

The "risk and culture" approach has paved the way for attending more closely to cultural variables such as *lifestyle, way of life, community, sociocultural quality of life, tribe,* and *values* in the discourse of risk science (e.g., Harris & Harper, 1997), especially in recognizing the systemic institutional relations that must change in remedying past injustices visited upon disadvantaged and marginalized peoples. No one's interests are served, however, when a risk evaluation has at its foundation an ill-conceived model of culture.

"RISK AND CULTURE" MODELS

In general, risk modelers appear to have two main choices about how to use the *culture* concept.

1. *Culture* constitutes one set of variables in an equation whose outcome is a measurement of "risk"—an adversarial approach that aims to allocate responsibility to various possible causal factors, or "affix blame" to individual actors (like polluters) within a territorial and economic system.
2. *Culture* is the encompassing context within which problems are framed—an approach that recognizes the spatial and economic interdependence of local and national interests and calls attention directly to the balance of national interests and local burdens.

Blame-Affixing Adversarial Model

The blame-affixing model treats *culture* as one set of variables in an equation that ultimately determines health risk. Two subspecies of this model exist, distinguished from one another by whether "risk" or "risk perceptions" are seen as the dependent variable. In the first variant of the blame-affixing adversarial model, what might be termed the *lifestyle variability* model, risk is a dependent variable. That is, variability in the risk of health hazards depends on lifestyle variability, and cultural group affiliation is directly and uniformly associated with lifestyle (see, for example, work by Harris & Harper, 1997, on Native Americans and Hanford and the Wisconsin Tribes Comparative Risk Project, United States Environmental Protection Agency, 1992). When this approach is used in the pursuit of risk attribution, a careful treatment of the concept *culture* is necessary if one is to properly characterize within-group variability in patterned behavior that may result in differential exposures.

In the second variant of the blame-affixing model, what might be termed the *perceptual distortions* model, it is perceptions of risk that are held up as the dependent variable because of heuristics, biases, and other cognitive sources of distortion in probabilistic reasoning that are associated with group affiliation. Prominently associated with this line of work are Paul Slovic, Baruch Fischhoff, and their colleagues; Vince Covello and his colleagues; Daniel Kahneman; and Amos Taversky; among others. If this approach is adhered to, primarily as a basis for designing educational campaigns and other information-based interventions aimed at adjusting public thinking about risk attribution, an explicit treatment of the culture concept is central to understanding the reasoning that people apply in arriving at or justifying their risk-related judgments.

Beyond-Blame Model

A contrasting model of risk employs the culture concept in a different way. This can be termed the "beyond blame" model. Rather than assuming *culture* to have a monolithic, static, one-to-one correspondence with a local population, culture is regarded as the more encompassing context in which local problems are framed (e.g., Douglas & Wildavsky, 1982; Rayner & Cantor, 1987). This culture concept recognizes the spatial and economic interdependence of local and national interests and explicitly brings to the surface such nontraditional risk-related notions as the balance of national interests and local burdens.

As highlighted in Table 9.1, the virtues of the beyond-blame model should be apparent. The ultimate goal in making decisions about how best to reduce risk is to do so *fairly*. Local values of fairness will prevail, and one should anticipate (rather than be surprised by or dismissive of) the potential that different local constituents will clash with respect to what they consider fair outcomes. If resolving conflicts over competing views of fairness is the outcome, then the problem to be structured is *not* one of affixing blame (who is at fault?). Instead, the problem is transforming an unproductive conflict into a productive one. To do so, specialists must relinquish sole authority on determining the legitimacy of problems raised, and it must be recognized that specialists' introspection is not an adequate substitute for direct observation of how potentially affected persons judge the burdens and benefits associated with deployment of risky technologies.

The relevant data that must be considered require an examination (rather than assumption) of the geographic extent of potential harm (e.g., Stoffle et al., 1991). One should not assume, a priori, that the potentially affected population is a monolithic group, the "culture-bearing" unit. For example, in the Columbia River Basin air, and watersheds contaminated by nuclear weapons fuel production, it would not be appropriate to lump together in a single cultural group all of Hanford's tribal neighbors (Wilkinson & Liebow, 1998). Instead, within-group variability should be examined empirically, with respect to knowledge and judgments concerning potential burdens and

Table 9.1
Three Dimensions of Contrast in Assessing Model Applications

Dimensions of Contrast	"Blame-Affixing"		"Beyond Blame"
	Lifestyle Variability	Perceptual Distortions	
Problem structuring techniques and degree of collaboration	• Refine assumptions about exposures but use conventional assumptions for estimating potency of contaminants. • Specialists guide exploration of exposure-related assumptions according to data input requirements.	• Subject assumptions about potency of contaminants to empirical investigation. • Apply introspection about "culture-bearing" unit associated with exposure variability. • Specialists determine relevant pathways, geographic extent of dispersion, and who should be concerned about that territory.	• Unproductive conflict is the problem; all assumptions and uncertainties need to be articulated. • Introspection is never an adequate substitute for observation. • Specialists *must* relinquish sole authority on determining the legitimacy of problems articulated.
Data input and analysis requirements	• Contaminant concentrations • Intake rates for contaminated media—often standardized for age- and gender-specific categories across broad populations • Exposure factors • Body weight—often standardized for age- and gender-specific categories across broad populations	• Potentially affected territory • Potentially affected population(s) • Within-group variability among affected populations—with respect to knowledge base and prompted judgments	• Potentially affected territory • Potentially affected population(s) • Within-group variability among affected populations—with respect to knowledge base and prompted judgments • Local observations regarding value orientations concerning time, consent, equity, liability • Protocols for local observation of chronic and cumulative exposure factors • Locally observed contaminant concentrations • Locally observed intake rates for contaminated media
Expected outputs	*Dose, Risk, and Uncertainty Estimates (Narrowly Construed)* • Reference doses • Standards (e.g., "No observed adverse effect levels" or "Lowest observed adverse effect levels") • Health outcome predictions • Clinical observations • Attribution	*Risk Communication Messages* • Tailored to vulnerable populations • Metamessage about attribution ("We share your pain but it's not our fault")	*Conflict Resolution* • Resource allocation versus survival issues • Use or ownership of resources • Precedent under conditions of uncertainty

benefits of the risky technologies, and also with respect to value orientations concerning:

- *Consent.* By what means are different sorts of joint actions agreed to? Different types of consent include, for example, implicit consent, agreement through deference to group leader authority, and explicit consent from "talking things out" or negotiating.
- *Equity.* By what principles of fairness are resources ideally allocated to address imbalances (e.g., proportionate to need, absolutely equal regardless of need, according to rank or status regardless of need).
- *Liability.* What happens if something goes wrong? Who will be held accountable for making restitution or compensation? Is this a shared responsibility, or placed at the feet of the party with the greatest ability to pay?
- *Time.* How far out into the future do contemporary events retain their salience? What constitutes locally relevant "everyday," "exceptional," and "in-between" events (Liebow, 1995).

Regardless of whether one adheres to the blame-affixing or beyond-blame models of risk and culture, one question concerning data relevance is of paramount importance: How well can aggregate behavioral data serve as a surrogate for local risk-inducing practices? As Giles and his colleagues (1988) demonstrated in the case of Australian aborigines and their traditional subsistence practices, Eurocentric assumptions about shelter, transportation, diet, and even children's games would divert attention away from potentially harmful pathways by which residual contamination might harm people who reoccupied ancestral lands adjacent to a former British nuclear test site. Specific attention needs to focus on localizing procedures (rather than taking national averages as representative of local practices) for observing chronic and cumulative exposures to multiple sources of environmental threat.

GROWTH AND SCARCITY

The fourth main theme of enduring interest to environmental anthropologists is the impact of population growth and mobility on natural resource scarcity. Some great puzzles in human history—for example, the decline of the Maya Empire, the Hohokam diaspora from the American Southwest—appear to have resulted from population growth and concentration outstripping the local resources. Recent analyses demonstrate how population growth is difficult to separate from a whole set of questions of economic and social development and from the environmental concerns related to the issues of production and consumption throughout the world (e.g., Lindahl-Kiessling & Landberg, 1994). Thus, factors underlying fertility changes are of interest not solely for their effects on family planning but also because of the implications for patterns of land use, settlement, and resource consumption. Further, anthropologists argue that certain patterns of environmental deterioration are affected not by market failures but by government policies, and it follows that the causes of these failures increasingly should be sought and addressed in the context of institutional analyses. They argue that the rapidly increasing stress on the world's natural resource base can, especially in the overpopulated areas of the world, create social tensions and conflicts between as well as within nations, and furthermore that such conflicts likely will occur before there is an ecological breakdown (Homer-Dixon, 1999; Homer-Dixon & Blitt, 1998; Poku & Graham 1998).

At the same time, it is scarcity that is the target phenomenon to be explained, not to be confounded with population growth. Resource scarcity is the product of an insufficient supply, too much demand, or an unequal distribution that forces some sector of a society into a condition of deprivation. These three sources of scarcity are in turn caused by variables such as population growth, economic development, and pollution. They interact in various ways—for example, declining supply can prompt one group to seize control of a resource, simultaneously forcing another group onto an ecologically marginal landscape.

Faced with growing scarcity, societies may experience health problems, social factionalism, and declines in agricultural and economic productivity. People may be compelled to move, often intensifying ethnic and other group identity tensions. Demands on government may increase while tax bases are being eroded. Violence may ensue or, if already present, worsen.

It is in this volatile, interactive, and complicated context that environmental scarcity can be described as a cause of conflict. Scarcity is not, Homer-Dixon stresses, likely to be a sufficient or necessary cause, but its growing presence in the causal network that generates violence is, he believes, clear and growing clearer.

SUMMARY AND CONCLUSIONS

From the anthropologist's perspective, there is much fertile ground for collaborative exploration with environmental psychologists. Although it appears that in the past, environmental psychologists have focused most heavily on intrapersonal processes and outcomes of individual cognition and decision making, solid new work has emerged in characterizing the interpersonal and social context in which individuals assign meaning to and, in turn, are influenced by natural forces. And while environmental anthropology has tackled some key questions of between-group variability, the field for the most part has avoided systematic examination of within-group or individual variability in traditional ecological knowledge, perceptions of risk and hazard, responses to such hazards, and choice making in fertility- and residential mobility-related decisions.

The practical payoff of an integrated approach, knowledge that makes a difference, can be seen in several policy domains already mentioned—bioconservation, disaster preparedness and response, and environmental health interventions. Management of natural resources for conservation's sake under fundamental conditions of uncertainty, rather than the previously presumed equilibrium of ecosystems, requires incremental responses with close monitoring by learning organizations. It suggests that research findings regarding organizational context can be applied to understanding how organizations "learn"—that is, structure problems, formulate plans, and incorporate monitoring observations into prescriptions for future action—and how people from different cultural backgrounds construct problems and monitor progress toward their resolution.

Disaster preparedness and response requires a clearer understanding of how vulnerability to hazards is socially produced, instead of assuming it to be randomly distributed across the landscape. Rather than blaming the victim for making bad choices (e.g., reoccupying flood-prone areas, clearcutting watersheds to the detriment of downstream settlements), these choices need to be linked to the context of more-encompassing institutions within which they are framed. Disputes over how best to reduce environmental health risks must be removed from the adversarial framework of seeking a polluter to blame and understood instead in the context of value orientations involving fairness, consent, time, and liability.

For applied researchers who have internalized the notion that context matters, it is appropriate to emphasize "problem structuring" because, especially in policy making, it is an article of faith that, if you start with the wrong formulation of the problem, you will end up with bad policy. In other words, *problem structuring is key to good policy.* And sound problem structuring is an important aim in adding an anthropologist to your policy-making team (Liebow, 1999). Anthropologists often fit quite comfortably in the role of "culture broker"—somebody who can act as a go-between in multicultural settings—and can help call attention to risks and impacts that might otherwise be discounted or ignored altogether.

In the case of environmental policy, the view of what causes degradation will have a great deal to do with how we try to avoid or mitigate the worst of these projected or observed impacts. As Tesh (1994) notes, at least three major arguments are advanced for environmental problems, each of which affixes responsibility to different agents. One view ascribes environmental degradation to population growth and consumerism, holding individuals responsible for destroying the environment because we do not see a link between our choices and their ecological impacts. The policy remedies are *educational*—if we teach people to consider the ecological consequences of their choices, we can save the Earth. Another view attributes environmental problems to the decisions made by owners and managers of industry and, more fundamentally, by the political and economic structure in which these decisions take place. The policy remedies here are *structural*—business owners and managers need to adopt different criteria for what to produce and how to produce it, and also become accountable to the public interest, not just their investors. And a third view holds government and technology responsible for environmental problems, because of inadequate laws and inefficient enforcement. The policy remedies derived from this view are *legal and organizational*—the institutions we trust to protect the public interest must have the tools and organizational capacity to wield them.

Selecting from among these alternative viewpoints a "right" and "wrong" notion of causality is beside the point. They each constitute an oversimplified model, whereas making a difference calls for just the opposite. What environmental anthropologists can contribute, in collaboration with our psychologist colleagues, of course, is an elaborated fund of knowledge that incorporates linked levels of institutional agency and temporal variability to take us beyond blame and towards productive conflict resolution.

REFERENCES

Agrawal, A. (1995). Dismantling the divide between indigenous and scientific knowledge. *Development and Change, 26,* 413–439.

Balée, W. (1999). Mode of production and ethnobotanical vocabulary: A controlled comparison of the Guajá and Ka'apor. In T. L. Grason & B. G. Blount (Eds.), *Ethnoecology: Knowledge, resources, and rights* (pp. 24–40). Athens: University of Georgia Press.

Barlett, P. (1982). *Agricultural choice and change: Decision making in a Costa Rican community.* New Brunswick, NJ: Rutgers University Press.

Barth, F. (1958). Ecological relationships of ethnic groups in Swat, North Pakistan. *American Anthropologist, 58,* 107–189.

Berlin, B. (1992). *Ethnobiological classification: Principles of categorization of plants and animals in traditional societies.* Princeton, NJ: Princeton University Press.

Biersack, A. (1999). From the "new ecology" to the new ecologies. *American Anthropologist, 101*(1), 5–18.

Carneiro, R. L. (1970). A theory of the origin of the state. *Science, 169,* 733–738.

Collier, G. A. (1975). *Fields of the Tzotzil: The ecological bases of tradition in highland Chiapas.* Austin: University of Texas Press.

Conklin, H. (1980). *Ethnographic atlas of Ifugao: A study of environment, culture, and society in northern Luzon.* New Haven, CT: Yale University Press.

Descola, P. (1994). *In the society of nature: A native ecology in Amazonia.* Cambridge: Cambridge University Press.

DeWalt, B., & Pelto, P. (Eds.). (1985). *Micro and macro levels of analysis in anthropology. Issues in theory and research.* Boulder, CO: Westview Press.

DeWalt, K., & DeWalt, B. R. (1992). Agrarian reform and the food crisis in Mexico: Microlevel and macrolevel processes. In J. J. Poggie Jr., B. DeWalt, & W. Dressler (Eds.), *Anthropological research process and application* (pp. 159–183). Albany: State University of New York Press.

Douglas, M. (1985). *Risk acceptability according to the social sciences* (Social Research Perspectives Occasional Report on Current Topics No. 11). New York: Russell Sage Foundation.

Douglas, M., & Wildavsky, A. (1982). *Risk and culture: An essay on the selection of technological and environmental dangers.* Berkeley: University of California Press.

Durham, W. (1995). The political ecology of environmental destruction in Latin America. In N. Painter & W. Durham (Eds.), *The social causes of tropical deforestation in Latin America* (pp. 249–264). Ann Arbor: University of Michigan Press.

Edgerton, R. (1992). *Sick societies: Challenging the myth of primitive harmony.* New York: Free Press.

Fischhoff, B., Svenson, O., & Slovic, P. (1987). Active responses to environmental hazards: Perceptions and decision-making. In D. Stokols & I. Altman (Eds.), *Handbook of environmental psychology* (pp. 1089–1133). New York: Wiley.

Folke, C., Berkes, F., & Colding, J. (1998). Ecological practices and social mechanisms for building resilience and sustainability. In F. Berkes & C. Folke (Eds.), *Linking social and ecological systems: Management practices and social mechanisms for building resilience* (pp. 414–436). Cambridge: Cambridge University Press.

Geertz, C. (1963). *Agricultural involution.* Berkeley: University of California Press.

Giles, M. S., Palmer, K., & Brady, M. A. (1988). Dose commitment estimates in an aboriginal community: Problem in rapidly changing social values. *Radiation protection in nuclear energy* (Vol. 1, pp. 173–179). Vienna, Austria: International Atomic Energy Agency.

Gottdiener, M. (1995). *Postmodern semiotics: Material culture and the forms of postmodern life.* Oxford: Blackwell.

Greaves, T. (1994). *Intellectual property rights for indigenous peoples: A source book.* Oklahoma City: Society for Applied Anthropology.

Green, E. C., Goodman, K. J., & Hare, M. (1999). Ethnobotany, intellectual property rights and benefit-sharing: The forest people's fund in Suriname. *Indigenous Knowledge and Development Monitor, 7*(1), 14–21.

Greene, L. S., & Danubio, M. E. (Eds.). (1997). *Adaptation to malaria: The interaction of biology and culture.* New York: Gordon and Breach.

Guha, R. (2000). *Environmentalism: A global history.* New York: Addison Wesley Longman.

Gunn, J. D. (Ed.). (1994). Global climate, human life: Physical contexts of historic landscapes [Special issue]. *Human Ecology, 22*(1).

Guyer, J., & Lambin, E. (1993). Land use in an urban hinterland: Ethnography and remote sensing in the study of African intensification. *American Anthropologist, 95*(4), 839–859.

Harries-Jones, P., Rotstein, A., & Peter, T. (1999). A signal failure: Ecology and economy after the Earth summit. In M. G. Schechter (Ed.). *Future multilateralism: The political and social framework* (pp. 101–135). Tokyo and New York: United Nations University Press.

Harris, S. G., & Harper, B. L. (1997). A Native American risk scenario. *Risk Analysis, 17*(6), 789–796.

Headland, T. (1997). Revisionism in ecological anthropology. *Current Anthropology, 38*(4), 605–625.

Homer-Dixon, T. (1999). *Environment, scarcity, and violence*. Princeton, NJ: Princeton University Press.

Homer-Dixon, T., & Blitt, J. (Eds.). (1998). *Ecoviolence: Links among environment, population, and security*. Lanham, MD: Rowman & Littlefield.

Hunn, E., & Selam, J. (1990). *Nch'iw·na, "the big river": Mid-Columbia Indians and their land*. Seattle: University of Washington Press.

Jacobs, M. E. (1993). *The green economy: Environment, sustainable development and the politics of the future*. Vancouver: University of British Columbia Press.

Kempton, W., Boster, J. S., & Hartley, J. A. (1995). *Environmental values in American culture*. Cambridge: Massachusetts Institute of Technology Press.

Kottak, C. (1999). The new ecological anthropology. *American Anthropologist, 101*(1), 23–25.

Kottak, C., & Colson, E. (1994). Multilevel linkages: Longitudinal and comparative studies. In R. Borofsky (Ed.), *Assessing cultural anthropology* (pp. 396–412). New York: McGraw-Hill.

Krech, S., III. (1999). *The ecological Indian: Myth and history*. New York: Norton.

Kroeber, A. L., & Kluckhohn, C. (1952). *Culture: A critical review of concepts and definitions*. New York: Vintage Books.

Latour, B. (1993). *We have never been modern* (C. Porter, Trans.). Cambridge, MA: Harvard University Press.

Leff, E. (1995). *Green production: Toward an environmental rationality* (M. Villanueva, Trans.). New York: Guilford Press.

Liebow, E. (1993). Who is expert at interpreting environmental hazards? A commentary on the disabling effects of an "expert/layperson" dichotomy. *The Environmental Professional 15*(3): 288–292.

Liebow, E. (1995). Inside the decision-making process: Ethnography and environmental risk management. In E. L. Cerroni-Long (Ed.), *Insider anthropology* (pp. 30–47). Washington, DC: American Anthropological Association.

Liebow, E. (1999, Spring). The heart of the problem: The local burden of national policies. *Common Ground*, 16–20.

Liebow, E. (2000). Environmental health. In L. Goldman (Ed.), *Social impact analysis: An applied anthropology manual* (pp. 233–256). Oxford: Berg Publishers.

Liebow, E., Bradbury, J. A., Branch, K. M., Heerwagen, J., Konkel, R. S., & Leyson, J. (1998). The landscape of reason: A scheme for representing arguments concerning environmental, health, and safety effects of chemical weapons disposal in the U.S. *High Plains Anthropologist, 18*(2), 115–126.

Lindahl-Kiessling, K., & Landberg, H. (Eds.). (1994). *Population, economic development, and the environment. The making of our common future*. Oxford: Oxford University Press.

Little, P. E. (1999). Environments and environmentalisms in anthropological research: Facing a new millennium. *Annual Review of Anthropology, 28*, 253–284.

Low, S. M. (1996). The anthropology of cities: Imagining and theorizing the city. *Annual Review of Anthropology, 25*, 383–409.

Martin, C. (1978). *The keepers of the game: Indian-animal relationships and the fur trade*. Berkeley: University of California Press.

Martin, C. (1992). *In the spirit of the Earth: Rethinking history and time*. Baltimore: Johns Hopkins University Press.

McGuire, T. (1997). The last northern cod. *Journal of Political Ecology, 4*, 41–54.

Mitchell, C. R. (1981). *The structure of international conflict*. New York: St. Martin's Press.

Moran, E. F. (1993). *Through Amazonian eyes: The human ecology of Amazonian populations*. Iowa City: University of Iowa Press.

Nabhan, G. P. (1982). *The desert smells like rain: A naturalist in Papago Indian country*. San Francisco: North Point Press.

Nabhan, G. P. (1985). *Gathering the dust*. Tucson: University of Arizona Press.

Nabhan, G. P. (1997). *Cultures of habitat: On nature, culture, and story*. Washington, DC: Counterpoint.

Nazarea, V. (1998). *Cultural memory and biodiversity*. Tucson: University of Arizona Press.

Netting, R. M. (1981). *Balancing on an Alp: Ecological change and continuity in a Swiss mountain community*. Cambridge: Cambridge University Press.

Oliver-Smith, A. (1996). Anthropological research on hazards and disasters. *Annual Review of Anthropology, 25*, 303–328.

Poku, N., & Graham, D. T. (Eds.). (1998). *Redefining security: Population movements and national security*. Westport, CT: Praeger.

Posey, D. A., & Balée, W. A. (Eds.). (1989). *Resource management in Amazonia: Indigenous and folk strategies* (Advances in Economic Botany Series, Vol. 7). New York: New York Botanical Garden.

Rappaport, R. A. (2000). *Pigs for the ancestors: Ritual in the ecology of a New Guinea people*. Prospect Heights, IL: Waveland Press. (Originally published 1968)

Rayner, S., & Cantor, R. (1987). How fair is safe enough?: The cultural approach to societal technological choice. *Risk Analysis, 7*(1), 3–9.

Rayner, S., & Malone, E. (Eds.). (1998). *Human choice and climate change*. Columbus, OH: Battelle Press.

Redford, K. H. (1990). The ecologically noble savage. *Orion, 9*(3), 22–37.

Ribeiro, G. L. (1994). *Transnational capitalism: Hydropolitics in Argentina.* Gainesville: University Press of Florida.

Ricoeur, P. (1980). *Hermeneutics and the human sciences.* Chicago: University of Chicago Press.

Rocheleau, D., Thomas-Slayter, B., & Wangari, E. (Eds.). (1996). *Feminist political ecology: Global issues and local experiences.* New York: Routledge.

Roosevelt, A. (1989). Resource management in Amazonia before the conquest: Beyond ethnographic projection. *Advances in Economic Botany, 7,* 30–62.

Ross, E. (1978). Food taboos, diet, and hunting strategy: The adaptation to animals in Amazon cultural ecology. *Current Anthropology, 19*(1), 1–36.

Sahlins, M. (1972). *Stone age economics.* Chicago: Aldine.

Said, E. (1983). *The world, the text, and the critic.* Cambridge, MA: Harvard University Press.

Scoones, I. (1999). New ecology and the social sciences: What prospects for a fruitful engagement? *Annual Review of Anthropology, 28,* 479–507.

Soulé, M., & Lease, G. (Eds.). (1995). *Reinventing nature?: Responses to postmodern deconstruction.* Washington, DC: Island Press.

Steward, J. (1955). *Theory of culture change: The methodology of multilinear evolution.* Urbana: University of Illinois Press.

Stoffle, R. W., Halmo, D. B., Evans, M. J., & Olmsted, J. E. (1990). Calculating the cultural significance of American Indian plants: Paiute and Shoshone ethnobotany at Yucca Mountain, Nevada. *American Anthropologist, 92*(2), 416–432.

Stoffle, R. W., Traugott, M. W., Stone, J. V., McIntyre, P. D., Jensen, F. V., & Davidson, C. C. (1991). Risk perception mapping. *American Anthropologist, 93*(3), 611–635.

Stokols, D. (1987). Conceptual strategies of environmental psychology. In D. Stokols & I. Altman (Eds.), *Hand-book of environmental psychology* (pp. 41–70). New York: Wiley.

Stonich, S. (1993). *"I am destroying the land": The political ecology of poverty and environmental destruction in Honduras.* Boulder, CO: Westview Press.

Tesh, S. (1994). Causal debates in environmentalism. *Journal of Public Health Policy, 15,* 298–309.

Townsend, P. (2000). *Environmental anthropology: From pigs to policies.* Prospect Heights, IL: Waveland Press.

United States Environmental Protection Agency. (1992). *Tribes at risk: The Wisconsin tribes comparative risk project* (Report No. EPA-230-R-92–017). Washington, DC: U. S. E. P. A., Office of Policy, Planning and Evaluation.

Vayda, A. P., & Walters, B. B. (1999). Against political ecology. *Human Ecology, 27*(1), 167–179.

Warren, D. M. (1993). Using IK for agriculture and rural development: Current issues and studies. *Indigenous Knowledge and Development Monitor, 1*(2), 6–7.

Wilkinson, J. R., & Liebow, E. (1998). Tribal involvement, tribal capacity, and historical dose reconstruction. In T. Takaro (Ed.), *Proceedings of the First Annual Health of the Hanford Site Conference, Richland, WA, December, 1997* (pp. 153–172). Seattle, WA: University of Washington School of Public Health.

Wittfogel, K. A. (1957). *Oriental despotism: A comparative study of total power.* New Haven, CT: Yale University Press.

Wolf, E. (1982). *Europe and the people without history.* Berkeley: University of California Press.

Wolfe, A. K., & Liebow, E. B. (Guest eds.). (1993). Communities at risk (Special issue). *The Environmental Professional, 15*(3), 237–333.

Wynne, B. (1996). May the sheep safely graze? A reflexive view of the expert-lay knowledge divide. In S. Lash, B. Szerszynski, & B. Wynne (Eds.), *Risk, environment, and modernity: Towards a new ecology* (pp. 44–83). Thousand Oaks, CA: Sage.

CHAPTER 10

Environmental Sociology

RILEY E. DUNLAP

ALTHOUGH THERE WAS SCATTERED sociological attention to both urban problems and natural resource issues prior to the 1970s, environmental sociology developed in that decade as sociology's own response to the emergence of environmental problems on the public agenda. At first, sociologists tended to limit their attention to analyzing societal response to environmental problems rather than examining the problems themselves. But as sociologists gradually paid more attention to environmental issues, a few began to look beyond societal attention to environmental problems to the underlying relationships between modern industrialized societies and the physical environments they inhabit as sources of these problems. The result was the emergence of environmental sociology as a recognized area of specialization.

This chapter provides an overview of this relatively new field. I will first discuss how and why environmental sociology represents a major departure from sociology's traditional neglect of environmental phenomena, then examine the key environmental foci of research in the field, next describe the field's institutionalization, and then review both traditional and more recent research emphases in the field. The former emphases involve analyses of societal awareness of environmental issues, while the latter involve work on the causes, impacts, and solutions of environmental problems. I end by briefly describing some current trends and debates within environmental sociology.

ENVIRONMENTAL SOCIOLOGY AND THE LARGER DISCIPLINE

Unlike the larger society, mainstream sociology in the 1970s was remarkably oblivious to the relevance of environmental matters. This disciplinary blindness stemmed from a long period of neglect of such matters stimulated by both the societal context and disciplinary traditions. The Durkheimian emphasis on explaining social phenomena only in terms of other "social facts" plus an aversion to earlier excesses of biological and geographical "determinisms" had led sociologists to ignore the physical world. These disciplinary traditions were further strengthened by sociology's emergence during an era of unprecedented growth and prosperity, which made limits to resource abundance and technological progress unimaginable, and increased urbanization, which reduced direct contact with the natural environment. With modern industrialized societies appearing to be increasingly independent of the biophysical world, sociology came to assume that the exceptional features of *Homo sapiens*—language, technology, science, and, more generally, culture—made these societies "exempt" from the constraints of nature (Catton & Dunlap, 1980). Thus, the task of sociology was to examine the uniquely social determinants of contemporary human life (Dunlap & Catton, 1979), but in the process the discipline adopted sociocultural determinism as its preferred form of explanation. Consequently, mainstream sociology offered infertile ground for planting sustained interest in the relations between societies and their biophysical environments.

It is not surprising, therefore, that efforts to establish environmental sociology as a legitimate and important area of inquiry included criticism of the larger discipline's blindness to environmental matters. Indeed, efforts to define and codify the field of environmental sociology were accompanied by explication and critique of the "human exemptionalism paradigm" (HEP) on which contemporary sociology was premised. While not denying that human beings are obviously an exceptional species, Catton and I argued that our special skills and capabilities nonetheless failed to exempt us from the constraints of the natural environment. Consequently, we suggested that the HEP should be replaced by a more ecologically sound perspective, a "new ecological paradigm" (NEP), that acknowledges the ecosystem dependence of human societies (Catton & Dunlap, 1978, 1980). We further argued that much of environmental sociology, particularly examinations of the relations between social and environmental phenomena, entailed at least implicit rejection of the HEP with its assumed irrelevance of nonsocial phenomena to modern societies (Dunlap & Catton, 1979, 1983).

Our call for replacing mainstream sociology's dominant paradigm with a more ecologically sound one has been a controversial feature of environmental sociology. Though regarded as a core element of the field's commitment to insuring that the material bases of modern societies are no longer neglected by sociology (Buttel, 1987), the call has been criticized for presumably deflecting efforts to utilize classical and mainstream theoretical perspectives in environmental sociology (Buttel, 1996, 1997). Fortunately, debate over the need for an ecological perspective versus the relevance of mainstream sociological theories has taken a new turn in recent years as several environmental sociologists have independently begun to develop ecologically informed versions of classical theoretical perspectives. Efforts to develop "green" versions of Durkheimian, Weberian, and especially Marxist macrosociologies as well as microlevel perspectives such as symbolic interactionism represent the integration of an ecological paradigm with classical theoretical traditions (see references in Dunlap, 1997).

Increasing awareness of the societal significance of ecological conditions has not only encouraged efforts to develop greener sociological theories but stimulated empirical research on societal-environmental relations. While the empirical thrust of environmental sociology thus represents at least implicit rejection of mainstream sociology's exemptionalist orientation by continually demonstrating the relevance of environmental phenomena in modern industrialized societies, the situation regarding adoption of an ecological paradigm or perspective is less clear. Some environmental sociologists follow Catton's (1980) lead in applying ecological theory and concepts to human societies (e.g., Fischer-Kowalski, 1997), and others employ an ecological perspective as an "orienting strategy" that encourages them to raise questions about issues such as the long-term sustainability of current consumption patterns in the wealthy nations (Redclift, 1996). However, other environmental sociologists express caution regarding the utility of ecological *theory* as a guiding framework for environmental sociology (Buttel, 1997) or disavow its utility altogether (Macnaghten & Urry, 1998). These differing orientations stem from the inherent ambiguities involved in applying concepts and findings from general ecology to human societies (Freese, 1997).

Environmental sociology is typically defined as the study of relations between human societies and their physical environments or, more simply, "societal-environmental interactions" (Dunlap & Catton, 1979). Such interactions include the ways in which humans influence the environment as well as the ways in which environmental conditions (often modified by human action) influence human affairs. Defining the field in this way, however, immediately raises the question as to what environmental sociologists take to be "the environment."

THE ENVIRONMENTAL FOCI OF THE FIELD

The environment is an enormously complex phenomenon and inherently difficult to conceptualize. This is reflected in work by environmental sociologists, who examine both "built" and "natural" environments (and the continuum in between) at levels ranging from the "micro," represented by housing, to the most "macro" of all—the global environment. This does not mean, however, that the diverse subjects studied by environmental sociologists are unrelated. As ecologists increasingly point out, the environment performs many services for human beings (Daily, 1997). At the risk of oversimplicity, we can sort these numerous services into three general types of functions that the environment or, more accurately, ecosystems serve for human societies (and all living species). Adopting this ecological perspective enables us to highlight the various aspects of the environment that environmental sociologists examine as well as to note some general trends in how these foci have changed over time (Dunlap, 1994).

To begin with, the environment provides us with the resources necessary for life, ranging from air and water to food to materials needed for shelter, transportation, and the vast range of economic goods we produce. Ecologists thus view the environment as providing the "sustenance base" for human societies, and we can also think of it as a "supply depot" for natural resources. Many environmental sociologists focus on issues surrounding the extraction, use, and/or conservation of various resources such as fossil fuels, forests, and fisheries. Second, in the process of consuming resources humans, like all species, produce "waste" products; indeed, humans produce a far greater quantity and variety of waste products than do any other species. The environment must serve as a "sink" or "waste repository" for these wastes, either absorbing or recycling them into useful or at least harmless substances. When the waste products exceed an environment's ability to absorb them, pollution results. A growing number of environmental sociologists examine social processes related to pollution problems, ranging from the generation of pollution to its social impacts. Finally, like all other species, humans must also have a place to live, and the environment provides our home—where we live, work, play, travel, and otherwise spend our lives. In the most general case, the planet Earth provides the home for our species. Thus, the third function of the environment is to provide a "living space" or habitat for human populations. Environmental sociologists have traditionally focused on a variety of living space issues ranging from housing to urban design.

When humans overuse an environment's ability to fulfill these three functions, "environmental problems" in the form of pollution, resource scarcities, and overcrowding and/or overpopulation are the result. Yet, not only must the environment serve all three functions for humans, but when a given environment is used for one function its ability to fulfill the other two is often impaired. Such conditions of functional competition often yield newer, more complex environmental problems (see Dunlap, 1994, for a more detailed analysis). Competition among environmental functions is obvious in conflicts between the living-space and waste-repository functions, since using an area for a waste site typically makes it unsuitable for living space. Similarly, if hazardous materials escape from a waste repository and contaminate the soil, water, or air, the area can no longer serve as a supply depot for drinking water or for growing agricultural products. Finally, converting farmland or forests into housing subdivisions creates more living space for people but means that the land can no longer function as a supply depot for food or timber (or as habitat for wildlife).

Understanding these three functions provides insight into the evolution of environmental problems and the major foci of environmental sociology. In the 1960s and early 1970s, when awareness of environmental problems was growing rapidly in the United States, primary attention was given to air and water pollution and the importance of protecting areas of natural beauty and recreational value. Sociological work on these topics thus joined the earlier emphasis on urban problems. The "energy crisis" of 1973 highlighted the dependence of modern industrialized nations on fossil fuels and raised the specter of resource scarcity in general, and the impacts of energy shortages became a major focus of sociologists. The living space function came to the fore in a new manner in the late 1970s when it was discovered that the Love Canal neighborhood was built on an abandoned chemical waste site that was leaking toxic materials, and this generated strong interest in local environmental hazards. More recently problems stemming from functional competition at huge geographical scales, ranging from deforestation and loss of biodiversity to the truly global-level phenomena of ozone depletion and global warming, have attracted increasing attention from sociologists.

The above examples of how human activities are harming the ability of the environment to serve as our supply depot, living space, and waste repository involve focusing on specific aspects of particular environments (e.g., a given river's ability to absorb wastes without becoming polluted). Technically, however, it is not "the environment" but "ecosystems" that provide these three functions for humans—and for all other living species. Furthermore, it is increasingly recognized that the health of entire ecosystems—including the global ecosystem—is being jeopardized as a result of growing human demands on them. Exceeding the capacity of a given ecosystem to fulfill one of the three functions may disrupt not only its ability to fulfill the other two but its ability to continue to function at all. Whereas historically the notion that human societies face "limits to growth" was based on the assumption that we would run out of food supplies or natural resources such as oil, nowadays the term *ecological limits* refers to the finite ability of the global ecosystem to serve all three functions simultaneously without having its own functioning impaired (see, e.g., Vitousek, Mooney, Lubchenco, & Melillo, 1997).

INSTITUTIONALIZATION OF ENVIRONMENTAL SOCIOLOGY

Sociological interest in the impact of energy and other resource scarcities accelerated the emergence of environmental sociology as a distinct area of inquiry by heightening awareness that "environment" was more than just another social problem and that environmental conditions could indeed have societal consequences (as well as the obvious fact that human activities could affect the environment). Studies of the societal impacts of energy shortages thus facilitated a transition from the early "sociology of environmental issues"—involving the use of standard sociological perspectives drawn from social movements, social psychology, social problems, and so forth to analyze societal responses to environmental issues—to a self-conscious "environmental sociology" focused explicitly on societal-environmental relations.*

The nascent environmental sociology of the 1970s was quickly institutionalized via formation of interest groups within U.S. national sociological associations. These groups provided an organizational base for the emergence of environmental sociology as a thriving area of specialization and attracted scholars interested in all aspects of the physical environment—from environmental activism to energy and

---

* Although Catton and I originally made the distinction between the sociology of environmental issues and environmental sociology to emphasize the need for studies of societal-environmental interactions (Dunlap & Catton, 1979), now that such studies have become common (Gramling & Freudenburg, 1996), we no longer feel the distinction is important and follow Buttel (1987) in equating environmental sociology with the work being done by self-identified environmental sociologists—regardless of its focus (Dunlap & Catton, 1994).

other natural resources, natural hazards and disasters, social impact assessment, and housing and the built environment (Dunlap & Catton, 1979, 1983). The late 1970s were a vibrant era of growth for American environmental sociology, but momentum proved difficult to sustain during the 1980s—as the Reagan era was a troublesome period for the field and social science more generally. Ironically, however, stimulated by major accidents such as those at Chernobyl and Bhopal, India, and growing evidence of global environmental change, sociological interest in environmental issues was taking root internationally. By the late 1980s and 1990s environmental sociology was not only reinvigorated in the United States but was being institutionalized in countries around the world and within the International Sociological Association (see Dunlap, 1997, and other chapters in Redclift & Woodgate, 1997).

SOCIETAL AWARENESS OF ENVIRONMENTAL PROBLEMS

The emergence of "environment" on the U.S. national agenda in the late 1960s and early 1970s led sociologists to study factors that contributed to environmental quality becoming recognized as a social problem. While there were a few early efforts to analyze the overall processes involved (e.g., Albrecht, 1975), most studies focused on specific factors such as environmentalism. The environmental movement played the major role in placing the environment on the nation's agenda, and studies of environmentalism were a primary emphasis of early sociological work not only in North America but subsequently in Europe, South America, and Asia as well. The growth of public awareness and concern stimulated by environmental activists also received a good deal of attention. These two emphases have continued over time, while in recent decades attention to the roles played by the media and especially science in generating societal attention to environmental problems has increased. In combination, such work has contributed to an improved understanding of the ways in which environmental problems are socially constructed.

ENVIRONMENTALISM

In the United States the modern environmental movement evolved out of the older conservation movement and the social activism of the 1960s, and sociologists helped document this evolution. Early studies focused heavily on what kinds of people joined environmental organizations. It was consistently found that large national organizations like the Sierra Club drew members who were above average in socioeconomic status, predominately white, and heavily urban. While this pattern led to charges of elitism, it was noted that most voluntary and political organizations have similar membership profiles and that environmental activists were hardly economic elites (Mertig, Dunlap, & Morrison, 2002).

Gradually sociologists shifted more attention to the organizational level and examined the large national organizations like the Sierra Club and Natural Resources Defense Council. Special attention was given to their strategies and tactics, especially their efforts to influence national policy making via lobbying and litigation and their successful use of direct mail advertising to recruit a large but only nominally involved membership base (Mitchell, 1979). Most of these organizations grew rapidly in the late 1960s and early 1970s and ended up following a typical pattern observed for social movement organizations: As they became larger and more successful in the political arena they also became more bureaucratic, professionalized, unresponsive to their memberships, willing to compromise, and conservative in their tactics (Mertig et al., 2002).

One result is that by the 1980s, as more and more communities discovered environmental hazards in their communities, a large number of local, grassroots organizations formed independently of the mainstream national organizations and generated a new strand of the environmental movement (Szasz, 1994). The discovery that a disproportionate share of environmental hazards often occurred in minority communities led to charges of environmental racism and emergence of an "environmental justice" movement distinct from the grassroots environmentalism centered in white, blue-collar communities (Taylor, 2000). And finally, frustration over mainstream environmentalism's tendency to compromise and work within the political system gave rise to a "radical" wing of environmentalism—epitomized previously by Earth First! and now by the Earth Liberation Front—that relies on direct action such as protests, sit-ins, and acts of "ecotage" (Mertig et al., 2002).

Besides describing and analyzing the organizational complexity and dynamics of contemporary environmentalism, sociologists have recently conducted long-term historical analyses of the growth of conservation/environmental organizations and of the increasingly diverse set of environmentally relevant discourses to document the evolution of modern environmentalism out of traditional conservation concerns (Brulle, 2000). Also receiving a good deal of attention has been the emergence of environmental movements and Green parties in Europe and, more recently, in Asia and Latin America (see Redclift & Woodgate, 1997, part III). In general these studies have shed light on how environmentalism has become a potent political force within many nations as well as at the international level.

ENVIRONMENTAL AWARENESS AND CONCERN

As environmental problems gained a foothold on the public agenda, both public opinion pollsters and social scientists began conducting surveys to examine levels of public awareness of environmental problems and support for environmental protection efforts. Initial efforts were confined to documenting growing levels of public awareness and concern for the environment among residents of the United States and other wealthy nations and to examining variation in environmental concern across differing sectors of society—comparing levels by education, age, and residence for example (Albrecht, 1975). Gradually a good deal of attention was paid to documenting the social correlates of environmental concern, and summaries of available findings indicated that age, education, and political ideology were the best predictors, with young adults, the well educated, and political liberals being more concerned than their counterparts. Urban residents and women were also often found to be more environmentally concerned than rural residents and men, although these relationships varied with the measure of environmental concern employed (Jones & Dunlap, 1992). Eventually longitudinal studies of environmental concern were conducted, tracking trends in public awareness of environmental problems and support for environmental protection over long periods of time. A few studies also examined correlates of environmental concern with longitudinal data, finding them to be relatively stable over long periods of time (Jones & Dunlap, 1992).

Although the above studies have provided useful information on the distribution and evolution of environmental concern among citizens of the United States and other developed nations, they often employ single-item indicators or other simple measures and shed little light on the nature of environmental concern. Gradually more attention was paid to the conceptualization and measurement of environmental concern, and sociologists and other scholars developed a wide range of measures of this concept (Dunlap & Jones, 2002). One set of measures grew out of efforts to conceptualize the emergence of environmentalism as representing a "new paradigm or worldview" that challenged the "dominant social paradigm" within industrialized nations. The "New Environmental Paradigm Scale," which measures core ecological beliefs such as the existence of ecological limits and the importance of maintaining the balance of nature, has become widely used both as a measure of endorsement of an ecological worldview and of environmental concern more generally (see Dunlap, Van Liere, Mertig, & Jones, 2000, for a revised NEP Scale).

Other sociological contributions have been the development of a norm activation model of environmental concern and behavior and insightful studies of the attitude-behavior relationship in the environmental domain. Such work has contributed significantly to current efforts to measure, predict, and explain proenvironmental attitudes and behaviors (Stern, 2000). A more recent contribution of sociologists has been to extend work on public attitudes toward the environment beyond North American and European nations to the international level, and a key finding is that citizen concern for the environment is not limited to wealthy nations as often assumed but has diffused throughout most of the world (Dunlap & Mertig, 1995).

In short, sociological studies of environmental concern have documented high levels of public awareness and concern over environmental quality, a crucial aspect of the emergence of environment as a social problem. These studies have shown that unlike most social problems, environmental problems have proved to have considerable staying power at least partly because the public's concern over them has not (despite ups and downs) faded away.

MEDIA AND SCIENCE

It is widely assumed that the media play a vital role in setting the policy agenda, and sociologists among others have examined the role of newspapers in generating societal attention to environmental problems. In general, it has been found that public newspaper coverage of environmental issues increased dramatically throughout the late 1960s and reached an early peak at the time of the first Earth Day in 1970, presumably contributing to the concomitant rise in public concern during the same period (Schoenfeld, Meier, & Griffin, 1979). More recently, Mazur (1998) has shown how changing patterns of media coverage of global environmental problems such as ozone depletion and global warming appear to have influenced the waxing and waning of attention given to such problems by policy makers.

It was common for sociologists to credit Rachel Carson's *Silent Spring* and other scientific contributions in accounting for the rapid emergence of societal attention to environmental problems in the 1960s, and Mitchell (1979) highlighted the dual emphasis on science and litigation in newer environmental organizations such as the Environmental Defense Fund and the Natural Resources Defense Council. However, detailed analysis of the significant role played by science in environmental issues has emerged as a major emphasis in environmental sociology only in the past decade or so. Yearley (1991), for example, has noted the ambivalent role of science vis-à-vis environmentalism: On the one hand, scientific discoveries are crucial in detecting and often in solving environmental problems; on the other hand, science-driven technological developments are often major generators of such problems. Furthermore, while some scientists are often strong allies of environmentalists, others end up as opponents defending government or industry. Such insights have led environmental sociologists to focus more broadly on the role of environmental science in generating societal interest in environmental issues, including analyzing how scientists frame the nature of the problems and thereby their presumed causes and potential solutions (Buttel & Taylor, 1992).

SOCIAL CONSTRUCTION OF ENVIRONMENTAL PROBLEMS

Sociologists have long argued that social conditions do not become social "problems" unless they are defined as such by claims makers—typically activists, scientists, or policy makers—who are then successful in having their definitions legitimated and publicized by the media and thereby placed onto the public agenda. Environmental sociologists have applied this "social constructionist" perspective to a wide range of environmental problems, highlighting the crucial roles played by environmental activists, scientists, and the media in getting the public and eventually policy makers to see environmental conditions as problems deserving attention and amelioration. Some have synthesized relevant work on environmentalism, environmental science, media attention, and public opinion into detailed models of the social construction of environmental problems, and in the process they have demonstrated why environmental quality has remained a significant social issue for over three decades (Hannigan, 1995; see also Albrecht, 1975; Yearley, 1991).

CURRENT RESEARCH EMPHASES

The foregoing work on societal awareness of environmental problems can technically be considered as exemplifying the sociology of environmental issues, but in recent decades it has become common to find research that clearly involves investigations of societal-environmental interactions or relations (Gramling & Freudenbrug, 1996; for more examples see Dunlap & Michelson, 2001). Rather than try to provide a comprehensive review of such work, in what follows I will focus on environmental sociologists' contributions to three particularly important theoretical and policy-relevant topics: the causes of environmental problems, the impacts of such problems, and the solutions to these problems.

CAUSES OF ENVIRONMENTAL PROBLEMS

Given that environmental sociology emerged in response to increased recognition of environmental problems, it is not surprising that a good deal of work in the field has been devoted to trying to explain the origins of environmental degradation. Much of the early work involved analyses and critiques of the rather simplistic views of the causes of environmental degradation that predominated in the literature, rather than original research. The need for such analyses stemmed from the fact that popular conceptions of the origins of environmental problems tended to emphasize the importance of single factors, such as population growth (emphasized by Paul Ehrlich) or technological development (stressed by Barry Commoner), rather than recognizing the multiplicity of factors involved, and also to ignore or simplify the distinctively social causes of environmental degradation. In this context, environmental

sociologists tended to explicate the competing range of explanations (Dunlap & Catton, 1983) and to criticize the most widely accepted ones for their shortcomings (Schnaiberg, 1980).

The most powerful sociological critique of common conceptions of the origins of environmental problems in general and of those by biologists such as Ehrlich and Commoner in particular was provided by Schnaiberg (1980). Schnaiberg criticized Ehrlich's view by noting the enormous variation in environmental impact between populations of rich and poor nations as well as between the wealthy and poor sectors within individual nations, and he emphasized that population growth is interrelated with factors such as poverty, which induces poor people to have more children for workforce and security reasons. Similarly, Commoner's perspective was criticized for viewing technology as an autonomous force, ignoring the degree to which technological developments are driven by political and especially economic forces—particularly the need for profit and capital accumulation.

Besides demonstrating the oversimplification involved in attributing environmental degradation to either population or technology, Schnaiberg also critiqued a third factor widely mentioned as a cause— the wasteful lifestyles of consumers. In particular, Schnaiberg distinguished between the production and consumption spheres of society and argued that the former is the more crucial contributor to environmental degradation. Attributing environmental degradation to the affluence of consumers ignores the fact that decisions made in the production realm (e.g., as to what types of transportation will be available to consumers) are far more significant than are the purchasing behaviors of individual consumers. Consequently, Schnaiberg emphasized the "treadmill of production," or the inherent need of market-based economic systems to grow and the powerful coalition of capital, state, and labor supporting such growth, as the most fundamental contributor to environmental degradation.

While Schnaiberg's analysis, which he has continued to update and refine (see, e.g., Schnaiberg & Gould, 1994), has become highly influential within environmental sociology (Buttel, 1987, 1996, 1997), it has proven difficult to translate into concrete empirical research beyond local case studies of organized opposition to treadmill processes (Gould, Schnaiberg, & Weinberg, 1996). Consequently, a new generation of sociological analyses, while cognizant of Schnaiberg's insights, has adopted a broader framework for investigating the causes of crucial environmental problems, particularly pressing global problems.

Ironically, one line of this new work has involved revisiting the Ehrlich-Commoner debate over the relative importance of population and technological factors in generating environmental degradation. As their debate progressed, both sides realized that they could not totally ignore the other's preferred cause, or more distinctively social factors, and the debate became encapsulated in differing interpretations of a simple formulation known as the "IPAT" equation. Both Ehrlich and Commoner came to agree that Environmental impact = Population × Affluence × Technology, although debate continued over which factor on the right side of the equation had the most impact on environmental degradation (see Dietz & Rosa, 1994, and Dunlap, Lutzenhiser, & Rosa, 1994, for more on this debate).

In recent years environmental sociologists have begun to reassess the IPAT model's utility, particularly for examining the causal forces generating global-level environmental problems such as tropical deforestation and climate change. Taking into account earlier critiques of the IPAT model, Dietz and Rosa (1994) have proposed a major revision that they label STIRPAT, for "stochastic impacts by regression on population, affluence, and technology." While this model can be applied to any environmental impact, the initial application has been to global climate change, where it was used to estimate CO_2 emissions (Dietz & Rosa, 1997). Tropical deforestation is another global-level problem that has attracted increasing attention by environmental sociologists seeking to understand its causes. Studies by Rudel and his colleagues (e.g., Rudel & Roper, 1997) employ a variety of theoretical models encompassing the elements of the IPAT model as well as other key sociological and environmental variables to predict national variation in deforestation.

Sociological studies of global-level problems such as deforestation and emissions of greenhouse gases, both of which directly contribute to global climate change, are yielding important findings as well as conceptual and methodological strategies for developing a better understanding of the driving forces producing global environmental change and other environmental problems. As such, they represent an important supplement to natural-science research programs on these topics and complement sociological work on local-level problems such as community hazards (Freudenburg, 1997).

IMPACTS OF ENVIRONMENTAL PROBLEMS

As noted earlier, environmental sociology was just emerging at the time of the 1973 to 1974 energy crisis, so it is not surprising that identifying real as well as potential social impacts of energy and other natural resources was emphasized in this early period. While diverse impacts—from regional migration to consumer lifestyles—were investigated, heavy emphasis was placed on investigating the "equity" impacts of both energy shortages and the policies designed to ameliorate them (Rosa, Machlis, & Keating, 1988). A general finding was that both the problems and policies often had regressive impacts, with the lower socioeconomic strata bearing a disproportionate cost due to rising energy costs (Schnaiberg, 1975).

Equity has been a persistent concern in environmental sociology, and researchers gradually shifted their attention to the distribution of exposure to environmental hazards (ranging from air and water pollution to hazardous wastes). A consistent finding has been that exposure to environmental hazards is generally negatively correlated with socioeconomic status. Many studies have also found that minority populations are disproportionately exposed to environmental hazards in part because of their lower-than-average socioeconomic levels but perhaps also because of conscious decisions to locate hazardous sites in minority communities. Such findings, which a few recent studies have challenged, have led to charges of "environmental racism" and efforts to achieve "environmental justice" (Taylor, 2000). At a broader level, international equity is attracting the attention of environmental sociologists who are investigating the export of polluting industries from wealthy to poor nations, the disproportionate contribution of wealthy nations to many global-level problems, and the consequent hurdles these phenomena pose for international cooperation to solve environmental problems (Redclift & Sage, 1998).

Sociologists have not limited themselves to investigating the equity impacts of environmental problems, and studies of communities exposed to technological or human-made hazards (such as Love

Canal) offer particularly rich portrayals of the diverse impacts caused by environmental and technological hazards. Whereas natural disasters—such as floods, hurricanes, and earthquakes—have been found to result in a therapeutic response in which communities unite in efforts to help victims, repair damage, and reestablish life as it was before the disaster struck, technologically induced disasters have been found to have very different impacts (Freudenburg, 1997). Although a putative hazard may appear obvious to those who feel affected by it, the ambiguities involved in detecting and assessing such hazards often generate a pattern of intense community conflict. Unlike those affected by *natural* hazards, these victims often find themselves at odds not only with public officials but also with other residents who fail to acknowledge the seriousness of the hazard (for fear of economic loss in terms of property values, jobs, etc.). In many cases, such conflicts have resulted in a long-term erosion of community life as well as exacerbation of the victims' personal traumas stemming from their exposure to the hazards (Couch & Kroll-Smith, 1985).

SOLUTIONS TO ENVIRONMENTAL PROBLEMS

As was true for research on the causes of environmental problems, early work by environmental sociologists interested in solutions to these problems often involved explications and critiques of predominant approaches. Early on, Heberlein (1974) noted the United States' predilection for solving environmental problems via a "technological fix," or developing and applying new technologies to solve problems such as pollution or energy shortages. Understandably popular in the United States, with its history of technological progress, such a solution is appealing because it makes it possible to avoid mandating behavioral and institutional change. Unfortunately, solving problems with new technologies sometimes creates even more problems, as illustrated by attempts to solve energy shortages with nuclear power. Consequently, as the seriousness and pervasiveness of environmental problems became more obvious, a variety of "social fixes," or efforts to change individual and institutional behaviors, have received attention.

Expanding on Heberlein's analysis, other sociologists (e.g., Dunlap, et al., 1994) have identified three broad types of social fixes or implicit policy types: (1) the cognitive (or knowledge) fix, which assumes that information and persuasion will suffice to produce the necessary changes in behavior—illustrated by campaigns encouraging energy conservation and recycling; (2) a structural fix, which relies on laws and regulations that mandate behavioral change—reflected in highway speed limits or mandatory water conservation; and (3) an intermediary behavioral fix that employs incentives and disincentives to encourage changes in behavior, as illustrated by pollution taxes (penalties) and tax credits (rewards) for installing pollution abatement technology (see Gardner & Stern, 1996, for a more refined typology of policy approaches and detailed examples of each).

Environmental sociologists in conjunction with other behavioral scientists have conducted a variety of studies that bear on the efficacy of these differing strategies for solving environmental problems, ranging from field experiments to test the effectiveness of information campaigns in inducing energy and water conservation to evaluations of alternative strategies for generating participation in recycling programs (see Gardner & Stern, 1996, for a good summary). A noteworthy sociological study was Derksen and Gartrell's (1993) investigation of recycling in Edmonton, Alberta, Canada, that found that individuals' level of environmental concern was not as important in predicting recycling behavior as was ready access to a curbside recycling program. While sociologists have conducted numerous field experiments and evaluations of community environmental and conservation programs, typically investigating the efficacy of one or more of the previously noted "fixes" (Lutzenhiser, 1993), they have generally left examinations of national and international environmental policy making to political scientists and economists. However, some sociologists have recently begun paying attention to efforts to negotiate international agreements to achieve reduction of greenhouse gases (Redclift & Sage, 1998), and we expect more sociological work along these lines.

CURRENT TRENDS AND CONTROVERSIES

As the foregoing illustrates, environmental sociology not only emerged in response to societal attention to environmental problems but has focused much of its energy on understanding these problems, especially their causes, impacts, and solutions. The field has proved to be more than a passing fad, becoming well institutionalized and also increasingly internationalized. But in the process, fundamental assumptions that once served to unify the field—agreement over the reality of environmental degradation; diagnoses of such degradation as inherent to modern, industrialized societies; and the sense that mainstream sociology is largely blind to the significance of environmental matters—have recently become matters of debate (Buttel, 1996).

The emergence of environmental problems provided the raison d'etre for environmental sociology, and the seriousness of such problems was seldom challenged. While environmental sociologists from the outset paid attention to how environmental problems are socially constructed (e.g., Albrecht, 1975), such efforts seldom questioned the objective existence of the problems. In recent years, however, environmental sociology has felt the effects of the larger discipline's turn toward more cultural/interpretative orientations. A growing number of scholars, particularly in Europe, have not only highlighted the contested nature of claims about environmental problems but—in the postmodern tradition—concluded that there is no reason for privileging the claims of any party to these debates—including those of environmental scientists (Macnaghten & Urry, 1998). Such work has led to the emergence of a strong constructionist orientation in environmental sociology that challenges the objectivist/realist perspective that has traditionally been dominant. These differing orientations have led to debate among environmental sociologists over the relative merits of the two approaches; fortunately, promising syntheses are beginning to emerge (Rosa, 1998).

Another source of current debate is the inevitability of continued environmental degradation. Whereas environmental sociologists have traditionally seen the drive toward capital accumulation inherent in industrialized societies as making environmental degradation inevitable (as epitomized by Schnaiberg's "treadmill of production" argument), recently European scholars have suggested that this may not be the case. Obvious successes in environmental amelioration within advanced European nations have led them to build upon economic models of "industrial ecology," which suggest that modernization of industrial processes can permit production with ever decreasing levels of material input and pollution output, to herald a new era of "ecological modernization" (Mol & Sonnenfeld, 2000). This perspective not only adopts a more sanguine image of the future of industrialized societies, but, as Buttel (1996) notes, involves a shift in focus for environmental sociology:

from a preoccupation with the origins of environmental degradation to efforts to explain the institutionalization of environmental amelioration (via technological innovation, policy incentives, pressures from citizens' groups, etc.). Ecological modernization has proven to be a controversial perspective that promises to stimulate continuing debate (Buttel, 2000).

The recent trends toward adoption of more-constructionist/interpretative frameworks and models of ecological modernization are related to a third trend in environmental sociology, the ongoing reassessment of its relationship to the larger discipline. As noted earlier, the emergence of environmental sociology was marked by criticism of mainstream sociology's neglect of the ecosystem dependence of modern industrialized societies and consequent inattention to the challenge posed by environmental problems. But in the past decade environmental problems, particularly global-level threats like climate change, have caught the attention of growing numbers of eminent sociologists, such as Giddens (1990), who have recognized that these problems cannot be ignored in analyses of the future course of industrial societies. Greater interaction between environmental and mainstream sociology has resulted, and this is producing considerable debate and self-reflection among environmental sociologists concerning the uniqueness of their field relative to the larger discipline. As a maturing and securely established field, environmental sociology will surely profit from this internal debate and the two prior ones as well.

REFERENCES

Albrecht, S. L. (1975). The environment as a social problem. In A. L. Mauss (Ed.), *Social problems as social movements* (pp. 566–605). Philadelphia: J.P. Lippincott.

Brulle, R. J. (2000). *Agency, democracy, and nature.* Cambridge, MA: MIT Press.

Buttel, F. H. (1987). New directions in environmental sociology. *Annual Review of Sociology, 13,* 465–488.

Buttel, F. H. (1996). Environmental and resource sociology: Theoretical issues and opportunities for synthesis. *Rural Sociology, 61,* 56–76.

Buttel, F. H. (1997). Social institutions and environmental change. In M. Redclift & G. Woodgate (Eds.), *The international handbook of environmental sociology* (pp. 40–54). Cheltenham, England: Edward Elgar.

Buttel, F. H. (2000). Ecological modernization as social theory. *Geoforum, 31,* 57–65.

Buttel, F. H., & Taylor, P. J. (1992). Environmental sociology and global environmental change: A critical reassessment. *Society and Natural Resources, 5,* 211–230.

Catton, W. R., Jr. (1980). *Overshoot: The ecological basis of revolutionary change.* Urbana: University of Illinois Press.

Catton, W. R., Jr., & Dunlap, R. E. (1978). Environmental sociology: A new paradigm. *The American Sociologist, 13,* 41–49.

Catton, W. R., Jr., & Dunlap, R. E. (1980). A new ecological paradigm for post-exuberant sociology. *American Behavioral Scientist, 24,* 15–47.

Couch, S. R., & Kroll-Smith, J. S. (1985). The chronic technical disaster: Toward a social scientific perspective. *Social Science Quarterly, 66,* 564–575.

Daily, G. C. (Ed.). (1997). *Nature's services: Social dependence on natural ecosystems.* Washington, DC: Island Press.

Derksen, L., & Gartrell, J. (1993). The social context of recycling. *American Sociological Review, 58,* 434–442.

Dietz, T., & Rosa, E. A. (1994). Rethinking the environmental impacts of population, affluence and technology. *Human Ecology Review, 1,* 277–300.

Dietz, T., & Rosa, E. A. (1997). Effects of population and affluence on CO_2 emissions. *Proceedings of the National Academy of Sciences, 94,* 175–179.

Dunlap, R. E. (1994). The nature and causes of environmental problems: A socio-ecological perspective. In Korean Sociological Association (Ed.), *Environment and development* (pp. 45–84). Seoul, South Korea: Seoul Press.

Dunlap, R. E. (1997). The evolution of environmental sociology. In M. Redclift & G. Woodgate (Eds.), *The international handbook of environmental sociology* (pp. 21–39). Cheltenham, England: Edward Elgar.

Dunlap, R. E., & Catton, W. R., Jr. (1979). Environmental sociology. *Annual Review of Sociology, 5,* 243–273.

Dunlap, R. E., & Catton, W. R., Jr. (1983). What environmental sociologists have in common (whether concerned with "built" or "natural" environments). *Sociological Inquiry, 53,* 113–135.

Dunlap, R. E., & Catton, W. R., Jr. (1994). Struggling with human exemptionalism: The rise, decline and revitalization of environmental sociology. *The American Sociologist, 25,* 5–30.

Dunlap, R. E., & Jones, R. E. (2002). Environmental concern: Conceptual and measurement issues. In R. E. Dunlap & W. Michelson (Eds.), *Handbook of environmental sociology.* Westport, CT: Greenwood Press.

Dunlap, R. E., Lutzenhiser, L. A., & Rosa, E. A. (1994). Understanding environmental problems: A sociological perspective. In B. Burgenmeier (Ed.), *Economy, environment, and technology* (pp. 27–49). Armonk, NY: M.E. Sharpe.

Dunlap, R. E., & Mertig, A. G. (1995). Global concern for the environment: Is affluence a prerequisite? *Journal of Social Issues, 51,* 121–137.

Dunlap, R. E., & Michelson, W. (Eds.). (2002). *Handbook of environmental sociology.* Westport, CT: Greenwood Press.

Dunlap, R. E., Van Liere, K. D., Mertig, A. G., & Jones, R. E. (2000). Measuring endorsement of the new ecological paradigm: A revised NEP scale. *Journal of Social Issues, 56,* 425–442.

Fischer-Kowalski, M. (1997). Society's metabolism. In M. Redclift & G. Woodgate (Eds.), *The international handbook of environmental sociology* (pp. 119–137). Cheltenham, England: Edward Elgar.

Freese, L. (1997). *Environmental connections.* In *Advances in human ecology* (Supplement 1 [Part B]). Greenwich, CT: JAI Press.

Freudenburg, W. R. (1997). Contamination, corrosion and the social order: An overview. *Current Sociology, 45,* 41–57.

Gardner, G. T., & Stern, P. C. (1996). *Environmental problems and human behavior.* Boston: Allyn & Bacon.

Giddens, A. (1990). *The consequences of modernity.* Stanford, CA: Stanford University Press.

Gould, K. A., Schnaiberg, A., & Weinberg, A. S. (1996). *Local environmental struggles: Citizen activism in the treadmill of production.* Cambridge: Cambridge University Press.

Gramling, R., & Freudenburg, W. R. (1996). Environmental sociology: Toward a paradigm for the 21st century. *Sociological Spectrum, 16,* 347–370.

Hannigan, J. A. (1995). *Environmental sociology: A social constructionist perspective.* London: Routledge.

Heberlein, T. (1974). The three fixes: Technological, cognitive and structural. In D. R. Field, J. C. Barron, & B. F. Long (Eds.), *Water and community development: Social and economic perspectives* (pp. 279–296). Ann Arbor, MI: Ann Arbor Science.

Jones, R. E., & Dunlap, R. E. (1992). The social bases of environmental concern: Have they changed over time? *Rural Sociology, 57,* 28–47.

Klausner, S. A. (1971). *On man in his environment.* San Francisco, Jossey-Bass.

Lutzenhiser, L. (1993). Social and behavioral aspects of energy use. *Annual Review of Energy and the Environment, 18,* 247–289.

Macnaghten, P., & Urry, J. (1998). *Contested natures.* London: Sage.

Mazur, A. (1998). Global environmental change in the news: 1987–90 vs. 1992–96. *International Sociology, 13,* 457–472.

Mertig, A. G., Dunlap, R. E., & Morrison, D. E. (2002). The environmental movement in the United States. In R. E. Dunlap & W. Michelson (Eds.), *Handbook of environmental sociology.* Westport, CT: Greenwood Press.

Mitchell, R. C. (1979). National environmental lobbies and the apparent illogic of collective action. In C. S. Russell (Ed.), *Collective decision making* (pp. 87–136). Baltimore, MD: Johns Hopkins University Press.

Mol, A. P. J., & Sonnenfeld, D. A. (Eds.). (2000). *Ecological modernisation around the world: Perspectives and critical debates.* Essex, England: Frank Cass.

Redclift, M. (1996). *Wasted: Counting the costs of global consumption.* London: Earthscan.

Redclift, M., & Sage, C. (1998). Global environmental change and global inequality: North/South perspectives. *International Sociology, 13,* 499–516.

Redclift, M., & Woodgate, G. (Eds.). (1997). *The international handbook of environmental sociology.* Cheltenham, England: Edward Elgar.

Rosa, E. A. (1998). Metatheoretical foundations for postnormal risk. *Risk Analysis, 1,* 15–44.

Rosa, E. A., Machlis, G. E., & Keating, K. M. (1988). Energy and society. *Annual Review of Sociology, 14,* 149–172.

Rudel, T. K., & Roper, J. (1997). The paths to rain forest destruction: Cross-national patterns of tropical deforestation, 1975–90. *World Development, 25,* 53–65.

Schnaiberg, A. (1975). Social syntheses of the societal-environmental dialectic: The role of distributional impacts. *Social Science Quarterly, 56,* 5–20.

Schnaiberg, A. (1980). *The environment: From surplus to scarcity.* New York: Oxford University Press.

Schnaiberg, A., & Gould, K. A. (1994). *Environment and society: The enduring conflict.* New York: St. Martin's Press.

Schoenfeld, A. C., Meier, R. F., & Griffin, R. J. (1979). Constructing a social problem: The press and the environment. *Social Problems, 27,* 38–61.

Stern, P. C. (2000). Toward a coherent theory of environmentally significant behavior. *Journal of Social Issues, 56,* 407–424.

Szasz, A. (1994). *Eco-populism: Toxic waste and the movement for environmental justice.* Minneapolis: University of Minnesota Press.

Taylor, D. E. (2000). The rise of the environmental justice paradigm. *American Behavioral Scientist, 43,* 508–580.

Vitousek, P. M., Mooney, H. A., Lubchenco, J., & Melillo, J. M. (1997). Human domination of Earth's ecosystems. *Science, 277,* 494–499.

Yearley, S. (1991). *The green case.* London: HarperCollins.

CHAPTER 11

Environmental Psychophysiology

RUSS PARSONS and LOUIS G. TASSINARY

Every scientific psychology must take into account whole situations, i.e., the state of both person and environment. This implies that it is necessary to find ways of representing person and environment in common terms as parts of one situation. We have no expression in psychology that includes both.

—Lewin, 1936, p. 12

In any concrete situation, one does not encounter man and his environment as separate but interacting; instead one finds a total situation which can be analyzed in a variety of ways. . . . Rather than defining the situation in terms of its components, the components, including man himself, can be defined only in terms of the situation in which they are encountered. . . . Man is never encountered independent of the situation through which he acts, nor is the environment ever encountered independent of the encountering individual. It is meaningless to speak of either as existing apart from the situation in which it is encountered. The word "transaction" has been used to label such a situation. . . .

—Ittelson, 1973, p. 18

The human brain and the rest of the body constitute an indissociable organism, integrated by means of mutually interactive biochemical and neural regulatory circuits. . . . The organism interacts with the environment as an ensemble: the interaction is neither of the body alone nor of the brain alone. . . . The physiological operations we call mind are derived from the structural and functional ensemble rather than from the brain alone: mental phenomena can be fully understood only in the context of an organism's acting in an environment.

—Damasio, 1994, p. xvi–xvii

The heart has its reasons that reason cannot understand.

—Pascal, 1660/1958, p. 50

THE FINAL QUOTATION ABOVE, by Pascal, expresses one variant of an old and commonly held belief: The body has its own wisdom or truth. We can confirm the current popularity of this and similar beliefs by scanning the Internet (use "body's own wisdom" or

We would like to thank Phyllis Sanchez, PhD, Carle Foundation Hospital, Urbana, Illinois, for helpful comments on earlier versions of this chapter.

"body's own truth" as search terms), where the sheer number and broad range of businesses, products, and personal philosophies capitalizing on the inherent wisdom of the human body is daunting. If we include terms such as "folk medicine" or "folk biology" and extend our search to more academically oriented databases, several interesting characteristics about beliefs in the wisdom of the human body emerge. First, many such beliefs are not about the body alone but involve the body's relationship to the sociophysical environment. This can be seen in familiar folk beliefs, such as the arthritic's belief that her pain presages a change in the weather, in common sayings such as "you are what you eat," or in aboriginal (as well as New Age) healers' use of herbal remedies to facilitate the body's own healing powers. A second interesting characteristic involves similarities among cultural beliefs about the body's wisdom, its ability to heal itself and its relationship to the environment. Folk medical practices throughout the world are structurally similar (Cattermole-Tally, 1998), as are the folk biologies upon which most of them are based (Atran, 1998). As an example, many cultures have historically developed similar notions of person environment balance as being important to good health (Cattermole-Tally, 1998). Understanding body-environment imbalances between such properties as hot and cold, moist and dry, internal and external pressure, and the like was critical to diagnosing diseases. In many cultures, then, and for a long time, people have believed that our bodies convey both environmentally oriented and environmentally generated knowledge that is worth knowing.

The other opening quotations give us the opportunity to compare these vernacular views with those of scientists regarding humans, their bodies, and their environments. The first two quotations, from Lewin (a social psychologist) and Ittelson (an environmental psychologist), reflect a certain unanimity between their respective disciplines regarding the study of humans and their environments: In a word, they are inseparable. To study one is to study the other. The third quotation, by Damasio (a neurobiologist), echoes this opinion but adds the conceptual wrinkle that the human mind, the central player in all psychology, cannot be fully understood independent of its physical substrate. Thus, as with the folk epistemologies mentioned earlier, a scientific understanding of humans and their environments focuses on the interdependencies between *embodied* humans and their sociophysical environments. From this quick comparison we can see that, if a field like environmental psychophysiology did not exist (however tentatively), we would have to invent it. It is a natural extension of the way scientists and laypersons alike understand humans and their environments.

Though environmental psychophysiology may be a natural extension of how we think about people and their environments, it is nevertheless a fledgling discipline that requires some definition. We begin with *psychophysiology*, a term that may only be vaguely familiar to many readers of this volume. As a subdiscipline of psychology, the ultimate aim of psychophysiology is to understand human behavior, and this is accomplished through the explicit integration of physiological constructs and processes into theoretical thinking (Cacioppo, Tassinary, & Berntson, 2000b). Stated more formally, *psychophysiology* is "the scientific study of social, psychological, and behavioral phenomena as related to and revealed through physiological principles and events" (Cacioppo & Tassinary, 1990). As the first part of this definition implies (and consistent with Ittelson's sentiments above), the level of analysis in psychophysiology is the organism-environment transactions that constitute human behavior, not isolated investigations of structure (anatomy) or function (physiology). As one of (at least) three subdisciplines within psychophysiology, *environmental psychophysiology* focuses on relationships between organism-place transactions and physiological events and can be distinguished from *social psychophysiology*, where the focus is on interorganismic information processing, and *cognitive psychophysiology*, which focuses on intraorganismic information processing.

Having specified what environmental psychophysiology is, we would like to provide some context for this definition by raising two important points regarding what environmental psychophysiology *is not*. First, the belief that the mind cannot be understood independently of its physical substrate is not without its naysayers, who variously regard this belief as either overly reductive (e.g., Allport, 1947; Caldwell, 1994) or beyond the ken of current (and foreseeable) research on the relationships between psychological and physiological processes (e.g., Kipnis, 1997). Second, and at the opposite end of the skeptic's scale regarding psychophysiology, is the often uncritical belief that physiological measures constitute more objective indications of psychological processes than more readily available measures, such as self-reports or behavioral observations (e.g., Jang, Ku, Shin, Choi, & Kim, 2000). Each of these positions distorts what psychophysiology has to offer environmental psychology (and psychology more generally). In the first instance, psychophysiologists typically do not regard measures of physiological response systems as the only data pertinent to theory building in psychology: As indicated in the previous definition, the reduction of mind to brain is not the aim of psychophysiology. Nor has psychophysiological research left us clueless with respect to psychological processes. Although there are certainly myriad behavioral complexities beyond the reach of current psychophysiological knowledge, our understanding of elemental (as well as some reasonably complex) psychological processes has been greatly enhanced by psychophysiological research (see the recent *Handbook of Psychophysiology,* by Cacioppo, Tassinary, & Berntson, 2000a).

In the second instance, there is no reason to regard physiological response data as any more objective than self-report data if the goal is to attribute psychological meaning to the findings. Both types of data can be collected more or less rigorously, both can be independently verified by multiple observers/ researchers, and both are subject to interpretive minefields laid by the idiosyncratic behavior of individual respondents. Whether we can attribute psychological meaning to verbal utterances or physiological responses depends not on the presumed subjectivity/objectivity of the respective data sources but on the strength of our experimental design, the psychometric properties of the measures, and the appropriateness of data analysis and interpretation (Cacioppo, Tassinary, & Berntson, 2000b). Thus, environmental psychophysiology is neither inherently reductive, unduly stymied by the complexities of psychological processes, nor more objective than other, more common approaches to research in environmental psychology. The psychophysiological approach complements other research approaches, and that complement is especially important when the psychological processes of interest are not completely available to or accurately represented by conscious recollection and behavioral observation. Environmental psychophysiology, then, can both inspire and constrain theory and research in environmental psychology by offering insights into psychological processes that might not otherwise be obtained.

Because the utility of a psychophysiological approach to theory building in environmental psychology depends critically on our ability to establish relationships between psychological processes and physiological events, we will begin by reviewing a simple taxonomy of possible psychophysiological relationships. However, the establishment of psychophysiological correlations, those "necessary monstrosities" (Gardiner, Metcalf, & Beebe-Center, 1937), does not in and of itself advance theory, and therefore, we will also specify the nature of the inferences that each type of relationship allows us to

draw. Armed with these inferential tools, we will then devote the remainder of the chapter to illustrating how research on the "embodied" nature of human behavior can be used to inspire, constrain, and thereby sharpen theory and research in environmental psychology.[1]

PSYCHOPHYSIOLOGICAL RELATIONSHIPS

Many theories and research questions in environmental psychology presume a relationship between psychological processes and physiological events. Work on environmental stressors (e.g., Evans, Bullinger, & Hygge, 1998), restorative environments (e.g., Parsons, Tassinary, Ulrich, Grossman-Alexander, & Hebl, 1998), topographic cognition (e.g., Maguire et al., 2000), environmental aesthetics (e.g., Ulrich, 1981), isolated environments (e.g., Carrere, 1991), and restricted environmental stimulation therapy (e.g., Suedfeld et al., 1994), to name but a few areas, has benefited from theoretical perspectives that regard human-environment transactions as embodied. To describe the range of possible psychophysiological relationships that might be fruitfully exploited in these (and other) environmental research areas, we begin with the assumption that all psychological events have some physiological referent—that is, there is no entity called "mind" that is independent of the central nervous system. This does not mean that psychophysiological relationships are necessarily one-to-one relationships, that every physiological event has psychological meaning, or that established psychophysiological relationships are invariant across situations or individuals. It means only that the mind has a physical substrate. A useful way to think about possibilities for these relationships is illustrated in Figure 11.1 (see also Cacioppo, Tassinary, & Berntson, 2000b).[2]

Five general psychophysiological relationships are shown: One-to-one relationships, in which one element from the psychological domain (Ψ) and one element from the physiological domain (Φ) are uniquely associated with each other; one-to-many

---

[1] Readers interested in a review of typical content areas in environmental psychophysiology should consult Parsons and Hartig (2000).
[2] The material in this section summarizes a fuller treatment of possible psychophysiological relationships and psychophysiological inferences presented in Cacioppo, Tassinary, and Berntson (2000b).

Psychophysiological Relationship	Domain	
	Ψ	Φ

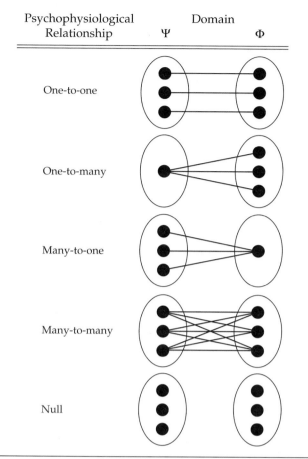

Figure 11.1 Possible relationships between elements in the psychological (Ψ) and physiological (Φ) domains. *Source:* Adapted from Cacioppo & Tassinary, 1990.

relationships, where one element in the psychological domain is associated with multiple physiological elements; many-to-one relationships, where multiple psychological elements are associated with the same physiological element; many-to-many relationships, where multiple psychological elements are associated with multiple (overlapping) physiological elements; and, null relationships, in which no association is observed between psychological and physiological elements.

Examining these five types of psychophysiological relationships, we can see that only the first two allow for the formal specification of psychological processes as a function of physiological events. This is important because in many areas of environmental psychology (see the previous discussion), changes in psychological processes due to human-environment transactions are presumed to be reflected in physiological response systems. To the extent that relationships between psychological states and physiological responses can be specified as one-to-one relationships,

inferences about the occurrence of a particular psychological state, given the observation of the appropriate physiological event, are strengthened. Accordingly then, our confidence in the psychological effects of human-environment transactions becomes stronger when we can establish one-to-one psychophysiological relationships. Unfortunately, one-to-one psychophysiological relationships occur relatively rarely (Coles, Gratton, & Gehring, 1987), leaving inferences about psychological processes based on physiological events problematic at best when we observe one-to-many, many-to-one, and many-to-many psychophysiological relationships.

It is possible to overcome some of the inferential limitations of these multiple-element relationships (i.e., multiple Ψ, multiple Φ, or both), however, if circumstances allow us to reconceptualize them as one-to-one relationships. For instance, in the one-to-many psychophysiological relationship, in which one psychological element is associated with multiple physiological elements, it may be possible to regard the set of physiological elements as a single response pattern or profile (Φ′), allowing the specification of a new one-to-one psychophysiological relationship. Depending upon the complexity of observed psychophysiological relationships, it may be necessary in some instances to augment this simple "co-occurrence" profiling (Φ′) by examining multiple physiological responses as they unfold over time (Φ″). Thus, even when multiple psychological states are associated with the same set of physiological responses (i.e., a many-to-many relationship), there may be distinct spatiotemporal profiles for the physiological responses that uniquely specify the observed psychological states. Figure 11.2 illustrates a concrete example of such a situation.

The many-to-many psychophysiological relationship depicted in the first panel of Figure 11.2 involves three psychological elements (orienting, startle, and defense responses) that are associated with changes in the same two physiological elements (heart rate [HR] and skin conductance responses [SCR], a measure of sweat gland activity). Simply knowing that changes have occurred in these two physiological response systems does not help us discriminate among orienting, startle, and defense responses. However, as Panel 2 in the figure shows, the specific nature of the HR response (acceleration vs. deceleration) does help us identify the orienting response, which is the only one of the three psychological states associated with increased SCR and a

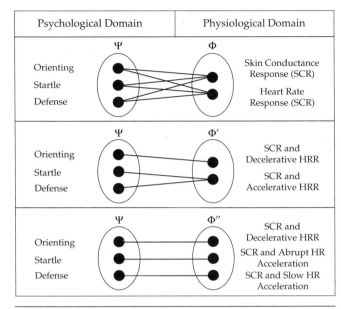

Figure 11.2 The logical relations between the psychological constructs orienting, startle, and defense and the physiological measures heart rate (HR) and skin conductance response (SCR). *Panel 1:* Links between psychological states and physiological responses. *Panel 2:* Links between psychological states and physiological response patterns. *Panel 3:* Links between psychological states and physiological response patterns over time. *Source:* Adapted from Cacioppo & Tassinary, 1990.

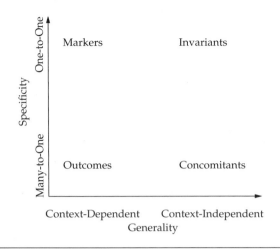

Figure 11.3 Two-dimensional space showing major classes of psychophysiological relationships. *Source:* Adapted from Cacioppo & Tassinary, 1990.

decelerating HR. The remaining psychological responses (startle and defense) are both associated with increases in SCR and HR acceleration. But, as Panel 3 shows, the *rate* of HR acceleration is abrupt in the former response and lingering in the latter, allowing us to uniquely associate specific patterns of HR and SCR with each psychological state. Thus, the original many-to-many psychophysiological relationship among these psychological and physiological elements has been parsed into three separate one-to-one relationships involving psychological states and spatial physiological patterns (Φ') or psychological states and spatiotemporal physiological patterns (Φ'').

A TWO DIMENSIONAL TAXONOMY OF PSYCHOPHYSIOLOGICAL RELATIONSHIPS

As we have seen, to the extent that we can establish spatiotemporal profiles of physiological responses that are uniquely associated with specific psychological elements (i.e., one-to-one relationships), we

are in a stronger inferential position with respect to identifying the occurrence of a given psychological state. But even when this is the case, the range of applicability for any particular psychophysiological relationship also limits the inferences we can draw regarding the occurrence of an associated psychological state. That is, not all psychophysiological relationships will be invariant across individuals or situations. Thus, just as the *specificity* of psychophysiological relationships ranges from one-to-one through many-to-one possibilities (as illustrated previously), their *generality* also ranges, from highly context dependent to completely context free.[3] When we consider these two dimensions (specificity and generality) of psychophysiological relationships together, four categories of possible relationships are implied, as illustrated in Figure 11.3.

OUTCOMES

In this taxonomy, context-specific many-to-one psychophysiological relationships are labeled "outcomes," and they are typically the first level of relationship established between psychological and physiological elements that are thought (or simply discovered) to be related. A psychophysiological

---

[3] Note that by *context*, we are referring to all those person-environment characteristics needed to specify the conditions under which the observed psychophysiological relationship holds. These may include both person-centered and sociophysical environment variables, such as "upper-middle-class African Americans in museum settings," "adolescent males in skateboard parks," "burn victims in virtual 'Snow-World' environments," and so forth.

outcome relationship indicates that a psychological state is reliably associated with a physiological response under a specified set of conditions. Although it may seem that we have a one-to-one relationship if we can establish that a given psychological state (e.g., stress) reliably elicits a particular physiological response (e.g., SCR), such a finding has no bearing on the relationships that other psychological states (e.g., orienting) may have with the same physiological response system. Thus, psychophysiological relationships are initially regarded as many-to-one until greater specificity can be established. Similarly, newly observed psychophysiological relationships are considered specific to the context in which they were established until greater generality can be demonstrated.

Both the many-to-one nature and the context specificity of outcome relationships have important implications for the inferences that can be made based on observed outcomes. Among psychologists, environmental psychologists are perhaps especially sensitive to the inferential limitations that context specificity imposes on theory and research, but the limitations imposed by many-to-one psychophysiological relationships may be less familiar. In particular, many-to-one relationships require a "negative" logic to develop research designs that can provide a strong test of competing theoretical models. This negative logic is required because, as we have seen, an observed many-to-one relationship does not allow us to confidently assert the presence of a psychological state, only its *absence*. That is, if the psychological state of interest reliably elicits a particular physiological response, but other psychological states may be present that also bring it about, when the physiological response occurs we cannot be certain which psychological state is implicated. However, if we *fail* to observe the physiological response (under the specified conditions), we can be sure that the associated psychological state also has not occurred. Of course, controls can be used to minimize the likelihood that competing psychological states are present, but this is not always possible, especially when all of the psychological states that might elicit the physiological response in question are not known. Thus, psychophysiological outcomes are good candidate variables for research when theoretical models predict the absence of a psychological state.

As an example of how an outcome relationship might be used, consider the psychophysiological research that has been done on the restorative effects of outdoor environments. In this work, various evolutionary theories about human transactions with outdoor environments (see chapters by Heerwagen and Hartig, this volume) have been used to predict that transactions with nature-dominated environments are aesthetically preferred and more restorative than transactions with heavily urbanized (i.e., artifact-dominated) environments. In some of this research, a simple methodological paradigm has emerged in which the elicitation of stress is followed by transactions with nature-dominated and artifact-dominated environmental surrogates while physiological response systems are monitored (e.g., Parsons et al., 1998). Restoration is defined in terms of the absence of stress, which is measured via psychophysiological outcome variables, such as skin conductance responses (SCR). Although interesting results have been obtained with this approach (e.g., Ulrich et al., 1991), we can see from the discussion above that the negative logic required to incorporate psychophysiological outcome variables has important limitations regarding the interpretation of findings. In particular, in those cases where null results are reported—that is, no differences in recovery for urban versus nature environments—it could be that there truly were no differences in the stress recovery experienced during different environmental exposures, but it could also be that other (nonstressful) psychological states associated with the same outcome variable were present. Thus, transactions with nature environments could well lead to greater recovery (i.e., absence of stress) relative to urban environments, but physiological evidence of recovery may be masked by the presence of increased interest in or attention paid to nature environments—alternative (nonstressful) psychological states that would also elicit increased SCR. Therefore, we see a need in this area of research for psychophysiological response profiles that clearly indicate stress recovery. That is, research on the restorative effects of environments would be greatly enhanced by the development of psychophysiological *markers* for "restoration."

Markers

A psychophysiological marker is a context-specific one-to-one relationship between a psychological state and a physiological response. As with an outcome relationship, the occurrence of a given psychological state reliably predicts the presence of a particular physiological response, but, for a psychophysiological marker, the obverse is also true: The occurrence of the physiological response reliably predicts the presence of the psychological state. The reciprocal predictability that characterizes psychophysiological markers is an inferential boon, albeit one that is relatively rarely experienced outside artificially induced relationships (e.g., classical conditioning). One reasonably good candidate for a "naturally occurring" marker comes from the literature in cognitive psychophysiology. Cacioppo, Martzke, Petty, and Tassinary (1988) recorded facial muscle activity while research participants were interviewed about themselves and found that ballistic muscle responses recorded from the brow region (paired with relatively quiescent facial muscle activity elsewhere) was reliably associated with the experience of negative emotions.

This example raises several interesting points about markers. First, markers are more apt to be identified when physiological response profiles (i.e., F′ or Φ″) are examined, because the more detailed the description of the physiological response, the less likely it is to be associated with multiple psychological elements. In this instance, the spatiotemporal profile of *ballistic* brow muscle activity and minimal responding elsewhere in the face is what predicts the occurrence of negative emotions. Second, though markers allow the reciprocal prediction of psychological and physiological elements, they have a restricted range of applicability. Here, the negative emotion-Φ″ marker relationship is limited to undergraduates being interviewed about their feelings while unaware that their facial muscle activity is being recorded. Third, this example nicely illustrates the fact that the distinction between many-to-one and one-to-one relationships is continuous, not categorical. We have characterized the negative emotion-Φ″ relationship in this example as a likely marker despite the fact that *negative emotion* implies multiple psychological states and thus precludes a true one-to-one relationship. Nevertheless, however broad we may imagine the class of negative emotions to be, the set of possible psychological states or processes that forms the *many* in such a many-to-one relationship is drastically reduced when everything other than negative emotions is eliminated. Further, because theory and research in broad areas of environmental psychology (e.g., prospect/refuge theory; Appleton, 1996) have reflected a tendency among emotions theorists to regard distinctions between positively and negatively valenced emotions as subjective components of more fundamental biobehavioral approach/avoid systems (Watson, Wiese, Vaidya, & Tellegen, 1999; Lang, 1995; but see also Buck, 1999; Ito & Cacioppo, 1999), a negative emotion marker is potentially very useful for environmental psychologists.

In sum, to propose a psychophysiological relationship as a marker, we must be able to (1) show that the presence of a physiological response reliably predicts the occurrence of a psychological state, (2) show that the physiological response is insensitive to (does not predict) the occurrence of other psychological states, and (3) specify the boundary conditions (context) under which the relationship applies. We note, as well, that even imperfect markers (less than true one-to-one status) may still constitute quite useful relationships, depending upon the psychological constructs of interest (e.g., positive vs. negative affects).[4]

Concomitants

Psychophysiological concomitants are many-to-one (Ψ/Φ) relationships that are context free. Though concomitants are many-to-one relationships, under certain circumstances they can be used to predict the *presence* of a psychological state given the observation of a physiological response. This is because, by definition, the Ψ/Φ relationship will have been observed in many contexts, presenting the opportunity to determine the relative frequency of pairings between the individual elements in the "many" psychological set and the physiological response in question. Given these base rates, in any given context where the physiological response is observed, we can estimate the probability that the psychological element in question has also occurred. Unfortunately, base rates such as these are not routinely gathered, and the establishment of actual concomitants lags behind claims for such relationships. As an example, consider the development of pupillary measures of psychological states over the past 40 years.

Several reports in the 1960s by Hess and his colleagues (Hess, 1965; Hess & Polt, 1960, 1964, 1966) of

---

[4] We are alluding here to the possibility of constructing psychological response profiles (Ψ′, Ψ″) analogous to the physiological response profiles (Φ′, Φ″) discussed earlier. An avoidance mindset, reflected by a specified set of negative emotions, could be one such psychological response profile. For simplicity's sake, we have restricted our discussion here to physiological response profiles.

a relationship between attitudes towards visually represented objects (or people) and pupillary dilation were seen as evidence that pupil size is a correlate (concomitant) of attitude. Subsequent research in different assessment contexts, however, has cast doubt on this conclusion. Wenger and Videbeck (1969), for instance, showed participants pictures of highly preferred (e.g., alpine lake/mountains) and disliked (e.g., logging debris) landscape scenes and found no relationship between scenic attractiveness and pupil size. And, researchers who have used non-visual attitude stimuli (e.g., Goldwater, 1972) have also failed to find a relationship between attitudes and pupil size. One explanation for the lack of correspondence between early reports of an attitude-pupil size relationship and later null results lies in the difficulties inherent in matching luminance levels across complex visual attitude stimuli. It is not enough to equate overall luminance levels across visual stimuli in a given study, because each fixation will present a different luminance level to the retina, depending upon where it lands on the image. Thus, when experimental procedures allow multiple fixations per image (as is typically the case), and when "bright" versus "dim" fixations across images are not controlled, the opportunity for specious relationships to emerge is great. This explanation is consistent with the record of some studies of visual attitude stimuli finding an attitude-pupil size relationship (e.g., Hess & Polt, 1960) while others do not (Wenger & Videbeck, 1969) and consistent as well with the repeated failure to find an attitude-pupil size relationship when nonvisual attitude stimuli have been used—that is, where researchers have been able to carefully control luminance levels (Goldwater, 1972). Despite hoary claims of sharp-eyed merchants and crafty poker players regarding what can be learned by studying someone's eyes (Stern & Dunham, 1990, p. 517), attitudes and pupil size do not appear to share a concomitant relationship.

INVARIANTS

"[R]eligion is a property of the brain, only the brain and has little to do with what's out there."[5] Such are the statements of a scientist in the thrall of a puta-tive psychophysiological invariant. What prompted this outburst was the discovery that 4 out of 5 research participants exposed to a particular pattern of electrocortical stimulation reported having a "mystical experience." Some wept, some felt God had touched them, and others simply experienced a presence in the room. That mystical experiences might be elicited by other patterns of excitation (or by other external means), that the specified electro-cortical stimulation might elicit other psychological phenomena (for at least 20% of the population), or that religion might consist of more than just mysti-cal experiences—these considerations seem to not have dampened the enthusiasm of this investigator.[6] Psychophysiological invariants, however, need to be more rigorously specified. Psychophysiological in-variants are context-free one-to-one relationships, and as such offer us the strongest basis for inferences about psychological states given the occurrence of physiological events. In a true invariant relationship, an element from the psychological domain and one from the physiological domain uniquely specify each other, regardless of conditions. That is, there is no danger of affirming the consequent here, because the relationship is truly reciprocal: Each element (Ψ or Φ) occurs if and only if the other is also present.

HOW PSYCHOPHYSIOLOGY CAN INSPIRE AND CONSTRAIN THEORY AND RESEARCH IN ENVIRONMENTAL PSYCHOLOGY: EXAMPLES FROM AN EMBODIED PERSPECTIVE

There are at least two senses in which a psychophys-iological approach might inspire research and theory in environmental psychology. First, constructs and theories developed in various subdisciplines of psychophysiology might be adapted for research

---

[5] Michael Persinger, professor of neuroscience at Laurentian University, as quoted in the June 16, 2001, issue of the *Washington Post*, online edition: www.washingtonpost.com/wp-dyn/nation/science/A10767-2001Jun16.html

[6] Which is not to say that the temporal lobe activations at issue have no psychological meaning. In previous work (Parsons, Tassinary, Bontempo, & Vanman, 1997), we have interpreted a linear association between temporal lobe activation and the sce-nic beauty of environmental stimuli as possibly reflecting feel-ings of wonder or awe elicited by spectacular landscape vistas. However, in this tentative interpretation of preliminary data, we have clearly regarded this relationship as an *outcome* of human-environment transactions of a particular sort, rather than an invariant produced via endogenous artifact.

questions in environmental psychology. Second, methodological approaches developed in psychophysiology to study psychological processes that are of interest to environmental psychologists (e.g., attention) could also inspire research when convergent operations are needed to understand the processes that a given class of environmental transactions engages. To illustrate both of these types of psychophysiological inspiration, we will examine recent research on the psychological treatment of pain. We use this example in part because the inspiration from psychophysiological constructs is particularly explicit, but this research is also conceptually similar to (and involves many of the same psychological processes as) work in environmental psychology on the restorative effects of environments. The second research example we will explore, spatial cognition, highlights the kinds of constraints an embodied perspective on human-environment transactions can exert on theory and research in environmental psychology.

PAIN CONTROL

Alternatives and adjuncts to the pharmacological treatment of pain have been popular for some time, especially in those situations where drugs are either contraindicated or do not provide sufficient relief. Pain associated with the care of burn wounds (e.g., changing dressings), for example, is often reported to be severe by 75% or more of those treated with pharmacological analgesics alone (Kibbee, 1984; Perry & Heidrick, 1982). Overwhelmingly, nonpharmacological adjunctive pain treatments have relied on distraction techniques, which are typically predicated on the assumptions that (1) pain perception requires attention to the nociceptive agent, (2) attention is a limited capacity, and (3) intervention stimuli that compete with pain for attention necessarily limit the amount of pain that can be perceived. Music (Good et al., 1999; Whipple & Glynn, 1992), guided mental imagery (Raft, Smith, & Warren, 1986), hypnosis (Rainville, Carrier, Hofbauer, Bushnell, & Duncan, 1999), disruptive tones (Crombez, Eccleston, Baeyens, & Eelen, 1996), and humor (Cogan, Cogan, Waltz, & McCue, 1987) are some of the many distractions that have been used to treat pain, often in conjunction with analgesic and/or anxiolytic drugs. Recently, pain researchers have also used both conventional (Lechtzin, Withers, Devrotes, & Diette, 2001) and virtual (Hoffman,

Doctor, Patterson, Carrougher, & Furness, 2000) environmental surrogates as distractors in pain control studies (in work that is directly analogous to restorative environments research; see Hartig, this volume) with encouraging results (see Figure 11.4).

Despite evidence for the effectiveness of various distraction techniques, the presumed attentional mechanism by which distraction works has not gone unchallenged. Several researchers have systematically varied the attention component of distraction tasks and found that, regardless of the attention required to successfully complete the tasks, cognitively oriented distractions did not relieve cold pressor pain (Hodes, Howland, Lightfoot, & Cleeland, 1990; McCaul, Monson, & Maki, 1992). These findings led McCaul and colleagues (1992) to suggest that previous work showing distraction to be an effective analgesic had actually capitalized on the co-occurrence of positive affects. Others, however, have found that both positive and negative affective distractions can increase pain tolerance (e.g., Greenstein, 1984; Weisenberg, Tepper, & Schwarzwald, 1995). As Meagher, Arnau, and Rhudy (2001) have suggested, because valence, arousal, and attention have often been confounded in this work, we cannot readily discern the relative importance of these characteristics for pain control. Although the independent work by Hodes, McCaul, and their respective colleagues strongly suggests that relatively "affectless" distraction is not sufficient to modulate pain perception and tolerance, taken as a whole the literature on pain control does not clearly indicate how affect may mediate the effects of distraction.

One possibility is that distraction is, in fact, a fundamentally attentional phenomenon, but because emotionally toned stimuli command attention more effectively than neutral stimuli (Robinson, 1998), distraction is effective only (or primarily) to the extent that it elicits affect. If this is true, the valence characteristics of a distraction technique should be relatively unimportant with respect to pain control—comparably strong positive and negative emotions should provide the same level of distraction from pain (see de Wied & Verbaten, 2001).[7] Alternatively, valence may also play an important role in the affective mediation of distraction, as suggested by several pain researchers who have examined the

---

[7] Note the implied one-to-one relationship in this hypothesis—the greater the affective arousal, the greater the distraction from pain.

Figure 11.4 Examples of conventional (top panel) and virtual (bottom panel) environmental surrogates used in pain control research.

utility of Lang's motivational priming model of emotions for pain research (see de Wied & Verbaten, 2001; Meagher et al., 2001).

According to Lang and his colleagues (Bradley & Lang, 2000; Lang, 1995), human emotions are behavioral action tendencies that subserve two opponent motivational systems, appetitive and aversive, the former disposing us toward approach behaviors and positive emotional responding, while the latter primes avoidance (defensive) behaviors and negative emotional responding. Activation of these systems

can be endogenous or exogenous, and, as opponent processes, rising activation in one system tends to be coupled with falling activation in the other. Much of the work Lang and his colleagues have done to develop the theory has focused on a particular defensive behavior, the startle blink response, owing to its simple and well-known neural circuitry. In multiple studies (see Lang, Bradley, & Cuthbert, 1997, for a review), they have demonstrated that when the avoidance system is activated (e.g., via exposure to negative emotional stimuli), the startle blink response is enhanced, whereas this defensive response is attenuated when the approach system (positive emotion) is activated.

Several characteristics of the motivational prime theory of emotions (and related research) make it a felicitous choice for adaptation to pain control research. First, if primed affective states can differentially modulate a defensive blink reflex, then they may well be able to influence the earliest stages of a perceptual response to pain. Second, primed affective states (i.e., moods) have also been shown to influence other cognitive processes, including stimulus evaluations, decision making, problem solving, and so forth (see Isen, 1999, for a review), and thus more-cognitively demanding stages of pain perception are also likely to be subject to affective modulation.[8] And third, there is an interesting overlap in the neural substrates underlying the startle reflex and the pain response—the amygdala and the periaqueductal gray are both critical components in the respective neural circuits that have been shown to modulate these responses (Davis, 1997; Fields & Basbaum, 1994). So, if positive emotions tend to inhibit and negative emotions tend to accentuate the startle blink reflex, we might expect the shared sensory gating circuitry of the pain response system to behave in a similar fashion. Recent evidence indicates that positive and negative emotional priming have differential effects on both pain perception and tolerance (de Wied & Verbaten, 2001; Meagher et al., 2001; Rhudy & Meagher, 2000), suggesting that the affective mediation of distraction is at least partially determined by valence.

Thus, the adaptation of this psychophysiological theory of motivational priming for use in the study of psychological pain control appears to have been fruitful. As intimated by the aforementioned emerging use of environmental surrogates in pain research,

this adaptation of motivational prime theory may also have a direct analogue in environmental psychology, especially with respect to the work being done on restorative environments. In fact, the indicated importance of affective valence for pain distraction may have immediate implications for the design of such places as "healing gardens," where some subset of those visiting the space can be presumed to be suffering from pain. At the very least, and despite the developing nature of this research, if we adopt a prudent approach to the design of health care settings, we can advise against designs for healing gardens that are less than unambiguously positive (see Figure 11.5).

Apart from immediate applications to design, this example also gives us the opportunity to consider the theoretical implications of the importance of affective valence for pain distraction, especially as the two most prominent theories of restorative environments are affect based (Ulrich, 1983) and attention based (Kaplan & Kaplan, 1989), respectively. One implication we might draw from the use of motivational prime theory in pain distraction research is that a complete theoretical account of restorative environments will likely have to explain how attention, affective valence, arousal, and environmental stimuli interact in human-environment transactions to achieve restoration. This is true to the extent that the psychological states targeted for restoration in these theories, stress and directed attention fatigue (DAF), activate the same aversive motivational system that pain does. Although this is a reasonable assumption to make with respect to stressful psychological states, DAF is presumed not to be stressful, though this has not been empirically verified (see Parsons & Hartig, 2000). DAF does motivate relief-seeking behavior (i.e., restoration), however, and thus it is unlikely to be affectively neutral.

We see an opportunity, therefore, for psychophysiological constructs and methods to help sharpen the theoretical distinctions between affectively and attentionally defined restoration. As an example, take the question of the affective neutrality of DAF. If we maintain our focus on the principles associated with the motivational prime theory described previously, we can propose that:

> If DAF is affectively neutral, then it should not prime the avoidance motivational system proposed to underlie negative affect and so should not enhance the startle blink reflex.

---

[8] These observations are hardly novel in the pain literature, where both cognitive and affective top-down modulations of pain perception have been acknowledged in theory (and subsequently empirically verified) since the introduction of the gate control theory of pain (Melzack & Wall, 1965). These observations hint as well at the interesting story of how a putative one-to-one psychophysiological relationship regarding the perception of pain held sway over Western thinking about pain for several hundred years. The specificity theory of pain perception, which was displaced by gate control theory and had its conceptual roots in Descartes's *Treatise of Man*, proposed that pain perception was directly proportional to the stimulus intensity of the nociceptive agent (see Eich, Brodkin, Reeves, & Chawla, 1999, for the full story).

Figure 11.5 A restored industrial landscape. Though landscapes like this have won numerous design awards, they would most likely not be suitable as healing gardens nor as distraction stimuli for the psychological treatment of pain. *Source: Piazza Metallica*, Duisburg, used with permission from Michael Latz.

Notice how we are capitalizing on a many-to-one psychophysiological relationship identified by motivational prime theory (multiple negative psychological states elicit a particular physiological response) to discriminate between two theories of restoration, one that predicts the presence and the other the absence of a negative psychological state (stress) under a specified set of conditions (attentional fatigue).[9]

As this example illustrates, it is a straightforward matter (conceptually) to incorporate psychophysiological principles to study questions in environmental psychology, especially those questions that hinge on commonly studied psychological states such as stress, attention, arousal, and valence. Multiple families of psychophysiological methods are available, as well, methods that provide continuously and noninvasively recorded data, allowing for the temporal resolution of dynamic psychological processes in ways that retrospective (and even more nearly continuous) self-reports cannot.[10] To illustrate the power of continuously recorded measures to illuminate

psychological processes that unfold over time, consider the measurement of DAF (one last time). DAF is typically elicited through the administration of vigilance tasks, which often are not very cognitively demanding but usually require protracted attention to the task before fatigue sets in. One such task involves searching for (and striking out) all instances of a particular letter (say, *e*) in a lengthy text. Although simple, such a task may elicit mild anxiety at the outset (either because of novelty or a desire to perform well), relatively little anxiety as we settle into a routine, and perhaps rising anxiety towards the end of the vigilance period as increasing frustration with the boredom of the task undermines our accuracy. Thus, if we wanted to construct a task that reliably elicits DAF (and not stress), this (hypothetical) U-shaped relationship between anxiety and attentional fatigue could easily be missed by discrete self-report measures of anxiety administered any time during the shallow part of the response curve.

Finally, beyond the advantage of continuous monitoring, psychophysiological methods that have been developed to study specific psychological phenomena might also inspire research and help to sharpen theory in environmental psychology. These include measures that can be used to help understand motivational and emotional phenomena, such as arousal and valence (see Bradley, 2000, for a review), as well as those useful for understanding more cognitively

---

[9] We are assuming that Ulrich's (1983) affect-based theory of restorative environments would predict that stress accompanies any state of DAF that is significant enough to elicit restoration-seeking behaviors.

[10] It is difficult, for instance, to continuously collect self-report data, either verbally or through electromechanical means (e.g., turning a dial, squeezing a dynamometer), without interfering with the psychological state of interest.

oriented phenomena, such as perceptual processing, spatial attention, working memory, alertness, and so forth (see Kramer & Weber, 2000, for a review). Measures assessing attention, for instance, would be a useful adjunct to those psychophysiological assessments of arousal already exploited in the pain research mentioned above, as well as being useful for sharpening the theoretical distinction between stress and DAF in restorative environments research (see Parsons & Hartig, 2000). More broadly, however, we can see how psychophysiological assessments of these basic psychological processes would be useful in many areas of environmental psychology reviewed in this handbook. In the next section, we will explore an area of research that illustrates how an embodied perspective on human-environment transactions can serve to constrain theory and research in environmental psychology.

SEXUALLY DIMORPHIC SPATIAL ABILITIES

Sex differences in human topographic and other spatial abilities have been observed in many diverse cultures (Mann, Sasanuma, Sakuma, & Masaki, 1990). Women have a better memory for the location of objects in a static visual array (Silverman & Eals, 1992) and for the recall of landmarks (Galea & Kimura, 1993), whereas men are better at spatial tasks that involve the mental rotation of objects (or a change in environmental perspective; Law, Pellegrino, & Hunt, 1993; Voyer, Voyer, & Bryden, 1995), route learning (Galea & Kimura, 1993), and geographic knowledge (Beatty & Troster, 1987). These differences tend to be largest for difficult mental rotation tasks performed in the laboratory (e.g., Vandenberg & Kuse, 1978), though there are real-world analogues of these differences, which are perhaps most evident in wayfinding behavior (e.g., Schmitz, 1999; Silverman et al., 2000). The nature of these differences has been addressed in various theories, including a recent interactionist perspective in the human geography and environmental psychology literatures (Kitchin, 1996; Schmitz, 1997, 1999). Several aspects of this perspective are highly commendable, such as its multidisciplinarity, and its focus on the methodological, social, cultural, and physical environmental contexts of spatial behavior. However, at least one version of this theoretical perspective (Schmitz, 1997) explicitly disregards the potential importance of biological contributions to sex differences in spatial behavior, primarily on the

basis of a presumptive causal ordering of correlational data. By exploring this presumption, we hope to illustrate how an embodied perspective on human-environment transactions can help to guide (constrain) theory building in environmental psychology.

Acknowledging that there are sex differences in neural lateralization (Witelson, 1988), Schmitz (1997, p. 225) assumes that they are an effect of differential spatial behaviors, not a cause. In particular, she cites multiple reports (Herman, Heins, & Cohen, 1987; Matthews, 1986, 1987) of differences in the size of home range between boys and girls to suggest that this is the reason for sex-differentiated brain lateralization. Although we agree that neural organization may indeed be shaped by environmental experience (see below), this possibility alone does not justify a causal attribution, nor does lateralization exhaust the possibilities for how biology may contribute to an explanation of sex differences in human spatial behavior. If we consider sex differences in home range in an evolutionary context, for example, we might come to a different conclusion regarding the cause-effect relationship between home range and brain lateralization. Both anthropological data (Gaulin & Hoffman, 1988) and archeological evidence of locomotion-induced changes in lower limb bone structure (Ruff, 1987) suggest that sex differences in home range is not a recent phenomenon but has probably characterized the species since at least the middle Paleolithic era. An embodied approach to environmental psychology thus requires more than a consideration of neuroanatomy (see the definition of *psychophysiology* given earlier) but should comprise all those biological forces (including evolutionary) that might influence human-environment transactions. The case of sex differences in spatial behavior is an especially good one to make this point because there is good evidence that biological differences between males and females play an important role in human spatial behavior.

In several recent reviews, Hampson and her colleagues (Hampson, 1995, 2000; Sherry & Hampson, 1997) have argued cogently for the importance of gonadal steroids in the sexual differentiation of human spatial cognition. Though a full review of the evidence is beyond the scope of this chapter, some specific aspects of this argument have interesting implications for theory and research in environmental cognition. Evidence for endocrine modulations of human spatial cognition is both *organizational* and *activational*, referring respectively to changes that are relatively long term (if not permanent) versus those that are relatively short term (i.e., reversible), which tend to track ordinary fluctuations of androgens and estrogens. An example of the first kind of evidence comes from studies of children with congenital adrenal hyperplasia (CAH) who are exposed in utero to unusually high levels of androgens. Girls with CAH are typically diagnosed soon after birth and concentrations of steroid hormones are normalized with replacement therapy. When CAH steroid imbalances are rectified early, any possible effects of elevated androgens are limited to the prenatal and early natal periods. Subsequent effects on prepubescent spatial abilities are assumed to be organizational.

Comparing such a sample of CAH girls with their unaffected same-sex siblings, Hampson and colleagues (Hampson, Rovet, & Altmann, 1998) found that the CAH girls outperformed their control sisters by a full standard deviation on tests of spatial relations but were no better on other (nonspatial) cognitive tasks. Data from girls exposed to subclinical elevations of androgens in utero provide convergent evidence for a link between sex hormones and spatial cognition. Girls with twin brothers, for instance, are normally exposed to slightly elevated levels of androgens, and they display better spatial abilities than girls from same-sex twin pairs (Cole-Harding, Morstad, & Wilson, 1988). And, the natural variability in prenatal exposure to testosterone among single-birth girls has been found to predict rotational spatial abilities reasonably well ($r = .67$) at age 7, though prenatal testosterone was not related to spatial play experience in boys or girls (Grimshaw, Sitarenios, & Finegan, 1995). Interestingly, in this same study (Grimshaw et al., 1995), prenatal exposure to testosterone was *negatively* related to spatial abilities in boys ($r = -.62$), which is consistent with Hampson and colleagues' (1998) sample of CAH boys, whose spatial abilities were depressed relative to control boys. Thus, it seems that prenatal exposures to androgens (including normal exposure levels) may well have an organizational effect on spatial abilities, though the relationship does not appear to be monotonic—when androgen levels are too high, spatial abilities suffer.

Evidence for activational (reversible) effects of sex hormones on spatial abilities suggests that fluctuations in adult levels of androgens and estrogens can influence the expression of spatial abilities. Several laboratories have repeatedly found small but reliable differences between the spatial performance of women in the menstrual (estrogen trough) and luteal (estrogen peak) phases of the menstrual cycle. High levels of circulating estrogens are associated with poorer performance on spatial tasks (Hampson, 1990a; Phillips & Silverman, 1997; Silverman & Phillips, 1993) but better performance on motor tasks, including verbal fluency (Hampson, 1990b). Comparatively few studies have been published regarding the influence of fluctuating androgens on spatial abilities, but they are suggestive. Among young men, both diurnal (Moffat & Hampson, 1996) and circannual (Kimura & Hampson, 1994) elevations of testosterone are associated with reduced performance on spatial tasks, whereas older men (60–75) undergoing testosterone replacement therapy saw improvements in their spatial cognition, though other cognitive abilities were unchanged (Janowsky, Oviatt, & Orwoll, 1994). As with the organizational data described above, this research suggests that there may be an optimal level of androgen exposure with respect to human spatial abilities (cf. Geschwind & Galaburda, 1987).

Though the endocrinological work sketched here indicates that sex hormones may have both organizational and activational effects on human spatial cognition, several additional points are warranted in this brief review. First, we must keep in mind that these are correlational data that have yet to reveal definitively whether and, if so, how androgens and estrogens modulate spatial abilities. We note, for instance, that even though Grimshaw and colleagues found that there was no relationship between spatial play experience on one hand and either prenatal testosterone or spatial rotational abilities on the other, their measure of spatial play experience had no component that solicited home range information (Grimshaw et al., 1995, Appendix). Thus, there may be some third factor (as yet unknown) that leads both to changes in hormone levels and improved spatial abilities, perhaps via increases in environmental curiosity and the concomitant expansion of home range. A study comparing prenatal androgen exposures to home range and spatial abilities might well be informative.

Second, although organizational effects are often regarded as permanent (e.g., Hampson, 1995), we have referred to them above as "relatively long term" because recent evidence from research in the neurosciences suggests that even adult neural structures are susceptible to experience-induced "sculpting."

Maguire and her colleagues (2000) compared the brain morphologies of experienced London taxi drivers and matched controls, and found that the taxi drivers had larger posterior and smaller anterior hippocampi, structural differences that correlated positively ($r = .5$) and negatively ($r = -.6$), respectively, with years on the job. Though these data suggest that cognitive demands of the environment can alter brain morphology, the relationship between hippocampal structure and spatial ability must be regarded as an outcome until we can rule out possible relationships between other (nonspatial) abilities and the hippocampus (Terrazas & McNaughton, 2000). We can see, however, how developing knowledge of this psychophysiological relationship will be invaluable in helping us to assess the role of learning in theoretical models of adult spatial abilities, especially given the aforementioned evidence of (putatively permanent) organizational endocrine effects.

A third caution regarding the endocrine research sketched above concerns the practical implications of this work, both for conducting research and for the directions that future research might take to make it most useful for designers and planners. With respect to conducting research, we can tentatively conclude from the evidence of fluctuating effects of circulating endocrines that researchers need to be mindful of biological rhythms. Those researchers focusing on questions of sex differences in adult human spatial abilities should routinely be collecting and reporting diurnal, circannual, and menstrual phase data to aid both intra- and interstudy interpretations. These data should also be collected when the sampled population includes both pre- and postpubescent participants.

With respect to directions for research, one critical question seems to be the extent to which organizational endocrine effects are truly permanent. If organizational effects are permanent (or very difficult to dislodge), then research regarding the specific environmental needs of people with differing spatial skills is clearly implicated. As noted above, sex differences in spatial skills tend to be magnified in the laboratory, both for rotational tasks involving abstract objects (Vandenberg & Kuse, 1978) and for wayfinding tasks in virtual environments (Waller, Hunt, & Knapp, 1998). Though differences in real-world environments tend to be less, they may still be magnified by the ways in which we design our buildings and larger scale environments. Informationally impoverished environmental surrogates, for instance, may have real-world counterparts in strip-mall developments that lack specific kinds of spatial cues (e.g., discernible landmarks) that aid navigation. Therefore, research regarding specific types of built environment elements that aid both landmark-based and more directionally based navigation is needed. Though this kind of research would have important practical value, it would also be beneficial to environmental psychologists concerned with building transactional theories of human-environment relations. For example, any transactional theory of the human mind would profit greatly from information regarding how people use their environments as "external cognitive scaffolding" for such basic cognitive processes as memory, to more sophisticated processes such as wayfinding and the modulation of social interactions (see Clark, 1997).

Finally, we note that our presentation lacks any reference to theoretical explanations for why sex hormones might be involved in the regulation of human spatial cognition. Given space limitations, we will mention only that a theoretical literature does exist for the sex endocrine-spatial cognition relationship and that it is dominated by evolutionary accounts (no fewer than seven, in fact; see Sherry & Hampson, 1997), some of which may well help to integrate biological findings that have been too easily dismissed (e.g., Schmitz, 1997) or largely absent from social learning models of spatial cognition (Baenninger & Newcombe, 1989).

CONCLUDING REMARKS

Though it had not emerged as a distinct area of research when the first edition of this handbook was published, environmental psychophysiology has been a part of environmental psychology virtually since its inception. We have used this chapter to help define environmental psychophysiology as a subdiscipline and to specify the conditions needed to make strong inferences about psychological states based on physiological events. Through two extended examples, we have tried to show how constructs and methods in psychophysiology can both inspire and constrain research and theory in environmental psychology. Though we harbor no illusions that hordes of environmental psychologists will now drop their current approaches and join the ranks of environmental psychophysiology, we hope that we have conveyed the potential power inherent in an embodied perspective on human-environment transactions.

REFERENCES

Allport, G. (1947). Scientific models and human morals. *Psychological Review, 54,* 182–192.

Appleton, J. (1996). *The experience of landscape.* London: Wiley.

Atran, S. (1998). Folk biology and the anthropology of science: Cognitive universals and cultural particulars. *Behavioral and Brain Sciences, 21,* 547–609.

Baenninger, M., & Newcombe, N. (1989). The role of experience in spatial test performance: A meta-analysis. *Sex Roles, 20,* 327–344.

Beatty, W. W., & Troster, A. I. (1987). Gender differences in geographical knowledge. *Sex Roles, 16,* 565–590.

Bradley, M. M. (2000). Emotion and motivation. In J. T. Cacioppo, L. G. Tassinary, & G. G. Berntson (Eds.), *Handbook of psychophysiology* (pp. 602–642). New York: Cambridge University Press.

Bradley, M. M., & Lang, P. J. (2000). Measuring emotion: Behavior, feeling and physiology. In R. D. Lane & L. Nadel (Eds.), *Cognitive neuroscience of emotion* (pp. 242–276). New York: Oxford University Press.

Buck, R. (1999). The biological affects: A typology. *Psychological Review, 106*(2), 301–336.

Cacioppo, J. T., Martzke, J. S., Petty, R. E., & Tassinary, L. G. (1988). Specific forms of facial EMG response index emotions during an interview: From Darwin to the continuous flow hypothesis of affect-laden information processing. *Journal of Personality and Social Psychology, 54,* 592–604.

Cacioppo, J. T., & Tassinary, L. G. (1990). Inferring psychological significance from physiological signals. *American Psychologist, 45*(1), 16–28.

Cacioppo, J. T., Tassinary, L. G., & Berntson, G. G. (Eds.). (2000a). *Handbook of psychophysiology.* New York: Cambridge University Press.

Cacioppo, J. T., Tassinary, L. G., & Berntson, G. G. (2000b). Psychophysiological science. In J. T. Cacioppo, L. G. Tassinary, & G. G. Berntson (Eds.), *Handbook of psychophysiology* (pp. 3–26). New York: Cambridge University Press.

Caldwell, A. B. (1994). Simultaneous multilevel analysis. *American Psychologist, 49,* 144–145.

Carrere, S. (1991). *Physiological and psychological patterns of acute and chronic stress during winter isolation in Antarctica.* Unpublished doctoral dissertation, University of California, Irvine.

Cattermole-Tally, F. (1998). Folk medicine. *Compton's encyclopedia online.* Available: www.comptons.com/encyclopedia

Clark, A. (1997). *Being there: Putting brain, body and world together again.* Cambridge, MA: MIT Press.

Cogan, R., Cogan, D., Waltz, W., & McCue, M. (1987). Effects of laughter and relaxation on discomfort thresholds. *Journal of Behavioral Medicine, 10,* 139–144.

Cole-Harding, S., Morstad, A. L., & Wilson, J. R. (1988). Spatial ability in members of opposite-sex twin pairs. *Behavioral Genetics, 18,* 710.

Coles, M. G. H., Gratton, G., & Gehring, W. J. (1987). Theory in cognitive psychophysiology. *Journal of Psychophysiology, 1,* 13–16.

Crombez, G., Eccleston, C., Baeyens, F., & Eelen, P. (1996). The disruptive nature of pain: An experimental investigation. *Behaviour Research and Therapy, 34*(11–12), 911–918.

Damasio, A. (1994). *Descartes' error: Emotion, reason and the human brain.* New York: G.P. Putnam.

Davis, M. (1997). The neurophysiological basis of acoustic startle modulation: Research on fear, motivation and sensory gating. In P. J. Lang, R. F. Simons, & M. T. Balaban (Eds.), *Attention and orienting: Sensory and motivational processes* (pp. 69–96). Hillsdale, NJ: Erlbaum.

de Wied, M., & Verbaten, M. N. (2001). Affective pictures processing, attention and pain tolerance. *Pain, 90,* 163–172.

Eich, E., Brodkin, I. A., Reeves, J. L., & Chawla, A. P. (1999). Questions concerning pain. In D. Kahneman, E. Diener, & N. Schwarz (Eds.), *Well-being: The foundations of hedonic psychology* (pp. 155–168). New York: Russell Sage.

Evans, G. W., Bullinger, M., & Hygge, S. (1998). Chronic noise exposure and physiological response: A prospective study of children living under environmental stress. *Psychological Science, 9*(1), 75–77.

Fields, H. L., & Basbaum, A. (1994). Central nervous system mechanisms of pain modulation. In P. D. Wall & R. Melzack (Eds.), *Textbook of pain* (3rd ed., pp. 243–257). Edinburgh: Churchill Livingstone.

Galea, L. A. M., & Kimura, D. (1993). Sex differences in route learning. *Personality and Individual Differences, 14,* 53–65.

Gardiner, H. N., Metcalf, R. C., & Beebe-Center, J. G. (1937). *Feeling and emotion: A history of theories.* New York: American Book.

Gaulin, S. J. C., & Hoffman, H. A. (1988). Evolution and development of sex differences in spatial ability. In L. L. Betzig, M. Borgerhoff Mulder, & P. W. Turke (Eds.), *Human reproductive behaviour* (pp. 129–152). Cambridge: Cambridge University Press.

Geschwind, N., & Galaburda, A. M. (1987). *Cerebral lateralization.* Cambridge, MA: MIT Press.

Goldwater, B. C. (1972). Psychological significance of pupillary movements. *Psychological Bulletin, 77,* 340–355.

Good, M., Stanton-Hicks, M., Grass, J. A., Anderson, G. C., Choi, C., Schoolmeesters, L. J., & Salman, A. (1999). Relief of postoperative pain with jaw relaxation, music and their combination. *Pain, 81*(1–2), 163–172.

Greenstein, S. M. (1984). Pleasant and unpleasant slides: Their effects on pain tolerance. *Cognitive Therapy & Research, 8,* 201–210.

Grimshaw, G. M., Sitarenios, G., & Finegan, J. K. (1995). Mental rotation at 7 years: Relations with prenatal testosterone levels and spatial play experiences. *Brain & Cognition, 29,* 85–100.

Hampson, E. (1990a). Estrogen-related variations in human spatial and articulatory-motor skills. *Psychoneuroendocrinology, 15*(2), 97–111.

Hampson, E. (1990b). Variations in sex-related cognitive abilities across the menstrual cycle. *Brain & Cognition, 14*(1), 26–43.

Hampson, E. (1995). Spatial cognition in humans: Possible modulation by androgens and estrogens. *Journal of Psychiatry and Neuroscience, 20*(5), 397–404.

Hampson, E. (2000). Sexual differentiation of spatial functions in humans. In A. Matsumoto (Ed.), *Sexual differentiation of the brain* (pp. 279–300). New York: CRC Press.

Hampson, E., Rovet, J. F., & Altmann, D. (1998). Spatial reasoning in children with congenital adrenal hyperplasia due to 21-hydroxylase deficiency. *Developmental Neuropsychology, 14,* 299–320.

Herman, J. F., Heins, J. A., & Cohen, D. S. (1987). Children's spatial knowledge of their neighborhood environment. *Journal of Applied Developmental Psychology, 8,* 1–15.

Hess, E. H. (1965). Attitude and pupil size. *Scientific American, 212*(4), 46–54.

Hess, E. H., & Polt, J. M. (1960). Pupil size as related to interest value of visual stimuli. *Science, 132,* 349–350.

Hess, E. H., & Polt, J. M. (1964). Pupil size in relation to mental activity during simple problem solving. *Science, 143,* 1190–1192.

Hess, E. H., & Polt, J. M. (1966). Changes in pupil size as a measure of taste difference. *Perceptual and Motor Skills, 23,* 451–455.

Hodes, R. L., Howland, E. W., Lightfoot, N., & Cleeland, C. S. (1990). The effects of distraction on response to cold pressor pain. *Pain, 41,* 109–114.

Hoffman, H. G., Doctor, J. N., Patterson, D. R., Carrougher, G. J., & Furness, T. A., III. (2000). Virtual reality as an adjunctive pain control during burn wound care in adolescent patients. *Pain, 85,* 305–309.

Isen, A. M. (1999). Positive affect. In T. Dalgleish & M. Power (Eds.), *The handbook of cognition and emotion* (pp. 521–539). New York: Wiley.

Ito, T. A., & Cacioppo, J. T. (1999). The psychophysiology of utility appraisals. In D. Kahneman, E. Diener, & N. Schwarz (Eds.), *Well-being: The foundations of hedonic psychology* (pp. 470–488). New York: Russell Sage.

Ittelson, W. H. (Ed.). (1973). *Environment and cognition.* New York: Seminar Press.

Jang, D. P., Ku, J. H., Shin, M. B., Choi, Y. H., & Kim, S. I. (2000). Objective validation of the effectiveness of virtual reality therapy. *CyberPsychology and Behavior, 3*(3), 369–374.

Janowsky, J. S., Oviatt, S. K., & Orwoll, E. S. (1994). Testosterone influences spatial cognition in older men. *Behavioral Neuroscience, 108*(2), 325–332.

Kaplan, R., & Kaplan, S. (1989). *The experience of nature: A psychological perspective.* Cambridge: Cambridge University Press.

Kibbee, E. (1984). Burn pain management. *Critical Care Update, 73,* 54–62.

Kimura, D., & Hampson, E. (1994). Cognitive pattern in men and women is influenced by fluctuations in sex hormones. *Current Directions in Psychological Science, 3*(2), 57–61.

Kipnis, D. (1997). Ghosts, taxonomies and social psychology. *American Psychologist, 52,* 205–211.

Kitchin, R. M. (1996). Increasing the integrity of cognitive mapping research: Appraising conceptual schemata of environment-behavior interaction. *Progress in Human Geography, 20,* 56–84.

Kramer, A. F., & Weber, T. (2000). Applications of psychophysiology to human factors. In J. T. Cacioppo, L. G. Tassinary, & G. G. Berntson (Eds.), *Handbook of psychophysiology* (pp. 794–814). New York: Cambridge University Press.

Lang, P. J. (1995). The emotion probe: Studies of motivation and attention. *American Psychologist, 50,* 372–385.

Lang, P. J., Bradley, M. M., & Cuthbert, B. N. (1997). Motivated attention: Affect, activation and action. In P. J. Lang, R. F. Simons, & M. T. Balaban (Eds.), *Attention and orienting: Sensory and motivational processes* (pp. 97–135). Hillsdale, NJ: Erlbaum.

Law, D. J., Pellegrino, J. W., & Hunt, E. B. (1993). Comparing the tortoise and the hare: Gender differences and experience in dynamic spatial reasoning tasks. *Psychological Science, 4,* 35–40.

Lechtzin, N., Withers, T., Devrotes, A., & Diette, G. (2001, May 18–23). *Distraction using nature sights and sounds reduces pain during flexible bronchoscopy.* Paper presented at the American Thoracic Society International Conference, San Francisco.

Lewin, K. (1936). *Principles of topological psychology* (F. Heider & G. M. Heider, Trans.). New York: McGraw-Hill.

Maguire, E. A., Gadian, D. G., Johnsrude, I. S., Good, C. D., Ashburner, J., Frackowiak, R. S. J., & Frith, C. D. (2000). Navigation-related structural change in the hippocampi of taxi drivers. *Proceedings of the National Academy of Sciences, 97*(8), 4398–4403.

Mann, V. A., Sasanuma, S., Sakuma, N., & Masaki, S. (1990). Sex differences in cognitive abilities: A cross-cultural perspective. *Neuropsychologia, 28,* 1063–1077.

Matthews, M. H. (1986). Gender, graphicacy and geography. *Educational Review, 38,* 259–271.

Mathews, M. H. (1987). Gender, home range and environmental cognition. *Transactions of the Institute of British Geographers, New Series, 12,* 43–56.

McCaul, K. D., Monson, N., & Maki, R. H. (1992). Does distraction reduce pain-produced distress among college students? *Health Psychology, 11,* 210–217.

Meagher, M. W., Arnau, R. C., & Rhudy, J. L. (2001). Pain and emotion: Effects of affective picture modulation. *Psychosomatic Medicine, 63,* 79–90.

Melzack, R., & Wall, P. D. (1965). Pain mechanisms: A new theory. *Science, 150,* 971–979.

Moffat, S. D., & Hampson, E. (1996). A curvilinear relationship between testosterone and spatial cognition in humans: Possible influence of hand preference. *Psychoneuroendocrinology, 21*(3), 323–337.

Parsons, R., & Hartig, T. (2000). Environmental psychophysiology. In J. T. Cacioppo, L. G. Tassinary, & G. Berntson (Eds.), *Handbook of psychophysiology* (pp. 815–846). New York: Cambridge University Press.

Parsons, R., Tassinary, L. G., Bontempo, D., & Vanman, E. J. (1997). Psychophysiology and judgments of landscape aesthetics: On the trail of awe, fascination and the sublime. In *ASPRS/ACSM Annual Convention Technical Papers: Vol. 4. Resource Technology* (pp. 288–301). Bethesda, MD: American Society for Photogrammetry and Remote Sensing/American Congress on Surveying and Mapping.

Parsons, R., Tassinary, L. G., Ulrich, R. S., Hebl, M. R., & Grossman-Alexander, M. (1998). The view from the road: Implications for stress recovery and immunization. *Journal of Environmental Psychology, 18,* 113–140.

Pascal, B. (1660/1958). *Pensées.* Translated by W. F. Trotter. Dutton, NY: Dutton Place.

Perry, S., & Heidrick, G. (1982). Management of pain during debridement: A survey of U.S. burn units. *Pain, 13,* 267–280.

Phillips, K., & Siverman, I. (1997). Differences in the relationship of menstrual cycle phase to spatial performance on two- and three-dimensional tasks. *Hormones and Behavior, 32,* 167–175.

Raft, D., Smith, R. H., & Warren, N. (1986). Selection of imagery in the relief of chronic and acute clinical pain. *Journal of Psychosomatic Research, 30*(4), 481–488.

Rainville, P., Carrier, B., Hofbauer, R. K., Bushnell, M. C., & Duncan, G. H. (1999). Dissociation of sensory and affective dimensions of pain using hypnotic modulation. *Pain, 82*(2), 159–171.

Rhudy, J. L., & Meagher, M. W. (2000). Fear and anxiety: Divergent effects on human pain thresholds. *Pain, 84,* 65–75.

Robinson, M. D. (1998). Running from William James' bear: A review of preattentive mechanisms and their contribution to emotional experience. *Cognition and Emotion, 12,* 697–713.

Ruff, C. (1987). Sexual dimorphism in human lower limb bone structure: Relationship to subsistence strategy and sexual division of labor. *Journal of Human Evolution, 16,* 391–416.

Schmitz, S. (1997). Gender-related strategies in environmental development: Effects of anxiety on wayfinding in and representation of a three-dimensional maze. *Journal of Environmental Psychology, 17,* 215–228.

Schmitz, S. (1999). Gender differences in acquisition of environmental knowledge related to wayfinding behavior, spatial anxiety and self-estimated environmental competencies. *Sex Roles, 41*(1–2), 71–93.

Sherry, D. F., & Hampson, E. (1997). Evolution and the hormonal control of sexually-dimorphic spatial abilities in humans. *Trends in Cognitive Neurosciences, 1*(2), 50–56.

Silverman, I., Choi, J., Mackewn, A., Fisher, M., Moro, J., & Olshansky, E. (2000). Evolved mechanisms underlying wayfinding: Further studies on the hunter-gatherer theory of spatial sex differences. *Evolution and Human Behavior, 21,* 201–213.

Silverman, I., & Eals, M. (1992). Sex differences in spatial abilities: Evolutionary theory and data. In J. Barkow, L. Cosmides, & J. Tooby (Eds.), *The adapted mind* (pp. 533–549). New York: Oxford University Press.

Silverman, I., & Phillips, K. (1993). Effects of estrogen changes during the menstrual cycle on spatial performance. *Ethology and Sociobiology, 14,* 257–270.

Stern, J. A., & Dunham, D. N. (1990). The ocular system. In J. T. Cacioppo & L. G. Tassinary (Eds.), *Principles of psychophysiology: Physical, social and inferential elements* (pp. 513–553). New York: Cambridge University Press.

Suedfeld, P., Steel, G. D., Wallbaum, A. B. C., Bluck, S., Livesey, N., & Capozzi, L. (1994). Explaining the effects of stimulus restriction: Hemispheric asymmetry hypothesis. *Journal of Environmental Psychology, 14*(2), 87–100.

Terrazas, A., & McNaughton, B. L. (2000). Brain growth and the cognitive map. *Proceedings of the National Academy of Sciences, 97*(9), 4414–4416.

Ulrich, R. S. (1981). Natural versus urban scenes: Some psychophysiological effects. *Environment and Behavior, 13*(5), 523–556.

Ulrich, R. S. (1983). Aesthetic and affective responses to natural environments. In I. Altman & J. F. Wohwill (Eds.), *Human behavior and environment: Vol. 6. Behavior and the natural environment.* New York: Plenum Press.

Ulrich, R. S., Simons, R. F., Losito, B. D., Fiorito, E., Miles, M. A., & Zelson, M. (1991). Stress recovery during exposure to natural and urban environments. *Journal of Environmental Psychology, 11,* 201–230.

Vandenberg, S. G., & Kuse, A. R. (1978). Mental rotations: A group test of three-dimensional spatial visualization. *Perceptual and Motor Skills, 47,* 599–604.

Voyer, D., Voyer, S., & Bryden, M. P. (1995). Magnitude of sex differences in spatial abilities: A meta-analysis and consideration of critical variables. *Psychological Bulletin, 117,* 250–270.

Waller, D., Hunt, E., & Knapp, D. (1998). The transfer of spatial knowledge in virtual environment training. *Presence, Tele-operators and Virtual Environments, 7*(2), 129–143.

Watson, D., Wiese, D., Vaidya, J., & Tellegen, A. (1999). The two general activation systems of affect: Structural findings, evolutionary considerations, and psychobiological evidence. *Journal of Personality and Social Psychology, 76*(5), 820–838.

Weisenberg, M., Tepper, I., & Schwarzwald, J. (1995). Humor as a cognitive technique for increasing pain tolerance. *Pain, 63*(2), 207–212.

Wenger, W. D., & Videbeck, R. (1969). Eye pupillary measurement of aesthetic responses to forest scenes. *Journal of Leisure Research, 1*(2), 149–161.

Whipple, B., & Glynn, N. J. (1992). Quantification of the effects of listening to music as a noninvasive method of pain control. *Scholarly Inquiry for Nursing Practice, 6*(1), 43–58.

Witelson, S. F. (1988). Neuroanatomical sex differences: Of consequence for cognition? *The Behavioral and Brain Sciences, 11,* 215–217.

CHAPTER 12

Environmental Psychology and Urban Planning: Where Can the Twain Meet?

ARZA CHURCHMAN

SINCE ITS INCEPTION, environmental psychology has focused its interdisciplinary discourse with those who design and plan the physical environment, toward architects (see, for example, Proshansky, 1971). This is exemplified in the fact that virtually all of the chapters in the application section of this handbook relate to aspects of the physical environment addressed by architects. We do not have a chapter on planning theory parallel to that of Groat and Despres (1991) on architectural theory and its significance for environmental design research. Most of the applied research in the field of environmental psychology has been on buildings, streets, parks, and neighborhoods. Postoccupancy evaluation research, for example, has not even reached the level of the neighborhood (Churchman & Ginosar, 1999). Crowding research has focused mainly on indoor crowding, much less on residential or urban crowding, and has not really attended concretely to the links between density and crowding (Alterman & Churchman, 1998).

We in environmental psychology are interested in environmental perception and cognition, in feelings, beliefs, and attitudes, in personality and the environment, in concepts such as personal space, territoriality, privacy, and crowding (see Bechtel, 1997; Gifford, 1997), all focused on the individual and his or her experience, and none intuitively or obviously relevant to urban planners.

Planners, on the other hand, talk about transportation systems (cf. Garrett & Wachs, 1996), central business districts (cf. Frieden & Sagalyn, 1992),

development and growth control, land uses and zoning issues (cf. So & Getzells, 1988), legal and institutional frameworks (cf. Cullingworth, 1993), environmental quality issues, economic efficiency and development (cf. Banister, Button, & Nijkamp, 1999), mixed-income housing (cf. Ayalon, Ben-Rafael, & Yogev, 1993), urban consolidation (Troy, 1996), urban sprawl (Ewing, 1997), or reurbanization (Berridge Lewinberg Greenberg Ltd., 1991), compact cities (Jenks, Williams, & Burton, 1996), and sustainable cities (Haughton & Hunter, 1994). All of these topics are not intuitively or obviously relevant to environmental psychologists.

To illustrate, in a review article of the multidisciplinary literature on density (Churchman, 1999), there was almost no overlap between the sources on different issues. In the lists of the advantages and disadvantages of (relatively) high densities, the potential environmental, transportation, physical infrastructure, urban form, and economic advantages and disadvantages all came from the planning literature (with two exceptions). The potential personal and social advantages and disadvantages came from both the planning and the environment behavior literature, while the potential personal and psychological disadvantages virtually all came from the environmental psychology literature. Interestingly, I could not find any relevant references for the potential psychological advantages of relatively higher densities.

It is fascinating that, in the list of planning skills and competencies suggested by Osawa and Seltzer

(1999) and reclassified by Alexander (2001) under the category of substantive knowledge that planners need to have, there is no subclassification of knowledge about people, their needs, and their preferences.

Nevertheless, some of the topics that the two fields deal with are common ones and are beginning to be even more so, particularly in the areas of sustainability, public participation, and community planning (cf. the chapters in this handbook by Pol; Bonnes & Bonaiuto; Horelli; Wiesenfeld & Sanchez).

My purpose in this chapter is to turn our attention to the planning field, to examine the commonalities and differences between the two fields, and to see what we can contribute to each other and how we have already done so. It is my contention that in relatively ignoring the field of planning we are missing out on a potentially important and willing partner and on the opportunity to make a difference in the real world. Planning is by definition a multidisciplinary endeavor that is open to social science and social science methods. It also focuses on the interrelationships between all the different aspects of the environment. Kaufman (1974), for example, recognized that, because of the mutual dependencies between the housing, service, and employment systems and the transportation system that links them, no one system can be planned separately without considering its relationship with the others. This is, of course, not to say that this ideal is achieved in every case, but it is recognized as an ideal.

Over the years, environmental psychology has become part of an interdisciplinary field, now called *environment behavior studies*, that includes anyone interested in the interface and the relationships between the physical environment and human behavior, and this definitely includes planners. The environment is understood to be an all-encompassing term, including all aspects of the world—physical, ecological, social, economic, cultural, political, institutional, technological, and individual.

One of the major differences between environmental psychology and planning is the inclusion by environmental psychologists of the individual level and its exclusion by planners, who usually think in terms of aggregations or collectives of people (Jones, 1996) or of systems and institutions beyond the people. The environment behavior approach focuses on different groups of people and the degree to which the environment "fits" their needs. This is a people-centered field that relates to people and their needs concretely, whereas planning relates to people in general and in the abstract. To use an image suggested by Kidder and Fine (1987), the lens used in planning is more a zooming-out one, and that used in environmental psychology is a zooming-in one.

Following is a statement written by Rachel Kallus and I (2001) in a forthcoming paper on the relationship between environmental psychology and urban design, but I think it exemplifies the situation in urban planning as well:

> Although the city is investigated and designed on the implicit premise of the necessity and importance of human experience, this experience is never specifically discussed or related to enough to make a difference. We seldom know who the persons in the space are, and what they are doing there. We never see their faces, let alone hear their voices.

The focus of environmental psychology is mainly on the microlevel and on relatively small-scale environments, whereas planning focuses mainly on the macrolevel and on relatively large-scale environments both in geographic terms and in social and economic terms. Their smallest unit would usually be the neighborhood (Jones, 1996), whereas for many environmental psychologists that might be the largest unit. In Bronfenbrenner's terms, we focus on the microsystem (the system of relationships between people and their immediate environment) and on the mesosystem (the interrelations between two or more settings that one experiences at a particular point in time) (Bronfenbrenner & Crouter, 1983). Planners focus on the exosystem, as described by Bronfenbrenner (1979), which includes such social and physical settings as the neighborhood, mass media, public institutions, and social program and policies, which affect or are affected by what happens in the setting containing the person; and on the macrosystem, which includes the institutions of the culture in which one lives—the economic, social, educational, legal, and political systems. It would seem that the exosystem would be the most obvious possible level of link between the two fields.

Another difference between the two fields is the relative weight given to the different aspects. Planners place much more emphasis on economic and political aspects than do we. As a result, they are also concerned about their own role within these systems and the manner in which these systems operate (Beauregard, 1998). Although in principle it is recognized by many in both fields that the environment is indivisible, that one cannot separate out various aspects from the whole, in practice it has been virtually impossible so far to do research or to practice in this manner. However, the ideal is there, and the striving to get closer to it is part of a relatively common zeitgeist.

There is a difference also in the time frame being dealt with: Planning's mandate is to focus on the future, whereas environmental psychology studies the past and the present and only sometimes is willing to hazard a guess as to what this means for the future. Planning also strives to be implemented—it is not a theoretical, knowledge-gathering field per se. Many of us in the field of environmental psychology have the luxury of undertaking research or developing theory without needing to be concerned about whether what we say will be accepted by decision makers or will be politically viable.

COMMON AND DIFFERENT ASSUMPTIONS

I have previously identified some very basic assumptions of the field of environmental psychology (Churchman, 2000). The first assumption, that the physical environment has implications for people's lives, is a given in planning and an even more basic assumption for them. However, the next assumptions are unfortunately not so well understood, acknowledged, or integrated into the planning field. These are the following: (1) People are different and have different needs. One cannot specify, identify, or posit one single model of the person environment relationship. (2) People are active and not passive—they interpret, evaluate, and use their environment in ways that they wish to or are able to. (3) Aggregates (or groups) can be identified who have some needs and characteristics in common, for example, by age, gender, health status, socioeconomic status, cultural background, and so forth (an idea acknowledged in planning but usually at a very general level and without knowing how to use this differentiation). (4) The purpose of the environment is to afford opportunities for achieving one's own definition of quality of life. The term *quality of life* is used to denote the subjective judgment by an individual as to the degree to which her or his needs in the various domains of life are met. These domains include the degree of self-actualization, health, family life, social relations, dwelling place, work situation, services, income level, security, environmental quality,

social justice, and equality (Churchman, 1993a). Only some of these domains are directly related to planning issues, but many others are indirectly related. (5) Just about everything is context dependent in one way or another (Rosnow & Rosenthal, 1989; Stokols, 1987).[1] Although we understand the importance of context intellectually, we don't always describe it or attend to it. Can we honestly say that we always follow Sinha's admonishments that psychological knowledge should (a) arise from within the culture, (b) reflect local behaviors, (c) be interpreted within a local frame of reference, and (d) yield results that are locally relevant (Adair, 1999, p. 405)?

Furthermore, our attention to context tends to stop before the level at which planners operate, and we tend to ignore the institutions or systems within which the environments that we study exist.

From the point of view of the field of environmental psychology, the goal of any field of planning is to enable people to achieve as high a level of quality of life as possible. Achieving this goal is not simple at all. It requires, among other things, an understanding of the way in which people perceive, think, learn, feel, and develop; an acceptance of the variability between people and between aggregates or groups of people; and an understanding of the ways in which the sociophysical environment can be an asset or a hindrance to this goal. Granted, planning cannot relate specifically to the particular needs and expectations of every individual. However, the opposite policy, too often adopted, of considering the population to consist of an "average" person or of a very few types is equally untenable. One cannot talk of *the* quality of life; one must talk of quali*ties* of lives, differentiating between groupings of individuals who have characteristics in common that have significance for their environmental and settlement needs.

This is a very important statement. However, in planning terms it is very easy to say but very difficult to apply in practice. It sounds much too subjective to be capable of application at all. Furthermore, some of the assumptions that, on the whole, we have rejected can still be found lurking in the words and sometimes deeds of planners (and perhaps also among some of us). Among these are (1) the notion

---

[1] In keeping with this assumption, I wish to note that many of my statements on planning may be contextually biased, and are likely to apply to the Israeli context more than to others. The relationship between the two fields may be different where the institutional, cultural, and normative contexts are different.

of the universal or generic human or the unspecified subject as applying to women as well as to men; (2) that various phenomena or concepts mean the same thing in different people's lives—leisure, work, home, family, and so forth; (3) that there is a single public good, a single public interest; (4) that there is a simple, unidirectional causal relationship between the environment and people's behavior, attitudes, and feelings; (5) that there is an average person or family; (6) that one can assume that everyone has a car or a computer or will work at home in the future.

Planners tend to be wary of the microlevel, because it will make things even more complicated than they already are. It is easier to work with macrolevel statistics that are readily available than to try to generate microlevel data. Furthermore, they are usually pressed for time and money and often do not have the luxury of being able to engage in specific research.[2]

This is not to say that there is no planning research that focuses on the attitudes of people toward planning issues (see, for example, Audirac & Smith, 1992; Heath, 2001; Takahashi, 1997). There is also growing recognition of the need to talk about differences and relate to them. However, they are the exception rather than the rule, and they are not informed by environmental psychology's theories, concepts, or knowledge.

Planners feel the lack of tools for applying the knowledge available in addition to the lack of knowledge that is in a form usable by them. Those planners who are aware of the importance of the microlevel do not always find partners to this understanding within the planning system and also do not find environmental psychologists there. We are not part of the interdisciplinary planning teams, our research is not readily accessible to them, nor does it necessarily present information that they consider relevant to the issues that they are dealing with.

It is instructive to compare some of the principles of feminist planning research with those of environment behavior research. One can find many similarities, even though they may not be stated in the same words (Churchman, 2000). What the feminist research adds is the political-ideological level, which is basically absent from the environment behavior field in general and from environmental psychology

in particular. The way we think about context could be extended to include this, but on the whole it isn't at the moment. Riger (1998) writes that a focus on the immediate social situation may overlook the larger social system, ignoring economic, political, or historical forces that shape women's and men's behavior. She argues that the ahistorical nature of social psychology relates to behaviors that are the product of contemporaneous conditions as if they were universal timeless principles of human behavior.

This could be said, too, about much of the work in environmental psychology. Despres (1991) found that most studies on the meaning of home overlook the impact of structural, societal, and formal forces on the individual's perceptions, judgments, behaviors, and experiences of and about the home. Schneekloth (1994) tried to link the two fields by arguing that the basis for the link exists in the historical fact that environment behavior studies started as a utopian project. However she sees us as having been captured by the scientific trap. Thus, in her words, we did not do this utopian work with what she terms as the critical self-reflection that acknowledges our locations within the culture, that criticizes our ways of working, and that attempts to be passionate and inclusive.

Feminist writing and research within the planning field has been more sensitive than other areas in planning to the variability of groups and individuals. There is growing recognition in the field of planning, fueled particularly by feminist planners, that "the dilemmas of difference, in all their cultural, social, spatial manifestations, are a challenge to the current way of thinking" (Sandercock, 1998, p. 3). McDowell (1993), for example, writes from a feminist position that we must get away from generalizations about women as an undifferentiated category toward more particular understandings of the historically specific processes that produce the particular range of gender relations in a range of places. Ritzdorf (1994) analyzes the issue of zoning in terms of its implications for the lives of women of different household types, rather than in macrolevel, land use terms.

Altman and I have argued that the distinction between private and public spheres that feminists have identified as problematic and as a political and value-laden act is also untenable within a transactional approach because individuals and groups function in contexts that are embedded in and

---

[2] I wish to thank Dr. Ronit Davidovitch-Marton and Michal Mitrany for their insights on the relationship between the two fields, based on their professional planning experience.

inseparable from all larger contexts relevant to their lives. Once we understand that women (and men) cannot be detached from their social, cultural, political, and physical environmental contexts, then it becomes clear that changes that take place only within the individual are not sufficient. Change must be eventually introduced throughout all levels of systems, including the physical environment (Churchman & Altman, 1994). This kind of recognition brings us close to the kind of thinking that characterizes many in the planning field.

Many planners understand that physical planning must incorporate the social and individual aspects of people's lives. However, there are two problems here: One is that there are no developed tools for how to accomplish this goal, so each planner tries to work out a strategy on his or her own. The second problem is that physical plans are usually expressed in two-dimensional drawings rather than in words, and it is very difficult to express the reasoning behind the plan and all of the considerations that went into the final product presented in this way.

BRIDGING ATTEMPTS

In an early article, Ginsberg and I identified the inherent difficulties arising in the attempt to use research findings in physical planning processes (Churchman & Ginsberg, 1984). We suggested that these could be divided into four categories: (1) the limitations of physical planning in terms of its ability to affect people's lives; (2) the tension, and possible conflict, between general societal goals and individual goals; (3) the relatively fixed, tangible physical planning solutions versus subjective, possibly conflicting, and changing user perceptions and behaviors; (4) planning for the future versus research on the past or present.

Jones (1996) makes an interesting attempt at bridging the fields of psychology and planning by applying Fishbein and Ajzen's (1975) theory of reasoned action to planning related to environmental issues. She sees the importance for planners of understanding individual processes of thinking and behavior so as to recognize the linkages between attitudes and perceptions of behavioral control and so as to change how they have traditionally thought of communities and groups and how they have identified them. She suggests that a more appropriate identification of the groups relevant to the people themselves could

enable the use of these groups to encourage acceptance of, or compliance with, particular (environmental) policies. In this way, one would know better how to provide system-level support for (positive) individually initiated and motivated behavior.

Davidovitch-Marton and Churchman (1997) based their bridging attempt on Altman and Rogoff's (1987) transactional theory. We argued that different planning models and theories attach great importance to the planning process, to its incorporation in decision-making processes, and to the politics of planning but give virtually no consideration to the content of the process or to the information necessary for relating to the needs of the people for whom the planning is ostensibly undertaken. We suggested an alternative model based on transactional and contextual principles that would define planning topics in terms of events and contexts. The event is defined as a series of activities conducted in an environment by a group of individuals, characterized in spatial, social, economic, and psychological terms. The context is a collection of events occurring in the same circumstances. Events are not defined by a demarcated geographical area but rather specifically by the manner in which they operate in the daily lives of the individuals involved. Such an approach requires the planner to begin the process on more of a microlevel and from there to build up to more of a macrolevel.

EXAMPLES

Let us look at some examples of the difference between the approach in environmental psychology and in planning as applied to various topics or concepts. With regard to the concept of disability, in environmental psychology we tend to look at the specific aspects of the physical environment that inhibit or enable persons with disabilities to conduct their lives, to have freedom of choice, and to be relatively independent (cf. Goltsman, Gilbert, & Wohlford, 1992; Null & Cherry, 1996). The planner Hahn (1986) looks at disability as a social and political phenomenon and examines the way attitudes toward disabled persons are reflected in policy. Gleason (2001) discusses sociopolitical theories that underlie the manner in which disability is, or should be, addressed in the planning of cities.

Another example of the particular approach in environmental psychology to a term common in urban planning is the issue of density. Three concepts are used by environment behavior researchers to address the issue of density and how density relates to people's lives: density, perceived density, and crowding. The distinctions were made by Stokols in 1972 and 1976, and by Rapoport in 1975, but only brought to the attention of planners by Alexander in 1993. *Density* is a term that represents the relationship between a given physical area and the number of people who inhabit or use that area. Density is an objective, quantitative, and neutral term. It is neutral in the sense that one cannot know immediately whether a given density level is positive or negative for the people involved. Some psychologists distinguish between spatial and social density. Spatial density is created by a given number of people within different size spaces. Social density is created by different numbers of people within the same space. The argument is that these two types of density are experienced differently (Altman, 1975; Baum & Paulus, 1987; Russell & Snodgrass, 1987). This distinction is similar to that made by the planner Hitchcock (1994) in his analysis of the difference between increasing density by reducing residential land area for the same number of people and by increasing the number of people in the same residential land area. The difference is that he does not conceive of these differences at all in terms of their implications for the people themselves, but rather for land uses, building types, and the impact on land consumption.

Perceived density and crowding are both based on the principle that the same density can be perceived and evaluated in very different ways, by different people, under different circumstances, in different cultures and countries. Thus, even though planners operate on the level of density, they must be, but are usually not, cognizant of the fact that people experience and live in a multilevel situation that manifests itself in interactions between a particular density and the perception and evaluation of that density.

Perceived density is defined as an individual's perception and estimate of the number of people present in a given area, the space available, and the organization of that space. Cues in the environment that represent people and their activities play critical roles in this perception of density (Rapoport, 1975). Perceived density is by definition subjective because it is determined by the individual, and neutral because it does not include an evaluative component.

Crowding is defined as the subjective evaluation by an individual that a given density and perceived density are negative. Crowding is also defined as a state of psychological stress that accompanies density that is evaluated as too high (Evans & Cohen, 1987; Sundstrom, 1978). It is a psychological state, the outcome of a subjective and experiential process that includes an appraisal of physical conditions, situational variables, personal characteristics, and coping assets (Altman, 1975; Baum & Paulus, 1987; Stokols, 1972). Thus, crowding represents a subjective, qualitative, and affective (emotion-laden) experience.

It should be noted that there is a need for a more general term than *crowding* for the subjective evaluation of density. Rapoport (1975) pointed out many years ago that research addresses the negative subjective aspects of high density (i.e., crowding) but virtually ignores the positive subjective aspects. Planning, however, recognizes the positive aspects of high densities and stresses them, particularly in relation to compact cities, sustainability, and so forth (Churchman, 1999). There has been some recent attention paid to this lacuna that hopefully will result at least in a term for positive evaluations of density (Mitrany & Churchman, 1998).

What lessons can be learned for environment behavior researchers and for planners, given the complexity of the meaning and use of the term *density* and the addition of the subjective concepts of perceived density and crowding? Real-world complexity and the interrelationships between variables and factors must be addressed in our research on density, as it is in practice. Real-world complexity includes a subjective element that is always present in people's behaviors, expectations, and attitudes (including those of decision makers, planning professionals, and researchers); thus, it must be taken into account. It is easier for planners to affect density and perceived density than to affect the subjective experience of crowding. However, planners have no choice but to try to address the implications of the intervening factors that are relevant to crowding.

The problem is that this is very easy for us to say but is certainly not sufficient information. The planners need to know which are the relevant intervening variables and characteristics of the environment, so that they can try to maximize the benefits and minimize the costs. They need to be alerted to the dangers of deterministic ways of thinking, which may creep into their plans. An obviously related lesson is that no one solution will meet the needs of every situation, context, person, or group. Therefore, a variety of solutions (different types of settlements, neighborhoods, housing, and transportation) are essential to meet the needs of different groups in different countries, regions, and towns. Solutions should be based on an understanding of the differences in needs and expectations of relevant groups so that they can offer choices that can meet these needs and expectations. Are we able at present to give substantive information related to these issues, not just general statements? Not really.

Environmental psychologists need to undertake research that links the physical aspects of the context to the subjective ones and describes the physical variables in terms that are relevant to planners. We need to understand the variables that planners deal with and the levels at which they can affect decisions and to focus research on those levels, too. Working with planners forces us to learn about the planning and governmental system and to expand our concept of context to include these aspects.

Many of the definitions of planning provided to me by my colleague Rachelle Alterman focus on the fact that planning is required to make decisions about the future (e.g., a definition by John Forester that planning is the guidance of future action, or an earlier one by Wildavsky that planning is the ability to control future actions). We in psychology are not really trained in this vein. We study the past and the present, sometimes attempt to learn about people's plans and desires for the future, and have the luxury when we make recommendations of knowing that others will have the responsibility for deciding whether, when, and how to act upon them.

Working with planners forces us to ask ourselves: Are we willing to make definite statements, to let go of our tendency to make contingent statements and take a stand, even if we don't really have enough information to do so. I have been convinced by my colleagues that it is better for me to take a stand based on partial information than to leave them to take a stand based on no information or on possibly erroneous assumptions. In one case, I was asked to state what amount of public space was necessary for playgrounds in neighborhoods. My initial response was to say that, based on the literature, playgrounds by themselves were not what was needed, but rather appropriate development of all of the outdoor spaces. My colleagues pointed out that, were we to say this, no space would be allocated for playgrounds and there would be none. As a result, I made a recommendation on the minimal size of playgrounds necessary for different age groups (Hill & Alterman,

1977), but I continue to teach my students that playgrounds in and of themselves are not the answer.

EXPERIENCE IN APPLICATION

What has been my experience in working as part of interdisciplinary planning teams on outline plans for two cities and on a plan for the whole country of Israel? At these levels, the challenge is to find a way to think in broad terms and yet still relate to the issues raised at a level relevant to the lives of the people who live there. In one case (that of the ultra-orthodox city of Bnai Brak), the input of Yona Ginsberg and myself (based on some specific empirical research we were able to conduct and our professional knowledge) focused on (1) the building types appropriate for the population, based on their lifestyle, culture, demographic characteristics, and economic circumstances; (2) the type and amount of open space required by the population; and (3) the types of streets appropriate for their circumstances (Churchman & Ginsberg, 1997). In another case (that of the city of Ashkelon), my contribution was to introduce a more differentiated and focused way of determining the nature, quantity, and location of public services for different neighborhoods within the city. In other words, to say that recognizing the differences in needs between groups within the city in terms of demographic and economic circumstances, lifestyle, and cultural factors requires the adjustment of the national prescriptions of which services are needed to fit the particular needs of particular neighborhoods.

Working on the national plan for the State of Israel in the year 2020 was a fascinating challenge because it required thinking in very different terms than when one is working on the neighborhood or even city level. However, I found that by approaching the issues from the microenvironmental level of residential buildings, streets, and neighborhoods and their implications for different age groups, genders, and cultural groups, I was able to move to the macrolevel and suggest recommendations that were based on our microlevel understandings, both in terms of planning principles and in terms of process principles (Churchman, 1993b, 1996). The fascinating aspect of this project was that my conclusions regarding density levels were the same ones arrived at by the planners from the totally different perspective of the land shortage in the country.

Similarly, all of the recommendations for improving the environment for women that we suggested in a different context are commensurate with what is considered "good" planning in general terms. We analyzed the needs of a particular group but found that none of the recommendations are detrimental to other groups; on the contrary, they are as positive for other population groups as for women. They are also clearly supportive of the principle of sustainability, whose goal is to balance concerns for the economy, the ecological environment, and the sociocultural integrity of the society with the attempt to ensure that future generations have the opportunity to do the same. The recommendations for relatively high housing densities, mixed land use policies, public transportation, open spaces, and walkable distances to services, all lead to savings of land and energy resources and less air pollution, thus contributing to sustainability (Churchman, Alterman, Azmon, Davidovitch-Marton, & Fenster, 1996).

The advantage of such work is the possibility of having a major impact on policy and practice. My colleague and I (Alterman & Churchman, 1998) were asked by the Israel Ministry of the Interior to suggest a policy for dealing with the need to intensify the use of land for housing purposes. This policy is necessary because Israel is a very small country with an expanding population, both from relatively high birth rates and from immigration, and with an increasing rise in the standard of living and in the size of dwellings. This results in pressure to use land that is presently used for agriculture or is open space for building purposes. We were very concerned that the policy be one in which higher densities could be achieved but without sacrificing the residents' quality of life, and we made that a basic principle of the policy we proposed. In the past year or two, parts of our policy are being increasingly used by planning commissions to evaluate plans that are brought before them and to argue for increased densities when the plans propose very low densities, but, very importantly, to argue for lower densities when the plans propose very high ones.

IMPLICATIONS

An important message from our field that has implications for planning alerts the planner to the complexities in people's behavior and attitudes and to the fact that people do not perceive, understand, or relate to the environment in the same way, nor do they necessarily do so in the way that the planner does or intends that they should. However, we need to do more than just state this; we need to present the specifics in a manner that planners can use. The challenge to them is to learn to consider the microlevel even when they are working on the macrolevel. The fact that the needs of many different groups (children, the elderly, some women, and probably others) complement each other mitigates the problem bedeviling many planners today—how to plan today for population changes over time. An environment that initially considers varied needs and preferences is likely to continue to fit the needs of different groups over a longer period of time, more than an environment tailored to only one group.

The movement in planning toward more participatory and empowering decision-making processes is a very positive step in the direction of accommodating the needs and preferences of different groups of people. Thus, one of the meeting points between the two fields is the area of public participation in planning. Introducing individuals into the decision-making process forces planners to consider the microlevel and to meet the people, see their faces, and hear their voices. Our interest in such processes will force us to consider the macrolevel and to understand the decision-making system and the constraints and pressures within which planners operate.

What are the challenges to environmental psychologists? Can we learn to use the language and concepts of planners? Do we want to? Are we prepared to translate our knowledge into quantitative terms to meet the perceived need of the economic or transportation planners, or can we convince them that quantitative terms may not be the most appropriate ones? Are we prepared to make definite statements, although based on partial or nonspecific knowledge?

One of the main challenges for both fields is how to learn to work together, to understand the concepts and concerns of the other. Given that each field has special strengths and qualifications, the potential benefits of such cooperation are manifold. From my personal experience, I can say that it is well worth the effort.

REFERENCES

Adair, J. (1999). Indigenization of psychology: The concept and its practical implementation. *Applied Psychology: An International Review, 48*(4), 403–418.

Alexander, E. (1993). Density measures: A review and analysis. *Journal of Architectural and Planning Research, 10*(3), 181–202.

Alexander, E. (2001). What do planners need to know? *Journal of Planning Education and Research, 20*(3), 367–380.

Alterman, R., & Churchman, A. (1998). *Housing density: A guide to increasing the efficiency of urban land use* [in Hebrew]. Haifa, Israel: Technion, Center for Urban and Regional Studies.

Altman, I. (1975). *The environment and social behavior.* Monterey, CA: Brooks/Cole.

Altman, I., & Rogoff, B. (1987). World views in psychology: Trait, interactional, organismic, and transactional perspectives. In D. Stokols & I. Altman (Eds.), *Handbook of environmental psychology* (Vol. 1, pp. 7–40). New York: Wiley.

Audirac, I., & Smith, M. (1992). Urban forms and residential choice: Preference for urban density in Florida. *Journal of Architectural and Planning Research, 9*(1), 19–32.

Ayalon, H., Ben-Rafael, E., & Yogev, A. (1993). *Community in transition: Mobility, integration, and conflict.* London: Greenwood Press.

Banister, D., Button, K., & Nijkamp, P. (Eds.). (1999). *Environment, land use, and urban policy.* Cheltenham, England: Wiley.

Baum, A., & Paulus, P. (1987). Crowding. D. Stokols & I. Altman (Eds.), *Handbook of environmental psychology* (Vol. 1, pp. 533–570). New York: Wiley.

Beauregard, R. (1998). Writing the planner. *Journal of Planning Education and Research, 18*(2) 93–101.

Bechtel, R. (1997). *Environment & behavior research: An introduction.* Newbury Park, CA: Sage.

Berridge Lewinberg Greenberg Ltd. (1991). *Guidelines for the reurbanisation of Metropolitan Toronto.* Toronto: Municipality of Metropolitan Toronto Corporate Printing Services.

Bronfenbrenner, U. (1979). *The ecology of human development.* Cambridge, MA: Harvard University Press.

Bronfenbrenner, U., & Crouter, A. C. (1983). The evolution of environmental models in developmental research. In W. Kessen (Ed.), *Handbook of child psychology: History, theory, and methods* (pp. 357–414). New York: Wiley.

Churchman, A. (1993a). A differentiated perspective on urban quality of life: Women, children and the elderly. In M. Bonnes (Ed.), *Perception and evaluation of environmental quality* (pp. 165–178). Rome: UNESCO Program on Man and Biosphere.

Churchman, A. (1993b). *Fitting spatial planning to the needs of various groups in the population of Israel* [in Hebrew]. Haifa, Israel: Technion, Israel 2020-A Master Plan for Israel in the 21st Century.

Churchman, A. (1996). Modeling the person-environment relationship through a gender lens: Implications for a master plan in Israel. *European Spatial Research and Policy, 3*(1), 87–93.

Churchman, A. (1999). Disentangling the concept of density. *Journal of Planning Literature, 13*(4), 389–411.

Churchman, A. (2000). Women and the environment: Questioned and unquestioned assumptions. In S. Wapner, J. Demick, T. Yamamoto, & H. Minami (Eds.), *Theoretical perspectives in environment-behavior research: Underlying assumptions, research problems, and methodologies* (pp. 89–106). New York: Kluwer Academic/Plenum Press.

Churchman, A., & Altman, I. (1994). Women and the environment: A perspective on research, design and policy. In I. Altman & A. Churchman (Eds.), *Women and the environment* (pp. 1–15). New York: Plenum Press.

Churchman, A., Alterman, R., Azmon, Y., Davidovitch-Marton, R., & Fenster, T. (1996). *Habitat II: Shadow report.* Jerusalem, Israel: Israel Women's Network.

Churchman, A., & Ginosar, O. (1999). A theoretical basis for the post-occupancy evaluation of neighborhoods. *Journal of Environmental Psychology, 19*, 267–276.

Churchman, A., & Ginsberg, Y. (1984). The use of behavioral science research in physical planning: Some inherent limitations. *Journal of Architectural and Planning Research, 1*(1), 57–66.

Churchman, A., & Ginsberg, Y. (1997). *A master plan for Bnai Brak: Social aspects* [in Hebrew]. Haifa, Israel: Technion, Center for Urban and Regional Studies.

Cullingworth, J. B. (1993). *The political culture of planning.* New York: Routledge.

Davidovitch-Marton, R., & Churchman, A. (1997). The event and the context: A theoretical approach to person-environment planning. In M. Gray (Ed.), *Evolving environmental ideals* (pp. 353–361). Stockholm: Royal Institute of Technology.

Despres, C. (1991). The meaning of home: Literature review and directions for future research and theoretical development. *Journal of Architectural and Planning Research, 8*(2), 96–115.

Evans, G., & Cohen, S. (1987). Environmental stress. In D. Stokols & I. Altman (Eds.), *Handbook of environmental psychology.* (Vol. 1, pp. 571–610). New York: Wiley.

Ewing, R. (1997). Is Los Angeles-style sprawl desirable? *Journal of the American Planning Association, 63*(1), 107–126.

Fishbein, M., & Ajzen, I. (1975). Belief, attitude, intention, and behavior. reading, MA: Addison-Wesley.

Frieden, B., & Sagalyn, L. (1992). *Downtown Inc.: How America builds cities.* Cambridge, MA: Massachusetts Institute of Technology Press.

Garrett, M., & Wachs, M. (1996). *Transportation planning on trial: The Clean Air Act and travel forecasting.* London: Sage.

Gifford, R. (1997). *Environmental psychology.* Boston: Allyn & Bacon.

Gleason, B. (2001). Disability and the open city. *Urban Studies, 38*(2), 251–266.

Goltsman, S., Gilbert, T., & Wohlford, S. (1992). *The accessibility checklist: An evaluation system for buildings and outdoor settings.* Berkeley, CA: MIG Communications.

Groat, L., & Despres, C. (1991). The significance of architectural theory for environmental design research. In E. Zube & G. Moore (Eds.), *Advances in environment, behavior, and design* (Vol. 3, pp. 3–52). New York: Plenum Press.

Hahn, H. (1986). Disability and the urban environment: A perspective in Los Angeles. *Environment and Planning D: Society and Space, 4,* 273–288.

Haughton, G., & Hunter, C. (1994). *Sustainable cities.* London: Jessica Kingsley.

Heath, T. (2001). Revitalizing cities: Attitudes toward city-center living in the United Kingdom. *Journal of Planning Education and Research, 20*(4), 464–475.

Hill, M., & Alterman, R. (1977). *Land allocation standards: Stage 1. Open spaces* [in Hebrew]. Haifa, Israel: Technion, Center for Urban and Regional Studies.

Hitchcock, J. (1994). *A primer on the use of density in land use planning.* Papers on planning and design, No. 41. Toronto: University of Toronto, Program in Planning.

Jenks, M., Williams, K., & Burton, E. (1996). A sustainable future through the compact city? Urban intensification in the United Kingdom. *Environments by Design, 1*(1), 5–20.

Jones, A. (1996). The psychology of sustainability: What planners can learn from attitude research. *Journal of Planning Education and Research, 16*(1), 56–65.

Kallus, R., & Churchman, A. (2001). *Urban space for multiple publics: An encounter between an urban designer and an environmental psychologist.* Manuscript in preparation.

Kaufman, J. L. (1974). An approach to planning for women. In K. Hapgood & J. Getzels (Eds.), *Planning, women and change* (Planning Advisory Service Rep. No. 301, pp. 73–76). Chicago: American Society of Planning Officials.

Kidder, L., & Fine, M. (1987). Qualitative and quantitative methods: When stories converge. *New Directions for Program Evaluation, 35,* 57–76.

McDowell, L. (1993). Space, place and gender relations: Part II. Identity, difference, feminist geometries and geographies. *Progress in Human Geography, 17*(3), 306–309.

Mitrany, M., & Churchman, A. (1998). *The conceptual framework for housing density research.* Paper presented at International Association for Person Environment Studies 15, Eindhoven, The Netherlands.

Null, R., & Cherry, K. (1996). *Universal design.* Belmont, CA: Professional Publications.

Ozawa, C. & Seltzer, E. (1999). Taking our bearings: Mapping a relationship between planning practice, theory, and education. *Journal of Planning Education and Research, 18,* 257–266.

Proshansky, H. (1971). *The role of environmental psychology for the design professions.* Paper presented at a symposium on architecture for human behavior, Philadelphia.

Rapoport, A. (1975). Toward a redefinition of density. *Environment and Behavior, 7*(2), 7–32.

Riger, S. (1998). From snapshots to videotape: New directions in research on gender differences. *Journal of Social Issues, 53* (2), 395–408.

Ritzdorf, M. (1994). A feminist analysis of gender and residential zoning in the United States. In I. Altman & A. Churchman (Eds.), *Women and the environment* (pp. 255–279). New York: Plenum Press.

Rosnow, R., & Rosenthal, R. (1989). Statistical procedures and the justification of knowledge in psychological science. *American Psychologist, 44,* 1276–1284.

Russell, J., & Snodgrass, J. (1987). Emotion and the environment. In D. Stokols & I. Altman (Eds.), *Handbook of environmental psychology* (Vol. 1, pp. 245–280). New York: Wiley.

Sandercock, L. (1998). *Towards cosmopolis: Planning for multicultural cities,* Chichester, England: Wiley.

Schneekloth, L. (1994). Partial utopian visions: Feminist reflections on the field. In I. Altman & A. Churchman (Eds.), *Women and the environment* (pp. 281–306). New York: Plenum Press.

So, F., & Getzells, J. (Eds.). (1988). *The practice of local government planning.* Washington, DC: International City Management Association.

Stokols, D. (1972). On the distinction between density and crowding: Some implications for future research. *Psychological Review, 79*(3), 275–278.

Stokols, D. (1976). The experience of crowding in primary and secondary environments. *Environment and Behavior, 8*(1), 49–86.

Stokols, D. (1987). Conceptual strategies of environmental psychology. In D. Stokols & I. Altman (Eds.), *Handbook of environmental psychology* (pp. 41–70). New York: Wiley.

Sundstrom, E. (1978). Crowding as a sequential process: Review of research on the effects of population density on humans. In A. Baum & Y. Epstein (Eds.), *Human response to crowding* (pp. 31–116). Hillsdale, NJ: Erlbaum.

Takahashi, L. (1997). Information and attitudes toward mental health care facilities: Implications for addressing the NIMBY syndrome. *Journal of Planning Education and Research, 17*(2), 119–130.

Troy, P. (1996). *The perils of urban consolidation,* Sydney, Australia: Federation Press.

SHARPENING METHODS

CHAPTER 13

Transactionally Oriented Research: Examples and Strategies

CAROL M. WERNER, BARBARA B. BROWN, and IRWIN ALTMAN

In the years since Altman and Rogoff (1987) compared the transactional world view with other of psychology's world views,[1] researchers have become more confident that this is a fruitful philosophical approach but often wonder how to implement it in their own work. This chapter reviews a variety of theoretical and research projects informed by the transactional world view, and derives a systematic approach for conducting research within this perspective. We stress that there is no single or best way to undertake a transactional analysis, but decisions should be based on the phenomenon being studied and the research goals and purposes. The chapter presents an explanation of our transactional world view, gives examples of research projects that illustrate this world view, and provides strategies for conducting research from a transactional perspective.

---

[1] Altman and Rogoff described three other world views: (1) trait, or an emphasis on people and personality as reasons for action; (2) interactional, in which people and context are separate elements, and change comes about by the "inter-action" of the independent elements; and (3) organismic, or systems approaches in which sets of independent elements interact in complex and often reciprocal ways, with the system evolving toward an ideal and homeostatic end state. Each worldview has strengths and weaknesses, and all are necessary to fully understand a phenomenon (see Altman & Rogoff, 1987; Dewey & Bentley, 1949; and Pepper, 1942, 1967, for more detailed descriptions and comparisons of various worldviews).

TRANSACTIONAL WORLD VIEW

There are three assumptions basic to our transactional world view. First is holism, or the view that phenomena should be studied as holistic unities composed simultaneously of people, psychological processes, the physical environment, and temporal qualities. Second is the idea that time and temporal qualities are integral to phenomena, not separate "markers" of events. And third is a unique philosophy of science that includes a search for formal causes in events. In this chapter, we emphasize two of these assumptions: One is holism, including deciding on the unit of analysis or scope of a research project, and the other is understanding "formal cause" as one type of causal explanation.

WHOLE PHENOMENA AS THE FOCUS OF STUDY

A fundamental assumption of the transactional world view is that phenomena should be treated as holistic unities rather than combinations of separate elements. As Werner, Altman, Oxley, and Haggard (1987) wrote:

There are no separate actors in an event; the actions of one person are understood in relation to the actions of other people, and in relation to spatial, situational, and temporal circumstances in which the actors are embedded. These different aspects of an event are mutually defining and lend meaning to one another, and are so intermeshed that understanding one aspect requires simultaneous inclusion of other aspects. (p. 244)

Altman and Rogoff used the term *aspect* rather than *part*, *component*, or *element*, to emphasize that the four qualities of phenomena are intrinsically interconnected, mutually defining, and not separable from one another. Understanding the whole, the relationships among aspects, and how they work in combination, is an important purpose of a transactional analysis.

People refers to both the participants of primary interest and the social milieu in which they are embedded. Indeed, in this chapter, we use the term *people* to refer generally to human beings and the terms *social participants* and *social milieu/social context* more specifically. *Social participants* refers to the people whose actions and mental processes are the primary target of study, and *social milieu* refers to people around the participants who have relevance to them. *People*—whether participants or milieu—can refer to individuals, dyads, and larger groups, and the particular "social unit" (particular individual, subgroup, or group) one studies depends on one's purposes. Social contexts can inform, constrain, and support the social units, such as when family members undermine or give legitimacy to a new marriage. *Psychological processes* include a complex array of human actions, emotional and affective experiences, cognitions, and the enactment of and response to social and cultural rules, norms, and so on. These psychological processes define relationships among different participants (friend, subordinate, relative, leader), define the connections between participants and their social milieu (Should I conform?), and also define participants' relationships to their physical environment (Is this place beautiful? What is its meaning? What should my actions be here?). The term *physical environment* is complex and can involve a wide variety of levels of scale, from objects in a home, to rooms, the home itself, the neighborhood, city, and beyond. The physical environment also includes nature and natural areas—flora and fauna of all types, scale, and degrees of immediacy to people. The physical environment is more than background. It shifts and changes, and its many forms provide constraints, challenges, and opportunities for participants. And as elaborated below, *time and temporal qualities* are integral to the meaning and definition of phenomena.

The lay public automatically understands familiar events in this integrated, mutually defining, and interdependent way. Birthdays are important events in most societies, and a lay person describing a birthday celebration would undoubtedly use holistic language. For example, the description would include particular participants (the celebrant and invited guests), engaging in particular behaviors, located in particular physical settings, and using particular objects (a birthday cake, perhaps gifts in special wrappings). The lay description would probably include temporal qualities (celebrant's age, birth date, an appropriate time frame for the celebration), and details that vary depending upon the celebrant's age.

Similarly, we believe it is useful to see psychological phenomena with a similar holistic eye. For example, our transactional analysis of celebrations (Werner, Altman, Brown, & Ginat, 1993) examined how rituals and celebrations serve important individual and cultural purposes and how they are composed, simultaneously, of participants and social context, physical environments, temporal qualities, and psychological processes. Our analysis focused on the psychological processes of identity development and showed how both individual and group identities were reflected in and strengthened by celebrations. Celebrations provide opportunities—and obligations—for people *simultaneously* to validate their uniqueness as well as their membership in different social groups. Through celebrations, participants can feel special and unique, such as at birthday parties, when the celebrant chooses a favorite place for the party, receives gifts, and celebrates with friends and family members. At the same time, the celebration brings people closer as a group, emphasizing family, group, and cultural identities. By engaging in family and group festivities, and by recalling previous similar group-oriented events, people feel supported by and bonded with their partners, families, and other important social groups, as well as feeling attached to the familiar settings that support these celebrations. Thus a transactional approach revealed the multilayered nature of celebrations. Our particular analysis focused on individual celebrants and the immediate social context of friends and families. Other researchers have studied celebrations holistically at the community level, such as how they support community identities and contribute to community social relations (Manning, 1983).

Time, Continuity, and Change Are Intrinsic to Phenomena

Time and temporal qualities are integral to events. At one level this means that phenomena are dynamic and contain both continuity and change. We cannot limit analyses to static snapshots but should try to understand different phases of phenomena and how they unfold. Another feature of this view is that time is not an external marker by which events are gauged but is instead a part of phenomena. Events vary in their temporal scale, pace, and rhythm and with respect to whether they are past-, present-, or future-oriented. Events unfold at their own pace and should be studied in their own time, such as how families celebrate each member's birthday and how events at a birthday party are sequenced and paced (see Werner, Altman, & Oxley, 1985, for more details on temporal qualities). These temporal qualities are part of the meaning and experience of activities but are often ignored by researchers.

A Distinctive Approach to Inquiry and Knowledge

The philosophy of science that guides our transactional world view has three main principles: (1) an emphasis on formal causality, an under-used form of causal explanation; (2) the importance of both unique and generalizable events; and (3) the utility of understanding phenomena from different perspectives and observers.

First, our transactional world view highlights Aristotle's "formal" cause, which focuses on understanding *patterns of relationships* among aspects of the transactional unity—how do the aspects fit together to form coherent or meaningful wholes? A researcher might study patterns in the sequences of events, such as how individual behaviors combine to create "place ballets" and "morning routines." We would not expect any event in the sequence to effect or "cause" another to occur; rather, we would expect that events unfold and combine in coherent ways. For example, the sequence of events in many European and U.S. weddings underscores the transition from two separate individuals to a married couple, as well as the

shift from two separate families to a larger "family of in-laws." The bride and groom are initially separated, then the bride's father accompanies her down the aisle where she ceremoniously joins the groom. The families sit on separate sides of the aisle during the ceremony but mingle together afterwards. Consistent with a formal cause analysis, the order of these events contributes to the larger social and interpersonal meaning of the wedding ceremony (Altman, Brown, Staples, & Werner, 1992). Indeed, in our research, we have been less interested in the more typically studied antecedent-consequent or "cause-effect" relations that Aristotle referred to as "efficient" cause. Similarly, although we adopt a holistic, systems-like view of phenomena, we are less interested in Aristotle's third type of determinism, "final" cause, the teleological view that systems evolve towards an ideal, homeostatic end state.

Second, our transactional world view also differs from traditional psychological approaches in its appreciation for both unique events and common principles. It assumes that events change and may or may not recur in their current form and that there is value in understanding this uniqueness. It also assumes that there are often generalizable underlying principles to unique events, and that one goal of research is to identify both unique and common features of phenomena.

And third, our transactional world view also assumes that phenomena actually "look" different from different temporal, physical, and psychological perspectives, similar to Einstein's ideas about relativity in time and space. Each perspective provides accurate and useful understandings of the phenomenon, and it is important to include the perspectives of multiple participants, not only that of trained researchers.

A Wealth of World Views

We do not suggest that any world view is better than others; rather, each makes valuable contributions to our understanding of phenomena. Indeed, many research projects contain elements of more than one world view, and scholars can learn much from these blends of perspectives. Furthermore, although we propose some strategies for conducting transactionally oriented research, we continue to explore additional ways of undertaking these analyses. The next section of the chapter presents brief overviews of our research projects that highlight transactional principles.

ILLUSTRATIONS OF RESEARCH GUIDED BY A TRANSACTIONAL WORLD VIEW

Three research projects illustrate the transactional world view and show how flexible it can be. These examples differ in methods, scope, degree of emphasis on design/policy issues, and substantive focus. They also illustrate that one cannot do everything in every transactional study—different projects highlight different features of a transactional approach. The following descriptions emphasize two principles of our transactional world view: (1) holism, or examination of the four aspects—people, psychological processes, physical environment, and temporal qualities—in combination and (2) formal cause and patterns of relationship, or how the four aspects fit together into coherent wholes and whether the patterns shift and change over time. We do not intend to define in a rigid way what is and is not a transactional approach but rather hope to provide a clear explanation of our vision while stimulating further exploration by other researchers.

ILLUSTRATION 1: "CHRISTMAS STREET" IN SUMMER AND AT CHRISTMAS

One example of a transactional approach is our analysis of "Christmas Street," a residential block in the United States that had a 40-year tradition of collectively decorating for and celebrating the Christmas holiday (Altman, Werner, Oxley, & Haggard, 1987; Kaplan, 1987; Oxley, Haggard, Werner, & Altman, 1986; Werner, Altman, Oxley, & Haggard, 1987). Christmas Street looks rather ordinary in summer, but, like many such streets in the United States, it is transformed at Christmas into a winter wonderland of lights and decorations. Starting in late November and running through January 1, an illuminated sign at the entrance to the cul-de-sac declares this as "Christmas Street." Typically all but a few homes are decorated, and almost every family contributes time and effort to various Christmas Street events.

A key research question was prompted by our interest in formal cause: How do the aspects of friendship, attachment to the block, and physical appearance fit together, and do the aspects fit together in similar patterns, summer and Christmas, or do the

patterns change with time and circumstance? To these ends, we collected data reflecting these aspects at two distinct points in time—in the summer and then again during the Christmas holiday season. Oxley and colleagues' (1986) analysis indicated that the differences in physical appearance between summer and winter were matched by differences in social relationships among the neighbors. Many people who didn't interact in summer began to interact just before and during the Christmas season, so social relationships were rather fluid and changed as events surrounding the Christmas season played out. In a more specific test of formal cause, Oxley and colleagues found differences between summer and Christmas in the patterns of correlations among social relationships, attitudes, and decorations. At Christmas, the three aspects were clearly interconnected: People who liked and interacted with their neighbors had the most attractive and extensive Christmas decorations and also reported the most favorable attitudes toward the Christmas Street tradition. Thus, during the Christmas season, there was a congruence among psychological processes, participants and their social context, and use of the physical environment. In contrast, the pattern of how the aspects fit together was quite different in summertime. The social networks were different, with a larger number of networks and less reciprocity in relationships within the networks and across the block. In contrast to Christmas, group membership and psychological attachment to the block were not related to having an attractive and well-maintained front yard. Instead, yard appearance was associated with individual factors reflecting time available to work in the yard (being older and retired), indicating a changing configuration among the aspects.

This study illustrates two basic principles of formal cause: The aspects fit together in holistic patterns, and relationships among aspects shift and change over time. In this case, the changes were gradual and emerged as events unfolded. Although there were two significant dates—when the decorations went up and came down—the events surrounding the Christmas celebration actually extended earlier and later in time (Werner, Haggard, Altman, & Oxley, 1988). We did not point to a particular event that led to the transformation, nor does the transactional researcher feel obligated to try to identify such critical moments. Instead, we focused on the unfolding patterns of relationships. Bih (1992) used a similar approach in his analysis of changing relationships between people and objects. By looking at a transition in students' lives (moving to a new country), he could put into relief the evolving meaning of cherished possessions, such as objects that took on greater significance as they helped students cope with the new world's stressful experiences. In a similar examination of transitions, Shumaker and Conti (1985) found that favorite objects retained their meaning and provided stability during otherwise turbulent changes of people, relationships, and settings. Thus, identifying periods of change can allow one to examine how relations among aspects shift and how these patterns and configurations relate to the meanings of events.

An additional feature of the Christmas Street study was our use of multiple observers—including ourselves—to provide different perspectives on historical practices as well as current activities related to the tradition. All residents completed extensive questionnaires at two different times, and we took extensive photographs of yard decorations and upkeep in order to content-analyze these uses of the physical environment. To expand our information, we used in-depth semi-structured interviews with key informants, contacted people who were leaders as well as those who were relatively disinterested about the activities, and tried to develop a multi-faceted ethnographic analysis of this block and its annual celebration (Werner et al., 1988). This work included, therefore, a variety of participant observers, quantitative and qualitative analyses, and multiple methodological instruments and procedures.

Illustration 2: New Urbanism and Front Porches

New Urbanism is a design and planning philosophy for blocks, neighborhoods, and regions that "offers an alternative to urban sprawl, urban decay and disinvestment, single-use zoning, and auto-only environments" (Calthorpe, 2000, p. 177). New Urban neighborhoods differ from traditional suburban developments by including a greater range of housing options and lot sizes and emphasizing affordable homes and small lots, so as to allow neighborhoods to be economically diverse and widely accessible. New Urban communities are growing in number and exist both as new developments (such as Seaside, Florida) and redevelopments, including publicly funded low- and moderate-income redevelopment

sites (such as Diggs Town, Virginia; see Leccese & McCormick, 2000, for a range of New Urbanist projects). New Urbanists hope to foster a renewed sense of place and community through design features that support social and physical diversity and pedestrian accessibility.

Brown and colleagues' transactional analysis of front porches on homes (Brown, Burton, & Sweaney, 1998) was stimulated in part by the desire to see how a transactional perspective might complement New Urbanists' claims about porch use. Whereas New Urbanists focus on how front porches encourage and support neighborhood social relationships, Brown and her colleagues hypothesized that a transactional view would broaden our understanding of the many ways in which this setting functions. This research example has several distinct features illustrative of transactional analyses. First, it does not attempt to examine all four transactional aspects in depth but focuses on three, with detailed data gathering on psychological processes and the social units or groups of participants, and a comparison of these two aspects at two distinct time periods. The research did not extensively examine *physical qualities*, such as variations in the design and extent of porches or the presence of natural areas around the porch. Second, multiple historical and contemporary perspectives on porch use were gathered so that these different points of view might enrich understanding of multiple motives for and patterns of porch use. Third, the research shows that transactional analyses can start with places or settings, illustrating that one can begin an analysis with any of the four aspects. The emphasis on place was also intended to be useful to architects and planners, thereby conveying the applicability of a transactional approach to design professionals. And fourth, the study was manageable, with goals and methodology chosen so the project could be completed in a consciously delimited time frame.

The study targeted the New Urbanists' assumption that porches and other pedestrian-friendly design elements (e.g., street trees, sidewalks, houses close to the sidewalk) are ways to encourage neighborly interactions between porch users and passers-by. In contrast, Brown and colleagues' (1998) interviews of porch users established that—in addition to supporting neighborly interactions—porches also serve many social units from individuals to large groups, such as single users, entire households and neighbors, sibling groups, parental dyads, cross-generational family units, and so on. The researchers also learned that porches provide private havens, magnets for social activity, good informal viewing posts, places to appreciate nature, and places for a variety of leisurely pursuits (eating, playing games, and gossiping).

Instead of attempting to cover all four aspects of the transactional unity, the study emphasized the psychological processes and social actors involved in porch use. In terms of temporal qualities, the study focused on a time contrast suggested by New Urbanism—the contrast between pedestrian-oriented and automobile-oriented eras. New Urbanists claim that the sociability of neighborhoods has been eroded by designs that emphasized the car over pedestrian friendliness (such as front-facing garages that overwhelm and often replace front porches, and streets without sidewalks, which make walking unpleasant and unsafe). This claim guided Brown and colleagues to contrast interviews of older people about past uses (1920 to 1955) with information from younger people about more contemporary eras (1986 to 1995). In terms of the physical environment, they found that usable porches need to be large enough to provide for seating areas and that porch use decline across eras is accompanied by increasing use of family rooms and backyard patios or decks. However, that was the extent of Brown's attention to environmental design. Although one could examine design variations in porches (front vs. wraparound, upper vs. ground floor, porches screened by shrubs vs. more visible porches), a conscious decision was made to focus on the aspects of porch use that seemed most neglected in contemporary debates about porches—who uses them, for what social purposes, and how such patterns have changed historically.

Thus, this study is a good example of a "manageable" project using a transactional analysis. However, one could expand the study to understand different aspects, such as the temporal phenomena of porches. Indeed, Wilson-Doenges (2001) used a lens of finer resolution by conducting direct observations of porch use and identified daily and weekly variations or "rhythms" in porch use. Furthermore, one could expand treatment of the environmental aspects examined so that a wider array of New Urbanist design features—porches, narrow setbacks, sidewalks, and alleys—can be related to degrees of neighboring and outdoor use of the neighborhood (Brown & Cropper, 2001). In terms of suiting the needs and interests of environmental professionals,

the study illustrates how one can begin with a place and examine the multiple processes, participants, and temporal patterns that involve the specific setting, much like studies that have been done on retirement communities (Parmelee & Lawton, 1990), plazas (Whyte, 1980), back alleys (Martin, 1996), farmers markets and grocery stores (Sommer, 1989), and communities (O'Donnell, Tharp, & Wilson, 1993). Thus, this study of porches used a delimited place but delved into the multiple processes, participants, and historical changes in order to understand the complex social purposes and uses of this important social setting.

ILLUSTRATION 3: CHANGING ENVIRONMENTAL BEHAVIORS

The final research example comes from an ongoing project on strategies for changing home owners' use of toxic home and yard chemicals. The project has been informed in a variety of ways by transactional principles (Werner, 2000). First, the project assumes a unity between people and the physical environment of their homes. Homes can reflect the dialectic tension between families and the larger society. Many people decorate their homes in ways that reflect their personal tastes, but they also use decorations that meet the aesthetic standards of their neighbors. The social group establishes the image of the ideal home, and people decorate and maintain their homes in order to achieve this image. Often, people use toxic chemical products as an easy way to achieve the ideal as well as to show their modernity and affluence.

A second and related assumption is that individuals' attitudes are embedded in and influenced by their social group. Concern for neighbors' opinions would make it difficult to change the individual's attitudes and behaviors unless the group also changed. In one phase of the project, trained group discussion leaders met with groups of 30 friends and neighbors to talk about using nontoxic products for home and yard care. The meetings were modeled after Lewin's (1952) use of group discussion to change behaviors. By hearing neighbors talk about their successful use of nontoxic alternatives, participants learned not only how to use the alternatives but also learned that their respected friends would not criticize them and might even regard them more positively if they also adopted a less toxic approach to decorating and maintaining their home and yard.

The third assumption is that behaviors are connected to the physical environment, and therefore persuasion and behavior-change efforts benefit from a clear articulation of how the target behavior fits into the physical environment. Persuasion researchers have not distinguished between abstract and behavioral messages, and most persuasive arguments have emphasized abstract principles such as "this is good for you" and "this is important." Certainly, persuasive messages should include such reasons for why behavior should change. But messages must also include information about *behavior,* such as *scripts* or *behavior streams,* that provide information about how the new behavior can fit into existing patterns of behavior. Persuasive messages should also include a connection to a *supportive physical environment.* That is, the message should include ideas for how the physical environment can be designed or changed to support the new behavior, such as by making it easier to perform the behavior or by providing reminders or prompts of the new behavior. A final assumption is that persuasive messages should emphasize the *positive phenomenal experiences* associated with actually doing the behavior, such as how interesting, fun, or pleasant it would be to use nontoxic alternatives. By conveying information about actually doing the new behavior in our persuasive messages, we expected to have more persuasive impact in both the short- and long term.

A variety of persuasive messages was introduced during the group meetings. The leaders affirmed residents' images of home and yard by saying "these nontoxic products are just as good as toxic ones" and "these nontoxic products are usually sufficient for the job." But the leaders also talked about a new image of home called "nature-friendly yard care"— yards designed as safe habitats for native wildlife, with native plants and nontoxic maintenance. The discussion leaders encouraged people to imagine how interesting it would be—and how fun for their children—to experience nature right in their own backyards. In this way, the leaders tried to change participants' ways of thinking about their yard in order to increase their interest in learning more about nontoxic home and yard care. In contrast to more traditional persuasion programs which focus exclusively on one aspect or one message, we aimed to destabilize multiple points in the total system— the image of home, the behaviors and products used in achieving this image, the social context of friends and neighbors—so that it could be reconfigured around more nature-friendly ideals and reduced use of toxins.

Time and temporal qualities are also evident in this project. First, a sensitivity to time led Werner deliberately to seek out and select strategies that would effect long-term change. The messages were designed to evoke thought and involvement by the audience so that they would rehearse and remember the message (Petty, Haugtvedt, & Smith, 1995). Werner also attempted to extend message impact by including handouts that reiterated the message (brochures, stick-on labels for nontoxic mixes) or that served as opportunities to rehearse the new information (a coloring and activity calendar that encourages people to practice new behaviors). "Institutionalization" was another way to extend the program's impact. Werner made special efforts to make the new behaviors a regular part of group activities, such as by involving one member of the group as a liaison, and by getting Boy Scout troops involved in helping people use up or properly dispose of their leftover toxic chemical products.

Much like other transactionally based research, this project used multiple strategies for gathering information. Werner and her team used focus groups initially to learn more about home and yard maintenance. They developed a preliminary presentation based on these initial groups and then observed audience reactions closely and talked to key participants to decide how to modify the meetings for optimum impact. In addition, once the basic procedures were determined, Werner used questionnaires and interviews to ascertain what participants thought about the meetings, how they could be improved, and what lifestyle changes appeared to result from the program. Thus, in both its open-ended and evolving form and in its final program evaluation, the project reflected a transactional orientation.

SUMMARY

These projects illustrate different ways of undertaking transactional analyses. The Christmas Street project illustrates a holistic approach to neighborhood relationships and shows that the aspects of people, physical environment, and psychological processes combine to define neighboring relationships and that the aspects combine in different ways at different times of year. The second project examines a single setting—the front porch—and asks how it functions for diverse purposes and diverse groups of participants at different historical periods. In addition to furthering our understanding of how people use their homes, the analysis has implications for designing and promoting this feature of homes. The third project is a holistic intervention using persuasion principles and transactional insights to effect long-term behavior change in the use of toxic home- and yard-care products. All three show how phenomena can be conceived more holistically but indicate considerable variability in conceptual and methodological details. They also show that it is sometimes necessary to limit the scope of a project so that it can be manageable and can yield a coherent story. We next propose a series of guidelines for framing research questions and gathering and analyzing information based on a transactional world view.

IMPLEMENTING A TRANSACTIONAL WORLD VIEW: AN ITERATIVE RESEARCH PROCESS

To some it appears daunting to approach research and theorizing from a transactional perspective. We suspect that this reaction reflects not inherent difficulties with this world view but the fact that social scientists are trained to use different world views and primarily read literatures informed by those world views. Based on our research experiences over the past 20 years and our readings of others' work, we next propose a series of principles or stages as guidelines for conducting transactionally oriented research. We do not suggest adhering strictly to the proposed sequence but rather recommend that one cycle through the steps in an iterative and intuitive way in order to home in on research ideas and ways of implementing them (see Wicker, 1989, for a similar dynamic interplay among theory, methods, and analysis).

STEP 1. BEGIN WITH A QUESTION THAT INTERESTS YOU

There is often a specific question or set of questions that prompts any study, regardless of one's philosophical world view. The three previous research illustrations began with questions such as: How are neighborhood relationships transformed during special Christmas Street celebrations? Are New Urbanists correct in assuming that porches primarily promote neighboring or do porches serve other functions as well? and How can we encourage people to be more conscientious in their use and disposal of toxic household chemicals? Other projects were stimulated by various questions, such as: How do physical and social aspects of weddings and new residences for married couples reflect and support dyad and family relationship processes? (Altman, Brown, Staples, & Werner, 1992). How do polygamous families manage unique husband-wife relationships in the context of complex plural families? (Altman & Ginat, 1996). Thus, like all projects, our research starts with initial questions that may or may not sound transactional and that can vary along a number of dimensions. Questions can be focused on a broad domain of human behavior, such as marital relationships; they can be oriented to particular design and intervention issues, like porch use and yard care; and research questions can be historical or contemporary in their time frame.

The starting point for any research reflects the researcher's interests and background. For example, Altman has a long history of research on relationship processes. Brown has a fascination with New Urbanist designs, so a place like a porch as a design feature can provide the starting point. Werner has an interest in preserving nature, so proenvironmental behaviors like recycling and toxics reduction draw her attention. Altman (1973) noted how design professionals often begin with an interest in a particular place they need to design, then try to understand all the processes that are relevant to the place. Often good research projects begin with vague and unformed notions not yet cast as transactional wholes. But most ideas provide good starting points that can evolve into comprehensive, transactionally based analyses.

STEP 2. THINK OF THE PHENOMENON AS A WHOLE AND IDENTIFY THE FOUR ASPECTS

Think about the question of interest holistically, with all four aspects of a transactional unity in mind—people, psychological processes, physical settings, and time. As your conceptualization grows richer, you will find yourself adding information about aspects as well as connections among the aspects. You will find yourself seeing how people, psychological processes, settings, and time are mutually defining and inseparable. In many ways, this process of thinking holistically is exactly like beginning an analysis of a behavior setting, especially in the way the setting program defines interconnections between people and setting (Barker, 1968; Wicker, 1987).[2] For example, the porch study started with a specific place and a focus on the social unit of householders and neighbors in relation to neighboring processes. The porch was conceptualized as a mutually defining whole. But the cast of participants who use porches and the kinds of processes supported by porches grew more complex. Eventually the holistic understanding of porch use that emerged was more complex than simply a setting to enhance neighborhood cohesion. Porches were used by individuals, siblings, parents, neighbors, and combinations of these groups for solitary retreat, as well as for family and neighborly interactions. The project illustrates the idea of using the transactional framework to identify all possible aspects of the issue you wish to study.

STEP 3. EXPLORE THE POSSIBLE BREADTH OF THE PROJECT

In the initial stages of a project, it is useful to be inclusive and flexible, open to a variety of ways of framing issues, gathering information, and defining the project's depth and breadth. Similar to a grounded theory or ethno-methodological approach, we encourage scholars to be open to different views of phenomena, to explore emerging information, and to avoid defining too rigidly the issues and scope of the investigation. This can be an exciting phase of the research process, as you discover unanticipated issues during data gathering and unanticipated information in the scholarly literature. For example, in the polygamy study, several topics relevant to our goals arose spontaneously during the course of our data collection and turned out to be important to our understanding of family functioning. These included how families managed their money and how they celebrated holidays, birthdays, anniversaries, and other special occasions. We had not thought about those beforehand, but they were quite revealing about husband-wife and wife-wife dynamics.

While it is important to be open and exploratory, it is also useful to be aware that you may eventually have to narrow the project's scope. Although it is possible to address all facets of the transactional world view in a single study, most often it will be necessary to limit specific projects in some way. As you explore a potential research opportunity, think about which aspects seem most interesting to you, have the most potential for theory building, or are most important at this stage of your research program. Also consider which aspects you wish to highlight for theoretical or practical purposes. As we begin a project, we maintain a broad focus on the four aspects of people, psychological processes, physical environment, and temporal qualities. But we also look for ways of limiting the scope of our inquiry or of organizing the information so that the project is manageable conceptually as well as practically. Often, we find we can narrow down some portions while expanding others. For the Christmas Street project for example, we decided to gather more information at two times of year instead of gathering less information more frequently. Thus, reducing the number of times we gathered data allowed us to expand the amount and complexity of information available to us. Another way to manage large amounts of information is to present different views of the phenomenon in different outlets. Each separate view retains its transactional flavor, but each has a different frame or story line. With respect to the Christmas Street project, the significance of temporal qualities leaped out at us as we examined the interviews and questionnaires. In order to highlight that information and really explore its features, we presented it in a separate article (Werner et al., 1988).

Sometimes the scope and focus of a project are decided very early on. In one analysis of home environments, we decided at the outset to highlight the rich array of temporal qualities apparent in the meanings and uses of homes (Werner et al., 1985). We did this because time and temporal qualities had been neglected in research on homes, and we wanted to illustrate their centrality and importance. We included information about people, relationships, and psychological processes, but we made these aspects subordinate so that we could explore the temporal underpinnings of homes and attachments to homes. Similarly, in the research on porches, priorities were set at the beginning of the project. Brown and her colleagues (Brown, Burton, & Sweaney, 1998) thought it was most important to find out by whom and how porches were used in contemporary life because

---

[2] Barker's behavior setting theory has elements of both transactionalism and organicism. In this chapter, we refer to its transactional features.

New Urbanist designers claim their porches primarily provide a pleasant setting for neighbors to interact with each other. Given these goals, it was deemed less important to track temporal qualities such as frequency, duration, and time-of-day porch use and, more important, to track who used porches and for what purposes. The research revealed that porches do support neighborly interactions but also support solitary and family activities as well, showing more complexity than had yet been claimed by the New Urbanists.

In contrast, in our study of courtship, weddings, and placemaking, the simplifying and organizing strategy emerged after considerable data gathering and discussion. We obtained voluminous information about relationship practices in many different societies, looking for information about the four aspects and how they fit together (e.g., whether the physical environment was used differently at different relationship stages). The material was almost overwhelming in its amount and complexity, and we struggled to find a way to organize the information in an interesting, meaningful, and coherent way. Our interest in dialectic processes in relationships (Altman, Vinsel, & Brown, 1981) led us to focus on tensions between the young couple and their families with respect to the couple's autonomy. We began to characterize some societies as *couple-autonomous* and others as *couple-dependent* and tested the emerging hypothesis that the four aspects would be instantiated differently and fit together differently in these two cultural types. By organizing the information around this dialectical theme, we were able to bring order to a diverse set of information. We could also focus on material relevant to this question and ignore other information. Additional manageability was provided by our decision to limit ourselves to the three stages of courtship, weddings, and placemaking, even though other life stages could be examined from a transactional perspective.

Sometimes, the decision of which features to emphasize is a practical matter, largely determined by what kinds of information can be found. Psychologists provide good information on individuals' psychological processes, though rarely grounded in a physical or social milieu. However, psychologists rarely provide information about time and temporal qualities, unless these happen to be the researcher's particular interest. Environmental psychologists, geographers, and anthropologists usually provide good details about how the physical environment is used and occasionally connect that use to psychological processes such as place attachment, satisfaction with the setting, restorative qualities of nature, or fear of crime. To capitalize on these different perspectives, we seek out articles in several disciplines to ensure a well-rounded and holistic understanding of phenomena.

STEP 4. SEEK MUTUAL DEFINITION BETWEEN ASPECTS

A transactionally oriented researcher's goal is to understand a phenomenon in its complexity, with as much coherence and integration as feasible. In part, this means understanding how the aspects are connected and mutually defining. Thinking about all four aspects at once can be overwhelming, so we typically go through a cycling of ideas where we focus on each aspect in turn and on the pairing of two or more aspects. We know it is artificial to break the phenomenon into aspects, but it is a useful device for clarifying our thinking about the research process. For example, in our study of Christmas Street, it was relatively easy to think of ways in which enthusiasm for the decorating tradition would be reflected in actual decorations of homes, that is, ways in which psychological processes and the physical environment would be mutually defining. There was a natural fit between attitudes toward Christmas Street celebrations and a resident's decorations: People who felt they were involved in the street's activities were more likely to decorate in elaborate ways. But when we shifted our focus to summertime, we had to develop new indices of how attachment to the neighborhood might be manifested in home and yard upkeep and decorating. By systematically pairing two aspects—in this case, psychological processes with the physical environment—we could focus on those two and develop measurements capable of tapping the union between them. Another example is the "social unit," or decision to understand how individuals fit into the neighborhood's social networks. We spent some time thinking about how social relationships among neighbors would be reflected in actions and how those actions might change with the season. To define different social networks, we incorporated social relationship scales that tapped different kinds of neighboring behaviors (Brown, 1983), but we adapted them for the two seasons in order to more accurately measure neighboring behaviors at the two times of year. In sum, by looking at different combinations of the four aspects, we were able to grasp and make sense of different combinations or aspects of the whole, and could ultimately connect them into a unified understanding.

Similarly, in a study of nineteenth-century Shaker and Oneida utopian communities (Isaac & Altman, 1998), a holistic analysis was made easier by looking at combinations of aspects. Among the Shakers, the cultural and religious beliefs of the founders were reflected in and supported by the design of the town and communal dwellings. Men and women used separate entrances to dwellings, used different stairways, lived in separate rooms, and ate in separate parts of the dining hall. This physical separation was also mirrored in prohibitions against men and women developing friendships or intimate relationships. Thus, pairing the physical environment with normative psychological processes revealed how these two aspects combined transactionally. Another combination of aspects links psychological processes with time. For example, as the Shaker community evolved, complaints from members led leaders to acknowledge that men and women members strongly desired interpersonal relationships. The community changed its practices but maintained ideological control by specifying very formalized dances and other public events that were consistent with the limited expression of dyadic attachment allowed in the Shaker community.

In general, when focusing on different pairs or other combinations of aspects, one should probe for many examples (e.g., the Shakers developed many mechanisms for controlling interaction between men and women), ask how the aspects lend meaning to one another, and how they illuminate the nature of the total phenomenon. In some cases, all the information may not fit together neatly, and this may be indicative of stress or disruption in the phenomenon, or it may simply indicate that the phenomenon is complex and inconsistent. Our goal has not been to smooth over inconsistencies but rather to use holistic analyses to understand them better.

Step 5. Gather Data "Reflexively"

We continue the iterative process as we gather data, whether our analyses are based on archival material or original data collection. Although our exploration begins with a guiding framework or set of issues, we try to be sensitive and open to new topics as they emerge during data gathering. With archival material and open-ended interviews, such "reflexivity" is easily achieved by simply continuing to seek information, by re-interviewing participants, or interviewing additional participants as needed. Even with paper and pencil measures, we try to include open-ended questions so that we can allow participants to express the complexity of their views and so that we can elicit unexpected information. In addition, similar to a grounded theory approach (Glazer & Strauss, 1967), we gather enough data to be sure the information is consistent and reliable and that we have captured multiple viewpoints about a phenomenon. Sometimes this occurs early in data collection; and other times, information is mixed and we continue to gather data until we are satisfied that we understand the various views on a phenomenon.

In a study of polygamous families, Altman and Ginat (1996) found consensus about some relationship issues but found that other topics required more extended investigation and a sensitivity to complex or contradictory information. In polygamous families, each husband-wife couple seeks to develop and maintain a traditional close dyadic relationship, but all of the families also ideally hope to develop and maintain a single group identity. Altman and Ginat traced how families used privacy regulation mechanisms and other processes to manage these often conflicting roles. During interviews, certain topics, such as wedding ceremonies, revealed a great deal of agreement among informants, so that fewer interviews were needed to understand them. However, spousal conflict took on many more varieties depending on how flexible or rigid the family processes were, the composition of the families, and so on. Thus, more interviewing was required to confidently describe the multiple experiences of plural family conflict. In addition, the idea that celebrations would have varied forms and meanings emerged during the interviews. Altman and Ginat pursued these issues and learned that some celebrations emphasized unique dyads (e.g., wives' birthdays, each dyad's anniversary), and others emphasized the whole family (e.g., husband's birthday, religious holidays). By cycling through information and staying alert to the unexpected, one can uncover a more nuanced understanding of phenomena.

Saegert (1989) also found that a combination of directed questions and careful listening was essential for her own richer understanding of the strengths of Black women who created meaningful lives and effective communities in low-income housing. Similarly, in a study of the positive and negative meanings of density in Israeli neighborhoods, Mitrany (2000) used questionnaires, cognitive maps, and intensive interviews. The interviews allowed her to be open to unanticipated facets of density, such as how certain dwelling designs and neighborhood contexts were related to negative density judgments, apart from objective levels of physical density.

Step 6. Draw on Multiple Perspectives and Participants to Gather Information

Another important part of the research process is to assume there will be multiple perspectives and participants to an event, and that all are useful and necessary for a complete understanding of the phenomenon. This may mean looking at a variety of historical sources to see how a phenomenon has been viewed over time. It may also mean reading contemporary accounts to understand the current ethos or the current varieties of explanations for a phenomenon. It may mean seeking out different voices and listening carefully to their unique point of view, and it may mean using unusual strategies for soliciting input. In their study of plural marriage, Altman and Ginat (1996) used many sources beyond interviews and observations to achieve a comprehensive understanding of the families. As they immersed themselves in the project, they examined anthropological material about polygamy around the globe and through the centuries. Within their target group of Fundamentalist Mormon polygamists, they read diaries from polygamous families from the 1800s to the present as well as scholarly treatises on Mormon polygamy. When they interviewed polygamous families in order to gather their own data, they made themselves available at many different venues with many combinations of family members in order to create a comfortable milieu for the conversation. They met at participants' homes, their own homes, restaurants—anywhere the families would feel comfortable. They also located women who had left polygamous relationships in order to tap that point of view. So in various ways, these researchers endeavored to identify many different kinds of informants and elicit from them honest accounts of their experiences.

Step 7. Apply Formal Cause to the Phenomenon

The next step in developing a transactionally based project is to critique how we think about causal explanations of events, or the relationships among the four aspects of a phenomenon. Are we thinking about efficient cause—antecedent-consequent relationships—or are we using formal cause to look for patterns of relationships among the aspects? While all of Aristotle's forms of determinism are useful, the transactional world view highlights and capitalizes on the unique strengths of formal cause. Most social science scholars have not had extensive experience with the formal cause approach, thereby limiting the social science perspective on phenomena. Our own exploration of how to use formal cause in research has taken three forms. One is the simple examination of *patterns of relationship among aspects*, and how those patterns shift or remain stable over time. A second is *coherence in a sequence of events*, or how actions unfold or are coordinated and staged in meaningful ways. Third is how we combined efficient with formal cause as a research strategy.

Our first research illustration, Christmas Street, was a classic example of formal cause and patterns of relationship. In that project, we used correlation coefficients in summer and at Christmas to ask how the aspects fit together—what was the pattern of intercorrelations among people/social context, psychological processes, and physical environment? And we compared the two patterns at two points in time to see if and how they shifted. As described previously, the patterns of correlation differed dramatically between summer and Christmas, such that the block was transformed and the aspects much more unified during the Christmas season.

Altman, Brown, Staples, and Werner's (1992) analysis of courtship, weddings, and placemaking provides a similar illustration of shifting patterns. In that analysis, we hypothesized that as a couple moved from courtship towards marriage and establishing their new home, these deepening bonds (psychological processes) would be reflected in and supported by the social and physical environments. Furthermore, we hypothesized that as the couple's relationship changed over time towards more commitment, there would be corresponding changes among other aspects in the system.

In addition to examining how individual relationships develop, our holistic analysis also compared societies and traced the multiple stages of relationship formation in different groups, some where couples are autonomous from their families and some where couples are dependent upon and integral with their families. In more couple-autonomous societies, contacts between partners began casually in public settings with many other friends around. Participants thought of themselves as a "group," and relationships among members were friendly rather than romantic. Family members were rarely, if ever, involved in these early, public stages of courtship. That pattern changed gradually over time as the couple decided to marry and began making arrangements for the wedding. Especially when they began preparing the apartment where they would live, the couple saw less and less of their friends and more and more of their families. The couple also began spending more and more time alone together, in private rather than public settings. Thus, the relationships among the aspects of people, social and physical contexts, and psychological processes (relationship commitment) shifted and changed, reflecting the changing nature of the couple's and families' relationship.

In contrast, in couple-dependent societies, courtship was largely controlled by the family and emphasized family members rather than the young couple. Marriage was viewed as a union of families rather than a young couple beginning a life together, separate from the families. The partners were chosen by parents or professional "marriage arrangers," family members and ancestors were consulted about the suitability of the match even before the young couple met, the couple's first meeting usually took place in a family home, and senior family members talked most and controlled events, not the couple. After the marriage, the young couple typically moved in with one or the other set of parents and were expected to behave as subordinate to the parents, even to the point of being servants in that family home.

The nature of relationships and how this played out in the social and physical environments was dramatically different between couple-autonomous and couple-dependent societies. In formal cause terms, although many practices are different in the two kinds of societies, the patterns of interconnection are the same. Who was involved, for how long, and where events took place all fit together coherently within each society. And all of these aspects contributed to defining the couple's relationship and their relationship to others. There is an internal consistency to these events that is revealed through a holistic, transactional analysis.

Our second use of formal cause shows how a *sequence* or *series* of events fits together into a meaningful whole. Werner et al. (1987) drew on Jacobs's (1961) and Seamon's (1979) concepts of sidewalk or place ballets to illustrate this type of formal cause:

> [O]ne might engage in a sidewalk "ballet" [composed of] a variety of behaviors done in a more or less regular order. Waving to neighbors does not "cause" one to pick up one's mail, nor does picking up the mail "cause" one to walk down the street to the coffee shop. . . . The "ballet" is an orderly pattern of behaviors that fit together in a meaningful way . . . the goal of formal cause is to understand the pattern as a coherent whole. (p. 248)

This focus on the coherence of a total pattern opens up a variety of research questions, many of which ask how participants view events rather than how researchers impose meaning on events. How aware are people of these place ballets, and what gives them meaning? When are place ballets improvised and when are they more carefully scripted? Do individuals have core events and optional events so that the ballet is only complete when events and their order are "right"? Are there personal psychological consequences for "successful" and "unsuccessful" place ballets? and so on.

Another kind of example is how individuals, families, and communities celebrate important events such as birthdays, anniversaries, and cultural holidays. What sequence of events is necessary for creating just the right meaning or spirit to events? A comparison between Christmas Street and the Zuni house-blessing celebration of Shalako revealed year-long cycles in both ceremonies (Werner et al., 1988). In many ways, the Shalako ceremony was much more specified and required stricter adherence to particular sequences of events throughout the year. Disruptions in the prescribed order could mean a serious flaw in the Shalako ceremony. Christmas Street residents adhered to some schedules and deadlines (e.g., coordinating the day when decorations are first displayed, and coordinating the turning on and off of the Christmas lights) but allowed variation in others (such as dates of parties). Understanding sequences and how they contribute to meaning is another domain of formal cause.

Altman and Ginat's (1996; Werner, Altman, Brown, & Ginat, 1993) analysis of celebrations in polygamous families revealed a great deal of variety in which events were included and their order and showed how families made the holiday "their own" through deliberate choices of activities and how these activities were ordered across the celebration.

Many polygamous families used Christmas as a time to emphasize family ties (in contrast to birthdays, when the individual or dyad was at the fore). Some families came together in a single home, prepared meals together, sang songs or had religious rituals together, and often exchanged gifts from one sister-family to another (gifts from mothers to their children were often given away from this collective celebration). Families worked out details and developed a familiar sequence or pattern to events that imbued the holiday with their family's special meaning. Consistent with principles of formal cause, one does not ask whether one event in the pattern "causes" another to occur, but rather what are the events, what is the sequence, and how do they fit together in a meaningful way?

Notice how these examples reveal both kinds of formal cause, each at a somewhat different level of analysis. For example, the holistic analysis of Christmas Street activities asks (1) how the four aspects fit together and how the configuration changes with time and circumstances and (2) how these changing configurations are part of a coherent sequence of events. Similarly, the analysis of courtships, weddings, and place making essentially examines a series of holistic unities and asks how coherently the aspects fit together at each step, as well as how coherently the total sequence unfolds.

A third way of thinking about formal cause is how efficient and formal cause might be combined. A useful strategy is to think of efficient cause as an event outside of the holistic system. Does the event change how the aspects of a phenomenon are configured? Does the event change the nature or coherence of actions in the phenomenon of interest? Territoriality theory provides an example of how to combine efficient with formal cause. Brown (1987) and Brown and Altman (1981) showed that primary, secondary, and public territories varied along five dimensions: how much control users could exercise, how much time they spent in the setting, how psychologically invested they were in the setting, how much they marked or decorated the setting, and how they would react to an intrusion. In a primary territory such as a home, these dimensions have a particular pattern or configuration: People have substantial control over, spend much time in, are psychologically invested in, claim and decorate their area and would show strong defense if others entered it. This pattern differs in a secondary territory, such as a neighborhood. Although people spend

time in, exercise control over, and are psychologically attached to the neighborhood and so on, these factors are not as strong in secondary as in primary territories. Furthermore, people tend to relate to the setting as a group rather than as individuals. Public territories are the least controlled and least psychologically meaningful settings. In large urban settings, the development of secondary territories has been associated with positive outcomes for local residents. In secondary territories, there is often a stronger sense of community, improved quality of life, and reduced crime when compared to neighborhoods that have qualities more typical of public territories.

Werner and Altman (1998) drew on the concept of strong secondary territories in their analysis of public housing developments. While recognizing that the features of secondary territories were not necessarily causally related—that the confluence of features had emerged together over time—Werner and Altman wondered if secondary territories could be encouraged to develop. Werner and Altman suggested that a number of activities could be used in a proactive way to *create* a secondary territory. In essence, they proposed a dynamic transactional approach whereby they could set in motion transformational processes. Such interventions have been successful, as when Newman diverted traffic around rather than through a neighborhood, resulting in more shared secondary territories and lower crime in the neighborhood (Donnelly & Kimble, 1997), supporting the idea of combining efficient with formal cause.

Another example of a dynamic transactional approach is a study assessing the impact of a neighborhood intervention on residents' attitudes and activities. In particular, Brown, Perkins, and Brown (2001) asked whether putting a new subdivision into a deteriorating neighborhood would help the neighborhood by improving attitudes towards the community and reducing fear of crime. That is, Brown and colleagues asked whether the outside intervention would be related to how the aspects of people, psychological processes, and physical environment fit together for the existing community. Results showed different patterns among the variables depending on how residents on the block felt about the new development. On blocks where neighbors perceived that the new housing intervention was in their neighborhood, individual residents were less fearful of crime; on blocks where neighbors perceived that the new housing was outside their neighborhood, there was no reduction in residents' fear of crime (with other variables controlled for individual and block levels of analysis). Thus, putting in a new subdivision had no overall effect on fear, but it was an effective intervention when it was psychologically "owned" by residents. This project indicated that it was important to take into account residents' consensual awareness of the new development and their feeling that it belonged to their neighborhood, thereby underscoring the importance of using formal cause to understand the impact of this intervention.

In sum, formal cause allows the researcher to pose questions such as: How do the four aspects of holistic unities fit together, and do the patterns of association change with time, circumstances, and society? How do sequences of events fit together in meaningful ways? In addition and just as significant, formal and efficient cause can be combined to add another dynamic quality to transactional analyses.

STEP 8. DECIDE ON THE SCOPE OF THE PROJECT

At some point, one must decide on the overall scope of the study, especially with respect to which of the four aspects to emphasize and de-emphasize and how much detail to provide about each. The most comprehensive transactional study would give equal emphasis to all four aspects of transactional unities, much like the study of polygamous families. The goal of the polygamy project was to see how people in plural marriages manage husband-wife dyadic relationships in the context of their other familial relationships. The project was organized around psychological processes, so multiple social relationship domains and interpersonal processes were assessed, such as the decision to add a new wife, her courtship by the husband and future sister wives, wedding practices, integration of new wives into the home, management of family conflict, management of resources, celebration of holidays, and so on. Consistent with a transactional view, these processes were investigated with respect to who participated and how, the temporal qualities of events, and the physical settings and objects that were integral to them.

The polygamy project was unusual in having both breadth and depth. It is more typical to see research that narrows the scope of analysis in some way, such as by emphasizing one or two aspects and subordinating the others or examining a limited number of events or processes. For example, in one paper, we

focused on celebrations as a way to explore the dialectic tensions between individual and group identity (Werner et al., 1993). We used material from the polygamy project to illustrate this dialectic process, but we used only the small amount related to celebrations. Our descriptions of celebrations were holistic and included all four aspects, but we were able to narrow our scope by examining only that one kind of relationship process. As noted in Step 3, another strategy for managing information is to carve the data into separate transactional wholes and present each in a separate forum.

The research scope can be purposely limited in any one study; but by emphasizing different aspects in different studies, one can ultimately achieve a broader transactional analysis. Every transactional research project does not have to address participants, processes, places, and time in depth, as long as all are included at some level, and the researcher has consciously decided what to emphasize.

SUMMARY

We proposed eight steps for conducting transactionally oriented research, stressing analyses that address all four aspects of people, psychological processes, physical environment, and temporal qualities. We suggested an iterative process of cycling through the steps: (1) beginning with a research question, (2) expanding the view to include a whole phenomenon, (3) selecting features to emphasize, and (4) carefully examining how those features are mutually defining and inseparable by looking at pairs of aspects and selecting research measures that capture those qualities. (5) We suggested gathering data as an iterative process so that the most accurate and comprehensive information could be found, and (6) we stressed including multiple perspectives when gathering data. (7) We explored three ways of using formal cause in research: simple examination of patterns of relationship, study of how those patterns shift and change with time and circumstance, and deliberate introduction of outside efficient causal events to instigate changes in the patterns of relationship. And (8) we ended by encouraging researchers to narrow the scope of analyses to manageable but meaningful portions. We suggested that researchers cycle and recycle through these steps, not in a lock-step and rigid way but rather as needed, perhaps focusing on some steps in one project and different steps in another.

A FINAL PERSPECTIVE

This chapter presented strategies for developing transactionally oriented theorizing and research that addressed the four aspects of people, psychological processes, physical environment, and time/temporal qualities. We used our and others' research to illustrate a variety of ways for undertaking transactional research projects and suggested an iterative process of eight steps for guiding the research process. We noted that there are many ways of shaping transactional analyses and that for every project the researcher needs to use judgment in selecting the topic, scope, and research strategies. We suggested that researchers should strive to understand a phenomenon in its complexity, with as much coherence and integration as feasible, but also to respect the existence of inconsistencies, anomalies, and unusual patterns among the four aspects.

We would not argue that transactionally oriented research is better than research based on other world views, but is simply different. Indeed, all three research illustrations in this chapter benefitted immensely from many research projects guided by other world views. That said, we turn to the issue of why we choose transactional approaches. What benefits do we and others see in this world view?

A primary advantage of the transactional world view is that it expands our understanding of basic conceptual and theoretical issues. The holistic approach of a transactional world view is often needed to capture the complexity of phenomena. Along these lines, Churchman and Ginosar (1999) attributed a dearth of evaluations of neighborhoods to a lack of sufficiently complex frameworks for capturing the full richness of these settings. They included a modified transactional approach (a transactional world view coupled with a naturalistic evaluation paradigm) as one way to develop a comprehensive picture of neighborhoods. As another example, Bonnes, Bonaiuto, and Ercolani (1991), found that perceptions of crowding and housing satisfaction were related to and qualified by the sociophysical context. In our terms, the four aspects fit together in different ways for different kinds of residents. Luke, Rappaport, and Seidman (1991) introduced the "setting phenotype" in order to expand behavior setting theory's concept of *genotypes* (taxonomically similar settings). Phenotypes include a more differentiated analysis of people, temporal qualities, and behaviors, thereby capturing more precisely the complex

nature of behavior settings. Fuhrer (1990) also expanded behavior setting theory to include more psychological aspects of person-place unities. And Hartig (1993) argued that most research on human-nature relations could benefit by a broader, more transactional analysis that would provide a different and more complex understanding of the myriad goals and meanings that draw people to nature.

Another reason for our preference is related to the social utility of our work. Unlike much psychological research, in which psychological processes are abstracted from their social and physical milieus and stripped of their temporal qualities, we find it useful to describe the rich complexity of everyday experiences. In addition, we find that nonpsychologist audiences such as architects and planners can understand our holistic descriptions of phenomena and see the implications for their own work. For many practitioners, studies of abstract, isolated, molecular psychological processes appear foreign and irrelevant. In contrast, using a transactionally guided approach, Brown and her students have been involved in a three-year user-participation project called "Envision Utah." In meetings, citizens, community leaders, elected officials, and civil servants gather to envision and discuss different growth scenarios for their local communities. By connecting alternative courses of development to larger social and physical environments, Brown has been able to create vivid images of how abstract growth patterns can be manifested in the physical environment (Brown & Brown, 1998).

A third reason for using a transactional approach is that the phenomena and problems of interest simply lend themselves to holistic analyses. For example, in the early 1990's, Werner participated in an education and persuasion campaign that put behavior change into one context (the grocery store) but did not do an adequate job of addressing other aspects of the total phenomenon. It did not address individual-level persuasion and memory, it did not involve any important reference groups, and it did not put in place behavioral and environmental mechanisms for helping people to maintain the new behavior over the long term (Gillilan, Werner, Olson, & Adams, 1996). That experience convinced Werner that a holistic, multilevel intervention is necessary for more substantial long-term impact.

As a fourth reason, some people find it important to study the dynamic and changing unity between people and context that is highlighted by a transactional approach. These scholars focus on the dynamic processes by which people engage their environments and the changes that occur in both person and setting as these transactions unfold. For example Gauvain (1993) drew on Vygotsky's activity theory to describe the complex interdependencies involved in children's acquisition of spatial knowledge. Sansone and Harackiewicz (1996) developed a dynamic model that describes how people transform boring tasks into interesting ones as a way to keep doing the task, transforming both the individual and the environment in the process. Reser and Scherl (1988, following Lazarus & Launier, 1978) detailed a "model of transactional feedback" to show how some tasks for some people represent a unity among people, place, and action, so that over time, people and setting are changed and a new unity is created. And Aitken (1992) noted that people and environments are constantly changing and therefore the *relationship* between people and setting always changes. For modest changes, people can ignore or reconstrue them so no action is necessary. However, for major changes, people will engage in deliberate cognitive, psychological, or physical strategies to adapt to the changed relationships.

A final reason for being attracted to the transactional world view is that there is considerable untapped potential to this world view, potential that can be captured by scholars from multiple disciplines. Our views about phenomena, how they should be studied, and what features to emphasize, are informed by our backgrounds as social-environmental psychologists. Our work tends to focus on small-scale social groups—individuals, dyads, families, and neighborhoods. Scholars from other disciplines should feel free to shift their own foci towards the social units of most interest to them—sociologists may wish to emphasize larger social groups, whereas political scientists and urban planners might want to emphasize the whole community, state, nation, and even larger regions.

Similarly, although we have understood in an implicit way that the physical environment is changing and dynamic, we have not made environmental changes the focus of the present analysis. Werner's (2000) research on toxic home and yard chemicals is essentially a study of how humans relate to myriad natural processes. How do humans respond to dust and bacteria deposited in their dwellings? How do they protect their home exteriors from naturally occurring sun, rain, and other weather damage? How

do they respond to natural events in their yards—do humans decide to coexist with or dominate insects and other natural wildlife (Altman & Chemers, 1980; Werner, Brown, & Altman, 1997)? As another example, Brown and Perkins (1992) studied how people respond to changes in the physical environment wrought by natural events such as earthquakes, floods, and hurricanes. Although psychologists call these "natural disasters," from a biologist's view they are necessary features of dynamic ecosystems (such as how floods and fires "clean out" nonnative and other species, providing habitat for different species). Scientists and scholars with other backgrounds might choose to undertake a transactional analysis more focused on and sensitive to humans' relationships with ever-changing natural systems.

As illustrated in this chapter, many researchers have begun to seek more complex ways of studying and describing phenomena, and many have developed frameworks by which to guide their thinking (e.g., Churchman & Ginosar, 1999; Fuhrer, 1990; Luke et al., 1991; O'Donnell et al., 1993; Wicker, 1989). Wapner and his colleagues (Wapner, Demick, Yamamoto, & Minami, 2000) have been leaders in this emerging shift towards more holistic analyses of phenomena. They have been instrumental in encouraging scholars to examine their underlying research assumptions and to articulate their guiding principles. We share their enthusiasm for this emerging trend, and hope that this chapter and our explanations for how we conduct research will make the transactional view more accessible and intriguing to others.

REFERENCES

Aitken, S. C. (1992). The personal contexts of neighborhood change. *Journal of Architectural and Planning Research, 9,* 338–360.

Altman, I. (1973). Some perspectives on the study of man-environment phenomena. *Representative Research in Social Psychology, 4,* 109–126.

Altman, I., Brown, B. B., Staples, B., & Werner, C. M. (1992). A transactional approach to close relationships: Courtship, weddings, and placemaking. In B. Walsh, K. Craik, & R. Price (Eds.), *Person-environment psychology: Contemporary models and perspectives* (pp. 193–241). Hillsdale, NJ: Erlbaum.

Altman, I., & Chemers, M. M. (1980). *Culture and environment.* New York: Cambridge University Press.

Altman, I., & Ginat, J. (1996). *Polygamous families in contemporary society.* New York: Cambridge University Press.

Altman I., & Rogoff, B. (1987). World views in psychology: Trait, interactional, organismic, and transactional perspectives. In D. Stokols & I. Altman (Eds.), *Handbook of environmental psychology* (Vol. 1, pp. 1–40). New York: Wiley.

Altman, I., Vinsel, A., & Brown, B. B. (1981). Dialectic conceptions in social psychology: An application to social penetration and privacy regulation. In L. Berkowitz (Ed.), *Advances in Experimental Social Psychology* (Vol. 14, pp. 107–160). New York: Academic Press.

Altman, I., Werner, C. M., Oxley, D., & Haggard, L. M. (1987). "Christmas Street" as an example of transactionally-oriented research. *Environment and Behavior, 19*(4), 501–524.

Barker, R. G. (1968). *Ecological psychology: Concepts and methods for studying the environment of human behavior.* Stanford, CA: Stanford University Press.

Bih, H. (1992). The meaning of objects in environmental transitions: Experiences of Chinese students in the United States. *Journal of Environmental Psychology, 12,* 135–147.

Bonnes, M., Bonaiuto, M., & Ercolani, A. P. (1991). Crowding and residential satisfaction in the urban environment: A contextual approach. *Environment and Behavior, 23,* 531–552.

Brown, B. B. (1983). *Territoriality, street form, and residential burglary: Social and environmental analyses.* Unpublished doctoral dissertation, University of Utah.

Brown, B. B. (1987). Territoriality. In D. Stokols & I. Altman (Eds.), *Handbook of environmental psychology* (Vol. 1, pp. 505–532). New York: Wiley.

Brown, B. B., & Altman, I. (1981). Territoriality and residential crime: A conceptual framework. In P. J. Brantingham & P. L. Brantingham (Eds.), *Environmental criminology* (pp. 55–76). Beverly Hills, CA: Sage.

Brown, B. B., & Brown, G. (1998). *Community options workshop: Results.* Salt Lake City, UT: Envision Utah.

Brown, B. B., Burton, J. R., & Sweaney, A. L. (1998). Neighbors, households, and front porches: New Urbanist community tool or mere nostalgia? *Environment and Behavior, 30,* 579–600.

Brown, B. B., & Cropper, V. L. (2001). New urban and standard suburban subdivisions: Evaluating psychological and social goals. *Journal of the American Planning Association, 67,* 1–20.

Brown, B. B., & Perkins, D. D. (1992). Disruptions in place attachment. In I. Altman & S. M. Low (Eds.), *Place attachment: Human behavior and the environment* (Vol. 12, pp. 279–304). New York: Plenum Press.

Brown, B. B., Perkins, D. D., & Brown, G. (2001). *Place attachment, incivilities, revitalization, and fear of crime.* Manuscript in preparation, University of Utah.

Calthorpe, P. (2000). Afterword. In M. Lecesse & K. McCormick (Eds.), *Charter of the New Urbanism* (pp. 177–180). New York: McGraw-Hill.

Churchman, A., & Ginosar, O. (1999). A theoretical basis for the post-occupancy evaluation of neighborhoods. *Journal of Environmental Psychology, 19,* 267–276.

Dewey, J., & Bentley, A. F. (1949). *Knowing and the known.* Boston: Beacon Press.

Donnelly, P. G., & Kimble, C. E. (1997). Community organizing, environmental change, and neighborhood crime. *Crime and Delinquency, 43,* 493–511.

Fuhrer, U. (1990). Bridging the ecological-psychological gap. *Environment and Behavior, 22,* 518–537.

Gauvain, M. (1993). The development of spatial thinking in everyday activity. *Developmental Review, 13,* 92–121.

Gillilan, S., Werner, C. M., Olson, L., & Adams, D. (1996). Teaching the concept of PREcycling: A campaign and evaluation. *Journal of Environmental Education, 28,* 11–18.

Glazer, B. G., & Strauss, A. L. (1967). *The discovery of grounded theory: Strategies for qualitative research.* New York: Aldine.

Hartig, T. (1993). Nature experience in transactional perspective. *Landscape and Urban Planning, 25,* 17–36.

Isaac, J., & Altman, I. (1998). Interpersonal processes in nineteenth century utopian communities: Shakers and Oneida Perfectionists. *Utopia, 9,* 26–49.

Jacobs, J. (1961). *The death and life of great American cities.* New York: Vintage Books.

Kaplan, R. (1987). Validity in environment/behavior research. *Environment and Behavior, 19,* 495–500.

Lazarus, R. S., & Launier, L. R. (1978). Person and environment. In L. A. Pervin & M. Lewis (Eds.), *Perspectives in interactional psychology* (pp. 287–327). New York: Plenum Press.

Leccese, M. & McCormick, K. (Eds.). (2000). *Charter of the New Urbanism.* New York: McGraw-Hill.

Lewin, K. (1952). Group decision and social change. In G. E. Swanson, T. M. Newcomb, & E. L. Hartley (Eds.), *Readings in social psychology* (pp. 459–473). New York: Holt.

Luke, D. A., Rappaport, J., & Seidman, E. (1991). Setting phenotypes in a mutual help organization: Expanding behavior setting theory. *American Journal of Community Psychology, 19,* 147–167.

Manning, F. E. (Ed.). (1983). *The celebration of society: perspectives on contemporary cultural performance.* Bowling Green, OH: Bowling Green University Popular Press.

Martin, M. (1996). Back-alley as community landscape. *Landscape Journal, 15,* 138–153.

Mitrany, M. (2000, July). *A transactional approach to subjective density.* Paper presented at the sixteenth bi-annual meeting of the International Association for Person-Environment Studies, Paris.

O'Donnell, C. R., Tharp, R. G., & Wilson, K. (1993). Activity settings as the unit of analysis: A theoretical basis for community intervention and development. *American Journal of Community Psychology, 21,* 501–520.

Oxley, D., Haggard, L. M., Werner, C. M., & Altman, I. (1986). Transactional qualities of neighborhood social networks: A case study of "Christmas Street." *Environment and Behavior, 18,* 640–677.

Parmelee, P. P., & Lawton, M. P. (1990). The design of special environments for the aged. In J. E. Birren & K. W. Schaie (Eds.), *Handbook of the psychology of aging* (3rd ed., pp. 464–488). New York: Academic Press.

Pepper, S. C. (1942). *World hypotheses: A study in evidence.* Berkeley: University of California Press.

Pepper, S. C. (1967). *Concept and quality: A world hypothesis.* La Salle, IL: Open Court.

Petty, R. E., Haugtvedt, C. P., & Smith, S. M. (1995). Elaboration as a determinant of attitude strength: Creating attitudes that are persistent, resistant, and predictive of behavior. In R. E. Petty & J. A. Krosnick (Eds.), *Attitude strength: Antecedents and consequences* (pp. 93–130). Mahwah, NJ: Erlbaum.

Reser, J. P., & Scherl, L. M. (1988). Clear and unambiguous feedback: A transactional and motivational analysis of environmental challenge and self-encounter. *Journal of Environmental Psychology, 8,* 269–286.

Saegert, S. (1989). Unlikely leaders, extreme circumstances: Older Black women building community households. *American Journal of Community Psychology, 17,* 295–316.

Sansone, C., & Harackiewicz, J. M. (1996). "I don't feel like it": The function of interest in self-regulation. In L. Martin & A. Tesser (Eds.), *Striving and feeling: Interactions between goals and affect* (pp. 203–228). Mahwah, NJ: Erlbaum.

Seamon, D. (1979). *A geography of the life world.* New York: St. Martin's Press.

Shumaker, S. A., & Conti, G. J. (1985). Understanding mobility in America: Conflicts between stability and change. In I. Altman & C. M. Werner (Eds.), *Home environments: Human behavior and the environment,* (Vol. 8, pp. 237–253). New York: Plenum Press.

Sommer, R. (1989). Farmer's markets as community events. In I. Altman & E. H. Zube (Eds.), *Public places and spaces: Human behavior and environment* (Vol. 10, pp. 57–82). New York: Plenum Press.

Wapner, S., Demick, J., Yamamoto, T., & Minami, H. (2000). *Theoretical perspectives in environment-behavior research: Underlying assumptions, research problems, and methodologies.* New York: Kluwer Academic/Plenum Publishers.

Werner, C. M. (2000). *Changing environmental attitudes and behaviors: A transactional approach.* Manuscript submitted for publication, University of Utah.

Werner, C. M., & Altman, I. (1998). A dialectic/transactional approach to neighborhoods: Children in secondary territories. In D. Gorlitz, H. J. Harloff, G. Mey, & J. Valsiner (Eds.), *Children, cities, and psychological theories* (pp. 123–154). Berlin: Walter de Gruyter.

Werner, C. M., Altman, I., Brown, B. B., & Ginat, J. (1993). Celebrations in personal relationships: A transactional/dialectical perspective. In S. Duck (Ed.), *Social context and relationships: Understanding relationship processes series* (Vol. 3, pp. 109–138). Newbury Park, CA: Sage.

Werner, C. M., Altman, I., & Oxley, D. (1985). Temporal aspects of homes: A transactional perspective. In I. Altman & C. M. Werner (Eds.), *Home environments: Human behavior and the environment,* (Vol. 8, pp. 1–32). New York: Plenum Press.

Werner, C. M., Altman, I., Oxley, D., & Haggard, L. (1987). People, place, and time: A transactional analysis of neighborhoods. In W. H. Jones & D. Perlman (Eds.), *Advances in personal relationships* (pp. 243–275). Greenwich, CT: JAI Press.

Werner, C. M., Brown, B. B., & Altman, I. (1997). Environmental psychology. In J. W. Berry, M. H. Segall, & C. Kagitcibasi (Eds.), *Handbook of cross-cultural psychology: Vol. 3. Social behavior and applications* (2nd ed., pp. 255–290). Needham Heights, MA: Allyn & Bacon.

Werner, C. M., Haggard, L. M., Altman, I., & Oxley, D. (1988). Temporal qualities of rituals and celebrations: A comparison of Christmas Street and Zuni Shalako. In J. E. McGrath (Ed.), *The social psychology of time: New perspectives* (pp. 203–232). Beverly Hills, CA: Sage.

Whyte, W. (1980). *The social life of small urban spaces.* New York: Conservation Foundation.

Wicker, A. (1987). Behavior settings reconsidered: Temporal stages, resources, internal dynamics, context. In D. Stokols & I. Altman (Eds.), *Handbook of environmental psychology* (Vol. 1, pp. 613–654). New York: Wiley.

Wicker, A. (1989). Substantive theorizing. *American Journal of Community Psychology, 17,* 531–547.

Wilson-Doenges, G. (2001). Push and pull forces away from front porch use. *Environment and Behavior, 33,* 264–278.

CHAPTER 14

Meta-Analysis

ARTHUR E. STAMPS III

IN 1976 GLASS COINED the term *meta-analysis* to describe "the statistical analysis of a large collection of results from individual studies for the purpose of integrating the findings." The utility of being able to synthesize a collective body of knowledge was clear as long ago as 1605, when Francis Bacon took up the question of how to improve upon information systems based on speculations about possibilities, personal experiences, or authority. Bacon (1605/1952), who was by training a lawyer, not an academic, suggested that learning could be advanced more efficiently if it were based on a collective tradition, if that collective tradition were based upon facts, and if the facts, the methods used to obtain them, and the circumstances under which the facts were collected were reported such that someone else could determine how reliable those facts were.

Bacon's ideas have undergone considerable refinement over the past 400 years. Research protocols were developed for creating experimental designs (Fisher, 1935/1971) and calculating statistical estimates of findings from individual experiments (Winer, Brown, & Michels, 1991). Versions of meta-analysis date back to 1805 when Legendre combined astronomical findings obtained by different laboratories (Cook et al., 1994, p. 6). A few researchers, such as Pearson (1904), Fisher (1932), and Cochran (1937), also worked on meta-analysis. Until Glass's 1976 article, however, statistical analyses largely stopped at the level of individual articles. When faced with many articles on an issue, the traditional method of summarizing a collective body of literature was reading the articles, forming an overall impression of the collective results, and reporting the collective results as a series of summaries of the papers together with an overall conclusion. In a meta-analytic review, the overall impressions of papers are replaced with actual estimates of an effect size and its sample size, the summaries of the papers are replaced by judgments whether or not the logic and experimental design were sound, and the overall conclusion is replaced by an empirical estimate of the magnitude of the relationship under inquiry. Table 14.1 shows a hypothetical example of traditional and meta-analytic reviews for five articles on the relationship between factors x and y.

In other words, if each article reports (1) a fact as a magnitude of an effect, and (2) the number of sampling units on which the effect was obtained, then statistical methods can be used across articles and the overall collective result could be expressed as "the current collective correlation between these two factors is $r =$ ____ with a confidence interval (ci) of [____, ____]." Other useful results include the following:

1. There is a meta-analytic test for homogeneity of findings. That test is useful for determining if a point estimate is appropriate for a collective effect size over a given series of findings.
2. The general linear model (regression, analysis of variance, contrast analysis) can be used across studies to investigate between-experiment factors.

Table 14.1
Hypothetical Example of Traditional and Meta-Analytic Reviews

Source	Traditional Review	Meta-Analytic Review	
		r	*n*
Author no. 1 (19xx)	There appears to be a moderate connection between *x* and *y*. but there might be a weakness in the choice of students as respondents.	.65	20
Author no. 2 (19xx)	There is a large number of respondents, and there is a strong connection between *x* and *y*.	.80	100
Author no. 3 (19xx)	This study employed a valuable research protocol and was fundamentally sound, but individual results varied and so no definite conclusion is possible at this time.	.75	30
Author no. 4 (19xx)	Results from this study suggested a relationship which is considered as "excellent" according to standards suggested by Author no. 7 (19xx).	.80	25
Author no. 5 (19xx)	Although this study is a valuable contribution to the literature, I would recommend caution in using its results.	.75	40
Overall conclusion:	Results appear to be mixed and so more work is needed on this topic.	$r = .77$ .05 ci = [.71, .82]	

3. There is a way of estimating whether an issue is (a) a dead end; (b) already pretty much settled, so more work would be a waste of time; or (c) the issue is ripe for additional work. These issues are quite useful for planning future research.

4. There is a way to estimate how much additional work would be needed to make the collective finding insignificant. This is useful for mediating scientific disputes with data, as opposed to mediating disputes with discourse.

These applications are described next in the detailed examples of meta-analyses in environmental psychology. I suggest that, if one is trying to understand an issue, trying to plan one's future research time, trying to select articles for publication, or trying to allocate research funding, the possible utility of meta-analytic results is clear.

Since Glass's article, use of meta-analysis has become widespread. A search on the term *meta-analysis* in the PsychInfo database during the summer of 2000 found 3,206 articles. Of the 3,206, 716 were about the method of meta-analysis, and the other 2,490 were applications of meta-analysis. However, meta-analysis has not yet been adopted in environmental psychology. Within the field of engineering and environmental psychology, the PsychInfo search

found only 25 articles, of which 8 were on the method and 17 were applications. When the engineering articles were excluded, the number of articles was reduced to 7. Of those 7, 5 were studies of conservation behavior (De Young, 1996; Hines, Hunderford, & Tomera, 1986–1987; Hornik, Cherian, Madansky, & Narayana, 1995; Winkler & Winett, 1982; Zelezny, 1999), one was a study of lighting levels on office task performance (Gifford, Hine, & Weitch, 1997), and the last was one of my studies on simulation effects (Stamps, 1990). Given the benefits of meta-analysis and its current underutilization in the field of environmental psychology, the time appears ripe to bring this technique to the attention of the environmental psychology community.

ORGANIZATION OF THE CHAPTER

The body of literature reviewed here includes all 716 abstracts on methodology identified in the PsychInfo search and Science Citation searches on articles used in my previous papers on meta-analysis (Stamps, 1990, 1993, 1997a, 1997b, 1997c). I organized the literature into three topics: general descriptions, methods, and possible weaknesses. The last topic made more sense if detailed examples of meta-analyses were presented first, and so the organization of this paper is (1) general descriptions of meta-analyses, (2) methods of meta-analyses, (3) examples of meta-analyses in environmental psychology, (4) possible weaknesses in meta-analysis, and (5) summary and conclusions.

GENERAL DESCRIPTIONS OF META-ANALYSIS

As was noted above, meta-analysis is a procedure for reviewing literature. As such, the basic steps in a meta-analysis are (1) defining a topic, (2) locating relevant material, (3) selecting articles for inclusion in a meta-analysis, (4) performing the quantitative analysis, and (5) writing the review. Relevant sources are Light and Pillemer (1984) and, on a slightly more detailed level, Cooper (1989). Topic definition and location of relevant material are no different in meta-analytic work than in other reviews, but meta-analysis does have different selection criteria: Both an effect size and its sample size must be available for a study to be included in a meta-analysis. Basic quantitative protocols are presented concisely by Rosenthal (1991) and Wolf (1986). Wachter and Straf (1990) and Rosenthal (1998) provide overviews and examples of meta-analyses, and the chapters in Cooper and Hedges (1994) discuss all the steps in meta-analysis at a somewhat more advanced level. Finally, Cook et al. (1994) present an annotated bibliography of books and journals on meta-analysis and a series of very high-quality meta-analytic articles. Dodd (2000) and Froese, Gantz, and Henry (1998) describe how to teach meta-analysis. For readers who are new to meta-analysis, I would recommend Cooper (1989) as the initial resource.

METHODS

There are many ways to perform the quantitative component of meta-analysis. Some methods are simple, others quite complex. Rosenthal (1991) describes techniques which can be used if articles report exact alpha (p) values or values of $t_{(1)}$, $F_{(1, dfe)}$, or $\chi^2_{(1)}$ from which exact alpha values can be calculated. Hedges and Olkin (1985) describe meta-analytic methods for articles that report standardized mean differences or correlations. They also describe how to compute homogeneity statistics for a series of studies and how to apply the general linear model to multiple studies. Each method is illustrated with a completely worked

example. Hunter and Schmidt (1990) extend the scope of meta-analysis to include study artifacts such as sampling error, dichotomization, and range variation in the independent variables. Fleiss (1994) and Haddock, Rindskopf, and Shadish (1998) extend meta-analysis to include categorical dependent variables. Schmidt (1992) indicates how meta-analysis can be applied to path analysis. If one had to select a single source for methods in meta-analysis, I would recommend Hedges and Olkin (1985).

CHOICE OF DEPENDENT VARIABLE

The dependent variable in a meta-analysis is an effect size[1] for a specific criterion. If articles are the boxcars in an intellectual train of thought, then effect sizes are the couplers which hold the train together. Typical measures of effect sizes are correlations, standardized mean differences (two means divided by a pooled standard deviation), odds ratios (for categorical dependent variables), and amount of variance. Alpha values or inequalities (the value typically reported as "$p < .05$" or "$p < .01$") are not measures of effect sizes. A finding with a tiny effect size can be highly significant and a huge finding can be nonsignificant, depending on the sample size. In addition, results are well-nigh uninterpretable if they are only reported in terms of p inequalities. Rosenthal and Rosnow (1991) devote the major portion of their book to this problem and how to solve it. The basic solution is to report the effect size.

To identify which effect measure would be of most interest to environmental psychologists, I conducted a survey of 511 articles published in five relevant journals (*Environment and Behavior*, Vols. 20[1] to 22[6]; *Journal of Environmental Psychology*, Vols. 6[1] to 10[4]; *Landscape Journal*, Vols. 3[1] to 8[2]; *Journal of Environmental Management*, Vols. 28[1] to 31[4]; and *Journal of Architectural and Planning Research*, Vols. 4[1] to 7[4]). The volumes were selected based on whether they were on the library shelf. Articles were coded for whether or not they used probability theory, what type of statistics they reported (the general linear model [correlations, R^2, analysis of

---

[1] Baseball provides an appropriate analogy: It is much more valuable to know a batter's hitting percentage than to know if he hits anything at all. The batting average is the effect size. A p value of 0.05 only means there is enough data to suppose that the batter hits anything at all.

variance, contrasts], chi-square, clustering [factor analysis, clustering, multidimensional scaling], or other), and whether they used three major components of contemporary practice in behavioral research: effect sizes, power analysis,[2] and meta-analysis. One hundred sixty-two of the articles (32%) used some sort of probability theory. Clustering was used in 19 studies, chi-square was used in 26, and variants of the general linear model were used in 100. Effect sizes were reported in 173 articles, while power analysis was reported in only 3 and meta-analysis in none at all. The most common statistic was the correlation (50 studies). Accordingly, this article will emphasize correlations.

In addition, effect sizes should come from independent samples. The simplest way to accomplish this is to use only one effect size per study. More elaborate techniques are available (see Rosenthal & Rubin, 1986, for suggestions), but with complication comes error; so for beginning meta-analytic studies, the prudent procedure is parsimony: one study, one result.

CHOICE OF SAMPLE SIZE

Meta-analysis requires two inputs from a study: an effect size and its corresponding sample size. Environmental psychologists typically take the number of respondents to be the sample size, but there are many circumstances when that is incorrect. For instance, if an article had a total of 1,000 respondents but a specific correlation were based on two groups of 10 respondents, then the appropriate n for that correlation would be 10, not 1,000. Likewise, if one is interested in generalizing over environments, the appropriate n is a function of the number of environments. The reason for this is that each respondent provides information on the same environment; therefore, the respondent effects are highly dependent, and after about 30 or so respondents, the central limit theorem takes hold and additional respondents contribute very little new information. For studies which report correlations between environments, the appropriate n is the number of pairs of environments. For technical reasons each study must include at least four environments, so studies of three or fewer environments cannot be included in a meta-analysis on differences between environments. On the other hand, if one were interested in differences between respondent groups, then the number of people in each group would matter. In that case, the appropriate n would be the harmonic mean of the number of respondents in each group.

CHOICE OF SOFTWARE

Several sources have reported computer software for performing meta-analysis, including Mullen's Basic program (Mullen, 1983), Hunter and Schmidt's (1990) program for meta-analysis with corrections for experimental artifacts (also in Basic), Rosenberg, Adams, and Gurevitch's program for Windows (1997), and Huttcutt, Arthur, and Bennet's (1993) program for SAS. Arthur, Bennet, and Huttcutt (1994) compared results from four meta-analytic programs and found that the results were identical to three or four decimal places. However, if one uses Hedges and Olkin (1985), nearly all the calculations can be done in a spreadsheet, and so using specialized software may not be cost-effective. The only calculation that my spreadsheet will not do is a weighted regression analysis, which can be done in any statistical computer package or in one's own routines.

To sum up: A meta-analysis is a literature review. Articles are selected if they address the topic, if the logic and experimental design are sound, and if they report an effect size and a corresponding sample size. The basic output for each article will be a single line: reference, an effect size (such as a correlation), and a sample size. At the end of the data-collection phase, all the pertinent information will fit into a very concise, even draconian, table, such as the ones next.

---

[2] Power analysis is the way to calculate the size needed in a study in order to detect a given effect size with given alpha and beta errors. The alpha level is the probability of obtaining a false alarm (the false positive). The p value typically used to report "significance" is the alpha probability; it is typically set at 0.05. The beta error is the probability of missing something (the false negative). It is typically taken to be 0.20. Power is the probability of finding something, and so it is $1 - \beta$. With power analysis, one can take estimates of effect sizes (small, medium, high, or actual numbers) and desired alpha and power (typically 0.05 and 0.80) and determine how large a sample would be needed. If the power of a future experiment is low, then it might be wise to refrain from doing the work. A useful analogy is mining: If the chances of hitting gold at one location were only 10%, would it be more worthwhile to go digging there or to find a place where the chances of getting rich were 80%? The key references for power analysis are Cohen (1988) and Cohen and Cohen (1993).

EXAMPLES OF META-ANALYSES IN ENVIRONMENTAL PSYCHOLOGY

Table 14.2 shows a basic meta-analysis on the topic of how well preferences from static color simulations correlate with preferences obtained on-site. The effect size is a correlation. The sample size is the number of pairs of environments. For each line in Table 14.2, both results for individual studies and collective results are shown. For example, in the first line, a 1972 study of four color photographs generated a correlation of $r = .88$ for preferences obtained on-site or through simulations. The values for the collective results were calculated following Hedges and Olkin (1985). As of 1972, there was only one article in the record, so the collective correlation was the same as the individual finding. With such a small n ($n = 4$), the .05 confidence interval (ci) on that correlation included 0.0, and so there was not yet sufficient data to suggest that there was any preference correlation between the on-site and simulated conditions. In 1973 a second study was reported with an r of .99 on an n of 6. Now the combined study was $r = .98$, and the .05 ci no longer included 0.0; so the collective finding was statistically significant. The last column in Table 14.2 (N_{over}) is the size of a study which would impeach the claim (i.e., make the collective finding nonsignificant). Technically, this can

be calculated by postulating a new study that reports an r of 0.0 and then finding how large that study would have to be before the collective ci included zero. This can be done by a root-finding routine or by hand. In 1973 it would have taken a study with 22 environments to impeach the claim that color simulations were valid for the prediction of environmental preferences. As more and more data became available, the size of the study required to impeach the claim increased. As of 1985, it would have taken a study with over 2,800 environments to overturn the validity of static color simulations.

Another very useful item in Table 14.2 is how the collective confidence interval changed over time. The initial studies made very large changes in the collective ci ([$-\infty$, $+\infty$] to [$-.59$, .99] for the first study, [$-.59$, .00] to [.87, 1.00] for the second study). However, by 1979 the collective ci was [.76, .90], and the next study made almost no change, [.75, .88]. The point here is that if the collective ci is already small, then future work is likely to have a tiny collective effect, and research resources would be better spent elsewhere. The implications for planning one's research time, allocating journal pages, or allocating public funds are obvious. For more information on this application see Brewer (1983).

Table 14.3 provides another example. In this table, the topic was whether scaling methods had much effect on measurements of preference. This table combines data from individual experiments and from a

Table 14.2
Meta-Analysis of Simulation Effects in Environmental Preference

| | Individual Results | | | Collective Results | | | |
| | | | | r^b | .05 ci[c] | | |
Year	Medium	n^a	r^b		Low	High	n_{over}^d
1972	Color photographs	4	.88	.88	.52	.99	—
1973	Slides	6	.99	.98	.87	1.00	22
1974	Slides	8	.71	.91	.70	.97	44
1975	Color photographs	8	.93	.92	.78	.97	116
1976	Slides	6	.99	.94	.86	.98	220
1976	Slides	18	.82	.90	.81	.95	555
1976	Color photographs	6	.77	.89	.80	.94	630
1979	Color photographs	10	.67	.87	.77	.93	780
1979	Slides	34	.79	.84	.76	.90	2,005
1985	Color photographs	20	.74	.82	.75	.88	2,808

Note: Sources are given in Stamps, 2000.

[a] Number of pairs of stimuli.
[b] Correlation.
[c] 0.05 confidence interval.
[d] Number of pairs of stimuli in a new experiment, with a finding of $r = 0$, which would make the collective .05 ci include 0.0.

Table 14.3

Studies of Environmental Scaling Methods

	Individual Results		Collective Results			
				.05 ci		
Methods	n	r	r	Low	High	n_{over}
Ratings and rank orders	8	.92				
Ratings and qsort	8	.89				
Ranks and qsort	8	.97				
Ranks and ranks of ratings	12	.89				
Ranks versus place on table	21	.97				
Raw score versus comparative judgment	900	.99				
Raw score versus true score	80	.93				
Raw score versus signal detection	113	.99				
Total:	1,150		.99	.99	.99	>10,000

Note: Sources are given in Stamps, 2000.

previous review paper. The results are that there is virtually no differences among the scaling methods ($r = .99$ on $n = 1,150$), that this correlation is highly reliable (.05 ci of [.99, .99]), and it would take a massive amount of new evidence (n over 10,000) to impeach the finding. Accordingly, environmental researchers can combine results obtained from any of these scaling methods without having to worry about possible experimental artifacts.

Meta-analysis can generate other useful information. For instance, it is worthwhile to know if a single estimate represents all the data. The homogeneity of a series of independent correlations can be estimated with a chi-squared variable, Q (Hedges & Olkin, 1985). If Q exceeds a critical value, then there is more than one story going on and a single estimate of the combined correlation would be misleading. For instance, although color photographs and slides may represent actual environments well, that might not be the case for other simulation media. Relevant findings are given in Table 14.4.

The homogeneity statistic is $Q = 15.3$ on $df = 4$ and $\alpha = .004$, and so there are differences among the findings. In fact, the difference is between the color and black-and-white simulations. That difference can be established by calculating the contrast between the first two findings ($r = .83$ for color) and the last three ($r = .58$ for black-and-white). The difference is quite significant $\chi^2 = 227$ on $df = 3$). More generally, any of the usual analysis of variance or regression tests that one can conduct on data from any one experiment can, with meta-analysis, be conducted on data from different experiments. The only conceptual difference is that meta-analysis tests for between-experiment factors. The utility of that capacity for research syntheses is clear.

Meta-analysis can also be used as a dispute resolution process. There are at least two ways this might be done. The way that follows Bacon most literally is for all interested parties to submit relevant data regardless of whether it supports or impeaches a particular claim and then use meta-analysis to

Table 14.4

Validities of Simulation Methods

				.05 ci	
Medium	Medium	r	n	Low	High
On-site	Slides/color photo	.83	185	.79	.87
Slides	Digitized slides	.84	309	.80	.87
Slides	B&W sketches	.69	23	.50	.81
On-site	B&W sketches	.56	18	.06	.83
Color photos	B&W photos	.41	18	−.12	.73

Note: Sources are given in Stamps, 2000.

calculate the current collective finding. This process would be no surprise to Bacon; it amounts to the legal requirement that all parties in a dispute are expected to present evidence. Thus, if one party supports a hypothesis with an r of .70 on an n of 100, and the other party impeaches that hypothesis with an r of −.10 on an n of 15, then the resulting meta-analysis would generate a collective finding of $r = .64$ with a .05 ci of [.52, .74]. In this example, the impeachment would not hold up. The appropriate way to impeach a finding scientifically would be to acquire more data. Again, meta-analysis can be helpful because the amount of data one would need to impeach a claim can be calculated as the N_{over}. If that number is readily within one's resources, it might be worthwhile to attempt impeachment, but if that number is larger than one's will or resources, it may be prudent to acknowledge the finding and move on. For the example in this paragraph, a critic would have to submit another 1,600 cases with an r of zero to make the objection stand up, and so acceptance would seem to be the better part of disputation.

Meta-analysis can also be used to manage scientific disputes even if only one party provides data. This is a fairly common occurrence in the behavioral sciences. Authors are required to substantiate their claims with data, but about a third of criticisms are supported only by speculations about possible difficulties. (The relevant literature on this topic is described by Speck's, 1993, compilation of 780 abstracts of articles on peer review.) An actual example of this use of meta-analysis can be found in a literature review on demographic effects in environmental preferences (Stamps, 1999). The universe of discourse was 107 articles with over 19,000 people and over 3,200 environments. During the peer review process, reviewers questioned the validity of the results on the grounds that I did much of the work (40 of those studies reported correlations or data from which correlations could be calculated, and of those 40, 5 were mine), or that simulation

media might have made a difference, or that only studies which had results with $p < .05$ were reported. No actual data were presented in support of these objections, so it was not possible to synthesize supporting and impeaching data in a combined meta-analysis. Instead, each objection was treated as a between-experiment factor, and each experiment was coded on the factor of laboratory (mine, others'), medium (color photographs or slides, other), and selective reporting (all results published, only results with $p < .05$ published). Table 14.5 shows the meta-analysis of variance. The resulting analysis of variance for these three criticisms produced an F of .017 on 3, 36 df, for an alpha of .99, and an eta (correlation) of .04. Clearly, these criticisms were not supported by the data and could safely be ignored.

Thus, application of even the simple meta-analytic techniques given in Hedges and Olkin (1985) will provide researchers with the ability to calculate the homogeneity of a series of findings; a collective effect size and collective confidence interval of a single estimate if appropriate and, if not appropriate, sources of heterogeneity; the amount of additional evidence necessary to impeach a collective result; and a scientific way to mediate scientific disputes.

POSSIBLE WEAKNESSES

Many authors have suggested that meta-analysis has serious weaknesses. I believe many of these objections are irrelevant because they address the wrong issue. For example, Sohn (1997) considers the issue of whether any literature review, qualitative or quantitative, will bring about scientific discovery to be a criticism of meta-analysis. I am inclined to consider that issue a general question about Bacon's program for the advancement of learning, not about meta-analysis. Strube and Hartmann (1982) list issues of biased selection of studies, reporting inaccuracies, poor data quality, various sources of invalidity, and lack of independence as problems in

Table 14.5
Anova of Objections to Demographic Findings

Source	df	SS	MS	F	alpha	eta
Constant	1	6.02				
Possible weaknesses	3	1.67	0.556	.017	.99	.038
Residual	36	1,148.00	31.89			
Total	40	1,155.00				

Note: Sources are given in Stamps, 2000.

meta-analytic reviews, but these problems are also present for non-meta-analytic reviews, and so also are irrelevant to the specific issue of meta-analysis. Ostroff and Harison (1999) and Sharpe (1997) also appear to confuse issues of scientific protocol or literature review in general with issues of meta-analysis (not specifying which population parameter is being investigated, sampling at different levels, mixing of dissimilar studies). Other discussions about possible flaws in meta-analysis can be found in Green and Hall (1984), Orwin and Cordray (1985), and Lipsey and Wilson (1993).

I was also able to locate three studies which published replications of meta-analyses. For example, Zakzanis (1998) presented 3 or 4 respondents with a topic, a copy of Wolf's (1986) book, access to *PsychInfo and Medline,* and asked them to go forth and return with an estimate of the standardized mean difference for their topic. The data are shown in Table 14.6. Overall, meta-analytic findings appear to be reproducible. However, the method cannot compensate for basic flaws in sampling, experimental design, or ambiguous writing. For example, in the third test for schizophrenia, one meta-analytic review reported a correlation of $r = .91$, while the other two reviews reported correlations of .48 and .35. What happened was that one reviewer included patients diagnosed as having schizophrenia, schizoaffective disorder, or schizophreniform disorder, while the other reviews included patients with only the first diagnosis. The discrepant finding in Matt's (1989) replications was due to the inability of new reviewers to understand how the original study

defined effect size. All reviewers used the same 25 studies, but the initial review reported 81 effects while the other reviewers found 159, 165, and 172 effects. In my opinion, this type of problem could be greatly reduced by enforcing the one sample-one result rule, by using parsimony in the design of the original study, or by writing more lucidly.

One relevant question raised by Sohn (1997) is whether there is a basis for claiming that meta-analysis is more accurate than traditional review. Cooper and Rosenthal (1980) had 41 respondents review seven papers on sex differences in task performance. Half of the respondents used meta-analysis and half used traditional review methods. 73% of the traditional reviews missed the correct conclusion that there was a difference, while only 32% of the meta-analytic reviews missed the conclusion. Cicchetti's (1991) studies of traditional reviews reported interrater reliabilities of .31 on overall quality for 6,794 journal reviews, .24 on strengths of parts of 1,947 articles, and .31 for 1,785 grant reviews. It would seem that, while certainly not perfect, quantitative reviews tend to perform better than traditional reviews.

On the other hand, meta-analytic reviews do emphasize some problems in scientific literature that are easy to overlook in a traditional review. For example, the current methods of meta-analysis require a measurement of an effect with a single degree of freedom. This implies that a research finding has to be highly focused. A mean difference between two groups (a contrast) has one degree of freedom, as does a correlation or any statistic from which a *t*

Table 14.6
Actual Replications of Meta-Analyses

Source	Variables	ES[a]	Replications of Findings[b]			
Zakzanis (1998)	Test for schizophrenia	*d*	1.02	0.96	0.92	0.95
	Test for schizophrenia	*d*	0.67	0.74	0.70	
	Test for schizophrenia	*d*	0.48	0.35	0.91	
Wanous, Sullivan, & Malinak (1989)	Job satisfaction vs. job performance	*r*	.14	.18	.15	.18
	Realistic job interviews vs. job survival	*r*	.06	.09	.07	
	Job satisfaction vs. absenteeism	*r*	.15	.07	.11	
Matt (1989)	Effectiveness of psychotherapy	*d*	.47	.68	.49	.90

[a] *ES* is effect size. Options are standardized mean difference *(d)* and correlation *(r).*
[b] The effect sizes reported in each of 3 or 4 meta-analyses.

value is reported. Claims in the behavioral sciences often have more than one degree of freedom (any F test with a $dfh > 1$), and these claims are not compatible with current versions of meta-analysis. The advantages of using focused claims (clarity, parsimony, reduced chance of mistakes) date back to William of Ockham in 1318 (Adams, 1987). Rosenthal and Rosnow (1985) make the same point in more contemporary terms, as do the discrepant data reported by Matt (1989). The problems of reporting unfocused results are not peculiar to meta-analysis, but use of quantitative methods for synthesizing a literature does tend to highlight this issue.

Another common difficulty in the behavioral literature is reporting many correlated findings. It is not uncommon to find articles that report dozens or even scores of tests from the same data. For instance, studies of environmental affect often use one set of stimuli and then make multiple tests over the stimuli for different emotions and different respondent groups. An analogy would be using a single set of patients to test for many diseases because a different clinical test or a different set of doctors was used for each disease. Clearly, findings about all the diseases would still be highly correlated because they were all tested on the same people. Likewise, multiple tests on a single set of environments would be correlated even if different affective responses or different groups of respondents were tested. In traditional reviews, such correlations are easy to overlook, but in meta-analysis, the collective confidence interval is simply invalid if the findings are dependent, and so meta-analytic review highlights this common problem. Simple solutions include using one result from each study and dividing a study's results so that they are based on independent samples. Other solutions can be found in Strube (1985); Meng, Rosenthal, and Rubin (1992); Timm (1999); Marascuilo, Busk, and Serlin (1988); and Hayes (1998).

A third problem that is more apparent in meta-analysis than in traditional review is the bias introduced by using alpha levels ($p < .05$) as a criterion for allowing publication. While a .05 level is a simple, easy-to-understand standard for distinguishing publishable from nonpublishable papers, it actually biases the collective record by excluding studies with either small effect sizes or small sample sizes. Here the use of a .05 criterion is not only misleading (the case when alpha levels are confused with effect sizes) but positively detrimental

to the creation of a collective body of reliable knowledge. If one is actually interested in a topic, it is just as worthwhile to know what did not work as to know what did work. Again, this problem is not specific to meta-analysis, just more obvious. Andersson (1999) and Greenwald, Gonzalez, Harris, and Guthrie (1996) discuss this issue in more detail. One solution is to adjust the meta-analytic calculations to truncated distributions (Hedges & Olkin, 1985). Another solution is to change the publication acceptance criteria to focusing of claims, soundness of logic, and correspondence of experimental design with the logic.

SUMMARY AND CONCLUSIONS

Meta-analysis is a statistical way to combine data from multiple studies. It is a direct implementation of Bacon's ideal of advancing knowledge by creating a reliable, collective body of information. Meta-analysis is appropriate when studies report focused ($df = 1$) effect sizes (correlation, standardized mean difference, odds ratio) and the sample size from which that effect was obtained. Typical outputs from a meta-analysis are the collective effect size, the collective confidence interval, and the size of a study needed to make the collective effect nonsignificant. Meta-analysis is highly useful in understanding literatures, planning future research, and mediating scientific disputes scientifically.

REFERENCES

Adams, M. M. (1987). *William Ockham* (Vol. 1). Notre Dame, IN: University of Notre Dame Press.

Andersson, G. (1999). The role of meta-analysis in the significance test controversy. *European Psychologist, 4*(2), 75–82.

Arthur, W., Bennett, W., & Huffcutt, A. (1994). Choice of software and programs in meta-analysis research: Does it make a difference? *Educational & Psychological Measurement, 54*(3), 776–787.

Bacon, F. (1952). *Advancement of learning.* New York: Collier. (Original work published 1605)

Brewer, J. K. (1983). Meta-analysis and the planning of future studies. *Florida Journal of Educational Research, 25*, 61–77.

Cicchetti, D. V. (1991). The reliability of peer review for manuscript and grant submissions: A cross-disciplinary investigation. *Behavioral and Brain Sciences, 14*, 119–186.

Cochran, W. G. (1937). Problems arising in analysis of a series of similar experiments. *Journal of the Royal Statistical Society, 4*(Suppl.), 102–118.

Cohen, J. (1988). *Statistical power analysis for the behavioral sciences.* Hillsdale, NJ: Erlbaum.

Cohen, J., & Cohen, P. (1993). *Applied regression/correlation analysis for the behavioral sciences.* Hillsdale, NJ: Erlbaum.

Cook, T. D., Cooper, H., Cordray, D. S., Hartman, H., Hedges, L. V., Light, R. J., Louis, T. A., & Mosteller, F. (Eds.). (1994). *Meta-analysis for explanation.* New York: Russell Sage.

Cooper, H. M. (1989). *Integrating research: A guide for literature reviews.* Newbury Park, CA: Sage.

Cooper, H. M., & Hedges, L. V. (Eds.). (1994). *The handbook of research synthesis.* New York: Russell Sage.

Cooper, H. M., & Rosenthal, R. (1980). Statistical versus traditional procedures for summarizing research findings. *Psychological Bulletin, 87,* 442–449.

De Young, R. (1996). Some psychological aspects of reduced consumption behavior: The role of intrinsic satisfaction and competence motivation. *Environment & Behavior, 28*(3), 358–409.

Dodd, D. K. (2000). Teaching meta-analysis in the undergraduate psychology course. *Teaching of Psychology, 27*(1), 54–57.

Fisher, R. A. (1932). *Statistical methods for research workers* (4th ed.). London: Oliver & Boyd.

Fisher, R. A. (1971). *The design of experiments.* New York: Hafner. (Original work published 1935)

Fleiss, J. L. (1994). Measures of effect size for categorical data. In H. Cooper & L. V. Hedges (Eds.), *The handbook of research synthesis* (pp. 245–260). New York: Russell Sage.

Froese, A. D., Gantz, B. S., & Henry, A. L. (1998). Teaching students to write literature reviews: A meta-analytical model. *Teaching of Psychology, 25*(2), 102–105.

Gifford, R., Hine, D. W., & Weitch, J. A. (1997). Meta-analysis for environment-behavior and design research, illuminated with a study of lighting level effects on office task performance. In G. T. Moore & R. W. Marans (Eds.), *Advances in environment, behavior and design* (Vol. 4, pp. 223–253). New York: Plenum Press.

Glass, G. V. (1976). Primary, secondary, and meta-analysis of research. *Educational Researcher, 5,* 3–8.

Green, B. F., & Hall, J. A. (1984). Quantitative methods for literature reviews. *Annual Review of Psychology, 35,* 37–53.

Greenwald, A. G., Gonzalez, R., Harris, R. J., & Guthrie, D. (1996). Effect size and *p* values: What should be reported and what should be replicated? *Psychophysiology, 33*(2), 175–183.

Haddock, C. K., Rindskopf, D., & Shadish, W. R. (1998). Using odds ratios as effect sizes for meta-analysis of dichotomous data: A primer on methods and issues. *Psychological Methods, 3*(3), 339–353.

Hayes, A. F. (1998). Within-study meta-analysis: Pooling the significance of doubly nonindependent (nonoverlapping) correlations. *Psychological Monographs, 3*(1), 32–45.

Hedges, L. V., & Olkin, I. (1985). *Statistical methods for meta-analysis.* Orlando, FL: Academic Press.

Hines, J. M., Hunderford, H. R., & Tomera, A. N. (1986–1987). Analysis and synthesis of research on responsible environmental behavior: A meta-analysis. *Journal of Environmental Education, 18*(2), 1–8.

Hornik, J., Cherian, J., Madansky, M., & Narayana, C. (1995). Determinants of recycling behavior: A synthesis of research results. *Journal of Socio-economics, 24*(1), 105–127.

Hunter, J. E., & Schmidt, F. L. (1990). *Methods of meta-analysis.* Newbury Park, CA: Sage.

Huttcutt, A. I., Arthur, W., & Bennet, W. (1993). Conducting meta-analysis using the PROC MEANS procedure in SAS. *Educational & Psychological Measurement, 53*(1), 119–131.

Light, R., & Pillemer, D. B. (1984). *Summing up: The science of reviewing research.* Cambridge, MA: Harvard University Press.

Lipsey, M. W., & Wilson, D. B. (1993). The efficacy of psychological, educational, and behavioral treatment: Confirmation from meta-analysis. *American Psychologist, 48*(12), 1181–1209.

Marascuilo, L. A., Busk, P. L., & Serlin, R. C. (1988). Large sample multivariate procedures for comparing and combining effect sizes within a single study. *Journal of Experimental Education, 57*(1), 69–85.

Matt, G. E. (1989). Decision rules for selecting effect sizes in meta-analysis: A review and reanalysis of psychotherapy outcome studies. *Psychological Bulletin, 105*(1), 106–115.

Meng, X.-L., Rosenthal, R., & Rubin, D. B. (1992). Comparing correlated correlation coefficients. *Psychological Bulletin, 111*(1), 172–175.

Mullen, B. (1983). A BASIC program for meta analysis of effect sizes using *r*, BESD, and *d. Behavior Research Methods & Instrumentation, 15*(3), 392–393.

Orwin, R. G., & Cordray, D. S. (1985). Effects of deficient reporting on meta-analysis: A conceptual framework and reanalysis. *Psychological Bulletin, 97*(1), 134–147.

Ostroff, C., & Harison, D. A. (1999). Meta-analysis, level of analysis, and best estimates of population correlations: Cautions for interpreting meta-analytic results in organizational behavior. *Journal of Applied Psychology, 84*(2), 260–270.

Pearson, K. (1904). Report on certain enteric fever inoculations. *British Medical Journal, 2,* 1243–1246.

Rosenberg, M. S., Adams, D. C., & Gurevitch, J. (1997). Metawin: Statistical software for meta-analysis with resampling tests. Sunderland, MA: Sinauer.

Rosenthal, R. (1991). *Meta-analytic procedures for social research* (2nd ed., Vol. 6). Newbury Park, CA: Sage.

Rosenthal, R. (1998). Meta-analysis: Concepts, corollaries and controversies. In J. G. Adair & D. Belanger (Eds.), *Advances in psychological science: Vol. 1. Social, personal, and cultural aspects.* Hove, England: Psychology Press/Erlbaum.

Rosenthal, R., & Rosnow, R. L. (1985). *Contrast analysis: Focused comparisons in the analysis of variance.* Cambridge: Cambridge University Press.

Rosenthal, R., & Rosnow, R. L. (1991). *Essentials of behavioral research: Methods and data analysis.* New York: McGraw-Hill.

Rosenthal, R., & Rubin, D. B. (1986). Meta-analytic procedures for combining studies with multiple effect sizes. *Psychological Bulletin, 99*(3), 400–406.

Schmidt, F. L. (1992). What do data really mean? Research findings, meta-analysis, and cumulative knowledge in psychology. *American Psychologist, 47*(10), 1173–1181.

Sharpe, D. (1997). Of apples and oranges, file drawers and garbage: Why validity issues in meta-analysis will not go away. *Clinical Psychology Review, 17*(8), 881–901.

Sohn, D. (1997). Questions for meta-analysis. *Psychological Reports, 81*(1), 3–15.

Speck, B. W. (1993). *Publication peer review: An annotated bibliography.* Westport, CT: Greenwood Press.

Stamps, A. E. (1990). Use of photographs to simulate environments: A meta-analysis. *Perceptual and Motor Skills, 71,* 907–913.

Stamps, A. E. (1993). Simulation effects on environmental preference. *Journal of Environmental Management, 38,* 115–132.

Stamps, A. E. (1997a). Advances in peer review research: An introduction. *Science and Engineering Ethics, 3*(1), 3–10.

Stamps, A. E. (1997b). Meta-analysis in environmental research. In M. S. Amiel & J. C. Vischer (Eds.), *Space design and management for place making: Proceedings of the twenty-eighth annual conference of the Environmental Design Research Association* [EDRA] (pp. 114–124). Edmond, OK: EDRA.

Stamps, A. E. (1997c). Using a dialectical scientific brief in peer review. *Science and Engineering Ethics, 3*(1), 85–98.

Stamps, A. E. (1999). Demographic effects in environmental preferences: A meta-analysis. *Journal of Planning Literature, 14*(2), 155–175.

Stamps, A. E. (2000). *Psychology and the aesthetics of the built environment.* Norwell, MA: Kluwer Academic.

Strube, M. J. (1985). Combining and comparing significance levels from nonindependent hypothesis tests. *Psychological Bulletin, 97*(2), 334–341.

Strube, M. J., & Hartmann, D. P. (1982). A critical appraisal of meta-analysis. *British Journal of Clinical Psychology, 21*(2), 129–139.

Timm, N. H. (1999). Testing multivariate effect sizes in multiple-endpoint studies. *Multivariate Behavioral Research, 34*(4), 457–465.

Wachter, K. W., & Straf, M. L. (Eds.). (1990). *The future of meta-analysis.* New York: Russell Sage.

Wanous, J. P., Sullivan, S. E., & Malinak, J. (1989). The role of judgment calls in meta-analysis. *Journal of Applied Psychology, 74*(2), 259–264.

Winer, B. J., Brown, D. R., & Michels, K. M. (1991). *Statistical principles in experimental design.* New York: McGraw-Hill.

Winkler, R. C., & Winett, R. A. (1982). Behavioral interventions in resource conservation: A systems approach based on behavioral economics. *American Psychologist, 37*(4), 421–435.

Wolf, F. M. (1986). *Meta-analysis: quantitative methods for research synthesis* (Vol. 59). Newbury Park, CA: Sage.

Zakzanis, K. K. (1998). The reliability of meta-analytic review. *Psychological Reports, 83,* 215–222.

Zelezny, L. C. (1999). Educational interventions that improve environmental behaviors: A meta-analysis. *Journal of Environmental Education, 31*(1), 5–14.

CHAPTER 15

The Experience Sampling Method: Measuring the Context and Content of Lives

JOEL M. HEKTNER and MIHALY CSIKSZENTMIHALYI

THE IMPORTANCE OF EXPERIENCE IN PSYCHOLOGICAL RESEARCH

IT IS CUSTOMARY to describe scientific psychology as a hybrid offspring of philosophy and natural science (Leahey, 1997). The methodological outcome of this mixed ancestry has been a schizophrenic tension between clinical and humanistic psychology on the one hand, which privileges subjective experience and personal meaning, and the more rigorous approaches of behavioral, biological, cognitive, and social psychologists on the other hand, which tend to recognize as data only results of controlled experiments. Largely ignored by either of these extremes has been a study of the physical activities and mental processes of normal people in their natural environments. It is our claim that psychology will not become a complete science unless it provides an accurate mapping of the experiences of everyday life in all their complexity.

One attempt in this direction has been the systematic phenomenology developed at the University of Chicago in the past 30 years (Csikszentmihalyi, 2000, pp. ix–xxviii). Basically this approach is a continuation of William James's insight to the effect that the paramount question of psychology is how a person's attention is allocated. The content of a person's life can be seen as the sum of billions of experiences—bits of information he or she has processed across the span of years (James, 1890). If such is the case, the main methodological challenge is to develop a reliable measure of the events occurring in the stream of consciousness over time (Csikszentmihalyi, 1978; Csikszentmihalyi & Csikszentmihalyi, 1988). It is as a response to this challenge that the experience sampling method was devised.

A recent special issue of *Applied Developmental Science* devoted to the uses of the ESM in research with adolescents shows some of the questions this method is equipped to answer: Do moods and self-esteem decline through the teenage years? (Moneta, Schneider, & Csikszentmihalyi, 2001); how do one-parent families facilitate the constructive use of teenagers' time? (Larson, Dworkin, & Gillman, 2001); does family context impact on adolescents' quality of experience over time? (Rathunde, 2001); what are the longitudinal effects of growth-producing environments? (Hektner, 2001); how do socialization practices affect the educational values of Asian and Caucasian American adolescents? (Asakawa, 2001).

THE EXPERIENCE SAMPLING METHOD

The experience sampling method (ESM) provides a means for collecting information about both the context and content of the daily life of individuals. This purpose is shared by other methods, but the unique advantage of the ESM is its ability to capture daily life as it is directly perceived in each moment, thus affording researchers an unsurpassed opportunity to examine the links between context and content. The method achieves this degree of immediacy by asking individuals to provide written responses to both open- and closed-ended questions at several random points throughout each day of a normal week. The questions can be fully tailored to the interests and goals of the researcher but often include queries focused on physical context (location, time of day), social context (number and description of others sharing the moment), activities, thoughts, feelings, and cognitive and motivational self-appraisals.

A more thorough understanding of the ESM can be derived from comparisons of the method to other means of data collection. In a naturalistic behavioral observation, information is obtained about the activities of people and the contexts within which these activities occur, but no information is gained on how people are actually experiencing those activities and contexts. The cognitive and affective dimensions of experience are lost. Further, observers are either limited to studying only the public activities of individuals or, in studying more private behavior, must consider how their presence is influencing the behavior they are observing.

Asking individuals to complete diaries of their experiences removes both of these problems and potentially allows for the gathering of the individual's perceptions, thoughts, and feelings about their behavior and contexts. However, researchers using diaries have rarely asked participants to provide reports of the subjective dimensions of their experiences. Major diary studies have typically focused on activity and time use (Hochschild, 1989; Robinson, 1977; Wheeler & Reis, 1991). Even for this limited purpose, diaries may not be the most accurate method of data collection. Research on how individuals reconstruct episodic memories calls into question the accuracy of recollected reports of experiences (Yarmey, 1979).

Because of the fallibility of memory, the use of diaries to collect information about behavior is an improvement over a one-time questionnaire in which questions might, for example, begin with "In the last month, how often have you . . ." (Sudman & Bradburn, 1982). The more profitable use of questionnaires has been in psychological research on individuals' self-related cognitions, affect, motivation, and personality traits. The psychometric precision and measurable reliability and validity of such instruments have been major advantages. Yet, by providing just one snapshot of the individual—one slice of time—questionnaires do not address the considerable variability that exists within individuals across situations and over time. A long-standing challenge to the ecological validity of questionnaire and interview data stems from their collection outside the context to which they are intended to refer (Willems, 1969). For example, asking college students on a questionnaire how they feel about the design of their dorm risks missing patterns of interaction and nuances of behavior that may lie beneath the residents' awareness.

In the ESM, information on these unique patterns and nuances would be collected. The ESM combines the ecological validity of naturalistic behavioral observation with the precision of scaled questionnaire measures. By sampling experience the moment it occurs, the method avoids the potential distortions associated with the use of daily or weekly retrospective diaries. Of course, the method is not without its limitations. One major drawback is its intrusiveness in respondents' lives, a burden that contributes to self-selection bias and selective nonresponse (Mulligan, Schneider, & Wolfe, 2000; Zuzanek, 1999). Another consideration is its high cost of implementation. Nevertheless, the burden for respondents and costs to researchers are well worth the richness of the data obtained through the ESM. For more extensive discussions of the strengths and limitations of ESM, see Alliger and Williams (1993) and Csikszentmihalyi and Larson (1987).

DESCRIPTION OF THE METHOD

Over the past 25 years, there have been numerous variations in the way that the ESM has been implemented. The diversity of implementations is appropriate for the wide range of applications and attests to the general utility of the method. Rather than being tailored to measure one dimension of reality, as IQ tests ostensibly measure intelligence, the ESM has been left unstructured to encourage researchers to use it for their own purposes (Kubey, Larson, & Csikszentmihalyi, 1996). This section will offer a brief overview of the most common approaches.

SIGNALING DEVICE, SCHEDULE, AND SELF-REPORT

In most studies, each participant is given an electronic signaling device, such as a pager or wristwatch.

The device can either be programmed ahead by the researcher or can respond to real-time signals sent from the research office. In either case, at each appointed time, the device signals the respondent by beeping or vibrating. Upon detecting the signal, the respondent can shut the signal off and then complete a brief self-report form. Blank forms are typically bound together in a booklet that respondents carry with them, along with the signaling device, as they carry out their daily activities. In most cases researchers tell the respondent to respond as soon as possible but not to fill out a form if more than 15 minutes have elapsed from the time of the signal.

The schedule of signals used in most studies attempts to generate a random sample of the respondents' waking hours. Several studies have signaled respondents once during each 2-hour block of time from early morning to late evening, resulting in six to nine signals each day. The specific minute chosen for the signal within each 2-hour block is determined randomly and varies from day to day so as not to allow the respondent to anticipate the next signal or to fall into a regular pattern of time usage. To minimize respondent annoyance, sometimes a stipulation is added that no two signals are scheduled within 30 minutes of each other. Studies using this schedule of daily signals usually continue for a full week to capture contexts and experiences that occur only on a weekly basis. However, both the frequency of signals and the duration of the signaling period can be fully tailored to the purposes of the researcher. For example, Hurlburt (1979) conducted a study of thought content in which participants were signaled every 30 minutes for 3 days, whereas LeFevre, Hendricks, Church, and McClintock (1992) signaled couples three times a day for one month in order to study mood changes during the woman's menstrual cycle. The distribution of signals also need not be uniform across the day. Larson and Richards (1994) sampled the experience of parents and adolescents every 90 minutes during the evening hours but only every 120 minutes during the workday, because they intended to focus on family interactions.

In response to each signal, respondents are to complete a brief self-report form. The structure of this form is determined by the researcher to best accomplish the goals of the research. Some researchers have used fully closed-ended items in which respondents circle a number on a scale to indicate their mood, motivation, and cognitive efficiency. To provide information on their location and activities, respondents can self-code, choosing a number on a preprinted list of possibilities (Hormuth, 1986). At the opposite extreme, others have asked respondents simply to take notes that were later coded by the researcher (Hurlburt, 1979) or the respondents (Brandstätter, 1983). Many studies have taken a combined approach to the structure of the self-report, asking subjects to note in open-ended format their location, activities, and thoughts and to indicate on rating scales the other internal dimensions of their experience (e.g., Csikszentmihalyi & Schneider, 2000). Social context (who the respondent is "with" at the moment) can be indicated on an open-ended item or on a check-off list of possible categories of people (stranger, spouse, classmate, friend, etc.). An example of this type of blended self-report form is reproduced in the Appendix to this chapter. However the self-report form is constructed, the researcher must strive to keep it as brief as possible so as to minimize the interruption of ongoing activities and the attention that might be drawn to the respondent during public or social situations. The willingness of respondents to complete all self-reports is dependent on such considerations.

A further consideration in the design of the self-report is the coding scheme that will be used to categorize the open-ended responses. Physical parameters such as time and date are exact enough to be used directly as the respondent reported them. The respondent's location will need to be coded into discrete categories, but the number and specificity of these codes are entirely dependent on the researcher's goals. For example, one study may be served simply by representing location as a small number of general types (school, work, public, home, other), whereas another may require a hierarchical system of categories (school: class: nonacademic: art class). Similarly, open-ended responses indicating the respondent's activities and thoughts will also require coding.

Scales measuring internal dimensions of experience typically focus on the respondent's quality of experience at the particular moment she or he was signaled. Three broad dimensions that are often measured include motivation, emotion, and cognitive efficiency. By asking respondents to indicate whether they wanted to do the activity or had to, whether the activity was important to them or not, or whether there was something else they would rather be doing, researchers can obtain measures of intrinsic motivation and perceived autonomy. Depending on the nature of the research, respondents indicate their mood on a set of bipolar semantic differential scales (e.g., happy-sad) or on scales measuring the strength of single dimensions (e.g., "How much were you enjoying the activity?"). Cognitive efficiency is tapped by items asking respondents to rate their level of concentration and how easy it was to concentrate.

The advent of the palm-top computer has made it possible to combine the signaling and data recording functions into one device. As early as 1982, researchers in one study used a similar type of "pocket microcomputer" in which participants typed in their coded responses to questions displayed on the screen (Pawlik & Buse, 1982). Such a device allows the direct transfer of data into larger computers, thus eliminating costly and time-consuming data entry. On the other hand, the researcher gives up control over coding the data and must rely on respondents to self-code. Finally, the cost of such devices makes them impractical for use with large samples.

WORKING WITH PARTICIPANTS

ESM research has been used with a diverse array of populations, ranging in age from 10 to 95 and in health from "normal" to physically disabled or schizophrenic. Often, a preexisting group is chosen from which to recruit participants. When participants are sought from schools or workplaces, initial permission should be requested from the appropriate institutional officials. Then, an individual or small-group meeting with potential participants is an ideal way to explain the goals of the research, the demands placed on the respondents, and the rewards they can expect from participation (intangible as well as monetary compensation, if offered). Other one-time questionnaires can be completed at this initial meeting (to collect demographic data, for example), and informed consent can be obtained from the participants once they have been reassured about their privacy and right to stop participating at any time. Of those invited to participate, rates of acceptance have varied widely, from 12% among unskilled blue-collar workers to 91% among 5th and 8th graders (Csikszentmihalyi & Larson, 1987).

During the signaling period, the researcher may simply step out of the picture or, depending on the competence of the sample, may want to provide participants with a phone number and/or a reminder call midway through so that any problems or questions can be addressed without missing an entire set of individual ESM data. At the end of the signaling period, a debriefing session is typically held with participants individually or in small groups. During this meeting, participants can inform the researchers of instances in which they turned their beeper off, and researchers can collect any other data they may need. In a recent study of adolescents, the debriefing session was structured as a one-on-one tape-recorded interview in which the interviewer asked for elaboration on particularly interesting moments (self-reports) in order to stimulate a conversation about specific issues (Csikszentmihalyi & Schneider, 2000).

DATA MANAGEMENT AND ANALYSIS

Considering that a typical self-report form may have 40 or more items and that respondents may complete 30 to 50 self-reports during the signaling period, a sample of even modest size generates a tremendous amount of data. Initially, data are entered and stored in a "beep-level" structure, meaning that each self-report comprises one case. Usually, researchers will also need to create a "person-level" data set, in which data from each person are aggregated by taking the mean across all observations or by calculating the percentage of the person's observations in each of several relevant categories of location, activity, and thought content. The creation of both of these types of data files allows the researcher to focus analysis on situations, on persons, and on the interactions between situations and persons. For example, one can examine whether people on the whole report more positive moods at work, at home, or while shopping at a mall. Comparisons can be made between groups of people on the overall quality of their daily life or on how they allocate their time among different activities (e.g., Do fathers in dual-earner couples spend more time doing housework than fathers who are their family's sole income-provider?). More complex analyses are possible when data are standardized (z-scored) within persons, so that individual differences in rating scale usage (favoring extremes versus middling responses, for example) are controlled. Larson and Richards (1994) made effective use of sequential analyses to examine the transmission of moods among family members. Finally, to deal with the nested nature of ESM data, analysts are increasingly turning to statistical strategies, such as hierarchical linear modeling (HLM; Bryk & Raudenbush, 1992), that take into account the nonindependence of observations within persons.

VALIDITY AND RELIABILITY

Rates of completion of ESM self-reports vary within and across samples. Csikszentmihalyi and Larson (1987) reported that adult workers responded to an average of 80% of the signals, whereas high school students responded to 70%. A more recent study of adolescents experienced somewhat lower rates of response, particularly among boys and older adolescents (Mulligan et al., 2000). Reasons for failure to complete a self-report include technical problems with the signaling device, failure to carry the device and/or the self-report booklet during all activities, and intentional nonresponse during such activities as swimming, napping, test taking, and attending religious services. Of the responses that are completed, the vast majority are answered within 10 minutes of the signal (Hormuth, 1986); responses delayed by 15 minutes or more are typically discarded. Further, in person-level analyses, individuals completing fewer than 25% of their self-reports are often excluded.

These levels of nonresponse do not appear to diminish the ability of the ESM to accurately reflect the daily life of individuals. In debriefing interviews, 80% to 90% of participants express belief that the method captured their week well. More systematic comparisons of the ESM with diary records show strong agreement between the methods on the allocation of time to different activities (Csikszentmihalyi & Larson, 1987). Mulligan et al. (2000) found ESM estimates of the amount of time adolescents spend at jobs to be remarkably similar to estimates from national survey data. Because the ESM is designed to capture the fluctuations in activities, moods, and thoughts inherent in daily life, perfect individual consistency on each question across multiple self-reports is not a goal, and thus the test-retest method would not provide an appropriate indication of reliability. One method that has proven useful for assessing the reliability of the ESM is to compare the first half of the signaling week to the second half. Using this approach, Csikszentmihalyi and Larson (1987) demonstrated strong consistency in activities and psychological states within persons.

The validity of the ESM for measuring psychological states has been shown in three ways. (See Csikszentmihalyi & Larson, 1987, for a more detailed discussion.) First, reported psychological states vary in expected ways with contextual factors. For example, feeling that one "has to" do an activity is strongest when that activity is work and weakest when it is watching television. Second, person-level means across all self-reports correlate with similar scales on one-time psychometric assessments. When the ESM self-report includes questions asking respondents to rate their self-esteem at the moment of the signal, respondents' overall means are correlated with their scores from more traditional questionnaire measures of self-esteem. Third, groups of people who can be expected to have different subjective experiences, such as people with and without psychopathology, actually do have different patterns of ESM data.

HOW ESM HAS BEEN USED

The research questions that have been addressed using the ESM center around the contexts of daily life, the experiential content of life, and the links between context and content. A third dimension to these investigations is added by the characteristics of the sample of participants. The cumulative impact of hundreds of ESM studies to date has been to produce a record of the contexts and content of the lives of people of many cultures, occupations, and ages.

TO DESCRIBE CONTEXT AND QUALITATIVE EXPERIENCES WITHIN EACH

Bronfenbrenner (1979) challenged psychologists to study the ecology of human development. The ESM allows the researcher to obtain detailed, systematic information on what he called *microsystems*, the contexts within which daily interactions take place. Much as a newspaper reporter would gather information on the who, what, where, and when, the ESM provides a record of what Csikszentmihalyi and Larson (1984) called the *external landscape* of daily life. In their ESM study of adolescents, they began by examining where teenagers spend their time, what they do with their time, and who they spend time with. As shown in the graph reproduced in Figure 15.1, locations can be lumped into broad categories (school, public, home) and also broken out into more detail. As in this graph, information on physical and social

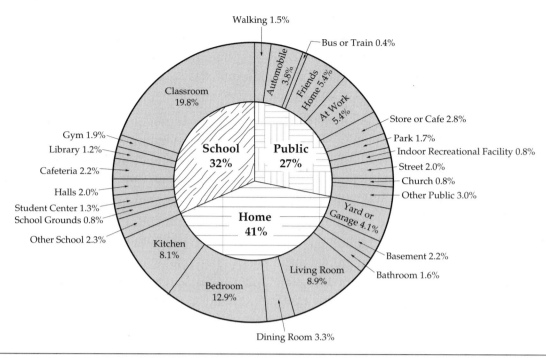

Figure 15.1   Where adolescents spend their time. This graph shows the percentage of self-reports in each location (*N* = 2,734). One percentage point is equivalent to approximately 1 hour per week spent in the given location. Reproduced from Csikszentmihalyi and Larson, 1984, p. 59.

context is often presented in terms of the percentage of (waking) time spent in each context, although conversions from this percentage to the actual number of hours spent can easily be accomplished by taking into account the sampling schedule. A more recent study of high school students showed that the proportion of time students spend in school but outside of class—about a third of their school time—has remained remarkably consistent (Csikszentmihalyi & Schneider, 2000). Similarly, adult workers report that although they are physically in the workplace, they are not actually working at their jobs about one third of the time (Kubey & Csikszentmihalyi, 1990). This time is spent eating, on the phone with friends and family, or in non-work-related conversations with coworkers.

These and other ESM investigations have also gone beyond cataloging which activities people engage in, where, and with whom, to focus on the psychological states individuals experience in each context. The unique combinations of emotion, motivation, and cognitive efficiency that accompany each moment of life have been called an individual's *internal landscape* or *quality of experience*. Some of the findings to emerge in this area are that adolescents feel the highest levels of intrinsic motivation when they are in public parks or at friends' homes and the

lowest levels when they are in class or at a job. They are happiest when with friends, have neutral affect on average when with their parents, and are least happy when alone (Csikszentmihalyi & Larson, 1984). Findings on adults have shown that men feel more anger and frustration at their jobs and report higher rates of absorbed attention than women. Men also experience more positive emotions at home than their wives do (Larson & Richards, 1994). Although adults typically rank working at their jobs as one of their least enjoyable activities on recall questionnaires, ESM data show that doing paid work is often experienced positively and is generally not one of the least enjoyed activities (Zuzanek, 1999). Across all ages, residents of developed countries report that while watching television they experience low levels of concentration, alertness, and activity; average moods; and high relaxation. Greater mental effort is experienced by those from less well developed countries who have had less experience with television (Kubey & Csikszentmihalyi, 1990).

One person-in-context system that has been widely studied with the ESM is the adolescent in the school. Beyond documenting the amount of time students spend in class and their generally lower levels of intrinsic motivation in school, ESM research has uncovered much more nuanced variations in student engagement during different classroom activities. Csikszentmihalyi and Schneider (2000) report that high schoolers spend over one-third of their class time listening to the teacher lecture or to audiovisual presentations but that they are actually thinking about the subject matter only 54% of the time during these activities. Students have the lowest levels of affect and motivation in history classes, which are heavily dependent on lectures, and the highest levels in computer science and vocational education classes such as drafting. The latter are usually elective classes that require much individual work at solving problems; indeed, choice, control, and student engagement in an individual or group project were the elements of a class period most likely to arouse both students' enjoyment and concentration.

To Study Patterns of Communication and Relationships in the Family

Given the importance of the social environment and social interaction to human development and behavior, much ESM research has focused on interpersonal communication and relationships. Kubey and Csikszentmihalyi (1990) found that conversation was one of the most enjoyable activities that people engage in. The most positive emotional states occur when people report that they are with friends; the least positive when they are alone. In between are interactions with classmates at school or colleagues at work (Brandstätter, 1983; Csikszentmihalyi & Larson, 1984; Larson & Bradney, 1988). Interaction with family members appears to carry the greatest potential for emotional transmission from one person to another. As Larson and Richards' (1994) ESM data show, emotions are often transmitted from husbands to wives, particularly when husbands return home from work. By having two parents and an adolescent complete ESM self-reports simultaneously, Larson and Richards were able to show that the perception of togetherness can vary across family members. A wife may report that she is "with" her husband, while in the same moment her husband reports that he was alone.

Other ESM studies have examined the daily interaction patterns of families to shed light on the processes that underlie adaptive versus maladaptive functioning. Kirchler (1988) found that happier couples are ones who are better able to estimate each other's mood, spend more time talking about personal topics, and experience a balance of power

more often. Studies of optimal family contexts and interaction patterns for facilitating adolescent development have focused on the role of emotional support and the provision of challenging opportunities and high expectations. If families provide consistent emotional support but no demands or challenges, children report being happy but do not engage themselves in activities that will stretch their abilities or move them toward a future goal. If families provide challenges without support, the opposite result occurs. An optimal family environment appears to be one in which children experience both strong emotional support and demanding challenges (Csikszentmihalyi & Rathunde, 1993; Csikszentmihalyi, Rathunde, & Whalen, 1993).

RECOMMENDATIONS FOR FUTURE ESM USE

By its very nature, the ESM is a research tool valuable to multiple disciplines, and it provides a way for researchers from specialized subfields of the human sciences to work together on projects that cross disciplinary boundaries. To date, the richest ESM studies have been those designed by multidisciplinary teams to answer questions relevant to human development, sociology, education, clinical/counseling psychology, family studies, communication, leisure studies, and environmental psychology. In the future, the most profitable use of the ESM will likely remain in these and other cross-disciplinary fields that deal with questions of human experience. What will evolve is the nature of the questions asked. Beyond documenting the contexts of life and individuals' inner experiences within each, future ESM studies will need to focus much more on the complex interactions among people and between people and their environment. The questions posed by such studies could range in scale from a focus on cultural evolution and mass communication processes to the dynamics of long-term interpersonal relationships and the generation of creativity.

Two research areas in particular illustrate the potential of the ESM to gather phenomenological data to address such questions. First, ESM studies need to be done to examine individuals' use and experience of the Internet. In recent years, e-mail, personal Web pages, and chat rooms have given rise to what some call "virtual communities." Paradoxically, initial (non-ESM) research into this greater level of interconnectedness has found that it leaves people more lonely (Kraut et al., 1998). Future ESM studies could go much further in documenting the dynamics of online communication and relationships and how they relate to individual mental health. Because of its interactive, user-directed nature, the Internet is also believed by some to be superior to traditional media such as television, movies, and books for both entertainment and serious information gathering. ESM research could not only describe how people use the Internet but also their levels of affect, motivation, and cognitive efficiency while doing so.

The second research area that is ripe for ESM research has had a much longer history, but because of rapid technological and social changes it seems almost as "undiscovered" to social scientists as the Internet. People spend a large portion of their lives at the workplace, devoting much energy and attention to an occupation or career. Globalization, greater gender equality, less hierarchical management styles, and, of course, information technology have all had a tremendous impact on the way work is performed

and experienced. Although workers in advanced nations are said to have more leisure time available than at any other point in history, there is also an increasing sense among many Americans, at least, of time pressure (Zuzanek, 1999). As organizational and social structures within the workplace continue on a rapid pace of change, ESM research will be needed to examine the dynamics and processes behind productivity, creativity, time use, and individual wellness. As with research on the Internet, this line of research has the potential to deliver new insights on questions ranging from intraindividual processes to cultural evolution.

Clearly, the adaptability of the ESM and the richness of the data it generates make it a powerful research tool. Still, it cannot stand alone. When used in a multimethod research design in conjunction with questionnaires, interviews, observations, or other methods, the ESM has a huge potential to help social scientists disentangle the complex interactions among people and their environment.

APPENDIX
Example of ESM Self-Report Form

Date _____   Time you were beeped _____ am/pm   Time you answered _____ am/pm

As you were beeped . . .

Where were you? _____

_____

_____

_____

What was on your mind? _____

_____

_____

_____

What was the main thing you were doing? _____

_____

_____

_____

What else were you doing? _____

_____

_____

_____

Was the main thing you were doing . . .

More like work ( )   More like play ( )   Both ( )   Neither ( )

	Not at All								Very Much	
How well were you concentrating?	0	1	2	3	4	5	6	7	8	9
Were you living up to expectations of others?	0	1	2	3	4	5	6	7	8	9
Was it hard to concentrate?	0	1	2	3	4	5	6	7	8	9
Did you feel self-conscious or embarrassed?	0	1	2	3	4	5	6	7	8	9
Did you feel good about yourself?	0	1	2	3	4	5	6	7	8	9
Did you enjoy what you were doing?	0	1	2	3	4	5	6	7	8	9
Were you living up to your expectations?	0	1	2	3	4	5	6	7	8	9
Did you feel in control of the situation?	0	1	2	3	4	5	6	7	8	9

Were you doing the main activity because . . .

You wanted to ( )   You had to ( )   You had nothing else to do ( )

Describe your mood as you were beeped:

	Very	Quite	Some	Neither	Some	Quite	Very	
Happy	☐	☐	☐	☐	☐	☐	☐	Sad
Weak	☐	☐	☐	☐	☐	☐	☐	Strong
Passive	☐	☐	☐	☐	☐	☐	☐	Active
Lonely	☐	☐	☐	☐	☐	☐	☐	Sociable
Ashamed	☐	☐	☐	☐	☐	☐	☐	Proud
Involved	☐	☐	☐	☐	☐	☐	☐	Detached
Excited	☐	☐	☐	☐	☐	☐	☐	Bored
Clear	☐	☐	☐	☐	☐	☐	☐	Confused
Worried	☐	☐	☐	☐	☐	☐	☐	Relaxed
Competitive	☐	☐	☐	☐	☐	☐	☐	Cooperative

Who were you with?

( ) alone
( ) mother
( ) father
( ) sister(s) or brother(s)
( ) other relatives
( ) others

( ) teachers
( ) classmates, peers
( ) strangers
( ) friend(s) How many? _____
   female ( ) male ( )

( ) If you were with friends, what were
their names?
_____
_____
_____
_____

Indicate how you felt about the main activity:

	Low								High
Challenges of the activity.	1	2	3	4	5	6	7	8	9
Your skills in the activity.	1	2	3	4	5	6	7	8	9

	Not at All								Very Much
Was this activity important to you?	1	2	3	4	5	6	7	8	9
How difficult did you find this activity?	1	2	3	4	5	6	7	8	9
Were you succeeding at what you were doing?	1	2	3	4	5	6	7	8	9
Did you wish you had been doing something else?	1	2	3	4	5	6	7	8	9
Was this activity interesting?	1	2	3	4	5	6	7	8	9
How important was it in relation to your future goals?	1	2	3	4	5	6	7	8	9

(continued)

If you had a choice . . .

Who would you be with? _____

What would you be doing? _____

Since you were last beeped, did you do any: (estimate to nearest quarter/hour)
(Please circle "0" if you haven't done the activity.)

TV watching	0	¼	½	¾	1	1¼	1½	1¾	2 Hours
Chores, errands	0	¼	½	¾	1	1¼	1½	1¾	2 Hours
Paid work	0	¼	½	¾	1	1¼	1½	1¾	2 Hours
Hanging out with friends	0	¼	½	¾	1	1¼	1½	1¾	2 Hours
Homework	0	¼	½	¾	1	1¼	1½	1¾	2 Hours

. . . has anything happened, or have you done anything which could have affected how you feel?

Any comments?

REFERENCES

Alliger, G. M., & Williams, K. J. (1993). Using signal-contingent experience sampling methodology to study work in the field: A discussion and illustration examining task perceptions and mood. *Personnel Psychology, 46*, 525–549.

Asakawa, K. (2001). Family socialization practices and their effects on the internalization of educational values for Asian and White American adolescents. *Applied Developmental Science, 5*(3), 184–194.

Brandstätter, H. (1983). Emotional responses to other persons in everyday life situations. *Journal of Personality and Social Psychology, 45*, 871–883.

Bronfenbrenner, U. (1979). *The ecology of human development: Experiments by nature and design.* Cambridge, MA: Harvard University Press.

Bryk, A. S., & Raudenbush, S. W. (1992). *Hierarchical linear models.* Newbury Park, CA: Sage.

Csikszentmihalyi, M. (1978). Attention and the wholistic approach to behavior. In K. S. Pope & J. L. Singer (Eds.), *The stream of consciousness* (pp. 335–358). New York: Plenum Press.

Csikszentmihalyi, M. (2000). *Beyond boredom and anxiety* (2nd ed.). San Francisco: Jossey-Bass.

Csikszentmihalyi, M., & Csikszentmihalyi, I. (Eds.). (1988). *Optimal experience.* New York: Cambridge University Press.

Csikszentmihalyi, M., & Larson, R. (1984). *Being adolescent: Conflict and growth in the teenage years.* New York: Basic Books.

Csikszentmihalyi, M., & Larson, R. (1987). Validity and reliability of the experience sampling method. *Journal of Nervous and Mental Disease, 175*, 526–536.

Csikszentmihalyi, M., & Rathunde, K. (1993). The measurement of flow in everyday life. *Nebraska Symposium on Motivation: Vol. 40.* (pp. 57–97). Lincoln: University of Nebraska Press.

Csikszentmihalyi, M., Rathunde, K., & Whalen, S. (1993). *Talented teenagers: The roots of success and failure.* New York: Cambridge University Press.

Csikszentmihalyi, M., & Schneider, B. (2000). *Becoming adult: How teenagers prepare for the world of work.* New York: Basic Books.

Hektner, J. M. (2001). Family, school, and community predictors of adolescent growth-conducive experiences. *Applied Developmental Science, 5*(3), 172–183.

Hochschild, A. R. (1989). *The second shift.* New York: Avon.

Hormuth, S. E. (1986). The sampling of experiences in situ. *Journal of Personality, 54*, 262–293.

Hurlburt, R. T. (1979). Random sampling of cognitions and behavior. *Journal of Research in Personality, 13*, 103–111.

James, W. (1890). *Principles of psychology* (Vol. 1). New York: Henry Holt.

Kirchler, E. (1988). Marital happiness and interaction in everyday surroundings: A time-sampling diary approach for couples. *Journal of Social and Personal Relationships, 5,* 375–382.

Kraut, R., Patterson, M., Lundmark, V., Kiesler, S., Mukopadhyay, T., & Scherlis, W. (1998). Internet paradox: A social technology that reduces social involvement and psychological well-being? *American Psychologist, 53,* 1017–1031.

Kubey, R., & Csikszentmihalyi, M. (1990). *Television and the quality of life: How viewing shapes everyday experience.* Hillsdale, NJ: Erlbaum.

Kubey, R., Larson, R., & Csikszentmihalyi, M. (1996). Experience sampling method applications to communication research questions. *Journal of Communication, 46,* 99–120.

Larson, R., & Bradney, N. (1988). Precious moments with family members and friends. In R. M. Milardo (Ed.), *Families and social networks* (pp. 107–126). Newbury Park, CA: Sage.

Larson, R., Dworkin, J., & Gillman, S. (2001). Facilitating adolescent's constructive use of time in one-parent families. *Applied Developmental Science, 5*(3), 143–157.

Larson, R., & Richards, M. H. (1994). *Divergent realities: The emotional lives of mothers, fathers, and adolescents.* New York: Basic Books.

Leahey, T. H. (1997). *A history of psychology.* Upper Saddle River, NJ: Prentice-Hall.

LeFevre, J., Hendricks, C., Church, R. B., & McClintock, M. (1992). Psychological and social behavior of couples over a menstrual cycle: "On-the-spot" sampling from everyday life. In A. J. Dan & I. L. Lewis (Eds.), *Menstrual health in women's lives* (pp. 75–82). Chicago: University of Illinois Press.

Moneta, G. B., Schneider, B., & Csikszentmihalyi, M. (2001). A longitudinal study of the self-concept and experiential components of self-worth and affect across adolescence. *Applied Developmental Science, 5*(3), 143–157.

Mulligan, C. B., Schneider, B., & Wolfe, R. (2000). *Time use and population representation in the Sloan Study of Adolescents.* Unpublished manuscript, Alfred P. Sloan/University of Chicago Center for the Study of Working Families.

Pawlik, K. & Buse, L. (1982). Rechnergestutzt verhaltensregistrierung im Feld: Beschreibung und erst psychometrische überprüfung einer neuen erhebungsmethode. *Zeitschrift für Differentielle und Diagnostiche Psychologie, 3,* 101–118.

Rathunde, K. (2001). Family context and undivided interest: A longitudinal study of family support and challenge. *Applied Developmental Science, 5*(3), 158–171.

Robinson, J. (1977). *How Americans use time: A social-psychological analysis of everyday behavior.* New York: Praeger.

Sudman, S., & Bradburn, N. (1982). *Asking questions: A practical guide to questionnaire design.* San Francisco: Jossey-Bass.

Wheeler, L., & Reis, H. T. (1991). Self-recording of everyday life events: Origins, types, and uses. *Journal of Personality, 59,* 339–354.

Willems, E. (1969). Planning a rationale for naturalistic research. In E. Willems & H. Raush (Eds.), *Naturalistic viewpoints in psychological research.* New York: Holt, Rinehart & Winston.

Yarmey, D. (1979). *The psychology of eyewitness testimony.* New York: Free Press.

Zuzanek, J. (1999). *Experience sampling method: Current and potential research applications.* Paper presented at the Workshop on Time-use Measurement and Research, National Research Council, Washington, DC.

CHAPTER 16

The Open Door of GIS

REGINALD G. GOLLEDGE

WHAT IS A GIS?

A GEOGRAPHIC INFORMATION SYSTEM (GIS) is a set of computer procedures for geocoding, storing, decoding, analyzing, and visually representing spatial information. Geocoding is the conversion of map or other spatial information into a digital form that is tied to an absolute or relative coordinate system or spatial reference frame (e.g., latitude/longitude or local street system, respectively). Marble (1999) identifies the following four major components of a minimal Geographic Information System:

1. A data input subsystem responsible for collecting or processing spatial data from existing digitizable information such as maps or remote sensing images.
2. A data storage and retrieval system (data structure) consisting of the logical and physical means for digitally encoding environmental features and attributes.
3. A data manipulation and analysis system.
4. A data-reporting system capable of displaying all or part of both the original database and the manipulated data.

This definition clearly differentiates between a complete GIS and software designed largely for data capture from documents which provide minimal storage retrieval capabilities and minimal representations.

Clarke (1999) suggests that definitions of *GIS* are numerous and different but can be collected under a limited set of headings such as:

1. A GIS as a toolbox containing a set of tools for analyzing spatial data: The tools are computer programs, and a GIS is a software package defining how these tools can be used on spatial data.
2. A GIS as a specialized information system: In this system, data are definable in space as points, lines, or areas. Point features include observations such as local elevations, individual buildings, and topographic features. Line features include linked sequences such as river systems and road systems. Area (polygon) features include one or more lines that form a loop, such as lake shorelines, neighborhood boundaries, and soil areas.
3. GISs as space-time systems: This identifies GISs' capability to deal with the events that include human activities such as shopping trips, criminal activities, and the spatial manifestation of historical events.
4. A GIS as an analytical instrument: To emphasize only GIS technology ignores one of the critical purposes, that is, to solve problems. This requires analysis, modeling, and prediction. Thus a GIS can be regarded as a problem-solving technology. As Goodchild (1987)

suggests, Geographic Information Science (GISc) has developed as a means of investigating basic research problems that improve the use of GIS technology, increase our understanding of its potential capabilities, and facilitate its further implementation and development.

In 1983, Dangermond summarized in tabular form some of the major responsibilities, data types, and functions that were supported by newly developing GISs. At that time, Dangermond's relations with landscape architecture, environmental science, and urban planning focused his suggestions for GIS use in areas such as natural resource exploitation, land taxation and ownership monitoring, land use infrastructure, land use zoning, facility record keeping and management, urban development, census statistics, event monitoring, environmental monitoring, and transportation monitoring. This was a very substantial group of activities that traditionally were strongly tied to hard-copy maps for records, management, and policy making. Dangermond stressed that digital data systems of geophysical events, topography, geology, vegetation, soils, land surveys, zoning records, land use surveys, population and housing censuses, police and fire protection, resource management, wildlife monitoring, and so on could all benefit substantially from computerizing their databases and using a GIS as the management, problem-solving, and display system. The databases developed for these areas consisted of encoded information used in a management system to produce maps and representations. Dangermond has been proved right in his predictions, and the result has been the rapid accumulation of spatialized databases for all manner of environmental and human-activity concerns. It has also encouraged the development of imaginative software for two- and three-dimensional representations of simple and complex phenomena that can be represented in graphic, map, or image formats. One has but to look at issues in the *Journal of Environmental Psychology* or *Environment and Behavior* over the last 5 years to see how many facets of environmental research would readily lend themselves to use of GIS (e.g., Adeola, 2000; Bergen, 1995; Berger, 1997; Binney, Mason, Martsolf, & Detweiler, 1996; Schultz, Oskamp, & Mainieri, 1995; as compared to Collins, 1997, and other articles in Couclelis & Craglia, 1997).

A GIS thus consists of an instantaneously queryable system that can house a variety of spatial data types from disparate sources and a set of analytical tools that can manipulate and analyze these data. Users can receive answers to questions that require access to multiple data sources in real time. Output usually contains the information required to solve a particular problem or to enlighten the decision-making process (in the latter case, it is called a *decision support system*).

GISs developed after it was realized that, when dealing with georeferenced data that involved points, lines, or areas, the process of map overlay could be undertaken more quickly and expertly by the computer than by doing it manually. The overlay process involved digitizing data and overlaying them to create new representations. Not only were separate stores of information merged in this manner, but patterns, associations, and relations that previously had to be inferred by glancing separately at map layers were made obvious from a single glance. Also, a map previously digitized could be dissolved or decomposed into component parts (e.g., land use, vegetation, slope, drainage, transportation systems). This process by itself frequently revealed new information. When accompanied by the application of various functions related to spatial analysis (e.g., calculating measures of spatial association, nearest neighbors, shortest paths, nodal or uniform regions), more complex and more powerful information could be revealed. Problems that had been solved for decades by careful manual and visual matching processes—such as associating soil, slope, and vegetation—could be performed quickly and effectively by the computer, with the results represented on screen for immediate visual inspection and analysis or produced in hard copy for display or dissemination or for policy enlightenment. This computerization of the overlay process produced a composite multifunction map, a representation that can be further aggregated or dissolved into its component parts, and a digital database that could be used for mathematical or statistical analysis based on spatially relevant formulae.

While the first GISs were developed in the 1960s by governmental agencies, particularly in response to increased awareness of complex environmental and natural resource issues, many attempts to build GISs during those early years failed because of poor system design that did not meet user needs. It was not until the 1980s that GIS technologies that appeared to handle many of the early limiting problems emerged and proliferated. By the 1990s, the

GIS had become a viable technology and today is used in multidisciplinary environments and complex management and policy situations at local, regional, national, and global scales. Simultaneously, there has been substantial cost reduction so that, instead of being the prerogative of governments, a few large businesses, and a few universities, GIS software has become available readily to local governments, private organizations, a wide range of educational institutions, and to individuals for home or business computing purposes.

Turk (1995a) suggests a number of broad categories of human-computer interface (HCI) issues that are relevant to a proposed use of GISs by environmental psychologists. They are: (1) classification and representation of phenomena; (2) identification and description of system functionalities; (3) differentiation between software development and user tasks; (4) the need for user spatial reasoning and other human factors in visualizing, interpreting, and using GIS output; (5) evaluations of the usability of data; (6) the development of help and training systems; and (7) the use of GIS as a decision support system. He goes on to suggest typical scenarios for potential GIS use, including data mining, discovering and analyzing relationships between data sets, visualization of material for ease of presentation to groups or individuals, and complementing and supplementing user mental models of problem scenarios.

GIS AND COGNITIVE MAPPING

The parallel between this concept and that of cognitive maps is obvious. Cognitive maps are our internal representations of the world as we know it. In decision-making and choice processes, cognitive maps are accessed to provide information for working memory relating to the task faced, the environment in which the solution must be developed and applied, and the behavior required by the selected solution procedures. A cognitive map contains information processed by the senses and internally represented in human memory that is brought into working memory as needed to solve problems. A GIS consists of sets of manipulation, analysis, visualization, and representation procedures that work on information stored in the computer's memory. Parts of both the GIS and the cognitive map consist of declarative information (i.e., the recorded facts) and procedural information (i.e., the rules for

processing information). These rules facilitate linking bits and pieces of data into strings, distributions, networks, clusters, patterns, shapes, hierarchies, routes, layouts, surfaces, and other meaningful orderings or groupings.

A useful theoretical framework for examining the relationship between GIS and spatial cognition in particular has been provided by Nyerges, Mark, Laurini, and Egenhofer (1995). They identify the two knowledge domains—problem domain and tool domain—that are essential to the building and successful use of GIS in any problem-solving context. The problem domain involves the ability to understand the spatial component of a task and the environment in which the task has to be performed. Tool domain knowledge involves understanding the manipulative and representational processes that are required to pursue a goal. Problem domain knowledge has spawned research on operations such as orientation, mental rotation, visualization, and spatial relations. The search for tool domain knowledge has produced a resurgence of Spatial Analysis and spatiotemporal problem solving (Egenhofer & Golledge, 1998). In particular, interest has focused on problems where GIS users are required to adopt new perspectives in two-dimensional and three-dimensional graphic representations (e.g., digital elevation models [DEM]) and on situations where spatial inferences regarding associations of shape, pattern, layer, network structure, or object orientation is a factor.

GISs AS JANUS

Janus was one of the most revered of Roman gods. He was often depicted as a bearded two-faced head (each profile facing in opposite directions) and was regarded either as the gatekeeper who opened the doors of heaven each morning and closed them each night (in his honor, the first month was named *January*) or as a god of light. He was worshipped under two aspects: as the god of all places, portals, or passages and as the god of all beginnings (or the god of enlightenment). Like Janus the gatekeeper, GIS has developed two complementary dimensions both of which provide an open door for environmental psychology researchers. The one face of this Janus is applied (Janus I), the other theoretical (Janus II). The former continues to be widely recognized and described by the term *GIS;* the latter adopts a small transformation of name and is referred to as

Geographic Information Science (GISc). This Janus characteristic has produced a line of distinction between, on the one hand, a GIS as a process for compiling a spatial database and for visualizing what is contained within that database and, on the other hand, GISc, which uses basic research to investigate the knowledge structures that allow associations and relations among bits of spatial data to be properly articulated and represented.

JANUS I: THE PURPOSE AND FUNCTIONS OF GISs

Data recorded digitally in absolute terms can be mapped. GIS software has, as its most primitive function, the compilation of such maps and their representation on screen or in hard copy for visual inspection. Beyond these basic mapping functions, however, most GISs have a substantial set of capabilities—called functionalities—that allow the user to manipulate, analyze, and represent the results of such activities. An examination of the range of functions available generally in a GIS reveals a remarkable similarity to the cognitive and perceptual processes associated with human spatial cognition. Typical functions are listed in Table 16.1.

EXAMPLES OF GIS FUNCTIONS

Layering, the process of integrating information learned from separate maps into a single one, is widely used in many environmental disciplines and is one of the most widely used operations in GISs. Most GISs allow separate patterns to be stored as layers or levels consisting of geocoded and digitized data that is place identified. The ultimate intention is to combine them into a single visual presentation. This process is a very powerful one. It lends itself to widespread use throughout the domain of environmental psychology. An implicit assumption of the GIS is that most of the procedures involved in its use represent fundamental components of naïve spatial experience or what may be called "commonsense spatial knowledge."

GIS usually performs actions that we do every day without realizing it. For example, we may observe and store a "layer" of shops, a "layer" of schools, a "layer" of residences, and a "layer" of roads as part of the process of building a cognitive image of a local environment. GIS similarly allows one to combine layers of different activities or objects into more complex representations for the

Table 16.1
Selected Functions Common to GIS and Spatial Cognition

• Location of points	• Dispersion
• Interpolation	• Connectivity
• Line drawing	• Mean areal center/centroid
• Line length estimation	• Modifiable areal unit/regionalization
• Search	• Perimeter, height, volume
• Buffering	• Shape
• Corridoring	• Similarity
• Overlaying	• Measurement of spatial association
• Area (polygon) definition	• Decomposing
• Slope and aspect	• Scanning/digitizing
• Viewshed/line of sight	• Georeferencing (encoding)
• Network structure	• Rubber sheeting
• Shortest path	• Generalization/smoothing
• Abstraction/symbolization	• Enhancement
• Proximity	• Aggregation
• Nearest neighbor/adjacency	• Scale change
• Diffusion/spread	• Filtering
• 2-D surface interpretation	• Boundary definition
• 3-D surface interpretation	• Data retrieval (decoding)

Source: Adapted and enhanced from J. Albrecht, 1995, pp. 15–20.

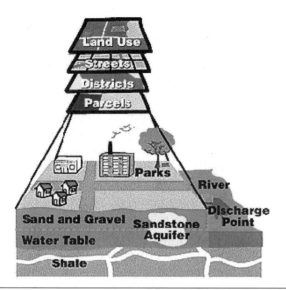

Figure 16.1 GIS overlay model. *Source:* Graphic image supplied courtesy of Environmental Systems Research, Inc. Copyright © 1996, Environmental Systems Research, Inc. *Note:* A GIS places several layers of map data on top of each other and compares these layers against one another. These comparisons are very powerful ways of analyzing data when "where" is important. For example, this factory may have been located because it needed two acres of flat land (slope less than 2°), proximity to two highways, proximity to a residential neighborhood, nearby parks, a low water table, underground water (well water), and/or a nearby perennial stream. A feasible location could be found using overlays of separate maps.

purpose of making spatial relationships clear or for providing a layer of information beyond common-sense understanding (see graphic image supplied courtesy of Environmental Systems Research Institute, Inc., Figure 16.1).

DIGITAL TERRAIN MODELS

For much research in environmental psychology, spatial representation of local relief can be fundamental to the understanding and interpretation of the questions being examined. Relief visualization is one of the strengths of a GIS (Lang, 1993). Representations of local topography, ground and underground water resources, vegetation types, wind directions, pollution levels, and temperatures, for example, can all be visually examined as layers in a GIS and combined in any way desired by the researcher. Combining different layers provides visualizable landscape models with high degrees of realism.

Despite this potential, there has as yet been very little use of GIS technology by researchers in environmental psychology.

VISUAL LANDSCAPE MODELS

Terrain visualization using two-dimensional or three-dimensional representational techniques conveys considerable information about the earth's surface and much more than is offered by conventional, two-dimensional, line-drawn diagrams or pictures. Often the phenomena being modeled using a GIS produces a level of visual realism that provides more insights into the spatial relationships among phenomena as well as allowing more thorough detection of data flaws and inconsistencies than other methods. In particular, the powerful integration of terrain models (digital elevation models [DEMs]) with auxiliary information such as sociodemographic characteristics, behavioral practices, or habits (e.g., recycling behaviors) provides representations with high degrees of realism. The results are referred to as visual landscape models (see Weibel & Heller, 1991, for a discussion of digital terrain modeling in GIS). Two-dimensional and three-dimensional landscape or relief modeling using a GIS has been discussed at length in Maguire, Goodchild, and Rhind (1991), Turner (1989), and Clarke (1999). When making use of GISs, environmental psychologists may have to develop specific user interfaces to allow terrain visualization to be used as a tool to assist modeling, manipulating, interpreting, and analysis of their data so presented. Examples of data representations that can be made using terrain modeling in GIS include distributions of spot heights, one-dimensional profiles, layouts, perspective views, dynamic views (i.e., obtained by rotating or translating viewing points), animations, simulations, and virtual environments.

As an example of the material that can be used when examining human reactions to air pollution, a GIS could provide layers such as local relief, land cover data, polluting sources, the distribution of pollutants, pollution maps, real-time monitoring and updating of pollution levels, localized (e.g., neighborhood) attitudes toward different pollution sources, emissions from transportation systems and traffic volumes, and so on. A GIS user now has a choice between dynamic and realistic modes of representation, versus static, cross-sectional, or abstract modes of visualization of landscape. Using simulations and virtual experiences, researchers can "participate" in walk-throughs and flyovers and obtain multisensory input (e.g., speech, touch, sound) and direct interaction with the computer representation of the problem area.

USING A GIS

Clarke (1999) argues that, to use a GIS effectively, one must learn how to use both the hardware and software comprising the system. One must also be able to comprehend how geographic information is going to help answer the problem being pursued. New GIS users must be aware of the abilities and liabilities of the system they plan to use. In particular, users need to understand what a GIS provides that is not available using other modes of analysis. Hearnshaw and Unwin (1994) suggests that new GIS users need to: identify and target changes in research activities as a result of using GIS; identify specific motivating factors that encourage the use of GIS; acquire the skills necessary to use a particular GIS; understand what spatial abilities will be needed to use GIS and interpret its output; develop a facility for understanding the limitations of GIS for a particular problem situation and recognizing potential sources of error; and be prepared to take advantage of any training or learning sessions offered by GIS vendors.

SPATIALIZING DATA

Most data can be allocated indicators of where they occur. This process is now called *spatialization*. Spatialized data is represented in an absolute way by adapting data to specific locations often identified by digital coordinates tied to some objective frame of reference (e.g., latitude and longitude). They also occur in a relational way in the form of places that are often locationally fuzzy but provide latent locational information (e.g., "the beaches of California").

JANUS II: GISc

GISc, according to Clarke (1999), is a discipline that uses GISs as tools to understand the world. Understanding is achieved by the processes of describing humankind's relationships to the many different environments that, in totality, make up the world we live in. Clarke suggests that GISs are important "entry points" for disciplines (like environmental psychology) where data spatialization has not previously been a significant factor.

GISc, Janus's other face, is a relatively recent development. Responding to numerous criticisms that GIS was "just another technique," researchers began examining, among other things, the cognitive basis of GIS functionalities. The resulting science involves concepts from cognitive science, spatial cognition, wayfinding, spatial perception, behavioral geography, visualization, spatial abilities, and internal representation. GISc has explored the contribution to GIS of computer graphics, image processing, computational geology, database management, and software engineering. In areas relating to artificial intelligence and cognitive science, it has explored spatial relations theory, expert systems, aggregation and generalization problems, exploratory data analysis, data mining, database queries, multimodal user interfaces, spatial data handling, and decision support systems. On the technical and engineering side, GISc has made substantial contributions in the area of map automation and database creation, error recognition, graphic display, animation, and two- and three-dimensional visualization.

The significant focus has been in discovering how well humans perform, use, and understand the different perceptual and cognitive processes necessary for informed use of GIS. Of particular concern have been: human abilities to encode and decode spatialized information (Lloyd, 1989a; MacEachren, 1992a, 1992b); distance estimation and reproduction (Montello, 1991); orientation (Presson & Montello, 1988; MacEachren, 1992a; and Golledge, 1992a, 1992b); direction giving (Couclelis, 1996; Ferguson & Hegarty, 1994; Sholl, 1987, 1992, 1995); direction or angle estimation (Golledge, Ruggles, Pellegrino, & Gale, 1993; MacEachren, 1992b; Loomis, da Silva, Fujita, & Fukusima, 1992; Loomis et al., 1993); adjacency or proximity analysis (Golledge, 1992a); wayfinding (Bovy & Stern, 1990; Golledge, 1999); layout learning (MacEachren, 1992a; Golledge, 1992b); and line of sight or viewshed analysis (Warren, Rossano, & Wear, 1990; Warren, Scott, & Medley, 1992).

Even the classic overlay problem has been studied in detail to examine how well people understand the cognitive processes involved. For example, Figures 16.2 and 16.3 illustrate how Albert and Golledge (1999) tested for recognition of the logical operators involved in the overlay process used in GISs to combine or dissolve different layers of information. In their tests of people's ability to recognize sets of the logical operators used in the GIS function of overlay/dissolve, they found no significant difference in

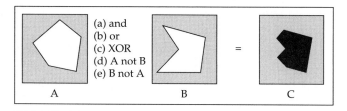

Figure 16.2 Example of Test 1: Subjects must select the correct logical operator. *Source:* Albert and Golledge, 1999, p. 12.

the performance of males and females or between trained and untrained GIS users. Results showed that map overlays in which visual correspondence can be made between the same polygons and the input and output map layers are cognitively less demanding than map overlays in which the shapes of the polygons have been radically transformed between the input and output map layers. They identified questions that are of continuing interest, such as: How do individuals mentally represent geographic information? How do individual differences play a role in understanding geographic information? How does the medium of presentation (numeration, maps, animation, simulation, navigation, audition) affect the mental representation of geographic information? How do people use natural language to describe complex geographic situations? What concepts do people use to reason about geographic space? How well do people understand spatial concepts? How well do people understand the spatial operations that they can access at the click of a mouse button in many GISs?

Montello (1993) has identified a variety of spaces ranging from body space to universal space. He

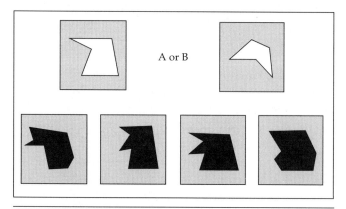

Figure 16.3 Example of Test 2: Subjects must select the correct output layer. *Source:* Albert and Golledge, 1999, p. 12.

argues that GISs have potential to be used in all these spaces. This is of importance to environmental psychologists, for in the early years of GIS development it was argued that GIS was suitable only for analyzing what Montello defines as *geographic spaces,* which are large and usually cannot be perceived by a single glance. Golledge, Loomis, Klatzky, Flury, and Yang (1991) argued that GIS could be used at very small scales (e.g., room size) or in imaginary domains, thus enriching the potential for GIS use in environmental psychology. In building a Personal Guidance System (PGS) for travelers without sight (or for sighted travelers in unfamiliar places), they combined a Global Positioning System (GPS, used for tracking movement) with a GIS (a spatial database on which the GPS tracking was plotted and which identified shortest paths and on- and off-route landmarks) with a virtual auditory interface (which gave the traveler information about obstacles, landmarks, and on-route choice points) to provide a unique and personalized wayfinding aid (Loomis et al., 1993).

GIS has advanced research on relevant theory well beyond the traditional cartographic concerns of representation, cartographic error, symbolization, and regionalization. The cognitive processes used in information-processing activities rely on the abilities of users or participants to recall and recognize spatial characteristics of point, line, and area distributions that constitute locational arrays of phenomena destined for overlay, representation, or spatial analysis. As such, this basic scientific approach differs from much of the early GIS literature that tended to focus on symbol perception and the manipulation of symbol dimensions of mapped information to allow stimulus processing and stimulus comparison (Goodchild, 1987). This new emphasis, therefore, focused a great deal of attention on the cognitive ability of people to comprehend layouts or arrangements of two- (and now three-) dimensional patterns represented on computer screens. It is in this area of GISc that some psychologists have become concerned with GIS. They continue to examine the extent to which GIS can perform functions similar to the internal cognitive functions of data coding, storage, manipulation, decoding, representation, and interpretation. A significant proportion of this literature is represented in the *Proceedings of the biannual Conference on Scientific Information Technology* (COSIT).

The concern of many psychologists with GIS and GISc lies in part in the distortions found in external representations of memorized information and the potential for eliminating many of these distortions by replacing human operations by those of computers. Interest of psychologists, computer scientists, and geographers in GISs increased dramatically during the 1990s. A particular emphasis has been placed on examining the cognitive factors involved in the construction and use of GIS (Egenhofer & Mark, 1995; Frank & Mark 1991; Medyckyj-Scott & Blades, 1992; Montello & Freundschuh, 1995; Nyerges et al., 1995; Turk, 1995a, 1995b). Since GIS involves a more complicated set of operations and decision-making processes relative to other information systems (Nyerges, 1993; Nyerges et al., 1995), knowledge and understanding of the cognitive factors involved in spatial information processing has become an important research topic. Within the GISc domain, interest by psychologists and behavioral geographers in particular has focused on how individuals are able to mentally encode, process, store, and retrieve digitized spatial information and on why certain individuals are better or worse than others at completing these activities (Fujita, Klatzky, Loomis, & Golledge, 1993; Fujita, Loomis, Klatzky, & Golledge, 1990; Golledge, Gale, Pellegrino, & Doherty, 1992; Lloyd, 1989a; Taylor & Tversky, 1992, 1995). Research into these questions has become increasingly important as attempts have been made to seamlessly join computer operations and human processes of thought and action (Montello & Freundshuh, 1995). To achieve this goal, it has been suggested that a GIS must take into account factors such as the natural use of spatial language (e.g., Mark, 1989), cross-cultural differences, and individual differences in spatial abilities, all of which allow the GIS user to store into memory geographic information in the form of spatial objects (or patterns of spatial objects) and to perform mental operations on those spatial objects. Such abilities are important when remembering what the specific maps look like; defining a spatial pattern, if it exists, among groups of objects recorded symbolically in a map or image; and determining the most appropriate sequence of operations to be carried out within a GIS domain in order to achieve a specific outcome.

GETTING SPATIAL DATA INTO THE COMPUTER

Conventionally, we think of maps as hard-copy units or drawings on paper. Clarke (1999) calls these "real" maps because they are touchable and portable. Computer maps, the main output of a GIS, can be both real and virtual. Maps on screen have, until recently, been regarded as virtual because they use visualization as the main sensory modality.

Following Clarke (1999), it can be suggested that, when using GIS, the digital map that is part of the process takes one of three forms: (1) The data already exists and can be purchased in digital form; (2) the data doesn't exist, so it has to be developed and geocoded; or (3) the data exists in an unrealized form, such as in remote sensing imagery or aerial photography. The bottom line, however, is that somehow a geocoded or digitized data set has to be obtained as the source material for use by a GIS. Sources of conventional digital data include mapping organizations (e.g., U.S. Geological Survey, U.S. Census, and the National Mapping Agency). Maps from these sources include digital elevation models (DEMs), digitized land use maps, and land cover data. Maps can be searched using search engines on America Online, Compuserve, and the Internet.

ENCODING DATA

Data prepared for use by a GIS is usually digitized or scanned. Both encoding processes may introduce error into the data set. But both scanning and digitizing appear to introduce less error than the traditional manual encoding by humans. Digitizing involves using the cursor tied to a sensitized digitizing tablet. Most introductory GIS texts have an explanatory section on digitizing. Scanning involves computer sensing of material (usually printed). Good quality scanners have very high degrees of reliability.

Digitizing involves geocoding by (1) tracing over a map with a cursor or (2) obtaining specific coordinates for mapped features using a digitizing tablet. Digitizing can take place on single maps or by digitally merging (zipping) multiple sheets. The coordinate system used in most GISs is UTM (Universal Transverse Mercator data) or latitude and longitude. Specific hardware coordinates can be used as desired.

HOW TO CHOOSE AN APPROPRIATE GIS

Clarke (1999) suggests the following steps when choosing a GIS that would be relevant to a particular research project:

1. *Data capture capability.* This includes the ability of the system to handle data collected in a variety of quantitative and qualitative formats. Different GISs have different requirements for the amount of preparation required for data capture. For example, examine whether the GIS supports scanning or mosaicing, digitizing, and editing procedures.

2. *Data storage.* Check to see if the GIS being considered facilitates integration of compression methods into its operating system.

3. *Data management.* Examine the GIS's capability of handling attribute data as well as object or feature data.

4. *Data retrieval.* Check to see if the GIS being considered can accurately retrieve locational, linear, and area data.

5. *Data analysis.* Check the adequacy of analytical procedures incorporated into the GIS and make sure they include methods of spatial analysis.

6. *Data display.* Examine the GIS capability to display information at various scales and levels of resolution and with its ability to add appropriate legend information such as titles, North lines, and symbol identifiers.

Clarke (1999) identifies "the big eight" of GIS. They are: (1) ARC INFO and its companion; (2) ARCVIEW; (3) AUTO CAD; (4) GRASS (Geographic Resources Analysis Support System), running on Unix systems; (5) IDRISI; (6) Map Info; (7) Maptitude; and (8) Microstation MGE.

SUMMARY AND SPECULATION ABOUT THE FUTURE

Environmental psychology is virgin territory for GIS use. But before it can be used it must be acquired. Obtaining and using a GIS involves planning for the selection of hardware and software. GISc is busy undertaking basic research that may considerably modify the GIS tool of the future. However, GISc has already brought new ideas into sciences such as oceanography, epidemiology, hazard research, environmental management, forest management, real estate planning, landscape architecture, urban planning, and crime analysis. Many of these areas have components of interest to environmental psychologists. The challenge, however, for environmental psychology, provided by the open book of GISs, is to determine what is relevant for each researcher and, potentially, to add new features and functionalities based on the different data types, management systems, and representation modalities needed by practitioners of environmental psychology. One question that must be answered is the ability of GISs to handle qualitative data. As long as this data can be place related or spatialized, then the representation and display power of GISs is available. But even more promise lies in the area of GISc. Research on the effectiveness of different representation modalities, the extension of simple on-screen displays into multimodal representations, the extent to which GISs can duplicate the laborious manual data capture and representation methods, and the appropriateness of visualization as the primary representation modality all raise interesting basic research questions. GISs have been touted as major potential users of image maps, but the images so far investigated are the satellite and photogrammetric images or remote sensing images from airplanes and satellites. Using a GIS to represent the images contained in people's minds, or cognitive maps, has been little explored. All the problems of representing and analyzing cognitively imaged information have yet to attract a reasonable number of researchers from psychology, although those interested in spatial cognition and cognitive science have already ventured down this path.

GISs could be the link between qualitative and quantitative analysis in the realm of environmental psychology. It could also provide an extremely valuable means for data exchange. Obviously, the exchange of digitized or scanned information is much easier to consider, and whether dealing with local, regional, or national cultural perspectives, the greatest hindrance to date in undertaking cross-cultural comparisons has been to capture data in such a way that direct comparison can take place. GIS has this capability and, as such, must be regarded as both an important future research area and a valuable tool for future generations of environmental psychologists.

USEFUL SOURCES

The history of GIS development can be obtained from textbooks such as those by Burrough (1986); Maguire, Goodchild, and Rhind (1991); Longley, Goodchild, Maguire, and Rhind (1999); Clarke (1997, 1999); Peuquet and Marble (1990); DeMeurs (1997); Raper (1993); and others.

RELEVANT PUBLICATIONS

Today a variety of national and international journals and magazines publish information on GISs. Academic research journals include: *International Journal of Geographic Information Science, Geographical Systems,* and *Transactions in Geographical Information Systems.* News and applications periodicals include: *Geo Info Systems, GIS World, Business Geographics, GIS Law, GrassClippings, GIS Asia/Pacific, GIS World Report/Canada, GIS Europe,* and *Mapping Awareness in the UK.* The revisions of the *Annals of the Association of American Geographers* in the year 2000 has identified GISc as a distinct subsection of each issue. Other journals include *Cartographica; Cartography and GIS; Computers, Environment, and Urban Systems; Computers and Geosciences; IEEE Transactions of Computer Graphics and Applications; Urban and Regional Information Systems Association Journal; Photogrammetric Engineering and Remote Sensing.* Books relevant to environmental modeling include those by the Environmental Systems Research Institute, 1995, 1997; Maguire et al., 1991; DeLepper, Scholten, and Stern, 1995; Haines-Young, Green, and Cousins, 1993; Burrough and McDonnell, 1998; Clarke, 1999; and Raper, 1993. The major professional societies that sponsor GIS and GISc include the Association of American Geographers, the American Congress of Surveying and Mapping, the American Society for Photogrammetry and Remote Sensing, and the Urban and Regional Information Systems Association. Web browsers can find a U.S. Geological Survey brochure on GIS at www.usgs.gov/research/gis/title.html. Much academic information can be obtained by a Web site of materials produced by the National Center for Geographic Information and Analysis (NCGIA; see Abler, 1987) located on the University of California Santa Barbara campus in the Department of Geography at www.ncgia.ucsb.edu.

In sum, to effectively use spatial data analysis and representation in Environmental Psychology, let Janus open the portals and be the guide.

REFERENCES

Abler, R. (1987). The National Science Foundation National Center for Geographic Information and Analysis. *International Journal of Geographical Information Systems, 1*(4), 303–326.

Adeola, F. O. (2000). Endangered community, enduring people: Toxic contamination, health, and adaptive responses in a local context. *Environment and Behavior, 32*(2), 209–249.

Albert, W. S., & Golledge, R. G. (1999). The use of spatial cognitive abilities in geographical information systems: The map overlay operation. *Transactions in GIS, 3*(1), 7–21.

Albrecht, J. (1995). *Universal GIS operations.* Unpublished doctoral dissertation, University of Vechta, Germany.

Bergen, S. D., Ulbricht, C. A., Fridley, J. L., & Ganter, M. A. (1995). The validity of computer-generated graphic images of forest landscape. *Journal of Environmental Psychology, 15*(2), 135–146.

Berger, I. E. (1997). The demographics of recycling and the structure of environmental behavior. *Environment and Behavior, 29*(4), 515–531.

Binney, S. E., Mason, R., Martsolf, S. W., & Detweiler, J. H. (1996). Credibility, public trust, and the transport of radioactive waste through local communities. *Environment and Behavior, 28*(3), 283–301.

Bovy, P. H. L., & Stern, E. (1990). *Route choice: Wayfinding in transport networks.* Dordrecht, The Netherlands: Kluwer Academic.

Burrough, P. A. (1986). *Principles of Geographic Information Systems for land resource assessment.* Oxford: Clarendon Press.

Burrough, P. A., & McDonnell, R. A. (1998). *Principles of Geographical Information Systems.* Oxford: Oxford University Press.

Clarke, K. C. (1997). *Getting started with Geographic Information Systems* (1st ed.). Upper Saddle River, NJ: Prentice-Hall.

Clarke, K. C. (1999). *Getting started with Geographic Information Systems* (2nd ed.). Upper Saddle River, NJ: Prentice-Hall.

Collins, S. (1997). Modelling urban air pollution using GIS. In M. Craglia & H. Couclelis (Eds.), *Geographic information research: Bridging the Atlantic* (pp. 427–440). London: Taylor & Francis.

Couclelis, H. (1996). Verbal directions for wayfinding: Space, cognition, and language. In J. Portugali (Ed.), *The construction of cognitive maps* (pp. 133–153). Dordrecht, The Netherlands: Kluwer Academic.

Couclelis, H., & Craglia, M. (Eds.). (1997). *Geographic Information Research: Bridging the Atlantic.* Bristol, PA: Taylor & Francis.

Dangermond, J. (1983). A classification of software components commonly used in geographic information systems. In D. J. Peuquet & J. O'Callaghan (Eds.), *Design and implementation of computer-based Geographic Information Systems* (pp. 70–91). Amherst, NY: IGU Commission on Geographical Data Sensing and Processing.

DeLepper, M. J., Scholten, H. J., & Stern, R. M. (Eds.). (1995). *The added value of geographic information systems in public and environmental health.* Boston: Kluwer Academic.

DeMeurs, N. (1997). *Fundamentals of geographic information systems.* New York: Wiley.

Egenhofer, M. J., & Golledge, R. G. (Eds.). (1998). *Spatial and temporal reasoning in Geographic Information Systems.* Oxford: Oxford University Press.

Egenhofer, M. J., & Mark, D. M. (1995). *Naive geography* (Tech. Rep. No. 95-8). Orono: National Center for Geographic Information and Analysis, University of Maine.

Environmental Systems Research Institute. (1995). *Understanding GIS: The ARC/INFO method.* New York: Wiley.

Environmental Systems Research Institute. (1997). *Getting to know ARCVIEW GIS.* Cambridge, England: Geoinformation International/Prentice-Hall.

Ferguson, E. L., & Hegarty, M. (1994). Properties of cognitive maps constructed from texts. *Memory & Cognition, 22*(4), 455–473.

Frank, A., & Mark, D. M. (1991). *Cognitive and linguistic aspects of geographic space.* Dordrecht, The Netherlands: Kluwer Academic.

Fujita, N., Klatzky, R. L., Loomis, J. M., & Golledge, R. G. (1993). The encoding-error model of pathway completion without vision. *Geographical Analysis, 25*(4), 295–314.

Fujita, N., Loomis, J. M., Klatzky, R. L., & Golledge, R. G. (1990). A minimal representation for dead-reckoning navigation: Updating the homing vector. *Geographical Analysis, 22*(4), 326–335.

GIS World. (1995). *GIS world source book.* Fort Collins, CO: Author.

Golledge, R. G. (1992a). Do people understand spatial concepts? The case of first-order primitives. In A. U. Frank, I. Campari, & U. Formentini (Eds.), *Theories and methods of spatio-temporal reasoning in geographic space* (pp. 1–21). (Proceedings of the International Conference on GIS—From Space to Territory: Theories and Methods of Spatio-Temporal Reasoning). New York: Springer-Verlag.

Golledge, R. G. (1992b). Place recognition and wayfinding: Making sense of space. *Geoforum, 23*(2), 199–214.

Golledge, R. G. (Ed.). (1999). *Wayfinding behavior: Cognitive mapping and other spatial processes.* Baltimore, MD: The Johns Hopkins University Press.

Golledge, R. G., Gale, N. D., Pellegrino, J. W., & Doherty, S. (1992). Spatial knowledge acquisition by children: Route learning and relational distances. *Annals of the Association of American Geographers, 82*(2), 223–244.

Golledge, R. G., Loomis, J. M., Klatzky, R. L., Flury, A., & Yang, X.-L. (1991). Designing a personal guidance system to aid navigation without sight: Progress on the GIS component. *International Journal of Geographical Information Systems, 5,* 373–396.

Golledge, R. G., Ruggles, A. J., Pellegrino, J. W., & Gale, N. D. (1993). Integrating route knowledge in an unfamiliar neighborhood: Along and across route experiments. *Journal of Environmental Psychology, 13*(4), 293–307.

Goodchild, M. J. (1987). A spatial analytical perspective on Geographic Information Systems. *International Journal of Geographic Information Systems, 1,* 327–334.

Haines-Young, R., Green, D. R., & Cousins, S. (1993). *Landscape ecology and Geographic Information Systems.* Bristol, PA: Taylor & Francis.

Hearnshaw, H. W., & Unwin, D. J. (1994). *Visualization in Geographic Information Systems.* New York: Wiley.

Lang, L. (1993, September). Terrain modeling. *Computer Graphics World, 16*(9), 23–43.

Lloyd, R. E. (1989a). Cognitive maps: Encoding and decoding information. *Annals of the Association of American Geographers, 79*(1), 101–124.

Lloyd, R. E. (1989b). The estimation of distance and direction from cognitive maps. *The American Cartographer, 16*(2), 109–122.

Longley, P. A., Goodchild, M. F., Maguire, D. J., & Rhind, D. W. (1999). *Geographic Information Systems* (2nd ed.). New York: Wiley.

Loomis, J. M., da Silva, J. A., Fujita, N., & Fukusima, S. S. (1992). Visual space perception and visually directed action. *Journal of Experimental Psychology: Human Perception and Performance, 18*(4), 906–921.

Loomis, J. M., Klatzky, R. L., Golledge, R. G., Cicinelli, J. G., Pellegrino, J. W., & Fry, P. A. (1993). Nonvisual navigation by blind and sighted: Assessment of path integration ability. *Journal of Experimental Psychology, General, 122*(1), 73–91.

MacEachren, A. M. (1992a). Application of environmental learning theory to spatial knowledge acquisition from maps. *Annals of the Association of American Geographers, 82*(2), 245–274.

MacEachren, A. M. (1992b). Learning spatial information from maps: Can orientation-specificity be overcome? *Professional Geographer, 44*(4), 431–443.

Maguire, D. J., Goodchild, M. F., & Rhind, D. W. (Eds.). (1991). *Geographical information systems: Principles and applications.* Harlow, England: Longman Scientific and Technical.

Marble, D. F. (1999). Geographic Information Systems: An overview. In T. J. Peuquet & D. F. Marble (Eds.), *Introductory readings in Geographic Information Systems* (pp. 8–17). London: Taylor & Francis.

Mark, D. M. (1988). *Cognitive and linguistic aspects of geographic space: Report on a workshop* (Tech. Rep. 88-6). Buffalo: National Center for Geographic Information and Analysis, State University of New York.

Mark, D. M. (Ed.). (1989). *Languages of spatial relations: Researchable questions & NCGIA research agenda* (National Center for Geographic Information and Analysis, Report 89-2A). Santa Barbara: University of California.

Medyckyj-Scott, D. J., & Blades, M. (1992). Human spatial cognition: Its relevance to the design and use of spatial information systems. *Geoforum, 23*(2), 215–226.

Medyckyj-Scott, D. J., & Hearnshaw, H. M. (1993). *Human factors in Geographical Information Systems.* London: Belhaven Press.

Montello, D. R. (1991). The measurement of cognitive distance: Methods and construct validity. *Journal of Environmental Psychology, 11*(2), 101–122.

Montello, D. R. (1993). Scale and multiple psychologies of space. In A. U. Frank & I. Campari (Eds.), *Spatial information theory: A theoretical basis for GIS* (pp. 312–321). Berlin: Springer-Verlag.

Montello, D. R., & Freundschuh, S. M. (1995). Sources of spatial knowledge and their implications for GIS: An introduction. *Geographical Systems, 2,* 169–176.

Nyerges, T. L. (1993). How do people use Geographic Information Systems? In D. J. Medyckyj-Scott & H. M. Hearnshaw (Eds.), *Human factors in Geographical Information Systems* (pp. 37–50). London: Belhaven Press.

Nyerges, T. L., Mark, D. M., Laurini, R., & Egenhofer, M. J. (Eds.). (1995). *Cognitive aspects of human-computer interaction for Geographic Information Systems.* Dordrecht, The Netherlands: Kluwer Academic.

Peuquet, T. J., & Marble, D. F. (Eds.). (1990). *Introductory readings in Geographic Information Systems.* London: Taylor & Francis.

Presson, C. C., & Montello, D. R. (1988). Points of reference inspatial cognition: Stalking the elusive landmark. *British Journal of Developmental Psychology, 6,* 378–381.

Raper, J. F. (Ed.). (1993). *Three-dimensional applications in Geographical Information Systems.* London: Taylor & Francis.

Schultz, P. W., Oskamp, S., & Mainieri, T. (1995). Who recycles and when? A review of personal and situational factors. *Journal of Environmental Psychology, 15*(2), 105–122.

Sholl, M. J. (1987). Cognitive maps as orienting schemata. *Journal of Experimental Psychology: Learning, Memory, and Cognition, 13*(4), 615–628.

Sholl, M. J. (1992). Landmarks, places, environments: Multiple mind-brain systems for spatial orientation. *Geoforum, 23*(2), 151–164.

Sholl, M. J. (1995). The representation and retrieval of map and environmental knowledge. *Geographical Systems, 2,* 177–195.

Taylor, H. A., & Tversky, B. (1992). Descriptions and depictions of environments. *Memory and Cognition, 20*(5), 483–496.

Taylor, H. A., & Tversky, B. (1995). Assessing spatial representation using text. *Geographical Systems, 2,* 235–254.

Turk, A. (1995a) An overview of HCI for GIS. In T. Nyerges, D. M. Mark, R. Laurini, & M. J. Egenhofer (Eds.), *Cognitive aspects of human-computer interaction for Geographic Information Systems* (pp. 9–17). Dordrecht, The Netherlands: Kluwer Academic.

Turk, A. (1995b). Cognitive ergonomics analysis methodology. In T. Nyerges, D. M. Mark, R. Laurini, & M. J. Egenhofer (Eds.), *Cognitive aspects of human-computer interaction for Geographic Information Systems* (pp. 393–404). Dordrecht, The Netherlands: Kluwer Academic.

Turner, J. (1989, October). Approximation algorithms for the shortest common superstring problem. *Information and Computation,* 1–20.

Warren, D. H., Rossano, M. J., & Wear, T. D. (1990). Perception of map-environment correspondence: The roles of features and alignment. *Ecological Psychology, 2,* 131–150.

Warren, D. H., Scott, T. E., & Medley, C. (1992). Finding locations in the environment: The map as mediator. *Perception, 21,* 671–689.

Weibel, R., & Heller, M. (1991). Digital terrain modelling. In D. J. Maguire, M. F. Goodchild, & D. Rhind (Eds.), *Geographic Information Systems: Principles and Applications* (Vol. 1, pp. 269–297). London: Longman Scientific & Technical.

CHAPTER 17

Structural Equation Modeling

VICTOR CORRAL-VERDUGO

STRUCTURAL EQUATIONS MODELING (SEM) combines two statistical approaches: On the one hand, *confirmatory factor analysis* (CFA), which allows the estimation of constructs or factors, and, on the other hand, *multiple regression* (MR) and its derivative *path analysis* (PA), which determine the degree of linear relationships between manifest or observed variables. This integrative feature of SEM makes it an attractive strategy for application in psychoenvironmental research. By using SEM techniques, it is possible to simultaneously elaborate theoretical constructions, such as "conservation attitudes," "environmental beliefs," or "proecological personality," and to estimate relationships between those constructs and other latent and observed variables. This virtue of structural modeling comes together with the possibility of measuring psychometric properties (i.e., reliability, validity) in the assessment of latent variables as well as the opportunity of detecting the pertinence (*goodness of fit*) of a theoretical model of relations among variables (Heck & Thomas, 2000). Therefore, in just one model of structural equations, a researcher should be able to (1) build factors or latent variables from manifest variables, (2) determine the consistency and validity of his or her observations or manipulations, (3) estimate relationships between variables in her or his model according to a predeter-

mined theory, and (4) test the goodness of fit of that theory, contrasting it against observed data.

The purpose of this chapter is to present a conceptual, nontechnical introduction to some applications of SEM strategies to the analysis of psychoenvironmental variables. The growing presence of psychoenvironmental models in the literature is a good reason for presenting and discussing SEM techniques as available for testing and estimating such models. The chapter focus is on application more than on theoretical elaboration or mathematical reasoning related to the use of structural equations. Examples are provided to illustrate how SEM helps researchers to specify and test their models.

MODELS OF PSYCHO-ENVIRONMENTAL DATA

Current research in environmental psychology is gradually becoming more characterized by the use of models. Models are theoretical representations of how a phenomenon is explained by a group of variables. Fishbein and Ajzen's (1975) theory of reasoned action (TRA) and Schwartz's (1977) norm activation theory (NAT), both applied to environmental behavior, are examples of such representations. In these models a criterion or dependent

Data for this chapter were extracted from a study funded by Mexico's National Council of Science and Technology (CONACyT), grant L0069-H. The author thanks Dr. A. J. Figuerdo for his suggestions in the writing of this chapter.

variable is "affected" or "explained" by one or more variables that in turn are affected by other independent variables.

For example, the TRA establishes that the criterion "proenvironmental behavior" is a function of a "behavioral intention," which is affected by a "subjective norm" and an "environmental attitude" (Goldenhar & Connell, 1993). Figure 17.1 shows the customary SEM representation of TRA. Circles represent latent variables or factors that are constructed from observed variables (the rectangles). The unidirectional arrows indicate causal influences. The symbol *d* represents a *disturbance* or error associated with the dependent latent variable "proenvironmental behavior." "Attitudes" and "subjective norms" are two exogenous variables that could relate to each other, as the double-arrowed line indicates.

Therefore, psychoenvironmental models usually specify (1) the effects of independent variables (also called *predictors*) on a criterion or dependent variable, (2) the effects of some predictors on other independent variables, (3) covariances among predictors, and (4) the amount of error ("d" in Figure 17.1) or unexplained variance in the dependent variables. Moreover, most psychoenvironmental models include constructs or latent variables as sets of dependent and independent variables that require the

specification and estimation of these latent variables within the model. The nature of these relationships makes necessary the use of a corresponding method, such as structural modeling.

A structural model is a more "ecological" way of analyzing relations between variables as compared with multiple regression or any other instance of the general linear model. In the real world, variables are interlinked in complex sets of relations in which variables are not only dependent *or* independent but also dependent *and* independent at the same time. Since environmental psychology studies interrelations between behavior and environmental factors, models of environment and behavior should be analyzed within an ecological framework of interdependence between those factors. Structural equation models represent such a framework. In these models a more realistic representation of environmental interactions can be achieved, getting closer to the actual ecological setting of environment and behavior relations.

STRUCTURAL EQUATIONS MODELING

The components of structural equations modeling are nothing new. Factor analysis was invented more than a century ago, and path analysis (PA)—an extension of multiple regression—is more than three-fourths of a century old (Byrne, 1994). However, the integration of both components—which results in what it is known as structural equation models—is no more than 30 years old (Hoyle, 1995). Ward Keesling and David Wiley, first, and then Karl Jöreskog and Dag Sörbom integrated factor analysis and P. A. Jöreskog and Sörbom (1989) created the first easy-to-use computer software to analyze SEM data: LISREL. This effort was complemented by Bentler (1993), who created the EQS program in the 1980s. Other programs devoted to SEM are RAM, COSAN, AMOS, and CALIS, to mention just some of them (see Loehlin, 1998).

Structural modeling involves a series of techniques intended to analyze complex sets of relations between multiple variables. *Complex* means relations other than single outcomes. In SEM, relations between variables are of three types: *association* or covariance, where the relation is conceived as nondirectional; *direct effect*, where the relation between two variables is directional; and *indirect effect*, where the effect of an independent variable on

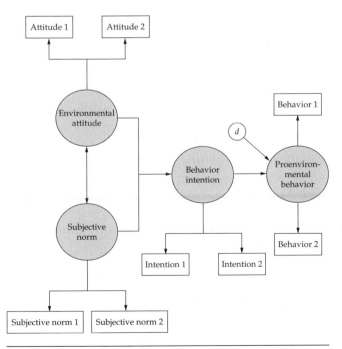

Figure 17.1 Structural representation of the Theory of Reasoned Action (Fishbein & Ajzen, 1975) applied to the explanation of proenvironmental behavior.

a dependent variable is mediated through an intervening variable (Hoyle, 1995).

The classical statistical tools, such as multiple regression, ANOVA, or factor analysis, allow the estimation of direct effects by means of bivariate correlations, regression's beta weights or factorial lambda loadings (Cohen & Cohen, 1983; Gorsuch, 1988; Grimm & Yarnold, 1998). Multiple regression is one way of estimating causal effects from multiple independent variables on a single criterion. The resulting statistics inform the effect size of each predictor on the criterion (i.e., *beta weights*) and its level of significance (*t* and its associate *p* level). These statistics provide details on the amount of the criterion's variance explained by each independent variable. Although the information provided by regression is valuable, it does not inform about nondirect effects or about correlations existing between some predictors.

There is another limitation of multiple regression: Criteria and predictors are observed variables, but most factors studied in environmental psychology are latent. For example, "conservation behavior," "environmental attitudes," "proecological beliefs," "environmental knowledge," and "conservation motives" are theoretical constructs, which have to be analyzed using a proper method, such as factor analysis, rather than regression or ANOVA. Thus, SEM combines MR and CFA (confirmatory factor analysis) in order to construct latent variables and to estimate their relations. In order to include categorical variables in SEM, one must first convert them to dummy or contrasted codes so that a structural model can combine latent and observed variables as well as categorical and continuous variables.

ELEMENTS OF THE SEM APPROACH

SEM comprises three basic elements: model specification, estimation, and fit evaluation. These elements are required in order to plan, estimate, and evaluate a due model.

Model Specification

Model specification is the exercise of formally stating a model (Hoyle, 1995). By specifying a model, direct, indirect, or nondirectional relations among variables are declared within the model. Also, variances of independent variables are to be considered (Chou & Bentler, 1993). In SEM, causal effects, variances and covariance are *parameters* that typically are specified as either fixed or free. *Fixed parameters* are not estimated from the data, and their values are usually fixed at zero or any other value. *Free parameters* are estimated from the data (Bentler, 1993). The pattern of parameters constitutes the two components of the general SEM: The *measurement model*, wherein latent variables are formed from observed indicators, and the *structural model*, which includes relations between latent variables and manifest variables that are not indicators of latent variables (Hoyle, 1995). Thus, the measurement model is a confirmatory factor analysis, whereas the structural model is a multiple regression or a path analysis.

Estimation

The purpose of estimation is to obtain numerical values for the unknown parameters (Chou & Bentler, 1995). Parameters in SEM can be estimated using the single-stage least squares (LS) method, such as the one used in ANOVA or multiple regression. However, iterative methods, such as maximum likelihood (ML) or generalized least squares (GLS), are preferred. Iterative methods consist of a series of attempts to obtain estimates of parameters from the covariance matrix (Hoyle, 1995). *Start values* are provided either by the user or the statistical package to begin the iterative process. These tentative values compute a theoretical or *implied covariance matrix* (representing the theoretical model to be tested) that is compared to the observed covariance matrix extracted from the data (Hoyle, 1995).

In comparing ML and GLS methods, it has been found that the GLS estimates are likely to be negatively biased (Jöreskog & Goldberger, 1972). Moreover, ML estimates have been found robust to the violation of normality. This means that estimates are good estimates even if the data are not normally distributed (Chou & Bentler, 1995).

Each estimation method provides estimates, standard error estimates, and a χ^2 test. Individual estimates of free parameters are evaluated according to their differences from zero. The ratio of each estimate to its standard error is distributed as a z statistic and, therefore, must exceed 1.96 to be considered a significant ($p < .05$) estimate.

Goodness of Fit

A model fits the data when the implied covariance matrix is equivalent to the observed covariance matrix. The degree of correspondence between the theoretical and the observed covariance matrices is indicated by the value of the *fitting function.* That value approaches zero as the implied matrix gets closer to the observed covariance matrix (Hoyle, 1995). Chisquare is the most common indicator of fit in SEM. It is the product of the value of the fitting function and the sample size minus one. A χ^2 value of zero, which results from a fitting function equal to zero, indicates a perfect fit. Therefore, large values of χ^2 indicates that the theoretical model is not a good representation of the observed data, while low and nonsignificant χ^2 values indicate a good fit (Hu & Bentler, 1995).

Doubts about the validity of χ^2 as a goodness of fit indicator have arisen (Chou & Bentler, 1995). Dissatisfaction with that indicator derives from violations of SEM assumptions, such as normal distribution of data, and a correct specification of models (Hoyle, 1995). In addition, χ^2 is known to be sensitive to increases in sample size: Its value becomes significant as N increases, which means that models evaluated with a large number of cases do not fit the data.

In response to these inconveniences, Bentler and Bonett (1980) generated *practical indices of fit:* The normed fit index (NFI) and nonnormed fit index (NNFI). Unlike the χ^2 statistical test, NFI and NNFI, among others, derive from comparing the fit of a theoretical model and an *independence* or *null model.* In the independence model, no relations among variables are specified and only variances are estimated. Practical indices reflect the improvement in fit of a theoretical model over the independence model. Most of these indexes vary between 0 and 1.0, where .90 is conventionally accepted as a value to exceed in order to accept a model's consistency with the data (Bentler, 1993; Loehlin, 1998). Another proposed fit index is the *root mean square error of approximation* (RMSEA), which focuses on estimated population fit. Values of RMSEA approaching zero are desired, and a value of .08 or less indicates a reasonable error of approximation (Browne & Cudeck, 1993).

STRUCTURAL MODELS IN ENVIRONMENTAL PSYCHOLOGY

SEM is not very commonly used in environmental psychology. Among the few studies using this approach, Harris, Brown, and Werner (1996) developed a theoretical model relating privacy regulation to place attachment in homes. They used path

analysis to test an effect of ease of privacy regulation on place attachment, mediated by sense of control. However, only the structural component of SEM was considered without including the measurement model integrated in their analysis. Similarly, Bonaiuto, Aiello, Perugini, Bonnes, and Ercolani (1999) used path analysis to test a model of neighborhood satisfaction predicted by a series of direct and indirect causes.

More studies are found in the subfield of environmental conservation behavior. Corral-Verdugo (1996, 1997) developed structural models of reuse and recycling behavior predicted by dispositional, contextual, and demographic variables. Kaiser and Shimoda (1999) constructed a model of general ecological behavior influenced by responsibility judgment that in turn was affected by responsibility feeling. Both guilt feeling and social desirability predicted this latter factor.

Goldenhar and Connell (1993), Jones (1990), and Taylor and Todd (1997) have reported SEM applications in studies testing the theory of reasoned action. In addition, Grob (1995) investigated the effect of a number of constructs (environmental knowledge, perceived control, emotions, and personal philosophical values) on the factor "environmental behavior"; and Bratt (1999) applied Schwartz's norm activation theory in modeling predictors of recycling behavior.

In a recent study, Corral-Verdugo and Figueredo (1999) developed a multitrait-multimethod model of reuse behavior. In this model, three different types of reuse were registered using three different methods. Combinations of these measures produced three constructs of method and three trait factors that were analyzed to assess reliability, convergent, and divergent construct validity.

A STRUCTURAL MODEL OF CONSERVATION BEHAVIOR

A model of conservation behavior will be used to illustrate SEM applications in psychoenvironmental studies. Within the field of proenvironmental behavior (PEB), several studies have been developed implying structural relations between predictors and criterion as well as interrelations between PEB predictors. Studies of PEB include motivational factors (Corral-Verdugo, 1996; De Young, 1996; Stern, Dietz, & Kalof, 1993) and systems of belief (Dietz, Stern, & Guagnano, 1998; Dunlap & Van Liere, 1978; Thompson & Barton, 1994), among others, as determinants of responsible environmental behavior. In the model presented here, four factors were assessed, including beliefs from the new environmental paradigm (NEP), beliefs from the human exemptionalism paradigm (HEP), conservation motives (CM), and reuse behavior (RB).

NEP and HEP are the most extensively used constructs indicating environmental belief systems (Bechtel, Corral-Verdugo, & Pinheiro, 1999). Dunlap and Van Liere (1978) first proposed and used this scale more than 20 years ago. According to them, HEP is a basic belief that humans are above nature and, therefore, do not have to regard it as they use up resources. By contrast, NEP is the belief that humans are part of nature, and so they have to take care of it, avoiding exploitation of resources. Thus, researchers have supposed that a positive relationship exists between NEP and PEB, and a negative link between HEP and PEB. Following this line of thought, Scott and Willits (1994) found significant relations between NEP and two kinds of proenvironmental behavior. Corral-Verdugo and Armendariz (2000) reported that NEP responses correlated with some instances of conservation behavior but failed to reproduce significant relations with every PEB instance they investigated. Moreover, others (Mainieri, Barnett, Valdero, Unipan, & Oskamp, 1997) have found that NEP does not predict environmentally responsible consumption. A possible reason for such discrepancies is that PEB is not a unitary construct but a set of different and independent kinds of conservation conducts (Berger, 1997; Corral-Verdugo, 1996; Lee, De Young, & Marans, 1995). Thus, NEP could be closely related to some but not all those types. Another possible reason is that NEP could be indirectly, not directly, predicting PEB through other factors. This hypothesis may be evaluated through SEM.

Conservation motives include reasons to engage in proenvironmental behavior (Corral-Verdugo, 1996; Stern et al., 1993), extrinsic (Hayes & Cone, 1981) and intrinsic (De Young, 1996; Vining, Linn, & Burdge, 1992) motives, as well as intentions to act (Goldenhar & Connell, 1993). Most PEB models produce significant and positive effects of conservation motives on conservation behavior. These models show that such an effect is direct. In addition, there are reasons to suppose that CMs are influenced by a variety of factors, including environmental beliefs (Goldenhar & Connell, 1993).

Several types of conservation behavior have been studied, including recycling and reuse of products (Corral-Verdugo, 1996; De Young, 1991); reduced consumption of products (Linn, Vining, & Feeley, 1994); and water (Aitken, McMahon, Wearing, & Finlayson, 1994; De Oliver, 1999), energy (Hayes & Cone, 1981), and ecosystem (Syme, Beven, & Sumner, 1993) conservation, among others. Reuse is one of the least investigated instances of PEB (De Young, 1991). It attempts to prevent pollution, avoiding generation of waste at its source. Sometimes, reuse involves using a potentially discardable object in a different way than was originally assumed when the object was acquired (e.g., reusing a wine bottle as a flowerpot). Yet, sometimes reuse involves using again the reused object for its original function, as a glass juice container that could be used to again serve juice made from concentrate (Corral-Verdugo & Figueredo, 1999). In this model, reuse of glass, newspaper, clothing, and boxes were used as instances of this kind of conservation behavior.

Based on the previously cited literature, the model depicted here represents reuse as directly predicted by the CM and indirectly influenced by NEP and HEP, which would affect conservation motives. Data representing such variables were collected and converted into a correlation matrix. This matrix was the input for a series of models illustrating SEM applications to psychoenvironmental models.

DATA

Generally, SEM uses a matrix of correlations as data input to produce its analyses. Table 17.1 shows the correlation matrix extracted from variables in this study.

Data were collected from a representative sample of 195 individuals (146 women, 49 men; age mean = 35 years) living in Hermosillo, a city in northwestern Mexico. Data consisted of 14 variables ($v1$ to $v14$): Six items from the original Dunlap and Van Liere (1978) scale were used. Three items were NEP statements: "There are limits to growth beyond which our industrialized society cannot expand" ($NP1$); "To maintain a healthy economy, we have to develop a 'steady state' economy where industrial growth is controlled" ($NP2$); and "The earth is like a spaceship with only limited room and resources" ($NP3$). The next three are HEP items: "Humans have the right to modify the natural environment to suit their needs" ($HP1$); "Mankind was created to rule over the rest of nature" ($HP2$); and "Humans need not adapt to the natural environment because they can change it to suit their needs" ($HP3$). All of these

Table 17.1
Correlation Matrix of Studied Variables*

	NP1	NP2	NP3	HP1	HP2	HP3	CM1	CM2	CM3	CM4	RB1	RB2	RB3	RB4
NP1	1.00													
NP2	.34	1.00												
NP3	.36	.33	1.00											
HP1	.11	.13	.10	1.00										
HP2	.15	.16	.20	.25	1.00									
HP3	.14	.17	.15	.26	.52	1.00								
CM1	−.02	.12	.11	−.13	−.09	−.11	1.00							
CM2	−.06	.09	.08	−.02	.03	−.10	.39	1.00						
CM3	−.05	.15	.10	−.16	−.01	−.16	.41	.37	1.00					
CM4	.07	.06	−.01	−.16	−.11	−.10	.47	.44	.48	1.00				
RB1	−.01	−.03	−.01	−.16	−.06	−.02	.08	.07	.16	.13	1.00			
RB2	−.01	−.06	.01	−.11	.06	−.10	.20	.20	.18	.39	.14	1.00		
RB3	.05	−.02	.05	−.07	.02	−.07	.35	.18	.13	.22	.21	.28	1.00	
RB4	.05	.04	.02	−.04	−.08	−.08	.16	.29	.16	.20	.21	.20	.29	1.00

*Variables are explained in the text.

items have a 4-point Likert scale: 4 (strongly agree), 3 (mildly agree), 2 (mildly disagree), 1 (strongly disagree).

The next four variables indicate conservation motives: reasons to reuse glass (CM1), reasons to reuse newspaper (CM2), reasons to reuse clothing (CM3), and reasons to reuse boxes (CM4). Every motive was expressed as the degree of agreement (0, total disagreement, . . . 10, total agreement) with a series of conservation reasons: "I reuse because I save money," "I like to reuse," "I keep the environment clean," "It is my custom," and "I avoid garbage." The addition of all these reasons conformed to an index for each particular kind of reuse (glass, newspaper, clothing, boxes).

Finally, reuse behavior is represented in the last four variables: RB1 (reuse clothing), RB2 (reuse boxes), RB3 (reuse glass), and RB4 (reuse newspaper). RBs were registered amounts of reused objects that each individual had conserved in his or her household for each product. All 14 variables were entered into a model where four latent factors were constructed and tested, and their interrelations estimated using the maximum likelihood (ML) method.

To test such a model, structural equations were used, and their particular applications were developed as examples to illustrate the use of SEM strategies. Those applications included: (1) factor construction, (2) assessment of psychometric properties, (3) the model's estimation, and (4) assessment of model pertinence. They implied the specification and testing of the four latent variables (1), the assessment of those latent variables' reliability and validity (2), the estimation of direct and indirect relations between variables (3), and the assessment of the model's goodness of fit (4).

FACTOR CONSTRUCTION

In environmental psychology, as well as in other psychological fields, researchers use latent variables (also called *factors* or *constructs*) and manifest (observed) variables or indicators. A manifest variable is directly recorded: It does not require more than its detection and observation. Latent variables are theoretical elaborations that must be inferred from indicators or observed variables. Usually, correlations among similar manifest variables produce a factor or latent variable. "Conservation behavior," for instance, is a latent factor that can be constructed from indicators such as observations of recycling, reusing, and composting. Correlations between manifest variables allow the inference and, hence, the construction of a factor. The statistical tool that makes this operation possible is factor analysis (FA).

Researchers use two types of FA: exploratory and confirmatory. Exploratory factor analysis (EFA) mainly consists of extracting factors from groups of observed variables purportedly measuring the same construct (Gorsuch, 1988; Kim & Mueller, 1991). EFA is a useful strategy, especially when researchers do not have a theory to be contrasted against data (i.e., when the nature of the subjacent latent variables is unknown). Then, EFA gives a provisional idea regarding the number of factors grouping the observed variables under study.

Conversely, the use of CFA (confirmatory factor analysis) requires the knowledge of the data factor structure. This means that the researcher has a theory determining how many factors there are and what is their nature (i.e., What does each factor mean?). Therefore, CFA's main objective is the confirmation or rejection of the proposed factor structure (Bryant & Yarnold, 1998). CFA is the most common factor analytical strategy used in the structural equation context. Thus, in this chapter, when the measurement component of structural equations is mentioned, it will be referring to CFA.

The relation between the factor "new environmental paradigm" (NEP; Dunlap & Van Liere, 1978) and their indicators (responses to items of NEP scale) can be represented in the structural equation manner. Figure 17.2 shows such a representation. As previously mentioned, the construct or factor is indicated as a circle, while the manifest variables are represented as rectangles. Direction of arrows goes from the factor to the observed variables, indicating that the factor "causes" its manifestations: NEP makes people agree with proecological statements. Figure 17.2 also shows the emergence of other arrows from external variables, denoted $e1$ to $e3$, which are errors. These e's are unexplained sources of variance that are not included in the model. For example, individuals could believe that we should impose "limits to industrial growth" not only because of NEP but also because it is necessary to rationalize the exploitation of Earth, or for other reasons. Since those reasons were not assessed, they are considered "errors" causing or explaining some portion of the studied observed variables.

Numbers besides the causal arrows represent correlation coefficients. A correlation coefficient between a factor and each indicator is known as "factor loading." The higher the value of each factor loading, the higher the relationship between each manifest variable and its factor. As in other statistical applications, it is expected that this value should be associated with a $p < .05$ to be accepted as a significant relation. The differential value of factor loadings indicates, besides the strength of a factor-indicator relationship, some properties of assessments, as will be further explained.

Latent variables for the psychoenvironmental model were constructed by using EQS, the statistical software developed by Bentler (1993). EQS programming involves the specification of *parameters*, equations in which dependent variables are explained by independent variables plus error variance, or equations used to calculate variances or covariances. For instance, the regression equation of variable 1 predicted by variable 2 is

/EQUATIONS

v1 = *v2 + e1;

This includes two parameters: $v1 = {}^*v2$ (a correlation between variable 1 and variable 2) and $e1$, which is the error associated to $v1$. The asterisk (*) indicates that $v1 = v2$ is a free parameter to be estimated.

Since factor analysis implies an equation in which the dependent variable is the indicator and the independent variable is the factor, the instruction for constructing the "NEP" factor from its three observed variables would be

/EQUATIONS

$v1 = {}^*f1 + e1; v2 = {}^*f1 + e2; v3 = {}^*f1 + e3;$

/VARIANCES

f1 = 1.0; e1 to e3 = *;

in which $f1$ is the factor predicting the three observed variables ($v1$ to $v3$). The equations produce factor loadings or *lambda weights*. These weights indicate the degree of relation between each observed variable and its factor. With */VARIANCES*, the variance of errors is estimated as free parameters (= *), while the value of the factor variance is fixed to 1 (fixed parameter). Instructions for constructing two factors (NEP, and HEP) would be

/EQUATIONS

$v1 = {}^*f1 + e1; v2 = {}^*f1 + e2; v3 = {}^*f1 + e3;$
$v4 = {}^*f2 + e4; v5 = {}^*f2 + e5; v6 = {}^*f2 + e6;$

/VARIANCES

$f1$ to $f2 = 1.0; e1$ to $e6 = {}^*;$

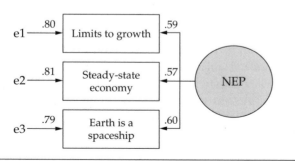

Figure 17.2 The latent variable "NEP" and its indicators.

/COVARIANCES

$f1, f2 = *;$

where the covariance between $f1$ (NEP) and $f2$ (HEP) is estimated as a free parameter.

RELIABILITY AND VALIDITY

Reliability indicates how *stable* a measure is throughout multiple assessments or how *consistent* that measure is (Nunnally & Bernstein, 1994). To observe the *stability* of a measure, it is usually compared against itself in a test/posttest situation where a high correlation (i.e., close to 1.0) would indicate that such a measure is reliable. By using structural equations it is possible to estimate not only the stability of a manifest variable but the stability of a factor as well, correlating a construct in moment A with the same construct in moment B. A high value for such correlation would indicate construct stability. Figure 17.3 shows an example where the construct "Conservation Motives," measured in time A is contrasted against itself in time B. These latent variables were constructed using instructions similar to those shown in the previous section, using a different matrix of correlations between the four observed variables for motives measured in a time and the same four variables assessed one week later. The bidirectional curved arrow is used to represent the fact that such relationship is not causal but a simple covariance. Since the value of such covariance is high (.87) it could be concluded that the assessment of motives is reliable.

Internal consistency, which traditionally is estimated using Cronbach's alpha, refers to the degree to which the indicators of a measure reflect a latent variable (Hoyle & Smith, 1994). In the SEM context, internal consistency is estimated by comparing the values of factor loadings against each other. If those loadings are of equivalent intensity (i.e., similar values), it can be concluded that measurement of that factor is consistent. In Figure 17.3, for example, it could be concluded that the construct "motives" has internal consistency (in both cases), since values of the lambda weights are very close to each other. (For simplicity, values for errors will not be subsequently shown in this and subsequent figures.)

Validity is a different story. This psychometric property has been defined, at least, in three aspects: (1) *content validity,* which generally considers whether a measure contains a representative sample of tasks or observations defining the content field to investigate (Marutza, 1977); (2) *construct validity,* which determines whether an instrument measures what it purportedly measures (Bechtel, Marans, & Michelson, 1990); and (3) *concurrent validity,* which refers to how much a due measure correlates with a different but, in theory, related measure assessed simultaneously (Nunnally & Bernstein, 1994). *Predictive validity* is similar to concurrent validity, in which a measure at time A correlates with (predicts) a different but theoretically related measure at time B. Construct and concurrent validity can be determined through SEM as follows.

Construct validity is obtained in two complementary ways, convergence and divergence (or discrimination). *Convergent construct validity* is obtained when independent measures of a latent variable are highly and significantly interrelated. This indicates that different forms of measurement grasp the same behavioral dimension. Such independent verification of constructs is called "convergent" because different indicators significantly converge on the same factor. In Figure 17.2, the latent variable "NEP" shows convergent validity because its indicators produced salient (.59, .57, and .60) and significant ($p < .05$)

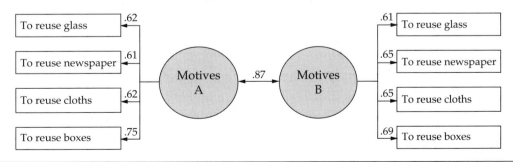

Figure 17.3   Reliability of a measure of conservation motives. The measure is stable since its covariation with itself, in a later assessment, is high. Values of lambda weights for each construct are similar, indicating internal consistency.

lambda loadings. Several researchers have previously shown this finding (Dunlap & Van Liere, 1978; Gooch, 1995; Noe & Snow, 1990).

Achieving convergence of independent measures on a factor is necessary to produce construct validity, but this is not enough. It is also necessary to demonstrate that what is assessed by the instrument is what was intended, not otherwise. Thus, an indication of *discriminant construct validity* is required. This is obtained when two presumably different constructs produce a correlation lower than values of their corresponding factor loadings. In order to test discriminant validity, at least two constructs should be compared. For example, the factor "HEP" can be contrasted against "NEP." Figure 17.4 shows that comparison.

As in the case of NEP, HEP produces evidence of convergent construct validity since its factor loadings are salient (.36, .73, and .71) and significant ($p < .05$). In addition, the covariance value was in every case but one lower than the values of the factor loadings for each construct. This is an indication of divergent construct validity since such lower covariation shows that both factors are different. Interestingly, although a negative covariance between HEP and NEP was expected, the present results indicate that NEP and HEP were positively related, which is probably a feature of Latin cultures, as Bechtel et al.

(1999) and Corral-Verdugo and Armendariz (2000) have argued. Anyway, these results seem to indicate discriminant validity.

In order to estimate concurrent validity, an additional measure is included in the model: "conservation motives" (CM). It is expected that NEP correlates significantly and positively with this construct, while HEP should exhibit a negative correlation with CM. Unidirectional (causal) correlations from a factor on another are called *structural coefficients*. If NEP is "factor 1" (with three indicators), and HEP is "factor 2" (three indicators), and CM is "factor 3" (four indicators), the instruction for calculating these relations would be

/EQUATIONS

$v1 = {}^*f1 + e1; v2 = {}^*f1 + e2; v3 = {}^*f1 + e3; v4 = {}^*f1 + e4;$
$v5 = {}^*f2 + e5; v6 = {}^*f2 + e6; v7 = {}^*f3 + e7; v8 = {}^*f3 + e8;$
$v9 = {}^*f3 + e9; v10 = {}^*f3 + v10;$
$\boldsymbol{f3 = {}^*f1 + {}^*f2 + d3;}$

/VARIANCES

$f1$ to $f2 = 1.0; e1$ to $e10 = {}^*; \boldsymbol{d3 = {}^*;}$

/COVARIANCES

$f1, f2 = {}^*;$

Now, $F3$ (motives) is a function of $F1$ (NEP) and $F2$ (HEP) and of its disturbance ($d3$), which is also calculated. Only variances of independent factors ($F1$, $F2$) are estimated, as well as their covariance.

Figure 17.5 shows results from this program. Indeed, NEP produced a positive (.26) and significant ($< .05$) structural coefficient on conservation motives, implying that the higher the level of agreement with NEP the higher the motives for reuse. Conversely, the structural coefficient from HEP to motives is negative (−.31): Individuals with higher levels of agreement with HEP statements present lower levels of motives to reuse. Therefore, both NEP and HEP exhibit, to some degree, the property of concurrent validity.

Included in the model is the result of the disturbance ($d1$) of motives. Its value (.95) allows the estimation of R^2 for this model. Since $R^2 = 1 - d^2$, the value of R^2 for motives is .10. This means that NEP and HEP together explain only 10% of motives' variance. Thus, additional predictors should be investigated in order to increase the explanatory power of a model of determinants of conservation motives.

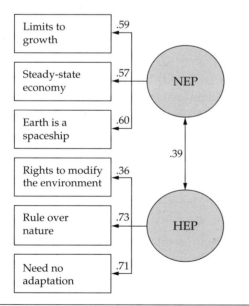

Figure 17.4 Convergent and divergent validity of NEP-HEP scale. Convergence is obtained from high and significant lambda weights, while divergence is indicated by a covariance lower than values of those lambda weights.

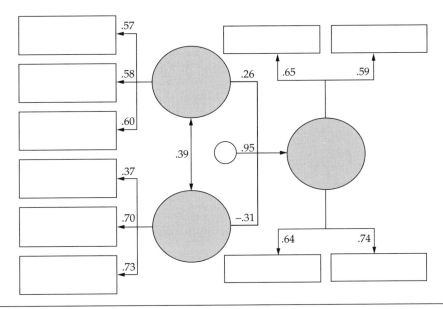

Figure 17.5 Concurrent validity of NEP-HEP constructs. As postulated by theory, NEP positively influences the related measure of conservation motives (CM), while HEP has a negative effect on CM.

ESTIMATION OF CAUSAL RELATIONS

In the latter example, the difference between a covariance and a causal relation is established. In a covariance, the correlation between two variables does not imply causation; they just covary (one changes when the other changes). Conversely, a causal relation implies that change in a factor is at least partially *determined* by change in another factor. From Figure 17.5 it can be derived that NEP and HEP covary, because one is not the cause of the other. However, since—in theory—NEP "produces" an increase in motivational levels for reuse and HEP decreases that motivation, these relations should be established as causal.

Of course, structural coefficients are just correlations between factors, and everybody knows the axiom that "correlation does not imply causation" (Cohen & Cohen, 1983). Therefore, the logic of the causal order (Davis, 1990) should be determined through extrastatistical procedures. In the context of experimentation, control of independent variables permits a substantial degree of certainty regarding causal relations.

However, when working with correlational (nonexperimental) data, special effort ought to be invested in (logically or theoretically) justifying the pertinence of causal relations. Davis (1990) presents some of these strategies.

Besides its factor analytical component, SEM "contains" a multiple regression component that allows the estimation of (supposedly) causal relations. As previously discussed, factor analysis in SEM constitutes the "measurement model," while MR is the "structural model" (Byrne, 1994). The measurement model was exemplified in the section of factor construction. The structural model is better understood as a *path analysis* (PA) where constructs (created in the measurement model) are used as interrelated variables. PA is a set of simultaneous regressions where multiple variables may be dependent or independent factors. Those variables shape causal networks where researchers, guided by theory, can estimate causal (direct and indirect) relations simultaneously (Klem, 1998).

Figure 17.6 presents the model of NEP, HEP, and CM predicting reuse behavior (RB). As in Figure 17.5, HEP and NEP directly affect CM. Since CM is the direct predictor of reuse, HEP and NEP are indirect "causes" of RB. The specification of this model is

/EQUATIONS

$v1 = {}^*f1 + e1$; $v2 = {}^*f1 + e2$; $v3 = {}^*f1 + e3$; $v4 = {}^*f2 + e4$; $v5 = {}^*f2 + e5$; $v6 = {}^*f2 + e6$; $v7 = {}^*f3 + e7$; $v8 = {}^*f3 + e8$; $v9 = {}^*f3 + e9$; $v10 = {}^*f3 + v10$; $v11 = {}^*f4 + e11$; $v12 = {}^*f4 + e12$; $v13 = {}^*f4 + e13$; $v14 = {}^*f4 + v14$; $f3 = {}^*f1 + f2 + d3$; $f4 = {}^*f3 + d4$;

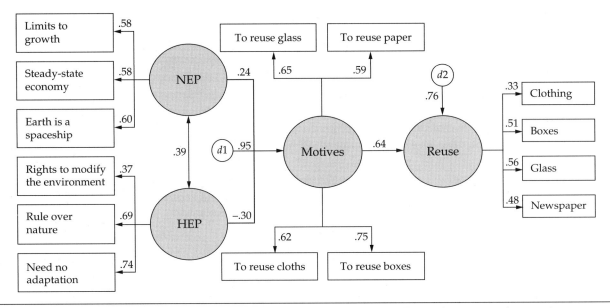

Figure 17.6 The full latent model of reuse predicted by NEP, HEP, and conservation motives.

/VARIANCES

$f1$ to $f2 = 1.0$; $e1$ to $e14 = *$; $d3 = .9$; **$d4 = .7$;**

/COVARIANCES

$f1, f2 = *$;

The "new" factor ($F4$) was created from $v11$ through $v14$ (reuse behaviors). In the */EQUATIONS* section, this factor was specified as affected by $F3$ and its disturbance ($d4$). As seen in the */VARIANCES* section, values of disturbs were fixed.

As in the previous models, latent variables coherently resulted from their measurement models. NEP, HEP, CM, and now RB had high and significant lambda weights. In addition, results of the structural model show that conservation motives significantly and positively affected reuse behavior: The more motives individuals had, the more they engaged in reuse practices. Reuse (R^2) equaled .43, meaning that motives explained 43% of reuse variance. Since HEP and NEP influenced motives, there was an indirect effect of these beliefs on reuse through CM. Such results confirmed the proposed hypotheses regarding those indirect effects. An indirect effect is calculated from multiplying values in the causal path. The net effect of NEP on RB is .15, because $.24 \times .64 = .15$. HEP has an indirect causal effect of $-.19$ on PB because $-.30 \times .64 = -.19$.

MODELS' GOODNESS OF FIT

A fundamental step in testing a structural model is the assessment of its *goodness of fit*. This property indicates how much the research data support a theoretical model under scrutiny. In other words, goodness of fit is an indicator of the pertinence of a theory, given by the correspondence between a model representing such a theory and the data used to test it. As mentioned earlier, in most cases correlation matrices are used as data input for structural models.

Structural equations include indicators of models' goodness of fit. The χ^2 test estimates the adequacy of a *restricted model* of relations between variables by contrasting it against an *inclusive model*. The inclusive model, also called *saturated*, is formed from the relations between all variables included in a study. This model has the highest explanatory power because it considers all possible direct and indirect paths, leaving no degrees of freedom (i.e., no correlation between variables is excluded). However, a saturated model could be an impractical representation of how things work. Very few researchers consider the possibility of specifying and testing a saturated model of interrelations between all variables in a model. Although extremely realistic and powerful, it is nonscientific, impractical, lacking simplicity and clarity, and thus devoid of parsimony.

Table 17.2
Goodness of Fit Indicators for Models Used as Examples in Figures 17.4 through 17.6

Model	χ^2	(df)	p	NFI	·NNFI	CFI
Confirmatory factor analysis (Figure 17.4)	1.61	(8)	.99	.99	1.08	1.00
Concurrent validity of NEP and HEP (Figure 17.5)	38.08	(32)	.21	.90	.97	.98
Structural model of reuse (Figure 17.6)	91.42	(73)	.07	.87	.94	.95

In contrast, researchers specify and test *restricted models*, that is, sets of variables where a selected group of correlations between those variables is analyzed. These are supposedly the most relevant ones. A scientific theory—represented by restricted models—is simple and provides a good number of degrees of freedom, making possible its rejection, unlike a saturated model, which is nontestable and unfalsifiable. However, a good theory, in addition to being simple, should exhibit a high explanatory power. How is this explanatory power determined (and, therefore, how can a model's goodness of fit be assessed)? An answer is, by contrasting the restricted model against the saturated one. Since the saturated model is the one having the highest explanatory power, if the restricted model is not significantly different from the inclusive model, then the restricted model has goodness of fit, in addition to being simpler.

This is what structural equations do: Comparison of the inclusive model (the whole correlation matrix) against the theoretical model (a selected number of correlations extracted from the matrix) is carried out by using the *statistical indicator* chi-square (χ^2). A high and significant (< .05). χ^2 value indicates that the restricted model is significantly different from the saturated one. Thus, it is expected that the χ^2 value estimating the relationship between these two models be low and nonsignificant (> .05).

By using practical indicators it is also possible to estimate goodness of fit of models. Unlike χ^2, these practical indices contrast the theoretical model against a null model. For example, the Bentler-Bonett normed fit index (NFI), the Bentler-Bonett nonnormed fit index (NNFI), and the comparative fit index (CFI) reflect the improvement of fit of the theoretical model over the null model. Values higher than .90 of these indicators are considered as evidence of goodness of fit. (Bentler, 1993).

In summary, a structural model is considered adequate if it presents a χ^2 nonsignificant to $p > .05$ and/or practical indices with values greater than .90. This indicates that the tested model, not necessarily the best one, is, at least, pertinent.

Goodness of fit indicators for models presented in Figures 17.4 through 17.6 are exhibited in Table 17.2.

In all cases, values of χ^2 were nonsignificant (p > .05). Since N (195) was rather small for these analyses, such values resulted as expected. Practical indices produced values higher than .90 in all cases but one (NFI for model of reuse). According to these results, it could be concluded that these models have goodness of fit: The theoretical models are supported by data.

EXAMPLE OF A PROGRAM

A structural equations program usually starts with a */TITLE* that, although optional, is useful for indicating to a researcher what study data is being analyzed. When writing a program, for example, in EQS, there is a required section of */SPECIFICATIONS* where, among others, the following elements must be included: */CASES*, which indicates the sample size (*N*); */VARIABLES*, determining the number of variables to analyze; and */MATRIX*, indicating whether a correlation or covariance matrix is being used. Also, the programmer must include */METHOD*, which determines the method to be used to estimate the required parameters. Instructions for reading external databases can be consulted in Bentler (1993). An optional section of /*LABELS* is also recommended to identify every observed and latent variable in the model. The next sections, */EQUATIONS*, */VARIANCES*, and */COVARIANCES* were already discussed in previous examples.

If the data are part of the program and these data are included in a covariance or correlation matrix, a */MATRIX* section should be incorporated, including correlations or covariances between all observed variables. If the database is a correlation matrix, a */STANDARD DEVIATIONS* section with standard deviations for each observed variable is included. The following instructions were used to specify and estimate the model of reuse predicted by HEP, NEP, and motives (referred to in Figure 17.6):

/TITLE

Reuse predicted by Motives, NEP, and HEP

/SPECIFICATIONS

Cases = 194; variables = 14; matrix = correlation; method = ml;

/LABELS

$v1 = np1$; $v2 = np2$; $v3 = np3$; $v4 = hp1$; $v5 = hp2$; $v6 = hp3$; $v7 = cm1$; $v8 = cm2$; $v9 = cm3$; $v10 = cm4$; $v11 = rb1$; $v12 = rb2$; $v13 = rb3$; $v14 = rb4$;
$F1$ = NEP; $F2$ = HEP; $F3$ = Motives; $F4$ = Reuse;

/EQUATIONS

$v1 = {}^*f1 + e1$; $v2 = {}^*f1 + e2$; $v3 = {}^*f1 + e3$; $v4 = {}^*f2 + e4$; $v5 = {}^*f2 + e5$; $v6 = {}^*f2 + e6$; $v7 = {}^*f3 + e7$; $v8 = {}^*f3 + e8$; $v9 = {}^*f3 + e9$; $v10 = {}^*f3 + e10$; $v11 = {}^*f4 + e11$; $v12 = {}^*f4 + e12$; $v13 = {}^*f4 + e13$; $v14 = {}^*f4 + e14$;
$f3 = {}^*f1 + {}^*f2 + d3$;
$f4 = {}^*f3 + d4$;

/VARIANCES

$f1$ to $f2 = 1.0$; $e1$ to $e14 = {}^*$;
$d3 = .9$; $d4 = .7$;

/COVARIANCES

$f1, f2 = {}^*$;

/MATRIX

```
1.00
 .34   1.00
 .36    .33   1.00
 .11    .13    .10   1.00
 .15    .16    .20    .25   1.00
 .14    .17    .15    .26    .52   1.00
-.02    .12    .11   -.13   -.09   -.11   1.00
-.06    .09    .08   -.02    .03   -.10    .39   1.00
-.05    .15    .10   -.16   -.01   -.16    .41    .37   1.00
 .07    .06   -.01   -.16   -.11   -.10    .47    .44    .48   1.00
-.01   -.03   -.01   -.16   -.06   -.02    .08    .07    .16    .13   1.00
-.01   -.06    .01   -.11    .06   -.10    .20    .20    .18    .39    .14   1.00
 .05   -.02    .05   -.07    .02   -.07    .35    .18    .13    .22    .21    .28   1.00
 .05    .04    .02   -.04   -.08   -.08    .16    .29    .16    .20    .21    .20    .29   1.00
```

/STANDARD DEVIATIONS

1.29 1.04 1.29 1.52 1.63 1.51 3.15 2.91 2.76 3.11 16.60 3.73 4.53 10.90

/END

FINAL COMMENTS

Structural equations constitute a useful analytical tool for psychoenvironmental research. Environmental psychology studies relations between environmental and behavioral factors within ecological frameworks. In these frameworks, some variables are, at the same time, both dependent and independent; therefore, multiple (direct and indirect) relations between variables simultaneously should be analyzed. SEM is a strategy for analyzing these complex sets of relations between latent and manifest variables and thus constitutes a more "ecological" way of modeling and analyzing psychoenvironmental variables. This ecological feature of SEM brings an environmental contribution to analysis of data: The more a model incorporates complex sets of direct and indirect effects, the more realistic (representative) it can be. This means that by analyzing complex relations between latent and manifest variables, a researcher can get closer to the environment she or he investigates.

In this chapter, SEM applications were discussed and exemplified. By themselves, these applications justify the use of structural equations in psychoenvironmental studies. However, this use is not limited to the instances here presented. Readers are encouraged to consult Bentler (1993), Heck and Thomas (2000), Hoyle and Smith (1994), Loehlin (1998), and McCallum and Austin (2000) for a review of additional SEM applications.

Although the use of SEM in the context of psychoenvironmental research is not yet extensive, it will likely be. This will represent an advantage for researchers since it allows factor construction, verification of measures' properties, elaboration and testing of causal and ecological models, and the assessment of models' adequacy, all simultaneously. This saves time and effort duplication and provides quick and precise answers to research questions. A limited use of SEM by psychoenvironmental researchers is already noticeable. By incorporating SEM into research routines, the effort of theoretical elaboration and model specification will be successfully complemented.

REFERENCES

Aitken, C. K., McMahon, T. A., Wearing, A. J., & Finlayson, B. (1994). Residential water use: Predicting and reducing consumption. *Journal of Applied Social Psychology, 24,* 136–158.

Bechtel, R. B., Corral-Verdugo, V., & Pinheiro, J. Q. (1999). Environmental belief systems: United States, Brazil, and Mexico. *Journal of Crosscultural Psychology, 30,* 122–128.

Bechtel, R. B., Marans, W. W., & Michelson, W. (1990). *Methods in environmental and behavioral research.* Malabar, FL: Krieger.

Bentler, P. M. (1993). *EQS: Structural Equations Program Manual.* Los Angeles: BMDP Statistical Software.

Bentler, P. M., & Bonett, D. G. (1980). Significance tests and goodness-of-fit in the analysis of covariance structures. *Psychological Bulletin, 88,* 588–606.

Berger, I. (1997). The demographics of recycling and the structure of environmental behavior. *Environment and Behavior, 29,* 515–531.

Bonaiuto, M., Aiello, A., Perugini, M., Bonnes, M., & Ercolani, A. (1999). Multidimensional perception of residential environment quality and neighborhood attachment in the urban environment. *Journal of Environmental Psychology, 19,* 331–352.

Bratt, C. (1999). The impact of norms and assumed consequences on recycling behavior. *Environment and Behavior, 31,* 630–656.

Browne, M. W., & Cudeck, R. (1993). Alternative ways of assessing model fit. In K. A. Bollen & J. S. Long (Eds.), *Testing structural equation models* (pp. 136–162). Thousand Oaks, CA: Sage.

Bryant, F. B., & Yarnold, P. R. (1998). Principal components analysis and exploratory and confirmatory factor analysis. In L. G. Grimm & P. R. Yarnold (Eds.), *Reading and understanding multivariate statistics.* Washington, DC: American Psychological Association.

Byrne, B. M. (1994). *Structural equations modeling with EQS and EQS/Windows.* London: Sage.

Chou, C.-P., & Bentler, P. M. (1993). Estimates and tests in structural equation modeling. In R. H. Hoyle (Ed.), *Structural equation modeling.* Thousand Oaks, CA: Sage.

Cohen, J., & Cohen, P. (1983). *Applied multiple regression/correlation analysis for the behavioral sciences.* Hillsdale, NJ: Erlbaum.

Corral-Verdugo, V. (1996). A structural model of reuse and recycling in Mexico. *Environment and Behavior, 28,* 665–696.

Corral-Verdugo, V. (1997). Dual "realities" of conservation behavior: Self-reports vs. observations of reuse and recycling behavior. *Journal of Environmental Psychology, 17,* 135–145.

Corral-Verdugo, V., & Armendariz, L. I. (2000). The "new environmental paradigm" in a Mexican community. *Journal of Environmental Education, 31,* 25–31.

Corral-Verdugo, V., & Figueredo, A. J. (1999). Convergent and divergent validity of three measures of conservation behavior: The multitrait-multimethod approach. *Environment and Behavior, 31,* 848–863.

Davis, J. A. (1990). *The Logic of Causal Order.* (Sage University Paper Series on Quantitative Applications in the Social Sciences). Beverly Hills, CA: Sage.

De Young, R. (1991). Some psychological aspects of living lightly: Desired lifestyle patterns and conservation behavior. *Journal of Environmental Systems, 20,* 215–227.

De Young, R. (1996). Some psychological aspects of a reduced consumption lifestyle: The role of intrinsic satisfaction and competence motivation. *Environment and Behavior, 28,* 358–409.

De Oliver, M. (1999). Attitudes and inaction: A case study of the manifest demographics of urban water conservation. *Environment and Behavior, 31,* 372–394.

Dietz, P., Stern, P., & Guagnano, G. A. (1998). Social structure and social psychological bases of environmental concern. *Environment and Behavior, 30,* 450–471.

Dunlap, R. E., & Van Liere, K. D. (1978). The new environmental paradigm. *Journal of Environmental Education, 9,* 10–19.

Fishbein, M., & Ajzen, I. (1975). *Belief, attitude, intention, and behavior.* Reading, MA: Addison-Wesley.

Goldenhar, L. M., & Connell, C. M. (1993). Understanding and predicting recycling behavior: An application of the theory of reasoned action. *Journal of Environmental Systems, 22,* 91–103.

Gooch, G. F. (1995). Environmental beliefs and attitudes in Sweden and the Baltic states. *Environment & Behavior, 27,* 513–539.

Gorsuch, R. L. (1988). Exploratory factor analysis. In J. R. Nesselroade & R. B. Cattel (Eds.), *Handbook of multivariate experimental psychology* (2nd ed.). New York: Plenum Press.

Grimm, L. G., & Yarnold, P. R. (1998). Introduction to multivariate statistics. In L. G. Grimm & P. R. Yarnold (Eds.), *Reading and understanding multivariate statistics* (pp. 1–18). Washington, DC: American Psychological Association.

Grob, A. (1995). A structural model of environmental attitudes and behavior. *Journal of Environmental Psychology, 15,* 209–220.

Harris, P. B., Brown, B., & Werner, C. M. (1996). Privacy regulation and place attachment: Predicting attachments to a student family housing facility. *Journal of Environmental Psychology, 16,* 287–301.

Hayes, S. C., & Cone, J. D. (1981). Reduction of residential consumption of electricity through simple monthly feedback. *Journal of Applied Behavior Analysis, 14,* 81–88.

Heck, R. H., & Thomas, S. L. (2000). *An introduction to multilevel modeling techniques.* Mahwah, NJ: Erlbaum.

Hoyle, R. H. (1995). The structural equation modeling approach: Basic concepts and fundamental issues. In R. H. Hoyle (Ed.), *Structural equation modeling* (pp. 1–15). Thousand Oaks, CA: Sage.

Hoyle, R. H., & Smith, G. T. (1994). Formulating clinical research hypotheses as structural equation models: A conceptual overview. *Journal of Consulting and Clinical Psychology, 67,* 429–440.

Hu, L.-T., & Bentler, P. M. (1995). Evaluating model fit. In R. H. Hoyle (Ed.), *Structural equation modeling* (pp. 76–99). Thousand Oaks, CA: Sage.

Jones, R. E. (1990). Understanding paper recycling in an institutionally supportive setting: An application of the theory of the reasoned action. *Journal of Environmental Systems, 19,* 307–321.

Jöreskog, K. G., & Goldberger, A. S. (1972). Factor analysis by generalized least squares. *Psychometrika, 37,* 243–260.

Jöreskog, K. G., & Sörbom, D. (1989). *LISREL 7: A guide to the program and applications* (2nd ed.). Chicago: Statistical Package for Social Sciences.

Kaiser, F. G., & Shimoda, T. A. (1999). Responsibility as a predictor of ecological behavior. *Journal of Environmental Psychology, 19,* 243–253.

Kim, J., & Mueller, C. (1991). *Factor analysis.* (Sage University Paper Series on Quantitative Applications in the Social Sciences). Beverly Hills, CA: Sage.

Klem, L. (1998). Path analysis. In L. G. Grimm & P. R. Yarnold (Eds.), *Reading and understanding multivariate statistics.* Washington, DC: American Psychological Association.

Lee, Y.-J., De Young, R., & Marans, R. W. (1995). Factors influencing individual recycling behavior in office settings. *Environment and Behavior, 27,* 380–403.

Linn, N., Vining, J., & Feeley, P. A. (1994). Toward a sustainable society: Waste minimization through environmentally conscious consuming. *Journal of Applied Social Psychology, 24,* 1550–1572.

Loehlin, J. C. (1998). *Latent variable models: An introduction to factor, path, and structural analysis.* Hillsdale, NJ: Erlbaum.

Mainieri, T., Barnett, E., Valdero, T., Unipan, J., & Oskamp, S. (1997). Green buying: The influence of environmental concern on consumer behavior. *The Journal of Social Psychology, 13,* 189–204.

Marutza, V. R. (1977). *Applying norm-referenced and criterion-referenced measurement in education.* New York: Allyn & Bacon.

McCallum, R. C., & Austin, J. T. (2000). Applications of structural equation modeling in psychological research. *Annual Review of Psychology, 51,* 201–226.

Noe, F. P., & Snow, R. (1990). The new environmental paradigm and further scale analysis. *Journal of Environmental Education, 21,* 20–26.

Nunnally, J. C., & Bernstein, I. H. (1994). *Psychometric Theory.* New York: McGraw-Hill.

Schwartz, S. H. (1977). Normative influence on altruism. In L. Berkowitz (Ed.), *Advances in experimental social psychology* (Vol. 10, pp. 221–279). New York: Academic Press.

Scott, D., & Willits, F. K. (1994). Environmental attitudes and behavior: A Pennsylvania survey. *Environment and Behavior, 26,* 239–260.

Stern, P. C., Dietz, T., & Kalof, L. (1993). Value orientations, gender, and environmental concern. *Environment and Behavior, 25,* 322–348.

Syme, G. J., Beven, C. E., & Sumner, N. R. (1993). Motivation for reported involvement in local wetland preservation: The roles of knowledge, disposition, problem assessment, and arousal. *Environment and Behavior, 25,* 586–606.

Taylor, S., & Todd, P. (1997). Understanding the determinants of consumer composting behavior. *Journal of Applied Social Psychology, 27,* 602–628.

Thompson, S., & Barton, M. (1994). Ecocentric and anthropocentric attitudes toward the environment. *Journal of Environmental Psychology, 14,* 149–157.

Vining, J., Linn, N., & Burdge, R. J. (1992). Why recycle? A comparison of recycling motivation in four communities. *Environmental Management, 16,* 785–797.

CHAPTER 18

Spatial Structure of Environment and Behavior

JOHN PEPONIS and JEAN WINEMAN

BUILT SPACE AND ITS SOCIAL FUNCTIONS

FROM A SOCIAL POINT OF VIEW, built space can be defined as a field of structured copresence, coawareness, and encounter. The boundaries that divide and the connections that reunite built space organize the way in which behaviors, activities, and people come together or remain apart. Boundaries are used to create relations of enclosure, contiguity, containment, subdivision, accessibility, and visibility. It follows that built space is to be understood as a relational pattern, a pattern of distinctions, separations, interfaces, and connections, a pattern that integrates, segregates, or differentiates its parts in relation to each other. To ask whether space has a "social logic" is to ask how such pattern becomes entailed in everyday behavior, in the structuring of social relationships, and in the way in which society and culture become intelligible through their spatial form.

In this chapter, some of the research agendas are examined that have developed from these premises over the last 20 years, particularly those associated with "space syntax." *Space syntax* can provisionally be defined as a set of analytical techniques associated with the theoretical ideas first presented by Hillier and Hanson (1984) in their book *The Social Logic of Space*. For the purposes of our argument, however, *space syntax* is a convenient way to refer to a relatively coherent body of literature.

Before this argument is developed, two basic theorems will be reviewed briefly. These theorems are chosen to illustrate two contrasting ways in which built space works socially. The first examines linear spaces, such as streets in urban areas or circulation in buildings, and the paths of movement along those spaces. This theorem suggests that, if the building or urban area is considered as a system that carries movement from every space to every other space within the system, certain spaces, those that are most directly connected to every other space in the system, will tend to attract higher densities of movement. Put simply, more direct universal accessibility implies a higher probability that a space will be used for movement. The theorem has three corollaries. First, it suggests that the distribution of movement is a function of spatial configuration—the theory of "natural movement" (Hillier, Penn, Hanson, Grajewski, & Xu, 1993). Second, it brings into focus a particular form of community that is based on the pattern of coawareness and copresence arising as a by-product of movement—the theory of "virtual community" (Hillier, 1989). For example, coffee shops and other gathering places typically take advantage of locations that provide greater exposure to "liveliness." Third, it sets the foundation for treating spatial systems as economies, where particular space uses locate according to their dependence, positive or negative, upon passing movement (Hillier, 1996). For example, retail business tends to

271

be located along the most directly accessible streets of a town. We will return to these issues below. For our present purposes it is important to notice that the first theorem endows space with a "generative" function: It suggests that extraneous social rules or practices do not need to be postulated in order to account for the distribution of movement according to spatial configuration. Social implication, or meaning, arises "from spatial configuration" itself.

The second theorem addresses the underlying spatial relationships that come into our common definition of building types. For any given building type there are some labels that are typically used to describe its component parts by activity (e.g., "dining room"), social rule (e.g., "private room"), or function (e.g., "reception"); it is intuitively known, however, that a list of component spaces is not a building. Buildings set component spaces into particular patterns of relationships. The precise patterns vary from design to design. The second theorem suggests that invariance resides in the statistical tendency for some labeled spaces to be more directly accessible, in the plan as a whole, than other labeled spaces (Hanson, 1999; Hillier & Hanson, 1984; Markus, 1993). For example, we would expect the "living room" to be more accessible than the "master bedroom" in the context of the plan of a house. The theorem endows space with a *reproductive* function. The fact that some set of labels that informs our understanding of the social program of a building sustains a stable, if abstract, spatial relationship suggests that space contributes to the reproduction of social schemas.

The basic premise of this work is that it is possible to identify certain underlying structures of space that are linked to observable patterns of behavior and that these patterns, in turn, create social function, whether *generative* as in the first example or reproductive as in the second example. The distinction between generative and reproductive functions is recurrent in the literature of space syntax, whether these functions are treated as complementary or as opposed to one another, according to subject matter or interpretative viewpoint. At present it is notable that the two kinds of function are rooted upon a property that we have loosely defined as *direct accessibility*. This implies that diverse social effects may share the same spatial foundation. We will turn our attention to this issue in slightly more detail.

DESCRIPTIVE THEORY: THE TOPOLOGY OF SOCIAL SPACE AND THE GEOMETRY OF BUILDINGS

How can built space be described as a relational pattern? In their earlier work, Hillier and Hanson (1984) sought to dissociate the socially significant properties of space from geometric shape. They have described their work as dealing with topological and numerical parameters. The measures of accessibility that they proposed are functions of the number of direction changes made, the number of boundaries crossed, or the number of spaces traversed. In this early work, metric distance was explicitly not factored in the measures. More recently, however, Hillier (1996) has sought to incorporate metric properties into a unified theoretical framework of description.

Hillier's measures of accessibility are reminiscent of Thiel's (1970) work on the description and scoring of attributes of the physical environment. Thiel codes patterns of behavior in terms of such elements as position, distance, and directional turns. His codes include perceptual awareness of Lynch's (1960) parameters of urban space: districts, nodes, edges, paths, and landmarks. A part of this notational system is the description of elements that define or establish space, relational patterns of these elements, and spatial connections. A significant difference in these two approaches to environment, and one that distinguishes Hillier's theory of description, is their basis of analysis. Hillier's theory rests on the purposeful separation of two underlying theoretical questions: First, what are the socially relevant properties of purely relational patterns? Second, how can we transcribe and represent two-dimensional plans of built space as purely relational patterns? In this sense, the methods of syntactic analysis derive from considerations of behavioral significance; however, their application is directed at the quantitative description of space apart from the users of that space. Once one has established these measures (in a sense they are descriptive of Gibson's, 1986, environmental "affordances"), they constitute a rich source of data for exploring and understanding behavior in space.

The most fundamental, socially significant properties of space evoked in the literature of space syntax can be stated in terms of graphs. A graph consists of a set of nodes, or vertices, and a set of lines, or edges. Each line makes a link between two of the nodes of the graph. Graphs may not necessarily be linked into a single complex. But very often, an architectural researcher will deal with a continuously linked graph representing the fabric of public space in a settlement or the interior of given premises in a building. For this purpose, simple continuously connected graphs will be considered as purely relational patterns: The area of nodes and the length of lines will not be taken into account, nor will directions be distinguished in the relationship between any two nodes. Each link will be treated as working in both directions.

Looking at simple graphs, three basic concepts can be defined, one simple and the other two a little more sophisticated. The simple concept is *depth*. Depth characterizes the relationship of a node to the graph that contains it. The depth of a node is the sum of the lines that are necessary in order to reach all other nodes in turn. Conceptually, for example, consider the graph of a building floor plan. Each node might be a space or room, and the links are connections between them. The depth of any particular node is the sum of the connections that must be traversed if one were to move from that space (node) to all other spaces (nodes) on the floor. It is easy to visualize the idea of depth by rearranging the graph in a particular way. The node under consideration is treated as a root. All other nodes are aligned in layers according to the number of lines that are needed to reach them. The rearranged graph is called "justified." Thus defined, depth becomes the basic syntactic measure of distance. In most graphs, different nodes will have different depth values. Associated with this, the same graph will look different when justified from different nodes. Thus, a graph can be thought of as a whole comprised of parts that are differentiated by the way in which they belong to the pattern of relations (see Figure 18.1). The part-whole relationship is thus defined in purely abstract terms. This constitutes a second fundamental concept. Now the graph can be changed by adding or removing a single line. This can be intuitively treated as a "local" change since it does not seem to involve more than two nodes. However, when depth values are recalculated and the justified graphs redrawn, the implications of this local change can be quite powerful and unexpected. The "local to global" dynamic is thus defined, also in purely abstract terms. This

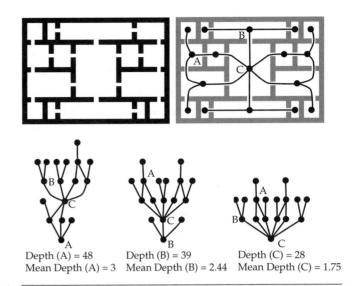

Depth (A) = 48 Depth (B) = 39 Depth (C) = 28
Mean Depth (A) = 3 Mean Depth (B) = 2.44 Mean Depth (C) = 1.75

Figure 18.1 A plan represented as a graph of connections. The graph is rearranged as seen from three positions within the plan. We are provided with a visual representation of the differentiation of parts by virtue of their position with respect to the whole.

constitutes the third fundamental concept. Taken together, these concepts define the idea of spatial configuration as it is used in space syntax. The word configuration refers to relations that take into account other relations. These concepts also exemplify what is meant by *topological* and *numerical* (relational) parameters. The clearest and most concise introduction of these ideas can be found in Hillier (1998).

Integration is the major graph-based measure used in the space syntax literature. Integration is an algebraic function of the mean depth of a node from all other nodes in a system. Referring to the previous example of a floor plan, Integration is a function of the mean depth (number of connections that must be traversed) if one were to move from every space (node) to every other space (node) on the floor. The higher the integration value of the node, the less its depth. Thus, Integration[1] is a measure of syntactic accessibility. If we agree that more accessible nodes are in some sense "syntactically central," then Integration is a measure of syntactic centrality. Depth values are transformed into Integration values so that systems of different sizes can be compared. While the "mean depth" of a complex from a node and the average mean depth of all nodes of a complex would

---

[1] Capitalized words refer to variables. When the word is used without capitalization it will refer to the common concept.

clearly increase with size, Integration tends to vary about 1. The original theoretical intention was to relativize depth values so that an Integration value of 1 represented the average for systems of a given size[2] (Hillier & Hanson, 1984). An alternative approach would be to relativize the depth values of individual systems with respect to the depth values of any number of ideal regular patterns treated as "benchmarks." For example, the depth values associated with a city with a given number of streets would be compared to the depth values associated with various kinds of regular grids with the same number of streets (Teklenburg, Timmermans, & Wegenburg, 1993). Integration can be computed to various radii so that the Integration value of a node takes into account only those other nodes that are accessible up to a given number of nodes (steps) away. It is conventional to treat the root node itself as "radius 1." Other graph-based measures are also used in the literature. Here we will only note that Connectivity refers to the number of links associated with a given node; it is, in other words, a simple and very local measure of connection. In the course of our discussion we will revisit graph-based measures and their uses.

The translation of a two-dimensional spatial layout into a graph is not an easy matter. To use Goodman's terms (Goodman, 1976), while a graph is treated as a "discrete system" where elements and relations can be clearly distinguished, a layout plan encompasses ambiguities and requires us to first acknowledge it as a "dense system," at least insofar as spatial relationships are concerned. Reading distinct spaces is much easier in cellular plans than in "free" or "open" plans. Deciding what counts as a boundary may require an effort of interpretation, especially if we allow ourselves to consider changes of floor or ceiling levels, deformations of shape, or other architectural devices. In principle, the question of the definition of distinct spaces can be addressed separately from the graph-based part of the theory. We could simply require that the conventions followed in transcribing a plan into a graph become explicit as a preliminary step toward the application of syntactic analysis. However, a number of techniques for reading plans as discrete systems have been proposed, and these are associated with fertile ideas and discussions.

Layout plans can be usefully read as discrete systems carrying social information only if we succeed in linking geometric intuition with our intuition regarding the human dimensions of inhabiting space. Movement and prolonged occupation are fundamental poles of our experience of space. Movement paths are essentially one-dimensional. Seeing beyond the present position in some particular direction is an aspect of how movement is possible. To capture the underlying spatial structure that is associated with movement, layouts can be represented as sets of intersecting lines. The "axial map" or "linear representation" (Hillier & Hanson, 1984) comprises the fewest and longest lines that are needed to cover all the ways of moving around a layout and to reach all the spaces (see Figure 18.2). Our prolonged occupation of a space is associated with our sense that there is a region of space within which we are located and to which we have reciprocal visual access to others located within that space (we see them, they see us). Both intuitions can be linked to the idea of convexity. By definition, each point on a convex space can be linked to all other points by a line that does not cross the boundary of the space. In perceptual terms, this means that all points of a convex space are visible from all other points and that, if several people occupy the same convex space, each will be aware of all others. Thus, the "convex map," which comprises the fewest convex spaces that are needed to cover a layout, is proposed as an appropriate method for identifying two-dimensional spatial units (Hillier & Hanson, 1984) (see Figure 18.3).

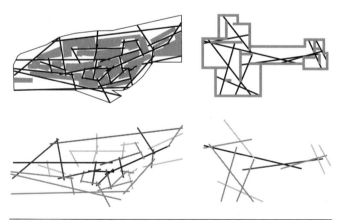

Figure 18.2 Linear representations (axial maps) of a settlement and a building plan. *Note:* More integrated lines are shown in darker shades.

---

[2] The reader must be warned that Integration is the reciprocal of the measure of "real relative asymmetry" (RRA) that is mentioned in the earlier literature. Terminology regarding measures has changed over the years, reflecting shifts in emphasis in the way graph-based properties were conceptualized.

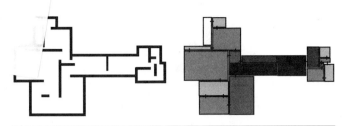

Figure 18.3 A plan and its partition into the minimum number of connected convex spaces. *Note:* More integrated spaces are shown in darker shades.

From any given position, our sense of space is neither limited to the convex area that contains us nor restricted to the lines of potential movement that direct us to other convex areas beyond. The "isovist" (Benedikt, 1979) comprises all the area that is visible around a particular position and offers us a way to study plans in terms of visual fields (see Figure 18.4). Archea's (1977) work on visual access and visual exposure established some of the early conceptual tools for exploring behavioral correlates with visual fields. He observed that people tend to position themselves in space on the basis of both the extent to which they can observe other occupants of space, "visual access," as well as the extent to which others can observe them, "visual exposure." Archea defines the behavior-related characteristics of the environment as the manner in which it concentrates or diffuses information. His discussion foregrounds the importance of conceptualizations of the environment that remain separate from the behaviors that take place within it.

On any given layout plan, a great many different isovists can be drawn, and to fully analyze the layout a convention must be followed to decide where

the isovists can be rooted. One convention is to cover the plan by a square grid of a given size, as if to tessellate it, and then to draw one isovist from each square unit (Batty, 2001; Turner, Doxa, O'Sullivan, & Penn, 2001). Another approach is to position isovists according to a partition that identifies small convex areas within which visual information remains relatively stable (Peponis et al., 1997). A third approach is to follow some independent convention, for example, to draw an isovist from each convex space or from each room.

The convex spaces that can be occupied, the lines along which we can move, and the visibility polygons that are available to us are three fundamental ways in which we may interpret plans as discrete patterns of relationships. If the nodes of a graph are taken to stand for lines, convex spaces, or visibility polygons from particular positions, the links of the graph will represent intersections, permeable adjacencies, and overlaps, respectively. The fact that Integration, a graph-based measure, becomes implicated in theorems such as those mentioned above seems to confirm that the social meaning of space is carried by relationships that are not shape specific but rather more topological in nature. This idea can be identified in a variety of background sources ranging from Piaget's studies of cognition (Piaget & Inhelder, 1967) to the earlier introduction of graph representations of plans by March and Steadman (1971). Such insights, at a minimum, cannot be operationalized without some engagement of questions of geometry. If socially and behaviorally meaningful spatial relationships are in essence shape independent, the research question is how to read plans with specific shape as realizations of such relationships. This question is not merely technical. As plans are read in discrete terms, the question arises as to how spatial relationships that can be understood, such as patterns of connections, interact with spatial relationships that can be perceived, such as the shape of boundaries. The graph-based and the geometry-based aspects of syntactic analysis complement each other.

The framework of Peponis, Wineman, and their associates (Peponis et al., 1997; Peponis, Wineman, Bafna, Rashid, & Kim, 1998; Peponis, Wineman, Rashid, Bafna, & Kim, 1998) is shape sensitive and derives from the critical parameters in the perception of shape as an occupant of space. Essentially it is argued that the occupant of a building becomes aware of building shape through an awareness of the

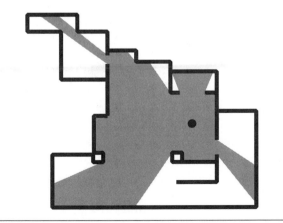

Figure 18.4 A plan and a visibility polygon (isovist) drawn from a point in it.

walls or partitions that define space and the corners or end points that define the discontinuities of these partitions. As an occupant moves through space, certain partitions and end points come into view, and others are no longer visible. These fundamental ideas of spatial awareness allow us to develop a geo-metrically coherent framework for describing spa-tial layouts as discrete systems. In essence, the framework develops from two concepts. The first concept is the idea of *threshold*. A threshold is de-fined every time a partition can be extended at a freestanding end point or at a concave corner. Cross-ing such a threshold brings the partition into view or removes it from the view of the moving occupant. The second concept is the idea of a visibility diago-nal perceptually coordinating any two end points or corners. Crossing the extension of a visibility diago-nal brings a new end point or corner into view or re-moves it from the view of the moving occupant. Thus, the extensions of visibility diagonals mark significant changes along the occluding edges (Gibson, 1986) of the visual field as we move through space. The re-gions of space contained by thresholds and the ex-tensions of visibility diagonals are "informationally stable" in the sense that the same corners and edges are visible from any position inside them (Figure 18.5). From these basic premises, more complex ideas are developed. For example, visibility diagonals and their extensions can be treated as a set of potential lines of movement crossing regions of space in all possible ways (Hillier, 1996, calls this an "all lines map"). From this set, it is possible to extract the more economic representation of the axes of linear move-ment, the axial map (Peponis, Wineman, Bafna, et al., 1998). The complex relationships between visibility fields and the interconnectivity of regions of space has been more systematically explored in recent liter-ature (Batty, 2001; Turner et al., 2001), which argues that the analysis of visual fields can subsume the analysis of lines of movement or convex spaces.

Before leaving the subject, we mention two addi-tional conventions for translating layout plans into graphs. The first convention is the interpretation of a plan as a tessellation, whereby each unit of two-dimensional area is linked to the surrounding units with which it shares a permeable edge. Hillier (1996) experimented with descriptions that also add a link from each tessellation unit to the boundary of the largest convex space that contains it. We point out this convention because it provides a way for incor-porating metric properties into syntactic analysis.

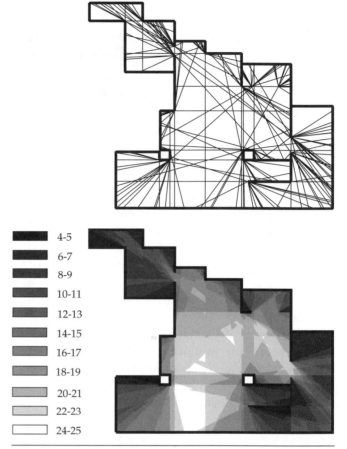

Figure 18.5 A plan partitioned into convex spaces, which are stable with respect to visual information. *Note:* Shading corresponds to the amount of visual information available from each space, lighter shades indicating more information.

The second convention is to divide spaces by social control thresholds, such as doors, without regard to their convex elaboration. This convention dominates some of the earlier work (Hillier & Hanson, 1984) and is associated with significant insights regarding the social logic of space. We can now return to a dis-cussion of such insights.

The origins of examining the essential functions of spatial layout are deeply rooted in studies of environ-ment and behavior. The theories of space syntax have also evolved from an understanding that relational patterns of built space have fundamental social con-sequences. Thanks to these foundations, the opportu-nity presents itself to identify characterizations of space and descriptive spatial variables that can be controlled and quantified in ways that are richer and more rigorous than is often the case with behavioral research associated with the design of environment.

SPATIAL CONFIGURATION AND MOVEMENT IN
URBAN AREAS: RECOGNIZING REGULAR PATTERNS
AND FORMULATING MORPHOLOGICAL PRINCIPLES

We will now examine the first theorem, presented earlier, in more detail. Hillier (1985) reports a correlation between Integration and the density of pedestrians (numbers of people per 100 meters) moving along street lines in Barnsbury, a residential area in London. The correlation is treated as a regularity, a consistent phenomenon, that needs explanation. It is suggested that the correlation results from the properties of urban layout. The most integrated spaces in Barnsbury, its "integration core," traverse its center and link it to the periphery, thus facilitating movement through the area. Thus, local movement within the area is interfaced with "through" movement. Furthermore, Integration is closely correlated with *Choice,* a graph-based measure that describes on how many internal routes each space lies; the difference between Integration and Choice can be simply understood by considering that even a cul-de-sac can be highly integrated (accessible) by virtue of being connected to a strongly integrated line, but it can never have a high Choice value because it does not lead to any other spaces. The correlation between Integration and Choice captures the continuity of spatial connections, the differentiation of parts through gradation of the potential use of spaces for movement, rather than the channeling of movement through imposition of discontinuities and boundaries.

Hillier and his associates (Hillier, Burdett, Peponis, & Penn, 1987) provide the first, more extensive formulation of the theorem based on four sets of studies. Pearson correlations of about .75 between Integration and the square root of moving pedestrians (numbers of people per 100 meters) are reported for four London urban areas. Less consistent correlations are reported for three suburban areas. In these areas, the observed number of pedestrians correlates more consistently with a computer-simulated pattern of movement driven to and from major streets with shops. The inferred orientation of observed movement to attractor spaces is attributed to the fact that the integration core does not cover the system but is biased toward a few dominant spaces. In a third sample of housing estates, integration is biased toward the periphery of the estate, and the pattern of movement inside the estates does not correlate to Integration values. For these estates, correlations become much stronger when the estate layout is analyzed as part of the larger urban context. This is taken to indicate that movement inside the estate is oriented toward the exterior, prioritizing those external spaces that are better correlated into the larger area. The analysis of a fourth sample, including many different local studies, reveals overall correlations as high as .88 to .95. More interestingly, the sample suggests that correlations between Integration and movement are better in areas that have a better correlation between Integration and Connectivity; *Connectivity* simply measures the number of intersections of each line to other lines. Thus, the degree of fit between the local and the global properties of layout affects the spatial logic of movement. These studies led to a critique of principles frequently found to apply to the design of housing estates in the United Kingdom. As the continuity of the urban fabric is interrupted, as integration shifts toward the periphery of the estate, and as the correlation between local and global spatial properties is weakened, movement no longer correlates with spatial layout. In addition, the rates of movement appear to be affected. Typical densities of about 2.6 people per 100 meters in normal residential areas are replaced by densities of about 0.4 to 0.7, an "urban desert" or "perpetual night" effect (Hillier, 1988).

A study of six Greek cities (Peponis, Hajinikolaou, Livieratos, & Fatouros, 1989) gave early corroboration of the general theorem as well as the insight regarding the "open" nature of urban, spatially based community. As originally suggested by Hillier, Burdett, et al. (1987), a given urban area for which movement data have been obtained can subsequently be analyzed as part of the surrounding urban context. If the correlation between Integration and movement density improves, we infer that movement inside an area is oriented to the spatial structure of the larger context. In the study of Greek towns, the correlations were consistently better when areas were treated as parts of much larger wholes. The inference is that movement, and the sense of "virtual community" that arises as a by-product of movement, is not territorially contained; local areas are merged into a global pattern of interface. The study led to additional findings. First, the effect of shops is to strengthen the correlation between Integration and movement (based on a comparison of patterns over periods when shops are open to periods when shops are closed). This implies that shops locate to take advantage of integration patterns. Second, movement densities are higher in cities where local integration cores overlap with global integration cores. Third, the correlation between movement and Integration is stronger where the Integration core is more spread into the fabric. A later study of 10 planned neighborhoods in Sweden and China by Min (1993) showed that, although movement densities were consistently correlated to integration, they were even more strongly correlated to "choice," a measure of the degree to which each space is used to make connections between other spaces (Hillier, Burdett, et al., 1987). The correlations reported by Min are not affected by the distribution of local facilities, including retail. However, they are affected by the distribution and shape of the integration core. Integration is a very good predictor of movement densities in neighborhoods whose core spreads around as a "deformed wheel."

The research problem definition that emerges from these studies has interesting aspects. Behavioral mapping is quite common in studies of environment and behavior. The work reviewed here takes the significant additional step from mere mapping to characterizing the spatial logic of the phenomena under observation. The regularity of the phenomena, the correlation between Integration and movement, is not treated as a conclusion in its own right. Rather, it is taken as a point of departure for further theory, seeking the principles that account for the regularity. The search for principles is only partly contained within the framework of graph-based measures. Of course, the hypothesis that the correlation between local and global spatial variables is a determinant of the correlation between Integration and movement is entirely encompassed within a graph-based framework. Much of the argument, however, goes beyond graph-based measures to deal with shape and configuration in more direct terms (this approach perhaps derives from classical sociological ideas of urban space such as the sector theory or the theory of concentric circles). Questions arise: How far is the integration core distributed across an area? What shape does it assume? What is the pattern of disjunction or overlap between local and global integration cores? In this way, the phenomena under investigation trigger two lines of inquiry. On the one hand, they point to sociological or psychological implication. On the other hand, they invite the development of a sharper theory of spatial form. This interaction between sociological and morphological insight is the most significant characteristic of the evolving problem definitions associated with syntactic research.

Some research programs that have emerged from this background will be discussed briefly. A further report of research on London areas suggests that the effect of retail land uses is to turn an otherwise linear correlation between Integration and movement into a logarithmic one (Hillier et al., 1993). This is based on comparing correlations for samples that included or excluded shopping streets. It is inferred that shops located according to the Integration of street segments. The same research suggests that some larger urban areas fuse their subareas into a consistent overall correlation between Integration and encounter, while other large areas seem to encompass subareas in which the patterns of correlation follow distinct regression lines. This provides quantitative and formal definition to the idea of the city as overlapping areas or "districts" (Lynch, 1960) with distinct identities, at least from the particular point of view of spatial layout. The most significant contribution of the report, however, is to propose the ideas of the "deformed grid" and of "sufficient axiality" as principles of a practically "intelligible" spatial organization; *Intelligibility* is defined as the correlation between local measures (such as connectivity) and global measures (such as integration). Intelligibility in practice is demonstrated by the strong correlation between patterns of movement and layout and suggests (although this is open to validation) that urban systems are more understandable if one can glean the structure of the global system on the basis of the structure of the local area. According to this theory, urban space evolves in such a way as to preserve an interface between local and global scales; smaller scales and more secluded areas are interspaced within a larger grid that maintains the continuity and coherence of the urban fabric as a whole. In London areas, one is never more than two or three syntactic steps away from the larger grid. The overall arrangement allows for local differentiation through deformation of what might otherwise have been a regular pattern. As systems grow larger, more axial continuity (longer lines, often intersecting at wide angles) is introduced to preserve a workable degree of integration globally as well as locally. When these principles are not followed, the spatial predictability of movement breaks down, as in the case of housing estates.

Subsequent studies in Atlanta indicate that the correlation between movement densities and Integration applies to vehicular traffic as well (Peponis, Ross, & Rashid, 1987). In addition, Downtown Atlanta, and the Peachtree Center complex more particularly, offers a demonstration that the pattern of pedestrian movement and copresence associated with urban liveliness cannot be produced by bringing together high densities, mixed land uses, transportation networks, and global accessibility without also respecting morphological design principles having to do with intelligibility and the interface of scales at a local level. In suburban Atlanta, on the other hand, the underlying pattern of correlation is much weakened when the level of pedestrian movement falls off to very low levels.

Much more thorough studies of vehicular movement are reported a little later by Penn, Hillier, Bannister, and Xu (1998), based on extensive data from six London areas. A strong correlation (.82) is identified between Integration-radius 3 (measured up to 3 steps away from each space) and the distribution of vehicular densities per street (the 4th root of vehicular densities is taken to normalize the distribution of density data). However, strong correlations are also obtained for net street capacity (.86) (street width available to traffic) and for the official designation of the street in the route hierarchy (−.81). More detailed analysis shows that vehicular densities on primary routes are better correlated with Integration-radius 7 while those on secondary routes are best correlated with Integration-radius 3. At the same time, the correlation with street capacity is stronger for primary routes as compared to secondary ones. Penn and his associates (Penn et al., 1998) infer that the Integration of street segments governs the "demand" that a given street will be chosen for vehicular movement, while street width determines whether the capacity "supplied" can accommodate that demand. A comparison of local areas taken as wholes leads the authors to conclude that, although average levels of vehicular density depend on overall Integration and street capacity, pedestrian densities depend on Integration-radius 3 and the density of development and land use pattern on a more local scale. Finally, Read (1999) found that in Dutch cities syntactic measures correlate not only with the intensity of occupation of individual spaces but also the average intensity of occupation of local areas, in spite of variations in population density.

Based on their findings, Penn and his colleagues discuss how integration, capacity, land use, and development density could be designed to work together in order to balance vehicular and pedestrian movement patterns. Given that different kinds of retail uses depend of different sizes of catchment areas and given that different scales of movement are better correlated to different radii of Integration, it is suggested that local areas that are characterized by a good correlation between global Integration and Integration-radius 3 will create a better interface between scales of spatial organization, movement, and land uses. This hypothesis is supported by the observation that, when areas with strong urban character, such as the City of London, are examined as parts of large spatial systems, a stronger correlation can be observed between Integration and Integration-radius 3 than the correlation prevailing for the larger urban system. Local areas, in other words, can be "recognized" as intensifiers of the interface between local and global scales of spatial organization. The theoretical outline of the argument is found in earlier work (Hillier, 1996, 1997). Consistent with paradigmatic tenets identified above, each successive development of empirical work is aimed not only at refining the reasoned mapping of spatial behaviors, as regular patterns, but also at formulating more sophisticated hypotheses about the morphological principles that may underpin the observed regularities.

Space syntax has contributed increasingly sophisticated ways for dealing with urban layouts as differentiated patterns of large-scale connections. This complements the emphasis on local attributes (such as the dimensional profile of street sections, the characterization of boundaries, or the attributes and qualities of individual open spaces) that is typical in many studies of urban space use (Caliandro, 1986; Whyte, 1980). Even when authors have emphasized the importance of configuration and overall connectivity to the culture and use of streets (Schumacher, 1986; Siksna, 1997; Southworth & Ben-Joseph, 1995; Southworth & Owens, 1993), descriptive concepts remain either qualitative or limited to mostly local variables, such as the various types of intersection between street segments, or the number of intersections per unit area, or the size of urban blocks. The ability of space syntax to describe global configurational properties as well as relationships of part to whole and the association between these properties and patterns of space use has made it a fruitful method used in a variety of broader fields ranging from the social characterization of modern sociospatial formations, such as Brasilia (Holanda, 1989), or traditional environments, such as the fortified towns of Anatolia (Kubat, 1997), to the historical evolution of cities such as London (Hanson, 1989).

Patterns of Movement and Copresence in Buildings

Movement, copresence, and coawareness in urban space are subject to a variety of independent programs of activity and space use. If the emergent pattern seems coordinated, this is largely due to its spatial regularities. Yet these regularities far exceed our ability to read overall purpose into the phenomena under observation. In this sense, movement can be understood more effectively with respect to properties of spatial layout than to programmatic purpose. Inside buildings, by contrast, activity and space use are regulated in a more coherent manner. They can be understood primarily in terms of specific purposefulness rather than spatial regularity. Correlations between the pattern of movement and the layout, if identified, could plausibly be attributed to the adaptation of layout to specific, not generic, programmatic function. The syntactic studies of movement and copresence inside buildings are, therefore, aimed at identifying critical issues arising at the interface between the spatial and the programmatic aspects of organization.

A study of six industrial settings (Peponis, 1985) suggested that layout and formal organization act to regulate encounter in different and sometimes in opposed ways. Layouts are described according to the relationships between the major convex spaces. Encounter is described as a set of networks, or graphs, representing the interactions of individual people at different frequency intervals. Over more limited time intervals, in this case the hourly interval, encounter is framed within local groups reflecting organizational structure or functional interdependence. Over more extended time intervals, most significantly at the daily interval, encounter is more clearly modulated according to overall spatial layout. The direction of the correlation, however, differs: In some settings higher encounter densities are associated with greater integration, while in other settings with greater segregation. This inconsistency may indicate inappropriate modeling of the relationship between encounter pattern and spatial setting. Alternatively, it can be hypothesized that in industrial settings integration works in two ways. First, it maximizes opportunities for encounter as a by-product of the interface between work positions and through movement; second, it amplifies exposure to surveillance and control. Thus it can be inferred that organizational cultures can be usefully characterized according to the way in which they work "with" or "against" the propensity of the layout to generate regular patterns of encounter, which may extend beyond the range formally specified by work routines or imposed by functional dependencies. Of course, the small number of case studies did not allow a proper test of this hypothesis.

An earlier article (Hillier, Hanson, & Peponis, 1984) drew a distinction between "strong" and "weak" program buildings. In strong program buildings, layout is used to ("strongly") control movement, interaction, and encounter in a prescribed manner. A courthouse would be an example where a programmatically prescribed layout is used to separate the three circulation systems of court employees, prisoners, and visitors. In weak program buildings the elements of accommodation come together in ("weak") less restrictive ways so that encounter is modulated according to the properties of layout rather than according to the stipulations of program. In a later article, the editorial floor of a major daily newspaper in London is used to exemplify a weak program building (Hillier & Penn, 1991). Copresence and encounter on this floor are strongly correlated ($r = .83$) to the degree of axial integration. In this work setting, where the unpredictability of environment disallows adherence to routines, decisions depend on frequent and multiple interactions involving people distributed across the floor. It is inferred that layout contributes to organizational function by sustaining encounter and awareness according to the pattern of integration. By implication, it is argued that we would expect the correlation between integration and copresence to be higher in weak program buildings.

The presence of people in buildings has been recorded according to behavioral categories such as moving, talking, or working. In describing the different culture of two research laboratories, Hillier and Penn (1991) suggest that the distribution of interaction relative to movement, practical work, and contemplative work is the crucial factor. Where movement occurs on the syntactically shallow side of work, near the spaces of movement, communication tends to spread across research groups. In the case where interaction occurs on the deeper side, away from the spaces of global movement, communication tends to reinforce the distinctions between research groups. Relating this finding to the previous work by Allen (1977) and Granovetter (1982) the authors suggest that in the former case layout has greater potential to work "generatively," that is, to sustain creative awareness on a more global scale. A study of two institutions for design education (Peatross & Peponis, 1995) develops similar themes and makes links to the theory of pedagogic codes of Basil Bernstein (1975). The study reports significant but not very strong correlations between integration measured on an axial map and movement densities (r = .4–.5). The comparison of the two institutions suggests two ways in which this function of layout may complement formal educational pedagogy: first, through creating opportunities for awareness and communication across the fields of study represented at a school; second, through qualifying the pedagogical process within a field by fostering a sense of comparison, definition through difference, and even creative competition between tutor-centered groups. The arrangement of furniture as well as behavioral maps is used as evidence of systematic responses to the propensities for awareness and communication generated by layout.

Grajewski (1993) reports strong correlations between interaction (the number of people talking as a proportion of the number of people observed) and integration in six office environments in the United Kingdom, the United States, and Sweden. After taking density into account, by splitting the sample into office segments with high (3 or more people observed per 100 m^2) and low density (less than 3 people observed per 100 m^2) and by analyzing each subsample separately, it was shown that more-integrated office segments (floors or relatively autonomous wings) are more interactive. Correlations between integration and interaction were also found within individual office complexes, such as the SAS (Scandinavian Airlines System) headquarters building in Stockholm. Recently, Serrato and Wineman (1999) investigated the relationship between the layout of two research and development facilities and communication patterns among research scientists. Although the layout of the two units was fundamentally different, the strongest predictor of communication for both units was found to be the extent to which scientists were linked to locally integrated corridors and the interface of this local system with the global spatial system. For both labs, the spatial layout supported localization. The major difference

occurred in the composition of the groups that were "localized." In one lab, localization reflected patterns of organizational subdivision by knowledge area, maintained apart from global spatial movement. In the other lab, localization mixed knowledge areas and created collaborative interface across the global spatial system. Penn and his colleagues (Penn, Desyllas, & Vaughan, 1999) trace the spatial culture of two organizations, an energy utility and an advertising agency, not only in detailed behavioral mapping but also in the nuances of behavior. For example, video analysis provides evidence of how distinct demeanors may signal availability or nonavailability for conversation while people are moving. In this sense, the study revives a connection between more quantitative aspects of behavioral mapping and the more qualitative observations that we associate, for example, with the work of Goffman (1959), Sommer (1966), or, in a very different context, Whyte (1980). The study also relies on questionnaires to establish frequencies of encounter and assessments of how useful each member of the organization is perceived to be by others, not only inside the workgroup but also outside it. While the study confirms that densities of movement are strongly correlated to integration, its main thrust is toward the systematic characterization of space use patterns. As the description of behaviors becomes richer, variables describing layout can potentially be linked to the patterns of correlation between behaviors, rather than to simple behavioral measures. The aim is to understand the mechanisms whereby the more generic functions of layout, such as the distribution of movement, affect the more critical and less easily observable aspects of function, such as useful communication. The study provides evidence that Integration is correlated to the perceived usefulness of people, based on a comparison between departments of a single organization as well as a comparison across a small sample of organizations.

Although not relying on direct observational data, Brown (1999) has argued that the techniques of space syntax could be introduced in real estate evaluations because they capture aspects of spatial function such as the modulation of movement and awareness. He compared two specialty shopping centers in Denver, one of which was a clear failure attributable to poor design. He argued that the failed shopping center was characterized by excessive convex and axial fragmentation that reduced the amount of visual information available to visitors from any one point. Second, the entrances were linked, Brown found, to fringe, not to integrated, areas. Third, the integration core did not reach out to the parts of the system, thus leaving large pockets of fringe space. The same variables, interpreted on a smaller scale, could account for the occurrence of locations that were harder to lease in the more successful shopping center.

The research reviewed above is aimed at identifying direct relationships between spatial layout and directly observable social behavior. Syntactic techniques of analysis, however, may also become useful when spatial layout is introduced as a variable in models of more complex social and psychological phenomena. For example, G. Evans, Lepore, and Schroeder (1996) found in a study of 200 college students that the effects of residential density on psychological distress were attenuated by syntactic depth. Based on their findings, they explained this by pointing to the fact that in homes with greater spatial depth, individuals were less likely to withdraw from their housemates. Supportive social contacts were thus better maintained.

By comparison to the analyses of urban layouts cited earlier, the syntactic analyses of buildings appear more fragmented and more speculative. To some extent, this arises from the attempt to link spatial morphology to the underlying issues or organization and function raised by different building types. The case study orientation, at least partly because of the inherent difficulty of obtaining data inside buildings, may also have rendered the identification of underlying regularities harder. Sharpening the research question may consequently have been more difficult than in the field of urban studies. Clear paradigmatic ideas do, however, emerge. First, the correlation between integration and movement patterns is treated as an underlying principle, perhaps less visible than in the case of urban form. Departures from the correlation are expected to arise from the way in which layouts and behaviors are constrained by a building program. This potentially leads not only to greater scope for divergence, but also to a greater need to develop theories about the modes of divergence themselves. Second, movement and coawareness as a by-product of movement are treated as a foundation on which particular patterns of encounter, interaction, or communication may develop. These need to be studied and spatially mapped in their own right. Third, a fundamental distinction is drawn between organizations that inhabit space generatively, so as to sustain otherwise

unprogrammed patterns of awareness communication, and interaction, and organizations that inhabit space in a programmatically restricted manner, so as to eliminate unprogrammed occurrences. Fourth, a distinction is drawn between "generic functions" such as the modulation of movement, coawareness, communication, and encounter and the "special functions" that correspond to particular programs and types of buildings (Hillier et al., 1984). Fifth, from the point of view of spatial morphology itself, a key issue is the distribution of the Integration core, the manner in which it is functionally and organizationally invested, the manner in which it is physically elaborated, and the manner in which it is linked to other parts of the building. Finally, the most fundamental theoretical idea is that buildings should be treated as mechanisms for creating spatial interfaces among categories of people, activities, behaviors, and functions. The idea of interface is the key toward understanding how building program, in the common sense of the word, translates into building layout.

The findings and theoretical ideas regarding the functions of building layouts are especially significant given that the relationship between space and behavior in organizational settings has proven to be elusive. In his pioneering work on the relationship between office design and organization, for example, Duffy (1974) challenged his own original hypotheses regarding the effects of spatial subdivision on interaction. His research led him to assert that the functions of layouts are mostly symbolic, linked to the projection of individual status and organizational identity. Similarly, Zimring, Weitzer, and Knight (1982) found that people labeled "severely and profoundly retarded" increased their positive socialization and decreased aggression when they were moved from open sleeping wards to more private quarters. These changes were recorded in observational, interview, and ethnographic data. The arrangements that offered the most support for regulating interaction had the greatest positive effects. Thus, naïve assumptions about the potential of an open plan to increase interaction were challenged in very different contexts. Based on qualitative rather than quantitative data, Beales (1978) found that layouts that were intended to break down the barriers between different professions and specializations in British health centers often had the opposite effect. He explained this by arguing for an inverse relationship between physical and behavioral boundaries in organizational settings: Where physical boundaries are removed, stronger behavioral boundaries are erected to ensure that organizational and professional identities are preserved. Bennett and his associates (Bennett, Andreae, Hegarty, & Wade, 1980) reported similarly puzzling findings indicating no clear and systematic connection between school layout and pedagogical practices. From a different point of view, historical studies such as the one by R. Evans (1982) on prisons indicated that building performance often contrasted with the intentions expressed in a building program. With historical hindsight, layouts could be understood as maps of intentions or expressions of ideas more than of actual function, as mechanisms triggering partly unintended consequences, and as fields contested by social practices. Against this background of persistent challenge to the heuristic behavioral assumptions that often guide design, space syntax supported more sophisticated models of spatial layout and, based on these, more sophisticated accounts of spatial behaviors in organizational settings. These, along with the associated theoretical ideas and research findings, offer a good foundation for extending and developing empirically testable, nondeterministic theories of spatial function in buildings.

Layouts as Codes

The labels that we use to describe built spaces (such as "conference room" or "dining room") encode information about the way building occupants understand how buildings are inhabited; they denote some of the categories of use, behavior, or function that apply to space use. However, the labels do not directly describe the configuration of space. If spatial configuration itself is an important dimension of social life, we may ask whether relatively typical labels get assigned to different areas in a layout so as to sustain typical spatial relationships. One way to do this is by looking at the position of labeled spaces within the graph that represents spatial relationships in a building. Hillier and Hanson (1984) propose that the depth of a label from the nearest building entrance is a measure of spatial asymmetry: Labels located deeper are asymmetrically related to labels located shallower in the spatial structure of a building. They also propose that the occurrence of rings, or potential circulation loops, in the pattern of connection between spaces is a function of control. Buildings with rings will tend to be associated with

less controlled patterns of communication or with patterns of communication diversified by category of user and regulated by regimes of control, negotiation, and institutional politics. These ideas are initially explored with reference to the labels that correspond to generic categories of building users: inhabitants and visitors. Inhabitants are the people who not only have rights over space use but are also in command of the social knowledge deployed in space use: doctors in a hospital, directors and actors in a theater. Visitors are those who have provisional rights over space use and are subject to the social knowledge deployed in space use: patients in a hospital, patrons in a theater. Hillier and Hanson proposed that in typical buildings inhabitants will be located deeper than visitors, and inhabitants of higher status deeper than inhabitants of lower status. Rings are often used to regulate the interface between inhabitants and visitors coming in from different directions, as in the courthouse, where judges face accused, or the theater, where actors face patrons, in a zoned space. This mode of locating labels is in contrast to an "inverted" alternative, which corresponds to buildings associated with regimes of discipline and with the treatment of pathology. In inverted buildings, inhabitants occupy and control the shallower structure and visitors are contained and often isolated in the deeper parts. Rings are used to provide inhabitants with options for movement and with the means to dominate the spatial structure, while visitors have restricted access to the system of connections. Hillier and Hanson developed these ideas with selective reference to evidence from the historical and anthropological record. A first thorough application of these ideas to the study of the evolution of modern building types is offered by Markus (1993). Markus used *space syntax* to describe "spatial structure" and discuss how it relates to architectural form and to the discourses that underlie the programs of modern building types.

The relationship between labels has also been studied in more abstract ways. Since the Integration value of a space describes its relationship to the layout as a whole, we may ask whether the spaces associated with different labels have Integration values that are similarly ordered from more to less integrated. Asking the question in this way is slightly counterintuitive because it does not directly address the relations of labeled spaces to each other. Instead, the relationships between labeled spaces are described as they are mediated through positioning within the whole pattern. Hillier and Hanson (1984) proposed that such a constant but more abstract relationship between the integration of labeled spaces could be treated as a spatial "genotype."

Integration genotypes have extensively been discussed with reference to domestic plans. In their earlier work Hillier and Hanson (1984) suggest that small English houses are characterized by the fact that the living room is more integrated than the kitchen, which is in turn more integrated than the "parlor," a space at the front of the house normally associated with formal occasions and the best furniture. Different cultural identities are manifested in the manner in which the genotype is realized. For example, traditional working-class houses strongly differentiated the Integration values associated with the internal labels but made a less sharp demarcation between interior and exterior. This was consistent with a culture of informal visits from neighbors. New middle-class conversions of these houses are typically associated with less strong differentiation of internal Integration values but a stronger differentiation between interior and exterior, consistent with receiving visitors who are members of "communities of interest" rather than local neighbors. Such visitors are entertained in a more open and spatially less differentiated plan, where social information is transmitted through the manner of displaying objects and behaviors. Another approach toward understanding genotypes is to focus on the syntactic position of a few, particularly significant labels rather than seek invariable Integration orders over many space labels. In a sample of seventeen farmhouses (Hanson, 1999; Hillier, Hanson & Graham, 1987), for example, a significant space label is the "common hall," a space associated with everyday living and dominated by women. In over half the sample, the common hall is shallow to the outside, the most Integrated space label in the house, a part of circulation rings, and a mediator between living functions and work functions. This characterizes half the sample. In the other half of the sample the most integrating space is a vestibule or other transition space. Previous interpretations of the cultural logic of these house plans identified "laterality" as a fundamental principle of spatial organization, whereby the living and the work areas of the house stood on opposite sides of the plan. Syntactic analysis indicates that the principle of laterality encompasses two distinct spatial realizations, one centered on a female-, the other on a male-dominated space. These are in turn associated with a distinction between "constitutive" and "representational" codes of space. The integrative, or constitutive, function of the common hall is available to experience both in terms of the activities it accommodates and in terms of strong visual connections to other spaces. Neither is true for integrated transition spaces that are occupied only transiently and afford no strong visual links to main use spaces. A similar approach has been applied to the analysis of a sample of 16 traditional Turkish house plans (Orhun, Hillier, & Hanson, 1995) where integration is either around an internal sitting space, the sofa, or around an external but highly used courtyard.

The approach has also been applied to the analysis of 20 small and 11 large Anasazi houses in Chaco Canyon, New Mexico (Bustard, 1999). The archeological record does not permit the assignment of special labels to all house areas, but based on the discovery of fixed floor features and other evidence, it is possible to draw a distinction between domestic and nondomestic use spaces. Analysis shows that spaces used for meals are frequently the most integrating interior spaces in small houses, while kivas as well as meal rooms are the most integrating interior spaces in larger ones. Furthermore, meal spaces seem associated with more than one dwelling unit. The analysis lends support to the hypothesis that economic cooperation in food processing occurs at a level higher than the individual household. According to this model, kivas are associated with integration through ritual, while meal rooms are associated with integration through economic cooperation. The study is of special interest because syntactic analysis is used to formulate and to some extent test interpretative hypotheses regarding culture by interrogating layout and physical evidence regarding its use.

The link between the analysis of coding and the analysis of observed or inferred patterns of space occupancy lies in the insight that space is socially used to differentiate statuses, roles, or categories and to generate or control the possibility of encounter or avoidance (Hanson, 1999). As suggested in preceding sections, configuration modulates probabilities of coawareness and copresence. The labels that are assigned to spaces offer a partial insight into the manner in which the underlying pattern of cohabitation is socially invested and regulated. Labeling spaces is an aspect of crystallizing and reproducing typical programs of function, behavior, and space use. The consistent configurational relationships between labels suggests that our naming, sanctioning, and representing of space use tacitly but powerfully interacts with the structuring potential of built space.

SPATIAL EXPLORATION AS COGNITIVE PROBLEM AND AS SOCIAL FUNCTION

The manner in which spatial relationships are explored and understood is a problem of cognitive science in its own right, but it is also an aspect of social and behavioral function: Access to space implies access to people, resources, or information; mapping spatial relationships can be used as a basis for making sense of social relationships and behavioral settings. Hillier and Hanson (1984) define intelligibility in terms of the correlation between local and global properties of spatial arrangements. Local properties tend to be more readily available to perception and understanding than global properties. However, as we have seen, global properties, such as integration, have a powerful effect on space use. It is inferred that layouts where local and global properties are strongly correlated will be more intelligible. Subsequent work has addressed the question of intelligibility as a research problem in its own right. Peponis, Zimring, and Choi (1990) have drawn a distinction between intelligibility and wayfinding. Intelligibility refers to our orientation within spatial configuration, wayfinding refers to our ability to reach particular destinations. A grid is intelligible as a system, but searching for a destination requires effort. A long meandering single sequence of spaces may be unintelligible as a system, but reaching a destination inside it represents no problem, at least in principle. In an "open search" exercise, subjects were asked to explore a medical building off working hours, when the volume of space use was almost insignificant, without a specific destination in mind, until they felt they understood it. In a subsequent "directed search" exercise they were asked to look for typical destinations, starting from particular origins. Analysis of their paths, which were recorded on the building plan, suggested that exploration paths, whether in open or in directed search, gravitate quite powerfully toward the most integrated spaces. This raised two lines of discussion, one theoretical, the other practical. The theoretically relevant finding is that Integration may govern the exploration of spatial environments as it seems to

govern normal patterns of movement and space use. This is a surprising finding because for a long time it has been suggested that configuration is understood at the end of a longer process of cognition (Hart & Moore, 1973). The possibility that a configurational property that takes the whole layout into account, such as integration, can be intuited within a short time interval is a challenging theoretical hypothesis. From a practical point of view, the research suggested that locating important destinations on the integration core would facilitate wayfinding and would minimize reliance on signage and other devices normally used to mitigate the effects of unintelligible layout.

Techniques of spatial analysis have been used to discuss the functions of museums (Peponis & Hedin, 1982; Wineman & Choi, 1991). Choi (1999) has subsequently analyzed visitors' paths in eight museum settings. Integration was significantly correlated with "tracking scores," the number of people that reached each convex space, while connectivity was correlated with "tracking frequencies," the number of times each space was visited, including multiple returns by the same person. These findings are particularly significant given that there were no correlations between scores or frequencies and the number of objects exhibited within each space; correlations with the total number of objects visible, including those visible beyond the boundaries of an individual space were better but inconsistent. Thus, spatial variables play an important role in structuring exploration even where the purpose of exploration is not to comprehend the layout itself but to view the displays in it. Choi also studied the distribution of people present in the museum, using normal behavioral mapping techniques. While the presence of people inside a space was not powerfully correlated with spatial variables, the presence of people visible from a space was correlated with Integration as well as with the area of the available visual field. By putting the findings based on tracking together with the findings based on behavioral mapping, we infer that as exploration paths gravitate toward more integrated spaces, museum space is experienced not only as a field of visual information but also as a field of spatially modulated social copresence.

The correlation between exploration paths and Integration suggests that there is indeed a link between the way layouts function and the manner in which they become intelligible. However, the cognitive mechanisms and the environmental cues whereby subjects reach an understanding of the integration pattern is open to further research, as is the way in which syntactic information may be stored in the mind. Earlier research (Appleyard, 1970; Evans, Smith, & Pezdek, 1982; Lynch, 1960) suggested multiple elements that enter into the mental image of physical environments without providing a configurational framework within which these elements could be systematically integrated. Where configuration has been an explicit consideration (and its importance has often been expressed in the literature—Gärling, Böök, Ergenzen, & Lindberg, 1981; Gärling & Golledge, 1989), configurational descriptors were based either on judgment rather than analytical computation (Weisman, 1981) or on simplified environments (G. Evans, Skorpamich, Gärling, Bryant, & Bresolin, 1984). Thus, syntactic research in this area since 1990 has addressed a commonly acknowledged problem in the field.

THEORETICAL COMMENTS

In this chapter, we have summarized some of the insights that can be gained by bringing explicit analytic theories of spatial configuration into social and psychological studies of environment. Our emphasis has been on theoretical propositions that are general or can potentially be generalized. We have not expanded on detailed spatial characterizations of individual settings, a matter that is of interest when spatial theory addresses particular problems in design, space allocation, or space management. We have also not expanded on questions of spatial morphology in its own right: what generative principles govern the emergence of the global properties of spatial arrangements; what are the relationships between geometric, topological, and graph properties; how we might classify layouts in morphological types that may cut across function types. These questions have only been touched upon when they intersected the development of theories of the social function, behavioral implications, or cultural significance of layouts.

We began by suggesting that, from a social point of view, built space can be defined as a field of structured copresence, coawareness, and encounter. In light of the foregoing discussion, we can distinguish three effects of structure: First, potential copresence, coawareness, and encounter arise as a by-product of movement. We have seen that movement is both generated and distributed according to configuration.

Second, copresence, coawareness, and encounter are framed according to the manner in which the labels that describe space use are distributed over layout configuration. Since the labels carry with them cultural assumptions about program, rules of behavior, social roles, and cultural meanings, we have suggested that copresence, coawareness, and encounter are framed by the social encoding of configuration. Third, the cognitive intelligibility of space is intertwined with the manner in which space becomes accessible to exploration and the contents of space become available to search.

Generative potential, cultural encoding, and the framing of exploration and search are fundamental functions involved with the social production and occupation of space. The underlying contribution of the literature of space syntax is to show how generation, encoding, and explorability are embedded in the arrangement of physical boundaries, the geometry of layouts, and the patterns of space as they are used, perceived, and understood. The construct that intervenes between the spatial, the social, and the behavioral dimensions of environment is the idea of configuration whereby these dimensions can be described in the common language of graphs once they have been diagrammed and mapped in particular ways. As we have seen, theory is involved in two stages. First, formal theory provides the conventions for mapping and diagramming the geometry of environment and the morphology of space use. Second, research tests theoretical hypotheses about the manner in which the geometry of environment is socialized, whether as generative resource, as cultural code, or as framing of exploration, through its configurational syntax.

This brings us to some final comments about the position of the literature of space syntax within the field of studies of environment, culture, and behavior. The research work discussed above addressed questions that are normally associated with diverse disciplinary emphases, including architectural theory; social, environmental, or cognitive psychology; sociology; organization theory; anthropology; or cultural studies. The interface between such bodies of inquiry and the literature of space syntax is unevenly developed. Even so, it is possible to ask whether the literature of space syntax represents a coherent body of ideas that may potentially integrate across such diverse fields. Our answer is in two parts. There is no doubt that the literature of space syntax has underscored the importance of developing descriptive theories of built space that allow us to systematically treat layouts as an independent variable. Studies of environment and behavior, in the broadest sense, are often stronger on describing behavior and dealing with intervening social, psychological, cultural, or organizational variables than they are on describing environment and the spatial structure of environment in particular. The literature of space syntax addresses this gap and provides a coherent but flexible framework for describing layouts at different scales and from different points of view: visual fields, lines of movement, areas of occupation, patterns of connectivity, choice of paths, control boundaries, and so on. Integration, as a well-defined measure of graphs, has consistently emerged as a significant property of spatial environment and one that can be diversely embedded in specific geometries and designs. In this sense, we may postulate that a descriptive theory of space, such as the one advanced in the literature on space syntax, may indeed cut across different fields of inquiry in terms of both analytical methodology and substantive findings.

This does not foreclose the larger question of whether the substantive hypotheses examined in the literature of space syntax can be brought within the purview of a single theory of space as a human artifact. To say that from a social point of view built space has generative potential, carries cultural encoding, and frames search and exploration is likely to open further questions rather than to close an area of inquiry. Questions of cognition, social organization, building function, cultural meaning, and design intentionality will continue to be asked in a manner that respects the problem situation and criteria for debate established in diverse and sometimes divergent disciplines. It is possible that bringing spatial configuration into the purview of explicit theory will have significant paradigmatic implications, as envisaged by Hillier and Hanson (1984). This issue is likely to remain open and should remain open. More than 15 years after the publication of *The Social Logic of Space* the literature of space syntax has as much to gain from critically engaging other lines of inquiry as the broader field of environment, culture, and behavior has to gain from the insights that have been systematically and copiously established within that literature. As usual with the history of knowledge, new insights bring about changes in the manner in which questions are asked and the manner in which their relationships are understood.

SOCIALLY SIGNIFICANT DESCRIPTIONS OF SPACE AND DESIGN

The impetus for studies of environment, culture, and behavior is, at least in part, to contribute to the knowledge base of the design disciplines involved with the production of the physical environment. It is commonplace that the design disciplines have an inherent social dimension: They contribute to sustaining patterns of behavior, understanding, and social relationships, even though they manipulate physical resources. Nevertheless, as Hillier and Leaman (1973) argued in the early days of environment behavior studies, this is not because the built environment can causally affect, significantly constrain, or conditionally enable *individual* behavior. This may be the overriding connection in special contexts only. Since its nineteenth-century elevation to a general principle, the dogma of "architectural determinism," has frustrated the development of theories of the social and behavioral significance of built space. Rather, the spatial structure of the built environment always embodies principles through which we make sense of social relationships and behaviors and learn to anticipate their normal flow; also, the spatial structure of the built environment produces or sustains statistical and collective effects of coawareness and copresence. In short, the pervasive effects of the spatial structure of environment upon behavior are indirect. They occur through the positioning of collective actors rather than through the prescription of action. With these caveats out of the way, the literature of space syntax has directly engaged questions of design.

This has occurred in several ways, practical and theoretical. In practice, the techniques of space syntax have been used to analyze design alternatives, to predict their likely effects, and to evaluate them; also to analyze context and to identify the constraints and possibilities that context imposes upon design. The application of space syntax to design has been more prominent at the urban scale. The relevant published documentation has not kept pace with the actual record. Here we will limit ourselves to reviewing some of the arguments presented by architect Sir Norman Foster (1997) at the First International Symposium on Space Syntax. Foster asserted that space syntax has worked to bridge the world of analysis, observation, and reason with the world of design passion and intuition. In the evolution of designs for the Kings Cross 52-hectare rail yard, space syntax contributed to design experimentation with layout, involving successive circles of proposals and evaluations aimed at integrating a difficult site into its surroundings and at turning the compositional heart of the scheme, an oval-shaped park, into a potentially well used space. Syntactic analysis specifically helped to generate a road through the site that Foster calls "Hillier way." This road and the connections that it made became critical to the development of traffic management, the assessment of retail potential, and the calibration of layout. The analytic arguments provided through the application of space syntax also helped maintain the confidence of the developer in the evolving design. Because of changes in the overall policies regarding the railway connection from the continent to London through the Channel Tunnel, the project was never realized. More recently, space syntax has been used to assist with developing new designs for Trafalgar Square and the larger Whitehall area in central London. In that project detailed mappings of behavior were correlated not only to the analysis of linear routes but also to the analysis of visual fields. The analysis, which was cross-checked against public consultation, helped to propose how the square could be reconfigured to create better interfaces between the paths used and the positions frequented by distinct categories of users including tourists and people working in the vicinity. The two projects used by Foster to illustrate the relevance of space syntax to his design practice offer an interesting contrast. They show the relevance of analytic theory to both large-scale design development and to smaller scale design fine-tuning. In both cases, spatial analysis seems to have contributed to a circle of development proceeding from the retrieval of descriptions of actual conditions and potential to the formulation of possibility, the prediction of implications, and the evaluation of design alternatives.

We would like to end our discussion taking up a theoretical argument that is very much connected to the observations made by Foster but looks upon the contributions of analytic theory to understanding design retrospectively rather than prospectively. One of the major divides within many schools of architecture in the United States and abroad is the divide between architectural history and criticism on the one hand and theories of the social functions and behavioral implications of design on the other. In his book, Markus (1993) proposes that bridging

this gap and bringing questions of programming and function into focus within architectural history and criticism is crucial to the knowledge base of the field and to the practice of design. The gap itself, he suggested, may partly originate in the predominant disciplinary influence exercised by art history and theory over the history and theory of architecture. We propose that one of the contributions of analytic theories of space and function, such as space syntax, can be sought in the reconstruction of the context of decisions and the reconstruction of intentionality in design. Art theorist and critic Baxandall (1985) has proposed a distinction between "charge" and "brief." *Charge* describes the programs, requirements, and known solution types that specify what is expected of design before design begins. *Brief* describes the additional aims, or inflections of aims, brought about by designers themselves in the course of design. In a way, *charge* refers to the aims of design that are known in advance, independent of the designed object, and *brief* to the aims of design that are intrinsic to the designed object and cannot be intimated before the design process itself. Curiously, a proposition that originates in the field of art history and criticism may provide us with a good way to conceptualize how analytic theories of space and function can contribute to design studies.

While questions of social function and behavioral implication may not be explicitly foregrounded in current architectural discourse that elucidates the brief, they are necessarily implied in the commissioning of designs, the charge. However, as Hillier (1996) has argued, spatial knowledge is largely nondiscursive, and as we have suggested earlier, the spatial correlates of programs are seldom explicitly and fully described in the commissioning documents. The contribution of analytic theories such as space syntax may be sought in the reconstruction of the underlying spatial aspects of charge through a systematic analysis of relevant precedent. The search for formal design innovation, the brief, always has to interact with the spatial aspects of charge, however implicitly, and this, ultimately, is one of the key criteria for the viability and sustainability of formal design innovations. In addition, we would like to observe that the spatial and functional aspects of charge should be thought not so much as a latent imposition but rather as a field of significant design choices that is more or less explicitly understood by designers. At any point in time, similar design problems are confronted in a relatively limited number of ways, whether we think of these as "stereotypical solutions" (Hawkes, 1976), "underlying design assumptions" (Duffy, 1974), "recurrent genotypes" (Hillier & Leaman, 1974), or "historically evolved types" (Colquhoun, 1981). The contribution of analytic theories of space and function is to make these choices explicit as well as to suggest the principles on the basis of which such received ranges of choices can be conditionally redrawn or overcome through deeper design innovations. This task brings together the potential contributions of analytic theories to the retrospective understanding of design intentionality, and the prospective involvement with design formulation.

REFERENCES

Allen, T. (1977). *Managing the flow of technology.* Cambridge: Massachusetts Institute of Technology Press.

Appleyard, D. (1970). Styles and methods of structuring a city. *Environment and Behavior, 2,* 100–116.

Archea, J. (1977). The place of architectural factors in behavioral theories of privacy. *Journal of Social Issues, 33,* 116–137.

Batty, M. (2001). Exploring isovist fields: Space and shape in architectural and urban morphology. *Environment and Planning (B): Planning and Design, 28,* 123–150.

Baxandall, M. (1985). *Patterns of intention.* New Haven, CT: Yale University Press.

Beales, G. (1978). *Sick health centres and how to make them better.* London: Pitman Medical.

Benedikt, M. L. (1979). To take hold of space: Isovists and isovist fields. *Environment and Planning (B): Planning and Design, 6,* 47–65.

Bennett, N., Andreae, J., Hegarty, P., & Wade, B. (1980). *Open plan schools.* London: Schools Council Publication.

Bernstein, B. (1975). *Class codes and control: Towards a theory of educational transmissions.* London: Routledge & Kegan Paul.

Brown, M. G. (1999). Design and value: Spatial form and the economic failure of a mall. *Journal of Real Estate Research, 17,* 189–225.

Bustard, W. (1999). Space, evolution and function in the houses of Chaco Canyon. *Environment and Planning (B): Planning and Design, 26,* 219–240.

Caliandro, V. (1986). Street form and use: A survey of principal American street environments. In S. Anderson (Ed.), *On streets* (pp. 151–185). Cambridge, MA: Massachusetts Institute of Technology Press.

Choi, Y. K. (1999). The morphology of exploration and encounter in museum layouts. *Environment and Planning (B): Planning and Design, 26,* 241–250.

Colquhoun, A. (1981). Typology and design method. In A. Colquhoun (Ed.), *Essays in architectural criticism.* Cambridge, MA: Massachusetts Institute of Technology Press.

Duffy, F. (1974). Office design and organizations. *Environment and Planning (B): Planning and Design, 1,* 11–118, 217–236.

Evans, G. W., Lepore, S. J., & Schroeder, A. (1966). The role of interior design elements in human responses to crowding. *Journal of Personality and Social Psychology, 70*(1), 41–46.

Evans, G., Smith, C., & Pezdek, K. (1982). Cognitive maps and urban form. *Journal of the American Planning Association, 48,* 232–244.

Evans, G., Skorpamich, M. A., Gärling, T., Bryant, K. J., & Bresolin, B. (1984). The effects of pathway configuration, landmarks and stress on environmental cognition. *Journal of Environmental Psychology, 4,* 323–335.

Evans, R. (1982). *The fabrication of virtue.* Cambridge: Cambridge University Press.

Foster, N. (1997). Opening address. In M. D. Major, L. Amorim, & F. Dufaux (Eds.), *Space syntax: First international symposium* [Proceedings of the First International Space Syntax Symposium] (Vol. 3, pp. xvii-xxii). London: Space Syntax Laboratory, Bartlett School of Graduate Studies.

Gärling, T., Böök, A., Ergenzen, N., & Lindberg, E. (1981). Memory for the spatial layout of everyday physical environment: Empirical findings and their theoretical implications. In A. E. Osterberg, C. T. Tiernan, & R. A. Findlay (Eds.), *Design-research interactions* [Proceedings of the Environmental Design Research Association] (Vol. 12, pp. 66–77). Washington, DC: Environmental Design Research Association.

Gärling, T., & Golledge, R. G. (1989). Environmental perception and cognition. In E. H. Szube & G. Moore (Eds.), *Advances in environmental behavior and design* (Vol. 2, pp. 203–239). New York: Plenum Press.

Gibson, J. J. (1986). *The ecological approach to visual perception.* Hillsdale, NJ: Erlbaum.

Goffman, E. (1959). *The presentation of self in everyday life.* London: Penguin.

Goodman, N. (1976). *Languages of art.* Indianapolis: Hackett.

Grajewski, T. (1993). The SAS head office—spatial configuration and interaction patterns. *Nordic Journal of Architectural Research, 2,* 63–74.

Granovetter, M. (1982). The strength of weak ties. In P. V. Marsden & N. Lin (Eds.), *Social structure and network analysis.* Beverly Hills, CA: Sage.

Hanson, J. (1989). Order and structure in urban design: The plans for the rebuilding of London after the Great Fire of 1666. *Ekistics, 56*(334/335), 22–42.

Hanson, J. (1999). *Decoding homes and houses.* Cambridge: Cambridge University Press.

Hart, R. A., & Moore, G. T. (1973). The development of spatial cognition. In R. M. Downs & D. Stea (Eds.), *Image and environment* (pp. 246–288). Chicago: Aldine.

Hawkes, D. (1976). Types, norms and habits in environmental design. In L. March (Ed.), *The architecture of form* (pp. 465–481). Cambridge: Cambridge University Press.

Hillier, B. (1985). The nature of the artificial: The contingent and the necessary in spatial form in architecture. *Geoforum, 16*(2), 163–178.

Hillier, B. (1988). Against enclosure. In N. Teymur, T. Markus, & T. Wooley (Eds.), *Rehumanizing housing* (pp. 63–88). London: Butterworth.

Hillier, B. (1989). The architecture of the urban object. *Ekistics, 56*(334/335), 5–21.

Hillier, B. (1996). *Space is the machine.* Cambridge: Cambridge University Press.

Hillier, B. (1997). Cities as movement economies. In P. Droege (Ed.), *Intelligent environments: Spatial aspects of the information revolution* (pp. 295–342). Amsterdam: Elsevier.

Hillier, B. (1998). A note on the intuiting of form: Three issues in the theory of design. *Environment and Planning (B): Planning and Design* (25th anniversary issue), 37–40.

Hillier, B., Burdett, R., Peponis, J., & Penn, A. (1987). Creating life: Or, does architecture determine anything? *Architecture and Comportment/Architecture and Behavior, 3*(3), 233–250.

Hillier, B., & Hanson, J. (1984). *The social logic of space.* Cambridge: Cambridge University Press.

Hillier, B., Hanson, J., & Graham, H. (1987). Ideas are in things. *Environment and Planning (B): Planning and Design, 14*, 363–385.

Hillier, B., Hanson, J., & Peponis, J. (1984). What do we mean by building function? In J. Powell, I. Cooper, & S. Lera (Eds.), *Designing for building utilization* (pp. 61–72). London: E. & F. N. Spon.

Hillier, B., & Leaman, A. (1973). The man-environment paradigm and its paradoxes. *Architectural Design, 8*, 507–511.

Hillier, B., & Leaman, A. (1974). How is design possible? *Journal of Architectural Research, 1*, 4–11.

Hillier, B., & Penn, A. (1991). Visible colleges: Structure and randomness in the place of discovery. *Science in Context, 4*(1), 23–49.

Hillier, B., Penn, A., Hanson, J., Grajewski, T., & Xu, J. (1993). Natural movement: Or, configuration and attraction in urban pedestrian movement. *Environment and Planning B: Planning and Design, 20*, 29–66.

Holanda, F. de (1989). Brasilia: The daily invention of the city. *Ekistics, 56*(334/335), 75–83.

Kubat, A. S. (1997). The morphological characteristics of Anatolian fortified towns. *Environment and Planning (B): Planning and Design, 24*, 95–123.

Lynch, K. (1960). *The image of the city.* Cambridge: Massachusetts Institute of Technology Press.

March, L., & Steadman, P. (1971). *The geometry of environment.* London: Royal Institute of British Architects.

Markus, T. (1993). *Buildings and power.* London: Routledge.

Min, Y. (1993). Housing layout design—Neighborhood morphology, pedestrian movement and strategic choices. *Nordic Journal of Architectural Research, 2*, 75–95.

Orhun, D., Hillier, B., & Hanson, J. (1995). Spatial types in traditional Turkish houses. *Environment and Planning (B): Planning and Design, 22*, 475–498.

Peatross, D., & Peponis, J. (1995). Space education and socialization. *Journal of Architectural and Planning Research, 12*(4), 366–385.

Penn, A., Desyllas, J., & Vaughan, L. (1999). The space of innovation: Interaction and communication in the work environment. *Environment and Planning B: Planning and Design, 26*(2), 193–218.

Penn, A., Hillier, B., Bannister, D., & Xu, J. (1998). Configurational modeling of urban movement networks. *Environment and Planning (B): Planning and Design, 25*(1), 59–84.

Peponis, J. (1985, April). The spatial culture of factories. *Human Relation, 38*, 357–390.

Peponis, J., Hajinikolaou, E., Livieratos, C., & Fatouros, D. A. (1989). The spatial core of urban culture. *Ekistics 56*(334/335), 43–55.

Peponis, J., & Hedin, J. (1982). The layout of theories in the Natural History Museum. *9H, 3*, 12–25.

Peponis, J., Ross, C., & Rashid, M. (1997). The structure of urban space, movement and co-presence: The case of Atlanta. *Geoforum, 28*(3–4), 341–358.

Peponis, J., Wineman, J., Bafna, S., Rashid, M., & Kim, S. H. (1998). On the generation of linear representation of spatial configuration. *Environment and Planning (B): Planning and Design, 25*, 559–576.

Peponis, J., Wineman, J., Rashid, M., Bafna, S., & Kim, S. H. (1998). Describing plan configuration according to the covisibility of surfaces. *Environment and Planning (B): Planning and Design, 25*, 693–708.

Peponis, J., Wineman, J., Rashid, M., Kim, S. H., & Bafna, S. (1997). On the description of shape and spatial configuration inside buildings: Convex partitions and their local properties. *Environment and Planning (B): Planning and Design, 24*, 761–781.

Peponis, J., Zimring, C., & Choi, Y. K. (1990). Finding the building in wayfinding. *Environment and Behavior, 22*(5), 555–590.

Piaget, J., & Inhelder, B. (1967). *The child's conception of space.* New York: Norton.

Read, S. (1999). Space syntax and the Dutch city. *Environment and Planning (B): Planning and Design, 26*, 251–264.

Schumacher, T. (1986). Buildings and streets: Notes on configuration and use. In S. Anderson (Ed.), *On streets* (pp. 133–149). Cambridge: Massachusetts Institute of Technology Press.

Serrato, M., & Wineman, J. (1999). Spatial and communication patterns in research & development facilities. *Space syntax: Second International Symposium* [proceedings of the Second International Symposium on Space Syntax] (Vol. 1, pp. 11.1–11.8). Brasilia, Brazil: Universidade de Brasilia.

Siksna, A. (1997). The effects of block size and form in North American and Australian city centers. *Urban Morphology, 1*, 19–33.

Sommer, R. (1966). Man's proximate environment. *Journal of Social Issues, 22*, 59–70.

Southworth, M., & Ben-Joseph, E. (1995). Street standards and the shaping of suburbia. *APA Journal, 61*(1), 65–81.

Southworth, M., & Owens, P. (1993). The evolving metropolis: Studies of community, neighborhood, and street form at the urban edge. *APA Journal, 59*(3), 271–287.

Teklenburg, J. A. F., Timmermans, H. J. P., & Wegenburg, A. F. van (1993). Space syntax: Standardized integration measures and some simulations. *Environment and Planning (B): Planning and Design, 20*, 347–357.

Thiel, P. (1970). Notes on the description, scaling, notation, and scoring of some perceptual and cognitive attributes of the physical environment. In H. M. Proshansky, W. H. Ittelson, & L. G. Rivlin (Eds.), *Environmental psychology* (pp. 593–619). New York: Holt, Rinehart and Winston.

Turner, A., Doxa, M., O'Sullivan, D., & Penn, A. (2001). From isovists to visibility graphs: A methodology for the analysis of architectural space. *Environment and Planning (B): Planning and Design, 28*, 103–121.

Weisman, J. (1981). Evaluating architectural legibility: Wayfinding in the built environment. *Environment and Behavior, 13*, 189–204.

Whyte, W. H. (1980). *The social life of small urban spaces.* Washington, DC: Conservation Foundation.

Wineman, J., & Choi, Y. (1991, December). Spatial/visual properties of zoo exhibition. *Curator, 34*(4), 304–315.

Zimring, C. M., Weitzer, W. H., & Knight, R. C. (1982). Opportunity for control and the built environment: The case of an institution for the developmentally disabled. In A. Baum & J. Singer (Eds.), *Advances in environmental psychology: IV. Environment and Health.* Hillsdale, NJ: Erlbaum.

CHAPTER 19

Behavioral-Based Architectural Programming

ROBERT HERSHBERGER

Architectural Programming is the definitional stage of design—the time to discover the nature of the design problem, rather than the nature of the design solution. It is the time in which the relevant values of the client, user, architect, and society are identified; important project goals are articulated; facts about the project are uncovered; and facility needs are made explicit.

—Hershberger, 1999

PROGRAMMING IS A CRUCIAL TIME in which serious mistakes can happen or insightful, formative decisions can be made. Indeed, many of the most important formative decisions are made before the architect begins to design. The decision may be reached to have only one building instead of two; an auditorium within the fabric of a larger building instead of a separate building; offices in a building separate from the classrooms, or vice versa. The budget can be set so low as to preclude any number of design opportunities, or the time span for completion of the design and construction can be so short that only the simplest of forms could be utilized to finish the project on schedule.

If the client and programmer are primarily interested in functional efficiency, organization and activity decisions may be made that could significantly affect the form of the building. If the client and programmer are more concerned with the social and psychological needs of the users, prescriptions for form may be inherent in the listed spaces, sizes, characteristics, and relationships. If they are concerned with

economics, it is possible that numerous material and system opportunities, as well as potentially unique spaces and places, will be eliminated from design consideration. Conversely, for any of the above situations, the lack of concern for important design issues may restrict the designer's options. The point is that the values and concerns of the client and the programmer have a significant impact because they decide both how the information is generated and how it is presented (see Figure 19.1).

HISTORY OF BEHAVIORAL-BASED ARCHITECTURAL PROGRAMMING

A number of social and behavioral scientists began to direct attention to the built environment in the 1960s. Indeed, a new social science specialization alternatively referred to as *environmental psychology, environmental sociology,* or *human ecology* began to emerge (Conway, 1973). Many of these social scientists became affiliated with the Environmental

This article is adapted from Chapters 1, 5, and 6 of the author's book: *Architectural Programming and Predesign Manager,* New York, McGraw-Hill, 1999 with permission from the publisher.

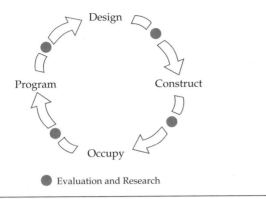

Figure 19.1 Architecture delivery process.

Design Research Association (EDRA), an organization in which architects, interior designers, and other design professionals began to interact with social scientists in the common concern that many buildings and other designed environments did not work particularly well for the people they were meant to serve. These interdisciplinary groups often chose to utilize research methods developed by social and behavioral scientists to study human attitudes regarding and behavior in the physical environment. These methods included literature search and review, systematic observation, controlled interviewing, questionnaires and surveys, population sampling, and statistical analysis.

Seminal studies of personal space and territoriality by Edward Hall (1966) and Robert Sommer (1969) were introduced to the architectural profession and influenced many architects, who gave consideration to their findings in both programming and design. Other behavioral scientists such as Altman (1975), Lawton, Windley, and Byerts (1982), Bechtel, Marans, and Michelson (1987), and Marcus (1975) followed with more directed studies on privacy, special needs of the elderly, survey research, and special building types. A number of architects including Horowitz (1966), Sanoff (1977, 1992), Moore (Moore & Golledge, 1976), Windley (Lawton et al., 1982), Spreckelmeyer (Marans & Spreckelmeyer, 1982), and the author (Hershberger, 1969) adopted some of the same methods to study problems of interest to them. Still other architects, such as Davis (1969), Farbstein (1976), Preiser (1978, 1985, 1993), Moleski (1974), Brill (Brill, Margulis, Konar, & BOSTI, 1984), and Hershberger (1985) began to utilize behavioral-based research in actual programming practice.

BENEFITS AND LIMITATIONS

Typically, these behavioral-based programming efforts have been of great benefit when applied to large, complex building types such as prisons, hospitals, airports, research facilities, government office buildings, and the like, where the architect or even the key administrators may not have a good understanding of the values, goals, and needs of persons in various divisions of the organization. In order to gain this understanding, it is necessary to interview key personnel in the various divisions about their values and goals and to observe how people use their current environments. It may also be helpful to review the research literature on special user needs, visit other facilities to see how they work, and devise questionnaires to discover typical user attitudes and ideas regarding furnishing and equipment requirements.

The information gained from the various research approaches is then assembled, statistically analyzed, and summarized in a program document that attempts to cover all of the human requirements of the organization. Indeed, space program sheets are often developed for every space in the proposed facility. Such a systematic approach to programming provides highly reliable information of considerable value to the designer in preparing plans to meet the needs of the client and the various user groups of the building.

Given the generally systematic approach to behavioral-based programming, there tend to be few problems with resulting programs. However, intensive focus on developing knowledge about users may tend to minimize consideration of other issues of importance to the design architect, such as cost and schedule. Similarly, if the design architect has yet to be hired, his or her expertise and values regarding areas such as site, climate, and technology may have no influence on the program. And utilizing high-powered research methods on comparatively easy problems can require excessive amounts of time and money that simply exceed the client's ability to cover them. Indeed, this is the primary problem with the behavioral-based approach to programming. It tends to consume large quantities of time in planning, making arrangements for the actual studies, doing the studies, and analyzing the large amounts of data generated. This is not a problem unless it leaves insufficient time or money to adequately consider the remaining environmental, technological, legal, temporal, economic, aesthetic, and safety issues in architecture. If something critical to the eventual architectural solution is not studied sufficiently or covered adequately in the program, the resulting building could fail in some way while succeeding admirably relative to environment/behavior issues.

METHODS

In a situation of unlimited time and resources, it would be ideal to devote an extensive systematic research effort on every relevant design issue so that no area of potential importance would be left unstudied. However, most programming endeavors are conducted under conditions where time and money are very limited and there is not enough of either to do the kind of job the programmer would prefer. It is, therefore, important that the programming team isolate the critical variables in whatever issue areas they are found and devote their more systematic research efforts on these variables. The high costs of research can then be focused where the cost of error is high, and less expensive programming approaches can be used to obtain other kinds of information. The following methods are useful in gaining needed information.

LITERATURE SEARCH AND REVIEW

The most obvious way to obtain information about a particular problem in behavioral-based programming is to see what others have discovered. Environmental design research findings are available covering territoriality, privacy, community, safety, and other social and psychological needs of various user groups: the elderly, young, handicapped, incarcerated, and so forth. This literature is typically available in major public and university libraries in such documents as the conference proceedings of the Environmental Design Research Association (EDRA), journals such as *Environment and Behavior*, the *Journal of Environmental Psychology,* and the *Journal of Architectural and Planning Research*; and in a variety of monographs such as *Tight Spaces* by Robert Sommer (1974), *Easter Hill Village: Some Social Indications of Design* by Marcus (1975), *Aging and the Environment: Theoretical Approaches* by editors Lawton et al. (1982), and *Using Office Design to Increase Productivity* by Brill et al. (1984).

A more difficult problem is to find behavioral-based literature that is particularly appropriate for the programming problem at hand. An organiza-

tion's library may include trade journals containing special information about similar organizations or have in-house documents that identify the principal purposes or "institutional values" of the organization as well as primary goals and directions for advancement and/or change. Guidelines for space size and use may also be available from the organization's headquarters or professional association(s) (see Figure 19.2).

Information on the site and its surroundings as well as on the urban infrastructure will be available from various governmental agencies. Cities also develop or adopt building codes (building, mechanical, plumbing, fire safety, etc.) containing important information. Current information on these topics is unlikely to be available in public or university libraries.

Table 19.1 lists 10 categories of printed materials that may contain useful information. How to find and use these information sources is covered extensively in Hershberger (1999).

Behavioral-based programming firms should have the more generally applicable books and journals in their libraries, while those wishing to program for particular building types should acquire appropriate monographs and applicable periodicals.

DIAGNOSTIC INTERVIEWING

Interviewing is the most frequently used method for gathering information in architectural programming. Indeed, as Preiser (1993) discovered, most architectural firms use interviews as practically their

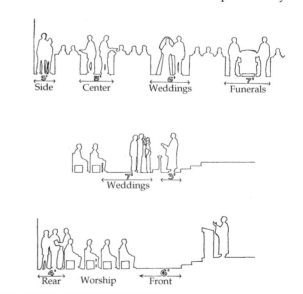

Figure 19.2 Organization design standards. *Source:* Board of Church Extension of Disciples of Christ.

Table 19.1
Literature Source List

1. Building and planning standards
2. Historical documents/archival materials
3. Trade publications
4. Research literature
5. Professional publications
6. Codes and ordinances
7. Government documents
8. Manufacturers' publications
9. Popular literature
10. World Wide Web

only information-gathering technique during architectural programming. Behavioral-based programming teams will also use them extensively along with other more objective methods of gathering information (see Figure 19.3).

The very first contact with the client, even before obtaining the commission, is an interview in which the client attempts to determine if the programmer is qualified to do the work and the programmer tries to obtain an initial understanding of the proposed project. After obtaining the commission, the programmer begins in earnest to interview the client and various users, expert consultants, and others who may have special knowledge about the facilities. The programmer tries to discover the reasons why a new facility is needed—the particular values and goals of the client; requirements for the master plan and first phase of development; expected growth and/or change; special conditions or restrictions relative to site, materials, and systems; the construction budget; and possibly the client's expectations

regarding the image or aesthetics. Thus, the programmer uses interviewing to obtain an understanding of the design problem to be undertaken.

If the project is quite large or complex, involving a sizable staff having important information to share or special users whose needs might be unknown, an extensive series of interviews may be needed to discover the special nature of the proposed project. The activity is like that of a doctor asking the patient about symptoms when trying to make a medical diagnosis. The programmer is looking for information that will help to define the architectural problem. We, therefore, refer to the process as *diagnostic interviewing.*

Continuing with the medical analogy, it is important to make the appropriate diagnosis before deciding upon the treatment. Understanding the values and goals of an organization changes architectural design from a puzzle-solving activity into an activity in which important goals can be achieved and important values can be expressed. It is therefore critical that behavioral-based programs first seek values and goals to set the direction for the balance of the research effort.

The interviewer will receive essentially five types of programmatic information from the interviewee: values, goals, facts, needs, and ideas. Each should be included in a *mental matrix* so that significant information can be gained, particularly with respect to important values and goals. The author uses the matrix in Table 19.2 to help catalog the information gained during an interview.

In a series of interviews, some of the value categories identified in Table 19.2 may not be mentioned

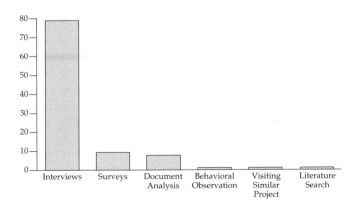

Figure 19.3 Methods of data gathering. *Source:* Preiser, 1993, pp. 17–20.

Table 19.2
Value-Based Interviewing Matrix

Values	Goals	Facts	Needs	Ideas
Human				
Environmental				
Cultural				
Technological				
Temporal				
Economic				
Aesthetic				
Safety				

by the person(s) being interviewed. This is okay! Only the programmer need be concerned about defining the whole problem. The programming approach should be flexible enough to admit new categories of information if they arise, leave out unimportant value categories, and especially allow "natural" categories to surface and be substituted for the initial value categories in the mental matrix.

If the project is a very simple one such as a home, it may be readily apparent who should be interviewed: the wife, husband, children, and grandparents—anyone who would ultimately live in the house. If the project is for a large institution, it may not be so apparent who should be interviewed. The programmer should request an organizational chart and identify the key officers, department heads, and other persons who are likely to be knowledgeable about and/or have the authority to make decisions regarding facility needs. The client should be asked about other persons inside and outside the organization who might have some special knowledge. For some projects this would include customers—the most important users of the facility.

It is not always advisable or even possible to interview only individuals. Group interviews have the advantage of time efficiency because they cover the interests of a number of persons with presumed similar concerns at one time. If they are "primed," the persons involved can meet and discuss their concerns prior to the interview and possibly arrive at a consensus on some issues. The danger in this approach is that some persons' viewpoints may be suppressed because others might dominate the exchange or because there may be fear of reprisal. The gain in efficiency in obtaining the views of larger numbers of people in this case must be weighed against the possible cost of error of obtaining biased information. There is no way to anticipate the size of this error, but if it seems the cost might be great, precautions must be taken. The groups might need to be re-formed. Or any individual wishing a personal interview should be granted one.

In any case, a listing of persons to be interviewed should be prepared for each new programming commission. If there are a large number of individuals, it may be necessary to interview only a representative sample of each category of user. The objective is not to see how *many* people can be interviewed but rather how *few* can be interviewed to obtain complete and reliable information (see Figure 19.4).

When possible, interviews should take place in the client's or user's existing environment. This

Figure 19.4   Small group interview.

tends to make the person more comfortable in answering questions and makes it easier to focus on his or her own architectural environment. The one exception to this is if the interviewee's environment is simply too uncomfortable: too noisy, cluttered, lacking in privacy, or otherwise unconducive to an interview.

The time of the interview is also important. Select a time when the interviewee is not being expected to produce work. Ideally, the client or someone on staff should arrange an interview appointment schedule. If this cannot be arranged, then the interviewer will simply have to be flexible and adjust the interview schedule as circumstances require.

The purpose of the interview is, of course, to obtain information that can be integrated with other information gathered in the programming process. It is necessary, therefore, to have a systematic way of recording the information for later retrieval and analysis. Specifics of this as well as many of the other diagnostic interviewing procedures are contained in the book by the author (Hershberger, 1999).

Contrary to the normal practice for "structured" interviews, it is important in behavioral-based interviews not to provide a number of specific questions on each page with a limited amount of space to record each answer. This does not allow the interviewee the flexibility to approach the subject from her or his point of view. Rather it forces him or her into the interviewer's framework. This can have disastrous results in terms of omitting important ideas and information that may have come out had the interviewee(s) been allowed to discuss the topic more freely. Conversely, if the interviewer has a restrictive recording format but allows the interviewee(s) to move from one topic to another freely, the interviewer is constantly required to search through the recording sheets to find the category into which the information should go. This may make it difficult for the interviewer to concentrate on the interview, and it is distracting to the interviewee. Finally, not everything discussed needs to be recorded, only the conclusions. If care is taken in this regard, the recorded information can be both understandable and manageable to analyze (see Table 19.3).

The purpose of diagnostic interviewing is to obtain an understanding of the most important design issues. It must be understood that this is only the beginning of information gathering. Controversial areas that might be settled through input from a larger sample of people can be followed up with additional focused interviews or a questionnaire-based survey. Questions of fact can be checked using observation techniques and by returning to the appropriate literature. Ultimately, the areas of importance and difference may be sorted out in a group session typically involving most of the interviewees. The results of the interviews are placed before the group and then discussed until a decision is reached about the inclusion and importance of each item.

The interviewing process involves six important steps: introduction, appraisal, diagnosis, recording, review, and open ending. The introduction, review, and open ending each occur just once during an interview. Appraisal, diagnosis, and recording, by contrast, occur numerous times as the interview shifts from one topic to another. This process is explained in detail in Hershberger (1999). It is important to note here that there are eight essential skills used in the diagnostic interview: direction, acceptance, reflection, clarification, amplification, redirection, interpretation, and summary. Acceptance, reflection, clarification, and amplification relate to

the appraisal portion of the interview and are known as "active listening" skills. Direction and redirection are management skills to keep the interview moving in an appropriate direction. Interpretation and summary relate to the diagnostic portion of the interview and bring closure to a portion of the interview. These skills are also covered extensively in Hershberger (1999).

DIAGNOSTIC OBSERVATION

While most programming commissions begin with an individual or group interview, it is not possible to understand the architectural problem fully until one has experienced the project site and the existing and/or other similar facility. Again, it is like a physician not only asking the patient about symptoms to discover important clues as to the nature of an illness but also observing the patient to find other, often more reliable, clues. Such observation includes visual inspection, listening to the heartbeat, and taking the patient's temperature, blood pressure, and so on to check for abnormalities. For the behavioral-based programmer, it is important to observe all areas of environment and human interaction to discover what works satisfactorily and where there are significant problems.

Observation and interviewing are at opposite ends of the spectrum in the way that information is obtained. With interviewing, the client or user is treated as a *subject.* Each person is considered as a potential source of information, knowing something that can be communicated to the interviewer. The interest is in the interviewee's values, feelings, beliefs, and attitudes as well as her or his perception of goals, facts, needs, and ideas related to the project being programmed. When being observed, the client or user is treated as an *object.* The interest is in his or her actual behavior. By careful observation the programmer can develop an understanding of how the activities of the client, user, or other building occupants are supported or inhibited by the architectural environment. Often the observer finds that what people say they do is not really true. Conversely, what one observes may not predict very well what the observed person is thinking or feeling.

Interviewing and observation are complementary. They serve to verify each other as reliability checks. Taken together they help the programmer diagnose the nature of a design problem. The interviewer is more effective in obtaining an understanding of a

Table 19.3
Typical Interview Analysis Summary Statement

Key Values and Goals

1. *Location.* Having lots of pedestrian traffic in area is essential.
2. *Visibility.* The store must be seen by passing pedestrians and vehicles.
3. *Image.* It must convey its purpose with signs, displays, materials, and colors.
4. *Inviting.* The entry must be convenient, ample, and protected.
5. *Display.* The merchandise must be displayed under the most favorable conditions.

person's strongly held beliefs, values, attitudes, ideas, and so forth. Observation is more effective in obtaining an understanding of the relationships of buildings to users, of buildings to their surroundings, and of patterns within the building itself. The point of both is diagnosis, to *understand* the nature of the architectural design problem (Deasy & Lasswell, 1985).

"An ounce of explanation," Ackoff (1967) has stated, "is worth a ton of description." It is possible to gather extensive amounts of description from either interviewing or observation, but to obtain understanding takes diagnostic skills. The objective of the behavioral-based program should not be to gather as much information as possible but to observe those things that have the potential to make important design differences and, thus, to obtain vital information.

There are several distinctly different types of observation, each of which should be included in behavioral-based programming. The extent of use of each will vary for any particular commission.

General Observation

As human beings and especially as architectural programmers, we are constantly involved in observing the world around us. This observation typically is simple and unstructured. We watch the world to understand it. The more we concentrate on the relationships of various things to the architectural environment, the more we build our intuition as to how architecture can best relate to and support the human activities to be accommodated. We also gain understanding of organizational and aesthetic principles and of which materials, systems, and forms respond best to external influences.

For example, it is easy to observe that the surface-mounted automobile bumpers are soon dislocated and present a very unsatisfactory appearance (see Figure 19.5). Similar, easily observed information could be obtained in many settings.

Walk-Through Observation

Observation and interviewing take place simultaneously in the building walk-through, an information gathering technique used frequently in architectural programming. If a client has come to the point of being unable to conduct operations satisfactorily in an existing facility, they seek out an architect to design an addition or new facility. The programmer

Figure 19.5   Dislocated parking bumpers.

for the architect first discusses the problem with the client in a diagnostic interviewing session, often in the client's office or conference room. But as various problems are discussed, the client invariably suggests that they go look at some of the problem areas. A walk-through observation has begun. They go together from place to place to observe and discuss the key issues and problems as the client sees them.

This approach to information gathering is very beneficial to the programmer in that it couples the objectivity of direct observation with the subjective viewpoint of the client as to the nature of each problem. It is an excellent way to begin preparation for more systematic observation. Visits to other projects of similar type and size to listen and observe how they work, perhaps in contrast to the client's facilities, can be useful (see Figure 19.6).

Space Inventory

After the initial walk-through, it is important to return to the same area to make an inventory of space, furnishings, and equipment. It is best to do this after a typical day but before janitors or maintenance personnel have come in to straighten things up. This will allow one to observe where objects are actually used. If available, take appropriately scaled plans and elevations of the area on which to sketch furnishings and equipment arrangements. If plans and elevations are not available, take a clipboard and paper to record this information. It is also important to take a tape measure to obtain sizes of objects and distances between the objects and the surrounding walls. Also take a camera to provide photo documentation. Polaroid or digital cameras are excellent for this purpose because you can determine if you obtained a satisfactory picture before leaving the space (see Table 19.4).

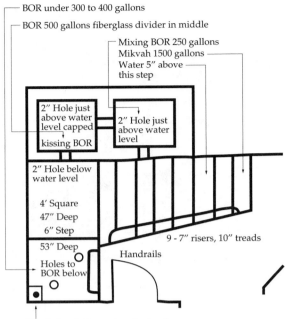

BOR under 300 to 400 gallons

BOR 500 gallons fiberglass divider in middle

Mixing BOR 250 gallons
Mikvah 1500 gallons
Water 5" above
this step

2" Hole just above water level capped

kissing BOR

2" Hole just above water level

2" Hole below water level

4' Square
47" Deep
6" Step

53" Deep

Holes to BOR below

9 - 7" risers, 10" treads

Handrails

Pipe below bottom of pool extends up behind boxing to drain Mikvah

Exhaust fan to room is set for humidity. Water at about 90° steams room up, so need to exhaust and to air condition. Set temperature of pool at 98°. If paint, must be very good epoxy to prevent peeling.

Fill and empty Mikvah with a timer, not a float, so must learn how long it takes and adjust. A reliable water level sensor would be better.

Two steps down before reach the water level of the Mikvah. There was no known reason why this was the case.

Grab bars must extend down into pool to prevent slipping. Sometimes another person assisting.

Figure 19.6   Walk-through observation/interview.

Trace Observation

Observation of physical traces is a very good and unobtrusive way of gathering information about how an existing facility has been used and abused, and it can often be accomplished as an adjunct to the space

Table 19.4
Space Inventory Categories

1. Dimensioned plan of space
2. Furnishings and equipment shown to scale on plan
3. Annotated elevations or perspective views (photographs or sketches)
4. Key to trace evidence of use and misuse of the space
5. Identification of key issues, good solutions, and problem areas

inventory effort. It involves observation of evidence left behind by users (Zeisel, 1980). Throughout the diagnostic observation process, the observer should not only be aware of the interactions of people and their environment in an overall or global sense but should also look carefully to see if clues about human-environment interaction have been left by previous users. Signs of rearrangement or remodeling can be important to diagnosis. What areas of the building have already been subjected to a number of changes? It may be likely that such areas will continue to be rearranged and modified, given their previous history. If chairs or tables are located in different places each time a room is visited, it may indicate that the room is used for more purposes than those indicated in an interview with the client. Signs in unusual places may indicate an inadequacy in the original design. For example, door signs such as "Do Not Open Quickly" or "Door Swings Out" or pavement markings may indicate a major problem in door location (see Figure 19.7).

Wear and tear on furnishings, floor surfaces, wall surfaces, and the like are good indicators of use, providing excellent clues as to where improvements could be made. Are there marks on the walls where the backs of chairs have rubbed against them? Perhaps a wainscot or a thicker base or base shoe is needed to keep the chair backs away from the wall, or perhaps another chair should be selected for the new building. Signs of pedestrian traffic, such as worn spots and smudge marks on carpets, can show where and how they have been used. Broken light fixtures, spray paint on walls, and the like may indicate areas of high vandalism where building security

Figure 19.7   Door swinging into a walkway.

Figure 19.8 Abrasion on masonry steps.

should not be underestimated. Freezing and thawing can cause abrasion on brick faces, especially at exposed edges and corners (see Figure 19.8).

There may also be examples of accretion rather than abrasion. This frequently happens on doors where inadequate space has been provided to post notices (see Figure 19.9). However, as in the case shown in Figure 19.10, if a conveniently located bulletin board is covered by a locked glass door, there are few people who will bother to get permission to have their notices posted there. They will simply post them on the door!

Unlike the more descriptive space inventory, the purpose of trace observation is to discover relationships

Figure 19.10 Notices in convenient location.

explaining how people behave in and use spaces. Just as the good physician does with a patient, it is necessary to look closely to make the correct diagnosis so that proper treatment or intervention can be prescribed. For example, heavy barricading and bolting of the required rear exit door of a gun shop is probably a good indicator that there are serious problems with burglary and theft that must be dealt with during design (see Figure 19.11).

Systematic Observation

As used in programming, systematic observation differs from other types of observation in several respects. First, it is planned or structured to obtain specific information about previously identified problems in the relationships between buildings and their human content, their physical surroundings, and elements of the buildings themselves. Second, it is structured to minimize bias and preconceptions by making certain that the observer takes into consideration all factors that may be influencing a particular environmental situation. It is an important supplement to the other forms of observation when some conflicting findings need to be resolved. It differs from the typical systematic observation of behavioral scientists only in that there is no need to generalize beyond the immediate environment to be designed. This does not reduce the need for rigor, because systematic observation should be used only in those cases where serious harm will come to someone if the wrong approach is taken.

Figure 19.9 Accumulation of notices.

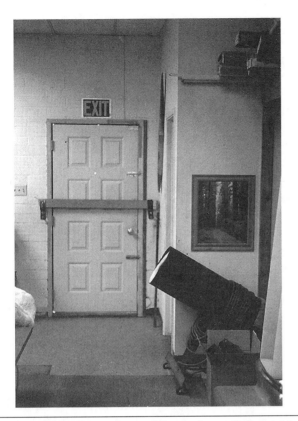

Figure 19.11 Rear door of gun shop. *Source:* Hine, 1987; School of Architecture, Arizona State University.

Systematic observation should be conducted to answer questions raised or to test specific hypotheses developed from the results of the other five forms of observation, the initial interviews, and the literature search and review activities. If the interviews conflict with the observations about how some space is used, it may be advisable to set up a specific study to discover the actual behavior in a space. For instance, if doctors and nurses have different perceptions of where they spend their time and on what kind of hospital activities, it may be possible to observe the doctors and nurses systematically over a period of time to confirm or refute the other findings. This would be important, of course, only if the results could make a design difference and impact some important human values. In the above example, this could involve the time it takes the doctor or nurse to get to a patient in a life-threatening situation. Survival comes into play. How far can the nursing station or the doctor's parking area be from a patient room and still maintain an acceptable margin of safety? Functional values could also be involved. How many times can nurses go between the nursing station and a distant patient's room in an 8-hour shift without exhaustion compromising their effectiveness?

Specific techniques and tools of systematic observation are discussed in Hershberger (1999) as well as in texts about behavioral science research (Bechtel et al., 1987; Ittelson, Rivlin, & Proshansky, 1970; Michelson, 1975) and numerous articles in the behavioral science literature (Collier, 1967; Cook & Miles, 1978; Davis & Ayers 1975; Whyte, 1988).

QUESTIONNAIRES AND SURVEYS

A questionnaire is an instrument that employs a predetermined set of questions to be answered by a respondent. A survey is the administration of such a questionnaire to a group of respondents. It can be administered by an interviewer who records the responses or given to the respondents to answer on their own (Berdie, Anderson, & Niebuhr, 1986; Blalock, 1972; Weisberg, Kronsnick, & Bowen, 1996).

The questionnaire survey is different from diagnostic interviewing because it relies on preestablished questions which each respondent is asked to answer. The questions typically are closed, that is, having a limited rather than an open-ended response format. The respondent is required to follow the line of questioning determined by the persons preparing the questionnaire.

Unlike observation, both interviews and questionnaires treat the respondent as a subject rather than as an object. They are also more intrusive than observation in that they require the respondent's full attention. The self-administered questionnaire is somewhat less intrusive than the interview in that the respondents can answer the questions at a time and place of their own choosing. However, the questionnaire requires respondents to accept the programmer's agenda rather than discussing areas of their own greatest personal interest. As a result, the diagnostic interview tends to be more effective in discovering issues of importance to the respondent, whereas questionnaires are usually more effective in obtaining factual information about specific facility and equipment needs.

The questionnaire can also be effective in determining if respondents share the viewpoints of those initially interviewed. Like the interview, and unlike observation, the questionnaire can be used to get at why people do what they do, what they think works well or poorly, and how they think something might be done better—but only within the limits of the alternatives actually provided in the questions. Just how effective the questionnaire is in this respect depends on the proficiency of the programmer in preparing, administering, and analyzing the results of the questionnaire.

A questionnaire should not be used in architectural programming until after literature review, diagnostic interviewing, and diagnostic observation have been completed. Even then, it should be used only if it would be more expensive to obtain additional information by continuing with the other information-gathering techniques. For most small- to medium-sized programming commissions, this is rarely the case. It is usually quicker and less expensive simply to reinterview someone for additional information or to count or measure something to obtain the missing data.

The time and effort to prepare, administer, and analyze a questionnaire intended to obtain information about respondent values, goals, needs, and ideas is warranted only when programming facilities for very large or complex organizations. On those occasions, it is advisable to employ a survey specialist to assist in developing and administering the questionnaire to ensure its reliability and validity. It is, however, useful if the programmer is able to develop and administer short questionnaires focusing on specific facility, furnishings, and equipment needs for mid-size projects.

While casual (unplanned) observation and interviewing are both effective ways of obtaining useful information about issues of importance to various user groups, there is no such usefulness to "casual" questionnaires. The effective use of questionnaires requires more preparation than any form of interviewing and most forms of observation. The programmer must first establish what information is needed and then use the questionnaire only if the information cannot be more easily obtained by searching the literature or through interviewing and/or observation. Having established that a questionnaire will be required, the programmer must determine the specific questions that should be asked to obtain the needed information. It must also be established who will receive the questionnaires and whether the selected respondents can provide reliable and valid answers. It should also be determined if there are enough funds and time available to administer and analyze the questionnaire.

The medical analogy might once again be used, even though it breaks down in several respects. Most physicians use a medical history form, a questionnaire that they use to ask each patient (or parent) to complete before interviewing or observing the patient. Such questionnaires ask about basic demographics: name, address, occupation, age, sex, and the like. They also ask about previous illnesses (even in the patient's family), whether related persons are still alive, current medications, allergic reactions to drugs, and so on. The reader might wonder why such a standard questionnaire is not appropriate in architectural programming. The answer is that most people are very much alike in terms of their basic anatomy, physiology, and types of medical problems. Most buildings are not! Each building type has fundamental differences in organization and structure as well as specific space needs. The doctor is trying to diagnose problems within a group of similar entities. The architectural programmer is trying to diagnose the nature of the entity itself, an entity which as yet does not exist (albeit an entity whose complexity is nowhere near the human body's).

There are, however, instances in which the medical analogy is appropriate regarding the use of questionnaires in programming. If a programmer has done numerous programs for a particular type of facility (offices, hospitals, schools), there are likely to be recurring questions. Questionnaires developed to provide such information on previous projects might be adapted for use on each new project. Such repetition has the advantage of developing standards of comparison and eventually, perhaps, of developing some general knowledge about the nature of a particular institution, user group, or activity area.

The process of preparing a good questionnaire is involved and time-consuming (see Table 19.5). Here again, an extensive discussion of questionnaire preparation, administration, and analysis for behavioral-based architectural programming is contained in Hershberger (1999).

WORK SESSIONS

The final method for gathering and analyzing information for behavioral-based architectural programming is the work session. This is a type of show-and-tell activity in which the programmer presents previously gathered information to the client/user group on a large wall-sized matrix or similar presentation method with the intention of defining the whole problem when completed. The client/users are asked to confirm or refute what is presented, generate new information, and reorganize the information to improve the matrix. It is an

Table 19.5
Ten Steps to Prepare a Questionnaire

1. List the goals and objectives of utilizing a questionnaire.
2. Determine who should be answering the questions: client, users, others.
3. Prepare a schedule for the types of questions to be asked.
4. Develop specific questions for each part of the questionnaire.
5. Analyze the questions to see if any can be combined or eliminated.
6. Answer the questions as if you were in each respondent group.
7. Revise the questions to make them clearer.
8. Attempt to tabulate the answers and summarize the results.
9. Revise the questions to make tabulation possible.
10. Pretest the questionnaire with your peers and members of the respondent group(s).

effective method for filling in gaps after using the other information-gathering methods. It is also effective in getting the client/users to make decisions regarding which of the previously suggested values, goals, facts, needs, and ideas should be retained in the architectural program.

Work sessions are the heart of any client/user group programming process where client/user agreement with the program is considered essential. The sessions are both the final step of information gathering and the first step of program preparation.

The work session is similar to diagnostic interviewing as an information-gathering process. It is similar in that the programmer is attempting to get the clients/users as a group to articulate what they think is important information. The same active listening skills utilized in the diagnostic interviewing process are helpful in getting the clients and users to identify their areas of concern. It is different from the diagnostic interviewing sessions in that the programmer will typically be presenting information obtained from the other information-gathering methods with the intent of securing agreement from the client/user decision makers as to its accuracy and importance.

Value areas as well as goals, facts, needs, and ideas that were identified in the literature search, interviewing, observation, and questionnaire-survey phases of information gathering need to be presented

and discussed. Do the decision makers agree that the preliminary list of values is complete? If an order of importance was identified earlier, do the decision makers agree with the order? Are the project goals appropriate? Are the decision makers willing to spend money to accomplish them? Which goals *must* be accomplished? Which could remain unaccomplished without seriously reducing the effectiveness of the organization? Are the previously identified goals, facts, or needs statements really important or just someone's pet project that the organization as a whole is unwilling to support?

In other words, the work session is a time for both active presentation and listening by the programmer and the client/user decision makers. If the first four areas of information gathering could be considered as primarily objective in their intent, designed simply to obtain the data, this phase could be considered as primarily subjective. It is a time for group decision making, a time for sorting out what is important from what is not. It is, as Peña (1969) said, a "problem seeking" situation, a time to resolve and agree on the design problem. Presentation, brainstorming, dialogue, and negotiation of agreement are the essential methods.

The effectiveness of work sessions is at least partially due to the presentation of everything that has been discovered in a clearly organized format such that the whole problem can be seen and understood by those present. It is also essential that the method of presentation be flexible to allow for change and augmentation by the work session participants.

PROSPECTS

The prospects for behavioral-based architectural programming are mixed. On one hand, some sophisticated clients like the General Services Administration (GSA), United States Postal Service (USPS), and a variety of universities, hospitals, and other major institutions have seen the value of behavioral-based architectural programs and are hiring consultants or developing in-house staff capable of producing them. A number of social/behavioral scientists and architects (who have done advanced study in the social sciences) are using behavioral research methods as an active component of their programming practices. Other architects offering programming services are at least searching the literature and interviewing or conducting work sessions with their clients to develop program information.

Less sophisticated and more profit-motivated clients often find behavioral-based programs to be too costly. They also believe that effective programming increases the costs of the resulting buildings. Worse, many architecture schools have been minimizing or even eliminating requirements in architectural programming, as if design can somehow stand alone, independent of the social and behavioral aspirations of the people for whom the designs are intended. It is no wonder that architects in general have developed a reputation for ignoring the legitimate values, goals, and needs of the users of their buildings. There also appears to be less current emphasis on human-environment concerns in schools of psychology, sociology, and anthropology than during what appears to have been the high-water mark of these concerns between 1960 and 1985.

One encouraging sign is the publication of several new texts on architectural programming (Cherry, 1999; Duerk, 1993; Hershberger, 1999; Kumlin, 1995). But only two of these texts advocate or provide instruction on effective behavioral-based methods of architectural programming. Hershberger has contributed a section on architectural programming for the *AIA Handbook of Professional Practice* (2001) that may have a positive impact on the profession. He also offers seminars and workshops at the American Institute of Architects National Convention on methods of interviewing, observation, and work session leadership that hopefully will increase the ability of membership in the AIA to do effective behavioral-based architectural programming.

REFERENCES

Ackoff, R. L. (1967). *Operations research lecture.* Philadelphia: University of Pennsylvania.

Altman, I. (1975). *The environment and social behavior: Privacy, personal space, territory, crowding.* Monterey, CA: Brooks/Cole.

Bechtel, R., Marans, R., & Michelson, W. (Eds.). (1987). *Methods in environmental and behavioral research.* New York: Van Nostrand Reinhold.

Berdie, D. R., Anderson, J. F., & Niebuhr, M. A. (1986). *Questionnaires: Design and use.* Metuchen, NJ: Scarecrow Press.

Blalock, H. M., Jr. (1972). *Social statistics.* New York: McGraw-Hill.

Brill, M., Margulis, S. T., Konar, E., & Buffalo Organization for Social & Technological Innovation. (1984). *Using office design to increase productivity.* Buffalo, NY: Workplace Design and Productivity.

Cherry, E. (1999). *Programming for design.* New York: Wiley.

Collier, J. J. (1967). *Visual anthropology: Photography as a research method.* New York: Holt, Rinehart and Winston.

Conway, D., (Ed.). (1973, October). *Social science and design: A process model for architect and social scientist collaboration and report of a conference.* Coolfront Conference Center, Berkeley Springs, WV.

Cook, R., & Miles, D. (1978). *Plazas for people: Seattle Federal Building Plaza: A case study.* New York: Projects for Public Spaces.

Davis, G. (1969). The independent building program consultant. *Building Research, 18*(2), 16–21.

Davis, G., & Ayers, V. (1975). Photographic recording of environment and behavior. In W. Michelson (Ed.), *Behavioral research methods in environmental design.* Stroudsburg, PA: Dowden, Hutchinson & Ross.

Deasy, C. M., & Lasswell, T. (1985). *Designing places for people.* New York: Whitney Library of Design.

Duerk, D. P. (1993). *Architectural programming: Information management for design.* New York: Van Nostrand Reinhold.

Farbstein, J. D. (1976). Assumptions in environmental programming. In P. Suedfeld & J. Russell (Ed.), *The behavioral basis of design: Proceedings of the Seventh International Conference of the Environmental Design Research Association, Vancouver, British Columbia, Canada* (Vol. 1, pp. 21–26). Stroudsburg, PA: Dowden, Hutchinson & Ross.

Hall, E. (1966). *The Hiddeno dimension.* Garden City, NY: Doubleday.

Hershberger, R. (1969). *A study of meaning and architecture.* Unpublished doctoral dissertation, University of Pennsylvania, Philadelphia.

Hershberger, R. (1985). Values: A theoretical foundation for architectural programming. In W. F. E. Preiser (Ed.), *Programming the built environment* (pp. 7–12). New York: Van Nostrand Reinhold.

Hershberger, R. (1999). *Architectural programming and predesign manager.* New York: McGraw-Hill.

Hershberger, R. (2001). *AIA handbook of professional practice.* Manuscript in preparation.

Hine, E. (1987). *Program for a gun shop.* Tempe, AZ: Unpublished work, Arizona State University, School of Architecture.

Horowitz, H. (1966). The architect's programme and the behavioural sciences. *Architectural Science Review, 9*(3), 71–79.

Ittelson, W. H., Rivlin, L. G., & Proshansky, H. M. (1970). The use of behavioral maps in environmental psychology. In H. M. Proshansky, W. H. Ittelson, & L. G. Rivlin (Eds.), *Environmental psychology: Man and his physical setting* (pp. 658–668). New York: Holt, Rinehart and Winston.

Kumlin, R. R. (1995). *Architectural programming: Creative techniques for design professionals.* New York: McGraw-Hill.

Lawton, P., Windley, P., & Byerts, T. (Eds.). (1982). *Aging and the environment: Theoretical approaches.* New York: Springer.

Marans, R., & Spreckelmeyer, K. (1982). *Evaluating built environments: A behavioral approach.* Ann Arbor: University of Michigan, Survey Research Center.

Marcus, C. C. (1975). *Easter Hill Village: Some social indications of design.* New York: Free Press.

Michelson, W. (Ed.). (1975). *Behavioral research methods in environmental design.* Stroudsburg, PA: Dowden, Hutchinson & Ross.

Moleski, W. (1974). Behavioral analysis in environmental programming for offices. In J. Lang, C. Burnette, W. Moleski, & S. Vachon (Eds.), *Designing for human behavior: Architecture and the behavioral sciences* (pp. 302–315). Stroudsburg, PA: Dowden, Hutchinson & Ross.

Moore, G., & Golledge, R. (Eds.). (1976). *Environmental knowing: Theories, research and methods.* Stroudsburg, PA: Dowden, Hutchinson & Ross.

Peña, W., & Focke, J. W. (1969). *Problem seeking: New directions in architectural programming.* Houston, TX: Caudill Rowlett Scott.

Preiser, W. F. E. (Ed.). (1978). *Facility programming.* Stroudsburg, PA: Dowden, Hutchinson & Ross.

Preiser, W. F. E. (1985). *Programming the built environment.* New York: Van Nostrand Reinhold.

Preiser, W. F. E. (1993). *Professional practice in facility programming.* New York: Van Nostrand Reinhold.

Sanoff, H. (1977). *Methods of architectural programming.* Stroudsburg, PA: Dowden, Hutchinson & Ross.

Sanoff, H. (1992). *Integrating programming, evaluation and participation in design: A Theory Z approach.* Brookfield, VT: Avebury.

Sommer, R. (1969). *Personal space: The behavioral basis of design.* Englewood Cliffs, NJ: Prentice-Hall.

Sommer, R. (1974). *Tight spaces: Hard architecture and how to humanize it.* Englewood Cliffs, NJ: Prentice-Hall.

Weisberg, H. F., Kronsnick, J. A., & Bowen, B. D. (1996). *Introduction to survey research and data analysis.* Thousand Oaks, CA: Sage.

Whyte, W. H. (1988). *The social life of small urban spaces* [Video recording]. Los Angeles: Direct Cinema Limited.

Zeisel, J. (1980). *Inquiry by design: Tools for environment-behavior research.* Monterey, CA: Brooks/Cole.

CHAPTER 20

Postoccupancy Evaluation: Issues and Implementation

CRAIG ZIMRING

THE UNITED STATES IS CONDUCTING the largest federal construction program since the Second World War, constructing some 160 new courthouses at the cost of $10 billion. After each project is completed, a postoccupancy evaluation team administers surveys, conducts interviews and observes activity in the building. These POEs are used to refine the *U.S. Courts Design Guide,* the document that has become the key document for judges, architects, project managers, and consultants in planning new courthouses (Administrative Office of the U.S. Courts, 1997).

Disney evaluates everything, all the time. The company assesses the experience of customers as they use the parks and other attractions, monitors the relationships between key design decisions and performance—such as how wide Main Street needs to be to feel comfortably busy during normal attendance levels—and records the performance of thousands of materials and products. The result is that the industrial engineering team can rapidly turn design goals into physical parameters. As a result, they have become key partners with the Imagineering group in planning and designing new properties (Weis, personal communication, March, 1999).

A group of UK architectural researchers and building scientists have teamed up with the *Building Services Journal* to conduct four evaluations annually of innovative sustainable office buildings. The buildings are published in the magazine when they are first opened and then evaluated three years later. Each evaluation involves questionnaires with users and technical assessment of energy use and building performance. The researchers have developed a growing set of benchmarks and the performance of individual buildings are reported with respect to the results for a large sample of similar buildings (Cohen, Standeven, Bordass, & Leaman, 2001a).

Postoccupancy evaluation (POE) grew out of the extraordinary confluence of interests among social scientists, designers, and planners in the 1960s and 1970s (see for example, Friedman, Zimring, & Zube, 1978; Preiser, Rabinowitz, & White, 1988; Shibley, 1982). Robert Bechtel has estimated that over 50,000 POEs have been completed; a recent Web search on *Google* turned up over 2,700 sites that mention "postoccupancy evaluation" by name. Whereas many POEs are conducted as academic studies, numerous large public agencies have developed POE programs, such as the U.S. General Services Administration, Administrative Office of the U.S. Courts, U.S. Department of State, U.S. Department of Commerce, U.S. Postal Service, Public Works Canada, California Department of Corrections, State of Minnesota, the government of New Zealand, and many

I would like to thank Bill Bordass, Arza Churchman, Joanne Green, Martin Symes, and Richard Wener for their thoughtful comments. Some of this material was presented in a different form to the Federal Facilities Council *Symposium on Building Performance Assessments: Current and Evolving Practices for Post Occupancy Evaluation Programs,* Washington, DC, March 2001.

others. The California Department of General Services is starting a large POE program and the European Community is initiating an effort called IANUS, linking building evaluation to the provision of public services and focusing on the specification of indicators that show the diversity of interests and perspectives related to different actors in policy-related built-environment evaluation (Symes & Robbins, 2001). The U.S. National Research Council's Federal Facilities Council recently conducted a symposium on POE in the federal sector (Stanley & Little, 2001). And, although they do not always call them "postoccupancy evaluations," many private clients have initiated programs where they systematically assess building performance.

POEs are conducted by a wide range of practitioners for many different purposes, and there is no common definition. I propose the following definition of POE, based on Weiss' (1997) definition of *program* evaluation. However, for this chapter I will adapt for POE the definition that Weiss proposed for program evaluation more generally (Weiss, 1997):

> *Post-occupancy evaluation* is the *systematic* assessment of the *process* of delivering buildings or other designed settings or of the *performance* of those settings as they are actually used, or both, as compared to a set of *implicit or explicit standards,* with the intention of *improving* the process or settings.

There are five key aspects of this definition:

1. By *systematic* I mean that the POE follows an explicit, accepted methodology developed for POE or derived from social science, building science, architecture, planning, or another discipline. This can be quantitative or qualitative.
2. Although POEs have often evaluated buildings, they may also evaluate the details of the *process* of building delivery, including planning, programming, design, value engineering, construction, facilities management, and reuse.
3. POEs assess buildings while they are actually in use and, hence, evaluators can assess performance. POE complements other practices such as programming, building modeling, preoccupancy evaluation, and others.
4. Performance standards are not always explicit. They might be implicit and embedded in the methodology used in the evaluation, but they are taken to be objective, or at least *intrasubjective* in the sense that they are shared. Most evaluators view performance as multidimensional, reflecting the needs or perspectives of a range of stakeholders, such as the organization that occupies the building and the individuals who use or are affected by the building. (The relationship among different performance standards is often a key aspect of POEs, such as understanding and reconciling first cost with life cycle cost, or first cost with user satisfaction.)
5. I am reserving the term *postoccupancy evaluation* for applied studies. Although POE projects might well yield conceptual understanding and some researchers label their theoretically driven field studies "POE," this blurs the focus of POE, which is ultimately aimed at improving the built environment. (However, I do argue that POE needs to be based on theories of building function and theories of organizational learning and change. This is explored further in the Discussion section.)

This chapter focuses on the last issue: how POE has contributed to improved buildings and building delivery processes. I focus on the distinction between two different kinds of applications of POEs: evaluations that are aimed at supporting a specific project (usually the project being evaluated, though sometimes another project) versus evaluations that are aimed at informing future projects (Zimring & Reizenstein, 1981). I emphasize this latter "feedforward" role of POE, which has not received as much discussion as the project support role (Horgen, Joroff, Porter, & Schon, 1996; Schneekloth & Shibley, 1995).

I pay particular attention to the potential difficulties faced by large building delivery organizations when using POE for organizational learning. Because the building industry is extremely fragmented among many small clients, design firms, consultants, and contractors, the relatively few large public and private organizations can have a disproportionately significant impact on the quality of buildings.

BACKGROUND

The following section provides a brief introduction to POE. More detailed discussions can be found elsewhere, such as Friedman et al. (1978); Grannis (1994); Horgen et al. (1996); Kincaid (1994); Parshall and Peña (1983); Preiser, Rabinowitz, and White (1988); Preiser and Schramm (1997); and Shibley, (1982).

HISTORY, TERMS, GOALS, AND METHODS

POE initially developed quickly as a result of the growth of environment and behavior research—pursued by social scientists, designers, and planners who were interested in understanding the experience of building users and in representing the "nonpaying" client (Zeisel, 1975). Early POEs were primarily conducted by academicians focusing on the settings that were accessible to them, such as housing, college dorms, and residential institutions (Preiser, 1994). During the 1980s, many large public agencies established more structured processes to organize information and decisions in their building delivery processes. As practices such as facilities programming became regularized and were accepted as routine, agencies such as Public Works Canada and the U.S. Postal Service added building evaluation as a further step in gathering and managing information (Kantrowitz & Farbstein, 1996).

This development of POE occurred while program evaluation was also rapidly growing. Campbell and many others had been arguing at least since the 1960s that public programs could be treated as social experiments and that rational, technical means could contribute to, or even replace, messier political decision making (Campbell, 1999). A similar argument was applied to POE, where statements of expected performance embedded in architectural programs could be viewed as hypotheses that POE could test (Preiser et al., 1988).

TERMINOLOGY

The term *postoccupancy evaluation* was intended to reflect that assessment takes place after the client has taken occupancy of a building. This was in direct contrast to some design competitions where completed buildings were disqualified from consideration and to other kinds of assessment such as "value engineering" that reviewed plans before construction. Over the years many theorists and practitioners have grown uncomfortable with the term *POE*. The literal meaning of the term seems to suggest that it occurs after people leave the building, and it seems to emphasize evaluation done at a single point in the process. Friedman et al. (1978) proposed the term *environmental design evaluation*. Other researchers and practitioners have suggested terms such as *environmental audits* or *building-in-use assessment* (Vischer,

1996). More recently, *building evaluation* and *building performance evaluation* have been proposed (Baird, Gray, Isaacs, Kernohan, & McIndoe, 1996). Despite the diversity of the practice, the term *postoccupancy evaluation* remains common for historical reasons, and I use it in this chapter for clarity.

THE SCOPE OF POE

Some researchers have argued that POE is only one component of an information- and negotiation-based approach to design decision making. For example, Bechtel has emphasized the importance of "preoccupancy evaluation" (Bechtel, personal communication, March 2000). Other authors have suggested that POE cannot be meaningfully discussed as a stand-alone practice but rather needs to be considered as one aspect of approaches that include "placemaking" (Schneekloth & Shibley, 1995) and "process architecture" (Horgen, Joroff, Porter, & Schon, 1999). (These are discussed later in the chapter.)

There have been several successful examples where POE has been incorporated into a broader program of user-based programming, discussion, and design guide development (Shibley, 1982). For example, the U.S. Army Corps of Engineers initiated an ambitious program of programming and evaluation that resulted in some 19 design guides for facilities ranging from drama and music centers to barracks and military police stations (Schneekloth & Shibley, 1995; Shibley, 1982, 1985). More recently, POE has been seen as part of a spectrum of practices aimed at understanding design criteria, predicting the effectiveness of emerging designs, reviewing completed designs, and supporting building activation and facilities management (Preiser & Schramm, 1997).

POE METHODS

As POE methods have become more sophisticated, at least two directions have emerged: (1) methods have become more diverse, and (2) standard methods packages have been developed.

GREATER DIVERSITY OF METHODS

With a few notable exceptions, many early POEs primarily focused on assessing user satisfaction, user assessment of building comfort and functionality, and user behavior using self-report methods such as questionnaires and interviews and direct observation of user behavior. More recent POEs now also assess the technical performance of building systems, cost, and other factors (Bordass & Leaman, 1996; Cohen, Standeven, Bordass & Leaman, 2001a, 2001b; Leaman, Cohen, & Jackman, 1995; Raw, Roys, & Leaman, 1990). Recently, Judith Heerwagen has suggested that POEs should employ a "balanced scorecard" approach that considers issues such as financial performance, impact of the building on the business process, growth and satisfaction of employees, and impact on other stakeholders (Heerwagen, 2001). The balanced scorecard approach is discussed in more depth later in this chapter.

DEVELOPING STANDARDIZED METHODS

Whereas most POEs assess the comfort and satisfaction of everyday building users, as POE methods have developed, more-standardized and -specialized evaluation approaches have been developed for specific building types such as schools (Ornstein, 1997), health care facilities (Carpman & Grant, 1993), environments for young children (Moore, personal communication, July 2000), retail settings (Foxall & Hackett, 1994; Underhill, 1999), housing (Anderson & Weidemann, 1997), and jails and prisons (Wener, Farbstein, & Knapel, 1993; Zimring, Munyon, & Ard, 1988). Not surprisingly, evaluation of the white-collar work environment has been one of the most active areas for evaluation (Brill, Margulis, Konar, Buffalo Organization for Social and Technological Innovation, & Westinghouse Furniture Systems, 1984; Cooper, 1992; Duffy, 1998; Francis, 1986; Ornstein, 1999; Raw et al., 1990; Spreckelmeyer, 1993; Stokols, 1988; Wineman, 1986). For example, Vischer created a standardized building-in-use survey that assesses self-reported satisfaction, comfort, and productivity (Vischer, 1996).

Some researchers have also developed standardized methods for assessing technical performance of buildings such as thermal and energy performance. The "Post-occupancy Review of Buildings and their Engineering" (PROBE) studies described above employ standard questionnaire and technical assessment techniques (Bordass, Bromley, & Leaman, 1995; Cohen et al., 2001a; Leaman et al., 1995). The PROBE team has conducted some 18 evaluations of buildings that were published in the *Building Services Journal* as representing technically innovative buildings. Approximately three years after commissioning, the team returns to the buildings and administers a standard building-in-use user questionnaire and monitors the performance of the heating, ventilating, and air-conditioning system, records energy use, and conducts pressure tests and other measures. The evaluation criteria are part of the standard methods package and allow the team to make links between building design and outcomes. The PROBE team has identified several variables that are good predictors of satisfaction and self-reported productivity. For instance, they have found that issues such as floor plans that offer more access to windows and higher levels of personal control over lighting, heating, and noise are strong predictors of self-reported satisfaction. Other standardized evaluation methods focus on more specific aspects of technical performance, such as the revised office environment survey (ROES) questionnaire, which assesses occupants' response to indoor air quality (Raw, 1995, 2000). The ROES survey focuses on occupants' reports of health, comfort, and productivity. The scale has been used many times and has established norms.

POE MODELS

POE methodologists have proposed several methodological and conceptual models of POE. For example, several authors have emphasized the importance of articulating different levels of POEs with different amounts of activity and resource requirements (Friedman et al., 1978; Preiser et al., 1988). In his influential book, Preiser advocated three levels of POEs: brief indicative studies, more-detailed investigative POEs, and diagnostic studies aimed at correlating environmental measures with subjective user responses (Preiser et al., 1988).

Although there have not been many theories of POE, many authors have used broader conceptual frameworks to organize their work. Some years ago, Friedman et al. (1978) suggested that POEs adopt an open systems framework that identifies a "focal problem" and "larger system" based on considering relationships among five elements of building delivery processes: building, users, design process, proximate-environmental context, and social-historical context. Preiser suggested that POE evaluation criteria be based on a habitability framework and has recently expanded this to include a focus on building performance evaluation and universal design (Preiser, 1994; Preiser & Schramm, 1997). As was mentioned earlier, Heerwagen has recently proposed that Kaplan and Norton's balanced scorecard approach (Kaplan & Norton, 1996) can be used in POE (Heerwagen, 2001). The balanced scorecard approach is a multistep process where organizational vision and strategy are translated into goals and objectives with quantifiable targets. The balanced scorecard is "balanced" in that it includes both financial and nonfinancial outcomes and focuses on both routine processes and "breakthrough" performance. Heerwagen has suggested that a balanced POE scorecard can focus on several outcomes: financial, business process, internal staff and professional development, and external stakeholders.

Recently, several authors have criticized approaches to building delivery and evaluation that emphasize standardization and accumulation of information. Rather, they argue that each decision-making process must be socially constructed by the participants. For example, Schneekloth and Shibley (1995) have proposed a dialogic "placemaking" process where a highly interactive process of building design and evaluation can help transform organizations and groups. They argue that programming, design, and evaluation can help organizations develop and change but only if consultants genuinely understand the values and perspectives of stakeholders rather than approaching projects with a preexisting model of correct solutions or approaches. For example, Schneekloth and Shibley have conducted many projects for the same large bank. Each of these has been different because the different participants in each project bring their own needs, values, and power relationships.

Horgen and her colleagues adopt a somewhat similar framework in their discussion of "process architecture" (Horgen et al., 1999). They criticize the prevailing "technical rational" approach to architecture and design and emphasize that the design process can be like a game where the role of consultants and evaluation is to help players clarify the impact of different moves for different players.

In sum, whereas many researchers are advancing the field by proposing specialized or standard methods that focus on a specific building type, others are suggesting that POE is most effective in a discursive framework that is different for each project.

SUMMARY

POE has become more diverse as it has developed. POEs now include a wider range of practices and have become embroiled in the larger debates about the development of knowledge and methods in the social sciences and humanities. However, as was discussed earlier, POE is by definition an applied practice, and it is not clear that it has always had the salutary impacts that were intended. Several large organizations have suspended their POE programs and many design practitioners discount their value. The following sections focus on the impacts POE has had on and particularly the roles that POE has had in individual and organizational learning.

LEARNING FROM POE

POE can both benefit a specific project and contribute to a more general knowledge base of lessons learned (Preiser et al., 1988; Shibley, 1982; Zimring, 1981). The next sections discuss these potential impacts in greater detail.

PROJECT-BASED LEARNING

POE can help clarify important decisions about the project that is being evaluated or can contribute to the programming or design for a subsequent project. At least five kinds of project-based decisions have emerged as important in POE: (1) fine-tuning, (2) diagnosing how to aid a troubled or problematic setting, (3) deciding whether to expand the scope of an innovative design or technology, (4) deciding how to address a key "strategic" programmatic decision, (5) maintaining quality such as by incentives for performance.

Fine-Tuning

The immediate experience of a new building can have a significant impact on the subsequent satisfaction of users and their organization. Small irritants can have a large and lasting influence. POE has recently been used as a way of understanding the move-in process and helping reduce problems and misfits. For example, project managers in Santa Clara County (CA) were tired of getting a storm of requests from building users when they initially moved in. In some cases, a few weeks' use of the building clarified how people would use their spaces, and they asked for additional small items such as extra shelves or bulletin boards. In other cases, there were problems with construction or the organization changed over the course of design and construction, and the space needed to be reconfigured to fit different patterns of use.

These requests came on an ad hoc basis and were difficult to direct to contractors, suppliers, and others. Santa Clara County contracted with consultants Cheryl Fuller and Craig Zimring to create a "quick response survey" (QRS) aimed at organizing and prioritizing user needs about three months after buildings were occupied. All building users fill out a one-page questionnaire, and project managers follow up with a half-day walk-through interview of the building with the facility manager and staff representatives. The project managers would then prioritize requests and meet with the client organizations. The State of California Department of General Services is further developing the QRS and will have evaluators enter results into a lessons-learned database.

POE as Diagnosis

Occasionally a building is the subject of complaints or controversy; a POE can help to diagnose the source of problems and prioritize solutions. For example, the new San Francisco central library was an architectural landmark when it opened in 1996 but aroused controversy. The project had been controversial since its inception—books were displaced to make room for computers, a hotly debated decision in the library community—but there were complaints by the public that it was hard to find books and other services and by staff that it was difficult to manage materials. As a result, the mayor appointed an audit commission that recommended a POE, led by architect Cynthia Ripley and accompanied by a blue-ribbon evaluation team including the director of the Los Angeles library system. After conducting focus groups with staff and users, observing the use of the facility, and analyzing records, the POE team found a number of serious problems. The configuration of the spaces made operations difficult. Related books were scattered among several buildings and much staff time was spent finding and retrieving them and some were damaged in transit. Poor signage and a confusing layout made it hard for users to find their way. The report commended the architecture but recommended a targeted $30 million multiphase renovation project to reorganize the book stacks and interiors (Flagg, 1999; Ripley Architects, 2000).

In another example, the architecture firm Hugh Stubbins and Associates was receiving complaints about a recently completed office building that they had designed. The offices were stuffy and hot. They conducted a POE and discovered that the ductwork had never been connected by the heating contractors, and they were able to resolve the problems to the client's satisfaction (Zimring & Welch, 1988).

In Ottawa a group of white-collar workers walked out of a large government office building, complaining that the building was "sick." Public Works Canada commissioned a very in-depth evaluation, including detailed interviews, questionnaires, and monitoring of air quality and lighting. The study showed that the workers' complaints were justified—the air quality was poor in some locations because of interior partitions that were added after the ventilating system was designed—but that many complaints were also due to other environmental qualities such as confusing layouts as well as building management and organizational factors (Vischer, 1996).

Using POE to Test Innovation

Evaluation can help decide whether innovative buildings or building components should be considered for broader application. For example, the State of Minnesota Department of Natural Resources (DNR) has recently changed the way in which it manages the environment. Rather than organizing their staff by discipline, they now use a matrix management system where decisions are made by a multidisciplinary group organized by ecosystem. The DNR is creating new regional centers that include wildlife biologists, air and water specialists, and others concerned with a given area. The centers are intended to encourage multidisciplinary collaboration and to be sustainable, with low energy use and low environmental impact. The DNR contracted with a university team led by Julia Robinson to evaluate two of the initial projects. Though the centers were generally successful, the team made numerous recommendations for retrofitting and for subsequent designs. When the budget request was made for the third center, the POE report was included as an appendix, resulting in full funding of a new project for the first time in DNR's history. DNR was told that the POE was a major reason: It showed a high level of understanding of the project. Though apparently successful, this project showed some of the tensions between POEs conducted by external consultants and by internal staff. An external evaluation can bring specialized POE skills and greater objectivity, but the results can sometimes be viewed as not addressing the needs of internal staff. In this project there was some concern by the internal staff about the sustainability recommendations. An additional team was hired to create design guidelines in close consultation with staff (Wallace, 2000).

Using POE to Support Strategic Decisions

Some design decisions are strategic in the sense that they influence many later decisions within a project. These are important targets of POE. For example, the California Department of Corrections (CDC) was considering adopting the practice of having two prison housing units share a common dining room and kitchen. This concept could save many millions of dollars statewide but might lead to greater difficulty in moving and controlling inmates. The CDC and the firm that was hired to manage the prison construction program, Kitchell CEM, performed a POE of a first example of the shared dining facility, interviewing staff and observing operations. The evaluation revealed that this shared arrangement worked well, and it was repeated several times in California (Fuller, 1988).

Whereas this POE, as with most others, focuses on how well strategic decisions achieve an accepted set of goals—what Argyris and Schon (1978) have called "single-loop learning,"—POE can also be used to examine the goals themselves, what has been termed "double-loop learning" (Argyris & Schon, 1978). For example, Zimring, Munyon, and Ard (1988) evaluated an innovative jail in Martinez, California, where inmate and guards spent all of their time in small housing units that included dining and exercise areas. In this case, the "strategic decision" was to decentralize services and bring food, visitors, and education to inmates rather than moving the inmates. The study included single-loop learning—how well the facility supported existing goals of high control and low maintenance—as well as considering how a less stressful facility can help shift the goals of incarceration toward rehabilitation rather than simply supporting custody or punishment.

Maintaining Quality

POE is sometimes used to maintain quality control. For example, the drug company Ciba-Geigy contracted with the architecture-engineering firm HLW and the contractor Sordoni Skansa Construction to put their design and construction profits ($300,000 and $1.2 million) at risk for the new $39 million Martin Dexter Laboratory in Tarrytown, NY. The profits were based equally on three issues: (1) the ability of the firms to deliver the building as scheduled, (2) their ability to deliver the building within the original budget, and (3) postoccupancy evaluation. The POE was based on responses to 14 survey questions concerning the following issues: HVAC, acoustics, odor control, vibration, lighting, fume hood performance, quality of construction (finishes), building appearance, and user-friendliness. The questions were binary choice (acceptable/not acceptable), and the building had to reach 70% satisfaction to pass the test. Some aspects such as sound transmission were also assessed using physical measures; if the user satisfaction measures didn't reach criterion, physical measures could be substituted (Gregerson, 1997). The designers and contractors consulted the scientists throughout the process, showing them alternatives of the facade design and full-scale mockups of the range hoods. The building passed on all criteria except satisfaction with the range hoods, which were modified after the evaluation as a response to user input. Sordoni Skansa has since used POE in several other projects.

Decision-focused evaluation as part of a design project can be performed in an attempt to rationalize decision making by shifting the criteria for decisions from politics to data: Which decision is likely to have the best outcome? However, as the Ciba-Geigy example illustrates, an equally important role of POE can be to set up a framework for discussion and negotiation that leads to greater clarity about goals and consensual strategies for building design.

POE AS ORGANIZATIONAL LEARNING

POE provides the opportunity for organizational learning about buildings. By *organizational learning,* I mean that organizations are able to constantly improve routine activities, such as more efficiently providing higher-quality standard office space for a white-collar work organization, and to respond to change quickly and effectively when needed (Argyris, 1992a). Learning is organizational if it concerns the core mission of the organization and is infused through the organization rather than residing in a few individuals.

For example, since the 1970s Disney Corporation has been evaluating everything it does. Disney has at least three evaluation programs and three corresponding databases: (1) They keep track of the performance of materials and equipment and record their findings in a technical database; (2) the guest services group interviews guests about facilities and services and records predictors of Disney's "key business drivers"—the intention to return; (3) a 40-person industrial engineering team conducts continuous research that is aimed at refining guidelines and rules of thumb. The industrial engineering team explores optimal conditions: When does Main Street feel pleasantly crowded but not oppressive? When are restrooms full without undue waiting? When are gift shops most productive? This research allows Disney to make direct links between "inputs," such as the proposed number of people entering the gates, to "outputs" such as the width of Main Street.

The Disney databases are not formally linked together but are used extensively during design and renovation projects. They have been so effective that the senior industrial engineer works as an equal with the Imagineering project manager during the programming of major new projects.

Disney's evaluation process is quite rare. It uses an evaluation program to do four processes that are key to organizational learning (Huber, 1991):

1. Monitoring changes in the internal and external business environment and assessing performance
2. Interpreting and discussing the implications of results
3. Consolidating results into an organizational memory
4. Widely distributing findings and conclusions

While POE potentially provides a methodology for all four of these processes, POE practice has historically focused on case studies and supporting decision making for individual projects rather than for more general lessons learned. Even when evaluators have been able to create databases of findings, they have often been used to benchmark single cases rather than to develop more-general conclusions.

Furthermore, organizational learning is hard to do. Most organizations spend a great deal of effort taking control of their environment and maintaining stability by doing things such as setting up functional divisions, establishing reporting arrangements, and creating policies that govern behavior. Most organizations are much poorer at fostering

learning and at nurturing the change that often results from learning. Learning requires the will to collect data about performance and the time to interpret and draw conclusions from it. To learn we have to expose mistakes so we can improve: Most organizations don't reward the exposure of shortcomings.

In a recent survey, Thierry Rosenheck and I examined the materials from some 18 POE programs, and wherever possible interviewed participants, to see if organizational learning had occurred and, if so, to see how they were able to overcome these barriers. These findings are discussed in a somewhat different way in another paper (Zimring & Rosenheck, 2001); I summarize them here.

Is There Evidence That Organizations Actually Use POE to Learn?

In looking at organizations that have active POE programs, Rosenheck and I found that members of project teams, including project managers, consultants, and clients, tend not to be aware of POEs unless a special evaluation has been conducted to address a problem that the team is facing. Where they are aware of the POEs, team members often do not have the reports from past POEs at hand and do not use POE results in daily decision making.

Midlevel staff tend to be more aware of POE results, and particularly midlevel staff responsible for developing guidelines and standards. For example, in the U.S. Postal Service, the staff who maintain guidelines also administer POEs. The POEs conducted by the Administrative Office of the U.S. Courts are directly used by the Judicial Conference to test and update the U.S. Courts Design Guide.

We were not able to identify situations in which senior management used POEs for strategic planning. As was mentioned earlier, POEs have the potential for supporting double-loop learning (Argyris & Schon, 1978): for not only evaluating how to better achieve existing goals but also to reflect on whether the goals themselves need to be reconsidered. But we were not able to find cases in which this actually occurred.

We were not able to find many compilations of POE findings, although several organizations, including the U.S. Army Corps of Engineers, U.S. Postal Service, Administrative Office of the U.S. Courts, U.S. General Services Administration, and others, have incorporated POEs into design guides. Disney and the U.S. Department of State have incorporated POE into databases of information. These are discussed in more detail later.

It does appear that POEs are not used to their full potential for organizational learning. There are undoubtedly sometimes issues with the POEs themselves if they are not credible or well constructed, but there are also at least three organizational reasons for this:

1. Learning is fragile and difficult and many organizations have not created the appropriate conditions for it. If learning is to be genuinely "organizational," a wide variety of staff must have the opportunity to participate and to reflect on the results in a way that enables them to incorporate those results into their own practice. Potential participants must see the value for themselves; there must be incentives for being involved. Most significantly, organizations cannot punish people when POEs reveal problems with projects.
2. Many organizations simply do not make information available in a format that is clear and useful to decision makers.
3. Many organizations have not created a coherent, integrated body of knowledge that is helpful in everyday decision making. Knowledge tends to be informal and individual.

Ways to Create the Appropriate Conditions for Learning through POE

Several organizations have overcome some of the difficulties in using POE to learn. They have used at least eight strategies: (1) Create opportunities for decision makers to participate and reflect; (2) provide access to knowledge for different audiences; (3) provide incentives; (4) reduce disincentives—create protected opportunities for innovation and evaluation; (5) reduce risk by upper management commitment; (6) focus on "learning moments; (7) tie POE to strategic design decisions and key business drivers; (8) create organizational memory for precedents.

Create opportunities for participation and reflection by decision makers. Our research suggests that POE-based knowledge is not widely shared within most organizations. One way to achieve this sharing is through direct participation in evaluations. Seeing how a facility works and hearing directly from users make for a memorable experience. And, the process of analyzing and writing up the results of an evaluation can help decision makers reflect on the implications of the results and make links to their own practice.

A lessons-learned program initiated in 1997 for New York City to examine the success of school projects in the state was aimed at creating change by having the architects themselves involved with the POEs. The School Construction Authority (SCA), whose membership is appointed by the governor, the mayor, and the New York City Board of Education, was charged with the program. To get the program approved, SCA, under the leadership of consultant Ralph Steinglass, adopted a simple methodology: require the architect/engineer of record to conduct the POE. The rationale was that this would guarantee that designers would confront how users responded to their designs and force a lessons-learned loop in the design process. About 20 POEs have been completed. To ensure reliability, SCA reviewed the results before approving the POEs. In some cases, the architects or engineers had to reschedule their interviews when they were suspected of introducing a bias or continue their investigation if they failed to include critical areas required in the study.

Provide access to knowledge for different audiences. Many organizations produce POEs as case study reports that are not widely distributed. Part of this may be due to the history of POE, which has focused on single case studies, and part may be due to the perceived disincentives to distributing information that might be seen as critical of internal efforts or individuals. Some of the problem is the simple technical difficulty of distributing printed information, which has become easier with the Internet and intranet and virtual private networks. NASA makes its lessons-learned database available to all authorized staff and contractors. In the UK, the PROBE team has created an interactive Web site for the 18 buildings they have evaluated as part of the PROBE project (Bordass & Leaman, 1997).

Some organizations have overcome these impediments by creating design guides and databases of POE information. Agencies such as the Administrative Office of the U.S. Courts, the U.S. Postal Service, and the U.S. General Services Administration have created design guides that are broadly distributed.

The growth of multimedia databases has allowed organizations to distribute information more broadly. For example, the U.S. Department of State's Office of Foreign Buildings Operations

(FBO) is responsible for the design and construction of U.S. posts overseas. From 1993 to 1999, FBO POE coordinator Thierry Rosenheck conducted 11 POEs of new embassies. The POEs were aimed at assessing both user response and technical performance of the buildings and building systems. Questionnaires, interviews, focus groups, site visits, and other measures were used to assess a wide range of issues, such as aesthetics, circulation, security, and maintainability. FBO contracted with Craig Zimring to develop an online database (called *LessonBase*) that consolidates all POE findings and makes them accessible for future decision making. The structure of LessonBase is aimed at confronting users with problematic situations that would cause them to reconsider their original assumptions or practices. LessonBase stories include problems, analyses of the problems, design or management solutions to the problems, and proposed guidelines or lessons for preventing the problems in the future. For example, while in many countries the ambassador's residence must be very secure, the use of institutional materials, equipment, and layouts has led to high cost and an unfriendly atmosphere. In one embassy, the ambassador initially refused to move into a multimillion-dollar facility. More careful attention to privacy and to a family setting can reduce problems and increase satisfaction.

One of the most popular features of LessonBase is the "Lessons-Learned" section where staff can add more informal lessons to the database. While LessonBase has not been fully implemented because of technical and management issues, it has been used in the planning of several new embassies and is being integrated into a comprehensive facilities management database called "Dr Checks" developed by the U.S. Army Corps of Engineers.

Design projects represent many different professional cultures. Engineers tend to take a technical problem-solving approach. Architects are often interested in form and materials. Clients might be interested in the usability and experience of the building. Senior managers might be searching for help in setting strategic directions, whereas project managers might be interested in lessons learned about specific materials or equipment. Part of the challenge in creating any database or report is translating between these different professional cultures, and evaluators have not always been successful at doing this.

Provide incentives. The California Department of General Services is considering including the results of POEs as part of the review of qualifications when selecting consultants and contractors. Even the consideration of this idea has strongly increased architecture firms' interest in POEs. I am unaware of any POE programs that provide incentives for internal staff members to participate in evaluations, though several programs have discussed such incentives, such as providing a free vacation day as a reward for adding data to the knowledge base or providing a minisabbatical for participating in evaluations or lessons-learned programs. Disney provides a powerful, if indirect, incentive: knowledge. Only the industrial engineers have access to key POE data, and they then become valuable members of the design team.

Reduce disincentives: Create protected opportunities for innovation and evaluation. Organizational learning consultants have long pointed to an inherent contradiction in many organizations. Whereas most organizations espouse innovation and learning, they behave in ways that actively limit it. One example is a recent meeting between project managers and senior management in a large public organization. The organization had used an innovative building delivery strategy but were not familiar with it and had left out a key review step. When this became clear, a senior manager turned to the project manager and said, "We would have expected someone at your level to do better." The message to everyone in the room was clear: Avoid innovation and avoid evaluation! This syndrome—focusing on the individual rather than the performance, blaming the innovator rather than learning from the innovation—is pervasive among organizations (Argyris, 1992b; Argyris & Schon, 1978). However, some building delivery organizations have used POE to at least partially overcome it.

Some organizations have done this by explicitly sanctioning "research" with the attendant acknowledgment that innovations might not succeed. For example, the U.S. General Services Administration (GSA) Public Buildings Service has recently appointed a "Director of Research." The first director, Kevin Kampschroer, has a budget to conduct, synthesize, and distribute research, including POE. The use of the term *research* carries with it the understanding that not all efforts are successful and the budget provides some time for reflection about findings. To date, much of the research is conducted by academic consultants who bring outside learning into GSA. However, GSA is also looking at ways to broaden internal ownership of the research program.

GSA has also created an active "officing" laboratory in its own headquarters building. The lab, supervised by Kampschroer, is one floor of actual workspace that includes an innovative raised-floor heating, ventilating, and air-conditioning system and several brands of modular office furniture systems. It also explores design to support teamwork, with many small conference rooms and meeting areas. The workers are frequently surveyed and observed, and the lab also becomes a place where clients can see alternative office layouts.

The U.S. Courts and the U.S. General Services Administration Courthouse Management Group are considering developing a different kind of laboratory: a full-scale courtroom mockup facility where new courtroom layouts and technologies can be tested and refined at relatively low cost and risk. This facility, to be constructed at the Georgia Institute of Technology, would allow mock trials to be conducted and would provide training for judges, staff, and lawyers.

Another way to reduce the personal and organizational cost of experimentation is by starting small with projects that have an experimental component. The innovation can be evaluated and considered for broader adoption. For example, the U.S. Department of State Office of Foreign Buildings Operations (FBO) tries out innovations on a limited number of projects before rolling out the innovation to the larger organization. FBO has recently used building serviceability tools and methods (ST&M) (Davis & Szigeti, 1996) for programming and design review for the new embassies in Dar es Salaam and Nairobi.

In many organizations, it is risky to be the first one to try an innovation. Massachusetts Institute of Technology organizational consultant Edgar Schein has proposed that, though organizations may benefit greatly from consultants, they often find the experience of peers more helpful when they actually move to implementing an innovation. Schein has called for "learning consortia" where people can get advice from peers in other organizations and learn from their experience (Schein, 1995). He argues that, though such learning consortia may be effective at all levels of an organization, they are particularly effective among CEOs or upper-midlevel managers.

Although the strategies described earlier—using prototypes, creating a laboratory, and developing a learning consortium—are quite different, all reduce the disincentives for innovation and evaluation by allowing innovation and evaluation at relatively low personal and organizational cost.

Reduce risk by securing upper management commitment. Participants in POE programs report that uncertainty about senior management's commitment to the program is a key disincentive to participation. A POE program takes 2 to 5 years to have an effect, and staff often have doubts about the depth and longevity of senior management's support. Support or lack of support can be manifest materially—through resources—as well as by more subtle means such as the use of POE in daily conversation, in performance reviews, and other ways.

Focus on "learning moments." The Administrative Office of the U.S. Courts (AO) conducts a POE program that informs design guidelines (the *U.S. Courts Design Guide*). However, the AO has achieved feedforward by linking the design guide to a "strategic learning moment" in the development of courthouses: the negotiation between judges and the building agent (the U.S. General Services Administration) about the scope and quality level for new courthouses. In the early 1990s the U.S. government initiated the largest civilian construction program since the Second World War, projecting to spend over $10 billion on 160 new courthouses. (The creation of new judgeships in the 1980s, concerns for increased security, and new technologies necessitated new courthouses or major renovations.) However, both the judiciary and GSA were being criticized by Congress for creating marble-clad "Taj Mahals." The AO initiated the POE program to identify necessary changes to the standards in the first edition of the *Design Guide,* to defend the judiciary against attack by documenting the efficacy of the design standards, and to inform the negotiation about issues such as the dimensions and materials of courtrooms and chambers. Information from POEs was also used in training workshops for judges and staff who were becoming involved in new courthouse design and construction. This program is run by the AO, but the design guide is actually created and vetted by a committee of the Judicial Conference, the group that sets broad policy within the federal judiciary. This program is quite unusual: It is the only case that we are aware of where a POE and design guide are developed by a client organization that does not build its own buildings.

Tie POE to strategic design decisions and key business drivers. POE can be particularly successful in feedforward if it links strategic facilities decisions to the "key business drivers" of the client organization. The U.S. Army Corps of Engineers design guide and POE program was motivated by the shift to an all-volunteer army. Potential recruits said that the aging facilities were a significant impediment to recruiting and retention and the Army sought to renovate or rebuild many of its buildings (Shibley, 1985).

In the 1980s the newly privatized U.S. Postal Service (USPS) was losing customers to competitors such as FedEx and UPS (Kantrowitz & Farbstein, 1996). Focusing initially on the customer experience with lobbies, the USPS contracted with Min Kantrowitz and Jay Farbstein and Associates to conduct focus group evaluations. This has led to a large and continuing program of evaluations and design guide development. New concepts of post office design are developed, such as the retail-focused "postal store"; innovative projects are designed; the projects are evaluated; and the ideas are refined and then incorporated into design guides. This program has sustained an ongoing process of testing and refining the design guides through evaluation and experience. More recently, the USPS has deemphasized on-site evaluations. According to POE manager Mark Nedzbala, most POEs now involve having facility managers fill out relatively brief mail-out surveys. Nedzbala has found that the open-ended responses to the questionnaire are often most valuable in refining the USPS's design guidelines because they are more specific than the scaled satisfaction responses.

Create organizational memory for precedents. A key part of organizational memory is simply knowing what the organization has done. Few building delivery organizations have good comprehensive databases that allow decision makers and clients to access past cases or to examine benchmarks. A potential use of POE is to consolidate such information and to tie it to evaluation.

CONCLUSIONS

A large number of POEs are being conducted, with a wide range of methods, goals, and heuristic frameworks. Some evaluators have created standard packages of methods, whereas others have argued that standardization can reduce the meaningfulness of evaluation and the ability of participants to take ownership of the results. Many evaluators have called for a broadening of the role of evaluation by focusing on its role in enabling a wide range of decisions about buildings and facilities management.

Despite the large number of POEs that have been conducted, POE has not had the impact that it could have on subsequent building delivery and management, partly because evaluators and their clients have not attended to the fit between POE and the organizational conditions that allow learning to go on. Though the goals of POE are inherently applied, part of this problem is actually a lack of *theory*. Somewhat adapting Weiss's model of program evaluation (Weiss, 1997), it is helpful to separate "evaluation implementation theory" from "setting operation theory." By *evaluation implementation theory* I mean a theory of action: how an organization or individual decision makers can implement the results of the POE. As was suggested earlier, this may range from creating design standards or guidelines to working intensively with a specific design team. Much of the previous section was devoted to beginning to sketch out a preliminary evaluation implementation theory and some actions based on this theory.

Much *setting operation theory*—theories about the links between design or process and other outcomes—has been only implicit in POE. However, several theories have begun to emerge. In their chapter in this volume focusing on space syntax, Peponis and Wineman present theories and evidence that the form of the environment interacts with issues such as culture, communication, movement, and wayfinding. Duffy has argued that one can link organizational characteristics, such as the number of professionals, to building characteristics, such as the length of the building perimeter that allows private cellular offices with windows (Duffy & Powell, 1997). Building serviceability tools and methods have adopted a similar approach by arguing that client requirements for office buildings can be defined in terms of some 100 scales about issues such as flexibility that are linked to specific building qualities (Davis & Szigeti, 1996).

An important role for environmental psychologists is to continue to develop both implementation and setting theories that can be incorporated into POE. Until this happens POE will continue to be a promising empirical exercise that all too often falls short of its potential.

REFERENCES

Administrative Office of the U.S. Courts. (1997). *U.S. Courts Design Guide.* Washington, DC: U.S. Government Printing Office.

Anderson, J. R., & Weidemann, S. (1997). Developing and utilizing models of residential satisfaction. In G. Moore & R. Marans (Eds.), *Advances in environment and behavior research and design* (Vol. 4, pp. 287–315). New York: Plenum Press.

Argyris, C. (1992a). *On organizational learning.* Cambridge, MA: Blackwell.

Argyris, C. (1992b). Teaching smart people how to learn. In C. Argyris (Ed.), *On organizational learning* (pp. 84–100). Cambridge, MA: Blackwell Business.

Argyris, C., & Schon, D. (1978). *Organizational learning.* Reading, MA: Addison-Wesley.

Baird, G., Gray, J., Isaacs, N., Kernohan, D., & McIndoe, G. (Eds.). (1996). *Building evaluation techniques.* New York: McGraw-Hill.

Bordass, W., Bromley, A., & Leaman, A. (1995). *Comfort, control and energy efficiency in offices.* Garston, England: Building Research Establishment.

Bordass, W., & Leaman, A. (1996). Future buildings and their services: Strategic considerations for designers and their clients. *Proceedings of the CIBSE/ASHRAE Joint National Conference, 1.*

Bordass, W., & Leaman, A. (1997). Future buildings and their services: Strategic considerations for designers and clients. *Building Research and Information, 25*(4), 190–195.

Brill, M., Margulis, S. T., Konar, E., Buffalo Organization for Social and Technological Innovation, & Westinghouse Furniture Systems. (1984). *Using office design to increase productivity.* Buffalo, NY: Workplace Design & Productivity.

Campbell, D. T. (1999). *Social experimentation.* Beverly Hills, CA: Sage.

Carpman, J. R., & Grant, M. A. (1993). *Design that cares: Planning health facilities for patients and visitors* (2nd ed.). Chicago: American Hospital.

Cohen, R., Standeven, M., Bordass, B., & Leaman, A. (2001a). Assessing building performance in use 1: The Probe process. *Building Research and Information, 29*(2), 85–102.

Cohen, R., Standeven, M., Bordass, B., & Leaman, A. (2001b). Assessing building performance in use 2: Technical performance of the Probe buildings. *Building Research and Information, 29*(2), 103–114.

Cooper, S. (1992). *We can learn from cross-cultural workplaces: A study of American executives in Japanese workplaces in the U.S.* New York: Environmental Psychology Program Graduate Center, City University of New York.

Davis, G., & Szigeti, F. (1996). Serviceability tools and methods (STM): Matching occupant requirements and facilities. In G. Baird, J. Gray, N. Isaacs, D. Kernohan, & G. McIndoe (Eds.), *Building evaluation techniques.* New York: McGraw-Hill.

Duffy, F. (1998). The new office. *Facilities Design and Management, 17*(8), 76–79.

Duffy, F., & Powell, K. (1997). *The new office.* London: Conran Octopus.

Flagg, G. (1999). Study finds major flaws in San Francisco main library. *American Libraries, 30*(9), 16.

Foxall, G., & Hackett, P. (1994). Consumer satisfaction with Birmingham's International Convention Center. *Service Industries Journal, 14*(3), 369.

Francis, J. (1986). *Office productivity: Contributions of the physical setting* (USA-CERL P-86/13). Washington, DC: U.S. Army Corps of Engineers.

Friedman, A., Zimring, C., & Zube, E. (1978). *Environmental design evaluation.* New York: Plenum Press.

Fuller, C. (1988). Post-occupancy evaluation: Fast feedback for planners. Corrections Today, 50(2), 213–214.

Grannis, P. (1994). Postoccupancy evaluation: An avenue for applied environment-behavior research in planning practice. *Journal of Planning Literature, 9*(2), 210–219.

Gregerson, J. (1997, August). Fee not-so-simple. Building Design and Construction, 30–32.

Heerwagen, J. H. (2001, March 13). *A balanced scorecard approach to post-occupancy evaluation: Using the tools of business to evaluate facilities.* Paper presented at the Federal Facilities Council Symposium on Building Performance Assessments: Current and Evolving Practices for Post Occupancy Evaluation Programs, Washington, DC.

Horgen, T. H., Joroff, M. L., Porter, W. L., & Schon, D. A. (1996). Post-occupancy evaluation of facilities: A participatory approach to programming and design. *Facilities, 14*(7/8), 16–25.

Horgen, T. H., Joroff, M. L., Porter, W. L., & Schon, D. A. (1999). *Excellence by design: Transforming workplace and work practice.* New York: Wiley.

Huber, G. P. (1991). Organizational learning: The contributing processes and the literature. *Organization Science, 2,* 88–115.

Kantrowitz, M., & Farbstein, J. (1996). POE delivers for the post office. In G. Baird, J. Gray, N. Isaacs, D. Kernohan, & G. McIndoe (Eds.), *Building evaluation techniques.* New York: McGraw-Hill.

Kaplan, R. S., & Norton, D. P. (1996). *The balanced scorecard: Translating strategy into action.* Boston: Harvard Business School Press.

Kincaid, D. (1994). Measuring performance in facility management. *Facilities, 12*(6), 17–21.

Leaman, A., Cohen, R., & Jackman, P. (1995). Ventilation of office buildings: Deciding the most appropriate system.

Heating and Air Conditioning(7/8), 16–18, 20, 22–24, 26–28.

Ornstein, S. W. (1997). Post-occupancy evaluation performed in elementary and high schools of greater Sao Paulo, Brazil: The occupants and the quality of the school environment. *Environment and Behavior, 29*(2), 236.

Ornstein, S. W. (1999). A post-occupancy evaluation of workplaces in Sao Paulo, Brazil. *Environment and Behavior, 31*(4), 435–462.

Parshall, S. A., & Peña, W. (1983). *Evaluating facilities: A practical approach to post-occupancy evaluation.* Houston, TX: CRS Group.

Preiser, W. F. E. (1994). Built environment evaluation: Conceptual basis, benefits and uses. *Journal of Architectural and Planning Research, 11*(2), 92–107.

Preiser, W. F. E., Rabinowitz, H. Z., & White, E. T. (1988). *Post-occupancy evaluation.* New York: Van Nostrand Reinhold.

Preiser, W. F. E., & Schramm, U. (1997). Building performance evaluation. In J. DeChiara, J. Panero, & M. Zelnik (Eds.), *Time-saver standards* (7 ed., pp. 233–238). New York: McGraw-Hill.

Raw, G. J. (1995). *A questionnaire for studies of sick building syndrome* (Building Research Establishment Rep. London: Construction Research Communications.

Raw, G. J. (2000). Assessing occupant reaction to indoor air quality. In J. Spengler, J. Samet, & J. McCarthey (Eds.), *Indoor air quality handbook.* New York: McGraw-Hill.

Raw, G. J., Roys, M., & Leaman, A. (1990). Further findings from the Office Environment Survey: Productivity. *Proceedings of Indoor Air '90.* Toronto, Canada: Building Research Establishment (BRE).

Ripley Architects. (2000). *San Francisco Public Library post occupancy evaluation final report.* San Francisco: Author.

Schein, E. H. (1995). *Learning consortia: How to create parallel learning systems for organization sets* [Working paper]. Cambridge, MA: Society for Organizational Learning.

Schneekloth, L. H., & Shibley, R. G. (1995). *Placemaking: The art and practice of building communities.* New York: Wiley.

Shibley, R. (1982). Building evaluations services. *Progressive Architecture, 63*(12), 64–67.

Shibley, R. (1985). Building evaluation in the main stream. *Environment and Behavior,*(1), 7–24.

Spreckelmeyer, K. (1993). Office relocation and environmental change: A case study. *Environment and Behavior, 25*(2), 181.

Stanley, L., & Little, R. (2001, March 13). *Introduction: Current and evolving practices for post-occupancy evaluation programs.* Paper presented at the Federal Facilities Council Symposium on Building Performance Assessments: Current and Evolving Practices for Post Occupancy Evaluation Programs, Washington, DC.

Stokols, D. (1988). *Developing standardized tools for assessing employees' ratings of facility performance.*

Symes, M., & Robbins, C. (2001). *"Literature Review" for "Indicators System for New Urban Services."* Paper presented at the European Union Framework 4 Research Programme: Key action 4 the City of Tomorrow.

Underhill, P. (1999). *Why we buy: The science of shopping.* New York: Simon & Schuster.

Vischer, J. (1996). *Workspace strategies: Environment as a tool for work.* New York: Chapman & Hall.

Weiss, C. H. (1997). *Evaluation* (2nd ed.). Upper Saddle River, NJ: Prentice-Hall.

Wener, R., Farbstein, J., & Knapel, C. (1993). Post-occupancy evaluations: Improving correctional facility design. *Corrections Journal, 55*(6), 96.

Wineman, J. (1986). Introduction. In J. Wineman (Ed.), *Behavioral issues in office design,* 6–31. New York: Van Nostrand Reinhold.

Zeisel, J. (1975). *Sociology and architectural design.* New York: Russell Sage Foundation.

Zimring, C., Munyon, W. H., & Ard, L. (1988). Reducing stress in jails. *Ekistics,*(332), 215–230.

Zimring, C., & Rosenheck, T. (2001, March 13). *Getting it right the second or third time rather than the sixth or seventh.* Paper presented at the Federal Facilities Council Symposium on Building Performance Assessments: Current and Evolving Practices for Post Occupancy Evaluation Programs, Washington, DC.

Zimring, C. M. & Reizenstein, J. E. (1981). A primer on post-occupancy evaluation. *Architecture (American Institute of Architects Journal), 70*(13), 52–59.

Zimring, C. M., & Welch, P. (1988, July). Learning from 20–20 hindsight. *Progressive Architecture,* 55–62.

SHARPENING APPLICATION

CHAPTER 21

Making a Difference: Some Ways Environmental Psychology Has Improved the World

ROBERT GIFFORD

THE EFFORTS OF WORKERS in the field of environmental psychology may be inexactly grouped into two complementary branches: experimental and applied. Of course, almost all environmental psychology is applied in the broad sense that its work is stimulated by the recognition of problems in interactions between people and their built and natural settings. Virtually all environmental psychologists hope eventually to help solve these problems.

Even the most experimental investigations typically conclude their articles with suggestions that "should be taken into consideration" in the design or management of offices, factories, homes, streetscapes, parks, or natural places. Nevertheless, this chapter mainly is concerned with environmental psychology that goes beyond the making of recommendations to actually changing environments: applied environmental psychology that does not merely consider problems, but in some way actually tackles them.

WHAT WE KNOW, WHAT WE CHANGE, AND WHO WE ARE

Experimental environmental psychologists have learned an enormous amount about person environment relations in the past 35 years. We know much about which features make a nature scene beautiful, how personal space changes with age, which sorts of people are more likely to hold proenvironmental attitudes, what the key environmental dimensions of personality are, how crowding affects social interaction, how noise harms learning, and how temperature is related to violence.

Many sound principles allow us to predict who will cooperate when resources are scarce, how cultures vary in their privacy-seeking, what meanings are conveyed to observers by which building facades, and to describe residents' strategies for dealing with spatial conflicts in their homes. Preferences, attitudes, spatial cognitions, and emotions in response to the built and natural environment: All are understood much better than they were three decades ago. And theories! Theoretical environmental psychologists have proposed theories of specific phenomena, such as defensible space, social physics, and affiliative conflict theories, not to mention transactional, organismic, and dialectical theories of everything.

But have the practitioners of environmental psychology and all our principles actually changed any setting or anyone outside the laboratory or field study setting? Have person environment relations "merely" (not that what follows is not in itself a great achievement) been observed, described, and explained as a series of correlations or significant differences between constructs A and B? Has environmental psychology changed the behavior of anyone except the participants in a given study and that only temporarily? Has it influenced policy in a way that has improved the lives of everyday persons or saved anyone from anything?

Yes, of course. In this chapter, a broad sample of these efforts will be presented. Not all such efforts can be gathered into one place, and many readers will know of some important work that changed the lives of a particular group, neighborhood, or entire city but is not acknowledged here. Many efforts that deserve a place in this chapter will be missed because no one wrote about them in an accessible publication or responded to my listserve call for suggestions. The works describe here, then, represents only a few of the efforts that have been made.

It must be admitted that not every effort to be described has had an effect large enough to warrant the phrase, "changed the world," but most have had at least a small, documented salutary effect on the lives of at least some people outside of the subjects in the study. Indeed, this was the working criterion for inclusion: Did the study, experiment, book, or article have a documented and presumably beneficial effect on individuals in the real, everyday world?

One further caveat: Not all persons who made the effort to be discussed would describe themselves as environmental psychologists. They include architects, urban planners, and others. Often these are the people who have their hands on the switch that controls actual changes in buildings, landscape, and natural places. But, in my view, they were using ideas, research, and principles that are at the core of environmental psychology when they made their differences.

Among some environmental psychologists, the desire to learn how some process worked—personal space and territoriality may be good examples—was sufficient motivation and justification to carry out a study. The emphasis was on the indisputable fact that most of psychology had ignored the very stage on which humans act and the sets among which we dance, as if we were players in a black vacuum. Merely to study people in settings was a joyful and worthy end in itself. With some notable exceptions, how the findings from those studies might relate to policy, architecture, or land-use planning were duly noted in discussion sections, but often this was pro forma, and few attempts to actually change the world were made.

For others, interest in work done out of pure intellectual curiosity was less attractive. It was not enough merely to know how it all worked; a study had to have practical implications. One major impetus for this desire to combine theory and change may be traced to Kurt Lewin. His idea of action research (Lewin, 1948) was perhaps the first major push in psychology toward linking scientific research with real social change.

An early example of research inspired by Lewin occurred in the late 1950s, when Robert Sommer and Humphrey Osmond began to systematically alter the physical elements of mental hospital buildings in Saskatchewan and to monitor the effects of these changes on patient behavior (Osmond, 1957; Sommer, 1969). By rearranging furniture and redesigning wards, they found they could increase communication among the patients.

A second general theoretical perspective that has change as its explicit goal is applied behavior analysis. Classically, in this approach, specific problematic behaviors are identified, and appropriate reinforcements are delivered when individuals engage in desirable behaviors. Some prime examples of problems that have been attacked with the ABA approach are recycling, littering, and residential energy wastage (Cone & Hayes 1980; Geller, Winett, & Everett, 1982). Applied behavioral analysts believe that positive or negative consequences for behavior are what count. Advocates assert that the way to change environment-related behavior may be summed up in the acronym DO-RITE, the letters of which stand for the following sequence (Geller, 1992):

Define the target behavior to be changed.

Observe the target behavior.

Record the rate of occurrence of the behavior.

Intervene with a program that changes the consequences of engaging in that behavior.

Test the impact of the program by comparing the frequency of the behavior before and after the program.

Evaluate the program. Was it cost-effective? Were the consequences appropriate and strong enough?

More recently, applied behavior analysts like Scott Geller (1995) have incorporated humanistic, or "actively caring," components that appeal to the social conscience.

In which settings and behaviors has environmental psychology made a difference? For the most part, this has occurred at five levels: the room, the building, the street, the neighborhood, and the city. In terms of behavior, efforts have been made in wayfinding; spatial behavior; residential, urban, and institutional design; hazard mitigation; and the promotion of environmentally responsible behavior.

ENVIRONMENTAL COGNITION IN EVERYDAY LIFE

Spatial cognition includes the notion of cognitive maps—pictorial and semantic images of how places are arranged (Kitchin, 1994). How have researchers used knowledge about cognitive mapping to improve the quality of life? At the building level, O'Neill (1991) showed how good signage significantly increases the rate of travel through complex buildings and reduces the number of wrong turns and backtracking by half or more. Others have used spatial cognition principles to help severely mentally ill people find their way around their communities (Taylor & Taylor, 1993).

Buildings may also be made more legible through the use of color-coded paths and carefully considered numbering systems. Painting the floors of a building different colors reduces wayfinding errors and improves comprehension of buildings by those who use them (Evans, Fellows, Zorn, & Doty, 1980). In hospitals, where many people visit only a few times and so are unfamiliar with the layout of these large buildings, Janet Carpman and her colleagues showed how a seemingly minor detail such as how the floors that are below ground level are numbered can seriously affect the wayfinding of patients and visitors (Carpman, Grant, & Simmons, 1983–1984).

At the street level, cognitive mapping research applied to everyday wayfinding is ubiquitous in the form of subway and bus maps, which depict routes in simplified ways rather than with cartographic accuracy. Removing unnecessary detail makes the maps more legible and thereby reduces both the cognitive effort required to understand them and the number of errors made as transit users, particularly tourists or new riders, select and use public transit routes (Downs & Stea, 1977).

At the city level, Lynch (1960) and Appleyard (1976) hypothesized that regular, clear paths and highly visible landmarks would improve the spatial cognition of cities, and research supports this contention (Tzamir, 1975) and has extended it. For example, distance judgments by people on the street are more accurate in cities with more regular traffic patterns (Canter & Tagg, 1975). In addition, the presence of strongly organizing features in cities such as rivers, roads, and railroads improve spatial cognition. Appleyard (1976) applied cognitive mapping principles to the urban design of Ciudad Guyana, a planned Venezuelan city that was created to centrally amalgamate several existing small towns.

Environmental psychologists also use cognitive mapping in crime fighting. Canter and Larkin (1993), for example, helped to construct cognitive map profiles of suspects based on their apparent plans and actual patterns of crime sites. The spatial patterns of serial rapists and murderers are not random; by understanding the spatial patterns in their crimes, their identity as well as the more likely locations of their next strike have become more knowable.

Environmental psychologists might even be said to have saved lives with their knowledge of cognitive mapping. Ed Cornell and Don Heth have, in a series of studies, shown how traditional grid-based search patterns for persons lost in the wilderness are less efficient than searches that take advantage of knowledge about the ways that lost persons tend to wander (Heth & Cornell, 1998). When searches are more efficient and take into account typical wandering patterns for different kinds of lost persons in different kinds of terrain, more lost persons will be found before it is too late for them.

IMPROVING THE QUALITY OF THE HUMAN DANCE

Environmental psychologists have studied human spatial behavior for over 40 years. Some of the original work in the area (Hall, 1959) was spurred by very real problems: misperceptions of diplomats as a result of cultural differences in interpersonal spacing. Once differences are understood, individuals who wish to interact more usefully with other cultures can consider learning to act like the other culture. Collett (1971) tested this idea by teaching English students how to act more like Arabs in their nonverbal behavior. Arabs who interacted with trained students liked them more than students who had not received training.

In some settings, crowding is a serious problem. Sometimes it can be alleviated by adding space, but often this is not feasible for economic or other reasons. When this is the case, more creative solutions must be found. One strategy involves the simple use of informative signs. Wener and Kaminoff (1983) used signs that offered simple directions and information to alleviate crowding in the lobby of a prison administration building that is often densely populated. Visitors felt significantly less crowded, confused, and angered after the signs were introduced, compared to visitors interviewed before the signs were introduced. The time required to complete the registration process was shorter and visitors made fewer navigational errors in the lobby. In another domain, Langer and Saegert (1977) found that merely providing shoppers with information about the effects of crowding made them feel better and helped them to shop more efficiently.

Baum and Davis (1980) followed up on a suggestion (Freedman, 1979) that where corridors are long, crowding might be reduced by shortening them. Baum and Davis' architectural intervention was simple. They arranged for a wall and double doors to be installed in the middle of a long dormitory corridor. After several weeks, residents on the divided-corridor floor felt significantly less crowded than did residents on a similar floor that remained undivided. Even though the double doors were not locked, the division of the floor into two halves seems to have reduced overload, encouraged separate use of public facilities (such as bathrooms) by the two groups of residents, and assisted in friendship formation.

Residential privacy can be achieved by building large houses, but what if the budget is very limited, yet privacy still should be regulated? Christopher Alexander devised what he called a privacy gradient in his designs for low-cost Peruvian residences (Zeisel, 1975). Based on interviews and careful consideration of cultural practices among the residents, Alexander arranged space in the houses from the most public (located near the entrance) to the most private (located farthest from the entrance).

BETTER LIVING THROUGH ENVIRONMENTAL PSYCHOLOGY

What if people could design their own homes at full scale? Architects learn to visualize spaces based on technical drawings, but many laypersons find this difficult. Rod Lawrence (1978) believes that the three spatial dimensions are all essential for the optimal representation of architectural space to the public. In his laboratory in Lausanne, Switzerland, a very large room with high ceilings is the site where residents have assembled their full-scale dream houses using lightweight polystyrene blocks and walls. Even two-storey simulated houses, complete with doors and windows, have been designed and "built" relatively quickly and easily. Then some of the houses have been actually constructed, based on

these designs that presumably reflect owner preferences that are discovered in three-dimensional, full-scale space.

One of the best-known applications of environmental psychology principles has been the work of Oscar Newman, whose ideas were based in part on the ideas of Jane Jacobs (1961). Defensible space theory predicts that certain changes in residential design that reduce apparently nonowned space and traffic by nonresidents and increase naturally occurring surveillance and a sense of ownership by the residents will reduce crime. For example, a neighborhood in Dayton, Ohio, with a high crime rate was altered to incorporate some defensible space features (Cose, 1994). Many entrances to the neighborhood were closed, speed bumps were installed to slow down traffic, gates with the neighborhood logo were installed, and the community was divided into five minineighborhoods with physical barriers. Two years later, traffic was down 67%, violent crime declined by 50%, and total crime declined by 26%.

In an earlier project, Newman (1972) oversaw the renovation of a low-income housing project adjacent to South Bronx, in New York. Clason Point consisted of rowhouse clusters housing from 12 to 40 families per cluster. The renovations assigned as much public space to the control of specific families, using both substantial and symbolic fencing, reduced the number of pedestrian routes through the project, improved lighting along the paths, improved the project's image, and encouraged a sense of personal ownership by resurfacing the dwellings and using different colors for individual units.

Residents took new pride in their dwellings, planted grass, added their own new modifications, and even swept the public sidewalks. According to Newman, maintenance costs and crime both were significantly reduced. Serious crimes such as burglary, assault, and robbery were said to drop by over 60%. The number of residents who said they felt that they had the right to question strangers in the project doubled. The results were not entirely positive (Kohn, Franck, & Fox, 1975), but the renovations appear to have had a generally beneficial effect on Clason Point.

MORE FUN DOWNTOWN

In one of the most widely utilized changes wrought by environmental psychology principles, the very fabric of many cities have been changed by a concept called density bonusing, which may be traced to the pioneering work of William Whyte. Recognizing the need for some open space in the city core, in 1961 the city of New York offered developers a deal: For every square foot of plaza they included in a new project, their new building could exceed normal zoning restrictions by ten square feet. Developers liked the idea, and this deal certainly increased New York's supply of open space downtown. Unfortunately, the new plazas tended to be vast empty spaces. So, in consequence, New York City revised its offers to developers. It would only allow extra floors in new buildings if developers offered plazas that included many of the amenities identified by Whyte that were associated with greater use and enjoyment of plazas, such as sittable space, water (fountains and pools), food stands, trees, accessible food outlets, and activities to watch (e.g., jugglers, mimes, and buskers) (Whyte, 1980). New plazas based on Whyte's amenities are markedly improved social spaces that increase the pleasantness not only of New York but also of many cities around the world.

Sidney Brower (1988) has spent years developing and testing ideas for enlivening urban neighborhoods in Baltimore. Some of his guidelines that have been used to improve the quality of life on the residential streets of that city include keeping the streetfront alive by encouraging residents to walk, stroll, and play on the sidewalks and finding a legitimate use for every public space, so that people routinely visit all areas of the neighborhood, and there are no "dead" or unowned spaces. Once some residents are outside, using the public space, others will feel safe doing so; security and socializing go hand in hand.

Brower encouraged more use of the streetfront by giving residents things to do and places to be. This may mean benches for some; for others it might be horseshoes, hopscotch, bocci, street vendors, or library vans. Recreation on public streets can be encouraged by blocking off streets, alleys, or parking lots to cars. Some areas, such as sidewalks themselves, must be preserved from fast, rough play for older people to enjoy walking or watching. To erase unsafe zones, recreation can be linked into a system of at least visually connected activities.

Brower reduced the speed and number of cars with speed bumps or temporary barricades; this reduces accidents by up to 30% and accidents with injuries by about 25%. Residents tend to accept the barriers because they feel safer and the neighborhood is quieter and more suitable for walking (Vis,

Dijkstra, & Slop, 1992; Zaidel, Hakkert, & Pistiner, 1992). However, cars should not be banned completely; residents in cars help to maintain a street presence. Parks are made more attractive to adults. Those relegated to juvenile use operate at juvenile developmental levels. Discover what adults might like to do in the park, and try to incorporate all age groups in all activities.

BETTER LEARNING THROUGH BETTER DESIGN

Changing the overall design of the learning setting can affect learning. For example, Wollin and Montagne (1981) changed a typical plain introductory psychology classroom into one with softer lighting, plants, posters, cushions, and rugs. Student exam scores after 5 weeks in the room were significantly higher than those of students who spent 5 weeks in a similar room that had not been modified. The renovations only cost a few hundred dollars and appear to have produced improved learning for many.

Robert Sommer and Helge Olsen (1980) redesigned a plain, thirty-seat college classroom. With a very small budget, they changed it into a soft classroom with semicircular, cushion-covered bench seating, adjustable lighting, a small carpet, and some mobiles. Compared to traditional classrooms of similar size, student participation increased markedly in the soft classroom. The number of statements per student tripled and the percentage of students who spoke in class approximately doubled.

The soft classroom, contrary to the expectations of some, was not damaged or vandalized even though some of its components were vulnerable to vandals. Besides the dramatic increase in participation, students using the room wrote many glowing comments about it in a logbook placed in the soft classroom. The room was still producing more student participation 17 years later (Wong, Sommer, & Cook, 1992). That is a lot of added discussion, considering the hundreds of students who have used the room in the quarter century since it was built! The room had suffered a bit aesthetically over the years because maintenance was wanting, so the room was renovated in postmodern style in 1995 (Rafter & Sommer, 1999). These efforts, together with Wollin and Montagne's work, suggest a tentative conclusion: College classrooms need not be plain and hard. In fact, the evidence shows that inexpensive changes to make them more pleasant have very tangible benefits.

ENVIRONMENTAL PSYCHOLOGY TO THE RESCUE

Environmental psychologists assist in formulating government policy on environmental hazards. They have, for example, investigated the stressfulness of living near a toxic waste dump or who in a community is likely to test their home for radon gas (Fischhoff, 1990). Research, for example, on which ethnic groups are more likely to adopt safety measures when dealing with pesticides can have a significant positive impact on government policies concerning pesticide use (Vaughan, 1993).

Architecture that is formed by observation and models can prevent minor and major problems with the eventual finished building. In one study of a mocked-up setting, social researchers investigating a design for a hospital room discovered a life-threatening flaw (Breu, 1984). During a drill simulating a cardiac arrest situation, a design research team found that one of two beds in the room could not fit past the other one; a patient who experienced a heart attack might lose valuable time while being transferred to intensive care. As a result of the drill, the designers enlarged the room to prevent the problem.

IMAGES, MEDIA, AND ENVIRONMENTALLY RESPONSIBLE BEHAVIOR

One of the most appropriate goals of environmental psychologists is to encourage proenvironmental behavior patterns. The most obvious technique for this has been educational campaigns, but educational approaches do not always work very well, except perhaps as priming agents to change attitudes (but not necessarily behavior). However, another form of educational approach is to use the pure dramatic power of the media.

For example, Hine and Gifford (1991) conducted a study designed to have an immediate, tangible payoff for the environmental movement. In one condition, we showed participants graphic environmental scenes, such as needles washing up on a beach (a control group was shown architectural images). As they left the study session, participants passed a table where a representative of a local group that was concerned with water pollution was sitting. Participants who saw the graphic environmental scenes

offered significantly more donations of their time and money to the representative than did participants in the control group.

An Australian study measured the effectiveness of a 30-second commercial that advocated conservation of gasoline (Syme, Seligman, Kantola, & MacPherson, 1987). It found that after 4 weeks of intensive airplay, the commercial had a small but significant effect on the conservation of gasoline.

In another campaign, environmental psychologists used a multimedia campaign to teach the concept of precycling to a large urban community that had never heard the term (Gillilan, Werner, Olson, & Adams, 1996). A survey showed that at least 65,000 citizens had probably learned the concept; many will have translated their new knowledge into behavior.

Other environmental psychologists see environmental problems as a marketing issue: They believe we should use the same arsenal of techniques to sell recycling as we do to sell commercial products. These *social marketers* note that relatively little attention has been paid to ensuring that psychological knowledge is accessible to those who design environmental programs. The goal of community-based social marketing is to make psychological knowledge relevant and accessible to program planners (McKenzie-Mohr, 2000).

COMMITMENT

Many studies have shown that asking people to make a public commitment or to set goals or that providing them with feedback improves the frequency of their proenvironmental behavior (Gardner & Stern, 1996). Taking this idea a step further, if commitment helps, will stronger commitment help even more? If public commitment leads to conservation, will stronger public commitment lead to even more energy conservation? Researchers invited 24 small businesses to participate in a conservation program (Shippee & Gregory, 1982).

All businesses were told that there was a community relations component to the program. They might be assigned, randomly, to a mild commitment condition (their business listed in a newspaper advertisement thanking firms in the small town where the study occurred for their participation), a strong commitment condition (nearly the same ad, except that newspaper readers could tell just how much each business had conserved or not), or a control condition (no ad exposure). The control condition produced the least conservation, as expected, but the strong commitment condition produced *less* conservation than did the mild commitment condition. Although a number of reasons for this might be advanced (too much pressure, feeling trapped), the study did produce conservation in all conditions even as it discovered that too much commitment is not as effective as moderate commitment.

FEEDBACK

Environmental psychologists who have investigated the effectiveness of feedback have offered energy use information to the consumer much more frequently—sometimes even an immediate, continuous read-out of how much energy is being used. In a typical study, householders were told four times per week how much electricity they had used in comparison to an amount predicted for them on the basis of outdoor temperature and other factors (Seligman & Darley, 1977). Compared to a no-feedback control group, the informed residents used 10.6% less electricity.

Other studies of feedback have reported savings in the range of 5% to 15% (Siero, Boon, Kok, & Siero, 1989). These savings may not sound very dramatic until they are multiplied by the number of residential units in a whole country; then the potential value of frequent feedback is clear. British Columbia Hydro, for example, has tested a device that offers a continuous display of the ongoing electrical use. Because the consumer may lose track of the overall meaning of a continuous display, usage rates for the past day and week are also displayed. A California study found that continuous displays combined with different rates for peak versus off-peak electricity use did not manage to reduce overall energy consumption but at least caused consumers to shift their electricity use to off-peak periods (Sexton, Johnson, & Konakayama, 1987).

GOAL SETTING

Energy savings are easier to achieve when individuals are also asked to meet relatively difficult, but voluntarily chosen goals—such as a 20% saving (L. Becker, 1978). When strategies are combined, savings are better. A Dutch study reports that daily feedback plus a commitment to save resulted in significant natural gas conservation (Van Houwelingen & Van Raaij, 1989).

MODELING

We learn from watching others. This principle has been shown to increase energy conservation behaviors in studies of university showering practices and home energy conservation. In the shower study, despite signs to the contrary, only 6% of students soaped up while the water ran and took short showers. A larger sign increased compliance to 19%, but the sign was a target for aggressive remarks and minor vandalism. When one student (a confederate of the experimenter) modeled the desirable behaviors, half of the others soaped up with the water off and took shorter showers. When two students modeled, 67% of the others complied (Aronson & O'Leary, 1977).

A similar strategy is to locate individuals on each block (or equivalent) who might encourage their neighbors to recycle (Hopper & Nielson, 1991). When these block leaders each approached several of their neighbors, recycling increased significantly; it even increased compared to recycling by other neighbors who received the same plea in written form instead of in person (Burn, 1991). In a similar approach, recycling also will increase when "significant others" are depicted recycling (Kahle & Beatty, 1987).

ENVIRONMENTAL AUDITS

Energy utility companies and governments also have tried to provoke conservation through programs in which a company representative visits the house and examines its energy-wasting capacity. Typically, the auditor points out problems, suggests that repairs be done, offers an attractive grant or loan for major refits, and suggests reputable contractors. The success of such programs is variable; a national average might be about 15% of householders who go on to make the necessary changes to weatherproof their houses.

Psychologists have improved that success rate by training auditors how to communicate with householders (Gonzáles, Aronson, & Costanzo, 1988). For example, auditors were told to use vivid examples, such as saying "If you were to add up all the cracks under these doors, it would be the same as if you had a hole the size of a basketball in your wall." The auditors were told to focus on loss rather than gain, such as saying "If you don't fix cracks, it's your hard-earned cash going right out the window."

The auditors were also trained to induce investment or commitment in the audit process by getting householders to follow them around the house, help take measurements, and actually look at the cracks. Together, these changes to the auditor's style produced a cooperation rate of about 60%, roughly four times the usual.

GREEN DESIGN

One way to integrate them is to build a small community composed of energy-conscious individuals and energy-saving houses. Michael and Judy Corbett are Davis, California, developers who have gone beyond merely adding solar panels to the houses in their project, Village Homes (Corbett, 1981). Davis can be very hot in the summer; their designs take advantage of natural ventilation patterns to reduce the need for air-conditioning. One ambient source of excess heat in some developments comes from broad expanses of pavement; in Village Homes, pavement area is reduced by narrowing streets and clustering homes (Sommer, 1983).

Village Homes incorporates these energy conservation features into an overall plan aimed at ecological soundness. There are water conservation features, defensible space features, and a community-constructed playground. Parts of a pre-existing orchard were retained; income from it goes into the homeowners' association coffers. The Corbetts reside in the development so that assistance with technical problems is close at hand.

Interior design can also support environmental goals. In the administration offices of a large university, three sort-as-you-toss designs were compared: (1) two wastebaskets, one for recyclable paper and one for non-recyclable garbage, (2) divided wastebaskets with one section for recyclable paper and one for nonrecyclables, and (3) a personal wastebasket for recyclables and a central (public) wastebasket for non-recyclables (Humphrey, Bord, Hammond, & Mann, 1977).

The first two designs resulted in proper recycling of over 92% of paper in the 10 weeks of the study. (Proper recycling was measured as the absence of nonrecyclables in wastebaskets designated for recyclables.) Even the less convenient (but presumably cheaper) alternative of a centralized container for non-recyclables resulted in 84% proper recycling.

Employees in half the 16 locations of the study received personal prompts on two occasions during the study. The prompts had only a small effect; they increased proper recycling from 88% to 92%. The vast bulk of the recycling was due to placement of the recycling containers in the office, a very simple design feature. More recent research confirms that nearby containers in offices produce dramatically increased recycling rates, compared to centralized containers (Brothers, Krantz, & McClannahan, 1994).

Another company has created a slightly more sophisticated sort-as-you-toss system (Geller, Winett, & Everett, 1982). This is a desktop system that places the paper separation process even closer to the point at which mail or old drafts of memos become garbage. This system is recommended by the U.S. Environmental Protection Agency (EPA), which lives up to its recommendation by using it in its Washington headquarters. The desktop system, used by about 2,700 people in the building, manages to outperform the divided wastebasket: Proper recycling reaches 97%. In the first year, EPA recovered 150 tons of high-grade paper. Designing the environment to encourage "mindless" recycling may be an important key to the promotion of recycling in the future.

SOCIAL DESIGN

Social design (Sommer, 1983) benefits the people who live or work in a building, or even visit it, by systematically incorporating their needs and ideas into the building. This can take many forms. One of the social designer's jobs is to advocate as many design considerations that benefit users as possible. In a large Michigan hospital project, over 500 design and policy changes were recommended (Carpman, Grant, & Simmons, 1986). Had these research-based suggestions not been made, the architect would have been forced to make intuitive decisions. As it happened, because of constraints and the political aspect of design, the social designers were "only" able to have about 60% of their recommendations adopted. However, that means about 300 social research-based design improvements were made to a hospital that has played a crucial, if brief, role in the lives of thousands of people who have been forced to stay in the hospital since it was built.

In one example of this social design research, the design of the hospital courtyard was studied (Carpman, Grant, & Simmons, 1986). A table-sized model of the courtyard was constructed so that it could be taken apart and reassembled in different patterns. After showing many possible variations of the courtyard to over 200 patients and visitors, the social researchers concluded that the courtyard should have densely planted trees, colorful plants, and seating arrangements that allowed for privacy or social interaction.

An example of the way social design can succeed—or almost fail—is illustrated in another story from this hospital. The architects planned to surface parts of the courtyard with brick (Carpman, Grant, & Simmons, 1986). Brick is attractive and other hospitals had used it frequently. But interviews at the other hospitals revealed that patients with recent injuries or surgery found it painful to be wheeled over brick surfaces, which are often bumpy. Although the decision was not popular with the aesthetics-minded architects, portions of the courtyard over which wheelchairs were expected to pass were redesigned with a smoother surface.

Research conducted after a building is completed can also benefit future building users and can show that interviews should be supplemented with systematic observations. In a study of a recently completed public library, Cheuk Ng and I learned that patrons believed there were not enough tables (Ng & Gifford, 1986). Yet behavior mapping revealed that many tables actually were unused. Instead of recommending to the library board that more tables be acquired, which would be logical had we merely interviewed the patrons, we recommended that the tables be rearranged. The reality was that there were enough tables, but too many popular activities were located in the same area of the library, so there was a shortage of tables *in that area.* Once the distribution of tables matched the rate of use for different areas of the library, the problem disappeared.

It is important to examine whether the suggested changes in a building have the hoped-for effects. Frank Becker and Donald Poe (1980) were involved in the renovation of a hospital wing. They had helped hospital users of all types (patients, staff, and visitors) to participate in the renovation decision-making. The changes made to the building represented those agreed on through a consensus-seeking process, although financial and administrative constraints restricted the changes slightly.

The effects of the changes were measured, using three methods, and the renovated hospital wing was compared with two similar but unchanged wings. The mood and morale of the hospital staff on the renovated wing increased dramatically after the design changes, in comparison to the mood and morale of staff who worked on the control wings. All user

groups rated the changed features of the renovated wing as better than comparable features of the unchanged wings. Behavior mapping showed that on the renovated wing the solarium was used significantly more than before the renovations, but solaria on the control wings were used slightly less than before. Users were also observed in conversation. Postrenovation conversation increased in the renovated wing but was essentially unchanged in the control wings.

Social designers cannot supply every wish and whim that building users might want. But that does not necessarily mean that clients must be left out of the decision-making process; indeed they can decide for themselves what is most important (Eisemon, 1975). In a housing complex in Madison, Wisconsin, low-income residents were guided through a set of procedures for designing their ideal apartment. They were also faced with the necessity of trade-offs: "If the costs of your ideal apartment rose, which features would you sacrifice?" Using models, the residents were asked to begin the design process by assessing how their present apartment met their needs. The ideal apartment grew out of needs unmet by their present apartment. The notion of trade-offs is central to an approach that emphasizes the user as an active design agent who is capable of adapting to some building features and changing others (Vischer, 1985). Merely determining users' needs and preferences is to regard users as passive, unable or unwilling to actively interact with the building.

A book devoted to social design applications (Preiser, Vischer, & White, 1991) was subtitled, *Toward a More Humane Architecture.* In it are many examples of housing and other structures designed with and for specific groups, such as single parents, the homeless, the terminally ill, and the elderly. Most chapters reflect the reaction of environmental psychologists and designers to Robert Sommer's statement that, in the usual course of things, the *affordability* of good design expertise is inversely proportional to the *need* for good design expertise.

One example is Rikard Kuller's work for people with dementia in Sweden. The dining room of a Swedish geriatric hospital was redecorated based on interviews with patients (Kuller, 1991; Kuller & Mattsson, 1984). The interviews revealed that the sterile hospital environment would best be replaced with one that resembled the patients' homes. The redecorated dining room was constructed to resemble a typical Swedish home of the 1930s or 1940s—the prime era of the patients' lives. The redecoration was very popular with the residents, which confirmed the value of the interviews.

Persons afflicted with multiple sclerosis (MS) represent an especially interesting design challenge. The disease causes such a variety of symptoms and problems that a sensitive designer must consider many different disabilities. In a project that I was fortunate enough to be part of (Gifford & Martin, 1991), the entire design cycle (Zeisel, 1975) from programing to postoccupancy evaluation (POE) was completed—and completed by the same team. An electronics warehouse and office complex was renovated into space for MS physiotherapy, counseling, social, and office space.

Over 80 interviews with MS patients, their families, and staff were completed. Perhaps the epitome of design for MS was the bathroom; the great variety of physical problems of people with MS lead not only to the need for bathrooms that go far beyond the building code for the disabled but also to much black humor about problems with this fundamental human process.

The bathrooms in the new center were the subject of a considerable proportion of the 150 recommendations made to the architect. Some recommendations were incompatible with others, so the three bathrooms were all different in some ways to provide something for everyone. Still, not every client's needs were met, but the POE showed that satisfaction with the building was very high.

Modern designers have begun to reach out to client groups in ever more embracing ways. A group including Ombretta Romice and Michael MacAulay at the University of Strathclyde in Scotland has brought its community design approach into a low-income project called Sighthill (www.hampden .arch.strath.ac.uk/Sighthill/startOK.htm).

Faculty and students even have a flat in the building, from which they engage the community in almost peer-level discussions about how to improve the setting and residents' quality of life. The designers have adopted a code of conduct that guides their approach as they interact with Sighthill residents. This code reflects their desire to work with the residents in a radically sincere and authentic manner:

- Don't use jargon.
- Be honest.
- Be enthusiastic.
- Listen to what groups have to say, no matter how it will be reported.
- Use diplomacy.

- Don't be patronizing.
- Be engaging.
- Don't raise false expectations.
- Keep promises.
- Involve everyone.
- Don't assume anything.
- Always make sure you have been understood.
- Work as a team with colleagues and with residents groups.

Social design research can even benefit the paying client (the developer or board of directors), who often is concerned with costs and assumes that social design is a net cost to the project. Instead, social research may cost less than other planning methods; studies have documented direct savings to building projects that may be attributed to social design research (Sommer, 1983). An Australian study suggests that information provided by social design research can help the paying client avoid mistakes that would cost considerable money indirectly over an extended period of the building's life (Reizenstein, 1982). These include chronic inefficiency in building maintenance, duplication of effort, user ignorance of building capabilities, overspending, and a design that is inappropriate for the activities housed by the building.

CONCLUSION

For a field of inquiry and action that is only 35 years old, environmental psychology has made some very significant improvements in the world. One wonders whether other branches of psychology, or even other disciplines, have so positively affected the quality of life of so many people within their first 35 years. From ubiquitous transit maps to international diplomacy, from more humane city plazas to the widespread acceptance of social design principles, from the encouragement of more environmentally responsible behavior to fighting crime, and from saving lost hikers to facilitating better learning in classrooms, environmental psychology has much to be proud of. It can truly say it has made a difference in the quality of life for millions of people.

REFERENCES

Appleyard, D. (1976). *Planning a pluralistic city*. Cambridge, MA: Massachusetts Institute of Technology Press.

Aronson, E., & O'Leary, M. (1977). The relative effectiveness of models and prompts on energy conservation: A field experiment in a shower room. *Journal of Environmental Systems, 12,* 219–224.

Baum, A., & Davis, G. E. (1980). Reducing the stress of high-density living: An architectural intervention. *Journal of Personality and Social Psychology, 38,* 471–481.

Becker, F. D., & Poe, D. B. (1980). The effects of user-generated design modifications in a general hospital. *Journal of Nonverbal Behavior, 4,* 195–218.

Becker, L. J. (1978). Joint effect of feedback and goal setting on performance: A field study of residential energy conservation. *Journal of Applied Psychology, 63,* 428–433.

Breu, J. (1984, April 20). Patients, visitors getting chance to help design new hospital. *American Medical News,* 10–11.

Brothers, K. J., Krantz, P. J., & McClannahan, L. E. (1994). Office paper recycling: A function of container proximity. *Journal of Applied Behavior Analysis, 27,* 153–160.

Brower, S. (1988). *Design in familiar places: What makes home environments look good.* New York: Praeger.

Burn, S. M. (1991). Social psychology and the stimulation of recycling behaviors: The block leader approach. *Journal of Applied Social Psychology, 21,* 611–629.

Canter, D., & Larkin, P. (1993). The environmental range of serial rapists. *Journal of Environmental Psychology, 13,* 63–70.

Canter, D., & Tagg, S. K. (1975). Distance estimation in cities. *Environment and Behavior, 7,* 59–80.

Carpman, J. R., Grant, M. A., & Simmons, D. A. (1983–1984). Wayfinding in the hospital environment: The impact of various floor numbering alternatives. *Journal of Environmental Systems, 13,* 353–364.

Carpman, J. R., Grant, M. A., & Simmons, D. A. (1986). *Design that cares: Planning health facilities for patients and visitors.* Chicago: American Hospital Publishing.

Collett, D. (1971). Training Englishmen in the nonverbal behavior of Arabs. *International Journal of Psychology, 6,* 209–215.

Cone, J. D., & Hayes, S. C. (1980). *Environmental problems/Behavioral solutions.* Monterey, CA: Brooks/Cole.

Corbett, M. N. (1981). *A better place to live: New designs for tomorrow's communities.* Emmaus, PA: Rodale.

Cose, E. (1994, July 11). Drawing up safer cities. *Newsweek,* 57.

Downs, R. M., & Stea, D. (1977). *Maps in minds: Reflections on cognitive mapping.* San Francisco: Harper & Row.

Eisemon, T. (1975). Simulations and requirements for citizen participation in public housing: The Truax technique. *Environment and Behavior, 7,* 99–123.

Evans, G. W., Fellows, J., Zorn, M., & Doty, K. (1980). Cognitive mapping and architecture. *Journal of Applied Psychology, 65,* 474–478.

Fischhoff, B. (1990). Psychology and public policy: Tool or toolmaker? *American Psychologist, 45,* 647–653.

Freedman, J. L. (1979). Current status of work on crowding and suggestions for housing design. In J. R. Aiello & A. Baum (Eds.), *Residential crowding and design.* New York: Plenum Press.

Gardner, G. T., & Stern, P. C. (1996). *Environmental problems and human behavior.* Needham Heights, MA: Allyn & Bacon.

Geller, E. S. (1992). Solving environmental problems: A behavior change perspective. In S. Staub & P. Green (Eds.), *Psychology and social responsibility: Facing global challenges* (pp. 248–268). New York: New York University Press.

Geller, E. S. (1995). Integrating behaviorism and humanism for environmental protection. *Journal of Social Issues, 51*(4), 179–195.

Geller, E. S., Winett, R. A., & Everett, P. B. (1982). *Preserving the environment.* New York: Pergamon.

Gifford, R., & Martin, M. (1991). A multiple sclerosis program and post-occupancy evaluation. In W. F. E. Preiser, J. C. Vischer, & E. T. White (Eds.), *Design intervention: Toward a more humane architecture* (pp. 197–222). New York: Van Nostrand Reinhold.

Gillilan, S., Werner, C. M., Olson, L., & Adams, D. (1996). Teaching the concept of precycling: A campaign and evaluation. *Journal of Environmental Education, 28*(1), 11–18.

Gonzáles, M. H., Aronson, E., & Costanzo, M. A. (1988). Using social cognition and persuasion to promote energy conservation: A quasi-experiment. *Journal of Applied Social Psychology, 18,* 1049–1066.

Heth, C. D., & Cornell, E. H. (1998). Characteristics of travel by persons lost in Albertan wilderness areas. *Journal of Environmental Psychology, 18,* 223–235.

Hine, D. W., & Gifford, R. (1991). Fear appeals, individual differences, and environmental concern. *Journal of Environmental Education, 23*(1), 36–41.

Hopper, J. R., & Nielson, J. M. (1991). Recycling as altruistic behavior: Normative and behavioral strategies to expand participation in a community recycling program. *Environment and Behavior, 23,* 195–200.

Humphrey, C. R., Bord, R. J., Hammond, M. M., & Mann, S. H. (1977). Attitudes and conditions for cooperation in a paper recycling program. *Environment and Behavior, 9,* 107–124.

Jacobs, J. (1961). *The death and life of great American cities.* New York: Vintage.

Kahle, L. R., & Beatty, S. E. (1987). Cognitive consequences of legislating postpurchase behavior: Growing up with the bottle bill. *Journal of Applied Social Psychology, 17,* 828–843.

Kitchin, R. M. (1994). Cognitive maps: What they are and why study them? *Journal of Environmental Psychology, 14,* 1–19.

Kohn, I. R., Franck, K. A., & Fox, A. S. (1975). *Defensible space modifications in row-house communities.* Report to the National Science Foundation. New York: Institute for Community Design Analysis.

Kuller, R. (1991). Familiar design helps dementia patients cope. In W. F. E. Preiser, J. C. Vischer, & E. T. White (Eds.), *Design intervention: Toward a more humane architecture* (pp. 255–268). New York: Van Nostrand Reinhold.

Kuller, R., & Mattsson, R. (1984). *The dining room at a geriatric hospital.* Paper presented at International Association for the Study of People and their Surroundings, West Berlin.

Langer, E. J., & Saegert, S. (1977). Crowding and cognitive control. *Journal of Personality and Social Psychology, 35,* 175–182.

Lawrence, R. J. (1978). *Housing, dwellings, and homes: Design theory, research and practice.* New York: Wiley.

Lewin, K. (1948). *Resolving social conflicts.* New York: Harper.

Lynch, K. (1960). *The image of the city.* Cambridge. MA: Massachusetts Institute of Technology Press.

McKenzie-Mohr, D. (2000). Promoting sustainable behavior: An introduction to community-based social marketing. *Journal of Social Issues, 56,* 543–554.

Newman, O. (1972). *Defensible space.* New York: Macmillan.

Ng, C. F., & Gifford, R. (1986). *Greater Victoria Public Library Esquimalt Branch): A Post-occupancy report.* Report to the Greater Victoria Public Library Board. Victoria, BC: Optimal Environments.

O'Neill, M. J. (1991). Effects of signage and floor plan configuration on wayfinding accuracy. *Environment and Behavior, 23,* 553–574.

Osmond, H. (1957). Function as the basis of psychiatric ward design. *Mental Hospitals, 8*(Architectural Supp.), 23–30.

Preiser, W. F. E., Vischer, J. C., & White, E. T. (1991). *Design intervention: Toward a more humane architecture.* New York: Van Nostrand Reinhold.

Rafter, K., & Sommer, R. (1999, August). *Postmodern design for a classroom.* Presentation at the 107th annual meeting of the American Psychological Association, Boston.

Reizenstein, J. E. (1982). Hospital design and human behavior: A review of the recent literature. In A. Baum & J. E. Singer (Eds.), *Advances in environmental psychology: Vol. 4. Environment and health.* Hillsdale, NJ: Erlbaum.

Seligman, C., & Darley, J. M. (1977). Feedback as a means of decreasing residential energy consumption. *Journal of Applied Psychology, 62,* 363–368.

Sexton, R. J., Johnson, N. B., & Konakayama, A. (1987). Consumer response to continuous-display electricity-use monitors in a time-of-use pricing experiment. *Journal of Consumer Research, 14,* 55–62.

Shippee, G., & Gregory, W. L. (1982). Public commitment and energy conservation. *American Journal of Community Psychology, 10,* 81–93.

Siero, S., Boon, M., Kok, G., & Siero, F. (1989). Modification of driving behavior in a large transport organization: A field experiment. *Journal of Applied Psychology, 74,* 417–423.

Sommer, R. (1969). *Personal space: The behavioral basis of design.* Englewood Cliffs, NJ: Prentice-Hall.

Sommer, R. (1983). *Social design: Creating buildings with people in mind.* Englewood Cliffs, NJ: Prentice-Hall.

Sommer, R., & Olsen, H. (1980). The soft classroom. *Environment and Behavior, 12,* 3–16.

Syme, G. J., Seligman, C., Kantola, S. J., & MacPherson, D. K. (1987). Evaluating a television campaign to promote petrol conservation. *Environment and Behavior, 19,* 444–461.

Taylor, B., & Taylor, A. (1993). Wayfinding training for the severely mentally ill. *Families in Society, 74,* 434–440.

Tzamir, Y. (1975). *The impact of spatial regularity and irregularity on cognitive mapping* (Technical Rep.). Haifa, Israel: Technion-Israel Institute of Technology, Center for Urban and Regional Studies.

Van Houwelingen, J. H., & Van Raaij, W. F. (1989). The effect of goal-setting and daily electronic feedback on in-home energy use. *Journal of Consumer Research, 16,* 98–105.

Vaughan, E. (1993). Individual and cultural differences in adaptation to environmental risks. *American Psychologist, 48,* 673–680.

Vis, A. A., Dijkstra, A., & Slop, M. (1992). Safety effects of 30 Km/H zones in The Netherlands. *Accident Analysis and Prevention, 24,* 75–86.

Vischer, J. C. (1985). The adaptation and control model of user needs: A new direction for housing research. *Journal of Environmental Psychology, 5,* 287–296.

Wener, R. E., & Kaminoff, R. D. (1983). Improving environmental information: Effects of signs on perceived crowding and behavior. *Environment and Behavior, 15,* 3–20.

Whyte, W. H. (1980). *The social life of small urban spaces.* New York: Conservation Foundation.

Wollin, D. D., & Montagne, M. (1981). College classroom environment: Effects of sterility versus amiability on student and teacher performance. *Environment and Behavior, 13,* 707–716.

Wong, C. Y., Sommer, R., & Cook, R. (1992). The soft classroom 17 years later. *Journal of Environmental Psychology, 12,* 337–343.

Zaidel, D., Hakkert, A. S., & Pistiner, A. H. (1992). The use of road humps for moderating speeds on urban streets. *Accident Analysis and Prevention, 24,* 45–56.

Zeisel, J. (1975). *Sociology and architectural design.* New York: Russell Sage Foundation.

CHAPTER 22

Bridging the Gap:
How Scientists Can Make a Difference

FRANCES E. KUO

ENVIRONMENTAL PSYCHOLOGISTS SEEK not only to understand human-environment relations but also to inform environmental design. Is this desire to "make a difference" in the larger world a realistic or quixotic quest? Can basic science make a difference outside academia? This chapter has three objectives: (1) to show the range of views on whether social science can inform environmental design, (2) to show the surprisingly large impacts that social science *can* have by examining the impacts a specific handful of studies *has* had, and (3) to propose a number of "best practices" for scientists wishing to maximize their work's impact.

CAN SOCIAL SCIENCE MAKE A DIFFERENCE? DIFFERENT VIEWS

Views on the role of research in environmental design range widely. The Environmental Design Research Association (EDRA) is the primary professional organization for many environmental psychologists, particularly those in the United States. A review of the introductions to EDRA conference proceedings over the past 31 years provides a sampling of different views on the relationship between social science and environmental design. Overall, the picture is decidedly mixed, and somewhat discouraging.

EDRA began on a note of high optimism, that social science should and could shape environmental design:

[S]olving environmental problems requires multi-disciplinary collaboration . . . a forum for discussion was needed . . . to bring individuals from the sciences together with environmental designers. To this end the first annual environmental design research association conference was held. (EDRA 1, Sanoff & Cohn, 1970, p. v)

We seek to emphasize the significance of research in design. . . . We encourage scientists concerned with the environment to direct their research interests to a responsive group [and] encourage environmental designers to be involved in research and incorporate those findings in their design efforts. (EDRA 3, Sanoff & Cohn, 1972)

Within four years of EDRA's inception, however, it was observed that despite the conferences and the increase in scientific activity, the gap between science and practice was still not being bridged:

As methodologies for environmental analysis are developed to higher degrees of sophistication, the question of applicability of research findings to environmental programming and design must be raised. (EDRA 4, Preiser, 1973, p. v)

This theme has emerged more than once in subsequent years:

In past conferences there has been a growing emphasis on the need for architects and planners to incorporate relevant contributions from the social sciences in their work . . . this synthesis has been more talked about than realized . . . basic research . . . has not been extensively translated into actual buildings. (EDRA 7, Suedfeld & Russell, 1976, p. vii)

The costs of inquiry without knowledge of practice are represented in the relative lack of impact that environment and behavior research has had on architecture. (EDRA 17, Wineman, Barnes, & Zimring, 1986, p. iii)

"Why don't designers heed research findings," some ask. "Why don't researchers address questions relevant to practice," others ask. (EDRA 26, Nasar, Grannis, & Hanyu, 1995, p. iii)

Perhaps in response to these discouraging observations, a few commentators have suggested that perhaps the gap between science and practice is simply not *meant* to be bridged. Some members of this school of thought distinguish social science research from "environmental design research," suggesting that social science isn't intended to influence practice:

Environmental design researchers share in the belief that through systematic research efforts, a knowledge base can be developed that will lead to the design of environments that are more successful in meeting users' needs . . . social scientists, on the other hand, have been conscientious in their objective of creating an empirically based understanding of human behavior. (EDRA 12, Campbell & Duerk, 1984, p. vii)

In recent years, another variation in the theme of "the twain shall never meet" has appeared. These observers seem to suggest that social science is inherently unsuited to informing practice. They draw stark distinctions between science and practice and suggest that making a difference in the larger world—informing design and reaching the general public—requires different methods than those used in science:

[W]hile science is concerned with finding factual knowledge about how the world works the other side—the "D" in EDRA—is concerned about how the world should be designed. And we have to keep reminding ourselves that validating design . . . guidelines . . . requires different methods and standards . . . than those appropriate to scientific research. (EDRA 30, Mann, 1999, p. 5)

[EDRA's] members certainly have interests and approaches so widely different that they constitute different cultures. . . . Which [method] to choose? It all depends on what you want to do. If one is helping to weave the web of collective knowledge, then knowledge of the reliability of each strand becomes very important. On the other hand, if one is applying knowledge to a specific case, then it may be more useful to reach for the widest, richest inputs possible rather than the fewest principles which account for most of the results. Likewise, if one is trying to communicate to the widest possible audience, then a credible story might well serve better than estimates of reliability of experimental findings. (EDRA 31, Stamps, 2000, pp. 1–4)

Since the first few years of EDRA, by far the most optimistic assessment of the hopes for bridging the gap comes from the 26th conference:

In previous conferences, participants have bemoaned the gap between research and practice. . . . Research directed at public policy bypasses the applicability gap. . . . We were pleased to have a distinguished group of keynote and plenary speakers who have played a vital role in making public policy through their research. (EDRA 26, Nasar et al., 1995, p. iii)

Even in this case, however, the hopeful examples came primarily from application-oriented research. Thus even this relatively optimistic assessment left open the question of whether basic science can have a real-world impact.

WHAT KINDS OF IMPACTS ARE POSSIBLE?

Can environment behavior (EB) social science research make a difference in the world beyond academia—beyond increasing our understanding of EB relationships and helping researchers achieve tenure? Contrary to many of the views above, the answer is yes. In this section I would like to demonstrate some of the impacts that social science research *can* have by examining the impacts some specific studies *have* had.

A number of studies that I have conducted with Bill Sullivan and our students have been notable in their impacts outside academia. Most of these pertain to the benefits of nature, especially the benefits of residential greenspaces. These studies, many conducted in inner-city Chicago, have linked residential greenspaces to: lower levels of intrafamily aggression and violence (Kuo & Sullivan, 2001); lower levels of crime (Kuo & Sullivan, 2001); more proactive, effective patterns of life functioning (Kuo, 2001); a greater sense of residential safety (Kuo, Sullivan, Coley, & Brunson, 1998); fewer incivilities (e.g., noise, litter, vandalism) (Brunson, Kuo, & Sullivan, in preparation); stronger ties between neighbors (Kuo et al., 1998); healthier patterns of play in children (Faber Taylor, Wiley, Kuo, & Sullivan, 1998); healthier patterns of adult supervision for children (Faber Taylor et al., 1998); milder attention deficit symptoms (Faber Taylor, Kuo, & Sullivan, 2001); and more vital neighborhood common spaces (Coley, Kuo, & Sullivan, 1997). Two additional studies documented the effectiveness (and ineffectiveness) of different techniques for communicating technical environmental information to the general public (Sullivan, Kuo, & Prabhu, 1996; Sullivan, Kuo, & Prabhu, 1997).

What follows is a description, based on our own experience with these studies, of the kinds of impacts social science EB research can have. This list is by no means complete in describing the full range of impacts; nonetheless, I find it remarkable and hopeful. I have been repeatedly surprised by the extent of these impacts—on the public, on practitioners and policy makers, and finally, on real places and policies. For more examples of EB research that has had substantial real-world impacts, the list of Environmental Design Research Achievement Awards and Career Awards as well as the EDRA/Places awards serves as a treasure trove of inspiring and wonderful examples.

What kinds of impacts can EB basic science have, beyond advancing scientific knowledge?

EB BASIC SCIENCE CAN REACH THE GENERAL PUBLIC

In addition to reaching academic audiences, scientific findings from EB research can reach both the general public and special interest audiences through media coverage—on radio and television, in newspapers and magazines, and increasingly on Internet news sources.

Our work has reached the general public through radio and television coverage both locally and nationally. A short list of the most widely familiar radio and television stations that have described our work includes National Public Radio's *All Things Considered; Good Morning, America;* and *The Today Show,* as well as a Public Broadcasting Service-produced documentary on the benefits of urban forests, *The Forests Where We Live.*

Our work has reached the general public via newspaper accounts as well, across the United States and even—without our help—internationally. U.S. newspapers that have provided accounts of our work include: the *Washington Post,* the *Chicago Tribune,* the *Chicago Sun-Times,* the *New Jersey Sentinel,* the *Richmond Times Dispatch,* the *Providence Journal-Bulletin,* the *Dallas Morning News,* the *Philadelphia Inquirer,* the *Albuquerque Tribune,* the *Manhattan Mercury,* and our local newspaper, the *Champaign News-Gazette.* International newspapers include the *Daily Herald, Scotsman,* and *Daily Telegraph* in the United Kingdom and the *Hamilton-Spectator* in Canada.

Our work has also reached targeted audiences, thanks to magazines and other publications, some on the Web. Examples include *Garden Design, Psychology Today, New Woman,* American Psychological Association's *Monitor, Self, New Age Journal,* the *Illinois Steward, Environment New Jersey, Communities and Forests, Inside Illinois, Illinois Research, Heart and Soul, Conscious Choice Magazine, Psychologie Magazine* (published in The Netherlands), and the *Southerner.*

It seems fair to conclude from this that the general public *can* be interested in social science EB research. Academic researchers can increase understanding of EB relationships not only within academia but also in the general public. As scientists, we have something to say not only to our colleagues but to our next-door neighbors.

EB BASIC SCIENCE CAN REACH PRACTITIONERS AND POLICY MAKERS

Findings from EB basic science can reach practitioners and policy makers at the local, state, and national level via briefs and technical bulletins, trade publications, indirect and direct requests, and presentations.

Our work has reached practitioners via a variety of outlets. A 2-page brief that was subsequently produced as a technical bulletin by the U.S. Forest Service has been perhaps one of the most effective single vehicles for reaching practitioners. This technical bulletin sold out in its first printing of 2,000 copies within about 2 years and prompted a second printing (G. Childs, personal communication, April, 1995).

A number of trade publications, including Internet publications, have allowed us to reach practitioners.

Because these publications, unlike peer-review outlets, are willing to publish already published work, many of them simply reprinted the original 2-page brief or abstracted it. Examples of these trade publications include: *Arbor Day, Arbor Age, Forestry Source, American Forests, American Nurseryman, Tree Scapes, The Landscape Contractor, Environmental News Network,* the U.S. Department of Energy's Center of Excellence for Sustainable Development Web site, and others.

Our work also reaches practitioners via direct and indirect requests. We receive multiple direct requests each month from landscape architects, advocacy organizations, city planners, and other individuals engaged in shaping the urban environment. Generally, the findings are being used to argue for the incorporation of natural elements in school settings, public housing, and urban environments. While we are aware of direct requests, it is more difficult to gauge the volume and nature of indirect requests. Certainly the U.S. Forest Service received a substantial number of requests for the technical bulletin described above. And Jim Skiera of the International Society for Arboriculture estimates that he personally receives an average of two calls per month about this body of work (personal communication, February, 1999).

Our work has also reached practitioners via presentations at conferences, for example at the Society of American Forests and National Urban Forestry conferences, a Governors' Conference on Urban Forestry, a talk to the Rhode Island Urban and Community Forestry Advisory Council, and so forth. Presentations constitute a relatively expensive way of reaching practitioners but can also have substantial impact (see, for example, the impact of a single presentation in Rhode Island in the next section).

Finally, our work has reached policy makers and agencies. Through a variety of vehicles, our work has reached such policy makers as U.S. Department of Agriculture Secretary Glickman, the U.S. Conference of Mayors, and congressional staff on Capitol Hill. And we have provided information for different federal or regional agencies, including the U.S. Department of Parks, U.S. Forest Service, Centers for Disease Control and Prevention, U.S. Environmental Protection Agency, U.S. Department of Energy, National Institutes of Health, and Tennessee Valley Authority.

Overall, our experience with reaching practitioners and policy makers has been extremely positive. It is clear that scientific EB research has the potential to reach the very individuals and institutions that can put the findings to use. It is also clear that much of this dissemination need not place inordinate demands on researchers' time and energy—a single 2-page brief can be extraordinarily effective. Moreover, a great deal of dissemination is undertaken by others: In our experience, various agencies and practitioner societies have taken it upon themselves to disseminate the findings—sometimes with our knowledge and involvement, sometimes without. In many instances, my collaborators and I have learned of a magazine or newspaper article on our work only by chance, through a distant friend's enthusiastic e-mail query, "Is this you?" Reaching relevant audiences with research findings seems to depend more on conducting policy-relevant research than on promoting and packaging the results. The right findings seem to largely disseminate themselves.

EB Basic Science Can Help Change Places and Policies

Not only can EB research reach the public, practitioners, and policy makers, but it can also help spark changes in real places and policies. While visible changes in specific places are extremely gratifying, it may be changes in policy that ultimately have the most impact, because a single policy generally shapes many specific places and continues to shape places for as long as it remains in effect.

Our experience suggests that social science research can help shape real places in ways both small and large. Our work has been cited in a $10 million tree planting initiative in the city of Chicago (Recktenwald, 1997), as well as in greening initiatives in Philadelphia and Rhode Island. Each of the public housing developments in Providence, Rhode Island, was newly landscaped within a few years after our findings were presented there. And on our own campus at the University of Illinois, our findings played a pivotal role in the decision to provide a green outdoor space for the university child-care center (B. McBride, personal communication, March 2000).

Social science can also affect policy. In Sweden, local codes are regularly changed to suit recent research, and EB labs at Texas A&M University and in Delft, The Netherlands, and Korea have all experienced success in influencing policy (R. Bechtel, personal communication, October 10, 2000). And from my own experience, Rhode Island's Urban and

Community Forestry Advisory Council has been extraordinarily successful in using our lab's findings to argue for new policies. Within a few years of receiving these findings, some two dozen or more communities in Rhode Island had adopted new municipal tree ordinances, and, increasingly, such ordinances are being adopted in communities throughout New England (J. Campanini, personal communication, April 2000). In addition, according to the U.S. Forest Service, the recent massive federal expenditures on rehabilitating public housing under the Hope VI program have been substantially shaped by our findings (P. Rodbell, personal communication, August 2000).

It is important to note that many of these impacts occurred in the absence of any direct contact with the policy makers involved. In most cases, other individuals and organizations have been responsible for taking our findings where they could make a difference—apparently with success.

Clearly, social science research has the capacity to impact real places and policies. There need be no fundamental distinction between basic and applied research. Each of the studies contributing to these impacts was intended to advance the field's understanding of EB relations in a scientifically defensible way, and each made a difference in the larger world.

WHAT CAN EB SCIENTISTS DO TO MAXIMIZE IMPACT?

The real-world impact of a particular piece of research undoubtedly depends on many factors; of these, some large proportion may lay entirely outside of the researcher's control. In the absence of the right prevailing winds and currents, even a perfectly constructed study may well fall on the shoals of oblivion. But outside factors are precisely that—factors that researchers have no control over. What can researchers themselves do to improve the chances of their research making a difference? What *besides* a favorable context distinguishes high-impact studies from other, well-constructed but unused pieces of research?

Here I offer five sets of ideas—hypotheses, really—regarding the characteristics that distinguish high-impact from low-impact studies. They are drawn from my own experiences with high- and low-impact research and from my understanding of other researchers' high-impact studies. None of these hypotheses have received systematic empirical testing. I offer them here as a way of generating discussion and, I hope, empirical study.

SELECTING A FUNDING SOURCE

Hypothesis 1: Research is more likely to make a difference when researchers seek funds from "applied" funding sources.

Applying to an "applied," as opposed to a "scientific," source of funding may be helpful in developing a high-impact research topic. For example, in writing to the National Science Foundation or National Institutes for Mental Health for a grant, one tends to focus on the methodological aspects of the proposed research, on the continuity of the research with the previous literature, and on choosing hypotheses with a very high probability of truth (e.g., hypotheses with encouraging pilot data). By contrast, in writing to a private foundation or an agency with an applied mission (e.g., Environmental Protection Agency, the Forest Service, the Kellogg Foundation), one tends to focus on the potential utility of the hoped-for findings, the extent to which these findings are new or surprising, and the connection of the proposed research to practice. Both types of funding agencies value all of these criteria, but the balance in their concerns is very different. And choosing to apply to a funding source with an applied mission may be helpful in prompting researchers to more thoroughly develop their thinking and research plans in the direction of application.

The next two categories of best practice I'd like to propose can be subsumed under a still more general claim: It matters what we study. I suggest that not all research topics are created equal and that some are more amenable to having an impact on practice than others. One implication of this is that having an impact is not simply a matter of clever packaging or self-promotion. Through the thoughtful selection of independent and dependent variables, researchers may be able to generate more useful, usable findings.

SELECTING AN INDEPENDENT VARIABLE

Hypothesis 2: Research is more likely to make a difference when researchers select independent variables that decision makers can control.

A number of possible "best practices" fall in the general category of selecting an independent variable.

Table 22.1 illustrates these best practices with a number of examples of independent variables that are more and less under decision makers' control. For ease of comparison, each of the examples is drawn from the same research domain; each of these variables is one a researcher might use if he or she were interested in the relationship between humans and nature. On the left are independent variables that decision makers cannot or do not control; on the right are independent variables that decision makers can control or have more control over. Each row illustrates a slightly different aspect of the more general point.

Compare these two independent variables—*individual differences in affinity for nature* and *number of trees outside an apartment building*—from the first row of Table 22.1. This comparison makes the point that, to affect policy, independent variables should be *environmental* factors (e.g., the number of trees outside apartment buildings, the color of interior paints in an office building, amount of lighting). Whereas a housing authority or developer can clearly control the number of trees outside an apartment building, it has essentially no control over whether the residents value trees. If a study shows that certain benefits are associated with the presence of trees outside an apartment building, it is fairly clear how that information might be applied: If the housing authority desires those benefits, they should try planting trees. In contrast, if a study shows that certain benefits are associated with having a strong affinity for nature, it is less clear how that information might be applied.

As a rule, individual-difference variables (e.g., affinity for nature, gender, environmental history, recreation habits) and psychological variables (e.g., stress, arousal, attentional fatigue) are not under the direct control of decision makers. If Hypothesis 1 is correct, EB researchers interested in application should avoid choosing individual-differences and psychological variables as their independent variables. Does this mean that EB researchers should not study individual differences? By no means. It is vitally important to know, for example, that the effects of an environmental factor (the presence of trees outside an apartment building) apply to nature lovers but not to city lovers. Similarly, it is extremely useful to know that mood rather than arousal mediates a given effect of a given environmental factor. But in these examples, the independent variables are still environmental factors; the individual differences and psychological variables are used as moderating or mediating variables.

Now compare *a wilderness outing* versus *a brief daily backyard outing*. This comparison, shown in the second row of Table 22.1, makes the point that not all environmental factors lend themselves equally to application. Simply from a practical standpoint, the finding that certain benefits are associated with brief daily backyard outings seems more likely to be widely applied than the finding that the same benefits are associated with wilderness vacations. All other things equal, inexpensive manipulations lend themselves more easily to application than expensive manipulations; thus a potential best practice is to favor relatively inexpensive manipulations.

It is important to note that this does not suggest that only inexpensive manipulations are worth studying. If, for instance, a study showed that having large windows in every office made a company substantially more productive, these would be important findings and could lead to a revolution in office building design. My guess is that there is a trade-off involved: The more expensive the recommended changes, the larger and more important the potential benefits might need to be to prompt implementation. The suggestion here is that, from an ap-

Table 22.1
Independent Variables That Decision Makers Can Control

Less Controllable Controllable IVs	More Controllable IVs
Individual differences in affinity for nature	Number of trees outside an apartment building
Wilderness outing versus no outing	Brief daily backyard outing versus no outing
Slides of green versus barren play settings	Actual green versus barren play settings

Note: No "good versus bad" dichotomy is implied here. It seems important for E-B researchers to use non-policy-oriented variables when the research questions they are grappling with require it. Moreover, there may be many cases in which the scientific goal of understanding and the practical goal of producing policy-relevant information can be simultaneously met by the thoughtful selection of independent variables.

plied standpoint, it only makes sense to study a ma-nipulation when its potential benefits outweigh the costs of implementation.

Note that wilderness outings and backyard out-ings are both operational definitions of the same conceptual variable—exposure to nature. Much of the difference between policy-oriented versus non-policy-oriented research may be in the operational definitions employed; if so, scientists can have sub-stantial latitude in the conceptual variables they choose and still conduct policy-relevant research.

Now compare using *slides of play settings* versus *ac-tual play settings* as the independent variables in a study. This comparison makes the point that, to af-fect policy, independent variables should represent real-world options. To affect policy, it may be more effective to study the effects of different real-world environmental configurations than the effects of different environmental proxies. For example, if a researcher is interested in affecting the design of ac-tual play settings, then at some point she may need to show that the effects she is interested in actually obtain in real play settings. A potential best practice is to study the outcomes associated with real-world options.

Note that studying real-world options does not preclude studying artificial stimuli. For instance, it is much more realistic to study the effects of nature posters on hospital patients in Manhattan than to study the effects of daily walks in Central Park on those patients. While nature posters are undeniably more artificial than a walk in Central Park, the prac-tical considerations surrounding installing nature posters in hospital rooms versus transporting ailing patients to Central Park are such that artificial stim-uli are the better real-world option.

An interesting corollary to the principle of study-ing real-world options is that the levels of our inde-pendent variables should be selected to include realistic levels. For example, in studying the effects of different levels of landscape maintenance, it may be scientifically useful to study the two ends of the con-tinuum (zero maintenance and "perfect" mainte-nance). But from a practical standpoint, since the decision makers controlling levels of landscape main-tenance are unlikely to consider either zero or "per-fect" maintenance, it seems important to include more intermediate, realistic options (e.g., once per week vs. twice per week) in one's research designs.

In essence, high-impact research is *decision-oriented research*. Decision-oriented research compares the impacts of different real-world choices that decision makers routinely confront—for example, between spending more or less on landscaping, between dif-ferent kinds of artwork in hospital rooms, or between retaining versus removing greenspace near schools.

To summarize, Hypothesis 2 suggests a number of best practices for scientists wishing to make a dif-ference in the larger world. Specifically, we should study environmental factors that decision makers can control, avoid using individual-difference or psychological variables as independent variables, study manipulations whose benefits could conceiv-ably outweigh their costs, and try to compare the ef-fects of real-world options.

SELECTING A DEPENDENT VARIABLE

Hypothesis 3: Research is more likely to make a difference when researchers select dependent variables that decision makers care about.

In conducting high-impact research, not only may the choice of independent variables matter, but so may the choice of dependent variables. Table 22.2 gives examples of typical EB dependent variables that seem more and less likely to prompt applica-tion. On the left are outcomes that seem less likely to be important to decision makers; on the right are outcomes that seem more likely to be important to decision makers.

Table 22.2 illustrates two points. The first is simply that decision makers care about some outcomes more than others. Mayors care a great deal about prevent-ing crime, reducing domestic violence, and enhanc-ing economic vitality. And hospital administrators care a great deal about whether medical staff make errors in writing prescriptions. In contrast, mayors and hospital administrators seem less likely to be moved by findings involving mood ratings, burglars' ratings, preference ratings, and digit span backwards performance. Each of these measures is likely to be unfamiliar to decision makers; each is likely to be only tenuously connected in decision makers' minds with the more familiar, concrete outcomes they are concerned with on a day-to-day basis.

A second point illustrated in Table 22.2 is that the same conceptual variable in a study may be opera-tionalized in more or less policy-oriented ways. Cer-tainly burglars' ratings of residential vulnerability are intended to serve as proxies for the probability a residence will be subject to burglary. It is entirely

Table 22.2

Dependent Variables That Decision Makers Care About

Less Important to Decision Makers	More Important to Decision Makers
Ratings of territorial defensibility	Burglary rate
Parental mood ratings	Number of times child is beaten up
Shoppers' preference ratings	Willingness to pay for parking
Digit Span Backwards performance	Errors made in writing prescriptions

Note: Again, no "good versus bad" dichotomy is implied here. Decision makers may place high importance on some outcomes that are trivial in the grand scheme of things; conversely, there may be outcomes that are genuinely important to human welfare that decision makers habitually ignore. Further, the scientific importance of a dependent variable may not always mirror its practical significance, or its centrality to policy makers.

plausible that the same underlying constructs could drive both mood ratings and incidents of violence. Similarly, some kind of affective response or preference probably influences willingness to pay for parking, and cognitive functioning should affect both digit span backwards performance and accuracy in writing prescriptions. Thus findings may *be* relevant to decision makers concerns, yet not *seem* relevant. The right outcome measures may be pivotal in determining how relevant findings seem.

This raises a question. Should researchers avoid well-established, valid, and reliable variables such as digit span backwards and study only situation-specific outcomes? Not at all. Science can serve both understanding and application. Many well-established scientific measures address outcomes of direct concern to decision makers. Moreover, in many circumstances it costs little to include both a standardized measure and an application-oriented measure in a study.

To summarize, Hypothesis 3 suggests a number of best practices. To maximize potential impact, we should choose outcome variables that address decision makers' concerns and operationalize them in ways that are concrete, vivid, and situation-specific.

DESIGNING THE RESEARCH

Hypothesis 4: Research is more likely to make a difference when researchers select compelling research methods.

Simply selecting policy-relevant research questions may not be sufficient to change the way buildings are built, cities are laid out, and landscapes are

shaped. Decision makers face many difficult choices and are accountable for their decisions. For example, how should the city's budget be spent? Should police protection receive less funding in order to allocate more money to parks? Should a health maintenance organization spend more on equipment, less on staff, or more on enhancing the physical setting for visitors? Should an architect design in bigger windows if it means cutting corners elsewhere?

One consequence of accountability in decision making may be that any decision that runs counter to common practice requires strong evidence. For EB researchers, this analysis suggests that, in order to *change* standard practices and policies, research findings must be not only relevant but compelling—even to a skeptical audience. If so, then here is a happy coincidence between what scientists and environmental decision makers demand from research.

Table 22.3 illustrates how decision makers might view different approaches to measurement and research design for parallel research questions. The first and second rows in the table illustrate that subjective measures and response scales may be less compelling to decision makers than objective measures and response scales. Compare two hospital administrators deciding how much of the budget to allocate to the landscaping for a new wing after the bids for construction have turned out far higher than original estimates. One administrator learns of a study that shows that a view of nature makes people "feel less stressed." Another administrator learns of a study that shows that a view of nature reduces patients' blood pressure. Even if self-ratings of stress were perfectly correlated with blood pressure, my sense is that most hospital administrators would feel

Table 22.3
Research Methods That Decision Makers Find Compelling

Less Compelling to Decision Makers	More Compelling to Decision Makers
Measuring feelings of stress	Measuring blood pressure
Subjective response scales "very often"	Anchored response scales "6 times a week"
Measuring projected behaviors "I will . . . ," "I would . . ."	Measuring actual behavior or performance
Studying beliefs about phenomena (e.g., Ps believe gardening makes people happy.)	Studying phenomena (e.g., Happiness is greater among gardeners than non-gardeners.)
Happiness is greater among gardeners than non-gardeners.	Ps randomly assigned to gardening versus similar activities are happier.

safer relying on a finding that involved physiological measures than on an equally valid measure of psychological state.

Similarly, there is something more tangible and concrete in objectively anchored estimates ("6 times a week or more") than in subjectively anchored estimates (e.g., "frequently"). I believe that, as a general rule, nonscientists find quantification compelling. Quantitative outcomes such as behavior frequencies, the number of days before hospital discharge, the number of milligrams of drug taken, sales per day, and standardized test scores, all have a reassuring sense of solidity that may help prompt decision makers to reassess entrenched practices.

The third row in Table 22.3 illustrates the notion that so-called behavioroid measures may be less compelling than measures of actual behavior in actual circumstances. A common technique in social and environmental psychology is to measure proxies of behavior—the intent or willingness to do X (e.g., vote, donate blood, recycle) under hypothetical scenarios. While these proxies are often inexpensive and easy to use, they may be best used in exploratory work and followed up with behavioral measures. The suggestion here is that skeptical policy makers will be more willing to rely on direct evidence of changes in behavior than on indirect evidence. Hence, for research to have a greater applied impact, researchers may wish to choose direct over indirect measures.

Along these lines, the fourth row in Table 22.3 illustrates the idea that individuals' descriptions or theories about the impacts of the environment may not be compelling as documentation of the actual impacts of the environment. For instance, gardeners may unanimously claim that gardening makes them happy—and they may be right. But this claim, by itself, seems less compelling than the finding that gardeners are on average significantly happier than nongardeners. By this I do not mean to imply that individuals' observations or beliefs about the impacts of the environment are uninteresting, unimportant, or unworthy of study. Certainly it is useful to know, for example, what aspects of a setting make people feel comfortable, or safe, or unsafe. The suggestion here is to study beliefs and phenomenology when those are the topic of interest—and not to study beliefs and phenomenology as proxies when the topic of interest is something else.

Finally, the fifth row in Table 22.3 illustrates the idea that a purely correlational study may not be as compelling to decision makers (and should not be!) as a study in which alternative explanations have been addressed. Skeptics are notoriously facile at generating alternative explanations of data; in order to reach such audiences, it may be crucial for researchers to build tests for confounds into their designs. Here I will speculate that random assignment may not be as compelling to the layperson as it is to the average scientist. Nonscientists may prefer concrete evidence that participants were matched on x, y, and z dimensions before being assigned to different conditions over the assurance of random assignment. This seems an especially fascinating potential area for research.

To summarize, Hypothesis 4 suggests a number of best practices for researchers wishing to make a difference in the world beyond academia. Specifically, we should choose objective measures and objectively anchored response scales over self-report and unanchored response scales, measure actual behaviors rather than proxies of behavior, and avoid studying beliefs about environmental impacts as a proxy for studying actual environmental impacts. In addition, it may be helpful to track and control for important confounding variables rather than simply trusting random assignment procedures to take care of them. Note that these suggestions are all old news for scientists wishing to conduct rigorous research. What is new is that these suggestions may also be vital for making a difference in the world of practice.

Presenting the Findings

Hypothesis 5: Research is more likely to make a difference when researchers present their findings in forms that decision makers find accessible.

While scientists may have much in common with skeptical decision makers in the kinds of evidence they find compelling, they may differ greatly in other ways. Specifically, effective communication with decision makers may require very different vehicles and formats than those typically used in the scientific discourse.

Consider the first row of Table 22.4. This comparison makes the point that while peer-reviewed journal articles may be the best vehicle for sharing findings with scientific audiences, these articles may fall short in reaching practitioners and policy makers. They may fall short because decision makers do not typically read scientific journals, and, ironically, they may fall short because these articles are too long. Decision makers generally do not have time to read journal article-length descriptions of studies, and even if decision makers had the time and interest to read such descriptions, "bite-sized" descriptions might be more effective. A bite-sized presentation—a 1-to-2-page brief, press release, or technical bulletin—may be clearer, more vivid, and more memorable and may even ultimately have more impact on more readers than a more lengthy

exegesis. Bite-sized presentations may be more easily grasped and therefore applied.

Just as the length of the presentation may matter, so may the writing therein. As the second row of Table 22.4 suggests, the standard scientific voice is likely to be no more appropriate in addressing decision makers than it is in addressing undergraduates. While decision makers typically have expertise in their own domain of operation, they are likely to be novices with respect to both the concepts and research methods in environment and behavior. Sound bites and "eye bites" are novice-friendly.

Presenting research in bite-sized sentences and photographs may not come easily. Scientists are unaccustomed to using anything other than the scientific voice in describing their findings, and it can be extremely difficult to describe research in a way that is accurate and yet makes sense to the novice. Fortunately, many academic social scientists have developed this skill in their teaching. The suggestion here is that it may be helpful to use the same skills employed in introducing new topics to undergraduates as when describing findings to policy makers.

In attempting to condense findings into bite-sized sentences, an important question may arise: How do you balance the need for caution with the need for comprehensibility? Brevity and concise writing serve both science and application well. At the same time, some practices that are necessary and valuable in communicating with fellow scientists may be unnecessary and even counterproductive in communicating with the public or with decision makers. The use of numerous qualifications, technical language, and relatively subtle (policy-irrelevant) distinctions are helpful in conveying messages precisely and accurately among scientists but can be hopelessly confusing for novice readers.

A final word on wording. The third row of Table 22.4 illustrates the notion that findings should be

Table 22.4
Dissemination Forms That Decision Makers Find Accessible

Less Accessible to Decision Makers	More Accessible to Decision Makers
Peer-reviewed journal article	1 to 2-page brief, press release, or technical bulletin
Long sentences filled with technical terms and qualifications	Short, novice-friendly sentences; graphs; photographs; diagrams
"An ANOVA indicated a highly significant condition difference, $F(1, 34) = 2.45$, $p < .01 \ldots$"	"Residents with a view of trees were more satisfied with their neighborhoods."

presented in standard English prose, not in statistical language. Decision makers are less concerned with what statistics were used and the degrees of freedom and *p*-value than with the content of the finding itself. Statistical details may be best omitted or sequestered in parentheses, so as not to detract from the central message.

To summarize, Hypothesis 5 posits that researchers should present their findings in forms that decision makers find accessible. A few specific best practices (and practices to avoid) are proposed for communicating findings to decision makers: shorter, 1-to-2-page descriptions of research may be more effective than longer descriptions, plain English and visuals may be more effective than "sciencese," and straightforward descriptions of findings may be more helpful than detailed descriptions of analytic techniques.

CONCLUSION

In closing, although the literature on the real-world impacts of social science research is somewhat discouraging, my own experience and the experience of numerous other researchers has been decisively positive. Success in having real-world impacts is clearly possible, even if we currently have little understanding of the factors underlying success. By studying what characteristics distinguish high-impact studies from other studies that are equally sound but have little impact, perhaps we can discover techniques for making success systematic.

I have presented five general hypotheses regarding the characteristics that distinguish high-impact research from low-impact research. Specifically, research is more likely to make a difference when researchers:

- Select "applied" rather than "basic" funding sources.
- Select independent variables that decision makers can control.
- Select dependent variables that decision makers care about.
- Select research designs that decision makers find compelling.
- Present findings in forms that decision makers find accessible.

My hope is that these hypotheses will serve other researchers in crafting more applicable studies. As with all hypotheses, however, these may be wrong, and readers should proceed with that possibility in mind. Fortunately, these hypotheses, as with all hypotheses, are testable. Someone needs only to independently assess the impact of a number of studies and the extent to which they fulfill the criteria proposed here, and see if the latter predicts the former. Thus even if these hypotheses are wrong, we as a field can determine them to be wrong.

Better yet, we are not restricted to this paltry handful. You, the reader, may have your own ideas. And other investigators pondering the differences between high-impact studies and low-impact studies will undoubtedly generate other hypotheses. For me, the excitement is in seeing impact as an empirical question. At base, I believe that social science research can have real-world impacts and that these impacts are not random. I believe there *are* principles governing high-impact research and that we as a field can discover them.

EXAMPLES OF HIGH-IMPACT RESEARCH

The impacts described in this chapter are associated with work conducted by me, Bill Sullivan, and our students at the Human-Environment Research Laboratory, University of Illinois, Urbana-Champaign. The following list gives the full citations for just those studies from our lab that have had a significant impact outside academia, from most recent to earliest. Although journal articles are not the primary vehicle through which these studies have had their impact, the titles of the articles give some indication of the topics, settings, and populations studied. Perhaps one of the most remarkable aspects of this experience is that the great preponderance of impacts I describe can be traced to a mere handful of studies; these three particularly high-impact studies are indicated with an asterisk (*).

Brunson, L., Kuo, F. E., & Sullivan, W. C. (in preparation). Planting the seeds of community: Greening and gardening in inner city neighborhoods.

Coley, R. L., Kuo, F. E., & Sullivan, W. C. (1997). Where does community grow? The social context created by nature in urban public housing. *Environment and Behavior, 29*(4), 468–494.

Faber Taylor, A., Kuo, F. E., & Sullivan, W. C. (2001). Coping with ADD: The surprising connection to green play settings. *Environment and Behavior, 33*(1), 54–77.

Faber Taylor, A., Wiley, A., Kuo, F. E., & Sullivan, W. C. (1998). Growing up in the inner city: Green spaces as places to grow. *Environment and Behavior, 30*(1), 3–27.

Kuo, F. E. (2001). Coping with poverty: Impacts of environment and attention in the inner city. *Environment and Behavior, 33*(1), 5–34.

*Kuo, F. E., & Sullivan, W. C. (2001). Environment and crime in the inner city: Does vegetation reduce crime? *Environment and Behavior, 33*(3), 343–367.

*Kuo, F. E., & Sullivan, W. C. (2001). Aggression and violence in the inner city: Impacts of environment via mental fatigue. *Environment and Behavior. Special Issue: Restorative Environments, 33*(4), 543–571.

*Kuo, F. E., Sullivan, W. C., Coley, R. L., & Brunson, L. (1998). Fertile ground for community: Inner-city neighborhood common spaces. *American Journal of Community Psychology, 26*(6), 823–851.

Sullivan, W. C., Kuo, F. E., & Prabhu, M. (1997). Communicating with citizens: The power of photosimulation and simple editing. *Environmental Impact Assessment Review, 17*(3), 295–310.

Sullivan, W. C., Kuo, F. E., & Prabhu, M. (1996). Assessing the impact of environmental impact statements on citizens. *Environmental Impact Assessment Review, 15*(3), 171–182.

REFERENCES

Campbell, D., & Duerk, D. (1984). *Proceedings of the Environmental Design Research Association Conference, USA, 15,* vii.

Mann, T. (1999). Introduction. *Proceedings of the Environmental Design Research Association Conference, USA, 30,* 5.

Nasar, J. L., Grannis, P., & Hanyu, K. (1995). Introduction. *Proceedings of the Environmental Design Research Association Conference, USA, 26,* iii.

Osterberg, A. E., Tiernan, C. P., & Findlay, R. A. (1981). Preface. *Proceedings of the Environmental Design Research Association Conference, USA, 12.*

Preiser, W. F. E. (1973). Preface. *Proceedings of the Environmental Design Research Association Conference, USA, 4,* v.

Recktenwald, W. (1997, May 25). Tree-dimensional: Chicago digs in for a record planting season. *The Chicago Tribune,* pp. 1, 7, 9.

Sanoff, H., & Cohn, S. (1970). Preface. *Proceedings of the Environmental Design Research Association Conference, USA, 1,* v.

Sanoff, H., & Cohn, S. (1972). The EDRA Conferences. *Proceedings of the Environmental Design Research Association Conference, USA, 3.*

Stamps, A. E. (2000). Bridging the many interests of the EDRA community. *Proceedings of the Environmental Design Research Association Conference, USA, 31,* 1–4.

Suedfeld, P., & Russell, J. A. (1976). EDRA-7 and its focus. *Proceedings of the Environmental Design Research Association Conference, USA, 7,* vii.

Wineman, J., Barnes, R., & Zimring, C. (1986). *Proceedings of the Environmental Design Research Association Conference, USA, 17,* iii.

CHAPTER 23

Women and Environment

KAREN A. FRANCK

THROUGHOUT THE WORLD, from birth onward, girls (and then women) are expected to act in a different manner, to assume different responsibilities, and to hold different attitudes than boys (and then men). For these and other reasons, the actions and experiences of men and women in the built environment and their attitudes toward it differ. Although exactly what these differences are varies historically and culturally and according to age, class, and many other circumstances, the existence of powerful gender differences is universal. What is important for any understanding of the built environment is recognition of how much these gender differences are enacted in space, how they generate different needs, and how assumptions of gender differences affect the design and planning of environments. What is important for any improvement in the lives of women is analysis of whether these assumptions of gender differences reflect the actual everyday lives of women and men, whether existing built environments do meet women's needs, and how alternatives could better do so. It is equally important to understand the roles that women have played and can play in creating and maintaining built environments.[1]

All of these concerns emerged in environmental psychology and related fields of architecture, planning, geography, anthropology, and sociology in the late 1970s and early 1980s with the publication of several books; the Canadian journal *Women and Environments;* special issues of the journals *Heresies* (1981), *Sociological Focus* (1985), and *Ekistics* (1985); and numerous individual articles and conference papers.[2] From the start the topic has been multifaceted, encompassing research about women's activities, experiences, and preferences; critiques of the difficulties women encounter in the built environment as it now exists; and descriptions of alternative environments and alternative ways of planning and designing.[3] From the beginning, a feminist perspective has

[1] This essay is dedicated to the memory of three contributors to the field of women and environment: architect Joan Forrester Sprague, architect and member of the New Everyday Life project Birgit Krantz, and planner Marsha Ritzdorf. We appreciate your contributions, and we miss you.

[2] The books are: *Women in American Architecture* (Torre, 1977); *The Suburban Environment and Women* (Rothblatt et al., 1979); *New Space for Women* (Wekerle, Peterson, & Morley, 1980); *Building for Women* (Keller, 1981); *Women and the American City* (Stimpson, Dixler, Nelson, & Yatrakis, 1981); *Women and Space* (Ardener, 1981); *Making Space: Women and the Man-Made Environment* (Matrix, 1984); *Her Space, Her Place* (Mazey & Lee, 1983); *From Sun to Sun: Daily Obligations and Community Structure in the Lives of Employed Women and their Families* (Michelson, 1985); *Redesigning the American Dream* (Hayden, 1984); and *The Unsheltered Woman: Women and Housing in the 80s* (Birch, 1985).

[3] Subsequent books include: *Women, Human Settlements and Housing* (Moser, 1987); *Women, Housing and Community* (van Vliet, 1988); *Architecture: A Place for Women* (Berkeley & McQuaid, 1989); *More than Housing: Lifeboats for Women and Children* (Sprague, 1991); *The Sphinx in the City: Urban life, the Control of Disorder and Women* (Wilson, 1991); *Discrimination by Design: A Feminist Critique of the Man-Made Environment* (Weisman, 1992); *Gendered Spaces* (Spain, 1992); *Feminism and Geography* (Rose, 1993); *Shelter, Women and Development* (Dandekar, 1993); *Women and the Environment* (Altman & Churchman, 1994); *Housing Women* (Gilroy & Woods, 1994); *Women and Planning* (Greed, 1994); *Changing Places: Women's Lives in the City* (Booth, Darke, & Yeandle, 1996); *Voices in the Street: Explorations in Gender, Media and Public Space* (Drucker & Gumpert, 1997b); and *Design*

framed the field of women and environment in two significant ways: First, gender has been an important category for analysis and, second, improving the lives of women and others has been an important goal.

For the most part, those of us writing and conducting research on women and environment have accepted the concept of gender first promoted in feminist research in the 1970s and early 1980s as a socially constructed and culturally and historically variable system of beliefs that gives meaning to sexual difference (Rubin, 1978; Thorne, 1982). And so we have made a sharp distinction between gender and sex, giving more importance to the former than the latter. When we have stated explicit definitions, we have treated gender as a social construct that is overlaid on the biology on sex (cf. Matrix, 1984, p. 7; Franck, 1985, p. 144; Ahrentzen, 1996, p. 72). This approach combats any essentialist assumptions that what a woman is or does is strictly determined by biology, a belief which stereotypes women, constrains their choices, and misrepresents society and culture.

In conducting research and developing proposals for change researchers have studied gender differences or, more frequently, focused on the particular activities and experiences of women. Women as a group have much in common resulting from societal expectations and organization; it is this exploration of commonality that stimulates interest and continues to guide the work on women and environment. At the same time, the experiences and needs of

and Feminism: Re-Visioning Spaces, Places and Everyday Things (Rothschild, 1999). In the early 1990s the _Journal of Architecture and Planning Research_ (1991) and _Design Book Review_ (1992) devoted special issues to the topic, and the geography journal _Gender, Place and Culture_ began publication (1994). In the late 1990s and 2000 several anthologies focused on the more historical and theoretical aspects of women and architecture: _The Architect: Reconstructing Her Practice_ (Hughes, 1996); _Architecture and Feminism_ (Coleman, Danze, & Henderson, 1996); _The Sex of Architecture_ (Agrest, Conway, & Weisman, 1996); _Desiring Practices: Architecture, Gender and the Interdisciplinary_ (Ruedi, McCorquodale, & Wigglesworth, 1996); _Gender, Space, Architecture_ (Rendell, Penner, & Borden, 2000), and _Gender and Architecture: History, Interpretation and Practice_ (Durning & Wrigley, 2000). _African Nomadic Architecture: Space, Place and Gender_ (Prussin, 1995) documents the art and architecture of several nomadic groups in northern Africa, which is produced primarily by women. Single women as clients of modern architects is the subject of _Women and the Making of the Modern House_ (Friedman, 1998), and women's contributions to urban development in the United States at the turn of the century is the subject of _How Women Saved the City_ (Spain, 2001). Joan Rothschild and Victoria Rosner (1999) provide a very detailed and well-documented history of work on women and the designed environment.

women vary significantly according to age, race, class, culture, lifestyle, sexual orientation, place of residence, and many other individual and environmental circumstances. Hence the interest also in difference and the attention researchers on women and environment give to these and other factors.

IDENTIFYING GENDER DIFFERENCES AND WOMEN'S NEEDS

Several key differences between men and women are apparent in their basic orientation to and engagement with the environment. These come about through socialization, through the development of male and female self-identity, and through the division of labor. From an early age girls are encouraged to be less exploratory, more fearful, and less physically active than boys. Various studies reviewed by Susan Saegert and Roger Hart (1978) indicate that in the United States the spatial range of girls' activities beyond the home is smaller than that of boys and that girls' play is less likely to involve active manipulation of the environment. Girls are also taught to take up less space and to cross their legs (Henley, 1977). Iris Marion Young notes that generally women are more restrained in their bodily occupation of space, keeping limbs closer to the body when moving and when still and putting less force and less movement into their engagement with things as in lifting, pulling, or throwing. "Feminine existence appears to posit an existential enclosure between herself and the space surrounding her, in such a way that the space that belongs to her and is available to her grasp and manipulation is constricted and the space beyond is not available to her movement" (Young, 1990, p. 151). In Marge Piercy's utopian novel, _Woman on the Edge of Time_ (1976), a woman from the future is so free and easy in her movements and so confident in her use of space that a woman from today's world mistakes her for a man.

On a larger scale, women's restricted movement is apparent in their constrained mobility outside the home in Western industrialized countries, and in some other societies even more so. Women are more frequently engaged in housekeeping and child care activities, in and outside the home, giving them less time for discretionary travel. When they are outside the home, they are also more likely to be accompanied by others, including small children, and to be engaged in necessary activities related to domestic responsibilities (Franck & Paxson, 1989). Women are more likely than men to rely on public transit and so are constrained by the schedules and paths that public transit offers. Women's fear of crime and the resultant precautionary measures they adopt also restrict where, when, and how they move about in public space (Day, 1995, 2000; Franck & Paxson, 1989; Gordon & Riger, 1989; Wekerle & Whitzman, 1995). Restrained bodily comportment and restricted movement are even greater for women in Muslim countries where women are expected to wear veils and not to venture outside the local neighborhood unless they are accompanied by male relatives (Fenster, 1999; Moser, 1987).

The kinds of actions women and men value may also differ, possibly along an instrumental/communicative dimension. Young realized that she had previously assumed a strongly "instrumentalist-purposive model" of action where a single activity is directed toward a single goal as being a universal model, whereas it may in fact be a masculinist model of action. A different model, more reflective of women's actions, could emphasize communicative activity and movement that is "plural and engaged, to and fro . . . rather than unified and singly directed" (Young, 1998, p. 289), as for instance in doing all the tasks of making and bottling jam while holding a crying baby. An emphasis on communication rather than instrumentality is apparent in women's attitudes toward the home and objects within it. There is some evidence that wives feel it is more important that the home express their personalities than do their husbands (Saegert & Winkel, 1980) and that husbands value objects of action such as TVs, stereo sets, sports equipment, vehicles, whereas their wives value objects of contemplation such as photographs, sculptures, plants, plates (Csikszentmihalyi & Rochberg-Halton, 1981). In the same study, men talked extensively about work they had done to the house, while women tended to see the house primarily as a place where people interact. Perhaps for many men the world is more a place to do things, while for women it is a place to relate to things (and to others).

This does not mean that women do not do things. Far from it, given their many responsibilities. Rather what women are likely to value and emphasize is their relationships to people and to things more than the completion of a task. Such a gender difference in orientation is consistent with the idea that women's underlying relationship to the world is one of connection while men's is one of separation. This idea is based on object relations theory and the work of Nancy Chodorow (1978), who holds that, since the daughter is of the same gender as the mother, development of the daughter's self-identity centers on attachment to the main parenting figure and thereby to the generalized "other" and the world. In contrast, development of the son's self-identity requires differentiation and separation from the mother, leading more generally to separation from the "other" and the world.

Male self-identity, at least in the West, may also be based on a tendency to degrade everyday life and the domestic sphere and instead to value abstraction, business, and the public world. Nancy Hartsock (1983) argues that the masculinity boys must achieve can only be reached by escaping domestic life. They see two worlds: one "valuable, if abstract and deeply unattainable, the other useless and demeaning, if concrete and necessary" (p. 241). This early opposition becomes the basis for a series of hierarchical dualisms—abstract/concrete, mind/body, culture/nature where the first member of each pair is associated with the male and the second with the female. In contrast, the female sense of self is achieved within the context of home and family and does require an opposition between concrete and abstract and hence embraces everyday life and a wide range of connections and continuities (Hartsock, 1983).

Women's early relationship of connectedness is further developed and strengthened by the division of labor by gender—that women assume most of the responsibility for child care, elder care, and house care. For example, in his detailed time-budget study of employed women and their families in Toronto, William Michelson (1985) found that when the obligatory activities of employment, commuting, shopping, house care, and child care were added together, mothers employed full time outside the home spent 11 hours per weekday on them. Shopping and trips associated with child care and the activities of children are more frequent for women than for men, and women are also heavily responsible for grocery shopping (Michelson, 1985).

This means that women have far less discretionary time than men and that, at any given time, they are more likely to be engaged in all kinds of caretaking activities. (It is also likely that they will be doing several things at once.) When men are not "at work" they are "off work," but women are much less frequently "off work" either at home or in public places (Duncan, 1996). One consequence touches again on separation and connection: "Men can separate themselves from their environments, live in a space that somebody else creates and maintains, 'tune out,' see in the space only what it pleases them to look at. . . . A woman's consciousness is more immersed in her surroundings, which she—more than a man—is likely to be monitoring for danger or for dust" (Kirby, 1996, p. 54).

For the most part researchers in the field of women and environment have not studied the reasons for the development of gender differences. Instead, our goal has been to identify differences and to learn how to make the environment more responsive to the specific needs of women that arise from those differences. This is the approach Arza Churchman describes: "[T]he fact is that the daily lives of women and men are different, and the question is how the environment can be congruent with those differences so that each person can achieve as positive a quality of life as possible" (Churchman, 2000, p. 100). This approach includes studying the needs that women have as well as analyzing existing environments to determine whether these needs are met and making proposals for alternatives.

Given their responsibilities for home care, child care, and elder care; their paid employment; and their greater dependence on public transportation, it is likely that women have different housing and neighborhood preferences from men. Research bears this out. Sylvia Fava (1985) reported that when describing the considerations that led to the choice of their present dwelling, women put greater emphasis on proximity to friends and relatives, convenient shopping, neighborhood safety, and mass transportation than did men. One study of women with children in different suburban communities demonstrated that women showed higher levels of satisfaction in denser communities that were closer to the city (Rothblatt, Garr, & Sprague, 1979). Many preferred multifamily housing with maintenance and security services in proximity to cultural and entertainment activities over single-family houses. Within the urban setting, women are more likely to praise the ease of accessibility to services and the ease of making social contacts (MacKintosh, 1985).

From her review of the literature, Rebecca Peterson (1987) concludes that the integration of services into housing and neighborhoods is a major need among women in many different circumstances. Many writers agree on the kinds of design and planning features

that benefit women: affordable housing, possibly with support services; higher density housing; possibility of home-based work; mixed land use at the neighborhood scale; easy access to safe public transit; and safe public space (cf. Churchman, 2000; Fox, 1985; Franck, 1985, 1987; Moser, 1987; Wekerle, 1985). Easy accessibility to different kinds of places, as provided by physical proximity, safe public space, or public transit, is the overarching need identified in the literature on women and environment.

RECOGNIZING THE FICTIONS AND THE SEGMENTATION

An age-old assumption divides the world into two spheres according to gender: Women properly "belong" in or near the dwelling, whereas men may have easy and frequent access to places distant from the dwelling where other people gather. The social and spatial organization of these two realms, the activities pursued, the meanings they have, and the degree to which women's movements are restricted all differ culturally and historically, but the tendency to divide the environment into sexually asymmetrical realms of the domestic (or private) and the public seems to exist throughout the world and continues today in a variety of forms from many Muslim countries to Greek villages (Hirschon, 1981), to Bedouin settlements in Israel (Fenster, 1999), to U.S. cities and suburbs (Franck & Paxson, 1989). This division helps restrict women's mobility in public space and prevents them from participating in it fully as workers and citizens.

Before the industrial revolution in the United States and other Western countries, home and production were closely related, and women were directly and frequently involved in activities of production in or near the home. Then men joined the paid labor force and began to work at a distance from home. While working-class women also joined the labor force (Stansell, 1986), society's ideal was that only men would do so and that women, certainly wives, would stay home. With the separation of the home from production (and "work" generally), the two realms of domestic and public took on additional expected characteristics. The home was to be a refuge of peace, affection, and morality, free of any appearance of work. Preferably in a rural location, it would be a retreat from the harsh, competitive, and immoral realm of business in the city (Davidoff, L'Esperance, & Newby, 1976). The wife would not only maintain this idyllic retreat for her husband but also act as comforter, nurse, and keeper of moral values for her husband and children (Welter, 1966). In this image a series of ideological dichotomies were mapped onto each other: private/public, home/work, female/male, and suburb/city (Franck, 1985; Saegert, 1981).

The image, which is still powerful, assumes a single idealized household composed of a stay-at-home wife responsible for all homemaking and child care, a wage-earning husband, and dependent children. Since the home is seen as a retreat from wage work, wage work cannot take place within it and the "housework" that does necessarily occur to maintain it is not recognized as work at all. Since the house is a retreat, it is presumed to be safe, even though it may be the site of serious abuse of women by their husbands. Since the home is viewed as a retreat for one family, preferably composed exclusively of husband, wife, and their children, it is best if the dwelling does not share any space or facilities with any other households and is as independent as possible from them. This requires that the wife and mother pursue her homemaking tasks independently of all her neighbors and spatially separate from them.

The building of the first suburbs made this ideal available for middle-class families in the United States. With the proliferation of suburbs and financing programs after World War II, the suburban house became affordable to the working class, as well. What has been promoted as ideal and is so frequently built is precisely the opposite of the kind of environment that would respond to women's multiple responsibilities of wage earner and homemaker. This environment separates, often at great distance, places of living from places of wage work, including commercial establishments and support services; it makes difficult or forbids by law wage-earning activities within the home; and it socially and spatially distances dwellings from each other. While this type of environment of social and spatial separations has been most fully realized in American suburbs, many of the same features, particularly the separation of land uses and the isolation of dwellings from each other, can be seen in other countries as well, including Scandinavia (Horelli & Vespä, 1994), Great Britain (McDowell, 1983, 1993; Roberts, 1991) and developing nations (Moser, 1987).

The ideology of separations by gender, activities, and space is apparent in planning and design principles and in zoning ordinances. In planning public transit, the man's economic role and his schedule may be the primary concern in locating and scheduling transit, with less, if any, attention given to women's employment and family care responsibilities and their scheduling throughout the day. The location of houses and their design may neglect women's needs to generate income either in the home or nearby (Moser, 1987). Marsha Ritzdorf's analysis (1994) of zoning ordinances throughout the United States demonstrates how they restrict housing types in many locations to those that best meet the ideal of "retreat" (a single family detached house); forbid accessory apartments, which could provide other housing options and income to the home owner; forbid various kinds of home-based work; and restrict access to child care through the separation of residential and commercial uses and through forbidding family-based child care in private houses.

While office parks and other places of employment are now located in suburbs, they are almost always separated by land use zoning from residential areas, as are hospitals, stores, and other services. The suburban ideal of separating activities, particularly private domestic life from the public realm of business and services, continues to be prominent. The various alternative housing schemes reviewed below are unlikely ever to be built in large numbers in the United States, precisely because they modify this separation and the spatial and social separation of individual households. Many women themselves may embrace these two characteristics of the American suburban ideal, despite the difficulties they cause, because that ideal is so widely held and because alternatives are so rarely seen.

Since women's "proper" place has historically been in or near the home, they have generally not been as welcome in public space as men, particularly when their reason for being there is not related to their homemaker role (such as shopping). During Victorian times, it was indecent for an unaccompanied woman to be on the street at all (Wilson, 1991), as it still is in many Muslim countries. This expectation made the necessary presence of working women in public space suspect, even into the twentieth century and even as the urban labor force depended on their participation (Meyerowitz, 1988). Although these expectations are no longer in effect in the United States and many other countries, women in public space are still vulnerable to bodily harm and verbal harassment (Bowman, 1993; Boys, 1984; Hayden, 1984; Wekerle, 1981). The harassment shows that once they are in public, unaccompanied by men, women cannot claim as much right to privacy as men can. Moreover, in looking at, commenting about, or molesting women in public places, men are associating a private activity, sex, with women's presence in public. As in Victorian times, when they are in public, women are still defined and perceived in terms of their sexuality (Franck & Paxson, 1989).

The one public activity that women are expected to pursue is shopping, which is also an extension of their private role as homemaker. Grocery shopping in many countries is the responsibility of women (Bowlby, 1984; Michelson, 1985). Even in Victorian times, when women alone could not enter even the most genteel restaurants, they could frequent the newly developed department stores (Wilson, 1991), which catered to women shoppers by providing reading rooms and dining rooms exclusively for them (Rothman, 1979). In many countries, the controlled, well-lit, and well-populated environment of the mall offers a safe and acceptable place for women to be (Drucker & Gumpert, 1997). Indeed, in Saudi Arabia, where women's movements and dress in public are so severely restricted, they are now allowed to frequent malls unaccompanied by male relatives and do so in great numbers. In a similar vein, women in Korea and other Southeast Asian countries enjoy the safe, clean, and predictable environment of McDonald's, which becomes a popular leisure center for both women and children.

Despite the evident frequency of women shopping, planning principles still assume the male-public-realm-versus-female-domestic-realm dichotomy, and so the design and planning of many public spaces has not fully addressed the needs of women or children. Until recently steps and revolving doors made access by people with small children or strollers difficult, and the absence of appropriate places to nurse or change babies' diapers ignored the existence of such needs. Now there is greater accessibility to public places, there are places to nurse and change babies, and there are play spaces in some large stores, but safety is still a serious concern. The design and planning of many transit stations, parking garages, streets, sidewalks, and other pedestrian circulation routes still do not adequately address women's need for safety. Traditionally, most places of wage work have also been designed for men, men free of family responsibilities such as child care, with the assumption that women are either not present or hold only subordinate positions such as secretary or nurse. In some cases even prominent work places did not have restrooms for women staff including, until recently, the U.S. Senate—women senators and staff had to use the women's restrooms for visitors.

Despite the symbolic dichotomies of female-reproductive life-private and male-productive life-public and their physical realization in the design and planning of housing, neighborhoods, and cities throughout the world, it is clear that they are a fiction in daily life. Women work extremely hard in the home to maintain the home and the household. For women, the home is not purely a retreat but a place of "housework" and frequently wage work as well. More and more women are also employed outside the home. And women, even full-time homemakers, do not remain at home all the time: To pursue homemaking and child care tasks, they must venture into the public realm. And the idealized household of two parents and their children is increasingly rare. Women do not always have children and, when old or young, may live alone or with others. Around the world an increasing proportion of women are single parents, bearing all domestic and economic responsibilities for their households.

The ideology of separations and the idealization of the nuclear family not only misrepresent the real circumstances and activities of many women but make those activities more difficult to pursue. When women have children and are employed, the difficulties multiply. Women's daily routines must connect all that has been physically separated. Indeed, those separations can only continue to exist because women spend so much time and effort connecting them. "A great deal of women's time and energy goes into the process of transforming the segmentation of these settings to yield something that resembles a coherent whole. This 'shadow work' brings about, however, the classic vicious circle. By compelling women to find individual solutions to collective problems, a situation is created where the women themselves assist in making the causes of the problem invisible and therefore unresolved" (Horelli & Vespä, 1994, p. 203).

PROPOSING ALTERNATIVES: MAKING CONNECTIONS

Analysis of existing environments and the actual domestic and employment circumstances of women reveals both the ideology behind the design and planning of these environments and the profound mismatch between these environments and women's lives. The former creates a highly segmented world; the latter is directed at making that segmentation work at great cost to women's time, energy, and quality of life. The first step toward change is recognition of this mismatch and the ways in which the symbolic dichotomies of public/private, male/female, work/home; the assumed division of labor by gender; and the idealized image of the nuclear family distort the daily reality of women's lives. The proposals for change that follow recognize that reality and its variety and suggest a variety of ways the environment can support that reality by reducing the segmentation of built environments that currently exists. The common theme in the alternatives, proposed or built, is to forge connections and to soften the boundaries between what has conventionally been considered private and public.

For communities to be designed with these connections and to provide housing for households that do not meet the model of a mother, father, and children, zoning in the United States and land use planning in many countries will have to be significantly changed. Planners, architects, and policy makers as well as women themselves need to recognize how existing laws and principles complicate women's daily lives (Horelli & Vespä, 1992; Moser, 1987; Ritzdorf, 1994). Marsha Ritzdorf (1994) points out that women need to see how "men and women's lives would be enhanced by residential neighborhoods that allow them the freedom to work at home, to have their children (or parents) watched at small neighborhood-based day care centers, to share living spaces within their homes as they choose" (p. 277). She reports some advances in the United States where suburban land use zoning has created such significant divisions: For example, movements led by women in 13 states have changed zoning regulations related to the location of family child care.

Design alternatives that incorporate connections also need to be pursued. Dolores Hayden (1984) proposed ways of redesigning a typical suburban block to join a part of each private yard to create a shared outdoor space and to incorporate space for day care, elderly care, or food service as well as space for children's play and gardening. In a similar vein, Leavitt and West's winning entry for the New American House competition comprised six units of housing that incorporate work spaces, with one unit offering the option of being a single-parent or an intergenerational house with space for family day care (Leavitt, 1989).

While neither of these proposals was realized, other cases have been built in the United States that, through design and the organization of daily life, bring households together and reduce the social and spatial isolation of the typical suburban house. The leading example is cohousing, an innovation adopted from Denmark (McCamant & Durrett, 1988). Cohousing combines complete single-family dwellings (usually houses) with shared pedestrian-oriented outdoor space and a "common house" that includes shared facilities (workshop, laundry, guest room, teen room) and a common kitchen and dining space where residents regularly eat together. Cohousing developments are designed and planned by the residents themselves, who seek this kind of alternative precisely for the greater sense of community it offers. Another clear advantage of cohousing (and a reason for its development in Denmark) is that through sharing the preparation of meals on a regular basis (several times a week in Denmark) the burden of meal preparation on each household and women in particular is reduced. The design of outdoor space also facilitates the joint play and supervision of children from different households. By 2000, a total of 51 cohousing developments had been built in the United States and Canada. In Denmark, this form of housing is so common now that it is no longer considered "alternative."

Cohousing is also a frequent housing choice in Sweden, where it joins another housing option that connects dwellings to a shared meal service and additional facilities. That is service-enriched housing where meals are provided to residents by a restaurant service (Woodward, 1989). In some cases, the housing and the dining service are for both families and elderly people, who live in separate buildings but share dining and many other facilities including all kinds of workshops and possibly a day care center for the families. The incorporation of a meal service into apartment living, in a restaurant and through room service, was once available in the United States for middle-class and upper-middle-class residents in cities (Cromley, 1990) and was also championed by women and men who worked, to reduce the housekeeping burden on women (Hayden, 1981). Today, however, this kind of service in the United States is limited to housing for the elderly (including expensive life care communities) and other special needs housing, including transitional housing for women who are homeless, recovering from substance abuse, or leaving abusive spouses. In this kind of housing a variety of social services is often provided on site, including counseling, training, and child care. The number and variety of this housing option for women has grown significantly in the United States, along with more shelters for battered women (Ahrentzen, 1989; Sprague, 1991). Transitional housing varies tremendously in design, policies, and services; all share the goal of providing the necessary support and services to enable women to move to permanent accommodations.

All of these housing alternatives either soften the conventional boundary between public and private or enlarge that boundary to include a variety of intermediate spaces. The housing may incorporate space for wage work or for services within or adjacent to individual dwellings; it may bring households together in outdoor and indoor spaces. Recommendations for the design of cohousing highlight the ways that site design can encourage chance encounters as well as planned activities among households (McCamant & Durrett, 1988). And Joan Forrester Sprague analyses the variety of sharing of spaces that can be designed in transitional housing within the personal, household, community, and neighborhood zones (Sprague, 1991).

The relationship, both spatial and structural, between the household and the larger world is a major concern of the New Everyday Life project. In their first conference, participants adopted the concept of the "intermediate level as a mediating structure" to stimulate and guide ideas for the greater integration of housing, work, and care (Horelli & Vespä, 1994). The intermediate level refers both to the missing structure between the state, the market, and the household and to a territory that may vary in size from a group of dwellings to a neighborhood or to part of a town. It makes the relationship between wage work (production) and care (reproduction) visible, as, for instance, in cohousing where the preparation of some meals occurs in the intermediate space of the common house. In a suburb of Helsinki the intermediate realm was realized in a "community living room," or combination cafe and community center open from 9 to 9 five days a week, offering lunch and a variety of activities for different age groups over the course of the day and the evening. Support for the value to women of this kind of homelike public space comes from a study of public space preferences among middle-class women in Orange County, California. The preferred spaces "graciously accommodated interaction with friends, family and strangers" (Day, 2000, p. 114), the best example being

Barnes & Noble bookstores with their sofas and chairs, restrooms, coffee, and warm and inviting ambience for both adults and children.

The Helsinki "living room" and the Barnes & Noble bookstores, despite their many differences, can be seen as illustrations of Dolores Hayden's idea (1984) of "domesticating urban space." Other ways of softening the conventionally sharp distinction between private domestic space and public urban space include the provision of changing rooms and play areas in public buildings (which are now more prevalent than in 1984). Physical accessibility is also increasing, primarily as a result of laws requiring changes to meet the needs of the handicapped. Domestication of the public realm also means the building of day care centers in or near places of wage work as well as in residential areas. Many companies throughout the United States are now including such facilities in their buildings. Possibly an even greater change, and a more radical softening of the separation between production and reproduction activities, is employees caring for infants in their offices; this also is happening in the United States (Belluck, 2000).

Connections between private dwellings and public space are also forged by adopting physical design features and other measures to improve public transit and to increase safety, allowing women and others to travel more easily, more frequently, and during various times of the day. Under one comprehensive approach to increasing safety, the "Safer Cities Initiative," citizens work closely with government agencies to develop social programs and to make community and design improvements to housing, streets, public transit, parks, and city centers. Gerda Wekerle and Carolyn Whitzman (1995) describe such worldwide initiatives with detailed attention to Toronto. They present tools for determining local safety needs and illustrate a great variety of design recommendations including: good lighting, unobstructed sightlines, elimination of entrapment opportunities, ability to find help from others, and visibility by others that derives from a mixture of land uses and activity generators.

MAKING AND MAINTAINING ENVIRONMENTS: WOMEN'S WORK

Understanding women's needs, analyzing existing environments, and proposing alternatives all depend upon a recognition of the importance of daily life, the practical needs it generates, and how planning and design can better meet these needs. The fields of both planning and architecture tend to demean daily life, privileging instead what is mistakenly viewed as either an independent realm of aesthetics in the case of architecture (Franck & Lepori, 2000) or of production-oriented activities and needs, where efficiency and economic gain are key objectives, in the case of planning (Horelli & Vespä, 1994; Milroy, 1991). Each of these approaches privileges the position and expertise of professionals who base decisions on aesthetic or technical grounds that are often several steps removed from the particular needs of specific kinds of people, including women. Inhabitants are viewed in very general terms, without specific needs relating to everyday life or with needs that are considered too trivial to be addressed. Indeed, the trivializing of the practical, the concrete, and the everyday appears to be an essential part of a masculinist orientation and possibly of male self-identity as it is constructed in the West.

Since most professional planners and architects have been men, they have had far more responsibility than women for deciding both the form of our environments and the general principles for their organization. Given their power, it is not surprising that the design and planning of so many built environments continue to follow the fiction that men engage in wage labor in public places while women stay home caring for house and family (Hayden, 1984; Spain, 1992; Weisman, 1992). As reviewed earlier, this social and spatial dichotomy neglects the fact that women often do productive work both in and outside the home and that reproductive work necessarily takes them into the public realm. In addition, the assignment of a purely reproductive role to women ignores a third responsibility they often assume: the managing and maintaining of their communities (Moser, 1987). In self-help settlements throughout the world women may be significantly involved in the building of houses and the organization, maintenance, and improvement of infrastructure and services.

Women in low-income neighborhoods in the United States assume this same kind of community responsibility. Jacqueline Leavitt and Susan Saegert (1990) documented the successful efforts of low-income residents in Harlem to renovate and convert their landlord-abandoned buildings to limited-equity cooperatives. Many of the most active and hardworking residents were older women. The authors outline a "community household" model for understanding such efforts and for building upon them in the development of social programs. The model "can be seen as an expanding circle of connection and support, building on the life of the household, but linking its strengths with those of tenants' associations, neighborhoods, cities, and the nation" (p. 172). Other contemporary examples of the community-household model in operation can be seen in the work of women in public housing in Chicago (Feldman & Stall, 1994), the work of various national women's organizations such as the National Congress of Neighborhood Women, the Center for Cultural and Community Development in the United States, and the Mothers' Centers movement in Germany (Belenky, 1996; Belenky, Bond, & Weinstock, 1997) and the decades long effort of women residents in public housing at Columbia Point in Boston to improve their community and to stay there once it was redeveloped (Breitbart & Pader, 1995).

In each case, the home extends beyond its confines into the community, transforming the larger realm into what bel hooks has called "homeplace" (1990). This larger realm may extend beyond the local neighborhood into the city at large and can include not just maintaining but also building. Between the Civil War and World War I middle-class women volunteers in cities throughout the United States produced hundreds of buildings to address the needs of immigrants and residents. These included boarding houses, settlement houses, vocational schools, playgrounds, hotels for transients, and public baths (Spain, 2001). In these many different ways, women have been working to domesticate the urban realm.

Martin Heidegger (1977) distinguished between two kinds of building: constructing and cultivating. Iris Marion Young, adopting the term *preservation* for the second kind of building, observes that construction has usually been the province of men and preservation the responsibility of women. The model for the second is cultivation in agriculture and so involves nurturing and caring (Young, 1997, p. 136). This is not only caretaking of places and things as in the community work of women described above; it is also preserving, within and beyond the home, the memory and the identity of groups and peoples (cf. Hayden, 1995). More women need to be engaged in the constructing kind of building as planners and architects; at the same time, building as preserving, as done by both women and men, needs to receive the appreciation it deserves. One way that can happen is by incorporating into government planning and development initiatives the values, skills, and insights women bring to grassroots efforts to improve their communities (Fenster, 1999; Horelli & Vespä, 1994; Moser, 1987). At the same time, grassroots efforts can be given additional resources and additional skills to support and strengthen their endeavors, and they can be invited to participate in community design and planning decisions rather than being forced only to contest them.

Citizen participation in those decisions requires a change in the predominant values and actions of many planning and architecture practitioners to give importance to the information, experience, and judgment of nonprofessionals who will or do occupy the places under consideration and to adopt the necessary techniques for doing so. Professional place makers can collaborate with place dwellers so that each group contributes its particular knowledge and expertise. This requires a level of care and commitment and a kind of vulnerability that is not typical of conventional planning and architecture practice. "[T]he responsibilities of placemaking extend beyond what is normally understood to be professional action and knowledge into the messy domain of human relationships, represented by words such as *caring, trust,* and perhaps even *love*" (Schneekloth & Shibley, 1995, p. 200). This approach, involving feelings of attachment and commitment among professionals and nonprofessionals alike, is similar to the approach manifested by many women in grassroots movements to maintain and improve their communities. In both cases, the relationship to the environment and others is one of connection, attachment, and care, not the usual professional relationship of separation, detachment, and control that is characteristic of architecture and planning and of a more masculinist orientation to the environment.

Such a masculinist orientation also characterizes architecture education, which promotes aesthetic concerns over everyday needs and an image of an architect as a male genius working alone and in competition with others. Even as the proportion of women faculty, students, and practitioners in architecture grows, these values remain and continue to shape both the architecture curriculum and the larger culture of architecture. Given the very different orientation women seem to have toward the environment and its occupants, it is understandable that architecture education, planned and carried out from a male orientation, is seen by women faculty as sexist (Ahrentzen & Groat, 1992). Significantly, the

recommendations that Sherry Ahrentzen and Linda Groat make for changing architecture education repeatedly refer to the making of connections and interrelations, as in establishing relationships between architecture and other disciplines, bringing different modes of thinking into the studio, and working collaboratively (Groat & Ahrentzen, 1996). Indeed, the authors propose a metaphor for architecture that plays out the notion of connectedness to its fullest: "a tapestry of cultural invention which comes to life through its diverse and interwoven threads" (Ahrentzen & Groat, 1992, p. 108). Many of their recommendations overlap with those generated by a Carnegie Foundation study of architectural education (Boyer & Mitgang, 1996).

TAKING RISKS: MAKING THE INVISIBLE VISIBLE AND IMPORTANT

The strengths of women and environment research lie in its analysis of daily life in the built environment and its development of recommendations for improving environments and for strengthening the role of women in making and maintaining them. These objectives reflect the original utopian goal of environmental design research (Schneekloth, 1994) and distinguish the work on women and environment from many other topics in environment behavior research. The generally applied orientation depends upon a keen analytical perspective. Employing the lens of gender, everyday life, and material conditions, researchers have been extremely effective in revealing what previously had been assumed, unknown, or ignored and in making the phenomena uncovered a basis for change. For professionals in design and planning, this takes courage. Articulating women's needs and making them a basis for recommendations for change is a radical position for professionals in planning and architecture to take and can lead to marginalization or hostile relations with colleagues (Ritzdorf, 1994).

Analysis has revealed the power of the symbolic, hierarchical dichotomies of public/private, male/female, work/home in the planning and design of built environments, which are intended to reproduce these dichotomies, and research has demonstrated how much these dualisms misrepresent and constrain women's lives. Feminist research and theory suggest that a masculinist worldview and male self-identity privilege separations and dualistic, stable categories, while the experience and self-identity of women center on connections and multiple, changing categories. Much of the research on women and environment demonstrates how the masculinist perspective has dominated the design of environments and how research, design, and planning from a feminist perspective can recognize and foster connections, intermediate and overlapping categories, and fluid boundaries. Indeed, those in the field of women and environment practice that approach in their work by crossing interdisciplinary boundaries, by applying their findings to planning and architecture recommendations, and by pursuing academically based research and community-based advocacy.

Once these dichotomous categories of private/home/female and public/work/male are put aside and women's everyday lives are studied, much is learned about the problems these dichotomies have generated and how these problems can be alleviated. Many times what is uncovered becomes the basis for change. Once the home is recognized as a place of paid and unpaid work, housing that incorporates options for paid work or for sharing the unpaid work of meal preparation makes sense. Documentation of women's work in community building suggests a model of community activism with important implications for social programs and for the practice of architecture and planning by professionals. Research on architecture education and the experiences of women faculty and students served as the basis for recommendations for changing that model and architectural curricula in the United States. Discovering what have been ways of thinking and doing that are particular to women can help us understand women's experience *and* suggest directions for change that will benefit both women and men.

Another dualism characteristic of a masculinist perspective is between the abstract and the concrete. This dualism makes certain phenomena important (production, politics, aesthetics, technology) and others (reproduction, family, everyday life) less so, if at all. It has helped render the lives and experiences of women invisible since they were associated with the concrete, and it has helped sustain an approach to architecture that prizes appearance over use. As demonstrated so well in the research reviewed in this essay, everyday life must be studied to understand the complete pattern of women's activities (Michelson, 1994), and it must be embraced as a concept and as a tool to propose changes that will

address the needs of women and men more fully (Franck, 1989; Horelli, Booth, & Gilroy, 2000; Horelli & Vespä, 1994). Everyday life is not only made visible but given importance in a normative sense.

Just as those of us engaged in women and environment research have made visible and subject to criticism the assumptions and categories used by others, so we need to examine and reflect critically upon the ones we employ ourselves. "We don't need a totality to work well, we don't even need to share a basic understanding of concepts. What we do need is the willingness to engage in the *conversation* about the construction and deconstruction of categories and knowledge" (Schneekloth, 1994, p. 301). One of the concepts we might question is gender.

There is legitimate concern that identifying gender differences or studying the particular activities and experiences of women will strengthen women's subordination, leading to more stereotyping of women and fewer choices for them (Ahrentzen, 1996) and for others. For instance, does recording the fear and the harassment women experience in public extend an image of women as victims and understate their frequent use and genuine enjoyment of public life (Lofland, 1984)? Does recognizing that women may feel safer in highly controlled, consumer-oriented public places such as shopping malls, Barnes & Nobles, or McDonald's strengthen their domestic role and contribute to the increased privatization and sanitization of public space and the loss of diversity, spontaneity, and unpredictability of urban life? Will proposing a model of community work that is based upon women's domestic role in the home (Leavitt & Saegert, 1991) serve to further restrict women to that role? Bringing women's ways of thinking and working to the fore, celebrating some of them, and making them a basis for change can be transformative, as this essay is intended to demonstrate. Recognizing their value does not mean they should remain only the province or responsibility of women; it can have liberating potential for all. But the double-edged potential of further constraint and future empowerment remains.

One gender difference that raises this risk is women's caretaking—of people and surroundings—and the orientation and values related to it. Carol Gilligan's research (1982) on moral development suggests that women and girls draw upon a "reflective understanding of care" in resolving moral dilemmas, which requires that no one be hurt and that one respond to the needs of others, whereas men and boys are concerned that everyone be treated fairly. Gilligan calls the first an "ethic of care" and the second an "ethic of justice." While the subject of much criticism, the ethic of care as a general orientation among women is supported by the research on women's community activism referred to earlier. It has been used as a basis for characterizing a feminist perspective in environmental design research (Ahrentzen, 1990) and a feminist approach to architecture (Franck, 1989). The ethic of care has also been used as a conceptual framework to analyze women's experience of public space and to generate recommendations for its design and for activism (Day, 2000). Members of the New Everyday Life project used an understanding of the ethic of care to propose a "rationality of responsibility" in planning, to be adopted by women and men, that includes both an expansion of the boundaries of care as well and a determination to fight for different material and social conditions (Horelli & Vespä, 1994).

There is also concern that being a woman is not always or for everyone the most important attribute, that the importance given to gender is misplaced and ignores other factors including age, race, class, sexual preference, ethnicity, and so on. Researchers on women and environment have identified significant differences in the attitudes and activities of women from different ethnic and economic backgrounds (cf. Day, 1999). Given the necessary brevity of this essay as a general overview, however, the influence of these other factors and the more fine-grained context of people's lives have not been described. Despite the lack of homogeneity of the category *women*, attention to women as a group is essential for "women and environment" to remain a viable research, design, and planning topic and for the efforts to improve the lives of women to continue.

One way to more fully represent the complexity of the category *women* and the differences that it always includes is to view women not as a group but as a collective or a series (Young, 1997). The concept of a series does not require that we identify the attributes all women have nor does membership in the series necessarily define one's self-identity. "*Woman* is a serial collective defined neither by any common identity nor by a common set of attributes that all the individuals in the series share but rather names a set of structural constraints and relations to practico-inert objects that condition action and its meaning" (Young, 1997, p. 36). Certainly many of those constraints and relations have been the topic

of women and environment research. Members of the series *women* may become a group when they choose to participate together as women whose particular goals are generated by specific social, historical, and cultural circumstances as well as by their gender. "While the gendered series *women* refers to the structured social relations positioning all biologically sexed females, groups of women are always *partial* in relation to the series—they bring together only some women for some purposes involving their gender-serialized experience" (Young, 1997, p. 35).

In research on women and environment, we continue, at least implicitly, to distinguish gender as a social construction from sex as a biological phenomenon. In doing so we seem to neglect the body in general and women as sexed bodies. The sharp distinction between gender and sex and a tendency to give all importance to gender and almost none to sex was once necessary to remove essentialist assumptions that what a woman is or does is biologically determined. That objective having been accomplished, it is now possible to move away from an abstracted view of the body that made it, as a concept and as an experience, nearly invisible. Indeed, in taking that stance we seem to have fallen prey to the mind/body and even the abstract/concrete dichotomies so pervasive in Western thought.

We could join other feminist researchers in adopting a view that posits a much greater intertwining of sex and gender.[4] It is not that gender as a cultural construct is an overlay on biological sex but that each helps constitute the other. To adopt this view and to try to avoid the pitfalls of biology as destiny, we need to recognize that the body is not an exclusively biological and fully determined entity but a complex, continuously changing, multifaceted phenomenon that overlaps and intertwines with other phenomena, including gender and culture.

We could give attention to both male and female bodies as Galen Cranz (1998) has done in her study of the physiology of sitting and the history of the

---

[4]This is a large and rich literature. A few key books are: *Gender Trouble: Feminism and the Subversion of Identity* (Butler, 1990); *Bodies That Matter: On the Discursive Limits of "Sex"* (Butler, 1993); *Unbearable Weight: Feminism, Western Culture and the Body* (Bordo, 1993); *Volatile Bodies: Toward A Corporeal Feminism* (Grosz, 1994); *Nomadic Subjects: Embodiment and Sexual Difference in Contemporary Feminist Theory* (Braidotti, 1994); *A Passion for Difference: Essays in Anthropology and Gender* (Moore, 1994); *Space, Time and Perversion: Essays on the Politics of Bodies* (Grosz, 1995); *The Eros of Everyday Life: Essays on Ecology, Gender and Society* (Griffin, 1995); *Imaginary Bodies: Ethics, Power and Corporeality* (Gatens, 1996).

chair and its disadvantages for the body. We could explore an approach to design that, like Galen Cranz's work, is more fully oriented to the body, as Bianca Lepori and I have recommended (Franck & Lepori, 2000). We could explore women's experience as sexed bodies as phenomenologists have done (Bigwood, 1998; Young, 1990), and we could explore the implications of this experience for design as Bianca Lepori has done for birthing rooms (Lepori, 1994). She began by studying the physiology of birth and the kinds of positions and movement reported by women who had given birth at home. She discovered that the most physiologically sensible position is squatting, which is the commonly assumed position in many cultures, and that women giving birth at home move about and try a variety of different positions during labor. Yet the conventional position in Western medicine is a prone position on a hospital bed with the medical staff taking the more active role and the mother being the recipient of the decisions and actions of others. Lepori's work integrates information from physiology, from an understanding of culture, and from women's own experiences of giving birth. Her prototype design of the space and furniture for a birthing room supports the woman's freedom of movement and her power to choose different positions and movements during labor. The design responds to the woman's body as well as to her emotions, her strength, and her vulnerability (Franck & Lepori, 2000, p. 44).

It is possible that, even with ample analysis of the role of culture, increased attention to the body and biology will be deemed by some to be essentialist and disempowering to women. This seems to be one of the risks we continually face in pursuing research on women and environments and in making proposals for change. The chances of discovering what we did not know before, of giving value to what is worthy but was previously ignored or treated with disdain, and of making changes that improve the lives of both women and men are well worth this risk. Let's take the risk while remaining ever vigilant of the pitfalls involved and always open to conversations about alternative approaches.

REFERENCES

Agrest, D., Conway, P., & Weisman, L. K. (Eds.). (1996). *The sex of architecture.* New York: Abrams.

Ahrentzen, S. (1989). Overview of housing for single parent households. In K. A. Franck & S. Ahrentzen (Eds.), *New households, new housing* (pp. 143–160). New York: Van Nostrand Reinhold.

Ahrentzen, S. (1990). Rejuvenating a field that is either "coming of age" or "aging in place": Feminist research contributions to environmental design research. In R. I. Selby, K. H. Anthony, J. Choi, & B. Orland (Eds.), *Coming of age: Proceedings of the twenty-sixth EDRA annual conference* (pp. 11–18). Oklahoma City, OK: Environmental Design Research Association.

Ahrentzen, S. (1996). The F word in architecture: Feminist analyses in/of/for architecture. In T. A. Dutton & L. H. Mann (Eds.), *Reconstructing architecture* (pp. 71–118). Minneapolis: University of Minnesota Press.

Ahrentzen, S., & Groat, L. N. (1992). Rethinking architectural education: Patriarchal conventions and alternative visions from the perspectives of women faculty. *The Journal of Architectural and Planning Research, 9,* 95–111.

Altman, I., & Churchman, A. (Eds.). (1994). *Women and the environment.* New York: Plenum Press.

Ardener, S. (Ed.). (1981). *Women and space.* New York: St. Martin's Press.

Belenky, M. F. (1996). Public homeplaces: Nurturing the development of people, families and communities. In N. R. Goldberger, J. M. Tarule, B. M. Clinch, & M. F. Belenky (Eds.), *Knowledge, difference and power* (pp. 393–430). New York: Basic Books.

Belenky, M. F., Bond, L. A., & Weinstock, J. S. (1997). *A tradition that has no name: Nurturing the development of people, families and communities.* New York: Basic Books.

Belluck, P. (2000, December 4). A bit of burping is allowed, if it keeps parents on the job. *New York Times,* pp. 1, 22.

Berkeley, E. P., & McQuaid, M. (Eds.). (1989). *Architecture: A place for women.* Washington, DC: Smithsonian Institution Press.

Bigwood, C. (1998). Renaturalizing the body (with the help of Merleau-Ponty). In D. Welton (Ed.), *Body and flesh: A philosophical reader* (pp. 99–114). Malden, MA: Blackwell.

Birch, E. (Ed.). (1985). *The unsheltered women: Women and housing in the 80s.* New Brunswick, NJ: Center for Urban Policy Research, Rutgers University.

Booth, C., Darke, J., & Yeandle, S. (Eds.). (1996). *Changing places: Women's lives in the city.* London: Paul Chapman.

Bordo, S. (1993). *Unbearable weight: Feminism, western culture and the body.* Berkeley: University of California Press.

Bowlby, S. R. (1984). Planning for women to shop in postwar Britain. *Environment and Planning (D): Society and Space, 2,* 179–199.

Bowman, C. G. (1993). Street harassment and the informal ghettoization of women. *Harvard Law Review, 106,* 517–581.

Boyer, E. L., & Mitgang, L. D. (1996). *Building community: A new future for architecture education and practice.* Princeton, NJ: Carnegie Foundation for the Advancement of Teaching.

Boys, J. (1984). Women and public space. In Matrix (Eds.), *Making space* (pp. 37–54). London: Pluto Press.

Braidotti, R. (1994). *Nomadic subjects: Embodiment and sexual difference in contemporary feminist theory.* New York: Columbia University Press.

Breitbart, M. M., & Pader, E. J. (1995). Establishing ground: Representing gender and race in a mixed housing development. *Gender, Place and Culture, 2,* 5–20.

Butler, J. (1990). *Gender trouble: Feminism and the subversion of identity.* New York: Routledge.

Butler, J. (1993). *Bodies that matter: On the discursive limits of "sex."* New York: Routledge.

Chodorow, N. (1978). *The reproduction of mothering.* Berkeley: University of California Press.

Churchman, A. (2000). Women and the environment: Questioned and unquestioned assumptions. In S. Wapner, J. Demick, T. Yamamoto, & H. Minami (Eds.), *Theoretical perspectives in environment-behavior research* (pp. 89–106). New York: Plenum Press.

Coleman, D., Danze, E., & Henderson, C. (Eds.). (1996). *Architecture and feminism.* New York: Princeton Architectural Press.

Cranz, G. (1998). *The chair: Rethinking body, culture and design.* New York: W.W. Norton.

Cromley, E. C. (1990). *Alone together: A history of New York's early apartments.* Ithaca, NY: Cornell University Press.

Csikszentmihalyi, M., & Rochberg-Halton, E. (1981). *The meaning of things.* Cambridge: Cambridge University Press.

Dandekar, H. (Ed.). (1993). *Shelter, women and development: First and third world perspectives.* Ann Arbor, MI: George Wahr.

Davidoff, L. J., L'Esperance, L., & Newby, H. (1976). Landscape with figures: Home and community in English society. In J. Mitchell & A. Oakley (Eds.), *The rights and wrongs of women* (pp. 139–175). London: Penguin.

Day, K. (1995). Assault prevention as social control: Women and sexual assault prevention on urban college campuses. *Journal of Environmental Psychology, 15,* 261–281.

Day, K. (1999). Embassies and sanctuaries: Women's experiences of race and fear in public space. *Environment and Planning (D): Society and Space, 17,* 307–328.

Day, K. (2000). The ethic of care and women's experiences of public space. *Journal of Environmental Psychology, 20,* 103–124.

Drucker, S. J., & Gumpert, G. (1997a). Shopping, women and public space. In S. J. Drucker & G. Gumpert (Eds.) *Voices in the street: Explorations in gender, media and public space* (pp. 119–136). Cressgill, NJ: Hampton Press.

Drucker, S. J., & Gumpert, G. (Eds.). (1997b). *Voices in the street: Explorations in gender, media and public space.* Cressgill, NJ: Hampton Press.

Duncan, N. (1996). Renegotiating gender and sexuality in public and private spaces. In N. Duncan (Ed.), *Bodyspace: Destabilizing geographies of gender and sexuality* (pp. 127–145). London: Routledge.

Durning, L., & Wrigley, R. (Eds.). (2000). *Gender and architecture: History, interpretation and practice.* New York: Wiley.

Fava, S. (1985). Residential preferences in the suburban era. *Sociological Focus, 18,* 109–117.

Feldman, R. M., & Stall, S. (1994). The politics of space appropriation: A case study of women's struggles for homeplace in Chicago public housing. In I. Altman & A. Churchman (Eds.), *Women and the environment* (pp. 167–200). New York: Plenum Press.

Fenster, T. (1999). Gender and human rights: Implications for planning and development. In T. Fenster (Ed.), *Gender, planning and human rights* (pp. 3–24). London: Routledge.

Fox, M. B. (1985). Access to workplaces for women. *Ekistics, 52,* 69–76.

Franck, K. A. (1985). Social construction of the physical environment: The case of gender. *Sociological Focus, 18,* 143–160.

Franck, K. A. (1987). Women's housing and neighborhood needs. In E. Huttman & W. van Vliet (Eds.), *Handbook of housing and the built environment in the United States* (pp. 285–300). New York: Greenwood Press.

Franck, K. A. (1989). A feminist approach to architecture: Acknowledging women's ways of knowing. In E. P. Berkeley & M. McQuaid (Eds.), *Architecture: A place for women* (pp. 201–216). Washington, DC: Smithsonian Institution Press.

Franck, K. A., & Lepori, R. B. (2000). *Architecture inside out.* London: Wiley-Academy.

Franck, K. A., & Paxson, L. (1989). Women and urban public space: Research, design and policy issues. In I. Altman & I. Zube (Eds.), *Public places and spaces* (pp. 121–146). New York: Plenum Press.

Friedman, A. (1998). *Women and the making of the modern house: A social and architectural history.* New York: Abrams.

Gatens, M. (1996). *Imaginary Bodies: Ethics, power and corporeality.* London: Routledge.

Gilligan, C. (1982). *In a different voice.* Cambridge, MA: Harvard University Press.

Gilroy, R., & Woods, R. (Eds.). (1994). *Housing women.* London: Routledge.

Gordon, M. T., & Riger, S. T. (1989). *The female fear: The social cost of rape.* Urbana: University of Illinois Press.

Greed, C. H. (1994). *Women and planning: Creating gendered realities.* London: Routledge.

Griffin, S. (1995). *The eros of everyday life: Essays on ecology, gender and society.* New York: Doubleday.

Groat, L. N., & Ahrentzen, S. (1996). Reconceptualizing architectural education for a more diverse future: Perceptions and visions of architectural students. *Journal of Architectural Education, 49,* 166–183.

Grosz, E. (1994). *Volatile bodies: Toward a corporeal feminism.* Bloomington: Indiana University Press.

Grosz, E. (1995). *Space, time and perversion: Essays on the politics of bodies.* New York: Routledge.

Hartsock, N. (1983). *Money, sex and power: Toward a feminist historical materialism.* Boston: Northeastern University Press.

Hayden, D. (1981). *The grand domestic revolution.* Cambridge, MA: Massachusetts Institute of Technology Press.

Hayden, D. (1984). *Redesigning the American dream.* New York: Norton.

Hayden, D. (1995). *The power of place.* New York: Norton.

Heidegger, M. (1977). Building dwelling thinking. In D. F. Krell (Ed.), *Martin Heidegger: Basic writings* (pp. 319–340). New York: Harper & Row.

Henley, N. (1977). *Body politics.* Englewood Cliffs, NJ: Prentice-Hall.

Hirschon, R. (1981). Essential objects and the sacred. In S. Ardener (Ed.), *Women and space* (pp. 72–89). New York: St. Martin's Press.

hooks, b. (1990). *Yearning: Race, gender and cultural politics.* Boston: South End Books.

Horelli, L., Booth, C., & Gilroy, R. (2000). *The Eurofem toolkit for mobilizing women into local and regional development.* Helsinki, Finland: Helsinki University of Technology, Centre for Urban and Regional Studies.

Horelli, L., & Vespä, K. (1994). In search of supportive structures for everyday life. In I. Altman & A. Churchman (Eds.), *Women and the environment* (pp. 201–226). New York: Plenum Press.

Hughes, F. (Ed.). (1996). *The architect reconstructing her practice.* Cambridge: Massachusetts Institute of Technology Press.

Keller, S. (Ed.). (1981). *Building for women.* Lexington, MA: D.C. Heath.

Kirby, K. M. (1996). Re: Mapping subjectivity. In N. Duncan (Ed.), *Bodyspace: Destabilizing geographies of gender and sexuality* (pp. 45–55). London: Routledge.

Leavitt, J. (1989). Two prototypical designs for single parents. In K. A. Franck & S. Ahrentzen (Eds.), *New households, new housing* (pp. 161–186). New York: Van Nostrand Reinhold.

Leavitt, J., & Saegert, S. (1990). *From abandonment to hope: Community-households in Harlem.* New York: Columbia University Press.

Lepori, B. (1994). Freedom of movement in birth places. *Children's Environments, 11,* 81–87.

Lofland, L. (1984). Women and urban public space. *Women and Environments, 6,* 12–14.

MacKintosh, E. (1985). Highrise family living in New York City. In E. Birch (Ed.), *The unsheltered woman* (pp. 101–119). New Brunswick, NJ: Center for Urban Policy Research.

Matrix. (Eds.). (1984). *Making space: Women and the man made environment.* London: Pluto Press.

Mazey, M. E., & Lee, D. R. (1983). *Her space, her place.* Washington, DC: Association of American Geographers.

McCamant, K., & Durrett, C. (1988). *Cohousing: A contemporary approach to housing ourselves.* Berkeley, CA: Habitat Press.

McDowell, L. (1983). Towards an understanding of the gender division of urban space. *Environment and Planning (D): Society and Space, 1,* 59–72.

McDowell, L. (1993). Space, place and gender relations: Part I. Feminist empiricism and the geography of social relations. *Progress in Human Geography, 17,* 157–179.

Meyerowitz, J. J. (1988). *Women adrift: Independent wage earners in Chicago, 1880–1930.* Chicago: University of Chicago Press.

Michelson, W. (1994). Everyday life in contextual perspective. In I. Altman & A. Churchman (Eds.), *Women and the environment* (pp. 17–42). New York: Plenum Press.

Michelson, W. (1985). *From sun to sun: Daily obligations and community structure in the lives of employed women and their families.* Totowa, NJ: Rowman & Allanheld.

Milroy, B. M. (1991). Taking stock of planning, space, and gender. *Journal of Planning Literature, 6,* 3–15.

Moore, H. (1994). *A passion for difference: Essays in anthropology and gender.* Cambridge, England: Polity Press.

Moser, C. (1987). Women, human settlements and housing: A conceptual approach for analysis and policy making. In C. Moser & L. Peake (Eds.), *Women, human settlements and housing* (pp. 12–32). London: Tavistock.

Peterson, R. (1987). Gender issues in the home and urban environment. In E. H. Zube & G. T. Moore (Eds.), *Advances in environment, behavior and design* (Vol. 1, pp. 187–220). New York: Plenum Press.

Piercy, M. (1976). *Woman on the edge of time.* New York: Fawcett.

Prussin, L. (1995). *African nomadic architecture: Space, place and gender.* Washington, DC: Smithsonian Institution Press.

Rendell, J., Penner, B., & Borden, I. (Eds.). (2000). *Gender space architecture.* London: Routledge.

Ritzdorf, M. (1994). A feminist analysis of gender and residential zoning in the United States. In I. Altman & A. Churchman (Eds.), *Women and the environment* (pp. 255–279). New York: Plenum Press.

Roberts, M. (1991). *Living in a man-made world: Gender assumptions in modern housing design.* London: Routledge.

Rose, G. (1993). *Feminism and geography: The limits of geographical knowledge.* Minneapolis: University of Minnesota Press.

Rothblatt, D. N., Garr, D. J., & Sprague, J. (1979). *The suburban environment and women.* New York: Praeger.

Rothman, S. M. (1978). *Women's proper place.* New York: Basic Books.

Rothschild, J. (Ed.). (1999). *Design and feminism: Re-visioning spaces, places, and everyday things.* New Brunswick, NJ: Rutgers University Press.

Rothschild, J., & Rosner, V. (1999). Feminisms and design: Review essay. In J. Rothschild (Ed.), *Design and feminism: Re-visioning spaces, places, and everyday things* (pp. 7–34). New Brunswick, NJ: Rutgers University Press.

Rubin, G. (1978). The traffic in women. In A. M. Jaggar & P. R. Struhl (Eds.), *Feminist frameworks* (pp. 154–166). New York: McGraw-Hill.

Ruedi, K., McCorquodale, D., & Wigglesworth, S. (Eds.). (1996). *Desiring practices: Architecture, gender and the interdisciplinary.* London: Black Dog.

Saegert, S. (1981). Masculine cities and feminine suburbs. In C. Stimpson, E. Dixler, M. Nelson, & K. Yatrakis, (Eds.), *Women and the American city* (pp. 93–108). Chicago: University of Chicago Press.

Saegert, S., & Hart, R. (1978). The development of environmental competence in girls and boys. In M. Salter (Ed.), *Play: Anthropological perspectives* (pp. 157–175). Cornwall, NH: Leisure Press.

Saegert, S., & Winkel, G. (1980). The home: A critical problem for changing sex roles. In G. R. Wekerle, R. Peterson, & D. Morley (Eds.), *New space for women* (pp. 41–63). Boulder, CO: Westview Press.

Schneekloth, L. H. (1994). Partial utopian visions: Feminist reflections on the field. In I. Altman & A. Churchman (Eds.), *Women and the environment* (pp. 281–306). New York: Plenum Press.

Schneekloth, L. H., & Shibley, R. G. (1995). *Placemaking: The art and practice of building communities.* New York: Wiley.

Spain, D. (1992). *Gendered spaces.* Chapel Hill: University of North Carolina Press.

Spain, D. (2001). *How women saved the city.* Minneapolis: University of Minnesota Press.

Sprague, J. F. (1991). *More than housing: Lifeboats for women and children.* Boston: Butterworth Architecture.

Stansell, C. (1986). *City of women: Sex and class in New York, 1789–1860.* New York: Knopf.

Stimpson, C., Dixler, E., Nelson, M., & Yatrakis, K. (Eds.). (1981). *Women and the American city.* Chicago: University of Chicago Press.

Thorne, B. (1982). Feminist rethinking of the family. In B. Thorne & M. Yalon (Eds.), *Rethinking the family* (pp. 44–68). New York: Longman.

Torre, S. (Ed.). (1977). *Women in American architecture.* New York: Whitney Library of Design.

van Vliet, W. (Ed.). (1988). *Women, housing and community.* Aldershot, England: Avebury.

Weisman, L. K. (1992). *Discrimination by design: A feminist critique of the man-made environment.* Urbana: University of Illinois Press.

Wekerle, G. (1981). Women and the urban environment. In C. R. Stimpson, E. Dixler, M. J. Nelson, & Y. B. Tarakis (Eds.), *Women and the American city* (pp. 185–211). Chicago: University of Chicago Press.

Wekerle, G. R. (1985). From refuge to service center. *Sociological Focus, 18,* 79–95.

Wekerle, G. R., Peterson, R., & Morley, D. (Eds.). (1980). *New Space for women.* Boulder, CO: Westview Press.

Wekerle, G. R., & Whitzman, C. (1995). *Safe cities: Guidelines for design, planning and management.* New York: Van Nostrand Reinhold.

Welter, B. (1966). The cult of true womanhood: 1820–1860. *American Quarterly, 18,* 151–174.

Wilson, E. (1991). *The sphinx in the city: Urban life, the control of disorder and women.* Berkeley: University of California Press.

Woodward, A. (1989). Communal housing in Sweden: A remedy for the stress of everyday life. In K. A. Franck & S. Ahrentzen (Eds.), *New households, new housing* (pp. 71–94). New York: Van Nostrand Reinhold.

Young, I. M. (1990). *Throwing like a girl and other essays in feminist philosophy and social theory.* Bloomington: Indiana University Press.

Young, I. M. (1997). *Intersecting voices: Dilemmas of gender, political philosophy and policy.* Princeton, NJ: Princeton University Press.

Young, I. M. (1998). Throwing like a girl: Twenty years later. In D. Welton (Ed.), *Body and flesh: A philosophical reader* (pp. 286–290). Malden, MA: Blackwell.

CHAPTER 24

Children's Environment

KALEVI KORPELA

SEVERAL RECENT WRITERS have emphasized the need to move forward from descriptive data toward theoretical conceptions in the studies of children's and adolescents' place preferences (Conn, 1994; Malinowski & Thurber, 1996; Wohlwill & Heft, 1987). Therefore, the main purpose of this chapter is to focus on empirical studies providing new insights and concepts that help in understanding the psychological dynamics underlying young people's preferential relationships with places. In particular, this chapter will focus on 4-to-19-year-old children's and adolescents' experience of place in terms of emotions and emotion and self-regulation. These issues have not been an explicit focus in the earlier reviews of environmental psychology (Holahan, 1986; Russell & Ward, 1982; Saegert & Winkel, 1990; Stokols, 1978; Sundström, Bell, Busby, & Asmus, 1996; Wohlwill & Heft, 1987).

In this chapter, studies on children's place preferences are reviewed first. The term *place preference studies* refers mainly to studies where children describe favorite (important, liked, valued) or unpleasant (disliked) places in their everyday surroundings. Thereafter, the development of place preferences and factors affecting the selection of favorite places, restoration, and self- and emotion regulation in favorite places are described. Some recent studies of place preferences suggest that self-regulation, place identity, place attachment, privacy regulation, and restorative effects of environments can be viewed as interrelated phenomena. Investigating their relations has the potential to provide new insights for research and theory of place preferences. Therefore,

some space at the end of the chapter is devoted to theoretical speculations. In order to limit the range of issues to be examined, topics such as design issues of children's environments and specific environments such as schools, kindergartens, and playgrounds are excluded.

PLACE PREFERENCES AND EMOTIONS

Studies of childhood memories of favorite places, such as Lukashok and Lynch (1956), Ladd (1977), Hester (1979), Cooper Marcus (1978, 1979), Wyman (1985), and Sobel (1990), and studies of children's place use, such as Hart (1979) and Moore (1986), have shown that strong emotions are attached to places. On the one hand, places can provide feelings of privacy, control, and security. The need to be alone and to escape from social pressures and the importance of hiding places is a general finding in these studies. By the end of the 1980s, the accumulated data on 4-to-12-year-old children suggested that outdoor environments have more emotional significance for children than could be expected from the actual time spent in those places and that certain special places such as hiding or lookout places, woods, or hills—even when forbidden to children—have emotional significance to attract them (R. Hart, 1979; Moore & Young, 1978). Pursuits like hanging out, talking with each other, or playing sedentary games constitute 19% to 30% of activities in places within the habitual range of children (Moore & Young, 1978). Places of solitary retreat may be important, and the loss of a favorite place or a part of it can be a difficult emotional experience to a child (Hart, 1979). By the mid-1990s, the studies on 11-to-19-year-olds revealed that freedom and control are important to teens in their valued outdoor places (Owens, 1988), adolescents long for solitary places as well as places for social interaction (Lieberg, 1994; Noack & Silbereisen, 1988; Owens, 1994), natural settings are valued in residential areas (Owens, 1988; Schiavo, 1988), and such settings are one of the best places to go for feeling better and getting things in perspective (Owens, 1988).

On the other hand, children also develop negative feelings toward their environment and identify places of fear and danger (Hart, 1979; M. H. Matthews, 1992). O'Brien, Jones, Sloan, and Rustin (2000) studied 10-to-14-year-old children in England and found that girls reported fears more frequently than boys. An in-depth case study showed how children cope with their fears when moving alone in their surroundings. For example, an 11-year-old inner-London girl made herself feel safe by repeating "don't worry" in her head over and over again when she passed places that made her feel anxious. In van Andel's (1990) study in the Netherlands, 6-to-12-year-old children assessed natural elements and settings in their neighborhood not only as attractive but as boring, scary, or dangerous, as well. Bixler and Floyd (1997) investigated urban and rural 8th-grade students in Texas and found that fear expectancy, disgust sensitivity, and desire for modern comforts were related to preferences for wildland environments represented by slides. Those with high fear expectancy; disgust sensitivity toward insects, dirt, or damp; and desire for modern comforts such as showers or a heater were more likely to prefer manicured park settings and urban environments. They also disliked wildland environments and expressed less interest in outdoor recreation activities such as backpacking or canoeing. Holaday, Swan, and Turner-Henson (1997) found in a multiethnic American sample that 10-to-12-year-old, chronically ill children (whose main diagnoses included asthma, congenital heart disease, neuromuscular disorder, and diabetes) liked friends and special adults most in their neighborhood and natural environments second. They most disliked unfriendly people and the absence of social relations, and secondly the absence of natural environments, excessive noise, lengthy distances, or environmental restraints such as hills.

CHILDREN'S FAVORITE PLACE SELECTIONS BY AGE AND GENDER

Some studies have reported age differences during childhood and adolescence in the frequency of selecting natural or private favorite places (Pihlström, 1992; Sommer, 1990), whereas other studies have found only slight or no age differences (Malinowski & Thurber, 1996; Schiavo, 1988; Silbereisen, Noack, & Eyferth, 1986). For example, Pihlström's (1992) data of an unpublished study of 7-to-12-year-old Finnish pupils' favorite places indicates that 7-to-9-year-olds selected natural settings as their favorite places more often than 10-to-12-year-olds. Sommer (1990) found that 11-to-13-year-old Estonian pupils preferred natural settings as their favorite places significantly more often than 15-to-17-year-olds. Silbereisen, Noack, and Eyferth (1986) found that 12-year-old German children in Berlin preferred natural settings as favorite leisure time places slightly more often than 15-year-olds. Home settings, sports locales, and shopping centers or shopping streets were the most preferred settings by both age groups. These European results indicate that 7-to-9-year-olds more than 11-to-13-year-olds and both groups more than 15-to-16-year-olds might favor natural outdoor settings.

In contrast, Schiavo's (1988) study in the United States did not reveal age differences between 10-, 13-, and 17-year-olds in their preference for nature sites as important places in the neighborhood. However, nature sites along with streets were the most popular choices. Malinowski and Thurber (1996) found also that there were only minor differences in the choices of favorite places between age quintiles in the group of 8-to-16-year-old U.S. boys during a 2-week summer camp located in New Hampshire. Natural settings, the lake or waterfront, and a private place, a cabin, were the most popular choices. It is possible that the nature-dominated research settings in studies by Schiavo (1988) and Malinowski and Thurber (1996) explain the difference in the results in comparison to the European studies mentioned above.

With regard to gender differences, the results from different countries suggest that boys tend to favor outdoor places, whereas girls tend to favor indoor places. Sebba (1991) found that 8-to-11-year-old Israeli boys chose outdoor favorite places more often than girls, who favored indoor places. Lieberg (1994) found that 13-to-17-year-old Swedish girls preferred private favorite places, whereas boys were more likely to prefer public places. In a similar manner, 5-to-12-year-old boys were more likely than girls to favor outdoor play in the clubs providing child care after school in England and Wales (Smith & Barker, 2000). In Sommer's (1990) study 11-to-12-year-old Estonian boys were more likely than girls to mention a natural setting as their favorite place.

In summary, studies done during the 1990s further strengthen the earlier findings of the importance of homes, natural settings, and social hangouts as well as commercial environments in childrens and youth's environmental preferences (cf. Chawla, 1992). Although not without exceptions, the evidence indicates that 7-to-9-year-olds more than 11-to-13-year olds, and both groups more than 15-to-16-year-olds, and boys more often than girls tend to favor natural outdoor settings. There is a lack of results about 17-to-19-year-olds in comparison to other age groups, but it is possible that natural settings gain increased attention during these years. In Korpela's (1992) study, homes were preferred most with natural and commercial settings ranking second in a sample of 17-to-18-year-old Finnish school pupils. Schiavo (1988) did not find a significant decrease in the preference for nature sites among 17-year-olds in comparison to 13- or 10-year-olds. Owens (1988) found that the most popular place type selected by 14-to-18-year-old teens was a natural park. In another study by Owens (1994), natural parks ranked not more than fourth among favorite places of Australian teens. However, only 6 of the 101 respondents were between ages 17 to 19, the majority being 13-to-16-year-olds. After the accumulation of such descriptive data it is important to ask—as Conn (1994) did—what are the dynamics underlying the observed place preferences? Why do these places matter to children and adolescents? Several answers became available during the 1990s. These include developmental descriptions of place preferences, analyses of the intervening variables affecting favorite place choices, analyses of restorative experiences in favorite places, and emotion- and self-regulative views of favorite place choice and use.

THEORETICAL GENERALIZATIONS ON DEVELOPMENTAL SHIFTS IN PLACE PREFERENCES

Theoretical generalizations of how place preferences develop with age are few in place preference litera-ture. This reflects the fact that the studies are few and they have generally compared age groups in cross-sectional designs. On the basis of a review of the studies of place use, place preferences, and behavior mapping done during the 1970s and 1980s, Chawla (1992) provides one of the two recent brief syntheses of the age shifts in children's place preferences. The development of place preferences is tied to the development of self-identity, needs of privacy, and social affiliations. Middle childhood, ages 6 to 11, is characterized by expansive local exploration, cooperation with others in exploring and in games, a self-identity determined by physical strength and dexterity, and creation of playhouses and forts in the nearby environment. After this expansive engagement with the local landscape in the company of same-sex friends, there comes a period of forming new mixed-sex groups and turning to the privacy of home or to more-distant commercial or downtown settings in adolescence, ages 12 to 17. Place preferences during childhood and adolescence are assumed to provide support for the developing self-identity, the need for security, social attachments to caregivers and to the peer group, and the practice of social roles. However, the pattern of preferences is not claimed to reflect universal developmental needs.

Malinowski and Thurber (1996) present another, preliminary developmental synthesis that suggests that there is a shift from social and commercial place preferences in early childhood to places selected on the basis of land use and activity preferences in late childhood. In teenage years, preferred places are selected on aesthetic and cognitive grounds. These shifts in place preferences are explained using R. A. Hart and Moore's (1973) model of the development of children's understanding of large-scale environments. Until the preschool age, children are presumed to view environments egocentrically, relating them only to themselves. Gradually, this mode is replaced by a fixed frame of reference in which the child orients in the environment in relation to some fixed landmarks. When abstract and formal reasoning develops in the later school years, a coordinated frame of reference begins to emerge. Fixed frames are synthesized to a coordinated view of the environment, and an understanding of cardinal directions becomes possible. Thus, Malinowski and Thurber (1996) suggest that the egocentrism of younger children might lead them to prefer places where gratification and protection is readily at hand. This would explain the preference for commercial and social places from 5 to 10 years of age.

Children's maturing understanding of fixed reference points at the age of 9 to 13 years might focus their attention to the purpose and use of places, producing preferences based on land use. Older children's (14 to 16 years) increasingly abstract view of the world might lead to place preferences on aesthetic or cognitive grounds, the latter meaning possibilities for reflection on personally important matters.

In summary, Malinowski and Thurber (1996) emphasize cognitive development as an important concomitant of the development of place preferences. Chawla (1992) combines development of place preferences to social development, the development of self-identity, and needs of privacy. Neither of the generalizations includes older teenagers, ages between 17 and 19. The concepts of self-identity and privacy implicitly indicate that motivational and emotional matters may also contribute to the development of place preferences. Emotions not only interact with cognitive development, as suggested by modern research on the integration of cognition and emotion (see Barnett & Ratner, 1997), but may also play an independent role in place preferences, as presented in the next section.

FACTORS AFFECTING FAVORITE PLACE SELECTION

Children select the favorite places within their territorial range. On one hand, Wohlwill and Heft (1987) propose that children's knowledge of their environment, predisposition to explore the environment, and curiosity might serve as possible intervening variables affecting the territorial range of children. On the other hand, restrictions, either social (parents' restrictions) or physical (traffic), can cut off the possibilities for children to have a broad range of environments from which to draw in forming place preferences. Parental restrictions are a result of familial negotiations where adults' fears, caretaking conventions, judgements about the degree of maturity and competence of their children, gender-related expectations, and cultural orientations are included (H. Matthews & Limb, 1999; O'Brien et al., 2000). For example, O'Brien et al. (2000) found that the cultural heritage of Moslem parents kept girls away from many public places in London, because the parents are protecting the honor of girls from the "public gaze." After studying children's outdoor place preferences in The Netherlands, van Andel

(1990) argues that children's environmental behavior and their environmental opinions are determined mainly by age- and gender-related characteristics in addition to the impacts of specific environments. For example, a small rural town and a large metropolitan area differ in the availability of behavior settings, opportunities for the development of specialized skills, amount and frequency of social contact, and levels of stimulation such as noise (Wohlwill & Heft, 1987).

Malinowski and Thurber (1996) list several intervening variables affecting the choice and evaluation of a favorite place:

- Prior exposure to different environments
- Rural versus urban upbringing
- Parental restrictions on environmental exploration
- Vicarious familiarity with diverse environments through the media
- Peers' preferences

Thurber's and Malinowski's (1999) study with 8-to-16-year-old boys from the United States is the first to show how emotional differences may be responsible for differences in place selections and use. They found that boys with higher levels of negative emotion were more likely to choose favorite places where they could be alone in a residential summer camp, whereas happier boys chose places where they could socialize. Boys with higher levels of negative emotion were also more likely to visit new places in camp than their less distressed peers.

In sum, it is suggested that emotions should be regarded as one factor among several others in the explanation of place preferences. Further evidence of the importance of emotional matters can be found in investigations of restorative experiences and self- and emotion-regulation in favorite places.

RESTORATION IN FAVORITE PLACES

In open-ended accounts, children's and adolescents' favorite places have been most often associated with being relaxed, calm, and comfortable. Frequent mention of being away from everyday life, forgetting worries, and reflecting on personal matters indicates that favorite places afford emotional release and restorative experiences (Korpela & Hartig, 1996). Another link between favorite places and restoration is provided by the general finding of the predominance of natural settings among favorite places. An accumulating body of evidence supports the notion that natural environments provide restorative benefits (Hartig, Böök, Garvill, Olsson, & Gärling, 1996; Hartig, Mang, & Evans, 1991; Kaplan & Kaplan, 1989; Ulrichet et al., 1991). Following negative antecedents such as stress or attentional deficit, natural settings compared to built environments produce larger physiological changes toward relaxation, for example, in muscle tension and blood pressure, and larger reductions in negative feelings such as fear, anger, and sadness, and they effectively hold attention and produce higher levels of restorative experiences labeled *fascination, being away, coherence,* and *compatibility.* Two main theories of restoration dominate the field: a theory focused on short-term recovery from acute psychophysiological stress (Ulrich et al., 1991) and one concerned with recovery from directed attention fatigue (Kaplan & Kaplan, 1989).

Several recent studies have also begun to analyze the effects of natural settings on children's imagination and attentional behavior. A. Taylor, Wiley, Kuo, and Sullivan (1998) found that there was significantly more play, more creative play, and more access to adults in high-vegetation public-housing outdoor spaces in comparison to barren spaces. The study was undertaken in Chicago, Illinois, in one of the ten poorest neighborhoods in the United States. Findings about Swedish schoolyards have shown that junior- and intermediate-level schoolyards with which the teachers were most satisfied ("good yards") had access to natural places, whereas the yards with which the teachers were least satisfied ("bad yards") did not. It was found also that children in the good schoolyards engaged in more activities than children in the bad ones. In particular, pretend play and teacher-led activities were concentrated in natural places (Lindholm, 1995). Wells (2000) studied 7-to-12-year-old, low-income urban children in the United States before and after relocation. She found that children whose homes improved the most in terms of natural views from home and naturalness of the home yard following the move tended to have the highest levels of attentional capacity. The change in the overall housing quality was not a significant predictor of the ability to focus attention. Taylor, Kuo, and Sullivan (2001) found that according to parents' assessments 7-to-12-year-old children with attention deficit disorder functioned better than usual after activities in green

settings and that the greener a child's play area, the less severe his or her attention deficit symptoms.

ENVIRONMENTAL SELF-REGULATION

Studies by Silbereisen and Eyferth (1986); Silbereisen, Noack, and Eyferth (1986); Noack and Silbereisen (1988); and Silbereisen and Noack (1988) in Berlin, Germany, were probably the first to adopt a self-regulative view of place selection. They consider development as action in context and suggest that adolescents regulate their own development by selecting and shaping appropriate outer contexts. For example, leisure time place preferences can be seen as one strategy of coping with developmental tasks such as forming a personal identity or peer-group relations. In a similar manner, using the concept of a person environment fit as a guiding principle, Cotterell (1991) has noted that the choice of a particular pavilion in Australia's World Expo 88 by 13-to-19-year-olds was based on an assumption that its atmosphere was compatible with their needs at the time.

A growing number of studies on children's and adults' favorite places (Korpela, 1989, 1992; Korpela, Hartig, Kaiser, & Fuhrer, 2001; Newell, 1997; Spencer & Woolley, 2000; Twigger-Ross & Uzzell, 1996; Wölfing, 1996) support a more detailed explanation of self-regulation as the underlying dynamic in favorite place preferences and experiences. The concept of environmental self-regulation holds that the physical environment itself can become an essential part of the process of regulating the experience of self and emotions.

Self-regulation implies that the psychological influences of any external factor such as sensory stimuli, visceral processes, or social norms are processed according to an individual's conscious or unconscious mental activity following certain basic principles of motivation. Cognitive-experiential self theory (CEST) (Epstein, 1985, 1991) describes these principles of self-regulation. The principles are basically similar in many recent theories of identity and self (Breakwell, 1986; S. Taylor, 1991; Tesser, 1986). CEST postulates that all people develop a preconscious theory of reality and self that is composed of a hierarchically organized set of schemas. Basic beliefs about the world and human nature represent the highest constructs in the hierarchy. As one descends the hierarchy, schemas become narrower in scope and more closely associated with direct experience. The lowest-order schemas are situation-specific cognitions that can readily change without affecting the higher-order structure. These preconscious conceptual systems or theories are not developed for their own sake but to make life as livable, meaningful, and emotionally satisfying as possible.

In cognitive-experiential self theory, principles governing cognition, motivation, and action are associated with the basic beliefs of a personal theory (Epstein, 1991). Maintaining a favorable pleasure-pain balance is a functional principle associated with the belief regarding the benevolence versus malevolence of the world. Assimilating the data of reality into a coherent conceptual system is associated with the belief that the world is meaningful versus meaningless. Maintaining a favorable level of self-esteem is associated with the belief that the self is worthy versus unworthy. Maintaining relatedness to others is associated with the belief that other people provide support and happiness versus insecurity and unhappiness. These four functional principles are of equal importance, and an individual's ongoing behavior involves compromise among them (Epstein, 1991).

Self-regulation proceeds with the application of mental, physical, social, and environmental strategies (Korpela, 1989, 1992). *Mental* strategies involve psychic operations with intentions, images, affects, and motives to maintain self-esteem. *Physical* strategies involve the use of the body with all of its somatic processes. For example, jogging may be a means of maintaining a positive self-image by controlling one's fitness. *Social* self-regulation strategies involve reliance on other people for achieving internal goals. These strategies have their roots in infancy, when a child needs help from a caretaker to reduce internal tensions such as hunger or pain (cf. Izard & Kobak, 1991). Social self- and emotion-regulation strategies thus imply extension beyond inner homeostatic processes to exchange with the environment, as in social attachments. *Environmental* strategies imply a similar extension and involve the use of places, place cognitions, and affects in the service of emotion- and self-regulation. For example, a study by Korpela (1992) found that 17-to-18-year-old adolescents often went to their solitary favorite places after emotionally negative events that threatened self-esteem and the coherence of the experience of self. Being in a favorite place helped them to relax, calm down, clear their minds, gain perspective on things, and face troublesome matters. Favorite places often afforded

escape from social pressures with concomitant freedom of expression and control. Thus, favorite places provide emotional release, restorative experiences, and possibilities for reflection in nondistracting circumstances. The results suggest that favorite places are used to regulate not only the experience of self but emotions as well.

In the context of environmental self-regulation, emotion-regulation implies that emotions are affected and modulated by some external regulator or factor such as a particular place (cf. Dodge & Garber, 1991). For example, people are sensitive in terms of emotional states and mood to particular locations, and entering or moving through a place may induce changes in a person's mood (Kerr & Tacon, 1999; Staats, Gatersleben, & Hartig, 1997). The concept of emotion-regulation—as well as self-regulation—is not a synonym for control, suppression, or elimination of emotions. The concept of regulation is neutral in this sense, and it can refer to enhancement or maintenance as well (Izard & Kobak, 1991). In summary, emotion regulation includes not only intra- but also extraorganismic factors by which emotional arousal is redirected, modified, and modulated in emotionally arousing situations (Cicchetti, Ganiban, & Barnett, 1991).

FUTURE PROSPECTS AND THEORETICAL SPECULATIONS

Self-regulation as a theoretical construct has the potential to integrate several phenomena related to place preferences. First, the cognitive and affective structures forming place identity (cf. Feldman, 1990; Proshansky, Fabian, & Kaminoff, 1983) can be seen as results of an active self-regulation process (Korpela, 1989, 1992). Such a process can be examined on different levels of analysis where different theories and concepts become useful (cf. Lalli, 1992). We can examine short-term or long-term regulation strategies and the products of these processes either on the behavioral or experiential level. Thus the concepts of place identity on the cognitive level, place attachment on the emotional level, and behavioral processes such as territoriality, personalization, and privacy become integrated in the environmental self-regulation point of view. Both Korpela (1991) and Newell (1994, 1997) have also proposed that theories involving processes of self-regulation are fruitful when explaining the restorative effects of favorite places.

PRIVACY

For children, emotional meanings of privacy and the consequences of not attaining privacy are quite profound. For example, Smith and Barker (2000) found that 5-to-12-year-olds frequently used den-making as a means of creating a private place in a large room outside the range of the watchful gaze of adult play workers in the out-of-school clubs in England and Wales. Violating children's needs for privacy, such as in crowded homes or day care settings, seems to result either in psychological withdrawal or aggression, depending on the length of crowding and individual characteristics (Maxwell, 1996). Maxwell's (1996) study in the United States of 3-to-5-year-old children found that children chronically exposed to high density in the home and child care center were more susceptible to behavioral disturbances such as aggression, anxiety, and hyperactivity.

On the positive side it can be said that, developmentally, the availability of privacy is closely related to the achievement of self-identity and self-esteem (Laufer & Wolfe, 1976; Newell, 1994). Personalization of private spaces provides children and adolescents with tangible signs that they are unique and different from others (Rivlin, 1990; Sobel, 1990). Solitude and opportunities for reflection in nondistracting circumstances and positive emotional outcomes have been mentioned at a noticeable frequency in favorite place studies (Korpela, 1992; Korpela & Hartig, 1996; Newell, 1997). Chawla (1991) summarizes that beginning as early as age 3, children highly value having a room of their own that they can name as the primary place where they feel most at home, that they can personalize, and where they retreat when they are upset or want to be undisturbed. Harden's (2000) study of Scottish children ages 9 to 15 also corroborates that many "ordinary" children experience their home as a safe and private haven and seldom describe the risks in the home. Feelings of insecurity such as being afraid of intruding thiefs were most keenly felt at night or when alone at home. However, when discussing risk and safety, the interviewed children mentioned not only the private sphere of home but also a local sphere. The local sphere included their neighborhoods and was identified in terms of proximity to home and familiarity with the surroundings and people. Within the local sphere children felt relatively safe. The local sphere was not associated with the same level of safety as home but included certain public areas such as railways or parks where interfering adults or teenagers were considered as potential risks, especially at night. The public space with which the children were not familiar was associated mainly with perceived risks. These included fears of being lost, judgements of risky areas, and concerns about strange adults and gangs of teenagers. However, children did not always accept these risks and the parental restrictions related to them but also expected there to be some negotiation with their parents for subverting restrictions.

In conclusion, the positive emotional outcomes related to the availability of private and favorite places suggest that the relations among privacy regulation, restoration, and self-regulation in children deserve further study (cf. Korpela et al., 2001; Newell, 1995).

TERRITORIALITY AND TERRITORIAL RANGE

Not only has territoriality been related to identity and self (Edney, 1976), but it has also been suggested that studies on children's territorial range might benefit from relating range to psychological processes such as the goal or motivation of a child's travel (Wohlwill & Heft, 1987). This would mean studying the correspondence between children's personal goals, emotions, and the extent to which they move around in their everyday surroundings. Korpela, Kyttä, and Hartig (2000) have begun to investigate how the use of favorite places as a means of self-regulation and territorial range might develop together.

PLACE IDENTITY, PLACE ATTACHMENT, AND RESTORATIVE EXPERIENCES.

The observation that people use particular places for self- and emotion regulation is common to research on place identity, place attachment, and restorative environments. Place identity is fundamentally formed by the experiences and cognitions in places that have a role in a person's emotion and self-regulation. Thus, place attachment is implicit in place identity (Korpela, 1989). Attachments are formed to places that fulfill people's emotional needs and enable them to develop and maintain their identities (Kaiser & Fuhrer, 1996). The developmental tasks of forming a self-identity and peer-group relations may be reflected in place preferences throughout childhood but particularly in later teenage years (ages 17 to 19) so that private and natural settings become predominant among favorite places. Recent studies reveal that such predominance is evident among adults (Korpela et al., 2001; Newell, 1997; Wölfing, 1996).

It has gone generally unnoticed in the literature of place identity that similar kinds of self-regulation principles as put forward in this chapter and earlier studies (Korpela, 1989, 1992) were implicitly present even in Proshansky and colleague's (1983) classic paper of place identity. These integrating or stabilizing principles are referred to in the description of the functions of place identity cognitions, which are to (1) recognize environments, (2) construct the meaning of the environment, (3) match the preferences of the person and the necessary requirements of the environment, (4) mediate change, and (4) serve as anxiety and defense mechanisms. The functions appear in the thoughts, behavior, and experience of the individual and meet the need for some level of integration of the individual's self-identity. Proshansky et al. (1983) assume further that place identity cognitions either define directly who the person is or do so indirectly by defending her or him and protecting her or him from those settings and properties that threaten who he or she is and what he or she wants to be. Defining, maintaining, and protecting the self-identity of the person implies that place identity cognitions help regulate anxiety and feelings of pain and threat. At root, what the person experiences is some level of self-worth or feelings of self-esteem. Thus, although Proshansky et al. (1983) emphasized the growth and change in place identity cognitions, they also postulated some functions of them. The functions reveal that humans strive for cognitive integration and consistency, anxiety reduction, and self-esteem maintenance, and they use places to achieve these goals.

Self-regulation and restoration in favorite places point also to the link between place studies and the psychology of health. For example, Korpela's (1992) study of 17-to-18-year-old Finnish adolescents found, and Wölfing's (1996) study of adult resettlers to Germany corroborated, that humanization—the act of ascribing humanlike attributes to a place such as "an understanding listener"—and control of a place are important aspects of the experience of a favorite place. The feeling of control and the humanization of the place can be interpreted as functional temporary illusions the maintenance of which guarantees that recovery from personal setbacks can happen in a favorite place. This interpretation is based on S. Taylor's (1983) theory of cognitive adaptation to threatening events. It holds that when individuals experience personal setbacks, they search for meaning in the experience, try to regain mastery over the event, and try to restore self-esteem. Succeeding in this depends on the ability to form and maintain a set of illusions—namely, overly positive self-evaluations, exaggerated perceptions of control or mastery, and unrealistic optimism. Illusions have functional significance in contributing to maintaining the self as a highly organized system, producing behavioral persistence, and promoting psychological well-being (Greenwald, 1981; S. Taylor & Brown, 1994; for a discussion of the role of positive illusions in mental health see also Block & Colvin, 1994; Colvin & Block, 1994). It would be worth studying how frequently these kinds of illusions in relation to places appear among children. It could also be investigated whether they are important to certain groups of children, such as socially or geographically isolated children or teenagers having difficulty in coping with social developmental tasks. The importance of control in favorite place experiences is noteworthy because of the relevance that the concept of control holds for the understanding of such health-related phenomena as stress and depression (Bechtel, 1992; Steptoe & Appels, 1989). Favorite place studies as a whole suggest that one thing that can potentially be controlled is the physical environment—a favorite place. Thus, it seems possible that in some life situations or stages of life, the sense of control may be derived from the physical environment. On the other hand, loss of control seems to characterize places that young adults experience as the most depressing in their lives (Bechtel, Fox, Korpela, & Parkkila, 1995).

In all, place identity, place attachment, privacy regulation, and restorative outcomes are interrelated phenomena within self- and emotion regulation. To give a concrete example, we might speculate that for an adolescent, entering a (possibly nicknamed) favorite place provides a first block to negative emotions prevailing just after a disappointment, mental fatigue, or stress by producing feelings of familiarity, security, and belongingness. An expectation or an illusion of the place's humanlike, nurturing, and ameliorating qualities may strengthen the positive feelings. After that, the feeling of being away from everyday routines may come into play and provide rest for directed attention, relaxation, and calmness. At the same time, personalizations or cues that elicit good memories of oneself may be seen in the surroundings. These, in turn, elicit positive memory associations about oneself, assisting psychic work in which the meaning of the disappointment is interpreted and evaluated. The sense of compatibility with the place accompanied by a feeling of control and engagement in psychic or behavioral activities may finally produce new insights about oneself and the situation that preceded the visit to the favorite place.

In conclusion, place preference studies reviewed in this chapter suggest that favorite places affect psychological well-being and eventually health. Thus, measuring well-being, health, coping, and the use of favorite places in different developmental stages would be a valuable strategy in future studies. The ideas from place preference studies might even now be applicable when, for example, psychologists try to diagnose children who are particularly vulnerable to forced relocation or try to support them through the period of change. Part of this diagnosing might include probing favorite places, writing environmental autobiographies (Cooper Marcus, 1979), and assessing a child's "place-identity status" (cf. Marcia, 1966), that is, her or his dependence on or commitment to the current living surroundings. Processes that are known to create belongingness and attachment to a place, such as naming, humanization, control, personalization, and fixing memory signs (Korpela, 1989) can be offered as conscious coping methods for children in the process of adapting to new environments (cf. Jalongo, 1985).

REFERENCES

Barnett, D., & Ratner, H. H. (1997). The organization and integration of cognition and emotion in development. *Journal of Experimental Child Psychology, 67*, 303–316.

Bechtel, R. (1992). Depressing and happy places. In A. Mazis, C. Karaletsou, & K. Tsoukala (Eds.), Socioenvironmental metamorphoses. *Proceedings of the Twelfth biennial IAPS conference* (Vol. 2, pp. 315–319). Thessaloniki, Greece: Aristotle University of Thessaloniki.

Bechtel, R., Fox, A., Korpela, K., & Parkkila, S. (1995). Most happy and most depressing places: A Finnish-U.S. comparison. In J. L. Nasar, P. Grannis, & K. Hanyu (Eds.), *Proceedings of the Twenty-Sixth annual EDRA conference* (pp. 80–86). Oklahoma City, OK: Environmental Design Research Association.

Bixler, R. D., & Floyd, M. F. (1997). Nature is scary, disgusting, and uncomfortable. *Environment and Behavior, 29*, 443–467.

Block, J., & Colvin, C. R. (1994). Positive illusions and well-being revisited: Separating fiction from fact. *Psychological Bulletin, 116*, 28.

Breakwell, G. M. (1986). *Coping with threatened identities.* London: Methuen.

Chawla, L. (1991). Homes for children in a changing society. In E. H. Zube & G. T. Moore (Eds.), *Advances in environment, behavior, and design* (Vol. 3, pp. 187–228). New York: Plenum Press.

Chawla, L. (1992). Childhood place attachments. In I. Altman & S. M. Low (Eds.), *Place attachment* (pp. 63–86). New York: Plenum Press.

Cicchetti, D., Ganiban, J., & Barnett, D. (1991). Contributions from the study of high-risk populations to understanding the development of emotion regulation. In J. Garber & K. A. Dodge (Eds.), *The development of emotion regulation and dysregulation* (pp. 15–48). Cambridge: Cambridge University Press.

Colvin, C. R., & Block, J. (1994). Do positive illusions foster mental health? An examination of the Taylor and Brown formulation. *Psychological Bulletin, 116*, 3–20.

Conn, M. (1994). The place of adolescents: Commentary to Eubanks Owens. *Children's Environments, 11*, 325–326.

Cooper Marcus, C. (1978). Remembrance of landscapes past. *Landscape, 22*, 35–43.

Cooper Marcus, C. (1979). *Environmental autobiography* (Working paper no. 301). Berkeley: University of California, Institute of Urban and Regional Development.

Cotterell, J. L. (1991). The emergence of adolescent territories in a large urban leisure environment. *Journal of Environmental Psychology, 11*, 25–41.

Dodge, K. A., & Garber, J. (1991). Domains of emotion regulation. In J. Garber & K. A. Dodge (Eds.), *The development of emotion regulation and dysregulation* (pp. 3–11). Cambridge: Cambridge University Press.

Edney, J. J. (1976). The psychological role of property rights in human behavior. *Environment and Planning (A), 8*, 811–822.

Epstein, S. (1985). The implications of cognitive-experiential self-theory for research in social psychology and personality. *Journal for the Theory of Social Behavior, 15*, 283–310.

Epstein, S. (1991). Cognitive-experiential self-theory: An integrative theory of personality. In R. C. Curtis (Ed.), *The relational self: Theoretical convergences in psychoanalysis and social psychology* (pp. 111–137). New York: Guilford Press.

Feldman, R. M. (1990). Settlement-identity: Psychological bonds with home places in a mobile society. *Environment and Behavior, 22*, 183–229.

Greenwald, A. G. (1981). Environmental structure and cognitive structure. In J. H. Harvey (Ed.), *Cognition, social behavior, and the environment* (pp. 535–553). Hillsdale, NJ: Erlbaum.

Harden, J. (2000). There's no place like home: The public/private distinction in children's theorizing of risk and safety. *Childhood, 7*, 43–59.

Hart, R. (1979). *Children's experience of place.* New York: Irvington.

Hart, R. A., & Moore, G. T. (1973). The development of spatial cognition: A review. In R. M. Downs & D. Stea (Eds.), *Image and environment: Cognitive mapping and spatial behavior* (pp. 246–288). Chicago: Aldine.

Hartig, T., Böök, A., Garvill, J., Olsson, T., & Gärling, T. (1996). Environmental influences on psychological restoration. *Scandinavian Journal of Psychology, 37,* 378–393.

Hartig, T., Mang, M., & Evans, G. (1991). Restorative effects of natural environment experiences. *Environment and Behavior, 23,* 3–26.

Hester, R. (1979, September). A womb with a view: How spatial nostalgia affects the designer. *Landscape Architecture,* 475–482.

Holaday, B., Swan, J. H., & Turner-Henson, A. (1997). Images of the neighborhood and activity patterns of chronically ill schoolage children. *Environment and Behavior, 29,* 348–373.

Holahan, C. J. (1986). Environmental psychology. *Annual Review of Psychology, 37,* 381–407.

Izard, C. E., & Kobak, R. R. (1991). Emotions system functioning and emotion regulation. In J. Garber & K. A. Dodge (Eds.), *The development of emotion regulation and dysregulation* (pp. 303–321). Cambridge: Cambridge University Press.

Jalongo, M. R. (1985). When young children move. *Young Children, 40,* 51–57.

Kaiser, F. G., & Fuhrer, U. (1996). Dwelling: Speaking of an unnoticed universal language. *New Ideas in Psychology, 14,* 225–236.

Kaplan, R., & Kaplan, S. (1989). *The experience of nature: A psychological perspective.* Cambridge: Cambridge University Press.

Kerr, J. H., & Tacon, P. (1999). Psychological responses to different types of locations and activities. *Journal of Environmental Psychology, 19,* 287–294.

Korpela, K. M. (1989). Place-identity as a product of environmental self-regulation. *Journal of Environmental Psychology, 9,* 241–256.

Korpela, K. M. (1991). Are favorite places restorative environments? In J. Urbina-Soria, P. Ortega-Andeane, & R. Bechtel (Eds.), Healthy Environments. *Proceedings of the Twenty-Second annual EDRA conference* (pp. 371–377). Oklahoma City, OK: Environmental Design Research Association.

Korpela, K. M. (1992). Adolescents' favourite places and environmental self-regulation. *Journal of Environmental Psychology, 12,* 249–258.

Korpela, K. M., & Hartig, T. (1996). Restorative qualities of favorite places. *Journal of Environmental Psychology, 16,* 221–233.

Korpela, K. M., Hartig, T., Kaiser, F. G., & Fuhrer, U. (2001). Restorative experience and self-regulation in favorite places. *Environment and Behavior, 33,* 572–589.

Korpela, K. M., Kyttä, M., & Hartig, T. (2000, July). *Restorative environments in the self-regulation of children.* Paper presented at the Twenty-Seventh International Congress of Psychology, Stockholm, Sweden.

Ladd, F. C. (1977). Residential history: You can go home again. *Landscape, 21,* 15–20.

Lalli, M. (1992). Urban-related identity: Theory, measurement, and empirical findings. *Journal of Environmental Psychology, 12,* 285–303.

Laufer, R., & Wolfe, M. (1976). The interpersonal and environmental context of privacy invasion and response. In P. Korosec-Serfaty (Ed.), *Appropriation of space* (pp. 516–535). Strasbourg, France: Institut Louis Pasteur.

Lieberg, M. (1994). Appropriating the city: Teenagers' use of public space. In S. J. Neary, M. S. Symes, & F. E. Brown (Eds.), *The urban experience. A people-environment perspective* (pp. 321–333). London: Spon.

Lindholm, G. (1995). Schoolyards: The significance of place properties to outdoor activities in schools. *Environment and Behavior, 27,* 259–294.

Lukashok, A. K., & Lynch, K. (1956). Some childhood memories of the city. *Journal of the American Institute of Planners, 22,* 142–152.

Malinowski, J. C., & Thurber, C. A. (1996). Developmental shifts in the place preferences of boys aged 8–16 years. *Journal of Environmental Psychology, 16,* 45–54.

Marcia, J. E. (1966). Development and validation of ego-identity status. *Journal of Personality and Social Psychology, 3,* 551–558.

Matthews, M. H. (1992). *Making sense of place: Children's understanding of large-scale environments.* London: Harvester Wheatsheaf.

Matthews, H., & Limb, M. (1999). Defining an agenda for the geography of children: Review and prospect. *Progress in Human Geography, 23,* 61–90.

Maxwell, L. E. (1996). Multiple effects of home and day care crowding. *Environment and Behavior, 28,* 494–511.

Moore, R. C. (1986). *Childhood's domain: Play and place in child development.* Berkeley, CA: MIG Communications.

Moore, R., & Young, D. (1978). Childhood outdoors: Toward a social ecology of the landscape. In I. Altman & J. F. Wohlwill (Eds.), *Children and the environment. Human behavior and environment* (Vol. 3, pp. 83–130). New York: Plenum Press.

Newell, P. B. (1994). A systems model of privacy. *Journal of Environmental Psychology, 14,* 65–78.

Newell, P. B. (1995). Perspectives on privacy. *Journal of Environmental Psychology, 15,* 87–104.

Newell, P. B. (1997). A cross-cultural examination of favorite places. *Environment and Behavior, 29,* 495–514.

Noack, P., & Silbereisen, R. K. (1988). Adolescent development and choice of leisure settings. *Children's Environmental Quarterly, 5,* 25–33.

O'Brien, M., Jones, D., Sloan, D., & Rustin, M. (2000). Children's independent spatial mobility in the urban public realm. *Childhood, 7,* 257–277.

Owens, P. E. (1988). Natural landscapes, gathering places, and prospect refuges: Characteristics of outdoor places valued by teens. *Children's Environmental Quarterly, 5,* 17–24.

Owens, P. E. (1994). Teen places in Sunshine, Australia: Then and now. *Children's Environments, 11,* 292–299.

Pihlström, N. (1992). *Oppilaiden mielipaikkakokemukset psyykkisen itsesäätelyn ilmentäjinä* [Favorite place experiences and self-regulation among school-children]. Unpublished master's thesis. University of Helsinki, Finland.

Proshansky, H., Fabian, A. K., & Kaminoff, R. (1983). Place-identity: Physical world socialization of the self. *Journal of Environmental Psychology, 3,* 57–83.

Rivlin, L. G. (1990). Home and homelessness in the lives of children. *Child and Youth Services, 14,* 5–17.

Russell, J. A., & Ward, L. M. (1982). Environmental psychology. *Annual Review of Psychology, 33,* 651–688.

Saegert, S., & Winkel, G. (1990). Environmental psychology. *Annual Review of Psychology, 41,* 441–477.

Schiavo, R. S. (1988). Age differences in assessment and use of a suburban neighborhood among children and adolescents. *Children's Environments Quarterly, 5,* 4–9.

Sebba, R. (1991). The landscapes of childhood: The reflection of childhood's environment in adult memories and in children's attitudes. *Environment and Behavior, 23,* 395–422.

Silbereisen, R. K., & Eyferth, K. (1986). Development as action in context. In R. K. Silbereisen, K. Eyferth, & G. Rudinger (Eds.), *Development as action in context: Problem behavior and normal youth development* (pp. 3–16). Berlin: Springer-Verlag.

Silbereisen, R. K., & Noack, P. (1988). Adolescence and environment. In D. Canter, M. Krampen, & D. Stea (Eds.), *Ethnoscapes: Environmental policy, assessment and communication* (Vol. 2, pp. 19–34). Aldershot, England: Avebury.

Silbereisen, R. K., Noack, P., & Eyferth, K. (1986). Place for development: Adolescents, leisure settings, and developmental tasks. In R. K. Silbereisen, K. Eyferth, & G. Rudinger (Eds.), *Development as action in context: Problem behavior and normal youth development* (pp. 87–107). Berlin: Springer-Verlag.

Smith, F., & Barker, J. (2000). Contested spaces: Children's experiences of out of school care in England and Wales. *Childhood, 7,* 315–333.

Sobel, D. (1990). A place in the world: Adults' memories of childhood special places. *Children's Environments Quarterly, 7,* 5–12.

Sommer, B. (1990). Favorite places of Estonian adolescents. *Children's Environmental Quarterly, 7,* 32–36.

Spencer, C., & Woolley, H. (2000). Children and the city: A summary of recent environmental psychology research. *Child: Care, Health, and Development, 26,* 181–198.

Staats, H., Gatersleben, B., & Hartig, T. (1997). Change in mood as a function of environmental design: Arousal and pleasure on a simulated forest hike. *Journal of Environmental Psychology, 17,* 283–300.

Steptoe, A., & Appels, A. (Eds.). (1989). *Stress, personal control and health.* Chicester: Wiley.

Stokols, D. (1978). Environmental psychology. *Annual Review of Psychology, 29,* 253–295.

Sundström, E., Bell, P. A., Busby, P. L., & Asmus, C. (1996). Environmental psychology. *Annual Review of Psychology, 47,* 485–512.

Taylor, A. F., Kuo, F. E., & Sullivan, W. C. (2001). Coping with ADD: The surprising connection to green play settings. *Environment and Behavior, 33,* 54–77.

Taylor, A. F., Wiley, A., Kuo, F. E., & Sullivan, W. C. (1998). Growing up in the inner city: Green spaces as places to grow. *Environment and Behavior, 30,* 3–27.

Taylor, S. E. (1983). Adjustment to threatening events: A theory of cognitive adaptation. *American Psychologist, 38,* 1161–1173.

Taylor, S. E. (1991). Asymmetrical effects of positive and negative events: The mobilization-minimization hypothesis. *Psychological Bulletin, 110,* 67–85.

Taylor, S. E., & Brown, J. D. (1994). Positive illusions and well-being revisited: Separating fact from fiction. *Psychological Bulletin, 116,* 21–27.

Tesser, A. (1986). Some effects of self-evaluation maintenance on cognition and action. In R. M. Sorrentino & E. T. Higgins (Eds.), *Handbook of motivation and cognition: Foundations of social behavior* (pp. 435–464). Chichester, England: Wiley.

Thurber, C. A., & Malinowski, J. C. (1999). Environmental correlates of negative emotions in children. *Environment and Behavior, 31,* 487–513.

Twigger-Ross, C. L., & Uzzell, D. L. (1996). Place and identity processes. *Journal of Environmental Psychology, 16,* 205–220.

Ulrich, R. S., Simons, R. F., Losito, B. D., Fiorito, E., Miles, M. A., & Zelson, M. (1991). Stress recovery during exposure to natural and urban environments. *Journal of Environmental Psychology, 11,* 201–230.

van Andel, J. (1990). Places children like, dislike, and fear. *Children's Environments Quarterly, 7,* 24–31.

Wells, N. M. (2000). At home with nature: Effects of "greenness" on children's cognitive functioning. *Environment and Behavior, 32,* 775–795.

Wohlwill, J. F., & Heft, H. (1987). The physical environment and the development of the child. In D. Stokols & I. Altman (Eds.), *Handbook of environmental psychology* (Vol. 1, pp. 281–328). New York: Wiley.

Wyman, M. (1985). Nature experience and outdoor recreation planning. *Leisure studies, 4,* 175–188.

Wölfing, S. (1996). The use of identity-relevant functions of things and places in the context of migration. *Swiss Journal of Psychology, 55,* 241–248.

CHAPTER 25

Design and Dementia

KRISTEN DAY and MARGARET P. CALKINS

RESEARCH ON AGING AND ENVIRONMENTS constitutes a well-developed field of scholarship within studies. Beginning with the work of early pioneers such as Powell Lawton (cf. Lawton, Liebowitz, & Charon, 1970) and Joachim Wohlwill (1966), aging-and-environment researchers have generated theory and research that addresses a range of settings that include workplaces, educational facilities, parks, and health care environments (see the review chapter on aging and environments by Carp, 1987, in the first edition of the *Handbook of Environmental Psychology*). Research and design application in environments for people with dementia constitutes an especially prolific and productive subset of this scholarship.

In the past two decades, environmental design emerged as a powerful therapeutic resource in the care of people with Alzheimer's disease and other dementias. Beyond decoration, environmental design is now considered a critical part of the care milieu. Thoughtful design is harnessed as a tool to help ameliorate the difficult symptoms—wandering, disorientation, agitation, social withdrawal, and others—associated with dementia. Design helps to promote quality of life and to maintain function among those who suffer from these conditions.

The importance of design in dementia care is evidenced by the burgeoning research on this topic and by the significant recent changes in the design of facilities for this population. Many factors explain this heightened attention to design and dementia. First, public and professional awareness and understanding of dementia have grown substantially in the past two decades. Likewise, diagnoses for Alzheimer's disease and other dementias have increased with greater awareness of the disease and with the aging of the population in many countries. Finally, interest in design and dementia is sparked by changes in the nature of long-term care in the United States and elsewhere.

This chapter summarizes advances in research and in application of research to design for people with dementia and addresses the following questions: (1) Based on existing research, what are the therapeutic impacts of design for people with dementia? And (2) how has design for dementia changed or evolved over the past several decades? Ideally, the chapter would also document the extent to which research findings influenced design changes. Unfortunately, this connection is extremely difficult to substantiate, because few published descriptions of facilities indicate the extent to which research findings informed the design process. This issue will be addressed later.

THE STATE OF RESEARCH ON DESIGN AND DEMENTIA

This section characterizes the state of research on design and dementia based on a recent review of existing research conducted by Day and colleagues (Day, Carreon, & Stump, 2000). The research review identified 71 English-language reports of empirical research that were published since 1980.[1] (The

---

[1] In this review, published empirical research reports on design and dementia were identified by searching four major databases.

reader should note that much additional research on design and dementia is not published but appears instead as masters and doctoral theses, conference presentations and proceedings, and so forth. Much research on design and dementia is also published in languages other than English. Japanese research, in particular, is prolific.)

The amount of research on design and dementia has increased significantly in recent years. The literature review identified six research reports from 1981 to 1985, 17 research reports from 1986 to 1990, 26 research reports from 1991 to 1995, and 21 research reports published between 1996 and 1999 (see Figure 25.1). A recent review of published and unpublished Japanese-language research on design and dementia identifies a similar increase in research over time (Adachi, Akagi, & Funahashi, 2000).

Research on design and dementia is widespread both in terms of where it is conducted and by whom. The research review identifies published English-language research on design and dementia conducted in Australia, Canada, Finland, Italy, Japan, Scotland, Sweden, The Netherlands, the United Kingdom, and the United States. Design and dementia research is conducted by scholars and practitioners in fields that include nursing, geriatrics, gerontology, research, cognitive science, psychiatry, medicine, occupational therapy, and health care management, among others.

Published English-language research on design and dementia focuses overwhelmingly on more institutional environments—special care units (SCUs), skilled nursing facilities, and other long-term care alternatives—rather than on less institutional options such as group homes, day care centers, or homes. Of the 71 studies identified in the literature review, 38 investigate SCUs, 22 examine other long-term care environments, and 9 examine psychogeriatric wards. A handful of studies investigate other options. The focus on institutional settings belies two important facts: (1) The vast majority of people with dementia in the United States and elsewhere

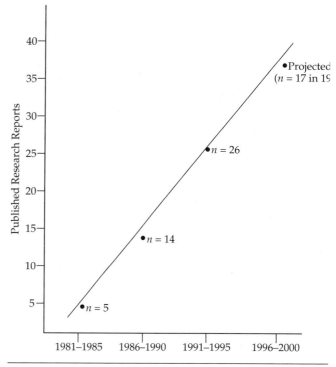

Figure 25.1 Published English-language research on design and dementia has increased significantly since 1980. *Source:* Day et al., 2000.

continue to live at home, and (2) alternatives to more institutional options, while not uniformly available, have become more prevalent in recent years.[2] Why, then, does research on design and dementia emphasize more institutional care settings? A possible explanation may be the comparative ease of conducting research in larger facilities that serve many people with dementia, that control multiple aspects of residents' lives (facilitating comparisons across individuals), and in which environmental characteristics are standardized across residents.

Research on design and dementia often exhibits shortcomings that are tied to the nature of the subject. One such weakness is that researchers rarely consider the first-hand experiences of people with dementia, because of the difficulty of collecting experiential information from those with cognitive

---

Research reports were also identified by reviewing all issues (1980–1999) of several journals in gerontology and in environment-behavior research and by reviewing reference lists for all identified research reports. The 71 research reports met the following criteria: published in 1980 or later; written in English; written with an emphasis on people with dementia or their families or staff caregivers; and written with a substantial emphasis on the relationship between the design of the physical environment and the well-being of people with dementia, their families, and/or staff.

---

[2] Japanese-language research reports also focus overwhelmingly on institutional rather than on residential or urban environments (Adachi et al., 2000). Adachi and colleagues do find an increase in investigations of group homes over time, possibly reflecting the fact that their review includes both peer-reviewed and non-peer-reviewed research. (Since it often constitutes a single case study, group home research may less often appear in peer-reviewed sources.)

impairments.[3] Instead, researchers typically conduct observations or interviews with staff or family members and extrapolate about the experiences of those with dementia. Another shortcoming is the difficulty of drawing firm conclusions and of generalizing from research findings on design and dementia because of the small sample sizes that are typically employed in these studies. Studies frequently involve fewer than 30 participants, and samples of less than 10 are not uncommon. These small sample sizes reflect the limited populations of residents at the single facility in which many studies were conducted, the high rates of resident mortality, and the limited numbers of residents in comparable stages of dementia at a facility at a single point in time. These methodological shortcomings make many findings tentative or preliminary, rather than conclusive.

THE RELATIONSHIP BETWEEN RESEARCH AND DESIGN

The relationship between research and design is complex. In trying to determine the extent to which research may have impacted design, one must first consider chronology. Design and construction are lengthy processes. Up to 2 years may pass between the beginning design development and the date a building is first occupied. Thus, to have informed the original design of a facility, research generally must have been conducted and published at least 2 years prior to the opening of that building. Second, one must acknowledge the limited documentation of the influence of research. Few published descriptions of projects specifically indicate whether research informed any design decisions, making the impact of research difficult to ascertain. Third, and perhaps most important, one must appreciate that research utilization is not always a one-to-one relationship between the findings of a particular study and their direct implementation in a specific facility design. Rather, design innovations often result from broad changes in thinking that are prompted in part by research (Seidel, 1985). The influence of

research may not be directly traceable, as this chapter demonstrates.[4]

In the case of design for people with dementia, research utilization has been aided by explicit efforts at design guidance—chiefly in the form of design guides—for dementia care environments. Beginning with early books by Calkins (1988) and Cohen and Weisman (1991), design researchers attempted to translate relevant information about dementia into practical design recommendations. Design guidance typically constitutes hypotheses for how the spatial organization and appointment of the physical environment might promote well-being in people with dementia. For instance, to respond to the symptom of sensitivity to overstimulation, design guides recommend environmental modifications such as the designation of quiet rooms with soft colors, the elimination of unnecessary clutter, and the removal of paging systems (cf. Brawley, 1997; Cohen & Weisman, 1991). Design guidance has been widely disseminated through books, articles, and conference presentations directed to facility administrators, staff, family members, and architects. Design guidance is also disseminated through design consultations by experts in dementia and design. The influence of design guidance is difficult to trace and virtually impossible to differentiate from the influence of published research reports.

Because of the rapid growth in specialized dementia care settings over the past decade and because of the incredible competition that facilities face in attracting residents (especially private-pay residents), numerous design features have "caught on" like fads, becoming so prevalent that a facility developed today without these features would be viewed as poorly designed. Some such features are supported by research demonstrating their effectiveness for people with dementia, although designers may not have been aware of the research. The prime example of this situation is the use of personalized cues at bedroom entries. This feature appears

---

[3] Some researchers argue that the quality and ethicality of research on design and dementia would be improved by directly examining the perceptions of people with dementia—especially those in the early to middle stages (Chaudhury, 1996).

[4] Seidel (1985) thus distinguishes between instrumental (or direct) research use and conceptual (or indirect) research use. Instrumental research use might include, for example, full documentation of specific design decisions that are based on behavioral research. Conceptual research use might include general application of notions learned through the popular press to the design of buildings. General use of research-based concepts and ideas gleaned from site visits or from conference presentations would fall midway in the continuum between these types of research utilization.

to have been first incorporated at Wesley Hall (Coons, 1985). Wesley Hall was evaluated over several years. Studies did not examine the impact of individual design features but rather adopted a global perspective to evaluate the impact of the whole setting. The idea of a personalized cue at the bedroom entry was then modified and included in the design of the Corinne Dolan Center (see Figure 25.2), which opened in 1989. Research demonstrating the efficacy of personalized cues at bedroom entrances was conducted at the Corinne Dolan Center in 1989 and published in 1991. In the interim period, numerous conference presentations were given in which both the design feature and the results of the research were described. It is impossible to determine who may have learned of this feature from conference presentations or site visits. Yet the feature—or one of its many design variations—is

Figure 25.2 Display cases at the Corinne Dolan Alzheimer's Center, Chardon, Ohio.

included in virtually every care setting for people with dementia built today.

Conversely, other design features are routinely recommended by design guides and are featured in designs but appear to have no basis in research. The prime example of such a feature is the "country kitchen." The country kitchen lacks conceptual, design, and functional/operational clarity and also lacks research to evaluate its effectiveness. Physical features described as country kitchens range from the simple presence of a large table for six to eight (which sometimes doubles as the staff work space) adjacent to a counter with a sink and microwave; to kitchen appliances, counter, and cabinets along a single wall in the dining room; to a separate room that may or may not have a work table. Similarly, use of the country kitchen also varies significantly, ranging from a weekly baking activity with residents with the kitchen locked at other times; to use for serving meals prepared in a different kitchen; to daily use for part or all of the meal preparations for the residents who live in that area. Despite the fact that there is virtually no research demonstrating any positive impact of the presence of a country kitchen, the vast majority of new and even renovated facilities include some form of country kitchen area.

In conclusion, it is often difficult or impossible to determine the extent to which the inclusion or design of specific features in a given facility is research based. Though it infrequently identifies direct linkages, this chapter discusses the potential relationships between research and design guidance on the one hand and design innovation on the other.

RESEARCH AND DESIGN FOR PEOPLE WITH DEMENTIA

This section reviews what is known about the therapeutic impact of design for people with dementia and examines related innovations in the design of dementia care environments. Research results are drawn from the research review described earlier (Day et al., 2000). Descriptions of related environmental features or characteristics were identified in a recent analysis of published citations describing care settings for people with dementia.[5] A total of 71

---

[5] Sources of descriptions of actual facilities included *Nursing Home Magazine* (1972-present), *Long Term Care Administrator* (1983–present), *Provider* (1987–present), and *Assisted Living*

articles describing specific dementia care facilities were identified.

This section organizes issues by scale, from the macroscale of entire facilities to the microscale of individual spaces within facilities. Each issue is first introduced as it concerns design for people with dementia (e.g., the hypothesized impacts of building configuration on residents' orientation). This brief introduction is followed by a summary of relevant findings from empirical *research* on that topic (e.g., research findings on the impact of building configuration for residents' orientation). Finally, innovations in *practice* or design related to this issue are discussed (e.g., changes over time in facility configurations that were intended to promote orientation among residents). Where appropriate, the possible relationships between research and practice innovations are considered.

CARE POPULATION

Facility administrators and researchers have debated over the appropriate population for facilities for people with dementia. By serving only people with dementia, they argue, facilities can specialize services and environments and can minimize embarrassment among dementia residents and conflict with cognitively intact residents. The argument in favor of integrated populations suggests that people with dementia might maintain function through regular contact with cognitively intact residents.

Physically and programmatically, dementia-specific facilities in the United States typically take the form of special care units (SCUs), which are segregated units that accommodate only cognitively impaired individuals. SCUs distinguish themselves by offering one or more special features, including dementia-appropriate activities, small groups of residents, special staff selection and training, family involvement, and specialized design (see Berg et al., 1991). In practice, SCUs vary enormously in their design, staffing, philosophy, activities, and so on, making comparisons of SCUs and integrated units nearly impossible, though researchers often attempt it.

Today (1993 to present). Additional sources include results of several national competitions ("Design for Aging," sponsored by the American Institute of Architects, and several competitions sponsored by the aforementioned trade journals) and design guide books for dementia care facilities.

Research

According to existing research, SCUs are associated with improvement or slowed decline in residents' communication skills, self-care skills, social function, mobility, and affective responses (Benson, Cameron, Humbach, Servino, & Gambert, 1987; Greene, Asp, & Crane, 1985; McCracken & Fitzwater, 1989; Skea & Lindesay, 1996) and with reductions in behavior disturbances, abnormal motor activity, apathy, and hallucinations among residents (Annerstedt, 1993; Bellelli et al., 1998; Benson et al., 1987; Greene et al., 1985; McCracken & Fitzwater, 1989; Swanson, Maas, & Buckwalter, 1993). SCUs are further associated with reduced emotional strain among relatives and with increased competence and satisfaction among staff (Annerstedt, 1993; Wells & Jorm, 1987).

In contrast, integrated units—including both cognitively intact and cognitively impaired residents—are associated with declines in mental and emotional status for cognitively intact residents who live in close residential proximity to people with dementia (Teresi, Holmes, & Monaco, 1993; Wiltzius, Gambert, & Duthie, 1981). These limited findings would appear to support separate environments for cognitively impaired and for cognitively intact older adults.

Practice

The number of units that call themselves SCUs or that constitute a physically separate space for residents with dementia has grown exponentially over the past 20 years (U.S. Department of Health and Human Services, 1987; Wagner, 1996). A 1987 report by the U.S. Office of Technology Assessment identified 100 SCUs and estimated that as many as 500 may exist in the United States (U.S. Department of Health and Human Services, 1987). By 1998, the number of SCUs had increased to 4,210 (National Institution on Aging, 1999). Some of the research conducted in the 1980s about the generalized positive benefits of segregated care settings for people with dementia may have helped to spur this rapid growth in SCUs. As mentioned earlier, however, numerous factors other than research stimulated the development of SCUs in many countries.

HOUSEHOLD OR GROUP SIZE

Care providers, designers, and researchers have hypothesized that living in smaller groups of residents—6 to 12 rather than 20 to 60—would be more familiar for people with dementia and would reduce their overstimulation by limiting the noise and the total number of people each resident encounters (Calkins, 1988; Cohen & Weisman, 1991). Research findings support this recommendation, though no consistent standard defines a large or a small unit.

Research

In research findings, larger units (ranging in size from 30 to 69 residents) are associated with higher resident agitation levels, increased intellectual deterioration and emotional disturbances, more frequent territorial conflicts and space invasions, and higher aggressiveness toward other residents (Annerstedt, 1994; Morgan & Stewart, 1999; Sloane et al., 1998). Smaller units (ranging in size from 9 to 19 residents), in contrast, are associated with benefits among residents such as less anxiety and depression; less usage of antibiotics and psychotropic drugs; higher motor functions; more mobility, social interaction, and friendship formation; and more supervision and interaction between staff and residents (Annerstedt, 1993, 1997; McAllister & Silverman, 1999; McCracken & Fitzwater, 1989; Moore, 1999; Netten, 1993; Skea & Lindesay, 1996). Smaller units appear to benefit family members and staff as well. Relatives with family members in smaller and less formal group living units report lower levels of strain and better attitudes toward dementia care as compared to relatives of residents in larger and more formal nursing homes (Annerstedt, 1993). Staff in group living units report greater competence, more knowledge in dealing with dementia, and greater job satisfaction than do their counterparts in nursing homes (Annerstedt, 1993).

Practice

The earliest setting in the United States specifically designed for people with dementia, the Weiss Pavilion at the Philadelphia Geriatric Center, was completed in 1972. The Weiss Institute distinguished itself from the traditional 60-bed nursing home unit, featuring instead a total of 25 resident rooms that accommodated 40 residents in 15 shared and 10 private rooms (Lawton, Fulcomer, & Kleban, 1984; Liebowitz, Lawton, & Waldman, 1979). A population of 40 was regarded as small enough to minimize overstimulation from too many people and too much activity while still providing sufficient numbers of

individuals to encourage spontaneous interaction (Cohen & Day, 1993; Lawton et al., 1984; Liebowitz et al., 1979).

The next generation of dementia-specific facilities opened in the late 1980s and early 1990s. These facilities adopted a much smaller scale. Three premiere and well-known facilities—Wesley Hall, the Corinne Dolan Center at Heather Hill, and Woodside Place—accommodated groups of 11 or 12 residents together in residential clusters (Cohen & Day, 1993; Coons, 1985). The vast majority of facilities built since this time have also grouped fewer numbers of residents together. Many articles describing these newer facilities provide no information on the size of the residential units. However, descriptions of nine facilities built prior to 1990 indicated unit sizes varying between 15 and 50 with a mean size of 30 beds. Of the 14 references that provided this data for facilities built between 1990 and 1994, unit size ranged from 12 to 35 but had a mean size of 19 beds per unit. The 20 facilities built between 1995 and 2001 for which there were data had unit sizes ranging from 8 to 34 beds with a mean size of 16 beds per unit. Descriptions of these facilities show a distinct trend away from larger- to smaller-scaled units.[6]

Clearly, the decision by designers and facility owners to create smaller units was not based primarily on the research reviewed earlier, most of which was conducted after 1993. Earlier design guidance (such as Calkins, 1988) may have been influential, however.

BUILDING CONFIGURATION

Prior to the development of SCUs for people with dementia, long-term care settings were designed around a few seemingly inviolate principles: 60 beds was the ideal unit size to maximize staff efficiency, large nursing stations should be centrally located with clear views down straight corridors, and day rooms that housed all activities and visiting were located across from the nursing station to facilitate staff's ability to easily monitor residents. Meals were provided in centrally located dining rooms that often served several hundred people at a time. Plan configurations varied but were often best described

---

[6] Certainly, facilities described in trade publications and entered in competitions are likely to be more "progressive" as a set than are their counterparts that receive no such attention. Analysis of descriptions of "published" facilities can therefore be used to indicate design trends but not the state of the art.

as a letter of the alphabet: *X, O, T, L, C, U,* or *E.* SCUs were among the first units to challenge these overarching principles.

Research

Design guidance for people with dementia has long suggested that building configuration may impact orientation, wandering, and social interaction among people with dementia (Calkins, 1988; Lawton et al., 1984). Limited research, however, examines this hypothesis. Findings suggest that simple building configuration is associated with resident orientation when residents are also provided with explicit environmental information (Passini, Rainville, Marchand, & Joanette, 1998). In findings from surveys and observations of 104 residents in several homes, cluster facilities (comprised of small units of residents' rooms and associated common spaces) were associated with higher levels of orientation than were larger scale communal facilities (common spaces separated from resident rooms and shared by larger groups of residents) (Netten, 1989). Additionally, L-, H-, or square-shaped buildings were associated with greater orientation among residents than were other facilities (Elmståhl, Annerstedt, & Åhlund, 1997).

Corridor designs were associated with higher degrees of restlessness and dyspraxia[7] and with reduced vitality and identity (Elmståhl et al., 1997). However, residents in units with a greater percentage of space dedicated to hallways displayed better relative orientation and higher relative vitality than did residents in units with a smaller percentage of space dedicated to hallways (Elmståhl et al., 1997); explanations for these findings are not provided.

Practice

The first unit specifically designed for people with dementia differed radically from the traditional nursing home unit, reflecting a conscious effort to design for a different set of priorities. Recognizing the challenges people with dementia experience with maintaining orientation, the team that created the Weiss Pavilion at the Philadelphia Geriatric Center arrayed bedrooms around a large, open central space (Liebowitz et al., 1979). They articulated the 8-foot corridors required by code with a change in floor color and ceiling height. The design team

believed that with a highly visible dining room, program space, and nursing station, residents would better orient themselves and more easily find desired locations.

Despite the radical nature of its design and the excellent evaluations conducted on the Weiss Pavilion, dementia design did not advance significantly over the next 15 years. The advances pioneered at the Weiss Pavilion were not examined or extended until the mid-1980s. The first of the next generation plans also adopted an open plan concept, although many other design features differed. The Corinne Dolan Center at Heather Hill, which opened in 1989, featured bedrooms arranged around an open central space that included the dining room and a kitchen. The design team (including Margaret Calkins) believed that this configuration would support residents' efforts to find the dining room for meals and to find their bedrooms, which were directly visible from the dining room. Only a few other facilities, such as Namaste (Cohen & Day, 1993) followed the same open plan style.

Woodside Place pioneered an alternative building configuration (Hoglund, Dimotta, Ledewitz, & Saxton, 1994). Here, instead of bedrooms arranged around an open central space, the plan comprises households of 12 residents. Households constitute short, double-loaded corridors with a kitchen and dining room located at the entrance to each. Numerous facilities have replicated Woodside's plan with slight modifications (see, for instance, "Looking Good," 1997; "Rethinking Regulation," 1995).

The other plan configuration common today—a hybrid solution—separates the bedroom wing(s) but keeps the shared social spaces more centralized, either as one large open space or as several smaller, more discrete spaces. Examples include New Perspective Home No. 4 and the Alzheimer Care Center (Cohen & Day, 1993). Other plan configurations exist, although the myriad variations make succinct description impossible (see the following discussion on noninstitutional design).

NONINSTITUTIONAL DESIGN

Early in the 1980s, advocates and researchers recognized that many people with dementia who lived in nursing homes did not require the skilled level of nursing care these facilities were designed, operated, and regulated to provide (Liebowitz et al., 1979; Snyder-Hiatt, 1978; U.S. Department of Health and Human Services, 1981). Instead of highly technical or

---

[7]Dyspraxia involves immaturity of the brain resulting in messages not being properly transmitted to the body.

sophisticated medical treatment, these individuals needed a caring, supportive environment that compensated for their decreasing cognitive capabilities. Care providers and researchers also recognized that, although the illness is progressive, living with dementia can be a long and drawn out process, often lasting 20 years or more. Thus, they argued, care settings should strive to be more nursing *homes* than *nursing* homes. As more and more facilities for people with dementia were developed, researchers and care providers sought ways to make settings less institutional and more like home.

Research

Research supports the value of noninstitutional design features, such as homelike furnishings and personalization, for residents' well-being. Noninstitutional environments characterized as having homelike or enhanced ambiance (personalized rooms, domestic furnishings, natural elements, etc.) are associated with improved intellectual and emotional well-being, enhanced social interaction, reduced agitation, reduced trespassing and exit seeking, greater preference and pleasure, and improved functionality of older adults with dementia and other mental illnesses (Annerstedt, 1994; Cohen-Mansfield & Werner, 1998; Kihlgren et al., 1992; McAllister & Silverman, 1999; Sloane et al., 1998). Compared with those in traditional nursing homes and hospitals, residents in noninstitutional settings are less aggressive, have better motor functions, require lower usage of tranquilizing drugs, and have less anxiety. Relatives reported greater satisfaction and less burden associated with noninstitutional facilities (Annerstedt, 1997; Cohen-Mansfield & Werner, 1998; Kihlgren et al., 1992). Staff also prefer less institutional, enhanced environments (Cohen-Mansfield & Werner, 1998).

Noninstitutional design offers reduced benefits, however, if not coupled with supportive caregiving practices. In an ethnographic study of one facility, inflexible and formal institutional caregiving practices were characterized as undermining the therapeutic potential of the homelike environment (Moore, 1999).

Practice

In the push to replace institutional concepts and language, progressive practitioners rejected the term *unit,* which signaled the old, traditional way of thinking. In the early 1990s, forward-thinking facilities instead developed "pods" or "clusters." These terms were meant to reflect smaller-scale units; facilities using these terms shared few other features in common. Some pods and clusters included all resident spaces (bedrooms, living room, dining room, kitchen) and staff support spaces, others located the staff support spaces off the unit, while still others served residents' meals in a dining room located away from the pod or cluster (Calkins, 1997). The arrangement of spaces varied as well. Some featured open plans while others included hallways (Doig, Scott, & Townsley, 1998; Hiatt, 1997; Hodgson, Nelson, Pellegrino, & Pruitt, 1998).[8]

---

[8] The following typology is proposed to provide additional clarity for the field. Because the primary focus of design should be the residents who live in the facility and because staff support systems can be changed and modified without altering the basic structure of the building, this typology does not differentiate unit type based on the location of staff support spaces. Nor does it specifically indicate how services are provided (i.e., whether meals are prepared in a kitchen on the unit or prepared in a central kitchen and brought to the unit). Rather, this typology categorizes spaces as residents experience them. Although the size of these spaces may vary, the maximum size typically does not exceed 25 residents living together and sharing living and dining rooms (except for the unit).

- *Unit* refers to the traditional, institutional design with long corridors and prominent, centrally located nurses' station and accommodations for 40 or more residents.
- *Pod* refers to an open plan unit for 24 or fewer residents with the majority of rooms opening directly onto the majority of shared spaces such as a dining room, living room, and/or kitchen. Additional program/activity rooms may be self-contained and may be located on or off the pod.
- *Cluster* refers to units, also for 24 or fewer residents, in which the majority of bedrooms open onto hallways, but the hallways are generally not longer than the width of five or six bedrooms. The shared social spaces may be grouped together or dispersed throughout the unit.
- *Household* refers to units in which the arrangement of spaces specifically reflects traditional residential design. The main entrance or front door to the unit opens onto shared public spaces such as a living room or dining room. Households include a kitchen, adjacent to the dining room, from which meals are served if not at least partially prepared. Bedrooms are somewhat separated from these spaces, reflecting traditional residential location of bedrooms upstairs or down a hallway. Households may also include a back door, often leading directly to an outdoor space. Typically, households are structured for 16 or fewer residents.
- *Neighborhood* refers to groupings of two to five of the previously described households in such a manner that households share some spaces that are typically found in neighborhoods (shops or deli, beauty/barber shop, library, etc.). Neighborhoods often feature some shared staff spaces (offices, medication rooms, supplies, and utility rooms). Staff and support spaces may be designed to resemble small office/retail spaces, which are also typical in neighborhoods.

Over a few short years, as facility operators, designers, and consumers became more knowledgeable and sophisticated, the terms *pod* and *cluster* were rejected as insufficiently residential. After all, it was argued, whales live in pods and grapes come in clusters (Oostendorp, 1996). People, however, live in households and neighborhoods. Hence, these latter terms became preferred. Here again, no consensus exists on the design features or characteristics that differentiate a space as being like a household versus a neighborhood. These terms are chiefly used for market advantage because of their intrinsic appeal to future residents and their families.

Along with unit scale, residents' right and ability to bring personal possessions from home has emerged as important in the move toward less institutional design (Calkins, 1997). Traditionally, nursing homes limited residents' personal possessions to a few pieces of art for the walls and some knickknacks for the dresser or windowsill. Early dementia care settings often eliminated these knickknacks (since residents frequently entered others' rooms and walked off with others' possessions, causing anger and mistrust among residents, family, and staff). This restrictive policy is gradually changing. Increasingly, facilities—especially assisted living facilities—actively encourage residents to bring some or all of their bedroom furniture and occasionally even furniture or other items for the shared living areas of the facility. However, in many states, fire codes limit the type of furniture (particularly upholstered chairs) that can be brought into facilities. Nursing home codes may further require facilities to provide a hospital bed for all residents.

SIGNAGE

Although the open plan configurations described earlier were designed specifically to support residents' ability to orient themselves within the facility, some spaces will inevitably be less than completely visible. In other plan configurations, desired locations may be almost completely hidden from view from hallways and bedroom entrances. Signage is therefore still necessary in dementia care facilities and may be required by codes.

Research

Research findings—though limited—support the use of signage to minimize disorientation among resi-

dents. For example, the use of room numbers and distinguishing colors for resident rooms and doors was associated with enhanced orientation among residents (Lawton et al., 1984). In several small-scale studies, large signs were associated with improvements in residents' orientation when orientation training was also provided (Hanley, 1981). As discussed earlier, personalized display cases outside resident rooms were associated with some improvements among residents in finding their rooms as compared to displays without personal significance (Namazi, Rosner, & Rechlin, 1991). The latter finding holds particularly true for residents with moderate dementia. Additional research on signage specifically for toilet rooms is described later.

Practice

Apart from published research reports, descriptions of actual facilities seldom indicate specific strategies used to orient residents. The Weiss Center design visually emphasized both the nursing station and the dining area so that these would be easily located by the residents (Lawton et al., 1984). This strategy involves creating "landmarks"—highly distinctive, visually unique elements to orient residents. Landmarks are frequently described in research and design guidance literature (Brawley, 1997; Calkins, 1989, 2001; Cohen & Weisman, 1991; Hiatt, 1991), yet they are referenced only occasionally in articles describing specific facilities (cf. Tames, 1992; Tetlow, 1995).

As discussed, the Corinne Dolan Center was the first long-term care setting to include designated space at the bedroom entry for displaying personal mementos that were specifically intended as orientation cues. Research demonstrating the efficacy of this feature was presented at several conferences in 1990 and published in 1992. The prevalence in most dementia facilities of some form of display case at the bedroom entrance (cf. Anders, 1994; "Best Practices," 1997; Cohen & Day, 1993; Kromm & Kromm, 1985; Tames, 1992; Tetlow, 1995) suggests that this research—along with widespread dissemination of information about the Corinne Dolan Center—may well have influenced designers and facility operators. A few facilities, such as the Helen Bader Center in Milwaukee, Wisconsin, acknowledge that the design of their bedroom orientation features were influenced by the research conducted at the Corinne Dolan Center.

Descriptions of existing facilities do not identify other specific signage strategies or solutions. When signage is mentioned, the description tends to be general (see Tetlow, 1995, however, for brief mention of one orientation strategy).

SENSORY STIMULATION AND LIGHTING

People with dementia face difficulties with sensory overstimulation, which may increase the distraction, agitation, and confusion associated with dementia. At the same time, sensory deprivation has been identified as a potential problem in many dementia care environments (Cohen & Weisman, 1991). The challenge is thus to maintain a balance such that residents suffer neither from environmental overstimulation nor from sensory deprivation.

Research

Research confirms the negative impact of noise on residents' functioning. In a study of 79 dementia residents at 13 long-term care facilities, quiet environments were associated with higher levels of orientation among residents (Netten, 1993). Researchers theorized that disorientation followed residents' attempts to shut out noisy environments. Loud noises (loud talking, singing, and clapping, etc.) were associated with overstimulation among residents (Nelson, 1995).

Overstimulation may impair residents' ability to concentrate. Limited-stimulation activity areas—made by hanging cloth partitions to eliminate views to ongoing activity—were found to reduce distractions among residents by up to two-thirds (Namazi & Johnson, 1992b). Use of these fabric partitions increased the ability to focus on a task among residents in all stages of dementia. Partitions worked by reducing visual distractions.

Design to minimize sensory stimulation appears to have some positive benefits for residents. Use of a neutral design and color scheme, elimination of stimulation, and consistent daily routines were associated with fewer behavioral disturbances, fewer catastrophic reactions, lower usage of physical and chemical restraints, more positive interactions, and more weight gain among residents (Bianchetti, Benvenuti, Ghisla, Frisoni, & Trabucchi, 1997; Cleary, Clamon, Price, & Shullaw, 1988; Swanson et al., 1993).

The effectiveness of design to maximize positive stimulation has received comparatively less attention by researchers. In a postoccupancy study of the Weiss Institute, residents were found to spend less time in their rooms and were more attentive to activity following relocation to the facility, which was designed as a more interactive open plan instead of the traditional hallway design (Lawton et al., 1984).

In research on the therapeutic impact of lighting, low lighting levels were associated with less successful wayfinding and with higher agitation levels among people with dementia but were not associated with increased psychiatric symptoms (Elmståhl et al., 1997; Netten, 1989; Sloane et al., 1998). Compared with other older adults, people with dementia are exposed to inadequate levels of bright light (described as light exceeding 2,000 lux, Campbell, Kripke, Gillin, & Hrubovcak, 1988.) No explanation for these findings was offered. Exposure to bright light treatment was found to consistently regulate circadian rhythms[9] and to improve sleep patterns among people with dementia (Mishima et al., 1994; Satlin, Volicer, Ross, Herz, & Campbell, 1992).

People with dementia face particular visual deficits including difficulty with color discrimination, depth perception, and sensitivity to contrast (Cronin-Golumb, 1995). These deficits exacerbate normal changes in vision that accompany aging, such as irritation from glare and changes in color perception (Brawley, 1997). Research infrequently examines the impacts of visual contrast in dementia care environments, though this strategy is often recommended to enhance legibility or clarity of the environment. In one study, 13 residents with dementia ate more and displayed less agitation when dining arrangements incorporated brighter light and heightened color contrast (i.e., high-contrast tablecloths, place mats, and the like) (Koss & Gilmore, 1998).

Practice

Though research reveals negative impacts of noise on residents with dementia, descriptions of actual facilities do not identify the use of specific strategies to reduce sources of noise, such as changing call systems to signal staff pagers instead of auditory alarms.

Facilities appear to differ in their stances on regulating visual stimulation. For instance, in their book of case studies of dementia care facilities, Cohen and Day (1993) identify several facilities (including

---

[9] Circadian rhythms are daily activity cycles based on 24-hour patterns.

Friendship Village, New Perspectives No. 4, Helen Bader Center, Namaste, Alexian Village, and Stonefield House) that include shared social spaces that are largely open to each other and the corridor (see also Adelsberg, 1995; Herin, 1998). Cohen and Day also include among their case studies other sites (including Alois Alzheimer Center, Alzheimer Care Center, Minna Murra, Woodside Place, and Corinne Dolan Center) that provide some combination of open and enclosed activity spaces (see also Parsons, 1996; "Renovation Architecture," 1996).

As with signage, descriptions of lighting in practice-oriented literature are typically nonspecific. Nonglare or no-shadow lighting was mentioned in several references (Anders, 1994; "Architectural Design Awards," 1994; Reeves & Cooper, 1987; Tetlow, 1995), though only one article specifically identified indirect lighting fixtures as a design solution (Reeve & Cooper, 1987). Inclusion of natural light was also mentioned in descriptions of several facilities despite the fact that natural light often causes glare.

Safety

Residents' attempts to leave facilities or homes present a major safety concern for staff and family caregivers. Design solutions to prevent unwanted exiting often do so by exploiting residents' cognitive deficits—for instance, by disguising doors or door handles to decrease the temptation to exit.

Research

Successful strategies that have been found to discourage residents' exit attempts include a full-length mirror placed in front of the exit door (Mayer & Darby, 1991); two-dimensional grids on the floor in front of doors (possibly interpreted by residents as three-dimensional barriers) (Hussian & Brown, 1987); cloth panels to camouflage door knobs or panic bars (Namazi, Rosner, & Calkins, 1989); and closed, matching miniblinds installed to restrict light and views through exit door windows (Dickinson, McLain-Kark, & Marshall-Baker, 1995). Disguised doors may be most effective in limiting exit attempts when disguises (blinds, etc.) also limit residents' views to attractive nearby locations (Chafetz, 1990; Morgan & Stewart, 1999; Namazi, Rosner, & Calkins, 1989).

Accommodating residents' exit attempts, rather than discouraging them, was also associated with

positive outcomes. In one small study, unlocking doors to allow access into secure outdoor areas was associated with significant decreases in agitation among residents (Namazi & Johnson, 1992c).

Staff consider surveillance important for maintaining safety in environments for people with dementia (Morgan & Stewart, 1999). Design interventions targeting other desired outcomes may unintentionally inhibit staff surveillance. In interviews with nine staff members and nine relatives associated with a newly designed SCU, staff reported that the new facility's low density, private resident rooms, enclosed charting spaces, and secluded outdoor area and activity spaces impeded opportunities for staff surveillance and increased time spent locating and monitoring residents (Morgan & Stewart, 1999). Ease of surveillance also has negative consequences, however. In an evaluation of the Weiss Institute, staff interaction with residents decreased following occupation of this new facility (Lawton et al., 1984). Since the facility's open design accommodated staff surveillance from the nurses' station, direct staff contact with residents declined.

Preventing falls among residents represents another key safety concern (cf. Morgan & Stewart, 1999; Pynoos & Ohta, 1991; Scandura, 1995). Design interventions have demonstrated some success in reducing residents' falls. A significant reduction in falls was reported in one SCU with the introduction of alternative furnishings that put residents closer to the ground (i.e., bean bag chairs, futons, and mattresses placed on the floor) (Scandura, 1995).[10] In other research, environmental modifications introduced into home environments to reduce falls were judged effective by 12 dementia caregivers at a 7-month follow-up (Pynoos & Ohta, 1991). Modifications included railings for tub and stairs, a nonskid bath mat, and a bath chair.

Practice

Though research frequently evaluates solutions to prevent unwanted exiting, descriptions of actual facilities rarely mention the use of any strategy to secure exits other than some form of lock or alarm. Tames (1992) describes one facility in which an exit

---

[10] Changes in furnishings were accompanied by changes in care plans to reduce demanding tasks (e.g., bathing) in the evenings, when most falls occurred. Complete research methods were not reported for this study.

door was relocated to be parallel with—not perpendicular to—the hallway. In this facility, the day room was intentionally placed at the end of the corridor to be more appealing to residents than the exit door. Beyond locks as a safety feature, these references reveal no consistent way of treating exit doors and no widespread adoption of the innovative control strategies examined by researchers.

In some facilities, exit doors are meant to be used by residents to exit to enclosed courtyards. For instance, in New Perspective Home No. 4 in Mequon, Wisconsin, the highly visible exit doors provide a tempting target for residents to exit to the enclosed courtyard (Cohen & Day, 1993). Several facilities (cf. Corinne Dolan Center, Woodside Place, and Alzheimer Care Center, referenced in Cohen & Day, 1993; "Copper Ridge," 1997) indicate that some exit doors are designed to provide residents with direct and highly visual access to outdoor spaces they may use, while other doors are either located to be less visible to the residents or designed specifically to minimize the view to the outdoors. Other facilities incorporated interior courtyards to allow residents access to outdoor spaces (cf. New Perspectives No. 4 in Cohen & Day, 1993; "Meadows Mennonite," 1999; "Parkcliffe Eldercare Community," 1999; "Westminster-Canterbury," 1999). This design strategy provides outdoor space from which residents cannot wander.

Outdoor Areas

Literature on design for dementia often mentions the importance of outdoor spaces, suggesting that outdoor space affords a familiar, homelike atmosphere and may increase exposure to light and sun. Researchers have documented that individuals with dementia living in long-term care settings (nursing homes) receive significantly less light exposure than do noninstitutionalized individuals (Lyketsos, Veiel, Baker, & Steele, 1999; Mishima et al., 1994; Satlin et al., 1992). Outdoor activity easily increases exposure to bright light, which helps maintain circadian rhythm and vitamin D absorption (cf. Ancoli-Israel et al., 1997; Rae, 1994).

Research

Limited research addresses the therapeutic value of outdoor spaces for people with dementia. In a longitudinal study of five facilities with and without outdoor spaces, researchers found that violent episodes among residents decreased over time in facilities with outdoor environments, whereas violent episodes increased during the same time period in facilities without outdoor environments (Mooney & Nicell, 1992). Residents walked outdoors more often (for short periods of time) in a facility with a special therapeutic garden (Mooney & Nicell, 1992).

Practice

Dementia care settings increasingly incorporate outdoor spaces directly adjacent to residential units. Of the 71 actual facilities described, 17 specifically mention an outdoor space adjacent to the unit (Cohen & Day, 1993; "Designing for Life," 1997; "Looking Good," 1997; Rajecki, 1992; Regnier, 1997; Tetlow, 1995). Many courtyard/outdoor spaces are described as inviting and highly visible, and most included a garden for the residents and a circular path that returned residents to the building entrance. Other features mentioned included a basketball hoop and laundry lines (Tetlow, 1995) and aromatic herbs and vegetable gardens ("Designing for Life," 1997).

The extent to which residents actually use these outdoor spaces is unclear. Concerns for safety, as mentioned earlier, often lead staff to secure exit doors, limiting residents' egress except when they can be accompanied outside. Nor does consensus exist concerning the specific outdoor design features that might benefit residents. The most commonly referenced element is the circular path to minimize disorientation and fear of getting lost outside (Cohen & Day, 1993).

Kitchens and Dining Rooms

Like outdoor spaces, kitchens are often characterized as key to a more homelike atmosphere. Since the vast majority of long-term care residents are women—many of whom have spent much of their lives caring for the home and family—the kitchen is targeted in design guidance for its potential to support familiar activities related to meal preparation and cleanup. (As an interesting aside, one might consider the relevance of kitchens and cooking/domestic activities for future cohorts of older adults, for whom these activities may have less salience. New forms, appropriate activities, and necessary design supports will certainly be needed for these groups.)

Research

Researchers have infrequently investigated the therapeutic impacts of kitchen or dining room design in dementia care environments. One study identifies increased social interaction and improved eating behavior among residents following the adoption of less institutional dining arrangements (i.e., substitution of family-style dining at small dining tables in a coffee room for dining from trays while seated in chairs in the corridor) (Götestam & Melin, 1987; Melin & Götestam, 1981).

Dining on the dementia unit itself—rather than in a centralized location in the facility—may also be linked to reduced aggression among residents. In one facility, assaults decreased by over 40% when residents dined on the unit itself rather than being crowded into elevators to reach the centralized dining room (Negley & Manley, 1990). (Elevators had been sites of frequent violations of personal space, which caused altercations.) The use of two separate dining areas on the unit may have further reduced assaults by separating higher-functioning residents (frequently assailants) from lower-functioning residents (typically victims of assault). Staff at this facility reported less anxiety and more time for assisting residents after dining was relocated to the dementia unit.

Practice

Despite the lack of research on their therapeutic effects, kitchens are increasingly included in newly designed or renovated dementia care settings. Here, design guidance may have been more influential than actual empirical research, since the incorporation of "country kitchens" was frequently recommended in design guidance as a strategy to ameliorate institutional appearance and to support familiar activities (cf. Brawley, 1997; Calkins, 1988; Cohen & Weisman, 1991). Broad dissemination of information on the Corinne Dolan Center and on Woodside Place—both with kitchens for resident use—may have also prompted the growing adoption of this feature. Eighteen of the references in practice-oriented literature included mention of some form of kitchen area (Anders, 1994; Cohen & Day, 1993; "Designing for Life," 1997; Parson, 1996). Kitchens discussed ranged from full working kitchens that are used on a regular basis related to meals (especially in the day care centers, as well as in a few long-term care units) to therapy kitchens used primarily for baking activities for the residents (Cohen & Day, 1993; French & Eamer, 1997; Kromm & Kromm, 1986; Parson, 1996).

Similarly, many facilities now serve meals on the smaller care unit rather than in a centralized dining room for 50 or more ("Sweet Life," 2000; "Outagamie County," 2000; "The Heritage," 2000; "Bethany Harvert Hills," 2000; "Westminster-Cantebury," 1999; "Parkcliffe," 1999). Research on dining, cited in a previous section, was conducted early enough to have influenced these design trends, although the paucity of studies on this issue makes the impact of research on changes in dining questionable.

RESIDENT ROOMS

The relative merits of private versus shared resident rooms remains a matter of debate (Cohen & Day, 1993). Widespread anecdotal evidence links shared bedrooms with significant anxiety and arguments between residents. Equally compelling, however, are the stories of people with dementia who fear being alone and of the deep and lasting friendships that can form among roommates (cf. Shoesmith, 1999).

Research

Existing research provides limited guidance on this issue. Facilities with and without private rooms typically manifest other architectural and programmatic differences as well, confounding attempts to determine the significance of resident room type (cf. Annerstedt, 1994, 1997; Skea & Lindesay, 1996).

Lawton and colleagues (1970) presented findings from a quasi-experiment involving 15 residents, which suggested that the number of residents and room design may affect levels of social interaction. This study evaluated the renovation of a long-term care unit—from two institutional-looking group rooms (four and five residents, respectively) to six less institutional-looking single rooms clustered around a common space. Following renovation, residents spent comparatively less time in their rooms and more time in motion and engaged in less interaction (perhaps by choice), compared to residents before the renovation (Lawton et al., 1970).

One area of bedroom design that has been studied is the design of closets to enhance residents' independence in dressing. In a quasi-experiment with eight SCU residents, specially designed clothes closets were found to increase autonomy in dressing for those with middle-stage dementia (Namazi & Johnson, 1992a). By presenting preselected clothing in an appropriate sequential order (undergarments first, followed by blouses, pants, etc.), modified closets reduced staff members' physical assistance in dressing and enhanced residents' independence.

Practice

The debate about private versus shared rooms is clearly manifested in design. Descriptions of actual facilities suggest a trend toward the provision of more private rooms, though this trend is by no means universal. References to existing facilities identified 10 facilities that were built prior to 1990 and that specified the number of private versus shared rooms. Eight of these (80%) had fewer than one-third private rooms, while two small facilities (20%) had 100% private rooms. Since 1990, the proportions have changed with significantly more facilities (73%) providing at least two-thirds private rooms (see Table 25.1).

The significance of resident room type is further complicated by the development of various shared bedroom layouts that provide considerable privacy to each individual, each of whom essentially shares a toilet but little else. No longer is a private room required for privacy.

Toilet and Bathing Rooms

Bathing is regarded as among the most stressful tasks in caring for people with dementia (Kovach & Meyer-Arnold, 1996; Pynoos & Ohta, 1991; Sloane et al., 1995). Language impairments that limit residents' ability to understand why they are being undressed, unfamiliar equipment, sterile tub rooms, and inability to control the flow and temperature of water combine to make bathing a frightening experience for many individuals (Briller, Proffit, Perez, Calkins, & Marsden, 2001).

Incontinence is another major problem among people with dementia. Incontinence may be exacerbated by facility design that includes few toilets in public areas and by building configurations that obscure toilet locations (cf. Hutchinson, Leger-Krall, & Wilson, 1996).

Research

Several studies examine aspects of bathing associated with high stress. Negative resident reactions are associated with unfamiliar or fearful equipment or procedures (bath tub lifts, specialized tubs, getting in and out of the water, high water levels in whirlpool baths); cold tub rooms (cold air or water temperature, chills from slow tub filling

Table 25.1
Changes over Time in the Provision of Private versus Shared Rooms

In references that describe the percentage of private versus shared bedrooms, a shift has occurred such that facilities appear to be providing a higher percentage of private rooms over time.

	Pre-1990	Post-1990	Pre-1990	Post-1990	Pre-1990	Post-1990
16						■
14						■
12						■
10						■
8	■					■
6	■					■
4	■	■				■
2	■	■		■	■	■
Facilities	0–33% Private rooms		34%–66% Private rooms		67%–100% Private rooms	

or draining); design features that impede bathing (poor lighting, inadequate mats or handrails); and distractions (noisy equipment, running water, or distracting activities outside the bathroom) (Kovach & Meyer-Arnold, 1996; Lawton et al., 1984; Namazi & Johnson, 1996; Sloane et al., 1995). Some evidence suggests that baths may be less upsetting than showers for residents, though findings are mixed (Kovach & Meyer-Arnold, 1996). In one study, the introduction of natural elements during bathing (e.g., animal and water noises, pictures of birds) had a calming effect on residents (Whall et al., 1997) perhaps because of the long-term positive association of these elements.

Research findings, though limited, support the effectiveness of design interventions to facilitate toileting. Early- and moderate-stage dementia residents were found to locate and use public toilets most often when cued by primary color signage affixed to the floor, comprising a series of arrows and the word *toilet* (Namazi & Johnson, 1991b).[11] Frequency of toilet use increased dramatically with direct visual access to toilets (Namazi & Johnson, 1991a). In an experiment with 14 residents, use of toilets increased by over 800% when curtains surrounding toilets (in lieu of doors) were left open, making public and private toilets clearly visible when not in use (Namazi & Johnson, 1991a).

Practice

The design of tub and toilet rooms does not appear to follow any clear trend. Despite the dramatic research findings showing increased use of highly visible toilets, few facilities appear to have incorporated this feature in their designs. Some facilities now place the bedroom toilet where it will be visible from the bed, though examples of this innovation are sparse (cf. Cohen & Day, 1993; Rajecki, 1992). Similarly, descriptions of actual facilities infrequently discuss tub rooms, perhaps suggesting a lack of innovation in this area, although a variety of tubs are now available that were designed to be less frightening to residents by not requiring a lift or special chair.

---

[11] Signage was affixed to the floor in response to residents' typically downcast gaze.

CONCLUSIONS

Dementia care settings have been at the forefront of research, although the direct application of this research to specific care settings is often difficult to determine. The past 2 decades have seen rapid, widespread, and positive change in the design of environments to promote greater well-being among this population. Research and research application are critical aspects of this success. Despite these advances, an analysis of empirical research on design and dementia suggests several shortcomings of the extant body of research. Future research on this topic should consider the following (see Day et al., 2000, for elaboration):

- *Enhance the methodological rigor of research and the usefulness of research reports.* Future studies should include larger sample sizes and equivalent comparison groups whenever possible. Research designs should isolate or otherwise control the design features being examined, and studies should incorporate explicit hypotheses on design-behavior relationships, to facilitate interpretation of findings. Research reports should include details on research methods, on the population being studied, and on the physical environment under examination.

- *Focus on multiple populations and diverse environments.* Future research should examine the impact of design not only on residents of dementia care environments but also on staff and on family members. Studies should examine environments other than long-term care units and SCUs, including alternatives such as day care centers, respite care, group homes, and others.

- *Target research and application to stage of dementia and to changing populations of older adults.* Researchers should carefully consider the stages of dementia during which design interventions are hypothesized to be of value and should examine design impacts for residents in various stages of dementia. Research should explicitly examine how design impacts and innovations might differ cross-culturally and also with new cohorts of older adults.

- *Focus on quality of life as well as on problem behaviors.* Future research should examine the potential for therapeutic design to enhance quality of life, as well as to ameliorate undesirable behaviors.

A significant barrier to the continued generation of empirical research is the additional burden it places on care facilities that already struggle with significant financial and staffing challenges. Few facilities are willing to commit the resources necessary to develop research centers that can produce the type of research needed in the field. Despite these challenges, a handful of facilities have made this commitment; these are primarily nonprofit religious-sponsored organizations.

The importance of the physical environment in creating successful care settings is increasingly recognized in the long-term care field. One indication of this change is the modest growth in the number of design competitions for residential and care facilities for the elderly (see Table 25.2). These competitions feature a greater number of project entries over time. Likewise, more projects are featured in these competitions, and more complete information is provided about each project.

As discussed, the precise impact of research on design is difficult to determine. Design guidance—the translation of research findings into design implications, rather than research on design impacts per se—may have had the greatest impact on design practice. Several factors increase the potential impact of design guidance on design practice. First, in the case of design for dementia care environments, design guidance preceded empirical research on design impacts in many instances. Design guidance did not require confirmatory findings to make recommendations. Thus, design guidance was available prior to and coinciding with the rapid growth of new dementia care environments and so could shape the planning of these facilities. Second, design guidance—by its nature—speaks directly to design audiences. Its intent is to translate research and clinical knowledge into novel and creative design implications. Unlike much empirical research, the language and the subject of design guidance addresses designers and facility administrators. Third, design guidance is disseminated in forums that directly target designers and facility staff and administrators. Such forums include consulting, presentations at professional conferences and meetings, and articles in trade journals, rather than articles in scholarly journals.

For these reasons, design guidance may have greater potential to influence design practice than do reports of research on design impacts. As this chapter notes, research is needed to confirm or modify the suggestions offered in design guidance—suggestions that may become standard practice with little or no evidence of their effectiveness. The model adopted at the Corinne Dolan Center—that of early small-scale studies of preliminary design guidance coupled with widespread dissemination of findings and recommendations—may be especially useful to bridge the gap between design guidance and full-scale evaluation, thus providing valuable direction for design practice in times of rapid development and innovation.

Features found effective in research or recommended by design guidance are not uniformly adopted in practice. A cursory review of those features that are most widely adopted—separate care population, small-size units, provision of outdoor space, incorporation of country kitchens, and use of personalized bedroom cues—seems to suggest that features likely to be adopted are those with high "face validity." Such features sound sensible to family and care providers and resonate with their experiences in dementia care. Popular features also appear to include those that provide a marketing advantage by appealing to families' desire for homelike residential environments.

Table 25.2

Changes over Time in the Number of Dementia Design Competitions

Recent years have seen an increase in the number of entries in design competitions for residential and care facilities for the elderly. Also growing are the number of dementia care facilities entered in these competitions.

Years	Number of Competitions	Number of Facilities	Number of Facilities That Included Dementia
1985–1989	9	31	1
1990–1994	8	51	9
1995–1997	5	51	14
1998–2000	4	125	22

The impact of dementia and design research and design guidance is not limited to dementia care environments. Several design principles that were originally conceived as supporting the needs of people with cognitive impairments are now widely applied to non-dementia-specific settings. For instance, the trend toward smaller units is also evidenced in nondementia facilities. In several nursing homes that were recently featured in design competitions sponsored by trade magazines, smaller numbers of residents (13 to 14) are grouped together in what are referred to as "households," with several such households combining to create "neighborhoods" ("Looking Good," 1997; "Outagamie County," 2000; "Parkcliffe," 1999; "Sweet Life," 2000). In 31 projects from the *Nursing Home and Long Term Care* magazine's design competitions (1997 to 2000, projects completed 1995 to 2001), the mean size for non-dementia-specific long-term care units was 21.5 residents, with a range from 8 to 40 residents.

Changes in long-term care cannot be entirely attributed to advances in designing for people with dementia. This decrease in unit size, however, reflects a substantial change from the traditional 60-bed units that prevailed in earlier decades—a change that coincides with a proliferation of dementia design guidance and with the rapid development of SCUs for people with dementia. Similarly, dining rooms and kitchens are increasingly found on all long-term care units/households, not only in those for people with dementia. In many ways, the impact of design for people with dementia has spread far beyond serving the needs of cognitively impaired individuals, and is considered more supportive for all residents of long-term care facilities.

REFERENCES

Adachi, K., Akagi, T., & Funahashi, K. (2000, May). *Japanese bibliographical research: Trends and issues on living environment for dementia*. Presentation at the 31st annual conference of the Environmental Design Research Association, San Francisco.

Adelsberg, R. (1995). The program room: The low-cost special dementia care. *Nursing Homes, 44*(4), 34–39.

Ancoli-Israel, S., Klauber, M., Jones, D., Kripke, D., Martin, J., Mason, W., Pat-Horenczyk, R., & Fell, R. (1997). Variations in circadian rhythms of activity, sleep and light exposure related to dementia in nursing home patients. *Sleep, 20*(1), 18–23.

Anders, K. T. (1994, February). Special care. *Contemporary Long Term Care*, 48–49.

Annerstedt, L. (1993). Development and consequences of group living in Sweden. *Social Science and Medicine, 37*(12), 1529–1538.

Annerstedt, L. (1994). An attempt to determine the impact of group living care in comparison to traditional long-term care on demented elderly patients. *Aging Clinical Experimental Research, 6*(5), 372–380.

Annerstedt, L. (1997). Group-living care: An alternative for the demented elderly. *Dementia and Geriatric Cognitive Disorders, 8*, 136–142.

Architectural Design Awards. (1994, June). *Contemporary Long Term Care*, 70.

Bellelli, G., Frisoni, G. B., Bianchetti, A., Boffelli, S., Guerrini, G. B., Scotuzzi, A., Ranieri, P., Ritondale, G., Guglielmi, L., Fusari, A., Raggi, G., Gasparotti, A., Gheza, A., Nobili, G., & Trabucchi, M. (1998). Special care units for demented patients: A multicenter study. *The Gerontologist, 38*(4), 456–462.

Benson, D. M., Cameron, D., Humbach, E., Servino, L., & Gambert, S. R. (1987). Establishment and impact of a dementia unit within the nursing home. *Journal of the American Geriatrics Society, 35*(4), 319–323.

Berg, L., Buckwalter, K. C., Chafetz, P. K., Gwyther, L. P., Holmes, D., Koepke, K. M., Lawton, M. P., Lindeman, D. A., Magaziner, J., Maslow, K., Sloane, P. D., & Teresi, J. (1991). Special care units for persons with dementia. *Journal of the American Geriatrics Society, 39*, 1229–1236.

Best practices. (1997). *Contemporary Long Term Care, 20*(8), 48–49.

Bethany Harvest Hills. (2000). *Design 2000, Nursing Homes Magazine, 4*(1), 76.

Bianchetti, A., Benvenuti, P., Ghisla, K. M., Frisoni, G. B., & Trabucchi, M. (1997). An Italian model of dementia special care unit: Results of a pilot study. *Alzheimer Disease and Associated Disorders, 11*(1), 53–56.

Brawley, E. C. (1997). *Designing for Alzheimer's disease: Strategies for creating better care environments*. New York: Wiley.

Briller, S., Proffitt, M., Perez, K., Calkins, M., & Marsden, J. (2001). Maximizing cognitive and functional abilities. In M. Calkins (Producer), *Creating successful dementia care settings*. Baltimore: Health Professions Press.

Calkins, M. P. (1988). *Design for dementia: Planning environments for the elderly and the confused*. Owing Mills, MD: National Health Publishing.

Calkins, M. P. (1989). Designing cues for wanderers. *Provider, 15*(8), 7–10.

Calkins, M. P. (1997). Home is more than carpeting and chintz. *Nursing Homes, 44*(6), 20–25.

Calkins, M. P. (2001). *Creating successful dementia care settings* (Vols. 1–4). Baltimore: Health Professions Press.

Campbell, S. S., Kripke, D. F., Gillin, J. C., & Hrubovcak, J. C. (1988). Exposure to light in healthy elderly subjects and Alzheimer's patients. *Physiology and Behavior, 42,* 141–144.

Carp, F. M. (1987). Environment and Aging. In D. Stokols & I. Altman (Eds.), *Handbook of environmental psychology* (Vol. 1, pp. 329–360). New York: Wiley.

Chafetz, P. K. (1990). Two-dimensional grid is ineffective against demented patients exiting through glass doors. *Psychology and Aging, 5*(1), 146–147.

Chaudhury, H. (1996). *Self and reminiscence of place.* Unpublished doctoral dissertation proposal. Department of Architecture, University of Milwaukee, Wisconsin.

Cleary, T. A., Clamon, C., Price, M., & Shullaw, G. (1988). A reduced stimulation unit: Effects on patients with Alzheimer's disease and related disorders. *The Gerontologist, 28*(4), 511–514.

Cohen, U., & Day, K. (1993). *Contemporary environments for people with dementia.* Baltimore, MD: Johns Hopkins University Press.

Cohen, U., & Weisman, G. D. (1991). *Holding on to home: Designing environments for people with dementia.* Baltimore, MD: Johns Hopkins University Press.

Cohen-Mansfield, J., & Werner, P. (1998). The effects of an enhanced environment on nursing home residents who pace. *The Gerontologist, 38*(2), 199–208.

Coons, D. (1985). Alive and well at Wesley Hall. *Quarterly: A Journal of Long Term Care, 21*(2), 10–14.

Copper Ridge. (1997). New construction, best in show. *Design '97, Nursing Home Magazine, 1*(1), 10–13.

Cronin-Golumb, A. (1995). Vision in Alzheimer's disease. *The Gerontologist, 35*(3), 370–376.

Day, K., Carreon, D., & Stump, C. (2000). The therapeutic design of environments for people with dementia: A review of the empirical research. *The Gerontologist, 40*(4), 397–416.

Designing for life. (1997). *Provider, 23*(4), 22–30.

Dickinson, J. I., McLain-Kark, J., & Marshall-Baker, A. (1995). The effects of visual barriers on exiting behavior in a demented care unit. *The Gerontologist, 35*(1), 127–130.

Doig, W., Scott, G., & Townsley, S. (1998). *Cluster design: Is there an optimum design?* Presentation at the American Association of Homes and Services for the Aging Thirty-Seventh Annual Meeting and Exposition, Los Angeles.

Elmståhl, S., Annerstedt, L., & Åhlund, O. (1997). How should a group living unit for demented elderly be designed to decrease psychiatric symptoms? *Alzheimer Disease and Associated Disorders, 11*(1), 47–52.

French, D., & Eamer, R. (1987). Choice is what matters in residential care. *Provider, 13*(11), 19–22.

Götestam, K. G., & Melin, L. (1987). Improving well-being for patients with senile dementia by minor changes in the ward environment. In L. Levi (Ed.), *Society, stress, and disease* (pp. 295–297). Oxford: Oxford University Press.

Greene, J. A., Asp, J., & Crane, N. (1985). Specialized management of the Alzheimer's disease patient: Does it make a difference? *Journal of the Tennessee Medical Association, 78*(9), 559–563.

Hanley, I. G. (1981). The use of signposts and active training to modify ward disorientation in elderly patients. *Journal of Behavioral Therapy and Experimental Psychiatry, 12*(3), 241–247.

Herin, S. (1998). Designing an active home life for Alzheimer's residents. *Nursing Homes, 47*(6), 31–34.

Hiatt, L. (1991). *Nursing home renovation designed for reform.* Boston: Butterworth.

Hiatt, L. (1997). *Secrets of good looking, effective environments for seniors (and how to apply them elsewhere).* Presentation at American Association of Homes and Services for the Aging thirty-sixth annual meeting and exposition, New Orleans, LA.

Hodgson, C. C., Nelson, G., Pellegrino, J., & Pruitt, C. (1998). *Design for Aging forum.* Presentation at American Association of Homes and Services for the Aging thirty-seventh annual meeting and exposition, Los Angeles.

Hoglund, J. D., Dimotta, S., Ledewitz, S., & Saxton, J. (1994). Long-term care design: Woodside Place—the role of environmental design in quality of life for residents with dementia. *Journal of Healthcare Design, 6,* 69–76.

Hussian, R. A., & Brown, D. C. (1987). Use of two-dimensional grid to limit hazardous ambulation in demented patients. *Journal of Gerontology, 42*(5), 558–560.

Hutchinson, S., Leger-Krall, S., & Wilson, H. S. (1996). Toileting: A biobehavioral challenge in Alzheimer's dementia care. *Journal of Gerontological Nursing, 22*(10), 18–27.

Kihlgren, M., Bråne, G., Karlsson, I., Kuremyr, D., Leissner, P., & Norberg, A. (1992). Long-term influences on demented patients in different caring milieus, a collective living unit and a nursing home: A descriptive study. *Dementia, 3,* 342–349.

Koss, E., & Gilmore, G. C. (1998). Environmental interventions and functional ability of AD patients. In B. Vellas, J. Fitten, & G. Frisoni (Eds.), *Research and practice in Alzheimer's disease 1998* (pp. 185–193). New York: Springer.

Kovach, C. R., & Meyer-Arnold, E. A. (1996). Coping with conflicting agendas: The bathing experience of cognitively impaired older adults. *Scholarly Inquiry for Nursing Practice: An International Journal, 10*(1), 23–36.

Kromm, D., & Kromm, Y. H. N. (1985). A nursing unit designed for Alzheimer's disease patients at Newton Presbyterian Manor. *Nursing Homes, 34*(3), 30–31.

Lawton, M. P., Fulcomer, M., & Kleban, M. (1984). Architecture for the mentally impaired elderly. *Environment and Behavior, 16*(6), 730–757.

Lawton, M. P., Liebowitz, B., & Charon, H. (1970). Physical structure and the behavior of senile patients following ward remodeling. *Aging and Human Development, 1,* 231–239.

Liebowitz, B., Lawton, M. P., & Waldman, A. (1979). Evaluation: Designing for confused elderly people. *American Institute or Architects Journal, 68,* 59–61.

Looking Good. (1997). *Contemporary Long Term Care, 20* (8), 42–47.

Lyketsos, C., Veiel, L., Baker, A., & Steele, C. (1999). A randomized, control trial of bright light therapy for agitated behaviors in dementia patients residing in long-term care. *International Journal of Geriatric Psychiatry, 14*(7), 520–525.

Mayer, R., & Darby, S. J. (1991). Does a mirror deter wandering in demented older people? *International Journal of Geriatric Psychiatry, 6,* 607–609.

McAllister, C. L., & Silverman, M. A. (1999). Community formation and community roles among persons with Alzheimer's disease: A comparative study of experiences in a residential Alzheimer's facility and a traditional nursing home. *Qualitative Health Research, 9*(1), 65–85.

McCracken, A. L., & Fitzwater, E. (1989). The right environment for Alzheimer's: Which is better—open versus closed units? Here's how to tailor the answer to the patient. *Geriatric Nursing, 10*(6), 293–294.

Meadows Mennonite. (1999). *Design 99, Nursing Home Magazine, 3*(1), 18.

Melin, L., & Götestam, K. G. (1981). The effects of rearranging ward routines on communication and eating behaviors of psychogeriatric patients. *Journal of Applied Behavior Analysis, 14*(1), 47–51.

Mishima, K., Okawa, M., Hishikawa, Y., Hozumi, S., Hori, H., & Takashi, K. (1994). Morning bright light therapy for sleep and behavior disorders in elderly patients with dementia. *Acta Psychiatry Scandinavia, 89,* 1–7.

Mooney, P., & Nicell, P. L. (1992). The importance of exterior environment for Alzheimer residents: Effective care and risk management. *Healthcare Management Forum, 5*(2), 23–29.

Moore, K. D. (1999). Dissonance in the dining room: A study of social interaction in a special care unit. *Qualitative Health Research, 9*(1), 133–155.

Morgan, D. G., & Stewart, N. J. (1999). The physical environment of special care units: Needs of residents with dementia from the perspective of staff and caregivers. *Qualitative Health Research, 9*(1), 105–118.

Namazi, K. H., & Johnson, B. D. (1991a). Environmental effects on incontinence problems in Alzheimer's patients. *American Journal of Alzheimer's Care and Related Disorders and Research, 6,* 16–21.

Namazi, K. H., & Johnson, B. D. (1991b). Physical environmental cues to reduce the problems of incontinence in Alzheimer's disease units. *American Journal of Alzheimer's Care and Related Disorders and Research, 6,* 22–29.

Namazi, K. H., & Johnson, B. D. (1992a). Dressing independently: A closet modification model for Alzheimer's disease patients. *American Journal of Alzheimer's Care and Related Disorders and Research, 7,* 22–28.

Namazi, K. H., & Johnson, B. D. (1992b). The effects of environmental barriers on the attention span of Alzheimer's disease patients. *American Journal of Alzheimer's Care and Related Disorders and Research, 7,* 9–15.

Namazi, K. H., & Johnson, B. D. (1992c, January/February). Pertinent autonomy for residents with dementias: Modification of the physical environment to enhance independence. *American Journal of Alzheimer's Care and Related Disorders and Research, 7*(1), 16–21.

Namazi, K. H., & Johnson, B. D. (1996). Issues related to behavior and the physical environment: Bathing cognitively impaired patients. *Geriatric Nursing, 17*(5), 234–239.

Namazi, K. H., Rosner, T. T., & Calkins, M. P. (1989). Visual barriers to prevent ambulatory Alzheimer's patients from exiting through an emergency door. *The Gerontologist, 29,* 699–702.

Namazi, K. H., Rosner, T. T., & Rechlin, L. (1991). Long-term memory cuing to reduce visuo-spatial disorientation in Alzheimer's disease patients in a special care unit. *American Journal of Alzheimer's Care and Related Disorders and Research, 6*(6), 10–15.

National Institute on Aging. (1999). *Progress Report on Alzheimer's Disease.* Washington DC: National Institute on Aging, National Institutes of Health.

Negley, E. N., & Manley, J. T. (1990). Environmental interventions in assaultive behavior. *Journal of Gerontological Nursing, 16*(3), 29–33.

Nelson, J. (1995). The influence of environmental factors in incidents of disruptive behavior. *Journal of Gerontological Nursing, 21*(5), 19–24.

Netten, A. (1989). The effect of design of residential homes in creating dependency among confused elderly residents: A study of elderly demented residents and their ability to find their way around homes for the elderly. *International Journal of Geriatric Psychiatry, 4*(3), 143–153.

Netten, A. (1993). *A positive environment? Physical and social influences on people with senile dementia in residential care.* Aldershot, England: Ashgate.

Outagamie County. (2000). *Design 2000, Nursing Homes Magazine, 4*(1), 24.

Parkcliffe Eldercare Community. (1999). *Design '99, Nursing Homes Magazine, 2*(1), 22.

Parsons, Y. (1996). Facilities in transition. *Contemporary Long Term Care, 19*(8), 8–12.

Passini, R., Rainville, C., Marchand, N., & Joanette, Y. (1998). Wayfinding and dementia: Some research findings and a new look at design. *Journal of Architectural and Planning Research, 15*(2), 133–151.

Pynoos, J., & Ohta, R. J. (1991). In-home interventions for persons with Alzheimer's disease and their care-givers. *Physical and Occupational Therapy, 9*(3–4), 83–92.

Rae, S. (1994, February/March). Bright light, big therapy. *Modern Maturity,* 36–38, 84–85.

Rajecki, R. (1992). Charting a new course in Alzheimer's care. *Contemporary Long Term Care, 15*(8), 41–47.

Reeves, J., & Cooper, B. (1987). Meeting residents' special needs through facility design. *Contemporary Long Term Care, 18*(9), 116–118.

Regnier, V. (1997). Design for assisted living. *Contemporary Long Term Care, 20*(2), 50–55.

Renovation architecture. (1996). *Contemporary Long Term Care, 19*(8), 49–50.

Rethinking regulations. (1995). *Contemporary Long Term Care, 18*(9), 16–18.

Satlin, A., Volicer, L., Ross, V., Herz, L., & Campbell, S. (1992). Bright light treatment of behavioral and sleep disturbances in patients with Alzheimer's disease. *American Journal of Psychiatry, 149*(8), 1028–1032.

Scandura, D. A. (1995). Freedom and safety: A Colorado center cares for Alzheimer's patients. *Health Progress, 76*(3), 44–46.

Shoesmith, J. (1999). *Redesigning the existing environment for Alzheimer's care.* Presentation at the Eighth National Alzheimer's Disease Education Conference, Long Beach, CA.

Seidel, A. (1985). What is success in E & B research utilization? *Environment and Behavior, 17*(1), 47–70.

Skea, D., & Lindesay, J. (1996). An evaluation of two models of long-term residential care for elderly people with dementia. *International Journal of Geriatric Psychiatry, 11,* 233–241.

Sloane, P. D., Honn, V. J., Dwyer, S. A. R., Wieselquist, J., Cain, C., & Myers, S. (1995). Bathing the Alzheimer's patient in long term care: Results and recommendations from three studies. *American Journal of Alzheimer's Disease, 10*(4), 3–11.

Sloane, P. D., Mitchell, C. M., Preisser, J. S., Phillips, C., Commander, C., & Burker, E. (1998). Environmental correlates of resident agitation in Alzheimer's disease special care units. *Journal of the American Geriatrics Society, 46*(7), 862–869.

Snyder-Hiatt, L. H. (1978). Environmental changes for socialization. *Journal of Nursing Administration, 18*(1), 44–55.

Swanson, E. A., Maas, M. L., & Buckwalter, K. C. (1993). Catastrophic reactions and other behaviors of Alzheimer's residents: Special unit compared with traditional units. *Archives of Psychiatric Nursing, 7*(5), 292–299.

Tames, S. (1992). Designing with residents in mind. *Provider, 18*(7), 17–28.

Teresi, J. A., Holmes, D., & Monaco, C. (1993). An evaluation of the effects of commingling cognitively and noncognitively impaired individuals in long-term care facilities. *The Gerontologist, 33*(3), 350–358.

Tetlow, K. (1995). Exercise by design. *Contemporary Long Term Care, 18*(3), 38–42.

The heritage. (2000). *Design 2000, Nursing Homes Magazine, 4*(1), 60.

The sweet life. (2000). *Design 2000, Nursing Homes Magazine, 4*(1), 20.

U.S. Department of Health and Human Services. (1981). *Progress report on senile dementia of the Alzheimer's type* (81–2342). Washington, DC: National Institute of Health.

U.S. Department of Health and Human Services. (1987). *Losing a million minds: Confronting the tragedy of Alzheimer's disease and other dementias.* (Vol. no. OTA-BA-323). Washington, DC: U.S. Government Printing Office.

Wagner, L. (1996). The special care touch. *Provider, 22*(12), 29–39.

Westminster-Canterbury. (1999). *Design '99, Nursing Homes Magazine, 2*(1), 90–91.

Whall, A. L., Black, M. E., Groh, C. J., Yankou, D. J., Kuperschmid, B. J., & Foster, N. L. (1997). The effect of natural environments upon agitation and aggression in late stage dementia patients. *American Journal of Alzheimer's Disease, 12*(5), 216–220.

Wiltzius, S. F., Gambert, S. R., & Duthie, E. H. (1981). Importance of resident placement within a skilled nursing facility. *Journal of the American Geriatrics Society, 29*(9), 418–421.

Wohlwill, J. (1966). The physical environment: A problem for a psychology of stimulation. *Journal of Social Issues, 22*(4), 29–38.

CHAPTER 26

Healthy Residential Environments

RODERICK J. LAWRENCE

UNTIL RECENTLY, HEALTH and environment were generally considered by scientists, practitioners, and policy makers working in different sectors. This common practice can be illustrated by major international charters and conferences beginning with the first international conference on the environment held in Stockholm in 1972 or the international conference on primary health care held in Alma-Alta in 1978. These traditional approaches to health and the environment were gradually replaced by more integrated ones during the 1990s. The World Summit on Environment and Development, held in Rio de Janeiro in 1992, endorsed a new approach to national and international development agendas and the consideration of the environment. This World Summit formalized a commitment to improving health and protecting the environment as two prerequisites for sustainable development that has been endorsed by the World Health Organization (1996b). (Note that here I refer to the commitment being endorsed not the prerequisites.)

During the 1990s, there was a growing interest in the interrelated nature of health and the environment across a wide range of geographical scales. At the global level, attention has focussed on carbon dioxide emissions, depletion of the ozone layer, and the incidence of cancer (McMichael, 1993). At the local level, ambient air conditions in residential neighborhoods and air quality inside buildings have been considered in relation to the incidence of allergies and respiratory diseases (Schwela, 2000). This chapter is not meant to provide a comprehensive review of a number of contributions across these geographical levels. Rather, it will consider healthy residential environments including indoor and outdoor conditions. It is noteworthy that the chapter on residential environments in the first *Handbook of Environmental Psychology* did not explicitly deal with health although the subject was addressed indirectly. Therefore, this chapter is not only meant to bridge that gap. It will also discuss the increasing attention given to health and housing during the 1990s by researchers both in and outside of the field of environmental psychology.

Today there is no widely shared consensus about the nature of the relationship between health status and living conditions (Corvalan, Nurminen, & Pastides, 1997). Some reasons for this lack of consensus include the environmental, geographical, and temporal complexity of the subject, as well as the diversity of ethnic, occupational, and other social groups living and working in residential neighborhoods. Furthermore, current disciplinary interpretations of health (including a wide range of theoretical and methodological approaches used to study it) do not facilitate the task. Apparently researchers and practitioners do not have the analytical tools or the measurement techniques that enable them to deal with the complexity of health in residential environments. In addition, this chapter shows that conceptual clarification and theoretical development is necessary. Current understanding can be improved if the following principles are borne in mind.

Residential environments are complex with many material and nonphysical constituents. The concentration of diverse kinds of human activities in urban areas leads to the discharge of large volumes of commercial, industrial, and household wastes (United Nations Commission on Human Settlements [UNCHS], 1996). This is one reason for the contamination of air, water, and soil. These negative impacts on the life support systems of cities have health effects that ought to be recognized and effectively dealt with by housing officers, urban planners, and public health officials. Other kinds of problems that have harmful effects on health are related to population density, housing conditions (including homelessness), imported foods, access to community services and health care, working conditions, as well as socioeconomic inequalities and spatial segregation in urban neighborhoods (Lawrence, 2000). In order to integrate all these dimensions, it is necessary to go beyond interpretations that rely solely on the biomedical model of health, and socioeconomic interpretations need to be replaced by interdisciplinary contributions. In this chapter, therefore, several concepts and methods from environmental psychology, epidemiology, human ecology, public health, social and policy sciences, and urban planning will be used in a complementary way.

The health status of populations in precise residential areas is the result not only of many material and nonphysical constituents but also of the interrelations between them (Raffestin & Lawrence, 1990). Hence, several conceptual and methodological questions need to be examined if the constituents and the interrelations between them are to be understood comprehensively. It is inappropriate to isolate a constituent from the contextual conditions in which it occurs. Instead, ecological approaches ought to be applied to understand both the constituents and the interrelations between them (Catalano, 1979). This chapter argues that although healthy residential environments have not been a high priority in environmental psychology, in-depth studies of people-environment relations can offer useful contributions to broaden our current understanding of this complex subject. The chapter begins with definitions of key concepts and an ecological perspective. Then a historical overview of the interpretations of housing, local environmental conditions, and health is presented and followed by interpretations of health, population density, and crowding. This chapter shows that although environmental psychologists and medical or public health researchers have not often collaborated, there are good reasons for them to share experience and

apply interdisciplinary approaches. The chapter concludes with some suggestions for future contributions in environmental psychology that are pertinent not only for theoretical development but also for health policy definition and implementation.

DEFINITIONS AND INTERPRETATIONS

The word *health* is derived from the old English word *hal* meaning whole, healed, and sound. Health is a difficult concept to define; therefore, it is not surprising that it has been interpreted in diverse ways. Nonetheless, health has an intrinsic value, which cannot be quantified only in monetary units. This stems from the fact that health is fundamentally different from other attributes of human life owing to the unique status of the human body. Unlike other objects, the body not only is possessed by an individual but also constitutes that person. There is no such thing as a disembodied person. Each individual may be a consumer of and an object to which health services are directed. Simultaneously, each person is an active producer of her or his health by following habits of diet, exercise, and hygiene and other lifestyle traits that may or may not be conducive to health promotion.

The ancient Greeks believed that *Asclepios*, the god of medicine, had two daughters: *Hygieia*, was responsible for prevention, whereas *Panacea* was responsible for cure (Loudon, 1997). This long-standing distinction between prevention and cure or treatment corresponds closely to the difference between public health interventions intended for entire populations and clinical interventions for individuals. The exception to this generalization can be prevention by immunization that is applied to individuals, but it does not necessarily involve the whole population in a country, city, or any precise geographical area. One key social policy issue should be to establish the appropriate scope and range of preventive and curative interventions to deal with specific health issues in precise localities.

HEALTH

The definition of the World Health Organization states that health is "not merely the absence of disease and infirmity but a state of optimal physical, mental and social well-being" (World Health Organization, 1946). This definition is idealistic, but it has the merit of not focusing on illness and disease, which have often been considered as either temporary or permanent impairment to health or as the malfunctioning of a single or several constituents of the human body. Given that the World Health Organization's definition of health includes social well-being, then the most common interpretations of health ought to be enlarged. The World Health Organization also states that the enjoyment of the highest attainable standard of health is one of the fundamental rights of every human being without distinction of race, religion, political, economic, or social condition.

Health is defined in this chapter as a condition or state of human beings resulting from the interrelations between humans and their biological, chemical, physical, and social environments. All these components of residential environments should be compatible with their basic needs and their full functional activity, including biological reproduction, over a long period. Health is the result of both the direct pathological effects of chemicals, some biological agents, and radiation, and the influence of physical, psychological, and social dimensions of daily life including housing, transport, and other characteristics of metropolitan areas (see Figure 26.1). For example, improved access to medical services is a common characteristic of urban neighborhoods that is rare in rural areas. In the field of health promotion, health is not considered as an abstract condition but as the ability of an individual to achieve her or his potential and to respond positively to the challenges of daily life. From this perspective, health is an asset or a resource for everyday life, rather than a standard or goal that ought to be achieved. This redefinition is pertinent for people-environment studies because the environmental and social conditions in specific residential environments do impact on human relations and induce stress and can have positive or negative impacts on the health status of groups and individuals. It also implies that the capacity of the health sector to deal with the health and well-being of populations is limited and that close collaboration with other sectors would be beneficial.

ENVIRONMENT

Environment derives from the word *environnement*, first used in the French language about the year 1300 by Godefroy. Initially it was used in the sense of a defining contour or the external boundary of an object. Then, during the sixteenth century, Estienne redefined the term to mean the group of natural and artificial things that condition human life (and notably not all living organisms). This definition is similar to that in a contemporary edition of the *Oxford English Dictionary* except that it includes all organisms: "the conditions under which any person or thing lives or is developed; the sum total of influences which modify and determine the development of life and character." Today the term *human environment* not only refers to those characteristics that people have constructed, modified, or perceived as components of human settlements but also interpersonal relations and social organization that affect both physical and mental health and psychological well-being.

The environment of any living species is multidimensional and extremely complex. Therefore, residential environments should not be interpreted as a neutral background for human behavior as it frequently has been in environmental psychology (Lawrence, 1987). The human ecology perspective applied in this chapter interprets the processes, patterns, products, and mediating factors that regulate human behavior in residential environments using a systemic framework explained in Raffestin and Lawrence (1990). A dialectical and integrated approach is therefore necessary in order to overcome the chasm dividing health professionals who blame environmental conditions for the incidence of ill health; environmental scientists who blame human individuals, groups, and enterprises for the deplorable state of the environment; and architects, housing administrators, and urban planners who

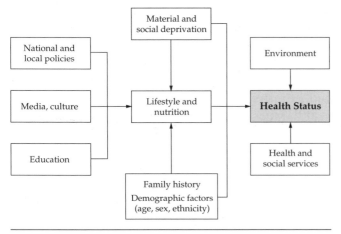

Figure 26.1 The multiple determinants and interrelations of health status are shown in this diagram.

still do not accept the reciprocal relationship between people and environment at either the small scale of the residential environment or any larger geographical scale (see Figure 26.2).

RESIDENTIAL ENVIRONMENT

In the first edition of the *Handbook of Environmental Psychology,* Tognoli (1987) used the words residential environment as "a neutral term to represent both home and housing, neighborhood and community." This interpretation can be reused here because it implies that the defining characteristics of residential environments include a composite set of natural and human-made components ranging from climate, topography, landscape, and vegetation to housing and building construction, infrastructure, community facilities, and services.

SUPPORTIVE ENVIRONMENTS

The concept of supportive environment has been used to emphasize that policy definition and implementation should focus on all the determinants of health, not just those within the health sector (Bistrup, 1991). Therefore, it includes the role of physical environmental factors that influence health and not just the lifestyle of individuals and groups in specific localities. In addition, it is not limited to the physical characteristics of the environment because it accounts for the cultural, social, economic, and political dimensions. When these dimensions are explicitly addressed then it is necessary to deal with equality and equity in societies and how these impact on health and well-being in precise residential environments.

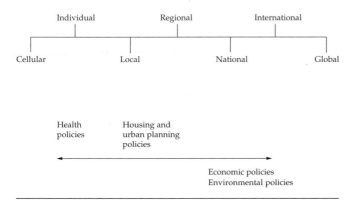

Figure 26.2 The spectrum of interrelated scales of health, economic, and environmental policies.

From this perspective the layout, design, and maintenance of residential environments should meet the requirements of all groups of the population including the increasing number of people with special needs—especially the most vulnerable in society, for example, the homeless, a group that comprises an increasing number of adolescents and young adults in industrialized countries; the elderly who need domiciliary care; people with disabilities who require easy access to and within housing units; single-parent households that may need access to special child care services; refugees and immigrants who have specific cultural customs in and outside their housing unit that should be accommodated (Organization for Economic Cooperation and Development [OECD], 1996).

HEALTH SYSTEMS AND SERVICES

Health systems include all the institutions, organizations, and resources that are devoted to promote, sustain, or restore health. A health system has important functions including the provision of services and the human, monetary, and physical resources that make the delivery of these services possible (World Health Organization [WHO], 2000). These resources can include any contribution whether in informal personal health care or public or private professional health and medical services. The primary purpose of all services is to improve health by preventive or curative measures. A health system should not only strive to attain the highest average level of the health status of the population but also strive simultaneously to reduce the differences between the health of individuals and groups. Hence the way that health systems are designed, managed, and financed affects peoples lives, contributes to inequalities in health, and influences how the situation of the underprivileged can be improved. Since all groups of the population, including the underprivileged, are confronted with their circumstances of daily life, they may need protection against health risks (Marmot & Wilkinson, 1999). In the case of the residential environment, housing may be an asset, but there is much evidence to show this is not usually the case for the poor (see following). Therefore, health care systems have the important responsibility to ensure that people are treated equitably, in an affordable manner and in accordance with human rights.

Interest in health care services applied in the home has grown during the 1990s in many industrialized countries. This follows changes in policies during the 1980s that were introduced to deinstitutionalize heath care for people with functional disabilities, or during periods of convalescence (Teeland, 1998). The policy to enable people to return to or stay at home, rather than being admitted to a hospital, is partly the result of a potential saving in the cost of health care services. However, Teeland notes that there is also an underlying humanistic perspective that is related to the view that people feel mentally and physically secure and satisfied in their homes, and perhaps more so than in hospitals. It is noteworthy that the financial savings have been debated by health administrators, whereas the affective ties between patients and their home environment has been largely overlooked by environmental psychologists. This gap in the current research agenda ought to be dealt with in the near future.

ECOLOGICAL PERSPECTIVE

The term *ecology* derives from the ancient Greek words *oikos* and *logos* and means "science of the habitat." It is generally agreed that this term was used first by Ernst Haeckel (1834–1919), a German zoologist, in 1866. The word *ecology* designates a science that deals with the interrelationships between organisms and their surroundings. Since the late nineteenth century the term *ecology* has been interpreted in numerous ways (Young, 1983). For example, in the natural sciences, botanists and zoologists use the term *general ecology* to refer to the interrelations between animals, plants, and their immediate surroundings. Human ecology explicitly deals with people-environment relations (Lawrence, 2001). It provides a conceptual framework for academics and practitioners from both the natural sciences (e.g., biology, chemistry, and geology) and the human sciences (e.g., anthropology, epidemiology, sociology, and psychology) to accept divergent disciplinary concepts and methods and develop an integrated approach.

The ecological perspective proposed herein maintains that four main sets of interrelated factors should be considered: the *individual,* who has a specific genetic code with a susceptibility and immunity to illness and disease, as well as lifestyle traits; the *agent* or *vector* of illness and disease, including not only biogeophysical components of the environment but also the social and psychological dimensions of human settings; the *physical* and *social environment* of the individual that affects the susceptibility of the host, the virulence of biophysical agents and the exposure, quantity, and nature of the contact between host and vector; the *available resources* used by the individuals and households including housing, nutrition, money, information, and access to health and medical services that ought to be affordable for all groups of the population.

The distinction between biomedical models and ecological interpretations of health is fundamental (Catalano, 1979). The germ theory, for example, is an incomplete explanation of human illness and disease because it ignores the contribution of numerous physical and social dimensions of the environment that can effect health. Ecological interpretations maintain that the presence of a germ is a necessary but not a sufficient condition for an individual to become ill. They accept that some individuals become more susceptible to certain illnesses because of their differential exposure to numerous environmental, economic, and social factors that can promote or harm health and well-being. This interpretation does not ignore the influence of genetics, individual behavior, or primary health care. However, it maintains that, alone, these do not address possible relations between social problems and illness (e.g., inequalities) or positive social dimensions and health promotion (e.g., public education). The distinction between potential and actual health status can be the foundation for a new interpretation of health that includes ecological, social, and psychological determinants. If this perspective is accepted then environmental psychology could contribute to an improved understanding of the health-environment relationship.

There are important conceptual and methodological questions that need to be examined if the relationships between conditions in human settlements and health are to be considered from a broad perspective. This kind of perspective implies that an analysis of the interrelations between multiple factors is necessary. Multifaceted interpretations of human illness and health have a long but chequered history. They can be traced back at least as far as the Hippocratic treatise *On Airs, Waters, and Places,* published initially about 2,600 years ago (Hippocrates, 1849).

Hippocrates applied an integrated approach that is far removed from much contemporary academic research and professional practice adopted by people who isolate variables from each other and from the contextual conditions in which they occur. For example, in recent decades, it has been common practice to study the relations between one indicator of environmental conditions (e.g., noise or air pollution in residential neighborhoods) or one indicator of housing quality (e.g., dampness in the building structure) and the health and well-being of the inhabitants. Alternatively, measures of the morbidity of resident populations (e.g., psychological strain) have often been examined only with respect to the number of persons per room or the number of persons per square meter of habitable floor space without controlling for other variables (see following).

HISTORICAL REVIEW

During the nineteenth century, in many Western European countries, professionals concerned about housing, urban planning, and public health shared a common goal. That goal was to reduce the transmission of infectious diseases, such as cholera and tuberculosis, which had a significant impact on mortality rates of populations, especially those in urban areas. In England, in the 1840s, the Public Health movement was founded after it was agreed that it was a responsibility of society to protect citizens from unsanitary housing and working conditions (Rosen, 1993). The contribution of Edwin Chadwick, secretary of the Poor Law Board, was instrumental because he established a correlation between the housing conditions and the health status of the population. In principle, those individuals who lived in sanitary houses generally lived longer than those who lived in slums; those persons from the same socioeconomic class who lived in the country generally lived longer than those who lived in urban areas (Chadwick, 1842).

Until the 1870s, the miasma theory—that noxious vapors transmit pathogens—was used to explain the transmission of diseases including cholera. Although the sanitary reform movement accepted this false interpretation, its activities resulted in improvements to the health status of urban populations by corrective and remedial measures. This approach argued that miasma ("bad air") had to be eradicated by improved exposure to sunlight and effective ventilation between and inside buildings (Lawrence, 1983).

Subsequently, the miasma theory was replaced by the germ theory—that specific agents including water transmit infectious diseases. The sanitary reform movement now identified direct links between specific agents and illnesses. A range of environmental components—water supply, sewage disposal, damp rooms, and mould growth in housing—were considered as the sources of illness and major health risks. These conditions were not limited to the physical fabric of housing units or the environmental conditions of their immediate surroundings. They also explicitly addressed the number of persons per habitable room. At that time the terms *unhygienic* and *unsanitary* were used in relation to "overcrowded" housing conditions and the high morbidity and mortality rates of the inhabitants (Chadwick, 1842). Several surveys and official enquiries examined the relationship between housing and living conditions and health. In general these contributions showed that the ill health of inhabitants resulted from unsanitary housing conditions with a relatively large number of persons per room (Lawrence, 1983). However, the mechanisms that underlie this cause-effect relation were not considered by many in-depth epidemiological studies.

A sanitary engineering approach based on corrective and remedial measures was used to remove unsanitary conditions by demolishing buildings and reconstructing neighborhoods (Rosen, 1993). Then the public concern in European countries about the health-housing relationship diminished in the twentieth century with the widespread provision of municipal water supply, drainage, and sewage disposal, as well as public immunization campaigns. Unfortunately, this is probably why there has been too little concern about the health impacts of housing conditions in the context of rapid urban development in European countries from the 1950s to the 1970s as well in as all other continents of the World in recent decades. According to the United Nations Commission on Human Settlements (1995), in Africa, Asia, and South America more attention has been given to lack of hygiene and sanitation, access to primary health care, and malnutrition in these regions than to the health impacts of housing occupancy conditions.

There has been a long debate about the reduction of mortality rates in many European countries from the late nineteenth century (McMichael, 1993; Rosen, 1993). It has been argued whether these reductions are more closely tied to the improvement of diet, the provision of a supply of safe water, and municipal waste disposal rather than progress in medicine and health care. This chapter considers this debate to be misguided, because it stems from a narrow interpretation of health and health systems. When the broader definitions of health and health systems are applied, then all actions including the nonpersonal, target area or population interventions including the promotion of healthy lifestyles and the provision of sewage disposal are integral components of interdisciplinary strategies to promote health in residential environments. Some of these kinds of interventions were used in the late nineteenth century following an improved understanding of how diseases, including cholera, spread in residential areas, even though the causes of such diseases remained unknown. This debate illustrates that an integrated, interdisciplinary understanding of how the health of populations in precise localities can be improved is essential if a range of interventions are to be applied effectively.

The preceding paragraphs show that conventional urban planning has successfully used reactive approaches to correct or remove inadequate housing and working conditions. However, today we know that infectious diseases stemming from unsanitary conditions are not the leading cause of morbidity and mortality in industrialized countries. Instead, noncommunicable illnesses having multiple causes are the main challenge for public health. Therefore, urban planning could shift from using reactive to proactive approaches. Urban planning should not only deal with removing negative health impacts but actively promote well-being (Barton & Tsourou, 2000). One example of an innovative approach would reconsider land use planning and transportation in and between residential neighborhoods from a broader ecological perspective. This approach would imply a shift from dealing with piecemeal approaches to road transport, car parking, and traffic safety. It would reinterpret accessibility and mobility in and between urban areas in terms not only of public and private modes of transport but also of air and noise pollution, consumption of nonrenewable resources, monetary costs and public investments, active and sedentary lifestyles, as well as health and well-being. This broader perspective not only raises questions about the high priority attributed to private motor cars during the twentieth century. It also shows that investments in efficient public transport systems and pedestrian precincts can be considered as investments to promote environmental quality and reduce energy consumption and air pollution while promoting health and well-being.

METHODOLOGICAL PRINCIPLES

The relation between the residential environment and health is multidimensional and complex. It is possible to determine not only whether housing impacts health but also how the health of an individual

can influence housing (UNCHS, 1996). Despite the contribution of a wide range of studies by environmental health officers, doctors, psychologists, physiologists, and housing researchers, some recent surveys of the literature on the health-housing relation indicate that there are few comprehensive, empirical studies that identify and measure those characteristics of housing that hinder or promote health and well-being (Fuller-Thomson, Hulchanski, & Wang, 2000; Martin, Kaloyanova, & Maziarka, 1976; Smith, 1989). These reviews show that contributions often lack a broad conceptual framework (including the societal context of housing); they have a restricted methodological approach (owing to a lack of multivariate techniques); and they rarely address practical guidelines or policy issues. The majority of contributions identify relations between illness and housing conditions without providing convincing evidence of the mechanisms linking them (Burridge & Ormandy, 1993). Empirical studies of the relationships between housing and health have commonly adopted this kind of approach by examining how one quantifiable characteristic of housing conditions in a precise situation (such as the presence of dampness in the building structure) effects the health and well-being of the inhabitants (Jacobs & Stevenson, 1981; Kasl & Harburg, 1975). Alternatively, proxy measures of the morbidity of resident populations (such as the number of visits to a doctor) are related to one aspect of the residential environment (such as floor level above the ground in high-rise housing) (Gillis, 1977; Mitchell, 1971). Irrespective of the simplifications inherent in these contributions, the findings of many studies have rarely been replicated in the same or different residential environments as Gabe and Williams (1986) have noted. Moreover, many studies have commonly examined the relationship between isolated variables at only one point in time. However, there is sufficient evidence from studies in environmental psychology indicating that the aspirations and preferences of people for housing change during the course of the life cycle (Stokols, 1982); that the health and well-being of people also change; and that the condition of the housing stock varies during the period of occupation.

Four categories of studies have been proposed by Fuller-Thompson et al. (2000):

1. Those that consider the impact of biological exposures (such as dampness and mould and the incidence of respiratory diseases)

2. Studies of the impact of chemical and physical exposure (such as urea formaldehyde foam insulation and its incidence on respiratory diseases)

3. Contributions that consider the physical conditions of the housing unit in relation to the risk of accidents or other characteristics of health and well-being

4. Studies that examine the cultural, economic, and other social characteristics of housing (such as housing cost or tenure) in relation to health and well-being

Despite numerous contributions in these four categories there is not a cumulative set of empirical findings that has identified and measured the mechanisms linking characteristics of residential environments to physical and mental health. A causal relation has no explanatory value unless the mechanisms linking the variables have been deciphered (Fuller-Thompson et al., 2000).

During the twentieth century the practice of prescribing minimum standards for the quality of a wide range of environmental constituents of residential environments—air, water supply, and building materials, for instance—has led to a significant improvement in site planning, building construction, and housing design in both industrialized and developing countries. However, when these standards are examined in terms of their rationale and objectives, it becomes clear that they have commonly been defined and applied with economic, technological, and political priorities in mind, whereas the lifestyle, domestic economy, health, and well-being of local populations have been largely undervalued (Lawrence, 1987). The human ecology perspective proposed in this chapter can correct this practice, because it enables the formulation and application of a more integrated and context dependent approach.

There are no static standards (such as an optimal household population density) that can be translated into optimal indoor and outdoor environmental conditions for human health and well-being. In particular, indoor domestic environments ought to be responsive to cultural, social, and individual differences as well as to annual, seasonal, and diurnal rhythms that not only influence acoustic, illumination, and thermal characteristics but also the physiological condition of the human organism (Lawrence, 1987). This perspective challenges the commonly practiced normative approach embodied in building

and environmental legislation. Therefore it is argued that people-environment studies can contribute to the improvement of current understanding and also help shift current emphasis from normative standards to contextual approaches that promote health and well-being. This kind of innovative approach will now be illustrated with respect to the health impacts of population density and crowding.

CONTRIBUTIONS OF ENVIRONMENTAL PSYCHOLOGY

In the 1950s and 1960s, pioneering studies in environmental psychology were meant to study the relationship between the attitudes and behavior of patients and staff and the physical conditions of hospital wards for psychiatric care. At the outset it is necessary to underline that health was not the subject of study. Rather, the behavior of patients in relation to the physical setting and other people with whom they had contact was observed systematically. The authors of these contributions noted that, in the discipline of psychology, there had been little concern about the relation between human behavior and the physical setting in which that behavior occurred. The goal of environmental psychology was to identify and explain this relation in order to generate findings that could be applicable in other settings, including schools, child care centers, offices, and housing (Proshansky, Ittelson, & Rivlin, 1970).

It is not unfair to affirm that since the 1950s and 1960s health has not been a mainstream topic in environmental psychology (or architectural psychology, environmental sociology, and social ecology). This does not mean that health has been completely ignored, as shown by comprehensive overviews of contributions about crowding (Baum & Paulus, 1987) and stress (Evans & Cohen, 1987) in the first *Handbook of Environmental Psychology*. According to Evans and Cohen (1987, pp. 590–591), contributions by environmental psychologists about the impact of high population density on human health are inconclusive for a number of reasons:

Human high density studies on cardiovascular data are too few in number to draw any conclusions, but several studies have found associations with poorer physical health. Many of these studies are static, correlational designs using aggregate levels of analysis and thus suffer from serious methodological limitations. Nevertheless there are evident

trends in the literature to suggest some link between residential density and poor physical health.
The data on high density and psychological health
are very contradictory and emanate primarily from
seriously flawed field studies. (p. 591)

In addition the authors note that

There is strong evidence that high density causes
elevated blood pressure, heart rate, and skin conductance, weaker data on catecholamines, and
contradictory findings on corticosteriods. The evidence on human task performances and high density is generally weak, with the only clear trend
showing more errors in multiple signal tasks during crowding. The data on density and self-reports
of negative affect as well as interpersonal behavior
are mixed. There is some evidence linking high
density and nonverbal indices of stress but contradictory findings on crowding and adaptation.
There are contradictory data on density and psychological health but reasonably consistent data
showing that high density is linked to greater ill
health in animals and possibly humans as well.
(p. 591)

It is noteworthy that the *Handbook of Environmental
Psychology* published in 1987 did not include a chapter on health. In that publication, however, Tognoli's
(1987, p. 671) review and synthesis on residential environments noted that there are many sociological
and psychological studies that interpret crowding in
terms of an individual's capacity "to adapt to negative conditions surrounding high social or low spatial density." Tognoli wrote that "crowded conditions
seemed to be strongly related to pathologies in mental and physical health, social relationships, and
child care, thus indicating a tendency toward maladaptive responses."

There are contributions on this topic that argue
that the sense of crowding can also mean a sense of
no personal control. This interpretation follows the
seminal contribution of Goffman (1959) who postulated that private space implies control and regulation of interpersonal contact. Many contributions
apply this kind of interpretation to institutional
kinds of housing such as student dormitories and
nursing homes for the elderly. In addition, a number
of cross-cultural studies were cited by Aiello and
Thompson (1980) to underline their thesis that
crowding is experienced negatively in a variety of
countries including Peru, Mexico, Puerto Rico.
Too often, there is a cultural bias in many studies

because the researchers assume that crowding implies negative impacts on well-being, without empirical proof that such impacts have occurred.

Since 1987, health still has not been accredited
the rank of a priority subject in environmental psychology whereas it has received increasing attention in a number of broad areas such as housing
and urban planning (Barton & Tsourou, 2000; Burridge & Ormandy, 1993; Lawrence, 2000). During
the 1990s there has also been a growing concern by
medical and social scientists about the influence of
global environmental change (e.g., depletion of the
ozone layer, the green house effect) as well as local
environmental conditions (e.g., air pollution in
neighborhoods, indoor air quality) on health and
well-being (McMichael, 1993). Given these trends,
this chapter presents arguments that may entice researchers of people-environment relations to explicitly consider health as a worthy subject for
systematic research and policy development. This
will be illustrated with respect to housing in general and household population density and crowding in particular.

Studies of human population density have a long
history stemming from a public concern about the
propagation of contagious diseases in densely populated residential areas, as well as Malthus's thesis
about the relation between available food resources
and population size. During the 1920s, empirical
studies at the Chicago School of Sociology interpreted population density as a causal explanation
for the incidence of social ills, including crime and
violence, in urban neighborhoods. The early studies
of sociologists at the Chicago School of Sociology
plotted the geographical distribution of some characteristics of the resident population of Chicago including their ethnic origin, socioeconomic status,
birth and mortality rates, delinquency, and mental
and other illnesses. These cartographic studies enabled the authors to overlay the maps of these characteristics in order to identify those that occurred in
the same urban area. This approach established
many so-called causal relations, such as the correspondence of cases of tuberculosis with the highest
incidence of delinquency. This finding led the authors to suggest that cities comprise "natural" areas
that are defined geographical, economic, social, and
cultural dimensions.

In the social sciences, the distinction between population density and crowding was made and has been
widely accepted (Baum & Paulus, 1987). However

this distinction is still not often used in the medical or public health sciences and the two terms are still used interchangeably. In contrast, in environmental psychology Stokols (1972) initiated an important theoretical contribution that distinguished between the physical condition of the population density (which can be measured by the number of persons in a given spatially demarcated area) and the subjective experience of crowding, which is variable according to cultural customs and values, the societal context of everyday life, and the experience, coping strategies, and preferences of individuals. Measurements of high density are not a determinant condition for crowding.

The innovative contribution by Stokols led other environmental psychologists in the 1970s to identify some typologies of population density. One basic typology concerned how population density could be modified in a specific location (Baum & Paulus, 1987). It is possible to increase density by increasing the number of people without changing the amount of space they occupy. This has usually been referred to as social density. Alternatively, density can be increased by keeping the number of people constant while reducing the amount of space they occupy. This is often referred to as spatial density. Although both these mechanisms for changing population density could have impacts on health and well-being (for reasons that will be explained below) this contribution from environmental psychology has not been recognized by medical and public health researchers.

Another typology of population density stems from the types of spatial unit of analysis. For example, at the microlevel, population density inside the housing unit can be measured in terms of persons per square meter or per habitable room. At a slightly larger scale the population density of a neighborhood or city can be measured in terms of persons per square kilometer. Likewise at the level of a state or country. This customary approach has led some authors to use the terms *internal* and *external density.*

In concluding their comprehensive overview of studies of population density and crowding Baum and Paulus (1987, p. 541) state that the overall results of experimental studies of the relation between urban density and crowding are not conclusive. The authors include an interesting discussion of the methodological limitations of a large number of contributions on this subject. It is noteworthy, for example, that many more studies have been completed in prisons and other institutional buildings rather than in residential neighborhoods.

CONTRIBUTIONS OF EPIDEMIOLOGICAL STUDIES

Studies about housing population density and ill health can be classified into two main classes. The first includes those studies of the relationship between measurements of population density in defined geographical areas and indirect accounts of health status (such as visits to a doctor or hospital admissions). This approach has a long history in the field of medical geography, beginning in the nineteenth century in Britain. It enables the spatial distribution of the incidence of illness or mortality to be mapped and interpreted in terms of certain variables. However, this kind of contribution does not identify whether household or neighborhood densities are correlates or root causes of ill health. Using this approach and a review of contributions of this kind Kellett (1993, p. 210), a medical professional, concludes that "the relation between crowding [sic] and mortality remains uncertain and there is little evidence to relate it to individual diseases."

The second approach includes those studies of individual's housing conditions and their relation to measurements of either objective or subjective assessments of ill health. This kind of approach uses the individual as the unit of analysis, but it often ignores the cultural and geographical context in which that individual lives. It usually does not distinguish between household population density (an objective calculation of the person-to-room ratio) and crowding, which is a subjective assessment of whether specific household occupancy conditions are overcrowded or not. Studies show that these assessments can vary significantly between people with different cultures and between people in the same society at the same time, such that age, gender, and socioeconomic status need to be addressed (Baum & Paulus, 1987).

In a survey in West London among a representative sample of British women aged 25 to 45 years, Gabe and Williams (1993) found a significant relation between household population density and psychological distress reported by women. Both very low and high household population densities were correlated with psychological ill health. These relationships remained even when employment status, presence of children, social class, and residential satisfaction were controlled for. Possible explanations are found in contributions by environmental psychologists about personal control and privacy regulation: For example, loneliness and lack of control of the desired amount of interpersonal interaction with other members of the household can be detrimental to psychological well-being (Altman, 1975). In the past two decades studies show that privacy regulation, the sense of insecurity, and access to communal amenities all promote mental and physical health (Halpern, 1995).

Other contributions show that the health of women is linked to their status in society. There is much evidence to show that women's health benefits from a livelihood founded on equality and equity, whereas it suffers in daily circumstances of discrimination. For example, the World Health Report for 1998, states: "In many parts of the world, discrimination against women begins before they are born and stays with them until they die. . . . Today girls and women are still denied the same rights and privileges as their brothers at home, at work, or in the classroom or clinic. They suffer more from poverty, low social status and the many hazards associated with their reproductive role." (WHO, 1998, p. 6). In particular, the health impacts of domestic violence, including physical, sexual, and psychological abuses against women have often been underestimated. Empirical studies have documented severe forms of abuse of women and girls in many countries (Heise, 1993).

Ironically, statistics also show that with respect to mortality, gender differences have existed throughout the twentieth century and they have always favored the female population across all age groups and in all countries that have available data. What needs to be stressed is that women live longer than men, but the quality of their lives has not received the same priority among policy makers. For example improvements in gender equality should be considered not only as a target for basic human rights but also as means of improving the health status of populations. There is evidence from several studies that confirm that low levels of education and limited access to resources depress the quality of life of women in many countries. Gender based discrimination is common in many developing countries even though women are a major part of the work force. According to the World Health Organization (1999) improvements in the educational level of women not only have a positive impact on their well-being but also account for a significant reduction in infant mortality. This finding clearly illustrates why it is important to adopt a broad interpretation of health.

INTEGRATING EPIDEMIOLOGICAL, PSYCHOLOGICAL, AND SOCIOLOGICAL INTERPRETATIONS

Bearing in mind the above contributions, housing occupancy conditions, specifically the number of persons per habitable room, can be analysed by survey methods that address cultural, social, and psychological variables in conjunction with those biological mechanisms that are responsible for the human-to-human transmission of infectious diseases. These biological mechanisms can be summarized from a report by the United Nations Commission on Human Settlements (1998):

1. High household population density increases the risk of multiple infections because the number of potential transmitters is increased. Consequently, if there is a relatively high number of persons per room, then the inhabitants will tend to have more infections than if there were lower numbers of persons per room.

2. High household population density increases proximity of people and the risk of disease transmission because not only the number of vectors but also the close contact may be a necessary condition for the human-to-human transmission of infectious diseases. Proximity can be measured in terms of the number of persons per habitable room, the floor area per person, or the number of persons sleeping in the same bed.

3. Housing occupancy conditions may affect the severity of the infection and the case fatality ratio because high household population density increases the risk of infection early in life. Infections early in life are one determinant of the severity of a disease.

4. Housing occupancy conditions affect the risk of prolonged intensive exposure to infections and, therefore, the severity of infection and the case fatality ratio. Given that high household population density influences the risk of contracting an infectious disease in the household, the number of susceptible individuals per household is an important risk factor for morbidity and mortality.

5. Housing occupancy conditions can increase the risk of the long-term negative impacts of

infections, especially childhood diseases such as measles. A high household population density is a key risk factor because long-term excess morbidity and mortality are related to the intensity of exposure during acute infection, being highest among children who contracted diseases at home at a young age at the time of exposure.

Another thesis that should be considered is that a high household population density can be beneficial for health and well-being because infections that do not require medical treatment stimulate the immune system to viral infections and, therefore, reduce the risk of morbidity and mortality from acute diseases (UNCHS, 1998).

One example of the application of the above principles is a field survey of housing occupancy conditions and the health status of residents conducted in Guinea Bissau from 1993 to 1995 in order to identify and measure epidemiological relationships (based on statistical significance) between house population density and the health status of children less than 3 years old and of pregnant women. The hypothesis was that higher household population density increases the risk and severity of ill health by the transmission of communicable diseases in the household. According to the United Nations Commission on Human Settlements:

> Overcrowding has usually been measured by the number of individuals of all ages per room—not the most adequate way of measuring potential negative crowding [sic]. For certain infections, it may be the number of individuals in susceptible age groups that is important, rather than the total number of individuals in the household. Therefore, it could be relevant to consider crowding [sic] for certain specific age groups. Space per person and the number of persons per bed may also be indicators of overcrowding, since they are connected with proximity and risk of transmitting infections. (1998, p. 10)

The results of the field survey show that after social, economic, and ethnic variables are controlled, household population density is a significant determinant of postperinatal infant mortality even when there is a high level of control for communicable diseases (such as measles, diphtheria, polio, whooping cough, and tuberculosis). Other predicators of high mortality were the level of formal education of the mother, the gender of the child, ownership of domestic pigs,

immunization, an internal bathroom in the house, and ethnicity-based behavioral customs including the duration of breast feeding. With respect to pregnancies this study did not find a relation.

The study in Guinea Bissau showed that the level of formal education of mothers and immunization coverage are preconditions for good health that warrant a higher priority than improved housing conditions in health promotion campaigns. One reason for this is that ethnic differences in the resident population are reflected in behavioral differences related to household hygiene and nurturing infants. Another reason is that different levels of household population density are pertinent for the transmission of different types of infectious disease, so that technical interventions can be more appropriate than other kinds of interventions in some situations. Finally, the study supports the viewpoint that the effect of interventions to improve health is dependent on the cultural context of each intervention. Various means and measures will only be implemented with a successful impact if an understanding of the cultural context is integrated into the intervention process.

RECENT DEVELOPMENTS AND CONDITIONS IN INDUSTRIALIZED COUNTRIES

The availability and affordability of habitable floor space is a crucial dimension of the qualitative aspects of housing. There are major differences in the amount of floor space per inhabitant in the world and even between European countries. Data on the housing size and occupancy conditions in central and eastern European countries show a housing deficit—the difference between the number of households and the number of housing units—that varies from 7.5% in the Baltic States to 20% in the Russian Federation. Only Bulgaria and Hungary have overall occupancy conditions in which there is less than one person per room. In Eastern Europe there is about 20 m^2 of habitable floor space per person, whereas in the Russian Federation it is only 16.4 m^2. In contrast, data for western European countries in 1993 indicate 32 m^2 in Italy and 45 m^2 in Norway.

There is some evidence that suggests there are links between habitable floor area per person and health. For example, there is a correlation between postneonatal infant mortality rates and habitable floor space per person in those countries that have available data. Also, a study of childhood tuberculosis in New York City found that there was a relation between the incidence of this disease and household population density in the Bronx, such that children living in overcrowded housing were six times more likely to develop active tuberculosis than their neighbors (de Cock, Lucas, & Mabey, 1995).

The official statistics and field studies presented in this chapter confirm that there is a growing amount of evidence that shows that housing programs and urban planning have yielded many improvements to living conditions in cities, but not all cities or neighborhoods benefit equally. Some deprived neighborhoods in France, for example, have levels of unemployment that are double the national average (OECD, 1996). These neighborhoods are also characterised by relatively large numbers of migrants from non-European countries, relatively large households, and a housing stock of many nonrenovated high-rise buildings constructed between 1949 and 1970. Recent events in cities highlight a range of contemporary problems including *environmental conditions* (e.g., summer and winter smogs, soil contamination, and water pollution), *socioeconomic deprivation* (e.g., poverty, homelessness, and unemployment), and *political problems* (e.g., social unrest, riots, and warfare). Since the 1980s a number of studies show that socioeconomic inequalities can be correlated with health inequalities in both urban and rural areas (Marmot & Wilkinson, 1999).

In principle, inequalities of professional status, income, housing, and work conditions are reflected in and reinforced by inequalities of health and well-being. Research has shown that loss of employment can be linked to as much as a twofold increase in risk of mortality from cancer and cardiovascular disease among men less than 60 years old (Morris, Cook, & Shaper, 1994). Other research found that black male residents in Harlem, a district of New York City, have a shorter life expectancy than black residents in other American neighborhoods; in addition, they are less likely to live beyond the age of 65 than men living in Bangladesh (McCord & Freeman, 1990). Although the economic, social, and physical characteristics of urban neighborhoods can be correlated with rates of morbidity and mortality, the lifestyle of groups and individuals cannot be ignored. Residents in deprived urban areas commonly have diets that contain relatively high levels of sugar, starch, and fats because foods high in protein, minerals, and

vitamins are relatively expensive. Smoking is also more prevalent, especially among women. In essence, when poverty is interpreted as a compound index of deprivation including lack of income and lack of access to education, employment, housing, and social support, then it is a significant indicator of urban morbidity and mortality.

Given that the growing extent of urban deprivation, poor health, and social inequalities are the outcomes of intentional decisions based largely on professional knowledge, technical expertise, and rationalism, it is appropriate to consider how and why such current dilemmas exist: Are inadequate responses to health challenges and environmental problems in residential neighborhoods due to a lack of knowledge, or to an inability to effectively use acquired knowledge in conjunction with innovative technology, or to some other circumstances? In other words, are there underlying problems of substance or procedure, or both?

There are no simple answers to current urban and global environmental problems. However, it should be acknowledged that policy makers have identified and isolated problems too narrowly. When environmental psychology was applied after the Second World War, it would have been difficult to predict the environmental, economic, and health problems that humanity is concerned about today. At the local level, from the 1950s, residential neighborhoods were supposedly planned rationally to overcome the unsanitary conditions of slum housing that they replaced. However, many of these modern residential neighborhoods now have multiple kinds of architectural, social, economic, and environmental problems (Ravetz, 1980). Nobody anticipated these outcomes. Today, it should be recognized that current problems cannot be solved by the same approaches that were used to construct residential environments in the last half of the twentieth century.

At the beginning of the twenty-first century, it is necessary to reconsider health and housing in a broader environmental, economic, social, and political context. Although it is commonly stated that there is a relationship between housing conditions and the health and well-being of residents, there is still no widely shared consensus about the nature of that relationship. Nonetheless, there are some pathological conditions that can be attributed to the quality of dwelling units and their surroundings (see the next section). Hence, residential environments can be evaluated by examining their characteristics in relation to the health and well-being of the occupants.

This section has suggested that a reorientation and a diversification of studies of the relations between residential environments, local environmental conditions, and health is required. Both theoretical and methodological developments are necessary to formulate and apply a more comprehensive approach. The following paragraphs discuss some theoretical and methodological principles that replace a biomedical model of housing and health by an ecological interpretation.

PRINCIPLES OF HEALTHY RESIDENTIAL ENVIRONMENTS AND POLICY IMPLICATIONS

Residential environments are known to be an important determinant of quality of life and well-being following the results of numerous studies in a range of disciplines cited earlier in this chapter. The multiple components of housing units and outdoor areas need to be considered in terms of their potential and effective contribution to physical, social, and mental well-being. In principle, there are eight main components that ought to be considered including:

1. The characteristics of the site in ensuring safety from "natural" disasters including earthquakes, landslides, flooding, and fires, and protection from any potential source of natural radon.
2. The residential building as a shelter for the inhabitants from the extremes of outdoor temperature; as a protector against dust, insects, and rodents; as a provider of security from unwanted persons; and as an insulator against noise.
3. The effective provision of a safe and continuous supply of water that meets standards for human consumption, and the maintenance of sewage and solid waste disposal.
4. Ambient atmospheric conditions in the residential neighborhood and indoor air quality both of which are related to emissions from industrial production, transportation, and fuels used for domestic cooking and heating, as well as the local climate and ventilation inside and around buildings.

5. Household occupancy conditions, which can influence the transmission of airborne infections including pneumonia and tuberculosis, and the incidence of injury from domestic accidents.
6. Accessibility to community facilities and services (for commerce, education, employment, leisure, and primary health care) that are affordable and available to all individuals and groups.
7. Food safety, including provision of uncontaminated fresh foods that can be stored with protection against spoilage.
8. The control of vectors and hosts of disease outdoors and inside residential buildings that can propagate in the building structure; the use of nontoxic materials and finishes for housing and building construction; the use and storage of hazardous substances or equipment in the residential environment.

Research in environmental psychology during the 1990s confirms that the relations between residential environments and health are not limited to the above eight sets of criteria. In addition, the housing environment can be considered in terms of its capacity to nurture and sustain social and psychological processes (Lawrence, 1987). For example, the capacity of the resident in her or his home environment to alleviate stress accumulated at school or in the workplace, and whether this capacity is mediated by views of nature or being in natural surroundings such as urban parks. The multiple dimensions of residential environments that circumscribe the resident's capacity to use her or his domestic setting for restorative processes is a subject that has been studied by a limited number of scholars during the past decade (Hartig, 2001).

Other contributions outside the field of environmental psychology confirm that achieving environmental quality across diverse geographical scales will depend as much on decisions about the use of resources including land, materials, and methods to construct residential environments, as on the layout and volume of services and energy sources used to secure environmental conditions in buildings and urban neighborhoods. The interrelations between indoor and outdoor environments are omnipresent. However, too frequently they are taken for granted. They are partly regulated by the activities and lifestyles of households. In the United Kingdom, for example, energy used in the building sector accounts for half of all energy consumption, and buildings contribute to the "greenhouse effect" because they emit carbon dioxide as well as other pollutants (Shorrock & Henderson, 1990). Studies in several industrialized countries show that more than half of all nonsleep activities of employed people between 18 and 64 years of age occur inside housing units. Children, the aged, and housewives spend even more time indoors (Szalai, 1972). Consequently, any shortcomings in the indoor residential environment (including high household population density) may have implications on human health and well-being (WHO, 1990).

If housing and the built environment are considered too narrowly then the interrelations between housing, health, and well-being may not seem important. In this chapter it has been suggested that an ecological perspective can provide a broad framework for comprehending the dimensions of housing and health that ought to be identified and studied. There is little doubt that the physical condition of housing units should be examined with respect to forms of housing tenure, household composition and income, the availability and cost of building materials, infrastructure and services, the levels of education, and the employment status of residents. In turn, these dimensions of housing environments and the health of residents cannot be isolated from their diet, lifestyle, type of employment, and the availability of health care (Marmot & Wilkinson, 1999).

Today, national and local authorities commonly aim to provide and maintain a healthy environment by the installation or improvement of infrastructure and by controlling environmental conditions through the enactment and administration of regulations. While there can be little doubt about the pertinence of supplying infrastructure for piped water, sewage, drainage, electricity, and other services, prescriptive regulations and absolute standards ignore socioeconomic inequalities that influence their availability and affordability for citizens in a specific city (Lawrence, 1993). In general, a reorientation of contemporary policy formulation and practice is required. An outline will now be given.

Contemporary environmental, housing, and health regulations are usually prescriptive principles. These kinds of principles specify what ought to be achieved; they imply a lack of individual choice in meeting required standards. In contrast, proscriptive

principles specify what should not be done; they imply that what is not forbidden is permitted, and therefore they may enable a range of solutions to housing requirements, as many studies of vernacular and self-help housing have shown (Lawrence, 1987). This chapter has argued that the control of residential environments by individuals or households ought to be increased in order to promote well-being. If this goal is to be attained then policy decision makers should accept that proscriptive principles replace prescriptive ones so that the initiative, skills, and nonmonetary resources of residents can be used during the course of time.

The World Health Organization (1990) has defined the health implications of certain kinds of local environmental conditions in terms of three levels of housing environment factors, the intensity and duration of exposure to these factors, and the vulnerability of particular groups (e.g., children, housewives, the aged). These three levels are:

1. "desirable levels of environmental conditions which promote human health and well-being"
2. "permissible levels of environmental conditions which are not ideal but which are broadly neutral in their impact on health and well-being"
3. "incompatible levels which, if maintained, would adversely affect health and well-being"

One major hurdle to overcome in order to implement a reorientation of contemporary policies and practices concerns the perception of decision makers, legislators, and public administrators. These persons not only have a limited, rather than a broad, interpretation of health and housing but also perceive a healthy residential environment as one that is controlled by them rather than the residents. Clearly, this is not necessarily the case. Bearing this in mind, it is suggested that an ecological perspective provides important cues for the definition of public health policies and programs founded on fundamental principles of:

1. preventive medical practice that helps to overcome recognizable health risks owing to inadequate employment, leisure and residential environments, adverse lifestyle, and a lack of health education
2. affordable housing policies that help to overcome recognizable health risks resulting from

homelessness, adverse indoor and outdoor environmental conditions, as well as the lack of household and personal control of these conditions

3. ecological environmental policies that help to identify and overcome the unforeseen and unacceptable consequences of urban and rural development, from the localized scale of harmful substances and conditions on or near specific sites to the impact of nonsustainable energy policies on global atmospheric conditions

These three sets of policies ought to be interrelated across traditional academic boundaries and between fields of professional practice. Both the principles and policies presented in this chapter can be applied in a complementary way.

PROSPECTS AND FUTURE DIRECTIONS

This chapter has argued that there is a need to reconsider the knowledge base that made possible the twentieth-century revolution in health in order to deal not only with many kinds of infectious diseases but also with the increasing burden of noncommunicable diseases. A recent report published by the World Health Organization (1996a) has identified critical gaps in knowledge to deal effectively with the growing incidence of allergies and respiratory infections, cardiovascular diseases, malignant neoplasms (commonly labeled "cancers"), intentional and unintended injuries (including suicide), and neuropsychiatric ill health (including depression, drug dependence, and other disorders). The report states that "among the many competing demands on the funds allocated to international assistance for health, those contributing to the generation of the new knowledge, products, and interventions that can be shared by all have special merit" (p. 6).

In order to move toward this goal, this chapter has argued that there is a need for conceptual clarification and methodological rigor using a combination of qualitative and quantitative approaches. It has also been argued that there is an urgent need for more coordination, because health and well-being are not limited to genetics or the medical sciences. In addition, a major barrier to the design and construction of residential environments that support health is the strong tendency for architects, planners, and policy makers to focus too strongly on technical information and applications without referring to a holistic framework, without understanding the contextual conditions of the site location, and without considering the dialectics of people-environment relations at the local and broader levels. This chapter has also shown that environmental psychology can contribute to broaden current understanding.

A restricted disciplinary interpretation of health has hindered the development of a broad understanding of the contextual conditions of human well-being in residential environments. Segmented interpretations could be replaced by studies of the mutual interrelations between humans, their residential environment, and the local ecosystem as a dynamic, regulated network that can be studied as a system and in terms of its components. From this perspective, studies of people detached from their surroundings can be replaced by studies of processes and relations that occur between the nonhuman and human components of open, dynamic residential environments that have a precise scale and location at the microlevel of a much larger ecosystem and biosphere (Raffestin & Lawrence, 1990).

Our capacity to deal with these complex subjects is insufficient for several reasons including the diversity and complexity of these problems; the difficulty of identifying and measuring the interrelations between them and their components; and the need to understand the relative importance of these components in precise localities, at different geographical scales and over time (Lawrence, 2001). Therefore, it is suggested that it is necessary to shift from multidisciplinary to interdisciplinary and transdisciplinary concepts and methods.

In this chapter disciplinarity refers to the specialization of academic disciplines especially since the nineteenth century (Klein, 1996). Multidisciplinary refers to collaborative research in which each specialist remains within his discipline and applies its concepts and methods without sharing the same goal. Interdisciplinary studies are those in which concerted action is accepted by contributors in different disciplines as a means to achieve a shared goal that usually is a common subject of study. In these studies one contributor will usually coordinate the research process and seek integration. In contrast, transdisciplinarity refers to an approach that incorporates a combination of concepts and methods from several disciplines, structured according to a hierarchy of tasks that are meant to lead to an objective (Klein, 1996). These contributions enable the cross-fertilization of contributions from different contributors and promote an enlarged vision of a subject, as well as new explanatory theories. Transdisciplinarity is a way of achieving innovative goals, enriched understanding, and a synergy of new methods, which are essential if current understanding of healthy residential environments is to be improved.

Multidisciplinarity, interdisciplinarity, and transdisciplinarity are complementary rather than mutually exclusive. Without specialized disciplinary studies there would be no in-depth knowledge and data. The interrelations between these approaches ought to be more systematic than they have been in people-environment studies in general and in human ecology in particular. To date, disciplinary contributions in people-environment studies have dominated the fewer interdisciplinary ones and the scarce number of transdisciplinary studies. In addition this chapter has argued that there still are too few multidisciplinary contributions about healthy residential environments.

Transdisciplinary research and practice require a common conceptual framework and analytical methods based on shared terminology, mental images, and common goals. Once these have been formulated, then the next requirement is to develop a research agenda based conceptually and pragmatically on diverse sources of data and information that can be organized in ways to help understand, interpret, and deal with problems. There are several ways of promoting transdisciplinary approaches. The problem-solving approach, for example, can be used. It is typically small scale and locality specific, and it is applicable for the study of health and housing in precise localities. This kind of approach can identify and explain what factors are pertinent in order to analyze and deal with problems that are frequently complex.

The relationship between researchers in different disciplines, including those who study health and housing, is often considered not to be conducive for collaboration. Nonetheless, this chapter has discussed and illustrated a multidisciplinary interpretation of health, population density, and crowding using the contributions from several disciplines and professions in a complementary way. This example shows how these kinds of contributions can lead to the development of new insights and knowledge about complex subjects. This means that there is an important challenge for environmental psychology and the health sciences at the beginning of this new millennium.

REFERENCES

Aiello, J. R., & Thompson, D. E. (1980). Personal space, crowding and spatial behavior in a cultural context. In I. Altman, A. Rapoport, & J. Wohlwill (Eds.), *Human behavior and environment: Advances in theory and research: Vol. 4. Environment and culture* (pp. 107–178). New York: Plenum Press.

Altman, I. (1975). *The environment and social behavior.* Monterey, CA: Brooks/Cole.

Baum, A., & Paulus, P. (1987). Crowding. In D. Stokols & I. Altman (Eds.), *Handbook of environmental psychology* (Vol. 1, pp. 533–570). New York: Wiley.

Barton, H., & Tsourou, C. (2000). *Healthy urban planning.* London: Spon.

Bistrup, M. L. (1991). *Housing and community environments: How they support health.* Copenhagen, Denmark: National Board of Health.

Burridge, R., & Ormandy, D. (Eds.). (1993). *Unhealthy housing: Research, remedy and reform.* London: Spon.

Catalano, R. (1979). *Health, behavior, and the community: An ecological perspective.* New York: Pergamon.

Chadwick, E. (1842). *Report on the sanitary condition of the labouring population of Great Britain.* London.

Corvalan, C., Nurminen, M., & Pastides, H. (1997). *Linkage methods for environment and health analysis: Technical guidelines.* Geneva, Switzerland: World Health Organization.

de Cock, K. M., Lucas, S. B., & Mabey, D. (1995). Tropical medicine for the 21st century. *British Medical Journal, 311,* 860–862.

Evans, G., & Cohen, S. (1987). Environmental stress. In D. Stokols & I. Altman (Eds.), *Handbook of environmental psychology* (Vol. 1, pp. 571–610). New York: Wiley.

Fuller-Thomson, E., Hulchanski, D., & Wang, S. (2000). The health-housing relationship: What do we know? *Reviews on Environmental Health, 15,* 109–134.

Gabe, J., & Williams, P. (1986). Is space bad for health? The relationship between crowding in the home and emotional distress in women. *Sociology of Health and Illness, 8,* 351–371.

Gabe, J., & Williams, P. (1993). Women, crowding and mental health. In R. Burridge & D. Ormandy (Eds.), *Unhealthy housing: Research, remedy and reform* (pp. 191–208). London: Spon.

Gillis, A. (1977). High-rise housing and psychological strain. *Journal of Health and Social Behavior, 18,* 418–431.

Goffman, I. (1959). *The presentation of self in everyday life.* New York: Doubleday.

Halpern, D. (1995). *Mental health and the built environment.* London: Taylor & Francis.

Hartig, T. (2001). Restorative environments. *Environment and Behavior, 33* (Special issue). Guest Editor's Introduction, pp. 475–479.

Heise, L. (1993). Violence against women: The hidden health burden. *World Health Statistics Quarterly, 46,* 78–85.

Hippocrates. (1849). On air, waters, and places. In F. Adams (Trans. & Commentary), *The genuine works of Hippocrates.* London: Sydenham Society.

Jacobs, M., & Stevenson, G. (1981). Health and housing: A historical examination of alternative perspectives. *International Journal of Health Services, 1,* 105–122.

Kasl, S., & Harburg, E. (1975). Mental health and the urban environment: Some doubts and second thoughts. *Journal of Health and Social Behavior, 16,* 268–282.

Kellett, J. (1993). Crowding and mortality in London boroughs. In R. Burridge & D. Ormandy (Eds.), *Unhealthy housing: Research, remedy and reform* (pp. 209–222). London: Spon.

Klein, J. (1996). *Crossing boundaries: Knowledge, disciplinarities, and interdisciplinarities.* Charlottesville: University Press of Virginia.

Lawrence, R. (1983). The sanitary house: An architectural interpretation of health and housing reforms in England c. 1840–1920. *Architectural Science Review, 26,* 39–49.

Lawrence, R. (1987). *Housing, dwellings, and homes: Design theory, research and practice.* Chichester, England: Wiley.

Lawrence, R. (1993). An ecological blueprint for healthy housing. In R. Burridge & D. Ormandy (Eds.) *Unhealthy housing: Research, remedy and reform* (pp. 338–360). London: Spon.

Lawrence, R. (2000). Urban health: A new research agenda? *Reviews on Environmental Health, 15*(special issue), 1–11.

Lawrence, R. (2001). Human ecology. In M. Tolba (Ed.), *Our fragile world: Challenges and opportunities for sustainable development* (Vol.1, pp. 675–693). Oxford: EOLSS Publishers & United Nations Educational, Scientific, and Cultural Organization.

Loudon, I. S. (Ed.). (1997). *Western medicine: An illustrated history.* Oxford: Oxford University Press.

Marmot, M., & Wilkinson, R. (Eds.). (1999). *Social determinants of health.* Oxford: Oxford University Press.

Martin, A., Kaloyanova, F., & Maziarka, S. (1976). *Housing, the housing environment, and health: An annotated bibliography.* Geneva, Switzerland: World Health Organization.

McCord, C., & Freeman, H. (1990). Excess mortality in Harlem. *New England Journal of Medicine, 322,* 173–177.

McMichael, A. (1993). *Planetary overload: Global environmental change and the health of the human species.* Cambridge: Cambridge University Press.

Mitchell, R. (1971). Some social implications of high density housing. *American Sociological Review, 36,* 18–29.

Morris, J., Cook, D., & Shaper, A. (1994). Loss of employment and mortality. *British Medical Journal, 308,* 1135–1139.

Organization for Economic Cooperation and Development. (1996). *Strategies for housing and social integration in cities.* Paris: Author.

Proshansky, H., Ittelson, W., & Rivlin, L. (1970). *Environmental psychology: Man and his physical setting.* New York: Holt, Rinehart and Winston.

Raffestin, C., & Lawrence, R. (1990). An ecological perspective on housing, health and well-being. *Journal of Sociology and Social Welfare, 27,* 143–160.

Ravetz, A. (1980). *Remaking cities: Contradictions of the recent urban environment.* London: Croom Helm.

Rosen, G. (1993). *A history of public health.* Baltimore: Johns Hopkins University Press.

Schwela, D. (2000). Air pollution and health in urban areas. *Reviews on Environmental Health, 15,* 13–42.

Shorrock, L., & Henderson, G. (1990). *Energy use in buildings and carbon dioxide emissions* (Info. Paper IP 18/88). Garston, England: Building Research Establishment.

Smith, S. (1989). *Housing and health: A review and research agenda* (Discussion Paper No. 27). Glasgow, Scotland: Centre for Housing Research.

Stokols, D. (1972). On the distinction between density and crowding: Some implications for future research. *Psychological Review, 79,* 275–277.

Stokols, D. (1982). Environmental psychology: A coming of age. In A. Kraut (Ed.), *The G. Stanley Hall Lecture Series* (Vol. 2, pp. 155–205). Washington, DC: American Psychological Association.

Szalai, A. (1972). *The uses of time.* The Hague, The Netherlands: Mouton.

Teeland, L. (1998). Home, sick: Implications of health care delivery in the home. *Scandinavian Journal of Housing and Planning Research, 15,* 271–282.

Tognoli, J. (1987). Residential environments. In D. Stokols & I. Altman (Eds.), *Handbook of environmental psychology* (Vol. 1, pp. 655–690). New York: Wiley.

United Nations Commission on Human Settlements. (1995). *Human settlement interventions addressing crowding and health issues.* Nairobi, Kenya: Author.

United Nations Commission on Human Settlements. (1996). *An urbanizing world: Global report on human settlements 1996.* Oxford: Oxford University Press.

United Nations Commission on Human Settlements. (1998). *Crowding and health in low-income settlements.* Nairobi, Kenya: Author.

World Health Organization. (1946). *Constitution.* Geneva, Switzerland: Author.

World Health Organization. (1990). *Indoor environment: Health aspects of air quality, thermal environment, light, and noise* (Pub. No. WHO/EHE/RUD/90.2). Geneva, Switzerland: Author.

World Health Organization. (1996a). *Investing in health research and development.* Report of the Ad hoc committee on health research relating to future intervention options (Pub. No. WHO/TDR/Gen.96.1). Geneva, Switzerland: Author.

World Health Organization. (1996b). *Our planet, our health: Report of the WHO commission on health and environment.* Geneva, Switzerland: Author.

World Health Organization. (1998). *The world health report 1998: Life in the 21st century—A vision for all.* Geneva, Switzerland: Author.

World Health Organization. (1999). *World health report 1999: Making a difference.* Geneva, Switzerland: Author.

World Health Organization. (2000). *World health report 2000: Health systems—improving performance.* Geneva, Switzerland: Author.

Young, G. (1983). *Origins of human ecology.* Stroudsberg, PA: Hutchinson Ross.

CHAPTER 27

Crime Prevention through Environmental Design (CPTED): Yes, No, Maybe, Unknowable, and All of the Above

RALPH B. TAYLOR

THE MAIN TITLE of this chapter conveys a simple idea. If we make correct choices in constructing, maintaining, and modifying the physical environments in which we live, work, travel, and recreate, we should be able to prevent some crimes from happening, either to us or to our property. The idea would seem to be supported by the commonsense observation that, to focus on urban neighborhoods as an example, those locations with high reported crime rates physically look very different from those with low reported crime rates. The high rate locales are likely to have denser housing designs, usually being older neighborhoods, and to have streets carrying more traffic and commercial or perhaps even industrial land uses mixed amongst the residences.

A chain of reasoning operates here as follows: There is more crime in some places than in others; physical design is different from place to place; design, therefore, is responsible for these place-to-place differences; consequently, if we change the design in high crime places, crime there will decline. In deference to two of the most popular shows currently on network television, *Who Wants to be a Millionaire* with Regis Philbin and *The Weakest Link* with Anne Robinson (Kellman, 2001), I have organized the bulk of the chapter as a series of multiple choice answers to the question: Is this chain of reasoning correct? Here are your possible responses:

a. No, it is incorrect;

b. Yes, it is correct;

c. Maybe—it is correct depending on certain other conditions;

d. Unknowable; it is something whose truth we are extremely unlikely to know; or

e. All of the above are true.

I will argue in this chapter that e is the best answer. Understanding how each of the first four different answers to the question may be valid highlights different ways the design-crime link has been conceptualized. The chapter starts by briefly noting one public policy area where the crime-design idea has had considerable influence. The material highlights the public relevance of this question about the chain of reasoning and the difficulties of answering it. The next sections review each of the terms in the title, clarifying the scope of each. Defining *prevent* forces us to closely examine the special challenges relevant to this area of work when we wish to establish causality. I then move on to review each of the possible answers to the question, Is the chain of reasoning correct? I close with a brief comment about how we need to know more about design-crime links given the profound transformations currently sweeping urban, suburban, and rural landscapes across the country.

AN EXAMPLE OF INFLUENCE BUT QUESTIONS

The assumption of a design-crime linkage has powerfully influenced some areas of public policy. Even though academics may still not be sure that design can prevent crime, in the area of public housing, planners have embraced this idea with a vengeance, resulting in massive demolitions of urban, high-rise, public housing communities through the 1990s.

In the wake of the urban disorders of the mid- and late 1960s, the U.S. federal government started funding research projects looking at design-crime connections in residential settings, particularly public housing communities (Kohn, Franck, & Fox, 1975; Newman & Franck, 1980; Taylor, Gottfredson, & Brower, 1984). City planner Oscar Newman, borrowing ideas from another planner, Jane Jacobs, coined the term *defensible space* and focused on a small number of design and site features that promoted crime. He generated enormous interest in the idea that changes in design of public housing communities could motivate residents to care for and watch over their locale and help prevent crime. Earning particular scorn from Newman were high-rise, minimalist design "towers" (Wolfe, 1981) built in large numbers in U.S. cities in the 1950s and 1960s as part of urban renewal projects whose origins dated to socialist architectural movements in the 1930s.

Although Newman's early research—but not the later work—was problematic in several respects and his assumptions about how people behave incorrect (Taylor, Gottfredson, & Brower, 1980), his ideas got attention from policy makers and held their interest through the 1980s and 1990s. In the mid-1990s, in part because of the impact of these ideas, these same places are being torn down in dozens of large cities, with federal financial support, and replaced by low-rise or scattered site housing (Popkin, Gwiasda, Olson, Rosenbaum, & Buron, 2000). Public high-rise communities, such as the Robert Taylor Homes in Chicago, are known as some of the most dangerous neighborhoods in American cities (Venkatesh, 2000). Will the new sites with different housing designs be safer? The main chapter title suggests so.

The focus on design, however, overlooks at least two key points. In the late 1950s or early 1960s, depending on the city, local housing authorities changed policies about who could live in public housing communities (Popkin et al., 2000). Perhaps as a result of this shift the fraction of two-parent households

with children living in these locales dropped. The timing of this change in policies and household composition in some places roughly coincided with the emergence of these locales as problem-ridden communities. In addition, the community contexts around these public housing communities changed dramatically as segregation of African-American communities and other populations of color into poor, core city locations increased dramatically throughout the 1970s and 1980s, at the same time that well-paying manufacturing jobs were migrating away from these locations (Kasarda, 1992; Massey & N. Denton, 1988; Massey & S. Denton, 1993; Wilson, 1996). These contextual shifts directly affect the prospects for community crime prevention and the possibilities of a crime-design prevention linkage (Hope, 1997). In short, when trying to explain crime changes, changes beyond physical environment features are crucial, especially issues related to selection effects (Tienda, 1991), or context (Weisburd, 1997).

This example is intended to illustrate two points. First, ideas about crime and design can have considerable public impact. In addition, what seems like a straightforward question—can design prevent crime?—even when we look at an obvious and widely cited example of "worst practices," is not simple at all.

DEFINITIONS

Before summarizing different answers to the question of design-crime connections, definitions are in order. *Design* refers to a wide range of physical environment features ranging from attributes of a single house or site to layout or design features of a small scale locale such as a streetblock or a public housing building, to physical features of neighborhoods. Design not only covers a range of levels but also covers an array of features (Zeisel, 1981). Of central interest of course are relatively permanent features explicitly decided upon by the architects or planners: How far is the house from the street? From the next house? How many windows are there in the house? How many floors are in the house? How long is the streetblock? Is the street straight or curved? How many lanes of traffic are accommodated on the street? What specific landuse types are present? How many entrances are there into the neighborhood? Is it a gated community? Are there trees? If you are thinking about convenience store design and commercial robbery relevant features might include: How much of the front of the store is glassed? Is the

cashier station located so it can be easily seen from outside the entrance? Semipermanent physical features that can be modified by users are also of interest. In a residential context these might include: fencing, other barriers between houses or between houses and the street, or physical features highlighting residents' involvement or vigilance (Taylor, 1988). Finally there also are behavioral traces, the physical features left behind as a result of human action or inaction. Two general clusters include evidence of a lack of caring, also called incivilities, that include graffiti, litter, sites in disrepair; sites not cared for or closed and abandoned cars (Taylor, 2000a); and signs of investment and involvement, usually labeled "signs of attachment" or "territorial functioning" (Taylor, 1988).

Crime refers to both Part I, or "serious," crimes and lesser, or Part II, crimes. Law enforcement agencies are required to report eight Part I crimes—four personal crimes (rape, robbery, homicide or nonnegligent manslaughter, and aggravated assault) and four property crimes (larceny, burglary, motor vehicle theft, and arson). These are compiled and reported yearly by the FBI. In addition there are a large number of Part II or "minor" crimes that include vandalism, prostitution, public drinking or drunkenness, and the like. This latter group is often referred to as "nuisance" or "quality of life" crimes.

At this current juncture, due to debates about the validity of the broken windows or incivilities thesis, researchers and policy makers are not sure that Part I crimes are a more important policy focus than Part II crimes (Taylor, 1999, 2000a). Many argue that the minor crimes are easier to prevent than the major crimes and that preventing the former has the happy result of helping prevent the latter (Bratton, 1998).

In addition to Part I and Part II crimes, I include police calls for service as well. The array of matters inspiring residents to call for police assistance is extremely broad, and there are no agreed upon classifications for calls for service that are similar from city to city. Typically these calls might include noise complaints, weapons complaints (man seen with a gun), requests for hospital transport, as well as reports of property damage, domestic violence, or simple assaults and fights. Calls to police, however, are far more numerous than reported crimes. Being more numerous, it may be easier to observe differences between settings using calls for service rather than reported crime data.

Most often researchers rely on crimes reported to police. It has been widely recognized that numerous crimes experienced or observed go unreported (Skogan, 1976). Researchers have subsequently mounted nationwide victimization surveys that can explore both reported and unreported crimes (Garofalo, 1990). But because serious victimizations are rare events, requiring large numbers of interviews to get stable rate estimates, and the survey methodology for correctly eliciting victimization accounts is lengthy, reported victimization data are rarely relied upon in studies on design-crime connections.

By *prevent* I mean decrease the number of crimes observed or experienced or reported in the time and space units of analysis used by the researcher, as indicated either through calls for service or reported crime data (Lab, 1992). (For a thumbnail sketch of crime prevention ideas see Lab, 1997.) Of course, it is possible that reported crime may increase even as occurring crime is decreasing if residents in a locale increase the portion of observed crimes they report, but we will overlook this point here.

Two key questions in defining if prevention has taken place are: (1) establishing causality and (2) documenting prevention rather than displacement.

The causality question is difficult because so much of the work in this area has been cross-sectional rather than longitudinal. Imagine a study comparing two sets of residential communities: those that are "gated" and those that are not. Gated communities have walls around them, gated entryways, and perhaps guards on duty. Traditionally associated with just the very wealthiest communities—Gibson Island (MD) or Ten Hills (CA)—their popularity has been increasing over the last two decades, and there are now many different types of gated communities (Blakely & Snyder, 1997; Wilson-Doenges, 2000); they can be found in center city as well as suburban or rural locations. Current estimates are that there are over 20,000 gated communities in the United States (Blakely & Snyder, 1997).

Suppose we find in a cross sectional study that gated communities have lower burglary rates than similar nongated communities; this does not mean that the gating is "causing" the lower crime rate because, as we all know, correlation, even a carefully partialled one with extraneous factors removed, does not necessarily mean causation. But if we change a number of communities from ungated to gated and find their burglary rates go down, while in matching ungated communities burglary rates stay level or increase, we can be somewhat more confident, depending on a host of potential threats to internal validity (Taylor, 1994), that the design change is partially causing the crime change. In fact the research on gated communities does suggest that initially crime rates do drop but that these reductions are transient (Blakely & Snyder, 1997).

Causality is difficult to establish generally in design-crime questions not only because cross-sectional rather than longitudinal studies predominate. In addition, if the design change involves a unit of analysis that is a community, or a portion of a community, such as a streetblock, the change needs to be implemented in a number of locations so we can learn how reliable the effects are across a range of contexts.

With design-crime questions, as soon as the unit of analysis extends from the individual or the individual household, to the streetblock or institution or community, study difficulty increases for three reasons. In either a longitudinal or cross-sectional study the researcher needs a large number of units of analysis if his or her quantitative analyses are to have sufficient statistical power. For example, a second-generation defensible space study of public housing communities included over 60 separate buildings, where each building included numerous households (Newman & Franck, 1980). To do a quasi-experimental study of the effects of gating communities, you would ideally like to have about 30 *communities* receiving the treatment and becoming gated and another 30 control communities. If the set of communities studied spans multiple police departments, we now have variations in crime reporting and recording practices that add a further source of variation to the outcome.

Further, with a longitudinal study where the unit of analysis is larger than the individual or the household or the single address, not only are a large number of units of analysis required, but researchers or planners need to implement design changes in a large number of those locations. These initiatives *necessarily* involve local residents and local leaders. Although one early study of a public housing community did overlook resident involvement and householders awoke one morning to find bulldozers tearing into the begonias and front lawns (Kohn et al., 1975), other longitudinal studies involving community-level design changes have actively involved local stakeholders (Donnelly & Majka, 1996, 1998; F. J. Fowler & Mangione, 1986). This is an extraordinarily

expensive and time-consuming process. Not surprisingly, many of the longitudinal studies in this area where design changes have been implemented and crime changes tracked, have focused just on one community. Given the apparent contextual dependence of some design-crime connections (see following), such a one-community study makes it extremely difficult to understand those dependencies.

Additionally, with larger units of analysis, selection problems become more challenging, making it extremely difficult to separate physical environment impacts from social or cultural or economic factors. In general, in many communities birds of a feather flock together. This means design features will relate with social and cultural factors such as racial or ethnic composition of a community, stability, family structure, and so on. But it also means, if we are talking for example about urban neighborhoods, that residents are drawn into a location in part because of the people who are living there and other features of the destination. Returning specifically to gated communities, one analysis suggested that houses in gated communities sell for a higher price (Bible & Hsieh, 2001). How can these economic impacts, that might also influence crime, be separated from the physical impacts of the gating per se? Or to take another example, those who are drawn to gated communities might be those who are more fearful of crime than those drawn to economically comparable nongated communities. If we find those in gated communities expressing higher fear rates, is that a cause of the gated features?; or were residents that way before they arrived?

In short, even with a longitudinal study design, causality in design-crime questions can be difficult to establish when the unit of analysis is more than the individual site or address or household because: Large numbers of units of analysis are needed for sufficient statistical power and to better understand how context conditions the design-crime connection; large numbers of sites are difficult to manage because in each site implementing design changes involves lengthy and often contentious local social and political dynamics; and selection problems make it exceedingly difficult to separate qualities of locale from qualities of those drawn to the locale.

The time and space unit of analysis is also crucial because how those units are defined influences whether crime displacement has taken place rather than crime prevention. Crime may be displaced spatially, temporally, or in several other ways (Barnes, 1995). Researchers looking at a particular family of design changes called situational crime prevention initiatives (see following) have successfully documented that crime displacement effects from situational crime prevention initiatives are less than one crime displaced for each crime prevented. They have proposed that in some instances adjoining areas may experience a diffusion of benefits (Clarke & Weisburd, 1994), enjoying enhanced safety just because they are near a prevention site. The debate about the volume of displacement, the quality of studies gauging such volume, and even the definition of displacement continues (Barnes, 1995). Nevertheless, the bulk of empirical work at this time demonstrates displacement effects at the least usually do not nullify prevention benefits, and diffusion benefits may sometimes outweigh displacement effects (Anderson & Pease, 1997; Green, 1995).

Deciding whether an outcome represents displacement or prevention depends on both the temporal and spatial unit. Imagine a program where a design change like a street closing is implemented on a number of streetblocks. (Such a program was put in place in the 1970s in San Francisco [Appleyard, 1981] although the purpose was to improve quality of life generally, not just prevent crime.) Imagine further that our unit of analysis is the streetblock, a viable social and physical unit (Taylor, 1997), and that the geographic distribution of streetblocks in the study is such that each control and experimental streetblock is at least a few blocks away from each other study unit. Suppose potential robbers, after the street closings were introduced, changed their behavior only slightly, moving just a block or two away from their original chosen locations. If we did not examine what was happening on streetblocks adjoining the sampled sites, we would not find evidence of this spatial displacement but would just conclude that crime had been prevented because of the street closings. If our unit of analysis was the streetblock and its immediately adjoining blocks, and we mapped robbery locations, we would see that displacement rather than prevention had taken place.

In the case of the temporal unit for study, potential street robbers may respond to the street closings by deferring their activities for a period of time, given the increased activities surrounding the street closing process. If the study data collection period ends before the potential robbers resume their activities, the results will suggest prevention rather than temporal displacement.

REVIEWING EACH POSSIBLE ANSWER

This section explains why each of the first four answers to our quiz question is an acceptable answer. If I can show that (1) through (4) each are valid, then (5) is our best (and final, thank you, Mr. Philbin) answer.

(1) WHY THE CHAIN OF REASONING IS INCORRECT

The chain of reasoning is incorrect if the crime-design relationship is built on the assumption of architectural determinism: the belief of many planners or architects that design features will determine or at least have the most substantial impact on the behaviors and feelings of those using that space (Broady, 1972). Despite the flaws in this assumption, it is widely adhered to by large numbers of planners and architects. One reason crime prevention through environmental design (CPTED) was so warmly embraced in the 1970s was because planners and policy makers thought they had found a "silver bullet" so powerful it would solve numerous crime problems at various locations (Murray, 1995). This enthusiasm was firmly grounded in the assumption of architectural determinism. According to this assumption, physical design characteristics will be a powerful if not the most powerful influence on crime in a locale, and correct changes in design will be both necessary and sufficient to achieve a crime reduction. Such a view is implicit in the previous chain of reasoning but is generally not applicable to a wide range of everyday settings.

Extensive work in interior and exterior spaces highlights how different groups of people use the same space, or physically similar spaces, in different ways (Rapoport, 1977). In the case of crime specifically, social, cultural, and economic factors almost always have far stronger impacts on how much crime is taking place in a locale than design features (Taylor, 2000b; Taylor et al., 1984). So if the crime-design chain of reasoning is assuming that design is the preeminent influence on the outcomes of interest, and therefore certain design changes are both a necessary and sufficient condition for prevention, it is incorrect. Empirical work has shown design is not the strongest connection with crime, when compared to social, cultural, or economic factors. Further, work has shown that design-crime connections (see following) are conditioned by context and highly malleable. In the case of defensible space, for example, undefended defensible spaces have been noted (Merry, 1981).

In short, the chain of reasoning of interest here is incorrect if by CPTED we mean that design is the most powerful determinant of local crime and victimization rates or patterns and that design changes will necessarily result in crime reductions.

(2) WHY THE CHAIN OF REASONING IS CORRECT

There is substantial empirical work on the design-crime link that is grounded in one of three generally rational perspectives about crime and victimization (Taylor, 1998). The rational offender perspective, which undergirds situational crime prevention initiatives, assumes that how potential offenders think about costs and benefits of various crimes or crime sites or crime times determine offending patterns. The behavioral geography perspective assumes that the places closer to where offenders work, recreate, live, and travel, are at higher victimization risk because they are more familiar to the potential offenders. This perspective undergirds initiatives emerging from environmental criminology. The routine activities or lifestyle perspective, although later modified in important ways, initially assumed that victimization is more likely in a location if there are more attractive targets for the offender, if there are more potential offenders close at hand, and if there are fewer or weaker potential guardians of the crime site (Felson, 1994). These three perspectives make claims that are so obvious they must be true. For example:

- If there are more potential burglars living near one neighborhood, all else equal, that neighborhood will have a higher burglary rate than another neighborhood with fewer potential burglars living nearby.
- If there is a neighborhood whose internal street layout makes it harder to get around, potential burglars from outside the locale are less likely to wander in and learn about potential targets.

Work in situational crime prevention focuses on how physical design features influence the costs and benefits perceived by potential offenders of committing crimes (Clarke, 1992; but see also Clarke &

Homel, 1997). A steady stream of studies over the past two decades have documented how specific setting features and/or changes in those features can deter offenders (for a review see Clarke, 1995; Clarke & Homel, 1997).

The driving rational offender framework naturally focuses our attention on property crimes or personal crimes for gain, such as robbery. It is when considering these crimes potential offenders are most likely to be motivated by potential benefits considered in the context of likely crime costs and to recognize opportunities for getting away with a crime—whether that crime be vandalizing a telephone, putting slugs in the subway, robbing a pedestrian, or stealing a car.

The situational crime prevention perspective will often recommend that crime can be reduced by making redesigns that "harden" the target and decrease the opportunities for successful crimes for gain in a setting. Some have criticized this perspective because the target hardening process seems obvious, costly, and likely to result in undesirable social consequences (Forrest & Kennett, 1997). But situational crime prevention is more than just target hardening. Although it does include a broad array of physical features (Crowe, 1991), it also has suggestions for those who manage and supervise public locations. Operations as well as design are important. A study of Washington, DC's Metro station designs and operations represents an example of situational crime prevention integrating a number of design, management, and operational features (La Vigne, 1996). Elsewhere I have provided a detailed description of the types of physical factors relevant to potential rational offenders at the site, block, and neighborhood levels (Taylor & Gottfredson, 1986) if we presume they are using a rational framework and focusing on potential costs and benefits.

The relevant costs and benefits imply four types of considerations made by the potential offender: how long it takes to get to the target, how quickly it takes to get away, what he or she can see about the value of the particular target or victim prior to deciding to commit a crime, and what the likelihood is that he or she will be spotted and/or recognized while preparing to commit the offense, actually committing it, or leaving the scene of the crime.*

---

*Most recently Clarke and Homel (1997) have expanded situational crime prevention to include setting features that may affect psychodynamics and social dynamics relevant to prevention,

The geographic perspective says design—and here we are using design to refer to macrolevel features such as landuse and circulation patterns—will influence how likely potential offenders are to learn about potential crime sites. If we consider distance an attribute of the physical environment, it is obvious that of two potential burglary sites, all else equal, the site located closer to a larger number of potential burglars, has a higher chance of being burglarized. An approach called environmental criminology or crime pattern theory, developed largely by the Brantinghams and their colleagues, relies on key concepts in behavioral geography. These include how daily activities of potential offenders structure activity space (the total set of locations they frequent) and awareness space (the total set of locations about which they are knowledgeable) and how these two spaces shape offenders' search space (the locations they will explore, consider, and evaluate as potential offending locations) when they have a particular crime in mind (Brantingham & Brantingham, 1981). Offenders go to jobs, visit friends, come home, shop at the store, and carry out other daily activities just like the rest of us. Within this activity space motivated offenders search for likely targets for the type of crime they hope to commit. For example, suburban burglars may look for worthwhile houses to burgle that are not too far off their route between home and work (Rengert & Wasilchick, 1985). Urban, drug-using burglars may choose sites near drug markets (Rengert, 1996). Crime pattern theory integrates ideas about offenders' movement through space with a consideration of target distributions through space (Eck & Weisburd, 1995). It links places with desirable targets and the context in which they are found by offenders. It focuses on the chances that the potential offender will even be likely to consider the site in the first place.

Therefore, design features prove most relevant as they influence both physical distance and functional distance. Physical distance between an offender and an offense site could be measured by looking at straight line or city block distance; functional distance could be measured by looking at the shortest route traveled, by foot, by car, or by public transport, between offender worksite—or home or shopping location—and an offense site.

Like the situational crime perspective, the behavioral geography perspective seems more or less applicable depending on the crime in question and depending on the locale in question. More specifically, applicability seems strongest when considering property crimes such as burglary, motor vehicle theft, and, although perhaps to a lesser extent, larceny. These are crimes where offenders often have particular types of targets or particular goals in mind, although they are certainly capable of changing their noncriminal plans when criminal opportunity arises (Rengert & Wasilchick, 1985). In addition, applicability seems strongest in communities where offenders and targets are not equally mixed. More specifically, the crime patterns in locations that are home to few offenders but are popular locations for committing offenses may be more easily understood given this view than the crime patterns in locations with large numbers of both targets and offenders.

Whereas the situational crime perspective seems most applicable for understanding microscale factors influencing target selection, crime pattern theory seems most helpful in understanding macroscale factors influencing access and familiarity. These help potential offenders build clear cognitive images of potential targets.

Neighborhood permeability is a case in point. I pick this case because it is one of the community-level design features most reliably linked to crime rates, and the connections operate consistently in the same direction across studies: more permeability, more crime. Several studies across several decades link neighborhood property crime rates with permeability versus inaccessibility of neighborhood layout (Beavon, Brantingham, & Brantingham, 1994; Bevis & Nutter, 1977; Frisbie, 1978; Greenberg, Williams, & Rohe, 1982; White, 1990). Neighborhoods with smaller streets or more one-way streets or fewer entrance streets or with more turnings have lower property crime rates. The findings seem to support the idea that as permeability increases the potential offender is more likely to include the neighborhood in her or his activity space and/or awareness space and therefore search space, and this increased availability results in clearer images of potential targets and higher burglary rates. Recognition that permeability creates a liability for residents is clearly one of the driving forces toward more gated communities in the United States.

Switching from cross-sectional to longitudinal perspectives leads to an obvious suggestion grounded in

focusing in particular on ways to induce guilt or shame. They are essentially merging the crime-design link with dynamics relevant to controlling the offender.

both the situational and the geographic frameworks: Change the layout of the neighborhood to make it harder for potential offenders to enter, or less likely that they will enter, or to keep them farther away from potential targets, and crime should go down. Longitudinal research in Hartford (F. J. Fowler & Mangione, 1986; F. Fowler, McCalla, & Mangione, 1979), Akron (Donnelly & Majka, 1998), and Dayton (Donnelly & Majka, 1996) and unpublished and published evaluations in Miami (Atlas & LeBlanc, 1994; Ycaza, 1992) suggest that physical changes to internal circulation patterns and boundaries were followed by lower crime rates. So our chain of reasoning appears to be correct even when applied at the community level. But such a confirmation is less resounding than we might like since the connection may be dependent on the organizational dynamics surrounding the implementation of physical changes.

In the studies involving redesign, local social or organizational dynamics have often accompanied planned changes (Donnelly & Majka, 1996). Although it seems likely that design changes themselves have at least been partially responsible for the impact observed (Donnelly & Majka, 1998), researchers have not yet precisely estimated their independent contribution to lowering crime. It is not known how much of the benefit has been due to the redesign and how much has been due to the social and organizational changes surrounding planning for the change. It seems extremely plausible, however, that design factors are contributing *partially* to the crime reduction.

There are several practical implications of this research at the neighborhood level. (1) Social and organizational conditions are important when changes in layout, traffic, or land use are being considered (Donnelly & Majka, 1998). Community involvement of residents, neighborhood organizations, and local businesspeople is essential for developing a plan free of adverse effects on major interest groups. (2) Local involvement may be an important precondition not only for rational, maximally beneficial change but also for achieving a redesign that will actually reduce crime. One study suggests that changes in layout, under conditions of community mobilization, appear to have been partially responsible for decreases in some crimes (F. J. Fowler & Mangione, 1986). But the crime preventive benefits of changes in layout appear to weaken as community mobilization wanes. (3) An early step in planning redesign to prevent crime is understanding offender location. For some offenses, such as auto theft,

offenders may come from other neighborhoods. For other offenses, such as drug dealing, offenders may live in the area. If they come primarily from outside the neighborhood, can residents readily distinguish between these potential predators and individuals who are in the neighborhood for legitimate purposes? If they can make the distinction, physical impediments to entry and circulation may result in less crimes committed by certain types of offenders. Under some conditions, restricting neighborhood entrances and making internal circulation patterns more difficult for outsiders should result in safer neighborhoods.

There are three important further caveats to such a circulation reduction approach. The limits cannot impair the ability of local public agencies to deliver services such as fire suppression, trash collection, and policing. In addition, the distinctions drawn between insiders and potential offenders from outside must have some empirical foundation and not be driven solely by residents' class- or ethnicity-based fears and concerns. Finally, these changes, even if they have an empirical foundation, can exacerbate between-neighborhood conflicts (Taylor, 2000a, chap. 8).

Of course such an implication needs to be tempered by the recognition that crime prevention is just one objective of land use planning. Other agendas such as economic development or equal housing opportunities may conflict at times with crime prevention or fear reduction goals.

Routine activities theory considers the confluence of potential victims or crime sites, potential offenders, and those who might prevent crime—natural guardians or site managers (Felson, 1995; Mazzerolle, Kadleck, & Roehl, 1998). At the site level this suggests the relevance of factors like surveillance opportunities and specific land uses likely to draw either potential offenders or potential victims, or both. So in a residential context, the nature, volume, and distribution of nonresidential land uses and the nature of associated local traffic patterns seem likely, from the routine activities perspective, to influence crime levels. Empirical work confirms this expectation. There are some nonresidential land uses, such as bars and schools, where crime will be higher (Roncek, 1981; Roncek & Bell, 1981; Roncek & Faggiani, 1985; Roncek & Maier, 1991; Roncek & Pravatiner, 1989). Sites like these are likely to be both crime generators and crime attractors. A crime generator generates lots of opportunities for crime as a byproduct of large volumes of pedestrian traffic—the potential victim flow is enhanced (Gardiner, 1976, p. 10). A crime attractor draws in lots of potential offenders because of the reputation of the site. Whether nonresidential land-uses that are not obviously crime generators or crime attractors cause higher or lower crime levels, however, appears to be less clear-cut and more contingent and will be addressed later.

In sum, at the site level we find numerous studies, many cross-sectional, and a few longitudinal, linking design and crime. At the community level we see very strong suggestions when considered cross-sectionally, and somewhat weaker confirmation when considered longitudinally, that reinforcing neighborhood boundaries may reduce crime rates. The two predominant theoretical perspectives affirming our chain of reasoning—situational crime prevention and behavioral geography—focus almost exclusively on the potential offenders movements, cognitions, and evaluations.

(3) Correct Depending on Certain Other Conditions

A third possible answer to our query is the economist's traditional favorite: It depends. The perspectives undergirding studies that generate this answer usually, in comparison to the rational perspectives described earlier: Pay greater attention to the behavioral and social dynamics of the users of the site or streetblock or community in question; and point out how offender cognitions and behaviors, user behaviors and cognitions, and physical and nonphysical features of the environment can be contingent upon one another in complex ways. The relevant theoretical models include territorial functioning, incivilities, informal social control, and others (for a detailed discussion of these perspectives see Taylor, in press). Here are some examples of contingent relationships.

- Recall from the previous discussion that nonresidential land uses such as bars and schools are usually associated with higher crime rates. The roles of such land uses in creating crime hot spots is well established (Taylor, 1998). But when we turn to other types of land uses more generally, it appears they may be associated with higher crime, or with lower crime, depending on other factors. A Canadian study found, as predicted by Jane Jacobs (1961) and her ideas about "eyes on the street," that crime was lower on mixed land use blocks if the streetblocks in

question were short (E. P. Fowler, 1987, 1992). But two U.S. studies, done in locations with varying length blocks, found nonresidential land use may weaken residents' ability to manage the street and deter criminal activity. In the first U.S. study, streetblock analyses in two cities—Baltimore and Philadelphia—confirmed strong connections between the relative dominance of nonresidential land use and assessed, on-site physical deterioration (Taylor, Koons, Kurtz, Greene, & Perkins, 1995). Blocks with more stores or small businesses or institutional uses, in a predominantly residential context, were more run down. It is not clear if this is a result of the higher foot traffic levels, lower levels of resident-based maintenance efforts as they withdraw, or both. In Baltimore this connection persisted even after controlling for status, race, and stability. In Philadelphia only one large neighborhood was included, Logan, but it was a racially mixed, lower-middle-income locale.

In the second study conducted solely in the Logan neighborhood, residents were surveyed about informal social control and territorial functioning. Results showed that nonresidential land use but not physical deterioration influenced residents' informal control and their willingness to call the police for assistance (Kurtz, Koons, & Taylor, 1998); more nonresidential land use went with more calls to police for social disturbances.

- Several authors, going back to the early 1970s, have described how physical deterioration in urban neighborhoods, often combined with disorderly behavior, can make residents fearful or even make a neighborhood go downhill or its crime rate increase. (For a review of these theoretical developments, see Taylor, 1999.) Several cross-sectional studies have looked at this connection (e.g., Brown & Perkins, 1992; Perkins, Florin, Rich, Wandersman, & Chavis, 1990; Perkins, Meeks, & Taylor, 1992). Only recently, however, have longitudinal, community-level data become available for examining the "grime causes crime" idea.

  The longitudinal data show that the grime-crime connection depends on two matters (Taylor, 2000a, chap. 5). How physical deterioration is measured determines whether initial grime levels, controlling for other neighborhood features, lead to later crime increases. Although the literature has presumed that asking residents "How much of a problem are vacant houses in your neighborhood?" would produce the same results as counting the vacant houses in the community, this presumption appears to be incorrect. A second contingency is the specific crime in question. Although the later incivilities theorists presume that physical incivilities will cause later increases in all violent street crimes, the longitudinal work showed that neither robbery nor rape were affected by earlier physical incivilities.

- Physical modifications to the residential setting suggesting resident involvement, care, or watchfulness can produce a safer setting (Brown, 1985; Brown & Altman, 1978, 1981). But the effectiveness of territorial signage may depend in part on the surrounding threat level; in more disorderly or dangerous settings redundant territorial cues may be needed to assure comparable safety (Brower, Dockett, & Taylor, 1983). One of the most empirically grounded models of territorial functioning explains in detail how connections between territorial functioning, such as physical changes initiated by residents or regular users, and social, psychological, and ecological outcomes are conditioned by the local socioeconomic, cultural, and social context (Taylor, 1988, chap. 5).

More examples could be supplied, but the main point here is that the design-crime linkage is conditioned by context. Elsewhere I have outlined how these contextual variations drive local microecological dynamics, that in turn moderate the design-crime connection (Taylor, 1997). Relevant contextual factors are numerous and include: stability of locale, socioeconomic levels, and dynamics in adjoining locales. But since too little research has been done systematically exploring connections between context and design-crime connections, the contingencies cannot be fully specified. "Substantial gaps still exist in the knowledge of how crime develops in specific contexts. . . . In part such gaps have developed from a lack of basic research examining the context of crime" (Weisburd, 1997, p. 13).

Suggesting the design-crime connections are sometimes contingent may prove troubling for decision makers. Policy planners far prefer the "one size fits all" approach when it comes to crime prevention (Rosenbaum, 1987, 1988). If the relationships are contingent, there is no point initiating design changes until one is assured the changes will have the intended positive impact. In other words, before deciding, from a practical perspective, where to try CPTED ideas, we must fully specify how context affects the design-crime link. We are currently unable to make such specifications because we know so little about which aspects of context influence the link, and why, and how design interacts with other nonphysical features of the setting to influence crime or victimization levels.

(4) ESSENTIALLY UNKNOWABLE

Understanding the design-crime link is essentially impossible if we mean by understanding: an ability to specify which community-level design features will influence which crimes in what situations because of what specific processual dynamics.

The answer is unknowable, if our unit of analysis is larger than the individual address or household, because the requisite number of longitudinal studies at the streetblock or community level would be extremely large and the scope of each study would be substantial; the costs associated with the requisite studies would verge on the astronomical; and the political difficulties surrounding each longitudinal intervention would be substantial and time-consuming.

We would need a large number of studies because we would need to implement each potential design change in a number of locations to obtain variation in surrounding contexts and sufficient statistical power. Even in the case of a simple examination of streetblock closures we would want at least 30 "treatment" sites and 30 "control" sites in each of several cities. Variation across cities is essential since political cultures around citizen involvement vary dramatically from city to city (Ferman, 1996), and these dynamics quite probably intertwine with design impacts (F. J. Fowler & Mangione, 1986).

It may be possible to "cross" different design changes in a single study and thus reduce the total number of studies needed. For example, a streetblock could receive either a closure or an increase in nonresidential landuses or both. But if we start adding different program elements to the study changes, we increase the number of sites needed in the study if we are to clarify the roles of context.

Further, it is not yet known what specific features of context are most likely to influence the design-crime relationship. As a preliminary step to be completed before initiating such studies, we need to delimit the most relevant contextual factors based on theories and findings in the field to date.

Some might counter that the increasing availability of crime maps and GISs using physical and crime data might reduce the cost of the needed studies. Although crime mapping and geographic information systems more generally are having an enormous impact on our abilities to analyze crime and identify crime patterns (Mazerolle, Bellucci, & Gajewski, 1996), we do not yet have widespread availability of site-level physical features, for entire cities, in geocoded databases. In addition, even were the latter widely available, studies linking geocoded crime data and geocoded physical environment data leave out crucial social, economic, and cultural variables that probably play big roles in both mediating and moderating (Baron & Kenny, 1986) the design-crime connections. So the proposed shortcuts will give us only partial answers.

CLOSING COMMENTS

The central question addressed here has been: Can we achieve crime prevention through environmental design? Researchers and policy makers have been studying this issue for over a quarter century and in several instances have acted on what they thought the answer to this question was. I have argued here that how you answer this question depends crucially on how you define key terms, how rigorous is the proof you demand, and how complete an answer you seek. If there is one thing we know it is that the design-crime connections are not simple but depend on other features of the site and the surround.

Unfortunately, policy makers have often insisted that the connections are simple. If we replace high-rise public housing communities with low rise ones crime will decrease, for example. Or, to take another example, at the time of this writing (June 2001), Philadelphia's Mayor John Street, in keeping with the current popularity of the "grime causes crime" idea, has launched an initiative to clean up 31,000 vacant lots in the city, proclaiming that such actions will help turn neighborhoods around. Although nearby residents certainly will enjoy the temporarily purified vacant lots, because this initiative is pursued without recognizing the complex connections between vacant lots and crime, it is likely to fail to provide any long-term benefits. Ethnographic work shows that these lots can serve local drug trade

activities (Simon & Burns, 1997). So it is important that local managers of these sites be put into place following the cleaning. But we also know that given residents' personal safety concerns in many of the lower income neighborhoods hosting such vacant lots, the residents are unlikely to assert control over the spaces unless the spaces are manageable and they have been authorized to manage the sites. Stated differently, the city needs to figure out how to transfer supervision of each site to the local block clubs, help develop those clubs as needed, provide secure enclosures for each site—fences and locking gates—so that legitimate place managers can control who has access to the sites, implement an incentive program that would reward residents' place management, and coordinate with public safety officials to respond quickly over lot conflicts that arise.

As viewers gather to watch fellow citizens gain fame and fortune, or fail in infamy on quiz shows like *Who Wants to Be a Millionaire* or *The Weakest Link*, the American landscape—city, suburban, and rural—is in the midst of profound physical transformations. In cities, planners are desperately trying to figure out how to remodel communities to accommodate lower neighborhood populations as many older cities continue to depopulate and vacant lots and vacant houses proliferate. City managers, often misunderstanding the person environment transactions relevant to these sites, have sometimes made foolish choices formulating policy responses. (For one case see Taylor 2000a, pp. 70–73.) Suburban locations, especially inner ring, older suburbs, are rapidly aging and deteriorating. And, at the suburban fringe, precious open space and farmland are being gobbled up by metropolitan sprawl. Sometimes jurisdictions, like Portland and the surrounding county, will initiate sweeping zoning changing so that suburban sprawl will be limited and in-city new housing will be dense to maximally use available city space. Across all three types of communities residents are bolting themselves inside more and more gated communities, believing they will be safer there. City depopulation, suburban aging, and metropolitan sprawl, as well as enclavization in all three types of settings, all imply dramatic physical changes in the locations where we live and work. It is imperative that we better understand design-crime connections so we can better plan for, respond to, and perhaps even strategically manage some of these processes.

REFERENCES

Anderson, D., & Pease, K. (1997). Biting back: From Kirkholt to Huddersfield, preventing repeat victimization. In R. V. Clarke (Ed.), *Situational crime prevention: Successful case studies* (2nd ed.). Albany, NY: Harrow & Heston.

Appleyard, D. (1981). *Livable streets.* Berkeley: University of California Press.

Atlas, R., & LeBlanc, W. (1994, October). Environmental barriers to crime. *Ergonomics in Design,* 9–16.

Barnes, G. S. (1995). Defining and optimizing displacement. In J. E. Eck & D. Weisburd (Eds.), *Crime and place* (pp. 95–114). Monsey, NY: Criminal Justice Press.

Baron, R. M., & Kenny, D. A. (1986). The moderator-mediator variable distinction in social psychological research: Conceptual, strategic and statistical considerations. *Journal of Personality and Social Psychology, 51,* 1173–1182.

Beavon, D. J. K., Brantingham, P. L., & Brantingham, P. J. (1994). The influence of street networks on the patterning of property offenses. In R. V. Clarke (Ed.), *Crime Prevention Studies* (Vol. 2, pp. 115–148). Monsey, NY: Willow Tree Press.

Bevis, C., & Nutter, J. B. (1977). *Changing street layouts to reduce residential burglary.* Paper presented at the annual meeting of the American Society of Criminology. Atlanta, Georgia. Minneapolis: Minnesota Crime Prevention Center.

Bible, D. S., & Hsieh, C. (2001). Gated communities and residential property values. *The Appraisal Journal, 69,* 140–146.

Blakely, E. J., & Snyder, M. G. (1997). *Fortress America: Gated communities in the United States.* Washington, DC: Brookings Institution Press.

Brantingham, P. L., & Brantingham, P. J. (1981). Notes on the geometry of crime. In P. L. Brantingham & P. J. Brantingham (Eds.), *Environmental criminology.* Beverly Hills, CA: Sage.

Bratton, W. (1998). *Turnaround.* New York: Random House.

Broady, M. (1972). Social theory in architectural design. In R. Gutman (Ed.), *People and buildings* (pp. 170–185). New York: Basic Books.

Brower, S., Dockett, K., & Taylor, R. B. (1983). Resident's perceptions of site-level features. *Environment and Behavior, 15,* 419–437.

Brown, B. B. (1985). Residential territories: Cues to burglary vulnerability. *Journal of Architectural Planning and Research, 2,* 231–243.

Brown, B. B., & Altman, I. (1978). Territoriality and residential burglary: A conceptual framework. In *Crime prevention through environmental design theory compendium.* Arlington, VA: Westinghouse.

Brown, B. B., & Altman, I. (1981). Territoriality and residential crime: A conceptual framework. In P. L. Brantingham & P. J. Brantingham (Eds.), *Environmental criminology.* Beverly Hills, CA: Sage.

Brown, B., & Perkins, D. (1992). Disruptions in place attachment. In I. Altman & S. Low (Eds.), *Place attachment* (pp. 279–304). New York: Plenum Press.

Clarke, R. V. (Ed.). (1992). *Situational crime prevention.* Albany, NY: Harrow & Heston.

Clarke, R. V. (1995). Situational crime prevention. In M. Tonry & D. Farrington (Eds.), *Building a safer society: Strategic approaches to crime prevention* (pp. 91–150). Chicago: University of Chicago Press.

Clarke, R. V., & Homel, R. (1997). A Revised classification of situational crime prevention techniques. In S. P. Lab (Ed.), *Crime prevention at a crossroads* (pp. 17–30). Cincinnati, OH: Anderson.

Clarke, R. V., & Weisburd, D. (1994). Diffusion of crime control benefits: Observations on the reverse of displacement. In R. V. Clarke (Ed.), *Crime prevention studies* (Vol. 2, pp. 165–184). Monsey, NY: Willow Tree Press.

Crowe, T. D. (1991). *Crime prevention through environmental design: Applications of architectural design and space management concepts.* London: Butterworth-Heinemann.

Donnelly, P., & Majka, T. J. (1996). Change, cohesion, and commitment in a diverse urban neighborhood. *Journal of Urban Affairs, 18,* 269–284.

Donnelly, P. G., & Majka, T. J. (1998). Residents' efforts at neighborhood stabilization: Facing the challenges of inner-city neighborhoods. *Sociological Forum, 13,* 189–214.

Eck, J. E., & Weisburd, D. (1995). Crime places in crime theory. In J. E. Eck & D. Weisburd (Eds.), *Crime Prevention Studies: Vol. 4. Crime and place* (p. 1034). Monsey, NY: Criminal Justice Press.

Felson, M. (1994). *Crime in everyday life.* Thousand Oaks, CA: Pine Forge Press.

Felson, M. (1995). Those who discourage crime. In J. E. Eck & D. Weisburd (Eds.), *Crime and place* (pp. 53–66). Monsey, NY: Criminal Justice Press.

Ferman, B. (1996). *Challenging the growth machine: Neighborhood politics in Chicago and Pittsburgh.* Lawrence: University Press of Kansas.

Forrest, R., & Kennett, P. (1997). Risk, residence and the post-Fordist city. *American Behavioral Scientist, 41,* 342–359.

Fowler, E. P. (1987). Street management and city design. *Social Forces, 66,* 365–389.

Fowler, E. P. (1992). *Building cities that work.* Montreal: McGill-Queens University Press.

Fowler, F. J., & Mangione, T. (1986). A Three pronged effort to reduce crime and fear of crime: The Hartford experiment. In D. Rosenbaum (Ed.), *Community crime prevention* (pp. 87–108). Newbury Park, CA: Sage.

Fowler, F., McCalla, M. E., & Mangione, T. (1979). *Reducing residential crime and fear: The Hartford neighborhood crime prevention program.* Washington, DC: U.S. Government Printing Office.

Frisbie, D. (1978). *Crime in Minneapolis.* Minneapolis: Minnesota Crime Prevention Center.

Gardiner, R. A. (1976). Crime and the neighborhood environment. *HUD Challenge.*

Garofalo, J. (1990). The National Crime Survey, 1973–1986: Strengths and limitations of a very large data set. In D. MacKenzie, P. Baunach, & R. Roberg (Eds.), *Measuring crime: Large scale, long range efforts* (pp. 75–96). Albany: State University of New York Press.

Green, L. (1995). Cleaning up drug hot spots in Oakland, California: The Displacement and diffusion effects. *Justice Quarterly, 12,* 737–754.

Greenberg, S. W., Williams, J. R., & Rohe, W. R. (1982). Safety in urban neighborhoods: A comparison of physical characteristics and informal territorial control in high and low crime neighborhoods. *Population and Environment, 5,* 141–165.

Hope, T. (1997). Inequality and the future of community crime prevention. In S. P. Lab (Ed.), *Crime prevention at a crossroads* (pp. 143–160). Cincinnati, OH: Anderson.

Jacobs, J. (1961). *The death and life of the American city.* New York: Vintage.

Kasarda, J. D. (1992). The severely distressed in economically transforming cities. In A. V. Harrell & G. E. Peterson (Eds.), *Drugs, crime and social isolation: Barriers to urban opportunity* (pp. 45–98). Washington, DC: Urban Institute Press.

Kellman, S. G. (2001, June 15). Who wants to be the weakest link? *Chronicle of Higher Education, 66,* B24.

Kohn, I. R., Franck, K. A., & Fox, A. S. (1975). *Defensible space modifications in row-house communities: A final report submitted to the National Science Foundation.* New York: The Institute for Community Design Analysis.

Kurtz, E., Koons, B., & Taylor, R. B. (1998). Land use, physical deterioration, resident-based control and calls for service on urban streetblocks. *Justice Quarterly, 15,* 121–149.

Lab, S. P. (1992). *Crime prevention: Approaches, practices and evaluations* (2nd ed.). Cincinnati, OH: Anderson.

Lab, S. P. (1997). Crime prevention: Where have we been and which way should we go? In S. P. Lab (Ed.), *Crime prevention at a crossroads* (pp. 1–17). Cincinnati, OH: Anderson.

La Vigne, N. (1996). Safe transport: Security by design on the Washington Metro. In R. V. Clarke (Ed.), *Crime prevention studies: Vol. 6. Preventing mass transit crime* (pp. 163–197). Monsey, NY: Criminal Justice Press.

Massey, D., & Denton, N. (1988). Suburbanization and segregation in U.S. metropolitan areas. *American Journal of Sociology, 94,* 592–626.

Massey, D., & Denton, S. (1993). *American apartheid: Segregation and the making of the underclass.* Cambridge, MA: Harvard University Press.

Mazerolle, L. G., Bellucci, C., & Gajewski, F. (1996, April). *Crime mapping in police departments: The challenges of building a mapping system.* Unpublished manuscript, University of Cincinnati, OH, Department of Criminal Justice.

Mazzerolle, L. G., Kadleck, C., & Roehl, J. (1998). Controlling drug and disorder problems: The Role of place managers. *Criminology, 36,* 371–404.

Merry, S. E. (1981). Defensible space undefended: Social factors in crime control through environmental design. *Urban Affairs Quarterly, 16,* 397–422.

Murray, C. (1995). The physical environment. In J. Q. Wilson & J. Petersilia (Eds.), *Crime* (pp. 349–362). San Francisco: Institute for Contemporary Studies.

Newman, O., & Franck, K. (1980). *Factors influencing crime and instability in urban housing developments.* Washington, DC: U.S. Government Printing Office.

Perkins, D. D., Florin, P., Rich, R. C., Wandersman, A., & Chavis, D. M. (1990). Participation and the social and physical environment of residential blocks: Crime and community context. *American Journal of Community Psychology, 18,* 83–115.

Perkins, D. D., Meeks, J. W., & Taylor, R. B. (1992). The physical environment of street blocks and resident perceptions of crime and disorder: Implications for theory and measurement. *Journal of Environmental Psychology, 12,* 21–34.

Popkin, S. J., Gwiasda, V. E., Olson, L. M., Rosenbaum, D. P., & Buron, L. (2000). *The hidden war: Crime and the tragedy of public housing in Chicago.* New Brunswick, NJ: Rutgers University Press.

Rapoport, A. (1977). *Human aspects of urban form.* New York: Pergamon Press.

Rengert, G. (1996). *The geography of illegal drugs.* Boulder, CO: Westview Press.

Rengert, G., & Wasilchick, J. (1985). *Suburban burglary.* Springfield, IL: Charles C. Thomas.

Roncek, D. W. (1981). Dangerous places: Crime and residential environment. *Social Forces, 60,* 74–96.

Roncek, D. W., & Bell, R. (1981). Bars, blocks and crime. *Journal of Environmental Systems, 11,* 35–47.

Roncek, D. W., & Faggiani, D. (1985). High schools and crime: A replication. *Sociological Quarterly, 26,* 491–505.

Roncek, D. W., & Maier, P. A. (1991). Bars, blocks, and crimes revisited: Linking the theory of routine activities to the empiricism of "hot spots." *Criminology, 29,* 725–753.

Roncek, D. W., & Pravatiner, M. A. (1989). Additional evidence that taverns enhance nearby crime. *Sociology and Social Research, 73,* 185–188.

Rosenbaum, D. P. (1987). The theory and research behind neighborhood watch: Is it a sound fear and crime reduction strategy? *Crime & Delinquency, 33,* 103–134.

Rosenbaum, D. P. (1988). A critical eye on neighborhood watch: Does it reduce crime and fear? In T. Hope & M. Shaw (Eds.), *Communities and crime reduction* (pp. 126–145). London: Her Majesty's Stationery Office.

Simon, D., & Burns, E. (1997). *The corner: A year in the life of an inner-city neighborhood.* New York: Broadway Books.

Skogan, W. G. (1976). Citizen reporting of crime: Some national panel data. *Criminology, 13,* 535–549.

Taylor, R. B. (1988). *Human territorial functioning.* Cambridge: Cambridge University Press.

Taylor, R. B. (1994). *Research methods in criminal justice.* New York: McGraw-Hill.

Taylor, R. B. (1997). Social order and disorder of streetblocks and neighborhoods: Ecology, microecology and the systemic model of social disorganization. *Journal of Research in Crime and Delinquency, 33,* 113–155.

Taylor, R. B. (1998). Crime in small scale places: What we know, what we can do about it. In *Research and Evaluation Conference 1997* (pp. 1–20). Washington, DC: National Institute of Justice.

Taylor, R. B. (1999). The incivilities thesis: Theory, measurement and policy. In R. L. Langworthy (Ed.), *Measuring what matters* (pp. 65–88). Washington, DC: National Institute of Justice, Office of Community Oriented Policing Services.

Taylor, R. B. (2000a). *Breaking away from broken windows: Evidence from Baltimore neighborhoods and the nationwide fight against crime, grime, fear and decline.* Boulder, CO: Westview Press.

Taylor, R. B. (2000b). Crime and human ecology. In R. Paternoster & R. Bachman (Eds.), *Explaining criminals and crime.* Los Angeles: Roxbury.

Taylor, R. B. (in press). Physical environment, crime, fear, and informal control. In J. Petersilia & J. Q. Wilson (Eds.), *Crime* (3rd ed.). Monterey, CA: Institute for Contemporary Studies.

Taylor, R. B., & Gottfredson, S. D. (1986). Environmental design, crime and prevention: An examination of community dynamics. In A. J. Reiss Jr. & M. Tonry (Eds.), *Communities and crime* (pp. 387–416). Chicago: University of Chicago Press.

Taylor, R. B., Gottfredson, S. D., & Brower, S. N. (1980). The defensibility of defensible space. In T. Hirschi & M. Gottfredson (Eds.), *Understanding crime.* Beverly Hills, CA: Sage.

Taylor, R. B., Gottfredson, S. D., & Brower, S. (1984). Understanding block crime and fear. *Journal of Research in Crime and Delinquency, 21,* 303–331.

Taylor, R. B., Koons, B., Kurtz, E., Greene, J., & Perkins, D. (1995). Streetblocks with more nonresidential landuse have more physical deterioration: Evidence from Baltimore and Philadelphia. *Urban Affairs Review, 30,* 120–136.

Tienda, M. (1991). Poor people in poor places: Deciphering neighborhood effects on poverty outcomes. In J. Huber (Ed.), *Macro-micro linkages in sociology* (pp. 244–262). Newbury Park, CA: Sage.

Venkatesh, S. A. (2000). *American project.* Cambridge: Harvard University Press.

Weisburd, D. (1997). Reorienting crime prevention research and policy: From the causes of criminality to the context of crime (Research Rep. No. NCJ165041). Washington, DC: National Institute of Justice.

White, G. F. (1990). Neighborhood permeability and burglary rates. *Justice Quarterly, 7,* 57–68.

Wilson, W. J. (1996). *When work disappears: The world of the new urban poor.* New York: Knopf.

Wilson-Doenges, G. (2000). An exploration of sense of community and fear of crime in gated communities. *Environment and Behavior, 32,* 597–612.

Wolfe, T. (1981). *From Bauhaus to our house.* New York: Farrar, Straus & Giroux.

Ycaza, C. (1992, May 17). Crime rate drops in Shores. *Miami Herald.*

Zeisel, J. (1981). *Inquiry by design.* Monterey, CA: Brooks/Cole.

CHAPTER 28

Wayfinding: A Broad View

JANET R. CARPMAN and MYRON A. GRANT

WAYFINDING—HOW LIVING ORGANISMS make their way from an origin to a destination and back—is an issue in which environment and behavior are indisputably intertwined. This chapter focuses on human wayfinding and its flip side, disorientation, which is a widespread problem in many environments—interior and exterior, large and small. Long a topic of interest to environmental psychologists, in the past few years wayfinding has been adopted, at least as a buzzword, by organizational administrators and facility managers as well as by graphic designers and architects, yet it is still narrowly and incompletely understood by each discipline.

This chapter, written from the vantage point of long-time interdisciplinary wayfinding consultants, seeks to broaden the view of wayfinding held by environmental psychologists. If design and behavior professionals are to play a role in improving wayfinding ease in a variety of settings, wayfinding needs to be conceived as a macro issue involving the physical and operational environments in which it occurs, rather than being understood as something dealing only with individual perception, cognition, and behavior.

WHAT IS WAYFINDING?

Wayfinding is behavior. Successful wayfinding involves knowing where you are, knowing your destination, knowing and following the best route (or at least a serviceable route) to your destination, being able to recognize your destination upon arrival, and reversing the process to find your way back out (Carpman & Grant, 1993). Wayfinding is not synonymous with "signage" as is often mistakenly thought

in the design fields, where sign fabrication firms advertise "Today's wayfinding solution" (Slatz, 1988).

Defining wayfinding is one thing, explaining it is another. Other definitions, such as Passini's (1984b), begin to describe the hierarchical series of decisions people make as they go about finding their way. Other writers and theorists explore the associated cognitive and perceptual processes in detail (see, for example, Golledge, 1999). Our approach views successful wayfinding as an outgrowth of a "wayfinding system": a combination of behavior, operations, and design (Weisman, 1982). This key idea of a wayfinding system will be discussed later in the chapter.

IMPORTANCE OF WAYFINDING EASE AND COSTS OF DISORIENTATION

One of the ironies present in the many relationships between the physical environment and human behavior is the seeming invisibility of environmental features well suited to users' needs; when there is a good "fit," most people don't notice. In this case, when users are able to find their way with ease, wayfinding is probably not even considered. However, when users become disoriented, negative aspects of the issue become apparent and wayfinding takes on more importance.

Disorientation has a number of costs. Not knowing where you are or how to get where you need to go is usually stressful and frustrating, resulting in negative physical and psychological effects. People may hyperventilate while running to catch a plane, because they can't find the right airport concourse;

feel their blood pressure rise as they think about the consequences of not finding the room for an important meeting; or exhaust themselves by walking long distances inside hospitals as a result of illogical room numbering. They may think less of themselves for not being able to find their way (Packard, 1994), or they may focus their anger on the organization or facility that has failed to provide necessary wayfinding aids like a logical corridor system or up-to-date signs.

Serious consequences can result from people being unable to find their way around complex places. They can be late for appointments, business meetings, planes, presentations, classes, or other important occurrences; resulting in loss of face, time, opportunities, and money. Wayfinding confusion in shopping malls, museums, and convention centers may cause visitors to fail to find the places they are seeking and to be unaware that other interesting destinations even exist (Carpman & Grant, 2001). Disorientation can even be deadly, as sobering news stories demonstrate: Some heart attack victims in Washington, D.C., arrived at local emergency rooms (ERs) too late to be helped when their ambulance drivers couldn't find their way (DeParle, 1989); several unlucky British tourists visiting Miami, Florida, became lost in a high-crime neighborhood and were shot when they asked directions ("Two British Tourists," 1991); a Texas man having an asthma attack died while searching for the Emergency Room in an out-of-state hospital (Tom Plastaras, personal communication, February 1992); and a young American teenager visiting Israel died of sunstroke after getting lost during a hike in the Judean Desert ("American Teen," 2000).

Disorientation is a problem for organizations, too. Lost late patients can disrupt hospital schedules, potential customers may avoid confusing shopping malls, and disoriented museum patrons may opt not to return. Staff at confusing facilities often spend considerable expensive, nonproductive time directing and escorting people to and from destinations (Zimring, 1990).

WAYFINDING PERSPECTIVES OF USERS, STAFF, ADMINISTRATORS

Though architects, interior designers, and graphic designers often make decisions that affect wayfinding ease and environmental psychologists study how the process of wayfinding occurs, three groups deal directly with the wayfinding outcomes in facilities: users, staff, and administrators. Their observations

and requests demonstrate that wayfinding needs to be understood as a complex issue. The following quotes and summaries are taken from several of the authors' unpublished wayfinding studies in health facilities, art museums, and educational facilities.

USERS

Unfamiliar users of complex facilities, those who are most likely to have trouble finding their way around, tend not to mince words when asked about wayfinding. While seeing it in the context of their own particular experience, it is obvious to them that wayfinding is important:

- *Being lost wastes time.*
  There might be something that has to be done right away; you can't wander around needlessly. I will not go to certain hospitals that I have found difficult to get around in.
- *Being lost is stressful.*
  If you're in a hospital, you're not usually there for a nice reason. You're nervous and your faculties aren't working right. You can't always pay attention.
- *Being lost is frustrating.*
  There's nothing more frustrating than wandering around a building for 15 minutes, not knowing where you're going or not finding someone to ask.
- *We expect organizations to help us find our way, and they often let us down.*
  I've noticed that when you follow signs, they lead you to the wrong place. There is often construction and no access. When someone gives you directions they say, "Turn right at the elevator," and there may be more than one elevator.

Users also need specific directions; including the best route, building name, parking location, building entrance, destination name, floor number, room number, elevator name or number, and stair name or number. They expect legible signs, accurate answers to their directional questions, and environmental features that differentiate one location from another (Carpman & Grant, 1997).

STAFF

Wayfinding is also a concern for those who work in complex facilities and outdoor environments. Not only do they need to find their own way around, they are also expected to assist and direct unfamiliar users. But confusing places can lead staff as well as visitors to become disoriented. Such disorientation causes them to lose face and become embarrassed when they are unable to direct visitors, and it can detract from their abilities to do their jobs:

- *We want to appear competent.*
  I was asked to take a patient over to a doctor's office in the Dillon Building. I took the elevators in this building, and I thought you could just walk straight across on the same floor, but you can't. This patient said, "Do you know where we're going?" And I said, "Oh yes we're going to get there." And then finally, I asked. It was kind of embarrassing for an employee to have to ask a question in front of a patient.
- *We want to be able to do our jobs.*
  I work in the STAT Lab, where we're supposed to give instant reports, and we have a real hard time finding patients. I'm still trying to figure out, standing in the Lab, where North, South, East, and West are. When you see 2 N on a label, you say, "Well let's see, is that 2100, 2200, 2300—what way am I facing?" It definitely slows us down and doesn't give us the information we need. We need room numbers. If we have room numbers we can find the floor.

Other wayfinding needs of staff include having initial and ongoing orientation to their ever changing physical environments, training in how to effectively give directions, information about wayfinding-related changes (where departments have moved, knowing which places have changed names, etc.), and knowledge about how to access up-to-date wayfinding information (Carpman & Grant, 1997).

ADMINISTRATORS

User and staff disorientation can cause administrative headaches. Administrators want to care for the customers they already have while attracting new customers and avoiding wayfinding problems.

- *Wayfinding ease is part of caring for users.*
  You want to make it as easy as possible so they don't have additional stress. If you're going to have a biopsy you are already up-tight about what it is, what it is going to be, and you can't even find where you are supposed to go to have

it done. I mean it's really tough on people. We've got to figure some way to make it better.
- *Wayfinding ease helps our organization market its facilities & services.*
  The object of the game is customer satisfaction, and if your customers aren't satisfied, they're going to go somewhere else. There are people who, if it made their life that difficult, they would go somewhere else where it was easier to find their way around.
- *Customer disorientation results in specific problems.*
  Deliveries can be somewhat sticky since the Ceramics Department has no sign. So unless they know where they are going or someone has given them pretty clear instructions, they can get lost easily. And there are several unidentified entrances to each building, so there is really no clue as to what door you need to use.

Wayfinding is often a "catalyst" issue for administrators, one that brings other organizational issues into focus, such as mission definition differences or staff discontent.

WAYFINDING LITERATURE

As a phenomenon affecting almost everyone, wayfinding is not only studied and written about by various academic disciplines and professions, it is also covered by the mass media. The popular press literature, design literature, and environmental psychology literature each offer differing perspectives.

POPULAR PRESS LITERATURE

People's inabilities to successfully negotiate both interior and exterior environments are widely documented in the popular press, including newspapers, magazines, and on the Internet (Carpman & Grant, 2001). Cartoons about getting lost, such as one featuring an angry-looking female passenger listening to a male driver saying "We have to be missing 24 hours before I consider us lost" (Cotham, 1998) appear regularly in the *New Yorker* magazine and other publications. Feature articles with lighthearted titles such as "Which Way Is Up? For Some It's Hard to Tell" (Packard, 1994) often describe the writer's struggle to find his or her way (Jordan, 1993; Pogrebin, 1998):

Getting lost for me comes in two basic forms: in a vehicle and on foot. In a vehicle I'm lost if N154, the route I am looking for, keeps appearing on road signs as C13871; on foot I'm lost if the Romanesque cloister I'm seeking out has pyramidal pagodalike stories. (Packard, 1994)

Other articles describe the wayfinding travails of celebrities, like golf pros who can't seem to find the next hole ("Way Off Course," 1985), or like former opera diva Beverly Sills, who, even after working there for 30 years, can't find her way around Lincoln Center (Blumenthal, 1996). Newspapers and magazines report on confusing subway station terminology (Feaver, 1978), indecipherable street names (Pearlman, 2000), blunders made when asking directions (Wetherell, 1990), and building types, like airports, that seem to regularly cause passenger disorientation (O'Brian, 1995). New wayfinding technology, like global positioning system (GPS) devices, has spawned much popular press coverage (for example, Hendrix, 1999; see also the chapter by Golledge in this handbook).

The anecdotal nature of much of this literature is both its strength and its weakness. More than almost any other environment behavior issue, wayfinding has found regular coverage in the American popular press, lending it familiarity as a widespread problem and demonstrating its multidimensionality. From this literature, we learn that disorientation is not limited to any one facility type. People lose their way indoors and outdoors, in large and small spaces, in complex and simple environments including hospitals and medical centers; colleges and universities; hotels; elementary, middle, and high schools; transit stations; shopping centers; sports complexes; expressways; office buildings; apartment complexes; and the like. It is also apparent that disorientation doesn't discriminate by age, sex, profession, or degree of fame. Most people become lost or disoriented at one time or another. However, since most popular-press wayfinding articles report on personal experiences, we really don't know how many people are "directionally challenged" or if feature writers are disproportionally represented among their ranks. We also don't get reports of environments where people *can* find their way with ease or particular wayfinding components, like you-are-here maps, that are well designed.

DESIGN LITERATURE

Designers write about wayfinding differently than do popular press writers. Articles written by or about architects and graphic designers tend to focus on showcasing wayfinding design "solutions" or approaches or featuring certain projects, building types, or designers (Finke, 1990; *Signs of the Times,* 1987). This literature is also usually anecdotal but less benignly so than popular press articles, since uncritical readers may not understand its subjectivity or question its constructs, assumptions, evaluation criteria, methodologies, or conclusions. The mere fact of being published lends these pieces and their subjects more credibility than they may merit.

ENVIRONMENTAL PSYCHOLOGY LITERATURE

Wayfinding theory and research have been explored in a large and growing body of environmental psychology literature. The following references, while only a tiny fraction of available sources, give a taste for the topics covered. As with other subjects discussed in this handbook, wayfinding is relevant to many different fields and perspectives, and the literature reflects this.[1] It is somewhat difficult, therefore, to grasp its full depth and breadth without considerable study.

The field does appear to be characterized, at least grossly, by a distinction between the interests of academics and practitioners. Some academics explore issues of how humans (and animals) perceive and "know" the environment (including developing "cognitive maps") and the detailed processes by which they are able to move from here to there and back again (Antes, McBride, & Collins, 1988; Golledge, 1999; Kaplan, 1978; Kuipers, 1982; Stea, 1974; Taylor & Tversky, 1996). Some theorize about the process of wayfinding itself (Blades, 1991; Passini, 1980b, 1984b), while others propose methodologies for analyzing wayfinding legibility within built environments (Peponis, Zimring, & Choi, 1990; O'Neill, 1991a, 1991b). Some researchers conduct experiments to test the usefulness of one wayfinding strategy over another (Vanetti & Allen, 1988). Others conduct research on the influence of environmental features, such as building configuration, on wayfinding (Dogu & Erkip, 2000; Moeser, 1988). Some researchers specialize in studies of wayfinding by particular age or gender groups (Blades & Spencer, 1994; Brown, Lahar, & Mosley, 1998; Devlin &

---

[1] Wayfinding is relevant to many fields including cognitive psychology, linguistics, graphic design, architecture, interior design, landscape architecture, site planning, urban planning, organizational behavior, facilities management, and marketing.

Bernstein, 1995; Foreman & Gillett, 1997; Heth, Cornell, & Albets, 1997; Kirasic & Mathes, 1990; Landau, 1986; Lawton, Charleston, & Zieles, 1996; Lawton & Morrin, 1999; Okabe, Aoki, & Hamamoto, 1986; Ward, Newcombe, & Overton, 1986), while others focus on wayfinding by those with physical limitations including vision impairments (Jacobson, 1998).

Applied researchers conduct postoccupancy evaluation (POE)-type studies in which wayfinding arises as an unexpected problem within buildings, or they examine wayfinding issues in detail within particular buildings (Brown, Wright, & Brown, 1997; Butler, Acquino, Hissong, & Scott, 1993; Olsen & Pershing, 1981; Passini, 1980b; Sanoff, 1999; Uzzell & Keaty, 1993). Others focus on examining the effectiveness of wayfinding aids, like maps and signs (Carpman, Grant, & Simmons, 1983–1984, 1985a, 1985b; Devlin & Bernstein, 1997; Kovach, Surrette, & Aamodt, 1988; Levine, Marchon, & Hanley, 1984; Talbot, Kaplan, Kuo, & Kaplan, 1993). Some practitioners publish applications of wayfinding theory and research in the form of wayfinding design guidelines (Carpman & Grant, 1993; Monahan, 1990).

A WAYFINDING *SYSTEM*

An important way for environmental psychologists to broaden their view of human wayfinding is to see it as a multidimensional, interconnected system involving behavior as well as environmental design and organizational policies and practices (Weisman, 1982). Each of these components is rich with activity, yet none is well researched or well documented.

BEHAVIORAL ELEMENTS

Wayfinding behavior is the outward manifestation of a host of complex cognitive and perceptual processes, as well as something rooted in people's own abilities and experiences. Such behavior may or may not help them get from point A to point B. Certain wayfinding *skills* are needed: asking and remembering directions, following a variety of signs (including highway identification signs, exterior directional signs, street identification signs, facility identification signs, parking structure or parking lot signs) and landmarks, comprehending special terminology, making sense of the layout of the place they're visiting, and reading handheld maps and/or you-are-here maps (Carpman & Grant, 2001).

Although there are a number of different approaches to finding one's way and individuals may change their own approaches depending on the situation, four wayfinding strategies or styles have been suggested (Weisman, 1982). The first strategy involves seeing one's destination and moving steadily toward it. This tends to be a more useful strategy outdoors than indoors, although views through buildings can help make interior wayfinding easier. The second wayfinding strategy involves following a path that leads to a destination. "Continuous cuing devices," such as colored floor lines have been used with mixed results to enable people to use this strategy in particularly large, complex places like hospitals. Such devices can work only when they lead to a very limited number of destinations. Otherwise, sensory overload is likely. The third strategy uses environmental elements, like signs and landmarks, to provide information along the way. These elements can supply reassurance that a person is on the right track and help clarify choices when decisions need to be made. The fourth strategy involves forming and using a mental image or cognitive map of the environment at hand. This means that someone has an understanding of how one place is spatially related to another place. It implies that she or he can use this understanding creatively to find alternative or more efficient ways of moving from one place to another (Carpman, 1991).

DESIGN ELEMENTS

A wide variety of environmental design elements can contribute to wayfinding ease or can lead to disorientation. Wayfinding design features like the following ones need to be carefully selected and legibly designed, act to support other wayfinding elements, and provide accurate and consistent information (Carpman, 1991):

- *Facility layout.* Components of layout that will affect wayfinding ease include the relationship of the main entrance to vehicular arrival and the parking area exit, relationships between common destinations ("functional adjacencies"), locations of elevators and stairways, and views to the outside.
- *Architectural and interior design differentiation.* It is much easier for people to tell where they are, on a campus or within a facility, if various areas do not look exactly alike. (See Figure 28.1.)
- *Landmarks.* Artwork is one type of interior and exterior landmark that can serve two purposes:

Figure 28.1 The numerous buildings at this medical center are so close together and are designed to look so much alike, that it is almost impossible to tell one from another or to single out a unique destination.

Figure 28.3 This exterior identification sign directs people to key destinations as well as marking a gateway to the facility.

beautifying the environment while giving people something to notice as they move in one direction and something to remember as they make their way back. (See Figure 28.2.)

- *Signs.* Signs are needed at "decision points" and at other places where people want to know where they are or how to reach their destination. Types of signs include directional signs, identification signs, and information signs. Sign design features such as sign placement, type style, type size, horizontal or vertical word orientation, spelling and punctuation, arrow design, contrast between copy and background, use of symbols, materials, and so forth can add to or detract from sign legibility. (See Figure 28.3.)

- *Maps.* Both handheld maps and fixed you-are-here maps must be designed to be useful to unfamiliar visitors. Clear, consistent information rendered in the simplest possible ways will help provide necessary details without overwhelming users.

- *Lighting.* If interior and exterior signs, landmarks, and decision points are well lit, they will add to users' wayfinding ease.

OPERATIONAL ELEMENTS

Neither wayfinding ease nor disorientation happen automatically. Organizations responsible for buildings and grounds make decisions that directly affect the ability of unfamiliar users to find their way. Organizations can make these decisions in a proactive way, they can react to wayfinding difficulties and try to fix problems as they arise, or they can take no responsibility at all and hope these issues will take care of themselves. While the first approach is obviously the most desirable, it involves committing precious resources of time, money, and staffing. Some of the most important operational areas where organizations can improve wayfinding ease for their staff and visitors include:

Figure 28.2 Unusual architectural features can act as wayfinding landmarks.

- *Terminology.* Many organizations have their own jargon, which is typically incomprehensible to outsiders like unfamiliar visitors. Add in abbreviations, acronyms, euphemisms, or proper names, and you have a recipe for confusion.
- *Wayfinding staff training.* Organizations need to teach staff how to find their own way around a complex facility so they can perform their jobs more efficiently. It is also helpful to give some training in direction giving, since staff are frequently asked for directions in complex facilities.
- *Previsit information.* Giving visitors accurate, consistent, useful information about where they need to go and how to get there is an important service complex facilities can offer their users. Such information may be conveyed in mailings, on Web sites, by phone, in written brochures, or in person.
- *Wayfinding system maintenance.* Many facilities like hospitals, shopping malls, and schools operate in an environment of almost constant change. Wayfinding system elements like signs and maps need to be capable of changing quickly and easily. Since almost no one can memorize every change in location or room numbering, staff need to be able to know how to access the latest wayfinding information.

OBSTACLES TO WAYFINDING EASE

Thinking about wayfinding as a system renders obstacles to wayfinding ease more identifiable. Rather than making disorientation seem like an unsolvable unilateral problem or seeing it as one-dimensional when it is really multidimensional, this three-way framework allows researchers and practitioners to carefully tease out wayfinding difficulties plaguing various organizations and facilities, and to make practical, interconnected recommendations for improvements.

BEHAVIORAL OBSTACLES AND "SENSE" OF DIRECTION

One's ability to navigate outdoor and indoor environments is usually called a "sense of direction." This sense, like a sense of humor or a sense of style, is different from the five human senses usually present at birth. A sense of direction is usually developed with practice, over time, and with attention to where one is in space and the relative locations of important destinations. There are considerable differences in people's senses of direction; some people always seem to know where they are and how to find their way using unfamiliar routes. These people can navigate in foreign countries when visiting for the first time. They are not stymied by detours or grids of one-way streets. They often use cardinal directions to describe locations. Other people, who berate themselves for being "directionally challenged," often cannot find their way even to familiar places. They become confused when trying to reverse automobile routes. They panic at the thought of navigating in a strange place (Carpman & Grant, 2001).

People with such chronic wayfinding difficulties are likely to lose their way even in well-designed environments. If their wayfinding skills (such as interpreting signs and reading maps) are not well developed, operational aspects of the wayfinding system need to help them compensate. For example, good "previsit information" will inform them about the location of their destination, valet parking will eliminate their need to negotiate potentially confusing parking structures, and escorts will not only lead them where they need to go but also be available to guide them back out.

DESIGN OBSTACLES

Design obstacles to wayfinding ease are often obvious. For instance, office buildings with circular or undifferentiated corridors, university complexes with indistinguishable buildings, or signs that blend into their surrounding environments, all make it difficult to tell where you are and how to get where you need to go. However, these examples of disorienting design result from faulty design *processes*. Both design processes and design features can act as obstacles to wayfinding ease. (See Figure 28.4.)

Some Design Process Obstacles to Wayfinding Ease

- *Not considering wayfinding as a high priority issue.* With so many other issues to consider and balance, designers and clients may relegate wayfinding to a low-status concern. Sometimes, it is only attended to by special request.
- *Not understanding relationships between design and wayfinding.* Unless they seek it out on their own, designers may not have been exposed to

Figure 28.4 One wayfinding-related design obstacle in this children's hospital is the lack of an obvious main entrance, as viewed from the parking area.

information about wayfinding and design. Wayfinding issues are rarely covered in depth in architecture and interior design programs, and they are infrequently considered as worthy of comment or awards in design publications.

- *Not conducting wayfinding design reviews. Wayfinding design review* means studying design and planning documents from a behavioral perspective to evaluate how well the proposed design scheme will accommodate users' wayfinding needs (Carpman & Grant, 2000). If existing schemes work well, nothing more is needed. If not, recommendations for change are made, changes occur, and the scheme is reviewed again. (See Figure 28.5.) It is most useful for reviewers to be wayfinding specialists,

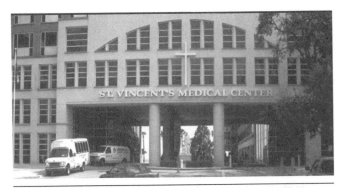

Figure 28.5 If design reviewers had seen the plans to use white sign letters on a white background, they would have recommended that contrasting color letters be used instead, in order to make this identification sign more legible during the day.

working independently from the design firms involved (see Case Study No. 2).

- *Being worried that wayfinding will "interfere" with design.* Sometimes designers see wayfinding elements as something that will detract from their design scheme. For instance, identification signage might be thought to mar the facade of a medical building, or directional signage might be thought to deface the inside of an art museum.

- *Considering wayfinding only as a signage issue.* If designers and clients don't understand that wayfinding has implications for every aspect of design, including urban planning, site planning, landscape design, architecture, interior design, and graphic design (as well as having many operational tie-ins), they may not consider it until the end of a project, when opportunities for optimum wayfinding design has been lost and when they will (unrealistically) expect all wayfinding problems to be solved by signs. Instead, wayfinding needs to be considered from the earliest stages of a design and planning project (during programming and schematic design) and throughout all its phases.

Some Design Obstacles to Wayfinding Ease

- *On-site exterior spaces*
  — Main building entrances not in view from the vehicular entrance to the site
  — Main building entrances not in view from related parking areas
  — Major buildings or building entrances not clearly identified
  — Not providing vehicular and pedestrian directional signs at appropriate decision points
  — Allowing landscaping to block views to important signs and entrances (See Figure 28.6.)

- *Interior spaces*
  — Not making places within a facility look unique
  — Connecting corridors at acute or obtuse angles (See Figure 28.7.)
  — Not providing lighting that will adequately illuminate intersections, entrances to major destinations, signage (overhead and wall mounted), and landmarks
  — Not providing appropriate wayfinding information at major building entrances and in elevator lobbies

Figure 28.6 Vegetation blocks views to this health facility's main parking structure and its entrance.

- *Signage*
  — Not making signage easy to read from appropriate distances
  — Not providing signs at decision points
  — Not placing signs perpendicular to the flow of vehicular and pedestrian traffic
  — Not designing signs to be noticeable within their environments

OPERATIONAL OBSTACLES

Operational decisions can impede wayfinding ease. For example, placing inexperienced volunteers at a museum information desk where they will need to answer directional questions, choosing to call a

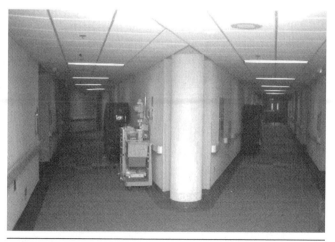

Figure 28.7 When corridors go off in odd directions, people are more likely to become disoriented than if corridors connect at right angles.

hospital admissions department by the ambiguous term "Patient Access Center," or not updating convention center maps even though they contain outdated information, all will lead to confusion. Again, it is important to understand operational decision-making *process* problems as well as problems with operational decisions themselves.

Some Operational Process Obstacles to Wayfinding Ease

- *Not being knowledgeable about codes and other sign-related governmental restrictions and requirements.* The sign portion of wayfinding implementation projects can become mired in red tape and radically changed from its original intent as a result of various regulations and need for official approvals. Being aware of these regulations and approval bodies early in the process will save time and money and reduce frustration (Sternlieb & Bairstow, 2000).

- *Not understanding the relationship between wayfinding ease and customer service.* Assisting unfamiliar people in finding the facility, locating parking, identifying the appropriate entrance, finding their destinations, and exiting with ease is all part of treating customers well. The frustration and anger that can result when customers became lost or disoriented reflect poorly on the whole organization and can be avoided.

- *Underestimating the need for wayfinding expertise.* Encouraged by organizations to take on wayfinding-related responsibilities, many staff come to think of themselves as wayfinding experts. Wayfinding decisions are often made by committees or by individuals without training or previous exposure to the issue. Some organizations incorrectly assume that all architects are highly knowledgeable about wayfinding and rely on them exclusively for wayfinding advice as well as sign and map design.

- *Underestimating the need for internal wayfinding leadership.* It is tempting for managers to think wayfinding problems can be completely solved by buying new signs. On the contrary, a wayfinding system includes much more than signs; it needs to be carefully planned with input from managers and staff and managed in a proactive way. Wayfinding leadership in the form of verbal, political, and financial support needs to emanate from the top officers in order to be felt throughout the organization.

- *Underestimating the long-term need for wayfinding system support.* With all of the pressing issues facing many organizations, it is tempting to want to deal with and dispose of each in turn. Unlike other issues, wayfinding is not trendy, time limited, nor able to be improved on only a temporary basis. Like many other facility infrastructure systems, such as air handling or communications, a healthy wayfinding system takes ongoing maintenance and updating of existing design elements, evaluation and improvement of operational elements, as well as both political and financial support.

- *Underestimating the importance of wayfinding system details.* As with other aspects of design and planning, "God is in the details" of wayfinding. Although it may seem time-consuming, for example, to mock up signs using different type faces and type sizes, it is important that resulting signs be legible. Though it takes time to review lengthy sign message schedules and mysterious-looking lighting-related and landscape-related wayfinding plans, it is important to make the most effective decisions possible.

Some Operational Obstacles to Wayfinding Ease

- *Confusing terminology.* Reserving certain lanes of an expressway for "HOV" vehicles, advising airport passengers to meet on the "North Concourse," or telling a hospital patient that her room will be cleaned by "Environmental Services," all may leave users scratching their heads. Part of finding your way is understanding the meaning of destination names and landmarks. When, for various reasons, organizations choose identifying terms that are mysterious or confusing, disorientation is more likely. (See Figure 28.8.)

- *Staff who don't know their own way around and who can't give good directions.* Orientation doesn't happen by osmosis. Staff who begin work at a large complex university, a sprawling hotel, or a gargantuan convention center don't know how to find their way around unless they are trained in how to do so. Such training takes time and can't occur in a single whirlwind tour. Since most people give directions that are either too short and devoid of critical information or too long and detail filled, staff also

Figure 28.8 Some terms, like the one shown here, create confusion by their lack of specificity.

need to be trained in how to give useful, concise directions.

- *Signs and maps that aren't kept up to date.* People expect signs and maps to contain correct, up-to-date information, and they get angry when maps direct them to destinations that have long since moved, or signs cause them to walk great distances in the wrong direction. Organizations need to periodically check messages on signs and copy on maps for accuracy and consistency and make updates as needed. (See Figure 28.9.)

- *Inconsistent or incorrect directions given to visitors.* It's difficult for people to find their way when they don't know where they need to go. For unfamiliar visitors as well as for those who are truly directionally challenged, traveling to a

Figure 28.9 When signs aren't kept up to date, users will take it upon themselves to fix them, sometimes with unaesthetic-looking results.

concert across town, a sports arena in another city, or even to a new local shopping center can be fraught with difficulties. At a minimum, "Pre-Visit Information" needs to contain accurate, useful, concise directions to the destination as well as details about where to park, where to enter, and where to go once inside.

USEFULNESS OF A BROAD VIEW OF WAYFINDING

The payoff of having a multidimensional view of wayfinding is being able to understand and solve existing wayfinding problems and avoid new ones. The following description of three general wayfinding problems at one large medical center shows recommendations for implementing various interconnected wayfinding design and operational elements.[2] In no case could a single wayfinding element solve the medical center's wayfinding problems: a wayfinding system approach was required.

MEDICAL CENTER WAYFINDING PROBLEM NO. 1:
MANY PATIENTS AND VISITORS ARE DISORIENTED

Design Recommendations

- Provide effective interior directional and identification signs.
- Enhance the appearance of the hospital and outpatient-building main entrances to look obvious.
- Enhance the appearance of the hospital's "functional" main entrance (from the parking garage) so that it looks obvious. (See Figure 28.10.)
- Provide well-designed, appropriately located interior you-are-here maps.

Operational Recommendations

- Train staff and volunteers to give accurate, useful directions to and around the medical center.
- Ensure that information desks at major entrances are staffed at all times when patients and visitors enter.

Figure 28.10 This photo shows a hospital's "functional" main entrance: the way visitors enter the hospital after parking in the adjacent structure, which is not nearly as attractive or noticeable as its formal main entrance.

- Assign oversight of the wayfinding system to a wayfinding manager.

MEDICAL CENTER WAYFINDING PROBLEM NO. 2:
MANY EXTERIOR AND INTERIOR DIRECTIONAL SIGNS
ARE INCOMPLETE, INCONSISTENT, HARD TO SEE,
CONFUSING, OR ABSENT

Design Recommendations

- Follow recommended guidelines for clear sign design (concerning sign size and placement, type style and type size, arrow design, organization of messages, etc.).
- Provide effective vehicular directional signs at all important decision points around the medical center.
- Provide effective institutional, building, and entrance identification signs.
- Improve directional and identification signage within the parking garages.
- Prune trees and shrubs to permit unobstructed views to building entrance areas and signs.
- Provide interior and exterior wayfinding-related lighting improvements.

Operational Recommendations

- Consider terminology changes.
- Provide ongoing wayfinding system maintenance.

---

[2] Although behavior needs to be considered as part of a wayfinding system approach, institutions generally do not have the interest, time, or resources to teach wayfinding skills to directionally challenged people. Instead, institutions must focus on improving both wayfinding design and operations.

Figure 28.11 Well-designed "You-Are-Here" maps enable people to easily find their own location in space and determine how they need to proceed to their destination.

MEDICAL CENTER WAYFINDING PROBLEM NO. 3: SOME STAFF ARE UNABLE TO GIVE CLEAR DIRECTIONS AND COMPENSATE BY ESCORTING PATIENTS AND VISITORS TO THEIR DESTINATIONS

Design Recommendations

- Improve interior and exterior signage.
- Provide well-designed handheld maps and you-are-here maps. (See Figure 28.11.)

Operational Recommendations

- Provide special training sessions for staff and volunteer information givers, including phone operators.
- Provide standardized written directions to major destinations.
- Provide wayfinding "help" phones.
- Consider instituting a volunteer escort corps.
- Consider a wayfinding recognition program for excellence in direction giving.
- Provide computerized wayfinding update information.

POTENTIAL CONTRIBUTIONS OF ENVIRONMENTAL PSYCHOLOGISTS TO WAYFINDING EASE

Wayfinding ease is a real-world environment behavior problem in great need of improvement. There are many potential roles for environmental psychologists who wish to study this issue in more breadth and depth and for those who wish to contribute in other ways. Theoretical work has primarily focused on issues of individual microprocessing. More broadly focused theory would be useful to help explain such phenomena as how people simultaneously make use of multiple wayfinding cues, how organizations make wayfinding-related decisions, and how people give and make sense of directions. Much more wayfinding-related research is needed in real-world settings to examine the various strategies people use to both find their way and compensate for wayfinding mistakes (see Case Study No. 1). The field would benefit from examinations of how people make sense of wayfinding graphics, including signs, maps, and GPS displays, as well as detailed systematic assessments of the effectiveness of various sign design features, map layouts, wayfinding kiosk displays, and the like. While some research-based wayfinding planning and design guidelines exist, more are needed at all levels of design from city scale to site planning, landscape architecture, architecture, interior design, and graphic design. Detailed performance criteria for operational decisions are also needed (Carpman & Grant, 1993). Detailed wayfinding-related design reviews of architectural and landscape design can be very effective and can make significant contributions (Carpman & Grant, 2000) (see Case Study No. 2). Postoccupancy evaluations that include wayfinding or specific wayfinding-focused POEs of a variety of large, complex building types would also add significantly to the existing knowledge base. Environmental psychologists should also consider broadening their pedagogical audiences to include graduate students in nondesign fields, like business and health administration, and decision makers, like facility managers.

ABOUT WAYFINDING DESIGN GUIDELINES

While it is tempting to end the chapter with a detailed list of widely applicable wayfinding design guidelines, the authors have chosen not to do so for several reasons. Wayfinding design guidelines vary tremendously with building type (e.g., a hospital and a theater will have very different requirements), building size and layout, rural versus urban versus suburban location, user requirements and preferences, and many other factors. Guidelines that are so generic as to be useful to every building and every user group will be pretty bland and not particularly helpful for any given project.

Specific, detailed, interior and exterior wayfinding design guidelines need to be based upon careful research, observation, and experience. Guidelines of this type pertaining to medical centers are available in the authors' book *Design That Cares: Planning Health Facilities for Patients and Visitors* (Carpman & Grant, 1993). Other sources likely contain wayfinding guidelines related to different building types.

Instead of design guidelines, the authors have chosen to conclude the chapter with two case studies showing how environmental psychologists can directly influence the physical environment. The first example describes how wayfinding design research can have a direct impact on design, and the second example demonstrates how detailed, informed wayfinding design review can change the shape of a project.

CASE STUDY NO. 1: WAYFINDING RESEARCH THAT INFLUENCED DESIGN

Early in the schematic design phase of the University of Michigan Medical Center, Ann Arbor (a $285 million project involving 1,250,000 ft^2 of new space, completed in 1986) there was a difference of opinion among design consultants concerning the optimum relationship between the entrance to the new parking structure and the circular drive for dropping people off at the hospital's main entrance.[3]

The circular drop-off drive and the parking structure were located immediately adjacent to one another, and the main road passed close by. Two alternatives were possible: having the parking deck accessed directly from the circular drop-off entrance drive or having the parking deck accessible only from the main road.

This was a critical decision since designers estimated that several thousand cars per day would be involved. In addition, there were only 2 weeks in which a decision could be made in order not to delay the "fast track" construction process. Environment behavior research was seen as a way in which these two differing views could be resolved.

This project used architectural simulation techniques and social science research protocols to design, execute, analyze, and present the study. In addition, careful pragmatism about the politics of the decision-making process were an integral component of the project's planning.

This study was undertaken as part of the Patient and Visitor Participation (PVP) Project, a research and advocacy project supported by the University of Michigan Medical Center as part of the Replacement Hospital Program. The PVP Project ran between 1980 and 1986 and involved over 3,200 patients and visitors in over 30 different studies looking at a wide variety of design-related needs and preferences of hospital consumers (Carpman & Grant, 1993).

Videotape simulations were made of a model of the entrance drive to the new hospital. These were used to evaluate the effect on turning behavior of two parking-deck entry options: constructing a parking deck entrance directly off the hospital's drop-off circle or providing an entrance only off the main road. In face-to-face interviews, 100 randomly sampled visitors were shown these simulations and asked where they would turn if they were coming alone to visit a patient and needed to park their car.

Several turn-off areas were located along the entrance drive before the parking deck turn-off. Each turn-off had a sign directing drivers to continue straight ahead for parking while listing destinations to the right, such as "Drop off" and "Main Entrance." Half the visitors saw a videotape in which there was an entrance to the deck from the drop-off circle, and half saw a tape in which the entrance from the drop-off circle was absent. Each visitor saw two scenarios: one having the drop-off circle crowded with cars and one uncrowded.

The results of the study showed that the presence of the entrance to the deck from the drop-off circle made a significant difference in reported turning behavior. Being able to see the entrance to the parking deck located adjacent to the drop-off circle lured a substantial percentage of drivers into the drop-off circle. Participants ignored the verbal cue of the signs that directed them to another entrance and instead followed the very powerful visual cue. However, if no entrance to the parking deck was visible from the drop-off circle—if the visual cue was absent—they were more likely to follow directional signs and go straight to the more appropriate parking structure entrance, bypassing the drop-off circle entirely.

The findings and subsequent recommendation—not to provide an entrance to the parking structure

---

[3] This case study is adapted from Carpman, Grant, and Simmons, 1985a; *Progressive Architecture*, 1995.

Figure 28.12 This is how the drop-off circle looked during the first few years of the hospital's operation, with no direct entrance to the parking structure. Many years later, in order to provide immediately accessible short-term parking, a direct entrance was created.

from the drop-off circle to the parking structure—directly influenced the design. (See Figure 28.12.)

A side benefit of the 1981 project was using a research method that showed designers and design decision makers their first moving three-dimensional image of the drive to the new hospital. In the days long before computer graphics, this was highly unusual.

CASE STUDY NO. 2: WAYFINDING DESIGN REVIEW THAT CHANGED DESIGN

During the process of designing and constructing many additions to an already large Midwestern medical center, the authors' firm was asked to perform a wayfinding-related design review of the emergency entrance and main entrance of the associated Children's Hospital. The request for this design review came while the project was under construction.

The two entrances in question were located close to one another on the site. Designers were uneasy about the design scheme they had proposed, but didn't really know why. Our review concluded that the two entrances were too close to one another and that the whole area was too constrained. We anticipated that parents bringing sick children to the emergency room might end up being caught in the congestion and be prevented from accessing the ER quickly enough for immediate medical attention.

We studied the site and saw an opportunity to gain some space from an adjacent courtyard area.

We recommended using the borrowed space to separate the main entrance area from the ER area and to create a more generous main entrance drop-off and valet parking area.

As a result of our recommendations, construction was stopped and the design was changed. Even though this was costly, the client recognized the value in creating main entrance and ER arrival areas that would function appropriately, and they saw the recommended changes as both potentially life saving and something that would forestall endless congestion problems.

REFERENCES

American teen dies of sunstroke. (2000, July 7). Available: Internet byline Jasmine Kelemen.

Antes, J., McBride, R., & Collins, J. (1988). The effect of a new city traffic route on the cognitive maps of its residents. *Environment and Behavior, 20*(1), 75–91.

Architectural research, comparing architectural and verbal wayfinding cues. (1995, February). *Progressive Architecture,* 81.

Blades, M. (1991). Wayfinding theory and research: The need for a new approach. In D. M. Mark & A. U. Frank (Eds.), *Cognitive and linguistic aspects of geographic space* (pp. 137–165). Dordrecht, The Netherlands: Kluwer Academic.

Blades, M., & Spencer, C. (1994). The development of children's ability to use spatial representations. *Advances in Child Development and Behavior, 25,* 157–199.

Blumenthal, R. (1996, February 13). Beverly Sills stars in her grandest role. *The New York Times,* p. B1.

Brown, B., Wright, H., & Brown, C. (1997). A post-occupancy evaluation of wayfinding in a pediatric hospital: Research findings and implications for instruction. *Journal of Architectural and Planning Research, 14*(1), 35.

Brown, L., Lahar, C., & Mosley, J. (1998). Age and gender-related differences in strategy use for route information: A "map-present" direction-giving paradigm. *Environment and Behavior, 30*(2), 123–143.

Butler, D., Acquino, A., Hissong, A., & Scott, P. (1993). Wayfinding by newcomers in a complex building. *Human Factors, 35*(1), 159–173.

Carpman, J. R. (1991). *Creating hospitals where people can find their way* (Plant Technology and Safety Management Series, No. 1). Oakbrook Terrace, IL: Joint Commission on Accreditation of Healthcare Organizations.

Carpman, J. R., & Grant, M. A. (1993). *Design that cares: Planning health facilities for patients & visitors* (2nd ed.). Chicago: American Hospital Publishing.

Carpman, J. R., & Grant, M. A. (1997). Wayfinding in healthcare facilities. In S. Marberry (Ed.), *Healthcare design: An introduction.* New York: Wiley.

Carpman, J. R., & Grant, M. A. (2000). *Taking a turn for the better: Wayfinding in health facilities.* Unpublished presentation at McGill University Health Center Design Conference in Montreal. Ann Arbor, MI: Carpman Grant Associates.

Carpman, J. R., & Grant, M. A. (2001). *No more mazes: Five learnable skills for finding your way around confusing places.* Unpublished manuscript. Ann Arbor, MI: Carpman Grant Associates.

Carpman, J. R., Grant, M. A., & Simmons, D. A. (1983–1984). Wayfinding in the hospital environment: The impact of various floor numbering alternatives. *Journal of Environmental Systems, 13*(4), 353–364.

Carpman, J. R., Grant, M. A., & Simmons, D. A. (1985a). Hospital design and wayfinding: A video simulation study. *Environment and Behavior, 17*(3), 296–314.

Carpman, J. R., Grant, M. A., & Simmons, D. A. (1985b). Sign spacing in a health care facility to increase wayfinding ease. *Proceedings of the 1985 International Conference on Building Use and Safety Technology.* Washington, DC: National Institute of Building Sciences.

Cotham, F. (1998, September 28). Cartoon. *New Yorker,* p. 69.

DeParle, J. (1989). The worst city government in America. *Washington Monthly, 20,* 33–45.

Devlin, A., & Bernstein, J. (1995). Interactive wayfinding: Use of cues by men and women. *Journal of Environmental Psychology, 15,* 23–38.

Devlin, A., & Bernstein, J. (1997). Interactive wayfinding: Map style and effectiveness. *Journal of Environmental Psychology, 17,* 99–110.

Dogu, U., & Erkip, F. (2000). Spatial factors affecting wayfinding orientation: A case study in a shopping mall. *Environment and Behavior, 32*(6), 731–755.

Feaver, D. B. (1978, November 27). What's in a subway station name? Sometimes less than you may think. *Washington Post,* p. C4.

Finke, G. (1990, Fall). Hospital hospitality. *Identity,* 28.

Foreman, H., & Gillett, R. (Eds.). (1997). *Handbook of spatial research paradigms & methodologies* (Vol. 1). Hove, England: Erlbaum.

Golledge, R. (1999). *Wayfinding behavior: Cognitive mapping and other spatial processes.* Baltimore: Johns Hopkins University Press.

Hendrix, S. (1999, June 18). Getting lost and found with GPS. *Washington Post,* weekend sec., p. 71.

Heth, C. D., Cornell, E. H., & Albets, D. M. (1997). Differential use of landmarks by 8- and 12-year-old children during route reversal navigation. *Journal of Environmental Psychology, 17,* 199–213.

Jacobson, R. D. (1998). Cognitive mapping without sight: Four preliminary studies of spatial learning. *Journal of Environmental Psychology, 18,* 289–305.

Jordan, E. H. (1993, March). Turn left at the dog. *Modern Maturity, 36*(1), 92.

Kaplan, S. (1978). On knowing the environment. In S. Kaplan & R. Kaplan (Eds.), *Humanscape: Environments for people* (pp. 54–58). North Scituate, MA: Duxbury Press.

Kirasic, K. C., & Mathes, E. A. (1990). Effects of different means for conveying environmental information on elderly adults' spatial cognition and behavior. *Environment and Behavior, 22*(5), 591–607.

Kovach, R. C., Jr., Surrette, M. A., & Aamodt, M. G. (1988). Following informal street maps: Effects of map design. *Environment and Behavior, 20*(6), 683–699.

Kuipers, B. (1982). The "map in the head" metaphor. *Environment and Behavior, 14*(2), 202–220.

Landau, B. (1986). Early map use as an unlearned ability. *Cognition, 22,* 201–223.

Lawton, C. A., Charleston, S., & Zieles, A. (1996). Individual and gender-related differences in indoor wayfinding. *Environment and Behavior, 28*(2), 204–219.

Lawton, C. A., & Morrin, K. A. (1999). Gender differences in pointing accuracy in computer-simulated 3D mazes. *Sex Roles, 40*(1,2), 73–92.

Levine, M., Marchon, I., & Hanley, G. (1984). The placement and misplacement of you-are-here maps. *Environment and Behavior, 16*(2), 139–157.

Moeser, S. D. (1988). Cognitive mapping in a complex building. *Environment and Behavior, 20*(1), 21–49.

Monahan, D. R. (1990, April). Parking structure signing & graphics. *Parking Professional,* 13–19.

O'Brian, B. (1995, March 28). Signs and blunders: Airport travelers share graphic tales: Way-finding, lost-getting are rites of passengers: Confusion seems by design. *Wall Street Journal,* p. A1.

Okabe, A., Aoki, K., & Hamamoto, W. (1986). Distance and direction judgment in a large-scale natural environment: Effects of a slope and winding trail. *Environment and Behavior, 18*(6), 755–772.

Olsen, R. V., & Pershing, A. (1981). *Environmental evaluation of the interim entry to Bellevue Hospital.* Unpublished manuscript.

O'Neill, M. (1991a). Effects of signage and floor plan configuration on wayfinding accuracy. *Environment and Behavior, 23*(5), 553–574.

O'Neill, M. (1991b). Evaluation of a conceptual model of architectural legibility. *Environment and Behavior, 23*(3), 259–284.

Packard, R. (1994, October 16). Which way is up? For some it's hard to tell. *New York Times,* p. 35.

Passini, R. (1980a). Wayfinding: A conceptual framework. *Man-Environment Systems, 10,* 22–30.

Passini, R. (1980b). Wayfinding in complex buildings: An environmental analysis. *Man-Environment Systems, 10,* 31–40.

Passini, R. (1984a). Spatial representations: A wayfinding perspective. *Journal of Environmental Psychology, 4,* 153–164.

Passini, R. (1984b). *Wayfinding in architecture.* New York: Van Nostrand Reinhold.

Pearlman, E. (2000, March 5). Tokyo, scrutable city: In the absence of street names, visitors must learn to find their way by relying on visual cues. *New York Times,* sec. 5, p. 33.

Peponis, J., Zimring, C., & Choi, Y. K. (1990). Finding the building in wayfinding. *Environment and Behavior, 22*(5), 555–590.

Pogrebin, L. C. (1998). Hansel and Gretel and me: Hiking in France an anxious traveler confronts her fear of getting lost. *Travel and Leisure, 28*(5), 100.

Sanoff, H. (1999). Student responses to architecture schools. In T. Mann (Ed.), *The power of imagination: Proceedings of the thirtieth annual Environmental Design Research Association [EDRA] conference* (188–195), Edmond, OK: EDRA.

Signs of the Times. (1987, October). Special issue on wayfinding.

Slatz (advertisement for Spandex USA). (1989, winter). *Identity, 2*(4), back cover.

Stea, D. (1974). Architecture in the head: Cognitive mapping. In J. Lang, C. Burnette, W. Moleski, & D. Vachon (Eds.), *Designing for human behavior: Architecture and the behavior sciences* (pp. 157–168). Stroudsburg, PA: Dowden, Hutchinson & Ross.

Sternlieb, J., & Bairstow, A. -M. (2000, December 29). All we wanted were directions. *Washington Post,* p. B1.

Talbot, J., Kaplan, R., Kuo, F., & Kaplan, S. (1993). Factors that enhance effectiveness of visitor maps. *Environment and Behavior, 25*(6), 743–760.

Taylor, H., & Tversky, B. (1996). Perspective in spatial descriptions. *Journal of Memory and Language, 35,* 371–391.

Two British tourists shot after losing way in Miami. (1991, August 31). *New York Times,* sec. 1, p. 8.

Uzzell, D., & Keaty, M. (1993). *A study of wayfinding and signage in the spectrum leisure centre, Guildford.* Unpublished manuscript, University of Surrey, England.

Vanetti, E., & Allen, G. (1988). Communicating environmental knowledge: The impact of verbal and spatial abilities on the production and comprehension of route directions. *Environment and Behavior, 20*(6), 667–682.

Ward, S., Newcombe, N., & Overton, W. (1986). Turn left at the church, or three miles North: A study of direction giving and sex differences. *Environment and Behavior, 18*(2), 192–213.

Way off course. (1985, July 22). *Sports Illustrated, 63,* 12.

Weisman, J. (1982). Wayfinding and architectural legibility: Design considerations in housing environments for the elderly. In V. Regnier & J. Pynoos (Eds.). *Housing for the elderly: Satisfaction & preferences* (441–464). New York: Garland.

Wetherell, W. D. (1990, November 18). Strangers in a strange town: A traveler's unerring instinct, when lost, for asking directions from the wrong person. *New York Times,* p. 41.

Zimring, C. (1990). *The costs of confusion: Non-monetary and monetary costs of the Emory University Hospital wayfinding system.* Unpublished manuscript, Georgia Institute of Technology, Atlanta.

CHAPTER 29

Work Environments

JANETTA MITCHELL MCCOY

WHAT WAS IT ABOUT the Quonset huts at Lockheed that made Skunkworks so creatively productive? And why did Mike West insist on an isolated basement for his team's development of the Eagle at Data General (Kidder, 1981)? If these are the workplaces ideal for creativity and performance, why do we bother designing elegant, organized offices for today's highly competitive organizations? Are there theories and concepts to be developed or lessons to be learned about the role of the physical workplace in the success of the changing organizational work environment?

The physical workplace is one component of the complex system of relationships in the changing work environment. While much research on human behavior in the workplace focuses on social dynamics, comparatively little attention has been paid to the role of the physical environment within the organization. Drawing on and expanding the previous work of Sundstrom (1987), this chapter emphasizes recent empirical findings on the relationship of the physical environment and the health, safety, and behavior of occupants of the workplace.

This chapter will present a framework for analyzing and understanding the complex relationships of the people, their experiential processes, and the physical features within the workplace. Analysis will be limited to the office work environment because in the Information Age[1] the office is the primary focus of research for understanding the workplace. This focus is appropriate because at this time more than 50% of working people in the United States work in offices. Seventy-five percent of these office workers are knowledge workers whose creative, innovative performance is often considered the measure of organizational success (Kao, 1996; Schrage, 2000).

The office is where individuals or groups of individuals congregate for handling information and making plans and decisions. It is a place where individuals are likely to be required to read and to think and to talk with others. It is a place where groups or teams are required to communicate and collaborate. The office is a place supplied by the organization to support individual and group contributions to the organizational mission and goals. The office is typically a physical place with features and properties that provide both functional opportunities and multiple levels of meaningful interaction and feedback for the people who work in them.

Traditionally, offices reflected the hierarchy or structure of the organization with the largest and most prominent or desirable office location and resources given to the highest-ranking member of the organization. In many traditional offices, job titles and office size and furnishings were indications of status. Increasingly, as corporate structure has changed, offices have become less well defined.

Recently, alternatives to the traditional office have developed as a result of new technologies and new economies. Some alternative offices include virtual offices, home offices, and hotelling, in which new

---

[1] The term frequently used to describe the postindustrial society in which information and information technology has been adopted as a primary focus of work.

mobile computers and telephone technologies allow work and communication to be done from locations remote from the traditional office. New concepts of flatter, less hierarchical organizational structure have supported the evolution of new ways of working, as well as new and different use of space. Responding to evolving technologies, economies, and markets, organizations are seeking more fluid ways of supporting constantly changing functional requirements of people working within the organization.

As described by Sundstrom (1987), performance and satisfaction of people in the organization have often been used to evaluate successful qualities of the physical office workplace. *Performance* refers to individual, team, or organization efficiency, accuracy, or other criteria of achievement. Job satisfaction is an individual's general evaluation of the job to be performed; satisfaction with the physical environment represents a component of job satisfaction. Behavioral outcomes discussed here will be the multiple components of satisfaction and performance and their relationship with the physical work environment of the office, including control, functional opportunities, and nonverbal self-expression.

STATUS OF EMPIRICAL RESEARCH

While the status of the current literature relevant to work environments is still, as Sundstrom (1987) described it, uneven, the focus of the literature has expanded and shifted as new economies and technologies have emerged. Increasingly, empirical research on work environments is included in programs of architecture and interior design with investigators from diverse disciplines such as organizational and environmental psychology, industrial design, human factors engineering, and business.

The primary research on the physical work environment focuses on organizational and business trends, especially organizational structure and strategies, workforce attitudes and preferences, and technology integration. Response to extreme and radical changes in organizations has prompted considerable interest in how the physical workplace can best support the new structure and strategies while helping to attract and retain the best people for the work to be done. The literature reviewed here is by no means comprehensive but is representative of the current literature relevant to the study of the work environment.

STRATEGIES OF RESEARCH

Research on work environments includes both qualitative and quantitative methods. While quantitative methods are preferred for more technological studies as might be relevant in engineering, increasingly qualitative methods compatible with social sciences are employed. Quantitative methods in work environments are used primarily in measurement and evaluation of thermal conditions, light, sound, and contents of indoor air quality on performance. Such methods include both field and laboratory experiments. Increasingly, field experiments are employed because, as Sundstrom (1987) suggested, generalizability of findings from laboratory conditions to actual work environments is open to question. Such methods are more useful when independent and dependent variables can be isolated so that cause and effect may be determined, which is rarely the case in the work environment.

Qualitative methods in research on work environments are used to capture a broad range of activities and responses that may require more complex explanations. Such methods include observations, interviews, and activity or behavior mapping as tools for understanding behavior of people in a work setting. Surveys and questionnaires, the systematic asking of questions, are popular tools for research in the work environment especially for determining user preference or attitude.

It is not uncommon to see programs of research use multiple methods of investigation to fully understand the many components of complex relationships within the workplace. Many of the studies described in this chapter used multiple methods to create comprehensive case studies for investigating human behavior in the work environment, understanding human behavior in response to changing environments, and describing human behavior in relation to multiple components of the work environment interacting with the physical workplace.

RECENT STUDIES

This review of current literature on the work environment involves several disciplinary and methodological approaches as well as multiple ontological priorities for understanding human experiences, processes, and behaviors. Within this review are diverse definitions and evaluations of environmental satisfaction, work performance, and organization success. What these studies have in common is their inquiry into the physical features and properties relevant to the behavior of people in the workplace. Thus, the literature is organized around the physical attributes of the workplace and each is examined for interactive qualities with the people of the organization.

SPATIAL ORGANIZATION

Spatial organization of the physical work environment is its most researched feature. The organization of space determines the level of enclosure, adjacencies, proxemics, and territoriality. It can provide needed privacy and control, variety and adaptability, flexibility, and legibility. Spatial organization can facilitate or inhibit communication and collaboration. Spatial organization may contribute to the efficiency and effectiveness of the organization.

An extensive study of the workplace as a physical environment has been the work of the Buffalo Organization for Social and Technological Innovation (BOSTI) (Brill, Margulis, & Konar, 1984; Brill, Weidemann, Alard, Olson, & Keable, 2001). In a long-term program of research, working closely with more than 80 different organizations, BOSTI researchers used a quasi-experimental research design. BOSTI manipulated the physical office environment of more than 13,000 office workers and administered pre- and posttest questionnaires to workers and control groups to make causal inferences regarding the influence of the physical environment on satisfaction and performance. Defining the workspace as a diverse collection of features and properties, including physical enclosure, aesthetics, privacy, furniture, status, communication, temperature control, and lighting, BOSTI has explored how changes in the identified features relate to changes in four measures—job performance, job satisfaction, ease and quality of communication, and satisfaction with the environment. Of these measures, job satisfaction and job performance of office workers were shown to have measurable economic consequences to the organizations.

BOSTI's studies are an important collection and organization of information and have generated many subsequent studies. Likewise, many organizations have used this research to justify significant, costly decisions. Although, BOSTI has not been forthcoming with precisely what changes were made, they do show us the proposed design solutions (objectively assessed by prominent design firms) but not what the original conditions were. Likewise, in their reports they do not discuss the multitude of other environmental conditions that might have influenced the outcomes, such as changes in organizational structure or systems of rewards. Perhaps most important, they do not track the influence of the new design solutions over time. Without this information it is somewhat difficult to fully assess the study—calling to mind the controversial Herzberg studies that produced the "hygiene factor"[2] and the studies coined the Hawthorne Effect.[3]

Subsequent studies by BOSTI (Brill, 1997) indicate that the success of team collaborations are correlated with four features:

1. Shared spaces that act as a team's "conceptual and technical playground"
2. Having and using multiple forms of representation and communication, such as conversation, physical models, whiteboards, computer screens, and drawings
3. Having a wide spectrum of formal and informal environments for random encountering, spontaneous meetings, and scheduled sessions
4. Easy access to team's spaces by coworkers "casually dropping-in or passing-by"

Most recently BOSTI (Brill et al., 2001) reported that the workplace quality with the "strongest effect on performance and satisfaction is the ability to do distraction-free solo work, support for impromptu interactions, and support for meetings and undistracted groupwork" (p. 19). BOSTI's research is important as a model for connecting the spatial organization of the physical environment to job performance. They found the physical environment relevant to communication, collaboration, and other issues relevant to teams and individual work satisfaction and performance.

---

[2] The "hygiene factor" comes from Herzberg's two-factor theory of job satisfaction. Never empirically documented, Theodore Herzberg's writings suggest that poor work conditions contribute to worker dissatisfaction but that an improved environment will not result in enhanced satisfaction, only in a reduction of dissatisfaction.

[3] Experiments at the Hawthorne plant of the Western Electric Company from 1924 to 1932 have been interpreted to suggest that changing the features or properties of the physical environment has an effect on work performance or satisfaction only because it signals to the worker the concern or interest of management.

The International Workplace Studies Program (IWSP) has conducted extensive case studies of numerous successful, creative organizations (i.e., Chiat/Day, Eastman Kodak, Xerox, DEC Finland, Lloyds of London). IWSP's methods and procedures are case studies utilizing interviews, observations, and questionnaires. The intention of this work is to understand how the physical work environment supports workplace initiatives that encourage high performance, such as teamwork, telecommuting, and cross-functional collaboration (Becker & Sims, 2000; Becker & Steele, 1995). IWSP's conclusions are reflected in five interdependent key criteria:

1. The physical environment must reflect the team's sense of identity. Physical features that support a team's sense of identity can include decorative styles, the location of offices, allocation of space, treatment of boundaries between the system and the outside world, signs, color codes, and artwork.
2. Features of the environment must facilitate communication. Physical features that facilitate communication include having a variety of places in which people come face to face, such as centrally located lounges or snack areas, "main street" corridors, well-planned adjacencies, communication technologies, patterns of meeting facilities, common facilities that serve as magnets to draw people together on an unplanned basis, shared eating facilities (as opposed to executive areas), and equal access to amenities such as fitness facilities.
3. Features of the environment must facilitate task accomplishment. This may be accomplished by adequate size and quality of workspaces, ergonomics, meeting spaces and other areas for joint activities, information and communication technologies, and logical adjacencies and proxemics.
4. Features of the environment must be adaptable to changes in the team and the organization. Designed features must be able to accommodate change quickly and without disruption. Solutions may include universal same-size offices making it easier to move people rather than offices, or work environments that have a variety of different types of activity spaces from which people can choose based on need for concentration or interaction.

5. Policies that govern the environment must support the team's ability to develop a sense of identity, facilitate communication, task accomplishment, and adaptation of spaces to team requirements. Conflict between team requirements and organizational policy will be detrimental to the goal of high productivity.

Although IWSP studies are insightful and significant in scale, like BOSTI, IWSP has not been forthcoming regarding procedures and participant recruitment. Nonetheless, they have been widely quoted and are influential in the practice of design and facilities management. These studies are useful as support for drawing parallels between team and organizational characteristics, social interactions, and the physical environment. They demonstrate how features and properties of the physical environment are associated with performance and satisfaction, communication and collaboration, and organizational culture and identity.

Duffy (1997) supports and extends these notions in his analysis of 20 case studies of large corporations. Focusing on evolving corporate cultures and new ways of working with information technology, Duffy suggests that the most vital function of an office building is to facilitate and accommodate change. Just as building and information technology have evolved dramatically since the Industrial Revolution, so too have patterns of work. New patterns of work require new conceptualizations of spatial organization and allocation. Duffy has defined four categories of office types, each with unique patterns of work and spatial requirements.

Hive   When work is broken down into small components and carried out by staff who are given precise instruction and little discretion, space required is satisfied by open, ganged cubicles easily defined by simple space standards. Little interaction and little autonomy are required.

Cell   High-level work carried out by talented, isolated individual knowledge workers is often allocated enclosed offices or individual workstations with high partitions. Individual concentration is paramount. Little interaction, high autonomy is required.

Den   Groups of people working together needing balance of different or interdependent skills require group rooms and continuous spaces incorporating meeting spaces together with individual work spaces. High interaction, little autonomy is required.

Club   High-level work carried out by talented independent individuals who need to work both collaboratively and individually. Work processes may be constantly evolving and require a diverse, complex, manipulable range of settings to accommodate a wide variety of tasks. High interaction, high autonomy is required.

Maximizing organizational efficiency and effectiveness through the designed physical environment, Duffy concludes, has measurable potential in improving organizational performance. Efficiency is achievable through the direct application of the designers' skill in space planning; effectiveness is achievable only through close collaboration of management and workers with the designer to effect features that reflect the workers' requirements. Duffy's case studies demonstrate that in any given organization, there may be need for each of these office types. He concluded that the most innovative groups were found in "club" offices.

While Duffy's historical analysis of evolving work patterns and spatial requirements is interesting and helpful for understanding significant change now being experienced in the physical work environment, his empirical basis for analyzing the "new offices" is somewhat narrow. He tells us what appears to work for 20 different new organizational facilities, but he does not make the comparative analysis that could tell us what might or might not have been working well in their previous offices. He prescribes interesting alternatives to different ways of working and associated corporate cultures, but he does not discuss how, or if, employees might participate in the design process, nor does he give but passing reference to the issue of individual or collective personalization of the work environment. His emphasis is primarily on spatial organization within a corporate environment; he does not address design process or how the space may change and evolve over time.

Duffy's study is important in making the association of the relationship between interaction and autonomy with the contribution of the physical work environment to work performance. By acknowledging that the physical environment offers potential for organizational effectiveness, he presents the concept of environmental quality as part of the appropriate balance between opportunity and cost associated with the physical environment.

Wineman and Serrato's (1999) review of best practices for workplace design supports Allen's (1977) proposition that communication is an important indicator of satisfaction and performance and that spatial organization of team workspace can enhance face-to-face communication. People in the workplace will talk with others who are in close proximity. Such social interaction encourages sharing of ideas and better coordination of activities. Proximity of workstations and informal gathering places, features that foster informal interaction, are considered important ingredients for supporting the longevity of the team (Sundstrom, Demuse, & Futrell, 1990).

Wineman and Serrato also demonstrate that shared team workspace is instrumental in encouraging the development of a "shared knowledge base" (p. 279). Such spaces may include conference areas allowing group members to lay out or display materials and equipment that are dedicated to their project and do not have to be removed at the end of each day. Whether enclosed or open, best practices suggest that a shared team workspace encourages team communication and collaboration. If an open space, the shared space should be supported by an enclosed conference room where more private or more formal conversations are encouraged. Easily accessible conference rooms located in close proximity to the teamwork spaces facilitate impromptu meetings and encourage collaboration.

McCoy's (2000) in-depth case study of seven teams in a large organization demonstrates that spatial organization permits and encourages informal communication and extended collaboration necessary for high levels of creative teamwork. Teams with no accessible areas for such communication and collaboration may not develop the characteristics or social abilities necessary for high levels of creative achievement or performance. Individuals in offices in which the spatial organization inhibits informal encounters between teammates may be less likely to develop open systems of communication and collaboration necessary for creative achievement of teams.

This research is important because it demonstrates the value of spatial organization and allocation of space in supporting satisfaction and performance of people in the workplace. It also links the physical environment with social activities of people within the organization. Spatial organization of the physical environment supports individual process as well as team communication and collaboration.

ARCHITECTONIC DETAILS

Architectonic details of the physical environment are sometimes overlooked, but as Becker and Steele's (1995) case studies suggest, decorative styles, and treatment of boundaries, signs, colors and artwork may encourage a sense of identity and purpose among the people in the workplace. Becker and Steele, however, are quick to point out that the interpretation of these architectonic details relies heavily on *how* they are used, rather than the specific item of use. In describing two highly successful firms in Silicon Valley they point out that "the rhetoric of creativity, freedom and nonconformity is perfectly reflected in break areas with comfortable sofas arranged in whatever way they were left by the last group to use them, walls painted with murals by adventurous programmers, and a variety of banners, posters, and knickknacks" (p. 39).

Becker and Steele (1995) also point out that "imaginative ways of allocating space and furnishings can support both individual identity needs and organizational cost concerns" (p. 28). They suggest that such ornamentation or display of artifacts is a "'non-verbal communication system' in which a wide range of messages are conveyed. Some messages may include status, identity of users, the history of the organization or the team itself, and expectation about what should and should not happen in the place" (p. 29). They suggest that in designing the architectonic details of workplaces to reflect the team's goals and work styles, the organization's own image will emerge. Alternately, requiring teams to conform to an organizational image may lead to confusion and stakeholders with an unclear focus.

BOSTI's (Brill et al., 1984) comprehensive report indicates that appearance of the environment is important to the extent that it reflects the values and norms of the people and the organization. Their investigation of office design and its influence on productivity also indicates that personalization (i.e., changes users make to enhance their capacity to do the work or to make some personal expression) serves to articulate and reinforce both individual and group identity, stake out group territory, make the environment more stimulating, and symbolize a commitment to a place and the purposes of that place.

Sundstrom (1987) points out that while personalization allows self-expression within a work environment, participatory design processes potentially allow self-expression through multiple features of the workplace: layout, furnishings, and decoration. Wineman and Serrato's (1999) review of best practices in corporate facilities design indicates that displays of artifacts or products of work are opportunities to share ideas or work-in-progress with other group members and with individuals in the larger organization. According to BOSTI (Brill et al., 1984) personalization and participation are significantly correlated with both environmental and job satisfaction. Rapoport (1990) suggests that some ornamentation may be cues to desired behavior.

McCoy's (2000) study of team work environments found that highly creative teams would collectively personalize their work areas with artifacts reflective of team goals and achievements. Less creative teams do not display team-oriented artifacts, though those individuals do tend to display items and photographs of personal interests. Likewise highly creative teams are more likely to actively participate in the design of new office space, whereas less creative teams do not express interest in, and even avoid, such participation, leaving design decisions to management.

Mazumdar's (1992) ethnographic study of organizational work life describes the intensity of the deprivation felt by those whose environment contains little or no architectonic detail. He found that in feeling deprived, members exhibited a range of responses: to distance oneself from other members, to groan and complain to reduce anxiety, to plead with those in authority to avoid or divert the deprivation, to fight for what they wanted, to quit the organization, or even to file a lawsuit for reinstatement or damages. His interviews and observations lead him to conclude that environmental deprivation in this context leads to loss of face and prestige and causes embarrassment, contributing to widespread alarm and apprehension that the team is in danger of elimination. This study is particularly significant in illustrating the importance of feelings and meanings attached to the physical environment of the workplace.

This area of research is significant because it demonstrates the value of occupants participating in the design and management of the physical office environment. It also illustrates the value of allowing or encouraging individual and team collective personalization of the space provided by the organization. If as Rapoport (1990) argues, the physical environment may provide cues to desired behavior by reflecting the level of satisfaction and performance of the occupants, it may also encourage increased levels of performance.

VIEWS

Views influence the individual's morale and environmental satisfaction. Views are evaluated based on scale and content. Views may have restorative value to stressful work (Heerwagen, 1990; S. Kaplan, Talbot, & Kaplan, 1988), they may relate an element of status (Becker & Steele, 1995, Brill et al., 1984), and they may be associated with health-giving affects of the physical environment (Ulrich, 1984).

Kaplan et al. (1988) report responses from a survey of three groups of office workers indicating that employees whose outdoor views included only built components (such as roads or buildings) experienced higher levels of job stress than others. In contrast, people who could see at least some natural elements outdoors (such as trees and grass) reflected higher job satisfaction levels than did either those with views of built elements outdoors or those with no outdoor views from their desks at all. These findings complement findings on view preferences. When asked to identify preferences for outdoor views from slides and photographs, R. Kaplan and Kaplan (1989) determined that people consider both content and spatial information. Making judgments from photographs, people preferred view content in which the natural environment was dominant though not exclusive.

Ulrich (1984) determined that views might also affect health and well-being of building occupants. In a hospital study of patients recovering from surgery, Ulrich determined that patients with a window view of a natural setting recovered more quickly than patients with a view of a parking lot. While there is only hypothetical speculation that people's affinity for a view of the natural environment is related to human evolutionary experience (Ulrich, 1993), the effect of our preference for outdoor views and windowlessness has been studied.

Heerwagen and Orians (1986) and Heerwagen (1990) examined the use of visual material to decorate windowed and windowless offices. Their detailed content analysis of existing corporate offices of accounting firms revealed that occupants of windowless offices used twice as many visual materials to decorate their offices. Further, materials in windowless offices were dominated by nature themes, displaying more landscapes and fewer cityscapes than did occupants of windowed spaces.

Admittedly, research on the influence of views on human performance is both scarce and limited by its focus on attitude and preference rather than behavioral observations. Nonetheless, the view from an office window is a well-known symbol of status (Becker & Steele, 1995; Duffy, 1992). Surveys on windows suggest that people value the opportunity for visual contact with the external environment and particularly welcome access to daylight and general environmental information such as weather and seasonal changes (Collins, 1975; Cuttle, 1983; Ludlow, 1976; Markus, 1967; Roessler, 1980).

RESOURCES

Amabile's (1988, 1993) interviews of office workers revealed that of nine qualities encouraging creative teamwork, 52% of respondents stated that it was very important to have "access to the necessary resources, including facilities, equipment, information, funds, and people" (p. 146). Similarly, BOSTI (Brill et al., 1984) suggests we reconceptualize the office as a tool, not just as a place to house tools. They argue that the office (the building, its furniture and equipment) is part of a larger information-handling system whose "goal is to add value to information in a managed process" (p. 28).

Becker and Steele (1995) identified two classes of resources pertinent to the corporations in their case studies. One class of resources is scarce, finite, and nonrenewable: time and money. The costs of buildings, furniture, equipment; costs for designers and consultants; cost of staff; and costs for maintenance and operation are finite. Time can be construed as an investment to gain familiarity and experience. The second class of resource is expandable and renewable: the interest and enthusiasm of members for the system, the energy of motivation. At this level, Becker and Steele are in accord with the psychoeconomic theories of creativity (Rubenson & Runco, 1992; Sternberg & Lubart, 1995): A corporation's level of commitment of resources is directly related to the level of commitment to the project. Conceptualizing the costs of physical environment and time as scarce, finite nonrenewable resources and the energy and motivation of the people of the organization as expandable and renewable resources is important because it helps to further define the contextual components of satisfaction and work performance.

Lipman-Blumen and Leavitt's (1999) study of "hot groups" found a strong association of dwindling resources with lowered performance of teams. While young entrepreneurial groups or teams may find challenge and motivation in having limited resources, the loss of resources has a strong negative association with work satisfaction and performance.

AMBIENT PROPERTIES

Thermal comfort, illumination, sound, and air quality can be evaluated both with objective measures and with more subjective responses of building occupants. A comprehensive review of published post-occupancy evaluation protocols (McCoy, 1996) found that ambient conditions and the systems that produce them are the most commonly measured features of the office environment. Whereas there are published "ideal" ambient conditions (for specific tasks), due to individual differences there may be no such thing as a single comfortable temperature, sound, or level of light. People are most comfortable if they can control the ambient properties of the environment to suit their own requirements (Gerlach, 1974). Conversely, inability to control the ambient properties of the workplace to satisfy those requirements is likely to result in some increased level of individual stress (Cohen, Evans, Stokols, & Krantz, 1991).

Thermal Comfort

Effective temperature, an index composed of air temperature, humidity, and air movement measures, is an indicator of thermal comfort. While heat and cold can affect both environmental satisfaction and performance, the effects are complex. Thermal comfort depends on the type of work being done, the amount of clothing being worn, and the length of time spent in high or low effective temperature. Thermal comfort may also depend on the age and the health of the occupant of the work environment.

Performance in manual labor tasks is compromised at thermal extremes. For heavy manual labor, high temperatures are quicker to impede performance. For fine motor skills, cold temperatures are more likely to cause performance to drop. Moderate variations in temperatures do not seem to influence social behavior. Studies have not been able to link heat and aggressive social behavior (Rule, Taylor, & Dobbs, 1987). Similarly, helping behavior, as might be important in teamwork or client-serving organizations, does not increase or decrease with moderate variations in behavior (Schneider, Lesko, & Garrett, 1980).

Illumination

Lighting research is dominated by investigations of the relationship between luminance and visual performance: how well we understand the relationship of light levels and visibility. Visibility is determined and described with four factors: luminance, task/background contrast, task size, and the age of the observer. Behavioral outcomes associated with lighting may be categorized as: task performance, communication and social interaction, mood, health and safety, and aesthetic judgments (Veitch & Newsham, 1998). Studies in lighting research include studies of light sources (lamp types and sunlight), fixtures, amount (illuminance), and arrangements (Gifford, 1997).

Light sources include natural daylight and electric lighting. Field studies and laboratory studies investigating lamp type (fluorescent, incandescent, sodium vapor) of electric lighting have generally failed to demonstrate an association with task performance. However, the luminous flicker associated with conventional magnetic ballasts of fluorescent lamps has been shown to have effects on neural activity, visual performance, saccadic eye movements, reading, and headaches (Kuller & Laike, 1998; Veitch & McColl, 1995; Veitch & Newsham, 1998).

Many believe that natural light, or daylighting, is superior to electric lighting in association with work performance; the research to support this notion is scarce. Access to natural light is highly desirable to office workers (Wineman, 1982), and full-spectrum fluorescent lamps have been developed with the premise that even mimicking daylight can enhance work performance (Veitch, Hine, & Gifford, 1993). Studies of the relationship of natural light and work performance are often confounded because of seasonal, diurnal, intensity, and chromaticity variations. The nature of natural light requires that it be supplemented with electric light, making it difficult to study and describe precisely which conditions people responded to if they were in rooms with windows.

There is limited evidence of adverse effects of windowlessness (Collins, 1975). Satisfaction with and performance in windowless rooms appears to depend on the function of the space, its size, and the duration of time spent there. However, as described previously, the preference for windows is notable. In The Netherlands, legislation mandates that no person be assigned a workspace further than 16 feet from a window (Duffy, 1997).

For most individuals, the eye is very adaptable, making a broad range of light levels acceptable and providing adequate quantity of illumination to see (Boyce, 1996). Preferences for low light levels have been noted in offices with video display terminals (VDT) in use. This may be due to the glare produced by the VDT, which is self-luminous. Recent research with the advent and increasingly common use of the VDT screen has shown that the degree of contrast between the viewed object and its background can mediate work performance through eye fatigue, glare, and job satisfaction (Sanders & Bernecker, 1990).

The ubiquitous use of the computer and VDT screen in the office workplace has changed primary office tasks from a horizontal to a vertical plain and raised some questions about acceptable luminance relations between the computer screen and paper documents. General, ambient, or indirect light that is required for a paper task becomes a veiling luminance, recognizable reflected images of light and other light sources on a VDT screen. Tests of proofreading found no effect of veiled luminance on work performance, specifically proofreading (Bernecker et al., 1994).

The system and quality of lighting in the workplace also can influence the health and well-being of building occupants. As noted above, glare can cause eyestrain and headaches; glare can also contribute to accidents and stress (Veitch, in press). Proper illumination can prevent accidents. As we age our eyes change and we need more illumination. Occupants with some control over their workspace lighting (and other building systems) report fewer building-related illnesses (Sterling, 1986).

Inadequate or improper lighting in the office may result in glare or shadows. BOSTI (Brill et al., 1984) reported that nearly half of the employees who have difficulty with light indicated that they have too much. And, while proximity to windows is often correlated with problems of glare, employees also feel that their workspaces are dark if they are unable to see windows from the workspace. Effect of artificial light versus natural light on work performance in laboratory tests has not been determined. However, some field studies suggest that the quality of light is an important determinant of satisfaction.

Rea, Oulette, and Kennedy (1985) noted that participants tend to modify their posture to maintain visual performance under lighting conditions that would otherwise reduce task visibility. Such awkward or slouching postures may lead to orthopedic or other health problems resulting in absenteeism, lost productivity, and increased health-care costs.

Claims that lighting quality or quantity can create or change moods are not well supported, but studies of light levels do tend to suggest that increased light expands arousal level, suggesting greater alertness for shift workers (Campbell & Dawson, 1990). When offices are darker, employees are more likely to leave when they have a choice, at lunchtime, breaks, and so forth (Oldham & Fried, 1987).

Research studies in lighting demonstrate that direct or objective measures of the ambient properties of the work environment may indicate or predict performance and satisfaction with the physical environment. They also indicate a clear connection between the physical environment and the psychosocial issues relevant to work performance.

Sound

The spectrum of sound in the office work environment ranges from pleasantly desirable to irritatingly undesirable and can be described as short bursts to continuous, predictable, and unpredictable. Noise is unwanted sound; desirable, beautiful sound is euphony (Gifford, 1997). Noise in the office workplace may include audible voices of other people, music, the sound of building mechanical systems or office equipment, and sounds coming from the street through open windows. The same sounds may be euphony for some people but noise to others in the workplace, depending on the individual and the situation. Unlike some work environments like factories, or airports, or street maintenance, sounds in the office are rarely loud enough to damage or cause hearing loss. Still, sounds in the office workplace are important and can influence work performance and satisfaction. As uncontrolled or uncontrollable sound becomes more relevant to an employee, it is likely to be branded distracting noise and considered a stressor detrimental to work performance (Brill et al., 2001; Cohen et al., 1991).

The relationship of noise to work performance is based on several factors: the task, characteristics of the employee, characteristics of the sound itself, unique employee-noise combinations, the relation between noise and person, and other contextual conditions. Noise may interfere with work performance depending on the relative simplicity or complexity of the task. A routine task with clear instructions and expectations is not likely to be affected by a loud continuous noise (Broadbent, 1982). Though noise may be a problem for complex tasks, it may improve performance of simple tasks, especially those that are routine and boring may improve if the sound is not too irritating.

Work performance may be affected by noise depending on the age, sex, and personality of the employee. Noise slows reaction time and concentration of older people more than younger people (Jennings, Nebes, & Brock, 1988; Lahtela, Nieme, Kuusela, & Hypen, 1986). Individual personalities may respond to noise in unique and complex ways. Some people are more sensitive to noise than others. More extraverted personalities may prefer more stimulation in general; others may find noise detrimental to reading comprehension (Standing, Lynn, & Moxness, 1990). Some people are just better at screening out noise than others (Toplyn, 1988).

In office environments noise is likely to come from equipment as well as the voices of others. Problems with such noise have increasingly become a source of stress with the use of open office or systems furniture. Paradoxically, reports BOSTI (Brill, 1997), with technological advances in highly absorptive ceilings, sound masking, carpet, and acoustically absorbent panels, there are also increasing complaints of too little sound in offices. Likewise, while there definitely are noise exposure limits physiologically, exposure to noise affects work performance less if it is predictable and controllable (Cohen et al., 1991; Glass & Singer, 1972; Smith, 1989).

Air Quality

In the interest of conserving energy, today's building design typically includes windows that do not open. In the interest of thermal comfort, such buildings are designed with centralized air-conditioning systems that rely on a controlled mixture of fresh and recycled air. We expect the air handling system of today's office building to be unnoticed. We expect the air to smell fresh, contain just the right

humidity, provide thermal comfort, and be economical to operate. When the air quality falls short of employee expectations, the discomfort is a distraction and can be detrimental to work performance.

Air quality can influence the health of building occupants (Abdout & Lorsch, 1994). Gas emissions from mechanical systems and office equipment can be toxic in tightly enclosed settings. Improperly installed mechanical equipment can encourage the growth and distribution of fungi and bacteria in the air. Buildings located close to major roadways may take in concentrations of toxic air pollutants. Studies of air quality and work performance often produce mixed results because individuals vary widely in sensitivity to such pollutants depending on age, sex, and general health.

Poor air quality may result in sick building syndrome symptoms for individuals in the work environment. These symptoms include physical complaints of headaches; tiredness; dry/itchy eyes; sore/dry throat; cough; cold/flu symptoms; irritability; skin rashes; and pains in the neck, shoulders, and back, among others. These symptoms also manifest increased psychological stress in the workplace (Jukes, 2000) that can significantly affect job satisfaction and work performance.

Studies of the relationship of the workplace and the ambient properties of the building are important to understanding the complex relationships that are the nature of the work environment. Evaluations of thermal comfort, illumination, sound, and air quality are influenced by the ability of the employee to control them in her or his own workspace and by how well they support the work to be done and are perceived as equitable in the organization.

INTERACTIONS OF PEOPLE AND THE WORKPLACE

From the foregoing review of the literature at least three important themes have emerged. The system of interactions of people and the physical environment of the workplace relevant to satisfaction and performance include control, functional opportunities, and nonverbal self-expression. For individuals, interactions with the features and properties of the physical work environment may be evaluated as levels of arousal, adaptation, fatigue, stress, safety, and security. For groups, they may be evaluated as levels of communication and collaboration, status and identity, and crowding or privacy. For the organization, these interactions may be evaluated in terms of economic success, such as effectiveness or profitability.

CONTROL

Control refers to autonomy and motivation in decision making. Control for people in the workplace may include participatory design processes, the ability to eliminate or reduce distraction, and the ability to personalize the workspace. Autonomy is the mastery or ability to take action, to alter or regulate the environment (Evans & McCoy, 1998). Motivation is the compelling reason for taking action; it is the internal process that makes people do what they do even if the path is difficult. The ability to make unique, creative decisions requires intrinsic motivation and the opportunity to take autonomous action, and this ability can be supported by the physical features of the workplace.

Spatial Organization

The size, shape, allocation, and division of office space may contribute to a sense of privacy and allow the individual to control distractions. Location of an individual's workspace within the division of space, furniture configuration, and circulation routes can support or inhibit an individual's control of visual distractions or coworkers' unexpected visits. Participation in the design process may allow the individual to control the size and configuration appropriate to assigned tasks and responsibilities.

Participation in the design process to determine size, shape, allocation, and division of space helps to insure that team requirements will be met. Spaces that support the requirements of the teams in the workplace encourage satisfaction and performance. Organization of space can encourage or inhibit team communication and collaboration and thus influence satisfaction and performance.

Architectonic Details

Ornament and materials intended to embellish the workplace may be indications of individual or team control in the workplace. Participation in the selection of artwork and other artifacts may provide people in the workplace the opportunity to personalize their workspaces, provide a sense of aesthetic control, and reduce the potential for dissatisfaction with the workplace. Individual personalization and collective team personalization of the workplace can be expressions of autonomy and motivation, thus encouraging both job and environmental satisfaction as well as work performance.

Views

While views from the workplace may constitute some distraction, some views may also provide important information for enhancing work performance. Some views provide a restorative quality to the workplace, thus enhancing satisfaction. Pleasing views of nature, for instance, may contribute to overall satisfaction, thus encouraging work performance. Views of coworkers in the workplace may be necessary for efficient, effective team performance, thus enhancing performance. On the other hand, a work area with no interior or exterior views may be appropriate for encouraging people to work with no distraction.

Resources

Access to adequate and appropriate resources available in the workspace can permit people to work efficiently and effectively and, thus, minimize distractions or frustrations. Individual participation in the specification of resources can insure adaptability and flexibility of resources for accommodating specific tasks, human factors, and ergonomic needs. Participation in acquisition and controlling access to resources relevant to the work can encourage satisfaction and performance.

Ambient Properties

Extremes of temperature, noise, air quality, and light quality or quantity can be distractions to work performance. Tolerance for extremes may vary with individual needs and characteristics. The extent to which people in the workplace can control the ambient properties of the workspace may minimize distractions while enhancing both job satisfaction and work performance. Accessible environmental controls may involve low technology, such as thermostats, operable windows, task lighting, or surface acoustical treatment or more high technology, such as personal environment modules giving individuals control over air quality, noise, and thermal conditions. High-performing teams engaged in the intense process of focused attention on the task at hand may not require specific conditions unless they fall into the extreme or individuals within the team have extenuating circumstances.

FUNCTIONAL OPPORTUNITY

Functional opportunity refers to physical and perceived support of the goals and the performance of the people in the organization (Gibson, 1966, 1976; McCoy, 2000; Shehayeb, 1995). Requirements of individual and team functioning include opportunities to communicate and to collaborate. Communication, the sharing of ideas, suggests some interaction between individuals. Collaboration, the blending and developing of ideas, suggests openness, acceptance, and respect for other new ideas. Functional opportunities in the workplace include places where people are encouraged to communicate and collaborate.

Physical features and properties of the workplace provide functional opportunities for people to work. Requirements of individual workspaces include opportunities to work quietly, focus on the computer, do telephone work, and have productive interaction with colleagues. Individuals may also require opportunities outside their workspace for meetings, informal interaction, and breaks.

Spatial Organization

Csikszentmihalyi (1996, p. 54) notes that a place for creative thinking processes requires "access to the domain and opportunities for interaction." Amabile (1993) posits that the social environment is key to creative performance of groups and teams and that includes positive communication—allowing collaboration to occur. Kraut, Galegher, Fish, and Chalfonte (1992) suggest that most collaboration begins as a consequence of unplanned and unintended interaction; if so, a floor plan and furniture arrangement that allows team members close proximity and sustained interaction may be the functional opportunities for capturing those ideas.

An individual's workplace can provide functional opportunities by providing a space of appropriate size and configuration for that person's required tasks. Functional opportunities may also be accommodated with flexible adaptable spaces as may be necessary for changing strategies and tasks.

Architectonic Details

Functional opportunities are provided by architectonic details that encourage communication and collaboration. Comfortable furniture styles and arrangements can encourage informal communication and may support sustained, meaningful communication and collaboration. Materials and finishes that are durable and sustainable may support such opportunities by encouraging the use of a space. Artwork and artifacts that stimulate conversation may encourage communication. Sustained, meaningful communication can encourage both job and environmental satisfaction and work performance.

Views

Natural views may contribute to the functional opportunities provided to the individual employee by encouraging the use of a space and providing stress relief. Restorative qualities provided by natural views may encourage more efficient or more effective work processes within the workplace. Visual contact with other people in the workplace may contribute to the individual's ability to identify new functional opportunities. Alternatively, a workspace with no views may provide opportunities for sustained collaboration.

Resources

Availability and access to the proper technology and equipment can mean functional opportunity for people in the workplace. The extent to which people can easily access and operate appropriate resources may encourage performance and enhance satisfaction. Resources that do not function well, such as being outdated or in need of repair, may cause frustration and dissatisfaction, thus inhibiting performance.

Ambient Properties

Functional opportunities are provided to people in the work environment by enhancing sensory function through thermal comfort, appropriate illumination, pleasant sounds, and comfortable air quality. In work areas in which such sensory functioning is enhanced, work performance may be encouraged. In work areas in which sensory functioning is uncomfortable, job satisfaction and environmental satisfaction may be compromised and work performance inhibited.

Nonverbal Self-Expression

Nonverbal self-expression is a system of indicating identity, territory, and focus. A system of self-expression in the physical work environment includes the nonverbal marking of territory and communication of focus and activities (Brown, 1987; McCoy, 2000; Taylor, 1988). It includes physical displays of interests and achievements. For an individual, such displays may communicate a sense of identity or encourage reflection on personal goals and ambitions. For a team, collective self-expression may also provide feedback conveying the quantity and quality of their activities.

The system of self-expression in the workplace includes nonverbal communication of focus and activities. Self-expression may include displays of artifacts that are meaningful to the individual or to the team as a whole. Such expressions include evidence of activities or systems of activities, such as posters, photographs, awards, and other memorabilia. If as Rapoport (1990) argues, these self-expressions are cues to desired behavior, the various artifacts displayed in the workplace may be reinforcement for performance at different levels. Such self-expression may provide feedback to the individual or team conveying the quantity and quality of the activities.

The artifacts of nonverbal self-expression may contribute to a sense of coherence, providing a cognitive consistency between how the team views itself and the physical environment (Festinger, 1957). This may account for why people have their own unique sense of appropriate expressions of identity and displays of past performance (Bennis & Biederman, 1997; Kidder, 1981; McCoy, 2000). People seek to make the environment coherent and congruent with their concept of self and display artifacts that reflect their own achievements.

Spatial Organization

The size and shape of an individual's workspace may provide symbols of identity or status; likewise, the location of the workspace in relation to other workspaces, conference rooms, or informal areas may also be expressions of organizational status.

Organization or arrangement of furniture may be the individual's own expression of a preferred method of interaction with others. Division and allocation of the workspace may suggest individual territorial markers within a team space.

The extent to which the symbolic interpretation of the spatial organization of the workplace is consistent with the individual or team's self-evaluation, job satisfaction, and environmental satisfaction may be encouraged and work performance enhanced. Inconsistency and incongruence between the sense of identity and features of the physical workplace may contribute to dissatisfaction and inhibited performance.

Architectonic Details

Displayed artifacts may be symbols of the individual's personal and professional status or goals. Photographs of family, hobbies, or vacation may suggest both personal commitment to the job and a balance between work and personal activities. Photographs or artifacts reminiscent of successful achievement in the workplace may be cues to desired future behavior.

For teams in the workplace, displayed artifacts may provide feedback regarding the quality of their activities. Artifacts reflecting activities in the professional domain may be cues to team member's expectations for future efforts. The absence of such expressions may be feedback encouraging the team to remain focused on the status quo, keeping team activities limited to the familiar tasks and systems. This is consistent with Amabile's (1993) assertion that an overemphasis on the status quo can inhibit creative achievement of teams, whereas emphasis on freedom to explore and the challenge of meaningful, important work stimulates creative achievement.

Views

Desirable views from the workspace may be considered symbols of status reflective of high achievement. Views from the office workplace may provide symbols of individual achievement, status, or identity. Such symbols of status may enhance satisfaction and encourage work performance. Dissatisfaction and compromised performance may occur if desirable views are reserved only for those of highest status.

Resources

Quality and quantity of resources provided to the team may be considered symbols of status, equity, or value reflective of high achievement. Such symbols of status may enhance satisfaction and encourage work performance. Dissatisfaction and compromised performance may occur if such resources are not consistent within the organization.

Ambient Properties

Like resources, quality of ambient conditions and availability of controls for these systems may be considered symbols of status reflective of high achievement, influencing satisfaction and encourage work performance. However, dissatisfaction and compromised performance is possible if ambient control and conditions are inadequate or are not consistent within the organization.

THE FUTURE OF THE WORK ENVIRONMENT

To paraphrase a great leader, the only sure thing in the changing work environment is change itself. The *informated* organization has changed our systems of working and our understanding of work (Zuboff, 1988). The speed with which information is exchanged and the great distances that information can travel continues to increase at rates faster than even our "smart machines" can track. The consequence of such change, the rate and depth of that change, are uncharted territory making predictions for the future of the work environment imprudent at best. However, some trends are evident.

Changes for the workplace of the future will include new, developing technologies and marketplaces. When people first accomplished a walk on the moon, who could have predicted that within 3 decades commercial applications of such knowledge and technology would already be considered obsolete; that children would play computer games with greater sophistication than it took to send those men to the moon; or that cyberspace would be the home of great and innovative organizations? Even the system with which organizations are formed is unprecedented. Dot-coms and e-commerce, in addition to changing our lexicon, have changed our concept of how, where, and the speed with which companies must design, build, and furnish workplace facilities.

Future workplaces will reflect new demographics of the people who deal with the added new stressors of changing cultural and educational demands. The work ethic and expectations of the most recent entrants into the workforce will be influenced by their life-long experiences with emerging technologies. Seniority and hierarchy are likely to become irrelevant; a fluid social and cultural mix of participants may question established roles and attitudes undermining loyalty and stability. New freedoms will create new tensions requiring increased tolerance for ambiguity and greater ability for adaptation.

Some recent responses to today's changing workplace include: virtual offices, home offices, telecommuting, hotelling, nonterritorial offices, and satellite offices. Each has demonstrated varying degrees of success.

Virtual offices imply only the need for a portable computer and a mobile phone; the physical environment of the virtual office is ubiquitous, wherever the worker happens to be—airport, hotel, home, or even at a client's worksite. The virtual office worker may have a more recognizable or traditional office in the organization's portfolio of workplaces, but with the right technology, the virtual office does not require the worker's physical presence in the main office.

The home office implies a specific area set up in the worker's home where most of his or her work is done. This may be a home-based business, or it may be that the work to be done does not require physical presence in the organizational workplace every day. In either case, computer and telephone technology contribute significantly to this business dynamic.

Satellite offices are a system of increasing efficiency of employees by providing alternative offices remote from the main offices and closer to the employees' other activities. The satellite office may use traditional dedicated offices or nonterritorial offices. Telecommuting, the use of technology to transfer information between remote locations and the organizational workplace, includes the virtual office, the home office, and satellite offices.

While telecommuting has become widely practiced and accepted as a new way of working, it is not without limitations. It does give the people of the workplace unprecedented control of communication and access to information. However, by definition, opportunities for face-to-face contact with colleagues and supervisors are minimized. Telecommuting is not universally appropriate for all personalities or all work tasks.

Nonterritorial offices imply that workspaces are available in the workplace on an as-needed basis but are not assigned. These workplaces are suitable for people who are out of the office at least half the time or for extended periods of time. They may be traditional private spaces or open office cubicles, each with the right communication technology. Hotelling is one form of nonterritorial office for those workers who are frequently away from the main office and therefore do not require a dedicated, personally assigned office. Similar to making a hotel reservation, when the worker does need to be in the main office, an empty available office and appropriate equipment may be reserved. This approach to the changing workplace is an efficient use of space and equipment but does not encourage displays of self-expression; likewise, it does not encourage familiarity between colleagues, which may be key to open communication and collaboration.

Universal plan offices have been developed for some organizations. *Universal plan* implies that all individual workspaces are identical, supporting all functions within the organization and de-emphasizing the allocation of space as a symbol of status. While the need for symbols of accomplishment and status may be met in other ways, such as financial reward or vacation time, ignoring essential differences between people, tasks, and ways of working may limit work performance.

The rate and complexity of technological, geopolitical, and social change within organizations have created a stressful and uncertain environment both at work and at home (Lipman-Blumen & Leavitt, 1999). Burnout, violence, and rage are no longer uncommon terms associated with the workplace. The physical environment of work should not exacerbate such problems. Indeed, it should provide methods of coping with and managing this stress. The physical workplace of the future can support the people who work there by acknowledging psychological and physiological needs specific to the individual, their tasks, and the social and cultural context of their work.

The physical workplace of the future can support the people who work there by acknowledging the stressors of change. Future workplaces that adapt to changing individual or team needs, that enhance

rather than inhibit autonomy, that promote communication and collaboration on complex problems, and that express the value of the individual in the organization are more likely to experience satisfied, high-performing people.

The workplace of the future will continue to be important, although we may not recognize its physical manifestation by today's standards. Decisions will continue to be made by people, though with increasingly greater assistance from technology. People will work in a place, and that place will have features and properties that can support or inhibit thinking, concentrating, and decision making. Working people will need to be able to communicate and collaborate; they will need to receive feedback on their value and their performance. Ways of working will evolve; change and ambiguity in the workplace are inevitable. Satisfaction with job and environment will influence work performance. Creativity and innovation will be measures of performance.

Finding ways to anticipate, manage, and respond to change is the challenge of the new work environment. Researchers, designers, and organizational managers are challenged with new ways of working together with a common language and common goals. Understanding the work environment of the future includes understanding the people and the organization of the future.

SUMMARY

This chapter provides a selective review of the current understanding of the environmental psychology of the office work environment. It draws on and expands the previous work of Sundstrom (1987), discussing recent empirical findings on the relationship of the physical environment with the health, safety, and behavior of people in the workplace. These findings are presented within a framework based on the conception of the work environment as a system of complex relationships between people and the physical features and properties of the workplace.

Interactions between the people in the workplace and the physical work environment are described based on their response to spatial organization, architectonic details, views, resources, and ambient properties of the workplace. Control of the workplace includes participation in the design process, as well as the ability to regulate distractions. Functional opportunities for communication and collaboration in the physical workplace are important for making complex decisions. Nonverbal self-expressions are symbols of status and identity that provide focus and feedback to the people in the organization for prioritizing activities.

Individuals and teams who can control the workplace sufficiently to support changing functional requirements experience greater satisfaction and enhanced performance. Workplaces that provide functional opportunities for individuals and teams support communication and collaboration and provide greater job satisfaction and enhanced performance. Symbols of status and identity as indications of previous successful achievement also support satisfaction and performance of the people in the organization.

In the future, key issues of work environment and workplace design will include human response to organizational change, ambiguity, and uncertainty. As technology evolves and new generations of people in the work environment emerge, concepts of work environments and workplaces will require unprecedented flexibility, adaptability, and responsiveness. Finding ways to anticipate, manage, and respond to change is the challenge of the new work environment.

REFERENCES

Abdou, O., & Lorsch, H. (1994). The impact of the building indoor environment on occupant productivity: Part 3. Effects of indoor air quality, *ASHRAE Transactions, 100*(2), 902–913.

Allen, T. (1977). *Managing the flow of technology.* Cambridge, MA: Massachusetts Institute of Technology Press.

Amabile, T. (1988). A model of creativity and innovation in organizations. *Research in Organizational Behavior, 10,* 123–167.

Amabile, T. (1993). Motivational synergy: Toward new conceptualizations of intrinsic and extrinsic motivation in the workplace. *Human Resource Management Review, 3,* 185–201.

Becker, F., & Sims, W. (2000). *Managing uncertainty: Integrating portfolio strategies for dynamic organizations* (Rep. of International Workplace Studies Program). Cornell University.

Becker, F., & Steele, F. (1995). *Workplace by design.* San Francisco: Jossey-Bass.

Bennis, W., & Biederman, P. (1997). *Organizing genius: The secrets of creative collaboration.* New York: Addison-Wesley.

Bernecker, C., Brainard, G., Fernsler, F., Rollag, M., Long, R., Tierney, S., & Gaddy, J. (1994). Biological effects of architectural lighting and their associated energy utilization. *Journal of the Illuminating Engineering Society, 23*(2), 31–39.

Boyce, P. (1996). Illuminance selection based on visual performance—and other fairy stories. *Journal of the Illuminating Engineering Society, 25*(2), 41–49.

Brill, M. (1997). *Now offices, no offices, new offices . . . wild times in the world of office work.* Toronto, Canada: Teknion.

Brill, M., Margulis, S., & Konar, E. (1984). *Using office design to increase productivity* (Vols. 1–2). Buffalo, NY: Workplace Design & Productivity.

Brill, M., Weidemann, S., Alard, L., Olson, J., & Keable, E. (2001). *Disproving widespread myths about workplace design.* Jasper, IN: Kimball International.

Broadbent, D. (1982). Recent advances in understanding performance in noise. In G. Rossi (Ed.), *Noise as a public health hazard, proceedings of the 4th international congress.* Milan, Italy: Centro Richerche Studi Amplifom.

Brown, B. (1987). Territoriality. In D. Stokols & I. Altman (Eds.), *Handbook of environmental psychology.* New York: Wiley.

Campbell, S., & Dawson, D. (1990). Enhancement of nighttime alertness and performance with bright ambient light. *Physiology and Behavior, 48,* 317–320.

Cohen, S., Evans, G., Stokols, D., & Krantz, D. (1991). *Behavior, health, and environmental stress.* New York: Plenum Press.

Collins, B. (1975). *Windows and people: A literature survey* (National Bureau of Standards REP. NO. 70). Washington, DC: U.S. Government Printing Office.

Csikszentmihalyi, M. (1996). *Creativity: Flow and the psychology of discovery and invention.* New York: HarperCollins.

Cuttle, K. (1983). People and windows in work places. In D. Joiner, G. Brimilcombe, J. Daish, J. Gray, & D. Kernohan (Eds.), *Proceedings of the Conference on People and the Physical Environment Research.* New Zealand: Ministry of Works and Development.

Duffy, F. (1992). *The changing workplace.* London: Phaidon Press.

Duffy, F. (1997). *The new office.* London: Conran Octopus.

Evans, G., & McCoy, J. (1998). When buildings don't work: The role of architecture in human health. *Journal of Environmental Psychology, 18,* 85–94.

Festinger, L. (1957). *A theory of cognitive dissonance.* Stanford, CA: Stanford University Press.

Gerlach, K. (1974). Environmental design to counter occupational boredom. *Journal of Architectural Research, 3*(3), 15–19.

Gibson, J. (1966). *The senses considered as perceptual systems.* Boston: Houghton Mifflin.

Gibson, J. (1976). *The theory of affordances and the design of the environment.* Paper presented at the annual meetings of the American Society for Aesthetics, Toronto.

Gifford, R. (1997). *Environmental psychology: Principles and practice* (2nd ed.). Boston: Allyn & Bacon.

Glass, D., & Singer, J. (1972). *Urban stress: Experiments on noise and social stressors.* New York: Academic Press.

Heerwagen, J. (1990). The psychological aspects of windows and window design. In *Coming of age: Proceedings of the twenty-first annual Environmental Design Research Association (EDRA) conference* (p. 269–280). Edmond, OK: EDRA.

Heerwagen, J., & Orians, G. (1986). Adaptations to windowlessness: A study of the use of visual decor in windowed and windowless offices. *Environment and Behavior, 18*(5), 623–639.

Jennings, J., Nebes, R., & Brock, K. (1988). Memory retrieval in noise and psychophysiological response in the young and old. *Psychophysiology, 25,* 633–644.

Kao, J. (1996). *Jamming: The art and discipline of business creativity.* New York: HarperCollins.

Kaplan, R., & Kaplan, S. (1989). *The experience of nature: A psychological perspective.* New York: Cambridge University Press.

Kaplan, S., Talbot, J., & Kaplan, R. (1988). *Coping with daily hassles: The impact of nearby nature on the work environment* (Proj. Rep., U.S. Forest Service, North Central Forest Experiment Station, Urban Forestry Unit Cooperative Agreement 23-85-08). Washington, DC: U.S. Government Printing Office.

Kidder, T. (1981). *The soul of a new machine.* Boston: Little Brown.

Kraut, R., Galegher, J., Fish, R., & Chalfonte, B. (1992). Task requirements and media choice in collaborative writing. *Human-Computer Interaction, 7,* 375–407.

Kuller, R., & Laike, T. (1998). The impact of flicker from fluorescent lighting on well-being, performance and physiological arousal. *Ergonomics, 41,* 433–447.

Lahtela, K., Nieme, P., Kuusela, V., & Hypen, K. (1986). Noise and visual choice-reaction time: A large-scale population survey. *Scandinavian Journal of Psychology, 27,* 52–57.

Lipman-Blumen, J., & Leavitt, H. (1999). *Hot groups: Seeding them, feeding them, and using them to ignite your organization.* New York: Oxford University Press.

Ludlow, A. (1976). The functions of windows in buildings. *Lighting Research and Technology, 8*(2), 57–65.

Markus, T. (1967). The function of windows—a reappraisal. *Building Science, 2,* 97–121.

Mazumdar, S. (1992). Sir, please do not take away my cubicle: The phenomenon of environmental deprivation. *Environment and Behavior, 24*(6), 691–722.

McCoy, J. (1996). *Assessing quality in the work environment* (Johnson Controls Institute for Environmental Quality in Architecture). Milwaukee, WI: University of Wisconsin.

McCoy, J. (2000). *The creative work environment: The relationship of the physical environment and creative teamwork at a state agency—A case study.* Unpublished doctoral dissertation, University of Wisconsin-Milwaukee.

Oldham, G., & Fried, Y. (1987). Employee reactions to workplace characteristics. *Journal of Applied Psychology, 72,* 75–80.

Rapoport, A. (1990). *The meaning of the built environment: A nonverbal communication approach.* Tucson, AZ: University of Arizona Press.

Rea, M., Oulette, J., & Kennedy, J. (1985). Lighting and task parameters affecting posture, performance, and subjective ratings. *Journal of the Illuminating Engineering Society, 14*(2), 231–238.

Roessler, G. (1980). The psychological function of windows for the visual communication between the interior of rooms with permanent supplementary artificial lighting and the exterior. *Light Research and Technology, 12*(3), 160–168.

Rubenson, D., & Runco, M. (1992). The psychoeconomic view of creative work in groups and organizations. *New Ideas in Psychology, 10,* 131–147.

Rule, B., Taylor, B., & Dobbs, A. (1987). Priming effects of heat on aggressive thought. *Social Cognition, 5,* 111–142.

Sanders, P., & Bernecker, C. (1990). Uniform veiling luminance and display polarity affect VDU user performance. *Journal of the Illuminating Engineering Society, 19*(2), 113–123.

Schneider, F., Lesko, W., & Garrrett, W. (1980). Helping behavior in hot, comfortable, and cold temperatures. *Environment and Behavior, 12*(2), 231–240.

Schrage, M. (2000). *Serious play: How the world's best companies simulate to innovate.* Boston: Harvard Business School Press.

Shehayeb, D. (1995). *Potential function opportunities in urban streets.* Unpublished doctoral dissertation, University of Wisconsin-Milwaukee.

Smith, A. (1989). A review of the effects of noise on human performance. *Scandinavian Journal of Psychology, 30,* 185–209.

Standing, L., Lynn, D., & Moxness, K. (1990). Effects of noise upon introverts and extroverts. *Bulletin of the Psychonomic Society, 28,* 138–140.

Sterling, E. (1986). Indoor air quality—Total environment performance: Comfort and productivity issues in modern office buildings. *The Canadian Journal of Real Estate, 18,* 21–25.

Sternberg, R., & Lubart, T. (1995). *Defying the crowd: Cultivating creativity in a culture of conformity.* New York: Free Press.

Sundstrom, E. (1987). Work environments: Offices and factories. In I. Altman and D. Stokols (Eds.), *Handbook of environmental psychology.* New York: Cambridge University Press.

Taylor, R. (1988). *Human territorial functioning: An empirical evolutionary perspective on individual and small group territorial cognitions, behaviors, and consequences.* New York: Cambridge University Press.

Toplyn, G. (1988). The differential effect of noise on creative task performance. *Dissertation Abstracts International, 48,* 3718.

Ulrich, R. (1984). View from the window may influence recovery from surgery. *Science, 224,* 420–421.

Ulrich, R. (1993). Biophilia, biophobia, and natural landscapes. In S. Kellert & E. Wilson (Eds.), *The biophilia hypothesis.* Washington, DC: Island Press.

Veitch, J. (in press). Psychological processes influencing light quality. *Journal of Illuminating Engineering Society.*

Veitch, J., Hine, D., & Gifford, R. (1993). End users' knowledge, preferences, and beliefs for lighting. *Journal of Interior Design, 19*(2), 15–26.

Veitch, J., & McColl, S. (1995). On the modulation of fluorescent light: Flicker rate and spectral distribution effects on visual performance and visual comfort. *Light Research and Technology, 27,* 243–256.

Veitch, J., & Newsham, G. (1998). Determinants of light quality I: State of the science. *Journal of the Illuminating Engineering Society, 27*(1), 92–106.

Wineman, J. (1982). The office environment as a source of stress. In G. W. Evans (Ed.), *Environmental stress.* New York: Cambridge University Press.

Wineman, J., & Serrato, M. (1999). Facility design for high-performance teams. In E. Sundstrom & Associates (Eds.), *Supporting work team effectiveness: Best management practices for fostering high performance.* San Francisco: Jossey-Bass.

Zuboff, S. (1988). *In the age of the smart machine: The future of work and power.* New York: Basic Books.

CHAPTER 30

Environmental Psychology in Museums, Zoos, and Other Exhibition Centers

STEPHEN C. BITGOOD

THE DEFINITION OF *MUSEUM*

THE WORD *MUSEUM* CONJURES varying images. Some might think of the natural history museum with dusty mounted animals that they visited occasionally as a child. Others might think of the architecture of museums as a defining characteristic—the palatial steps leading into a huge columned entrance designed to create a feeling of awe and reverence in the visitor. Still others might reminisce about family visits to a science center with hands-on science exhibits and an Omnimax movie. Still others might recall a local history museum crammed with Native American artifacts or old farming tools. Those who have more aesthetic tastes might think of an art museum filled with artworks, some of which are comprehensible, while others seem to stretch the definition of art.

A museum can, of course, be all of the above. However, for purposes of this chapter, the focus will be on a museum as an exhibition center whose primary mission is education. This includes (but is not limited to) aquariums, art museums, history museums, botanical gardens, science centers, nature centers, and zoos. The concept that connects these facilities is *educational exhibition*. While theme parks such as Sea World and EPCOT have educational

exhibitions, their major goal is profit rather than education. Theme parks may also be distinguished from museums in terms of willingness to share data collected about their visitors, collections, and programs, thus minimizing their scientific contributions to environmental design research.

Live animal exhibits create an additional consideration for environmental psychology since the design of the animal habitats must be considered. Zoos and aquariums are not the only exhibition centers using live animals. Many, if not most, natural history museums and science centers now exhibit a variety of live animals.

FORMAL VERSUS INFORMAL EDUCATION

Museums are informal learning institutions. As educational institutions, museums share several characteristics with formal education (regular classrooms). For example, both usually formulate objectives or teaching points. Both employ common media (e.g., lecture, film, slides, computers, demonstrations), although the frequency of use may differ between formal and informal practice. In addition, both tend to organize the subject matter into academic chapter headings. Both rely to a greater or lesser degree on text materials to deliver their messages.

Despite these similarities, informal educational environments differ markedly from formal

Thanks to Harris Shettel and Arlene Benefield for their comments on an earlier draft of this manuscript.

institutions (e.g., Bitgood, 1988; Brown, 1979; Screven, 1986). These differences include but are not restricted to:

- *Instructional stimuli.* In formal education, the instructional stimuli are usually verbal, whereas in informal setting they are more likely to be visual or multisensory. Formal education emphasizes sustained exposure to the education material (usually called studying), while informal education is characterized by a brief exposure to the material as the visitor moves through the exhibit space.

- *The physical environment.* A classroom in formal education usually attempts to minimize distractions (e.g., bare walls, lack of competing sounds). The focus of attention is usually on the instructor and/or audiovisual presentations. In informal education, the environment is flooded with competing stimuli, many of them distracting the learner from focusing on a single educational message.

- *Overt behaviors.* Formal education is usually teacher paced and responses are explicitly prescribed (study the text, take a test, etc.). In informal education, behavior is less explicitly prescribed or under the influence of external factors. The visitor is generally considered to make choices (Do I go here or there? Should I read this label?).

- *Social contacts.* In formal settings, social contact is highly controlled and socialization among group members is discouraged. In informal learning settings, on the other hand, social contacts are sometimes the most important part of the experience (or at least a very important aspect).

- *Learning consequences.* In formal education, consequences of behavior are coercive. Powerful rewards and punishers (earning good grades, failing, social ridicule) are the usual consequences of academic performance. In informal education, the consequences are minimal. You are not admonished if you fail to read an exhibit label or understand the exhibit's message. In museums the less coercive consequences include the delight in discovering new knowledge or reminiscing about old artifacts and/or the pleasure of social interaction with family and/or friends.

THE EMERGING FIELD OF VISITOR STUDIES

While there may still be debate over whether or not there is a distinct discipline (Loomis, 1988), "visitor studies" has become the name of the field for those who study the visitor perspective to environmental design issues in museums. Those who practice visitor studies come from a variety of fields and only a few would consider themselves environmental psychologists. Some come from an educational background, some from museum studies programs, some from content area disciplines (history, science, etc.). There is no higher education degree in visitor studies at this time, although there has been increasing interest in establishing such a program (e.g., Friedman, 1995).

The field now has an association (Visitor Studies Association, established in 1991), an annual conference (which began in 1988), and a newsletter (*Visitor Behavior* from 1986 to 1997 and *Visitor Studies Today* from 1998 to present) and has a Standing Professional Committee within the American Association of Museums. A journal (*International Laboratory for Visitor Studies Review*), devoted exclusively to visitor studies, was published from 1988 to 1992. Other journals (*Curator, The Journal of Interpretive Research, Environment and Behavior, Museum Management and Curatorship*) also publish articles on visitor studies.

There are other organizations with overlapping interests in exhibition centers, but visitor studies is the only group strongly dedicated to applying psychological and educational research methods to environmental problems within the museum setting.

THE METHODOLOGY OF VISITOR STUDIES

The methodology of visitor studies is not unlike the field of enviornmental psychology in general. It deals with diverse audiences and uses eclectic methods borrowed from other disciplines.

TARGET AUDIENCES

Research and evaluation in museums have included three general audiences: leisure (unscheduled visitors or groups of family and friends), school groups, and nonvisitors.

Leisure Visitors

The bulk of visitor studies has focused on unscheduled, on-site (leisure) visitors. This, of course, makes sense since leisure visitors (groups of families and friends) comprise the largest museum audience. Leisure visitors tend to be very heterogeneous groups, often comprised of multigenerational members.

School Groups

In addition to the individuals and groups that show up at the door, a large segment of museum audiences include school groups, which differ substantially from the leisure visitor (e.g., Bitgood, 1989, 1991b). School groups are usually guided by teachers, parents, and/or docents and generally focus on specific content areas (usually associated with its relevance to the school curriculum). Unlike the usual visitor, school groups also have supplementary educational material sometimes presented in the formal classroom or workbook-type tasks to complete within the museum.

Nonvisitors

There are also times when nonvisitors are selected (e.g., Hood, 1983). Nonvisitors are studied to attempt to understand why many people do not visit or to identify differences in leisure values or demographics between visitors and nonvisitors.

Quantitative versus Qualitative Methodology

There is some debate within the field on the appropriateness of qualitative and quantitative methodologies. Some have argued that the nature of the informal learning environment dictates a qualitative approach (e.g., Wolf, 1980); others argue that both types of methodology may be fruitful, each contributing some valuable information (Bitgood, Serrell, & Thompson, 1994; Screven, 1990).

Observational Methods

Observational methods typically include tracking visitors through an entire exhibition or exhibit area, conducting a time sampling at specific areas, or doing intensive or focused observations of a single exhibit or small exhibit area.

Tracking Studies

This method is used to study an entire exhibition when it is important to identify how people move through the exhibition, where the "hot" and "cold" spots are, and so forth. A selected visitor and/or group is observed throughout the exhibition noting where visitors stop, for how long, and what they do when stopping. This method allows comparisons among exhibit elements. It assesses the circulation patterns and gives a "big picture" analysis of how visitors distribute their attention in an exhibition.

Time Sampling

This method records visitor behaviors at selected times in each of the specific areas of the exhibition. Similar to tracking studies, all areas are generally sampled, but the focus here is on all visitor activity in each area rather than a record of an individual visitor's behavior. This is another way to assess how visitors distribute their attention without having to examine every exhibit element for every visitor.

Focused Observations

When only one exhibit (or a small number) is being studied, focused observations can provide a cost-effective way to collect observational data. If a problem exhibit display has been identified, intensive assessment of the impact of this exhibit on visitors can be conducted.

Automatic Recording

Although rarely used in museum settings, automatic recording devices have considerable potential. Bechtel (1967) described a "hodometer" device in which pressure-sensitive pads were placed under the floor of an art gallery. This device allowed indirect measures of the number of visitors, rate of movement, and pattern of movement through the gallery. More common examples of automatic recording include the use of audio and video recording devices. For example, McManus (1989) audio recorded visitors' verbal responses at exhibits and later compared them with observations of label reading.

Self-Report Methods

Self-report methods include both surveys and focus groups. Surveys are used to measure a variety of things including attitudes, free recall, and/or recognition of information and the visitor's ability to apply or generalize what he or she has learned. Here are a few typical examples of museum surveys:

- A museum exit survey designed to measure overall visitor satisfaction for the entire museum experience
- A survey to obtain visitor reactions to a specific exhibit or exhibition
- A front-end survey during the planning stage of an exhibition designed to assess the potential audiences preknowledge, attitudes, and preferences for media, topics, and so forth
- A survey to identify possible visitor orientation problems

Focus groups have also become a popular way to collect information about visitors, especially when marketing is involved. Groups may be asked to respond to questions about the museum's image, about their experiences at the museum, or about exhibits or programs still in the planning stage.

CRITIQUE OF MEASUREMENT IN MUSEUMS

The most accepted form of evaluating an exhibition combines observational and self-report data recognizing that observational data has more validity for assessing what visitors actually do and that self-report data are necessary to assess thoughts, feelings, and attitudes associated with the visitor experience.

There are currently several major problems with data collected in museums. First, many evaluators and consumers of the data lack the knowledge and skills to collect and use the information in a reliable and valid manner. Second, there have been very few studies reporting reliability and validity of the instruments used to collect the data. A third problem is that the museum stakeholders (e.g., directors and boards) lack the knowledge to judge the reliability and validity of the data collected. These problems should be reduced as professionals and consumers become more knowledgeable in evaluation.

THE HISTORY OF VISITOR STUDIES

Visitor studies in informal learning settings has a short history and will be given a very brief treatment here. Interested readers are referred to Shettel (1989), Schiele (1992), and Bitgood and Loomis (1993) for more detailed descriptions of this history.

THE 1920s AND 1930s: FOCUS ON ENVIRONMENTAL DESIGN

While a few isolated studies of visitors were conducted prior to the 1920s, the first systematic research was conducted by Edward Robinson and Arthur Melton at Yale University (e.g., Melton, 1933, 1935, 1972; Robinson, 1928, 1930, 1931). Robinson and Melton were primarily interested in studying how the physical design of the museum environment influences visitor behavior. Among their major contributions were a systematic study of factors that influence visitor attention and patterns of visitor circulation through exhibit galleries. While environmental design may have been the primary focus of Robinson and Melton, they were not oblivious to the fact that the museum is a learning environment. Melton, Feldman, and Mason (1936) reported a series of studies examining the effects of instructional design variables (e.g., previsit activities) on the learning of school children in museums.

THE 1960s AND EARLY 1970s: THE APPLICATION OF BEHAVIORAL LEARNING APPROACHES

During the two decades following the work of Robinson and Melton, only a few scattered studies were conducted. In the 1960s, however, a renaissance of visitor studies activity began in museums. The most prominent leaders were Harris Shettel (e.g., Shettel, 1967, 1976; Shettel, Butcher, Cotton, Northrup, & Slough, 1968; Shettel & Schumacher, 1969) and Chan Screven (e.g., 1969, 1974, 1975). Screven and Shettel's backgrounds in behavioral learning and programmed instruction were readily applied to the assessment of cognitive and affective learning that results from exposure to exhibits.

THE LATE 1970s AND 1980s

Until the late 1970s, visitor studies were conducted primarily by outside professionals (Melton, Robinson, Screven, and Shettel were not museum employees). The locus of evaluation projects began to change in the 1970s when visitor evaluation started to become an internal process. The British Museum of Natural History (London) under the leadership of

Roger Miles, Mick Alt, and Steve Griggs became the first museum to adapt an internal, systematic approach to visitor evaluation during the 1970s (e.g., Alt, 1980; Griggs, 1981; Miles, 1986; Miles & Alt, 1979; Miles & Tout, 1978).

Also during this time period, the Lawrence Hall of Science at Berkeley (University of California) began a series of studies on exhibit effectiveness (e.g., Eason & Friedman, 1975; Eason & Linn, 1976; Friedman, Eason, & Sneider, 1979; Sneider, Eason, & Friedman, 1979). Minda Borun at the Franklin Institute of Science (Philadelphia) was another key early investigator in visitor learning during this period (e.g., Borun, 1977; Borun, Flexer, Casey, & Baum, 1983; Borun & Miller, 1980).

In the late 1970s, Robert Wolf and his associates (e.g., Wolf, 1980; Wolf & Tymitz, 1978) developed an approach, called "naturalistic evaluation," that used qualitative methods of data collection and attempted a holistic approach to the museum experience. Much of their work was completed at the museums of the Smithsonian Institution.

The Exploratorium, in San Francisco, under the direction of Frank Oppenheimer developed the science center concept most prevalent today. This concept involves almost exclusive use of hands-on, interactive exhibit devices (e.g., Duensing, 1987; Oppenheimer, 1968, 1975, 1986). The importance of the Exploratorium model is evident by the fact that so many science exhibits mimic those developed at the Exploratorium. Oppenheimer's philosophy (people will learn what they want and when they want, and what visitors learn is less important than the fact that they learn something) has become a major view of informal science education.

John and Mary Lou Koran at the University of Florida, applying a cognitive approach, began their museum work during this period (e.g., J. Koran, Lehman, Shafer, & Koran, 1983). John Falk and his colleagues (e.g., Falk & Balling, 1980, 1982; Falk, Martin, & Balling, 1978) were also active during this period; they reported a series of studies on factors influencing field trip learning by school groups.

Another methodological approach was introduced to visitor studies in the late 1970s and early 1980s. A group of researchers using an ethological approach (e.g., Diamond, 1980, 1982, 1986; Gottfried, 1979, 1980; Rosenfeld, 1979; Rosenfeld & Turkel, 1982; Taylor, 1986) provided a series of dissertations at the University of California, Berkeley. Their studies conducted at the Lawrence Hall of Science offer excellent examples of the value of descriptive research in visitor learning.

THE CURRENT PERIOD: THE ERA OF ECLECTICISM

In the late 1980s a large number of new investigators joined the visitor studies movement and the amount of research has increased dramatically. A number of different approaches (cognitive developmental, information processing, behavioral, ethological, etc.) are applied and melded into multimethod evaluation systems. Piaget's cognitive developmental theory has been adopted by several educators (e.g., Boram, 1991). Norman's (1988) information processing approach has been applied to the design of interactive exhibits (e.g., Bitgood, 1991a; Kennedy, 1990). The contributions of the behavioral, cognitive, and ethological approaches have all been integrated into the arsenal of visitor studies methodology. Although philosophical arguments are still common (e.g., Bitgood, 1997; Hein, 1997; Miles, 1993, 1997; Shettel, 1990b; St. John, 1990), there are probably more similarities than differences in the application of methodology.

The interested reader can find an increasing number of sources for the visitor literature. Publications include: *Curator, Visitor Studies Today, Current Trends in Audience Research* (an annual publication by the American Association of Museums' Committee on Audience Research and Evaluation), *Journal of Museum Education, International Journal of Museum Management and Curatorship, ILVS Review, Visitor Behavior, Visitor Studies: Theory, Research and Practice* (the annual collected papers from the Visitor Studies Conferences). There have also been two related special issues of a Sage publication, *Environment and Behavior*—one on visitor studies in zoos and the other on museums. Conference presentations on visitor studies can be found at the annual meetings of the American Association of Museums, the Association of Zoos & Aquariums, the Association of Science-Technology Centers, Visitor Studies Association, at many regional conferences, and at a surprising number of one-time conferences on special topics.

THE SCOPE OF VISITOR STUDIES

Several areas of visitor studies can be identified, although it is important to emphasize that they must all work together to make a successful museum environment. For a more detailed discussion, see Bitgood and Loomis (1993) and Bitgood and Shettel (1996).

AUDIENCE RESEARCH

One approach to visitor studies has been called "audience research" (e.g., Hood, 1983). This area is concerned with: why people visit or why they stay away, people's impressions of the museum, how leisure values relate to visitation patterns and satisfaction. This area is most clearly associated with marketing and publicity, and professionals who conduct these types of studies are often marketing firms or marketing departments within a museum.

EXHIBIT AND PROGRAM EVALUATION/DEVELOPMENT

The bulk of activity in visitor studies has focused on exhibition development and assessment. Fewer visitor studies have been conducted on program development, although it is not uncommon particularly for school group programs to be evaluated.

Exhibition evaluation can be implemented during all three major stages of development (planning, preparation, and installation). Visitor input during the planning stage is called front-end evaluation; during the preparation stage it is called formative evaluation; and after installation it is called either remedial or summative evaluation (Bitgood & Loomis, 1993; Screven, 1990). Perhaps there has not been enough concern with the predictive validity of these evaluation types, but some efforts have been made (e.g., Griggs & Manning, 1983).

ORIENTATION AND CIRCULATION

"Conceptual orientation" refers to information and delivery devices that give visitors advance organizers about the museum and the exhibitions within. Some information such as architectural style may communicate visually. "Wayfinding" (sometimes called physical or geographical orientation) is what it sounds like—the ability to navigate through the museum. "Circulation" is related to patterns of movement through museum settings. A number of variables have been identified that influence this movement or these pedestrian traffic patterns (e.g., Bitgood & Lankford, 1995).

VISITOR SERVICES

Another area of concern is related to the "front-line" staff. "Customer relations" is recognized as a critical area in museums, theme parks, hotels, and retail stores (e.g., Hayward, 1996; Hill, 1996; Hood, 1993; Stokes, 1996).

SETTING FACTORS

One way to describe environmental design in museums from the visitor perspective is to focus on the major settings found within a museum—the entrance/lobby, exhibitions, areas with amenities (rest rooms, gift shop, and food service), and, finally, the macroarchitecture of the museum. These settings will be discussed individually.

ENTRANCE AND LOBBY

The design of the facility's entrance and lobby is of critical importance especially for infrequent visitors or first-time visitors who are unfamiliar with the museum (e.g., Bitgood & Tisdal, 1996). The museum must ensure that the "hard architecture" and orientation systems meet the needs of visitors. "Hard architecture" includes the physical environment (placement of doors, windows, ticket booths/windows, information desks, etc.). Foremost of the visitors' needs are: (1) *conceptual orientation* (knowledge about what to see and do and how to plan the visit) and (2) *wayfinding* (knowing how to find the rest rooms, exhibit galleries, gift shop, cafeteria). Based on lobby information (entrance fee, information about exhibitions, etc.), visitors sometimes make the decision not to pay the entrance fee and leave the museum. In addition to visitor needs, the museum must communicate to the visitor the rules of behavior, choices, special programs, and the like. Unfortunately, very little research has focused on this area, although museums tend to spend considerable energy dealing with these problems.

One of the difficulties in designing the entrance/lobby is political—a number of different museum stakeholders want some control. For example, in science centers, the lobby usually contains an information desk, a membership desk, ticket windows for Omnimax or Imax movies and the planetarium shows, local tourist information, and so forth. Each of these entities competes for the ideal location for their particular function. Thus, the resulting lobby configuration may be more political than practical.

CONCEPTUAL ORIENTATION

Information about what to do, alternative choices, where to go, and so forth is often provided in a visitor guide, on orientation signage, or by museum staff. Several generalizations can be abstracted from the literature:

- On-site staff to provide orientation information is inadequate since visitors rarely ask staff for orientation information (visitors are more likely to ask for content) (Cohen, Winkel, Olsen, & Wheeler, 1977).
- You-are-here maps are generally not used for wayfinding purposes but for conceptual orientation or to provide information about which exhibits were located in the museum (Cohen et al., 1977).
- When a combination of visitor guide and orientation slide show are available in the lobby, visitor questions to staff may substantially decrease, suggesting improved visitor orientation (Birney, 1989).
- If possible, visitors should have visual access to rest rooms, gift shops, and entrances to exhibition galleries when they are orientating themselves in the lobby.
- Location of functions in the lobby should meet visitor expectations (e.g., rest rooms, phones, coat rooms are expected to be adjacent to each other).

WAYFINDING

Wayfinding information is also critical at the beginning of the visit. Hand-held maps (usually in the form of a visitor guide), fixed you-are-here maps, directions signs, and museum staff are all used to decrease the confusion.

- A visitor guide may increase the total time visitors spend in the museum and/or exhibitions viewed and result in overall increased satisfaction with the visit (Bitgood & Richardson, 1986; Bitgood & Tisdal, 1996).
- Redundant wayfinding cues (hand-held maps, direction signs, you-are-here maps, etc.) are

helpful to visitors because such cues provide a feeling of security, give the visitors a choice of options, and are more likely to be noticed.
- Maps should be simple but give enough information so that visitors can locate where they are at any moment (Levine, 1982; Talbot, Kaplan, Kuo, & Kaplan, 1993).
- You-are-here maps should follow the Levine's principles of forward-up equivalence, a you-are-here symbol, and some landmark that is visible in the environment and present on the map (Levine, 1982).
- Wayfinding information should be placed at the point it is needed (e.g., choice points).
- Visitors prefer hand-held maps over other wayfinding devices (e.g., Bitgood & Richardson, 1986).

Orientation and wayfinding principles applied to exhibitions are also important. Griggs (1983) provides some useful guidelines. Hayward and Brydon-Miller (1984) have examined visitor orientation at an outdoor history museum (Old Sturbridge Village in Massachusetts) and have identified some important issues.

EXHIBITIONS

It has been about 70 years since the ground-breaking studies of Robinson (1928) and Melton (1935). After reporting a series of studies in museums, Melton suggested the following:

> The obvious recommendation which flows from these studies is that there should be a branch of museum research which is wholly concerned with the psychological problems of museum architecture. (p. 267)

Melton's reference to "museum architecture" is what is more commonly called "exhibit design." There has been much effort in the last 30 years or so toward realizing Melton's recommendation. However, there are few theoretical formulations to tie together the growing body of empirical observations.

Bitgood (2000b) has suggested that three interrelated principles of attention explain and help organize what we know about visitors' reactions to exhibitions:

Principle No. 1. Attention to exhibits is selective, visitors attend to one thing at a time, and what gets attention is determined by distinctiveness or salience of the element/object and by whether or not the visitor's pathway is close to the element/object.

Principle No. 2. Visitors must be motivated in order to focus their attention on exhibits. Motivation is a function of cognitive-emotional arousal (e.g., interest level), the amount of perceived work, and the number and intensity of distractions.

Principle No. 3. The resources for attending to exhibitions have a limited capacity and are depleted by mental and physical effort. The rate of depletion and renewal is dependent upon the total amount of effort expended, the amount of cognitive-emotional arousal, and the amount of time.

SELECTIVITY

Attention is selective in the sense that some things capture our attention while others do not, and in the sense that we can attend (generally) to only one thing at a time. If visitors can attend to only one exhibit element at a time, what will it be? Capturing visitor attention is the first step in the process of communicating the educational message. Visitors must first pay attention to a label before it has any chance of delivering any kind of message.

Two obvious factors in capturing attention are the salience or distinctiveness of the exhibit element and the traffic flow patterns in the environment. The more salient the element, the more likely it will be noticed. Traffic flow also influences whether an exhibit element will be detected: Objects in locations along the pathway taken by visitors have a reasonable chance of being seen, whereas those outside the pathway have almost no chance of receiving attention.

Stimulus Salience (Distinctiveness)

Following are some of the major factors that influence visitor attention in terms of detecting exhibit elements:

- *Isolation.* An object isolated from other objects is likely to get the undivided attention of visitors (e.g., Melton, 1935, 1972). The greater the number of stimuli surrounding an element, the

less likely it will be noticed, especially if it lacks other salient factors.

- *Size.* Larger objects receive more attention than smaller ones (e.g., Bitgood & Patterson, 1993).

- *Contrast with setting background.* Objects that blend into the background may be ignored because they lack attention-getting power. In the parlance of signal detection theory, background "noise" makes it more difficult to detect a stimulus.

- *Multisensory characteristics.* Adding sound, smell, or touch to an exhibit attracts more attention (sometimes at the cost of less attention to surrounding objects) (e.g., Melton, 1972).

- *Lighting.* The overall level of lighting is, of course, important in determining whether or not an object will be noticed. In addition, the contrast in lighting between the object and its surrounding produced by spot lighting is another way to make it more detectable.

- *Line-of-sight placement.* An object that falls easily within a viewer's line of sight is easier to detect. One consideration is the distance from the floor. Objects placed more than 6 or 7 feet above the floor often go unnoticed because people tend not to look up (Bitgood, Benefield, & Patterson, 1989; Bitgood, Conroy, Pierce, Patterson, & Boyd, 1989). Another consideration is where visitor attention usually is focused, that is, on the object. If a label is not close to the object it describes (e.g., on the railing in front of the object), the label is less likely to be noticed and read (Bitgood, Hines, Hamberger, & Ford, 1991).

Circulation/Traffic Flow

Many exhibit objects are ignored because of the traffic flow. If visitors do not pass by an object, it will not attract attention. Consequently, it is critical to understand the factors that influence traffic flow in exhibit environments. Rarely do visitors pass by all objects in a gallery (Bitgood et al., 1991; Melton, 1935). Factors that influence traffic flow are:

- *Attraction of a salient object.* A large object (such as an exhibit display) will influence the traffic flow by creating a tendency for visitors to move toward or approach after entering the environment (Bitgood et al., 1991). Landmark objects influence pathway, which in turn influences whether or not other objects receive attention. For example, visitors are likely to bypass and consequently ignore a less salient object in order to approach and view a more salient one.

- *Attraction (or distraction) of an open door.* Melton (1935) reported that there was a strong tendency for visitors to enter a gallery, move along the right-hand wall, and exit by the first open door. When the door was closed so that visitors had to exit by the same door as they entered, visitors circulated more completely through the gallery giving attention to more objects on exhibit.
- *Arrangement of objects/displays.* The arrangement of objects within the environment determine how people will move through the environment (e.g., Bitgood et al., 1991). In every exhibit space, there are "hot" and "cold" spots of visitor attention that are at least partially influenced by the circulation patterns of visitors. A myriad of exhibit islands creates a chaotic traffic flow in which some displays receive a high level of attention and others receive a low level. When the flow is chaotic, visitors are more likely to miss a display unintentionally. If there is a clear pathway or order of viewing displays, each object is more likely to get attention.
- *Inertia.* Visitors tend to continue along a straight-line path unless some force (e.g., landmark exhibit object) pulls them away. Melton's (1935) proposed "exit gradient" is a special case. Melton defined *exit gradient* as the tendency to take the shortest distance between the entrance and exit when moving through a gallery.
- *Right-turn bias.* In the absence of other forces (see earlier discussion), visitors have a tendency to turn right when entering an interpretive space (e.g., Melton, 1935).

MOTIVATING FOCUSED (SUSTAINED) ATTENTION

The second principle of attention in exhibitions is that focused attention requires motivation. Motivating visitors to focus on labels and objects is the most challenging task in exhibition design. Rand (1990) has suggested some intriguing ideas on how to "hook" readers with the use of language. Screven (1992) has identified many of the variables that seem to increase visitors' motivation to read labels. Motivating interest results in focused visitor attention on the exhibits.

There appear to be three general factors involved in motivating visitors to focus their attention on exhibits: (1) Minimize the perceived effort to obtain information, (2) increase cognitive-emotional arousal (provoke interest in the subject matter if it is not already there), and (3) minimize distracting factors.

Minimize Perceived Effort

In terms of the processes of attention, mental effort may do two things: (1) It decreases motivation to attend and (2) it depletes the resources of attention. The first of these will be discussed here, and the latter (depletion of the resources of attention) later. By reducing mental effort, more cognitive resources for attending to exhibits are available, and presumably, this increases motivation to focus. Since most of the effort is mental and involves making sense of interpretive labels, the following principles deal primarily with label design:

- *Number of words per label chunk.* Bitgood and Patterson (1993) demonstrated that breaking down a long label into three smaller ones (chunks), resulted in increased reading.
- *Proximity of label to object.* The least amount of effort in label reading occurs when a visitor can look at the exhibit object and read a label at the same time. Thus, placing a label on a railing in front of the object viewed is more effective than on the side of the exhibit or away from the exhibit (e.g., Bitgood, Benefield, & Patterson, 1989). Placement closer to the exhibit object is apparently important in a recessed exhibit display as well (Bitgood et al., 1992). There is a common approach to interpretation (especially in natural history museum and naturalistic zoo exhibits) that places interpretive labels away from the naturalistic exhibits. The assumption is that the immersion experience will be compromised by the presence of text, which is unnatural to the setting. Instead, interpretative labels are often placed in a central area away from the exhibit. Evaluations of such exhibits suggest that this is a mistake if one wants to motivate visitors to read labels.

- *Ease of cognitive processing.* Visitors are more likely to read if information is arranged in a manner that minimizes effort. One way to accomplish this is to bullet a list of items rather than embedding it in a paragraph format. Another way to decrease cognitive processing is to provide small chunks of text close to a visual image on a diagram/illustration/graphic.

- *Figure-ground contrast.* Not only is it easier to attract attention with figure-ground contrast, but it is easier to read text when the letters and the background have high contrast (Bitgood, 1990a).

- *Sensory overload (density of labels/objects).* The greater the number of labels in an area, the less attention any one label is likely to receive. While this relates to attention, it may also relate to perceived effort. That is, an overabundance of text in any form (number of words per label or number of labels) may be perceived as too much work.

Increase Cognitive-Emotional Arousal

One of the more difficult tasks that exhibits attempt is to provoke interest and/or thought in the visitor. Once stimulated, visitors usually become more "mindful" and are more willing to read and think about the exhibit content. Thus, increasing cognitive-emotional arousal motivates mental focusing on interpretive objects. Provoking interest may also be a way to renew the resources of attention (see principle No. 3, capacity of attention).

Following are brief descriptions of, and the evidence for, many of the variables that seem to stimulate cognitive-emotional arousal:

- *Asking questions.* Among others, Rand (1990) has suggested that labels should ask questions rather than just tell the facts (e.g., "Which jaws could crush a crab?"). Several studies suggest that labels that ask questions can be effective at provoking label reading (Hirschi & Screven, 1988; Litwak, 1996). The content of the question is likely to be critical. If the question raises issues/information that are not interesting to visitors, it is not likely to be motivating.

- *Confront and correct misconceptions.* Once a misconception about a subject has been identified by a visitor study during the planning stage (front-end survey), directly confronting this misconception may provoke greater interest. Rand (1990) provides an example: "They may look empty, but mudflats crawl with life." At present there does not appear to be any studies that have examined the effectiveness of addressing misconceptions explicitly, although Borun and her colleagues (Borun, Massey, & Lutter, 1993) have documented the difficulty in overcoming misconceptions about gravity in a series of exhibits at the Franklin Institute of Science. Here is another example: "Not all fishes need a buoyancy regulator; when a wolf-eel or sculpin swims, it doesn't go too far from the bottom. But what do you suppose happens when a wolf-eel stops swimming?" (Rand, 1990). There is a danger in taking this approach. If the question is too difficult, the reader may lose interest and is unlikely to try additional challenges. It is also important to provide the correct answer once visitors' interest has been stimulated.

- *Writing style.* Rand (1990) has listed a number of label objectives that translate to good writing style. These include:
  —Draw analogies ("Flatfishes are quick-change artists.")
  —Use a reader-relevant approach to explain things ("Orca clans take care of their own.")
  —Communicate in a conversational tone that is approachable, familiar, often humorous, but not flippant or formal ("See the rock with ruffles? That's the hornmouth, one of the more ornamental snails.")
  —Address the reader directly ("The tentacles you see are sensitive to touch and help locate drifting algae.")

- *Identify high-interest content.* A survey during the planning stage can often identify information that is of interest to visitors (and it's not always what the museum staff thinks visitors are interested in).

- *Mental imagery.* Mental imagery can help create a feeling of immersion by encouraging the visitor to put her- or himself in a particular time and place (e.g., Bitgood, 1990b). Screven (1992) described this as "encouraging visitors to fantasize or project themselves into an exhibit situation."

- *Handouts.* Robinson (1928) used a handout giving more detailed descriptions of selected paintings than found on wall labels. Those who used this handout showed decreased "museum fatigue" (i.e., increased total amount of time in museum and attention to artwork). Others have found similar findings (Bitgood & Davis, 1991).

- *Presence of 3-D objects.* Two-dimensional labels by themselves attract less attention than labels associated with three-dimensional objects (e.g., Peart, 1984).

- *Format of label.* Labels can be designed using several formats (graphic panel with blocks of text, flip labels that can be raised to reveal an answer to a question or additional information, auditory labels either self-activated or visitor activated, etc.).

- *Instructions on what to look for or what to do.* Assuming visitors are at all curious about the objects they are seeing, they generally welcome information that tells them what they should look for or do.

- *Hands-on flips.* Arndt, Screven, Benusa, and Bishop (1993), in a zoo study at a lion exhibit, found that flip labels increased the percentage of visitors who stopped, viewing time, and learning. Flip labels, when carefully designed, are capable of sparking considerable curiosity.

- *Clarifying the message.* Written text can help to clarify the message. Bitgood et al. (1996) found a dramatic increase in attention and total time in the gallery when text was placed on life-size photos. The text clarified both what was being said and who said it in recorded voices conducted over speakers.

- *Social interaction.* Interpretive experiences are primarily social in nature. Design should consider how to motivate visitors to share information and ideas. Parents often read labels to children, and it is not uncommon for one adult to read to other adults in a group. Labels are likely to encourage social interaction if they are interesting, challenging, prompt parents to ask questions of their children, and so forth.

Minimize Distractions

Sensory distractions such as sounds from outside the interpretive area can take attention away from labels. In one of the first studies of label reading at a zoo, my colleagues and I (Bitgood, Patterson, & Benefield, 1988) observed that each time the zoo train blew its whistle as it passed, visitors would stop reading labels. Once interrupted, visitors did not go back to complete reading of a label. They moved on to the next exhibit. This phenomenon was observed for almost every visitor:

- *Sounds.* Sounds of all types can distract visitors from reading. Sound bleed from other exhibits is a common distracter in museums, zoos, and science centers.

- *Competition from other exhibit elements.* Frequently, two elements of the same exhibit compete with one another for attention. An object may compete with a label, a label with another label, and so forth.

- *Novelty of the surroundings.* The work of John Falk and his colleagues (e.g., Balling & Falk, 1980; Falk & Balling, 1980, 1982) suggests that, at least for school groups, a novel setting distracts students from the programmed interpretation. To some extent, this may also apply to all visitors in interpretation settings. Visitors may be concerned with where to go next, and so forth. Good orientation (visitor guides, direction signs, etc.) will minimize the distractions.

LIMITED CAPACITY OF ATTENTION

The third principle of attention states that the resources of attention have a limited capacity in the sense that there appears to be only so much available and they appear to become depleted with physical and mental effort. The reserves are renewed slowly over time and, to some extent, by cognitive-emotional arousal. Consequently, three factors are of critical importance to this principle of attention: the size of the reserve, the rate of depletion, and the rate of renewal.

Evidence for this depletion effect is provided by several studies of "museum fatigue" (Falk, Koran, Dierking, & Dreblow, 1985; Melton, 1935; Robinson, 1928). Robinson (1928) compared decreases in attention across time during visits to four museums that differed in size as well as other characteristics. He found similar decrements in attention (as measured by average viewing time per painting) at all museums. He found an even greater decrement in attention across viewing in a laboratory study in which subjects were asked to view 100 prints of paintings. Subjects were allowed to view each print as long as they wanted. Dividing the prints into tenths, Robinson found that there was a systematic decrement from the first to the last tenth of the prints. Melton (1935) found a similar decrement in attention (as measured by average viewing time per painting) when the number of paintings in a gallery was systematically increased from 6 to 36 in increments of six.

Falk et al. (1985) reported evidence for a decrement in attention across time in a study at the Florida State Museum of Natural History. They monitored visitors' attention to exhibits, to the setting, to self, and to other people throughout the visit. They found that visitors' attention to exhibits dropped rapidly after 30 to 45 minutes in the museum. "The primary change in visitor behavior during the observations was a change from moving slowly from exhibit to exhibit and reading labels to 'cruising' through the halls, stopping occasionally and only very selectively" (p. 254).

Serrell (1998) reported viewing time measures and overall usage in exhibitions at a number of museums conducted by a number of different investigators. Visitors spent less than 20 minutes in 82% of the 110 total exhibitions included in the study. Many of these exhibitions were large, which didn't seem to make a lot of difference. The median stops in these exhibitions was 33.9% of the total possible exhibit elements. These findings can be easily interpreted as support for the limited capacity of attention.

Size of Reserve

The total capacity of the attention reserve is assumed to be limited, based on the physical energy available to the individual, condition of health, mental attitude, and so forth. Obviously, the capacity would vary for different individuals and for each individual from one time to another.

Rate of Depletion and Renewal

How quickly the reserves of attention are depleted is assumed to be influenced by the amount of mental effort, by the number and strength of distractions (both setting and social), information overload, by cognitive-emotional arousal, by physical fatigue, by time pressures, and by rate of pacing through the exhibition (e.g., rest periods allow renewal).

Several design factors may reduce this attention decrement:

- Design heterogeneous exhibits rather than monotonous displays with similar objects all in a row. Displays of similar objects or animals all in a row create a rapid decrement in attention. By varying the displays in terms of content and appearance, greater interest is maintained.
- Minimize mental effort every way possible. As noted earlier, there are many ways to decrease the amount of mental effort required by visitors.
- Increase interest level with methods described earlier under "Provocation." Provoking interest

by the methods described previously should also help to hold off object satiation.

Renewal rate refers to how fast the reserves of attention are replenished. It is assumed that a recovery period will renew these resources. Thus, taking a break to have a snack or eat lunch will rejuvenate the resources of attention. Increasing cognitive-emotional arousal (stimulating interest) also acts to renew the reserves. Thus, entering a new museum gallery on a new topic (especially one that is interesting) generally results in increased attention to exhibits.

Interpretive labels can come in many forms and, in the form of hand-held guides, may be used to slow down the rate of depletion of attention. Robinson (1928) reported a study (study No. 4) in which pamphlets were used as a visitor guide to artwork in a small museum. Those who used the guide spent more time in the museum (28 vs. 17 minutes); viewed a larger number of artworks (46 vs. 30), and viewed a larger percentage of the artworks (25 vs. 17). Those who did not use the guide showed the usual decrement in viewing time across their visitation. Thus, the hand-held guide appeared to counteract the fatigue effect usually observed.

SOME IMPLICATIONS AND RELATED CONCEPTS

Several implications follow from the previous discussion. Following is a brief discussion of four such implications.

Redistribution of Attention

Any change to the interpretive setting creates a change in the pattern of visitor attention to the whole milieu. According to the attention framework, this redistribution is the result of a combination of moment-to-moment selectivity, motivated focusing, and depletion of the reserves of attention. In an interpretive environment dense with stimulation, the capacity of attention is likely to be depleted before all elements have received an adequate level of attention. Also, in a densely stimulating environment, only the most distinctive elements are likely to receive attention because of the selectivity principle.

The limitations of attention require that designers plan the interpretive experiences carefully so that visitors distribute their attention to focus on important messages and objects. This is a difficult task. In addition to considering the moment-by-moment distribution of attention, the designer must, throughout the interpretive area, attempt to minimize mental demands that sap visitors of their resources for attending.

Redistribution of attention was demonstrated in a study by Melton (1935, 1972) in which the number of artworks in a museum gallery were systematically varied. When the number of artworks was increased, the attention to each one was decreased. Although this study did not examine interpretive labels, it seems a safe guess that the finding would generalize to text.

A more detailed analysis of the distribution of attention can be found in a study by Bitgood and Patterson (1993). Their study, conducted over a 2-year period, systematically varied label characteristics and locations. The study was conducted in a small Egyptian mummy gallery at the Anniston Museum of Natural History. Labels were systematically changed and a bronze bust added to the gallery during the course of the study. Each change in the gallery resulted in a redistribution of visitor attention to all objects in the gallery. For example, when more labels were added, the percentages of stops at labels increased, but the total reading time decreased. In addition, when the percentage of label readers increased by label changes, average total time in the gallery for label readers declined, suggesting that the new label readers produced by making the labels more attractive didn't influence the overall time in the gallery of these new readers. However, when a three-dimensional object (bronze bust of a mummy) was added to the gallery, the total gallery time as well as time viewing other objects in the gallery increased.

The Complementary Role of Interpretive Labels

The structural limits of attention prevent visitors from simultaneously attending to both label and objects. When given a choice, visitors look at objects rather than read labels. Since the focus of visitor attention is primarily on three-dimensional visual experiences, this is where interpretation should start. Rarely do visitors start their viewing experience by reading text. In study after study, two-dimensional graphic panels not associated with some three-dimensional objects receive very little attention. (This is one reason why it is difficult to get visitors to read introductory labels.) Label reading cannot compete with the visual experience. It follows that labels are most effective when they complement the objects. They complement by focusing attention on important characteristics or explaining phenomenon, or serving some other such function. Visitors generally want to know what they should look for, how to focus their attention, and so forth. How do you design for this supplementary role for labels? Here are a few suggestions to provide visual reference to the label:

- Focus attention on important ideas or relevant features associated with the object.
- Create a symbolic dialogue between the label and the object.
- Answer the visitors' questions first, then tell them what you think they should know.
- Ask what is most notable or important about the object(s).

Since interpretive labels are less attention getting than objects, it is predicted that there will be a greater decrement in attention to label reading than to object viewing as the resources for attention are depleted. I don't know of any data that relates to this prediction.

Communicating Educational Messages

Focused attention is necessary, but not sufficient for the interpretive messages to be communicated. Once visitors attend to the label and are motivated to read, the final task is to ensure that the interpretive message is communicated. The critical factor here is difficulty of comprehension. Anything that makes comprehension more difficult is going to increase mental effort, deplete the resources of attention, and consequently decrease the chances of delivering interpretive messages. It seems that many of the variables associated with interpretive labels seem to influence both motivation and communication. Text that is difficult to understand impedes visitor motivation to read.

Here are a few principles from the literature that, when followed, facilitate the delivery of the interpretive message:

- *Syntactic complexity.* Screven (1992) described a group of variables he termed "syntactic complexity." They include sentence length and number of sentences with phrases that lack any new information (e.g., in summary). As Rand (1990) points out, "every word counts." It is easier to understand if short, simple sentences are used.

- *Semantic complexity.* According to Screven (1992), semantic complexity includes: "number and level of propositions, causal structures, vague, abstract language, concept density (ratio of concrete to abstract concepts)."
- *Vocabulary.* Difficult-to-understand vocabulary has been frequently noted as a problem in communicating interpretive messages (Bitgood, 1990a; Screven, 1992; Serrell, 1983, 1996). The best advice is to keep it simple and test any questionable words/phrases on the target audience.
- *Writing style.* Clarity, conciseness, and simplicity will usually facilitate understanding of the interpretive message. In addition, Rand suggests using an active voice, vivid language, and addressing the reader directly.
- *Presence of labels.* It may seem obvious to most, but objects rarely (if ever) speak for themselves. Without interpretation at the critical location where it will be used, visitors are likely to get the wrong message, a trivial message, or none at all.
- *Literary techniques.* Rand (1990) has suggested drawing analogies and using a conversational tone to "hook" readers. Serrell (1996) suggests that labels tell stories. Both of these techniques, when used intelligently, are likely to increase label effectiveness.
- *Conflicting messages.* At times what visitors see and what they read are in conflict. If a sign at a zoo exhibit implores visitors not to feed the bears, it is inconsistent for a keeper to throw an apple to the bear when the bear begs.

Visitors can more readily attend to the educational messages if the labels are designed to minimize mental effort, increase interest level, and help visitors focus their attention on easy-to-understand information.

Response Facilitation

In the case of "hands-on" (interactive) exhibits, the device must be designed such that it facilitates an appropriate response (one that is consistent with or aids in the understanding of the objectives of the exhibit). Norman's (1988) principles of design provide a useful guide for such interactive exhibits (Bitgood, 1991a; see also Kennedy, 1990):

- *Visibility.* It should be obvious what to do by looking at the device.
- *Feedback.* All responses should receive immediate and continuous feedback.
- *Conceptual model.* The visitor conceptual model of how something works must match the designer's model.
- *Natural mapping.* When appropriate, controls should be mapped out in the same pattern as what they are controlling. For example, in the Pacific Science Center there is an exhibit in which visitors attempt to identify the smell from bottles. The smells are identified by flip labels that are laid out in the same pattern as the bottles. It is clear which flip goes with which bottle simply by seeing the natural mapping.
- *Navigation.* It should be easy to navigate through instructions (or software programs).
- *Instructions.* Instructions must be simple and placed close to the things they are describing.

When interactive exhibits are designed, visitor testing is crucial. We have not reached the point where we can predict with any certainty how all of the design variables are going to work together.

VISITOR SERVICES AND AMENITIES

When people spend several hours in a facility, amenities such as food and rest rooms take on significant importance. Perhaps even more important for a satisfying visit is the human contact visitors have with staff.

CUSTOMER RELATIONS

The way front-line staff interact with visitors is recognized by many organizations including the Disney theme parks, the hotel industry, and the Wal-Mart organization. A friendly greeting sets the tone for the visit. Dealing with complaints can also lead to more or less visitor satisfaction.

REST ROOMS

In surveys of visitor satisfaction, one of the consistently important factors is cleanliness and availability of rest rooms.

FOOD SERVICE

It seems logical that if a visit is of sufficient length, providing food is likely to keep visitors in the museum longer. However, there is apparently no data to support this assumption. Nor do there appear to be any studies on the impact of quality of food as an incentive to visit or remain in the museum. The tendency to provide fast food chain restaurants in museums may reflect the preference of children.

GIFT SHOP

Many visitors (especially families) expect to purchase a souvenir of their visit. It is unclear how this affects visitor satisfaction or motivation to visit. Unfortunately, few published studies have examined the role of the gift shop in museum visitation. However, there is no doubt that the income from gift shops plays a significant role in the finances of the museum!

MACROARCHITECTURE

The architectural style of the building may also convey meaning to visitors (e.g., Bitgood, 2000a; Thompson, 1993). The architectural difference between art museums and children's museums illustrates this point. Art museums tend to be designed as temples with large columns, palatial stairs to the entrance, and large atriums, all designed to create a feeling of awe and reverence. Both written and unwritten messages command the visitor not to touch. It is ironic that the outside entrance to the Philadelphia Museum of Art is used quite differently than originally intended. Skateboarders fly down the stairs while would-be Rocky imitators run up the stairs and jump up and down as Rocky did in the movie.

A children's museum is designed with quite the opposite intentions. The message here is "come in and enjoy, play, touch, have fun." Bright colors, attractive objects, and easy-to-do activities are the norm.

VISITOR VARIABLES

The environmental factors described earlier (lobby, exhibitions, amenities, macroarchitecture) are only part of the museum formula. Visitor variables also play an important role. In addition, environmental and visitor variables invariably interact.

DEMOGRAPHICS AND LEISURE VALUES

As one might suspect, age, gender, and educational level are important variables in understanding the museum environment. In addition, Hood (1983) has provided evidence that leisure values are strongly correlated with visitation patterns.

SOCIAL INFLUENCE

The overwhelming percentage of visitors come in groups—usually with families or friends unless they are part of a school group. Consequently, museum visitation is, to a large extent, a social experience. Groups typically approach an exhibit together and discuss the exhibit, point to exhibit elements, and try as a group to make sense of the display. Provocative exhibits tend to stimulate group discussion and pointing.

Exhibit design often interacts with visitor variables. For example, some exhibits allow only one individual access, while others encourage group participation.

PREKNOWLEDGE AND ATTITUDES

Visitors enter the museum with knowledge and attitudes that influence their interests and how they cognitively process their museum experience. Some type of misconceptions for any subject matter can be found in visitor studies. These preconceptions are important to identify at an early stage of exhibition development so that the exhibition can be designed to correct them. For example, Borun (1988) found that visitors held several misconceptions about the concept of *gravity*. She then designed and tested exhibits to correct these misconceptions.

ANIMAL HABITAT DESIGN

The design of live animal exhibits has also received increasing attention in the last several years with the development of more naturalistic exhibitions (Shepherdson, Mellen, & Hutchins, 1998). What is "naturalistic" in the viewers' eyes is not always "naturalistic" to the animal (e.g., Shettel-Neuber, 1988; Swift, 1986).

One of the dilemmas for habitat design is to create a rewarding experience for visitors as well as to promote animal welfare (e.g., Bitgood, 1999). If animals are stressed by close proximity to visitors, the design conflict between animal needs and visitor preference to see animals up close is obvious, but the solution not so obvious. Changing individual animals on display to the public and having multiple animals in the display are two ways to deal with this problem.

One of the major debates in zoo exhibit design seems to center around the importance of a "naturalistic" habitat. Quick (1984) has summarized this controversy. On one end of the spectrum, Hutchins, Hancocks, & Calip (1978) argued that exhibit habitats should replicate the animal's natural environment to produce naturalistic behavior. This approach is against the use of technological devices such as feeling devices that animals must trigger. Operant conditioning of animals to elicit "natural" behaviors is contrary to the concept of *natural*. Markowitz (1982) and his followers, on the other hand, argue that operant conditioning of "naturalistic behaviors" such as prey behaviors not only has value for the education of visitors but provides stimulation for the animal in an artificial environment. No matter how faithfully one tries to duplicate the natural environment, it would be impossible. The animal's welfare is best served by providing healthy stimulation.

Another issue in habitat design is animal usage of the exhibit enclosure (e.g., Maple & Finlay, 1986, 1987; Ogden, Lindburg, & Maple, 1993; Stoinski, Hoff, & Maple, in press). Zoo Atlanta, under the direction of Terry Maple, has conducted postoccupancy evaluations of gorilla exhibits. Ogden et al. (1993) and Stoinski et al. (in press) examined the relationship of patterns of space use and environmental structures as well as the effect of temperature and social factors on space use. These studies found: (1) Gorillas spent more time near the holding building than in other areas of the exhibit; (2) animals avoided the buildings when it was cold and sought them out when it was warm; (3) a single gorilla's habitat use influenced the habitat use of other animals.

FINAL THOUGHTS

Environmental design in museums is still in its infancy and suffers from a lack of competent researchers. However, practitioners do not suffer from a lack of enthusiasm, and it is expected that improved education and training will continue to develop. Despite the limitations, there are a number of empirical principles that seem to have generality across museums and visitors. It is difficult to predict the degree to which these principles will be able to guide museum design. At worst, they provide a set of heuristics that, combined with front-end, formative, and remedial evaluation, can greatly improve the chances of success.

REFERENCES

Alt, M. (1980). Four years of visitor surveys at the British Museum (Natural History). *Museums Journal, 80,* 10–19.

Arndt, M., Screven, C., Benusa, D., & Bishop, T. (1993). Behavior and learning in a zoo environment under different signage conditions. *Visitor studies: Theory, research, and practice* (Vol. 5, pp. 245–251). Jacksonville, AL: Visitor Studies Association.

Balling, I., & Falk, J. (1980). A perspective on field trips: Environmental effects on loaning. *Curator, 23*(4), 229–240.

Bechtel, R. (1967). Hodometer research in museums. *Museum News, 45*(7), 23–26.

Birney, R. (1989). *Colonial Williamsburg Foundation Orientation Study* (Tech. Rep. No. 89-10). Jacksonville, AL: Center for Social Design.

Bitgood, S. (1988). *A comparison of formal and informal learning* (Tech. Rep. No. 88-10). Jacksonville, AL: Center for Social Design.

Bitgood, S. (1989). School field trips: An overview. *Visitor Behavior, 4*(2), 3–6.

Bitgood, S. (1990a). The ABCs of label design. In S. Bitgood, A. Benefield, & D. Patterson (Eds.), *Visitor studies: Theory, research, and practice* (Vol. 3, pp. 115–129). Jacksonville, AL: Center for Social Design.

Bitgood, S. (1990b). *The role of simulated immersion in exhibition* (Tech. Rep. No. 90-20). Jacksonville, AL: Center for Social Design.

Bitgood, S. (1991a). Suggested guidelines for designing interactive exhibits. *Visitor Behavior, 6*(4), 4–11.

Bitgood, S. (1991b, January/February). What do we know about school field trips? *ASTC Newsletter,* 5–6.

Bitgood, S. (1992). The anatomy of an exhibit. *Visitor Behavior, 7*(4), 4–14.

Bitgood, S. (1997). The Hein-Miles debate: An introduction, explanation, and commentary. *Visitor Behavior, 12*(3–4), 3–7.

Bitgood, S. (1999). Zoo exhibit design: Impact of setting factors on visitors. *Visitor Studies Today, 2*(2), 1–5.

Bitgood, S. (2000a). *The psychology of museum architecture.* Paper presented at the Annual Meeting of the American Association of Museums, Baltimore, MD.

Bitgood, S. (2000b). The role of attention in the design of interpretive labels. *Journal of Interpretation Research, 5*(2), 31–45.

Bitgood, S., Benefield, A., & Patterson, D. (1989). The importance of label placement: A neglected factor in exhibit design. In *Current trends in audience research* (Vol. 3, pp. 49–52). Washington, DC: American Association of Museums Visitor Research and Evaluation Committee.

Bitgood, S., Benefield, A., Patterson, D., & Litwak, H. (1990). Influencing visitor attention: Effects of life-size animal silhouettes on visitor behavior. In S. Bitgood, A. Benefield, & D. Patterson (Eds.), *Visitor studies: Theory, research, and practice* (Vol. 3, pp. 221–230). Jacksonville, AL: Center for Social Design.

Bitgood, S., Campbell, R., Desmidt, E., Gunnip, K., Hawerott, M., & Johaneson, H. (1992). Formative evaluation of a Pepper's ghost exhibit device. In *Current trends in audience research* (Vol. 6, pp. 15–18). Baltimore, MD: American Association of Museums Visitor Research and Evaluation Committee.

Bitgood, S., Cleghorn, A., Cota, A., Crawford, M., Patterson, D., & Danemeyer, C. (1996). Enhancing the Confrontation Gallery at the Birmingham Civil Rights Institute. In S. Bitgood, A. Benefield, & D. Patterson (Eds.), *Visitor studies: Theory, research, and practice* (Vol. 7, pp. 48–56). Jacksonville, AL: Center for Social Design.

Bitgood, S., Conroy, P., Pierce, M., Patterson, D., & Boyd, J. (1989). Evaluation of "attack and defense" at the Anniston Museum of Natural History. In *Current trends in audience research* (Vol. 3, pp. 1–4). Washington, DC: American Association of Museums Visitor Research and Evaluation Committee.

Bitgood, S., & Davis, J. (1991). Self-guided handouts in museums and zoos: An annotated bibliography. *Visitor Behavior, 6*(3), 7–10.

Bitgood, S., Hines, J., Hamberger, W., & Ford, W. (1991). Visitor circulation through a changing exhibits gallery. In A. Benefield, S. Bitgood, & H. Shettel (Eds.), *Visitor studies: Theory, research, and practice* (Vol. 4, pp. 103–114). Jacksonville, AL: Center for Social Design.

Bitgood, S., & Lankford, S. (1995). Museum orientation and circulation. *Visitor Behavior, 10*(2), 4–6.

Bitgood, S., & Loomis, R. (1993). Introduction: Environmental design and evaluation in museums. *Environment and Behavior, 25*(6), 683–697.

Bitgood, S., & Patterson, D. (1992). Using handouts to increase label reading. *Visitor Behavior, 7*(1), 15–17.

Bitgood, S., & Patterson, D. (1993). The effects of gallery changes on visitor behavior. *Environment and Behavior, 25*(6), 761–781.

Bitgood, S., Patterson, D., & Benefield, A. (1988). Exhibit design and visitor behavior: Empirical relationships. *Environment and Behavior, 20*(4), 474–491.

Bitgood, S., Pierce, M., Nichols, U., & Patterson, D. (1987). Formative evaluation of a cave exhibit. *Curator, 311*(1), 31–39.

Bitgood, S., & Richardson, K. (1986). *Validation of visitors self-reports in a zoo* (Tech. Rep. No. 86-30). Jacksonville, AL: Center for Social Design.

Bitgood, S., Serrell, B., & Thompson, D. (1994). The impact of informal science education on visitors to museums. In V. Crane, H. Nicholson, M. Chen, & S. Bitgood (Eds.), *Informal science learning: What research says about television, science museums, and community based projects* (pp. 61–106). Dedham, MA: Research Communications.

Bitgood, S., & Shettel, H. (1996). An overview of visitor studies. *Journal of Museum Education, 21*(3), 6–10.

Bitgood, S., & Tisdal, C. (1996). Does lobby orientation influence visitor satisfaction? *Visitor Behavior, 11*(3), 13–16.

Boram, R. (1991). What are school-age children learning from hands-on science center exhibits? In A. Benefield, S. Bitgood, & H. Shettel (Eds.), *Visitor studies: Theory, research, and practice* (Vol. 4, pp. 121–130). Jacksonville, AL: Center for Social Design.

Borun, M. (1977). *Measuring the immeasurable: A pilot study of museum effectiveness.* Washington, DC: Association of Science Technology Centers.

Borun, M., Flexer, B., Casey, A., & Baum, L. (1983). *Planets and pulleys: Studies of class visits to a science museum.* Washington, DC: Association of Science Technology Centers.

Borun, M., Massey, C., & Lutter, T. (1993). Naive knowledge and the design of science museum exhibits. *Curator, 36*(3), 201–219.

Boron, M., & Miller, M. (1980). *What's in a name?* Philadelphia, PA: Franklin Institute and Science Museum.

Brown, W. (1979). The design of the informal learning environment. *Gazette,* 4–10.

Carlisle, R. (1935). What do children do at a science center? *Curator, 28*(1), 27–33.

Cohen, M., Winkel, G., Olsen, R., & Wheeler, F. (1977). Orientation in a museum: An experimental visitor study. *Curator, 20*(2), 85–97.

Diamond, J. (1980). *The ethology of teaching: A perspective from the observations of families in science centers.* Unpublished doctoral dissertation, University of California, Berkeley.

Diamond, J. (1982). Ethology in museums: Understanding the learning process. *Journal of Museum Education: Roundtable Reports, 7*(4), 13–15.

Diamond, J. (1986). The behavior of family groups in science museums. *Curator, 29*(2), 139–154.

Duensing, S. (1987). Science centres and exploratories: A look at active participation. In D. Evered & M. O'Conner (Eds.), *Communicating science to the public* (pp. 131–142). New York: Wiley.

Eason, L., & Friedman, A. (1975). Elevator exhibit. *The Physics Teacher, 13*(8), 492–493.

Eason, L., & Linn, M. (1976). Evaluation of the effectiveness of participatory exhibits. *Curator, 19*(1), 45–62.

Falk, J., & Balling, J. (1980). The school field trip: Where you go makes the difference. *Science and Children, 17*(6), 6–8.

Falk, J., & Balling, J. (1982). The field trip milieu: Learning and behavior as a function of contextual events. *Journal of Educational Research, 76*(1), 22–28.

Falk, J., Koran, J., Dierking, L., & Dreblow, L. (1985). Predicting visitor behavior. *Curator, 28*(4), 249–257.

Falk, J., Martin, W., & Balling, J. (1978). The novel field trip phenomena: Adjustment to novel settings interferes with task learning. *Journal of Research in Science Teaching, 15*, 127–134.

Friedman, A. (1995). Creating an academic home for informal science education. *Curator, 38*(4), 214–220.

Friedman, A., Eason, L., & Sneider, G. (1979). Star games: A participatory astronomy exhibit. *Planetarium, 8*(3), 3–7.

Gottfried, J. (1979). *A naturalistic study of children's behavior in a free-choice learning environment.* Unpublished doctoral dissertation, University of California, Berkeley.

Gottfried, J. (1980). Do children learn on school field trips? *Curator, 23*(3), 165–174.

Griggs, S. (1981). Formative evaluation of exhibits at the British Museum. *Curator, 24*(3), 189–202.

Griggs, S. (1983). Orienting visitors within a thematic display. *International Journal of Museum Management and Curatorship, 2*, 119–134.

Griggs, S. (1990). Perceptions of traditional and new style exhibitions at the Natural History Museum (London). *International Laboratory for Visitor Studies Review, 1*(2), 78–90.

Griggs, S., & Manning, J. (1983). The predictive validity of formative evaluation of exhibits. *Museum Studies Journal, 1*(2), 31–41.

Hayward, J. (1996). The whole visitor experience: An introduction to three papers about visitor services. In S. Bitgood (Ed.), *Visitor studies: Theory, research, and practice* (Vol. 7, pp. 1–2). Jacksonville, AL: Visitor Studies Association.

Hayward, U. G., & Brydon-Miller, M. L. (1984). Spatial and conceptual aspects of orientation: Visitor experiences at an outdoor history museum. *Journal of Environmental Education, 13*(4), 317–332.

Hein, G. (1997). A reply to Miles' commentary on constructivism. *Visitor Behavior, 12*(3/4), 14–15.

Hill, K. (1996). The role of research in the opening of the United States Holocaust Memorial Museum. In S. Bitgood (Ed.), *Visitor studies: Theory, research, and practice* (Vol. 7, pp. 7–11). Jacksonville, AL: Visitor Studies Association.

Hirshi, K., & Screven, C. (1988). Effects of questions on visitor reading behavior. *International Laboratory for Visitor Studies Review, 1*(1), 50–61.

Hood, M. (1983). Staying away: Why people choose not to visit museums. *Museum News, 61*(4), 50–57.

Hood, M. (1993). Comfort and caring: Two essential environmental factors. *Environment and Behavior, 26*(6), 710–724.

Hutchins, M., Hancocks, D., & Calip, T. (1978). Behavioral engineering in the zoo: A critique. *International Zoo News, Part I, 25*(7), 18–23.

Kennedy, J. (1990). *User friendly: Hands-on exhibits that work.* Washington, DC: Association of Science-Technology Centers.

Koran, J., Lehman, J., Shafer, L., & Koran, M. L. (1983). The relative effects of pre- and post-attention directing devices on learning from a "walk through" museum exhibit. *Journal of Research in Science Teaching, 20*(4), 341–346.

Levine, M. (1982). You-are-here maps: Psychological considerations. *Environment and Behavior, 14*(2), 221–237.

Litwak, J. M. (1996). Visitors learn more from labels that ask questions. In *Current trends in audience research* (Vol. 10, pp. 40–50). Minneapolis, MN: American Association of Museums Committee on Audience Research and Evaluation.

Loomis, R. (1988). The countenance of visitor studies in the 1980s. In S. Bitgood, J. Roper Jr., & A. Benefield (Eds.), *Visitor studies, 1988: Theory, research, and practice* (pp. 12–24). Jacksonville, AL: Center for Social Design.

Maple, T., & Finlay, T. (1986). Evaluating the environments of captive non-human primates. In K. Benirschke (Ed.), *Primates: The road to self-sustaining populations* (pp. 479–488). New York: Springer-Verlag.

Maple, T., & Finlay, T. (1987). Post-occupancy evaluation in the zoo. *Applied Animal and Behavioral Science, 18*, 5–18.

Markowitz, H. (1982). *Behavioral enrichment in the zoo.* New York: Van Nostrand Reinhold.

McManus, P. (1989). Oh, yes, they do: How museum visitor read labels and interact with exhibit texts. *Curator, 32*(3), 174–189.

Melton, A. (1933). Studies of installation at the Pennsylvania Museum of Art. *Museum News, 10*(14), 5–8.

Melton, A. (1935). *Problems of installation in museums of art* (New Series No. 14). Washington, DC: American Association of Museums.

Melton, A. (1972). Visitor behavior in museums: Some early research in environmental design. *Human Factors, 14*(5), 393–403.

Melton, A., Feldman, N., & Mason, C. (1936). *Experimental studies of the education of children in a museum of science* (New Series No. 15). Washington, DC: American Association of Museums.

Miles, R. (1986). Lessons in "Human biology": Testing a theory of exhibition design. *International Journal of Museum Management and Curatorship, 5*, 227–240.

Miles, R. (1993). Grasping the greased pig: Evaluation of educational exhibits. In S. Bicknell & G. Farmelo

(Eds.), *Museum visitor studies in the 90s* (pp. 24–33). London: Science Museum.

Miles, R. (1997). No royal road to learning: A commentary on constructivism. *Visitor Behavior, 12*(3/4), 7–13.

Miles, R., & Alt, M. (1979). British Museum (Natural History): A new approach to the visiting public. *Museums Journal, 78*(4), 158–162.

Miles, R., & Tout, A. (1978). Human biology and the new exhibition scheme in the British Museum (Natural History). *Curator, 21*(1), 36–50.

Norman, D. (1988). *The psychology of everyday things.* New York: Basic Books.

Ogden, J., Lindburg, D., & Maple, T. (1993). The effects of ecologically-relevant sounds on zoo visitors. *Curator, 36*(2), 147–156.

Oppenheimer, F. (1968). A rationale for a science museum. *Curator, 11*(2), 206–209.

Oppenheimer, F. (1975). The role of science museums. In E. Latrobe (Ed.), *Museums and education* (pp. 167–178). Washington, DC: Smithsonian Institution Press.

Oppenheimer, F. (1986). Exhibit conception and design. In L. Klein (Eds.), *Exhibits: Planning and design* (pp. 208–211). New York: Madison Square Press.

Peart, R. (1984). Impact of exhibit type on knowledge gain, attitudes and behavior. *Curator, 27,* 220–227.

Quick, D. L. (1984). An integrative approach to environmental engineering in zoos. *Zoo Biology, 3,* 65–77.

Rand, J. (1990). *Fish stories that hook readers: Interpretive graphics at the Monterey Bay Aquarium* (Tech. Rep. No. 90-30). Jacksonville, AL: Center for Social Design.

Robinson, E. (1928). *The behavior of the museum visitor* (New Series No. 5). Washington, DC: American Association of Museums.

Robinson, E. (1930). Psychological problems of the science museum. *Museum News, 8*(5), 9–11.

Robinson, E. (1931). Exit the typical visitor. *Journal of Adult Education, 3*(4), 418–423.

Rosenfeld, S. (1979). The context of informal learning in zoos. *Journal of Museum Education: Roundtable Reports, 4*(2), 1–3, 15–16.

Rosenfeld, S., & Turkel, A. (1982). A naturalistic study of visitors at an interpretive mini-zoo. *Curator, 25*(3), 187–212.

Schiele, B. (1992). Creative interaction of visitor and exhibition. In D. Thompson, A. Benefield, H. Shettel, & R. Williams (Eds.), *Visitor studies: Theory, research, and practice* (Vol. 6, pp. 54–81). Jacksonville, AL: Center for Social Design.

Screven, C. G. (1969). The museum as a responsive learning environment. *Museum News, 47*(10), 7–10.

Screven, C. G. (1974). *The measurement and facilitation of learning in the museum environment: An experimental analysis.* Washington, DC: Smithsonian Press.

Screven, C. G. (1975). The effectiveness of guidance devices on visitor learning. *Curator, 18*(3), 219–243.

Screven, C. G. (1986). Exhibitions and information centers: Some principles and approaches. *Curator, 29*(2), 109–137.

Screven, C. G. (1990). Uses of evaluation before, during, and after exhibit design. *International Laboratory for Visitor Studies Review: A Journal of Visitor Behavior, 1*(2), 36–66.

Screven, C. G. (1992). Motivating visitors to read labels. *International Laboratory for Visitor Studies Review, 2*(2), 183–211.

Serrell, B. (1983). *Making exhibit labels: A step by step guide.* Nashville, TN: American Association for State and Local History.

Serrell, B. (1996). *Exhibit labels: An interpretive approach.* Walnut Creek, CA: Altamira Press.

Serrell, B. (1998). *Paying attention: Visitors and museum exhibitions.* Washington, DC: American Association of Museums.

Shepherdson, D., Mellen, J., & Hutchins, M. (1998). *Second nature: Environmental enrichment for captive animals.* Washington, DC: Smithsonian Institution Press.

Shettel, H. (1967). *Atoms in Action Demonstration Center impact studies: Dublin, Ireland and Ankara, Turkey* (Rep. No. AIR-l 58-1 1/67-FR). Washington, DC: American Institutes for Research.

Shettel, H. (1976). *An evaluation of visitor response to "Man in his environment"* (Report No. AIR-43200-7/76-FR). Washington, DC: American Institutes for Research. (Also Tech. Rep. No. 90-10. Jacksonville, AL: Center for Social Design.)

Shettel, H. (1989). Evaluation in museums: A short history of a short history. In D. Uzzell (Ed.), *Heritage interpretation: Vol. 2. The visitor experience* (pp. 129–137). London: Belhaven Press.

Shettel, H. (1990a). Research and evaluation: Two concepts or one? In S. Bitgood, A. Benefield, & D. Patterson (Eds.), *Visitor studies: Theory, research, and practice* (Vol. 3, pp. 33–39). Jacksonville, AL: Center for Social Design.

Shettel, H. (1990b). There's a worm in my corn. *Visitor Behavior, 5*(3), 11–14.

Shettel, H., Butcher, M., Cotton, T., Northrup, J., & Slough, D. (1968). *Strategies for determining exhibit effectiveness.* (Rep. No. AIR E-95-4/68-FR). Washington, DC: American Institutes for Research.

Shettel, H., & Schumacher, S. (1969). *Atoms in Action Demonstration Center impact studies: Caracas; Venezuela and Cordoba, Argentina* (Report No. AIR-F58-3/69-FR). Washington, DC: American Institutes for Research.

Shettel-Neuber, J. (1988). Second and third generation zoo exhibits: A comparison of visitor, staff, and animal responses. *Environment and Behavior, 20,* 452–473.

Sneider, C., Eason, L., & Friedman, A. (1979). Summative evaluation of a participatory science exhibit. *Science Education, 63*(1), 25–36.

St. John, M. (1990). New metaphors for carrying out evaluations in the science museum setting. *Visitor Behavior, 5*(3), 4–8.

Stoinski, T., Hoff, M., & Maple, T. (in press). Habitat use and structural preferences of captive western lowland gorillas (Gorilla g. gorilla): The effect of environmental and social variables. *International Journal of Primatology.*

Stokes, E. (1996). Through the eyes of the guest: How guest services can influence the visitor studies agenda. In S. Bitgood (Ed.), *Visitor studies: Theory, research, and practice* (Vol. 7, pp. 3–6). Jacksonville, AL: Visitor Studies Association.

Swift, J. (1986). How natural is "naturalistic"? *Visitor Behavior, 1*(1), 3.

Talbot, J., Kaplan, R., Kuo, F., & Kaplan, S. (1993). Factors that enhance effectiveness of visitor maps. *Environment and Behavior, 25*(6), 743–760.

Taylor, S. (1986). *Understanding processes of informal education: A naturalistic study of visitors to a public aquarium.* Unpublished doctoral dissertation, University of California, Berkeley.

Thompson, D. (1993). *Considering the visitor: An interactional approach to environmental design.* Unpublished doctoral dissertation, University of Wisconsin, Milwaukee.

Wolf, R. (1980). A naturalistic view of evaluation. *Museum News, 58*(1), 39–45.

Wolf, R., & Tymitz, B. (1978). *A preliminary guide for conducting naturalistic evaluation in studying museum environments.* Washington, DC: Smithsonian Institution, Office of Museum Programs.

CHAPTER 31

Climate, Weather, and Crime

JAMES ROTTON and ELLEN G. COHN

FEW ISSUES HAVE PROVOKED as much concern as global warming. There can be little doubt that atmospheric temperatures are rising (Gaffen & Ross, 1998; Oskamp, 2000). The prospect of global warming serves as a harsh reminder of the often unrecognized role that meteorological variables play in our lives. At the risk of sounding like climatic or geographical determinists, it is worth noting that people take weather and climate into account when they decide where they want to live, the type of domicile they inhabit, and where they vacation (Bass & Alexander, 1972; Rubinstein, 1982). For example, it is no accident that most theme parks can be found in the southern part of the United States (Weiss, 1994). Those who desire other examples of the role that climate and weather play in everyday lives should consult P. Parker's (1995) annotated bibliography, which lists 3,397 works on the societal and economic effects of meteorological variables.

This chapter focuses on research that has explored relations between meteorological variables and criminal behavior. The terms *weather* and *climate* are sometimes used interchangeably to describe changes in meteorological conditions; however, as far back as 1904, Dexter pointed out that the terms imply very different ways of looking at variations in meteorological conditions. *Weather* describes momentary or temporal variations in meteorological conditions, whereas *climate* refers to spatial or geographical variations. The predictor in a weather study is typically a monthly, daily, or hourly average of conditions in a city or particular geographical region; in contrast, climatic measures are based on data that have been averaged over no less than 35

years but may be as long as 75 years (see www .worldclimate.com).

CLIMATE AND CRIME: IS THERE A RELATIONSHIP?

This section will be brief because it is difficult to separate effects that can be attributed to climate from the effects of culture, history, and social class (Rotton, 1986). For example, in the United States, temperatures are higher in southern than northern states, and it has long been known that homicide rates are also higher in the South than the North (Hawley & Messner, 1989; C. Wilson & Ferris, 1989). Shall we attribute regional differences in violence to temperature? The answer is that, if we do, we run the risk of ignoring historical and cultural factors that have shaped southern life. Rotton (1993b), for example, found that correlations between temperature and violent crimes did not attain significance in analyses that controlled for southern culture and variations in socioeconomic conditions, such as education level.

Anderson, Anderson, Dorr, DeNeve, and Flanagan (2000) presented a model that suggests that temperature exerts effects on violence after one controls for southernness and socioeconomic factors. Their model includes four measures of temperature (e.g., number of days with temperatures over 91°F, heating degree days) and three measures of southern subculture, such as Gastil's (1971) well-known index of southernness. However, a factor analysis disclosed that their 7 measures loaded on a single factor (Rotton, Cohn, Peterson, & Tarr, 2000). This implies that one cannot assess the effects of both climate and southernness in a single analysis without committing Gordon's (1968) partialling fallacy. Using data from the 1990 census (www.census.gov) and other government Web sites, Rotton et al. found that the correlation between composite indices of temperature and rapes shrank to nonsignificance when they controlled for percentage of the population born in southern states (an obvious measure of southernness). The correlation with homicide rates lost its significance when they controlled for southernness and city size. Finally, temperature's correlation with assaults did so when they controlled for southernness, city size, poverty rates, and percentage of high school graduates. Essentially, the analysis indicated that regional and socioeconomic variables, rather than temperature, are responsible for southern violence. In order to avoid the confound that region introduces, Rotton et al. also examined correlations between annual temperatures and violent crime rates (homicide, assault, and rape, separately) in 81 nations and 45 capital cities. None of the correlations attained significance.

It would be unfortunate if the reader concluded that we believe that nothing is to be gained from further research on climate and crime. Quite the contrary! We suspect that climate acts as a moderator that determines the size of relationships between weather variables and crime. This expectation is based on theories that emphasize adaptation (Wohlwill, 1974) or, as it is known in this area, acclimatization (Frisancho, 1979; Newman, 1970). It is consistent with results from a study (Humphreys, 1976) that examined the effects of monthly temperatures on thermal comfort. Humphreys developed the nomogram reproduced in Figure 31.1 to predict the combined effects of monthly and current temperatures on mood. Given that it rarely takes more than 10 days to adapt to a new climate (Parsons, 1993), it is reasonable to assume that this nomogram can also be used to predict the combined effects of climate and current temperature. Its equations suggest that high temperatures exert stronger effects in cold than temperate regions; conversely, low temperatures should exert stronger effects in warm regions. Of course, this prediction is subject to the usual caveat: It is likely that climate's moderating effects will be reduced by the coping strategies (e.g., clothing, staying indoors, air conditioning) that Bell, Greene, Fisher, and Baum (2000) term *adjustment*.

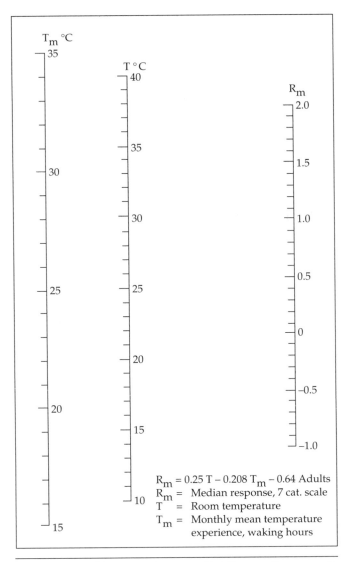

$$R_m = 0.25\,T - 0.208\,T_m - 0.64\ \text{Adults}$$
R_m = Median response, 7 cat. scale
T = Room temperature
T_m = Monthly mean temperature experience, waking hours

Figure 31.1 Nomograph to predict the median warmth of adults. *Source:* Reproduced from Humphreys, 1976.

WEATHER AND CRIME: WHAT ARE THE RELATIONSHIPS?

Much more consistent results have been obtained in research on weather than climate. In particular, as might be expected, several studies have uncovered a positive relationship between temperature and crime. However, taking a closer look at individual studies, we find that relationships between temperature and violence are not as ubiquitous as some have suggested. For example, as Table 31.1 shows, nonsignificant results have been obtained in studies that have looked at homicide rates (Cheatwood, 1995).

Referring to Table 31.1, it can be seen that most of the positive correlations are based on studies whose time period spanned a duration of 12 months. This

Table 31.1
Summary of Results Obtained in Research on Weather and Crime

Study	Period	Time	Place[a]	Temp.	Humid.	Wind	Sun	Press.	Rain.
Aggressive/Violent Crimes									
Anderson & Anderson (1984)[b]	Oct.–Sep.	311 days	11	+					
Cotton (1986)	Jul.–Aug.	62 days	8[c]	+	0				
	June–Aug.	184 days	12[d]	+	+				
Hagelin et al. (1999)[e]	Jan.–Dec.	260 weeks	21	+	0		0		0
Assault (Total or Aggravated)									
Cohn & Rotton (1997)	Jan.–Dec.	5,687 periods	13	+[f]	0	–	+		
Feldman & Jarmon (1979)	Jan.–Dec.	365 days	15	+	0			0	–
Harries & Stadler (1983)	Mar.–Oct.	245 days	6	+[g]					
Harries & Stadler (1985, 1988)	Mar. 1980–Oct. 1981	610 days	6	+[g,h]					
Lab & Hirschel (1988)	Jul.–Dec.	1,460 periods	4	+	–	0	0	0	0
Rotton & Cohn (2000a)	Jan.–Dec.	5,840 periods	6	+[f]	–	0		0	
Rotton & Frey (1985)	Jan.–Dec.	731 days	7	+	0	0	0	0	
Disorderly Conduct									
Rotton & Cohn (2000b)	Jan.–Dec.	2,742 periods	13	+[f]	–	–			
Domestic Violence									
Auliciems & DiBartolo (1995)	Jan.–Dec.	365 days	3	+	0	0	0	–	0
Cohn (1993)	Jan.–Dec.	5,687 periods	13	+[f]	0	–	+		
LeBeau (1994)	Mar.–Oct.	1,894 periods	4	+[g]					
Mitchell (1991)	Jul.–Dec.	2,920 periods	4	+					
Rotton & Frey (1985)	Jan.–Dec.	731 days	7	+	0	–	0	0	
Homicide									
Cheatwood (1995)	Jan.–Dec.	1,462 days	1	0[i]	0[i]	0	0	0	0
Feldman & Jarmon (1979)	Jan.–Dec.	365 days	15	0	0			0	0
Maes et al. (1994)	Jan.–Dec.	468 weeks	2	0	0	0	0	0	0
Valentine et al. (1975)	June–Sept.	92 days	16	0	0		–	0	0
Yan (2000)	Jan.–Dec.	14 years	10	0	0[i]	0		0	+[k]
Horn Honking									
Baron (1976)	June–Aug.	100 Ss	22	+					
Kenrick & MacFarlane (1986)	Apr.–Aug.	73 Ss	20	+					
Sex Offenses									
Rotton (1993a):									
Indecent Exposure	Jan.–Dec.	731 days	7	+	0	0	0	0	
Other[l]			7	0	0	0	0	0	
Miscellaneous Crimes[m]									
Anderson & Anderson (1984)	June–Aug.	90 days	5	+					
Obscene Phone Calls									
Rotton (1993a):	Jan.–Dec.	731 days	7	0	0	0	0	0	
Thefts				+	0	–			0
Burglary				+	0	0			0
Cotton (1986)	Jul.–Aug.	62 days	8[o]	0	0				
	June–Aug.	184 days	12[p]	0	+				
Lab & Hirschel (1988)[q]	Jul.–Dec.	1,460 periods	4	0	–	+	0	0	0
Public Intoxication									
LaRoche & Tillery (1956)	Jan.–Dec.	365 days	19	0	0			0	
Psychiatric Problems									
Lucero et al. (1965)	Jul.–Dec.	183 days	13	0	0	+			
Rotton & Frey (1984)	Jan.–Dec.	731 days	7	+	0	0	0	0	

(continued)

Table 31.1   (Continued)

Study	Period	Time	Place[a]	Temp.	Humid.	Wind	Sun	Press.	Rain.
Rape									
Cohn (1993)	Jan.–Dec.	5,687 periods	13	+	0	0	+		
Rotton (1993)	Jan.–Dec.	731 days	7	+	−	0	0	0	
Riots									
Baron & Ransberger (1978); Carlsmith & Anderson (1979)	Jan.–Dec.	102 episodes	23	+					
Tyson & Turnbull (1990)	Jan.–Dec.	24 years	17	0					
Robbery									
Cohn & Rotton (2001)	Jan.–Dec.	2,901 periods	13	+	0	0			0
van Koppen & Jansen (1999)	Jan.–Dec.	2,557 days	14	0		0	0	0	
Total Calls for Service									
Cohn (1996)	Jan.–Dec.	5,687 periods	13	+	0	−	+		
Feldman & Jarmon (1979)	Jan.–Dec.	365 days	15	0	0			0	−
Heller & Markland (1970)	Jul.–Dec.	140 weeks	5	+			+		
	Jul.–Dec.	156 weeks	9	+			+		
	Jul.–Dec.	112 weeks	18	+			+		
LaRoche & Tillery (1956)	Jan.–Dec.	365 days	19	0	0			0	
LeBeau & Corcoran (1990); LeBeau & Langworthy (1986)	Jan.–Dec.	1,461 days	5	+[r]					
Lucero et al. (1965)	Jul.–Dec.	183 days	13	+	0			0	

Note: Temp. = Temperature; Humid. = Humidity; Wind. = Wind speed; Sun = Sunshine; Press. = Barometric pressure; Rain = Rainfall.
[a] Places: (1) Baltimore, MD; (2) Belgium; (3) Brisbane, Australia; (4) Charlotte, NC; (5) Chicago, IL; (6) Dallas, TX; (7) Dayton, OH; (8) Des Moines, IA; (9) Detroit, MI; (10) Hong Kong; (11) Houston, TX; (12) Indianapolis, IN; (13) Minneapolis, MN; (14) The Netherlands; (15) Newark, NJ; (16) Philadelphia, PA; (17) South Africa; (18) St. Louis, MO; (19) Tallahassee, FL; (20) Tempe, AZ; (21) Washington, DC; (22) West Lafayette, IN; (23) U.S.A.
[b] Murder and rape.
[c] Assault, assault and battery, molestation, rape, murder, robbery, and terrorism.
[d] Assault, robbery, rape, and murder.
[e] Homicides, rapes, and assaults.
[f] During evening but not other hours.
[g] Discomfort index or temperature-humidity index.
[h] In low and medium but not high socioeconomic neighborhoods.
[i] But discomfort point (days of temperature > 79°) attained significance.
[j] Operationalized as dew point.
[k] For females but not males.
[l] Prostitution, molesting a minor, voyeurism, public sex.
[m] Murder and arson.
[n] Robbery and arson.
[o] Burglary, theft, and vandalism.
[p] Larceny, burglary, and vandalism.
[q] Tests of significance inferred from table in Lab & Hirschel (1987).
[r] Operationally defined as a warm front (increase in temperature).

means that the data included crimes committed during cold days of the winter as well as hot days of the summer. Thus, a positive correlation between temperature and violence cannot be used to assert that heat causes people to behave more violently. As Rotton and Cohn (1999a) observed, the same correlation can be interpreted as showing that cold weather inhibits violence. For example, Rotton and Frey (1985) uncovered a strong and robust correlation between temperature and violence even though none of the days in their study had a temperature over 79°F.

It might be noted that most of the correlations in Table 31.1 are based on daily totals and 24-hour averages. A recent analysis of assaults in Dallas, Texas, indicates that a very different pattern of results is obtained when one examines crime during more frequent (e.g., 3-hour) intervals. As the graph in Figure 31.2 shows, Rotton and Cohn (2000a) found that daily totals (i.e., data averaged over 24-hour intervals) for assaults were a linear function of temperature; however, a curvilinear (inverted-shaped) curve emerged when the data were disaggregated into

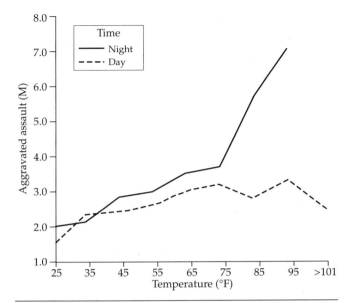

Figure 31.2 Aggravated assault in Dallas, Texas, as a function of temperature during 3-hour and 24-hour periods. *Source:* Reproduced from J. Rotton and E. G. Cohn, 2000a.

3-hour intervals. They traced the attenuating effects of averaging to the fact that temperatures equaled or exceeded 91°F on 365 occasions when analyses were based on 3-hour averages. The number of periods over 91°F shrank to four when the analyses were based on daily totals.

Finally, temperature's correlation with violence is highest during evening hours, which are typically the coolest time of day (LeBeau & Corcoran, 1990). The previously noted analysis of assaults in Dallas revealed that violence was an accelerated function of temperature between the hours of 12:00 A.M. and 2:59 A.M., but temperature's correlation with assaults did not attain significance during the warmest hours of the day (i.e., 12:00 P.M. to 5:59 P.M.). An earlier study of assaults in Dallas (Harries & Stadler, 1988) revealed that the relationship between temperature and assaults also depends on the socioeconomic status (SES) of the neighborhoods studied. After their initial analyses failed to uncover any relationship for temperature, Harries and Stadler divided the city into high-, medium-, and low-SES neighborhoods. Their more detailed analyses indicated that it was only in the medium- and low-SES neighborhoods that temperature predicted assaults; a nonsignificant relationship was obtained for temperature in the high-status neighborhoods. More recently, Mitchell (1991) found that the relationship between temperature and domestic violence was stronger in poor than affluent neighborhoods in Charlotte, North Carolina.

In sum, relationships between temperature and antisocial behavior are not as pervasive as prior reviews suggest. Rather than ask *if* temperature and violence are related, we need research aimed at determining *when* and *why* the two are correlated. We will take up the question of why in the section that deals with theories of weather and crime.

HUMIDITY, WIND, AND OTHER WEATHER VARIABLES

It is a well-known fact that humidity contributes to discomfort (Rohles, 1974). Thus, it is not surprising that several investigators (e.g., Harries & Stadler, 1983) have employed measures that reflect the combined effects of temperature and humidity, such as the temperature-humidity index (THI). It is important to note that these indexes are only applicable when temperatures exceed 58°F. Because the THI cannot be used to assess the effects of low temperatures, investigators have to throw out a great deal of interesting and useful data; for example, Cohn and Rotton (2000b) found that if they had used the THI, they would have had to discard 53% of their data (1,577 out of 2,224 periods) when temperatures fell below 59°F.

There are other reasons for having reservations about measures that combine temperature and humidity. First, it has yet to be shown that these indexes would attain significance if temperature and humidity were the first variables entered into a hierarchical regression analysis. Second, the idea that humidity contributes to discomfort is based solely on results obtained in laboratory studies; it is not supported by studies that have examined thermal comfort in field settings (Humphreys, 1976). Third, rather than presume that temperature and humidity combine in a particular way, we believe that much more can be learned by testing for temperature's interaction with humidity in a moderator-variable regression analysis. For example, Cohn and Rotton (1997) obtained a significant bilinear interaction for temperature and humidity in their analysis of assaults; however, the interaction shrank to nonsignificance when they controlled for time of day. It is of course possible that a more complicated form of the interaction (say, linear × quadratic or quadratic × linear) would have retained its significance after we controlled for temporal variables such as time of day.

Of greater concern, the THI and other measures assume that the correlation between humidity and crime is positive. This assumption is contradicted by the results from several studies (see Table 31.1) that indicate that violence is more likely to occur at low than at high levels of humidity. Rotton and Cohn (2000a) proposed alcohol consumption as a possible explanation for this unexpected finding. It is reasonable to assume that dry weather (low humidity) gives rise to dry throats; and if people quench their thirst by drinking alcohol, they will be more likely to engage in aggression. Laboratory studies leave little doubt that consuming alcohol causes aggressive behavior (Ito, Miller, & Pollock, 1996), and alcohol consumption is associated with violence in field settings (Gerson & Preston, 1979; R. Parker & Auerhahn, 1998). However, we should caution that this post hoc explanation is not supported by the only published report (LaRoche & Tillery, 1956) that examined public intoxication. It is also contradicted by results from climate studies (London & Teague, 1985; Room, 1983; Welte & Russell, 1982) that indicate that more distilled liquor is consumed in cold than warm regions of the United States. Nonetheless, further research needs to be done to determine if temporal measures of alcohol consumption (e.g., public intoxication, driving under the influence) might mediate relationships between temperature and violence.

Another variable that combines with temperature to affect comfort is air velocity or wind speed. On one hand, wind cools us off when temperatures are high; so also, winds might blow away pollutants that cause irritation and discomfort (Cavalini, 1992; Rotton & Frey, 1985). On the other hand, the wind-chill index reminds us that wind adds to discomfort when temperatures are low (Parsons, 1993; Tacken, 1989). However interesting these possibilities may be, most studies have failed to uncover any relationship with wind speed.

Mixed results have also been obtained in studies that have included sunlight as a predictor. This may be due to the fact that there is little consistency in how sunlight has been operationalized. In one study or another, sunlight has been defined as a percentage (amount of sun divided by minutes of sunlight), cloud cover, and time of day (e.g., dark vs. light). The first and third are probably better measures of seasonal differences in the length of the day (e.g., longer days during summer than winter months) than how sunny the day happens to be. Less ambiguous results can be drawn from studies

that have used cloud cover as a predictor; for example, Cohn and Rotton (1997) found that less violence occurs on cloudy (overcast) than sunny days.

It might be thought that the results obtained for cloud cover could be generalized to predict the effects of rainfall. However, only two studies obtained any effect for precipitation or rainfall, and the results of these studies (Feldman & Jarmon, 1979; Yan, 2000) were in opposite directions. Thus, as Cohn and Rotton (2000b) concluded, there is very little support for the idea that "rainfall is a police officer's best friend." The results in Table 31.1 also contradict what appear to be widely held beliefs about the effects of barometric pressure. Regardless of how barometric pressure is measured—either in absolute terms or changes in pressure—it does not appear to be correlated with antisocial behavior (Cyr, 1995).

The reader may have noticed that the variables in Table 31.1 are continuous. A much larger table would be required if we had included every discrete variable (e.g., snow, fog, thunderstorms) that has been employed as a predictor in one or another investigation. However, we doubt that including more variables would alter the major conclusion that can be drawn from our tally: Temperature is the only variable that has consistently emerged as a correlate of criminal activity. This conclusion is much more conservative than ones found in prior reviews, which typically highlight results from a single study that happened to obtain a significant result while ignoring the many studies that failed to uncover reliable relationships. Of course, there may be some who feel that the entries in Table 31.1 should be replaced with the effect sizes found in a meta-analysis. However, there are so many zeroes in our table that we are inclined to conclude that, except for temperature, relationships in this area are as erratic, unpredictable, and capricious as the weather itself.

SEASONAL DIFFERENCES

Table 31.1 does not include studies that examined seasonal differences in meteorological conditions and crime (Field, 1992; Linkowski, Martin, & De Maertelaer, 1992; Michael & Zumpe, 1983, 1986; Perry & Simpson, 1987). A much larger table would reveal support for the first half of Quetelet's thermic law of delinquency: Violent crimes are much more common during summer than other months (Baumer & Wright, 1996). The second half of Quetelet's law predicts that property crimes are more common during winter months. While this portion of Quetelet's law still holds in European nations, studies in the United States (Cohn & Rotton, 2000b; Dodge, 1988) indicate that property crimes are also more common during summer than other months.

Although it is tempting to attribute seasonal differences to meteorological variables, especially temperature, we would be remiss if we failed to point out that there are seasonal differences in behaviors that have little or nothing to do with weather. They include monthly and quarterly differences in gift giving, employment, automobile purchases, the school year, television programming, drug consumption (which peaks on April 15, when taxes are due in the United States), and even the purchase of contraceptives (Aschoff, 1981; Barnett & Cho, 1996; Kevan, 1979; MacMahon, 1983). There are two reasons why we believe that it is a mistake to attribute seasonal differences to meteorological conditions. First, relationships between weather variables and violent crimes attain significance in analyses that include controls for months and quarterly divisions of the year (Cohn & Rotton, 1997, 2000b; Harries & Stadler, 1983; Rotton & Cohn, 2000a, 2000b; Rotton & Frey, 1985). There are some (Anderson et al., 2000) who have argued that temperature and seasonal trends are so highly correlated that it is impossible to separate the two. This argument is contradicted by results obtained in studies (Rotton & Cohn, 1999a) that have employed standard procedures for assessing multicollinearity (i.e., excessively high correlations among predictors). Second, the relationship between temperature and assault varies across seasons (Rotton & Cohn, 2000a, 2000b). As Figure 31.3 shows, assaults were a curvilinear function of temperature during most months; however, when we controlled for other temporal variables (e.g., time of day, day of the week), it was only during spring and summer months that the curvilinear relationship attained significance.

THEORY: EXPLAINING THE RELATIONSHIPS

Early research on weather and criminal behavior was largely atheoretical. Its goal was often to determine if weather predicted calls for service so that police officers could be scheduled more efficiently (Cohn, 1993; Heller & Markland, 1970). Unlike research on climate, where one is limited to examining concomitant relationships, the longitudinal (time-series) nature of data on weather allows investigators to use

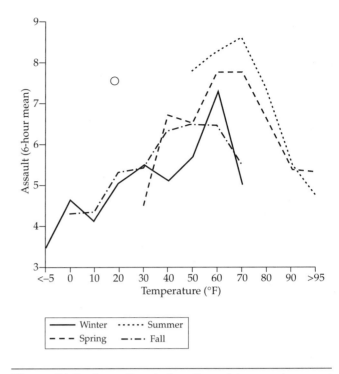

Figure 31.3 Assault as a function of temperature and season of the year in Minneapolis, Minnesota. *Source:* Reproduced from J. Rotton and E. G. Cohn, 2000b. *Note:* The circle denotes an outlier during spring months that would distort this graph if a line was drawn to it; the score was retained in statistical analyses.

current meteorological conditions to forecast criminal activities. Several investigators have found not only that outdoor temperatures are correlated with concurrent levels of violent crimes but that increased temperatures also precede increases in domestic violence by 6 and 12 hours (LeBeau & Langworthy, 1986; Rotton & Cohn, 1999b), assaults by 12 and 24 hours (Rotton & Cohn, 1999b; Rotton & Frey, 1985), and disorderly conduct by 48 hours (Rotton & Cohn, 1999b).

More recent research has been guided by theoretical issues and concerns. As might be expected, psychologists have favored theories that emphasize emotional states (e.g., arousal and negative affect), whereas criminologists have placed more emphasis on overt patterns of behavior (e.g., interaction rates and routine activities).

NEGATIVE AFFECT MODELS

Psychological theorizing can be traced to unexpected results obtained in a series of laboratory experiments on the effects of heat on aggressive behavior (Baron, 1978; Baron & Bell, 1976). Contrary to expectations, heat combined with other affect-inducing manipulations (e.g., provocation) to reduce rather than facilitate aggression. Baron and Bell advanced what is now termed the *negative affect escape* (NAE) model in order to explain results from their surprising findings. According to this model, moderate departures from comfortable temperatures (both heat and cold) increase the probability of aggressive behavior, but people try to escape and engage in behavior aimed at reducing their discomfort (e.g., swimming) when environmental conditions become extremely aversive. As the first diagram in Figure 31.4 shows, the NAE model suggests that the relationship between temperature and violence can be described by a butterfly-shaped curve.

Very different predictions can be derived from Anderson and colleague's (2000) general affective aggression model (GAAM). Anderson and colleagues have repeatedly argued that aggression is a linear function of high temperature: The hotter it is, the angrier we get. Their model suggests that both high and low temperatures facilitate aggression; that is, as the second diagram in Figure 31.4 shows, violence should be a U-shaped function of temperature. The GAAM incorporates predictions from earlier models that suggested that the relationship between aversive stimuli (including extreme temperatures) is mediated by affective states, such as anger (Berkowitz, 1993) and arousal (Zillmann, 1988).

The NAE model can explain results obtained in research on air pollution (Asmus & Bell, 1999) and crowding (Matthews, Paulus, & Baron, 1979) as well as extreme temperatures. Thus, the NAE model is somewhat broader than the GAAM. However, despite their differences, the GAAM and the NAE model share one thing in common: Both assume that the relationship between environmental conditions (e.g., temperature) and aggression is mediated by negative affect. The most convincing evidence for the mediating effects of negative affect can be found in a study conducted by Bell and Baron (1976). They found that aggression was a curvilinear (inverted U-shaped) function of levels of the amount of negative affect reported by subjects. To date, however, those who favor affect-based theories have not performed tests that are necessary for establishing mediation (Evans & Lepore, 1997).

There can be little doubt that weather extremes such as heat and cold cause discomfort. However, if one excludes a study conducted in the equatorially hot city of Calcutta, India (Ruback & Pandey, 1992), empirical support for this seemingly obvious proposition is based entirely on the results obtained in laboratory studies (Griffitt, 1970; Griffitt & Veitch, 1971; Vrij, van der Steen, & Koppelaar, 1994), where subjects have little else to do but reflect on their emotional states. Further, even in laboratory settings, extreme temperatures do not always affect people's mood (Anderson et al., 2000).

The picture becomes even hazier (pun intended) when we move from the laboratory to the field. This is somewhat surprising because cross-cultural research (Pennebaker, Rimé, & Blankenship, 1996) indicates that most people believe that meteorological conditions affect their own moods and other people's emotions. As might be expected, people who have an external locus of control are more likely to believe that weather affects their behavior (Jorgenson, 1981a, 1981b). T. Wilson, Laser, and Stone (1982) found that weather was ranked above food, exercise, work, and sleep when students were asked to rate

Negative Affect Escape (NAE) Model

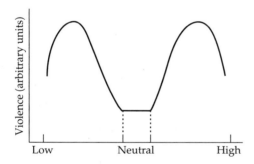

General Affective Aggression Model (GAAM)

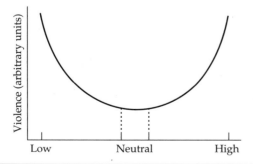

Figure 31.4 Contrasting predictions of the Negative Affect Escape Model and the General Affective Aggression Model.

factors that affected their mood. However, a non-significant correlation was obtained when the same group of subjects rated each day's weather and how they felt at the end of the day over a 5-week period.

It is difficult to draw conclusions from most studies that have examined relationships between weather and mood, because their authors (Barnston, 1988; Brandstätter, Frühwirth, & Kirchler, 1988; Howarth & Hoffman, 1984; Whitton, Kramer, & Eastwood, 1982) have used procedures that confound differences between people with differences observed over time.[1] However, if one were to do a simple count of the number of correlations that attained significance, the literature suggests that people report less vigor and energy when humidity levels are high (Goldstein, 1972; Sanders & Brizzolara, 1982), and they describe their moods as more positive on sunny than cloudy or rainy days (Cunningham, 1979; Parrott & Sabini, 1990; Persinger & Levesque, 1983; Schwarz & Clore, 1983; Sinclair, Mark, & Clore, 1994). Unfortunately, as Watson (2000) observed, many of these correlations are based on small numbers of observations; for example, Persinger's (1975) frequently cited study had a sample of only 10 students.

One would expect that more impressive results would emerge from studies that employed larger samples and covered longer periods of time. However, Watson (2000) obtained nonsignificant results when he had 8 samples of students in Dallas (a total of 478 subjects in all) rate their moods over 3-month periods. He concluded that mood was "not strongly or consistently related to *any* of the assessed weather variables, including temperature, barometric pressure, and level of sunshine" (p. 95, italics in the original). However, this conclusion is based on ratings that were made during evening hours when, in all probability, students were indoors and consequently not experiencing the factors (e.g., sunshine) that might have affected their moods earlier in the day. In addition, the ratings were obtained during fall and spring terms of the academic year; they did

not include reports obtained during the notoriously hot summers that characterize Dallas. The same criticism cannot be applied to studies conducted in Miami, Florida (Rotton, Shats, & Standers, 1990; Standers, Rotton, & Schlossberg, 1992). In the first study, students gave almost identical ratings of mood when they were tested at an outdoor shopping center (where temperatures ranged between 88°F and 92°F) or inside an air-conditioned mall (78°F). In a follow-up experiment, Standers et al. tried to make temperature salient by leading half of the students to believe that the study was being conducted by a professor who was interested in the effects of heat on memory. (Subjects were drawn from a class entitled Memory and Memory Improvement.) Once again, temperature did not have any effect on ratings of mood, nor did it matter if temperature had been made salient. We do not believe that these failures can be attributed to either insufficient sample size (e.g., $n = 89$ in the follow-up experiment) or instrument failure. Both studies employed reliable and widely used scales for assessing affective states.

In sum, the effects of weather on mood are considerably weaker than commonly supposed. It seems to us that the burden of proof now lies with those who have argued that relationships between meteorological variables (especially temperature) and aggression are mediated by negative affect. They need to present evidence that shows that weather variables exert appreciable effects on moods in natural settings. One possibility would be to use thought-listing procedures: We could ask people in warm, cool, sunny, and other settings what they are thinking. It would be interesting to determine how many thoughts people list before they mention the weather. Even more interesting is the question of whether people who mention heat or cold also mention feelings (e.g., "angry" or "irritated") that are supposed to mediate relationships between temperature and violence.

THEORIES OF SOCIAL CONTACT AND AVOIDANCE

Sociologists and criminologists have favored theories that can be traced to Durkheim's (1897/1951) classic work on suicide. Durkheim proposed that pleasant weather during spring months of the year increases the probability of social contact, which has the paradoxical effect of leading individuals to consider taking their own lives. According to Durkheim, people are more likely to experience

---

[1] It would take us far afield to explain why between-subject (or cross-sectional) and within-subject (time-series) variation cannot simply be pooled (Bryk & Raudenbush, 1992; Firebaugh, 1978). However, the reader may begin to understand some of the problems that arise by considering the following paradox: Time-series analyses indicate that exercise (or any kind of exertion) causes a person's blood pressure to rise, but cross-sectional studies indicate that the blood pressure is lower among people who exercise regularly than those who are sedentary.

social isolation and normlessness (a condition he termed *anomie*) during spring than other months of the year. Building on Durkheim's theory, Cohen and Felson (1979) proposed that crime is more likely to occur when events bring motivated offenders and victims into contact with each other in the absence of capable guardians. This proposition lies at the heart of routine activity theory (Felson, 2000). Building on Cohen and Felson's theory, Cohn (1990) identified weather in general and temperature in particular as factors that determine when and where offenders and victims come into contact. Specifically, she suggested that victims are more likely to leave their homes and stray into dangerous areas during pleasant than during inclement weather. As the theory predicts, Cohn and Rotton (1997) found that relationships between temperature and assaults in Minneapolis were strongest during evening and early hours of the night. In another study, Cohn and Rotton (2000b) found that temperature also predicted burglaries, larceny, and robberies. The correlations between temperature and property crime would be hard to explain in terms of theories that emphasize negative affect, but they can be traced to the fact that homes are less likely to be secured (e.g., open windows) on warm than cool or cold nights, and victims are more likely to venture into places that bring them into contact with motivated offenders when the weather is pleasant.

However, routine activity theory has three drawbacks as an explanation of weather-crime relationships. First, although the theory was originally developed to explain predatory crimes, such as larceny and theft, Cohn and Rotton (2000b) found that temperature is a much better predictor of violent crimes (affective aggression) than it is of property crimes (instrumental aggression). Second, criminologists have not obtained separate measures of the theory's three principal elements (victims, offenders, and guardians); that is, when a crime is recorded, we do not know if it is because the victim was in the wrong place at the wrong time, the offender set out to find the victim, or there were no guardians in the vicinity of the crime. Third, the theory cannot explain nonlinear relationships between temperature and violence; as Figure 31.2 shows, Rotton and Cohn (2000a) found that more violence occurs at moderately high than low or very high levels of temperature.

Rotton and Cohn (2000b) have tried to integrate predictions from psychological and contact models.

They have proposed that uncomfortably hot and cold weather keeps people apart. Instead of suggesting that people leave settings that they find aversive, as the NAE model posits, Rotton and Cohn proposed that individuals do not enter them in the first place; that is, individuals make a conscious decision to avoid very high as well as low temperatures by, for example, staying indoors. As a result, victims are less likely to come into contact with motivated offenders on cold and very warm days. This prediction has received some support from analyses that examined disorderly conduct, which includes many of the less savory aspects of social contact (e.g., complaints about loud parties, mischievous conduct, barking dogs). Rotton and Cohn found that the curvilinear relationship between temperature and violence shrank to nonsignificance when they controlled for disorderly conduct. This finding is consistent with the idea that social contact mediates the relationship between temperature and violence. Moreover, the previously noted interaction between temperature and seasons (see Figure 31.3) vanished when the authors controlled for the mediating effects of social conduct.

Rotton and Cohn's (2000b) findings suggest that individuals not only try to escape from unpleasantly high and low temperatures, as the NAE model predicts, but people also avoid conditions that are expected to cause discomfort. This integration brings research on weather in line with psychological theories (Aldwin, 1994; Lazarus, 2000; Moos & Tsu, 1976) that include avoidance as a strategy for coping with stress. It also highlights the proactive nature of our attempts to cope with extreme temperatures and adverse weather conditions: People rely on second-hand information (e.g., weather reports, the sight of snow on the ground; cf. Rind, 1996) as well as brief exposures (e.g., opening the front door) to decide whether they want to encounter or avoid weather extremes.

The proposed integration of the NAE model and routine activity theory is consistent with results obtained in studies that have examined activities in parks and outdoor plazas. For example, Li (1991) observed people in New York parks during winter and transitional months (October and March). His observations indicated that hardly anybody visited parks during winter months; however, during transitional months, there were more people in parks on warm than cool or cold days. Li (1994) subsequently found that temperature not only predicted the number of persons in plazas but also how long each person remained: The warmer the weather, the more time that individuals spent in plazas and the more likely they were to sit down. Westerberg (1994) obtained similar results when he used an automatic camera to register outdoor activity in a Swedish housing project; as might be expected, more people were recorded outdoors on clear than overcast or rainy days. He also presented graphs that suggest that children are more likely to be observed outdoors on moderately cool than cold or, surprisingly, warm days. Rotton, Cohn, and Paulson (2001) found that temperature also influences the number of fans attending major league baseball games: Even after controlling for month of the year, the warmer the day, the higher the attendance.

Models that emphasize escape, contact, and avoidance are also supported by results obtained in studies (Hoel, 1968; Walmsley & Lewis, 1989) that have examined pedestrian tempo. As might be expected, people walk faster in cold than warm or comfortable temperatures. This finding might be dismissed as "pedestrian," because rapid walking is a physical activity that raises the body's temperature. However, Rotton et al. (1990) found that people also walk faster on hot days in Miami than they do in climate-controlled malls. They explained this counterintuitive result by suggesting that people walked faster to get out of the heat. Much the same explanation can be advanced for the faster movement that is observed when it is raining (Gifford, Ward, & Dahms, 1977).

However interesting these results may be, they do not answer the question of where people are and what they are doing when they happen to be victims of crime. The real question is, do people gravitate to so-called "hot spots" (i.e., places where a disproportionate number of crimes occur, such as bars and convenience stores) when temperatures are comfortably warm? And do uncomfortable temperatures lead individuals to stay indoors and thereby reduce their chances of being victimized? In the following section, we consider new ways of answering these and related questions.

FUTURE DIRECTIONS: DISCOVERING NEW RELATIONSHIPS

The research we have reviewed suggests that there has been a resurgence of interest in the effects of meteorological variables on behavior. Research on weather and climate fell into disrepute during the 1920s and 1930s, largely as a consequence of the excessive claims made by those we now term climatic and geographical determinists (for a historical review, see Sommers & Moos, 1976). For example, the first edition of this handbook did not include a chapter on weather and climate. Only one of its chapters (Evans & Cohen, 1987) did more than mention weather and climate in passing. Although Evans and Cohen dealt with the effects of heat, their 3-page section was primarily concerned with physiological reactions rather than criminal behavior. There are three reasons why we are optimistic about further advances in this area. Two of them can be traced to opportunities afforded by personal computers. First, these tools have made it much easier to access data needed to answer both theoretical and applied questions. Second, they have increased the amount of data we can handle and, more importantly, the amount of information we can extract from the data we have obtained. As we shall discuss, our third reason for optimism relates to changing attitudes about how research can and should be conducted.

ARCHIVAL DATA

The Internet has taken much of the drudgery out of collecting data on meteorological variables and behavior. To illustrate, we began this chapter by referring to problems caused by global warming. These include more frequent heat waves, drought, coastal flooding caused by melting ice in polar regions, forest fires, hurricane activity, and deaths caused by heat stroke (Oskamp, 2000). Anderson and colleagues (2000) have suggested that we should also be worried about the prospect of a dramatic increase in murder and assault rates. They reached this conclusion after copying data on yearly averages for temperature and serious assaults (including homicide) in 50 U.S. cities from several printed sources. This was obviously a Herculean task that consumed a considerable amount of time. Unfortunately, such tasks are prone to transcription and coding errors (Rosenthal, 1978). Nevertheless, based on these data, Anderson et al. predicted that an increase of 2°F will generate an additional 24,000 homicides and assaults in the United States. This prediction is hard to reconcile with the much heralded decline in crime rates in recent years. Therefore, as part of a larger project, Cohn and Rotton (2000a) assembled a more complete file on national temperatures and homicide rates by downloading material from two Web sites. They obtained a listing of homicide rates from 1950 through 1998 from the Bureau of Justice Statistics (www.ojp.usdoj.gov/bjs/homicide/hmrt.htm), which are averages for the United States as a whole, not just 50 of its largest cities. They imported area-weighted averages for annual temperatures from the National Climatic Data Center (www.ncdc.noaa .gov/ol/climate/online/doe/doe.html); each average was based on data aggregated across more than 500 recording stations. The two series were then converted into standard scores so that temperature and homicide rates could be plotted on a single graph (see Figure 31.5).

At first glance, the trends in Figure 31.5 seem to suggest that homicide rates have declined as temperatures have begun to rise. This finding would have provided interesting support for the NAE model of aggression. However, the interocular (eyeball) test fails to take into account the fact that homicide rates drift in a purely stochastic fashion that economists term a *random walk* (Rotton, 1985). Because our goal was to predict changes over time, we addressed this problem by taking first differences (i.e., lagging and then subtracting rates from the preceding year from the current year); after all, like investors, we are not interested in absolute values during any one year. We found that the transfer function (a type of

regression coefficient) for temperatures did not attain significance ($p > .25$). This finding brings research on yearly temperatures and homicides in line with prior studies (see Table 31.1) that have failed to uncover any relationship between temperature and homicide.

Handling Data

In the process of tracking down data on annual temperatures and homicide rates, we ran across a Web site that indicates that there is very little consistency nationwide in yearly trends for homicide rates (www.ojp.usdoj.gov/bjs/homicide/city.htm). While homicide rates have declined in Tampa, Florida, they have increased in Richmond, Virginia, and remained fairly steady in Miami, Florida. This recommends the use of recently developed procedures for handling multilevel data, such as Bryk and Raudenbush's (1992) hierarchical linear model (HLM) program. Using this program, investigators will be able to answer a question raised in the section on climate: Does the relationship between temperature and violence depend on a region's climate?

One of our graduate students, Frank Paulson, is using HLM to assess the generality of results obtained on an interesting form of aggression: pitchers hitting batters during baseball games. Reifman, Larrick, and Fein (1991) found that temperature was correlated with the number of batters hit by pitched balls. Paulson will use HLM to determine if similar or different trends are observed in northern and southern cities. This study illustrates how access to large archives and advances in statistical analyses go hand in hand: Paulson obtained his data from an archive on the *USA Today* Web site.[2] It is worth noting that multilevel analyses will also enable investigators to make sense of data on how several people respond (e.g., mood ratings) during different times of the day and days of the week. As we noted, past investigations have employed procedures that confounded variation due to how different people responded (between-subject) with variation that reflected responses on different days (within-subject).

Perhaps the most serious problem facing investigators is the sheer complexity of relationships in

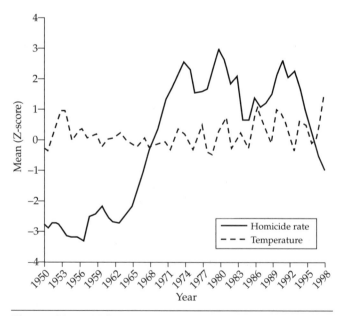

Figure 31.5 U.S. annual mean temperatures and homicide rates (standard scores).

---

[2] We are grateful to Alan Reifman for calling this Web site to our attention.

this area. As Persinger (1980) observed, five weather variables (e.g., temperature, humidity, barometric pressure, wind speed, and sunshine) can give rise to 120 main effects and interactions. This fact has led some (e.g., Gifford, 1997) to suggest that it may not be possible to separate out the influence of individual variables. However, Aiken and West (1991) have described fairly straightforward procedures for making sense of interactions between continuous variables, such as temperature and humidity. This is not to deny that high correlations between the predictors may sometimes present a problem, but Rotton and Cohn (1999a) showed that the problem is not as serious as Gifford and Persinger have suggested. The more serious problem facing researchers is conceptual rather than analytical: Even readers involved in the same area of research are reluctant to wade through the verbiage needed to describe three-way interactions (let alone higher interactions). The availability of massive amounts of data on weather and behavior present investigators with something of an embarrassment of riches. More often than not, a single set of data requires more than one article for presentation and proper interpretation.

FIELD SETTINGS AS NATURALISTIC (AND REALISTIC) LABORATORIES

Research on weather and behavior raises questions about the generalizability (or external validity) of results obtained in laboratory settings. For example, laboratory studies suggest that cold causes people to behave aggressively (Boyanowsky, 1999; Boyanowsky, Calvert, Young, & Brideau, 1981–1982). However, as we have seen, one of the most consistent findings in this area is that fewer violent crimes are reported to the police during cold than during temperate periods of time. This inconsistency raises the possibility that beliefs about the weather, expectations, and demand characteristics are responsible for results obtained in laboratory settings. Dubitsky, Weber, and Rotton (1993) addressed this issue by exposing subjects to comfortable and moderately high temperatures in a room that had been designed to convey one of two impressions. Half of the subjects came to an unadorned room where heating units were visible and there was a sign on the door describing it as a "Heat Chamber." The other half entered a room that had been constructed to resemble a sauna (complete with rocks and wooden slats). They found that actual temperatures did not affect

feelings, but subjects tested in the sauna reported less hostility than individuals tested in the heat chamber.

It would be a mistake to conclude that we are suggesting that the problems of demand characteristics, stereotypes, and subject expectancies are insurmountable. They are not. However, it will be necessary for investigators in this area to accept the idea that a psychological laboratory is only one of many types of environment where experiments can be conducted. For example, this chapter's authors could capitalize on the fact that they are at a university where many classes are held in double-wide trailers. These classrooms are cooled by individual air conditioners that frequently malfunction. Thus, we are fairly confident that we could expose research participants to varying levels of heat without arousing suspicion.

APPLICATIONS

While we are optimistic about the prospect of developing more complete and comprehensive theories in this area, we are somewhat skeptical about overly enthusiastic attempts to apply the knowledge that has been acquired. Our skepticism can be traced to the excesses of those we now term geographical determinists. A good example is Huntington's (1949) ozone hypothesis. After reviewing a tremendous amount of evidence, Huntington concluded that the invigorating properties of ozone contributed to the vigor, energy, and productivity of people living in the northeastern part of the United States (which just happened to be where Huntington was living at the time). This hypothesis was widely accepted by other scientists and by members of the general public, as shown by the existence of towns with names like Ozone, Texas, and Ozona, Florida (Chappell, 1968). Indeed, at one time, the makers of ion generators advertised that their machines produced ozone as a healthy by-product. Of course, we now know that even low levels of ozone are irritating and a threat to human health. Huntington's hypothesis illustrates the dangers of the premature application of findings from a small knowledge base.

REFERENCES

Aiken, L. S., & West, S. G. (1991). *Multiple regression: Testing and interpreting interactions.* Newbury Park, CA: Sage.

Aldwin, C. M. (1994). *Stress, coping, and development: An integrative perspective.* New York: Guilford.

Anderson, C. A., & Anderson, D. C. (1984). Ambient temperature and violent crime: Test of the linear and curvilinear hypotheses. *Journal of Personality and Social Psychology, 46,* 91–97.

Anderson, C. A., Anderson, K. B., Dorr, N., DeNeve, K. M., & Flanagan, M. (2000). Temperature and aggression. In M. P. Zanna (Ed.), *Advances in experimental social psychology* (Vol. 32, pp. 63–133). New York: Academic Press.

Aschoff, J. (1981). A survey of biological rhythms. In J. Aschoff (Ed.), *Handbook of behavioral neurobiology: Biological rhythms* (Vol. 4, pp. 475–487). New York: Plenum Press.

Asmus, C. L., & Bell, P. A. (1999). Effects of environmental odor and coping style on negative affect, anger, arousal, and escape. *Journal of Applied Social Psychology, 29,* 245–260.

Auliciems, A., & DiBartolo, L. (1995). Domestic violence in a subtropical environment: Police calls and weather and Brisbane. *International Journal of Biometeorology, 39,* 34–39.

Barnett, G. A., & Cho, S. H. (1996). Predicting television viewing: Cycles, the weather, and social events. In J. H. Watt & C. A. Van Lear (Eds.), *Dynamic patterns in communication processes* (pp. 231–254). Thousand Oaks, CA: Sage.

Barnston, A. G. (1988). The effect of weather on mood, productivity, and frequency of emotional crisis in temperate continental climate. *International Journal of Biometeorology, 32,* 134–143.

Baron, R. A. (1976). The reduction of human aggression: A field study of the influence of incompatible reactions. *Journal of Applied Social Psychology, 6,* 260–274.

Baron, R. A. (1978). Aggression and heat: The "long hot summer" revisited. In A. Baum, J. E. Singer, & S. Valins (Eds.), *Advances in environmental psychology: The urban environment* (Vol. 1, pp. 57–84). Hillsdale, NJ: Erlbaum.

Baron, R. A., & Bell, P. A. (1976). Aggression and heat: The influence of ambient temperature, negative affect, and a cooling drink on physical aggression. *Journal of Personality and Social Psychology, 33,* 245–255.

Baron, R. A., & Ransberger, V. M. (1978). Ambient temperature and the occurrence of collective violence: The "long, hot summer" revisited. *Journal of Personality and Social Psychology, 36,* 350–360.

Bass, B. M., & Alexander, R. A. (1972). Climate, economy, and the differential migration of white and nonwhite workers. *Journal of Applied Psychology, 56,* 518–521.

Baumer, E., & Wright, R. (1996). Crime seasonality and serious scholarship: A comment on Farrell and Pease. *British Journal of Criminology, 36,* 579–581.

Bell, P. A., & Baron, R. A. (1976). Aggression and heat: The mediating role of negative affect. *Journal of Applied Social Psychology, 6,* 18–30.

Bell, P. A., Greene, T. E., Fisher, J. D., & Baum, A. (2000). *Environmental psychology* (4th ed.). New York: Holt, Rinehart and Winston.

Berkowitz, L. (1993). *Aggression: Its causes, consequences, and control.* Philadelphia: Temple University Press.

Boyanowsky, E. O. (1999). Violence and aggression in the heat of passion and cold blood: The Ecs-TC syndrome. *International Journal of Law and Psychiatry, 22,* 257–271.

Boyanowsky, E. O., Calvert, J., Young, J., & Brideau, L. (1981–1982). Toward a thermoregulatory model of violence. *Journal of Environmental Systems, 11,* 81–87.

Brandstätter, H., Frühwirth, M., & Kirchler, E. (1988). Effects of weather and air pollution on mood: An individual difference approach. In D. Canter, J. C. Jesuino, L. Soczka, & G. M. Stephenson (Eds.), *Environmental social psychology* (pp. 149–159). Boston: Kluwer Academic.

Bryk, A. S., & Raudenbush, S. W. (1992). *Hierarchical linear models: Applications and data analysis methods.* Newbury Park, CA: Sage.

Carlsmith, J. M., & Anderson, C. A. (1979). Ambient temperature and the occurrence of collective violence: A new analysis. *Journal of Personality and Social Psychology, 37,* 337–344.

Cavalini, P. (1992). *It's an ill wind that brings no good: Studies on odour annoyance and the dispersion of odorant concentrations from industries.* Unpublished doctoral thesis, University of Groningen, The Netherlands.

Chappell, J. E., Jr. (1968). *Huntington and his critics: The influence of climate on civilization.* Unpublished doctoral thesis, University of Kansas, Lawrence.

Cheatwood, D. (1995). The effects of weather on homicide. *Journal of Quantitative Criminology, 11,* 51–70.

Cohen, L. E., & Felson, M. (1979). Social change and crime rate trends: A routine activity approach. *American Sociological Review, 44,* 588–608.

Cohn, E. G. (1990). Weather and violent crime: A reply to Perry and Simpson, 1987. *Environment and Behavior, 22,* 280–294.

Cohn, E. G. (1993). The prediction of police calls for service: The influence of weather and temporal variables on rape and domestic violence. *Journal of Environmental Psychology, 13,* 71–83.

Cohn, E. G. (1996). The effect of weather and temporal variations on calls for police service. *American Journal of Police, 15,* 23–43.

Cohn, E. G., & Rotton, J. (1997). Assault as a function of time and temperature: A moderator-variable time-series analysis. *Journal of Personality and Social Psychology, 72,* 1322–1334.

Cohn, E. G., & Rotton, J. (2000a). *Serious questions about "Hot years and serious and deadly assaults:" A failure to replicate.* Unpublished manuscript, Florida International University, Miami.

Cohn, E. G., & Rotton, J. (2000b). Weather, seasonal trends, and property crimes in Minneapolis, 1987–1988: A moderator-variable time-series analysis of routine activities. *Journal of Environmental Psychology, 20,* 252–272.

Cotton, J. L. (1986). Ambient temperature and violent crime. *Journal of Applied Social Psychology, 16,* 786–801.

Cunningham, M. R. (1979). Weather, mood, and helping behavior: Quasi experiments with the sunshine Samaritan. *Journal of Personality and Social Psychology, 37,* 1947–1956.

Cyr, K. A. (1995). *Mental health, mood, and perceptual responses to meteorological conditions.* Unpublished doctoral thesis, Union Institute, Chicago.

Dexter, E. G. (1904). *Weather influences.* New York, NY: Macmillan.

Dodge, R. W. (1988). *The seasonality of crime victimization* (Rep. No. NCJ-111033). Washington, DC: Bureau of Justice Statistics.

Dubitsky, S., Weber, R., & Rotton, J. (1993). Heat, hostility, and immune function: The moderating effects of gender and demand characteristics. *Bulletin of the Psychonomic Society, 31,* 534–536.

Durkheim, E. (1951). *Suicide: A study in sociology* (G. Simpson, Trans.). New York: Free Press. (Original work published 1897)

Evans, G. W., & Cohen, S. (1987). Environmental stress. In D. Stokols & I. Altman (Eds.), *Handbook of environmental psychology* (Vol. 1, pp. 571–610). New York: Wiley.

Evans, G. W., & Lepore, S. J. (1997). Moderating and mediating processes in environment-behavior research. In G. T. Moore & R. W. Marans (Eds.), *Advances in environment, behavior, and design* (Vol. 4, pp. 255–285). New York: Plenum Press.

Feldman, H. S., & Jarmon, R. G. (1979). Factors influencing criminal behavior in Newark: A local study in forensic psychiatry. *Journal of Forensic Sciences, 24,* 234–239.

Felson, M. (2000). The routine activity approach as a general crime theory. In S. S. Simpson (Ed.), *Of crime and criminality* (pp. 205–216). Thousand Oaks, CA: Pine Forge Press.

Field, S. (1992). The effect of temperature on crime. *British Journal of Criminology, 32,* 340–351.

Firebaugh, G. (1978). A rule for inferring individual-level relationships from aggregate data. *American Sociological Review, 43,* 557–572.

Frisancho, A. R. (1979). *Human adaptation: A functional interpretation.* St. Louis, MO: Mosby.

Gaffen, D. J., & Ross, R. J. (1998). Increased summertime heat stress in the US. *Nature, 396,* 629–630.

Gastil, R. D. (1971). Homicide and a regional culture of violence. *American Sociological Review, 36,* 412–427.

Gerson, L. W., & Preston, D. A. (1979). Alcohol consumption and the incidence of violence crime. *Journal of Studies on Alcohol, 40,* 307–312.

Gifford, R. (1997). *Environmental psychology: Principle and practice* (2nd ed.). Boston: Allyn & Bacon.

Gifford, R., Ward, J., & Dahms, W. (1977). Pedestrian velocities: A multivariate study of social and environmental effects. *Journal of Human Movement Studies, 3,* 66–68.

Goldstein, K. M. (1972). Weather, mood, and internal-external control. *Perceptual and Motor Skills, 33,* 786.

Gordon, R. A. (1968). Issues in multiple regression. *American Journal of Sociology, 73,* 592–616.

Griffitt, W. (1970). Environmental effects on interpersonal affective behavior: Ambient effective temperature and attraction. *Journal of Personality and Social Psychology, 15,* 240–244.

Griffitt, W., & Veitch, R. (1971). Hot and crowded: Influences of population density and temperature on interpersonal affective behavior. *Journal of Personality and Social Psychology, 17,* 96–98.

Hagelin, J. S., Rainforth, M. V., Orme-Johnson, D. W., Cavenaugh, K. L., Alexander, C. N., Shatkin, S. F., Davies, J. L., Hughes, A. O., & Ross, E. (1999). Effects of group practice of the Transcendental Meditation program on preventing violent crime in Washington, DC: Results of the National Demonstration Project, June–July 1993. *Social Indicators Research, 47,* 153–201.

Harries, K. D., & Stadler, S. J. (1983). Determinism revisited: Assault and heat stress in Dallas, 1980. *Environment and Behavior, 15,* 235–256.

Harries, K. D., & Stadler, S. J. (1985–1986). Aggravated assault and the urban system: Dallas, 1980–81. *Journal of Environmental Systems, 15,* 243–253.

Harries, K. D., & Stadler, S. J. (1988). Heat and violence: New findings from Dallas field data, 1980–1981. *Journal of Applied Social Psychology, 18,* 129–138.

Hawley, F. F., & Messner, S. F. (1989). The southern violence construct: A review of arguments, evidence, and the normative context. *Justice Quarterly, 6,* 481–511.

Heller, N. B., & Markland, R. B. (1970). A climatological model for forecasting the demand for police service. *Journal of Research in Crime and Delinquency, 7,* 167–176.

Hoel, L. A. (1968). Pedestrian travel rates in central business districts. *Traffic Engineering, 38,* 10–13.

Howarth, E., & Hoffman, M. S. (1984). A multidimensional approach to the relationship between mood and weather. *British Journal of Psychology, 75,* 15–23.

Humphreys, M. A. (1976). Field studies of thermal comfort compared and applied. *Building Services Engineer, 44*(5), 5–27.

Huntington, E. (1949). *Mainsprings of civilization.* New York: Wiley.

Ito, T. A., Miller, N., & Pollock, V. E. (1996). Alcohol and aggression: A meta-analysis on the moderating effects of inhibitory cues, triggering events, and self-focused attention. *Psychological Bulletin, 120,* 60–82.

Jorgenson, D. O. (1981a). Perceived causal influence of weather: Rating the weather's influence on affective states and behavior. *Environment and Behavior, 11,* 239–256.

Jorgenson, D. O. (1981b). Superstition and the perceived causal influence of the weather. *Perceptual and Motor Skills, 52,* 111–114.

Kenrick, D. T., & MacFarlane, S. W. (1986). Ambient temperature and horn honking: A field study of the heat/aggression relationship. *Environment and Behavior, 18,* 179–191.

Kevan, S. M. (1979). Season of life—season of death. *Social Science and Medicine, 13,* 227–232.

Lab, S. P., & Hirschel, J. D. (1988). Climatological conditions and crime: The forecast is . . . ? *Justice Quarterly, 5,* 281–299.

LaRoche, E., & Tillery, E. (1956). Weather and crime in Tallahassee during 1954. *Journal of Criminal Law, Criminology, and Police Science, 47,* 218–219.

Lazarus, R. S. (2000). Toward better research on stress and coping. *American Psychologist, 55,* 665–673.

LeBeau, J. L. (1994). The oscillation of police calls to domestic disputes with time and the temperature humidity index. *Journal of Crime and Justice, 17,* 149–161.

LeBeau, J. L., & Corcoran, W. T. (1990). Changes in calls for police service and changes in routine activities and the arrival and passage of weather fronts. *Journal of Quantitative Criminology, 6,* 269–291.

LeBeau, J. L., & Langworthy, R. H. (1986). The linkages between routine activities, weather, and calls for police service. *Journal of Police Science and Administration, 14,* 137–145.

Li, S. (1991). A study of winter plaza use in New York City. *Proceedings of the Environmental Design Research Association, 22,* 253–265.

Li, S. (1994). Users' behaviour of small urban spaces in winter and marginal seasons. *Architecture & Comportment, 10,* 95–109.

Linkowski, P., Martin, F., & De Maertelaer, V. (1992). Effect of some climatic factors on violent and non-violent suicides in Belgium. *Journal of Affective Disorders, 25,* 161–166.

London, W. B., & Teague, G. B. (1985). Alcohol consumption and latitude in the United States. *American Journal of Psychiatry, 142,* 656–657.

Lucero, R. J., Brantner, J. P., Brown, B. W., & Olson, G. W. (1965). Weather, crime, and mental illness. *Journal of the Minnesota Academy of Science, 32,* 223–226.

MacMahon, K. (1983). Short-term temporal cycles in the frequency of suicides, United States, 1972–1978. *American Journal of Epidemiology, 117,* 744–750.

Maes, M., de Meyer, F., Thompson, P., Peeters, D., & Cosyne, P. (1994). Synchronized annual rhythms in violent suicide rate, ambient temperature, and the light-dark span. *Acta Psychiatrica Scandinvica, 90,* 391–396.

Matthews, R. W., Paulus, P. B., & Baron, R. A. (1979). Physical aggression after being crowded. *Journal of Nonverbal Behavior, 4,* 5–17.

Michael, R. P., & Zumpe, D. (1983). Annual rhythms in human violence and sexual aggression in the United States and the role of temperature. *Social Biology, 30,* 263–278.

Michael, R. P., & Zumpe, D. (1986). An annual rhythm in the battering of women. *American Journal of Psychiatry, 143,* 637–640.

Mitchell, M. F. (1991). *The effects of weather and routine activity on domestic disputes across ecological areas in Charlotte, North Carolina: 1986.* Unpublished master's thesis, Southern Illinois University, Carbondale.

Moos, R. H., & Tsu, V. D. (1976). Human competence and coping. In R. H. Moos (Ed.), *Human adaptation* (pp. 3–16). Lexington, MA: D.C. Heath.

Newman, R. W. (1970). Why man is such a sweaty and thirsty naked animal: A speculative review. *Human Biology, 42,* 12–25.

Oskamp, S. (2000). A sustainable future for humanity? How can psychology help? *American Psychologist, 55,* 496–508.

Parker, P. M. (1995). *Climatic effects on individual, social, and economic behavior.* Westport, CT: Greenwood Press.

Parker, R. N., & Auerhahn, K. (1998). Alcohol, drugs, and violence. *Annual Review of Sociology, 24,* 291–311.

Parrott, W. G., & Sabini, J. (1990). Mood and memory under natural conditions: Evidence for mood incongruent recall. *Journal of Personality and Social Psychology, 59,* 321–336.

Parsons, K. C. (1993). *Human thermal environments.* London: Taylor & Francis.

Pennebaker, J. W., Rimé, B., & Blankenship, V. E. (1996). Stereotypes of emotional expressiveness of northerners and southerners: A cross-cultural test of Montesquieu's hypothesis. *Journal of Personality and Social Psychology, 70,* 372–380.

Perry, J. D., & Simpson, M. E. (1987). Violent crimes in a city: Environmental determinants. *Environment and Behavior, 19,* 77–90.

Persinger, M. A. (1980). *The weather matrix and human behavior.* New York: Praeger.

Persinger, M. A. (1975). Lag responses in mood to changes in the weather matrix. *International Journal of Biometeorology, 19,* 108–114.

Persinger, M. A., & Levesque, D. F. (1983). Geophysical variables and behavior: XII. The weather matrix accommodates large portions of variance of measured daily mood. *Perceptual and Motor Skills, 57,* 868–870.

Reifman, A. S., Larrick, R. P., & Fein, S. (1991). Temper and temperature on the diamond: The heat-aggression relationship in major league baseball. *Personality and Social Psychology Bulletin, 17,* 580–585.

Rind, B. (1996). Effect of beliefs about weather conditions on tipping. *Journal of Applied Social Psychology, 26,* 137–147.

Rohles, F. H., Jr. (1974). The modal comfort envelope and its use in current standards. *Human Factors, 16,* 314–322.

Room, R. (1983). Region and urbanization as factors in drinking practices and problems. In B. Kissen & H. Begleiter (Eds.), *The pathogenesis of alcoholism: Psychosocial factors* (Vol. 6, pp. 555–604). New York: Plenum Press.

Rosenthal, R. (1978). How often are our numbers wrong? *American Psychologist, 33,* 1005–1008.

Rotton, J. (1985). Astrological forecasts and the commodity marker: Random walks as a source of illusory correlation. *Skeptical Inquirer, 9,* 339–346.

Rotton, J. (1986). Determinism *redux*: Climate and cultural correlates of violence. *Environment and Behavior, 18,* 346–368.

Rotton, J. (1993a). Atmospheric and temporal correlates of sex crimes: Endogenous factors do not explain seasonal differences in rape. *Environment and Behavior, 25,* 625–642.

Rotton, J. (1993b). Geophysical variables and behavior: LXXIII. Ubiquitous errors: A reanalysis of Anderson's (1987) "Temperature and Aggression." *Psychological Reports, 73,* 259–271.

Rotton, J., & Cohn, E. G. (1999a). Errors of commission and errors of omission: Comment on Anderson and Anderson's (1998) "temperature and aggression." *Psychological Reports, 85,* 611–620.

Rotton, J., & Cohn, E. G. (1999b, August). *The long and short of "the long hot summer effect."* Paper presented at the annual meeting of the American Psychological Association, Boston.

Rotton, J., & Cohn, E. G. (2000a). Violence is a curvilinear function of temperature in Dallas: A replication. *Journal of Personality and Social Psychology, 78,* 1074–1081.

Rotton, J., & Cohn, E. G. (2000b). Weather, disorderly conduct, and assaults: From social contact to social avoidance. *Environment and Behavior, 32,* 649–671.

Rotton, J., & Cohn, E. G. (2001). Temperature, routine activities, and domestic violence: A reanalysis. *Victims and Violence, 16,* 203–215.

Rotton, J., Cohn, E. G., & Paulson, F. L. (2001). *Stately pleasure domes: Baseball stadiums, attendance, and performance.* Paper presented at the annual convention of the American Psychological Association, San Francisco.

Rotton, J., Cohn, E. G., Peterson, A., & Tarr, D. (2000). *Temperature and crime rates in U.S. cities and U.N. countries: Destructive testing in philosophical context.* Manuscript under review, Florida International University, Miami, FL.

Rotton, J., & Frey, J. (1984). Psychological costs of air pollution: Atmospheric conditions, seasonal trends, and psychiatric emergencies. *Population and Environment, 7,* 3–16.

Rotton, J., & Frey, J. (1985). Air pollution, weather, and violent crimes: Concomitant time-series analysis of archival data. *Journal of Personality and Social Psychology, 49,* 1207–1220.

Rotton, J., Shats, M., & Standers, R. (1990). Temperature and pedestrian tempo: Walking without awareness. *Environment and Behavior, 22,* 650–674.

Ruback, R. B., & Pandey, J. (1992). Very hot and really crowded: Quasi-experimental investigations of Indian "tempos." *Environment and Behavior, 24,* 527–554.

Rubinstein, C. (1982, February). Regional states of mind. *Psychology Today, 16,* 22–30.

Sanders, J. L., & Brizzolara, M. S. (1982). Relationships between weather and mood. *Journal of General Psychology, 107,* 153–156.

Schwarz, N., & Clore, G. L. (1983). Mood, misattribution, and judgments of well-being: Informative and directive functions of affective states. *Journal of Personality and Social Psychology, 45,* 513–523.

Sinclair, R. C., Mark, M. M., & Clore, G. L. (1994). Mood-related persuasion depends on (mis)attributions. *Social Cognition, 12,* 309–326.

Sommers, P., & Moos, R. H. (1976). Weather and human behavior. In R. H. Moos (Ed.), *The human context: Environmental determinants of behavior* (pp. 73–107). New York: Wiley.

Standers, R., Rotton, J., & Schlossberg, R. (1992). *Effects of heat and cognitive demands on ambulatory movement.* Paper presented at the Symposium on Walking and Bicycling Issues, Orlando, FL.

Tacken, M. (1989). A comfortable wind climate for outdoor relaxation in urban areas. *Building and Environment, 24,* 321–324.

Tyson, G. A., & Turnbull, O. (1990). Ambient temperature and the occurrence of collective violence: A South Africa replication. *South African Journal of Psychology, 20,* 159–162.

Valentine, J. H., Ebert, J., Oakey, R., & Ernst, K. (1975). Human crises and the physical environment. *Man-Environment Systems, 5*(1), 23–28.

van Koppen, P. J., & Jansen, R. W. J. (1999). The time of rob: Variations in time of number of commercial robberies. *Journal of Research in Crime and Delinquency, 36,* 7–29.

Vrij, A., van der Steen, J., & Koppelaar, L. (1994). Aggression of police officers as a function of temperature: An experiment with the fire arms training system. *Journal of Community and Applied Social Psychology, 4,* 365–370.

Walmsley, D. J., & Lewis, G. J. (1989). The pace of pedestrian flow in cities. *Environment and Behavior, 21,* 123–150.

Watson, D. (2000). *Mood and temperament.* New York: Guilford.

Weiss, M. J. (1994). *Latitudes & attitudes.* Boston: Little, Brown.

Welte, J. W., & Russell, M. (1982). Regional variations in the consumption of alcohol in the U.S.A. *Drug and Alcohol Dependence, 10,* 243–249.

Westerberg, U. (1994). Climatic planning—physics or symbolism? *Architecture and Behavior, 10,* 49–71.

Whitton, J. L., Kramer, P., & Eastwood, R. (1982). Weather and infradian rhythms in self-reports of health, sleep, and mood measures. *Journal of Psychomatic Research, 26,* 231–235.

Wilson, C. R., & Ferris, W. (Eds.). (1989). *Encyclopedia of southern culture.* Chapel Hill: University of North Carolina.

Wilson, T. D., Laser, P. S., & Stone, J. I. (1982). Judging the predictors of one's own mood: Accuracy and shared theories. *Journal of Experimental Social Psychology, 18,* 537–556.

Wohlwill, J. F. (1974). Human adaptation to levels of environmental stimulation. *Human Ecology, 2,* 127–146.

Yan, Y. Y. (2000). Weather and homicide in Hong Kong. *Perceptual and Motor Skills, 90,* 451–452.

Zillmann, D. (1988). Cognition-excitation interdependencies in aggressive behavior. *Aggressive Behavior, 14,* 51–64.

CHAPTER 32

Noise Pollution: A Hazard to Physical and Mental Well-Being

ARLINE L. BRONZAFT

TOO OFTEN INDIVIDUALS ERR in using the words *sound* and *noise* synonymously. Sound, when received by the human ear and interpreted by the listener, may be judged to be either pleasant or unpleasant; noise, on the other hand, defined by the listener as unwanted and disturbing is very likely to be judged as unpleasant. There is a general consensus that very loud sounds can impair hearing. With respect to other than very loud sounds, the finding that "one person's music may be another's noise" has generated the often quoted assumption that one cannot study the impacts of noise on the physiological and psychological well-being of people, other than that of hearing. Yet, with the world growing increasingly noisier and more and more people worldwide claiming that noise is robbing them of a decent quality of life, as well as their health, it is imperative that we define noise in a way that permits the examination of its impacts on the health and well-being of people. By defining noise as unwanted, uncontrollable, and unpredictable sound, researchers have been able to examine its effects, producing a body of studies that indeed suggests that noise is hazardous to good health.

SOUND AND HEARING

Sound begins as the movement of air molecules. A vibrating object sets up alternating bands of compression and expansion in the surrounding air. The outer part or the external portion of the ear responds to these vibrations and transmits them to the three bones of the middle ear. The middle ear then pushes the sound to the inner ear, which contains hair cells that respond to the patterns of vibrations. These vibrations are converted into specific codes in the inner ear, which then sends on the sounds to the temporal lobe of the brain. Here the sounds are decoded, and with additional information provided by the brain, these sounds take on both meaning as to what they are as well as being judged wanted or unwanted, pleasant or annoying.

Sound, which travels in waves, has two major physical properties: the speed at which the waves vibrate, called the frequency, and the intensity of each vibration. If one were to compare sound waves to the ocean waves, one could identify the distance between the waves as characterizing the speed and the crests of the waves as the intensity. Humans react to these two physical properties as follows: Frequency accounts for the psychological interpretation of pitch, and intensity accounts primarily for the human response to loudness, recognizing that frequency also contributes to the interpretation of loudness, with higher-pitched sounds perceived as louder.

Loudness is measured on a decibel scale, but to better assess human responses to sound, the scale has been modified to compensate for the effect of higher-pitched sounds. This modified scale, known as the A scale and measuring loudness in dBAs, more accurately reflects the ways people actually hear the different volumes of sound. The typical dBA scale ranges from 0, approximating the softest sound humans can hear, to 200 dBA, with 180 decibels closely representing the loudness of a rocket being launched. The A scale increases logarithmically so that an increase of 10 decibels represents a doubling of the volume heard. Here are the decibel levels of some common sounds: whispers at 20 decibels, average conversation at 60 decibels, household appliances and noisy restaurants around 80 to 90 decibels, New York City subway trains over 90 decibels, rock concerts and discos at 110 to 120 decibels, and jet take-offs at 150 decibels.

LOUD SOUND AND HEARING LOSS

Loud sounds can impair hearing, even if the listener deems these sounds to be pleasurable. Pete Townshend of The WHO music group enjoyed playing loud music but now reports that the music that made him a recording giant also caused a serious hearing deficit. Mr. Townshend is not alone in acknowledging the damage of loud music to hearing ability. Kathy Peck of San Francisco founded an organization (Hearing Education and Awareness for Rockers, HEAR) that is dedicated to the prevention of hearing impairment in musicians and listeners who enjoy amplified music.

Hearing loss can come about after many years of listening to loud music, but it can also happen after a single exposure to an intensely loud sound. Former President Bill Clinton, who complains of his hearing loss (Sanger & Lacey, 2000) and had been fitted with small hearing aids at the start of his second term, has a hearing deficit that is greater than one would expect of a man in his early fifties. It is very likely the result of his exposure to loud music as a member of the "baby boom" generation as well as his love for his saxophone, which he probably plays without hearing protection. On the other hand, it has been reported that former President Ronald Reagan suffered some hearing damage after one explosive gun shot that rang out near his ear while he was shooting a movie.

The literature on the relationship between exposure to loud sounds and hearing loss is substantial (Fay, 1991; Kryter, 1994; Passchier-Vermeer & Passchier, 2000; see also the Web site for the League for the Hard of Hearing: www.lhh.org/noise). The National Institutes of Health (1990) has reported that approximately 28 million people in the United States suffer some hearing loss and attributes approximately 10 million of these impairments to damage from exposure to loud sounds. Undoubtedly a large number of these people who are suffering hearing loss are or were employed in occupations dominated by loud sounds, such as factory workers, firefighters, and military personnel.

How loud must a sound be to cause hearing loss? It is generally accepted that continuous exposure to sounds over 85 dBA for about 8 hours a day will very likely lead to some hearing loss over time, and exposures at higher levels require shorter periods of time before hearing loss occurs. The U.S. Occupational Safety and Health Administration (OSHA) has established 90 dBA as the allowable exposure level for an 8 hour day and recommends that workers wear hearing protection if the exposure is greater. However, retrospective studies have demonstrated that even when industries have lowered noises to reach OSHA standards, workers still have shown some hearing loss (Wilson, 1998), indicating that OSHA has set too high a standard for acceptable sound exposure. Furthermore, not all workers wear the recommended ear mufflers, making them more vulnerable to hearing loss.

However, with the advent of stereos, video arcades, outdoor recreational vehicles, and personal headsets, as well as the idea that "it has to be loud to be fun," very loud sounds are no longer simply limited to the working environment. Today many people are hearing very loud sounds in their homes and in recreational settings. Children's toys have been measured as high as 125 decibels (Nadler, 1997), and movies emit sounds as high as 117 decibels (Sawhill & Brown, 1998). Stopping people on the street to measure the level at which they were listening to their headsets, Jane Madell (1986) found that may headsets were set beyond 110 decibels. Plakke (1983) reported that the two video arcades he visited had games measuring as high as 111 dBA.

Thus, it is not surprising that hearing loss has been identified as one of the leading disabilities in the United States nor to learn that hearing loss starts earlier than what would be expected if hearing deficits were largely a function of the aging process. Nearly 30 years ago, Lipscomb (1972) already found a significant increase in the prevalence of high frequency hearing impairment among the more than 14,000 college freshmen he tested. Cozad, Martson, and Joseph (1974) also found a steady increase in the number of students, from age 6 to 18, suffering sensorineural hearing loss. More recently Niskar et al. (2001) reported that nearly 12.5% of the children in the United States between the ages of 6 and 19 have noise-related hearing problems. The hearing data collected by the League for the Hard of Hearing over the past 19 years (Bat-Chava & Schur, 2000) also indicated a downtrend in hearing ability for older adults, as well. Taking hearing measurements of over 27,000 New Yorkers for three different age groups (60 to 69, 70 to 79, 80 to 89), Bat-Chava & Schur report that a higher percentage of individuals failed the hearing screening test with each passing year.

With respect to the high-frequency loss found in so many young people, it would be safe to hypothesize that this loss is rooted in increased exposure to loud sounds in their environment. In discussing the older population she tested, Dr. Bat-Chava attributes a large part of their hearing loss to living in a city that has grown increasingly louder with each passing year. The following are reasons why New York has become louder: the increase in high-rise buildings, greater airport and highway traffic, more outdoor facilities, and a lessening of civil respect for people's rights to quiet. New Yorkers call the loud sounds that they experience noise because they are unwanted and unwelcomed.

Yet one should not conclude that only large cities provide the loud sounds that endanger their residents to potential hearing loss. Broste, Hansen, Strand, and Stueland (1989) reported "that teenaged school children who are actively involved in farm work have increased prevalence of mild hearing loss and early noise-induced hearing loss." Living near a very loud airport may also affect hearing. Chen, Chen, Hsieh, and Chiang (1997) found that hearing ability was worse in individuals exposed to high-frequency aircraft noise. In this case, the sounds to which these people were exposed could be called noise because they were indeed unwanted sounds. Similarly, Hiramatsu and his colleagues (1997) found evidence for noise-induced hearing loss in their study of a group of individuals exposed to continuous aircraft noise. However, Chen et al. acknowledged that their results conflicted with those of other investigators who found no relationship between permanent hearing damage and aircraft noise, clearly calling for further studies in this area.

In summing up the effect of loud sounds on hearing loss, there appears to be sufficient evidence to demonstrate this relationship, whether the loud sounds are enjoyed by the listener or not. It would be wise to protect oneself from these loud sounds by wearing the appropriate hearing protection. Ear plugs are a very inexpensive way to guard a very valuable asset.

NOISE AND STRESS

The human ear is the organ of the body that directly responds to sound and can be damaged if the sounds are too loud. Unwanted, uncontrollable, and unpredictable sounds, whether soft or loud—labeled *noise*—can be annoying and very disturbing. The body reacts to the annoyance of these unwanted sounds, or noises, through a complex set of physiological responses that are collectively labeled *stress*. These physiological responses can include: a rise in blood pressure, excessive secretion of certain hormones, a change in heart rhythm, or a slowing down of digestion. Should the noise continue to be disturbing and the stress reaction sustained, then permanent ailments may occur in the circulatory, cardiovascular, or gastrointestinal system. Thus, noise mediated by stress can affect many organs of the body indirectly.

Examples of continuous exposure to noise include: the overhead jets that both awaken you each morning and prevent you from falling asleep before midnight; the neighbor playing her television set late at night or refusing to put soft coverings on her floors. Although it is true that not all people respond to the same sounds in a similar fashion, there are sizeable numbers of residents who complain about aircraft noise, and there are many dwellers who complain about their neighbors' noises. Even workers in noisy occupational settings have complained that noise bothers them physically, not just affecting their ears. There appears to be sufficient literature to indicate that noise has become a major environmental pollutant worldwide, annoying and disturbing millions of people in a manner that may in time bring about physiological and psychological disorders (Bronzaft & Madell, 1991). In fact Berglund and Lindvall (1995) state that "noise is one of the most frequent reasons for public protest."

Annette Zaner (1991) lists many sources of annoying noises, with urban traffic noise being the most significant source of annoyance. Citing a 1977 National Academy of Sciences report, Ms. Zaner reports that over 40 million residents in the United States alone are disturbed by traffic noise and about 14 million complain about aircraft noise. In the past 20 years, aircraft have been equipped with quieter engines, allowing airlines to indicate that fewer residents are probably being disturbed by overhead jets. However, the rapid increase in air travel these past years and the growth of smaller airports has very likely negated the effect of the Stage 3 quieter airplanes, and so it is doubtful that the numbers of individuals bothered by planes has significantly decreased. With the method airports use to assess annoyance being criticized as underestimating the numbers of people disturbed by aircraft noise, it is very likely that even more people today are probably annoyed by overhead aircraft (Stenzel, 1996).

Along with the expansion of airports there has been a considerable increase in highway traffic and with it an increase in the numbers of people bothered by traffic noise. A more recent survey on an international sample, with Americans comprising the largest number of respondents (Bronzaft, Deignan, Bat-Chava, & Nadler, 2000), concurred with the Zaner findings in that highway vehicles and aircraft were still the most bothersome noises. The Bronzaft et al. study provides a long list of bothersome noises: loud music, loud movies, restaurants, garden and lawn equipment, recreational vehicles, bars, nightclubs, and neighbors. According to Stansfeld, Haines, and Brown (2000), neighbor noises have become a major source of disturbance, and complaints of such noises have increased sharply in recent years. The list of surrounding noises that disturb people is growing.

Since many of the subjects queried in the Bronzaft et al. (2000) study indicated that their noise complaints did not result in an alleviation of the problem, we can assume that they will continue to be annoyed by the noises. Contributing to the stress originally brought on by the noise is the person's feeling that nothing can be done to "stop the noise." This feeling, in which the person does not think anything can be done to solve the noise problem and that one has to learn to live with the noise, has been cited as an example of "learned helplessness." The individual is expected to "just sit back and take it." This feeling of helplessness also serves to exacerbate the physiological responses associated with stress.

With stress potentially the precursor to illness, we should examine the nonauditory health effects of noise.

NOISE AND PHYSICAL HEALTH

The Office of Noise Abatement's brochure entitled *Noise: A Health Problem* (U.S. Environmental Protection Agency, 1978) left no doubt that noise was not just a nuisance but a health hazard. The brochure linked noise to disorders such as hypertension, heart disease, and ulcers as well as sleep disturbance. The following extensive reviews of studies on the nonauditory effects of noise on workers in noisy occupations and people living in communities disturbed by noises from nearby highways, railroads, and airports also point to the dangers of noise to physical well-being: Berglund and Lindvall, 1995; Fay, 1991; Kryter, 1985, 1994; Passchier-Vermeer, 1993; Stansfeld et al., 2000; Tempest, 1985. Passchier-Vermeer and Passchier (2000), after examining the noise and health literature, conclude that, "Exposure to noise constitutes a health risk." Yet, they are quick to point out that the scientific evidence is strongest only for hypertension and ischemic heart disease. Tomei et al. (1995) also believe that the relationship between noise exposure in the workplace and cardiovascular disorders are the easiest to confirm.

With the field of immunology expanding, the effects of noise on the immune system should prove of interest. For now, both Raymond (1991) and Passchier-Vermeer and Passchier (2000) find that the small number of studies in this area prevents them from drawing any conclusions on the relationship of noise to the immune system. However, Peters et al. (1999), using noise as the uncontrollable variable in a laboratory setting, found that uncontrollability affected a "wide range of immunological functions." With noise frequently viewed as a factor over which one has no control, the Peters et al. findings indicate that this is an area that calls for further exploration.

In a study that asked people to evaluate their own health, Bronzaft, Ahern, McGinn, O'Connor, and Savino (1998) found that residents living within the path of planes from a nearby airport perceived themselves to be in poorer health than a matched group who did not live with aircraft noise. Personal evaluations of current health status have proven useful in detecting illnesses. The Bronzaft et al. (1998) subjects also complained that the aircraft noise interfered with their right to open their windows, listen to radio and television, talk on the telephone, and converse with others in the home. Okinawa residents living near two air bases (Hiramatsu, 1999) also reported that aircraft noise disturbed their daily activities in a similar way. Essentially the quality of life for the community residents in both these studies had been diminished by the intrusive airplane noise.

The finding that children exposed to noises in their environment may be especially vulnerable (Evans & Lepore, 1993) has been singularly disturbing. Evans and Lapore in their review of nonauditory effects of noise concluded that children who lived near or attended school near a major airport were more likely to have elevated blood pressure. With the opening of a new airport in Munich, Evans and his colleagues were able to demonstrate a relationship between chronic noise exposure and elevated neuroendocrine and cardiovascular measures (Evans, Hygge, & Bullinger, 1995).

Even before living in a community that may expose its children to extremely noisy conditions, infants exposed to continuous noises in neonatal intensive units may suffer some hearing loss or be slow in their growth and development (American Academy of Pediatrics, 1997). When Jones and Tauscher (1978) reported that infants born to mothers living near the Los Angeles Airport had lower birth weights and greater numbers of birth defects, such as cleft palates, this study and similar ones led the United States National Research Council (1982) to issue a report urging pregnant mothers to avoid working in noisy industrial settings. However, in their latest article Passchier-Vermeer and Passchier (2000) state that more recent investigations have not "shown statistically significant effects of occupational or environmental exposure of pregnant women to noise in the course of pregnancy and congenital defects in babies, with the exception of high-frequency hearing damage" (p. 127). The studies cited above clearly demonstrate the importance of continued research into the noise-health relationship. Whereas scientists today, unlike those in the 1970s, are demanding more evidence to solidify the view that noise is hazardous to physical health, they would still concur that the current data are sufficient to warn people of the potential harm of noise exposure. With noise on the increase, a strong warning should be issued. Furthermore, it is also possible that we have relied too heavily on the development of physical symptoms in determining the noise-health link. Good health is not merely the absence of symptoms. It should also include the absence of extreme stress and discomfort as well as the assurance of a decent quality of life. If we were to broaden the definition of health to include quality of life, there would be far more evidence to support the deleterious effects of noise.

NOISE AND SLEEP DISRUPTION

Individuals living beneath the roar of overnight jets complain that they do not get a good night's sleep (Bronzaft et al., 1998; Hiramatsu, 1999). Sleep is required for physiological and psychological recuperation and the inability to reinvigorate oneself during sleep after a day of chores may lead to physiological disorders. Passchier-Vermeer and Passchier (2000) noted in their review of epidemiologic studies that nighttime noise disturbances change sleep patterns, increase awakenings, and affect heart rate. Yet Pollak (1991) reported that the data on the long-term health consequences of sleep interference are inconclusive. However, Pollak points out a possible secondary effect brought about by sleep disruptions: Sleep-deprived individuals may become more dependent on tranquilizers and other drugs to induce sleep, and these may adversely affect physical health.

Both Pollak and Passchier-Vermeer and Passchier also discuss the impacts of noise on performance, and both agree that noise-induced sleep loss may impair task performance the next day. Sleep loss may also cause one to be less attentive and, as a result, less receptive to cues of danger and more accident prone. Furthermore, the resentment expressed by individuals deprived of sleep by overhead jets or the loud music from a nearby restaurant precipitates a less than pleasant mood the next day. Representatives of the U.S. Federal Aviation Administration speaking at community meetings are often confronted by angry residents whom they would generally label "extremely moody."

NOISE AND MENTAL WELL-BEING

Residents who live near airports are continually exposed to noises both day and night from aircraft above their homes, and undoubtedly many of these individuals are feeling annoyed, distressed, and unhappy. The Bronzaft et al. study (2000) identified six emotional responses to noise, with the majority of their respondents reporting feelings of annoyance. Anger was identified by somewhat less than 50%. Without a doubt, people who are bothered by noise are annoyed, but could this annoyance lead to serious mental health problems?

Early studies (Abey-Wickrama, a'Brook, Gattoni, & Herridge, 1969; Herridge & Chir, 1972; Meecham & Smith, 1977) found higher admissions to mental hospitals for people who lived near airports. However, the methodology of these studies was subsequently questioned. Recently residents living near an air base, exposed to intense noises, evidenced greater mental instability, depression, and overall nervousness (Hiramatsu, Yamamoto, Taira, Ito, & Nakasone, 1997) as determined by a survey they completed. Still, there is a strong need for further investigation of the relationship between noise and mental health.

Mental stress can also be expressed in other ways, namely through aggressive acts. Laboratory findings (Donnerstein & Wilson, 1976; Geen & O'Neal, 1969) indicate that subjects exposed to noise were more likely to administer shocks (shocks were not actually given) to other subjects. Anger, as noted above in the Bronzaft et al. study (2000) is a frequent response when an individual is disturbed by noise, and anger often elicits aggression. Thus, one should not be surprised at newspaper stories of individuals attacking noise-making neighbors. The Noise Pollution Clearinghouse provides many of these newspaper accounts on its Web site (www.nonoise.org). In New York City, the former director of the Victim Services Mediation Program, Janice Tudy-Jackson, has noted at several public talks that many of the disputes they are asked to mediate involve noise that too often escalated to aggressive behavior.

In the 15 years I've served in New York City as the mayor's appointee to the Council on the Environment, chairing its noise committee, many New Yorkers have called me to help them with noise problems. They had already sought assistance from the New York Department of Environment and the Police Department but to no avail. The anguish and distress expressed by these people clearly spoke to their mental state. These callers were upset not only by the noises that have robbed them of the "quiet enjoyment" of their homes but also by their inability to resolve the problem. Meeting with community groups around the country who are battling aircraft and other neighborhood noises has also put me into contact with many people who are desperate, agitated, and unhappy.

John Dallas in his poignant essay titled "No More Jerichos!" (1995) writes that when a person cannot find peace and quiet in his surrounding environment, he or she will find it difficult to find quiet within. Dallas believes that people are entitled to develop themselves to the fullest and to do so requires some inner sense of peace. Noise robs the individual of achieving this inner peace, because too much time is spent reacting to outside stimuli, preventing one from focusing on and developing one's own individuality.

Dallas, who had considered becoming a priest, now spends much of his time combating noise pollution in his South Bronx community. Though his writings reflect his religious beliefs, he has still captured the feeling that frequently overcomes people who are unable to go on with their lives because noise has so overwhelmed them. When people cannot get their neighbors to stop blasting the television or cannot persuade the nearby store owner to repair the noisy cooling unit, they feel they are no longer in control of their own lives. They begin to center their daily activities around the parts of their homes that are further from the noise source or stay out later on evenings that their neighbors have loud parties. One might wonder why these people have not asked for some assistance with the noise problem. Why haven't they contacted the landlord, the police, or the department of environmental protection? Many report they have but to no avail.

In their survey on community noises, Bronzaft et al. (2000) learned that less than 20% of the people who complained about the noise actually had the noise stopped or reduced. Thus, when people complain to the authorities, too often they discover that no one can do anything about the noise. This can lead to a feeling of "learned helplessness" in which the person accepts the noise, believing that nothing can be done. However, living with the noise in this way does not reflect a healthy lifestyle. Too much time and too much energy is devoted to avoiding the noise or at least trying to cope with the noise.

As a psychologist, I wondered whether the people who have sought my assistance were in good mental health before the noise problem. I have concluded that most were, based largely on the thank-you calls received after the problems were resolved from people who sounded cheerful, in a good state of mind, and who informed me that they were once again able to get on with their lives. Yet in the past few years, more calls have been received from individuals who appear to be very disturbed and unusually agitated by the noise. Even when helped, they continue to call me just to stay in touch "in case the noise reappears." These individuals appear to be suffering from emotional problems independent of the noise problem, but the noise problem appears to have exacerbated the condition.

These numerous personal encounters plus the stories in the media linking noise to violence, in some cases against oneself because of the stress, leads me to conclude that noise, even identified as an annoyance rather than a health hazard, can adversely affect the mental stability of individuals who "cannot stop the noise."

CHILDREN'S LANGUAGE DEVELOPMENT, COGNITION, AND LEARNING

As stated earlier, noise may affect the development of the child within the womb. It is not known whether the cause is the mother's stress elicited by the noise that harms the child or the drugs the mother takes so that she can get a good night's sleep in spite of the surrounding noise. That the Hospital for Sick children (Adkins, 1998) instituted quiet times, with radios turned off or tuned to soft music and certain therapies not scheduled, indicates the awareness of members of the medical profession that young children require silent periods.

Unfortunately, too many young children are being reared in homes that are too noisy because of loud television playing, parental shouting, and overcrowding from within and the sounds of traffic from the outside. Then, many of these same children attend schools within the flights of aircraft or adjacent to noisy elevated trains or horn-honking vehicles.

How does a noisy home or school affect the mental development of the child? Wachs and Gruen (1982) informed us that noisy households impair a child's cognitive and language development. By contrast, Bronzaft (1996) interviewed a large number of older academic high achievers, all Phi Beta Kappa graduates, and discovered that they were reared in homes that respected quiet. They informed her that their parents provided quiet times and places for them to read, think, and do their homework. These academic achievers also related that they could sit and talk with their parents with no radio or television in the background. Discipline was generally done with strong looks and low voices rather than shouts and loud voices. One could readily surmise that the quiet that these academic achievers experienced contributed to their academic success, as well as later in life to their personal and professional success. Quiet also contributes to creative performance, as was demonstrated by Kasof's (1997) laboratory study and the examples he cites from the writings of recognized authors who commented on how important quiet was to their creative works.

In their critical review of the nonauditory effect of noise on children, Evans & Lepore (1993) conclude that residential noise delays early cognitive development and that chronic noise exposure in classroom settings has been associated with poorer reading, especially in the higher elementary grades. The authors also point out that children with lower aptitude appear to be more susceptible to the harmful influence of noise. To explain these findings the author considered the strong possibility that noise exposure interfered with auditory discrimination and attentional mechanisms, thus making it more difficult for the child to learn to read. Evans and Lepore stress the need for additional research, particularly longitudinal studies, to tease out the factors that actually account for the deficits in reading.

New York City has three major airports, a noisy elevated train system, and a vast highway system that shower noise upon many communities, and so it has been the field laboratory for a number of studies examining the impacts of noise on children. Cohen, Glass, and Singer (1973) found that children who lived in apartments on the lower floors of a large apartment complex, and thus were more impacted by traffic noise from a highly traveled highway, had poorer reading scores than children who lived in the same building but on higher floors. In 1982, Green, Pasternak, and Shore reported that children attending schools near New York's major airports had poorer reading ability than children who went to school further from the airports. Hambrick-Dixon (1986), working with preschool children attending day-care centers near New York's noisy elevated trains, reported that these children were impaired in psychomotor performance.

I was afforded an excellent opportunity when I was allowed to examine the reading scores of children who attended a school where half of the children's classes faced a noisy elevated train structure and the other half of the classes were located on the quiet side of the school building (Bronzaft & McCarthy, 1975). Many experimental controls were in place because of the school setup. Eighty trains passed the school during the school hours and were responsible for raising the average noise level of 69 dBA in the nearby classrooms to an average of 89 dBA. At least 11% of teaching time was lost because of passing trains. Reading scores for 2nd, 4th, and 6th graders were compared for several years and it was found that by the 6th grade, children on the noisy side of the building were nearly a year behind their counterparts on the quiet side. The children on the elevated train side of the school also complained that the subway trains bothered them and made it hard for them to think.

The results of the above study brought pressure on the New York City Transit Authority and the Board of Education to employ technology that would lower the decibel level in the school. The Transit Authority agreed to select the track near the school to test out its new resilient rubber pads and the Board of Education installed noise-absorbing materials in the rooms facing the tracks. Noise levels were significantly reduced in the noisy classrooms, by 6 to 8 dBAs, after these two noise abatements were in place. I was then asked by the transit agency to investigate whether or not the quieting of the classrooms near the tracks brought about improved reading scores. The results of this second investigation (Bronzaft, 1981) demonstrated that lessening noise in a school environment improves reading scores—children on both sides of the building were now reading at the same level. This latter study contributed significantly to the Transit Agency's decision to install resilient rail fasteners along the entire track line, imposing less noise on the many people who live, go to school, and work near New York's elevated train tracks.

Too many children in New York City reside and attend school near the city's airports, and the growth in air travel during these past 10 years has been accompanied by a significant increase in the noise engulfing these children. Evans and Maxwell (1997) selected children who resided and attended school within the flight path of one of New York's major airports and compared their reading scores with those of a sample of children not exposed to aircraft noise either at home or in school. They found that 1st- and 2nd-grade children chronically exposed to aircraft noise have significant deficits in reading; this was partially attributed to problems in language acquisition. There has been much interest in the relationship between aircraft noise and learning. A London study by Haines, Stansfeld, Job, Berglund, and Head (2001) also found that chronic aircraft noise exposure was "associated with impaired reading comprehension."

Schools in New York City and elsewhere, even when not located near highways, railroads, or airports, often lack the appropriate design for maximum learning to take place. Classrooms can be overcrowded and may have faulty electrical duct work, ceilings that are too high, or doors that are not well-sealed—all of these increase the noise within the classrooms. In order to be heard above the din,

teachers frequently raise their voices and shout; at other times they may use loud bells or whistles to quiet down the children.

A symposium sponsored by the U.S. Federal Interagency Committee on Aviation Noise (FICAN) was held in San Diego, California, in February 2000. Researchers from the United States and Europe indicated that there was strong evidence that aircraft noise impeded the child's ability to read and do math (Airport Noise Report, 2000). At this symposium two members of the Acoustical Society of America discussed recommendations for lowering tolerable sound levels in classrooms, from 46 dBA to 35 dBA. Following this conference, FICAN issued a report (2000) acknowledging the findings that aircraft noise interferes with children's learning. The evidence provided by researchers that noise is indeed hazardous to children's learning, the acceptance of a U.S. government agency of these findings, and the recommendations by the Acoustical Society for better classroom acoustics should, hopefully, in the long run bring about policies that will result in quieter classrooms and improved reading and math scores in the United States.

NOISE: NOT A NEW PROBLEM BUT A MORE UBIQUITOUS ONE TODAY

The Industrial Revolution and the rise of cities have been very much responsible for the rapid growth in noise pollution this past century. With modern technology advancing more noise-producing tools, vehicles, and products, the twenty-first century will be even noisier. The expected increase in air traffic alone will be a major factor in the rise in the world's decibel level. Yet noise did not emerge as an intrusive pollutant for the first time during the Industrial Revolution. Stories of loud music appear in the Old Testament; noisy delivery wagons along cobblestone streets of ancient Rome were disturbing; stories of barking dogs and squealing pigs have been found in literature for hundreds of years (Zaner, 1991). Noise is not a recent problem; it has just grown into a more pervasive one.

Noise has generally been associated with urban living. Large cities such as New York, Rome, Athens, and Cairo are frequently characterized as much too noisy. These cities and many others like them became major financial and entertainment centers providing work for millions of people. So that the workers in these cities could retreat to quieter surroundings at the end of their work day, suburbs arose near these major urban centers. However, as we moved into the latter part of the twentieth century, things began to change for many residents of these once quiet suburban communities. Their once quiet homes were now beneath the paths of noisy overhead jets or being invaded by the loud sounds of their neighbors' leaf blowers or lawn mowers.

Rural areas were once thought of as very quiet places in which to live, but we now know that these isolated areas can also be intruded upon. New airports have arisen or are planned for parts of the United States that are far removed from the urban environment. Industrial facilities are relocating in rural parts of the country. A Massachusetts farmer found his once quiet lifestyle drastically changed with the building of a plastic company at the edge of his farm and has filed a complaint in the Superior Court department in the Commonwealth of Massachusetts (personal communication, March 9, 1998).

National parks and beach environments have been traditionally viewed as ideal places for vacationers to find peace and solace. However, these wonderful areas have also been overrun by noise. Sightseeing planes and helicopters are plaguing visitors to the Grand Canyon (Jaroff, 1995), but, hopefully, the restrictions recently imposed by federal law on the numbers of flights over the canyon will serve to lessen the noise problem. Jet skis have become a popular vehicle for travel across the water, and Komanoff and Shaw in their book *Drowning in Noise* (2000) have estimated that 1.3 million jet skis operate in the United States today. The authors, using a quantitative model that translates noise into dollars of "disamenity," have calculated that beachgoers lose over 900 million dollars annually because of the "roar and whine of a jet ski." Komanoff and Shaw were only estimating the loss of vacation dollars. They neglected the distress and suffering experienced by vacationers because of the jet ski noise and the cost to the health and welfare of these individuals who failed to get the requisite rest they needed and expected.

People should know that no one is safe from the "noise intruder." Aircraft routes can be changed; helicopter pads can be set down in grassy fields; the "neighbors from hell" can move in next door or into the apartment above; noisy bars or restaurants can open in the residential neighborhoods; cars with loud boom boxes can travel down quiet streets; and

factories can be built near farms. There is no assurance that a quiet home or a quiet community will remain that way.

Based on the data supplied by the United States Federal Aviation Administration, it is expected that international passenger traffic will double by the year 2010 and domestic passenger traffic will double within the next 20 years (Stenzel, 1996). This growth will result in the demand for additional air flights and for the expansion of airports. Automobile travel is also expected to increase during this period, creating a similar demand for new and expanded highways and roads. Although Komanoff and Shaw (2000) report some bans and operating limits on jet ski use, they note that these are the exceptions. Thus, they predict more jet skis on waterways. The economic boom experienced by the United States during this last decade has revitalized the building industry. Many high-rise buildings have risen in major urban centers for both business and personal use. The result—overcrowding, traffic jams, and, of course, more noise.

There is also another factor that has brought about the growth of noise, namely, a lack of civility. In his thoughtful article, "Noise, Sovereignty, and Civility" (2000), Les Blumberg addresses the relationship between noise pollution and the right of the individual "to make noise." According to Blumberg, noise makers don't care about the impact of their sounds on others. He singles out businesses as the worst offenders but also recognizes that ordinary people can be equally rude. Businesses are, he claims, often allowed to continue to make noise, whereas a college student hosting a late-night party might be told to break up the party. The rationale for tolerating business noise, according to Blumberg, is that if "someone is making money they can also make noise."

Blumberg believes that low-income communities are the most victimized by noise. This would be supported by John Dallas's (1995) description of his South Bronx neighborhood as one filled with music-blasting vehicles, loud-playing stereos, children playing late into the night beneath residents' windows, and lots of loud-talking mothers and fathers. Whether or not low-income communities have greater exposure to noise pollutants, both higher-income and lower-income communities have complained about noise. In fact, some of our largest airports impose noise on the most expensive neighborhoods. The call by both Dallas and Blumberg to respect the right of one's neighbors to peace and quiet in the homes applies to all neighborhoods.

THE ROLE OF GOVERNMENT AND THE CITIZEN IN NOISE ABATEMENT

Passchier-Vermeer and Passchier (2000) conclude that noise is on the increase in industrialized nations and in developing nations. They further conclude that noise exposure will be a major public health problem in the twenty-first century. If this be the case, then governments around the world as well as individual citizens must assume a role in curtailing the noises around them. Now, in the twenty-first century, it is time for governments to assess the noises within their countries and put into place legislation and policies that will address the growing noise problem. In the 1970s the U.S. federal government demonstrated some interest in abating noise, but by 1982 the federal government had for the most part lost its interest in protecting citizens from the dangers of noise (Bronzaft, 1998). The withdrawal of federal support for noise abatement activities meant that states and cities had to rely more heavily on local ordinances and local dollars to curtail the ever increasing noises (see Noise Pollution Clearinghouse Web site on U.S. noise laws, www.nonoise.org). However, even when local noise laws are in place, citizens too frequently complain that they are not readily enforced.

In 2000, the U.S. Congress passed legislation calling on the National Academy of Sciences (NAS) to conduct a study on the effects of noise on health and on children's learning. The demand for this noise-health study came from activist citizens, many of them members of antinoise organizations, who pressured their public officials to do something about the intrusive noises, especially from aircraft, that have robbed them of the "peaceful enjoyment of their homes." This study, however, has not yet been funded and so Americans are left to wonder whether their government will once again become involved in the issue of noise pollution. Antinoise groups have been established around the world and similar demands are being made in other countries as well.

Governments have not been alone in failing to treat noise as a serious pollutant. Well-established environmental organizations have not yet viewed noise as an environmental concern. For too many people, noise still remains a personal issue, with the single individual believing she or he alone is being bothered by the intrusive noise. While antinoise groups are reaching out to citizens to assist them with their noise problems and to enlist them in combating the noise pollutant, these antinoise organizations have not yet attained the status that is needed to bring the noise issue to the forefront.

At a recent noise conference, a third-world representative resented the fact that one of the speakers from a highly developed nation appeared to be dictating future noise policies. For some nations, namely, third-world countries who have lagged behind in development, curtailment of noise may be viewed as an attempt to restrain them from becoming urbanized and industrialized nations. Lessening environmental noises should be the aim of governments and citizens around the globe, but it is urged that the position taken by this third-world citizen be included in discussions of how we go about limiting noise. Even in the area of noise abatement, diplomacy is needed.

NOISE: A DANGER TO OUR HEALTH!

Though scientists are correct in demanding more rigorous evidence to link noise to health, one need not wait for all the pertinent data to be collected before cautioning people about the adverse impacts of noise on health. Dr. William H. Stewart, the former Surgeon General of the United States, when asked to speak of noise as a health hazard at a 1969 conference, said the following:

> Must we wait until we prove every link in the chain of causation? . . . In protecting health, absolute proof comes late. To wait for it is to invite disaster or to prolong suffering unnecessarily. (United States Environmental Protection Agency, 1978)

Dr. Stewart's advice was sound in 1969, and it is still sound in the year 2001. In assessing the effects of noise on our physiological and psychological health, one would have to conclude that there is enough evidence to justify warnings that noise may be dangerous to our health and well-being.

REFERENCES

Abey-Wickrama, I., a'Brook, M. F., Gattoni, F. W. G., & Herridge, C. F. (1969). Mental hospital admissions and aircraft noise. *Lancet, 2,* 1275–1277.

Adkins, C. L. (1998, September 28). Alarming: Findings of hospital noise studies are loud and clear. *Advance for Speech-Language Pathologists & Audiologists,* 30–31.

Airport Noise Report. (2000, February 25). Ashburn, VA. p. 28.

American Academy of Pediatrics, Committee on Environmental Health. (1997). Noise: A hazard for the fetus and newborn. *Pediatrics, 4,* 724–727.

Bat-Chava, Y., & Schur, K. (2000, November). *Longitudinal trends in hearing loss: Nineteen years of public screenings.* Paper presented at the 128th annual meeting of American Public Health Association, Boston.

Berglund, B., & Lindvall, T. (1995). *Community noise.* Stockholm: Center for Sensory Research.

Blumberg, L. (2000). Noise, sovereignty, and civility. *Hearing Rehabilitation Quarterly, 25,* 10–14.

Bronzaft, A. L. (1981). The effect of a noise abatement program on reading ability. *Journal of Environmental Psychology, 1,* 215–222.

Bronzaft, A. L. (1996). *Top of the class.* Greenwich, CT: Ablex.

Bronzaft, A. L. (1998). A voice to end the government's silence on noise. *Hearing Rehabilitation Quarterly, 23,* 6–12, 29.

Bronzaft, A. L., Ahern, K. D., McGinn, R., O'Connor, J., & Savino, B. (1998). Aircraft noise: A potential health hazard. *Environment and Behavior, 30,* 101–113.

Bronzaft, A. L., Deignan, E., Bat-Chava, Y., & Nadler, N. (2000). Intrusive community noises yield more complaints. *Hearing Rehabilitation Quarterly, 25,* 16–22, 34.

Bronzaft, A. L., & Madell, J. R. (1991). Community response and attitudes toward noise. In T. H. Fay (Ed.), *Noise and health* (pp. 93–99). New York: New York Academy of Medicine.

Bronzaft, A. L., & McCarthy, D. (1975). The effect of elevated train noise on reading ability. *Environment and Behavior, 7,* 517–528.

Broste, S. K., Hansen, D. A., Strand, R. L., & Stueland, T. (1989). Hearing loss among high school farm students. *American Journal of Public Health, 79,* 619–621.

Chen, T., Chen, S., Hsieh, P., & Chiang, H. (1997). Auditory effects of aircraft noise on people living near an airport. *Archives of Environmental Health, 52,* 45–50.

Cohen, S., Glass, D., & Singer, J. (1973). Apartment noise, auditory discrimination and reading ability in children. *Journal of Experimental Social Psychology, 9,* 422–437.

Cozad, R. L., Martson, L., & Joseph, D. (1974). Some implications regarding high frequency loss in school-age children. *Journal of School Health, 44,* 92–96.

Dallas, J. (1995). No more Jerichos. *Hearing Rehabilitation Quarterly, 20,* 9–11.

Donnerstein, E., & Wilson, D. W. (1976). Effects of noise and perceived control on ongoing and subsequent aggressive behavior. *Journal of Personality and Social Psychology, 34,* 774–781.

Evans, G. W., Hygge, S., & Bullinger, M. (1995). Chronic noise and psychological stress. *Psychological Science, 6,* 333–338.

Evans, G. W., & Lepore, S. J. (1993). Nonauditory effects of noise on children: A critical review. *Children's Environments, 10,* 31–51.

Evans, G. W., & Maxwell, L. (1997). Chronic noise exposure and reading deficits: The mediating effects of language acquisition. *Environment and Behavior, 29,* 638–656.

Fay, T. H. (Ed.). (1991). *Noise and health.* New York: New York Academy of Medicine.

Federal Interagency Committee on Aviation Noise. (2000, September). *FICAN position on research into effects of aircraft noise on classroom learning.* Washington, DC: Author.

Geen, R. G., & O'Neal, E. C. (1969). Activation of cue-elicited aggression on general arousal. *Journal of Personality and Social Psychology, 11,* 289–292.

Green, K. B., Pasternak, B. S., & Shore, R. E. (1982). Effects of aircraft noise on reading ability of school-age children. *Archives of Environmental Health, 37,* 24–31.

Haines, M. M., Stansfeld, S. A., Job, R. F. S., Berglund, B., & Head, J. (2001). Chronic aircraft noise exposure, stress responses, mental health and cognitive performance in school children. *Psychological Medicine, 31,* 265–277.

Hambrick-Dixon, P. J. (1986). Effects of experimentally imposed noise on task performance of Black children attending day care centers near elevated subway trains. *Developmental Psychology, 22,* 259–264.

Herridge, C. F., & Chir, B. (1972). Aircraft noise and mental hospital admission. *Sound, 6,* 32–36.

Hiramatsu, K. (1999). *A report on the aircraft noise as a public health problem in Okinawa.* Okinawa, Japan: Okinawa Prefectural Government, Department of Culture and Environmental Affairs.

Hiramatsu, K., Yamamoto, T., Taira, K., Ito, A., & Nakasone, T. (1997). A survey of health effects due to aircraft noise on residents living around Kadena air base in the Ryukyus. *Journal of Sound and Vibration, 205,* 451–460.

Jaroff, L. (1995, July 3). Crunch time at the canyon. *Time,* 40–48.

Jones, F. N., & Tauscher, J. (1978). Residence under an airport landing pattern as a factor in teratism. *Archives of Environmental Health, 33,* 10–12.

Kasof, J. (1997). Creativity and breadth of attention. *Creativity Research Journal, 10,* 303–310.

Komanoff, C., & Shaw, H. (2000). *Drowning in noise.* Montpelier, VT: Noise Pollution Clearinghouse.

Kryter, K. D. (1985). *The effects of noise on man.* Orlando, FL: Academic Press.

Kryter, K. D. (1994). *The handbook of hearing and the effects of noise.* San Diego, CA: Academic Press.

Lipscomb, D. M. (1972). The increase in prevalence of high frequency hearing impairment among college students. *Audiology, 11,* 231–234.

Madell, J. R. (1986). A report on noise. *Hearing Rehabilitation Quarterly, 11,* 4–13.

Meecham, W. C., & Smith, H. G. (1977). Effects of jet aircraft noise on mental health admissions. *British Journal of Audiology, 11,* 81–85.

Nadler, N. (1997). Noisy toys—some toys are not as much fun as they look. *Hearing Rehabilitation Quarterly, 22,* 8–10.

National Institutes of Health. (1990). Noise and hearing loss: Consensus conference. *Journal of the American Medical Association, 263,* 3185–3190.

Niskar, A. S., Kieszak, S. M., Holmes, A., Esteban, E., Rubin, C., & Brody, D. J. (2001). Estimated prevalence of noise induced hearing threshold shifts among children 6 to 19 years of age: The third national health and nutrition examination survey, 1988–1994. *Pediatrics, 108,* 40–43.

Passchier-Vermeer, W., & Passchier, W. F. (2000). Noise exposure and public health. *Environmental Health Perspectives, 108,* 123–131.

Peters, M. L., Godaert, G. L. R., Ballieux, R. E., Brosschot, J. F., Sweep, F. C. G. J., Swinkels, L. M. J. W., van Vliet, M., & Heijnen, C. J. (1999). Immune responses to experimental stress: Effects of mental effort and uncontrollability. *Psychosomatic Medicine, 61,* 513–524.

Plakke, B. L. (1983). Noise levels of electronic arcade games: A potential hearing hazard to children. *Ear and Hearing, 4,* 202–203.

Pollak, C. P. (1991). The effects of noise on sleep. In T. H. Fay (Ed.), *Noise and health* (41–60). New York: New York Academy of Medicine.

Raymond, L. W. (1991). Neuroendocrine, immunologic, and gastrointestinal effects of noise. In T. H. Fay (Ed.), *Noise and Health* (pp. 27–40). New York: New York Academy of Medicine.

Sanger, D. E., & Lacey, M. (2000, January 19). It's very late, the phone is ringing, must be that lonely president. *New York Times,* p. A12.

Sawhill, R., & Brown, C. (1998, July 6). Pumping up the volume: Movie sound has been getting better—and louder. *Newsweek,* 66.

Stansfeld, S., Haines, M., & Brown, B. (2000). Noise and health in the urban environment. *Reviews of Environmental Health, 15,* 43–82.

Stenzel, J. (1996). *Flying off course.* New York: New York Natural Resources Defense Council.

Tempest, W. (Ed.). (1985). *The noise handbook.* London: Academic Press.

Tomei, F., Tomao, E., Papaleo, B., Baccolo, T. P., Cirio, A. M., & Alfi, P. (1995). Epidemiological and clinical study of subjects occupationally exposed to noise. *International Journal of Angiology, 4,* 117–121.

United States Environmental Protection Agency, Office of Noise Abatement and Control. (1978). *Noise: A health problem.* Washington, DC: Author.

United States National Research Council. (1982). *Prenatal effects of exposure to high level noise* (Rep. of Working Group 85). Washington, DC: Author.

Wachs, T., & Gruen, G. (1982). *Early experience and human development.* New York: Plenum Press.

Wilson, C. E. (1998). Noise. In J. R. Pfafflin & E. N. Ziegler (Eds.), *Encyclopedia of environmental science and engineering* (855–862). Amsterdam: Gordon and Breach Science.

Zaner, A. (1991). Definition and sources of noise. In T. H. Fay (Ed.), *Noise and health* (pp. 1–14). New York: New York Academy of Medicine.

CHAPTER 33

The History and Future of Disaster Research

LORI A. PEEK and DENNIS S. MILETI

THE PURPOSE OF THIS CHAPTER is to inform the reader of what is known in the field of natural hazards and disaster research. The chapter begins with an outline of the history of disaster research, which is followed by a brief synopsis of the hazards adjustment paradigm. Disaster impacts are then examined, with a focus on deaths, injuries, and dollar losses as well as psychological, short-term, and long-term impacts. Next, warning systems and public response to warnings are detailed. Preparedness activities and response to disasters are also described as well as the factors that influence them. The topics of recovery and reconstruction are then detailed. The chapter concludes with a discussion of the impact of disaster research on planning and helping people and a brief statement on the likely future of disaster research.

DEFINITION OF DISASTER

Considerable change has taken place in theorizing about the characteristics of hazards and disasters over the past several decades. These changes have influenced research that has been conducted and the knowledge that has been accumulated; they have redirected policy decisions at all levels.

Until recently, most people generally agreed with the initial definition of disaster developed by Charles Fritz (1961) over 40 years ago. Using a functionalist viewpoint, he defined a disaster as:

an event, concentrated in time and space, in which a society, or a relatively self-sufficient subdivision of society, undergoes severe danger and incurs such losses to its members and physical appurtenances that the social structure is disrupted and the fulfillment of all or some of the essential functions of the society is prevented. (p. 655)

In today's social and political climate, opinions diverge about what constitutes a disaster. In fact, entire books and journal issues have been dedicated to further exploring the concept of disaster (cf. "What is a disaster?" *International Journal of Mass Emergencies and Disasters,* 1995; Quarantelli, 1998). Current theorizing is based on diverse orientations, for example, social constructionism, postmodernism, and conflict-based and political economy theories. Kreps (1995) takes the stance that Fritz's position should be retained with the modification that disasters are social constructions; essentially, disasters do not exist in and of themselves but are the products of how people agree to define them. Hewitt (1995) criticizes mainstream approaches for focusing on the physical characteristics of disasters because that tends to locate the source of the disaster outside of society rather than within it. Porfiriev (1995) defines *disaster* as a breaking of the routines of social life in such a way that extraordinary measures are needed for survival. Another description characterizes natural disasters as infrequent, unexpected, and traumatic events that are threatening to societal well-being and overwhelming to the coping resources of individuals and communities (Ursano, McCaughey, & Fullerton, 1994).

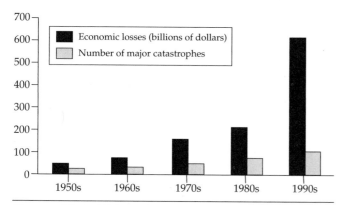

Figure 33.1 Rising losses from natural disasters. *Source:* Munich Reinsurance Company (as cited in Abramovitz, 2001).

Even though opinions differ, a common element that can be detected in almost all definitions is that disasters and the losses that result from them are the consequence of the interaction between the natural, social, and constructed environments and are initiated by some extreme event in the natural world. Moreover, one thing is strikingly clear: The world is becoming increasingly vulnerable to natural disasters. As the human population increases and as more people migrate to hazard-prone areas such as the coastlines, the human and economic costs of natural disasters are increasingly reaching catastrophic proportions. On average, natural disasters claimed the lives of over 84,000 people each year from 1973 to 1997, and more than 140 million people were impacted in a significant way (International Federation of Red Cross and Red Crescent Societies, 1999). There has also been a dramatic increase in economic losses from natural catastrophes over the past 50 years (see Figure 33.1). In the United States alone, an estimated $500 billion in losses resulted from natural disasters during the 1975 to 1994 period (Mileti, 1999).

THE HISTORY OF DISASTER RESEARCH

Many of the disciplines that address hazards and disasters today had their origins in the school of thought known as human ecology, which was a developing subdiscipline in the social sciences at the University of Chicago at the turn of the last century. The human ecological perspective was philosophically explored by John Dewey, who wrote that the

fact that humanity exists in a natural world that is innately hazardous results in human insecurity. Individuals and societies are thus compelled to seek security through the comfort of perceived absolute truths, such as religion, science, and philosophy (Dewey, 1929/1984). More importantly, environmental perils such as floods and earthquakes do not exist independently of society, because these perils are defined, reshaped, and redirected by human actions. Dewey's perspective was that "environmental problems stimulate inquiry and action, which transform the environment, engendering further problems, inquiries, actions, and consequences in a potentially endless chain" (Dewey, 1938, p. 28).

Dewey's ideas have been attributed with the profound distinction of having shaped a generation of social scientists who in turn shaped the young mind of geographer Gilbert F. White while he was a student at the University of Chicago over 50 years ago. White is known today as the father of natural hazards research and management (see Wescoat, 1992). White himself (1973) traces the origins of his ideas along a different path, but, like Dewey, he has consistently maintained that hazards and disasters are the result of the interaction of natural and social forces and that hazards and their impacts can be reduced through individual and social adjustment (White, 1945; White et al., 1958; White, Platt, & O'Riordan, 1997).

An alternative current developed in the discipline of sociology, independent of the human ecological heritage, during the early twentieth century. "Disaster research" began with Prince's (1920) dissertation on a technological disaster and was followed by investigations of natural disasters and inquiry into the conditions of panic. Disaster research received attention during the 1950s because of national anxiety over the Cold War. With federal funding, the National Research Council embarked on a series of investigations of disasters to learn lessons transferable to civil defense in the event of nuclear war with the Soviet Union. The specialty area, originally labeled *social disorganization*, was based on expectations about what the research would discover. The findings from that research program have been synthesized in the social psychology of collective behavior and theories of social organization. (For a summary of the history of the field, see Quarantelli, 1995; for an assessment of the impacts of disaster research on social policy, see Dynes & Drabek, 1994; for a discussion of methods, see Stallings, 1997).

Both theories are extraordinarily different from those of the human ecologists. The collective behaviorists offered explanations for human adjustment and behavior in the minutes, hours, and days after a disaster's impact. Scholars of social organization offered similar conclusions about the behavior of organizations. The "social disorganization" label for the research area was dropped as disasters were observed to strengthen rather than paralyze the communities that they affected. For example, after studying a tornado that hit Topeka, Kansas, in 1966, Drabek and Key (1984) could find no long-term negative impacts (pp. 365, 366), leading the researchers to develop the concept of the therapeutic community.

By the 1970s, natural hazards research in geography (with its human ecological heritage and emphasis on loss reduction) and disaster research in sociology (with its collective behavior perspective and emphasis on disaster response and emergency preparedness) were both entrenched in their respective disciplines. Beginning in 1972, these approaches were mixed with the perspectives of climatology, economics, engineering, geology, law, meteorology, planning, psychology, public policy, seismology, and others. Geographer Gilbert White and sociologist Eugene Haas (1975), assisted by many others, began the nation's first assessment of research on natural hazards—an effort to take stock of the nation's knowledge regarding hazards in order to suggest directions for national policy and to inventory research needs. That project lowered the walls that had separated many of the disciplines involved with hazards and paved the way for the interdisciplinary approaches to hazards research and management that the nation employs today.

Research into the psychological aspects of disasters, as in other disciplines, emerged independently. Early work characterized impacts on individuals that included people being "dazed" and experiencing "hyperactivity." In the 1950s, a model called "the disaster syndrome" was proposed by Wallace (1956) which was constructed as a psychologically determined defensive reaction in which people are: (1) dazed and immobile, followed by (2) extreme suggestibility and altruism, (3) euphoric identification with the damaged community, and, eventually, (4) return to predisaster ambivalent attitudes. More contemporary psychological models (cf. Green, Grace, & Gleser, 1985) begin with exposure to the traumatic event. This includes the experience a person brings to the event and specific aspects of the event experience. Exposure leads to "immediate appraisal" of the event and "initial emotional reactions," followed by attempts to process the information and put it into perspective given one's present world view. Most models now take both personal and socioenvironmental characteristics into account. Contemporary views were greatly influenced by the call for psychological research resulting from the accident at the Three Mile Island nuclear power generating station in the late 1970s (cf. Bromet, Parkinson, & Dunn, 1990). Psychological research now utilizes diverse approaches including adult and child studies regarding topics that include rates of disorder, longevity of impact, risk factors, and post-traumatic stress disorder (PTSD), and incorporates other variables such as severity of exposure, gender, age, pre-existing conditions, and family factors (cf. Green, 1996, for a summary of research findings).

In the early 1990s, a second national assessment of hazards and disasters was begun at the University of Colorado's Natural Hazards Center as part of the nation's activities in the Decade for Natural Disaster Reduction (see Mileti, 1999). The project summarized knowledge in all fields of science and engineering (psychology was the only discipline in the nation not to participate), evaluated U.S. approaches and programs over the last quarter century to judge what has worked and what has not, and made recommendations regarding a shift in approach and perspective. Over 130 of our nation's leading scientists and engineers participated in the project, which was overseen largely by members of the White House's Subcommittee on Natural Hazards in the Committee on the Environment in the Office of Science and Technology Policy. One result of this effort was to create a holistic model for future programs and research on hazards and disasters that links hazards mitigation, planning response, recovery, and reconstruction to sustainable development. The holistic and interdisciplinary approach recommended in the second assessment has attracted global attention, and it now serves as the basis for several national and international interdisciplinary programs. It is most likely that future research and policy approaches for hazards and disasters will be less limited by the boundaries of traditional disciplines and more influenced by the need to approach problems with teams representing the range of skills and knowledge areas needed to impact a solution to the problem.

THE HAZARDS ADJUSTMENT PARADIGM

Research on hazards conducted over the past 30 years has been based on the notion that individuals and groups choose how to cope with or adjust to hazards in their natural and constructed environment. This paradigm used the bounded rationality model of decision making, which says that individuals make decisions based on limited knowledge and within constraints set by the social system in which they live. This allows for acceptable, although often not optimal, adjustments and outcomes. This decision-making model, paired with the adjustment concept, generated the following five-step strategy for coping with hazards: (1) assess hazard vulnerability, (2) examine possible adjustments, (3) determine the human perception and estimation of the hazard, (4) analyze the decision making process, and (5) identify the best adjustments, given social constraints, and evaluate their effectiveness.

Public and private policies that have been developed based on this paradigm have generated a management strategy with the goal of reducing hazard-related losses, such as lives, injuries, dollars, and social and economic disruption. This strategy is organized conceptually around a four-stage cycle of preparedness, response, recovery, and mitigation, which is described in what follows. Current policy implementation relies on "loss reduction" activities in all four stages, fostered at the societal level but carried out locally or individually.

PREPAREDNESS

Preparedness involves developing an emergency response and management capability before a disaster strikes, in an effort to promote effective response as needed. This requires a vulnerability and risk analysis to identify potential problems that an extreme meteorological or geological event could impose. Furthermore, preparedness involves hazard detection and warning systems, identification of evacuation routes and shelters, maintenance of emergency supplies and communication systems, procedures for notifying and mobilizing key personnel, and preestablished mutual aid agreements with neighboring communities. Training and educating response personnel, citizens, and community leaders are also crucial to the preparedness process.

RESPONSE

Response refers to the actions taken immediately before, during, and following a disaster. The intent of an effective response to disaster is to save lives, minimize property damage, and to enhance the recovery process. The activities typically carried out during a response effort are hazard detection and warning, evacuation and shelter of victims, medical care, search and rescue operations, and security and protection of property. The effectiveness of the response effort is directly related to the activities carried out during the predisaster preparedness phase.

RECOVERY

Disaster recovery efforts involve short-term activities such as restoring vital support systems as well as long-term endeavors aimed at returning life to normal. The initial recovery phase involves an assessment of the damage to help prioritize the recovery efforts. The recovery stage involves repairing and rebuilding homes, public buildings, lifelines, and infrastructure; organizing volunteers and donations; delivering disaster relief; restoring vital community services; coordinating government activities; and expediting permitting procedures. The recovery process can take weeks or even years, depending on the magnitude of the disaster, available resources, and the effectiveness of community and governmental efforts.

MITIGATION

The fourth stage, mitigation, refers to the policies and activities aimed at reducing an area's vulnerability to damage from future disasters. These mitigative measures are typically in place before a disaster occurs. Generally, mitigation activities are characterized as structural, infrastructural, and nonstructural. Structural and infrastructural mitigation measures attempt to keep hazards away from people and buildings, to construct buildings more able to withstand disaster, and to strengthen elements of the constructed environment that are exposed to hazards. Nonstructural mitigation measures try to distribute the population and the constructed environment such that their exposure to disaster losses is limited.

A CONTEMPORARY RECONCEPTUALIZATION

Over the past several decades, a vast amount of theoretical, empirical, and policy work has been conducted, all in an attempt to reduce vulnerability to losses from natural and related technological disasters. While these efforts have led to many accomplishments, including stronger infrastructures, safer buildings, and better warning systems, just to name a few, there is still a need for improvement. Many policy makers are troubled by the fact that more progress does not appear to have been made in reducing losses from hazards: The staggering monetary losses from disasters continue to increase at alarming rates; some mitigation measures may only be postponing losses onto future generations; and short-term thinking has resulted in environmental degradation and ecological imbalance, which not only is detrimental to society but also contributes to the severity of the next disaster. Given this, the contemporary hazards adjustment paradigm needs to further evolve to begin to deal with the complex factors that contribute to natural disasters in today's world and especially tomorrow's.

DISASTER IMPACTS

Some impacts of disaster can be readily quantified, such as dollars lost or the number of deaths and injuries. Other more indirect and less easily quantified impacts of disaster are more difficult to measure, such as increased stress levels or a loss of community cohesiveness. The following sections describe disaster impacts in terms of deaths, injuries, and dollar losses; psychological impacts; and economic impacts.

DEATHS, INJURIES, AND DOLLAR LOSSES

It is estimated that natural hazards killed over 24,000 people (about 24 per week) and injured at least four times that many in the United States and its territories between January 1, 1975, and December 31, 1994 (Mileti, 1999). Almost 2 million households per year (24.5 per 1,000) experienced injuries or damages from natural hazards including floods, storms, tornados, hurricanes, earthquakes, and fire (Rossi, Wright, Weber-Burdin, & Pereira, 1983). Furthermore, about one-seventh of the population reports feeling threatened by natural hazards (Norris,

1992). In the 1975 to 1994 period, dollar losses to property and crops from natural hazards and disasters were between $230 billion and $1 trillion (Mileti, 1999). A conservative estimate of the actual average dollar losses from natural hazards and disasters in the nation from 1974 to 1994 is $500 billion (Mileti, 1999).

PSYCHOLOGICAL IMPACTS

It is now widely recognized that disasters can cause emotional distress and trauma. This distress often results in both short- and long-term effects. Most of the psychological research following a disaster has been on the short-term impacts. For example, Bland, O'Leary, Farinaro, Jossa, and Trevisan (1996, p. 18) found that in the short-term, disasters are associated with an increased prevalence of severe psychiatric symptomatology, PTSD, anxiety, depression, somatic complaints, and nightmares. While the long-term effects have been studied less extensively, reports do suggest that there may be a latency period, or delayed onset of some symptoms, symptoms can come and go, and significant psychiatric symptomatology may remain for as long as 14 years (Bland et al., 1996, p. 18). Although there is little supporting psychological research, most disaster intervention programs have identified certain population subgroups to be at greater risk of emotional distress than others. Most often identified as special risk groups are children, the elderly, the poor, those with a previous history of emotional disability, and those with a marginalized predisaster existence.

Research on gender shows mixed results. Some researchers have found that females exhibit more short-term mental health problems following a disaster, including stress, depression, PTSD symptoms, and anxiety (Fothergill, 1996). Other studies state that men experience greater decreases in mental and physical well-being and have increased rates of depression and alcohol abuse after a disaster (Fothergill, 1996). Some studies have concluded that women may be able to cope in disasters because of their "flexibility" and "adaptability" skills and because the traditional role division in nuclear families better prepares women for disaster (Clason, 1983). An early but still common claim is that both males and females suffer from emotional distress, but females report and express types of psychological upset more than males (Moore & Friedsam, 1959).

516 HANDBOOK OF ENVIRONMENTAL PSYCHOLOGY

Research on race and ethnicity and the psychological impacts of disaster is limited. The work that has been conducted has found important associations. Aptekar (1990) reports that social class and race contribute to differing psychological reactions to the disasters. In a study regarding stress and disaster relocation, J. L. Garrison (1985) reported a correlation between minority status and increased stress levels. In another study of fear associated with earthquakes, it was found that Hispanics, women, and the poor reported the highest levels of fear from the risk of disaster. Shoaf (1998) reported that blacks and Latinos suffered the most emotional injuries in a survey done after the Northridge earthquake. In a follow-up study of the Buffalo Creek dam collapse disaster, 14 years after the event, Green et al. (1990) found that more blacks had delayed PTSD symptoms than whites.

Socioeconomic status may impact emotional vulnerability, yet very little research has been conducted on this topic. The studies that have been done overwhelmingly show that higher-income victims suffer less psychological damage than do lower-income victims. Importantly, the psychological impacts could be caused by the poverty, the disaster, or a combination of the two. Yet, no matter if the poverty causes the psychological conditions, the disaster exacerbates the situation. The financial devastation of a disaster creates mental stress (J. L. Garrison, 1985). After a disaster, people generally have "increased debt burdens," and poor people are more likely to be financially devastated by the disaster and subsequent relocation than are wealthy or middle-class people, thus increasing the likelihood of mental stress. Bolin (1993) found that higher-income victims reported fewer stress symptoms than lower-income victims. Aptekar (1990) states that the working class were embittered by the losses they sustained. Furthermore, if these residents knew they were not going to be compensated for their losses, they are said to have been less likely to resolve psychological issues. Another study found that poorer people and those with larger families are more likely to report emotional problems following a disaster (Bolin & Bolton, 1986). Rossi et al. (1983) agree, finding that those respondents with higher incomes reported fewer feelings of depression after the disaster.

Age also influences impacts, with the young and elderly being the most vulnerable (Bolin & Klenow, 1988). For example, after Hurricane Hugo, children were more impacted than adults, with girls more emotionally affected, while boys experienced some behavioral difficulties, such as attention problems (Shannon, Lonigan, Finch, & Taylor, 1994). Essentially, girls seemed to suffer more from PTSD, while boys acted out more and had increased sleep disturbances. Other studies of Hugo indicated that adolescent females communicated somewhat higher PTSD symptoms than adolescent males (C. Z. Garrison, Weinrich, Hardin, Weinrich, & Wang, 1993).

ECONOMIC IMPACTS

In general, most disasters affect relatively small proportions of communities, and consequently, those communities as a whole tend to bounce back quickly with available forms of assistance (Friesema, Caporaso, Goldstein, Lineberry, & McCleary, 1979). There is additional evidence that suggests that, though disasters may be manageable in most events, about 1 in 10 events results in losses that are truly catastrophic (Burby et al., 1991, p. 46). However, the issue regarding economic impacts is more complicated. For example, a key question regarding economic impacts seems to be if a certain type and magnitude of disaster is anticipated and planned for in a community: If so, the disaster, when it occurs, would have no long-term economic impacts, but if not, larger local economic impacts can be expected (Yezer & Rubin, 1987). Additionally, economic impacts can vary widely across different subpopulations in a local community, and some are affected proportionately more than others; small businesses, for example, are particularly vulnerable.

WARNINGS

Warning systems detect impending disaster, give that information to people, and help people to take protective actions prior to a disaster. This definition is simple, but warning systems are complex because they link many specialities and organizations, such as science, engineering, technology, government, news media, and the public. The most effective warning systems integrate the subsystems of "detection of extreme events," which use knowledge from the natural and physical sciences and engineering; "management of hazards information," which applies what is known in disciplines like public administration, planning, and political science; and "public response," which is informed by disciplines like psychology and sociology.

THE CHARACTER OF PUBLIC RESPONSE

Public response to warnings of disaster involves the interruption of the routine of daily ongoing life. Responses vary by hazard type and involve such things as community evacuation during a hazardous chemical spill, sheltering in-place in case of a rapidly developing nuclear power plant accident, or bolting water heaters to help mitigate the impact of a predicted earthquake. Additionally, during the warning period, people invariably actively seek out further information on their own and in response to getting a warning in order to verify and confirm what they heard. This information search is typically referred to as "warning confirmation" (Drabek & Stephenson, 1971; Mileti & Sorensen, 1990; Quarantelli, 1984). The result can be variation in risk perception about what to do about the warning (Bellamy & Harrison, 1988; Flynn & Chalmers, 1980; Nigg, 1987; Perry, Lindell, & Greene, 1981).

THE WARNING RESPONSE PROCESS

A fairly thorough understanding of public warning response has been developed by social scientists. It is generally understood that public warning response is a process with several stages: (1) hearing the warning, (2) believing the warning is credible, (3) confirming that the threat does exist and others are heeding it, (4) personalizing the risk to oneself, (5) determining if protective action is needed and if it is feasible, and (6) deciding what action to take and then taking it (Lindell & Perry, 1992; Mileti & Sorensen, 1990). Many research studies exist on the factors that influence the process of public response to disaster warnings. Findings point to two general categories of factors that influence response: the form of the warning information itself and variation in the personal characteristics of the people who receive it. Moreover, some factors are more important in shaping people's response to warnings than others.

Information Factors

Warning information can play a more important role in influencing public response than the characteristics of the people warned if the information is well-crafted; however, the converse is likely the case when warnings are not well designed. Table 33.1 includes a list of the key warning variables that impact public response.

Table 33.1
Key Warning Variables That Impact Public Response

1. Credibility of source
2. Consistency
3. Accuracy
4. Clarity
5. Perceived confidence and certainty
6. Clear guidance
7. Frequency

The channels and mechanisms through which warnings are disseminated also have an impact on public response. Warnings communicated over multiple channels—such as printed and electronic media or personally delivered—enhance people's understanding, belief, and response (Mikami & Ikeda, 1985; Mileti & Beck, 1975; Rogers, 1985).

Public and Personal Factors

The perceptions that people form in response to warnings and their reactions to the warnings also covary with their diverse personal and social characteristics. Table 33.2 lists the important factors that influence response to warnings. It is important to note that the weight of these variables in impacting behavior decreases as the quality of warning information, as described earlier, increases.

In summary, the communication of risk information to the public in warnings is a dynamic process. Seeking additional information and engaging in protective actions is a direct result of the understanding, belief, and personalization of risk that a person comes to possess in the context of receiving a warning. Risk perception is a product of people interacting with risk information and each other. These interactions are directly influenced by the content

Table 33.2
Factors That Influence Public and Individual Response to Warnings

1. Environmental cues interacting with warning information to influence perception and response
2. Social setting
3. Social ties
4. Position in the social structure
5. Psychological attributes
6. Preconceived ideas about risk

and style of the warning message(s) communicated. Perceptions are simultaneously influenced by the context people are in when the warning is received, as well as by personal psychosocial characteristics.

PREPAREDNESS AND RESPONSE

The following sections detail what is known about emergency preparedness and disaster response and the factors that influence them. Preparedness is an important phase in the disaster cycle. Better prepared communities are more able to respond effectively to catastrophic events. In turn, the more effective the response is, the more lives can be saved, injuries can be reduced, and damage and disruptions can be lessened.

PREPAREDNESS

The purpose of emergency preparedness is to anticipate problems in disasters so that plans can be devised to address the problems effectively and so that the resources needed for an effective response are in place prior to the event. Preparedness may include activities like formulating, testing, and exercising disaster plans; providing training for disaster responders and the general public; and communicating with the public and others about disaster vulnerability and what to do to reduce it. Preparedness activities occur at varied levels including families and households, organizations, communities, states, and at the national level. Factors that influence preparedness at each of these levels are discussed in what follows.

All other things being equal, households of higher socioeconomic status and nonminorities are better prepared than others, but those who do prepare are doing relatively little. "Prepared" households may undertake any of the following activities: purchasing insurance, making structural changes to the home, assembling first aid kits, storing food and water, rearranging furniture, establishing a household disaster plan. According to Cuny (1983), disaster preparation efforts should be primarily geared towards designing and building secure housing because most individuals are injured or killed due to unsafe housing. Unfortunately, however, many people take no action at all. Although some of the factors that affect preparedness are known, there is still no thorough understanding of

the social-psychological processes involved in making the decision. In other words, researchers know who prepares, but not why (Mileti & Fitzpatrick, 1993). A good deal is known about how public education can overcome obstacles to foster significant amounts of household preparedness. Less is known about the incentives that will motivate people to increase and sustain preparedness efforts during periods of relative normalcy.

Knowledge about organizational preparedness and the factors that impact it is still lacking. More is known about preparedness among public-sector organizations than the private sector, but what is known is far from comprehensive. Preparedness among local emergency management agencies in the nation has improved significantly, but little is known about fire and police department disaster preparedness. Hospitals and health care organizations are not prepared to advise people or to treat victims of chemical hazards and disasters, and, until recently, private sector business preparedness was virtually never investigated by researchers (see Mileti, 1999). The research that does exist indicates that private firms are less than enthusiastic about disaster preparedness, even in disaster-prone areas.

Numerous studies have shown that local support for disaster preparedness is low in most communities and that relatively few resources are allocated to disaster preparedness and response. This low priority of disasters tends to occur because disasters are locally infrequent, the benefits are not immediately apparent, responders tend to overgeneralize from experiences with routine emergencies, and nonspecialists tend to either underestimate the magnitude of disaster demands (resulting in unrealistic optimism) or grossly overestimate them (resulting in fatalism).

States possess broad authorities and play a key role in disaster preparedness and response, both supporting local jurisdictions and coordinating with the federal government on a wide range of disaster-related tasks. In light of the important roles that states play in the management of hazards and disasters, the small amount of research that is focused on state-level disaster preparedness activities is surprising. What states do undoubtedly makes a difference at the local level; however, without research that takes an in-depth look at what states and localities are actually doing, researchers can conclude little about their role in the preparedness process.

The picture is scarcely better at the national level. Much of the knowledge in hand about federal government preparedness comes from detailed case studies that either focus on the federal government at a particular point in time or assess changes in federal policies and programs that have taken place over time. It is known that national-level preparedness initiatives tend also to be shaped by dramatic events, such as the Three Mile Island nuclear accident. One key message in the research literature is that federal preparedness is influenced and constrained not only by institutional power differentials but also by the nature of the intergovernmental system itself—the nature of federalism; the complexity of agencies, responsibilities, and legislation; and the difficulty of effective interagency coordination.

RESPONSE

Disaster response activities include the following: emergency sheltering, search and rescue, care of the injured, firefighting, damage assessment, and other emergency measures. Disaster responders must also cope with response-generated demands such as the need for coordination, communications, ongoing situation assessment, and resource mobilization during the emergency period. The response period has been the most studied phase of disasters. In general, response research has a good deal in common with preparedness research. Conceptual frameworks, research designs, and the variables included in analyses range widely across studies, making generalizations difficult. Some response topics, such as emergency sheltering, social solidarity, group emergence, and organizational response have been studied extensively, while others have received little attention.

Research findings associated with the more widely studied response topics are generally consistent. For example, we know that preexisting social inequities, including differences in income and household resources, home ownership, insurance, and access to affordable housing have a significant impact on housing options in the postdisaster response phase. Furthermore, the literature on U.S. disasters consistently shows that social solidarity remains strong in even the most trying of circumstances. Disasters engender prosocial, altruistic, and adaptive responses during the emergency period immediately after a disaster's impact. Research regarding group emergence during the response phase shows that new groups invariably

form during and after disasters (Drabek & Key, 1984), usually in situations characterized by a lack of planning, ambiguity over legitimate authority, exceptionally large disaster search and rescue tasks, a legitimizing social setting, a perceived threat, a supportive social climate, and the availability of certain nonmaterial resources. Political and social inequality may also drive group emergence. Finally, disaster research concerning organizational response has most often looked at the following groups: local emergency management agencies; medical, fire, and police departments; the private sector; and the news media.

FACTORS THAT INFLUENCE PREPAREDNESS AND RESPONSE

Broad social, political, economic, cultural, and institutional contexts shape disaster preparedness and response. At the personal and household levels, ethnic and minority status, gender, language, socioeconomic status, social attachments and relationships, economic resources, age, and physical capacity, all have an impact on the propensity of people to take preparedness actions, to evacuate, and to take further mitigation measures. In addition, people use a wide variety of decision-making processes, not all rational.

Household preparedness activities are more likely to be undertaken by those who are routinely most attentive to the news media; are more concerned about other types of social and environmental threats; have personally experienced disaster damage; are responsible for the safety of school-age children; are linked with the community through long-term residence, home ownership, or high levels of social involvement; have received some sort of disaster education; and can afford to take the steps necessary to get prepared. For organizations, governments, and people in general, mandates and legal incentives can in some instances induce preparedness, proper response, and other actions. However, there is a wide body of literature that indicates that politicians are often resistant to disaster prevention activities (cf. Burby & French, 1980; Kunreuther et al., 1978; Mader et al., 1980; Turner, Nigg, Paz, & Young, 1980). Disaster planning and prevention can be politically troublesome because, to most politically influential people in most states and local communities, natural hazards problems are not especially serious ones, absolutely and relative to other problems (Rossi, Wright, & Weber-Burdin, 1982, p. 65). Thus, hazards preparedness efforts often take a back seat to other pressing political matters.

In sum, three clear conclusions can be made regarding preparedness and response. First, effective preparedness and response activities help save lives, reduce injuries, limit property damage, and minimize all sorts of disruptions that disasters cause, and research into preparedness and response has done much to effectively inform how we plan for and respond to disasters. Second, the theoretical approach to disaster preparedness and response has changed dramatically over the years. It has moved from a "functional" view of disasters to a much broader one that recognizes the tremendous influence social norms and public perceptions and expectations have on the occurrence, effects of, and recovery from disasters. Finally, a great deal has been learned about who prepares for disasters, but why they do so is still somewhat of a mystery.

RECOVERY AND RECONSTRUCTION

While early views of recovery almost exclusively saw it as reconstruction of physical damage, researchers have recently begun to view recovery as a process and an opportunity to address long-term material problems in local housing and infrastructure. In this light, reconstruction is recast into a developmental process of reducing vulnerability and enhancing economic capability (Anderson & Woodrow, 1989). Moreover, the contemporary perspective is that recovery is not just a physical outcome but a social process that encompasses decision making about restoration and reconstruction activities. Thus, recovery is often driven as much by the human interest to resurrect predisaster patterns of culture and human interaction as by interests in reconstructing purely the physical environment (Mileti & Passerini, 1996).

Most research has examined how recovery is affected by a family's socioeconomic status and other demographic characteristics, position in the life cycle, race or ethnicity, real property losses, employment loss, loss of wage earner(s), the family's support, and the use of extrafamilial assistance programs. Researchers have found that linkages to extended family are strengthened immediately after disasters, and this lasts well into the recovery phase. Extended kin groups provide assistance to relatives.

Socioeconomic status, race, ethnicity, and gender are interrelated in complex and different ways. Ethnic and racial minority groups are typically disproportionately poor and thus disproportionately more vulnerable to disaster and to the negative impacts of long-term recovery. Poorer families have more difficulty recovering from disasters and also have the most trouble acquiring extrafamilial aid.

Businesses have many of the same characteristics as households: They vary in size, income, and age; they are typically housed in structures that are more or less vulnerable; and they differ in the resources they demand and control. Some businesses are less vulnerable to disaster and more capable of recovering. Although businesses play vital community roles, research to date has not documented the effects of business closures on family and community recovery.

There are several components of community recovery, including residential, commercial, industrial, social, and lifelines, and there are various degrees of recovery. Some aspects of community life, such as tax revenues and community values, may take years to return to normal. When the fundamental look of the community has been altered, it has been argued that other aspects, such as a sense of community, will not return. Thus, researchers have discovered that communities try to rebuild in forms similar to predisaster patterns and that the resulting continuity and familiarity in postdisaster reconstruction may enhance psychological recovery.

PLANNING FOR RECOVERY AND RECONSTRUCTION

With each new disaster, more is learned about how to plan more effectively for recovery and reconstruction. However, this information has yet to be systematically collected or synthesized into a coherent body of knowledge. Perhaps because of this lack of synthesized knowledge, planning for recovery has been minimal in the United States. However, this is changing, largely because of attempts at the federal level to educate and train public officials to cope effectively with recovery in their jurisdictions.

The notion of predisaster planning for postevent recovery is a relatively new and powerful concept. When further researched, developed, tested, and evaluated, such knowledge may help many communities mitigate current hazards before a disaster and recover more quickly and safely afterwards. Predisaster planning is key because planning dramatically reduces the unintended longer-term consequences of hasty disaster response actions (Mileti & Passerini, 1996). Thus, whereas recovery is characterized by wanting to rapidly return to normal, increase safety, and improve the community, planning must reflect an effort to balance certain ideal objectives with reality.

According to Arnold (1993), to be effective, recovery plans require the following information: (1) the characteristics of the hazards and the geographic areas likely to be impacted; (2) a demographic analysis of the population's size, composition, and distribution; (3) data on the local economy; (4) the resources likely to be available in the postdisaster environment; (5) knowledge of the powers, programs, and responsibilities of local, state, and federal governments; (6) existing land use patterns and building stock location and characteristics; and (7) an inventory of local infrastructure, for example, water, power, communication, and transportation lifelines (p. 7). Finally, recovery involves a process of interaction and decision making among a variety of groups and institutions including households, organizations, businesses, the broader community, and society and thus requires extraordinary flexibility and teamwork.

THE FUTURE OF DISASTER RESEARCH

Rooted in the origins of human ecology at the University of Chicago at the beginning of the last century, disaster research in today's social and behavioral sciences began in earnest in the middle of the last century. Researchers in disciplines such as sociology, geography, psychology, and others have spent decades in pursuit of knowledge that both advanced discipline-specific theories and contributed to practical applications to mitigate future losses, prepare for disaster response, and recover from the impacts of disasters experienced. In the last quarter century, interdisciplinary approaches have been increasingly used to develop more effective approaches and solutions to disaster-related problems. The future of disaster research will likely be closer to Dewey's (1938) holistic and philosophical claims, discussed earlier, than to that which is familiar to contemporary researchers.

Many disaster losses—rather than stemming from unexpected events—are the predictable result of interactions between the physical environment, which includes hazardous events; the social, demographic, and psychological characteristics of the people in communities that experience them; and the buildings, roads, bridges, and other components of the constructed environment. Growing disaster losses result partly from the fact that capital stock is expanding, but they also stem from the fact that all these systems—and their interactions—are becoming more complex with each passing year.

Three main influences are at work. First, the earth's physical systems are constantly changing—witness the current warming of the global climate. Scientists expect a warming climate to produce more dramatic meteorological events such as storms, floods, drought, and extreme temperatures. Second, recent and projected changes in the demographic composition and distribution of the nation's population mean greater exposure to many hazards. The number of people residing in earthquake-prone regions and coastal counties subject to hurricanes, for example, is growing rapidly. Worsening inequality of wealth also makes many people more vulnerable to hazards and less able to recover from them. Third, the built environment, including public utilities, transportation systems, communications, and homes and offices buildings, is growing in density, making the potential losses from natural forces larger.

Settlement of hazardous areas has also destroyed local ecosystems that could have provided protection from natural perils. The draining of swamps in Florida and the bulldozing of steep hillsides for homes in California, for example, have disrupted natural runoff patterns and magnified flood and landslide hazards. In fact, many mitigation efforts themselves degrade the environment, only contributing to the heightened intensity of the next disaster. For example, levees built to provide flood protection can destroy riparian habitat and increase the magnitude of downstream floods.

Another major problem has become clear over the last several decades: Some efforts to head off damages from natural hazards only postpone them. One case is communities that are built below dams or behind levees may avoid losses from flood that those structures were designed to prevent. However, such communities often have more property to lose when those structures fail, because additional development occurred that counted on protection. Thus, it is important to recognize that it is often difficult to anticipate the long-term impacts for future generations of decisions that are made today. Attempting to plan for disaster in order to lessen the impact is psychologically and politically difficult, as are all long-range efforts, because the effects and benefits are not immediately apparent.

In conclusion, the future of disaster research will likely be linked to broad issues like these and focus on the link between sustainable development and natural hazards. Although discipline-specific research will undoubtedly continue, as will research into disaster impacts and recovery, a likely future research direction will focus on how to mitigate losses from future disasters in ways that enhance sustainable development. From the viewpoint of disasters, sustainability means that a locality can tolerate—and overcome—damage, diminished productivity, and reduced quality of life from an extreme event without significant outside assistance. To achieve sustainability, communities must take responsibility for choosing where and how development proceeds. Toward that end, each locality evaluates its environmental resources and hazards, chooses future losses that it is willing to bear, and ensures that development and other community actions and policies adhere to those goals. Future disaster research in the social and behavioral sciences will likely shift from their current emphases to ones that explore the human dimensions of how to mitigate impending disaster losses in a sustainable way. Furthermore, future research in the varied disciplines that study hazards and disasters will likely target research on hazards-related sustainability dependent variables.

REFERENCES

Abramovitz, J. M. (2001). Averting unnatural disasters. In L. Starke (Ed.), *State of the world 2001* (pp. 123–142). New York: Norton.

Anderson, M., & Woodrow, P. (1989). *Rising from the ashes: Development strategies in times of disaster*. Boulder, CO: Westview Press.

Aptekar, L. (1990). A comparison of bicoastal disasters of 1989. *Behavior Science Research, 24,* 73–104.

Arnold, C. (1993). *Reconstruction after earthquakes: Issues, urban design, and case studies*. (Final Report to the National Science Foundation). Palo Alto, CA: Building Systems Development.

Bellamy, L. J., & Harrison, P. I. (1988). *An evacuation model for major accidents*. Paper presented at the International Building Council Conference on Disaster and Emergencies, Washington, DC.

Bland, S. H., O'Leary, E. S., Farinaro, E., Jossa, F., & Trevisan, M. (1996). Long-term psychological effects of natural disasters. *Psychosomatic Medicine, 58,* 18–24.

Bolin, R. (1993). *Household and community recovery after earthquakes*. Boulder: Natural Hazards Research and Applications Information Center, University of Colorado.

Bolin, R., & Klenow, D. J. (1988). Older people in disaster: A comparison of black and white victims. *International Journal of Aging and Human Development, 26*(1), 29–33.

Bolin, R. C., & Bolton, P. A. (1986). *Race, religion, and ethnicity in disaster recovery*. Boulder: Institute of Behavioral Science, University of Colorado.

Bromet, E., Parkinson, D., & Dunn, L. (1990). Long-term mental health consequences of the accident at Three Mile Island. *International Journal of Mental Health, 19,* 48–60.

Burby, R. J., Cigler, B. A., French, S. P., Kaiser, E. J., Kartez, J., Roenigk, D., Weist, D., & Whittington, D. (1991). *Sharing environmental risks: How to control governments' losses in natural disasters*. Boulder, CO: Westview Press.

Burby, R. J., & French, S. P. (1980). The U.S. experience in managing flood plain land use. *Disasters, 4*(4), 451–457.

Clason, C. (1983). The family as a life-saver in disaster. *Journal of Mass Emergencies and Disasters, 1*(1), 43–62.

Cuny, F. C. (1983). *Disasters and development*. New York: Oxford University Press.

Dewey, J. (1938). *Logic, the nature of inquiry*. New York: Holt, Rinehart and Winston.

Dewey, J. (1984). The quest for certainty. In J. Boydston (Ed.), *The Later Works: 1925–1953* (Vol. 4, pp. 3–20). Carbondale: Southern Illinois University Press. (Original work published 1929)

Drabek, T. E., & Key, W. H. (1984). *Conquering disaster: Family recovery and long-term consequences*. New York: Irvington.

Drabek, T. E., & Stephenson, J. S., III. (1971). When disaster strikes. *Journal of Applied Social Psychology, 1*(2), 187–203.

Dynes, R. R., & Drabek, T. E. (1994). The structure of disaster research: Its policy and disciplinary implications. *International Journal of Mass Emergencies and Disasters, 12*(1), 5–23.

Flynn, C. B., & Chalmers, J. A. (1980). *The social and economic effects of the accident at Three Mile Island*. Tempe, AZ: Mountain West Research and Social Impact Research.

Fothergill, A. (1996). Gender, risk, and disaster. *International Journal of Mass Emergencies and Disasters, 14*(1), 33–56.

Friesema, H. P., Caporaso, J., Goldstein, G., Lineberry, R., & McCleary, R. (1979). *Aftermath: Communities after natural disasters*. Beverly Hills, CA: Sage.

Fritz, C. (1961). Disaster. In R. K. Merton & R. A. Nisbet (Eds.), *Contemporary social problems* (pp. 651–694). New York: Harcourt Press.

Garrison, C. Z., Weinrich, M. W., Hardin, S. B., Weinrich, S., & Wang, L. (1993). Post-traumatic stress disorder in adolescents after a hurricane. *American Journal of Epidemiology, 138*(7), 522–530.

Garrison, J. L. (1985). Mental health implications of disaster relocation in the United States: A review of the literature. *International Journal of Mass Emergencies and Disasters, 3*(2), 49–65.

Green, B., Grace, M., & Gleser, G. (1985). Identifying survivors at risk: Long-term impairment following the Beverly Hills Supper Club fire. *Journal of Consulting Clinical Psychology, 53*, 672–678.

Green, B. L. (1996). Traumatic stress and disaster: Mental health effects and factors influencing adaptation. In F. L. Mak & C. C. Nadelson (Eds.), *International review of psychiatry* (pp. 177–210). Washington, DC: American Psychiatric Press.

Green, B. L., Lindy, J. D., Grace, M. C., Gleser, G. C., Leonard, A. C., Korol, M., & Winget, C. (1990). Buffalo Creek survivors in the second decade: Stability of stress symptoms. *American Journal of Orthopsychiatry, 60*(1), 43–54.

Hewitt, K. (1995). Excluded perspectives in the social construction of disaster. *International Journal of Mass Emergencies and Disasters, 13*(3), 317–339.

International Federation of Red Cross and Red Crescent Societies. (1999). *World disaster report 1999.* Geneva, Switzerland: Continental Printing.

Kreps, G. A. (1995). Disaster as systemic event and social catalyst: A clarification of subject matter. *International Journal of Mass Emergencies and Disasters, 13*(3), 255–284.

Kunreuther, H., Ginsberg, L., Miller, P., Sagi, P., Slovic, P., Borkan, B., & Katz, N. (1978). *Disaster insurance protection: Public policy lessons.* New York: Wiley.

Lindell, M., & Perry, R. (1992). *Behavioral foundations of community emergency planning.* Washington, DC: Hemisphere.

Mader, G. G., Spangle, W. E., Blair, M. L., Meehan, R. L., Bilodeau, S. W., Degen Kolb, H. J., Duggar, G. S., & Williams, N., Jr. (1980). *Land use planning after earthquakes.* Portola Valley, CA: William Spangle.

Mikami, S., & Ikeda, K. (1985). Human response to disasters. *International Journal of Mass Emergencies and Disasters, 3*(1), 107–132.

Mileti, D. S. (1999). *Disasters by design: A reassessment of natural hazards in the United States.* Washington, DC: Joseph Henry Press.

Mileti, D. S., & Beck, E. M. (1975). Communication in crisis: Explaining evacuation symbolically. *Communication Research, 2*, 24–49.

Mileti, D. S., & Fitzpatrick, C. (1993). *The great earthquake experiment: Risk communication and public action.* Boulder, CO: Westview Press.

Mileti, D. S., & Passerini, E. (1996). A social explanation of urban relocation after earthquakes. *International Journal of Mass Emergencies and Disasters, 14*, 97–110.

Mileti, D. S., & Sorensen, J. S. (1990). *Communication of emergency public warnings: A social science perspective and state-of-the-art assessment.* Oak Ridge, TN: Oak Ridge National Laboratory.

Moore, H. E., & Friedsam, H. J. (1959). Reported emotional stress following a disaster. *Social Forces, 38*, 135–139.

Nigg, J. M. (1987). Communication under conditions of uncertainty: Understanding earthquake forecasting. In R. R. Dynes, B. DeMarchi, & C. Pelanda (Eds.), *Sociology of disasters* (pp. 103–117). Milan, Italy: Franco Angeli Libri.

Norris, F. (1992). Epidemiology of trauma: Frequency and impact of different potentially traumatic events on different demographic groups. *Journal of Consulting Clinical Psychology, 60*, 409–418.

Perry, R. W., Lindell, M. K., & Greene, M. R. (1981). *Evacuation planning in emergency management.* Lexington, MA: Lexington Books.

Porfiriev, B. N. (1995). Disasters and disaster areas: Methodological issues of definition and delineation. *International Journal of Mass Emergencies and Disasters, 13*(3), 285–304.

Prince, S. H. (1920). *Catastrophe and social change: Based upon a sociological study of the Halifax disaster.* New York: Columbia University Press.

Quarantelli, E. L. (1984). *Organizational behavior in disasters and implications for disaster planning.* Emmitsburg, MD: National Emergency Training Center, Federal Emergency Management Agency.

Quarantelli, E. L. (1995). What is a disaster? *International Journal of Mass Emergencies and Disasters, 13*(3), 221–229.

Quarantelli, E. L. (1998). *What is a disaster?* New York: Routledge.

Rogers, G. O. (1985). *Human components of emergency warning.* Pittsburgh, PA: Center for Social and Urban Research, University of Pittsburgh.

Rossi, P. H., Wright, J. D., & Weber-Burdin, E. (1982). *Natural hazards and public choice: The state and local politics of hazard mitigation.* New York: Academic Press.

Rossi, P. H., Wright, J. D., Weber-Burdin, E., & Pereira, J. (1983). *Victims of the environment: Loss from natural hazards in the United States, 1970–1980.* New York: Plenum Press.

Shannon, M. P., Lonigan, C. J., Finch, A. J., Jr., & Taylor, C. M. (1994). Children exposed to disaster: I. Epidemiology of post-traumatic symptoms and symptom profiles. *Journal of the American Academy of Child and Adolescent Psychiatry, 33*(1), 80–93.

Shoaf, K. (1998). Psychological effects of the Northridge earthquake. Poster session presented at the Twenty-Third Annual Hazards Research and Applications Workshop, Boulder, CO.

Stallings, R. A. (1997). *Sociological theories and disaster studies* (Preliminary Paper No. 249). Newark: University of Delaware, Disaster Research Center.

Turner, R. H., Nigg, J. M., Paz, D. H., & Young, B. S. (1980). *Community response to earthquake threat in southern California: Part eight, grass roots organization and resistance.* Los Angeles: Institute for Social Science Research, University of California, Los Angeles.

Ursano, R. J., McCaughey, B. G., & Fullerton, C. (1994). *Individual and community responses to trauma and disaster: The structure of human chaos.* Cambridge: Cambridge University Press.

Wallace, A. (1956). *Tornado in Worcester* (National Academy of Sciences/National Research Council Disaster Study No. 3). Washington, DC: National Academy of Sciences.

Wescoat, J. L. (1992). Common themes in the work of Gilbert White and John Dewey: A pragmatic appraisal. *Annals of the Association of American Geographers, 82*(4), 587–607.

What is a disaster? Six views of the problem. (1995). *International Journal of Mass Emergencies and Disasters, 13*(3) [Special issue].

White, G. F. (1945). *Human adjustment to floods* (Res. Paper No. 29). Chicago: Department of Geography, University of Chicago.

White, G. F. (1973). Natural hazards research. In R. J. Chorley (Ed.), *Directions in geography* (pp. 193–216). London: Metheun.

White, G. F., Calef, W., Hudson, J., Mayer, H., Sheaffer, J., & Volk, D. (1958). *Changes in urban occupancy of flood plains in the United States.* (Res. Paper No. 57). Chicago: University of Chicago Press.

White, G. F., & Haas, J. E. (1975). *Assessment of research on natural hazards.* Cambridge, MA: Massachusetts Institute of Technology Press.

White, G. F., Platt, R. H., & O'Riordan, T. (1997). Classics in human geography revisited: Commentary on human adjustment to floods. *Progress in Human Geography, 21,* 423–429.

Yezer, A. M., & Rubin, C. B. (1987). *The local economic effects of natural disasters.* (Working Paper No. 61). Boulder, CO: Institute of Behavioral Science, University of Colorado.

CHAPTER 34

The Challenge of Increasing Proenvironment Behavior

E. SCOTT GELLER

MY CONTRIBUTION TO THE FIRST *Handbook of Environmental Psychology* (Stokols & Altman, 1987) attempted to show the potential for constructive collaboration between environmental psychology and applied behavior analysis (Geller, 1987). With a few notable exceptions (Everett & Watson, 1987; Stern & Oskamp, 1987), most researchers and teachers in environmental psychology at the time defined this subdiscipline as the systematic study of how environmental factors affect behavior and cognition. Thus, changes in environmental qualities such as noise, physical space, and architectural design were the independent variables; while behavior, perception, or cognition were dependent variables (cf. Altman, 1975).

Applied behavior analysts advocate another perspective. They consider behavior an independent variable influencing the environment and have attempted to change certain target behaviors in order to sustain the environment. More specifically, human behavior can protect or destroy the environmental conditions and resources that support life on Earth, and applications of behavior analysis can reduce environment-destructive behaviors and increase environment-protective behaviors (Cone & Hayes, 1980; Dwyer, Leeming, Cobern, Porter, & Jackson, 1993; Geller, 1986, 1987, 1992, 1994; Geller, Winett, & Everett, 1982).

While many textbook discussions of environmental psychology still focus on the initial and traditional definition of the field (e.g., Feldman, 2001; Kenrick, Neuberg, & Cialdini, 1999; Lahey, 2000),

recent textbooks consider the second definition and give considerable attention to the topic of changing behavior in order to protect the environment (Aronson, Wilson, & Akert, 1999; Bell, Greene, Fisher, & Baum, 2001; Gerow, 1995; Howard, 1997; Winter, 1996). Moreover, the issue of preserving the environment through behavior change was a theme of the May 2000 issue of the *American Psychologist*.

Thus, it seems that applied behavior analysis and environmental psychology are no longer "strange bedfellows," as I proposed in the first *Handbook of Environmental Psychology* (Geller, 1987). The expanded definition of environmental psychology proposed in 1987 has been adopted by some, and the need to address human behaviors related to environmental sustainability has been receiving increased attention by psychologists. Unfortunately, it seems we've not moved beyond the research demonstration in applying the principles and procedures of behavior analysis for environmental protection.

My chapter in the first *Handbook* reviewed a variety of studies conducted from 1970 to 1986 that demonstrated successful applications of behavior analysis to increase environment-preserving behaviors (e.g., litter pick-up, the purchase of returnable bottles, carpooling, delivery of recyclable newspaper to collection sites, and use of public transportation) and to decrease environment-destructive behaviors (e.g., littering, vehicle miles driven and vehicle speed, and electricity consumption). Also, since that time a myriad of additional community-based studies have shown the value of applying behavior analysis principles to improve patterns of human behavior related to environmental protection (see reviews by Dwyer et al., 1993; Geller, 1992, 1995; Huffman, Grossnickle, Cope, & Hoffman, 1995; Porter, Leeming, & Dwyer, 1995). However, the "marriage" of these two disciplines has not been as productive as it could be from the perspective of environmental sustainability. There have been few if any large-scale implementations of the most effective behavior change strategies for environmental protection.

While many utility companies push conservation, they don't apply the most effective behavior change techniques defined by research. Likewise, water suppliers and municipalities periodically ask residents to avoid certain water-wasting behavior; but such requests are usually reactive (i.e., when a water shortage is imminent) rather than proactive, and it seems strategic applications of behavior analysis techniques are rare except for education, prompting, and policy enforcement. It's encouraging that most major appliances are sold with an "Energy Guide," but the impact of these "activators" could be significantly enhanced if behavior analysis and self-management principles had been considered when they were designed.

LACK OF ENVIRONMENTAL IMPACT

There are a variety of possible reasons for the failure of these behavioral community studies to have any notable impact on environmental preservation. Most obvious is the audience of these demonstration projects. The research is published in professional journals and books read almost exclusively by other psychologists. The authors give convincing demonstrations of the efficacy of their behavior change techniques to people who have little interest or influence in large-scale dissemination and application. In other words, the critical social marketing aspects of behavior change technology have not been addressed (Geller, 1989).

Bailey (1991) comments on this dissemination problem: "We have a great science (the experimental analysis of behavior) and a pretty good technology (applied behavior analysis) but no product development or marketing" (p. 39). He explains further that "we do not value marketing" and have "neglected to develop socially acceptable terminology for presenting our concepts to consumers . . . we have, in our zest for science and technology, taken the human concerns out of behavior analysis" (p. 39).

Another problem may be the selection of target behaviors to change. Oskamp (2000) and Howard (2000), for example, identify overpopulation and overconsumption as the key threats to environmental sustainability, not litter control nor recycling, which have been prime targets for applied behavior analysts. Gardner and Stern (1996) distinguish between curtailment behaviors (such as reducing consumption) and efficiency behaviors (which reduce the resource consumption of equipment and machinery). They emphasize that people can do more to save environmental resources by purchasing energy-efficient water heaters and vehicles than by carpooling or insulating their current water heater. In addition, efficiency behaviors require a one-time purchase of more environmentally friendly commodities (from vehicles and major appliances to home heating and cooling systems), whereas curtailment behaviors typically involve repeating inconvenient or sacrificial action (from collecting recyclables and carpooling to turning back thermostats and reducing water use). Behavior analysts have typically targeted curtailment behaviors rather than one-shot efficiency behaviors.

Of course, efficiency behavior requires efficiency options, and such availability is greatly determined by organizations and government policy. In the first *Handbook,* Stern and Oskamp (1987) emphasized that "corporations make a greater direct contribution to environmental problems than individuals, and it is worth examining whether more can be done to alleviate these problems by modifying corporate rather than individual behavior" (p. 1050). Thirteen years later, Stern (2000) makes the same point, reminding us that "organizations usually do more to degrade the environment than individuals and households" (p. 522), and, "If manufacturers adopt 'greener' production technologies and product designs, this will further increase the potential to help solve environmental problems without sacrificing well-being" (p. 525).

Another reason for the lack of environmental impact from applied behavior analysis is the fact that long-term maintenance and institutionalization of behavior change strategies has rarely been studied. All of the applications of behavior analysis to change environment-related behavior have been short-term demonstration projects, conducted to show that a particular intervention procedure has a desired effect. Methods to sustain the environmental impact of a behavior change technique have not been addressed. This is not critical for one-time efficiency behaviors but is absolutely necessary for the regular repetition of curtailment behaviors.

Boyce and Geller (in press) recently addressed this challenge of maintenance by reviewing the research literature related to applying behavior analysis techniques to improve occupational safety. They found that relatively few studies evaluated behavioral maintenance by including a lengthy evaluation period after an intervention process was withdrawn. In addition, they found no systematic study of variables related to successful institutionalization of an effective behavior change process. However, they did identify some factors conducive to sustaining a successful behavior change process, and these have been verified by practitioners (McSween & Mathews, in press). For example, the following factors contribute to the long-term impact of behavior change interventions in industrial settings:

- Each level of an organization (from management to line workers) needs education and training to understand the rationale behind an intervention and to realize their specific roles in making the process work (cf. DePasquale & Geller, 1999).
- Indigenous staff need to implement the intervention procedures and thus have substantial input into intervention design (Geller, 2001; McSween, 1995).
- A formal accountability system is required, which is best handled by an employee-manned steering committee that monitors intervention results and develops action plans for enhancing intervention impact (Geller, 1998b; McSween & Mathews, in press).
- A formal procedure for collecting, reviewing, and using behavioral results is needed to support the accountability system and enable continuous improvement (Krause, 1995; Krause, Hidley, & Hodson, 1996).
- Group and individual rewards are needed to support ongoing participation in the process as well as to recognize exemplary achievements (Geller, 1996, 1997).

Although these conclusions were derived from large-scale applications of behavior analysis to improve safety performance in organizations, they are certainly relevant to sustaining environmental protection interventions, especially in organizational settings, which should be a prime target (Stern, 2000; Stern & Oskamp, 1987).

With regard to the design of behavior change interventions, Boyce and Geller (in press) reached the following conclusions from their comparison of behavior-based interventions that resulted in substantial versus minimal behavioral maintenance:

- Reward schedules that are just sufficient to initiate behavior change are more likely to produce longer-term behavior change than more powerful rewards.
- Global or general representations of desirable behavior results in more behavioral maintenance than references to specific behavior.
- Behavioral commitment strategies accompanied by information regarding the rationale for performing a target behavior can have long-term effects.

More specifics regarding these intervention recommendations for behavioral maintenance are covered later in this chapter, including theoretical rationale and specific examples. First let's retreat a bit and review the behavior analysis approach to environmental protection, beginning with a definition and rationale for three basic principles.

PRINCIPLE 1: FOCUS INTERVENTION ON OBSERVABLE BEHAVIOR

The behavior analysis approach to intervention design and evaluation is founded on behavioral science as conceptualized and researched by B. F. Skinner (1938, 1953, 1974). Experimental behavior analysis and, later, applied behavior analysis emerged from Skinner's research and teaching. He laid the groundwork for numerous therapies and interventions to improve the quality of life of individuals, groups, and entire communities (Geller, Winett, & Everett, 1982; Goldstein & Krasner, 1987; Greene, Winett, Van Houten, Geller, & Iwata, 1987). Whether working one-on-one in a clinical setting or with work teams throughout an organization, the intervention procedures always target specific behaviors in order to produce constructive change. In other words, the behavior-based approach focuses on observing what people do, analyzes why they do it, and then applies a research-supported intervention strategy to improve what people do.

Behavior varies according to factors in the external world, including equipment design, management systems, the behaviors shown by others, and various social dynamics. An open discussion about the physical and interpersonal determinants of environment-protective versus environment-destructive behavior can lead to practical modifications of conditions or contingencies to encourage behavior that supports environmental sustainability.

Behavior-based intervention *acts people into thinking differently*, whereas person-based intervention *thinks people into acting differently*. The person-based approach is used successfully by many psychiatrists and clinical psychologists in professional therapy sessions, but it is not cost-effective in a group, organizational, or community setting. To be effective, person-focused intervention requires extensive one-on-one interaction between a client and a specially trained intervention specialist. Even if time and facilities were available for an intervention to focus on internal and nonobservable attitudes and person states, few relevant agents of change for environmental protection have the education, training, and experience to implement such an approach. Internal person factors can be improved indirectly, however, by directly focusing on behaviors in certain ways.

PRINCIPLE 2: LOOK FOR EXTERNAL FACTORS TO IMPROVE PERFORMANCE

Internal person dimensions like attitudes, perceptions, and cognitions are difficult to define objectively and change directly. So stop trying! Most of us don't have the education, training, experience, nor time to deal with people's attitudes or person states directly. Instead, look for external factors influencing behavior independent of individual feelings, preferences, and perceptions. When you empower people to analyze behavior from a systems perspective and to implement interventions to improve behavior, you will indirectly improve their attitude, commitment, and internal motivation.

In the first widely used American textbook in psychology, *Principles of Psychology*, William James (1890) explained the reciprocity between behavior and attitude as follows:

> Sit all day in a moping posture, sigh, and reply to everything with a dismal voice, and your melancholy lingers. . . . If we wish to conquer undesirable emotional tendencies in ourselves, we must . . . go through the outward movements of those contrary dispositions which we prefer to cultivate.

Careful observation and analysis of people's ongoing activities at home, at work, and in the community can pinpoint many potential causes of excessive or destructive uses of environmental resources. Those causes external to people—including reward and punishment contingencies, policies, or supervisory behaviors—can often be altered for the improvement of both behavior and attitude. In contrast, internal person factors are difficult to identify, and if defined, they are even more difficult to change directly. So with applied behavior analysis the focus is placed on external factors—conditions, contingencies, and behaviors—that can be changed to benefit environmental sustainability.

PRINCIPLE 3: FOCUS ON POSITIVE CONSEQUENCES TO MOTIVATE DESIRED BEHAVIOR

The ABC contingency is a basic tenet of behavior-based safety. "A" stands for *activator*, or the antecedent events that direct behavior, "B." And "C" refers to *consequence*, or the extrinsic stimuli and events that motivate behavior. We do what we do to gain a positive consequence or to escape or avoid a negative consequence. And we stop doing what we're doing when our behavior results in immediate negative consequences.

The most powerful motivating consequences are "soon" and "certain." That's why most environment-destructive behavior occurs. It provides the performer with such soon and certain consequences as comfort, convenience, and perceived efficiency.

As this third principle indicates, using positive over negative consequences is critically important. It's relevant to *attitude* and many other internal dimensions of people. As detailed elsewhere (Geller, 1997, 1998c, 2001), when positive recognition is delivered correctly, it does more than increase the frequency of the behavior it follows. It also increases the likelihood that other desirable behaviors will occur and that positive recognition will be used more often to benefit both behavior and attitude.

The popular commonsense belief that we learn more from our mistakes than our achievements is wrong. We learn more from our successes. So recognizing people's environment-protective behavior will facilitate more learning and positive motivation than will criticizing people's environment-destructive behavior (cf. Flora, 2000). Consider that only with positive consequences can both behavior and attitude be improved at the same time.

Recent research by Boyce and Geller (2001) applied these principles in an attempt to increase proenvironment behaviors throughout a university campus. In two field studies, large numbers of students were given "Actively Caring Thank-You" cards and instructed to give them to others (university faculty, staff, or students) when they saw them do something that protected the environment (e.g., pick up litter, use a trash receptacle, carpool, or use public transportation) or helped another person.

This intervention plan was well received but was used more often when direct and indirect reward strategies were added to motivate delivery of the thank-you cards. A commitment or indirect reward strategy, whereby students received raffle coupons for promising to hand out two thank-you cards, was most effective at increasing the number of students who distributed at least one card. In contrast, a direct reward strategy, which gave students one opportunity to win prizes in a raffle for each card delivered, was most influential at increasing the number of Actively Caring Thank-You Cards used per student.

THE DO IT PROCESS

The DO IT process is a general behavior analysis method for solving the behavioral dimensions of environmental sustainability. It provides objective data for exploring why certain environment-related behaviors occur or don't occur, and for evaluating the impact of interventions designed to increase environment-protective behavior or decrease environment-destructive behavior. If an intervention does not produce a desired effect, it is either refined or replaced with a completely different behavior change approach.

"D" FOR DEFINE

The process begins by defining certain behaviors to work with. These are the targets of the environmental sustainability intervention. They are environment-protective behaviors to increase or environment-destructive behaviors to decrease. The proenvironment behavior might be a curtailment activity that needs to be repeated (such as collecting recyclables, purchasing products with less packaging, composting, walking or riding a bicycle instead of using a motor vehicle, or wearing more outer garments in lieu of turning up the thermostat). Alternatively, the target behavior could be a one-time efficiency behavior (such as purchasing a more environmentally friendly appliance or heating/cooling system, installing a shower-flow restrictor, or insulating a water heater).

To define the variety of possible target behaviors for a comprehensive plan to protect the environment, Geller et al. (1982) used a $2 \times 3 \times 5$ matrix with the following factors: (1) two intervention approaches (physical vs. behavioral); (2) three community sectors requiring an intervention process (residential/consumer, government/institutional, and commercial/industrial); and (3) five target areas for intervention within each sector (i.e., heating/cooling, solid waste management, transportation, equipment efficiency, and water use and disposal). Obviously, these five targets do not cover the entire domain of environmental protection. For instance, problems related to population explosion, air pollution, land misuse, hazardous waste, and mineral depletion were not addressed by Geller et al. and have not been researched by behavior analysts. Cone and Hayes (1980) did include population control and noise pollution in their text on behavioral approaches to environmental protection, but the behavior change research in these additional areas has been minimal.

Practically all of the behavior change research for environmental protection has targeted individual and group behaviors in the residential/consumer sector rather than the governmental/institutional or commercial/industrial sectors, where the potential for large-scale benefit is greatest. Moreover, as indicated above, most of the targeted behaviors have been curtailment behaviors that need to be repeated rather than efficiency behaviors that require a one-time occurrence. However, the principles and intervention strategies developed from demonstration projects in the residential/ consumer sector are relevant for designing interventions and policy in the corporate and governmental sectors of society that target both efficiency and curtailment activities.

"O" FOR OBSERVE

After defining one or more target behaviors to influence, a baseline level of the behavior(s) is obtained by observing how often the target behavior occurs under natural conditions. With the ABC contingency in mind (as described above in Principle 3), conditions are recorded which hinder proenvironment behavior or support environment-destructive behavior. This observation stage is not a faultfinding but a fact-finding process to facilitate the discovery of behaviors and conditions that need to be changed or continued in order to protect the environment. There is not one generic observation procedure for all situations. It is necessary to customize and refine a process for a particular target behavior and setting.

"I" FOR *INTERVENE*

During this stage, interventions are designed and implemented in an attempt to increase proenvironment behaviors or decrease environment-destructive behavior. As reflected in Principle 2 above, intervention means changing external conditions in order to make environment-sustaining behavior more likely. When designing interventions, Principle 3 is your guide. Specifically, the most motivating consequences are soon, certain, and sizable. And positive consequences are usually preferable to negative consequences.

The variety of intervention procedures applied successfully to increase environment-protective behavior and decrease environment-destructive behaviors are described in several review documents (e.g., Dwyer et al., 1993; Geller, 1986, 1987, 1992, 1995; Huffman et al., 1995; Porter et al., 1995). The interventions that included only activators (e.g., media messages, signs, demonstrations, and goal setting) were effective at increasing environment-protective behaviors when the instructions were behavior specific and given in close physical and temporal proximity with opportunities to emit the target behavior and when performing the behavior was relatively convenient (like turning off lights in unoccupied rooms, using a particular trash receptacle or recycling container, or purchasing drinks in returnable bottles).

When target behaviors are relatively inconvenient, behavior change interventions have usually required consequences in order to have substantial beneficial impact. A notable exception has been the application of "promise card commitment" activators referred to above (cf. Boyce & Geller, 2001). Field researchers, for example, have markedly increased participation in community recycling programs by asking residents to sign cards promising their participation (e.g., Burn & Oskamp, 1986; Pardini & Katzev, 1984; Wang & Katzev, 1990), and there is some evidence that behavior change following this type of commitment strategy is more durable than incentive/reward techniques (Boyce & Geller, in press; Geller, Rudd, Kalsher, Streff, & Lehman, 1987; Katzev, 1986).

Consequences for Environmental Protection

Skinner (1987) claimed that behavior is determined by its consequences, and we should not expect many people to modify their behavior as the result of information or advice alone (i.e., activators), especially when the information pertains to a distant future—the case with environmental sustainability. Although people will often follow advice when the advisor's information (or activator) previously led to reinforcing consequences, this situation requires people to experience the reinforcing consequences of following the advisor's message or rule. This type of learning (or response selection by reinforcing consequences) is especially difficult when the future consequences (reinforcing or punishing) are unclear, uncertain, or remote.

Each of these characteristics of weak consequences is usually present when environmentally protective behaviors are advocated. People have typically not conserved water or gasoline until experiencing punishing consequences (e.g., inconvenience and increased monetary costs) of water and gas shortages. And the behavior of collecting recyclables has not usually become standard practice until after people experienced (directly or vicariously) the consequences of excessive solid waste (as in media reports of problems finding suitable landfill space or a port to dock a garbage barge).

Rewards versus Penalties

Incentives and disincentives are activators that announce the availability of a rewarding or penalizing consequence, respectively, in order to motivate behavior change. Traditionally, local, state, and federal governments have used disincentives and penalties to motivate environment-preserving behaviors. These attempts to protect the environment usually take the form of ordinances or laws (e.g., fines for littering, illegal dumping, or using excessive water or for polluting land, water, or air); and to be effective, these disincentive/penalty interventions usually require extensive promotion (activators) and enforcement (consequences). Behavior analysts have de-emphasized this approach, primarily because negative affect, feelings, or attitudes typically accompany attempts to mandate behavior change through disincentive/penalty tactics.

When a positive attitude is linked to one's change in behavior, the probability that the desired behavior will become a social norm increases. Positive attitudes are more likely to follow an incentive/reward approach than a disincentive/penalty intervention because the former approach is more likely to be perceived as "voluntary" and no threat to individual freedom (Skinner, 1971). In fact, perceiving a threat to one's freedom can lead to behavior contrary to compliance with a mandate (Brehm, 1972).

Types of Reward Contingencies

The reward contingencies implemented for environmental sustainability have been diverse. Some rewards have been given after the performance of a desired target behavior, whereas other rewards have been contingent upon a particular outcome (e.g., for reaching a designated level of environmental cleanliness, energy conservation, or water savings). The rewards themselves have varied widely, including such consequences as monetary rebates, verbal commendations, merchandise discount coupons, raffle tickets, self-photographs, soft drinks, recognition on an "energy efficient" honor roll, as well as opportunities to engage in a valued behavior (e.g., attend a special event, use a preferred parking space, or tour a mental health facility).

As reviewed in several documents (e.g., Cone & Hayes, 1980; Dwyer et al., 1993; Geller, 1992; Porter et al., 1995), most of the reward contingencies produced dramatic increases in the desired behaviors; but unfortunately, the behaviors usually returned to preintervention baseline levels when the reward contingencies were withdrawn. Although some have used such reversals to demean incentive/reward strategies to motivate behavior change (De Young, 1993; Kohn, 1993), it's noteworthy that most of the intervention phases in this research were relatively short term and likely did not allow sufficient time for natural consequences (e.g., social approval, media recognition, visible environmental improvement) to gain control. Moreover, many of the rewarding consequences (e.g., raffle coupons for prizes donated by community merchants) were inexpensive enough to keep in place for a long time. In some cases it is cost effective to maintain a consequence strategy indefinitely. Many feedback strategies, for example, are cheap and effective and do not have to be withdrawn.

Feedback Techniques

Most of the feedback research for environmental protection addressed residential energy consumption, and the feedback was usually given to residents (e.g., see reviews by Shippee, 1980; Winett, 1980). The more labor-intensive procedures included the delivery of feedback cards with amount of kilowatt hours or cubic feet of gas used (and the cost) for a particular time period. The technology is currently available to deliver this sort of feedback directly and automatically to homes equipped with appropriate displays. Analogous devices, including a hygrothermograph giving continuous readings of room temperatures and humidity (Winett et al., 1982), an electronic feedback meter with a digital display of electricity cost per hour (McClelland & Cook, 1979–1980), and a special device with a light that illuminates whenever electricity use exceeds 90% of a household's peak level (Blakely, Lloyd, & Alferink, 1977), have been tested and have shown much promise for dramatic energy savings.

A few field studies of feedback intervention for environmental protection addressed the conservation of transportation energy. One study showed a decrease in vehicular miles of travel (vmt) after publicly displaying the vmt of individuals in a work group (Reichel & Geller, 1980). Lauridsen (1977) found vehicular miles per gallon (mpg) to increase with a fuel flow meter that displayed continuous mpg or gallons-per-hour consumption; and Runnion, Watson, and McWhorter (1978) increased mpg among short-run and long-haul truck drivers with a public display of each employee's mpg. More feedback research is certainly needed in the transportation domain, including the development of vehicle feedback displays that give continuous readouts of mpg.

Even with feedback technology for home and vehicle energy use, however, a momentous challenge remains. How can we get substantial numbers of these devices in people's homes and vehicles? And how can we get people with these devices to attend to them regularly, and respond appropriately to the feedback? Increases in the cost of energy (e.g., electricity and petroleum) could motivate attention and reaction to consumption feedback, but usually such increases are gradual and thus are barely noticed. A more proactive approach is to enroll intervention agents to activate environment-protecting lifestyles among friends, neighbors, and coworkers and to apply basic behavior change consequences (e.g., social approval and disapproval) to motivate energy-protective behaviors (cf. McKenzie-Mohr, 2000). In other words, large-scale increases in environment-protective behavior requires large numbers of people to apply the DO IT process as intervention agents (cf. Boyce & Geller, 2001).

"T" FOR *TEST*

The test phase of DO IT provides behavior change agents with the information they need to refine or replace a behavior change intervention. If behavioral observations during this phase indicate lack of significant improvement in the target behavior, the behavior change agents analyze and discuss the situation, and then refine the intervention or choose another intervention approach. On the other hand, if the target reaches the desired frequency level, the change agents can turn their attention to other environment-relevant behaviors.

Every time behavior change agents evaluate an intervention approach, they learn more about how to improve behavior. They have essentially become behavioral scientists using the DO IT process to: (1) diagnose a human dynamics problem, (2) monitor the impact of a behavior change intervention, and (3) refine interventions for continuous improvement. The results from such testing provide motivating consequences to support this learning process and keep the participants involved.

Let's consider some basic principles about behavior and behavior change techniques that can facilitate the development of the most effective intervention for a particular situation. This will lead to the notion that the ABC contingency of Principle 3 can be internalized for self-persuasion and self-management intervention. In other words, people can use activators and consequences on themselves for self-direction and self-motivation. First, it's important to distinguish between other-directed, self-directed, and automatic behavior (Watson & Tharp, 1993).

THREE STAGES OF BEHAVIOR

Most voluntary behavior starts out as other directed, in the sense that we follow someone else's instructions.

Such direction can come from a training program, operations manual, or policy statement. After learning what to do, essentially by memorizing or internalizing the appropriate instructions, our behavior enters the self-directed stage. In other words, we talk to ourselves or formulate an image before performing a behavior in order to activate the right response. Sometimes we talk to ourselves after performing a behavior to reassure ourselves we performed correctly or to figure out ways to do better next time. We are internalizing the ABC contingency. At this point we're usually open to corrective feedback if it's delivered well.

After performing some behaviors frequently and consistently over a period of time, we find they become automatic. A habit is formed. Some habits are good and some are not good, depending on their short- and long-term consequences. If implemented correctly, rewards, recognition, and other positive consequences can facilitate the transfer of behavior from the self-directed stage to the habit stage.

Of course our self-directed behavior is not always desirable. When we intentionally waste environmental resources, we are choosing to disregard environmental sustainability in order to achieve a soon, certain, and positive consequence or avoid an immediate, probable, and negative consequence. In this state, we are "consciously incompetent." Attempts to change self-directed behavior from incompetent to competent is often difficult because it usually requires a relevant change in personal motivation.

Before an environment-destructive habit (or routine) can be changed to an environment-protective habit, the target behavior must become self-directed. In other words, people need to become aware of their undesirable habit before adjustment is possible. Then, if the person is motivated to improve (perhaps as a result of an incentive/reward program), his or her new self-directed behavior can become automatic.

Let's see what kinds of behavior-based interventions are appropriate for the three transitions alluded to:

1. Turning an unintentional environment-destructive habit (when the person is "unconsciously incompetent") into environment-productive self-directed behavior
2. Changing self-directed environment-destructive behavior (when the person is "consciously incompetent") to environment-productive self-directed behavior

3. Turning environment-productive self-directed behavior (when the person is "consciously competent") into an environment-protective habit ("unconscious competence")

THREE BASIC INTERVENTION APPROACHES

The activators and consequences of the ABC contingency described earlier in Principle 3 are external to the performer, or they are internal (as in self-instructions or self-recognition). They can be intrinsic or extrinsic to a task, meaning they provide direction or motivation naturally as a behavior is performed (as in a computer game), or they are added to the situation extrinsically in order to improve performance. An incentive/reward program is external and extrinsic. It adds an activator (an incentive) and a consequence (a reward) to the situation in order to direct and motivate desirable behavior (Geller, 1996).

INSTRUCTIONAL INTERVENTION

An instructional intervention is typically an activator or antecedent event used to get new behavior started or to move behavior from the automatic (habit) stage to the self-directed stage. Or it is used to improve behavior already in the self-directed stage. The aim is to get the performer's attention and instruct her or him to transition from unconscious incompetence to conscious competence. You assume the person wants to improve, so external motivation is not needed—only external and extrinsic direction.

This type of intervention consists primarily of activators, as exemplified by education sessions, training exercises, and directive feedback. Since your purpose is to instruct, the intervention comes before the target behavior and focuses on helping the performer internalize your instructions. As we've all experienced, this type of intervention is more effective when the instructions are specific and given one-on-one.

SUPPORTIVE INTERVENTION

Once a person learns the right way to do something, practice is important so the behavior becomes part of a natural routine. Continued practice leads to fluency and in many cases to automatic or habitual behavior. This is an especially desirable state for behavior that needs to be repeated to benefit the environment. But practice does not come easily and benefits greatly from supportive intervention. We need support to reassure us we are doing the right thing and to encourage us to keep going.

While instructional intervention consists primarily of activators, supportive intervention focuses on the application of positive consequences. Thus, when we give people rewarding feedback or recognition for environment-sustaining behavior, we are showing our appreciation for their efforts and increasing the likelihood they will perform the behavior again. Each occurrence of the desired behavior facilitates fluency and helps build an environment-protective routine.

Thus, after people know what to do, they need to perform the behavior many times before it can become a habit. Therefore, the positive regard we give people for their proenvironment behavior can go a long way toward facilitating fluency and a transition to the automatic or habit stage. Such supportive intervention is often most powerful when it comes from one's peers—as in peer support.

Note that supportive intervention is typically not preceded by a specific activator. In other words, when you support self-directed behavior, you don't need to provide an instructional antecedent. The person knows what to do. You don't need to activate desired behavior with a promise (an incentive) or a threat (a disincentive). The person is already motivated to do the right thing.

MOTIVATIONAL INTERVENTION

When people know what to do but don't do it, a motivational intervention is needed. In other words, when people are consciously incompetent about proenvironment behavior, they require some external encouragement or pressure to change. Instruction alone is obviously insufficient because they are knowingly doing the wrong thing.

We usually waste environmental resources because we perceive the natural positive consequences of the behavior to be more powerful than the environment-destructive consequences. This is because the positive consequences of environmental waste or degradation are immediate and certain, while the natural negative consequences of proenvironment behavior seem improbable and remote. Furthermore, the proenvironment alternative is usually relatively inconvenient, expensive, uncomfortable, or inefficient; and these negative consequences are immediate and certain. As a result, we often need to add both activators and consequences to the situation in order to move people from "conscious incompetence" to "conscious competence." This is when an incentive/reward program is useful, as defined above. Such a program attempts to motivate a certain target behavior by promising people a positive consequence if they perform it. The promise is the incentive and the consequence is the reward.

Motivational intervention is clearly the most challenging, requiring enough external influence to get the target behavior started without triggering a desire to assert personal freedom. Remember the objective is to motivate a transition from conscious incompetence to a *self-directed* state of conscious competence. Powerful external consequences might improve behavior only temporarily, as long as the behavioral intervention is in place (Geller, 2001a). Hence, the individual is consciously competent, but the excessive outside control makes the behavior

entirely other directed. Excessive control on the outside of people can limit the amount of control or self-direction they develop on the inside (cf. Lepper & Greene, 1978).

A long-term implementation of a motivational intervention coupled with consistent supportive intervention can lead to a good habit. In other words, with substantial motivation and support, other-directed proenvironment behavior can transition to unconscious competence without first becoming self-directed.

SUMMARY

Figure 34.1 reviews this intervention information by depicting relationships between four competency states (unconscious incompetence, conscious incompetence, conscious competence, and unconscious competence) and four intervention approaches (instructional intervention, motivational intervention, supportive intervention, and self-management). When people are unaware of the proenvironment

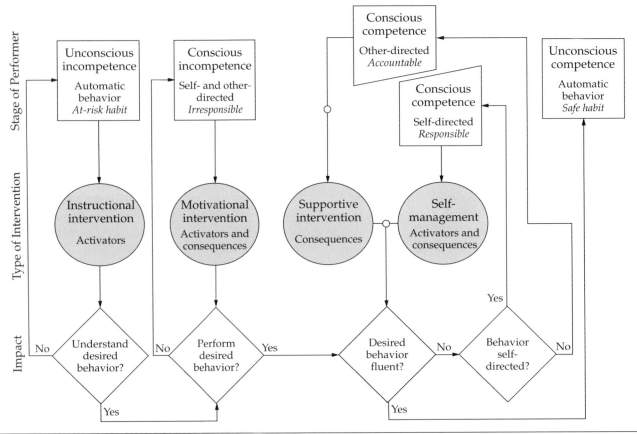

Figure 34.1   The flow of behavior change model helps to match intervention approach with needs of the target individual(s).

practice desired (i.e., they are "unconsciously incompetent"), they need repeated instructional intervention until they understand what to do.

Then, as depicted at the far left of Figure 34.1, the critical question is whether the desired proenvironment behavior is performed. If the desired behavior occurs, the question of behavioral fluency is relevant. A fluent response becomes a habit or part of a regular routine enabling the individual to reach a state of "unconscious competence."

When people know how to protect the environment but don't, they are considered "consciously incompetent" or irresponsible. This is when an external motivational intervention can be useful, as discussed earlier. Then, when the desired behavior occurs at least once, supportive intervention is needed to make the behavior more fluent and, eventually, habitual.

Most people need supportive intervention for their proenvironment behavior. In other words, most people already know what they can do at home, at work, and on the road to protect environmental resources, and they have likely performed such proenvironment behavior at least once. But the proenvironment approach might not be habitual. The individual is "consciously competent" but needs supportive recognition or feedback for increased fluency and response maintenance.

Figure 34.1 illustrates a distinction between conscious competence/other-directed and conscious competence/self-directed. If an environment-protective behavior is self-directed, the individual is considered responsible and a fourth type of intervention is relevant—self-management. As detailed elsewhere (Watson & Tharp, 1997), the methods and tools of effective self-management are derived from applied behavior analysis research and are perfectly consistent with the principles and procedures reviewed here.

In essence, self-management involves the application of the DO IT process described above to one's own behavior. An individual defines one or more target behaviors to improve, monitors these behaviors, manipulates relevant activators and consequences to increase desired behavior and decrease undesired behavior, and tracks continual change in the target behaviors to determine the impact of the self-management process (cf. Geller, 1998b; Geller & Clarke, 1999). The critical challenge is to help people get so personally committed to environmental protection that they would use self-management

techniques to increase their proenvironment behavior. This requires a shift from being accountable to feeling responsible, as discussed next.

ACCOUNTABILITY VERSUS RESPONSIBILITY

From the perspective of large-scale environmental sustainability, the differentiation in Figure 34.1 between accountable and responsible is critical. People often use the words *accountability* and *responsibility* interchangeably. Whether you hold someone accountable or responsible for getting something done, you mean the same thing. You want that person to accomplish a certain task, and you intend on making sure it happens. However, let's consider the receiving end of this situation. How does a person feel about an assignment—does he or she feel accountable or responsible? Here's where a distinction is evident.

When you are held accountable, you are asked to reach a certain objective or goal, often within a designated time period. But you might not feel responsible to meet the deadline. Or, you might feel responsible enough to complete the assignment, but that's all. You do only what's required and no more. In this case, accountability is the same as responsibility.

There are times, however, when you extend your responsibility beyond accountability. You do more than what's required. You go beyond the call of duty as defined by a particular accountability system. This is often essential when it comes to protecting environmental resources. Long-term proenvironment behavior requires that people extend their responsibility for the environment beyond that for which they are held accountable. They need to transition from an other-directed state to a self-directed state. This requires a consideration of self-persuasion (Aronson, 1999), or intervention techniques that facilitate a supportive link between overt behavior and self-perception (Bem, 1972). In this regard, a direct attempt to motivate behavior change might not be optimal.

DIRECT PERSUASION

Advertisers use direct persuasion. They show us people enjoying positive consequences or avoiding negative consequences by using their products. As such, they apply the ABC contingency of behavior analysis discussed above to sell their wares or services. The activator (or the "A" of the ABC contingency) announces the availability of a reinforcing consequence (the "C" of the ABC contingency) if the purchasing behavior is performed (the "B" of the ABC contingency).

Advertisers also apply research-based principles from social psychology to make their messages more persuasive. Specifically, social scientists have shown advantages in using highly credible communicators and in arousing their audience's emotions (Aronson, 1999; Hovland & Weiss, 1951). Therefore, sales pitches are often given by authority figures and attempt to get viewers emotionally involved with product-related issues. It's noteworthy, however, that these attempts at direct persuasion are not asking for behavior that is inconvenient or difficult. Normally, the purpose of an advertisement is to persuade a consumer to select a certain brand of merchandise. This boils down to merely choosing one commodity over another at the retail store. While shopping, consumers only need to move their hands a few inches to select one product over another. This is hardly a burdensome change in lifestyle.

Environmental protection behavior is usually much more inconvenient and requires more effort than switching brands at a supermarket. It often requires significant adjustment in a highly practiced and regular routine at work, at home, or on the road. Thus, adopting a proenvironment way of doing something might first require the elimination of an efficient and convenient habit that uses excessive environmental resources. Furthermore, participation in an environment-sustaining effort usually requires the regular performance of several inconvenient proenvironment behaviors.

Consequently, direct persuasion might not be the most effective approach for increasing proenvironment behavior. Since other people are not usually around to hold us accountable for selecting the most proenvironment behavior available, we need to hold ourselves accountable.

Direct attempts to persuade people to make inconvenient changes in their lifestyles often yield disappointing outcomes. For example, communication strategies have generally been unsuccessful when designed to persuade smokers to quit smoking (Elder, Geller, Hovell, & Mayer, 1994), drivers to stop speeding (Geller, 1998a), homeowners to conserve water (Geller, Erikson, & Buttram, 1983) or insulate their water heaters (Geller, 1981), bigoted individuals to cease prejudicial behavior, or sexually active people to use condoms (Aronson, 1999). Similarly, the "Just Say No to Drugs" campaigns have not influenced much long-term behavior change.

The problem with direct persuasion is that it's direct. It comes across as someone else's idea, and it could give the impression that the behavior is actually for someone other than the performer. It reflects other-directed accountability rather than self-directed responsibility. This can cause a disconnection between the behavior and self-perception.

BEHAVIOR-BASED SELF-PERCEPTION

Bem (1972) prefaces his classic and innovative presentation of self-perception theory by asserting that "individuals come to 'know' their own attitudes, emotions, and other internal states by inferring them from observations of their own overt behavior and/or the circumstances in which this behavior occurs" (p. 2). In other words, we write mental scripts or make internal attributions about ourselves from our observations and interpretations of the various ABC contingencies that enter our lifespace. And "if external contingencies seem sufficient to account for the behavior, then the individual will not be led into using the behavior as a source of evidence for his self-attributions" (p. 19).

Thus, children who had the excuse of a severe threat for not playing with a "forbidden toy" did not internalize a rule and, therefore, played with the forbidden toy when the threat contingency was removed (Lepper & Greene, 1978). Similarly, college students who were paid $20 (a substantial sum in 1959 when Festinger and Carlsmith conducted their classic study) for telling other students a boring task was fun did not develop a personal view that the task was enjoyable. The reinforcement contingency made their behavior incredible as a reflection of their belief or self-perception.

In contrast, participants who received a mild threat or low compensation (only $1) to motivate their behavior developed a self-perception consistent with their behavior. The children avoided playing with the forbidden toy in a subsequent situation with no threat, and the college students who lied for low compensation decided they must have liked the boring task. In theory, these participants viewed their behavior as a valid guide for inferring their private views, since their behavior was not under strong ABC contingency control.

In an instructive follow-up experiment, Lepper (as cited in Bem, 1972) tempted young boys (with an attractive prize) to falsify their scores on a test he gave them. Three weeks earlier in another setting, these same subjects had resisted playing with the forbidden toy following a mild or severe threat. Those boys who had earlier received the mild threat were significantly less likely to cheat than those in the severe threat condition. Presumably, the boys who earlier complied with only a mild threat were more likely to develop the self-perception that "I'm a good boy who resists temptation," and this internal dialogue or personal rule influenced resistance to temptation to cheat 3 weeks later.

I have only summarized a small sample of the research that supports the notion that self-directed behavior or self-persuasion is more likely when the extrinsic control of the ABC contingency is less obvious or perhaps indirect. In other words, when there are sufficient external consequences to justify the amount of effort required for a proenvironment behavior, the performer does not have to develop an internal justification for the behavior. There is no self-persuasion (Aronson, 1999), and performing the behavior does not alter self-perception (Bem, 1972). Under these circumstances the maintenance of environment-protective behavior is unlikely, unless it's possible to keep a sufficient accountability system (e.g., incentives or disincentives) in place over the long term.

External contingencies are not usually available to motivate proenvironment behavior. Therefore, it's often necessary to implement an intervention process to motivate environment-protective behavior on a large scale. However, to promote self-persuasion and self-directed behavior it's critical for the ABC contingency to be strong enough to get the behavior started but not powerful enough to provide complete justification for the effort. But, of course, this is only relevant for curtailment behaviors or proenvironment practices that need to be regularly repeated in order to have substantial beneficial impact on the environment. In the case of one-shot efficiency behaviors (Gardner & Stern, 1996), a single application of the ABC contingency can motivate the purchase of certain equipment or machinery which saves environmental resources whenever it's used.

CONCLUSION

This chapter addressed the challenge of changing behaviors related to environmental protection. Since improving behavior is the primary focus of applied behavior analysis, this approach was reviewed. A basic framework for implementing a behavior-based intervention process was introduced. It was referred to as DO IT for the four basic procedural steps: (1) Define target behaviors to support or improve. (2) Observe critical behaviors in order to help people become more mindful of environment-protective versus environmental-destructive behaviors and provide constructive behavioral feedback. (3) Intervene for instruction, support, motivation, or self-management. And (4) test the impact of the intervention process to verify the beneficial behavioral influence and learn how to have greater environmental impact through behavior change.

The subsequent introduction of a "flow of behavior change" model and a distinction between accountability and ways to develop personal responsibility went beyond applied behavior analysis. The issues of mental scripting or self-persuasion were considered in order to handle the issue of long-term behavior change. In other words, when external contingencies cannot remain in place to hold people accountable for performing proenvironment behaviors (which is usually the case), it's necessary to consider ways to increase self-directed behavior. This is when people feel responsible for environmental protection and hold themselves accountable to consistently perform proenvironment behavior. In this regard, the research reviewed indicated that the more obvious the external control or accountability, the greater the disconnection between behavior and self-perception and the less self-persuasion and sustained participation when the behavior change intervention is removed.

Thus, it seems the basic challenge regarding the large-scale improvement of environment-relevant behavior is as follows: (1) Define specific curtailment and efficiency behaviors that can contribute to environmental sustainability; (2) rank order this list from most to least critical with regard to environmental impact; (3) develop and implement a behavior-based intervention process to instruct, support, or motivate the desired proenvironment behavior(s) depending on whether participants are "unconsciously incompetent," "consciously incompetent," or "consciously competent"; (4) if motivational contingencies must eventually be withdrawn, then make them only strong enough to get the behavior started but not powerful enough to provide complete justification for the effort and thereby hinder self-persuasion and feelings of personal responsibility for environmental protection; (5) derive a marketing plan for large-scale dissemination and implementation of the behavior change intervention.

Strategies for putting the large-scale dissemination step in place could not be covered in this chapter. To date, the research literature offers little advice regarding practical connections between behavioral intervention and social marketing. Thus, these two disciplines are the new strange bedfellows which need a productive marriage in order to meet the challenge of increasing proenvironment behavior on a large scale and over the long term.

REFERENCES

Altman, I. (1975). *The environment and social behavior.* Monterey, CA: Brooks/Cole.

Aronson, E. (1999). The power of self-persuasion. *American Psychologist, 54,* 875–884.

Aronson, E., Wilson, T. D., & Akert, R. M. (1999). *Social psychology* (3rd ed.). New York: Addison Wesley Longman.

Bailey, J. S. (1991). Marketing behavior analysis requires different talk. In E. S. Geller (Ed.), *Science, theory, and technology: Varied perspectives* (Monograph No. 6, pp. 37–40), Lawrence, KS: Society for the Experimental Analysis of Behavior.

Bell, P. A., Greene, T. C., Fisher, J. D., & Baum, A. (2001). *Environmental psychology* (5th ed.). New York: Harcourt.

Bem, D. J. (1972). Self-perception theory. In L. Berkowitz (Ed.), *Advances in experimental social psychology* (Vol. 6, pp. 1–60). New York: Academic Press.

Blakely, E. Q., Lloyd, K. E., & Alferink, L. (1977). *The effects of feedback on residential electrical peaking and hourly kilowatt consumption.* Unpublished manuscript, Drake University, Des Moines, IA.

Boyce, T. E., & Geller, E. S. (2001). Encouraging college students to support pro-environment behavior: Effects of direct versus indirect rewards. *Environment and Behavior, 33,* 107–125.

Boyce, T. E., & Geller, E. S. (in press). Applied behavior analysis and occupational safety: The challenge of response maintenance. *Journal of Organizational Behavior Management.*

Brehm, J. W. (1972). *Responses to loss of freedom: A theory of psychological reactance.* New York: General Learning Press.

Burn, S. M., & Oskamp, S. (1986). Increasing community recycling with persuasive communication and public commitment. *Journal of Applied Social Psychology, 16,* 29–41.

Cone, J. D., & Hayes, S. C. (1980). *Environmental problems/Behavioral solutions.* Monterey, CA: Brooks/Cole.

DePasquale, J. P., & Geller, E. S. (1999). Critical success factors for behavior-based safety: A study of 20 industry-wide applications. *Journal of Safety Research, 30*(4), 237–249.

De Young, R. (1993). Changing behavior and making it stick: The conceptualization and management of conservation behavior. *Environment and Behavior, 25,* 485–505.

Dwyer, W. O., Leeming, F. C., Cobern, M. K., Porter, B. E., & Jackson, J. M. (1993). Critical review of behavioral interventions to preserve the environment: Research since 1980. *Environment and Behavior, 25,* 275–321.

Elder, J. P., Geller, E. S., Hovell, M. F., & Mayer, J. A. (1994). *Motivating health behavior.* Albany, NY: Delmar.

Everett, P. B., & Watson, B. G. (1987). Psychological contributions to transportation. In D. Stokols & I. Altman (Eds.), *Handbook of environmental psychology* (Vol. 2, pp. 987–1008). New York: Wiley.

Feldman, R. S. (2001). *Social psychology* (3rd ed.). Upper Saddle River, NJ: Prentice-Hall.

Festinger, L., & Carlsmith, J. M. (1959). Cognitive consequences of forced compliance. *Journal of Abnormal and Social Psychology, 58,* 203–210.

Flora, S. R. (2000). Praise's magic reinforcement ratio: Five to one gets the job done. *The Behavior Analyst Today, 1*(4), 64–69.

Gardner, G. T., & Stern, P. C. (1996). *Environmental problems and human behavior.* Boston: Allyn & Bacon.

Geller, E. S. (1981). Evaluating energy conservation programs: Is verbal report enough? *Journal of Consumer Research, 8,* 331–334.

Geller, E. S. (1986). Prevention of environmental problems. In L. Michelson & B. Edelstein (Eds.), *Handbook of prevention* (pp. 361–383). New York: Plenum Press.

Geller, E. S. (1987). Applied behavior analysis and environmental psychology: From strange bedfellows to a productive marriage. In D. Stokols & I. Altman (Eds.), *Handbook of environmental psychology* (Vol. 1, pp. 361–388). New York: Wiley.

Geller, E. S. (1989). Applied behavior analysis and social marketing: An integration to preserve the environment. *Journal of Social Issues, 45,* 17–36.

Geller, E. S. (1992). Solving environmental problems: A behavior change perspective. In S. Staub & P. Green (Eds.), *Psychology and social responsibility: Facing global challenges* (pp. 248–270). New York: New York University Press.

Geller, E. S. (1994). The human element in integrated environmental management. In J. Cairns Jr., T. V. Crawford, & H. Salwasser (Eds.), *Implementing integrated environmental management* (pp. 5–26). Blacksburg, VA: Virginia Polytechnic Institute & State University.

Geller, E. S. (1995). Integrating behaviorism and humanism for environmental protection. *Journal of Social Issues, 51,* 179–195.

Geller, E. S. (1996). The truth about safety incentives. *Professional Safety, 41*(10), 34–39.

Geller, E. S. (1997). Key processes for continuous safety improvement: Behavior-based recognition and celebration. *Professional Safety, 42*(10), 40–44.

Geller, E. S. (1998a). *Applications of behavior analysis to prevent injury from vehicle crashes* (2nd ed.). Monograph published by the Cambridge Center for Behavioral Studies, Cambridge, MA.

Geller, E. S. (1998b). *Beyond safety accountability: How to increase personal responsibility.* Neenah, WI: J.J. Keller.

Geller, E. S. (1998c). *Understanding behavior-based safety: Step-by-step methods to improve your workplace* (2nd ed.). Neenah, WI: J.J. Keller.

Geller, E. S. (2001). *The psychology of safety handbook.* Boca Raton, FL: CRC Press.

Geller, E. S. (in press). Dream—operationalize—intervene—test: If you want to make a difference—Just DO IT. *Journal of Organizational Behavior Management.*

Geller, E. S., & Clarke, S. W. (1999). Safety self-management: A key behavior-based process for injury prevention. *Professional Safety, 44*(7), 29–33.

Geller, E. S., Erikson, J. B., & Buttram, B. A. (1983). Attempts to promote residential water conservation with educational, behavioral, and engineering strategies. *Population and Environment: Behavior and Social Issues, 6,* 96–112.

Geller, E. S., Rudd, J. R., Kalsher, M. J., Streff, F. M., & Lehman, G. R. (1987). Employee-based programs to motivate safety belt use: A review of short and long-term effects. *Journal of Safety Research, 18,* 1–17.

Geller, E. S., Winett, R. A., & Everett, P. B. (1982). *Environmental preservation: New strategies for behavior change.* New York: Pergamon Press.

Gerow, J. R. (1995). *Psychology: An introduction* (4th ed.). New York: HarperCollins.

Goldstein, A. P., & Krasner, L. (1987). *Modern applied psychology.* New York: Pergamon Press.

Greene, B. F., Winett, R. A., Van Houten, R., Geller, E. S., & Iwata, B. A. (Eds.). (1987). *Behavior analysis in the community: Readings from the Journal of Applied Behavior Analysis.* Lawrence, KS: Society for the Experimental Analysis of Behavior.

Hovland, C., & Weiss, W. (1951). The influence of source credibility on communication effectiveness. *Public Opinion Quarterly, 15,* 635–650.

Howard, G. S. (1997). *Ecological psychology: Creating a more Earth-friendly human nature.* South Bend, IN: University of Notre Dame Press.

Howard, G. S. (2000). Adapting human lifestyles for the 21st century. *American Psychologist, 55,* 509–515.

Huffman, K. T., Grossnickle, W. F., Cope, J. G., & Huffman, K. P. (1995). Litter reduction: A review and integration of the literature. *Environment and Behavior, 27,* 153–183.

James, W. J. (1890). *Principles of psychology.* New York: Holt.

Katzev, R. D. (1986). The impact of commitment in promoting consumer energy conservation. In E. Monnier, G. Gaskell, P. Ester, B. Joerges, B. Lapillonne, C. Midden, & L. Puiseux (Eds.), *Consumer behavior and energy policy: An international perspective* (pp. 280–294). New York: Praeger.

Kenrick, D. T., Neuberg, S. L., & Cialdini, R. B. (1999). *Social psychology: Unraveling the mystery.* Needham Heights, MA: Allyn & Bacon.

Kohn, A. (1993). *Punishment by rewards: The trouble with gold stars, incentive plans, A's, praise and other bribes.* New York: Houghton Mifflin.

Krause, T. R. (1995). *Employee-driven systems for safe behavior: Integrating behavioral and statistical methodologies.* New York: Van Nostrand Reinhold.

Krause, T. R., Hidley, J. H., & Hodson, S. J. (1996). *The behavior-based safety process: Managing involvement for an injury-free culture* (2nd ed.). New York: Van Nostrand Reinhold.

Lahey, B. B. (2000). *Psychology: An introduction* (7th ed.). New York: McGraw-Hill.

Lauridsen, P. K. (1977). *Decreasing gasoline consumption in fleet-owned automobiles through feedback and feedback-plus-lottery.* Unpublished master's thesis, Drake University, Des Moines, IA.

Lepper, M. R., & Greene, D. (1978). *The hidden costs of reward: New perspectives on the psychology of human motivation.* Hillsdale, NJ: Erlbaum.

McClelland, L., & Cook, S. W. (1979–1980). Energy conservation effects of continuous in-home feedback in all-electric homes. *Journal of Environmental Systems, 9,* 169–173.

McKenzie-Mohr, D. (2000). Fostering sustainable behavior through community-based social marketing. *American Psychologist, 55,* 531–537.

McSween, T. E. (1995). *The values-based safety process: Improving your safety culture with a behavioral approach.* New York: Van Nostrand Reinhold.

McSween, T. E., & Matthews, G. A. (in press). Maintenance in organizational behavior management. *Journal of Occupational Behavior Management.*

Oskamp, S. (2000). A sustainable future for humanity? How can psychology help? *American Psychologist, 55,* 496–508.

Pardini, A. U., & Katzev, R. A. (1984). The effect of strength of commitment on newspaper recycling. *Journal of Environmental Systems, 13,* 245–254.

Porter, B. E., Leeming, F. C., & Dwyer, W. O. (1995). Solid waste recovery: A review of behavioral programs to increase recycling. *Environment and Behavior, 27,* 122–183.

Reichel, D. A., & Geller, E. S. (1980, March). *Group versus individual contingencies to conserve transportation energy.* Paper presented at the twenty-sixth annual meeting of the Southeastern Psychological Association, Washington, DC.

Runnion, A., Watson, J. D., & McWhorter, J. (1978). Energy savings in interstate transportation through feedback and reinforcement. *Journal of Organizational Behavior Management, 1,* 180–191.

Shippee, G. (1980). Energy consumption and conservation psychology: A review and conceptual analysis. *Environmental Management, 4,* 297–314.

Skinner, B. F. (1938). *The behavior of organisms: An experimental analysis.* Acton, MA: Copley.

Skinner, B. F. (1953). *Science and human behavior.* New York: Macmillan.

Skinner, B. F. (1971). *Beyond freedom and dignity.* New York: Alfred A. Knopf.

Skinner, B. F. (1974). *About behaviorism.* New York: Knopf.

Skinner, B. F. (1987). *Upon further reflection.* Englewood Cliffs, NJ: Prentice-Hall.

Stern, P. C. (2000). Psychology, sustainability, and the science of human-environment interactions. *American Psychologist, 55,* 523–530.

Stern, P. C., & Oskamp, S. (1987). Managing scarce environmental resources. In D. Stokols & I. Altman (Eds.), *Handbook of environmental psychology* (Vol. 2, pp. 1043–1088). New York: Wiley.

Stokols, D., & Altman, I. (Eds.). (1987). *Handbook of environmental psychology* (Vols. 1–2). New York: Wiley.

Wang, T. H., & Katzev, R. (1990). Group commitment and resource conservation: Two field experiments on promoting recycling. *Journal of Applied Social Psychology, 20,* 265–275.

Watson, D. L., & Tharp, R. G. (1997). *Self-directed behavior: Self-modification for personal adjustment* (7th ed.). Monterey, CA: Brooks/Cole.

Winett, R. A. (1980). An emerging approach to energy conservation. In D. Glenwick & L. Jason (Eds.), *Behavioral community psychology.* New York: Praeger.

Winett, R. A., Hatcher, J. W., Fort, T. R., Leckliter, I. N., Love, S. Q., Riley, A. W., & Fishback, J. F. (1982). The effects of videotape modeling and daily feedback on residential electricity conservation, home temperature and humidity, perceived comfort, and clothes worn: Winter and summer. *Journal of Applied Behavior Analysis, 24,* 71–86.

Winter, D. D. (1996). *Ecological psychology: Healing the split between planet and self.* New York: HarperCollins.

CHAPTER 35

Emerging Theoretical and Methodological Perspectives on Conservation Behavior

JOANNE VINING and ANGELA EBREO

ALTHOUGH ENVIRONMENTAL CONCERN has remained strong since the first edition of the *Handbook of Environmental Psychology* (Stokols & Altman, 1987), recent studies show that the strength of environmental concern and proenvironmental attitudes may be declining (though they are still positive). Sand (1999) reported that 69% of Americans were satisfied with governmental environment protection efforts in 1999 versus 52% in 1993. She also found that the number of individuals who felt that the government, members of the public, or businesses that were not worried enough about the environment had declined. Perhaps more important, her survey results showed that, other than recycling, self-reported conservation behaviors had not changed since 1993.

Encouraging signs are few and primarily couched in terms of slower rates of growth in consumption. For example, Brown, Renner, and Halweil (1999) noted that the growth rate of fossil fuel use and population slowed somewhat in the late 1990s, though rates were still positive. They also found strong increases in the development of alternative energy sources, but the proportion of energy generated by these sources is still miniscule. Given that environmental attitudes are still strong and most agree that conservation is a good thing, why isn't there more conservation behavior? In this chapter we review theoretical and methodological approaches to the study of conservation behavior that may help to answer this question.

THEORETICAL APPROACHES TO CONSERVATION PROBLEMS

Darley and Gilbert (1985) stated that, because of its focus on the solution of a range of important social problems, theoretical advancement in environmental psychology would most likely be represented by "theories of the middle-range." Environmental psychologists have most often been trained in another area of psychology such as cognitive, social, or experimental, and thus bring with them the methodologies and theories of their subdisciplines. This is clearly evident in the work of environmental psychologists who have studied conservation behavior.

Rather than reviewing the conservation psychology literature, we decided to examine the status of literature in terms of the range of theories that have been applied to this topic. We present the constructs from these theories and then present studies that serve as examples of how the theory has been applied to conservation behavior. We then examine additional approaches that could be used to study this phenomenon. In our discussion, we use the term *theory* more loosely to include models of conservation behavior.

LEARNING THEORY: OPERANT CONDITIONING (APPLIED BEHAVIORAL ANALYSIS)

With operant conditioning one seeks to demonstrate that behavior can be modified if one changes its antecedents and consequences. Briefly, people increase the frequency of behaviors that are reinforced and decrease the frequency of behaviors that are not reinforced. In addition, people perform behaviors when they are presented with environmental stimuli that serve as cues or facilitators of the target behaviors. Thus, researchers with a behavioral orientation seek to modify behavior by changing the antecedents and consequents of the behaviors of interest.

Examples of behavioral-based interventions to increase environmentally responsible behaviors have frequently appeared in the conservation literature. Useful general overviews of behavioral approaches are given by Geller (1986) and De Young (1993). Behavioral approaches have most often been used to encourage behavior change in the solid waste management literature. Porter, Leeming, and Dwyer (1995) reviewed this literature and found 31 published experiments, two-thirds of which reported manipulations of behavioral antecedents such as providing prompts (Hopper & Nielson, 1991), obtaining some form of commitment to perform the behavior (Burn & Oskamp, 1986; Wang & Katzev, 1990), or introducing some facilitating condition into the environment (Jacobs, Bailey, & Crews, 1984). In another third of the behaviorally oriented recycling literature, consequences were manipulated by providing informational feedback (Katzev & Mishima, 1992), rewards (Diamond & Loewy, 1991), or penalties (Levitt & Leventhal, 1986). Behavioral approaches have also been used in office, work-site, and other institutional settings (Austin, Hatfield, Grindle, & Bailey, 1993; Howard, Delgado, Miller, & Gubbins, 1993; Ludwig, Gray, & Rowell, 1998). Other recent studies using the behavioral approach include Cobern, Porter, Leeming, and Dwyer's (1995) study of residential grass recycling and Werner and colleague's (1995) studies of curbside recycling. Energy and water conservation studies have also employed operant approaches especially with respect to metering and feedback (Brandon & Lewis, 1999).

Although behavior modification approaches are effective in promoting short-term behavioral change, they are costly to use as long-term solutions to maintaining proenvironmental behavior. Several studies have indicated that the approaches by themselves do not lead to permanent changes in behavior: When the antecedents or consequences that lead to increases in the behavior are withdrawn, the behavior diminishes over time. Moreover, Deci & Ryan's (1985) research suggests that providing rewards for behavior that might otherwise have occurred through intrinsic or altruistic motivations weakens intrinsic motives and may ultimately lower the frequency of altruistic behavior.

Thus, motivating people to engage in conservation behavior solely through the use of external means is not a viable permanent solution to conservation problems. Other researchers have examined ways in which intrinsic motives can be influenced or, alternatively, how people can act in ways that are consistent with motives, values, and attitudes that are already favorable.

MOTIVATIONAL, MORAL, AND VALUE THEORIES

Several researchers have examined the categories of motives that might be related to conservation behavior. In the solid waste management literature, for instance, DeYoung (1986a; 1986b, 1996), Oskamp, Burkhardt, Schultz, Hurin, and Zelezny (1998), and Vining and her colleagues (Vining & Ebreo, 1990; Vining, Linn, & Burdge, 1992) have examined motives related to participation in various recycling programs, including curbside recycling. The categories that these researchers have developed, although they may be labeled differently, are very similar. Categories that frequently appear include the environmental or social benefits of recycling, costs or financial concerns, social constraints or pressures, and matters of personal inconvenience. Despite the empirically replicated finding that these motives are related to people's endorsements of public policies (Ebreo & Vining, 2000) and to their proenvironmental behavior, these individual studies have not really incorporated motives into a theoretical framework.

Norm Activation Model

In his norm activation model Schwartz (1968, 1977) proposed a set of factors that are related to the performance of altruistic behavior. Applications of this theory to conservation assume that conservation behavior is at least in part altruistic. According to this model, people are motivated to engage in conservation efforts when they hold personal norms that are favorable to these efforts. In addition, these personal norms are a result of two factors: (1) awareness that performing the particular behavior (or not) has certain consequences and (2) feelings of responsibility for carrying out the behavior.

Schwartz's norm activation model and several variants of it have been applied to many conservation issues. These include a composite measure of proenvironmental behavior (Widegren, 1998), recycling (Bratt, 1999; Hopper & Nielsen, 1991; Vining & Ebreo, 1992; Vining, Linn, & Burdge, 1992), support for public policies related to conservation (Stern, Dietz, & Black, 1986), off-road vehicle use (Noe, Hull, & Wellman, 1982), willingness to pay for environmentally friendly products (Guagnano, Dietz, & Stern, 1994), and ratings of the environmental aspects of consumer goods (Ebreo, Hershey, & Vining, 1999). Additional evidence that self-ascribed responsibility is related to conservation behavior has been provided by Belk, Painter, and Semenik (1981) and Kaiser and Shimoda (1999).

Geller's Model of Actively Caring

In his model of altruistic behavior, Geller (1995) proposed that people act in proenvironmental ways when they actively care about performing these altruistic behaviors. In order to actively care, however, people must be able to think beyond the satisfaction of their own immediate needs to the well-being of other people and their community. Geller also proposed that actively caring, an altruistic motive, mediates the relation between proenvironmental behavior and the five individual needs for self-esteem, belonging, personal control, self-efficacy, and optimism. In a study of Geller's assertions, Allen and Ferrand (1999) showed that the effects of personal control on self-reported proenvironmental behavior were mediated by feelings of sympathy for others (a proxy measure of actively caring).

Schwartz's Value System

Relative to the number of studies that have examined attitudes and their relation to proenvironmental behavior, the number of studies focusing on personal values as predictors of this behavior is small. Findings from an early study of values and their role in energy conservation (Neuman, 1986) suggested that values were weakly related to conservation behavior and might primarily have their effect through their influence on conservation beliefs, such as the belief that conservation behavior is effective in solving environmental problems. More recently, McCarty and Shrum (1994) found that although values do not directly influence behavior, they do affect attitudes. In fact, values are important because they are more distal determinants of attitudes (Olson & Zanna, 1993).

Schwartz (1994) recently developed a measure of the dimensions of values that can be considered to be universal across cultures. The measure assesses 10 different types of values that can ultimately be categorized into four major groups: self-transcendence, self-enhancement, openness to change, and conservatism. Self-transcendence includes values related to universalism and benevolence; self-enhancement includes values related to power and achievement; openness to change includes values related to self-direction, stimulation, and hedonism; and conservatism includes values related to tradition, conformity, and security.

Several authors have attempted to link values to attitudes by postulating that universalistic values should be related to environmental concerns, and self-enhancement values to concerns for the effects of environmental problems on the self, a more egoistic basis for performing proenvironmental behaviors. In their model of the value basis of environmental concern Stern and Dietz (1994), for example, proposed that environmental attitudes have their basis in three possible sets of values: egoistic, social-altruistic, or biospheric. Stern, Dietz, and Guagnano (1998) developed a brief inventory of values and demonstrated that the measure is predictive of environment-related political activities, consumer behavior, and economic sacrifices made to protect the environment. Additional support for these authors' assertions is found in survey research conducted by Karp (1996) and in cross-national studies conducted by Schultz and Zelezny (1998, 1999). Most recently, Stern, Diete, Abel, Guagnano, and Kalof (1999) have developed a model that integrates their value model with Schwartz's earlier theory of altruistic norms.

Lifestyles

Concerns about the effects that lifestyle choices have on the environment are not new and can be demonstrated by the emergence of terms such as *voluntary simplicity,* which refers to lifestyles that are directed toward low consumption of natural resources. However, voluntary simplicity has not often appeared in the research literature in models of conservation behavior. Perhaps this is due to the difficulty in operationalizing the construct itself. One documented measure of voluntary simplicity (Leonard-Barton, 1981) consists of endorsements of various lifestyle choices assessed by behaviors such as biking instead of using a car, making gifts rather than buying them, and growing vegetables. Despite this problem, there is evidence that voluntary simplicity lifestyles are related to proenvironmental behavior (e.g., Iwata, 1990, 1999; Leonard-Barton, 1981).

Self-Determination Theory

According to Deci and Ryan's (1985) self-determination theory, three broad types of motives underlie behavior. The types vary by the degree of self-determination involved, with intrinsic motivation indicating the highest level of self-determination. First, people may act because they choose to do so, enjoying behaviors for their own sake. Intrinsically motivated people derive satisfaction from performing the behavior itself. Second, people may act because by engaging in the behavior they can achieve positive outcomes or avoid negative ones. The behavior of extrinsically motivated persons can be regulated by their attention to external rewards or punishments or to internal feelings such as guilt, shame, or self-esteem. Third, people might act in circumstances of amotivation, in which they are unsure of the positive or negative consequences of their behavior. According to the theory, the performance of a particular behavior is a function of the level of a person's self-determination, with high levels of self-determination leading to increases in the performance of desirable behavior.

Green-Demers, Pelletier, and Menard (1997) examined the relationship between self-determination, the perceived difficulty of performing various proenvironmental behaviors, self-reported recycling behavior, purchase of environmentally friendly consumer products, and efforts to gain knowledge about environmental problems. They found that, consistent with the theory, self-determination was positively related to the frequency of proenvironmental behavior. In addition, the magnitude of this relation was greater for behaviors that were considered difficult to perform.

Self-Regulation

Other theories that fall within the motivational domain focus on the factors that determine how people regulate their own behavior by changing their cognitions, emotions, or perceptions of their behavior. In a model of how people induce themselves to perform boring or uninteresting tasks, Sansone and colleagues (Sansone & Harackiewicz, 1996; Sansone, Weir, Harpster, & Morgan, 1992) proposed that those who have reasons to persist at a boring, mundane task will create ways of making the task more interesting. That is, they reframe their experience of performing the behavior so that it is more positive.

Werner and Makela (1998) applied Sansone's self-regulatory model in a longitudinal study of recyclers. Consistent with the model, these authors found that although respondents often spoke of recycling as routine and even unpleasant, some spoke of the personal and societal benefits of performing the task, thus directing their own attention away from the mundane aspects of the task toward something positive. In addition, respondents who had positive attitudes toward recycling were also more likely to report that they had reasons for engaging in the behavior, had figured out ways of making the task interesting or easier to perform, and were continuing to recycle over time.

THEORIES OF ATTITUDE, BELIEF, OR INTENTION

Before we summarize the contributions of attitude theories to the study of conservation behavior, it is useful to note that the models presented here move beyond the simpler information models, which proposed that the provision of information would lead to changes in attitudes that in turn would lead to modifications in behavior. It is not that information does not contribute to behavior change. Rather, as suggested by several authors (e.g., De Young, 1989; Gamba & Oskamp, 1994; Nyamwange, 1996; Sivek & Hungerford, 1990; Vining & Ebreo, 1990), the type of information provided should have direct implications for the performance of the target behavior. There is also some evidence that perception of the knowledge that one has may have different relations to proenvironmental behavior than actual knowledge (P. S. Ellen, 1994). In addition, research (e.g., Moore, Murphy, & Watson, 1994) suggests that conservation knowledge is only weakly related to conservation behavior.

Many studies of the relations between environmental attitudes and proenvironmental behavior have focused on the prediction of behavior from general attitudes about the environment, that is, from environmental concern. However, measures of environmental concern have generally been found to be only weakly related to the performance of proenvironmental behaviors. For example, the New Environmental Paradigm instrument (Dunlap & VanLiere, 1978; Dunlap, VanLiere, Mertig, & Jones, 2000) assesses the general worldview that growth should be limited, that economic growth should be controlled to ensure that the environment is protected, and that humans should live in harmony with nature. Although many people endorse the items on this measure, their overall score on the instrument has small correlations with their behavior (Scott & Willits, 1994; Vining & Ebreo, 1992).

Although several nonpsychological explanations exist for the lack of a correspondence between generalized attitudes such as environmental concern and behavior, research psychologists suggest that this result can be attributed to both theoretical and methodological issues. Fishbein and Ajzen (1975), for instance, argue that measures of attitudes and behaviors should be at similar levels of specificity, and that it cannot be expected that general attitudes would be strongly related to individual behaviors. Schultz, Oskamp, and Mainieri's review (1995) of the recycling literature indicated that many studies support the assertion that relevant attitudes that are specific to recycling have consistent relations with recycling behavior, whereas general attitudes appear to be important predictors only when recycling takes greater effort.

Direct experience with attitude objects, in contrast to vicarious experience, and the existence of strong social norms can also affect the degree to which expressed attitudes match actual behaviors (Newhouse, 1990). With these considerations in mind, we now turn to the consideration of the role attitude theories have played in the conservation literature.

Theory of Reasoned Action

Fishbein and Ajzen (1975; also Ajzen & Fishbein, 1980) developed the theory of reasoned action (TRA) in an attempt to explain factors that are related to intentions to perform behaviors. Research guided by this theory has repeatedly shown that intentions, measured close to the time when the behavior is performed, are often the strongest predictors of the behavior. According to this theory, behavioral intentions are determined by two factors: attitudes toward the behavior and subjective (perceived) norms. In turn, these factors mediate beliefs. Attitudes toward the behavior mediate the effects of beliefs that performing the behavior will lead to a particular set of consequences. Subjective norms mediate the effects of beliefs that important others will approve or disapprove of the behavior.

Although the TRA has been widely applied to other types of behavior, it has received differing amounts of attention in the conservation literature. For example, in the recycling literature, Bagozzi and Dabholkar (1994) studied the effects of goal importance on attitudes and subjective norms. Goldenhar and Connell (1992–1993) and Jones (1990) provide other examples of the application of the TRA to recycling behavior. The theory has also been applied to water conservation (Kantola, Syme, & Nesdale, 1983) and to participation in programs to preserve natural areas (Luzar & Diagne, 1999).

Theory of Planned Behavior

The theory of planned behavior (TPB) is a derivative of TRA (Ajzen, 1991). In this theory, behavioral intentions are determined by three factors: attitudes toward the behavior, perceptions of social norms, and perceptions of behavioral control. As in the TRA, attitudes toward the behavior and perceived norms mediate particular sets of beliefs. The TPB differs from the TRA in the addition of perceived behavioral control as a predictor of behavioral intentions. This factor mediates the effect of beliefs that certain conditions facilitate or inhibit behavioral performance.

The TPB, in comparison to the TRA, has had somewhat less attention in the conservation literature.

However, it has been applied to studies of general proenvironmental behavior (Kaiser, Wolfing, & Fuhrer, 1999) and to individual conservation behavior (Harland, Staats, & Wilke, 1999). In a water conservation study, Lam (1999) used a modified TPB model to predict intentions to conserve water. As the model would predict, attitudes toward water conservation, perceived norms, and perceived behavior control over water use were all found to be related to the respondents' intentions.

The model has also been compared with the TRA. In a study of the predictors of composting behavior that compared the TRA, the TPB, and an environmental belief-behavior model (Taylor & Todd, 1997), the TPB exhibited greater predictive power than the other models, thus supporting the idea that perceptions of control over one's behavior is an important factor to consider. The TPB constructs have also been found to be more predictive of farmers' adoption of water-conserving technology than the TRA (Lynne, Casey, Hodges, & Rahmani, 1995).

Attitude Change

Feedback was mentioned earlier as an environmental manipulation used by applied behavior analysts. It is also true, however, that feedback can have an effect through its impact on beliefs and social norms, concepts included in the attitude theories described above. Research on recycling (e.g., Schultz, 1998) suggests that the provision of information about both individual- and group-level norms can result in beneficial behavioral changes, especially in cases where there are large discrepancies between the normative information and actual behavior.

One limitation of the attitude theory approaches, at least in terms of how they have been represented in the conservation literature, is that they have primarily focused on the cognitive aspects of attitude rather than on the emotional or affective aspects. We now turn to a discussion of those aspects of conservation behavior.

THEORIES OF EMOTION AND AFFECT

In the pursuit of cognitive structures that predict conservation behavior, emotion has largely been ignored. However, there is strong potential for both positive and negative emotions to be both predictors of conservation behavior as well as mediators of predictor variables. Smith, Haugtvedt, and Petty (1994)

proposed that, because conservation behavior is altruistic, assessments of affective reactions may play a more significant role in predicting behavior than more cognitively based attitude measures. They suggested that affect may be a strong predictor of behavior when attitudes are weak. Grob (1995) also argued for the inclusion of emotions in models of conservation behavior. Although it is likely that emotions are an important part of conservation behavior, we found few examples of studies examining the relationship between emotion and conservation attitudes or behavior.

In the mid- to late twentieth century, emotion was often viewed as a separate and often undesirable part of thought. Recently theorists have begun to conceive of emotion as an integral and adaptive part of cognition. Most emotion theorists now view emotion in terms of its adaptive and instrumental advantages (e.g., Fischer & Tangney, 1995; Frijda, 1986; Lazarus, 1991; Mandler, 1997; Scherer, 1994). We describe three functions of emotion and their importance for the understanding of conservation behavior.

Emotion and Motivation

Emotion can be a fundamental part of motivation. Consider, for example, the emotional foundations of cognitive dissonance. Originally formulated by Festinger (1957), cognitive dissonance theory proposes that people experience a negative affective state, called cognitive dissonance, when they hold two cognitions that are inconsistent. Once in this negative state, people are motivated to reduce their discomfort by either changing their cognition or their behavior. For example, if our attitudes are proenvironmental but we don't perform conservation actions, a dissonant state is created with accompanying negative emotions. One way to resolve this dissonance and relieve the negative emotion is to find a way to act in accordance with our attitudes, that is, perform a conservation action.

Aronson (1980) argued that persuasive attempts that generate dissonance through challenges to a person's self-concept or self-evaluations are more effective than persuasive communications that are merely informational in nature. Other researchers (e.g., Dickerson, Thibodeau, Aronson, & Miller, 1992) demonstrated how behavior change might be accomplished through interventions designed to cause cognitive dissonance. In a field study of water conservation, Dickerson et al. (1992) showed that a dissonance-arousing manipulation involving commitments to conserve after being reminded of one's past (non)conserving behavior led to decreases in the length of their respondents' showers. Other examples of cognitive dissonance-based interventions are found in Aitken, McMahon, Wearing, and Finlayson (1994) and Kantola, Syme, and Campbell (1984).

Kals, Schumacher, and Montada (1999) suggested that both positive and negative emotions serve as predictors of attempts to conserve resources. They found that an emotional affinity for nature was positively related to self-reported conservation behavior. They also reported that emotions such as resentment and indignation were negatively associated with conservation behavior. These studies demonstrate that an emotional affinity for nature is a significant motivational force for activities that protect nature.

Vining (1992) made a similar point, arguing that the emotional affinity for natural resources is a strong motivational force for individuals who entered careers in environmental and resource management. Kellert and Wilson (1993) have suggested that biophilia, an innate positive regard for living things, is a fundamental force in human psychology. Others (Kaplan & Kaplan, 1989; Ulrich, 1983) proposed that a positive affective affiliation with certain environments could confer adaptive advantages. Conversely, negative emotions may occur when treasured natural resources and environments are threatened. Kals et al. (1999) showed that resentment and indignation regarding others' failure to protect nature predicted conservation activities and attitudes.

The self-conscious or self-evaluative emotions, such as pride, shame, and guilt, are central to conservation motivations. However, environmental psychologists have rarely studied these emotions except as they relate indirectly to cognitive constructs such as personal or social norms. We argue that moral and social norms often function through the pressures of pride, guilt, and shame. This is illustrated by a story told to us by the recycling coordinator of Champaign, Illinois. When the curbside recycling programs first began in Champaign, recycling buckets were distributed to residents. One resident was using his bucket to wash his car when his daughter came home from school and sternly informed him that the bucket was for recycling, not washing the car. The embarrassed citizen retired the recycling bucket from car washing duty and used it for its intended purpose.

Pride, guilt, and shame are self-conscious emotions in that they result from evaluations of the self and one's behavior with respect to either internal or external standards. Thus, pride may result from compliance with a standard, and guilt or shame result from defiance of a standard. Guilt and shame are further distinguished by being based on behavior and identity, respectively. Thus, guilt results from behavior that defies an individual's values or societal norms. Shame results when an individual interprets the entire self negatively (Barrett, 1995; Fischer & Tangney, 1995).

The behavioral consequences of the negative self-evaluative emotions are of interest in finding ways to encourage conservation behavior. There are three self-control procedures associated with the emotion of guilt: One may change the target behavior, deny it, or disguise it (Lindsay-Hartz, de Rivera, & Mascolo, 1995). For example, if an individual feels guilty for not recycling, he or she might seek out ways to relieve this negative emotion by increasing recycling behavior. An individual might also relieve the guilty feelings through denial or rationalization. This can be seen in studies of recycling behavior in which individuals believe that they do not generate enough materials to make recycling worthwhile (Vining & Ebreo, 1990, 1992). Finally, a person might try to disguise her or his behavior. An example of this can be found in a story related to us by a city official. When curbside recycling programs were started in Urbana, Illinois, recycling buckets were made available to all residents. On recycling pickup days the streets were lined with these buckets, which served as prompts or reminders as well as normative indicators. One resident who had not been setting aside recycled materials left his home to discover that he was in violation of the norm. He resolved his guilt, and his dissonant state, by disguising his behavior: He removed materials from a neighbor's container and placed them in his own bucket at the curb.

These analyses of the self-evaluative emotions offer numerous avenues for promoting conservation behavior. Instilling pride, for example, might take the form of feedback on energy use or littering or persuasive messages designed to promote civic or national pride. Providing a convenient means for performing a conservation behavior (such as curbside pickup of recyclables or energy tax credits) could help to alleviate guilt. Relieving shame is more problematic since self-worth is at stake. Perhaps the best conclusion to be drawn from the literature on shame is that it is better not induced in the first place.

Structure of Emotions

A second functional role of emotion is structural or organizational. In contrast to midcentury theories suggesting that emotions and cognition were fundamentally separate mental activities, many researchers and theorists now propose that emotions are stored and retrieved in much the same way as, and along with, cognitive structures (Bower, 1981). For example, emotions associated with a particular conservation activity would be stored and retrieved along with cognitions regarding the same activity. If negative emotional experiences are associated with a particular event, information about that event would best be recalled and stored when an individual is in a congruent emotional state. Moreover, mood-incongruent information would probably not be stored or retrieved. Thus, if a conservation behavior is associated with negative emotions, information with a more positive emotional valence would likely be ignored. For example, if an individual conserves water out of fear of drought, information regarding water conservation and drought would be stored along with the associated negative affect. Information with a more optimistic outlook would be incongruent with the individual's fear-based associations and thus likely be ignored.

Conversely, complacency associated with a sense of progress on environmental issues, as was reported by Sand (1999), may inhibit fear-based appeals. However, Fredrickson (1998) has found that positive emotions result in greater openness to new information. These theories have important consequences for the study of conservation information processing and decision making but have received little attention to date.

Emotion and Communication

Finally, emotion plays a role in communication and persuasion. Emotion is an important signal of importance or relevancy (Clore, 1994; Lazarus, 1991). Also, facial expressions and animation of voice or body can indicate the importance of a message (Ekman, 1982). This function of emotion has received little attention in the conservation behavior literature. An exception is Lord's (1994) study of the effects of message source and framing (positive versus negative) on recycling behavior and attitudes. While all types and sources of messages increased recycling behavior and improved attitudes, Lord found that positively framed messages tended to engender positive attitudes and belief in the message. However, negative fear-based appeals from personal acquaintances were the most effective means of increasing recycling behavior. Also, Mobley, Painter, Untch, and Unnava (1995) found that positive affective evaluations of recycled products were associated with support for those products.

LESS FREQUENTLY USED APPROACHES

There are a number of other approaches to conservation behavior that are useful but that have been under-represented in the literature. These approaches offer a number of productive avenues for additional research.

Personality and Individual Differences

The person-centered approach has not been well represented in the conservation literature as a whole. An exception is the early work on conservation behavior that examined the relationship between locus of control and behavior. Examples of this work include Sherman, Perez, and Sherman's study (1981) of gasoline conservation, Huebner and Lipsey's study of environmental activism (1981), and Bergsma and Bergsma's study of energy conservation (1978). More recent studies (Allen & Ferrand, 1999; Hamid & Cheng, 1995; Schwepker & Cornwell, 1991; Smith-Sebasto, 1995) have continued to examine this concept and its relation to conservation behavior. Other individual difference characteristics that have been examined include dogmatism and self-perceptions (Pettus & Giles, 1987) and perceived consumer effectiveness, the belief that individual consumer actions have an effect (P. M. Ellen, Wiener, & Cobb-Walgren, 1991).

Procedural Justice Theories

In contrast to a focus on the evaluation of outcomes as central to people's reactions and behaviors in social situations, procedural justice theories focus on the fairness of the decision-making processes through which valued outcomes are allocated. Procedural justice theories fall into two main categories. Some theorists attempt to explain the beneficial effects of fair processes in terms of their role in obtaining fair and/or favorable outcomes. Other theorists take a more social normative approach and examine how people interpret procedures to have meaning for their status in important social groups or in society as a whole. According to the theories in the first category (Thibaut & Walker, 1975, 1978), perceptions of having some control or influence over decision-making processes are related to judgments of the fairness of procedures, which are then related to behavior. Theories in the second category (Lind & Tyler, 1988; Tyler, 1989; Tyler & Lind, 1992) also posit that perceptions of control are important but consider relational variables (e.g., equality of status, trust) as being valuable predictors of procedural fairness.

Procedural justice theories have not been widely applied to environmental issues. There is some evidence (Syme & Fenton, 1993) to indicate that judgments of fairness are important predictors of the public's endorsement of conservation policies. However, other researchers (e.g., Ebreo, Linn, & Vining, 1996) have shown that procedural justice concepts are not powerful predictors of the public's opinions of public policy.

Social Influence and Diffusion Models

Diffusion models are based on the notion that ideas and behavior are transmitted through communications over time between different people in a social system or network. Rogers (1983) identified five groups of people who adopt new ideas or behavior at various points in time: innovators, early adopters, early majority adopters, late majority adopters, and laggards. In order to understand dissemination, adoption, implementation, and maintenance of an innovation, researchers strive to identify the characteristics of the innovation, the populations involved, the social systems within which they are embedded, and the communication channels through which people learn about innovations (Oldenbrug, Hardcastle, & Kok, 1997).

The study of opinion leaders is an example of diffusion-based research. Opinion leaders are people who influence the opinions and behavior of others in their social system by learning about innovations and then passing information on to their friends

and/or coworkers. In a study of proenvironmental consumer behavior, Flynn and Goldsmith (1994) were able to identify a group of women who performed as opinion leaders. This group of women felt that they knew more about environmentally friendly consumer goods and engaged in proenvironmental consumer behavior more frequently than other women.

Another example of diffusion-based research is that which examines communication networks in a target population. In network studies, it is assumed that diffusion is related to the quantity of links between people in the network as well as to the characteristics of the individual people and the quality of the relationships among them. Weenig (1993) provided examples of network studies in the area of energy conservation.

Health Belief Model

The health belief model (HBM) (Janz & Becker, 1984; Rosenstock, 1990; Rosenstock & Kirscht, 1974) is similar to the attitude-intention-behavior models presented earlier. The HBM describes factors that are related to the performance of volitional behavior. However, in the case of behavior related to health and the environment, the behaviors are usually performed to avoid some negative consequence that may occur in the future. In the original HBM, the likelihood that a person would engage in a behavior is a function of two factors: perceived threat and outcome expectancies. Perceived threat is composed of two beliefs: the likelihood that negative consequences will occur and the judgment of the severity of these consequences. Outcome expectancies consist of the belief that performance of the behavior will prevent or affect the negative consequence and the belief that there are costs or barriers associated with the behavior. In more recent formulations of the model, Rosenstock (1990) added the concept of self-efficacy, the belief that one is capable of performing the behavior.

The HBM provides a useful framework for integrating several of the findings in the conservation literature, particularly studies that show a positive relationship between behavior and appraisals of the severity of environmental problems (e.g., Olsen, 1983) or perceptions of barriers to performing proenvironmental behavior (Lansana, 1992; Margai, 1997). Lindsay and Strathman (1997) applied the HBM model to the study of recycling behavior.

Consistent with the model, perceived barriers, the likelihood of negative consequences, and judgments of self-efficacy related to recycling predicted respondents' recycling behavior.

POLITICAL ACTION

So far, we have emphasized theories that focus on individual behavior change. We close this section by discussing political action, an area that could benefit from frameworks provided by existing models or theories but that has received little attention from environmental psychologists.

Kempton (1993) noted that in comparison to individual proenvironmental actions, engagement in political activities related to the environment is less common. Although many of his respondents indicated that a political candidate's stand on environmental issues affected their voting patterns, very few of the same people said that they had talked to candidates about their opinions or written a letter to the editor about these issues.

Studies that examine the factors that contribute to environment-related political action are relatively rare. Research has focused on understanding the characteristics of environmental activists (Herrera, 1992; Manzo & Weinstein, 1987), examining how perceptions of threats to the environment contribute to political action (Syme, Beven, & Sumner, 1993), examining how the attitudes of environmentalists differ from those of government officials (Vining, 1992; Vining & Ebreo, 1991; West, Lee, & Feiock, 1992), studying the types of actions taken by individuals, including voting behavior (Gill, Crosby, & Taylor, 1986), and examining protests regarding the siting of waste disposal and other types of facilities (Lober, 1995; Simmons & Stark, 1993).

In an attempt to develop a model that integrates the variables that have been shown to be determinants of environmental activism, Pelletier, Legault, and Tuson (1996) developed the Environmental Satisfaction Scale. This scale assesses satisfaction with the condition of the environment and with environmental policies. Seguin, Pelletier, and Hunsley (1998) built a model of environmental activism that related motives, perception of responsibility to prevent health risks, perceived importance of environmental problems, and knowledge of health risks to perceptions of health risks, which are seen as the most proximal determinant of activist behavior.

METHODOLOGICAL APPROACHES TO CONSERVATION PROBLEMS

Although qualitative methods have gained increasing acceptance in psychology in general, they have not often been put to work in the conservation psychology literature. This may be due to the training and/or preferences of the majority of environmental psychologists currently conducting research in this area, or it may directly be a result of the theory-testing and modeling focus of the research itself. In any case, the methods currently used in conservation research have been largely quantitative in nature (i.e., survey research methods, field studies that are primarily observational, quasi-experiments, and, in a few instances, "true" experiments that involve random assignment of participants or the units of analysis to experimental conditions). Nonetheless, there has been good progress in the development of measures of concepts that are crucial to our understanding of conservation behavior.

METHODOLOGICAL CHALLENGES

Many of the methodological concerns voiced in earlier articles on conservation behavior and environmental psychology are repeated here to reiterate the point that some of the more fundamental problems of the field are yet to be resolved.

Validity of Behavioral Self-Reports

Survey research has produced relatively robust findings regarding the relationship between behavior-specific norms, intentions, attitudes, and beliefs and self-reported conservation behavior. However, the validity of self-reported behavior as an indicator of actual behavior is still problematic (De Oliver, 1999; McGuire, 1984). In addition, some research (e.g., Obregon-Salido & Corral-Verdugo, 1997) suggests that the predictors of self-reported behavior and observed behavior are different. For example, researchers who have been able to collect both self-reports and either direct or indirect measures of recycling behavior have shown that the two assessments do not always correspond. In fact, since recycling is perceived as socially approved, respondents often systematically overestimate the extent to which they perform this behavior. Additional research on the accuracy of respondents' self-reports might result in the development of a "correction factor" by which overestimations could be adjusted. We also recommend that researchers collect direct measures of behavior if possible and that, in those instances where this is difficult, they develop innovative means of assessing behavior indirectly.

Assessing Behavior as a Dependent Variable

Another methodological issue concerns the selection of the item or items used to assess behavior, particularly when information is collected through behavioral self-reports (Heinen, 1995). The performance of a behavior can be described in several different ways. It can be represented by a dichotomous variable, in which performance is either there or it is not. One can also describe behavior in terms of the frequency, duration, or intensity with which it is performed. In a review of the recycling literature, Schultz, Oskamp, and Mainieri (1995) reported that almost all studies employed single rather than multiple measures of recycling behavior and that interventions designed to increase recycling may have had differential effects on the various behavioral measures.

The choice of a measure is not always clear-cut, and research findings can sometimes be misleading, depending on what behavioral measure is reported. For example, Lober (1996) reported that source reduction of waste was widely practiced, as over 50% of his respondents performed at least one type of waste reduction activity. However, he also reported that respondents engaged in source reduction activities infrequently and that relatively little material was saved through these activities. Thus, source reduction is not having as great an effect in diverting material from the waste stream as it might seem.

At this time, theories about conservation behavior are not developed to the point that the relations between various psychosocial variables and specific types of measures of behavior can be specified. Thus, we recommend that these relations be examined in more detail.

Single Behaviors versus Categories of Behaviors

Ambiguity in the interpretation of some research findings exists partially as a result of the choice of single behaviors versus categories of behaviors as dependent variables. Sometimes researchers have assumed that the antecedents and concomitants of a single behavior are the same as those of other, similar behaviors and have designed interventions based on one behavior and applied them to other behaviors. This assumption may be rooted in the notion that a generalized attitude toward the environment underlies all types of proenvironmental behavior. However, it has been shown that different behaviors are likely to have different antecedents and that no single dimension describes different proenvironmental behavior (Cook & Berrenberg, 1981; Oskamp et al., 1991; Stern & Oskamp, 1987). In a study of solid waste management behavior, Berger (1997) showed that recycling was not strongly related to energy conservation, water conservation, or other consumer behaviors. Similarly, Ebreo and Vining (1994) and Linn, Vining, and Feeley (1994) showed that recycling and household purchasing behavior were not as strongly related as might be assumed.

In other work, Tracy and Oskamp (1983–1984) found that people who engaged in one form of proenvironmental behavior often did not engage in others, and McKenzie-Mohr, Nemiroff, Beers, and Desmarais (1995) showed that no common set of variables predicted a wide range of proenvironmental behavior. In addition, Reams, Geaghan, and Gendron (1996) showed that "spillover or carryover effects," that is, the generalization of one type of proenvironmental behavior to a slightly related one, might be limited to closely related behavior. Other research (e.g., Thøgersen, 1999) suggests that, instead of a positive spillover effect, the performance of one proenvironmental behavior may actually inhibit the performance of other behaviors perhaps by diminishing perceptions of personal responsibility. Seligman and Finegan (1990) proposed a model of conservation behavior in which the difficulty of conserving and the public or private nature of the behavior combine to determine the likelihood of a conservation behavior occurring.

Some authors (e.g., Kaiser, 1998) have recently begun to address the problems inherent in developing a general measure of environmental behavior. Kaiser uses Rasch modeling to show how, if one takes into account differences in the difficulty of performing various proenvironmental behaviors, a general measure of proenvironmental behavior comprising several categories of behavior can be developed. Rasch modeling is a psychometric procedure that allows for inconsistency among participants' responses to the items across different domains of behavior.

Levels of Analysis

Social psychology's continuing influence can also be seen in terms of the levels researchers select to develop and examine their models and theories. Despite attempts to examine differences in conservation behavior across communities, the majority of the research conducted has examined behavior at the level of individuals. Very few approaches have included systematic analyses of variables that are related to differences in the contexts, such as the neighborhoods and communities, in which these individuals reside. Some researchers have compared contexts in a broad sense. For example, Lansana (1993) examined differences between urban and suburban settings, and Axelrod and Lehman (1993) studied motives to protect the environment among students versus community members. In addition, few studies have examined the interactions between differences at the level of individuals and differences at the level of the neighborhood or community. The recent development and more widespread availability of statistical software programs for hierarchical linear modeling provide opportunities for researchers to design studies that incorporate more than one level of analysis. To date, however, we are not aware of any conservation studies that have used this procedure.

CONCLUSION

Studies of recycling behavior dominate the conservation behavior literature, as was true in 1987. However, it appears to be relatively easy to get people to recycle by making it convenient. There are relatively few studies that attack consumption at its source by studying purchasing behavior and attempts to reduce consumption. Moreover, the studies that have examined these behaviors show discouraging results. Also, there is little relationship between reduced consumption and other conservation behaviors: Even recycling, which is conceptually close to the idea of reducing waste, has been only weakly related to reduction in consumption of products in the first place.

We have made good progress with recycling waste. Self-reported recycling is often greater than 90% (Sand, 1999). However, there is little evidence that recycling generalizes to other conservation behaviors. As noted earlier, it is possible that recycling waste may perform a compensatory inhibition role:

An individual who recycles may feel that this justifies more consumption. Does the act of recycling somehow absolve us of the duty to perform other, more demanding conservation behaviors? Or, as has been suggested, are we erroneously linking recycling with other conservation behaviors?

Relatively little attention has been given to energy and water conservation issues. This may be due to a psychology of scarcity in the developed countries in which most of the conservation behavior research has been conducted. Landfill space has become scarce, so waste reduction has received greater attention. In developed nations, energy and water are still relatively plentiful and inexpensive, so perhaps there is not yet a sense of urgency about these issues (though that may be changing as this chapter goes to press). This raises the question of the human propensity for short- versus long-term thinking. In his landmark article on the tragedy of the commons, Hardin (1968) drew attention to this issue, arguing that individual short-term gains would outweigh concerns for longer-term and societal consequences. Compounding this problem is the fact that individual action to conserve resources often accrues collective rather than individual benefits and abstract rather than concrete gains. That is, an individual who recycles or reduces energy use will typically not see concrete evidence of the results of these actions on an individual basis. From a psychological perspective, commons dilemmas can be viewed in terms of reinforcement theory. It is generally recognized that behavior with only long-term consequences, whether positive or negative, is difficult to encourage, whereas shorter-term consequences produce rapid changes in behavior. According to this analysis, because most conservation behaviors produce consequences that occur primarily in the distant future they will be altruistically based and rare.

Finally, there has been little in the way of new environmental psychological contributions to theories of conservation actions. Much of the research that we reviewed was predictive rather than explanatory and focused on concrete applications rather than overarching theory. As we noted at the beginning of this chapter, theoretically based research on conservation behavior employs theories drawn from other subdisciplines of psychology, most notably social and cognitive. This is not necessarily a disadvantage, but it surely does beg the question of the contribution that might be made by environmental psychologists to a more comprehensive theory of human-environment interactions.

REFERENCES

Aitken, C. K., McMahon, T. A., Wearing, A. J., & Finlayson, B. L. (1994). Residential water use: Predicting and reducing consumption. *Journal of Applied Social Psychology, 24,* 136–158.

Ajzen, I. (1991). The theory of planned behavior. *Organizational Behavior and Human Decision Processes, 50,* 179–211.

Ajzen, I., & Fishbein, M. (1980). *Understanding attitudes and predicting social behavior.* Englewood Cliffs, NJ: Prentice-Hall.

Allen, J. B., & Ferrand, J. L. (1999). Environmental locus of control, sympathy, and proenvironmental behavior: A test of Geller's actively caring hypothesis. *Environment and Behavior, 31,* 338–353.

Aronson, E. (1980). Persuasion via self-justification: Large commitments for small rewards. In L. Festinger (Ed.), *Retrospection on social psychology* (pp. 3–21). Oxford: Oxford University Press.

Austin, J., Hatfield, D. B., Grindle, A. C., & Bailey, J. S. (1993). Increasing recycling in office environments: The effects of specific informative cues. *Journal of Applied Behavior Analysis, 26,* 247–253.

Axelrod, L. J., & Lehman, D. R. (1993). Responding to environmental concerns: What factors guide individual action? *Journal of Environmental Psychology, 13,* 149–159.

Bagozzi, R. P., & Dabholkar, P. A. (1994). Consumer recycling goals and their effect on decisions to recycle: A means-end chain analysis. *Psychology and Marketing, 11,* 313–340.

Barrett, K. C. (1995). A functionalist approach to shame and guilt. In J. P. Tangney & K. W. Fischer (Eds.), *Self-conscious emotions* (pp. 25–63). New York: Guilford Press.

Belk, R., Painter, J., & Semenik, R. (1981). Preferred solutions to the energy crisis as a function of causal attributions. *Journal of Consumer Research, 8,* 306–312.

Berger, I. (1997). The demographics of recycling and the structure of environmental behavior. *Environment and Behavior, 29,* 515–531.

Bergsma, L. C., & Bergsma, H. M. (1978). Internal-external control and attitudes toward energy conservation and Warren Commission Report. *Journal of Psychology, 99,* 255–257.

Bower, G. H. (1981). Mood and memory. *American Psychologist, 36,* 129–148.

Brandon, G., & Lewis, A. (1999). Reducing household energy consumption: A qualitative and quantitative field study. *Journal of Environmental Psychology, 19,* 75–85.

Bratt, C. (1999). The impact of norms and assumed consequences on recycling behavior. *Environment and Behavior, 31,* 630–656.

Brown, L. R., Renner, M., & Halweil, B. (1999). *Vital Signs 1999.* New York: Norton.

Burn, S. M., & Oskamp, S. (1986). Increasing community recycling with persuasive communication and public commitment. *Journal of Applied Social Psychology, 16,* 29–41.

Clore, G. C. (1994). Why emotions are felt. In P. Ekman & R. J. Davidson (Eds.), *The nature of the emotions* (pp. 103–111). New York: Oxford University Press.

Cobern, M. K., Porter, B. E., Leeming, F. C., & Dwyer, W. O. (1995). The effect of commitment on adoption and diffusion of grass cycling. *Environment and Behavior, 27,* 213–232.

Cook, S. W., & Berrenberg, J. L. (1981). Approaches to encouraging conservation behavior: A review and conceptual framework. *Journal of Social Issues, 37,* 73–107.

Darley, J. M., & Gilbert, D. T. (1985). Social psychological aspects of environmental psychology. In G. Lindzey & E. Aronson (Eds.), *Handbook of social psychology* (Vol. 2, 3rd ed., pp. 949–991). New York: Random House.

Deci, E. L., & Ryan, R. M. (1985). *Intrinsic motivation and self-determination in human behavior.* New York: Plenum Press.

De Oliver, M. (1999). Attitudes and inaction: A case study of the manifest demographics of urban water conservation. *Environment and Behavior, 31,* 372–394.

De Young, R. (1986a). Some psychological aspects of recycling: The structure of conservation satisfactions. *Environment and Behavior, 18,* 435–449.

De Young, R. (1986b). Encouraging environmentally appropriate behavior: The role of intrinsic motivation. *Journal of Environmental Systems, 15,* 281–291.

De Young, R. (1989). Exploring the difference between recyclers and non-recyclers: The role of information. *Journal of Environmental Systems, 18,* 341–351.

De Young, R. (1993). Changing behavior and making it stick: The conceptualization and management of conservation behavior. *Environment and Behavior, 25,* 485–505.

De Young, R. (1996). Some psychological aspects of reduced consumption behavior: The role of intrinsic satisfaction and competence motivation. *Environment and Behavior, 28,* 358–409.

Diamond, W. D., & Loewy, B. Z. (1991). Effects of probabilistic rewards on recycling attitudes and behavior. *Journal of Applied Social Psychology, 21,* 1590–1607.

Dickerson, C. A., Thibodeau, R., Aronson, E., & Miller, D. (1992). Using cognitive dissonance to encourage water conservation. *Journal of Applied Social Psychology, 22,* 841–854.

Dunlap, R. E., & VanLiere, K. D. (1978). The "new environmental paradigm": A proposed instrument and preliminary results. *Journal of Environmental Education, 9,* 10–19.

Dunlap, R. E., VanLiere, K. D., Mertig, A. G., & Jones, R. E. (2000). Measuring endorsement of the new ecological paradigm: A revised NEP scale. *Journal of Social Issues, 56,* 425–442.

Ebreo, A., Hershey, J., & Vining, J. (1999). Reducing solid waste: Linking recycling to environmentally responsible consumerism. *Environment and Behavior, 31,* 107–135.

Ebreo, A., Linn, N., & Vining, J. (1996). The impact of procedural justice on opinions of public policy: Solid waste management as an example. *Journal of Applied Social Psychology, 26,* 1259–1285.

Ebreo, A., & Vining, J. (1994). Conservation-wise consumers: Recycling and household shopping as ecological behavior. *Journal of Environmental Systems, 23,* 109–131.

Ebreo, A., & Vining, J. (2000). Motives as predictors of the public's attitudes toward solid waste issues. *Environmental Management, 25,* 153–168.

Ekman, P. (1982). *Emotion in the human face.* Cambridge: Cambridge University Press.

Ellen, P. M., Wiener, J. L., & Cobb-Walgren, C. (1991). The role of perceived consumer effectiveness in motivating environmentally conscious behaviors. *Journal of Public Policy and Marketing, 10,* 102–117.

Ellen, P. S. (1994). Do we know what we need to know? Objective and subjective knowledge effects on pro-ecological behaviors. *Journal of Business Research, 30,* 43–52.

Festinger, L. (1957). *A theory of cognitive dissonance.* Stanford, CA: Stanford University Press.

Fischer, K. W., & Tangney, J. P. (1995). Self-conscious emotions and the affect revolution: Framework and overview. In J. P. Tangney & K. W. Fischer (Eds.), *Self-conscious emotions* (pp. 3–24). New York: Guilford Press.

Fishbein, M., & Ajzen, I. (1975). *Belief, attitude, intention and behavior: An introduction to theory and research.* Reading, MA: Addison-Wesley.

Flynn, L. R., & Goldsmith, E. (1994). Opinion leadership in green consumption: An exploratory study. *Journal of Social Behavior and Personality, 9,* 543–553.

Fredrickson, B. L. (1998). What good are positive emotions? *Review of General Psychology, 2,* 300–319.

Frijda, N. H. (1986). *The emotions.* Cambridge: Cambridge University Press.

Gamba, R. J., & Oskamp, S. (1994). Factors influencing community residents' participation in commingled curbside recycling programs. *Environment and Behavior, 26,* 587–612.

Geller, E. S. (1986). Prevention of environmental problems. In B. A. Edelstein & L. Michelson (Eds.), *Handbook of prevention* (pp. 361–383). New York: Plenum Press.

Geller, E. S. (1995). Actively caring for the environment: An integration of behaviorism and humanism. *Environment and Behavior, 27,* 184–195.

Gill, J. D., Crosby, L. A., & Taylor, J. R. (1986). Ecological concern, attitudes, and social norms in voting behavior. *Public Opinion Quarterly, 50,* 537–554.

Goldenhar, L. M., & Connell, C. M. (1992–1993). Understanding and predicting recycling behavior: An application of the theory of reasoned action. *Journal of Environmental Systems, 22,* 91–103.

Green-Demers, I., Pelletier, L. G., & Menard, S. (1997). The impact of behavioural difficulty on the saliency of the association between self-determined motivation and environmental behaviours. *Canadian Journal of Behavioural Science, 29,* 157–166.

Grob, A. (1995). A structural model of environmental attitudes and behaviour. *Journal of Environmental Psychology, 15,* 209–220.

Guagnano, G. A., Dietz, T., & Stern, P. C. (1994). Willingness to pay for public goods: A test of the contribution model. *Psychological Science, 5,* 411–415.

Hamid, P. N., & Cheng, S. (1995). Predicting antipollution behavior: The role of molar behavioral intentions, past behavior, and locus of control. *Environment and Behavior, 27,* 679–698.

Hardin, G. H. (1968). The tragedy of the commons. *Science, 162,* 1243–1248.

Harland, P., Staats, H., & Wilke, H. A. M. (1999). Explaining proenvironmental intention and behavior by personal norms and the theory of planned behavior. *Journal of Applied Social Psychology, 29,* 2505–2528.

Heinen, J. T. (1995). A review of, and research suggestions for, solid-waste management issues: The predicted role of incentives in promoting conservation behavior. *Environmental Conservation, 22,* 157–166.

Herrera, M. (1992). Environmentalism and political participation: Toward a new system of social beliefs and values? *Journal of Applied Social Psychology, 22,* 657–676.

Hopper, J. R., & Nielson, J. M. (1991). Recycling as altruistic behavior: Normative and behavioral strategies to expand participation in a community recycling program. *Environment and Behavior, 23,* 195–220.

Howard, G. S., Delgado, E., Miller, D., & Gubbins, S. (1993). Transforming values into action: Ecological preservation through energy conservation. *The Counseling Psychologist, 21,* 582–596.

Huebner, R. B., & Lipsey, M. W. (1981). The relationship of three measures of locus of control to environmental activism. *Basic and Applied Social Psychology, 2,* 45–58.

Iwata, O. (1990). Relationships of proenvironmental attitudes to wildernism-urbanism and pro-preservation attitudes toward historical heritages. *Psychologia, 33,* 203–211.

Iwata, O. (1999). Perceptual and behavioral correlates of voluntary simplicity lifestyles. *Social Behavior and Personality, 27,* 379–386.

Jacobs, H. E., Bailey, J. S., & Crews, J. I. (1984). Development and analysis of a community-based resource recovery program. *Journal of Applied Behavior Analysis, 17,* 127–145.

Janz, N. K., & Becker, M. H. (1984). The health belief model: A decade later. *Health Education Quarterly, 11,* 1–47.

Jones, R. E. (1990). Understanding paper recycling in an institutionally supportive setting: An application of the theory of reasoned action. *Journal of Environmental Systems, 19,* 307–321.

Kaiser, F. G. (1998). A general measure of ecological behavior. *Journal of Applied Social Psychology, 28,* 395–422.

Kaiser, F. G., & Shimoda, T. A. (1999). Responsibility as a predictor of ecological behaviour. *Journal of Environmental Psychology, 19,* 243–253.

Kaiser, F. G., Wolfing, S, & Fuhrer, U. (1999). Environmental attitude and ecological behaviour. *Journal of Environmental Psychology, 19,* 1–19.

Kals, E., Schumacher, D., & Montada, L. (1999). Emotional affinity toward nature as a motivational basis to protect nature. *Environment and Behavior, 31,* 178–202.

Kantola, S. J., Syme, G. J., & Campbell, N. A. (1984). Cognitive dissonance and energy conservation. *Journal of Applied Psychology, 69,* 416–421.

Kantola, S. J., Syme, G. J., & Nesdale, A. R. (1983). The effects of appraised severity and efficacy in promoting water conservation: An informational analysis. *Journal of Applied Social Psychology, 13,* 164–182.

Kaplan, R., & Kaplan, S. (1989). *The experience of nature.* Cambridge: Cambridge University Press.

Karp, D. G. (1996). Values and their effect on proenvironmental behavior. *Environment and Behavior, 28,* 111–133.

Katzev, R. D., & Mishima, H. R. (1992). The use of posted feedback to promote recycling. *Psychological Reports, 71,* 259–264.

Kellert, S. R., & Wilson, E. O. (1993). *The biophilia hypothesis.* Washington DC: Island Press.

Kempton, W. (1993). Will public environmental concern lead to action on global warming? *Annual Review of Energy and the Environment, 18,* 217–245.

Lam, S. (1999). Predicting intentions to conserve water from the theory of planned behavior, perceived moral obligation, and perceived water right. *Journal of Applied Social Psychology, 29,* 1058–1071.

Lansana, F. M. (1992). Distinguishing potential recyclers from nonrecyclers: A basis for developing recycling strategies. *Journal of Environmental Education, 23,* 16–23.

Lansana, F. M. (1993). A comparative analysis of curbside recycling behavior in urban and suburban communities. *Professional Geographer, 45,* 169–179.

Lazarus, R. S. (1991). *Emotion and adaptation.* New York: Oxford University Press.

Leonard-Barton, D. (1981). Voluntary simplicity lifestyles and energy conservation. *Journal of Consumer Research, 8,* 243–252.

Levitt, L., & Leventhal, G. (1986). Litter reduction: How effective is the New York State bottle bill? *Environment and Behavior, 18,* 467–479.

Lind, E. A., & Tyler, T. R. (1988). *The social psychology of procedural justice.* New York: Plenum Press.

Lindsay, J. J., & Strathman, A. (1997). Predictors of recycling behavior: An application of a modified health belief model. *Journal of Applied Social Psychology, 27,* 1799–1823.

Lindsay-Hartz, J., de Rivera, J., & Mascolo, M. F. (1995). Differentiating guilt and shame and their effect on motivation. In J. P. Tangney & K. W. Fischer (Eds.), *The self-conscious emotions* (pp. 274–300). New York: Guilford Press.

Linn, N., Vining, J., & Feeley, P. A. (1994). Toward a sustainable society: Waste minimization through environmentally conscious consuming. *Journal of Applied Social Psychology, 26,* 1259–1285.

Lober, D. J. (1995). Why protest? Public behavioral and attitudinal response to siting a waste disposal facility. *Policy Studies Journal, 23,* 499–518.

Lober, D. J. (1996). Municipal solid waste policy and public participation in household source reduction. *Waste Management and Research, 14,* 125–143.

Lord, K. R. (1994). Motivating recycling behavior: A quasi-experimental investigation of message and source strategies. *Psychology and Marketing, 11,* 341–358.

Ludwig, T. D., Gray, T. W., & Rowell, A. (1998). Increasing recycling in academic buildings: A systematic replication. *Journal of Applied Behavior Analysis, 31,* 683–686.

Luzar, E. J., & Diagne, A. (1999). Participation in the next generation of agriculture conservation programs: The role of environmental attitudes. *Journal of Socio-Economics, 28,* 335–349.

Lynne, G. D., Casey, C. F., Hodges, A., & Rahmani, M. (1995). Conservation technology adoption decisions and the theory of planned behavior. *Journal of Economic Psychology, 16,* 581–598.

Mandler, G. (1997). *Human nature explored.* New York: Oxford University Press.

Manzo, L. C., & Weinstein, N. D. (1987). Behavioral commitment to environmental protection: A study of active and nonactive members of the Sierra Club. *Environment and Behavior, 19,* 673–694.

Margai, F. L. (1997). Analyzing changes in waste reduction behavior in a low-income urban community following a public outreach program. *Environment and Behavior, 29,* 769–792.

McCarty, J. A., & Shrum, L. J. (1994). The recycling of solid wastes: Personal values, value orientations, and attitudes about recycling as antecedents of recycling behavior. *Journal of Business Research, 30,* 53–62.

McGuire, R. H. (1984). Recycling: Great expectations and garbage outcomes. *American Behavioral Scientist, 28,* 93–114.

McKenzie-Mohr, D., Nemiroff, L. S., Beers, L., & Desmarais, S. (1995). Determinants of responsible environmental behavior. *Journal of Social Issues, 51,* 139–156.

Mobley, A. S., Painter, T. S., Untch, E. M., & Unnava, H. R. (1995). Consumer evaluation of recycled products. *Psychology and Marketing, 12,* 165–176.

Moore, S., Murphy, M., & Watson, R. (1994). A longitudinal study of domestic water conservation behavior. *Population and Environment, 16,* 175–189.

Neuman, K. (1986). Personal values and commitment to energy conservation. *Environment and Behavior, 18,* 53–74.

Newhouse, N. (1990). Implications of attitude and behavior research for environmental conservation. *Journal of Environmental Education, 22,* 26–32.

Noe, F. P., Hull, R. B., & Wellman, J. D. (1982). Normative response and norm activation among ORV users within a seashore environment. *Leisure Sciences, 5,* 127–142.

Nyamwange, M. (1996). Public perception of strategies for increasing participation in recycling programs. *Journal of Environmental Education, 27,* 19–22.

Obregon-Salido, F. J., & Corral-Verdugo, V. (1997). Systems of beliefs and environmental conservation behavior in a Mexican community. *Environment and Behavior, 29,* 213–235.

Oldenburg, B., Hardcastle, D. M., & Kok, G. (1997). Diffusion of innovations. In K. Glanz, F. M. Lewis, B. K. Rimer (Eds.), *Health behavior and health education: Theory, research and practice* (pp. 270–286). San Francisco: Jossey-Bass.

Olsen, M. E. (1983). Public acceptance of consumer energy conservation strategies. *Journal of Economic Psychology, 4,* 183–196.

Olson, J., & Zanna, M. (1993). Attitudes and attitude change. *Annual Review of Psychology, 44,* 117–154.

Oskamp, S., Burkhardt, R. L., Schultz, P. W., Hurin, S., & Zelezny, L. (1998). Predicting three dimensions of residential curbside recycling: An observational study. *Journal of Environmental Education, 29,* 37–42.

Oskamp, S., Harrington, M. J., Edwards, T. C., Sherwood, D. L., Okuda, S. M., & Swanson, D. C. (1991). Factors influencing household recycling behavior. *Environment and Behavior, 23,* 494–519.

Pelletier, L. G., Legault, L. R., & Tuson, K. M. (1996). The environmental satisfaction scale: A measure of satisfaction with local environmental conditions and government environmental policies. *Environment and Behavior, 28,* 5–26.

Pettus, A. M., & Giles, M. B. (1987). Personality characteristics and environmental attitudes. *Population and Environment, 9,* 127–137.

Porter, B. E., Leeming, F. C., & Dwyer, W. O. (1995). Solid waste recovery: A review of behavioral programs to increase recycling. *Environment and Behavior, 27,* 122–152.

Reams, M. A., Geaghan, J. P., & Gendron, R. C. (1996). The link between recycling and litter: A field study. *Environment and Behavior, 28,* 92–110.

Rogers, E. M. (1983). *The diffusion of innovations* (3rd ed.). New York: Free Press.

Rosenstock, I. M. (1990). The health belief model: Explaining health behavior through expectancies. In K. Glanz, F. M. Lewis, & B. K. Rimer (Eds.), *Health behavior and health education* (pp. 39–62. San Francisco: Jossey-Bass.

Rosenstock, I. M., & Kirscht, J. P. (1974). The health belief model and personal health behavior. *Health Education Monographs, 2,* 470–473.

Sand, L. K. (1999, April). 1999 Earth Day poll: Environmental concern wanes. *The Gallup Poll Monthly,* 38–44.

Sansone, C., & Harackiewicz, J. M. (1996). "I don't feel like it": The function of interest in self-regulation. In L. Martin & A. Tesser (Eds.), *Striving and feeling: Interactions between goals and effect* (pp. 203–228). Mahwah, NJ: Erlbaum.

Sansone, C., Weir, C., Harpster, L., & Morgan, C. (1992). Once a boring task always a boring task? Interest as a self-regulatory mechanism. *Journal of Personality and Social Psychology, 63,* 379–390.

Scherer, K. R. (1994). Emotion serves to decouple stimulus and response. In P. Ekman & R. J. Davidson (Eds.), *The Nature of Emotion* (pp. 127–130). New York: Oxford University Press.

Schultz, P. W. (1998). Changing behavior with normative feedback interventions: A field experiment on curbside recycling. *Basic and Applied Social Psychology, 21,* 25–36.

Schultz, P. W., Oskamp, S., & Mainieri, T. (1995). Who recycles and when? A review of personal and situational factors. *Journal of Environmental Psychology, 15,* 105–121.

Schultz, P. W., & Zelezny, L. (1998). Values and proenvironmental behavior: A five-country survey. *Journal of Cross-Cultural Psychology, 29,* 540–558.

Schultz, P. W., & Zelezny, L. (1999). Values as predictors of environmental attitudes: Evidence for consistency across 14 countries. *Journal of Environmental Psychology, 19,* 255–265.

Schwartz, S. H. (1968). Words, deeds, and the perception of consequences and responsibility in action situations. *Journal of Personality and Social Psychology, 10,* 232–242.

Schwartz, S. H. (1977). Normative influences on altruism. In L. Berkowitz (Ed.), *Advances in experimental social psychology* (Vol. 10, pp. 221–279). New York: Academic Press.

Schwartz, S. H. (1994). Are there universal aspects in the structure and content of human values? *Journal of Social Issues, 50,* 19–45.

Schwepker, C. H., & Cornwell, T. B. (1991). An examination of ecologically concerned consumers and their intention to purchase ecologically packaged products. *Journal of Public Policy & Marketing, 10,* 77–101.

Scott, D., & Willits, F. K. (1994). Environmental attitudes and behavior: A Pennsylvania survey. *Environment and Behavior, 26,* 239–260.

Seguin, C., Pelletier, L. G., & Hunsley, J. (1998). Toward a model of environmental activism. *Environment and Behavior, 30,* 628–652.

Seligman, C., & Finegan, J. E. (1990). A two-factor model of energy and water conservation. In J. Edwards & R. Tindale (Eds.), *Social influence processes and prevention* (pp. 279–299). New York: Plenum Press.

Sherman, M. F., Perez, M. E., & Sherman, N. C. (1981). Motorists' locus of control, behavioral intentions regarding gasoline conservation, and confidence in measures to promote it. *Perceptual and Motor Skills, 52,* 115–118.

Simmons, J., & Stark, N. (1993). Backyard protest: Emergence, expansion, and persistence of a local hazardous waste controversy. *Policy Studies Journal, 21,* 470–491.

Sivek, D. J., & Hungerford, H. (1990). Predictors of responsible behavior in members of three Wisconsin conservation organizations. *Journal of Environmental Education, 21,* 35–40.

Smith, S. M., Haugtvedt, C. P., & Petty, R. E. (1994). Attitudes and recycling: Does the measurement of affect enhance behavioral prediction? *Psychology and Marketing, 11,* 359–374.

Smith-Sebasto, N. J. (1995). The effects of an environmental studies course on selected variables related to environmentally responsible behavior. *Journal of Environmental Education, 26,* 30–34.

Stern, P. C., & Dietz, T. (1994). The value basis of environmental concern. *Journal of Social Issues, 56,* 121–145.

Stern, P. C., Dietz, T., Abel, T., Guagnano, G. A., & Kalof, L. (1999). A value-belief-norm theory of support for social movements: The case of environmentalism. *Human Ecology Review, 6,* 81–97.

Stern, P. C., Dietz, T., & Black, J. S. (1986). Support for environmental protection: The role of moral norms. *Population and Environment, 8,* 204–222.

Stern, P. C., Dietz, T., & Guagnano, G. A. (1998). A brief inventory of values. *Educational and Psychological Measurement, 58,* 984–1001.

Stern, P. C., & Oskamp, S. (1987). Managing scarce environmental resources. In D. Stokols & I. Altman (Eds.), *Handbook of environmental psychology* (Vol. 2, pp. 1043–1088). New York: Wiley.

Stokols, D., & Altman, I. (Eds.). (1987). *Handbook of environmental psychology* (Vols. 1–2). New York: Wiley.

Syme, G. J., Beven, C. E., & Sumner, N. R. (1993). Motivation for reported involvement in local wetland preservation: The roles of knowledge, disposition, problem assessment, and arousal. *Environment and Behavior, 25,* 586–606.

Syme, G. J., & Fenton, D. M. (1993). Perceptions of equity and procedural preferences for water allocation decisions. *Society and Natural Resources, 6,* 347–360.

Taylor, S., & Todd, P. (1997). Understanding the determinants of consumer composting behavior. *Journal of Applied Social Psychology, 27,* 602–628.

Thibaut, J., & Walker, L. (1975). *Procedural justice: A psychological analysis.* Hillsdale, NJ: Erlbaum.

Thibaut, J., & Walker, L. (1978). A theory of procedure. *California Law Review, 66,* 541–566.

Thøgersen, J. (1999). Spillover processes in the development of a sustainable consumption pattern. *Journal of Economic Psychology, 20,* 53–81.

Tracy, A. P., & Oskamp, S. (1983–1984). Relationships among ecologically responsible behaviors. *Journal of Environmental Systems, 13,* 115–126.

Tyler, T. R. (1989). The psychology of procedural justice: A test of the group value model. *Journal of Personality and Social Psychology, 57,* 830–838.

Tyler, T. R., & Lind, E. A. (1992). A relational model of authority in groups. In L. Berkowitz (Ed.), *Advances in experimental social psychology* (Vol. 25, pp. 115–191). New York: Academic Press.

Ulrich, R. S. (1983). Aesthetic and affective response to natural environment. In I. Altman & J. F. Wohlwill (Eds.), *Behavior and the natural environment* (pp. 85–126). New York: Plenum Press.

Vining, J. (1992). Environmental emotions and decisions: A comparison of the responses and expectations of forest managers, an environmental group, and the public. *Environment and Behavior, 24,* 3–34.

Vining, J., & Ebreo, A. (1990). What makes a recycler? A comparison of recyclers and non-recyclers. *Environment and Behavior, 22,* 55–73.

Vining, J., & Ebreo, A. (1991). Are you thinking what I think you are? A study of actual and estimated goal priorities and decisions of resource managers, environmentalists, and the public. *Society and Natural Resources, 4,* 177–196.

Vining, J., & Ebreo, A. (1992). Predicting recycling behavior from global and specific environmental attitudes and changes in recycling opportunities. *Journal of Applied Social Psychology, 22,* 1580–1607.

Vining, J., Linn, N., & Burdge, R. J. (1992). Why recycle? A comparison of recycling motivations in four communities. *Environmental Management, 16,* 785–797.

Wang, T. H., & Katzev, R. D. (1990). Group commitment and resource conservation: Two field experiments on promoting recycling. *Journal of Applied Social Psychology, 20,* 265–275.

Weenig, M. W. H. (1993). The strength of weak and strong communication ties in a communication information program. *Journal of Applied Social Psychology, 23,* 1712–1731.

Werner, C. M., & Makela, E. (1998). Motivations and behaviors that support recycling. *Journal of Environmental Psychology, 18,* 373–386.

Werner, C. M., Turner, J., Shipman, K., Twitchell, F. S., Dickson, B. R., Bruschke, G. V., & Von Bismarck, W. B.

(1995). Commitment, behavior, and attitude change: An analysis of voluntary recycling. *Journal of Environmental Psychology, 15,* 197–208.

West, J. P., Lee, S. J., & Feiock, F. C. (1992). Managing municipal waste: Attitudes and opinions of administrators and environmentalists. *Environment and Behavior, 24,* 111–133.

Widegren, O. (1998). The new environmental paradigm and personal norms. *Environment and Behavior, 30,* 75–100.

CHAPTER 36

Contamination:
The Invisible Built Environment

MICHAEL R. EDELSTEIN

WHEN KURT LEWIN FIRST conceptualized the region of free movement offered by different life contexts, he was reflecting upon his experiences as a soldier in World War I. At the front, one could not stand up without drawing sniper fire. In contrast, behind the lines, soldiers faced an incredible lack of restraint on their behavior. Clearly different conditions afforded the person widely variant degrees of freedom (Heider, 1959). Erving Goffman would later take the notions of front and back region to symbolize being in the public eye versus enjoying the freedoms of privacy; home, where many exercise the greatest control over intrusions from others, offers perhaps our most protected region of free movement (Goffman, 1971).

The field of environmental psychology emerged during the environmental era of the late 1960s and early 1970s, contemporary to the U.S. National Environmental Policy Act's call for the study of newly recognized environmental impacts using a "systematic, interdisciplinary approach which will insure the integrated use of the natural and social sciences and the environmental design arts."[1] Yet its dominant roots were shaped by the humanistic bias of psychology, socially constructed in the manner of the front and back region as a human and social sphere and organized principally around the indulgence of self afforded by the correct setting (i.e., meeting human needs through a responsive built environment). As a result, the field has shown a historic disinterest in the crisis of the physical environment, the lost integrity of the natural systems upon which human life depends and their replacement by a largely invisible synthetic "post-natural world" that has come to threaten our health and the health of our surround.[2] This chapter addresses part of this realm, the *contaminated* surround. Contamination represents a second invisible layer of the built environment, "socially constructed" around houses and communities from undesirable baggage, the left overs of the modern way of life. Contamination might be microscopic, affect a room in a building, a single home or workplace, a neighborhood, a municipality, a bioregion (i.e., a watershed), a contrived catchment area, or the entire hemisphere or globe. Small isolated pollution events can be unique or can reflect a broad pattern repeated in many places. I focus here on one of these contexts, "contaminated communities," defined as "any residential area located within

[1] The National Environmental Policy Act of 1969 as amended in July and August 1975, Title 1, Sec. 101(c)a.

[2] "Post-natural world" is Kroll-Smith, Brown, and Gunter's (2000) homage to McKibben's *End of Nature*. Although the author's do not clearly define their terms, we can presume that the postnatural world reflects McKibben's haunting observations about how human interference has intruded into every vestige of what used to be thought of as nature, so that we can no longer delude ourselves that such an unspoiled realm exists. Moreover, the postnatural world not only is tainted with human finger prints but has been rendered hazardous to us, to other forms of life, and even to its own continuing viability. In my definition, the postnatural world is therefore not merely a synthetic world but a contaminated world as well.

or proximate to the identified boundaries for a known exposure to pollution" (Edelstein, 1988, forthcoming; for a discussion of unbounded contaminations, see Edelstein, forthcoming).

Scholarly attention to the psychosocial impacts of toxic exposure in such communities dates from the efforts of Levine to document and analyze the Love Canal disaster (Levine, 1982). Reflecting the discovery that schools and residences had been built over an old canal filled with toxic wastes, this heavily publicized event signaled the realization that toxic exposure can destroy a neighborhood (see also Fowlkes & Miller, 1982, 1987; L. Gibbs, 1982b, 1998; Mazur, 1998). With the subsequent publication of Edelstein's *Contaminated Communities,* in 1988, a basic theory of contamination was proposed and demonstrated in the case study of Legler, a section of Jackson, New Jersey, where groundwater supplying wells used by residents of a subdivision had been contaminated by leachate from the nearby municipal landfill (Edelstein, 1988). The emerging field originally drew upon the literature on natural disasters, although there was little that was natural about the human-caused Buffalo Creek flood, the subject of model litigation and studies of stress and trauma influential for later consideration of toxic events (Erikson, 1976; Gleser, Green, & Winget, 1981; Green, Grace, et al., 1990; Green, Lindy, et al., 1990; Titchner & Kapp, 1976). Other early and influential works in the field included Vyner's analysis of the impacts of radioactive exposure, with a particular emphasis upon the resulting medical uncertainties (Vyner, 1988); P. Brown and Mikkelson's demonstration of the "popular epidemiology" employed by parents who discovered a potential cause of their children's leukemia in the industrial solvents found in Woburn, Massachusetts's groundwater (P. Brown & Mikkelson, 1990, 1999);[3] Kroll-Smith and Couch's description of social turmoil in the Pennsylvania coal town of Centralia, eventually abandoned because of high carbon monoxide concentrations, potential explosions, and unpredictable subsidence caused by a subterranean fire started in a nearby landfill (Kroll-Smith & Couch, 1990); and Picou and Gill's longitudinal study of the stressful consequences for both native and nonnative Alaskans of the 1986 oil spill of

the Exxon *Valdez* into Prince William Sound in Alaska (see Picou, Gill, & Cohen, 1997).

It has been common to distinguish between acute events, such as the Exxon *Valdez* spill, and chronic events, such as Love Canal and Legler. An acute event may result in immediate death and destruction, whereas a chronic event is more often associated with slow and insidious effects. However, regardless of how sudden the event, toxic disasters are invariably followed by chronic and protracted impacts. Thus, the "accident" at Three Mile Island, which caused thousands of residents from areas nearby to Harrisburg, Pennsylvania, to temporarily abandon their homes in the wake of a governor's advisory for pregnant women, entailed continuing effects evidenced in residents' fear of the subsequent restart of the twin reactor (see, for example, Goldsteen & Schorr, 1991; Sorensen, Soderstrom, Copenhaver, Carnes, & Bolin, 1987). The worst acute toxic incident to date globally, the release of methyl icocyanate in 1984 from the Union Carbide plant over a sleeping Bhopal, India, killed thousands and affected thousands more whose lives have continued to be haunted by their injuries (see Bogard, 1989; Edelstein, 1995; Shrivastava, 1987; Wilkins, 1987). And the world's worst nuclear disaster, at Chernobyl in 1985, unleashed continuing consequences felt around the northern hemisphere but particularly by victims from the former Soviet Union (see Edelstein, 1995; Ginzburg, 1993; Marples, 1988, V. Rich, 1991; Schroeder, 1990). Events at Times Beach, Missouri, where flooding spread prior dioxin contamination thoughout the community, resulting in permanent relocation of residents, mixed the categories of acute and chronic as well as natural and caused (see Miller, 1984; Reko, 1984; Smith, Robins, Prybeck, Goldring, & Solomon, 1986).

These incidents from the late 1970s through the mid-1980s, served as "signal events" (Slovic, 1990), calling society's attention to a novel pattern that Kai Erikson later termed a "new species of trouble" (Erikson, 1991, 1994). Such events are hardly rare even if people are loath to treat them as commonplace; there is exposure to toxic and radioactive materials at home and in the workplace, as consumers, and even in the act of meeting the most basic needs. Reflecting but a drop in the toxic bucket, some 600,000 contaminated sites in the United States were identified by the former Office of Technology Assessment. Of these, 1,266 have been designated or proposed by the Environmental Protection Agency

---

[3] This incident gained notoriety through the best selling book *A Civil Action,* made into a popular movie about the lawsuit filed on residents' behalf (Harr, 1995).

(EPA) for priority cleanup under the Superfund program established through the 1980 Comprehensive Environmental Response, Compensation, and Liability Act (CERCLA), with another 41,000 sites under review. Another additional 400,000 municipal landfills, 100,000 liquid waste impoundments, millions of septic tanks, hundreds of thousands of deep-well injection sites, and some 300,000 leaking underground gasoline storage tanks threaten groundwater, much as hundreds of municipal and hazardous waste incinerators and millions of other combustion sources threaten the air. More than abstract statistics, such numbers reflect the likelihood of widespread human exposures. For example, it is estimated that one in six (i.e., some 40 million) Americans live within 4 miles of a chemical dump or suspected other hazardous waste site.[4]

A new and shared identity defines a community of interest for those living within designated boundaries of contamination, or more broadly, within the resulting "risk perception shadow" (Stoffel at al., 1991). Bounding a contamination event presents an aura of certainty and manageability on an otherwise ambiguous situation and often more represents political expediency than scientific precision. Thus, at Love Canal, a "habitability study" was done to justify resettling part of the area from which residents had been moved. Instead, the study redrew boundaries of exposure, suggesting that some residents had been relocated unnecessarily, while others continued to occupy dangerous areas (New York State Department of Health, 1988). In Legler, NJ, boundaries changed over time so that people who thought they were safe might suddenly find themselves within the contaminated zone. And, in the Essex County, New Jersey, radium-contaminated soil case, the boundaries of the affected area have been continually expanding for more than a decade (Edelstein, 1988, 1991, forthcoming; Edelstein & Makofske, 1998). Thus, a temporal dimension to contamination exists beyond the spatial. Designation as a "Superfund site" in the United States not only sets boundaries of suspected contamination but also draws the affected community into a predetermined sequence of events commonly lasting 20 years before some form of "cleanup" has been achieved, to be followed

by some 30 years of monitoring (U.S. General Accounting Office, 1997). This schedule applies only to communities "fortunate" enough to have their sites listed for priority cleanup. The temporal spectrum involved can encompass multiple generations and victims' entire lifespans.

Overall, community contamination brings about a deterioration in the relationship between humans and their ecological surround (Couch & Kroll-Smith, 1985). As with naturally occurring disasters such as floods and hurricanes, victims of toxic exposure experience stress because their way of life is disrupted and society may not readily restore what was lost. Trauma associated with the disaster affects the family and community as well as the individual. Threats to health and safety, social relationships, and the prevailing world view are likely to enhance the perceived extent of the disaster (Barton, 1969; Couch & Kroll-Smith, 1985; Erikson, 1976; Janis, 1971). However, toxic disaster adds additional sources of stress. The exposure is generally not voluntary; in fact it can be blamed on human action, perhaps deliberate. The definition of the situation as exposure to a contaminant implies bodily contact with some invisible harmful agent, yet most aspects of the situation are likely to be unclear, uncertain, or unavailable for consideration. Courses of action to remedy the situation may not be easily defined. Thus, intrinsic sources of stress come from a combination of the given uncertainties of the situation as well as from the "certainties," namely what is known or believed to be true about the exposure, including its cause, consequences, and courses of possible response (Edelstein, forthcoming).

TOXIC SHOCK AND ADAPTATION

Edelstein describes the intrusion of toxic exposure into people's lives with his theory of environmental turbulence. In brief, the theory recognizes that toxic incidents may spend extended periods of time in "incubation," while toxic exposure is occurring undetected and unrecognized. During this time, victims continue to live their prior lives. Like most people, they are comparatively oblivious to changes for which they lack a personal baseline of comparison, exhibiting the human adaptation to incremental and gradual change that has more globally resulted in a collective "environmental generational amnesia" that accounts for people allowing the environment to

---

[4] For example, see Faber, 1998; Freeze, 2000; Lewis, Keeting, & Russell, 1992; U.S. Congress, Office of Technology Assessment, 1983; Ottum, 1984; Ridley, 1987; Robertson, 1983; Szasz, 1994; and Toth, 1981.

degrade to a perilous state (Kahn, 1999, p. 7). When a personal baseline becomes evident, people become very sensitive to changes that contradict established points of adaptation and expectation (see Wohlwill & Kohn, 1973). Thus, both discovery of previously unknown contamination and local environmental resistance to proposed hazardous facilities reflect the threat to baseline assumptions and conditions, often more clearly recognized and valued in the face of the threat (Edelstein, 1988, forthcoming).

Thus, the obliviousness has to end for the psychosocial impacts of contamination to commence. It is only after the contaminant has been disclosed—discovered and announced—that victims are confronted with a whole new set of realities and challenges (Edelstein, 1988, forthcoming; Edelstein & Wandersman, 1987). However, even after victims learn of their potential exposure, it may be some time before most come to accept this change of fortune. People generally give up their assumptions of normalcy with reluctance. Thus, entry into environmental turbulence requires an acceptance of change in the prior assumptive world. This generally occurs when there is an unambiguous announcement or notification of contamination and exposure or when an uncertain situation is interpreted by the victims as indicating a toxic threat. Of course, some potential victims never accept that they are at risk because of exposure. Accordingly, it is often useful to distinguish between "believers" and "nonbelievers" within a contaminated community (Fowlkes & Miller, 1982).

Several categories of variables have emerged in the literature associated with either the tendency to believe in one's vulnerability to a toxic hazard or the tendency to discount this threat. Historical variables or cues reflect having seen or heard of illegal or dangerous behavior at the site, having detected changes in water quality, having seen abnormalities in plants or animals, and importantly, having experienced in oneself or family and friends unusual illness or patterns of illness. Spatial factors include general location, proximity, and direction and being within sight/smell/sound of and along a transportation corridor to. Temporal or life-cycle vulnerability indicators range from being young enough to have children in the home or to be planning to have children and to be concerned about long-term developments in one's own life, on the susceptible side, to being old enough that children are long gone and to not care about long latency diseases, on the other extreme. Length of residence is another potential factor.

Women are also more likely to respond to potential contamination, in part because they are more likely to be engaged in child care and in part because they are less likely to be associated with a polluting industry. Economic factors reflect dependence on a polluting industry, a perceived lack of resources to be mobile, and a fear of any threat to real estate values. Education is another factor, particularly where the person has enough understanding of the situation to comprehend the nature of the threat.[5]

In the end, it is likely that some perceive themselves to be victims yet were never exposed, while others deny any threat but actually came in contact with toxins. Short of somatopsychic symptoms, it is the former group—the believers—that evidence psychological impacts to the contamination. However, both may receive psychosocial impacts because, beyond the issues of toxic exposure per se, there are stresses due to the ways that the exposure is addressed over time by society. Therefore, since at least half of the psychosocial impact is due to the postdiscovery chain of events and not the exposure itself, impacts need not correlate with actual exposure nor even with belief in exposure. Ironically, nonbelievers may be heavily impacted by the response to contamination despite their denial of risk (Fowlkes & Miller, 1982; Kroll-Smith & Couch, 1990). Cuthbertson and Nigg attempt to capture these distinctions in their typology of victims based upon Cuthbertson's early, in-depth examination of a contaminated community for her 1987 dissertation. In Globe, Arizona, a mining town where asbestos had been discovered beneath a mobile home subdivision, about half the "primary victims," those exposed or living proximate to the hazard, were "hazard-endangered" residents who believed in the threat from asbestos. The remaining primary victims were divided between "hazard-disclaimers," dismissing either a threat or personal vulnerability from this common feature of the local environment; the "hazard-ambivalent"; and the "hazard-tolerant." "Secondary victims," those injured by the public response to the disaster, included "bystanders," those outside the contaminated area but still affected in some manner, and "perpetrators," blamed for causing the accident (Cuthbertson, 1987; Cuthbertson & Nigg, 1987).

---

[5] See Cuthbertson, 1987; Cuthbertson & Nigg, 1987; Edelstein 1981, 1988, 2001; Evans & Jacobs, 1981; Fowlkes & Miller, 1982; Francis, 1983; Hamilton, 1985; Krause, 1993, 1994; Levine, 1982; Vissing, 1984.

In the theory of environmental turbulence, the period of incubation, discovery, and announcement is followed, for believers, by a sense of shock, as a formerly assumed sense of protection is lost (see Wolfenstein, 1957). The reaction of toxic victims as they learn of their families' contamination was well captured by Creen (1984, p. 52): "We kept hearing phrases like 'possible carcinogen' or 'suspected mutagen.' These phrases strike a person like the rattling of a chain—with a sense of dread" (see also Fowlkes & Miller, 1982; N. Freudenberg, 1984a; Levine, 1982). The theory recognizes that individuals are not the only level of social process impacted. Family, other relational groups, neighborhood and community, the institutional environment, and society as a whole are all potentially affected in a mutually synergistic manner. According to the theory, victims initially try to deal with contamination through conventional means. At first treating the problem as a private family issue, they attempt to resolve emergent problems using their own resources. Failing, they at some point turn to their social network for help, only to discover that family, friends, and coworkers may be of little assistance in this novel situation and may even offer blame and ridicule. McGee aptly terms this absence of support by family and others in the victims' social network as "social undermining" (McGee, 1996). Turning instead to their institutional network, victims are routinely disappointed with the level of assistance they receive from government. Community conflict and rejection of the victims by the larger community is not uncommon. Thus spurned, victims finally turn to their spatial network, those who live in their neighborhood and share the same threat from contamination (Edelstein, 1988, forthcoming). Here, an extensive grassroots response has been noted, as victims draw information, support, and power from collective action (Cable & Cable, 1995; Camacho, 1998; Edelstein, 1988, forthcoming; Freudenberg, 1984a, 1984b; Geiser, 1983; Schwab, 1994; Szasz, 1994). This neighborhood dynamic helps to explain Stone and Levine's comment, based upon their Love Canal analysis, that only one-third of their residents reported losing friends while half reported making new friends (Stone & Levine, 1985).

According to the theory of environmental turbulence, such dynamics of social process exist within an eco-historical context made up, on one hand, by the perceived health of the environment and, on the other, of the chronology of locally important events or key milestones that shape the identity, coping capacity, concerns, and relationships for every level of social process (Edelstein, 1988, 1993, forthcoming). The baseline for any pollution event thus involves identifying the prior status of the community on social, ecological, and historical dimensions (see also Soliman, 1996). And for the contamination event itself, the challenge to any observer is not only to understand the event studied at that discrete point in time but to place it into the evolving eco-historical context for meaning in that setting. As Shkilnyk correctly notes, toxic impact combines in complex ways with prior insults to produce "cumulative injuries" for the community (Shkilnyk, 1985). Edelstein assesses these injuries according to two categories of impact—the behavioral "lifestyle" and the cognitive "lifescape" (Edelstein, 1988, forthcoming).

LIFESTYLE

Normal life before a contamination event provides a lifestyle baseline against which we can compare later behavioral and cognitive changes. *Lifestyle* refers to people's way of living, including their pattern of activities and the relationships, places, and props needed to sustain these activities. Lifestyle embodies the core assumptions of a society as reflected in the pursuit of personal goals. The achievement of these goals and related social expectations allows the attainment of "quality of life," encompassing such factors as economic security, secure family life, personal strengths, friendships, enjoyment of home and property, and an aesthetic physical environment (see Campbell, 1981).

Patterns of living in a community reflect numerous factors, including the degree of sociability and privacy found in the relationships of neighbors. Thus, analogous to the normative behavioral patterns identified by ecological psychologists for different settings, it is possible to map the patterns of activity that comprise private life in and away from home, as well as the basic patterns of community life. Lifestyle impacts represent a disruption of these basic patterns, as illustrated by the recommendations of EPA officials in response to widespread soil contamination by heavy metals in Washington state. Officials told one Rushton family to take precautions with gardening, to wear gloves outdoors, and to prevent small children from eating dirt, the recollection of which prompted the father to tell Edelstein, "I started to realize how this was going to affect small day to day decisions" (Edelstein, forthcoming).

Adverse community impacts may predate a contamination incident. The construction and operation of a waste facility or noxious industry or even a land use change of lesser disruption may itself involve a significant change from the baseline qualities of local life and serve as a source of stress or upset for local residents. Ironically, later residents arriving after the change has occurred may disregard or even accept it as a given. Thus, Evans and Jacobs found that old-timers who predated construction of a mill in a small town were more disturbed by it than were newcomers who moved in knowing about the industry (Evans & Jacobs, 1981). Similarly, Edelstein found that residents living near the Jackson Township, New Jersey, municipal landfill whose residency predated the facility were more likely to understand the potential hazards than were those who arrived after the facility was open (Edelstein, 1981, 1988, 2000).

Noxious facilities by definition cause direct stressors for local residents. Among the local impacts found with landfills, for example, are problems with odors. Foul odor is a uniquely intrusive stimulus, capable of spoiling the enjoyment of home and the use of one's property as well as curtailing the use of public amenities. While odors may or may not indicate exposure to hazard, there is the sense that, if one can smell the facility, one is breathing contaminated air. Indeed, a series of studies of residents living near three California hazardous waste sites found positive relationships between environmental worry and odor detection and between odors and physical symptoms including nausea, eye and throat irritation, and especially headaches. The authors found that stress-related illnesses are cued by odors. Instructively, even after remediation of the landfills, people living in the areas where odors had been previously detected continued to suffer from headaches and other symptoms (Shusterman, Lipscomb, Neutra, & Satin, 1991).

Noise is a well-established stressor considered to be disruptive of thought and emotionally debilitating (see, for example, Cohen & Weinstein, 1980; Evans & Jacobs, 1987; M. Gibbs et al., 1997; Glass & Singer, 1972; Reim, Glass, & Singer, 1971; Staples, 1996; Weinstein, 1982b). Facility noise comes from both traffic and equipment. Truck traffic includes diesel engines, shifting of gears, breaking, horns, and the banging of metal bodies on often ruined roads. Likewise, in landfills, heavy equipment is used to move dirt and cover garbage. Resulting noises are likely to be both high-decibel and also erratic in pattern, as found with back-up beepers. Beyond the potential for hearing damage, the disturbance value of noise should be considered as well as its meaning. People are more likely to tolerate noises that they associate with a desirable outcome than the opposite (Edelstein, 1988).

Traffic to and from a facility can alter the character of surrounding areas and along routes used to reach the site. Typical concerns with traffic in residential areas include safety, intrusion on local roads by cut-through traffic, noise, congestion, litter, and air pollution (see Edelstein, Kameron, Colombotos, & Lehman, 1975). There is often concern about the interface of children, pedestrians, the elderly, and pets with facility traffic. Transit is often considered to be a point of particular vulnerability for a facility in terms of the potential for both traffic accidents involving facility traffic per se and the release of contaminants through shipping mishaps. Such concerns are perhaps maximized in considerations of the shipment of high-level nuclear wastes (Flynn, Slovic, & Mertz, 1993).

Other direct stressors associated with noxious facilities include litter and dust, visual and aesthetic impacts, and the attraction of vectors and nuisance species of rodents and birds. Further intrusions to lifestyle may involve fencing in of open spaces and other restrictions on movement through the community. Beyond the actual direct impacts, these intrusions may serve as secondary stressors altering the patterns and meaning of daily life. Particularly where residential, community, or recreational expectations are violated as a result of these impacts, they easily become a source of anger and loss. Direct stressors often serve as cues that something is not right with the environment during the period of incubation.

A contamination event itself adds to the above lifestyle impacts. Depending upon the medium and the source of exposure, the lifestyle impacts of contamination may vary. For example, in the Legler study of water pollution, tap water was distrusted, and such activities as showering, bathing, gardening, cooking, and cleaning were curtailed (Edelstein 1988, forthcoming). A successful 2-year effort to reduce exposures to lead in Broken Hills, New South Wales, illustrates some of the lifestyle impacts of soil contamination. Parents were told to discourage children from eating soil, have them play in sand rather than dirt, reduce the number of times carpets were vacuumed to once a week, wet mop floors 2 hours after vacuuming, repair cracks in ceilings and walls, make sure children's hands were washed before meals, stop children from sleeping or eating on the floor or eating outside, keep kids particularly clean, and use a low-fat, nutritious diet including lots of fruit. Residents were also advised to seek consultation prior to renovating or painting their houses or altering their gardens (McGee, 1996).

Lifestyle closely correlates with the analysis of exposure pathways in health risk assessment. For example, a survey conducted by the Ohio Department of Health in the communities along the Middle Fork of Little Beaver Creek confirmed the strong overlap between the lifestyle of local rural residents and the known exposure pathways for the pesticide mirex, which had contaminated a 30-mile stretch of the river, its banks, and flood plain, affecting dairy cattle and their milk and meat, crops, fish, and wildlife. The reported potential pathways for physical contact with the creek and sediments were from swimming and wading (reported by 40.5% of residents), game consumption (by 32.5%), fish consumption (by 17%), irrigation of crops (by 9%), and consumption of animal products (by 5%) (Rouse, Shelley, & Mortensen, 1990; see also Edelstein, 1990, forthcoming). Addressing these pathways to reduce exposure and risk could not but have serious lifestyle impacts.

Other contamination scenarios promise yet different lifestyle impacts. Radon and other gasses may render basements uninhabitable (Edelstein & Makofske, 1998). Cleanup of contamination may result in new direct impacts because of removal activities or construction, continuing operations of remedial facilities, and other noxious conditions and activities. Residents may be forced from their homes for the duration of remediation or even permanently relocated (Edelstein, forthcoming).

LIFESCAPE IMPACTS

Beyond our routine activities, the precontamination baseline also reflects our normal assumptions about life, what Edelstein has termed the "lifescape."[6]

---

[6] The construct *lifescape* draws upon Lewin's concept of "lifespace" (Lewin, 1936), reflecting all the factors that influence behavior, the sociological work on the social construction of reality (see Berger & Luckmann, 1966), and Kuhn's (1962) examination of paradigms (see Harmon, 1976; Milbrath, 1984, 1989; Olsen, Lodwick, & Dunlap, 1992; Orr, 1994; Pirages, 1978; and, in psychology, Janoff-Bulman & Frieze, 1983). Lifescape reflects

Lifescape is organized around five core assumptions identified in the analysis of interviews with toxic victims, concerning health, personal control, home, environment, and social trust. Lifescape combines unique individual interpretive frameworks with shared social paradigms used for understanding the world. As with other cognitive paradigms, lifescape is generally invisible until it is disconfirmed by an anomaly, in this case the contamination events. Lifescape disconfirmation thus results in a paradigm crisis, another reflection of environmental turbulence.

At the societal level, disconfirmation of the lifescape can be discussed in light of work on the dominant social paradigm of Western society. Toxic exposure directly contradicts core social beliefs of this paradigm: human dominion over nature; personal control over one's destiny; belief in progress at any cost; the belief that growth is a natural and desirable occurrence; the belief that technology is necessary, benevolent, and capable of solving all problems; the acceptability of risks necessary to support the lifestyle; belief in justice; respect for expert knowledge; marketplace self-regulation; the sanctity of the home and right to private property; and trust in government to help those in need (Milbrath, 1984, 1989; Olsen, Lodwick, & Dunlap, 1993). It is not easy to discard such beliefs unless they have previously been cast into doubt. Some may so strongly adhere to these assumptions that they deny, rationalize, or ignore issues of toxic exposure in order to maintain their existing lifescape. Others recognize the anomaly and accept the need for a paradigm shift. Theorists such as Beck have focused on the broader societal lifescape impacts of contamination, the emergence of the often unseen, uncertain, and human-caused "risks" resulting from modern life as the principle cause of postmodern insecurity and psychological distress (Beck, 1992, 1995; Beck, Giddens, & Lash, 1994). In contrast, most environmental social scientists have tended to focus on the local level of individual, family, and community, where a great deal of empirical data is available. This evidence is reviewed for each of the five lifescape indicators.

---

the invisible assumptions underlying daily life. These are midrange paradigms in that they are highly personal, influenced by personal experience and the lifestyle or daily pattern of behaviors, yet they are also socially normative paradigms, as well, in the sense suggested by Kuhn.

LOSS OF HEALTH OPTIMISM

Health has been identified as a central variable in people's sense of well-being (Campbell, 1981; see also Dohrenwend & Dohrenwend, 1974). The Western lifescape is normally characterized by a basic tendency to be optimistic rather than pessimistic about health prospects (Weinstein, 1982a, 1984, 1989). Contamination, or even its threat, inverts this optimism, in part because of its association with the most dreaded disease—cancer (Berman & Wandersman, 1990). Beyond carcinogeneity, toxins are also known to be mutagenic, teratogenic, somatogenic, neurotoxic, and endrocrine disruptive (Colbern, Dumanoski, & Peterson, 1996; Freeze, 2000; L. Gibbs, 1995). Many of these conditions are long in latency and hard to attribute to a specific cause (Vyner, 1988). It has been argued that the fetus is the point of earliest reliable detection for exposures (see Levine, 1982).

Perceptions of contamination are influenced both by what is known and what is uncertain about the exposure. Government pronouncements about a contaminant are likely to make reference to what Edelstein terms the "risk personality" of the contaminant, including the possible consequences, an understanding of the cause of the exposure, and expectations for whether cures or remedies are available (Edelstein, 1984, forthcoming). The facts of risk personality are determined in no small degree by media coverage. Yet, the media are characterized by error and bias. They are likely to depict institutions as actors and individuals as helpless victims (Wilkins, 1986; Wilkens & Patterson, 1987) and to be devoid of critical content, mindlessly balancing different points of view according to form, regardless of their merit (Nelkin, 1987; see also Wilkins, 1986). Furthermore, studies demonstrate substantial inaccuracies in coverage of risk-related events, including omissions of qualifying statements, methodological detail, and significant results (Singer & Endreny, 1993). Press often serves to amplify risks having low probability of occurrence (Wilkins & Patterson, 1990) and to create an "availability heuristic," whereby observers vicariously apply images associated in the media with one incident to others of a seemingly like nature (Slovic, Fischhoff, & Lichtenstein, 1980; see also Mazur, 1981; Molotch & Lester, 1975). Substantive information contained in stories may be less impactful, however, than the sheer quantity of coverage (Mazur, 1989). The risk personality of a contaminant determines its appraisal as a stressor (see Edelstein, 1984; also Edelstein & Makofske, 1998).

The "facts" established by government, the media, and other sources about risk personality do not offset what Vyner calls "medical invisibility," or the inherent uncertainties surrounding exposure, which include past, present, and future medical conditions, dose of exposure and its effect, the latency before the effect manifests itself, what actually causes the effects, how one detects the symptoms and ties them to causal factors, the prognosis, what treatment will cost, and the potential consequences for future generations (Vyner, 1988; see also Kroll-Smith & Floyd, 1997). Uncertainties are compounded by the frequent inability of the medical system to recognize, describe, and treat symptoms of exposure and thus to "legitimize" victims' concerns as rational (Fowlkes & Miller, 1982). To provide some evidence of consequences, citizens are often forced to engage in "popular epidemiology," grassroots initiatives to document family and community health patterns and identify their causes (P. Brown, 1992, 1987; see also P. Brown & Mikkelson, 1990, 1999).[7] Uncertainty invites differing interpretations between those believing and those disbelieving the threat and is thus divisive of the community, as seen at Love Canal (Fowlkes & Miller, 1982). Even 20 years after this heavily studied incident, serious dispute continues over the health effects, as social scientists have observed (contrast Levine, 1982, and Gibbs, 1995, with Mazur, 1998).

Under such circumstances, believers easily become preoccupied with health concerns. As they reassess their health, past and current symptoms, particularly ones that lack conventional explanation, are readily attributed to exposure. And given the delayed onset of environmental health problems, these contemporary concerns are often outweighed by anxiety over the likelihood for future illness, a shortened lifespan, and genetic damage (Edelstein, 1988, forthcoming). Dilemmas are created over just what behaviors are "healthy." For example, in the Michigan PBB contamination case, many mothers grew to fear the consequences for their infants of breast-feeding, creating a dilemma because they otherwise viewed it as a superior means of providing sustenance (see Hatcher,

---

[7] In general, the concept of popular epidemiology fits within the broader frame of local knowledge or practical epistemology described by the anthropologist Geertz (1983; see also Kroll-Smith & Floyd, 1997, and Kroll-Smith et al., 2000).

1982). In Legler, New Jersey, some parents allowed their children to play under sprinklers drawing contaminated water, while others forbade such play. And in various instances of soil contamination discussed in this chapter, parents are forced to define pockets of perceived safety for their children—can they play in the yard and, if so, how and where? (Edelstein, 1988, forthcoming).

There is convergent evidence of health anxiety among toxic victims. Levels of perceived health and cancer risk were significantly greater for South Carolina residents living closest to a hazardous waste landfill, and present and future health risk was found to be their dominant concern (Hallman & Wandersman, 1995; Wandersman, Hallman, & Berman, 1989). Health concern and fear of cancer were documented at significant levels 20 months after a train derailment in Livingston, Louisiana, that caused a toxic spill; greatest concern was found for those living closest to the spill who had members of their family evacuated for longer periods of time and who were separated during the accident from family members (Gill & Picou, 1991). And New Jersey toxic victims were found to score significantly on the MMPI scale for hypochondria (M. Gibbs, 1982, 1986). Reviewing their research on three types of contamination events, including the acute toxic disaster in Livingston, Louisiana, the Brio Superfund site located near a new suburban residential community south of Houston, Texas, and the Exxon *Valdez* oil spill in Alaska, Gill and Picou conclude that there is a significant relationship between perceived threat to health and elevated levels of chronic community stress (Gill & Picou, 1998). Stress is enhanced in the interpretation of health consequences because these human-caused disasters are perceived to have been avoidable and involuntary (Creen, 1984).

LOSS OF PERSONAL CONTROL

If there is one core postulate in the social psychology of Western society, it is the belief that people need to understand, feel in control of, and be effective in producing changes in their physical and social environment (e.g., see DeCharms, 1968; Heider, 1958; Kelley, 1972). Environmental disaster, much as disaster more broadly, breaks down this ability to believe in a predictable and controllable world and shatters key assumptions, leaving behind a sense of threat,

insecurity, and doubt (M. Gibbs, 1989; Janoff-Bulman, 1986; Janoff-Bulman & Frieze, 1983). The ability to shape a desired future is lost. The sense of fairness and justice is violated (Janoff-Bulman & Frieze, 1983; Lerner, 1980; Peterson & Seligman, 1983), and the ability to protect one's family from harm is called into question. The general cultural sense of immunity and invulnerability is lost, and no longer is there a belief that "bad things won't happen to me" (Wolfenstein, 1957, p. 153; see also Janoff-Bulman & Frieze, 1983). Furthermore, toxic contamination is an involuntary victimization. By robbing the victim of his or her sense of agency, self-esteem is also attacked. Health concern itself can challenge the sense of control, and uncertainty is control's anathema. Adding to these issues, victims' lives are now in the control of experts who can detect the invisible, define risks, and martial public resources to respond. Edelstein adopts Illich's term "disabled" to describe the loss of control experienced by toxic victims who suddenly find that they have lost their ability to participate directly in understanding and determining courses of action important to their lives, becoming dependent upon professionals to "expertly" handle these decisions (Edelstein, 1986–1987, 1988, forthcoming; Illich, 1977).

The loss of control in the face of contamination is well documented. For example, in Edelstein's 1981 study of Legler, New Jersey, most residents reported feeling in control prior to the contamination issue, but only a fifth felt in control subsequently. The reasons for this were clear. Virtually every element of the situation robbed residents of control. Their predicament was human caused: Others acted to disrupt their lives. It was an involuntary situation. Management of the threat was controlled by outside forces. And residents were forced to abandon use of their private wells and shift to an expensive municipal water source (see also M. Gibbs, 1982, 1986).

Stress and Psychopathology as Indications of Loss of Control

Much of the research on loss of control in toxic disaster has employed quantitative studies focusing on indicators of stress and psychopathology. In the aftermath of the Three Mile Island (TMI) accident, feelings of helplessness were associated with persistent higher levels of stress. Longitudinal sampling after the TMI accident by Baum and colleagues revealed significantly more psychophysical symptomatology among TMI residents than in a comparison population at a year, at a 17-month interval, and again at five years; a marker of urinary catecholamines, an indication of stress, was prevalent in the TMI sample, along with various physical and mental symptoms and decreased task performance. Threatening events at the reactor, such as the venting of radioactive gasses, served to produce acute effects for these chronic problems (Baum, Fleming, & Singer, 1983; Baum et al., 1990; Davidson, Fleming, & Baum, 1986; Fleming et al., 1982; Gatchel, Schaeffer, & Baum, 1985; Schaeffer & Baum, 1984). When these researchers also compared stress for residents around TMI with those living within a mile of a hazardous waste landfill, the landfill sample evidenced even greater self-reported emotional, somatic, and cognitive distress (Davidson et al., 1986). And significantly higher levels of intrusive thought and higher levels of avoidance thinking were evident for both the TMI and landfill samples. These post-traumatic stress disorder (PTSD) indicators correlated significantly with other chronic stress measures (Fleming & Baum, 1984; Fleming, O'Keefe, & Baum, 1991).

Margaret Gibbs found Legler, New Jersey, residents to have comparatively high scores on indicators of health concern, an above-normal amount of hostility toward authority, and clinical levels of paranoia and depression. A disproportionate number of Legler residents evidenced serious psychological problems several years after the period of acute stress, suggesting that stresses were both powerful and pervasive. In this and another study of toxic exposure, lowered levels of self-control were evident for victims and pathology correlated with loss of control. In a third study by Gibbs of opposition to a hazardous facility, perceived control correlated with the emotional response and evidence of psychological symptoms (Gibbs, 1982, 1986, 1989).

As noted, Gill and Picou studied the persistent effects a year and one half after an acute disaster in Livingston, Louisiana, caused by the derailment of a train carrying toxic chemicals. Later fears for health and desire for relocation were greatest for victims most proximate to the spill, those evacuated the longest, and those separated from loved ones during the chaotic aftermath of the event (Gill & Picou, 1991; see also Gill, 1986). These stress impacts were particularly strong for women, the elderly, adolescents, and younger children. Even though the physical effects of the spill were quickly dissipated, except at the actual site, lasting social and psychological consequences occurred for residents (Picou & Rosenbrook, 1993). And demoralization was evident for both victims of the Chemical Control fire in Elizabeth, New Jersey, and victims of a malathion pesticide release at an American Cyanamid plant in Linden, New Jersey (Markowitz & Gutterman, 1986).

In a small poor, rural, and cohesive community whose water was polluted by a nearby hazardous waste landfill, Foulks and McLellen found residents to have suffered significantly impaired personal functioning in such areas as daily living, work, parenting, and overall social adjustment. Psychiatric symptoms, somatic complaints, obsession, depression, and anxiety were also significantly greater than in a control community. The symptoms found in the contaminated community were similar to those found for depressed and anxious individuals receiving treatment in an outpatient clinic (Foulks & McLellen, 1992).

In one of the largest U.S. toxic disasters, the "Cotton Poison," methyl parathion (MP), was illegally used indoors by exterminators to combat cockroach infestations in a poor minority area of Jackson County, Mississippi. Some 1,800 homes had to be remediated on an emergency basis in the mid-1990s. More than half the victims tested as significantly depressed, particularly the poorest victims, amongst whom African Americans and women were overrepresented. Because MP causes severe physiological and neurotoxic reactions and exposure data was available for buildings and individuals, the case offered a unique opportunity to see if the depression was physiological in origin. However, length rather than level of exposure proved to be predictive of depression. Level of contamination was useful in identifying the cause of the depression, however; residents of highly contaminated homes faced stressful relocation, whereas residents of less contaminated buildings had to deal with continued occupation of a tainted building. Because heads of household had hired the exterminators, often selecting the cheapest, blame and self-blame also contributed to the overall levels of depression (Rehner, Kolbo, Trump, Smith, & Reid, 2000).

Bowler and colleagues used clinical interviews to document residual fears of long-term adverse health outcomes and continuing symptoms of PTSD among minority residents living near chemical factories. After the release of an organic chemical in California, for example, they found evidence of PTSD in more than half of the respondents. Not only were

PTSD symptoms elevated, but so were scales of depression, anxiety, and anger. More than two-thirds of their respondents suffered also from memory and cognitive functioning impairments, and almost all from dysphoric mood (Bowler, Hartney, & Ngo, 1998).

Studies comparing natural and technological disasters demonstrate that stress impacts from toxic disaster are comparatively resistant to recovery, resulting in long-lasting and chronic stress. The most fortuitous comparison of natural and toxic disaster was made by Smith and her colleagues, who gathered data on Missouri victims of flooding before it was learned that some of the flood victims additionally suffered from massive dioxin contamination. Against 3.6 symptoms for people not exposed to either disaster, the mean number of psychiatric symptoms was 4.5 for flood victims, 5.3 for dioxin victims, and 5.9 for victims of both disasters. All disaster victims showed significantly elevated levels of depression, somatization, phobia, generalized anxiety, and post-traumatic stress disorder, as well as alcohol abuse. Almost a third of Times Beach victims suffered symptoms of PTSD, 6% at a diagnostic level. While other symptoms often had historical precedents in affected individuals, PTSD was likely to be a new condition for victims (Smith et al., 1986; Smith, North, & Price, 1988).

The previous findings by M. Gibbs and others of clinical levels of psychopathology for toxic victims must be reconciled with the subclinical "daily hassle" findings of chronic stress by Baum and his colleagues (Davidson et al., 1986; Gatchel & Newberry, 1991). In both cases, long-term stress is found but at significantly divergent levels of severity. Several possibilities exist to explain the discrepancy. On one hand, different approaches used by different researchers might yield different findings. On the other, there may be wide fluctuations in the degree of psychological damage between communities studied by the two viewpoints. Edelstein argues for a third interpretation, namely that the findings are actually consistent overall but the apparent differences are due to sampling over space and time. On one hand, the Baum group has used large populations living within a certain proximity to a hazardous waste site (e.g., Davidson et al., 1986). However, as noted previously, there is no reason to assume that proximity to such a site is the only or best indicator of stress. Furthermore, highly stressed individuals in such random samples are easily watered down by the less stressed individuals, resulting in a finding of overall moderate levels of stress. On their part, M. Gibbs and other clinical researchers are more likely to be working with litigation groups or others somewhat self-selected for greater impacts. Rather than a mix of believers and nonbelievers, the sample includes mostly believers, those with the greatest impacts. Moreover, the temporal issues also may contribute to the divergent findings. Data collected at the time of a major new community confrontation or toxic discovery or around the time of trial in a toxic tort lawsuit are likely to reflect the acutely stressful events of that period. In contrast, data collected during a relative period of calm may indeed reflect the ongoing daily challenges of contamination but not the adrenaline-pumping points that occur around important milestone events. While the Baum data might be collected at a quiet point in the unfolding events of a toxic site, M. Gibbs always collects her data during a period of relative stress, the preparation for trial. Thus, Edelstein concludes that a toxic incident longitudinally includes periodic extreme acute stress points interspersed with chronic stresses at a more modest level (Edelstein, 1988, forthcoming).[8]

These symptoms of stress and psychopathology reflect a fundamental loss of control experienced by toxic victims. Gibbs offers evidence that depression and other psychopathology is due to the loss of control caused by environmental stress. While a subset of the Legler residents were uncommonly likely to take control over events affecting them, the majority of Legler residents in her sample scored lower on measures of control than did comparison populations. Further support for these findings can be drawn from Gibbs' later studies of toxic victims near two other New Jersey sites, one a landfill and the other the scene of a gasoline spill (M. Gibbs, 1982, 1986). And the comparative studies of populations near TMI and a hazardous landfill by the Baum group found that feelings of helplessness were significantly correlated with measures of chronic stress, and feelings of future uncertainty and uncertainty about future illness correlated significantly

---

[8] Baum and colleagues have also recognized the relationship between acute and chronic disaster, suggesting that any given stressful event be judged according to the duration (i.e., acute or chronic nature) of three levels: the event, the threat, and the response. Any given stressful event may combine chronic and acute characteristics (Baum, O'Keefe, & Davidson, 1990, pp. 1649, 1651).

with measures of depression (Davidson et al., 1986; see also Baum, Cohen, & Hall, 1993).

Despite the fact that testing of toxic victims frequently reveals problems normally dictating a need for psychological help (Gibbs, 1982), most receive neither psychological nor clerical assistance (M. Gibbs, personal communication, August 1987; see also M. Gibbs, 1986). Recently, the matter has begun to receive attention from social workers (Rogge, 1995), church groups such as the Church World Service, and government agencies such as the Agency for Toxic Substances and Disease Registry of the Centers for Disease Control. Becker has recently written a comprehensive overview of the issues involved in responding to the psychosocial impacts of contamination (Becker, 1997). Both Edelstein and M. Gibbs have written about the environmental rather than personal causality of stress and symptomology for toxic victims and the resulting challenge to normal models of therapy based upon the assumptions of personal control and the efficacy of individual change (Edelstein, 1988, forthcoming).

The Enabling Response

One approach for regaining some control in the face of contamination is to engage in active coping by attempting adaptive protective actions. For example, McGee found that compliance with guidelines intended to minimize exposure to ambient lead in Broken Hill, New South Wales, allowed parents to regain a sense of partial control over their children's exposures (McGee, 1996). However, in the complex dilemmas posed by contamination events, denial may be selected over protective action. For example, more than half of some 100 recent mothers tested in the 1970s for the chemical PPB in their breast milk evidenced conflicted feelings about whether to breast-feed their children; half felt guilt over endangering their children. Only about one-third of the group attempted to master the situation by changing their behaviors in order to reduce their infants' exposure to the PPB. Their responses included actively searching for alternatives, altering diet, changing where food was purchased, changing the frequency of nursing, switching to bottle-feeding, moving away, and consulting experts about what to do. The remainder engaged in denial, as indicated by a lack of protective actions, forgetfulness about their levels of exposure, and inability to articulate their feelings. Mothers with the highest PPB levels

were found to engage in the most extensive denial (Hatcher, 1982). Denial may have predominated in this instance because the contaminants were inside the mothers already and had already been fed to the child, no good alternative to breast-feeding may have been perceived, and, given the importance of breast-feeding in the relationship of mother to child, it may have been too traumatic to sever this mutual dependency. In short, protective actions may even have represented a loss of control to outside circumstances over choices made for the most intimate of relationships. Even in the soil contamination case, protective adaptations involve this admission of lost control. One must stretch further to change the circumstances.

Under the theory of environmental turbulence, as toxic victims exhaust their hopes that personal actions or social and institutional help will fundamentally change their victimizing situation, they turn to a spatial network consisting of their neighbors similarly affected by the same contamination issue. Edelstein describes an "enabling effect" of local grassroots organizations that form around contamination and siting issues and that, at least for a time, help residents to find the information, support, and power otherwise lacking in the situation (Edelstein, 1981, 1988, forthcoming; see also Baas, 1986; Brown & Masterson-Allen, 1994; de Boer, 1986; L. Gibbs, 1982b, 1985; Levine, 1982; Stone & Levine, 1985; van Eijndhoven & Nieuwdorp, 1986). An early study of 21 toxic sites found that "*ad hoc* groups were formed, often quite rapidly, at every site studied with significant public participation" (ICF, 1981, p. 34). There is substantial corroboration of the psychological benefits of this enabling effect (M. Gibbs, 1989; see also Baas, 1986; Creen, 1984; de Boer, 1986; Edelstein, 1981; N. Freudenberg, 1984b; L. Gibbs, 1982b; ICF, 1981; Levine, 1982; Shaw & Milbrath, 1983; Stone & Levine, 1985; van Eijndhoven & Nieuwdorp, 1986). For example, at Love Canal, activists were less likely to report being negatively affected and held higher self-regard and personal efficacy (Stone & Levine, 1985).

Enablement helps victims to regain control but is not necessarily less stressful. For example, activists responding to a proposed hazardous waste site in Arizona were less emotionally upset than less involved individuals but they had more intense emotions (Bachrach & Zautra, 1986). Emotion-focused approaches (especially reappraisal of the threat) were found to be more successful in reducing stress for TMI neighbors than were problem-solving approaches (Collins, Baum, & Singer, 1983). And M. Gibbs (1989) found a positive correlation between activism and psychological symptoms for residents of a New Jersey neighborhood targeted for disposal of radium-contaminated soil. Gibbs correctly explains that an active approach to coping provides control over the situation but not necessarily less symptomatology. She further notes that both active and passive coping styles may prove to be functional, depending upon the point in the disaster and how much change the victim can actually accomplish (M. Gibbs, 1989).

Who actually becomes enabled through grassroots activism? Local grassroots involvement appears to be an avenue particularly for enablement of women, who predominate in leadership positions and comprise some 70% of the activists at the local level (see Blocker & Eckberg, 1989; P. Brown & Ferguson, 1995; L. Gibbs, 1982a; ICF, 1981; Krause, 1993, 1994; Milbrath, 1984; Shaw & Milbrath, 1983). Krause interviewed women toxic activists, concluding that their involvement is a response to tangible family issues, notably illness and fear of illness (DiChiro, 1998; Krause, 1993, 1994). Other salient features of a toxic activists' profile to emerge in the literature include being under age 40, fairly new to the community but in residence long enough to be place attached, a homeowner with young children yet having a smaller family, dependent upon a single wage earner not from the polluting industry, and having at least a moderate income and level of education (ICF, 1981; Stone & Levine, 1985).

The theory of environmental turbulence recognizes as a cohesive force for local toxic victims the major challenge of the abnormal informational context characterized by an extreme degree of uncertainty (see Edelstein, 1992; Fleming & Baum, 1985; N. Freudenberg, 1984a; Levine, 1982; Slovic et al., 1990). Victims in a contaminated community are further drawn together in the face of unsupportive and even hostile reactions from the surrounding community of disbelievers. Early in the issue, community groups are commonly forced into a confrontational mode with government, using the media and direct action to apply political pressure to override the regulators (e.g., L. Gibbs, 1982a, 1982b; Levine, 1982). This is a period with great potential for emergent internal community cohesion and consensus. That Love Canal activists underwent the greatest overall change from the incident was explained because they tended to be the most heavily impacted

by the disaster. Thus, Love Canal activists came to rely on their community group for social support, while those least involved continued to rely on their families and relatives. As noted, activists exceeded nonactivists in the loss of friends as well as in finding new friendships (Stone & Levine, 1985).

The enabling response of local environmental action restores lost control to those involved (Edelstein, 1992; Levine, 1992; R. Rich, Edelstein, Hallman, & Wandersman, 1995; Stone & Levine, 1985). In drawing help from neighbors, believers often opened up lines of communication and support previously kept to a minimum (Edelstein, 1988, forthcoming). Emergent grassroots organizations quickly become a source of trusted information (Baas, 1986; Edelstein, 1988, forthcoming; L. Gibbs, 1982a), sometimes by attracting experts to work with them in an advisory role (see Fowlkes & Miller, 1982; L. Gibbs, 1982b; Levine, 1982; van Eijndhoven & Nieuwdorp, 1986). Community organizations are also able to serve as a base for community participation (L. Gibbs, 1982a). Through their collective activities and ability to attract resources, these organizations provide a means for attaining the power needed to address the complex issues resulting from toxic exposure (Baas, 1986). Moreover, N. Freudenberg found that 83% of the community groups he sampled perceived themselves to be at least somewhat successful. Half reported the elimination or reduction of the hazard that was the group's main focus (1984a). Leaders of Love Canal groups experienced enhanced self-control, self-worth, and personal efficacy (Shaw & Milbrath, 1983). Such growth outcomes reflect the enhanced competence of the community group but also its active members.

Unlike permanent community organizations, grassroots groups that develop in response to toxic exposure are temporary organizations formed only for the duration of their problem-solving effort (Bennis & Slater, 1968). The cohesiveness and collective strength found in grassroots organizations in contaminated environments is often short-lived. N. Freudenberg reported disharmony in one-third of the communities he studied (N. Freudenberg, 1984a, 1984b). Edelstein observed that, while extracommunity conflict and the resulting isolation initially invite consensus within the community of shared victims, over time intracommunity conflict is likely. As a result, any local community organization will range along a continuum from consensus to dissensus, its place heavily influenced by where the group falls in its lifecycle (Edelstein, 1988, forthcoming). At the Lipari Landfill Superfund site in New Jersey, for example, the initial condescending response of officials so angered the public as to spur the early acceptance of community organizers (Kaminstein, 1995). The formation of a local organization (van Eijndhoven & Nieuwdorp, 1986) and its ability to forge a consensus is influenced by the legitimacy now accorded the group by government (Baas, 1986; van Eijndhoven & Nieuwdorp, 1986; see also ICF, 1981). However, the conditions for cohesiveness wane. Temporary organizations are forced to address protracted issues stretching way beyond the staying power of most temporary alliances. The Lipari Landfill site required three sets of RIFS (Remedial Investigation and Feasibility Studies) and RODs (Records of Decision): for the original emergency action waste containment plan, cleaning the site, and cleaning adjacent areas. Residents involved in this protracted process ended up having to oppose proposals for on-site treatment of wastes, implying to them that government had not been listening to them anyway. When EPA subsequently sought to remedy its bad relationships at the Lipari site, it funded the citizen's group PALLCA to hire an expert and to set up an advisory committee (Kaufman, 1995). In carrying out these programs, however, PALLCA became closely aligned with government and lost its public legitimacy. As a result, the leadership split apart over differences in tactics (Kaminstein, 1995). In short, the group was destroyed by its success in entering the very process it had been united in opposing.

Grassroots tactics may also vary over time, from approaches dependent upon the direct action of members to more focused and instrumental approaches, such as law suits. As a result, a spent or divided group may be forced to remain together involuntarily in order to support litigation or other long-term activities. Meanwhile, litigation is itself a major source of stress while offering only partial success in remedying the source of the original stress (Edelstein, 1989; Harr, 1995; Picou, 1996, 2001; Thornton & Edelstein, 1999).[9] Because local grassroots organizations are grafted onto the preexisting lives of the active members, they are themselves a source of continuing disruption. Adding to the organizational strain, in later stages of a toxic incident,

personal rather than community issues may predominate, possibly contributing to a loss of the strong ties of mutual interdependence found earlier.

Similar dynamics of conflict and temporary organization have occurred in community after community. Moreover, there has been a synergy between communities. Szasz notes that the media coverage of local empowerment at Love Canal literally spawned hundreds of similar groups around the country as people found their own feelings and situation reflected in the publicized events from Niagara Falls (Szasz, 1994). Once the story became national, through coverage in the *New York Times* and television, it had to be kept newsworthy for coverage to continue, which was achieved by Lois Marie Gibbs, president of the Love Canal Homeowner's Association, who was persistent and creative in generating news. An eventual coalition of such local groups created a national toxics movement a decade after the issue reached national prominence in the late 1970s (Mazur, 1981). Notably, the movement has been highly decentralized, involving the participation and networking of local activists and groups but eschewing national leadership (N. Freudenberg, 1984b; ICF, 1981). Lois Marie Gibbs, now president of the Center for Environmental Health and Justice, is a notable exception.

Over the past decade and a half, the national toxics movement has been overtaken and merged with a second movement. While minorities have traditionally not chosen to be active in the American environmental movement (Cutter, 1981), the confluence of numerous developments in the mid-1980s called attention to environmental racism, the toxic victimization of African Americans (Bullard, 1984; Commission for Racial Justice, 1987; see also Bullard, 1993, 1994, 2000). As a result, a new civil rights movement based upon environmental justice began. The basis for this movement was the research of Robert Bullard on racial disparity in the siting of hazardous facilities, the results of which were quickly corroborated by the U.S. General Accounting Office and then the Commission on Racial Justice (Bullard, 1984; Commission for Racial Justice, 1987; U.S. General Accounting Office, 1983; see also Brown, 1995; Zimmerman, 1993). Beyond race, class has also been cited as a factor in siting decisions (Pollock & Vittas, 1995; Yandle & Burton, 1996). There is also evidence that does not support environmental racism (Napton & Day, 1992; Rogge, 1996; U.S. Government Accounting Office, 1995), although

---

[9] For a more general overview of litigation and contamination, see Hartsough, 1985, 1989; Hartsough and Savitsky, 1984; Savitsky and Hartsough, 1986.

methodological issues easily confound findings (Edelstein, forthcoming). Overall, the combined environmental justice movement represents what Szasz has called a "radical environmental populism" (Szasz, 1994, pp. 80–81). This movement indicates the importance of enabling actions that offset the loss of control due to contamination for individuals and emergent communities.

Conclusion to Loss of Control

In the wake of natural disaster, it is common to find a therapeutic community forming a protective shield around victims, bringing in assistance and help, support and encouragement (Drabeck & Key, 1983). As our discussion of community response to contamination indicates, this therapeutic shield is missing because outsiders aren't deeply sympathetic with a costly situation beyond their comprehension. Victims are forced to look within the community for such support or to network with others elsewhere who have shared similar victimization. The result of these emergent new movements around environmental justice has been a fundamental tool for reshaping policy in a significant way.

INVERSION OF HOME

Edelstein describes the complete transformation of toxic victims' feelings about home as "the inversion of home." The inversion of home involves the negation of the hopes, dreams, and expectations that surround the institution of home. When it is revealed to be a point of toxic exposure, all the diverse and vital roles played by home are threatened—as a place for privacy, as a center of activity and family life, for intimacy, for display and protection of possessions, for investing our equity, for indicating status, for achieving feelings of security, and for anchoring our sense of self and expressing our identity and our attachment to place (Edelstein, 1986, 1988, forthcoming; Fitchen, 1989; for the importance of home per se, see Altman & Chemers, 1980; Becker, 1977; P. Brown & Perkins, 1992; Cooper, 1971; Fried, 1963; Goffman, 1971; Hayword, 1976, 1977; Perin, 1977). Lifescape impacts must be considered in light of such residential expectations held by victims.

In his study of Legler, New Jersey, Edelstein encountered a neighborhood of mostly young homeowners with children who felt that their new homes were not "starter homes" but rather represented the achievement of their residential ideals. When asked what home meant to them, Legler residents gave Edelstein a range of answers: a place where they were in control and had achieved independence; a place of security and permanence; a refuge; a place to relax, be yourself, and escape from the pressures of life; the orienting point for scattered lives; a place to "feel at home" and be comfortable; a place for enjoyment and to entertain friends; a place for solitude, tranquility, and seclusion; a repository of memories; a place for observing changes over time and for attaining a sense of achievement; a place for raising children and gathering family; a place for avoiding crowding; and a focus for ownership, responsibility, and investment. After water contamination was discovered, the invisible and uncertain nature of the contaminant made it hard for residents to again feel secure. Their "home-centered" repertoire of activities was converted from a primary source of pleasure to a cause for dread (Edelstein, 1981, 1986, 1988, forthcoming).

Home facilitates mobility when its value can easily be traded in; conversely, it provides for continuity and long-term relationship to place. While Americans continue to dream about ownership of a house on an acre of land, many of the same needs and issues arise for those living in alternative structures or in rentals. An important feature of the owned unit is the importance of its salability for residential mobility. When the desirability of the house is altered, its value and ability to attract a buyer are affected. Thus, Edelstein has found that a frequent consequence of contamination is that the economic value is as impacted as is the psychological value—in fact the two are symbiotic. As the contaminated property becomes unsalable or of greatly diminished value, the residents are trapped by their indebtedness and investment in the now undesired structure. The real essence of the inversion dynamic is the simultaneous desire to leave the home and inability to sell it (Edelstein, 1988, forthcoming).

One of the dilemmas for toxic victims is that anything that makes their plight visible to the public makes them vulnerable to stigma. Without publicity, residents might have no means of pressuring government for assistance, yet this same publicity marks the community as tainted. In the case of Legler, Edelstein documented how not only the neighborhood but the entire town of Jackson was impacted by a real estate slowdown even at a point that the surrounding county was experiencing a growth boom (Edelstein,

1988, forthcoming). In instances where relocation becomes an option, such as Love Canal and Times Beach, believers in the contamination leave, although nonbelievers may remain (see Fowlkes & Miller, 1982; Levine, 1982, for the former and Reko, 1984, for the later case). The process of valuing and purchasing property represents a trying time during community relocation (Edelstein, 2002; Reko, 1984).

Inversion of home has also been documented for the collective fabric of community. The cohesive community of Times Beach maintained relationships to the final moments, when a ceremony attended by virtually all residents marked its abandonment (Reko, 1984). Following in the steps of Herbert Gans's description of a lost ethnic community in Boston because of redevelopment (1962) and of Kai Erikson's classic description of the loss of community after the Buffalo Creek Flood (1976), a series of studies have documented the destruction of community in the face of contamination. As a group, these studies suggest that contamination tends to make communities become "corrosive," divided and conflictive (W. Freudenburg & Jones, 1991). Classic examples of community corrosion include Kroll-Smith and Couch's documentation of how an underground mine fire ripped apart the formerly cohesive community of Centralia, Pennsylvania (1990). Also of significance is Anastasia Shkilnyk's description of how the combination of forced governmental relocation and mercury contamination caused by the forestry industry shattered the life of the Grassy Narrows Ojibwa and severed their attachment to place (1985). Gill and Picou found related dynamics in the aftermath of the Louisiana train derailment they studied (Gill, 1986; Gill & Picou, 1991).

Beyond inversion of home and community, Edelstein further points to circumstances where home and livelihood are combined and contamination brings about an inversion of livelihood (Edelstein, 1988, forthcoming).

INVERSION OF THE ENVIRONMENT

Edelstein notes that the environment is also subject to inversion as the former assumption of a benign backdrop to human activity is reversed so that now the focus is on ground and not figure; the ground has become the figure. He describes the fear toxic victims have of the invisible threats in their environment whose presence cannot easily be confirmed or disconfirmed and whose consequences are even

more obscure. This anticipatory fear extends beyond the contaminated home and community to become a distrust or general suspicion of the environment as harboring danger. Victims are forced to recognize the vulnerability of natural systems and their intimate interconnectedness and interrelatedness with their surround, suddenly perceiving threats not previously in awareness. Environment is now central to their understanding of life. Confronted with the realities of contamination, victims find themselves suddenly and acutely aware of the ambient surround, almost as a revelation.[10]

Regulatory agents try to teach people to fear the environment, as when "no fishing" advisories are posted around contaminated lakes and rivers. And parents are also forced to teach their children to fear the environment, as well, so that children grow up with a concept of contamination and a distrust of the environment (Edelstein, 1988, forthcoming). This later situation represents a major demand on normal parenthood. In Legler, residents had to teach their children not to drink the water. As a result, children distrusted the water everywhere they went (Edelstein, 1988, forthcoming). Similarly, at the Asarco Superfund site in Rushton and Tacoma, Washington, residents faced the challenge of teaching their children to live without coming in contact with soils contaminated by arsenic and lead. Parents were told not to let their children come in contact with soil outside, so swing sets were removed from yards and blankets were laid out on the ground. Because soil is tracked inside on feet and blown in, there were additional demands to keep children off the floor, to make them wear shoes and layered clothes, and to wash the children and the sheets and clothes continually. One single parent of two young daughters recounted that his 3-year-old kept taking her shoes off despite his efforts to teach her not to. She would then sit on the floor to put them back on, violating a second rule. And when he would tell her that the floor was "dirty" (his euphemism for "contaminated"), she would look at the freshly shampooed rug and say, "It doesn't look dirty" (Edelstein, 1994).

Vulnerability to the inversion of environment is increased for people whose lives are most directly tied to their surround. Thus, after the 1989 Exxon *Valdez* accident in Alaska, Picou and Gill focused

---

[10] It is in this context that victims undertake what Edelstein calls a "de facto environmental education" (see Edelstein, 1988, forthcoming).

their research on "Natural Resource Communities," native and nonnative inhabitants of the region culturally and physically dependent upon the utilization of renewable natural resources and thus extremely vulnerable to ecological disaster (Dyer, Gill, & Picou, 1992). As a result, the kinds of stresses and psychopathology discussed previously could be found even in the absence of concerns about direct toxic exposures. In a longitudinal research project, these researchers collected data in the fishing town of Cordova at 5, 18, and 30 months after the accident, at the latter two times in Valdez, and also in a control community unaffected by the spill at each point (Picou & Gill, 1996; Picou, Gill, Dyer, & Curry, 1992). Social disruption (disruption at work, change in personal plans, and changes to the community) was elevated after the disaster, decreasing somewhat over time but remaining significantly above the control community. Stress, as measured on the Impact of Events Scale, was significantly higher in the impacted community than the control and only partially diminished over time. Global stress remained higher in the affected communities than in the comparison community but decreased over time, except for fishers, who remained highly stressed. Loss of tradition led to cultural chaos in affected native communities that had relied upon natural cycles, social cooperation, and sharing (Dyer, 1993). An update of these findings given in March 2001 extends the longitudinal comparison across seven data collection points from 1989 through 2000. This data shows continuing intrusive stress effects for commercial fishers at a rate more than half that found in the immediate wake of the accident. Some 60% of the sample reported more emotional health problems over time and nearly 40% maintained the same level after more than a decade. Half reported that their relationships with nonrelatives have suffered or ended in this period. More than half were found to suffer depression, PTSD, or depression and PTSD. While being a fisher correlated with intrusive stress strongly immediately after the accident, over time, participation in litigation has emerged as the primary stressor (Picou, 2001).

The severity of the Exxon *Valdez* impact was confirmed by an independent project conducted by Impact Assessment, Inc., for the "oiled mayors" of 13 affected communities. This research team identified uncertainty over resource availability in the future as the primary source of impact and the cleanup as the second major source. Despite the fact that a boom economy occurred during the cleanup, this period was associated in nonnative communities with increased demand for mental health care, an increase in problems requiring police intervention, and increased community conflict. Native communities lost key members during the cleanup effort and were forced upon their return into a cash economy. For both natives and nonnatives, there was a direct relationship between exposure to impacts and depression, suffered by one out of six at a year from the accident. In addition to depression, anxiety and posttraumatic stress disorder were found, particularly in natives, women, and younger adults. Women showed particular vulnerability. Overall, a year after the spill, some 20% of the sample of highly exposed individuals evidenced a prevalence of generalized anxiety and just less than 10% evidenced PTSD. These scores indicated 3.6 times the likelihood of having high anxiety and 2.9 times the likelihood of having PTSD as a control community unaffected by the spill. Problems with increased drinking, drugs, and domestic violence were evident after the spill, and there was an increase in doctor-diagnosed medical conditions (Palinkas, Downs, Petterson, & Russell, 1993; Palinkas, Petterson, Russell, & Downs, 1993; Palinkas, Russell, Downs, & Petterson, 1992; Rodin, Downs, Petterson, & Russell, 1992; see also Russell, Palinkas, & Downs, 1993).

Similarly, long-term psychosocial impacts have been evident for survivors of the 1986 Chernobyl nuclear power plant accident in what is now Ukraine. A study done by the International Atomic Energy Agency (IAEA) several years after the accident examined both health and psychological issues for residents continuing to live in the contaminated areas and for residents of control communities from the same republics. While the IAEA team did not believe that health complaints reported by residents were due to radiation, they took note of many psychological issues. Levels of anxiety and stress greatly exceeded actual exposures. More than 90% of the residents of the contaminated villages believed that they had an illness related to radiation (against three-fourths of the control community residents). Half of both samples believed that milk was still contaminated. More than 40% of the contaminated villagers believed that the level of radiation was not diminishing (against half that for the control). Two-thirds of the contaminated village sample and half of the control sample reported being too tired in the morning to get up. More than 70% of those living in the contaminated villages wanted to be relocated (against 17% of the controls). Of course, relocation was also disruptive, with neighbors often being separated permanently. These responses, collected several years after the disaster, suggest that recovery is hampered by distrust of the environment, belief in prior exposures, perceived continuing health effects, avenues for new exposure, depression, and perhaps by relocation (Ginzburg, 1993). The responses of control villagers suggests considerable impact, as well, implying that these people may also have believed that they were exposed to radiation from the accident even though their village was not classified as contaminated.

Adverse impacts on indigenous peoples, namely Sami reindeer herders from Lapland whose herds became contaminated from consuming radioactive lichen, have also been identified for the Chernobyl accident (Beach, 1990; Stephens, 1987). These impacts have also persisted over time (Beach, personal communication, June 2001).

SOCIAL DISTRUST

Distrust is an inherent consequence of contamination events (Edelstein, 1988, 1991–1992; Finsterbusch, 1987; Flynn, Burns, Mertz, & Slovic, 1992; Flynn & Slovic, 1993; Goldsteen & Schorr, 1991; Slovic, 1991, 1993). Edelstein's theory of environmental turbulence predicts a chain of breakdowns of social trust. Toxic victims come to believe that they have been wrongfully harmed, and they seek to restore meaningful control over their lives. Yet, as they make efforts to cope with contamination over time, the victims' trust in their social and institutional support systems is tested again and again (Edelstein, 1988, forthcoming; see also Edelstein & Wandersman, 1987). By the very nature of their victimization, they first reject the polluter as a source of trusted information and assistance. Meanwhile, their social and relational networks—the family, friends, kin, and coworkers that they have always looked to for support and help in times of need— either prove inadequate or unwilling to address the situation. Fellow residents outside the boundaries of contamination may blame them for their costly demands and for stigmatizing the community. Turning to their institutional network for assistance, victims confront delay, unclarity, and uncertainty. It was earlier noted that physicians are usually seen as unresponsive. And official actions often exacerbate rather than ameliorate the victims' distress (see

Fowlkes & Miller, 1982; L. Gibbs, 1982b, Levine, 1982; Miller, 1984; Paigen, 1982; Reko, 1984; Shaw & Milbrath, 1983; Stone & Levine, 1985).

Besides the issue of help seeking, there is the question of whom to hold responsible. Victims search for explanations to human-caused disaster in a manner not demanded by natural disasters, questioning whether government, industry, or others had the ability either to cause or prevent the exposure and whether they attempted or intended to do so. Freudenburg notes that, in contrast to danger from large accidents, most environmental exposures result from mundane events, the less dramatic but more socially divisive risks of ordinary nuclear and other hazardous technologies in the hands of those who purport to be friends—the government officials, industry public-relations people, and experts involved in selling and permitting the hazardous trade-offs needed to be made if modern society is to work (W. Freudenburg, 2000, p. 114; see also Wynne, 1996). After the Times Beach, Missouri, disaster, where flooding spread dioxin through the community, 92% of the dioxin victims blamed others for what occurred. While government agencies were blamed for their failure to regulate waste disposal, in this instance blame was also directed to the businesses that improperly disposed of the hazardous wastes, a waste oil recycler named Bliss who spread dioxin-laced oils on roads as a dust suppressant (Smith et al., 1988).

Despite the Times Beach data, it is frequently the case that industry is not the principal focus of post-contamination blame. Forgiveness of the polluting industry reflects such factors as local economic dependence, allegiance of workers, offsets for past civic responsibility, benefit of the doubt for the fact that chemicals were dumped prior to knowledge and regulation, active public relations management of information by the polluter, the belief that government and not private business must assure the public's safety, and a tolerance for "elite deviance" (Fowlkes & Miller, 1982; Francis, 1983; Paigen, 1982; Shrivastava, 1987; Vissing, 1984).

In contrast, government is not only expected to be technically competent but to have a moral obligation to act on the public's behalf (Goldsteen & Schorr, 1991). Allowing pollution to occur can be seen as a breaking of this promise (see Easterling & Kunreuther, 1990; Goldsteen & Schorr, 1991). Freudenburg terms the failure of government to fulfill its fiduciary responsibility in such instances as "recreancy" (W. Freudenburg, 1991, p. 15). As a result, even when government is not blamed for causing the contamination, it is frequently blamed both for inadequate prevention and inadequate response (Edelstein, 1988, after Brickman et al., 1982). Such distrust is magnified further in the postcontamination experience, where government is expected to remedy the situation. Contributing to this distrust of government are the inbuilt dynamics of contamination events that frustrate both citizens and officials attempting to cope with the catastrophe from their respective positions.

A Dialectic of Double Binds

The relationship of citizens and officials is characterized by what Edelstein (1988, forthcoming) terms a "dialectic of double binds." On their part, the victims' double bind stems from the fact that they are frequently made to bear the burden of proof that instances of poor health are caused by an environmental source (see Reich, 1983; Thornton & Edelstein, 1999). Generally, they lack sufficient evidence of imminent danger to force fast and definitive action by government, yet neither are they free of risk and able to return to normal life. Meanwhile, the government officials working with them have their own double bind. They are expected to be responsive to the public's concerns yet agree to no actions that would exceed their regulatory authority, budgets, professional norms, or political realities and to make rational decisions that maximize net overall benefits (Edelstein, 1988, forthcoming; Fiorino, 1989b, commenting on the work of Reich, 1985; Fowlkes & Miller, 1982; L. Gibbs, 1982b; Levine, 1982; van Eijndhoven & Nieuwdorp, 1986; for the concept of double bind, Bateson, 1972). Confounding this position is the role of government in discovering the problem, the inherent uncertainties, and the pervasiveness of exposure (Miller, 1984). Citizens use media to create a climate of belief to which government must respond. At the same time, because government action and language shape later understandings of the event, agencies are very deliberate and cautious (Szasz, 1994, p. 52). Furthermore, official response may be bound by seemingly arbitrary yet rational criteria. Their response may be limited: to certain routes of contamination, to only those issues directly linked to health threats, and to circumstances where resources and technology are readily at hand (van Eijndhoven & Nieuwdorp, 1986).

A common path by which the dialectic of double binds is played out involves victims becoming increasingly alarmed by the potential for health effects, while health officials attempt to play down their fears so as to avoid panic while conserving public resources for higher priority problems (see Creen, 1984; Levine, 1982; Paigen, 1982; also N. Freudenberg, 1984a). The regulatory response, purporting to be careful science, is more likely to reflect a combination of bureaucratic rigidity and political expediency (Levine, 1982; Reich, 1983). Government routinely fails to offer confirmation or reassurance about the hazard or safety of the situation (Fowlkes & Miller, 1982). The increasing use of risk benefit-analysis thinking in agencies has contributed greatly to their inability to communicate with the public in such situations (Bela, Mosher, & Calvo, 1988; Edelstein, 1988, forthcoming; Fiorino, 1989a, 1989b; Heiman, 1996; Kaufman, 1995; Miller, 1984; Shrader-Frechette, 1985). Pressures to avoid precedent-setting costly actions are well supported by the risk assessment approach. Similarly, the norms of conventional science, most notably the bias against making Type I error, support conservative decision making, implying caution in concluding that a place is *unsafe* (Brown & Mikkelson, 1990; Edelstein, 1982, 1988, forthcoming; Levine, 1982; Paigen, 1982). Such scientific rationalizations may often indicate political decisions hidden behind the rationale of technical standards set by experts (Edelstein & Makofske, 1998; Levine, 1982; Reich, 1983, 1991). Numerous agencies may become involved, each with its own experience and expectations (see Shaw & Milbrath, 1983). Government organizations may also be subject to "regulatory capture" in the sense of having a built-in conflict of interest in favor of one side of a controversy, most often corporate, not citizen, interests (see Reich, 1983).

As a result of their dilemma, victims not responsible for causing their predicament are stuck with the consequences. For this reason, considerable recent effort has gone into articulating the "precautionary principle" as an alternative paradigm for scientific and government action more reflecting a bias toward Type II error (O'Riordan & Cameron, 1994; Raffensperger & Tickner, 1999). Victims are likely to be stressed as much by their encounters with government as they are by the knowledge of the exposure itself. Thus, the social reaction to contamination—and particularly governmental response—becomes a major source of the psychosocial impact. As part of the dialectic, each side rejects the other. While the public evidences a tendency to dismiss scientists and officials for their conservative positions, there is a counterdialectic, as well, by which the public is derogated as chemophobics, radiophobics, and "NIMBYs" (sufferers of the "not in my backyard" syndrome) (Edelstein, 1988, 1990, 1992, forthcoming; W. Freudenburg & Pastor, 1991; Hilgartner, 1985; Mitchell, 1984).

Tosteson (1995a, 1995b) stresses the importance for scientists to give toxic victims back some sense of control, for example, by validating their beliefs. The challenge is that some victims look to scientists to prove unconfirmed exposures or effects with the hope that, made real, such dreaded fears become more controllable. Conversely, others may expect scientists to prove that all are safe and everything can return to normal. Moreover, Tosteson observes that officials are forced to make decisions under uncertainty, even though this means that sometimes they will err; this uncertainty exacerbates the lack of confidence scientists already feel given their practice of a new environmental science in a highly politicized arena. Thus vulnerable, they experience the community's distrust as a personal attack on their credibility. As a result, they may act in a highly detached manner, relying all the more upon method and professionalism as a way of compensating for this uncertainty (see also Levine, 1982). By playing objective scientist, these officials try to place themselves outside the social context of the contamination victims. Answers within the value system of science are projected onto the community, as if the community shared these values. "Thus," Tosteson writes, "they refuse to provide an adequate context or interpretive frame to permit the community to understand what actions they can take to reduce the level of threat they feel, a threat compounded of not only scientific uncertainty but also of broader social and philosophical uncertainty" (Tosteson, 1995b, pp. 6–7).

The dialectic of double binds is further compounded by the common divergence of expert and public opinion (see, for example, Fischhoff, Slovic, & Lichtenstein, 1982; Irwin, 1995; Slovic et al., 1990). In part this is a difference of emphasis about what is important. For example, Superfund managers have tended to be interested in the technical site issues of a cleanup and not sensitive to the overriding public interest in the health implications (Powell, 1988). But there are also dramatic differences in the rating of risks. Flynn, Slovic, and Mertz compared responses to a 1989 public survey about the siting of a high-level nuclear waste facility and a sample of nuclear waste professionals responding to the same questions (Flynn et al., 1993). Beyond agreement on local employment opportunities and other economic benefits from the facility, perceptions of risk and stigma diverged. The public overwhelmingly assumed that the U.S. nuclear program had caused and would cause local health problems, while the experts assumed it had not and would not. The public was less likely than experts to recognize the potential to make the repository safe and considerably less trusting of the Department of Energy to manage the repository. And the public, much more than experts, anticipated that a dump would stigmatize the identity of the area. Negative images reported by the public reflect dangers of high-level nuclear wastes and their disposal; nuclear experts' negative images focus on public fears and the NIMBY opposition to the repository.

The fact that the only risk category rated by experts as highly negative in the above study was the transportation of nuclear wastes is interesting in light of an analysis by environmental attorney Michael Gerrard of regulatory systems for preventing toxic contamination. Gerrard concluded that, of the three laws he compared, the greatest savings of life was due to the Hazardous Materials Transportation Act (HTMA), which regulates the transportation of hazardous materials by truck, rail, ship, and plane. An order of magnitude fewer lives are saved by CERCLA (i.e., Superfund), focused on cleanup of already contaminated sites, and the Resource Conservation and Recovery Act (RCRA), used to manage current hazardous materials. Yet, HTMA is hardly known, perhaps because, Gerrard conjectures, it involves familiar activities, such as hauling of fuel, witnessed by people on a daily basis. Meanwhile, CERCLA receives dramatically more attention than RCRA despite RCRA's importance for preventing future waste problems. As a striking indicator of social attention to these three statutes, Gerrard reports that a poll of environmental attorneys found more than 3,000 specializing in CERCLA litigation, a little more 1,000 on RCRA cases, and only 5 working on HTMA (Gerrard, 1998).

In sum, the dialectic of double binds distances citizens and officials, even though both ostensibly share the same objectives. The dialectic contributes to the breakdown of trust that accompanies contamination.

Environmental Stigma

Another inherent element in the lifescape shift of distrust is stigma. Following Goffman's exposition of social stigma, Edelstein has adopted this construct to describe "environmental stigma," the social and economic devaluing that results from being recognized as "contaminated." Environmental stigma involves a victim—affected residents, objects, places, animals, and products—identified by an observer as marked (deviant, flawed, limited, spoiled, or generally undesirable). When the mark is noticed, it changes in a negative and discrediting way how the observer sees the victim, whose identity is now spoiled (see Edelstein, 1981, 1984, 1987, 1988, 1991, 1991–1992, 1992, 1993, 2000a, forthcoming; Flynn, Slovic, & Kunreuther, 2000; for the theory of social stigma, see Goffman, 1963; Jones et al., 1984). Blaming of victims is common (Barton, 1969; Ryan, 1971). Jones and his colleagues suggest criteria used by observers for evaluating a stigma: its disruptiveness, its concealability, its aesthetic effects, its prognosis, the degree of peril it portends, and whether the victims deserve blame (Jones et al., 1984). Once contaminated, many exposure victims view themselves differently, in part because they fear dreaded health impacts such as cancers, threats to unborn children, and cross-generational genetic effects. Victims also discover that others see them differently, as well. And their homes and neighborhood are downgraded by observers who exhibit "anticipatory fears" about the place.

Many examples of environmental stigma are found in the literature. Stigma has played a major role in the opposition to the proposed high-level nuclear waste repository at Yucca Mountain (Slovic et al., 1990; Slovic, Layman, & Flynn, 1990a, 1990b). Victims of Chernobyl were openly shunned in parts of Russia (Edelstein, 1995; Marples, 1988). At Love Canal, nonbelievers derided believers as abnormal and thus illegitimate (Fowlkes & Miller, 1982). Kroll-Smith and Couch report various ways that Centralians were stigmatized (J. S. Kroll-Smith & S. Couch, personal communication, August 1984). One of the dynamics of the "adversary disaster culture" described by Cuthbertson in her study of the Globe, Arizona, asbestos contamination was the creation by regional Tucson media coverage of "a true victimization perspective," exacerbating local nonbelievers who labeled subdivision residents as "opportunists." While the community sought to downplay the stigma caused by publicity of the incident and repair the damage, hazard-endangered residents (believers) courted the view that they were being victimized in order to win relocation (Cuthbertson, 1987, quotes from pp. 83, 177).

CONCLUSION TO LIFESCAPE CHANGE

The theory of environmental turbulence describes how most toxic victims are marginalized as they face a situation of uncertainty and regulatory abandonment, living on the line delineating safe from nonsafe areas (Coyer & Schwerin, 1981; Edelstein, 1988, forthcoming; Levine, 1982; Reich, 1983). As a broader frame for the above dialectic of double binds, Edelstein argues that patterns of trust and stigma result in a mutually unsupportive dialectical relationship between "insiders" and "outsiders," reflecting the fact that contamination is understood by those who share the experience and ill understood by others (Edelstein, 2000b, forthcoming). When such toxic victims inevitably complain that outsiders don't understand their plight, what do they mean? Such victims have come to accept that they, and perhaps family, home, and community, as well, have been exposed to health-threatening environmental contamination. The step into this nonnormative reality now separates their experience from that of friends, kin, coworkers, and even from the government officials with whom they must now deal, all of whom are still living in the previous reality of the "noncontaminated" person. The result is an insider/outsider divide. Except for those neighbors or others who also perceive themselves to be toxic victims, other people are not privy to the meaning of contamination. They are ill-prepared to be supportive, informative, or helpful because their reality is drastically different (Edelstein, 2000b). Mired in distrust, it appears that contamination involves a loss of civility itself (Kroll-Smith, 1995). The degree of distrust found among toxic victims reflects a breakdown of the assumption that others, the polluter, the community, and particularly those in government, will restore justice and aid innocent toxic victims to make their lives once again whole (Levine, 1982).

We see that, with the loss of social trust, as in the other four areas of lifescape inversion, contamination fundamentally changes the victims' assumptive worlds. Not only is daily life different in concrete ways necessitated by avoiding further contamination or addressing its remediation, but now the very expectations for what life can reasonably offer have been changed in largely negative ways. It is surprising neither that these impacts are associated with significant stress and emotional damage nor that these effects are often long lasting.

CONCLUSION

The Gestalt psychologist Jacob von Uexkull, as interpreted by his nephew Thure, distinguished between two frames of understanding. One, signified by the term *environment,* connotes an abstract realm, effectively separate from people, that is described by scientists and manipulated by engineers. We act toward this abstract environment nonchalantly, "as though we have another environment in the boot" (i.e., a spare one in the trunk). The second, the *ambient,* refers to our immediate and intimate surround. While we can be objective and distanced in considering the environment, what happens to the ambient happens to us. We live *in* the ambient environment. It is our surround. We swim in it like a fish in water. Any changes to our ambient environment causes us to reflexively respond as we would to some direct attack on our bodies. This environment begins at the boundaries of ourselves, forming what von Uexkull termed our "second skin." And as living organisms, we have a total interdependence with this surround (von Uexkull, 1984; see also Hornborg, 1996). Perhaps the major implication of an environmental psychological examination of contamination is that we can not view the topic as "outsiders" after all.

The contaminated community is not the only context for examining our polluted world. Our bioregional, regional, and global environments have been affected by persistent organic chemicals with direct and secondary, short- and long-term, isolated and cumulative effects. Tropospheric ozone affects our lungs, while holes in the stratospheric ozone layer allow excessive exposures to ultraviolet radiation. And excesses of greenhouse gases, most notably carbon dioxide, represent a form of global climate-change agents unleashed by our actions. Neither ozone nor carbon dioxide is considered to be a pollutant in all contexts; in the right place they are beneficial. Thus, they illustrate the unanticipated consequences of our way of life that, even when understood, we continue to live anyway (see Edelstein, 2001; Stern, Young, & Druckman, 1992). Clearly, the contaminated environment is a constructed environment. We have built it. And now we must live in it. This second, "shadow" built environment is a factor in the life of modern people that deserves full

attention from environmental psychologists. And there are more than enough issues raised by contamination to preoccupy the field for a long time to come.

REFERENCES

Altman, I., & Chemers, M. (1980). *Culture and Environment.* Monterey, Brooks/Cole.

Baas, L. (1986). Impacts of strategy and participation of volunteer organizations of involved inhabitants in living quarters on contaminated soil. In H. Becker & A. Porter (Eds.), *Impact assessment today* (Vol. 2, pp. 835–842). Utrecht, The Netherlands: Jan van Arkel.

Bachrach, K., & Zautra, A. (1986). Assessing the impact of hazardous waste facilities: Psychology, politics, and environmental impact statements. In A. H. Lebovits, A. Baum, & J. E. Singer (Eds.), *Advances in environmental psychology* (pp. 71–88). Hillsdale, NJ: Erlbaum.

Barton, A. (1969). *Communities in disaster.* Garden City, NY: Doubleday.

Bateson, G. (1972). *Steps to an ecology of mind.* New York: Ballantine.

Baum, A., Cohen, L., & Hall, M. (1993). Control and intrusive memories as possible determinants of chronic stress. *Psychosomatic Medicine, 55,* 274–286.

Baum, A., Fleming, R., & Singer, J. (1983). Coping with victimization by technological disaster. *Journal of Social Issues, 39*(2), 117–138.

Baum, A., O'Keeffe, M., & Davidson, L. (1990). Acute stressors and chronic response: The case of traumatic stress. *Journal of Applied Social Psychology, 20,* 1643–1654.

Beach, H. (1990). Perceptions of risk, dilemmas of policy: Nuclear fallout in Swedish Lapland. *Social Science and Medicine, 30*(6), 729–738.

Beck, U. (1992). *Risk society: Towards a new modernity.* Newbury Park, CA: Sage.

Beck, U. (1995). *Ecological enlightenment: Essays on the politics of the risk society.* Atlantic Highlands, NJ: Humanities Press.

Beck, U., Giddens, A., & Lash, S. (1994). *Reflexive modernization: Politics, tradition, and aesthetics in the modern social order.* Stanford, CA: Stanford University Press.

Becker, F. (1977). *Housing messages.* Stroudsburg, PA: Dowden, Hutchinson & Ross.

Becker, S. (1997). Psychosocial assistance after environmental accidents: A policy perspective. *Environmental Health Perspectives, 105*(6), 1557–1563.

Bela, D., Mosher, C., & Calvo, S. (1988). Technocracy and trust: Nuclear waste controversy. *Journal of Professional Issues in Engineering,* 27–39.

Bennis, W., & Slater, P. (1968). *The temporary society.* New York: Harper & Row.

Berger, P., & Luckmann, T. (1966). *Social construction of reality: A treatise on the sociology of knowledge.* New York: Anchor.

Berman, S., & Wandersman, A. (1990). Fear of cancer and knowledge of cancer: A review and proposed relevance to hazardous waste sites. *Social Science and Medicine, 31*(1), 81–90.

Blocker, T. J., & Eckberg, D. L. (1989). Environmental issues as women's issues: General concerns and local hazards. *Social Science Quarterly, 70*, 586–593.

Bogard, W. (1989). *The Bhopal tragedy: Language, logic, and politics in the production of a hazard.* Boulder, CO: Westview Press.

Bowler, R., Hartney, C., & Ngo, L. H. (1998). Amnestic disturbance and PTSD in the aftermath of a chemical release. *Archives of Clinical Neuropsychology, 13*(5), 455–471.

Brickman, P., Rabinowitz, V. C., Karuza, J., Jr., Coates, D., Cohn, E., & Kidder, L. (1982). Models of helping and coping. *American Psychologist, 37*(4), 368–384.

Brown, B., & Perkins, D. (1992). Disruptions of place attachment. In I. Altman & S. Low (Eds.), *Place attachment: Human behavior and environment, advances in theory and research* (pp. 279–304). New York: Kluwer Academic.

Brown, P. (1987). Popular epidemiology: Community response to toxic waste-induced illness in Woburn, Massachusetts. *Science, Technology and Human Values, 12*, 78–85.

Brown, P. (1992). Popular epidemiology and toxic waste contamination: Lay and professional ways of knowing. *Journal of Health and Social Behavior, 33*, 267–281.

Brown, P. (1995). Race, class, and environmental health: A review and systematization of the literature. *Environmental Research, 69*, 15–30.

Brown, P., & Ferguson, F. (1995). Making a big stink: Women's work, women's relationships and toxic waste activists. *Gender and Society, 9*, 145–172.

Brown, P., & Masterson-Allen, S. (1994). Citizen action on toxic waste contamination: A new type of social movement. *Society and Natural Resources, 7*, 269–286.

Brown, P., & Mikkelson, E. (1990). *No safe place: Toxic waste, leukemia, and community action.* Berkley: University of California Press.

Brown, P., & Mikkelson, E. (1999). *No safe place: Toxic waste, leukemia, and community action* (2nd ed.). Berkley: University of California Press.

Bullard, R. (1984, August). The politics of pollution: Implications for the black community. Paper presented at the annual meeting of the Association of Black Sociologists, San Antonio, TX.

Bullard, R. (Ed.). (1993). *Confronting environmental racism: Voices from the grassroots.* Boston: South End.

Bullard, R. (Ed.). (1994). *Unequal protection: Environmental justice and communities of color.* San Francisco: Sierra Club.

Bullard, R. (2000). *Dumping in Dixie: Race, class, and environmental quality* (3rd ed.). Boulder, CO: Westview Press.

Cable, S., & Cable, C. (1995). *Environmental problems/grassroots solutions: The politics of environmental conflict.* New York: St. Martin's Press.

Camacho, D. (Ed.). (1998). *Environmental injustices, political struggles: Race, class, and the environment.* Durham, NC: Duke University Press.

Campbell, A. (1981). *The sense of well-being in America.* New York: McGraw-Hill.

Cohen, S., & Weinstein, N. (1980). Nonauditory effects of noise on behavior and health. *Journal of Social Issues, 17*(1), 36–70.

Colbern, T., Dumanoski, D., & Myers, J. P. (1996). *Our stolen future: Are we threatening our fertility, intelligence, and survival?—A scientific detective story.* New York: Penguin Books (Dutton).

Collins, D., Baum, A., & Singer, J. (1983). Coping with chronic stress at Three Mile Island: Psychological and biochemical evidence. *Health Psychology, 2*(2), 149–166.

Commission for Racial Justice. (1987). *Toxic wastes and race in the United States: A national report on the racial and socioeconomic characteristics of communities with hazardous waste sites.* Report by the United Church of Christ.

Cooper, C. (1971, May). *The house as a symbol of self* (Working paper No. 120). Berkeley: Institute of Urban and Regional Development, University of California.

Couch, S., & Kroll-Smith, J. S. (1985). The chronic technical disaster: Toward a social scientific perspective. *Social Science Quarterly, 66*, 564–575.

Coyer, B. W., & Schwerin, D. (1981). Bureaucratic regulation and farmer protest in the Michigan PBB contamination case. *Rural Sociology, 46*(4), 703–723.

Creen, T. (1984). The social and psychological impact of NIMBY disputes. In A. Armour (Ed.), *The not-in-my-backyard syndrome* (pp. 51–60). Downsview, Ontario, Canada: York University Press.

Cuthbertson, B. (1987). *Emotion and technological disaster: An integrative analysis.* Unpublished doctoral dissertation, Arizona State University, Tempe.

Cuthbertson, B. J., & Nigg, J. M. (1987). Technological disaster and the nontherapeutic community: A question of true victimization. *Environment and Behavior, 19*, 462–483.

Cutter, S. (1981). Community concern for pollution: Social and environmental influences. *Environment and Behavior, 13*, 105–124.

Davidson, L. M., Fleming, I., & Baum, A. (1986). Posttraumatic stress as a function of chronic stress and toxic exposure. In C. Figley (Ed.), *Trauma and its wake* (Vol. 2, pp. 57–77). New York: Brunner/Mazel.

de Boer, J. (1986). Community response to soil pollution: A model of parallel processes. In H. Becker & A. Porter (Eds.), *Impact Assessment Bulletin* [Special issue], *4*,(3/4), 187–200.

DeCharms, R. (1968). *Personal causation.* New York: Academic Press.

DiChiro, G. (1998). Environmental justice at the grass roots: Reflections on history, gender and expertise. In D. Faber (Ed.), *The struggle for ecological democracy: Environmental justice movements in the United States* (pp. 104–136). New York: Guilford Press.

Dohrenwend, B. S., & Dohrenwend, B. P. (1974). *Stressful life events: Their nature and effects.* New York: Wiley.

Drabek, K., & Key, I. (1983). *Conquering disaster: Family recovery and long-term consequences.*

Dyer, C. L. (1993). Tradition loss as secondary disaster: Long-term cultural impacts of the Exxon Valdez oil spill. *Sociological Spectrum, 13*(1), 65–88.

Dyer, C., Gill, D., & Picou, S. J. (1992). Social disruption and the Valdez oil spill: Alaskan natives and a natural resource community. *Sociological Spectrum, 12*(2), 105–126.

Easterling, D., & Kunreuther, H. (1990, October 2). *Siting strategies to install trust and legitimacy: The case of radioactive waste repositories.* Paper presented at the symposium on Hazardous Materials/Wastes: Social Aspects of Facility Planning and Management, Toronto, Ontario, Canada.

Edelstein, M. R. (1981). *The social and psychological impacts of groundwater contamination in the Legler section of Jackson, New Jersey.* Report prepared for the law firm Kreindler & Kreindler for Ayers v. Jackson Township.

Edelstein, M. R. (1986). Toxic exposure and the inversion of home. *Journal of Architecture and Planning Research, 3,* 237–251.

Edelstein, M. R. (1986–1987). Disabling communities: The impact of regulatory proceedings. *Journal of Environmental Systems, 16*(2), 87–110.

Edelstein, M. R. (1987). Toward a theory of environmental stigma. In J. Harvey & D. Henning (Eds.), *Public environments* (pp. 21–25). Ottawa, Canada: Environmental Design Research Association.

Edelstein, M. R. (1988). *Contaminated communities: The social and psychological impacts of residential toxic exposure.* Boulder, CO: Westview Press.

Edelstein, M. R. (1989). Psychosocial impacts on trial: The case of hazardous waste disposal. In D. Peck (Ed.), *Psychosocial effects of hazardous toxic waste disposal on communities* (pp. 153–176). Springfield, IL: Charles Thomas.

Edelstein, M. R. (1990, November). The psychological basis for the "NIMBY" response. In J. Andrews, L. Askew, J. Bucsela, D. Hoffman, B. Johnson, & C. Xintaras (Eds.), *Proceedings of the Fourth National Environmental Health Conference: Environmental Issues—Today's Challenge for the Future* (pp. 271–278). Washington, DC: U.S. Department of Health and Human Services, Public Health Service.

Edelstein, M. R. (1991). Ecological threats and spoiled identities: Radon gas and environmental stigma. In S. Couch & J. S. Kroll-Smith (Eds.), *Communities at risk: Community responses to technological hazards* (pp. 205–226). Worster, MA: Peter Lang.

Edelstein, M. R. (1991–1992). Mitigating environmental stigma and loss of trust in the siting of hazardous facilities (Yucca Mountain Studies Series). Washington, DC: U.S. Department of Energy.

Edelstein, M. R. (1992). NIMBY as a healthy response to environmental stigma associated with hazardous facility siting. In G. Leitch (Ed.), *Hazardous material/wastes: Social aspects of facility planning and management* (pp. 413–431). Winnipeg, Manitoba, Canada: Institute for Social Impact Assessment.

Edelstein, M. R. (1993). When the honeymoon is over: Environmental stigma and distrust in the siting of a hazardous waste disposal facility in Niagara Falls, New York. In W. Freudenburg & T. Youn (Eds.), *Research in social problems and public policy* (Vol. 5, pp. 75–96). Greenwich, CT: JAI Press.

Edelstein, M. R. (1995). Disaster revisited: Bhopal and Chernobyl—What are the lessons? In W. J. Makofske & E. Karlin (Eds.), *Technology and global environmental issues* (pp. 305–336). New York: HarperCollins.

Edelstein, M. R. (1999, January 7). Psychosocial impacts associated with the contamination of the Middle Fork of Little Beaver Creek. Report prepared for the law firm Murray & Murray for Bettis v. Reutgers-Nease.

Edelstein, M. R. (2000a). Crying over spoiled milk: Contamination, visibility, and expectation in environmental stigma. In J. Flynn, P. Slovic, & H. Kunreuther (Eds.), *Risk, media, and stigma* (pp. 41–68). London: EarthScan.

Edelstein, M. R. (2000b). Outsiders just don't understand: Personalization of risk and the boundary between modernity and postmodernity. In M. Cohen (Ed.), *Risk in the modern age: Social theory, science and environmental decision-making* (pp. 123–142). New York: St. Martin's Press.

Edelstein, M. R. (forthcoming). *Poisoned places.* Boulder, CO. Westview Press. Manuscript in preparation.

Edelstein, M. R. (forthcoming). *Contaminated communities: Residential toxic exposure as psycho-social disaster, the search for environmental justice in a contaminated world* (2nd ed.). Boulder, CO: Westview Press. Manuscript in preparation.

Edelstein, M. R., Kameron, J., Colombotos, M., & Lehman, S. (1975). Psychological impact of traffic and attendant factors of air pollution, noise and safety. In R. Graham & S. Posten (Eds.), *An applied natural resource inventory of the borough of Paramus, New Jersey.* Paramus, NJ: Paramus Environmental Commission.

Edelstein, M. R., & Makofske, W. (1998). *Radon's deadly daughters: Science, environmental policy and the politics of risk.* Lanham, MD: Rowman & Littlefield.

Edelstein, M. R., & Wandersman, A. (1987). Community dynamics in coping with toxic exposure. In I. Altman & A. Wandersman (Eds.), *Human behavior and the environment: Vol. 9. Neighborhood and community environments* (pp. 69–112). Plenum Press.

Erikson, K. (1976). *Everything in its path*. New York: Simon & Schuster.

Erikson, K. (1991). A new species of trouble. In S. Couch & J. S. Kroll-Smith (Eds.), *Communities at risk: Community responses to technological hazards* (pp. 12–29). New York: Peter Lang.

Erikson, K. (1994). *A new species of trouble: Explorations in disaster, trauma and community*. New York: Norton.

Evans, G., & Cohen, S. (1987). Environmental stress. In D. Stokols & I. Altman, *Handbook of environmental psychology* (Vol. 1, pp. 571–611). New York: Wiley.

Evans, G., & Jacobs, S. (1981). Air pollution and human behavior. *Journal of Social Issues, 37,* 95–125.

Faber, D. (1998). The struggle for ecological democracy and environmental justice. In D. Faber (Ed.), *The struggle for ecological democracy: Environmental justice movements in the United States* (pp. 1–26). New York: Guilford Press.

Finsterbusch, K. (1987, June). *Typical scenarios in twenty-four toxic waste contamination episodes*. Paper presented at the annual meeting of the International Association for Impact Assessment, Barbados.

Fiorino, D. (1989a). Environmental risk and democratic process: A critical review. *Columbia Journal of Environmental Law, 14,* 501–547.

Fiorino, D. (1989b). Technical and democratic values in risk analysis. *Risk Analysis, 9*(3), 293–299.

Fischhoff, B., Slovic, P., & Lichtenstein, S. (1982). Lay foibles and expert fables in judgments about risk. *The American Statistician, 36*(3, Pt. 2), 240–255.

Fitchen, J. (1989). When toxic chemicals pollute residential environments: The cultural meanings of home and homeownership. *Human Organization, 48*(4), 313–324.

Fleming, I., & Baum, A. (1984). *Stress in residents living near a toxic waste site*. Paper presented to the Eastern Psychological Association, Baltimore, MD.

Fleming, I., & Baum, A. (1985). The role of prevention in technological catastrophe. In A. Wandersman & R. Hess (Eds.), *Beyond the individual: Environmental approaches and prevention* (pp. 139–152). New York: Haworth.

Fleming, I., Baum, A., Giesriel, M., & Gatchel, R. (1982). Mediating influences of social support on sterss at Three Mile Island. *Journal of Human Stress, 8,* pp. 14–22.

Fleming, I., O'Keeffe, M., & Baum, A. (1991). Chronic stress and toxic waste: The role of uncertainty and helplessness. *Journal of Applied Social Psychology, 21*(23), 1889–1907.

Flynn, J., Burns, W., Mertz, C. K., & Slovic, P. (1992). Trust as a determinant of opposition to a high-level radioactive waste repository: Analysis of a structural model. *Risk Analysis, 12,* 417–429.

Flynn, J., & Slovic, P. (1993). Nuclear wastes and public trust. *Forum for Applied Research and Policy, 8,* 92–100.

Flynn, J., Slovic, P., & Kunreuther, H. (Eds.). (2000). *Risk, media, and stigma*. London: EarthScan.

Flynn, J., Slovic, P., & Mertz, C. K. (1993). Decidedly different: Expert and public views of risks from a radioactive waste repository. *Risk Analysis, 13*(6), 643–648.

Foulks, E., & McLellen, T. (1992). Psychologic sequelae of chronic toxic waste exposure. *Southern Medical Journal, 85*(2), 122–126.

Fowlkes, M., & Miller, P. (1982). *Love Canal: The social construction of disaster*. Report to the Federal Emergency Management Agency.

Fowlkes, M., & Miller, P. (1987). Chemicals and community at Love Canal. In B. Johnson & V. Covello (Ed.), *The social construction of risk: Essays on risk selection and perception* (pp. 55–78). Boston: D. Reidel.

Francis, R. S. (1983). Attitudes toward industrial pollution, strategies for protecting the environment, and environmental-economic trade-offs. *Journal of Applied Social Psychology, 13,* 310–327.

Freeze, A. (2000). *The environmental pendulum: A quest for truth about toxic chemicals, human health, and environmental protection*. Berkeley: University of California Press.

Freudenberg, N. (1984a). Citizen action for environmental health: Report on a survey of community organizations. *American Journal of Public Health, 74*(5), 444–448.

Freudenberg, N. (1984b). *Not in our backyards*. New York: Monthly Review Press.

Freudenberg, N., & Steinsapir, C. (1992). Not in our backyards: The grassroots environmental movement. In R. E. Dunlap & A. Murtig (Eds.), *American environmentalists: The U.S. environmental movement 1970–1990* (pp. 27–38). Philadelphia: Taylor & Francis.

Freudenburg, W. (1988). Perceived risk, real risk: Social science and the art of probabilistic risk assessment. *Science, 242,* 44–49.

Freudenburg, W. (1991, August 24). *Risk and recreancy: Weber, the division of labor, and the rationality of risk perception*. Paper presented at the annual meeting of the American Sociological Association, Cincinnati, OH.

Freudenburg, W. (2000). The "risk society" reconsidered: Recreancy, the division of labor, and risks to the social fabric. In M. Cohen (Ed.), *Risk in the modern age: Social theory, science and environmental decision-making* (pp. 107–122). New York: St. Martin's Press.

Freudenburg, W. R., & Jones, T. (1991). Attitudes and stress in the presence of technological risk: A test of the Supreme Court hypothesis. *Social Forces, 69*(4), 1143–1168.

Freudenburg, W. R., & Pastor, S. K. (1991). Public response to technological risks: Toward a sociological perspective. *Sociological Quarterly, 33,* 389–412.

Freudenburg, W. R., & Youn, T. I. K. (Eds.). (1993). *Research in social problems and public policy* (Vol. 5). Greenwich, CT: JAI Press.

Fried, M. (1963). Grieving for a lost home. In L. J. Dahl (Ed.), *The urban condition* (pp. 151–171). New York: Basic Books.

Gans, H. (1962). *The urban villagers: Group and class in the life of Italian-Americans.* New York: Free Press of Glencoe.

Gatchel, R. J., & Newberry, B. (1991). Psychophysiological effects of toxic chemical contamination exposure: A community field study. *Journal of Applied Social Psychology, 21,* 1961–1976.

Gatchel, R., Schaeffer, M., & Baum, A. (1985). A psychophysiological field study of stress at Three Mile Island. *Psychophysiology, 22*(2), 175–181.

Geertz, C. (1983). *Local knowledge: Further essays in interpretive anthropology.* New York: Basic Books.

Geiser, K. (1983, February). The emergence of a national anti-toxic chemical movement. *Exposure, 7.*

Gerrard, M. (1998). Demons and angels in hazardous waste regulation: Are justice, efficiency, and democracy reconcilable? *Northwestern University Law Review, 92*(2), 706–749.

Gibbs, L. M. (1982a, August 24). *Community response to an emergency situation: Psychological destruction and the Love Canal.* Paper presented at the annual meeting of the American Psychological Association, Washington, DC.

Gibbs, L. M. (1982b). *Love Canal: My story.* Albany: State University of New York Press.

Gibbs, L. M. (1985). The impacts of environmental disasters on communities. Report by the Citizens Clearinghouse for Hazardous Wastes, Arlington, VA.

Gibbs, L. M. (1995). *Dying from dioxin: A citizen's guide to reclaiming our health and rebuilding democracy.* Boston: South End Press.

Gibbs, L. M. (1998). *Love Canal: The story continues. . . .* Gabriola Island, British Columbia, Canada: New Society.

Gibbs, M. (1982). *Psychological dysfunction in the Legler Litigation Group.* Report to the law firm of Kreindler & Kreindler for Ayers v. Jackson Township.

Gibbs, M. (1986). Psychological dysfunction as a consequence of exposure to toxics. In A. Lebovitz, A. Baum, & J. Singer (Eds.), *Health consequences of exposure to toxins* (pp. 47–70). Hillsdale, NJ: Erlbaum.

Gibbs, M. (1989). Factors in the victim that mediate between disaster and psychopathology: A review. *Journal of Traumatic Stress, 2*(4) 489–511.

Gibbs, M., Staples, S., & Cornelius, R. (1997, May). *Factors relating to neighborhood satisfaction near a small developing airport.* In *Proceedings of the annual Environmental Design Research Association (EDRA) conference.* Edmond, OK: EDRA.

Gill, D. (1986). *A disaster impact assessment model: An empirical study of a technological disaster.* Unpublished doctoral dissertation, Texas A&M University, Department of Sociology.

Gill, D. A., & Picou, J. S. (1991). The social psychological impacts of a technological accident: Collective stress and perceived health risks. *Journal of Hazardous Materials, 27*(1), 77–89.

Gill, D. A., & Picou, J. S. (1998). Technological disaster and chronic community stress. *Society and Natural Resources, 11,* 795–815.

Ginzburg, H. (1993). The psychological consequences of the Chernobyl accident: Findings from the International Atomic Energy Agency study. *Public Health Reports, 108*(2), 184–192.

Glass, D., & Singer, J. (1972). Behavioral aftereffects of unpredictable and uncontrollable aversive events. *American Scientist, 60,* 457.

Gleser, G. C., Green, B. L., & Winget, C. (1981). *Prolonged psychological effects of disaster: A study of Buffalo Creek.* New York: Academic Press.

Goffman, E. (1963). *Stigma: Notes on the management of spoiled identities.* Englewood Cliffs, NJ: Prentice-Hall.

Goffman, E. (1971). *Relations in public.* New York: Harper & Row.

Goldsteen, R., & Schorr, J. (1991). *Demanding democracy after Three Mile Island.* Gainesville: University of Florida Press.

Green, B., Grace, M., Lindy, J., Gleser, G., Leonard, A., & Kramer, T. (1990). Buffalo Creek survivors in the second decade: Comparison with unexposed and nonlitigant groups. *Journal of Applied Social Psychology, 20*(13), 1033–1050.

Green, B., Lindy, J., Grace, M., Gleser, G., Leonard, A., Korol, M., & Winget, V. (1990). Buffalo Creek survivors in the second decade: Stability of stress symptoms. *American Journal of Orthopsychiatry, 60*(1), 43–54.

Hallman, W., & Wandersman, A. (1995). Present risk, future risk or no risk? Measuring and predicting perceptions of health risks of a hazardous waste landfill. *Risk: Health, Safety & Environment, 261,* 261–280.

Hamilton, L. (1985). Who cares about pollution: Opinions in a small-town crisis. *Sociological Inquiry, 55*(2), 170–181.

Harmon, W. (1976). *An incomplete guide to the future.* San Francisco: San Francisco Book.

Harr, J. (1995). *A civil action: A real-life legal thriller.* New York: Random House.

Hartsough, D. M. (1985). Measurement of psychological effects of disaster. In J. Laube & S. Murphy (Eds.), *Perspectives on disaster recovery* (pp. 22–61). Norwalk, CT: Appelton-Century-Crofts.

Hartsough, D. M. (1989). Legal issues and public policy in the psychology of disasters. In R. Gist & B. Lubin (Eds.), *Psychological aspects of disaster* (pp. 283–307). New York: Wiley.

Hartsough, D. M., & Savitsky, J. C. (1984). Three Mile Island: Psychology and environmental policy at a crossroads. *American Psychologist, 39*(10), 1113–1122.

Hatcher, S. L. (1982). The psychological experience of nursing mothers upon learning of a toxic substance in their breast milk. *Psychiatry, 45,* 172–181.

Hayword, G. (1976). Home as an environmental and psychological concept. *Landscape, 20,* 2–9.

Hayword, G. (1977, April). *An overview of psychological concepts of "Home."* Paper presented at the Environmental Design research Association Conference, Champaign Urbana, IL.

Heider, F. (1958). *The psychology of interpersonal relations.* New York: Wiley.

Heider, F. (1959). On perception, event structure, and the psychological environment: Selected papers. *Psychological Issues,* 112–113.

Heiman, M. (1996). Race, waste, and class: New perspectives on environmental justice. *Antipode, 28*(2), 111–121.

Hilgartner, S. (1985). The political language of risk: Defining occupational health. In D. Nelkin (Ed.), *The language of risk: Conflicting perspectives on occupational health* (pp. 25–65). Beverly Hills, CA: Sage.

Hornborg, A. (1996). Ecology as semiotics: Outlines of a contextualist paradigm for human ecology. In P. Descola & G. Palsson (Eds.), *Nature and society: Anthropological perspectives* (pp. 45–62). New York: Routledge.

ICF, Inc. (1981, July). *Analysis of community involvement in hazardous waste site problems.* A report to the Office of Emergency and Remedial Response, U.S. Environmental Protection Agency.

Illich, I. (1977). Disabling professions. In I. Illich, I. Zola, J. McKnight, J. Caplan, & H. Shaiken (Eds.), *Disabling professions.* London: Marion Boyars.

Irwin, A. (1995). *Citizen science: A study of people, expertise and sustainable development.* New York: Routledge.

Janis, I. (1971). *Stress and frustration.* New York: Harcourt, Brace & Jovanovich.

Janoff-Bulman, R. (1986). The aftermath of victimization: Rebuilding shattered assumptions. In C. Figley (Ed.), *Trauma and its wake* (Vol. 2, pp. 15–35). New York: Brunner/Mazel.

Janoff-Bulman, R., & Frieze, I. H. (1983). A theoretical perspective for understanding reactions to victimization. *Journal of Social Issues, 39*(2), 1–17.

Jones, E., Farina, A., Hastorf, A., Markus, H., Miller, D., & Scott, R. (1984). *Social stigma: The psychology of marked relationships.* New York: W.H. Freeman.

Kahn, P. (1999). *The human relationship with nature: Development and culture.* Cambridge, MA: Massachusetts Institute of Technology Press.

Kaminstein, D. (1995). A resource mobilization analysis of a failed environmental protest. *Journal of Community Practice, 2*(2), 5–32.

Kaufman, S. (1995). Conflict and conflict resolution in citizen participation program: A case study of the Lipari Landfill Superfund site. *Journal of Community Practice, 2*(2), 33–55.

Kelley, H. (1972). Attribution in social interaction. In E. Jones, D. Kanouse, H. Kelley, R. Nisbett, S. Valins, & B. Weiner (Eds.), *Attribution: Perceiving the causes of behavior* (p. 197). Morristown, NJ: General Learning Press.

Krause, C. (1993). Blue-collar women and toxic-waste protests: The process of politicization. In R. Hofrichter (Ed.), *Toxic struggles: The theory and practice of environmental justice* (pp. 107–117). Gabriola Island, British Columbia, Canada: New Society Press.

Krause, C. (1994). Woman of color on the frontline. In R. D. Bullard (Ed.), *Unequal protection: Environmental justice and communities of color* (pp. 256–271). San Francisco: Sierra Club.

Kroll-Smith, J. S. (1995). Toxic contamination and the loss of civility. *Sociological Spectrum, 15,* 377–396.

Kroll-Smith, J. S., Brown, P., & Gunter, V. (2000). *Illness and the environment: A reader in contested medicine.* New York: New York University Press.

Kroll-Smith, J. S., & Couch, S. (1990). *The real disaster is above ground: A mine fire and social conflict.* Lexington: University of Kentucky Press.

Kroll-Smith, J. S., & Floyd, H. H. (1997). *Bodies in protest: Environmental illness and the struggle over medical knowledge.* New York: New York University Press.

Kuhn, T. (1962). *The structure of scientific revolutions.* Chicago: University of Chicago Press.

Lerner, M. J. (1980). *The belief in a just world: A fundamental delusion.* New York: Plenum Press.

Levine, A. (1982). *Love Canal: Science, politics and people.* Boston, MA: Lexington Books.

Lewin, K. (1936). *Principles of topological and vector psychology.* New York: McGraw-Hill.

Lewis, S., Keeting, B., & Russell, D. (1992). *Inconclusive by design: Waste, fraud, and abuse in federal environmental health research.* Boston: National Toxics Campaign Fund, and Harvey, LA: Environmental Health Network.

Markowitz, J., & Gutterman, E. (1986). Predictors of psychological distress in the community following two toxic chemical incidents. In A. H. Lebovits, A. Baum, & J. E. Singer (Eds.), *Advances in environmental psychology* (pp. 89–107). Hillsdale, NJ: Erlbaum.

Marples, D. R. (1988). *The social impact of the Chernobyl disaster.* New York: St. Martin's Press.

Mazur, A. (1981). *The dynamics of technical controversy.* Washington, DC: Communications Press.

Mazur, A. (1989). Communicating risks in the mass media. In D. Peck (Ed.), *Psychosocial effects of hazardous toxic waste disposal on communities* (pp. 119–138). Springfield, IL: Charles Thomas.

Mazur, A. (1998). *A hazardous inquiry: The Rashomon effect at Love Canal.* Cambridge, MA: Harvard University Press.

McGee, T. (1996). *Shades of grey: Community responses to chronic environmental lead contamination in Broken Hill, New South Wales.* Unpublished doctoral dissertation, Australian National University.

McKibben, B. (1989). *The end of nature.* New York: Doubleday.

Milbrath, L. (1984). *Environmentalists: Vanguard for a new society.* Albany: State University of New York Press.

Milbrath, L. (1989). *Envisioning a sustainable society: Learning our way out*. Albany: State University of New York Press.

Miller, R. (1984, August). *"I'm from the government and I'm here to help you": Fieldwork at Times Beach and other Missouri dioxin sites*. Paper presented at the annual meeting of the Society for the Study of Social Problems, San Antonio, TX.

Mitchell, R. C. (1984). Rationality and irrationality in the public's perception of nuclear power. In W. R. Freudenburg & E. Rosa (Eds.), *Public reactions to nuclear power: Are there critical masses?* (pp. 137–179). Boulder, CO: Westview Press.

Molotch, H., & Lester, M. (1975). Accidental news: The great oil spill as local occurrence and national event. *American Journal of Sociology, 81*, 235–260.

Napton, M. L., & Day, F. A. (1992). Polluted neighborhoods in Texas: Who lives there? *Environment and Behavior, 24*(4), 508–526.

Nelkin, D. (1987). *Selling science: How the press covers science and technology*. New York: W.H. Freeman.

New York State Department of Health. (1988). *Love Canal emergency declaration area: Decision on habitability*. New York: Author.

Olsen, M., Lodwick, D., & Dunlap, R. (1993). *Viewing the world ecologically*. Boulder, CO: Westview Press.

Orr, D. (1994). *With Earth in mind: On education, environment and the human prospect*. Washington, DC: Island Press.

Ottum, M., & Updegraff, N. (1984). Local residents: Perception of the Williamstown pollution problem. Unpublished research summary.

Paigen, B. (1982). The ethical dimensions of scientific conflict: Controversy at Love Canal. *Hastings Center Report*, 29–37.

Palinkas, L. A., Downs, M., Petterson, J. S., & Russell, J. (1993). Social, cultural, and psychological impacts of the Exxon Valdez oil spill. *Human Organization, 52*(1), 1–13.

Palinkas, L. A., Petterson, J. S., Russell, J., & Downs, M. A. (1993). Community patterns of psychiatric disorders after the Exxon Valdez oil spill. *American Journal of Psychiatry, 150*(10), 1517–1523.

Palinkas, L. A., Russell, J., Downs, M. A., & Petterson, J. S. (1992). Ethnic differences on stress, coping and depressive symptoms after the Exxon Valdez oil spill. *Journal of Nervous and Mental Disease, 189*(5), 287–295.

Perin, C. (1977). *Everything in its place: Social order and land use in America*. Princeton, NJ: Princeton University Press.

Peterson, C., & Seligman, M. (1983). Learned helplessness and victimization. *Journal of Social Issues, 39*(2), 103–116.

Picou, J. S. (1996). Toxins in the environment, damage to the community: Sociology and the toxic tort. In P. Jenkins & S. Kroll-Smith (Eds.), *Witnessing for sociology: Sociologists in court* (pp. 211–224). Westport, CT: Praeger.

Picou, J. S. (2001, March 9–11). *Twelve years of uncertainty and the changing configuration of the "corrosive community."* Paper presented at the risk workshop, New Orleans, LA.

Picou, J. S., & Gill, D. (1996). The Exxon Valdez oil spill and chronic psychological stress. In F. Rice, R. Spies, D. Wolfe, & B. Wright (Eds.), *Proceedings of the eighteenth Exxon Valdez Oil Spill (EVOS) Symposium* (pp. 879–893).

Picou, J. S., Gill, D., & Cohen, M. (Eds.). (1997). *The Exxon Valdez disaster: Readings in a modern social problem*. Dubuque, IA: Kendall-Hunt.

Picou, J. S., Gill, D. A., Dyer, C. L., & Curry, E. W. (1992). Stress and disruption in an Alaskan fishing community: Initial and continuing impacts of the Exxon Valdez oil spill. *Industrial Crisis Quarterly, 6*(3), 235–257.

Picou, J. S., & Rosebrook, D. (1993). Technological accident, community class-action litigation and scientific damage assessment: A case study of court-ordered research. *Sociological Spectrum, 13*(1), 117–138.

Pirages, D. (1978). *The new context for international relations: Global ecopolitics*. North Scituate, MA: Duxbury Press.

Pollock, P. H., & Vittas, M. E. (1995). Who bears the burdens of environmental pollution? Race, ethnicity and environmental equity in Florida. *Social Science Quarterly, 76*(2), 294–310.

Powell, J. D. (1988). A hazardous waste site: The case of Nyanza. In S. Krimsky & A. Plough (Eds.), *Environmental hazards: Communicating risks as a social process* (pp. 239–297). New York: Auburn House.

Rehner, T., Kolbo, J., Trump, R., Smith, C., & Reid, D. (2000). Depression among victims of South Mississippi's methyl parathion disaster. *Health and Social Work, 25*(1), 33–40.

Reich, M. (1983). Environmental politics and science: The case of PBB contamination in Michigan. *American Journal of Public Health, 73*(3), 302–313.

Reich, M. (1991). *Toxic politics: Responding to chemical disasters*. Ithaca, NY: Cornell University Press.

Reko, H. K. (1984). *Not an act of God: The story of Times Beach*. Unpublished manuscript.

Reim, B., Glass, D., & Singer, J. (1971). Behavioral consequences of exposure to uncontrollable and unpredictable noise. *Journal of Applied Social Psychology, 1*, 44.

Rich, R., Edelstein, M., Hallman, W., & Wandersman, A. (1995). Citizen participation and empowerment: The case of local environmental hazards. *American Journal of Community Psychology, 23*(5), 657–676.

Rich, V. (1991, May 4). USSR: Chernobyl's psychological legacy. *The Lancet, 337*, 1086.

Ridley, S. (1987). *The state of the states*. Washington, DC: Fund for Renewable Energy and Environment.

Robertson, J. (1983). Geohydrologic aspects of hazardous waste disposal. In D. Wiltshire & D. Hahl

(Eds.), *Information needs for tomorrow's priority water issues.* Albany, NY: U.S. Geological Survey.

Rodin, M., Downs, M., Petterson, J., & Russell, J. (1992). Community impacts resulting from the Exxon Valdez oil spill. *Industrial Crisis Quarterly, 6,* 219–234.

Rogge, M. (1995). Coordinating theory, evidence, and practice: Toxic waste exposure in communities. *Journal of Community Practice, 2*(2), 55–76.

Rogge, M. (1996). Social vulnerability to toxic risk. *Journal of Social Service Research, 22*(1/2), 109–129.

Rouse, M. A., Shelley, T. L., & Mortensen, B. K. (1990, October 4). *Assessment of exposure to Mirex associated with the Nease Chemical Company Superfund site in Salem, Columbiana County, Ohio.* Columbus: Ohio Department of Health.

Russell, J. C., Palinkas, L. A., & Downs, M. (1993). *Social, psychological and municipal impacts related to the Exxon Valdez oil spill.* OR: Briker, Nodland, Studenmund.

Ryan, W. (1971). *Blaming the victim.* New York: Pantheon.

Savitsky, J., & Hartsough, D. (1986). Use of the environment and the legal impacts of resulting emotional harm. In C. Figley (Ed.), *Trauma and its wake* (Vol. 2, pp. 378–397). New York: Brunner/Mazel.

Schaeffer, M., & Baum, A. (1984). Adrenal cortical response to stress at Three Mile Island. *Psychosomatic Medicine, 46*(3), 227–237.

Schroeder, K. (Ed.). (1990, August 17). *Chernobyl: The intangible catastrophe continues.* Report of the World Council of Churches, Commission on Inter-Church Aid, Refugee and World Service Team Visit to Moscow and Byelorussia from June 23 to July 4, 1990. New York: World Council of Churches.

Schwab, J. (1994). *Deeper shades of green: The rise of blue-collar and minority environmentalism in America.* San Francisco: Sierra Club Books.

Shaw, L. G., & Milbrath, L. W. (1983). *Citizen participation in governmental decision making: The toxic waste threat at Love Canal, Niagara Falls, New York* (Working Paper No. 8). New York: Rockefeller Institute.

Shkilnyk, A. (1985). *A poison stronger than love.* New Haven, CT: Yale University Press.

Shrader-Frechette, K. S. (1985). *Risk analysis and scientific method: Methodological and ethical problems with evaluating societal hazards.* Boston: Reidel.

Shrivastava, P. (1987). *Bhopal: Anatomy of a crisis.* Cambridge, MA: Ballinger.

Shusterman, D., Lipscomb, J., Neutra, R., & Satin, K. (1991). Symptom prevalence and odor-worry interaction near hazardous waste sites. *Environmental Health Perspectives, 94,* 25–30.

Singer, E., & Endreny, P. (1993). *Reporting on risk.* New York: Russell Sage Foundation.

Slovic, P. (1990). A risk communication perspective on an integrated waste management strategy. In H. Kunreuther & M. V. R. Gowda (Eds.), *Integrating insurance and risk management for hazardous wastes* (pp. 195–216). Boston: Kluwer Academic.

Slovic, P. (1991). Perceived risk, trust, and the politics of nuclear waste. *Science, 254,* 1603–1607.

Slovic, P. (1993). Perceived risk, trust and democracy. *Risk Analysis, 13,* 675–682.

Slovic, P., Fischhoff, B., & Lichtenstein, S. (1980). Facts and fears: Understanding perceived risk. In R. Schwing & W. A. Albers Jr. (Eds.), *Societal risk assessment: How safe is safe enough?* (pp. 181–214). New York: Plenum Press.

Slovic, P., Layman, M., & Flynn, J. (1990a, November). *Images of place and vacation preferences: Implications of the 1989 surveys for assessing the economic impacts of a nuclear waste repository in Nevada.* Unpublished paper prepared for the Nevada Agency for Nuclear Projects, Yucca Mountain Socioeconomic Project, Phase IV-B, Tasks 8.5 and 8.6.

Slovic, P., Layman, M., & Flynn, J. (1990b, November). *What comes to mind when you hear the words "nuclear waste repository"? A study of 10,000 images.* Unpublished manuscript prepared for the Nevada Agency for Nuclear Projects, Yucca Mountain Socioeconomic Project, Phase IV-B, Tasks 8.5 and 8.6.

Slovic, P., Layman, M., Kraus, N., Flynn, J., Chalmers, J., & Gesell, G. (1990, August). *Perceived risk, stigma, and potential economic impacts of a high-level nuclear waste repository in Nevada.* Unpublished manuscript. Eugene, OR: Decision Research.

Smith, E., North, C., & Price, P. (1988). Response to technological accidents. In M. Lystad (Ed.), *Mental health response to mass emergencies* (pp. 52–95). New York: Brunner/Mazel.

Smith, E. M., Robins, L. N., Prybeck, T. R., Goldring, E., & Solomon, S. D. (1986). Psychosocial consequences of a disaster. In J. H. Shore (Ed.), *Disaster stress studies: New methods and findings* (pp. 50–76). Washington, DC: American Psychiatric Press.

Soliman, H. (1996). Community responses to chronic technological disaster: The case of the Pigeon River. *Journal of Social Service Research, 22*(1/2), 89–107.

Sorensen, J., Soderstrom, J., Copenhaver, E., Carnes, S., & Bolin, R. (1987). *Impacts of hazardous technology: The psycho-social effects of restarting TMI-1.* Albany: State University of New York Press.

Staples, S. (1996). Human response to environmental noise: Psychological research and public policy. *American Psychologist, 31*(2), 1–8.

Stephens, S. (1987, December). Lapp life after Chernobyl. *Natural History,* 33–40.

Stern, P., Young, O., & Druckman, D. (Eds.). (1992). *Global environmental change: Understanding the human dimensions.* Washington, DC: National Academy Press.

Stoffle, R., Traugott, M., Stone, J., McIntyre, P., Jensen, F., & Davidson, C. (1991). Risk perception mapping: Using ethnography to define the locally affected population for a low-level radioactive waste storage facility in Michigan. *American Anthropologist, 93*(3), 611–635.

Stone, R., & Levine, A. (1985). Reactions to collective stress: Correlates of active citizen participation at Love Canal. In A. Wandersman & R. Hess (Eds.), *Beyond the individual: Environmental approaches and prevention* (pp. 153–178). New York: Haworth.

Szasz, A. (1994). *Ecopopulism: Toxic waste and the movement for environmental justice.* Minneapolis: University of Minnesota Press.

Thornton, S., & Edelstein, M. R. (1999). Citizen enforcers or bothersome meddlers? A plaintiff's perspective on the Orange County Landfill case. *Environmental Law in New York, 10,* 81, 88–96.

Titchner, J. L., & Kapp, F. T. (1976). Family and character change at Buffalo Creek. *American Journal of Psychiatry, 133*(3), 295–299.

Tosteson, H. (1995a, June 5–8). *Communication and negotiation at hazardous waste sites: Some psychological and sociological influences on scientific debate.* Paper presented at the International Congress on Hazardous Waste: Impact on Human and Ecological Health, Atlanta, GA.

Tosteson, H. (1995b, March 30-April 1). *Improving communication in a climate of uncertainty.* Paper presented at the Communication and the Environment Conference, Chattanooga, TN.

Toth, R. (1981). Life without chemicals: Does bad outweigh good? In *Training manual on toxic substances, Book One.* San Francisco: Sierra Club.

U.S. Congress, Office of Technology Assessment. (1983, March). *Technologies and management strategies for hazardous waste control.* Washington, DC: U.S. Government Printing Office.

U.S. General Accounting Office. (1983). *Siting of hazardous waste landfills and their correlation with racial and economic status of surrounding communities.* Washington, DC: U.S. Government Printing Office.

U.S. General Accounting Office. (1995). *Hazardous and nonhazardous waste: Demographics of people living near waste facilities.* Washington, DC: U.S. Government Printing Office.

U.S. General Accounting Office. (1997). *Superfund: Times to complete the assessment and cleanup of hazardous waste sites.* Washington, DC: U.S. Government Printing Office.

van Eijndhoven, J. C. M., & Nieuwdorp, G. H. E. (1986). Institutional action in soil pollution situations with uncertain risks. In H. Becker & A. Porter (Eds.), *Impact assessment today* (Vol. 11, pp. 267–278). Utrecht, The Netherlands: Jan van Arkel.

Vissing, Y. (1984, August). *The difficulties in determining elite deviance: Dow Chemical Company and the dioxin controversy.* Paper presented at the annual meeting of the Society for the Study of Social Problems, San Antonio, TX.

von Uexkull, T. (1984, July 25–29). *Ambient and environment—or which is the correct perspective on nature?* Paper presented at the annual meeting of the International Association for the Study of People and Their Physical Surroundings, West Berlin, West Germany.

Vyner, H. (1988). *Invisible trauma: The psychosocial effects of the invisible environmental contaminants.* Boston: Lexington Books.

Wandersman, A., Hallman, W., & Berman, S. (1989). How residents cope with living near a hazardous waste landfill: An example of substantive theorizing. *American Journal of Community Health, 17*(5), 575–583.

Weinstein, N. (1982a). Unrealistic optimism about susceptibility to health problems. *Journal of Behavioral Medicine, 5*(4), 441–460.

Weinstein, N. (1982b). Community noise problems: Evidence against adaptation. *Journal of Environmental Psychology, 2,* 87–97.

Weinstein, N. (1984). Why it won't happen to me: Perceptions of risk factors and susceptibility. *Health Psychology, 3*(5), 431–457.

Weinstein, N. (1989). Optimistic biases about personal risks. *Science, 246,* 1232–1234.

Wilkins, L. (1986). Media coverage of the Bhopal disaster: A cultural myth in the making. *International Journal of Mass Emergencies and Disasters. 4*(1), 7–33.

Wilkins, L. (1987). *Shared vulnerability: The media and American perceptions of the Bhopal disaster.* Westport, CT: Greenwood Press.

Wilkins, L., & Patterson, P. (1987). Risk analysis and the construction of news. *Journal of Communication, 37*(3), 80–92.

Wilkins, L., & Patterson, P. (1990). The political amplification of risk: Media coverage of disasters and hazards. In J. Handmer & E. Penning-Roswell (Eds.), *Hazards and the communication of risk* (pp. 101–106). Aldershot: Gower Technical.

Wohlwill, J., & Kohn, I. (1973). The environment as experienced by the migrant: An adaptation-level view. *Representative Research in Social Psychology, 4,* 135–164.

Wolfenstein, M. (1957). *Disaster: A psychological essay.* Glencoe, IL: Free Press.

World Commission on Environment and Development. (1987). *Our common future.* New York: Oxford University Press.

Wynne, B. (1996). May the sheep safely graze? A reflexive view of the expert-lay knowledge divide. In S. Lash, B. Szerszynski, & B. Wynne (Eds.), *Risk, environment & modernity* (pp. 44–83). Thousand Oaks, CA: Russell Sage.

Yandle, T., & Burton, D. (1996). Reexamining environmental justice: A statistical analysis of historical hazardous waste landfill siting patterns in metropolitan Texas. *Social Science Quarterly, 77*(3), 477–492.

Zimmerman, R. (1993). Social equity and environmental risk. *Risk Analysis, 13*(6), 649–666.

CHAPTER 37

Environmental Conflict
and Its Resolution

TAMRA PEARSON D'ESTRÉE, E. FRANKLIN DUKES, and JESSICA NAVARRETE-ROMERO

RESIDENTS IN VIRGINIA'S COAL country were angry. In an effort to recover more coal than traditional underground "room and pillar" methods allowed, companies were shifting to "longwall" mining. In longwall mining, powerful machines remove long sections of coal and allow the mined area to collapse. This "subsidence" can and does damage structures built above the mined area; however, such damage usually can be anticipated and prevented or compensated for. What is more difficult to anticipate and almost impossible to prove is damage to water supplies.

Damage to water supply from subsidence can occur in many ways. Streams dry up, captured through cracks in streambeds. Aquifers may be disturbed and groundwater contaminated. Well and spring dewatering and degradation occurs. Even where there is no significant groundwater disturbance, damage to buildings, septic drainfields, and well casings may occur. There is also some concern about the long-term effects of subsidence, since the entire hydrologic regime may be altered in watersheds.

Compounding the problems are technical and scientific uncertainties. Repair of the geologic damage is impossible, and there is disagreement about whether natural repair occurs (i.e., whether fractures reseal, allowing recovery of water level). More than one operator claims that abandoned mines actually serve as an underground reservoir, improving water quantity, and there have been some preliminary studies confirming that in some circumstances.

Very little information exists about premining quality and quantity of water supplies for landowners to use as a basis for damage claims. The effects on water quality appear to be slight, but there is no research into the significance of such effects. Science cannot yet, and may never, provide accurate answers as to the causes, extent, delay in onset, and duration (permanence) of water loss through subsidence, and design methods which may prevent or mitigate the damage.

The U.S. Surface Mining Control and Reclamation Act did not require water replacement or compensation for the effects of underground mining. State law did not require replacement or compensation in all cases, either. The companies, in effect, determined their own policy about who and when to reimburse.

Residents, therefore, largely depended on the goodwill of the coal companies for replacement of or compensation for lost water. Not surprisingly, such dependence resulted in a number of disputes between the companies and individual water users and even entire communities. Citizens and surface owners claimed that even the coal operators with voluntary compensation or replacement policies did not always treat them fairly. The climate was one of antagonism, mistrust, and anger. Conflict in "coal country" is particularly intense because of the extreme dependence upon coal mining for the economic health of the communities.

Regulatory responsibility in Virginia is given to the Division of Mined Land Reclamation (DMLR) of the Department of Mines, Minerals, and Energy. In effect, the state is responsible for regulation, with federal oversight and review. DMLR has considerable leeway to determine what is and is not acceptable. This leeway may be one reason why the citizens of this particular "coal county" accused DMLR of collusion with the mining companies, deception, and outright fraud.

Complicating this situation is the competitiveness among the coal companies themselves. Several companies with replacement and compensation policies complain that unscrupulous operators take advantage of the regulatory laxity and scientific uncertainty to, in effect, take the coal and run. Not only does this reflect poorly on other mining companies, who may be blamed for damage they did not cause and who certainly suffer from the distrust this practice engenders, it gives those companies who don't offer compensation a competitive pricing advantage. Thus, many of the companies in the state do favor some regulations that would require all operators to meet standards similar to those they voluntarily accept.

Considerable political and legal activity by all parties has occurred, including lobbying for changes in state law, picketing and demonstrations, litigation against individual companies by angry residents, and challenges to state agencies responsible for administering mining and water law. All parties agree that the current situation creates ill will between surface owners and operators and generates community and political conflict. It is an unstable situation that is totally unsatisfactory to all parties.

Environmental conflicts are known for their complexity, their breadth of scope, and their enduring nature—they seem to be "never over" as parties return for the next round of litigation. Some examples include:

- Angry residents
- Defensive industry and/or government agencies
- Confusion and debates over scientific and technical information
- Fears of permanent damage and of losses of ways of life
- Litigation and threats of litigation

Conflicts involving federal and state agencies on issues of the environment represent an enormous financial and social drain on our communities. Yet new practices, rooted in psychology as well as other sources, have evolved to address these difficult conflicts. This chapter reviews the nature of environmental conflicts, the formal processes that have been classically used for environmental dispute settlement, and the newer processes emerging to address more stable and thorough resolution of issues. Finally, future directions for applied psychological research are discussed.

ENVIRONMENTAL CONFLICT

Conflict occurs whenever two or more parties interact, directly or indirectly, over goals they perceive to be mutually incompatible. Rubin, Pruitt, and Kim (1994) define conflict as the perception that goals cannot be reached simultaneously. In addition to perceived incompatibility among goals, conflict can also arise from perceived differences in priorities or values.

Environment refers to interconnected biophysical, economic, political, and social systems and encompasses both natural and human systems (Glavovic, Dukes, & Lynott, 1997). *Environmental conflict* arises when a party perceives that its goals regarding either the protection, maintenance, or use of a natural resource run counter to the goals of another party. Environmental conflict is usually conceived to be part of a larger category of conflicts involving public issues such as race, health and health care, and economic development. Many environmental conflicts include elements of these larger public issues. Because many of these conflicts involve questions of policy, they are often grouped as a category into "public policy conflicts."

TYPES OF ENVIRONMENTAL CONFLICT

While environmental conflicts are stereotypically conceived as face-offs between environmentalists and industry, such as the controversy over the spotted owl and the logging of old-growth forests on the U.S. West Coast, they actually involve many different types of parties, issues, and resources. In fact, environmental conflicts may be less likely to be conflicts between environmentalists and industry than between one or both of these parties and federal and/or state agencies. Environmental conflicts typically occur over landuse, water quality and/or quantity, air quality, or toxic cleanup, and they often involve a combination of two or more such issues.

Landuse

Land conflicts revolve around issues of ownership or use. While disputes over land ownership are important and often passion filled, leading to violence and even war, they are not typically considered "environmental" conflicts unless they involve other dimensions discussed later in this chapter. Environmental conflicts over land wrestle with the uses to which land is put, the impact these uses have on others, and rights that determine who makes these decisions. Typical landuse conflicts include interests of farmers and ranchers, mining and timber companies, developers, "small" businesses, environmentalists, governments, local communities, and agencies charged with public mandates to provide public goods such as water and transportation.

Landuse conflicts may involve *private* or *public* lands. Conflicts over private land uses typically involve *nuisance* issues caused by growth and development and the relative role of public regulation versus private property rights. Common nuisances pitting private property rights against public protection include odor from confined animal feeding operations, airport or construction noise, encroachment of views, siting of businesses or subdivisions and attendant concerns over increased traffic or loss of natural areas, and impacts of development on water supply.

With public lands, conflict is ubiquitous. Recent decades have seen a shift away from management of public lands primarily for resource extraction to management of public lands for health of the land and for recreation. That shift has come gradually and continues to spark fierce debate, particularly in the western United States. Such conflicts may involve issues such as cattle grazing rights, the amount of timber allowed for harvesting, mining permits, and road construction for access to property or one of these activities.

Water

Water conflicts involve two dimensions: quality and quantity. Water's essential nature for basic sustenance of life adds a psychological dimension of entitlement, security, and vulnerability to these conflicts (d'Estrée, 1993). Conflicts over quality involve "acceptable" levels of pollutants that can be added to the water before some degradation causes harm to habitat or indicator species.

Conflicts over quantity stem from water's finite and often scarce nature (as opposed to air, discussed later). This limited and valuable resource is in demand for multiple uses. First, it "feeds" human growth and development, and it is in demand for various purposes from agriculture to mining to industry to power generation. In short, economic growth is not possible without water. Other water uses, less preferred historically by U.S. policies and laws but increasing in influence, involve water's use for ritual and recreational purposes and its necessity for maintaining natural habitat. Water quantity also can affect water quality as pollutants and their effects are diluted by larger amounts of water, but when water is scarce, even small amounts of toxins (natural or artificial) can represent unacceptable levels for sustaining life.

Issues emerge around how much life needs to be sustained and trade-offs between needs of agriculture, industry, municipalities, the health of the habitat, and the basic sustainability of the resource. Examples of common water-focused conflicts include dam construction and relicensing, harvesting and protection of certain species (e.g., salmon, blue crab), water allocation among localities or interests (e.g., agriculture versus industry), and dewatering of groundwater supplies.

Air Quality

In contrast to land or water, air is not scarce or limited; thus, quantity and allocation issues do not emerge. Therefore, the defining issue in conflicts over air involves its quality. Emissions from industrial processes, automobiles, and even recreational activities such as boating or lawn mowing all introduce pollutants into the air. At issue is the level and type of pollution or, more specifically, the maximum concentrations of various pollutants that pose a health risk. Federal regulation standards such as the U.S. National Ambient Air Quality Standards (NAAQS) mandated by the Clean Air Act reflect the maximum concentrations that can exist "and not harm the health of the most sensitive parts of the population (such as the elderly or people with respiratory conditions)" (O'Leary, Durant, Fiorino, & Wieland, 1999, p. 27). Regulations in this area also set technology-based rules such that new sources of pollution must meet emission limits that are linked to "the best available and most affordable technology" (p. 27).

Common issues found in conflicts over air quality include impacts of acid rain on public lands and water, ozone/air quality alerts in urban areas in summer heat, lead paint dust in older housing, asbestos removal, and hazardous waste incineration.

Toxic Site Regulation and Remediation and Waste Disposal

Conflicts over wastes, hazards, pesticides, or toxic substances often involve a combination of landuse, water, and even air quality issues, as well as other policy issues such as health and even race. The term *environmental racism* originated in the discovery that a disproportionate number of waste facilities were located in communities of color (Bullard, 1983; U.S. General Accounting Office, 1983).

Such conflicts may involve issues of the amount and expense of remediation compared to anticipated use, siting and operation of waste facilities, safety procedures at chemical manufacturing plants, identification of potentially responsible parties for remediation, and the need for and expense of pollution prevention measures.

CHARACTERISTICS OF ENVIRONMENTAL CONFLICTS

Environmental conflicts have a number of characteristics that have implications for whether and how conflicts are resolved (d'Estrée & Colby, 2001). First, they inevitably consist of multiple rounds of interaction. One reason they are "never over" is because nature is dynamic and the parties must regroup to deal with drought, flood, pest infestations, and other unanticipated changes in natural systems. Moreover, scientific understanding and human culture and values always are in flux and so the parties must grapple with new technical knowledge about resources and with new social values and concerns regarding the environment.

The ongoing nature of resource conflicts has implications for conflict resolution. The parties have incentives for different behavior than in a one-time dispute. They know they will meet again. They have the opportunity to learn cumulatively over time as they respond to changing conditions, and they may have an incentive to build trust so that the next round of problems can be solved more easily.

Second, resource conflicts always are multicultural—in the broadest sense. They involve urban and rural interests; Native American (many diverse tribal cultures), Hispanic, and Anglo communities;

loggers, miners, ranchers (traditional resource users) and anglers, mountain bikers, backpackers (new resource users); newcomers and old-timers. Consequently, one of the ever present challenges is for the parties to acknowledge and learn to respect cultural differences.

Third, multiple parties are involved. Given the importance of outcomes of environmental conflicts in setting precedent and policy as well as impacting local economic and quality of life conditions, several citizen groups are usually concerned in addition to the standard players of government and industry. The involvement of many parties means the interaction of many agendas and many alternative framings of the scope and dimensions of the conflict. These are often difficult to accommodate within a litigation context.

Each of the multiple parties involved has diverse values and stakes in the outcome of the conflict and differing legal rights and legal strengths if the conflict is litigated. Moreover, the parties may have different capabilities to reach internal consensus and to bind their constituents to an agreement through established internal decision processes. For example, governments (cities, counties, states, tribes, and irrigation districts) usually have a formal decision process that may or may not be functioning adequately over the course of the conflict. Citizen and neighborhood groups, environmentalists, and an angry but diffuse public likely do not have a clear internal consensus-building process. Consequently, it may be difficult for these groups to define their positions and to commit to a proposed agreement. A key to the success of multiparty negotiations is the authority of representatives at the bargaining table to make binding agreements on behalf of the group they represent. Some disputants may need help with their internal decision process.

The parties likely also will have diverse financial capabilities that affect the sharing of costs of a conflict resolution process and of solving technical problems, if agreement on a solution is reached. The parties have differing abilities to hire experts and to access authoritative legal and technical information. Their financial status also affects their staying power in the conflict resolution process, lending credence to the adage, "the one with the deepest pockets wins."

Fourth, legal, economic, and technical information are enormously influential in resource conflicts. The role of information is complex because parties inevitably have differing perceptions regarding: the technical nature of the problem; who has what legal rights; the likely outcome of litigation; costs to solve technical problems; and who should pay how much ("fair" cost sharing). The widespread use of "dueling" experts and attorneys to gain bargaining power in negotiations adds to the complex (and often confusing) role of technical and legal information.

Fifth, environmental conflicts are complex with conflict arising from many sources. According to Bacow and Wheeler (1984), a primary source of conflict is the diversity of different views on what constitutes good environmental policy. People also may have very different stakes in the outcome. Finally, environmental policy decisions involve a good amount of uncertainty. Not only may people be unclear on how they value alternatives, but those alternatives themselves may be highly uncertain. For example, upon considering options for disposing of municipal solid waste, a community must weigh not only the potential pollution costs but also probabilities of system failure. People may look at the same data, but depending on their assessment of risks or on their notion of acceptable risk, they may come to very different conclusions about the meaning of that data.

According to Dukes (1996), many lingering problems of public policy merit the designation "wicked." Rittel and Webber (1973) distinguish "wicked" from "tame" problems in that "wicked" problems have no definitive formulation and no finite set of potential solutions. Other aspects of environmental and public policy conflicts that support the "wicked" designation include the interrelatedness of many problems, scientific and technical complexity and uncertainty, resistance to monocausal explanations and solutions, and transcendence of political jurisdictions (Dukes, 1996). Thus authority and responsibility are not clear, multiple causes must be addressed, multiple problems must be addressed at once, and knowledge resources are typically insufficient.

When conflicts stem in part from assessing risks, predicting future trends, or valuing options, it is fairly standard procedure to enlist experts to resolve the issue. Scientific and technical information can be brought in to focus the area of disagreement and/or generate options. However, new options bring with them their own uncertainties, so even with extensive technical support, differences may still arise with regard to assessing and valuing options. In addition, even when there are no disagreements over facts, many conflicts still involve legitimate differences in priorities, values, and attitudes

toward risk. Scientists are often ill-cast to resolve such differences.

What often results in such conflicts is a "battle of the experts." True differences over policy are confounded with differences in models and theoretical assumptions. Rather than utilizing the expertise available to problem solve and generate new options ("expanding the pie"), expertise is used to justify previously held competing positions. Scientists find themselves engaged in a process with values that contradict scientific epistemology. This approach also incurs considerable expense, as each group must hire its own experts.

Other characteristics classic to environmental conflicts typically emerge in the various types of conflicts outlined above. These issues arise from the legal, constitutional, and regulatory frameworks in which environmental conflicts are embedded.

First, environmental conflicts are typically *interjurisdictional*. Water and air flows do not obey political boundaries, transportation often cuts across jurisdictions, and often more than one regional governance entity will have to be involved. In addition, issues involve policies, regulations, and responsibilities at the city/county, state, regional, federal/national, and international levels.

Second, environmental conflicts and their solutions are often constrained by *rights reserved by the federal government* in historic laws and executive orders. For example, federal reserve land and water rights stem from the U.S. federal government's need to guarantee promises made in treaties with Native American tribes and nations, to fulfill international treaty obligations, and to provide for national defense.

Third, environmental conflicts are often influenced by, and may even be in part caused by, an extensive regulatory and administrative structure produced by federal and state acts. Examples include the National Environmental Policy Act (NEPA), the Clean Air Act, the Clean Water Act, and the Endangered Species Act (for an excellent overview of this legal and regulatory framework, see O'Leary et al., 1999). Environmental conflict resolution processes must often include among the issues to be considered whether or not solutions will address or violate these broad (and sometimes vague) guidelines for public policy.

In sum, natural resource and environmental conflicts have characteristics that make resolution challenging. Traditional procedures for resolution may fall short; however, newer processes similarly have their drawbacks (d'Estrée & Colby, 2001). Continued research should enlighten the most likely combinations of processes that will best resolve these complex and difficult problems.

SOURCES OF ENVIRONMENTAL CONFLICT

Environmental conflicts have both structural and psychological sources, which must both be considered in understanding these complex conflicts.

Structural

As explicated in Dukes (1999), despite considerable attention devoted to environmental conflict, misconceptions of its sources abound. One common notion is that such conflict is caused primarily by miscommunication and misunderstanding. Within this particularist view, each such conflict stands on its own, with its sources and dynamics a feature of particular circumstances and personalities. Sociological elements such as race and class are ignored or viewed merely as impediments to resolution. And there is little or no recognition that individual disputes may be embedded in larger social conflicts reflecting structural forces and divisions common to all such disputes. A competing but equally incomplete view is that environmental conflict may be entirely explained by fundamental inherent or acquired characteristics such as class, political affiliation, or race. The sources of conflict then rest with particular individuals or interests, either business, environmental advocates, or government officials, depending on which group the observer holds in greatest disfavor. Circumstances such as individual and group identity certainly play a considerable role in environmental conflicts and are discussed later. But particular conflicts also exist within a larger framework of social structures and social conflict, and many such disputes are the product of forces beyond the control of individual disputants.

At its most fundamental source, environmental conflict involves the competition and balancing of human rights, basic physical human needs, and biophysical constraints, all played out within a context of social, political, and scientific uncertainty (Glavovic et al., 1997). This competition is reflected globally in many local disputes involving the stewardship, use, and distribution of various types of natural resources. Because these disputes are fought in myriad ways, their outcomes are many and varied, including advancement or blockage of economic development, persistence or cessation of environmental degradation, the development or diminishment of group or community identity, and transaction and opportunity costs. To fully understand any particular environmental dispute, even one as localized as a group of neighbors trying to shut down a landfill, one needs to account for these larger forces at play. In the case of the landfill, particularist circumstances may include the density of the neighborhood, the personalities of the neighbors and the landfill operators, the geography and hydrogeology of the area, and the political makeup of local governing bodies. Structural elements are those factors that are beyond the intentions or control of any one individual or group. Structural elements in this case may include national or state policies that determine the scope of local discretion for landfill regulation, the state's inclinations toward importation of out-of-state trash, the attention to waste issues paid by state or national environmental and business organizations, and even the economic system that produces or avoids certain kinds of waste. Such structural elements would, to varying degrees, influence all such conflicts of this type.

Psychological

Psychological sources of environmental conflicts include those stemming from individuals' cognitive processes (perceptions, schemas, decision making) and those arising from aspects of the interaction between individuals or groups (communication, social dilemmas).

Perceptions and Schemas. As in any conflict, schema-driven processing can bias parties toward limited understanding of both other parties and the problems at hand. Preexisting cognitive structures affect the perception of all new information, the memory of the information, and the inferences made from this information (Fiske & Taylor, 1991). When the information is ambiguous, like most social information, it is most likely to be shaped by these preexisting expectations.

Each party applies his or her own schemas in order to "make sense" of a conflict and its other parties. By design, this cognitive process adaptively reduces one's choices for interpretation and narrows one's perceived options for behavior, so that one can act. However, one's schemas can often foreclose likely options for behavior as well as predispose one toward negative expectations of other parties to the conflict. Stereotypes and other negative expectations can result in two typical cognitive patterns in conflict: worst-case thinking and self-fulfilling prophecies.

In *worst-case thinking,* each action or statement by another party is interpreted in its worst possible light. Negative behaviors of the other such as threats or defensiveness are viewed as "validation" of the perceiver's negative image, rather than as justified behaviors, and even the other's neutral behaviors such as asking questions can themselves be considered attempts to trap or deceive. In *self-fulfilling prophecies,* negative actions by the perceiver towards the other party elicit the very negative behaviors or characteristics expected by the perceiver. In their classic study of expectancy effects, Rosenthal and Jacobsen (1968) demonstrated that randomly assigned high or low expectations of children "produced" subsequent achievement levels that confirmed the initial expectation. Bronfenbrenner (1961) and others (Deutsch, 1986) have described this process in terms of *self-confirming images.* Although none of these have been explicitly studied in environmental conflicts as they have in other conflict realms, environmental conflict resolution practitioners have provided numerous examples of their occurrence and of the relevance of this psychological research.

Decision-making. In addition to the likelihood that parties have different stakes in the outcome of an environmental conflict and stand to lose or gain differently, the uncertainty surrounding many aspects makes these conflicts particularly thorny. Choices are not clear, and in fact must be considered in light of the uncertainties involved. Outcomes are uncertain. Alternative courses of action cannot result in guaranteed outcomes, given the complexity and dynamic nature of the natural environment and the social environment. Therefore, each outcome is only probabilistic.

Probabilistic outcomes might not lead to conflict were it not for some additional accompanying characteristics. Bacow and Wheeler (1984) expand on the role of individual judgment and decision-making sources of conflict: First, not only are outcomes uncertain, but the probabilities of these outcomes are uncertain as well. Thus, parties may have very *different probability estimates* of, for example, a system failure or the impact of certain actions. These estimates may be based on different sets of data since parties rarely have access to all relevant data. Even when looking at the same data, parties may generate different conclusions.

Second, parties value outcomes differently, or in other words, parties have *different values.* In addition to the uncertainty around outcomes, one party may consider a given outcome (e.g., water pollution, degradation of a habitat) to be a minor inconvenience that another party may consider a tragedy. As Bacow and Wheeler (1984) point out, *differing assessments of impacts* are really conflicts over values.

Third, parties may have *differences in their definition of the scope* of the dispute. Parties may seek to define the scope narrowly in terms of a few locally affected parties, while others may define the scope broadly to include others in the region (i.e., the whole watershed), other, more distant parties that may have interests (e.g., protecting wildlife), or even future generations.

Fourth, parties may have *differences in their attitudes toward risk.* If combining differing probabilities of outcomes with differing assessments of impact were not already enough to produce conflict, this fourth factor would be reason enough. Parties may view a particular probability of an outcome as an acceptable risk that others would consider to be a high risk, for example, "one person may be comforted by the fact that there is only one chance in a thousand of a serious accident at a proposed nuclear power plant, whereas another may be terrified by the same statistic" (Bacow & Wheeler, 1984, p. 9). General research in judgment and decision making on attitudes toward risk (Kahneman & Tversky, 1979; Lopes, 1997) has much research that is relevant to the environmental conflict domain.

Incentive Structure. Much has been done in the areas of organizational psychology, social psychology, and political science on how incentives or perceived incentives in a given situation shape strategic behavior in an interaction between parties. In addition to valuing their own alternatives, parties must also engage in *reflexive reasoning,* that is, they must predict the other parties' reaction when structuring their own action.

The models for this interaction are familiar to most. One is the notion of the "tragedy of the commons" (Hardin, 1960), where behavior by each individual in a collective acts in her or his self-interest and ends up harming the self-interest of each when others engage in the same behavior. This was first applied, appropriately enough for this chapter, to a landuse example:

> Picture a pasture open to all. It is to be expected that each herdsman will try to keep as many cattle as possible on the commons. Such an arrangement may work reasonably satisfactorily for centuries because tribal wars, poaching, and disease keep the numbers of both man and beast well below the carrying capacity of the land. Finally, however, comes the day of reckoning, that is, the day when the long-desired goal of social stability becomes a reality. At this point, the inherent logic of the commons remorselessly generates tragedy.
>
> As a rational being, each herdsman seeks to maximize his gain. Explicitly or implicitly, more or less consciously, he asks, "What is the utility *to me* of adding one more animal to my herd?" . . . The rational herdsman concludes that the only sensible course for him to pursue is to add another animal to his herd. And another, and another . . . But this is the conclusion reached by each and every rational herdsman sharing a commons. Therein lies the tragedy. Each man is locked into a system that compels him to increase his heard without limit—in a world that is limited. (Hardin, 1960, p. 1244)

Its characteristics fit well with most if not all environmental conflicts, including overfishing and pollution. While pursuit of self-interest may be rational, its consequences can be tragic (Schelling, 1978).

The other model of incentive structure useful for understanding environmental and many other conflicts is the classic "prisoners' dilemma" (Luce & Raifa, 1957), where situational incentives and lack of trust between parties seem to suggest less than optimal solutions. In this model, two prisoners must independently choose between confessing or keeping silent. It is best if they both remain silent, but worst if both confess. But for each individual the incentive is to confess to gain leniency, and so both often do, and both obtain the worst outcome. The model represents the situation, apropos for environmental conflicts, where each party favors a certain course of action that is in its self-interest while at the same time hoping that other parties will do the opposite. In this sense a multiparty prisoners' dilemma resembles a commons dilemma. For example, each consumer of electricity may wish that other consumers would cut back, allowing his or her increased use to go unnoticed. "Payoffs" to any given party depend on what the other parties do. In the absence of communication or trust between parties, no incentive exists to improve joint welfare, and in fact costs

suggest against it. For review of other situational factors affecting negotiation behavior, consult Druckman (1977).

Communication. Finally, communication factors may if not produce then at least exacerbate environmental conflicts. As noted earlier, incentives are often such that when there is lack of communication and no ability to share information, parties will assume the worst behavior from other parties and plan their responses accordingly.

Conflict escalation typically stems from miscommunication between parties. A substrate of tension may exist prior to a crisis, but schemas and assumptions shape behaviors that then are misinterpreted. Parties may intentionally alter their communication from that which would be most direct and unambiguous in order to retain ability for maneuver. Such strategic considerations make it difficult to say clearly what was "miscommunication" versus what was intentionally ambiguous communication (Coupland, Giles, & Wiemann, 1991).

Finally, the structure of interaction in most environmental conflicts is such that, at least prior to intervention (see section on resolution, following), parties have little opportunity to share information or to coordinate joint strategy or problem solving. Given the complex nature of information in these conflicts, the nature of (or lack of) information sharing can significantly influence the quality of the solutions that are developed and considered.

INSTITUTIONAL WAYS OF RESOLVING ENVIRONMENTAL CONFLICT

Societies have evolved various general mechanisms for managing conflicts (Gulliver, 1979; Nader & Todd, 1978). Often these mechanisms and procedures have been codified and formal institutions created for their execution. In the United States, it is typically assumed that if people cannot resolve a dispute informally, the next step is "taking it to court." Bringing a conflict to a local, state, or federal court accesses one branch of government that has been specifically set up to resolve disputes. Less obvious, perhaps, are the conflict resolution roles played by the other two branches of government, the legislative and the executive/administrative. All three branches of government have formal procedures for hearing the concerns of parties, for weighing in other concerns they may be responsible for protecting, and for producing a decision that then must be adhered to by all parties.

JUDICIAL: ENFORCING LAWS

In theory, there are two major areas of law in the United States—criminal and civil. Both areas fall under the judicial branch of government. The third area of law less familiar to the layperson is administrative law. What makes administrative law unique is that it falls under the executive branch rather than the judicial branch. The U.S. judicial court system has two levels, state and federal, and the systems often run parallel.

Environmental conflicts are typically handled in administrative law proceedings, but certain types of issues go to traditional judicial courts. These cases usually are tried as civil cases, although examples of criminal violations do exist. Civil cases involve issues of systemic and consistent regulatory violations as well as issues of "standing." Criminal cases involve issues of gross negligence, where employees or others have suffered serious medical/health consequences, and corporate officers are tried for criminal negligence. Examples have included requiring employees to clean out toxic tanks without protective gear or hiding safety and health information. Senior corporate officers are sometimes held criminally liable for intentionally harming the environment. Examples include dumping toxins or hiding data from the Environmental Protection Agency (EPA) to prevent the discovery of noncompliance with federal regulations, such as those stemming from the Clean Air Act (CAA) or Clean Water Act (CWA). Such actions are perceived as similar to conspiracy.

ADMINISTRATIVE: CREATING AND ADMINISTERING REGULATIONS

More commonly, parties who are involved in an environmental conflict may also find that their dispute is one where a government agency has been given administrative responsibility and accompanying adjudicative powers. Most laws and legislative acts designed to protect air and water quality or influence landuse are cast in broad and vague language that must be further interpreted or operationalized to apply. This task falls to the administrative branch. For example, while an act may state that air quality must be protected, it is the responsibility of the administering agency to specify the limit on how many parts per billion of a given pollutant will be allowed

to be discharged into the air. Similarly, many acts establish programs (and authorize funding for them), such as the program to regulate what is dumped into U.S. waters, but it is up to the agency to set up and administer these programs. Agencies develop regulations, assess and monitor impacts, and issue permits and licenses. These processes are accompanied by public hearings.

Thus, common environmental conflicts develop when one of these existing regulations may be violated. Examples might be a neighborhood that fears its water or air is being polluted by leaking tanks at a nearby business or an environmental group that fears the negative impact on wildlife habitat of a new highway under construction. When parties feel they are suffering a form of harm that regulations are supposed to protect against, they take their conflict to an administrative rather than a judicial hearing.

Other common environmental conflicts handled in this way include ones where proposed future changes or actions by one party are felt likely to threaten existing limits or standards, one where existing standards are felt by parties to be either inadequate or too stringent, or ones where it is felt that regulations are not being adequately or consistently enforced. Conflicts also occur when an agency, in its role of administering law, must develop and propose a new regulation ("promulgate a rule") that interprets and enforces new standards or limits. Until recent innovations in procedure (see "regulatory negotiation" later in this chapter), this was typically a highly litigious process, involving suits by all parties potentially affected by the new regulation.

Agencies must respond to existing federal and state laws as they plan to implement a project. In the United States, the National Environmental Policy Act (NEPA) requires all federal agencies to conduct an environmental impact analysis and a detailed statement for any actions they plan to take. These environmental documents are then available for public review. The act defines fairly stringent requirements on public participation in agency decision making. As a result, agencies are placed less into an adjudicatory role than a mediative role. However, public hearings often have functioned ineffectively as a forum for the airing and integration of the concerns of diverse parties with differing values. Public officials and agencies have often found themselves unable to take action using traditional administrative procedures alone; fortunately, innovations in consensus building, discussed later, have provided new process tools (Susskind & Cruikshank, 1987; Susskind, McKearnan, & Carpenter, 1999).

LEGISLATIVE: CREATING MANDATES FOR REGULATION

Often controversy and conflict may arise because no clear legal framework exists for deciding who is "right." Laws are a way of formalizing and codifying a society's values and priorities, and when public values change or become divided on an issue, the representative framework set up by the U.S. Constitution provides a mechanism for (theoretically) assessing the "will of the people" and enacting new law to shape future judicial and administrative decisions.

An example of a legislature being used to resolve such a conflict is the passing of the Clean Air Act in 1963. Increasing scientific evidence emerging in the 1960s suggested the deleterious effects of pollution on human health, biodiversity, and so forth. The publication of Rachel Carson's *Silent Spring* in 1962 convinced an increasing number of U.S. citizens that policies allowing unregulated polluting by industry, agriculture, and even individuals was producing a potential toxic and dangerous environment. While opinions across the society were (and still are) divided, and scientific evidence disputed, the relative "weight" of the "majority" argued for a shifting of priorities in the legal framework that guides policies and decision making (O'Leary et al., 1999).

INTERACTIONS

Because the three branches of the U.S. government are part of an interrelated system, sometimes conflicts will set in motion processes/actions that cross all three branches of government. For example, in "friendly litigation," an environmental advocate may sue a federal agency to compel it to perform its role (e.g., to designate critical habitat for a listed endangered species), possibly forcing the legislative branch to allocate more resources so that the agency may discharge its responsibility.

LIMITATIONS OF TRADITIONAL LEGISLATIVE, JUDICIAL, AND ADMINISTRATIVE INSTITUTIONS

Critics argue that many aspects of environmental litigation are inefficient. Horowitz (1977) outlines several concerns. First, adjudication is focused on rights and addressing "wrongs," deferring any discussion of

alternatives and virtually ignoring any discussion of costs. "If a person possesses a right, he possesses it whatever the cost" (p. 34). The judiciary has little flexibility to experiment or to adjust its techniques to the problems it faces. Adjudication is also "the supreme example of incremental decisionmaking," able to focus on problems only piecemeal. The judge can rule only on those specific issues before the court. This results in an unrealistic separation of interrelated policy questions, often with unfortunate consequences. Because courts respond only when litigants come to them, litigants may be unrepresentative of the affected parties, and cases may be unrepresentative of modal cases. The adversarial process encourages litigants to argue their positions on priorities with exaggerated vigor, possibly misleading the judge on public preferences. Finally, as a result of the focus on rights and duties rather than alternatives, judges must focus their decision on "antecedent facts," behavior in the past, rather than on "consequential facts," the impact of the decision on behavior in the future. The concept of planning seems to be in contradiction to the nature of adjudication.

Finally, the conflictual and adversarial nature of traditional environmental litigation means that parties remain at odds once a settlement is achieved. The "losers" either continue to appeal or work to erode support for the decision. Most solutions are ultimately short term in that seeds are planted for related conflicts in the future.

Administrative processes, as well, until recent modifications, were often seen as causing more conflicts than they resolved. The addition of procedures to "regulate the regulators" and give legitimacy to administrative decision-making processes ended up burdening the process and making it time-consuming, cumbersome, and susceptible to judicial challenge (Susskind & Cruikshank, 1987). Administrative agencies became more bureaucratized, leading to indecision, delay, and stalemate.

Such challenges to traditional formal processes have proved an impetus to the development of alternative methodologies for addressing environmental and public policy conflicts.

PUBLIC CONFLICT RESOLUTION

While legislative, judicial, and administrative processes all represent formal and institutionalized ways of managing environmental conflicts, extralegal ways of resolving these and other public conflicts also have evolved. Mediation is the classic form of "alternative dispute resolution" (ADR), although many other processes for addressing environmental conflicts are often mistakenly lumped together under this rubric. These varied processes represent ways of fashioning alternatives to what is often perceived as the drawbacks of litigation. Though seemingly new, several of these processes have antecedents that are quite old (Dukes, 1996; Shonholtz, 1987).

Antecedents and Development

It is generally acknowledged that environmental and public policy conflict resolution (as well as the larger conflict resolution "movement") has emerged from three sources: labor-management mediation, social psychology's facilitated encounters and conciliation work in international and race relations, and community development/empowerment (Dukes, 1996; Moore, 1996).

Labor-management relations evolved a process for mediating disputes that was directive and orderly, under time pressure, operated within legal and administrative procedures, with defined parties who were in a long-term relationship. Those doing early work on environmental conflicts and on public conflicts involving race and health saw analogs to community organizing in labor organizing and saw similar negotiation processes operating in these conflicts. Early efforts to mediate public disputes drew on procedures from labor-management mediation (Bellman, Sampson, & Cormick, 1982; Laue & Cormick, 1974).

Social psychologists were drawing on work in group dynamics and intergroup relations to propose techniques for exploring group tensions and for changing attitudes and behaviors. In workshops in Ethiopia, Northern Ireland, and Cyprus, Doob and Foltz (Doob, 1970, 1971, 1974; Doob & Foltz, 1973, 1974) applied experiential learning techniques (derived from sensitivity training and T-groups in North America). The objectives were to increase self-awareness and understanding of group processes among workshop participants so that they would better be able to manage their own conflict. Similarly, Kelman and colleagues (1972, 1986, 1992; Kelman & Cohen, 1976) developed "problem-solving workshops" to facilitate changes in perceptions and attitudes held by the individual influential workshop participants and to generate new ideas and

policy options that could ultimately be fed back into policy processes and decision making.

The third source for conflict resolution practice came not from earlier forms of conflict management or conciliation but from the traditions of community organizing (cf. Alinsky, 1972; Friere, 1970). The civil rights movement, the women's movement, and the environmental movement overlapped in their pursuit of social justice goals. These goals were not being addressed by the more distributive bargaining approaches coming out of the labor movement. Early models used by these social justice-seeking movements were explicitly confrontative. However, the nonviolent strands, in the tradition of Gandhi and Martin Luther King Jr. drew on negotiation and mediation as well, particularly as less militant leadership emerged. Also, after an early focus on "professional" organizers and mediators, there came a shift toward organizing communities from the bottom up with volunteer leadership. Such grassroots organizing empowered communities to experiment with processes that returned power for decision making (including conflict resolution) back to their communities.

Current Practice

Dukes (1996) reviews several types of current practice in what he calls "public conflict resolution." These practices fall into two general categories: (1) *mediation,* practices that are directed toward reaching agreement on a specific issue or set of issues and (2) *facilitation,* practices that are educational, exploratory, and directed toward "gathering information and developing understanding short of agreement" (p. 43).

Mediation, probably the most well-known, emerged from labor relations and attempts "to identify—through negotiation—the limited but real cooperative actions possible for mutually interdependent parties having different long-term interests and objectives" (Cormick, 1987, p. 29). Dukes (1996) argues that, because of the nature of public conflicts (not easily defined, blurring public and private; see earlier "characteristics" section), no single process can be identified for mediation in this realm. However, he offers the following "working definition": Mediation involves two or more groups negotiating, with process guidance from a third party, in order to clarify, understand, and eventually agree on public issues. These negotiations are direct and face to face among all the affected parties, with a focus on collaborative or nonadversarial interaction and a decision rule (ideally) of consensus. Moore (1996) details the mediation process and the roles and activities of mediators.

Variants of this process exist; three of the most well-known are ad hoc mediation, regulatory negotiations, and policy dialogues. Because so much of public policy mediation is ongoing, *ad hoc mediation* can be distinguished by its focus on particular circumstances and its typically one-time nature. *Regulatory negotiations*, also called "reg-neg" or *negotiated rule making*, supplement existing agency decision-making processes by convening mediated discussions among parties that may have a stake or interest in a proposed rule or regulation. Bacow and Wheeler (1984), Haygood (1988a), and Dukes (1996) provide summaries of this process. Finally, *policy dialogues* are convened to bring together government and industry, or sometimes government agencies and other interested parties, to a form of an ongoing round-table discussion. These discussions are not directly tied in to agency decision making as are regulatory negotiations, but they are convened around issues where policy action is under consideration and involve participants such that agreements and other inputs from such a process are expected to have significant impact.

Facilitation, in contrast to mediation, focuses less on achieving agreement and more on increasing capacities of parties for dialogue, reflection, and understanding on public issues. Older forms of public participation such as study circles and salons have been revived, while newer forms of public participation have been developed. The goals of these processes, according to Dukes (1996), are:

- Educating disputants, stakeholders, and/or the general public about the issues under consideration
- Discovering public interest in, concern with, and ideas about particular issues
- Raising the level of awareness among a particular audience about an issue
- Demonstrating to adversaries that even on the most divisive issues there are items which can be discussed and people on the other side(s) worth talking to
- Reducing the risk of violent confrontation
- Building public support for consequential decisions (pp. 63–64)

Public participation processes often take the form of either the "blue ribbon panel," "public hearing model," or "community-based working group" (Potapchuk, 1988). Processes may vary on the role of experts and they also will vary on their legitimacy based on the consideration actually offered to views of the public. A recent development is the process of *visioning*, where substantial portions of the community are included in a process of "imagining their desired future" and then goals are set for how to achieve it. This usually includes acknowledging the need to move beyond existing processes and the need to build a community-wide consensus for change. This differs from traditional planning processes in that it is focused on the long term and on the values of the community rather than exclusively those of its leadership and/or professional planners. Like other public participation processes, it can be manipulated as a public relations exercise, but when done with commitment by leaders it can enhance public participation in governance (Dukes, 1996).

Facilitated dialogue has a long history in applied psychology, and much of this work has informed the development of dialogue processes that address public issues. Convening a discussion among two or more parties that is controlled by a moderator has many variants, and three have been chosen for mention here (for a full elaboration, see Dukes, 1996). First, the tradition of dialogues on race can be traced back to work by Lewin and colleagues and the early work of the Community Relations Service. Recent years have seen the development of "diversity training" and "prejudice reduction," intensive workshops designed not to reach agreement on issues but to develop insight into one's own identity and respect and understanding for the identities of others. Second, the Kettering Foundation has sponsored the development of the National Issues Forum (NIF) to increase public discussion of major policy issues. Leaders of forums are trained, and communities are provided with issue books and discussion guidelines. Finally, organizations such as the "Public Conversations Project" convene public and private discussions on contentious issues, again without any intent to reach agreement but rather so that new understanding and awareness of common ground on positions may be discovered.

Many types of practitioners, both individuals and institutions, exist in the United States and abroad. These include private individuals and organizations, academic institutions, branches and agencies of the federal government, state offices of dispute resolution, and, with increasing frequency, conflict resolution mechanisms internal to organizations themselves. Further information on this range of practitioners can be found in Dukes (1996).

PROCESS AND OUTCOME GOALS

Throughout the field of conflict resolution generally, recent years have seen an increased interest in assessment and evaluation (Ross & Rothman, 1999). As with other interventions such as psychotherapy, social work, or education, those practicing, researching, or paying for such interventions want to know what works and what does not (and, hopefully, why). Engaging in the task of evaluation brings with it a certain logic that can help to clarify the assumptions and goals of practice, isolate effective behaviors, and build in useful feedback (Patton, 1997).

d'Estrée and Colby (2000; d'Estrée, Beck, & Colby, 1999) identify the various goals addressed or attempted by environmental conflict resolution. Building on literature reviews, interviews with practitioners, and case analyses, they identify six categories of criteria for successful environmental conflict resolution that reveal the many goals these processes often hope to address. These categories include: (1) reaching an agreement or other form of outcome desired by and/or acceptable to the parties; (2) using a quality process (fair, satisfactory, inclusive, economical, etc.); (3) achieving a quality outcome (economically sound, environmentally sustainable, culturally sustainable, clear, feasible, etc.); (4) obtaining a desirable relationship between the parties and the outcome (compliance, satisfaction with the outcome, stability, flexibility); (5) obtaining a desirable relationship between the parties themselves (reduced hostility, increased trust, increased capacity for cooperation, changes in attitudes and behavior); and finally (6) increases in social capital (community problem-solving capacity, increased coordination, and system integration).

In sum, the goals of environmental conflict resolution are many. Improvements to practice will be informed by evaluation research on individual cases of resolution but also through comparative studies on the relative benefits of various forms of environmental conflict resolution, including litigation, legislation, and administrative processes (d'Estrée & Colby, 2001).

RELATED PSYCHOLOGICAL RESEARCH

In order to better sense the nature and variety of psychological research done on environmental conflict and its resolution, we sample and profile two particular applied research programs. We then review general categories of psychological research on environmental conflicts.

KENNETH HAMMOND AND COLLEAGUES ON THE ORME DAM CONFLICT (ARIZONA)

Hammond, Harvey, and Hastie (1992) believe that one major obstacle to effective utilization of scientific results in science-related policy comes from the inability to manage uncertainty or perhaps even recognize its presence in policy decisions. Hammond et al. discuss the importance of separating fact from value in alleviating the confusion that arises in policy decision processes. They cite Thibaut and Walker's distinction between the aim of science (truth) and the aim of policy (justice) and the need for a "two-tiered solution" with first stage designed to resolve issues of fact and the second stage to resolve policy questions.

Hammond et al. applied psychological research methods to develop a schematic summary of the application of social judgment theory to separate, estimate, and then systematically recombine value and scientific judgment in the formation of public policy surrounding the central Arizona Orme Dam conflict.

In this model, social value judgments (policy judgments) are obtained separately from the public, while scientific judgments are obtained from experts. Then the social value judgments and scientific judgments are combined using the following equation: $Y_s = W_1X_1 + W_2X_2 + W_3X_3$, where Y_s is the overall degree of acceptability of the object in dispute; W represents the weight or relative importance of the social value judgments; X represents the experts' scientific judgments of predicted magnitude on outcome dimensions.

In the case of the Orme Dam, value identification was compiled through the distribution of a fact book and a series of public meetings. The representatives from 60 public groups assigned the "importance" weight to 14 factors that reflected their own values. The scientific-technical collection phase was initiated after the value importance analysis was completed. The importance weights were then combined with the scientific performance predictions to produce the global acceptability ratings of the plans.

The results of the analysis revealed that none of the plans involving the Orme Dam received a high rating. Regardless of the long-standing public promotion by both the water development representatives and the representatives for flood control, the analysis revealed other alternatives that fit more closely with their value positions. In the end, an alternative to the Orme Dam was created.

In this example, it was through the specification of different judgment tasks for policy makers and scientists and also the systematic recombination of value and fact that helped alleviate the confusion in the policy decision process that often accompanies resource conflict.

LINDA PUTNAM AND COLLEAGUES ON THE EDWARDS AQUIFER CONFLICT (TEXAS)

The Edwards Aquifer is the sole source of water for a seven-county region that includes San Antonio, Texas. The dispute over water rights in this area dates back before the 1950s.

Putnam and Wunsch (1999), via an analysis of interviews conducted with different stakeholder groups involved in the conflict, consider the role of how the representatives of particular stakeholder groups frame tier identities, characterizations of other parties, and views about conflict management in this intractable environmental dispute. The interview data are analyzed by focusing upon the ways that stakeholder groups cast identity, characterization, and conflict management frames. For Putnam and Wunsch *framing* refers to the world views, interpretations of experiences, and perspectives that stakeholders have on the situations they encounter. The frames provide participants with accounts for inclusion and exclusion of issues in a dispute, ways of acting and reacting, and ways to interpret the actions of other parties in the dispute.

Identity frames reflect how stakeholders describe their own roles in conflict and include references to societal roles, ethnic or cultural orientation, place identity, institutional identity, and interest-based references. Analysis of the interviews indicates institutional identity is the dominant frame in this dispute. Putnam and Wunsch note that when stakeholders are asked to characterize what the conflict is about, they respond with a strong institutional bias.

Characterization frames focus on the labels and potential stereotypes that disputants hold for particular groups. Conflict management frames refer to the disputants' preferences for how the conflict should be managed and reflect their opinion of how they think it has been managed in the past.

Putnam and Wunsch analyze each of the aforementioned frames in relation to conflict intractability, and it appears that frames are closely tied to perceptions of the conflict itself with conflict management frames contributing to the nature and definition of this conflict. Putnam and Wunsch also point out that a full analysis of the dispute will need to intertwine the three frames with the descriptions of intractability to unpack the relationship between institutional frames and the way the dispute develops over time.

Putnam and Peterson focus their analysis of this dispute by analyzing the way four key events in the dispute alter or produce a shift in identity, characterization, and conflict management frames.

Identity frames shifted from interest-based frames early in the dispute to place-based (urban/rural) and then to institutional identity frames. Characterization frames shifted as the conflict evolved according to shifting identity frames. In the earlier stages of the dispute, conflict management frames were aligned with consensus recommendation and joint problem solving. However, as litigation began to dominate the Aquifer dispute, adjudication became the reactionary tactic.

Putnam and Peterson (2000) discuss how officials can identify frames, apply them to an analysis, and use them in dealing with stakeholders. Putnam and Peterson write that agency officials can identify frames by talking with spokespeople of various stakeholder groups and that the grammar in which the stories are told offers clues as to the way stakeholders see the identities and the roles of the other stakeholders. These stories can also reveal stakeholder perception of conflict management.

Putnam and Peterson also discuss the importance of key events or turning points and how they may signal frame changes. The authors consider frame changes to be important because they alter the patterns of relationships and move the conflict to a different level. The authors propose that intervention may be more effective when identities shift or as the disputants shift their conflict management frames. Understanding stakeholder frames can help agency officials avoid premature judgments and enable them to be more informed of how participants interact with the resource.

Putnam and Thompson (1999) performed a language analysis of newspaper articles to examine the identity and characterization frames and to explore the role of the media in framing the situation. The authors concluded that since parties in the conflict were separated both geographically and organizationally, the media may assume a very important role in documenting the events, representing environmental concerns to the public, and forming images of the conflict management frames.

ADDITIONAL PSYCHOLOGICAL RESEARCH ON ENVIRONMENTAL CONFLICTS

In addition to the psychology research reviewed above (schemas, risk perception, social dilemmas, decision making) that helps inform us about the processes taking place both individually and within groups during resource conflicts, research relevant to environmental conflicts has also been done in the areas of environmental behavior, justice perception, and computer-assisted negotiations.

Because research on environmental attitudes and behavior has been reviewed elsewhere, it is not repeated here. This large research literature examines prediction and change of environmental attitudes and behavior ranging from encouraging conservation actions to the most effective means of environmental awareness education. For additional examples of this type of research see Paul C. Stern (2000) and Stephen Kaplan (2000).

Research on environmental justice represents a new and developing area of psychological research. As Clayton (2000) states in her article concerning models of justice in the environmental debate, it is a significant trend that environmental issues are being evaluated in terms of justice and fairness and that researchers have found that perceived justice is not only a good predictor of environmental attitudes and willingness to compromise but also an important factor in the successful resolution of environmental conflict. Clayton's research addresses the question of which justice principles are preferred in resolving environmental conflicts. The results from two questionnaire studies confirm that environmental justice—defined as the responsibility to other species, to future generations, and the rights of the environment as an entity of its own—emerges as the most highly rated consideration in resolving environmental conflicts.

Clayton (2000) also suggests that environmental justice is distinct from traditional procedural and distributive justice factors. Distributive justice evaluations are generally made by considering norms as the basis for the allocation of scarce resources while procedural justice evaluations focus upon the "fairness" of the process by which those decisions are made. For an in-depth review of the psychological literature concerning procedural justice and its theoretical and applied implications that process judgments are important determinants of attitudes and behavior, see Lind and Tyler (1988).

Syme and Fenton (1993) investigated the applicability of procedural justice theory to allocation decision making for the purpose of providing information about how people view current mechanisms for decision making and what alternatives are seen as fair. The authors found that the concepts of equity and procedural justice had greater significance as competition for water resources increased and that the most preferred procedure was arbitration regardless of high- or low-intensity conflict.

Opotow and Clayton (1994) summarize the importance of justice research in understanding environmental debates by stating that the way we answer the fundamental questions surrounding justice perception—rights, entitlements, fairness, and ethics—determines many of our attitudes and much of our behavior.

Finally, while negotiations and computer-assisted negotiations have long been studied outside the environmental domain, recent efforts have brought these methodologies to environmental conflict. Thiessen, Loucks, and Stedinger (1998) describe an interactive computer-assisted negotiation support (ICANS) system. Based upon the information provided to the program by each party, it can help all parties identify feasible alternatives, if any exist, that should be preferred to each party's proposal. If such alternatives do not exist, the program can help to develop counterproposals. Thiessen, Loucks, and Stedinger (1998) present results from limited experiments involving water resource system development. Since water resource development is a highly complex multiobjective process, the developing real-time computer programs could benefit decision makers by assisting them in making favorable decisions. The results of their experiments suggest that programs like ICANS can help negotiators find agreements that parties in conflict will judge superior to those that they might have reached without the use of computer assistance. However, Thiessen et al. also acknowledge that the procedures incorporated in the ICANS are not designed to address equity or subjective judgments concerning relative worth of benefits.

Zigurs, Reitsma, Lewis, Huebscher, and Hayes (1999) investigated whether increased accessibility of computer-based simulations models would increase the quality of decisions and satisfaction of negotiators. The negotiation task was based upon a real-life problem in Colorado River water management. Zigurs et al. designed their study to address the question of whether accessibility to simulation models is likely to improve negotiation processes and outcomes. Zigurs et al. concluded that the increased accessibility of computer-based simulation models was not worth the cost of its development and deployment under the conditions examined in their study. Zigurs et al. also discussed the input-output relationship of the computer model and lack of process factors. The authors discuss several factors for the lack of expected improvement results. How and whether the information exchanged is used by the disputants is a factor, as well as the possibility of the higher accessibility conditions that might have been offset by the negotiators' inability to handle the increased information load.

As computer-assisted negotiation programs become more sophisticated, their role in information-heavy resource conflicts will be greatly improved if they can assist not only in providing necessary information exchange but also by assisting in the management and use of the information.

FUTURE DIRECTIONS FOR RESEARCH AND PRACTICE

In addition to social complexity, the complexity of the scientific and technical information contributes to the difficulty of resolving these environmental conflicts. Psychological research is particularly well-suited to addressing questions of information collection/perception, management, and integration. Recent research reviewed earlier has begun to address ways to assist in the management of large amounts of technical information. Another difficulty in such conflicts is uneven access to resource information that should be shared by all parties.

Information hoarding only leads to less than efficient solutions, and adds to perceptions of injustice. Future research on processes and mechanisms for information-sharing and the potential benefits would support the creation of optimal solutions.

As described earlier, environmental conflicts are usually, at some fundamental level, conflicts over values. Psychological traditions of research both on values and on emotions and decision making provide sources for the development of more sophisticated processes for integrating values. Research, such as that reviewed earlier, on processes for the identification of value components should be further developed. As parties become able to separate "fact" from value, the options for addressing values become clearer. Such processes may be achieved through assisted decision making, as in Hammond's work. More attention could also fruitfully be paid by researchers to the processes used by conflict resolution practitioners who achieve this same separation through facilitated discussion, such as the process used by the Public Conversations Project.

Further work on framing in complex environmental disputes also will likely lead to important insights. Putnam's work on institutional frames and the role of framing in creating turning points seems particularly valuable. Work reviewed at various points in this chapter suggests the need for the application of frame analysis to questions of framings that are most likely to elicit fears of risk or fears of threats to values.

Finally, several questions for social-science research generally arise from the continuing evolution and even institutionalization of the newer processes developed to address environmental conflict. (For further investigation of these questions, consult Dukes, 2001.) As processes that were often initially grassroots supported are funded more and more by government agencies, what influence does this have on the form of the practice? These processes are now being "mainstreamed," and offices for environmental conflict resolution are being established within state governments and federal agencies. How is this changing the processes used? Is this changing the perceptions of the parties using them? What are the institutional arrangements that "best" support various conflict resolution processes? As is common in the professionalization of any field, calls are often made for practitioner standards. Beyond the question of what these will include, what will be the impact of imposing standards on the practice and process? Finally, as various new models emerge under an even newer movement of *collaboration*, questions are again being raised of what may be sacrificed in exchange for collaboration (Dukes & Firehock, 2001). How do and should such processes interact with existing legal, political, and social frameworks?

In closing, as environmental issues continue to increase in prominence, they will more often be seen as part of most major conflicts. For example, it has been said that the international conflicts of the next century will be fought over water. Further attention by researchers to the sources, dynamics, and processes for change in environmental conflicts may contribute to more sustainable and just solutions.

REFERENCES

Alinsky, S. D. (1972). *Rules for radicals: A pragmatic primer for realistic radicals.* New York: Vintage.

Bacow, L. S., & Wheeler, M. (1984). *Environmental dispute resolution.* New York: Plenum Press.

Bellman, H. S., Sampson, C. S., & Cormick, G. W. (1982). *Using mediation when siting hazardous waste management facilities: A handbook.* Washington, DC: United States Environmental Protection Agency.

Bronfenbrenner, U. (1961). The mirror image in Soviet-American relations. *Journal of Social Issues, 17,* 45–56.

Bullard, R. D. (1983). Solid waste sites and the black Houston community. *Sociological Inquiry, 53,* 273–288.

Clayton, S. (2000). Models of justice in the environmental debate. *Journal of Social Issues, 56*(3), 459–474.

Cormick, G. (1987). Environmental mediation: the myth, the reality, and the future. In D. J. Brower & D. S. Carol (Eds.), *Managing land-use conflicts* (Case Studies in Special Area Management, Duke Press Policy Studies). Durham, NC: Duke University Press.

Coupland, N., Giles, H., & Wiemann, J. M. (Eds.). (1991). *"Miscommunication" and problematic talk.* Newbury Park: Sage.

d'Estrée, T. P. (1993, May). *Psychological dimensions of water conflicts.* Paper presented at the biannual meeting of the National Conference on Peacemaking and Conflict Resolution, Portland, OR.

d'Estrée, T. P., Beck, C. A., & Colby, B. G. (1999). *Criteria for evaluating successful environmental conflict resolution.* Unpublished manuscript.

d'Estrée, T. P., & Colby, B. G. (2000). *Guidebook for analyzing success in environmental conflict resolution* (ICAR Rep. No. 3). Fairfax, VA: Institute for Conflict Analysis and Resolution.

d'Estrée, T. P., & Colby, B. G. (2001). *Evaluating success in environmental conflict resolution: Case studies of Western water conflicts.* Unpublished manuscript.

Deutsch, M. (1986). Folie à deux: A psychological perspective on Soviet-American relations. In M. P. Kearns (Ed.), *Persistent patterns and emergent structures in a waving century.* New York: Praeger.

Doob, L. (1970). *Resolving conflict in Africa: The Fermeda Workshop.* New Haven, CT: Yale University Press.

Doob, L. (1971). The impact of the Fermeda Workshop on the conflicts in the Horn of Africa. *International Journal of Group Tensions, 1,* 91–98.

Doob, L. (1974). A Cyprus workshop: An exercise in intervention methodology. *Journal of Social Psychology, 94,* 164–178.

Doob, L., & Foltz, W. (1973). The Belfast Workshop: An application of group techniques to a destructive conflict. *Journal of Conflict Resolution, 17,* 489–512.

Doob, L., & Foltz, W. (1974). The impact of a workshop upon grass roots leaders in Belfast. *Journal of Conflict Resolution, 18,* 237–256.

Druckman, D. (Ed.). (1977). *Negotiations: Social-psychological perspectives.* Beverly Hills, CA: Sage.

Dukes, E. F. (1996). *Resolving public conflict: Transforming community and governance.* Manchester, England: Manchester University Press.

Dukes, E. F. (1999). Structural forces in conflict and conflict resolution in democratic society. In H.-W. Jeong (Ed.), *From conflict resolution to peacebuilding.* London: Ashgate.

Dukes, E. F. (2001, Fall). Integration in environmental conflict. *Conflict Resolution Quarterly, 19*(1), 103–115.

Dukes, E. F., & Firehock, K. (2001). *Collaboration: A guide for environmental advocates.* Institute for Environmental Negotiation, The Wilderness Society, National Audubon Society.

Fiske, S. T., & Taylor, S. E. (1991). *Social cognition* (2nd ed.). New York: McGraw-Hill.

Friere, P. (1970). *Pedagogy of the oppressed.* New York: Seabury Press.

Glavovic, B., Dukes, E. F., & Lynott, J. (1997). Training and educating environmental mediators: Lessons from experience in the United States. *Mediation Quarterly, 14*(4), 269–292.

Gulliver, P. H. (1979). *Disputes and negotiations.* New York: Academic Press.

Hammond, K. R., Harvey, L. O., Jr., & Hastie, R. (1992). Making better use of scientific knowledge: Separating truth from justice. *Psychological Science, 3*(2), 80–87.

Hardin, G. (1960). The tragedy of the commons. *Science, 162,* 1244.

Haygood, L. V. (1988). Negotiated rule making: Challenges for mediators and participants. *Mediation Quarterly, 20,* 77–91.

Horowitz, D. (1977). *Courts and social policy.* Washington, DC: Cato Institute.

Kahneman, D., & Tversky, A. (1979). Prospect theory: An analysis of decision under risk. *Econometrica, 47,* 263–291.

Kaplan, S. (2000). Human nature and environmentally responsible behavior. *Journal of Social Issues, 56*(3), 491–508.

Kelman, H. (1972). The problem-solving workshop in conflict resolution. In R. Merritt (Ed.), *Communication in International Politics* (pp. 168–204). Champaign-Urbana: University of Illinois Press.

Kelman, H. (1986). Interactive problem solving: A social-psychological approach to conflict resolution. In W. Klassen (Ed.), *Dialogue toward inter-faith understanding* (pp. 293–314). Jerusalem: Ecumenical Institute for Theological Research.

Kelman, H. (1992). Informal mediation by the scholar-practitioner. In J. Bercovitch & J. Z. Rubin (Eds.), *Mediation in international relations: Multiple approaches to conflict management* (pp. 64–96). New York: St. Martin's Press.

Kelman, H., & Cohen, S. P. (1976). The problem-solving workshop: A social-psychological contribution to the resolution of international conflicts. *Journal of Peace Research, 13,* 79–90.

Laue, J. H., & Cormick, G. W. (1974). The ethics of intervention in community disputes. In G. Bermant, H. C. Kelman, & D. Warwick (Eds.), *The ethics of social intervention.* Washington, DC: Hemisphere Publishing.

Lind, E. A., & Tyler, T. R. (1988). *The social psychology of procedural justice.* New York: Plenum Press.

Lopes, L. L. (1997). Between hope and fear: The psychology of risk. In W. M. Goldstein & R. M. Hogarth (Eds.), *Research on judgment and decision making: Currents, connections, and controversies.* Cambridge: Cambridge University Press.

Luce, R. D., & Raifa, H. (1957). *Games and decisions: Introduction and critical survey.* New York: Wiley.

Moore, C. (1996). *The mediation process.* San Francisco: Jossey-Bass.

Nadar, L., & Todd, H. F. (1978). *The disputing process: Law in ten societies.* New York: Columbia University Press.

O'Leary, R., Durant, R. F., Fiorino, D. J., & Weiland, P. S. (1999). *Managing for the environment.* San Francisco: Jossey-Bass.

Opotow, S., & Clayton, S. (1994). Green justice: Conceptions of fairness and the natural world. *Journal of Social Issues, 50*(3), 1–11.

Patton, M. Q. (1997). *Utilization-focused evaluation.* Thousand Oaks, CA: Sage.

Potapchuk, W. (1988). Building forums for the cooperative resolution of disputes in communities. *National Civic Review, 77,* 342–349.

Putnam, L. L., & Peterson, T. (2000). *The Edwards aquifer dispute: Shifting frames and conflict intractability.* Unpublished manuscript, Texas A&M University, College Station.

Putnam, L. L., & Thompson, C. (1999). *Media framing of the Edwards aquifer case: The fate of the Edwards underground water district.* Paper presented at the meeting of the Academy of Management, Chicago, IL.

Putnam, L. L., & Wunsch, J. (1999). *Organizational framing of the Edwards aquifer dispute.* Unpublished manuscript, Texas A&M University, College Station.

Rittel, H. W. J., & Webber, M. W. (1973). Dilemmas in a general theory of planning. *Policy Sciences, 4,* 155–169.

Rosenthal, R., & Jacobson, L. (1968). *Pygmalion in the classroom.* New York: Holt, Rinehart & Winston.

Ross, M. H., & Rothman, J. (1999). *Theory and practice in ethnic conflict management: Theorizing success and failure.* New York: St. Martin's Press.

Rubin, J. Z., Pruitt, D. G., & Kim, S. H. (1994). *Social conflict: Escalation, stalemate, and settlement* (2nd ed.). New York: McGraw-Hill.

Schelling, T. (1978). *Micromotives and macrobehavior.* New York: Norton.

Shonholtz, R. (1987). The citizens' role in justice: Building a primary justice and prevention system at the neighborhood level. *Annals, 494,* 45–52.

Stern, P. (2000). Toward a coherent theory of environmentally significant behavior. *Journal of Social Issues, 56*(3), 407–424.

Susskind, L., & Cruikshank, J. (1987). *Breaking the impasse: Consensual approaches to resolving public disputes.* New York: Basic Books.

Susskind, L., McKearnan, S., & Carpenter, S. (Eds.). (1999). *Consensus building handbook.* Thousand Oaks, CA: Sage.

Syme, G. J., & Fenton, D. M. (1993). Perceptions of equity and procedural preferences for water allocation decisions. *Society and Natural Resources, 6,* 347–360.

Thiessen, E. M., Loucks, D. P., & Stedinger, J. R. (1998). Computer-assisted negotiations of water resources conflict. *Group Decision and Negotiation, 7*(2), 109–129.

U.S. General Accounting Office. (1983). *Siting of hazardous waste landfills and their correlation with economic and social status of surrounding communities.* Washington, DC: U.S. General Accounting Office.

Zigurs, I., Reitsma, R., Lewis, C., Huebscher, R., & Hayes, C. (1999). Accessibility of computer-based simulation models in inherently conflict-laden negotiations. *Group Decision and Negotiation, 8*(6), 511–533.

CHAPTER 38

A Methodology of
Participatory Planning

LIISA HORELLI

THE AIM OF THIS CHAPTER is to present for discussion a methodological approach to participatory planning from the perspective of environmental psychology. The presentation seeks to explain: why environmental psychology should be interested in this type of planning, what participatory planning is like in some of its varieties, and how and with what methodological tools this activity might be conducted. Finally, the likely impact on both behavior and the environment will be discussed.

THE PROBLEMATIC NATURE OF PARTICIPATORY PLANNING

The previous *Handbook of Environmental Psychology* (Stokols & Altman, 1987) ignored rather conspicuously the theme of participation in spite of the many movements and trends in action research and participatory planning and design from the 1960s on. Student riots in Europe and political protests in favor of civil rights and against nuclear weapons and the Vietnam war as well as the rise of the neighborhood movement and the grassroots organizations in the United States and Canada paved the way for seeing planning as a form of political action directed at realizing certain values (Castells, 1983; Connor, 1996; Taylor, 1998). Some of the early planning theorists who were sensitive to the value-laden and political nature of planning sought to promote forms of participatory planning that would simultaneously improve democracy as a whole. Davidoff (1965) not

only stressed the necessity of making and debating choices during the phases of planning but also pointed out that it was the duty of planners to act as "advocates" for client groups whose interests were not adequately represented. Alinsky (1972, cited in Sanoff, 1999) utilized various methods to mobilize citizens on the neighborhood level to grasp local control and consumer power. Sherry Arnstein (1969, p. 216) claimed that "participation without redistribution of power is a frustrating process for the powerless." She formulated her much cited "ladder of participation," which raised the question concerning the degree to which the public should be given a say over and have power to decide their affairs.

Several experiments in participatory planning around housing and community building took place in Europe during the 1960s and 1970s (Bernfeld, Mayerl, & Mayerl, 1980). Hungarian-born Yona Friedman (1970) not only created popular utopias for ordinary people about cities in France but also designed serial cartoons to enable residents in poor areas of Europe and in developing countries to improve their neighborhoods and towns (Y. Friedman, 1975). After the student riots of the late 1960s, there was a wave of interest in cohousing in Denmark. Collective construction and living were seen as a solution to the demands of raising children since both women and men were working. "Every child should have 100 parents" was the slogan that inspired an interdisciplinary Nordic women's group to create the utopia of a "new everyday life" and its supportive structures (Forskargruppen, 1987; Horelli &

Vespä, 1994). Johannes Olivegren (1975) created his method of user planning for collective groups of dwelling in Sweden. The corresponding Finnish version of participation was a system of self-planning for housing, developed by Heikki Kukkonen (1984), which was, however, too radical for that stage of societal development in Finland. The United Kingdom had several early promoters of participation. Among the most influential internationally were Colin Ward (1976) and John Turner (1976), who inspired many followers in their native country and abroad to promote the role of residents, including children, in the development of housing and living environments.

Public participation was nurtured in the 1980s and 1990s both by the theories of planning as communicative action (Forester, 1999; Healey, 1997) and by innovations in the practical tools for participatory endeavors (Hamdi & Goethert, 1997; Sanoff, 1999; Wates, 2000; Wilcox, 1994).

Currently, participatory planning enjoys a varying status in different parts of the world depending on the political, economic, and administrative culture of the country, the prevailing planning system, and the stage of transformative empowerment of citizens, enabled by the interactive application of information and communication technology (Castells, 1996). Many of the most inspiring participatory tools have been created in the developing countries (Worsley, 1967). Several Western industrialized nations still have complex planning systems, full of rules and regulations, that have been created for the governance of an industrial society (European Commission, 1997). Thus, they have had difficulties in shifting from an expert-led, top-down system of planning to one that would grant a voice to different partners and the networks of citizens. Phenomena like NIMBY (not in my backyard) or LULU (locally unwanted land uses) have made the implementation of participatory results difficult, especially in the better-off neighborhoods. In addition, signs of manipulation—co-option of participatory projects by powerful local interests (Francis, 1988; Hester, 1996)—and even exploitation of poor people as cheap labor for housing construction have not been infrequent (Hamdi & Goethert, 1997).

Many kinds of participatory planning seem to exist, the names of which vary according to the taste of the author. Some of the examples are advocacy planning (Davidoff, 1965), self-planning (*autoplanification*, Y. Friedman, 1970; *itsesuunnittelu*, Kukkonen, 1984), transactive planning (J. Friedman, 1973), user planning (*brukarplanering*, Olivegren, 1975), community action planning (Hamdi & Goerthert, 1997), deliberative planning (Forester, 1999), communicative or collaborative planning (Healey, 1997; Innes & Booher, 1999a), community planning and design (Sanoff, 1999).

The naming of the phenomenon is not the only difficulty. Participatory planning is in fact a typical "mess" of late modern times that seems to involve a set of interconnected problems that are difficult to conceptualize and analyze (Chisholm, 1998). Some of the problems are the access to planning arenas, the eligibility of participants, and the selection of appropriate methods and techniques to be used. The core problem lies in the fuzzy relationship between participatory planning and decision making or in that between direct and representative democracy.

Little focus has so far been granted to the methodology of participatory planning, perhaps because of the complexity of its conceptualization. This is not alleviated by the gap in scope and level of abstraction that seems to exist between the approaches of theoreticians and practitioners of participatory planning (Forester, 1999; Taylor, 1998; Wates, 2000). However, both expert groups seem to have in common the focus on the process of planning at the expense of the outcomes and their internal or external evaluation. Consequently, it is difficult to assess the real impact of participatory planning and design on people and their settings.

The methodological approach presented here is based on a meta-analysis of theoretical and practical planning literature, on an analysis of some 30 case studies sent in by members of the Environment Design Research Association (EDRA) and the International Association for People-Environment Studies (IAPS), as well as on the author's personal involvement with participation for nearly 3 decades.

FRAMING THE METHODOLOGICAL APPROACH

The methodological approach to participatory planning from the perspective of environmental psychology is constructed from three sources:

- Concepts of environmental psychology and environment behavior design research, which provide the basis for the argumentation regarding why participation is important for environmental psychology

- Concepts of collaborative planning and approaches, including enabling tools, as described by the practitioners of community design and action planning, that help to define what participatory planning is
- Concepts and strategies of action research, which assist in defining how participatory planning can be methodologically approached

WHY SHOULD ENVIRONMENTAL PSYCHOLOGY BOTHER ABOUT PARTICIPATORY PLANNING?

Several arguments exist to explain why participation in planning and decision making by citizens is necessary and desirable. Participation is a human, moral, and democratic right, a duty in the new type of welfare society, and a necessary resource for mastering the problems of "glocalization" (the tensions between the globalization of markets and the local efforts of survival; Healey, 1997). But what is the argument for why participatory planning should be important for environmental psychology?

There is no consensus on the definition and scope of environmental psychology (EP). According to a review of six textbooks by Sime (1999), some of the authors regard EP as a subdiscipline within psychology or social psychology (Bonnes & Secchiaroli, 1995). Others see it as part of the multidisciplinary field of environment behavior (EB) research (Bechtel, 1997). Sommer (2000) prefers a dual approach in which EP is both a subdiscipline within the behavioral sciences and a field of study involving people from a variety of disciplines and professions. The author of this chapter is in favor of an interdisciplinary approach to the field, the (delete and add) foci of which are the psychosocial and behavioral processes of different individuals and groups of people in diverse settings in the varying phases of the cycle of research, policy planning, design, implementation, and evaluation (cf. Moore, 1987). Thus, the approach is close to that of environment behavior design research but with a special focus on the environment behavior transactions that are interpreted from the perspective of individual, communal, and societal regulation (Horelli, 1999). Communal regulation means the opportunity of a group or local collective to influence environmental issues, for instance, through participatory planning. Societal regulation takes place as regional policy,

zoning laws, or urban policy programs. Individual regulation can be seen as the subjective appropriation of the environment and the processing of this experience in which the setting and its cues are used as a means of psychic self-regulation (Horelli, 1993, 1995; Korpela, 1995). The latter comprises the construction and maintenance of self through psychic work (mental operations with images, intentions, thoughts, dreams), use of the body, and through behavior or activities in the social and the built environment as well as in nature. Environmental transactions can be examined both as verbal and nonverbal communication (cf. Rapoport, 1982). They also involve a form of internal communication in which the participant processes meaningful emotions, cognitions, and symbols (Noschis, 1988). The approach is in fact an expansion of the transactional perspective to environmental psychology (Altman & Rogoff, 1987) in the sense that it lays more emphasis on both the psychological interpretations of and the societally mediated nature of environmental transactions (Bronfenbrenner, 1993; Horelli, 1999).

Planning and design are regarded in this framework as supporters of environmental transactions that enhance the fit or congruence between the needs and intentions of the users and their settings. The approach sets requirements for the quality of the planning content. The approach also implies a demand for methods that enhance the communicative nature of the planning process. The latter means that the procedural theories of planning should explain how participation can be organized in such a way that the planning cycle becomes an arena for learning and capacity building of citizens, experts, and decision makers.

Thus, *the argument for participatory planning within environmental psychology is based on the conception that participatory planning can be a medium that supports successful communicative transactions benefiting women and men, young and old, from varying ethnic groups and social classes, in different environments.*

WHAT IS PARTICIPATORY PLANNING?

Different disciplines or fields, such as political science, community organization, or environment behavior studies, tend to define *citizen* or *public participation* in varying ways (Churchman, 1987, 1990). Therefore, defining *participatory planning* requires an examination of the literature on planning theories and of the writings of practitioners.

The history of urban planning theories after the Second World War has been characterized, especially in the Anglo-American countries, by two significant changes (Taylor, 1998). The first one took place in the 1960s, when the tradition of *planning as urban design* was transformed into a *systems and rational process view of planning.* This ended the centuries-long tradition of seeing planning as mostly physical design of human settlements aiming at the production of master plans and blueprints for the construction and implementation of settings of high aesthetic quality. The systems view of planning saw its object, whether neighborhood, town, or region, as a system of interrelated activities in a constant state of flux. The focus of planning was, besides the physical environment, the social, cultural, and economic aspects that affected the lives of people and institutions. Consequently, urban planning was conceptualized as an exercise in systems analysis the results of which were reflected mostly in strategic plans (local planning went on as usual). This shift also meant that the geographical and morphological conception of space was replaced by a sociological and even an economic one (Harvey, 1973, cited in Taylor, 1998). Planning itself was thought of as a rational process of decision making the goals of which were not an end state. Faludi (1973) distinguished substantive theories, dealing with the subject matter or content, from procedural theories, focused on the process of planning. In fact, he understood planning as a process of rational action comprising the definition of problems and goals, identification and evaluation of alternative plans and policies, implementation, and monitoring of the effects.

However, the rational model of instrumental (means-end) reasoning and the comprehensiveness of the plans soon met with criticism. On one hand, Lindblom (1959, cited in Taylor, 1998) argued for a noncomprehensive and *incremental approach to planning* in his famous article "The Science of Muddling Through." On the other hand, Davidoff (1965) and others criticized the technical fallacy of the approaches that hid the value-laden and, hence, political nature of planning. *The role of the planner should be that of an advocate.*

The second significant change took place in the 1970s and 1980s, when the gradual shift in the role of the planner became conspicuous. It was a shift to *viewing the planner, not as a technical expert, but as a negotiator, communicator, or facilitator who enables various participants or stakeholders to express themselves and make planning value judgments* (Taylor, 1998). This communication model of urban planning has dominated the academic discussions of the 1990s.

The *communicative or collaborative "turn"* in planning became a term to denote the types of practice whose emphasis is on interaction and communication among various stakeholders. On one hand, it draws on the American pragmatism developed in the philosophy of John Dewey and Richard Rorty. On the other, it is based on the theory of communicative rationality or action by Jürgen Habermas (Feinstein, 2000). Collaborative planning is heavily based on a consensus-building tradition in which stakeholders of different interests are guided through the phases of the planning cycle by facilitators. They apply a variety of methods to animate the discourses, which might turn into collaborative tinkering (Innes & Booher, 1999b; Susskind, McKearnan, & Thomas-Larmer, 1999). Judith Innes approaches the content of planning through concepts borrowed from complexity science. The latter sees the world as a self-organizing and adaptive learning system in which new solutions and patterns of action emerge, if space is made for them. Consensus building can provide the necessary information flow and links that help the complex adaptive system move to higher levels of performance (Innes & Booher, 1999a).

Patsy Healey (1997) brings an institutional approach to collaborative planning by focusing on, besides communicative planning practices with individuals (the soft infrastructure), the institutional frames of planning systems within which the planning takes place (the hard infrastructure). She argues for planning systems that will encourage more collaborative and inclusionary forms of planning practice. This might bring about individual and institutional capacity, which assists in dealing with the social, economic, environmental, and spatial problems of "fragmented societies." Healey is more interested in the transformative influence upon existing structures, whereas the U.S. version of collaborative planning focuses more on agency and the informal negotiations between the participating stakeholders.

The positive aspect of collaborative planning is that it brings new participants into the theory and practice of planning and seeks to care for and value a range of knowledges and reasoning from different sources (Healey, 1997). The outcome of such a process might be consensus over the planning solutions or decisions as well as much needed social and political capital for communities (Innes & Booher, 1999a). Schneekloth and Shibley (1995) elaborate a similar kind of approach to design by placing architecture into the practice of collaborative placemaking.

The main criticism of collaborative planning focuses on the neglect of power, especially in the American, individualist version (cf. Flyvbjerg, 1998). An other criticism is the nonempirical treatment of structure and agency (Allmendinger, 1999). Collaborative planning also pays too much attention to the role of the planner as the central element of communication, at the expense of dealing with the visions, content, and distribution of the outcomes of planning (Campbell & Marshall, 1999a). Last but not least, collaborative planning has so far been surprisingly gender neutral or even gender blind, even though several pioneers of collaborative planning have been women.

The latest directions in planning theory are the "New Urbanism" with its focus on the physical image (although not placemaking; cf. Shibley, 1998) of the desirable town, and the "just city," with its model of spatial relations based on equity (Feinstein, 2000). They corroborate Taylor's (1998) claim that there cannot be just one theory of town planning. There are different kinds of urban planning theories that answer different questions. Procedural theories, such as the rational process view and incremental and collaborative planning, provide answers concerning the process of planning. Questions concerning the content and outcomes are answered by the substantive theories of the traditional design approach and the New Urbanism but also by some forms of pragmatic and advocacy planning. There seems to be a shortage of adequate substantive theories, although some of the ecological ones around Local Agenda 21 are promising.

Some planning theories are more explicit about their normative elements than others. The rational process view and collaborative planning include prescriptions of how to carry out the process properly or fairly. Ethical concerns comprising both good outcomes and fair actions, in the service of both individuals and the community, are taken up only in the theories of participatory planning, such as advocacy planning (Campbell & Marshall, 1999a).

Academic adherents of collaborative planning concentrate on the nature of participatory planning, whereas the practitioners focus on how participatory planning should be carried out in specific contexts. The code of ethics of the International Association of Public Participation Practitioners (Michaelson, 1996) provides a model of behavior for inclusive participatory practice. The code implies that people should have a say in decisions about actions that affect their lives. Participation should provide necessary information for and facilitate the involvement of those potentially affected. Participation should also include the promise that the public's contribution will influence the decisions and that the authorities will communicate to participants how their input was, or was not, utilized.

The differences between theoreticians and practitioners are conspicuous in their varying approaches to planning arenas. According to Voogd (1998), planning arenas can be categorized by their territorial level (local or regional), the level of legal regulations (formal or relaxed), the power structure of the actors (hierarchical or mixed), the level of integration of planning (sectoral or comprehensive), and the level of abstraction (strategic or operational).

The planning arenas that seem to concern theoreticians of collaborative planning are characterized by local or regional territorial levels and by strategic and comprehensive, rather than operational and sectoral, planning. The practitioners of participatory planning, on the contrary, seem to be most active on the local level. The planning is operational and sectoral or transsectoral, and it takes place in either hierarchical or mixed power structures. Practitioners also tend to focus on the application of a wider palette of enabling tools than theoreticians.

If urban or community and regional planning are not a science but rather a form of social, ethical, and political action and practice directed at shaping the physical environment (Taylor, 1998), what is participatory planning? Because of the abundance of different kinds of participatory planning, the definition has to be so generic that it refers to planning in a wide variety of contexts. It should be based on both procedural and substantive theories, with normative and ethical tones in terms of fair implementation of the participatory process and just distribution of outcomes for the individual and the community. It should also take an explicit stance on the desired level of decision making in the specific context. Thus, *participatory planning is a social, ethical, and political practice in which individuals or groups, assisted by a set of tools, take part in varying degrees at the overlapping phases of the planning and decision-making cycle that may bring forth outcomes congruent with the participants' needs and interests.* Although the users or the residents are a necessary stakeholder group in participatory planning, a distinction is not made here between the participation of residents and the involvement of authorities or professionals, as Churchman (1987, 1990) has done, because participation increasingly involves a great variety of stakeholder groups.

Participatory planning as defined above might support the communicative transactions of participants in the overlapping phases of the planning cycle (cf. Figure 38.1). It might also bring forth, in addition to the geographical, economic, and sociological space, a psychological and behavioral space that is congruent with the needs and interests of the participants and the community. This is a hypothesis needing testing and assessment that the methodological approach to participatory planning should take into account.

HOW CAN PARTICIPATORY PLANNING BE APPROACHED METHODOLOGICALLY?

Methodology refers to the aims, concepts, and principles of reasoning and action of some discipline or practice, including its strategy and mode of research or implementation. Methodology is closely connected to one or several paradigms. Paradigms are general concepts or worldviews of a discipline, associated with a certain ontology and epistemology. The chosen methodological approach is usually set by the problem under examination. The core problem here is: How can (with what strategy and methods) participatory planning support the communicative transactions of the participants in specific contexts, and what is the impact of the process on varying groups of people and their environments?

Participatory planning involves, however, besides the practical problems mentioned in the introduction to this chapter, a set of interconnected problems that relate to the intermingling of normative and explanatory statements about the planning process and its outcomes. *Normative* means that the description of the issue implies a value statement or that the phenomenon is expressed in a prescriptive mode of what ought to be done or what good results should be like.

Epistemologically problematic is the fact that environment behavior design-design research has and still is operating mostly within the postpositivist paradigm, in which the explanatory mode of inquiry dominates. Participatory planning, on the other hand, like postmodern architecture, represents a multiparadigmatic and fragmented phenomenon that combines several conflicting elements (cf. Groat & Despres, 1991). Locating participatory planning in the borders between modern and postmodern theories of knowledge and social practice might be one solution to the dilemma. Schneekloth and Shibley (1995) argue that the complex realm of borders between modern (either-or positions and standpoints) and postmodern thought (embracing contradictions) provides places for dialogue between multiple and partial knowledges of professionals, politicians, and lay people in each site of intervention.

The most suitable methodological approach that recognizes the creation of both change and knowledge is provided by action research (AR). It is a fairly loose methodological orientation and strategy. AR can be applied from various theoretical perspectives (psychological, social, critical, feminist) since it is not tied to one specific theory. AR acquires its substance from the object and context where it is applied, whether in education, working life, organizational development, waste management, or urban and rural planning (cf. Wisner, Stea, & Kruks, 1991). Currently, the differences between the two main strands of action research are being blurred (Stringer, 1996). The individually or psychosocially

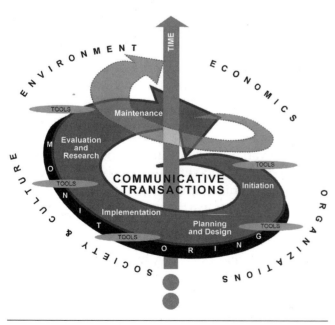

Figure 38.1 A schema of the methodological approach to participatory planning.

oriented Anglo-American strand has its roots in the pragmatism of John Dewey. It was explicitly formulated into action research by Kurt Lewin (1948) and later on developed into reflective action science (Argyris & Schön, 1991) and participatory action research (Whyte, 1991) including participatory evaluation (cf. Horelli & Roininen, 2000; Sabo, 1999). The societally oriented strand of AR draws from the critical theory of the German philosophers Adorno and Horkheimer in the 1930s. Their thought was expanded by Jürgen Habermas (1979, 1984, 1994), whose writings on the value-laden basis, conditions, and legitimacy of knowledge production have influenced both participatory planning and critical action research. This critical strand of AR focuses on questioning and changing the underlying value structure of society, institutions, and daily praxis. Its tenets have been adopted and further elaborated by the Deakin school of action research in Australia (Carr & Kemmis, 1986) but also by some U.S. researchers of planning and design (Sabo, 1999; Schneekloth, 1987; Wisner et al., 1991).

The shared characteristics of different types of action research include the involvement of many participants in a change process and even in knowledge production (Whyte, 1991). Most AR also implies an adherence to democratic values and a critical attitude to the object of change. Collaborative learning plays a central role, which is enhanced by the creation of arenas for dialogue and by the application of enabling tools. The latter may create favorable conditions for the circle of reflexive or even double-loop learning (Kolb, 1984, p. 42; see also Argyris & Schön, 1991; Horelli, 1997). Thus the social and material change caused by the action might also result in local theory (a new shared framework), which is cocreated by participants who test it when acting on it (Elden & Levin, 1991).

Carr and Kemmis (1986), on the basis of the earlier work of Habermas (1979), suggest three types of action research the appropriateness of which depends on the object and context of the project. In the *technical type*, the researcher is an independent outsider who concentrates on the empirical analysis of the phenomenon undergoing change. In the *practical type*, the researcher collaborates with the participants and urges them to perceive and reflect on the action and its goals. In the *emancipatory or critical type*, the researcher is a change agent and coordinator who shares the responsibility for the process and project with the participants. The latter are urged to

question the conditions and power structure of the project as well as its societal and historical context. Wisner et al. (1991) prefer to speak about instrumental and transformative AR. The latter seeks to change the social consciousness of the participants and the social structures of the context, whereas the former is concerned with the effectiveness of the endeavor.

Habermas (1984, 1994) turned his interest from critical theory to the development of the conditions for and validity claims of ideal discourse—communicative rationality and authentic dialogue. The principles of the latter mean, for instance, that the participants in collaborative planning should speak in its ideal form with sincerity, legitimacy, accuracy, and comprehensibility (Innes & Booher, 1999a, 1999b).

The differences and similarities of varying knowledges produced during participatory planning and design, such as place knowledge (material and physical), local knowledge (people's subjective interpretations), and situational knowledge (partial contextual visions), require continuous negotiation of meaning and position (Schneekloth & Shibley, 1995). Also the externalization of tacit knowledge into explicit knowledge requires special techniques (Nonaka & Takeuchi, 1995). All these, consensus-building tools included, can be regarded as knowledge-making technologies that assist in determining what constitutes legitimate knowledge and how the knowledge will or should be used.

Action research and participatory planning share the iterative and spiral-like flow of evolvement in which perception, reflection, and new orientation (planning) unfold throughout the process (cf. Horelli, 1997). Thus, it is possible to integrate AR as part of the methodological approach to participatory planning. Figure 38.1 presents the methodological schema of participatory planning, at the center of which lie the communicative transactions of participants in a specific environmental, organizational, economic, cultural, and temporal context. The transactions are supported by appropriate tools during the overlapping phases of the planning process—initiation, planning, design, implementation, evaluation, and maintenance. Both participatory planning and action research initiate the process with a preliminary analysis of and reflection on the context, after which the dialectical and hermeneutic spiral of action research runs more rapidly. The latter is integrated with the phases of planning through continuous self-monitoring and evaluation. Monitoring provides the participants with feedback on the quality of the change process and its results as well as on the advances in collaborative learning leading to knowledge creation. Evaluation might take the form of research in which the impact of participation can be examined in depth. Research is then conducted from a chosen theoretical perspective in accordance with the problem in question.

The application of enabling tools and methods for the promotion of action and knowledge creation plays a significant role in this methodological approach. Sabo (1999) argues that participation becomes a transformative relational activity if its methods grow out of group activity. Especially young participants and women seem to profit from the creation of their own enabling tools (Horelli, Booth, & Gilroy, 2000; Owens, 1997; Svane, 2001). There are, however, certain conditions that should be taken into consideration in the choice and appropriation of tools for participatory planning and design in practice, which are described in the next section.

CONDITIONS FOR SELECTING TOOLS AND METHODS IN PARTICIPATORY PLANNING

Practitioners of various types of participatory planning seem to agree that the following issues, which should be addressed at the initial stage of the planning cycle, will condition the choice of tools and methods in participation (Hamdi & Goethert, 1997; Sanoff, 1999; Wates, 2000; Wilcox, 1994):

- Clarification of the context (situational culture; geographic scale; topics and goals of policy, program, or project; extent of intended action; access to resources)
- Eligibility of participants (representation of users, professionals, politicians)
- Definition of the level of participation (information—full control)
- Definition of the phases in which participation occurs (initiation—maintenance of results)
- Availability of various types of techniques, methods, or tools

The methodological approach described in Figure 38.1 will structure the following exposition of the conditions for selecting tools and methods for participatory planning.

An Abundance of Enabling Tools for Participatory Planning

A great variety of techniques, methods, and tools exist within participatory planning, but awareness and use of them are not widespread (Sharpe, 1999). Traditional research methods, such as surveys or paper and pencil tests, can be applied at the beginning and at the end of the planning cycle. They do not, however, enhance the communicative process of planning. Therefore, it is important to distinguish another category of techniques that are called enabling tools (Horelli, 1997). A collection of 40 enabling tools, most of which comprise several techniques, is presented in the Appendix of this chapter. Enabling tools *refers to any techniques, even traditional research methods, that enhance the transactions and knowledge creation of the stakeholders during the phases of participatory planning*. Tools can also be created by the participants themselves.

Requirements for the development of enabling tools derive from the nature of person-environment transactions, from the needs of knowledge management, and from the logic and nature of the planning process. Consequently, tools are needed to support the communication of the participants with the psychosocial and physical environment. The stakeholders have to be able to recognize their own important symbols and to *express* themselves adequately. Therefore, expressive tools are necessary and enable even children or elderly people to get involved. The participants also need to be able to *diagnose* the context and the quality of the evolution of the process and outcomes (diagnostic tools). Participation involves extensive *organizing* of resources, events, and processes as well as the mastering of social situations and conflicts that demand organizational and consensus building tools. Last but not least, participation is always connected to power issues and to the *political* networks that might demand the application of political tools.

These enabling tools have been classified into four types: diagnostic, expressive, organizational, and political (Horelli, 1997; for another type of classification see Dürrenberger & Behringer, forthcoming). The varying types of enabling tools presented in the Appendix of this chapter are, however, overlapping in the sense that most tools belong to two or three categories, even if the main focus is on one particular issue. The collection of tools also includes a few "methodological packages," such as *charettes* (special design workshops) or community action planning (CAP), the scope of which covers all the phases and most issues of participatory planning. Since they require a great deal of organizing, they have been put into the category of organization.

This long list of enabling tools, which is far from exhaustive, offers a good range of choices for dealing with diagnostic, expressive, and organizational tasks. Nevertheless, the list lacks tools for managing political issues that reflect the problematic relationship that participatory planning has with power and politics.

CLARIFICATION OF THE CONTEXT OF PARTICIPATION

Any participation project, regardless of its size or significance, should start by discussing its context. Some of the critical questions to be discussed with the participants at the initiation of the project or process are the following:

- What is the cultural (political) context?
- What is the geographic scale or territorial level of participation?
- What are the topic and goals of the project, program, or policy?
- What is the extent of action in which the participants will be involved?
- What will the levels of integration and abstraction of planning be?
- What will the available resources (money, time, personnel, spaces) be?

The cultural and political context, a complicated social issue, can initially be reflected upon by analyzing the regulations level (formal or relaxed regulations concerning the process and product of planning) or the type of power structure (hierarchical—top-down—or mixed; Voogd, 1998). The mixed and less formally regulated power structure allows space for "autonomous participation." This means that the forms of organization are determined by the participants, in contrast to "mobilized participation," which is initiated by external actors to the community (cf. Churchman, 1987). The latter is typical of a hierarchical and formally regulated culture.

Awareness of the geographic scale or territorial level of participation in planning is important. Local planning is closer to citizens and is often operational and implementation oriented. Regional planning deals with strategic (long-term) and comprehensive planning, which is less frequently open to meaningful public participation. The strengths, weaknesses, opportunities, and threats (SWOT) analysis is a simple method for involving various citizen groups in the assessment of the cultural and political context, especially if the SWOTs are conducted from the point of view of women and men, young and old, or varying ethnic groups (see Appendix this chapter; Horelli et al., 2000).

The topic and the goals of the project or program are also determinants of the attractiveness of participation. Sustainable development and waste management may attract different participants from those interested in housing or social issues. The goals of the project, which usually evolve during the process and require several redefinitions, can at the initial stage be quickly diagrammed as problem and goal trees or conceptualized with simple charts (Appendix this chapter; Chambers, 1992; Wates, 2000). Later on, the goals might be checked through visioning and the making of scenarios. Special planning assistance kits with sheets for prioritizing concerns and conflicts, the setting and choosing of goals, strategies, options, and trade-offs have been created for participatory purposes (Hamdi & Goerthert, 1997). Visioning can also take place through online social networks and computer-mediated discussions (Kimball & Rheingold, 2001).

Participation also varies in terms of the extent of action. Action can be high and intensive at the individual or communal level, such as recycling or tree planting, whereas it is low at the institutional level, for instance as a member of urban policy committees. The impact of the latter is, however, greater and potentially has a wider impact (cf. Sharp & Connelly, 2000).

The availability of resources should also be mapped from the very beginning, as participation always requires human, material, and temporal resources. Later on, the mapping of resources can take the form of profiling, auditing, or even photographing (see Appendix this chapter; Martin, 2000). The application of information and communication techniques (ICT) provides a promising participatory tool if the access to it is organized in a communal way. For instance, Al-Kodmany (2000) has applied a Web-based survey, linked through a server to a GIS (geographic information system) program, to map residents' concerns, preferences, and resources in a Chicago neighborhood. Similar experiments have been conducted with Finnish young people (Horelli & Kaaja, 2000).

ELIGIBILITY OF PARTICIPANTS

Some of the critical questions concerning the eligibility of participants are:

- Can everybody participate in the project or process?
- Who decides who can participate, if the participation is limited?
- What are the criteria of representation for citizenship or the public?

Openness of participation depends on the situational context as well as the goals and initiators of the project. In small-scale projects of direct participation, all those interested can get involved. Sometimes, however, people are not motivated to get involved for one reason or another. In more complex contexts, one criterion for involvement might be the degree of threat participants represent for the established system. Those groups that are unlikely to challenge the existing policy are considered safe, whereas networked and well-informed participant groups might be dangerous (Sharp & Connelly, 2000).

According to Pitkin (1967, cited in Churchman, 1990) the criteria for representing "the public" in participation can be formal, as in elections or similarity in terms of demographics, attitudes, or behavioral characteristics. The criterion might also be symbolic, as when the representative is an object of identification by the others, or it may be the sharing of interests with the constituency. Practitioners tend to divide the participants into politicians, professionals (both planning and business experts), and lay people or citizens. The latter are further classified into activists, local groups, residents in general, or end users (Wilcox, 1994). Participation projects often underrepresent minority groups, women, and young and elderly people. What ever the case is, an effort should be made to tap a large variety of representatives of the community, based on both demographics, interest, and geographical location through mapping techniques or stakeholder analysis (see Appendix this chapter).

CHOICE OF THE LEVEL OF PARTICIPATION IN TERMS OF THE OVERLAPPING PHASES OF THE PROCESS

The opportunity to participate and the role of the participants will also vary according to the level and phase of participation.

Some of the critical questions concerning the level and phases of participation are:

- What are the varying phases of participatory planning?
- What are the different levels of participation?
- Will the stakeholders participate in all the phases equally?

Planning and development, placemaking included, imply cyclical processes that can be classified for analytic purposes into phases or stages. The latter are not separate from one another in practice but overlapping and iterative. The phasing, described in Figure 38.1 and Table 38.1, has been chosen from several sources (Hamdi & Goerhert, 1997; Moore, 1987; Wates, 2000). *Initiation* refers here to the beginning of the process in which the preliminary clarification of the context, the definition of participants, the choice of the level of participation, and the preliminary selection of tools are made. *Planning* comprises the programming or briefing of the project in which the details and specific activities are defined. *Design* involves technical expertise that develops the details of the plans. *Implementation* means the execution of the project through constructing the buildings, installing the infrastructure, or putting up some training or social programs. *Evaluation* (and research) consists of the analysis and assessment of the monitored data gathered throughout the project. *Maintenance* means the transference of results and nurturing them in a long-term perspective.

The level of participation is connected to the goals of participation. The latter are not, however, the same as the goals of the project or program, although they might be associated with one another. Churchman (1987) distinguished six higher order goals of participation in her seminal study of Israel's Project Renewal: the furthering of democratic values; bringing about political, social, or personal change; legitimizing planning solutions; educating the public; and achieving congruence with the preferences of different groups

Table 38.1
A Matrix of Level and Phase of Participation with Examples of Appropriate Enabling Tools and Research Methods

| Indicative Levels of Participation | Overlapping Phases of the Cycle of Participatory Planning | | | | |
	Initiation	Planning and Design	Implementation	Evaluation/ Research	Maintenance
Community control	Paper and pencil tests, visioning	Modeling, games, trade-offs	Contracted and self-building	Internal and external evaluation	Contracted or self-maintenance
Partnership	Future workshops, mapping, stakeholder analysis	Planning workshops, consensus building	Contracted and self-building, training workshops	Self-evaluation portfolios, citizen panels	Collaborative maintenance
Consultation	Surveys, meetings campaign demonstrations	Communication and information techniques (ICT)	Displays	POE	Surveys, ICT
Information	Leaflets, lobbying	Media	Videos	Traditional research methods	Traditional research methods

through planning. The latter is a typical goal of environmental psychology, whereas the furthering of democratic values and the promotion of political and social change belong to the sphere of politics or political science. Because of the great variety of goals of participation, they might be incompatible with and even contradictory to one another.

Inherent in the goals of participatory planning is the power of the public to have an impact on decision making. Sherry Arnstein's (1969) ladder, which is a visual metaphor depicting the balance of power between the participants and decision makers, has been criticized for being too simplistic and not empirically valid. The rungs of the ladder, starting from nonparticipation (manipulation and therapy) and moving through tokenism (informing, consultation, and placation) to degrees of citizen power (partnership, delegated power, and citizen control) are overlapping and do not recognize the complexities of the varying interests of different players in the participation processes (Sharp & Connelly, 2000).

Nevertheless, Arnstein's ladder is ethically illuminating (Forester, 1993) in that it takes a stance in favor of the powerless. It also indicates, even if metaphorically, the level of influence or control and space for action by the citizens in specific projects. For instance, in the hierarchical and formally regulated planning contexts of continental Europe, full citizen control is rarely achieved since the legislation only recognizes the decision making of political representatives. Partnership then means the collaboration with the planner or other professional

gatekeepers of planning issues but not partnership with political decision makers.

In spite of the defects in the ladders of participation, it is important to be able to indicate what level of control the users or residents have in specific projects. Therefore, a five-level scale of participation is adopted here. The levels, which are only indicative, since the borders of the levels cannot be exactly defined, include (cf. Hamdi & Goerthert, 1997; Wates, 2000):

- *No participation.* No involvement of users or the community; authorities are in charge.
- *Information.* Authorities are still in charge, but one-way flow of information exists either as informing or retrieving data from the public, for instance, through surveys. The community is treated in the abstract.
- *Consultation.* Authorities are in charge of the project, but they ask opinions about the presented options (in North America, consultation may sometimes mean almost partnership). The role of the community is that of an interest group.
- *Partnership.* Shared working and decision making with the authorities (not necessarily politicians in formally regulated planning cultures). The role of the community is that of stakeholders who have a stake in the project.
- *Community control.* The community (users and residents) decides and the experts or practitioners are used as resources.

The level of participation often varies in terms of the phases of the planning cycle. There are examples of the involvement of the public in all the phases at the highest levels (Horelli, 1993), although they are rare. Wates (2000) and Hamdi and Goerthert (1997) argue that the criterion for real participation lies, at least, at the partnership level of the planning phase.

Table 38.1 provides a matrix that can be used to analyze and even to outline participatory projects, such as playgrounds, schools, small housing communities, or local agendas. As neighborhood rehabilitation or regional planning often includes a set of different "projects" or subelements, each of them requires a matrix of its own.

SELECTION OF APPROPRIATE TOOLS AND METHODS

After examining the context, the eligibility of participants, the level and phase of participation, it is time to choose the appropriate tools and methods. The critical question will then be: What enabling tools and methods should be applied in the different phases in terms of the varying levels of participation?

Table 38.1 can assist in answering the previous question. The varying phases of participatory planning tend to require different types of enabling tools and research methods. Diagnostic tools dominate the initiation phase, whereas the planning phase abounds with expressive and organizational tools. Implementation, which is quite seldom dealt with in the case studies of participatory planning, lacks enabling tools. Implementation rather consists of the organizing of concrete actions, as is also the case with the phase of maintenance. The evaluation phase comprises again mainly diagnostic tools and traditional research methods.

The different levels of participation imply not only varying degrees of influence and control by the stakeholders but also different amounts of personal and collective involvement. Therefore, *the higher the level of participation, the larger the spectrum of tools and methods that can be applied or created.* Examples of community control or partnership, such as the participatory planning of a school (Sanoff, 1999) or of a cohousing community (Horelli, 1993) or participatory urban risk reduction and disaster management (Bhatt, Gupta, & Sharma, 1999), and environmental rehabilitation (Stea & Rodriguez, 2001) display the application of a wide set of tools. They include modeling and simulation (Kukkonen, 1994; Lawrence, 1993), games and trade-offs (Sanoff, 1979, 1999), and a great

variety of consensus-building techniques (Susskind et al., 1999). This is the level where all kinds of planning and design workshops or charettes, lasting from one to several days, are appropriate (see Appendix this chapter; Clitheroe, 2000; Hamdi & Goerthert, 1997).

Participatory programming or project briefing for spatial redesigning (cf. Vischer, 2001) or accessible design often comprise and invent new tools, which are sensitive to the special needs of groups, like senior citizens or handicapped people (Luck, Haenlein, & Bright, 2001 in press). However, if the level of participation is only information or consultation, false expectations concerning the effect upon decision making should be avoided, as by involving the public with deeply mobilizing enabling tools such as workshops of community action planning.

The chosen level of participation has political consequences. Churchman's study (1990) indicates that although government-initiated projects do not necessarily lead to co-option, they seldom result in radical change. Nevertheless, if the public is not content with the granted minor level of participation, it might start applying political tools that are outside the consensus-building spirit (Susskind et al., 1999). Campaigning or organizing demonstrations might grant the citizens a higher level of participation opportunities (cf. Flyvbjerg, 1998) or paralyze it altogether, as in the demonstrations around the WTO negotiations. Consequently, *the choice of tools and methods for participation depends not only on the phase of the planning cycle but also on the adopted level of participation in a specific context.*

THE IMPACT OF PARTICIPATORY PLANNING— A DOMAIN FOR SYSTEMATIC RESEARCH

There are at least two reasons why the question concerning the impact of participatory planning is difficult to answer. First, monitoring and evaluation are not among the key issues taken up by practitioners. Participatory planning, which is enhanced by enabling tools, produces a great deal of data in both visual and verbal form. The data is, however, seldom systematically documented, gathered, analyzed, and interpreted, perhaps because of the intensity of the action-oriented process.

The practical knowledge may remain tacit or underdeveloped unless the knowledge creation processes are integrated with evaluation or action research. The creation of a monitoring and evaluation system at the initiation phase, is a way to connect the application of the chosen enabling tools to systematic knowledge creation (cf. Figure 38.1). This kind of monitoring might take the form of self-evaluation portfolios containing assessment sheets for the tasks of different phases that the stakeholders can manage collectively (Horelli & Roininen, 2000; Sabo, 1999). Or the monitoring and evaluation can be organized by internal or external consultants.

At the end of the participatory project, a summative evaluation is often made. Some postoccupancy evaluations (POEs) are close to research and they are frequently conducted by outside experts (cf. Preiser, Rabinowitz, & White, 1988). For instance, the POE conducted by a group of researchers on the participatory creation of Davidson Elementary School in North Carolina, United States, included observations, interviews, and surveys accompanied by quantitative and qualitative analysis. The results disclosed that the new school provides interactive and aesthetically pleasing learning spaces, as was hypothesized, and it enhances the well-being of students and teachers alike (Sanoff, 1999). However, participatory POEs that connect the process to the assessed outcomes (cf. Vischer, 2001) are quite rare.

Second, in-depth evaluation is only recently being taken up in the academic literature of collaborative planning (cf. Khakee, 1998). Innes and Booher (1999a) focus on the results of the planning process and expand the evaluation criteria for desired outcomes and impact to include intellectual, social, and political capital as first-order effects. In addition, second- and third-order effects include joint learning, changes in practices, and results on the ground in the form of improvement of services or accessibility of urban parks. In-depth evaluation and research share many characteristics, but evaluation is always tied to the requirement of utility for the clients, in contrast to traditional research (cf. Patton, 1997).

Some research on the impact of participatory planning has been conducted within environmental psychology. Churchman (1987, 1990) found that residents are mainly interested in tangible issues and that those who participate directly benefit most from the event. Both the process and outcomes of participation seem to be important, but the significance depends on the interests and perspective of the participant. Churchman's report did not, however, mention the methods of participation used.

Horelli (1993, 1995) studied the impact of a participatory process in which 21 families planned their dwellings and communal spaces at the outskirts of Helsinki by using three-dimensional models and dollhouse furniture (Kukkonen, 1984). The results indicated that most of the self-planners succeeded in creating psychologically supportive and even restorative spaces for themselves and the family but that the community as a whole did not produce social capital to the extent that was expected (see also Lawrence, 1993; Noschis, 1988). Questions, such as, how does the participatory process enhance environmental competence and self-efficacy of children and young people (Chawla, 2000; Kyttä, Kaaja, & Horelli, 1998) or empower women and self-builders in derelict neighborhoods (Feldman & Westphal, 1999; Wiesenfeld, forthcoming), have recently been answered by applying a great variety of research methods and enabling tools.

Most of the research on the impact of participatory planning indicates that participation often brings forth favorable effects, such as the increase of individual competence and satisfaction or social capital, if the process has been organized and facilitated appropriately. There are also clear tangible results in the form of dwellings, schools, or neighborhood infrastructure that meet the criteria of environmental congruence. Nevertheless, these results remain methodologically fragmented as long as there is no shared framework of evaluation and research. Therefore, the impact of participatory planning remains a domain for systematic research that would observe the key issues of participatory planning, namely the clarification of the context, eligibility of participants, the choice of the level of participation, and the selection of tools that are integrated into a monitoring and evaluation system.

CONCLUSIONS AND DISCUSSION

The aim of this chapter was to present a methodological approach to participatory planning from the perspective of environmental psychology. The specific questions that were dealt with were: Why should environmental psychology be interested in this type of planning? What is participatory planning like in some of its varieties? With what methodological tools might this activity be conducted? In addition, the likely impact on both behavior and the environment was discussed.

Participatory planning was defined here as "a social, ethical, and political practice in which individuals or groups, assisted by a set of tools, take part in varying degrees at the overlapping phases of the planning and decision-making cycle that may bring forth outcomes congruent with the participants' needs and interests." The chosen methodological approach consists of concepts from environmental psychology, planning theories, and action research. It was condensed into a schema (Figure 38.1) that guided the analysis of case studies on participation and the argumentation concerning the tools and methods for participatory planning. The schema is based on the idea that participatory planning will support the communicative transactions of participants in a specific environmental, organizational, economic, cultural, and temporal context. Action research is integrated with the overlapping phases of planning through continuous self-monitoring and evaluation that provides the participants feedback on the quality of the change process and its results.

The application of enabling tools for the promotion of action and knowledge creation plays a significant role in this methodological approach. Enabling tools, or new participatory instruments, as they are sometimes called, are not yet widely known nor applied, although the lengthy list of enabling tools in the Appendix of this chapter might suggest the opposite (Sharpe, 1999). However, managing the complex conditions that should be taken into consideration before choosing the appropriate tools might be problematic (cf. Dürrenberger & Behringer, forthcoming). The analysis of the case studies indicates that enabling tools are not knowledge-making technologies in the true sense unless they are integrated with a monitoring and evaluation system or even with some type of action research.

Has participatory planning succeeded in producing psychological and social spaces that are congruent with the environmental needs of the participants? POEs and some research indicate that participatory planning might have favorable results, such as an increase in the environmental competence of children and young people and in the satisfaction with self-constructed dwelling solutions and neighborhood improvements, if the projects have been properly conducted. The results remain, however, fragmentary because of the lack of a shared methodological framework and the complexity of the issue of participation.

The chosen perspective regarding participation here has been based on the assumption that public participation can be complementary to and an expansion of representative democracy. Thus the adopted approach lies within the borders between the "system" and the "life-world" of the users (Habermas, 1984). The focus is on the opportunities of the users to have an impact on their environment, but their participation is seen as constrained by the culturally and politically conditioned planning systems as well as by the traditions of public production of space.

Participation is entwined in power issues in varying ways. The multiple rationalities embodied in the various knowledges of the participants are infused with particular power relations, not only with decision makers but also within and between different user groups. Consequently, communicative transactions become micro-political processes through which policy meanings, symbols and material forms are constructed and distributed (Healey, 1997). Power in itself is neither good, nor bad. Its quality depends on how and for what purpose it is exercised. It is evident that citizens are tired of being puppets in systems- or government-led participation. On the other hand, some community-led initiatives in the United States in which the unsuccessful (nonfacilitated) balancing of personal interests and the public good, have resulted in paralyzing the local decision making them keep them altogether (Campbell & Marshall, 1999b).

However, Innes and Booher (1999c) suggest, on the basis of several positive American examples that "network power," which links players who develop shared perceptions of problems, agendas for needed action, norms, and heuristics to guide their actions on a reciprocal basis, could increasingly supplant traditional forms of power. Promising signs of network power and even innovations in dynamic participation (Catterall, 1997) are being provided by the place-based politics of women in some developing countries. In the pursuit of humanizing globalization, their unexpected political strategies imply the linking of identity, body, place, nature, and culture at local, regional, national, and transnational levels into a powerful virtual and real network (Escobar & Harcourt, forthcoming; also Staffans, 2001).

Research on participatory planning in the future would profit from a closer collaboration between users, practitioners, decision makers, and researchers. Users can bring forth issues and strategies of everyday life that are not as tied to the planning system as those of planners and decision makers but are in need of critical analysis. Planners and decision makers could test this methodological approach and provide answers, whether the application of enabling tools can assist in the reconciliation of community-led initiatives and the structures of representative democracy? Also the role of the tools in the creation of supportive settings or social capital, and the application of aggressive instruments, such as demonstrations, in the pursuit of higher levels of participation, require further studies. As the presented methodological approach to participatory planning has mostly been discussed in the light of local cases, it should also be examined on regional and strategic levels, where other issues might be critical (Langer, 2000).

The core question concerning the role of participatory planning as a means to support the communicative transactions of the citizens is not only scientific but also ethical and political. Providing support and balancing power relations are, of course, not merely a methodological issue. As such, however, they require a transdisciplinary approach in which EB concepts and methods could play a significant role.

Nevertheless, it is evident that participatory planning has not succeeded in getting into the mainstream of planning despite its 40 years of history. Successful shifting of power from the strong to the weak seems to require significant political and civic will as well as cultivation of democratic values and procedures in planning. The trend is, however, toward an increase in participation or varieties of it since the evolving network society of the information age is deeply embedded in participatory processes.

APPENDIX

List of Types of Enabling Tools for Participatory Planning with Examples

Types and Examples of Enabling Tools	Description of Enabling Tools
Diagnostic Observation	Most forms of observation (structured/unstructured, obtrusive/unobtrusive, participant/nonparticipant), focusing on traces, places, or EB relations, can be used as enabling tools (Bechtel, Marans, & Michelson, 1987).
Survey methods	Simple questionnaires, interviews (individual or focus groups; Zeisel, 1981), and checklists are useful survey techniques for finding out potential resources (people, spaces, equipment, organizations) for the planning process.
Paper and pencil tests	A vast array of standardized and specifically tailored self-administrative assessment sheets (tests) exist that can be collectively discussed as the basis for negotiation: semantic differential, adjective checklists, scales, "Who am I," "Our family," visual appraisals, etc. (Bechtel et al., 1987).
Mapping	Behavioral mapping, cognitive mapping, mapping with colored labels (favorite places) can all be used for finding out how people view their settings in different ways and as a basis for collective solutions (Wates, 2000). Mapping of problems can be displayed in the form of problem trees.
Behavioral plan analysis	Analysis and annotation of the floor plan or the layout of the neighborhood from the perspective of the participants provide a good basis for discussions (Zeisel, 1981).
Walking tours, visits	Sensory walks or walk-throughs with preplanned guidance and after-tour discussions often function as a kick-off event for a project (Sanoff, 1999). They might also serve as the first phase of a future workshop (a three-phase session of critique, fantasy, and planning).
SWOT-analysis	The SWOT sheet of strengths, weaknesses, opportunities, and threats is one of the quickest ways to conduct a contextual analysis. The analysis can be conducted from women's and men's perspectives. It can also be combined with a community risk assessment comprising hazard and risk mapping, threat ranking, vulnerability, and capacity analysis (Wates, 2000).
Stakeholder analysis	Charting the stakeholders in the various phases of the project is one of the basic steps in participatory planning. It reveals the different players with their interests and possible roles. Different kinds of sheets can be tailored and used (Horelli et al., 2000).

(continued)

Types and Examples of Enabling Tools	Description of Enabling Tools
Engendering statistics	Instead of expert-produced statistics, women and men can participate in the collection of relevant numbers and indicators in local and regional development (Hedman, Perucci, & Sundström, 1996).
Audits and appraisals	Many versions of audits exist. A step-wise safety audit, created by Women's Design Service in London, is a technique to involve ethnic women in the planning of their neighborhood (Horelli et al., 2000). PAR (Participatory Rapid Appraisal; Chambers, 1992), initially developed for rural areas, comprises a family of techniques with community collection of information.
Profiling	Community profiling is a methodological package to build up collectively the picture of the nature, needs, and resources of the community. It comprises techniques, such as activity charts, building surveys, walks, mapping, household livelihood analysis, and so forth (Wates, 2000).
POE	Postoccupancy evaluation, which comprises a set of evaluation techniques (observation, interviews, simulations) for the assessment of the utility of the building or setting, can also be conducted in a participatory manner (Preiser et al., 1988).
Self-evaluation portfolios	Internal or self-evaluation can be made easier for the participants if they have access to a collection of self-assessment sheets for the tasks in the varying phases of the project (Horelli & Roininen, 2000; Wates, 2000).
Expressive	
Photographing and filming	Participants taking photos or making a video of the area under change may have a mobilizing effect, especially on children and young people (Martin, 2000).
Diagramming	Diagrams and charts are effective visual techniques to collect and display information for discussion during the participation process. Types of diagrams are calendars, flows, matrix, mind maps, networks, organization, pie charts, and timetables. The Venn diagram focuses on the roles of and interrelations among different organizations (Wates, 2000).
Drawing and designing	Architect's drawings and designs might become tools for participative design, if they are used as a medium of communication (Stea, 1988). Children's drawings tend to enhance their involvement in the planning process.
Modeling and simulating	Most children and adults like to build models, ranging from room layouts to house, street, and neighborhood structures. Scrap material provides inexpensive models. Full-scale environmental simulation techniques (LEA modeling kit in Lausanne) that are both perceptual and dynamic offer an effective medium for participatory design practice (Lawrence, 1993). Simulation can also be used to try out a real event or to test draft plans.
Role playing and drama	Residents can take part in role playing or in sociodrama depicting the future construction and living process (Kukkonen, 1984).
Visioning	Visioning is a tool for thinking about and creating the future. Several mobilizing techniques exist for eliciting shared visions: "I have a dream," community visioning (Horelli et al., 2000), and even computer-aided visioning.
Scenarios	Scenarios for optional futures of community centers, derelict neighborhoods, or town centers can be created with participants. Wates (2000) illustrates how methods can be combined in an overall strategy (including logistics, timescale, and actions) to realize a scenario in a specific context.
Brainstorming	Classical brainstorming is a group problem-solving method that encourages generation of ideas from which solutions can be elaborated. Brainstorming is usually complemented by some other techniques, such as the nominal group technique, pin card, and so forth (Sanoff, 1999).
Games and trade-offs	Games are simulations of real situations allowing the participants to have an experience of the future process or end product. A variety of games exist around housing, design, participation, role play, trade-offs. The latter compares competing alternatives according to the types of amenities offered (Sanoff, 1979, 1999).

Types and Examples of Enabling Tools	Description of Enabling Tools
ICT techniques	CAD (computer aided design), GIS (geographical information system), electronic maps, and the use of interactive WWW will be the key simulation, communication, and design devices in the participatory planning of the future (Al-Kodmany, 2000; Horelli & Kaaja, 2000; Kimball & Rheingold, 2001).
Exhibits and interactive displays	Exhibits are a medium to raise the awareness of the issues to be planned or to prepare for political panel discussions. Interactive displays allow participants to alter the plans or add new solutions.
Organizational	
Information dissemination	Leaflets, posters, newsletters, presentations, advertising, and briefing the media are tools to spread information about the participatory process or project. Capacity building is also an effective way of spreading out information that leads to mastering of soft outputs—community confidence and social capital (Booth, 1996).
Lobbying	Influencing decision makers through individual or group persuasion is sometimes necessary, especially in policy processes. Lobbying requires good contacts, a sense of timing, knowledge of the context and subject area, as well as good communication skills.
Networking	A network is a set of autonomous individuals and organizations that come together to reach goals that none of them can reach separately. Networking is important for all citizens but especially to groups with small resources. The Internet can effectively support the networking of future participants (Baker, 1994; Chisholm, 1998; Levy, 1996).
Time planning	Coordinating the activities of daily life—work and care—in unsupportive urban structures has encouraged women in Italy to focus on the planning of time (opening hours of services and institutions) instead of places (Belloni & Rampazi, 1996).
Consensus building	Consensus building is an approach to problem solving through which groups can forge agreements that satisfy everyone's primary interests and concerns. The preconditions include facilitation, formalized commitment (ground rules), sufficient time, and a clear map of how to build consensus (Susskind et al., 1999).
Workshops and forums	Workshops can be considered as the basic tool of participatory planning. A variety of different kinds of workshops exists: Future workshops, stadtforum, charrette. The basic idea is to arrange a place and a social process in which the planning cycle and its outcomes can be collectively discussed. Some workshops last only a few hours, whereas most of them last for a day or several days. Workshops often comprise many participatory tools focusing on varying competences (Dürrenberger & Behringer, forthcoming).
Community action planning	CAP is an active, intense community-based workshop carried out over a period of 2 to 5 days. The output is a development plan that includes a list of prioritized problems, strategies, and options and a work program. It involves a shared relation between the professional technical inputs and the community. CAP also comprises an elaborate package of tools (Hamdi & Goethert, 1997).
Planning for real	Planning for real is a community-built model focusing on public inputs and initiating workshop sessions with card and chart techniques. The length of the workshop is 2 to 4 days. A special kit is often applied that provides basic instructions on how to conduct sessions, a sample model, and cutout masters for physical items and nonphysical attributes (problems and opportunities). The three-phase process is effective in mobilizing community interests (Gibson, 1988; Hamdi & Goethert, 1997).
ZOPP	ZOPP, or GOPP—goal oriented project planning in a workshop setting—provides a systematic structure for identifying, planning, and managing projects for principal interest groups. It produces a logical project framework that summarizes and structures the main elements of a project and highlights logical linkages between intended inputs, planned activities, and expected results. The workshop lasts 2 to 5 days and deals with all the phases of the project cycle (European Commission, 1993; Hamdi & Goethert, 1997).

(continued)

Types and Examples of Enabling Tools	Description of Enabling Tools
UCAT (design charette)	The urban community assistance team belongs to a larger family of tools that comprises task forces and workshops (design charettes). The methodology is based on community mobilization and project definition by outside professional assistance teams who work with local officials, volunteer agencies, and residents (Hamdi & Goethert, 1997; Sanoff, 1999). The workshops last 2 to 4 days.
Political	
Fund raising	Collective fund raising by the participants also requires a systematic plan of action—timeline, budget, stakeholder analysis—to be effective.
Goal setting and prioritizing	Setting goals and ranking them on the basis of needs and on what has to be done is an aspect of decision making that involves all the participants. Prioritizing techniques comprises the "wheel of fortune" (Wates, 2000), "giving hearts," and application of worksheets (Hamdi & Goethert, 1997).
Strategic choice	Strategic choice enhances decision making and developing action plans in situations with many options. It can be applied in workshops and by using a special software (STRAD). The latter comprises modules: shaping, designing, comparing, and choosing (Friend & Hickling, 1987).
Panels	Many types of panels exist, but the citizen panel is a highly political tool in which well-informed lay people ask politicians or experts questions concerning the project or policy.
Demonstrations	Demonstrations are a way to raise public awareness that is not normally included in consensus-building procedures.

REFERENCES

Alinsky, S. (1972). *Rules for radicals*. New York: Vintage Books.

Al-Kodmany, K. (2000). Using Web-based technologies and geographic information systems in community planning. *Journal of Urban Technology, 7*(1), 1–31.

Allmendinger, P. (1999, July). *Beyond collaborative planning*. Paper presented at the thirteenth Association of European Schools of Planning Conference, Bergen, Norway.

Altman, I., & Rogoff, B. (1987). World views in psychology: Trait, interactional, organisimic, and transactional perspectives. In D. Stokols & I. Altman (Eds.), *Handbook of environmental psychology* (Vol.1, pp. 1–40). New York: Wiley.

Argyris, C., & Schön, D. A. (1991). Participatory action research and action science compared: A commentary. In W. F. Whyte (Ed.), *Participatory action research*. London: Sage.

Arnstein, S. R. (1969). A ladder of citizen participation. *Journal of the American Institute of Planners, 35*, 216–224.

Baker, W. E. (1994). *Networking smart. How to build relationships for personal and organizational success*. New York: McGraw-Hill.

Bechtel, R. B. (1997). *Environment and behavior: An introduction*. Thousand Oaks, CA: Sage.

Bechtel, R. B., Marans, R. W., & Michelson, W. (Eds.). (1987). *Methods in environmental and behavioral research*. New York: Van Nostrand Reinhold.

Belloni, C., & Rampazi, M. (Eds.). (1996). *Luoghi e Reti. Tempo, spazio, lavoro nell`era della comunicazione telematica* [Places and networks. Time, space, work in the age of telecommunication]. Messina, Italy: Rubbetini.

Bernfeld, D., Mayerl, M., & Mayerl, R. (1980). *Architecture et Urbanisme participatifs. Expériences francaises dans le contexte européen* [Architecture and participatory urban planning. French experience in the European context]. Venise, Italy: Editions du Ciedart.

Bhatt, M., Gupta, M., & Sharma, A. (1999). Action planning from theory to practice. *Open House International, 24*(3), 16–23.

Bonnes, M., & Secchiaroli, G. (1995). *Environmental psychology: A psycho-social introduction*. London: Sage.

Booth, C. (1996). Women and consultation. In C. Booth, J. Darke, & S. Yeandle (Eds.), *Changing places: Women's lives in the city*. London: Paul Chapman.

Bronfenbrenner, U. (1993). Ecology of cognitive development: Research models and fugitive findings. In R. H. Wozniak & K. W. Fischer (Eds.), *Development in context:*

Acting and thinking in specific environments. Hillsdale, NJ: Erlbaum.

Campbell, H., & Marshall, R. (1999a). Ethical frameworks and planning theory. *International Journal of Urban & Regional Research, 23*(3), 464–479.

Campbell, H., & Marshall, R. (1999b). Public involvement and planning: Looking beyond the one to the many. *International Planning Studies, 5*(3), 321–344.

Carr, W., & Kemmis, S. (1986). *Becoming critical: Education, knowledge and action research*. London: Falmer.

Castells, M. (1983). *The city and the grassroots: A cross-cultural theory of urban social movements*. London: Aldershot.

Castells, M. (1996). *The information age: Economy, society and culture: Vol 1. The rise of the network society*. London: Blackwell.

Catterall, A. (1997). Citizen movements, information and analysis: An interview with Manuel Castells. *City, 7*, 140–155.

Chambers, R. (1992). *Rural appraisal: Rapid, relaxed and participatory* (Institute of Development Studies Discussion Paper 311). Sussex, England: University of Sussex.

Chawla, L. (2000). *Participation as a means of self-development: Self-efficacy, self-esteem and other measures of personal change*. Paper prepared for the Oslo Symposium on Children's Participation in Community Settings, Oslo, Norway.

Chisholm, R. E. (1998). *Developing network organizations: Learning from practice and theory*. Reading, MA: Addison Wesley.

Churchman, A. (1987). Can resident participation in neighborhood rehabilitation programs succeed? Israel's Project Renewal through a comparative perspective. In I. Altman & A. Wandersman (Eds.), *Neighborhood and community environments* (pp. 113–162). New York: Plenum Press.

Churchman, A. (1990). Resident participation issues through the prism of Israel's Project Renewal. In N. Carmon (Ed.), *Neighbourhood policy and programmes* (pp. 164–178). London: Macmillan.

Clitheroe, C. (2000). *An analysis of an innovative community planning method*. Unpublished manuscript.

Connor, D. M. (1996). Public participation in Canada: Development, current status and trends. *Interact: The Journal of Public Participation, 2*(1), 31–49.

Davidoff, P. (1965). Advocacy and pluralism in planning. *Journal of the American Planning Institute of Planners, 31*, 277–296.

Dürrenberger, G., & Behringer, J. (forthcoming). New participatory instruments. In M. Flury & M. U. Geiser (Eds.), *Local environmental management in a North-South perspective: Issues of participation and knowledge management*. Basel, Switzerland: Birkhäuser.

Elden, M., & Levin, M. (1991). Cogenerative learning: Bringing participation into action research. In W. F. Whyte (Ed.), *Participatory action research* (pp. 127–142). London: Sage.

Escobar, A., & Harcourt, W. (forthcoming). Power, culture, identity: Women and the politics of place, an introduction for discussion. *Development, 45*, 1.

European Commission. (1993). *Manual: Project cycle management: Integrated approach and logical framework*. Brussels, Belgium: Author.

European Commission. (1997). *The EU compendium of spatial planning systems and policies*. Brussels, Belgium: Author.

Faludi, A. (1973). *Planning theory*. Oxford: Pergamon Press.

Feinstein, S. S. (2000). New directions in planning theory. *Urban Affairs Review, 35*(4), 451–479.

Feldman, R., & Westphal, L. M. (1999). An agenda for community design and planning: Participation and empowerment in practice. *Places, 12*(2), 34–37.

Flyvbjerg, B. (1998). *Rationality and power: Democracy in practice*. Chicago: University of Chicago Press.

Forester, J. (1993). *Critical theory, public policy and planning practice*. Albany: State University of New York Press.

Forester, J. (1999). *The deliberative practitioner: Encouraging participatory planning processes*. London: Massachusetts Institute of Technology Press.

Forskargruppen för det nya vardagslivet. (1987). *Veier till det nye verdagslivet* [Ways to the New Everyday Life]. Oslo, Norway: Nord.

Francis, M. (1988). Proactive practice: Visionary thought and participatory action in environmental change. *Places, 12*(1), 60–62.

Friedman, J. (1973). *Retracing America: A theory of transactive planning*. Garden City, NY: Doubleday.

Friedman, Y. (1970). *L'Architecture mobile, vers une cite concue par ses habitants* [Mobile architecture, toward a city planned by her residents]. Paris: Casterman.

Friedman, Y. (1975). *It's your town: Know how to protect it*. Strasbourg, Germany: Council of Europe.

Friend, J., & Hickling, A. (1987). *Planning under pressure: The strategic choice approach*. New York: Pergamon Press.

Gibson, T. (1988). *Planning for real: Users' guide*. Telford, England: Neighbourhood Initiatives Foundation.

Groat, L., & Despres, C. (1991). The significance of architectural theory for environmental design research. In E. H. Zube & G. T. Moore (Eds.), *Advances in environment, behavior, and design* (Vol. 3, pp. 3–52). New York: Plenum Press.

Habermas, J. (1979). *Communication and the evolution of society*. Boston: Beacon Press.

Habermas, J. (1984). *The theory of communicative action: Vol. 1. Reason and the rationalization of society*. London: Heinemann.

Habermas, J. (1994). Diskurssietiikka [Discourse ethics]. In J. Kotkavirta (Ed.), *Järki ja kommunikaatio* [Reason and communication] (pp. 98–164). Tampere, Finland: Gaudeamus.

Hamdi, N., & Goethert, R. (1997). *Action planning for cities: A guide to community practice.* Chichester, England: Wiley.

Harvey, D. (1973). *Social justice and the city.* London: Arnold.

Healey, P. (1997). *Collaborative planning: Shaping places in fragmented societies.* London: McMillan.

Hedman, B., Perucci, F., & Sundström, P. (1996). *Engendering statistics: A tool for change.* Stockholm: Statistics Sweden.

Hester, R. T., Jr. (1996). Wanted: Local participation with a view. In J. Nasar & N. Brown (Eds.), *Public and private places: Proceedings of the 27th annual Environmental Design Research Association (EDRA) conference* (pp. 42–52). Salt Lake City, UT: EDRA.

Horelli, L. (1993). *Asunto psykologisena ympäristönä* [The Dwelling as a psychological environment]. Espoo, Finland: Helsinki University of Technology.

Horelli, L. (1995). Self-planned housing and the reproduction of gender and identity. In L.Ottes, E. Poventud, M. van Schendelen, & G. Segond von Banchet (Eds.), *Gender and the built environment* (pp. 22–28). Assen, The Netherlands: Van Gorcum.

Horelli, L. (1997). A methodological approach to children's participation in urban planning, *Scandinavian Housing & Planning Research, 14,* 105–115.

Horelli, L. (1999, October 22–23). *Finnish environmental psychology as a participatory trajectory.* Paper presented at the Second East-West Colloquium in Environmental psychology, Tallinn, Estonia.

Horelli, L., Booth, C., & Gilroy, R. (2000). *The EuroFEM toolkit for mobilising women into local and regional development* (Rev. ed.). Helsinki, Finland: Helsinki University of Technology.

Horelli, L., & Kaaja, M. (2000, July). *Opportunities and constraints of Internet-assisted urban planning for young people and the neighborhood.* Paper presented at the International Association for People-Environment Studies conference, Paris.

Horelli, L., & Roininen, J. (2000, September 17–19). *Self-evaluation instruments as mobilisers of women and young people into regional policy.* Paper presented at the fourth Conference on Evaluation of the Structural Funds, Edinburgh, Scotland.

Horelli, L., & Vespä, K. (1994). In search of supportive structures for everyday life. In I. Altman & A. Churchman (Eds.), *Women and the environment: Human behavior and environment* (Vol. 13, pp. 201–226). New York: Plenum Press.

Innes, J., & Booher, D. E. (1999a). Consensus building and complex adaptive systems: A framework for evaluating collaborative planning. *APA Journal, 65*(4), 412–423.

Innes, J., & Booher, D. E. (1999b). Consensus building as role playing and bricolage: Toward a theory of collaborative planning. *APA Journal, 65*(1), 9–26.

Innes, J., & Booher, D. E. (1999c, February 25–26). *Planning institutions in the network society: Theory for collaborative planning.* Paper presented at the Revival of Strategic Spatial Planning colloquium, Royal Netherlands Academy of Arts and Science, Amsterdam.

Khakee, A. (1998). The communicative turn in planning and evaluation. In N. Lichfield, A. Barbanente, D. Borri, A. Khakee, & A. Prat (Eds.), *Evaluation in planning: Facing the challenge of complexity* (pp. 97–111). Dordrecht, The Netherlands: Kluwer Academic.

Kimball, L., & Rheingold, H. (2001). *How online social networks benefit organizations* [On-line]. Available: www.rheingold.com/Associates/onlinenetworks.html

Kolb, D. A. (1984). *Experiential learning: Experience as a source of learning and development.* Englewood Cliffs, NJ: Prentice-Hall.

Korpela, K. (1995). *Developing the environmental self-regulation hypothesis.* Tampere, Finland: Acta Universitatis Tamperiensis.

Kukkonen, H. (1984). *A design language for a self-planning system* (Acta polytechnica scandinavica, ci 82). Helsinki, Finland: Helsinki University of Technology.

Kyttä, M., Kaaja, M., & Horelli, L. (1998, August 9–14). *Neighborhood density as part of the creation of child-friendly environments.* Paper presented at the Twenty-Fourth International Congress of Applied Psychology. San Francisco.

Langer, K. (2000). *Organizing and designing citizen participation processes in the field of urban and regional planning.* Unpublished manuscript. Württemberg, Germany: Center of Technology Assessment in Baden.

Lawrence, R. (1993). Simulation and citizen participation: Theory, research, and practice. In R. W. Marans & D. Stokols (Eds.), *Environmental simulation: Research and policy issues* (pp. 133–161). New York: Plenum Press.

Levy, C. (1996). *The process of institutionalising gender in policy and planning: The web of institutionalisation.* London: Development Planning Unit, University College of London.

Lewin, K. (1948). *Resolving social conflicts.* New York: Harper.

Lindblom, C. E. (1959, spring). The science of "muddling through." *Public Administration Review, 19,* 79–88.

Luck, R., Haenlein, H., & Bright, B. (in press). Project briefing for accessible design. *Design Studies, 22*(3), 297–315.

Martin, F. E. (2000). *Picturing the campus: Participatory photography as a tool for campus involvement in master planning*. Paper presented at the conference of the Society of Campus and University Planners, Denver, CO.

Michaelson, L. (1996). Core values for the practice of public participation. *Interact: The Journal of Public Participation, 2*(1), 77–82.

Moore, G. T. (1987). Environment and behavior research in North America. In D. Stokols & I. Altman (Eds.), *Handbook of environmental psychology* (Vol. 2, pp. 1371–1410). New York: Wiley.

Nonaka, I., & Takeuchi, H. (1995). *The knowledge-creating company*. New York: Oxford University Press.

Noschis, K. (1988). Le language de notre interieur [Our internal language]. *Les cahiers médio-sociaux, 32*(3–4), 187–191.

Olivegren, J. (1975). *Brukarplanering* [User-planning]. Göteborg, Sweden: Technical University of Gothenburg.

Owens, P. E. (1997). Youth in design decision making: The context, some strategies, their concerns. In *International Urban Design Conference Proceedings*. Nagoya, Japan: Nagoya International Urban Design Forum.

Patton, M. Q. (1997). *Utilization focused evaluation: The new century text* (3rd ed.). London: Sage.

Pitkin, H. (1967). *The concept of representation*. Berkeley: University of California Press.

Preiser, W. F. E., Rabinowitz, H. Z., & White, E. T. (1988). *Post-occupancy evaluation*. New York: Van Nostrand Reinhold.

Rapoport, A. (1982). *The meaning of the built environment: A nonverbal communication approach*. Beverly Hills, CA: Sage.

Sabo, K. (1999). *Young people's involvement in evaluating the programs that serve them*. Unpublished doctoral dissertation, City University of New York.

Sanoff, H. (1979). *Design games*. Los Altos, CA: William Kaufmann.

Sanoff, H. (1999). *Community participation methods in design and planning*. New York: Wiley.

Schneekloth, L. H. (1987). Advances in practice in environment, behavior, and design. In E. H. Zube & G. T. Moore (Eds.), *Advances in environment, behavior, and design* (Vol. 1, pp. 307–334). New York: Plenum Press.

Schneekloth, L. H., & Shibley, R. G. (1995). *Placemaking: The art and practice of building communities*. New York: Wiley.

Sharp, L., & Connelly, S. (2001). *Theorising participation: Pulling down the ladder*. In Y. Rydin & A. Thornley (Eds.), Planning in the UK. The Proceedings of the Planning 2000 conference, 27–29 March, 2000, London School of Economics. London: Ashgate.

Sharpe, T. (1999). Participatory design methods in Glasgow. *Nordic Journal of Architectural Research, 12*(2), 99–109.

Shibley, R. (1998). The complete new urbanism and the partial practices of placemaking. *Utopian Studies, 9*(1), 80–102.

Sime, J. (1999). What is environmental psychology? Texts, content and context. *Journal of Environmental Psychology, 19,* 191–206.

Sommer, R. (2000). Discipline and field of study: A search for clarification. *Journal of Environmental Psychology, 20,* 1–4.

Staffans, A. (2001). *Strategic networks in urban planning: Competing for local knowledge*. Unpublished manuscript.

Stea, D. (1988). Participation, planning and design in intercultural and international practice. In D. Canter, M. Krampen, & D. Stea (Eds.), *New directions in environmental participation* (pp. 50–67). Gower, England: Aldershot.

Stea, D., & Rodriguez, V. C. (2001). *Community action, public participation, and environmental planning in a Mexican colonia*. Unpublished manuscript.

Stokols, D. I., & Altman, I. (Eds.). (1987). *Handbook of environmental psychology* (Vols. 1–2). New York: Wiley.

Stringer, E. (1996). *Action research: A handbook for practitioners*. London: Sage.

Susskind, L., McKearnan, S., & Thomas-Larmer, J. (Eds.). (1999). *The consensus building handbook: A comprehensive guide to reaching agreement*. London: Sage.

Svane, F. (2001). *On young people's participation* [Online]. Available: www.home.c2i.net/swan

Taylor, N. (1998). *Urban planning theory since 1945*. London: Sage.

Turner, J. (1976). *Housing by people*. London: Marion Boyers.

Vischer, J. (2001). User participation in re-designing the space and the organization of Hypertherm Inc., Lebanon, New Hampshire. In J. Zeisel (Ed.), *Inquiry by design* (Rev. ed.). Cambridge: Cambridge University Press.

Voogd, H. (1998). The communicative ideology and ex-ante planning evaluation. In N. Lichfield, A. Barbanente, D. Borri, A. Khakee, & A. Prat (Eds.), *Evaluation in planning: Facing the challenge of complexity* (pp. 113–126). Dordrecht, The Netherlands: Kluwer Academic.

Ward, C. (1976). *Housing: An anarchist approach*. London: Freedom Press.

Wates, N. (2000). *The community planning handbook: How people can shape their cities, towns & villages in any part of the world*. London: EarthScan.

Whyte, W. F. (Ed.). (1991). *Participatory action research*. London: Sage.

Wiesenfeld, E. (forthcoming). Auto-construcction y satisfaccion residencial: una aproximacion psicosocial [Self-building and residential satisfaction: a psychosocial approach]. In G. Francescato & T. Gärling (Eds.), *Residential environments*. New York: Greenwood.

628   Handbook of Environmental Psychology

Wilcox, D. (1994). *The guide to effective participation.* Brighton, England: Partnership Books.

Wisner, B., Stea, D., & Kruks, S. (1991). Participatory action research methods. In E. H. Zube & G. T. Moore (Eds.), *Advances in environment, behavior, and design* (Vol. 3, pp. 271–296). New York: Plenum Press.

Worsley, P. (1967). *The Third World.* Chicago: University of Chicago Press.

Zeisel, J. (1981). *Inquiry by design: Tools for environment-behavior research.* Monterey, CA: Brooks/Cole.

CHAPTER 39

Sustained Participation:
A Community Based Approach to
Addressing Environmental Problems

ESTHER WIESENFELD and EUCLIDES SÁNCHEZ

THE STATE'S APPROACH to environmental issues in Latin America, the context for this chapter, has traditionally been characterized by the adoption of measures that ignore people's points of view despite their importance for adapting environmental policies to human needs. Centralized environmental planning and management policies have included urban renewal projects that often involve the razing of inner-city or destitute urban satellite housing and its replacement by shopping centers and middle-class high-rises, frequently ignoring the critical issues of public safety, health, and public transportation. In addition, Latin American poverty is often concentrated in the urban periphery in which squatters build shacks under precarious circumstances. These marginal areas are bereft of any kind of planning strategies at all.

But in recent decades, procedures that incorporate people's points of view have been adopted to a greater or lesser extent. Polls provide a way to know what people think but do not allow them to participate in determining the methods to be used to discover their opinions or in the interpretation and expression of this information in environmental intervention programs. This is a task left mainly to government authorities. Community participation is another way to factor in people's perceptions, but unlike polling, it not only allows the members of the community to state their needs and values in their own terms but also permits them to participate in decisions on environmental issues. Community participation is thus a channel for directly involving communities in addressing environmental problems and, hence, a strategy whereby they can comanage the solution of those problems.

Moreover, since the community is a level of citizen organization that stands midway between the individual and society as a whole, wherein there is frequent interaction among the members and certain values, feelings, needs, and resources are shared in a given space and time, it is in our view the social scale at which mobilization for participation is most viable.

Given the importance of bringing in the community as a key participant in environmental planning and management, we believe the definition and implementation of both should be grounded in a conception that incorporates community participation as a strategy for involving the communities. Naturally, the application of a strategy of this kind requires a set of principles to make it feasible.

To achieve that purpose, in this chapter we present the conditions that encourage sustained community participation, in the hope that it will contribute to guiding the actions of professionals interested in fostering the development of community participation in environmental planning and management. But before presenting these conditions, we would like to describe the socioeconomic and political conditions associated with the emergence of community participation in the Latin American countries that form the social context in which this process has come into being.

THE CONTEXT IN WHICH PARTICIPATION AROSE IN LATIN AMERICA

According to Cunill (1991), important changes in Latin America in recent years have occurred in the political, economic, and social spheres. In the political arena, the restoration of democratic government in a number of countries (Ecuador, Bolivia, Honduras, Argentina, El Salvador, Uruguay, Brazil, Guatemala, Paraguay, and Chile) has brought with it a new respect for citizen rights, such as the right to organize political parties or freedom of the press. But it has also worsened the social and economic problems that had already prevailed under the military regimes. Furthermore, both in the countries mentioned above and in others with a stronger democratic tradition (such as Colombia, Mexico, and Venezuela), there has been a loss of confidence in the ability of institutions such as elected legislatures or political parties to properly represent the citizens' interests. That loss of confidence is reflected in the decline of electoral support for the traditional parties' electoral platforms and in growing support for alternative political options.

In the economic and social sphere, we see a steadily worsening deterioration of the population's quality of life and a reduction in public funding to respond to the different social problems (Kliksberg, 2000; Lustig & Legovini, 2000; Wacquant, 2000). To illustrate, according to Gabaldón (2000), in 1998 it was estimated that 15% of the Latin American population suffered from human poverty, that is, lack of access to basic resources such as food, medical care, formal employment, shelter, and education (United Nations Development Programme, 1997), whereas 24% faced income poverty, defined as the amount of monetary units received daily or the cost of the basic diet (United Nations Development Programme, 1997). These numbers increased in the 1990s as a result of the combination of low economic growth, high demographic growth rates, and unequal distribution of resources. The World Bank and the International Labor Organization state that Latin America has one of the worst income distribution patterns in the world. The poorest fifth of the population receives only 3.1% of total national income, as against 6.5% received by the poorest fifth in a sample of nations from other regions (Mitchell, 2000).

These conditions have induced governments to adopt economic adjustment programs, which have only intensified the economic and social problems and have also, according to Reed (1996) and Ortiz (1997), been oblivious to their impact on the environment. The growing poverty provoked by these measures has forced large numbers of rural poor to migrate to the cities, further increasing the cities' already very high population density, overloading their already deficient infrastructure, and generating still more pollution and unhealthful conditions (Reed, 1996). This finding coincides with a United Nations estimate that 75.4% of the population of Latin America and the Caribbean—mostly poor—would be living in cities in the year 2000 (United Nations Environment Programme, 1999).

A positive social development in the context of this set of conditions is the emergence of community organizations through which communities have themselves taken responsibility for the defense of interests vital to them and have attempted to influence political decisions that may affect them. The assumption of these responsibilities reveals a growing awareness among the citizens of the need for them to take an active role in the formulation of public policies for the satisfaction of their basic needs.

In relation to environmental issues, specifically, communities have learned that the environment is a key dimension for social development and as such is mediated by power relations that bias environmental plans towards the benefit of certain interests in society. For example, in Venezuela recently there has been considerable debate about the exploitation of rain forests in the southern part of the country to take advantage of mineral, lumber, and other resources, and proposals have been made that would fragment the area through the construction of roads, energy transmission lines, and ranching. In addition to these influences, the exploitation in question will involve the production of toxic pollutants from mining enterprises and will ultimately endanger the sustainability of Venezuela's economy. Environmental groups and the indigenous communities that live in the forest have challenged these proposed changes, but strong economic interests continue to promote them.

THE COMMUNITY PARTICIPATION CONCEPT

We pointed out above that the influence of communities on decision making is an important aspect of participation. We will now focus on other characteristics of participation to complete the concept of community participation on which we rely.

Sánchez (2000), comparing definitions of *community participation* put forward by researchers with those expressed by the members of different communities, specifies the following characteristics of community participation that are common to the two groups:

1. Community participation is a process that takes place at different stages of a community's activity, when the community seeks to achieve goals whose importance to the group's interests motivate its members to take actions that vary according to the goals to be achieved and the sociopolitical circumstances in which the community acts. However, given the tension between the citizens' needs and values on one hand and the state's control over the resources needed to satisfy them on the other, as well as the fact that the state makes its own appraisal of those needs, community participation reflects an attempt to exert influence over decisions relevant to the achievement of community goals.

2. Participation is a voluntary act that occurs when people become conscious of the value of participatory action and view it as desirable for all the members of the group to become involved in the different activities undertaken in a participatory project or initiative.

3. The development of community participation varies according to context and time. That is to say, community participation is built on the foundation of interaction between the characteristics of the participating community, the nature of the project or initiative in which it becomes involved, access to and control over the resources needed to achieve the stated goals, and political conditions that form a context conducive to participation.

It is the participants themselves, then, who in ongoing interaction among themselves and with the other parties to the process gradually determine the nature of their participation. The significance of the participation that is forthcoming will be affected by the quality of the participatory experience and, hence, will differ from one experience to another.

Participation, then, is a social construction, and hence, it has multiple meanings and is subject to the contextual values and circumstances that prevail at a given time.

4. The contribution of the participants to decision making is established in the course of the community participation. That is to say, it is during the construction of the participation that it becomes possible to predict when and how a given activity will contribute inputs that will significantly influence decisions. In this respect, it may be just as important to foster neighbors' attendance at community meetings, teach others to read so that they can themselves gain access to the written information circulating in their group, or put forward ideas on how to be more efficient in pursuing the stated goals. Moreover, experience shows that not every participatory process starts with a maximum of influence by the participants over the decision-making process; it is more common for them to gradually gain control over decisions, mobilizing further in response to demonstrated efficacy.

SOME FORMS OF COMMUNITY PARTICIPATION

We will now examine certain forms of community participation that illustrate differing degrees of community involvement in the solution of environmental problems.

A form of community participation is the public hearing, a type of participation that has been adopted in several Latin American and Caribbean countries as a nonbinding channel through which communities can express their opinions in connection with initiatives to obtain resources or the approval of programs that may affect the environment. The aim of a public hearing, which may be called by the public administration or by nongovernmental organizations, is to involve community members in an evaluation of the environmental impact that an action by government or private institutions might have on the environment. It can also be used to search for solutions to an existing environmental problem (Santandreu, 2000).

Uruguay's legislation, for example, treats public hearings as a consultative channel for environmental impact evaluations. The opinions expressed at these events serve as inputs for the public administration to use. One successful case of a public hearing was the one called by the Uruguayan Housing,

Territorial Organization, and Environment Ministry as part of the environmental authorization process for a hospital waste incineration plant at Estación Pedrera in Canelones Department. The members of the Canelones community, who opposed the plant's construction, organized and formed a "Clean Canelones Committee." They collected over 9,000 signatures in support of their initiative, held a series of meetings near the proposed plant site, and called for participation in the hearings, which approximately 1,000 people eventually attended. The residents' arguments were based on environmental considerations (generation of dioxins and furanes), economic considerations (agricultural and tourist activities were located nearby), and sociocultural considerations (charges that the plant would have a negative emotional impact on the local residents).

Stakeholder negotiation is another way of handling environmental problems, a form of bargaining procedure in which environmentalists, industry, governmental agencies, inhabitants of particular localities, and neighborhood groups become the main actors. McCloskey (1996) mentions groups such as watershed councils, consensus groups, and coordinated resource management groups in which individual and shared concerns are aired.

Similarly, various participatory planning strategies such as participatory research, mutual inquiry, participatory action research, and, more recently, empowerment evaluations are being increasingly employed to address a number of environmental issues (Minkler, 2000). Participatory planning has been conceived as a collective intervention process, decided and assumed by all the participants, that requires articulation of the participants' activities and organization throughout diverse contexts and moments of the process (Meira, 1996). These approaches have been characterized by Minkler (2000) as follows:

1. They employ ground-up rather than top-down approaches that grow in part out of a recognition of the limitations of expert knowledge and narrow, single-discipline approaches to complex human problems.
2. They emphasize the need for the use of democratic participatory processes to understand the meanings that different actors ascribe to the problems of concern to communities, with the aim of overcoming these problems.
3. They tend to be driven by community priorities rather than those of outside experts.

4. They emphasize the strengths of people and communities, including, importantly, their capacity for problem solving.

Wiesenfeld (1997, 2000) asserts that participatory processes in which the community plays a leading role not only contribute to overcoming adverse conditions but also stimulate the construction of the community itself by strengthening the ties among its members, their feeling of belonging to the group and the place, their commitment to the projects of common interest, and their feelings of achievement and self-esteem.

This characteristic, in essence, refers to community empowerment (Rappaport, 1987). However, Sadan and Churchman (1997) add that participatory planning strategies contribute to the empowerment of both community members and professionals involved in community participatory projects.

The forms of participation described are appropriate for addressing environmental problems whose solution requires short-term community involvement. However, these problems vary in their complexity and in the degree of participation required for their solution. Following is a description of two cases that illustrate sustained community participation in two different environmental problems.

"LAS LAJITAS": AN AGRICULTURAL COMMUNITY

In this example, we will discuss an environmental and community intervention set in the context of a sustained participatory process that predates the arrival of professional or student facilitators. More than 20 years ago, rural day workers from a community near Bojó in Lara State, Venezuela, were living in substandard conditions. This community is located in the southeastern part of the country and consists of about 400 families (with an average of 4 members each). Their chief concerns were high unemployment, high illiteracy, and poor health care. In spite of these problems, the people had a strong sub-Andean family-based culture distinguished by the values of self-reliance and personal dignity. The local priest (Father Mario) began working with these people, at first in informal conversations about their economic situation and later in more structured discussions about how to change things.

This first nonacademic "intervention" cannot be described as a formal attempt to achieve empowerment, grassroots organization, environmental improvement, social awareness, or any of the other goals that community and environmental facilitators usually envisage. The intervention model can perhaps be described (ex post facto) as participatory action intervention. Conceivably Father Mario would say that he has been following the dictates of the ideology called liberation theology in the Brazilian Catholic Church. He began with a strong commitment to cultural, social, and economic self-determination, and from there he and the community he organized developed a successful and innovative social experiment.

The first step was to found a cooperative together with a group of these day workers. In the course of his activities with the community, a strong sense of community was developed, and today the members are likely to be more identified with the cooperative than they are with the towns in which they live.

The members continued to work on other people's farms for day wages, but they did so from a stronger power base and could ask for uniform wages and a certain stability of working conditions. In addition, at that time, Venezuela had a stable currency that allowed them to save some of their earnings in a collective fund. This money formed a reserve for buying acreage that went on sale from time to time, thus permitting the group to slowly accumulate their own farmland.

From the beginning Father Mario's commitment to self-determination influenced the group. Committees were organized for administrative purposes, with frequent rotation of tasks and responsibilities. They also met and made decisions from time to time in a general assembly of all the members. This meant that all members had to be aware of the cooperative's activities and that all members needed basic administrative skills. Nevertheless, Father Mario's presence as a leader could be identified as the principle driving force for the participatory process, and he continues to play an important leadership role.

The cooperative has had, from the beginning, a strong ideological commitment to a healthy, "natural" environment. This can be considered an environmental attitude or a progressive social construction in relation to the environment that is of special interest to environmental psychologists. The members began to use organic agricultural techniques, producing their own fertilizers and insecticides from compost and cultivating crops like basil, stinging nettle, and hot peppers. They have rejected the use of industrial insecticides and fertilizers, partly because of the possibility of poisoning the human consumers of their products and also because of the danger of poisoning the workers themselves. Another reason

for this rejection can be found in the cooperative's desire to maintain economic independence from the companies that produce and sell seed and other agricultural inputs. Besides the natural insecticides, they began to use other mechanisms for insect control, including:

1. Crop alternation to avoid large extensions of the same crop (because monoproduction stimulates the reproduction of insects that feed on particular plants)
2. Seeding of selected insect predators (following a study on the effect of the introduction of nonnative species to the ecological system)

The search for expert advice to improve farming and food production techniques was an important goal for the group. It is interesting to see how the group used this advice. The members learned about the recommended techniques, such as different methods of producing compost and adding nutrients to the soil and chose the most appropriate ones for their own purposes. This can be considered an excellent example of self-directed empowerment. Expertise was sought from varied sources including a group of French experts in organic agriculture. The group learned how to make cheese and yogurt and established a commercial relationship with these advisors. The cooperative still purchases the starter bacteria from these French sources and several members of the cooperative have participated in production workshops in France. In addition, local technical expertise was found at the Lisandro Alvarado University in relation to soil chemistry, production of organic topsoil, and prevention of wind and water erosion. The cooperative has also received help from the Venezuelan Ministry of Health and from the Venezuelan Central University in the form of group dynamics workshops and an environmental psychology project (Cronick, 2000) designed to determine how the members come into contact with the insect that transmits a disease endemic to the area called leishmaniasis.

With time the group's original goals, restricted to the planting, cultivation, and sale of vegetables, have been diversified to include:

1. a group of women who conserve and package vegetables for commercialization
2. a supplementary school for children and adolescents where courses and workshops are given after the official school day ends

3. an adult education program
4. a computer lab
5. a group that transports the products made by the cooperative to market

The environmental psychology project is of special interest for this paper. This project was inspired in a particular conception of the ecological environmental factors that influence people's behavior, well-being, productivity, and even survival. It was proposed that the relationship that exists among the different species in a given habitat constitutes part of the environmental influences for each of these species. Thus, the presence of sand fly vectors for a disease called leishmaniasis could be considered an environmental component for the humans that live in the same area. Leishmaniasis is a common tropical disease. It is found in different forms in Asia, Africa, and Latin America and is caused by a parasite that infects vertebrates and is transmitted by a sand fly called the flebotome. There are three types of leishmania: (1) the cutaneous variety, which produces ulcers leaving the victim permanently scarred and causing generalized disability; (2) the mucocutaneous form, which leads to disfiguring lesions of the nose, mouth, and throat; and (3) the more dangerous, visceral form that may be fatal if left untreated.

The people who coexist with these sand flies are not the passive victims of this relationship. The project was elaborated on the supposition that both the insects and the human inhabitants of the affected areas have an important role in its development. Thus people's ways of working, sleeping, dressing, constructing, cultivating, and recreating are closely related to their vulnerability to this disease. Cronick (2000) proposed that a study in which people reflected on this vulnerability and in which a regular interchange of ideas about the causes and cures of leishmaniasis was facilitated would be useful in arresting (or at least limiting) epidemiological aspects of contagion.

Considering the sand fly a component of people's environments, a project was elaborated to examine the relationship between these vectors and the members of the cooperative (Cronick, 2000).

To this end Cronick, together with a number of students of an environmental psychology undergraduate course (Central University of Venezuela), have carried out group dynamics sessions, focus groups, observation, and informal interviews with the members of the community, in addition to extensive conversations with two priests who currently act as agricultural advisors and community and spiritual guides. Since the community is organized into committees for the cooperative's management, these committees have met with the environmental facilitators to discuss the leishmaniasis project. Thus, the final planning of the project represents both the observations of the facilitators and the expressed needs of the community members. For example, the community members rejected an epidemiological study of those people already infected with leishmaniasis, because they did not want to be exposed to contagion by injection (under the skin) of substances they did not understand. From an environmental point of view, the facilitators felt that it was important to know who the potential reservoirs of the disease were. This is important because the vector only transmits the disease if it becomes contaminated from having fed on an infected vertebrate (often a human being). This means that both vectors and reservoirs are environmental factors in disease transmission. Because of this rejection of an initial epidemiological study, the intervention was planned without it. This decision-making process is of interest from a participatory standpoint. The community members have employed participatory strategies (such as asking for clarification of technical terms, offering alternatives, and rejecting options until they are fully understood) with the intervening team that are similar to the ones learned in the development of the agricultural cooperative. That is, they use the expertise critically in developing their own agenda for addressing their problems.

These diagnostic activities were carried out over a one-year period as a prelude to a more involved intervention in which the community members will be filmed as they work and perform domestic activities. The films will then be used as a basis for "problematization," a term coined by Paulo Freire (1972) that means collective critical reflection about everyday practices and oppressive living conditions that are assumed as natural, to determine when and how the people in the community come into contact with the infected vectors. In addition, the community members have been participating in the collection of vector samples (using light traps) that then undergo morphological analysis at a local research institution (Venezuelan Institute for Scientific Research [IVIC]).

This environmental diagnosis has been focused around the identification and employment of alternative appropriate or soft technologies in this community. The need to examine the relationship between community activities and the conduct of the vector population can be viewed as an environmental problem whose solution can be conceived within a community-problematizing framework. Problematization aims at empowering the members by facilitating their (critical) access to information on the appropriate technologies for the solution of their environmental problems. This experience is an example of the combination of environmental and community intervention techniques in which "environment" is considered in an ecological context. Intervention and environmental research form part of a single participatory process.

Another example of the need for sustained community involvement is the Catuche case, described by Giuliani and Wiesenfeld (2000), which we will now summarize.

THE CATUCHE PROJECT

Barrio Catuche, a spontaneous squatter settlement founded over 40 years ago in Caracas, covers an area of 483 hectares and is comprised of nine distinct residential sectors and occupied by approximately 10,000 inhabitants, mostly members of the lower socioeconomic strata. Catuche is crossed by a stream that flows down from the mountain and whose mouth is several kilometers below in a totally urbanized part of the city.

The origin of the project we will refer to lies in years of pastoral work done by Christian organizations composed of community residents acting with the support of Jesuit priests. At that time, the community faced serious problems of violence and extreme social decomposition. But the work that was done increasingly generated conditions for community organization that led to the creation of an environmental project. At the outset its purpose was a "cleanup of the river," which was then badly polluted, chiefly by garbage dumped into it by upstream residents. The stream also posed a danger of flooding, especially for the houses built along its banks.

To address this problem, the community began to formulate a project that initially included an engineering works to channel the stream and modify its direction. Then the community launched an environmental education project accompanied by the installation of garbage dumps. This in turn required the planning and construction of a street grid to allow the garbage trucks to reach the dumps. In

third place came a housing substitution project to replace a set of houses built on the stream bank. These houses not only ran the greatest risk of flooding, which had happened many times and had taken the lives of several residents, but also posed a grave risk for the entire community since a serious overflow could knock down those houses, blocking the stream and causing far wider destruction to the entire barrio.

An urban project was needed that would require the intervention of the municipal authorities as well as the participation of architects and urban planners; but the community demanded to participate in the process as well. Therein lay the origin of a Social Consortium, comprised of the community itself, a group of independent architects and urban planners, a nongovernmental organization (NGO) concerned with local development (Foundation for the Development of a Popular Economy, [FUDEP]), and a Popular Education Movement (Fe y Alegría). All these participants jointly drew up a master plan covering both the community and the larger urban area and submitted it to the municipal authorities, which approved and supported it. The consortium was divided into a community organization and participation unit (COPU), a project unit, and a management and development unit, among which the different responsibilities and activities were distributed. In addition, the consortium was answerable to a community general assembly empowered to approve or reject the projects and their execution. This assembly is the community's representative and is comprised of delegates from each sector.

The housing substitution project, identified as the principal problem to be addressed, consisted of the construction of two buildings within the community for 33 families who lived in high-risk areas. The criteria that oriented the development of this project included the following: (1) relocation within the community; (2) agreement with the community and the families to be relocated. The use of the resources needed for the project was approved by the community through a participatory process in which the inhabitants of the barrio came to understand the common need for the project, even though only 33 families were direct beneficiaries. We might say that it reflected a true labor of consciousness raising that made it possible to achieve a community-wide commitment with the project. (3) Community participation in the project through the construction of "microbusinesses": The project created work for many unemployed residents, who were given training to organize microbusinesses that took on the construction of the buildings. (4) Input by the families to be relocated, as regards the criteria for assignment of apartments: This meant consultation with the architects to ensure an apartment design suited to each family's needs based on its size, as well as respect for each family's preference in the creation of floor groups of families who were related, were good friends, or had previously been next-door neighbors. And (5) a commitment by the relocated families to participate in the development of a new form of neighborliness, adapted to the space they would occupy, that required training for the organization of a condominium board and for collective management of public utilities, maintenance and janitorial work, and neighborhood relations.

The construction work took approximately 11 months, and after the families moved to their apartments, case study research was undertaken in order to understand, interpret, and evaluate the experiences that took place in the community (Giuliani & Wiesenfeld, 2000). In-depth interviews and focus group discussions were performed with three types of participants who had been involved in the relocation project in different ways: (1) the relocated families; (2) the social promoters (community members organized into committees) and members of the Catuche Consortium's COPU; and (3) members of the technical team. The sample was comprised of 33 informants representing each of the 33 relocated families (18 women and 15 men), 5 social promoters (3 men and 2 women), and an architect from the team.

Next, we mention the most interesting topics brought up by the interviewees.

Critical Reflection on the Taken for Granted

In our opinion, modifying the perception of the consequences of living in risk and turning the community's condition into a problem to be solved were of critical importance since, if people do not understand or view a situation as problematic, they are unlikely to mobilize in support of a project that, though it may be beneficial to them, does not respond to their felt needs. Dialogue and collective critical analysis of oppressive living conditions promote consciousness raising (Freire, 1972) and, hence, can lead to the community residents preserving their habitat, appropriating it, and strengthening their group and place identity (Wiesenfeld, 2000).

The opposite happens when relocations are not negotiated but imposed by the authorities.

Participation and Appropriation

Participation has been a key factor in this project. The approach of the community initiative in Catuche has always relied on people's participation in that initiative, and this project was no exception. But in addition to that, we can see in this experience an interesting association between the process of participation and that of appropriation. This association stems from the effort to achieve a linkage with the people from the project's inception and to involve them in the initial discussions of the risk and the need to relocate the houses. That approach continued during later stages including designing the new housing units, selecting the residents, and even constructing the buildings.

From the standpoint of participation, we can say that this process was successful because it responded, as shown earlier, to an issue that was identified as a problem together with the community. But another source of its success was the type of participation that was elicited and that, in addition to ensuring the project's development on the basis of the people's commitment, advanced the processes of appropriation of place that normally do not occur until people have taken up residence in their new housing units.

It is also interesting to see how the importance of housing, conceived not only as a physical construction that shelters the family but also as a resource for the development of the individual, the family, and the community, has continued over the entire length of the process, always operating as a fundamental core of meaning for the people involved. The project successfully incorporated this factor, using participation to generate the conditions needed for people to visualize not only the solution to a problem of risk but also the attainment of an improved quality of housing.

The Community's Commitment to the Project

Though the relocation project directly involved only the 33 families living on the stream bank, it can be described as a community project in the sense that the barrio provided all of the support needed for its execution. It did so basically because the people understood that the risk posed by the stream bank houses was shared by all the residents and that the elimination of that risk would benefit the entire community.

Enhanced Sense of Community

The sense of community, that is, "a spirit of belonging together, a feeling that there is an authority structure that can be trusted, an awareness that trade and mutual benefit come from being together, and a spirit that comes from shared experiences that are preserved as art" (McMillan, 1996, p. 315), was reinforced in the process. The links between the sector where the housing substitution project was carried out and the rest of the barrio were strengthened. Both reaffirmed their commitment to the project as a whole, and the networks of cooperation and solidarity were strengthened.

Involvement of Different Actors

The experience described above clarifies the need to incorporate a range of participants into a process of this kind. An urban transformation of such magnitude could not conceivably be undertaken without the contribution of a broad gamut of resources: technical, political, economic, professional, community, and so forth. In this case professionals, NGOs, the community, and government agencies all participated, making it possible to act on the basis of sustainability criteria and carry out the project in a comprehensive fashion.

In addition, there are at least two issues on which it is important to reflect and that derive from the experience of the social psychologists involved in the project.

COMMUNITY SOCIAL PSYCHOLOGY AND ENVIRONMENTAL PSYCHOLOGY: THE NEED FOR INTEGRATION

From the point of view of our activity as community and environmental psychologists, the experience described provides interesting contributions to a "community-environmental" approach. It would seem clear that the boundaries of those two areas melted away in this case. The psychosocial processes identified, such as attachment and rootedness, become especially important when examined in the light of the community, especially in the context of the barrios. In like manner, the construction of a

community, the development of a sense of community, and the creation of a social identity among the inhabitants can never ignore the place as a key determinant thereof (Wiesenfeld, 2000).

Along these lines, the most interesting factor for us may have stemmed from the interaction between the process of participation and that of appropriation, as illustrated by the experience described herein. The fact that people participated on the basis of their commitment to the project and that it met a need felt by the community also strengthened the people's sense of appropriation. They even began to relate to the new place as their own before it was built. That strikes us as being of enormous interest for experiences of this kind, in which participation is not limited to the levels studied in the context of community social psychology. In other words, it is not just a process in which people take part in decisions and initiatives, but in addition, the process as such can be understood as a catalyst or a facilitator of the process of psychological appropriation of place.

It is the same process that takes place in connection with self-help building of houses in the barrios; a process that generates a strong psychological appropriation of housing units and place. But in this case it also includes planned collective participation facilitated by technical assistance. This can be best approached by applying the methodology developed by community social psychology and incorporating the aspects stemming from environmental psychology into its focus on participation, thereby strengthening the community-based processes of urban initiative.

DECEMBER 1999

On December 15, 1999, Venezuela was hit by a natural disaster that killed thousands of people and caused material damages that are still difficult to quantify. Vargas State, Caracas's neighbor to the north of the Avila Mountain, was so devastated that it has still not recovered. At the southern foot of the mountain, the city of Caracas suffered localized flooding and mudslides in some areas, one of which was Catuche. In a matter of hours, a gigantic river several meters high flowed through the center of the barrio carrying tree trunks, rocks, and mud and sweeping away everything in its path. Fourteen lives were lost and approximately 800 houses were destroyed.

The forecasts of the risk posed by the stream were thus borne out years later and in the most dramatic possible way. But in spite of the devastation actually suffered, the importance of projects of this kind was demonstrated. The community organization, with which work had been under way for several years, proved its mettle at the time of the evacuation, which was conducted quickly and efficiently, thereby avoiding a larger number of deaths. The same organizational support also allowed the community to remain together at the shelters where its members were temporarily housed.

The buildings put up as substitute housing were among the few structures that remained standing, though they had to withstand the river's attack for several hours. Several floors were flooded and their inhabitants were quickly evacuated. The structure suffered no serious damage, and the apartments could be reoccupied following minor repairs. According to experts, had the original houses still been standing along the bank at the time of the December 1999 disaster, not only would all their occupants have been killed but the destruction of those houses would have created a gigantic dam that would have changed the river's course, sending the water into an adjacent urbanized area and then down into the city center.

A reconstruction program is now under way in the Catuche community with the core goal of building housing units for all the inhabitants who lost their homes. Once again, the community is launching a new project. It is doing so in an organized way and in the hope that one day its members can inhabit a decent place, free of risks, in the city to which they belong.

It is clear that the solution to many environmental problems through community involvement lies, as in the cases described previously, in sustained community participation. That makes the community participation process more complex and accordingly requires knowledge for external agents to understand that complexity and for the community, or internal agent, to generate proposals that will help foster its continuity. It therefore becomes appropriate to examine what psychological research on community participation has contributed to the subject.

THE CURRENT STATUS OF RESEARCH IN COMMUNITY PARTICIPATION

Research in community participation can be classified into research done to understand the variables that influence the initiation of participation or that divide participants from nonparticipants and research aimed at specifying the variables related to the continuity of participation. But despite the clear importance of knowing which factors foster the maintenance of community participation over time, the first approach has received far more attention from researchers.

In reviewing both types of research, Sánchez (1999) points out the following:

1. The study of demographic variables gave rise to the distinction between participants and nonparticipants, but this approach was not very successful in view of its meager ability to explain what motivates community participation. The exception is the set of indicators of attachment to the place of residence, possibly because rootedness in a place is associated with greater familiarity with its problems and more emotional and social awareness for the person.

2. Inclusion of psychological variables in research on participation was done from the perspective of intrapersonal characteristics in spite of the interpersonal nature of participation, but the meager explanatory value of the results persuaded researchers to focus more on the variables relating to the participants' interaction with their physical (place of residence) and social (community) environment.

3. This change of focus began to reveal that participation is highly related to aspects of the participants' perception of their situation in terms of the quantity and importance of their felt needs and their identification with and confidence in the organization and cohesion of the community with which they involve themselves. The participating subject also perceives him- or herself and others as efficacious, both in working together with others, as is required for participatory action and in influencing those who control the resources needed to satisfy the community's needs. This points to the importance of the relationship between the community's sense of participation and the participants' sense of efficacy, in managing both internal community issues and relations with the outside including contacts with other organizations. The latter is a key activity given the support networks with external agents that can be created for the benefit of a participation project.

4. There are other organizational factors that can either encourage or block participation, such as distribution of benefits among participants and

reduction of costs (time, economic costs), and that are undoubtedly present in all participatory projects. But of greatest interest is the coincidence between the collective value of participation and the feeling of solidarity that is generated by it, on one hand, and the meaning the participants attribute to the benefits classified as social and their low perception of costs of the same type, on the other hand.

5. There is little research on continuity of participation, but some of the results of the research done to date coincide with the conclusions expressed above. It should be added, however, that the continuation of participation over time is also related to the creation of a climate of participatory democracy within the organization that keeps the leaders accessible and under the participants' control.

6. Most of the research has been done in the framework of a model characterized by a dualistic epistemology that maintains a separation between the researcher and the participant; this is thought to enhance objectivity (Lincoln & Guba, 1985). But it is also characterized by the use of quantitative research methods in which the community members role is reduced to that of informants or suppliers of responses to researchers questions, an approach that denies the contribution that the participants can make on the basis of their experience to the design of research instruments capable of examining the conditions that influence the participatory experience in greater detail.

AN EXPLANATORY FRAMEWORK FOR CONTINUITY OF COMMUNITY PARTICIPATION

In view of the absence of research on the conditions for continuity of participation, Sánchez (2000) studied those conditions using a qualitative research methodology that emphasized the meanings attributed to those conditions by the participants themselves. Based on that research, Sánchez put forward the following propositions:

1. Community participation should be conceptualized as a dynamic process that varies with the circumstances and the time when the participatory project is carried out. The specificity of community participation is socially constructed within the framework of the participatory experience, in view of which the intervention undertaken to foster it must reflect the entire set of particular conditions in which it takes place.

2. These conditions, the community's organization and leadership, the goals that orient the community project, the support the community receives from external agents, the community climate that is created during the course of the participation, and the struggle the community must wage to achieve its goals, all change during the evolution of the participatory experience, as a result of the dynamic of the pattern of relationships that comes into being during the community's mobilization. Community participation is influenced by these variations, but it is no less true that the amount and quality of community participation affects the conditions in question as well.

3. The organization of a participatory community is not imposed; it emerges in response to the requirements for community participation, and hence, the organizational structure that is adopted should be congruent with the values that inspire the participation. This means that the structure of the organization must consider involvement of the community in both decision making and the execution of those decisions. Moreover, the community's organization must be flexible enough so that it can be modified to preserve the fit between the organization's design and the changes occurring in the participants' needs. Finally, the organization must provide opportunities for reflection on the participatory experience itself, thereby facilitating the cycle of praxis, or the circular relationship between action and reflection (Fals Borda, 1996; Kieffer, 1984). In a nutshell, the organization must be democratic because it abides by the decisions of its members and participatory because it is a product of those decisions.

4. Leadership is participatory and is characterized by the leader's attributes and her or his ability to spur the organization's development and motivate the community's mobilization, by his or her accessibility and visibility in the community, and above all, by her or his skill in creating the conditions required to induce broad participation in the formulation and execution of decisions. This quality stimulates the feeling of a shared leadership, such that any member of the community sees him- or herself as being capable of taking over the leadership role if necessary. In other words, in a participatory community there is a leader-follower relationship but within a model in which their respective functions are not totally separated but often overlapping.

Both the community's leaders and its other members become involved in what Sagie and Koslowsky (1996) have called strategic decisions (those related to the definition of the organization's purposes) and tactical decisions (those made to put the strategic decisions into operation).

To sum up, by its own nature participatory action requires that the decisions made and the means chosen to implement them be collective ones. That is why the relationship between the leaders and the rest of the community has been described as a shared one. The foregoing does not mean, however, that the status of leader in a participatory process is unimportant. On the contrary, leadership is required, but to perform a facilitation role that Sagie (1997) has called framework-substance, meaning that leadership in the participatory decision-making model moderates the production of ideas and the formulation of problems within a given time frame. These are the inputs for subsequent decision making or creation of the substance of those decisions. But that substance is a collective function, as is its implementation, implying no distance between leaders and followers.

5. The core goal of a community participation project may be unclear at the outset of the project in question, but as time goes on it comes into sharper focus through the collectivity's interaction with the support of external agents. For example, a community's wish for housing may change from acceptance of the traditional—and generally unsatisfactory—public housing offered by governments to an initiative for housing units better than those the government provides. With this kind of participation, which induces changes in official policies, the community adds a political connotation to the original action in pursuit of a concrete aspiration.

It is clear that the community's reformulations of the initial goal will depend in large measure on the success the community achieves in obtaining the resources (economic, material, information, or psychological support) needed to achieve the new goal from other organizations. In the housing example stated above, that meant access to funding and materials provided by public agencies, access to technical support from academic institutions such as universities that can orient the community in the design and construction of housing, and strengthening of the community's organization.

The definition of the main goal, however, does not prevent the community from posing other goals related to that core goal; the community's actions can

be aimed simultaneously at multiple goals. Teaching community members to read so that their participation need not be constrained by their lack of that skill and training them to use construction tools or equipment for the conservation of their environment are associated goals whose achievement can facilitate that of the main goal.

6. Obtaining a range of resources from the environment external to the community is essential for both the commencement and the continuity of a participatory project. Resources are inputs that strengthen the participatory process and help shape the achievements to which the community aspires. But getting resources does not depend solely on the community's efficacy; it also depends to a great extent on the attitudes toward community participation that prevail among the external agents with which the community interacts.

In other words, the external agents can foster or impede community participation, or they may act in both ways at different stages of the participatory process, depending on their changing attitudes toward cooperation with community participation.

7. The community climate, defined as the intra- and intersubjective atmosphere that characterizes a community during the successive stages of its participatory experience, may be conducive to community participation or may discourage it, depending on the behavior of the other conditions, but especially on organization, leadership, and relations with external agents.

8. Community participation must undergo a process of overcoming impediments or obstacles that are costs for community participation. Consciousness of the additional effort needed to overcome the barriers to participation is known as struggle.

Struggle can energize the community and induce its members to continue participating, especially when what some communities call "control over fear" is achieved. But it can also destroy participation, as occurred with a Venezuelan community that stopped work after striving for several years to complete a self-construction housing project. When people were asked for the reason for this failure, the answer was: "The people threw in the towel. The fight has been very hard." The relationship between the conditions described above and community participation is illustrated in Figure 39.1.

As the figure shows, the continuity of community participation is influenced by the kind of organization and leadership built by the community, the

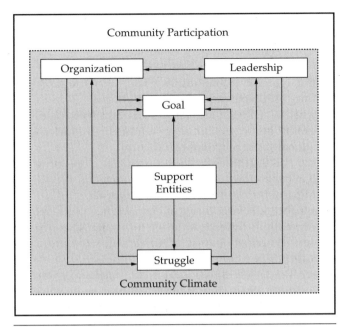

Figure 39.1 Psychosocial conditions for the maintenance of community participation. *Source:* Adapted from Sánchez, 2000.

collective nature and importance of the goal, the pattern of relationships between the community and the support entities, the struggle in which the community must engage to achieve its goals, and the community climate that is built up over the course of the community project. Community participation is, in turn, a process that influences these conditions. This dual linkage is illustrated in the figure through the placement of the dotted line, whose spaces represent the idea of permeability. The community climate, which is in turn affected by the other five conditions, changes over the successive stages of the participatory process.

Community organization and leadership are two conditions of special importance for the continuity of community participation; they are closely interlinked by the requirement for the congruence that must prevail between them. That is, a community's organization under a democratic participatory model must be matched by a leadership of the same kind to ensure the community's internal coherence. In addition, organization and leadership are two conditions that have a decisive impact on the definition and scope of the project's goal and on the actions taken to minimize the costs of participation that are inherent in the struggle. However, the definition and achievement of the goal are also influenced by the kind of support the community receives from external entities and by the total

amount of struggle in which the community must engage.

The support agents are a condition of enormous importance for the continuity of community participation since the resources they manage are usually essential for completion of the community's project. Accordingly, these entities can influence the community's organization and leadership, its goal (as discussed earlier), and the amount of struggle present in the community participation experience.

CONCLUSION

To encourage and reinforce community participation in environmental planning and management projects, it is necessary to understand participation as a collective action process whereby the community performs a role of crucial importance in the joint formulation and execution of decisions that may have an enormous impact on the environment. This also implies that community participation takes place in conjunction with the particular characteristics of the context, whose identification is necessary to allow the professionals working with the community to act in concert with it.

Moreover, since the community is also an important actor in the definition of the specific forms that will be taken by the conditions that influence the continuity of community participation (described earlier), the professional must act as a facilitator who—through his or her expertise—contributes to the formulation of those definitions. From this point of view, the professional can, for example, help judge the degree to which the community's leadership fosters a shared direction of the project, such that the other members of the community will feel themselves to be jointly responsible for the decisions made in it. He or she can also help examine how to reduce the costs of community participation to help increase the participants' interest in participation.

In a word, the scheme presented here provides an integration of the basic conditions that influence the development of community participation. It may help professionals to channel their work in communities along the lines envisaged in this chapter as community participation's "way of being."

REFERENCES

Cronick, K. (2000). *La evaluación diagnóstica de un problema ambiental en una cooperativa agrícola en el Estado Lara* [Diagnostic evaluation of an environmental problem in a agricultural cooperative in Lara State]. Unpublished manuscript.

Cunill, N. (1991). *Participación ciudadana. Dilemas y perspectivas para la democratización de los Estados latinoamericanos* [Citizen participation: Dilemmas and perspectives for the democratization of Latin American States]. Caracas, Venezuela: Centro Latinoamericano de Administración para el Desarrollo.

Fals Borda, O. (1996). A north-south convergence on the quest for meaning. *Qualitative Inquiry, 2,* 76–87.

Freire, P. (1972). *Pedagogy of the oppressed.* New York: Herder & Herder.

Gabaldón, A. J. (2000). Sustainable development in Latin America and the Caribbean: Perspectives and future [Online]. Available: www.eolss.co.uk/46.htm

Giuliani, F., & Wiesenfeld, E. (2000, July). Promoting sustainable communities: theory, research and practice. In E. Pol (Chair), *Cities, identity and sustainability (CIS Project).* Symposium conducted at the sixteenth annual conference of the International Association for People-Environment Studies (IAPS), Paris.

Kieffer, C. (1984). Citizen empowerment: A developmental perspective. *Prevention in Human Services, 3,* 9–36.

Kliksberg, B. (2000). La situación social de América Latina y sus impactos sobre la familia y la educación [Social situation in Latin America and its impacts on family and education]. In B. Kliksberg (Ed.), *La lucha contra la pobreza en América Latina: deterioro social de las clases medias y experiencias de las comunidades judías* [The fight against poverty in Latin America: Social decay of the middle classes and experiences of Jewish communities] (pp. 37–74). Buenos Aires, Argentina: FCE, BID, Congreso Judío Latinoamericano.

Lincoln, Y., & Guba, E. (1985). *Naturalistic inquiry.* Beverly Hills, CA: Sage.

Lustig, N., & Legovini, A. (2000). Crisis económicas y protección social para los pobres: la experiencia latinoamericana [Economic crises and social protection for the poor: Latin American experiences]. In B. Kliksberg (Ed.), *La lucha contra la pobreza en América Latina: deterioro social de las clases medias y experiencias de las comunidades judías* [The fight against poverty in Latin America: Social decay of the middle classes and experiences of Jewish communities] (pp. 17–36). Buenos Aires, Argentina: FCE, BID, Congreso Judío Latinoamericano.

McCloskey, M. (1996). A systematic assessment of community-based resource management partnerships: Memoir to the Board of Directors of the Sierra Club [Online]. Available: www.umich.edu/~crpgroup/proposal.html

Meira, M. E. (1996). The struggle of the city and for the citizenship: Participation and social innovation. In J. C. Bolay, D. Kullock, M. Cruz, M. E. Meira, & T. Bolívar (Eds.), *New opportunities: Participating and planning* (pp. 99–119). Caracas: Institut de Recherche aur l'Environnement Construit, École Polytechnique Féderéle de Lausanne, Fondation pour le Progrés de l'Homme, Universidad Central de Venezuela.

Minkler, M. (2000). Using participatory action research to build healthy communities. *Public Health Reports* [Online]. Available: www.northernlight.com

Mitchell, C. (2000). Latin America at century's end: From grassroots to globalization [Online]. Available: www.globaled.org/curriculum/laa.htm

Ortiz, P. (1997). *Globalización y conflictos socio ambientales* [Globalization and socioenvironmental conflicts]. México, D.F: Editorial Manaral, Ayayala.

Rappaport, J. (1987). Terms of empowerment/examplar of prevention: Towards a theory for community psychology. *American Journal of Community Psychology, 15,* 121–145.

Reed, D. (1996). *Ajuste estructural, ambiente y desarollo sostenible* [Structural adjustment and sustainable development]. Caracas: Fondo Mundial para la Naturaleza, CENDES, Nueva Sociedad.

Sadan, E., & Churchman, A. (1997). Process focused and product focused community planning: Two variations of empowering professional practice. *Community Development Journal, 32*(1), 3–16.

Sagie, A. (1997). Leader direction and employee participation in decision making: Contradictory or compatible practices? *Applied Psychology: An International Review, 46,* 387–452.

Sagie, A., & Koslowsky, M. (1996). Decision type, organizational control, and acceptance of change: An integrative approach to participative decision making. *Applied Psychology: An International Review, 45,* 85–92.

Sánchez, E. (1999). Participación comunitaria para la solución de problemas ambientales: Un marco explicativo de su continuidad en el tiempo [Community participation for the solution of environmental problems: An explanatory framework for its continuity]. In J. Guevara, A. M. Landázuri, & A. Terán (Eds.), *Estudios de psicología ambiental en América Latina* [Studies of environmental psychology in Latin America] (pp. 97–116). México, D.F: Benemérita Universidad Autónoma de Puebla, Universidad Nacional Autónoma de México, Instituto Mexicano de Investigaciones Psicosociales, Consejo Nacional de Ciencia y Tecnología.

Sánchez, E. (2000). *Todos con "La Esperanza": La continuidad de la participación comunitaria desde la perspectiva de la psicología* [All with "The Hope": On the continuity of community participation from the perspective of psychology]. Caracas: Consejo de Estudios de Postgrado, Universidad Central de Venezuela.

Santandreu, A. (2000). Audiencias públicas y conflictos sociales [Public hearings and social conflicts]. *Relaciones: Revista al tema del hombre* (No. 45) [Online]. Available: www.uyweb.com.uy/relaciones/9705

United Nations Development Programme. (1997). *Human Development Report*. New York.

United Nations Environment Programme. (1999). *Global Environmental Outlook 2000*. London: Earthscan Publications.

Wacquant, I. (2000). Urban marginality in the coming millennium. *Urbana, 5*, 73–80.

Wiesenfeld, E. (1997). From individual need to community consciousness: The dialectic between land appropriation and eviction threat. *Environment and Behavior, 29*, 198–212.

Wiesenfeld, E. (2000). *La autoconstrucción: Un estudio psicosocial del significado de la vivienda* [Self-help building: A psychosocial study on the meaning of housing]. Caracas, Venezuela: Consejo Nacional de la Vivienda (CONAVI).

THE FUTURE

CHAPTER 40

Personal Space in a Digital Age

ROBERT SOMMER

> There seems to be less respect these days for personal space. People are crowding each other in movie lines, elevators, subways and on the streets.
>
> —*New Yorker*, p. 70

THE LANGUAGE OF HUMAN RELATIONSHIPS is rich in spatial metaphor. We speak of looking up to or down upon another person, appearing distant or close, needing elbow room, and keeping another person at arm's length. The term *personal space* (PS) was introduced into the social psychological literature to describe the emotionally tinged zone around the human body that people feel is "their space" (Sommer, 1959). The dimensions of the emotionally tinged zone are not fixed but vary according to internal states, culture, and context.

This chapter will describe the history of the PS concept, theoretical underpinnings, measurement techniques, research findings, areas of application, and PS in the digital age; clarify terminology; and list some unanswered questions. Related topics on which considerable research has been done, such as territoriality, crowding, and privacy, are mentioned only in passing, leaving their definitions, theories, and research findings to other chapters.

PRECURSORS AND RELATED CONCEPTS

The PS concept has its roots in animal studies, particularly the work of ethologists and zoologists. Katz (1937) compared PS to the shell of a snail, Von Uexkull (1957) made the analogy of individuals surrounded by soap bubble worlds, and Stern (1938) likened the "personally near" to an aura surrounding the body. Ethology at the time included many descriptive studies where terminology was not used precisely. The concept of personal space overlapped with several existing concepts and some that came afterward, including the following terms:

Individual distance: The amount of space between organisms and their conspecifics. This concept is useful in interpreting naturalistic studies of human spacing.

Flight distance: The amount of space between individuals and members of other species seen as potential predators. When used in human studies this became the basis of invasion studies of personal space.

Proxemics: Term introduced by Hall (1959, 1966) for the study of spatial relationships. Hall identified four interaction zones: intimate distance (0–18 in.), personal distance (1.5 ft.–4 ft.), social distance (4 ft.–12 ft.), and public distance (12 ft.–25 ft.).

Territory: A fixed geographical space marked and defended by an organism and used for life-sustaining activities. Although personal space has occasionally been described as a temporary or portable territory, there are important differences between the two concepts. *Territory* refers to a fixed geographic location, whereas *PS* does not. The boundaries of territory are marked, whereas those of PS are invisible. PS has the body at its center, whereas territory has the home or nest as center.

Distancing: To put physical distance between self and others in order to gain privacy (Buslig, 1999).

Defensible space: Introduced by Newman (1972) to describe the ways in which well-marked territories and good surveillance can increase the safety of residential housing. The concept has been widely applied in city planning and urban design.

Body buffer zone: Term introduced by Horowitz, Duff, and Stratton (1964) with a meaning very similar to that of personal space. It can be used as a synonym.

UTILITY OF THE CONCEPT

A search was made on the PsycINFO database using "personal space" as the subject. From 1970, when the term first appeared on the database, through 1999, there were 873 abstracts of articles and chapters and 233 dissertations. These numbers are undercounts since they exclude all the pre-1970 research undertaken before "personal space" became a separate index term and all dissertations outside the United States and Canada.

Personal space has become a common term in social psychology and communications textbooks and a chapter heading in environmental psychology textbooks, often in concert with *territory* and *crowding.* Demonstrations of PS invasions are included as exercises in psychology classes. Applications of the PS concept in design, education, government standards, and in the courts will be described later in this chapter.

SEARCH FOR THEORY

When the personal space concept was developed in the 1950s, there was very little published research on interaction distances among humans. The most relevant experimental studies had been done by ethologists using animal species under the rubric of *individual distance* (Hediger, 1950; Tinbergen, 1953). Most animals in the wild maintained defined distances from conspecifics, and these distances were influenced by the animal's age, size, gender, and other factors. Particularly relevant were the theories of Hediger, which had come directly out of his efforts to improve zoo environments, illustrating the reciprocal relationship between applied research and theory. Research can be based on theory but it may also lead to new theories.

Using these animal studies as a model, Sommer and Ross (1958) undertook research on interpersonal spacing in humans as part of a larger effort to improve mental hospital conditions. It was expected that information about human spatial needs would assist in designing suitable living quarters for patients. The work began on this atheoretical basis and continued this way for many years. Evans and Howard (1973) noted the paucity of theoretical discussion of PS. Other writers responded to the absence of a satisfactory theory by importing explanatory concepts from social psychology, based either on considerations of protection or communication (Bell, Greene, Fisher, & Baum, 1996). Within the category of protection, the *overload* theory of Scott (1993) maintained that distance from others was needed to prevent overstimulation. Horowitz et al. (1964) and Dosey and Meisels (1969) saw the body buffer zone protecting individuals from threat. Altman (1975) described PS as a boundary regulation mechanism intended to achieve desired levels of privacy. In a similar vein, Aiello (1987) proposed a *comfort* model based on the *equilibrium* or *affiliative-conflict model* (Argyle & Dean, 1965) in which a person seeks an optimal level of closeness with others. If this equilibrium is disturbed by people coming too close or staying too far away, compensatory behaviors will be used, such as decreased or increased eye contact. Hayduk (1994) explained the results of stop-distance spatial invasions as a dynamic readjustment of the participants. Using Lewin's (1951) field theory, Knowles (1989) interpreted interpersonal spacing as gradients of attraction and avoidance. Other writers spoke of the protection function in terms of reduced *arousal* (Patterson, 1976). The *behavioral constraint* perspective suggested that PS increases personal autonomy and helps maintain control in social situations (Edney, Walker, & Jordan, 1976). Hall (1959, 1966) viewed interpersonal distance as a type of nonverbal communication that conveys information about the nature of participants relationship both to themselves and to observers.

Since the concept of personal space was an outgrowth of ethological research, there have also been evolutionary theories. Evans and Howard (1973) suggested that a more thorough understanding of personal space could be achieved by viewing it in functional terms. They proposed that PS is a mediating cognitive construct that allows human beings to operate at acceptable stress levels and aids in the control of intraspecies aggression. By maintaining a minimum distance from their fellows, humans are exhibiting adaptive, stress-reducing behavior, and this has selective advantages in the evolutionary process. Burgess (1981) sees similarities between spacing in human aggregations that are "close but not too close" and the protective function of grouping in other species following the "selfish herd" concept (Hamilton, 1971).

As environmental psychologists have begun to study the natural as distinct from the human-made environment, the heuristic value of evolutionary explanations has become more evident (S. Kaplan, 1992). Studies of human response to the landscape draw heavily from Orians's savanna theory (1986), Appleton's prospect-refuge theory (1990), and the biophilia hypothesis proposed by Kellert and Wilson (1993) and developed by Ulrich (1993). The new evolutionary theories are more sophisticated than earlier ones. They do not neglect culture but include it in a lengthy process of gene-culture coevolution through natural selection (Wilson, 1998). Testable Darwinian explanations will promote *consilience*, defined by Wilson (1998) as "the linking of facts and fact-based theories across disciplines to create a common groundwork of explanations" (p. 8). Specifically, a Darwinian framework of PS will bring together studies of human spatial behavior by environmental psychologists with the much larger body of studies by ethologists and zoologists on animal spatial behavior and reawaken interest in collaborative research between psychologists and biologists in this area. It will also suggest new research questions. Hamilton (1964) has revised Darwin's original formulations to focus more attention upon kinship selection as a force in evolution. Gaulin and McBurney (2001) apply Hamilton's neo-Darwinism to social psychology. Although traditional human societies are organized around kinship, they note that the vast majority of studies in social psychology employ unrelated individuals. This is certainly true of personal space research. Apart from developmental studies of parent-child spacing, there has been virtually no attention to kinship issues.

In many respects, the choice of populations (familiars or strangers) rests on whether one is doing basic or applied research. Designing a metro car for French commuters requires knowledge of their space use. Learning why they might cluster more tightly than English metro riders is not particularly relevant and certainly would not be a priority issue. Surveys and observational studies of unacquainted French metro riders would certainly be appropriate here. However if one's goal is to understand *species-typical behavior*, then it is important to use familiar individuals as subjects since our species lived in small groups of familiar individuals throughout most of its evolutionary history.

Darwin's (1859/1909) evolutionary theory emphasizes reproductive success as a force in natural selection. Behaviors that bring a competitive advantage in reproductive success will be favored over those that do not. Social theorists such as Herbert Spencer (1898) maintained that natural selection was the mechanism by which cultural traits evolve. Darwinian theory goes directly to the "Why?" questions that most environmental psychologists (including myself) have avoided. It is time to remedy this oversight and address the functional basis of the needs for privacy, affiliation, and equilibrium mentioned in the social psychological theories of personal space. An evolutionary perspective in environmental psychology can increase its influence in the biological sciences. A Darwinian perspective puts major emphasis on the reproductive fit between organisms and the environment. Formulations about environmental influences are directly relevant to understanding the sources of natural selection favoring some adaptations over others. Testable formulations based on evolutionary theory as applied to human spatial behavior will be proposed. Some of the research has already been done outside this framework. The task now is to move in the direction of consilience and integrate what have been social-psychological concepts and research into an evolutionary framework. Other studies remain to be completed, such as examining approach distances between siblings according to age and gender (see Table 40.1).

METHODS OF MEASUREMENT

Methods of measurement include both field studies and simulations.

Table 40.1
Predictions of Spatial Behavior in a Functional Framework

Rationale: Ample high quality space enhances reproductive success and child-rearing. From this assumption, various derivations can be made. This list can be added to and revised by other researchers.

Adults will seek proximity to:

- Desirable mates

- Noncompeting own offspring in need of protection

- Similar conspecifics, especially kin, who will make future allies

Adults will maintain distance from:

- Stigmatized individuals who will adversely affect survival or reproduction

- Strangers and other unpredictable individuals

- Any individual who is perceived as a threat

- Family members subject to incest taboos

Other predictions relate to social organization (including dominance orders), territory, crowding, and the immediate response to invasions of personal space:

- High status, dominant individuals will be allocated more high quality space than will low status individuals.

- Unwanted proximity will produce signs of discomfort and hasten withdrawal.

- Approaches from the rear are potentially more dangerous and will be more threatening than approaches from the front or side.

- As territory is used for vital, life-sustaining activities, a spatial invasion in a person's territory will provoke greater resistance than an invasion in other settings.

- Crowding produces unwanted proximity and thereby shrinks personal space boundaries. It can also be viewed as a threat to reproductive success, in terms of a surfeit of competitors in limited space. Crowding therefore results in discomfort, lower helpfulness, and various compensatory behaviors.

- During stages of dependence, children will remain close to the primary care provider. As the child develops, this distance increases.

- When the child reaches puberty, distance to opposite sex parent and post-pubertal siblings will increase because of incest taboos.

- As humans evolved in kinship groups, preferred spatial closeness should parallel genetic similarity, taking into account incest taboos.

- Reciprocity is a successful reproductive strategy within social groups. This will produce a stigma against non-reciprocating, unhealthy, and non-reproducing individuals and those not carrying similar genes. This leads to a prediction of closeness between group members, particularly those who will make good reproductive mates or allies.

- Humans can adapt to living in the close presence of strangers, as in the modern city, but there will be a psychological cost. There may also be benefits, as in increased variety of stimulation and learning opportunities related to high density.

FIELD STUDIES

Anonymous individuals in natural settings are unaware that their behavior is being recorded. The dependent variable may be measured during the invasion (e.g., faster departure) or afterward (e.g., less helpfulness in a subsequent encounter):

- *Unobtrusive observation in natural settings.* Quantification of data from photographs, video, or seating charts. This method is especially useful in cross-cultural studies since language is not a barrier.

- *Staged invasions in natural settings.* A confederate stands too close to an unwitting subject while an observer records the subject's response.

- *Blocked access.* In one variant of this method, pairs of confederates stage a conversation that partially blocks a corridor or sidewalk. An observer records whether people walk through or around the conversing pair (Schiavo et al.,

1995). Another variant of this approach stations a confederate unusually close to a drinking fountain to see if this discourages usage of the fountain by others (Ruback & Snow, 1993). The confederates can be varied by gender, ethnicity, dress, or status.

SIMULATIONS

The participants are aware that they are being observed or tested, although the particular variables of interest to the researcher may not be specified:

- *Spatial preference.* These are studies of how people place themselves under various laboratory conditions, that is, high- and low-anxiety situations or after success or failure.
- *Stop distance.* A confederate approaches the subject who tells the other person to stop when the confederate comes uncomfortably close.
- *Approach distance.* Subjects are asked to move toward another person or a person surrogate, such as a photograph of a person showing a specific emotional expression, and to stop at a comfortable interaction distance. A variation suitable for three individuals at a time is the family approach-stop measure (Larson & Lowe, 1990). Family members are asked to stand approximately 10 feet from each other in a triangular formation and move toward each other and stop "at a comfortable distance."
- *Retreat.* C. Albas (1991) employed retreat rather than invasion. When the confederate moved the chair farther away from the subject during a staged interview, the subject moved forward to maintain a comfortable conversation distance.
- *Figure placement tests.* Respondents place surrogate human figures in conversational or other social arrangements. Stimuli have included silhouettes (Greenberg, Strube, & Myers, 1980), photographs (Strayer & Roberts, 1997), felt cutouts (Kuethe, 1962), manikins (Ruggieri & Frondaroli, 1989), and dolls (Summit, Westfall, Sommer, & Harrison, 1992),
- *Paper and pencil tests.* These have included the Comfortable Interaction Distance Scale (Duke & Nowicki, 1972), the Psychological Distance Map (Kogawa, 1983), Figure-Drawing Tests (Holmes, 1992), the Individuation-Attachment Questionnaire (K. Kaplan, 1988), and the Interpersonal Distance Measure (Pedersen, 1973).

- *Physiological recording.* Researcher records the subject's eye-blink rate, heart rate, or other physiological measures as a function of interpersonal distance (Omori & Miyata, 1998).

RESEARCH FINDINGS

There are too many studies on the determinants of interpersonal distance to describe them all in terms of subject population, treatment, and results. There are some excellent reviews available, particularly Aiello (1987); Bechtel (1997); Bell et al. (1996); Gifford (1996); and Knowles (1989). Recent research has broadened the populations and sites studied and include samples from Turkey (Kaya & Erkip, 1999), Japan (Yamaguchi, 1997), South Africa (Akande, 1997), India (Sinha & Mukherjee, 1996), England, France, Netherlands, Italy, Greece, Scotland, and Ireland (Remland, Jones, & Brinkman, 1995), Canada (Gifford & Sacilotto, 1993), and Nigeria (Balogun, 1991). Observational sites extend to elevators and bars (Hewitt & Henley, 1987), ATMs (Kaya & Erkip, 1999), telephone booths (Ruback, Pape, & Doriot, 1989), preschools (Burgess & Fordyce, 1989), dentist waiting rooms (Ajdukovic, 1988), water fountains (Ruback & Snow, 1993) and busses (Rivano-Fischer, 1988). Specialized subgroups of respondents involved in the research, either as subjects or confederates, have included visually impaired persons (Eaton, Fuchs, & Snook-Hill, 1998), hearing-impaired persons (Jones, 1985), maladjusted children (Dawson & Scarborough, 1994), pregnant women (Davis & Lennon, 1983), and employees working in isolation (Gifford & Sacilotto, 1993). New combinations of participants whose spatial behavior has been observed are attorney-witness (Brodsky, Hooper, Tipper, & Yates, 1999), police-suspect (Winkel, Koppelaar, & Vrij, 1988), salesperson-customer (McElroy & Morrow, 1994), manager-employee (Smeltzer, Waltman, & Leonard, 1999), husband-wife (Sinha & Mukherjee, 1996), photographer-subject (Hosch & Himelstein, 1982), and nurse-patient (Smith & Cantrell, 1988).

Table 40.2 summarizes those findings that seem best substantiated within this copious body of research. These have come from field studies, simulations, or both. For the most consistent findings based upon numerous studies (e.g., spatial invasions are stressful, or friends interact at closer distances than strangers), a review chapter summarizing the findings is cited. For conclusions based on a limited number of studies, only one or two original articles

Table 40.2

Influences upon Interpersonal Distance: Summary of Research Findings

(−) decreases distance
(+) increases distance
(A > B) A has larger space than B

attractiveness: (−) (Gifford, 1996)

acquaintanceship, friendship: (−) (Bell, Kline, & Barnard, 1988; Gifford, 1996)

cooperation: (−) (Mehrabian, 1968; Tedesco & Fromme, 1974)

similarity: (−) (Gifford, 1996)

family cohesion: (−) (DeCarlo, Sandler, & Tittler, 1981)

dark glasses or eyes closed: (−) (Argyle & Dean, 1965)

stigma: (+) (Conigliaro, Cullerton, Flynn, & Roeder, 1989; Stephens & Clark, 1987)

threat, anxiety, insult: (+) (D. Albas & Albas, 1989; O'Neal, Brunault, Carifio, Troutwine, & Epstein, 1980; Skorjanc, 1991)

inappropriate staring: (+) (Tobiasen & Allen, 1983)

mental disorder: (+) (Srivastava & Mandal, 1990; Gifford, 1996)

child's age: (+) (Larson & Lowe, 1990; Sigelman & Adams, 1990)

smoking: (+) (Kunzendorf & Denny, 1982)

approach angle: Side < front in terms of preferred distance in invasion studies; long distances in approach from the rear are particularly marked in studies with violent offenders (Wormith, 1984).

cultural factors: Most studies support Hall's contention that people from contact cultures (Mediterranean and Latin backgrounds) sit and stand closer together than people from noncontact Anglo Saxon cultures (Aiello, 1987).

gender: Female pairs < male pairs (Daigle, 1996; Gifford, 1996). Findings with opposite sex pairs appear to depend on level of acquaintance or relationship (Bell et al., 1988).

participants' height: (+) (Caplan & Goldman, 1981)

isolation: (+) (Worchel, 1986; Gifford & Sacilotto, 1993)

environmental variables: Studies have been done on the effects of room size and shape, location in the room, and room density (Evans, Lepore, & Schroeder, 1996), ceiling height (Cochran & Urbanczyk, 1982), indoors versus outdoors (Cochran, Hale, & Hissam, 1984), and lighting (Adams & Zuckerman, 1991).

personality variables: Researchers have examined the relationship between PS and numerous personality variables. Gifford (1996) provides a good review of the studies. Probably the most consistent findings are that people who are extroverted, field dependent, affiliative, and cooperative tend to interact at a closer distance than those who are anxious, maladjusted, and introverted. A favorable attitude toward touching is also associated with reduced personal space (Andersen & Sull, 1985).

---

are listed. More-detailed accounts can be found in the review articles and chapters mentioned earlier.

APPLICATIONS

In addition to studies in the technical literature, another test of the importance and durability of a concept lies in its application. How have professionals whose concerns include interpersonal distance used the concept during the past 30 years? Several areas of application are identified.

DESIGN USES

Studies have attempted to define the optimal layout of furnishings for maintaining individuals' feelings of adequate space and for allowing people to regulate their interaction distance from others to reduce unwanted closeness. The PS concept has been used in the design of offices, stores, banks, and other building types, but its greatest applicability is in mass transit and institutional settings with fixed seating and little opportunity for personal mobility. The U.S. space agency NASA used the results of PS research to improve habitability in the space station (Harrison, Clearwater, & McKay, 1991; Price, 1996).

TEACHING USES

Hall (1966) taught classes for diplomats and corporate executives being posted to different cultures, describing the different ways that people around the globe used space and time. Others applied these ideas to interactions between salespeople and customers, police interrogations, nurse-patient relationships, and interactions among family members.

LEGAL USES

In the United States, the concept of PS had almost as much application in the courtroom as in design. Space usage became a pivotal issue in lawsuits on sexual harassment, as unwanted closeness was interpreted as a form of harassment toward individuals considered to lack power. Consultants in jury selection evaluate space usage by potential jurors, noting how far people stand and sit from one another and observing their postures and gestures as they respond to questions asked during the selection process.

Hall (1959, 1966) and LaFrance (LaFrance & Mayo, 1978) testified as expert witnesses on interpersonal distance in a case where a city government enacted a "body buffer" ordinance to protect women entering an abortion clinic. The court considered angry protesters' deliberately getting unusually close to anxious and vulnerable clients to be a form of harassment. The judge upheld a minimum distance to be maintained between demonstrators and clinic patients (Hern, 1991).

PERSONAL SPACE IN A DIGITAL AGE

When a new technology is introduced, there will be contrasting predictions from proponents and opponents regarding its impacts on society. The negative response from those wedded to earlier technologies will be most apparent at the outset, before the bugs have been worked out of the innovation and displacements of people and activities occur. As the benefits of the new technology become evident and the early problems are resolved, oppositional tendencies diminish and a reasoned appraisal of overall costs and benefits becomes possible.

There is a dystopian literature about the effects of computers on human relationships (e.g., Roszak, 1986; Stoll, 1995). There is a burgeoning literature on Internet addiction with symptoms checklists that enable people to judge if they are "hooked" or just casual users, along with online recovery groups (Young, 1998). "Technotherapists" offer counseling on methods for combating "technostress," citing ways in which people can limit the intrusion of cell phones, beepers, and remote e-mail into their lives (Weil & Rosen, 1998). Sprandel (1982) reported that "computer addicts" can lose touch with the real world, feel a loss of control, and feel dehumanized. A survey of undergraduates found that they regard the computer as efficient and enjoyable but also desocializing (Kerber, 1983). College officials are concerned about the amount of time some students are spending on the Internet (DeLoughry, 1996). Others see it fostering solipsism (Levy, 1984) and reduced interest in the body and physical appearance (Travers, 2000). Virtual images can crowd out real-world interactions, distancing people from direct physical information about the world. In a detailed study of 73 households during their first years online, Kraut et al. (1998) found greater use of the Internet associated with a decline in participants' communication with family members in the household, a decrease in the size of their social circles, and increased feelings of loneliness. Some researchers report a change in modes of communication following interest in computers (Orcutt & Anderson, 1977), with heavy users becoming less social and less able to communicate effectively with other people and with reduced interest in interpreting nonverbal aspects of communication (Simons, 1985). In his book *The Technological Society*, Ellul (1964) maintains that new technology separates people from nature. Simons (1985) only half-jokingly suggests that computer documentation should include a warning from the U.S. Surgeon General: "Only to be set up near a window where you can preferably see one tree" (p. 100). This proposal is consistent with research documenting the benefits of viewing nature (Ulrich, 1984).

On the opposite side of the argument, there are activists who see computer networks as tools for building community, overcoming alienation and anomie, and empowering the disenfranchised (Agre & Schuler, 1997). There is a movement dedicated to socially responsible computing intent on building bridges between computer professionals and non-technical people. The Berkeley Community Memory Project placed computer terminals in public locations in working-class neighborhoods (Farrington & Pine, 1997). The manager of an interactive online service compares himself to an innkeeper or resort manager, describing groups such as The Well or The Gate as villages, communities, and safe places (Coate, 1997). Kode is a wireless phone service, with connections to the Web and e-mail, oriented to teenagers worldwide.

This section considers the implications of a largely aspatial technology on human spatial interactions. People no longer need to live close to where they work or physically commute to work; they can telecommute and telework. They do not need to see or even know the people with whom they interact in an online group. They can physically be in one location, such as an airport or sidewalk corner, surrounded by people, and talk on a cell phone or send e-mail messages to someone else. In an online group, they find people with similar interests, drawing from a wider pool than exists in their own neighborhoods (Sproull & Faraj, 1995). Relative to face-to-face communication, online communication lacks cues from facial expressions, eye contact, body language, and interpersonal spacing. Some people change their personas online, especially if they can remain anonymous, becoming more assertive and willing to say what might cause an irrevocable rupture in face-to-face interaction. Physical appearance, age, and dress have less meaning in online interactions, but this may change as two-way viewing is integrated into computer technology. Although the videotelephone is not yet commercially successful, Kraut and Fish (1997) found that many customers appreciate its enhancement of the social aspects of communication. Heath and Luff (1993) provide an excellent discussion of interactional problems in existing video-mediated communication and how these are being resolved. Bolt (1984) believes that future computer interfaces will become even more like face-to-face conversations, responding directly to user gestures, movements, and gaze, as some virtual reality transmitting devices are able to do.

As with other design-related terms appropriated by computer users (e.g., *rooms, architecture, portals, exits, habitats,* and *furniture*), personal space possesses a metaphorical meaning in virtual space related to privacy and regulation of the intensity of interaction. It is important to remember that, at some point, this virtual world intersects with the real world. All messages are composed and read in real settings where the principles of environmental influence and interpersonal spacing still apply. Individuals interacting electronically may eventually meet face-to-face. The manager of an online group notes that members like to see each other socially, and the groups sponsor potlucks, parties, and other social events for members in which the virtual and real personas collide. A SeniorNet book club reading Chaucer decides to meet in England for a tour and more-personal discussion. The face-to-face meeting will influence subsequent online communication (Coate, 1997). Because of the newness of the technology, most of these issues have not been addressed by researchers.

CELL PHONES

The cell phone has removed the requirement of a fixed location to receive messages. One can be in a public place with several other people each of whom is engaged in an independent conversation with others not present. Those nearby, unable to shut out the various cell phone conversations, feel as if their space has been invaded. Some professionals use cell phones to communicate on a regular basis with clients at work or on vacation. The "office in the saddle" consists of a car, a briefcase, and a cell phone (Weigel, 1998). New technologies are linking the cell phone to the Internet in the form of a Wireless Web that is likely to encourage more, albeit weaker, interactions. Courts are currently adjudicating issues of cell phone privacy, considering whether this new mode of communication over public airwaves carries an expectation of privacy and whether intercepted conversations (a type of invasion and capture) can be made public by others.

There is little or no published research on how cell phones affect human spacing. It would be feasible to conduct both field and simulation studies on this issue. A desire for increased personal space may be one of the motivations for using a cell phone in a public place. Observations can be made in public locations at times of low density to see how close people sit in relation to those engaged in cell phone conversations. Simulations can be conducted on preferred conversational distance from someone holding a cell phone, with the control condition involving an object of similar size and shape.

Informal invasions I have conducted in public locations suggest that sitting close to people talking on cell phones increases signs of discomfort, reduces conversational length, and hastens departure.

THE INTERNET

With digital media, a distinction must be made between surfing the Web, which is interaction with media rather than specific individuals, and conversation through e-mail and chat rooms, which are conversations with individuals who happen not to be physically present. Surfing the Web is a virtual rather than real encounter with other people, although it can be used to find people's location and thereby lay the basis for subsequent physical or e-mail contact. In contrast, e-mail can be a real, although aspatial and asynchronous, interaction with another person. There are many testimonials to the closeness e-mail brings to physically distant family members, friends, and colleagues. For the homebound and their caregivers, the Internet offers the possibility of virtual encounters with family, friends, support groups, and work sites. This has produced an explosion of interest in computers among older adults in the United States. Many senior centers and retirement homes offer computer instruction, access to computers and peripherals, and provide electronic lists of health-related support groups and Web sites. A senior with Parkinson's or diabetes is no longer isolated and dependent on infrequent medical appointments for information and advice. Virtual encounters leap over distances between distant family members. There is no evidence that they replace actual encounters between people who would rarely see one another under any circumstances. Common sense would suggest the reverse; that virtual encounters between distant individuals will increase the likelihood of spatial contact at some future time.

On the debit side, there are reports of individuals in the same office or household leaving messages for one another on e-mail rather than having a face-to-face conversation. Electronic mail can discourage telephone calls that provide real-time contact with additional voice cues available for interpretation. It also facilitates telecommuting that reduces face-to-face contact among office workers (Simons, 1985).

The Web is aspatial in that the participants' locations are irrelevant, but it "houses" spatial environments, or at least environments that resemble and act like spatial environments. The Palace is a client/server program that is the subject of an online case study (Suler, 2000). It is a visual, spatial, and auditory environment whose most heavily populated site is "the main mansion," which consists of approximately 30 rooms through which visitors can move freely and converse with one another. They can secretly communicate even if others are "present" in the room using a technique called "whispering" or communicate with distant people using a Palace version of ESP. One moves from room to room by clicking on an icon. Visual space can be transcended by passing through walls or through the ceiling. The laws of gravity and physics do not apply in hyperspace. Yet the palace remains both a visual and a spatial environment, an indication of the interactive multimedia environments that can be created and used for graphical multiuser konversations (GMUKs).

Internet technology is developing so rapidly that it is too early to gauge its effects on the amount and quality of social interaction. Now is the time to collect the naturalistic baseline data. How many people do we interact with each day and for how long, and what is the content of these interactions? The logistics, expense, and privacy implications of data collection make this a daunting task, probably not practicable on a large scale, although Kraut et al. (1998) came close to this detail in a study of 73 households in a single city. Research has not addressed context effects on Internet use. Important questions of workplace quality lie at the heart of this issue. Does it matter that messages are sent or received in a bare cramped cubicle or in a well-lit spacious, attractively furnished office? To what degree are the flat keyboard and flickering screen of a TV monitor the only significant realities for the office worker? These questions can be answered experimentally by comparing messages composed in different types of settings. Following Maslow and Mintz (1956), one would predict shorter messages in an ugly setting along with subtle content differences.

Do previous virtual encounters with another person reduce the distance between them in subsequent face-to-face interaction? An affirmative prediction can be made following the well-documented finding that friends converse at smaller distances than do strangers. How are message senders and receivers affected by the proximity of other people, including those who sit or stand too close for comfort? Will messages typed by those whose space has been invaded show signs of discomfort and tension, not only in behavior but also in message content and length, including fewer positive and more negative terms and more typing errors? My prediction is that typing on a keyboard, like reading, is a silent, self-absorbed activity that would be only minimally affected by the close presence of other people. The absorption in the virtual encounter would protect the individual against the effects of a spatial invasion. It is hypothesized that an airport traveler typing on a laptop will be less likely to show discomfort or move in the event of a spatial invasion than a person without a laptop and that reading would have the same protective effects as the laptop in a public environment by providing a psychological escape from unwanted social proximity.

INVASIONS OF CYBERSPACE

In an aspatial technology, there can be aspatial invasions. Hackers are cyberspace invaders who attack not only corporate and government security but also personal-computer files and sometimes take personal identities. There are also serious concerns about the protection of e-mail messages that can be read and stored by operators at both ends of a system. Most system operators have the right to read messages, and government agencies can intercept and read them. In 1986 the United States Congress passed the Electronics Communication Privacy Act to address some of these issues.

Domain names are territorial markers in cyberspace. It takes only a small fee to buy a domain name and hold it for two years. The U.S. Congress passed the Cybersquatter Act to prevent a person appropriating domain names that steal the identity of another person or company. There is also legislative concern with computer viruses inserted to deliberately overload a system and "invade" a computer network. Recipients of some of the most notorious viruses, such as the 2000 "I love you" message that originated in the Philippines, felt overloaded (I personally considered it humorous to receive multiple "I love you" messages from highly placed university administrators), whereas individuals whose computers were taken over by the virus and who became the inadvertent source of further messages felt personally affronted. Is Milgram's (1970) list of responses to potential stimulus overload among city residents applicable to digital overload? Little research has been done about the psychological consequences of

these and other cyberspace intrusions that are virtual in their electronic format but very real in terms of costs and consequences.

OVERVIEW AND FUTURE DIRECTIONS

Problems of definition continue to trouble those who review research studies on personal space. This seems less of a problem for researchers who employ operational definitions. My own view is that *personal space* should be reserved for the emotionally charged zone around the individual's body. Analogies to a soap bubble or snail shell can be misleading since the shape of this zone is more like an hourglass than a circle, with longer distances in front and rear than at the sides. The term *personal space* seems particularly suited for interpreting the results of simulated invasions, especially when the approach is arbitrary and unnatural, such as a side or rear invasion with the subject facing ahead. It is difficult to call the chosen distance in these cases "interaction space" since the unusual arrangement was not selected by the actors.

A different term is required for the space between two or more interacting people, what Goffman (1971) labeled *interactional space*. I would be content to use Hall's *zone system* or Lewin's *field terminology*, although I prefer a parsimonious term like *interaction distance*. Clearly this concept has wider applicability than *personal space*, especially in social psychology, which is concerned with group interaction.

My recommendation is as follows: When the measurement involves the space surrounding a single individual's body, the use of *personal space* seems appropriate. This preserves an index term in psychological data bases with an extensive background literature. When the measurement involves the space between two or more interacting individuals, then *interaction distance* should be used. With this nomenclature, personal space is a mental construction, similar to body image in its subjectivity and individual centeredness. In contrast, interaction distance is an objective concept, measured in terms of distances between two or more people.

The lack of functional theories attempting to explain why people maintain distance from others (or why people seek privacy, comfort, reduced arousal, or equilibrium, to cite several of the current social-psychological theories) has hindered consilience in keeping separate the research with humans from the larger body of work on animal spatial behavior. There need to be more studies of spacing among acquainted and related individuals. Research on spacing of strangers has applied value in an increasingly urban world, whereas research on familiars will provide theoretically useful information about species-typical behaviors. Hopefully the framework presented in Table 40.2 will have some heuristic value. Comparing preferred interaction distances between pre- and postpubertal siblings and between them and same- and opposite-sex parents will test certain aspects of Wilson's consilience model. There is a developing literature relating interaction distance to attitude toward touching. The taboos surrounding haptic research in which people touch one another at the experimenter's direction suggest another interesting, albeit difficult and risky, test of consilience in this area.

There is a developing research literature on interpersonal spacing in human services fields such as nursing, psychotherapy, social work, and family counseling. Much of this research is found in dissertations and unpublished presentations. There is also a proliferation of how-to books describing appropriate spacing in various interpersonal encounters. Some of this is directed to protection from lawsuits, but other books deliberately recommend the aggressive appropriation of space in areas of sales, management, and dating as a form of impression management. There continues to be a flourishing cross-cultural literature stimulated by Hall's proxemic theory.

Is has been interesting to observe *personal space* enter the popular culture. Airlines advertise more of it in their seating, homeless shelter residents complain that they have too little of it, and corporate training manuals warn employees to respect each others' personal space. Whether this usage is good or bad for research and theory building in this area is debatable. What is clear is that the concepts of personal space and interaction distance have lasted four decades and show no signs of disappearing even in a digital age when communication is increasingly aspatial. The verdict is still out as to whether the Internet is a technology like the telephone that increases social participation (Fischer, 1992) or is more like television in reducing it (Brody, 1990). Probably the answer will be that under some circumstances, the Internet can enhance interaction and, in other cases,

it will reduce it, and an overall conclusion independent of context is of little value.

REFERENCES

Adams, L., & Zuckerman, D. (1991). The effect of lighting conditions on personal space requirements. *Journal of General Psychology, 118,* 335–340.

Agre, P. E., & Schuler, D. (Eds.). (1997). *Reinventing technology, rediscovering community.* Greenwich, CT: Ablex.

Aiello, J. R. (1987). Human spatial behavior. In D. Stokols & I. Altman (Eds.), *Handbook of environmental psychology* (Vol. 1, pp. 505–531). New York: Wiley.

Ajdukovic, D. (1988). A contribution to the methodology of personal space research. *Psychologische Beitrage, 30,* 198–208.

Akande, A. (1997). Determinants of personal space among South African students. *Journal of Psychology, 131,* 569–571.

Albas, C. (1991). Proxemic behavior: A study of extrusion. *Journal of Social Psychology, 131,* 697–702.

Albas, D., & Albas, C. A. (1989). Meaning in context: The impact of eye contact and perception of threat on proximity. *Journal of Social Psychology, 129,* 525–531.

Altman, I. (1975). *The environment and social behavior.* Monterey, CA: Brooks/Cole.

Andersen, P. A., & Sull, K. K. (1985). Out of touch, out of reach. *Western Journal of Speech Communication, 49,* 57–72.

Appleton, J. (1990). *The symbolism of habitat.* Seattle: University of Washington Press.

Argyle, M., & Dean, J. (1965). Eye-contact, distance, and affiliation. *Sociometry, 28,* 289–304.

Balogun, S. K. (1991). The influence of sex and religion on personal space among undergraduate students. *Indian Journal of Behaviour, 15,* 13–20.

Bechtel, R. B. (1997). *Environment and behavior.* Thousand Oaks, CA: Sage.

Bell, P. A., Greene, T. C., Fisher, J. D., & Baum, A. (1996). *Environmental psychology* (4th ed.). Fort Worth, TX: Harcourt Brace.

Bell, P. A., Kline, L. M., & Barnard, W. A. (1988). Friendship and freedom of movement as moderators of sex differences in interpersonal spacing. *Journal of Social Psychology, 128,* 305–310.

Bolt, R. A. (1984). *The human interface.* Belmont, CA: Lifelong Learning.

Brodsky, S. L., Hooper, N. E., Tipper, D. G., & Yates, S. B. (1999). Attorney invasions of witness space. *Law and Psychology Review, 23,* 49–68.

Brody, G. H. (1990, April). Effects of television viewing on family interactions. *Family Relations, 29,* 216–220.

Burgess, J. W. (1981). Development of social spacing in normal and mentally retarded children. *Journal of Nonverbal Behavior, 6,* 89–95.

Burgess, J. W., & Fordyce, W. K. (1989). Effect of preschool environments on nonverbal social behavior. *Journal of Child Psychology and Psychiatry and Allied Disciplines, 30,* 261–276.

Caplan, M. E., & Goldman, M. (1981). Personal space violations as a function of height. *Journal of Social Psychology, 114,* 167–171.

Coate, J. (1997). Cyberspace innkeeping. In P. E. Agre & D. Schuler (Eds.), *Reinventing technology, rediscovering community* (pp. 165–190). Greenwich, CT: Ablex.

Cochran, C. D., Hale, W. D., & Hissam, C. P. (1984). Personal space requirements in indoor versus outdoor locations. *Journal of Psychology, 117,* 121–123.

Cochran, C. D., & Urbanczyk, S. (1982). The effect of availability of vertical space on personal space. *Journal of Psychology, 111,* 137–140.

Conigliaro, L., Cullerton, S., Flynn, K., & Roeder, S. (1989). Stigmatizing artifacts and their effects on personal space. *Psychological Reports, 65,* 897–898.

Daigle, V. L. (1996). Sex differences in personal space: A meta-analytic review of the sex effect literature. Unpublished doctoral dissertation, Syracuse University (New York).

Darwin, C. (1909). *On the origin of species.* New York: P. F. Collier. (Original work published 1859)

Davis, L. L., & Lennon, S. J. (1983). Social stigma of pregnancy. *Psychological Reports, 53,* 997–998.

Dawson, R., & Scarborough, J. (1994). Space invaders will be spat at: The personal space needs of anti-social and neurotic children. *Therapeutic Care and Education, 3,* 270–276.

DeCarlo, T., Sandler, H., & Tittler, B. (1981). The role of personal space in family therapy. *Family Therapy, 8,* 255–266.

DeLoughry, T. J. (1996, March 1). Snared by the Internet. *The Chronicle of Higher Education, 42,* A25.

Dosey, M., & Meisels, M. (1969). Personal space and self-protection. *Journal of Personality and Social Psychology, 11,* 93–97.

Duke, M. P., & Nowicki, S. (1972). A new measure and social learning model for interpersonal distance. *Journal of Experimental Research in Personality, 6,* 119–132.

Eaton, S. B., Fuchs, L. S., & Snook-Hill, M. (1998). Personal space preference among male elementary and high school students with and without visual impairments. *Journal of Visual Impairments and Blindness, 92,* 769–782.

Edney, J. J., Walker, C. A., & Jordan, N. L. (1976). Is there reactance in personal space? *Journal of Social Psychology, 100,* 207–217.

Ellul, J. (1964). *The technological society.* New York: Knopf.

Evans, G. W., & Howard, R. B. (1973). Personal space. *Psychological Bulletin, 80,* 334–344.

Evans, G. W., Lepore, S. J., & Schroeder, A. (1996). The role of interior design elements in human responses to crowding. *Journal of Personality and Social Psychology, 70,* 41–46.

Farrington, C., & Pine, E. (1997). Community memory. In P. E. Agre & D. Schuler (Eds.), *Reinventing technology, rediscovering community* (pp. 219–228). Greenwich, CT: Ablex.

Fischer, C. S. (1992). *America calling.* Berkeley: University of California Press.

Gaulin, S. J. C., & McBurney, D. H. (2001). *Psychology: An evolutionary approach.* Saddle River, NJ: Prentice-Hall.

Gifford, R. (1996). *Environmental psychology* (2nd ed.). Boston, MA: Allyn & Bacon.

Gifford, R., & Sacilotto, P. A. (1993). Social isolation and personal space. *Canadian Journal of Behavioral Science, 25,* 165–174.

Goffman, E. (1971). *Relations in public.* New York: Basic Books.

Greenberg, C. I., Strube, M. J., & Myers, R. A. (1980). A multitrait-multimethod investigation of interpersonal distance. *Journal of Nonverbal Behavior, 5,* 104–114.

Hall, E. T. (1959). *The silent language.* New York: Doubleday.

Hall, E. T. (1966). *The hidden dimension.* New York: Doubleday.

Hamilton, W. (1964). The genetical evolution of social behaviour, II. *Journal of Theoretical Biology, 7,* 17–52.

Hamilton, W. D. (1971). Geometry for the selfish herd. *Journal of Theoretical Biology, 31,* 295–311.

Harrison, A. A., Clearwater, Y. A., & McKay, C. P. (Eds.). (1991). *From Antarctica to outer space: Life in isolation and confinement.* New York: Springer.

Hayduk, L. A. (1994). Personal space: Understanding the simplex model. *Journal of Nonverbal Behavior, 18,* 245–260.

Heath, C., & Luff, P. (1993). Disembodied conduct. In G. Button (Ed.), *Technology in working order* (pp. 35–54). London: Routledge.

Hediger, H. (1950). *Wild animals in captivity.* London: Butterworth.

Hern, W. M. (1991). Proxemics: The application of theory to conflict arising from antiabortion demonstrations. *Population and Environment, 12,* 379–388.

Hewitt, J., & Henley, R. (1987). Sex differences in reaction to spatial invasion. *Perceptual and Motor Skills, 64,* 809–810.

Holmes, R. M. (1992). Children's artwork and nonverbal communication. *Child Study Journal, 22,* 157–166.

Horowitz, M. J., Duff, D. F., & Stratton, L. O. (1964). Body buffer zone. *Archives of General Psychiatry, 11,* 651–656.

Hosch, H. M., & Himelstein, P. (1982). Factors influencing the violation of personal space between a photographer and subject. *Journal of Psychology, 111*, 277–283.

Jones, E. E. (1985). Interpersonal distancing behavior of hearing impaired vs. normal-hearing children. *Volta Review, 87*, 223–230.

Kaplan, K. J. (1988). Teaching individuals to live together. *Transactional Analysis Journal, 18*, 220–230.

Kaplan, S. (1992). Environmental preference in a knowledge-seeking, knowledge-using organism. In J. H. Barkow, L. Cosmides, & J. Tooby (Eds.), *The adapted mind* (pp. 581–598). New York: Oxford University Press.

Katz, D. (1937). *Animals and men.* New York: Longmans, Green.

Kaya, N., & Erkip, F. (1999). Invasion of personal space under conditions of short-term crowding. *Journal of Environmental Psychology, 19*, 183–189.

Kellert, S. R., & Wilson, E. O. (Eds.). (1993). *The biophilia hypothesis.* Washington, DC: Island Press.

Kerber, K. W. (1983). Attitudes towards specific uses of the computer. *Behaviour and Information Technology, 2*, 197–209.

Knowles, E. S. (1989). Spatial behavior of individuals and groups. In P. B. Paulus (Ed.), *Psychology of group influence* (2nd ed., pp. 53–86). Hillsdale, NJ: Erlbaum.

Kogewa, M. (1983). A microgenetic developmental study of interpersonal cognition during transition to a new environment. *Japanese Journal of Psychology, 53*, 330–336.

Kraut, R. E., & Fish, R. S. (1997). Prospects for videotelephony. In K. E. Finn, A. J. Sellen, & S. B. Wilbur (Eds.), *Video-mediated communication* (pp. 546–561). Mahwah, NJ: Erlbaum.

Kraut, R. E., Patterson, M., Lundmark, V., Kiesler, S., Mukopadhyay, T., & Scherlis, W. (1998). Internet paradox. *American Psychologist, 53*, 1017–1031.

Kuethe, J. L. (1962). Social schemas. *Journal of Abnormal and Social Psychology, 64*, 31–38.

Kunzendorf, R. G., & Denney, J. (1982). Definitions of personal space: Smokers versus nonsmokers. *Psychological Reports, 50*, 818.

LaFrance, M., & Mayo, C. (1978). *Moving bodies: Nonverbal communication in social relationships.* Monterey, CA: Brooks/Cole.

Larson, J. H., & Lowe, W. (1990). Family cohesion and personal space in families with adolescents. *Journal of Family Issues, 11*, 101–108.

Less respect. (1995, July 24). *New Yorker,* p. 70.

Levy, S. (1984). *Hackers.* New York: Anchor Press.

Lewin, K. (1951). *Field theory in social science.* New York: Harper.

Maslow, A., & Mintz, N. (1956). Effects of aesthetic surroundings. *Journal of Psychology, 41*, 247–254.

McElroy, J. C., & Morrow, P. C. (1994). Personal space, personal appearance, and personal selling. *Psychological Reports, 74*, 425–426.

Mehrabian, A. (1968). Relation of attitudes to seating posture. *Journal of Personality and Social Psychology, 10*, 26–30.

Milgram, S. (1970). The experience of living in city. *Science, 167*, 1461–1468.

Newman, O. (1972). *Defensible space.* New York: Macmillan.

Omori, Y., & Miyata, Y. (1998). The effect of interviewer distance on eyeblinks and heart rate of interviewee. *Japanese Journal of Psychology, 69*, 408–413.

O'Neal, E. C., Brunault, M. S., Carifio, M. S., Troutwine, R., & Epstein, J. (1980). Effect of insult upon personal space preferences. *Journal of Nonverbal Behavior, 5*, 56–62.

Orcutt, J. D., & Anderson, R. E. (1977). Social interaction, dehumanization, and the "computerized other." *Sociology and Social Research, 61*, 380–397.

Orians, G. H. (1986). An ecological and evolutionary approach to landscape aesthetics. In E. C. Penning-Rowsell & D. Lowenthal (Eds.), *Landscape meanings and values* (pp. 3–25). London: Allen & Unwin.

Patterson, M. L. (1976). An arousal model of interpersonal intimacy. *Psychological Review, 83*, 235–245.

Pedersen, D. M. (1973). Prediction of behavioral personal space from simulated personal space. *Perceptual and Motor Skills, 37*, 803–813.

Price, S. K. (1996). Psychological effects of personal habitability space aboard the space station and its implications for counseling. Unpublished doctoral dissertation, Texas Southern University, Houston.

Remland, M. S., Jones, T. S., & Brinkman, H. (1995). Interpersonal distance, body orientation, and touch. *Journal of Social Psychology, 135*, 281–297.

Rivano-Fischer, M. (Ed.). (1988). *Psychological Research Bulletin, Lund University, 28.*

Roszak, T. (1986). *The cult of information.* New York: Pantheon.

Ruback, R. B., Pape, K. D., & Doriot, P. (1989). Waiting for a phone. *Social Psychology Quarterly, 52*, 232–242.

Ruback, R. B., & Snow, J. N. (1993). Territoriality and nonconscious racism at water fountains. *Environment and Behavior, 25*, 250–267.

Ruggieri, V., & Frondaroli, C. (1989). Styles of interpersonal contact and some prosodic features. *Perceptual and Motor Skills, 68*, 947–953.

Schiavo, R., Kobashi, K., Quinn, C., Sefscik, A., & Sunn, K. M. (1995). Territorial influences on the permeability of group spatial boundaries. *Journal of Social Psychology, 135*, 27–29.

Scott, A. L. (1993). A beginning theory of personal space. *Perspectives in Psychiatric Care, 29*, 12–21.

Sigelman, C. K., & Adams, R. M. (1990). Family interactions in public. *Journal of Nonverbal Behavior, 14*, 63–75.

Simons, G. (1985). *Silicon shock.* Oxford: Basil Blackwell.

Sinha, S. P., & Mukherjee, N. (1996). The effect of perceived cooperation on personal space requirements. *Journal of Social Psychology, 136,* 655–657.

Skorjanc, A. D. (1991). Differences in interpersonal distance among nonoffenders as a function of perceived violence of offenders. *Perceptual and Motor Skills, 73,* 659–662.

Smeltzer, L., Waltman, J., & Leonard, D. (1999). Proxemics and haptics in managerial communication. In L. K. Guerrero & J. A. DeVito (Eds.), *The nonverbal communications reader* (2nd ed., pp. 184–191). Prospect Heights, IL: Waveland Press.

Smith, B. J., & Cantrell, P. J. (1988). Distance in nurse-patient encounters. *Journal of Psychosocial Nursing and Mental Health Services, 26,* 22–26.

Sommer, R. (1959). Studies in personal space. *Sociometry, 22,* 247–260.

Sommer, R., & Ross, H. (1958). Social interaction on a geriatrics ward. *International Journal of Social Psychiatry, 4,* 128–133.

Spencer, H. (1898). *First principles.* New York: Appleton.

Sprandel, G. (1982). A call to action. *Computing and Society, 12,* 12–13.

Sproull, L., & Faraj, S. (1995). Atheism, sex, and databases: The Net as a social technology. In B. Kahin & J. Keller (Eds.), *Public access to the Internet* (pp. 62–81). Cambridge, MA: Massachusetts Institute of Technology Press.

Srivastava, P., & Mandal, M. K. (1990). Proximal spacing to facial affect expressions in schizophrenia. *Comprehensive Psychiatry, 31,* 119–124.

Stephens, K. K., & Clark, D. W. (1987). A pilot study on the effect of visible physical stigma on personal space. *Journal of Applied Rehabilitation Counseling, 18,* 52–54.

Stern, W. (1938). *General psychology.* New York: Macmillan.

Stoll, C. (1995). *Silicon snake oil.* New York: Doubleday.

Strayer, J., & Roberts, W. (1997). Children's personal distance and their empathy. *International Journal of Behavioral Development, 20,* 385–403.

Suler, J. (2000). Life at the Palace: A cyberpsychology case study [Online]. Available: www.rider.edu/users/suler/psycyber/palacestudy.html

Summit, J. E., Westfall, S. C., Sommer, R., & Harrison, A. A. (1992). Weightless and interaction distance. *Environment and Behavior, 24,* 617–633.

Tedesco, J. F., & Fromme, D. K. (1974). Cooperation, competition, and personal space. *Sociometry, 37,* 116–121.

Tinbergen, N. (1953). *Social behaviour in animals.* London: Methuen.

Tobiasen, J. M., & Allen, A. (1983). Influence of gaze and physical closeness: A delayed effect. *Perceptual and Motor Skills, 57,* 491–495.

Travers, A. (2000). *Writing the public in cyberspace.* New York: Garland.

Ulrich, R. (1984). View through a window may influence recovery from surgery. *Science, 224,* 420–421.

Ulrich, R. S. (1993). Biophilia, biophobia, and natural landscapes. In S. R. Kellert & E. O. Wilson (Eds.), *The biophilia hypothesis* (pp. 73–137). Washington, DC: Island Press.

Von Uexkull, J. (1957). A stroll through the worlds of animals and men. In C. Schiller (Ed.), *Instinctive behavior* (pp. 5–76). New York: International Universities Press.

Weigel, R. G. (1998). A day of office in the saddle. *Consulting Psychology Journal, 50,* 190–194.

Weil, M. M., & Rosen, L. D. (1998). *TechnoStress.* New York: Wiley.

Wilson, E. O. (1998). *Consilience.* New York: Vintage.

Winkel, F. W., Koppelaar, L., & Vrij, A. (1988). Creating suspects in police-citizen encounters. *Social Behaviour, 3,* 307–318.

Worchel, S. (1986). The influence of contextual variables on interpersonal spacing. *Journal of Nonverbal Behavior, 10,* 230–254.

Wormith, J. S. (1984). Personal space of incarcerated offenders. *Journal of Clinical Psychology, 40,* 815–827.

Yamaguchi, H. (1997). The effects of spatial arrangement on one's feelings under concealed gaze. *Japanese Journal of Experimental Social Psychology, 37,* 109–118.

Young, K. S. (1998). Internet addiction. *CyberPsychology and Behavior, 1,* 237–244.

CHAPTER 41

Toward an Environmental
Psychology of the Internet

DANIEL STOKOLS and MARIA MONTERO

A DEFINING FEATURE of environmental psychology relative to other areas of behavioral and environmental science is its explicit focus on human-environment transactions—the processes by which people come to understand, evaluate, modify, and respond to their everyday physical and social environments (Craik, 1973; Proshansky, Ittelson, & Rivlin, 1976). This core concern with the nature of people-environment relationships is reflected in the multiple research paradigms of the field, including studies of environmental stress, cognitive mapping, environmental assessment, human spatial behavior, resource conservation behavior, and ecological psychology, among others (Craik, 1977; Stokols, 1995). Although these research traditions emphasize different facets of human-environment transaction (e.g., environmental cognition, evaluation, and behavior), they are guided by at least two common assumptions. The first is that people's relationships with their physical and social environments are psychologically important to them and substantially influence their development and well-being (Ittelson, Proshansky, Rivlin, & Winkel, 1974). The second is that people ideally strive to optimize, or at least enhance, the degree of fit between their own (or their group's) goals and needs, on one hand, and conditions of the environment that either support or constrain those needs, on the other (Michelson, 1970; Stokols, 1978).

The premise that people's transactions with their place-based environments are psychologically important and influential was regarded as a fundamental truth among environmental psychologists when the field coalesced during the late 1960s and was still taken for granted two decades later when the first *Handbook of Environmental Psychology* was published (Stokols & Altman, 1987). As this handbook goes to press in 2002, however, the psychological significance of people's attachments to their proximal environments has been called into question by the societal transformations that have occurred during the 14 years separating the publication of the two handbooks—especially the dramatic social and environmental changes spawned by the desktop-computing revolution of the 1980s (Kling & Iacono, 1991) and the proliferation of the Internet, World Wide Web, and related digital communications technologies (e.g. cellular phones, hand-held computers) during the 1990s (Castells, 1998; Wellman, 1999). The rapid influx of computers into people's workplaces, homes, and educational environments not only altered the physical landscape of interior environments but also made possible the establishment of high-speed digital communication networks that have substantially eased the constraints of physical distance and time on many forms of social interaction.

The research literature in environmental psychology provides ample evidence that (1) spatial propinquity fosters social contacts and friendship formation (Festinger, Schachter, & Back, 1950), (2) individuals' experiences with particular places constitute an important part of their self-identity (Cooper, 1974; Proshansky, Fabian, & Kaminoff, 1983), and (3) involuntary relocation from a familiar neighborhood often provokes emotional distress and illness symptoms among the dislocated individuals (Fried, 1963). A major question addressed in this chapter is whether or not these "foundational" findings from earlier programs of environment behavior research are generalizable to the Internet Society of the twenty-first century. Scholars from urban sociology and other fields have concluded that human communities no longer are place based but reside instead within highly personalized, digital communication networks unbounded by space and time. For instance, Wellman (in press) has written that:

> Computer-supported communication will be *everywhere*, but because it is independent of place, it will be situated *nowhere*. The importance of a communication site as a meaningful place will diminish even more. The person—not the place, household, or workgroup—will become even more of an autonomous communication node. Contextual sense and lateral awareness will diminish. (p. 4)

He further states:

> People usually obtain support, companionship, information, and a sense of belonging from those who do not live within the same neighborhood or even within the same metropolitan area. People maintain these community ties through phoning, writing, driving, railroading, and flying. . . . Neighborhoods are not important sources of community. They have become variably safe and salubrious milieus from which people sally forth in their cars, telephone from their kitchens, or email from their dens. (p. 7)

Certainly not all individuals or groups in North America and other regions of the world are sufficiently affluent to own computers and personal digital assistants, nor do they possess the requisite technological knowledge to establish and maintain digital communication networks (National Telecommunications and Information Administration, 2000). We discuss the implications of this "Digital Divide" later in the chapter (cf. Garces, 2000). Nonetheless, Wellman's observations about contemporary society and those of other scholars who regard the Internet as a means of promoting social support and community cohesion (cf. Cole et al., 2000; Horan, 2000; Negroponte, 1995) must be taken seriously by environment behavior researchers because their perspectives on the Internet Society offer a provocative counterpoint to the more traditional view—predominant in environmental psychology—that people's attachments to particular places are essential to their emotional and physical well-being.

The rapid growth of the Internet, World Wide Web, and digital communications technologies over the past decade poses several challenges for future studies of human-environment transaction. First, new measures and methods must be developed for characterizing the variety of cyberspaces that now exist on the Web (e.g., Web-based chat rooms and electronic bulletin boards). For instance, the visual and interactive qualities of these virtual sites remain to be assessed not only in terms of their objective qualities (e.g., informational complexity and accuracy, multimedia components), but also for their perceived attractiveness (Nasar, 1988), legibility, imageability (cf. Downs & Stea, 1973; Lynch, 1960), and capacity to influence participants' behavior, development, and well-being (Gackenbach, 1998; Kiesler, 1997). Second, several questions concerning the impact of the Internet and Web on people's attachments to their proximal environments and their commitments to place-based relationships remain to be addressed (Stokols, 1999, in press). These research questions and challenges are likely to catalyze novel theories of environment and behavior in the coming years.

In the next section of the chapter, we examine key features of the Internet and Web and document their tremendous growth during the 1990s. We then consider certain conceptual questions posed by the rise of the Internet and sketch the broad contours of a newly emerging field, the *environmental psychology of the Internet* (cf. Stokols & Montero, 2001).

DIMENSIONS, GROWTH, AND BEHAVIORAL IMPACTS OF THE INTERNET

The Internet encompasses the vast array of electronic connections that link millions of computers and their users throughout the world. The Internet is a highly diversified technology in that it supports multiple forms of computer-mediated communication (CMC) such as electronic mail, e-mail listserves (groups of e-mail users organized around certain topics), electronic bulletin boards and newsgroups, and sites on the Web that range from noninteractive to interactive displays of textual, graphical, and auditory information and media. Among the most interactive of these Web sites are the multiuser domains (MUDs), which offer visitors and members opportunities to enter virtual chat rooms, communicate with each other in real time, and manipulate graphical objects displayed at the site. Individuals gain access to the Internet using their desktop or hand-held computers and cable TV systems. But in contrast to TV programming, which is passively received by viewers once a particular channel is selected, the Internet offers unprecedented opportunities for interactive exploration of electronic Web sites, MUDs, bulletin boards, and data archives (Rheingold, 1993; Schuler, 1996).

Over the past decade, the Web and the Internet have grown exponentially. According to a recent survey of Web usage, the number of recorded sites on the Web grew from 10,022 in December 1993 to 109,574,429 in January 2001 (Internet Software Consortium, 2001). An independent report on *The State of the Internet 2000* estimated that, in 1993, fewer than 90,000 people worldwide used the Internet on a regular basis, but by summer 2000, the number of regular Internet users had expanded to more than 300 million people worldwide—a 3,000-fold increase in the online population (International Technology and Trade Associates [ITTA], 2000). And by the year 2005, the number of Internet users worldwide is expected to surpass the 1 billion mark. The rapid growth of the Internet during the 1990s has dramatically altered the ways in which people live and work. For instance, the increasing prevalence of desktop computing and access to the Web have made telecommuting and home-based work more feasible for large segments of the population (Internatonal Telework Association and Council, 2001). Also, the development of instantaneous interactive communications via the Internet, incorporating multiple media such as text, graphics, video, and audio, have given computer users much greater access to geographically distant people and places than ever before (Mitchell, 1995; Negroponte, 1995).

THEORETICAL QUESTIONS CONCERNING ENVIRONMENT AND BEHAVIOR IN THE AGE OF THE INTERNET

The capacity of the Internet to bring geographically distant information sources and electronically simulated "virtual" places to one's computer or TV screen raises several intriguing questions about the changing ecology of human-environment transactions. Some of these questions pertain, for example, to: (1) the relative influence of "proximal" versus "distal" processes on individuals' behavior, development, and well-being; (2) the bivalent nature of the Internet—that is, its capacity to enhance or impair individuals' development and well-being and to strengthen or weaken people's attachments to their proximal environments; and (3) the behavioral and health implications of the Internet's exponential growth in light of humans' limited capacities for coping with information overload and accelerating rates of environmental change (cf. Cohen, 1980; Emery & Trist, 1972; Lyman & Varian, 2000).

Research in environmental psychology has focused largely on the conditions in one's immediate environment that influence his or her behavior and well-being. This explicit focus on the behavioral influence of the proximal environment is rooted in Lewin's (1936) conceptualization of the *psychological lifespace*—the totality of psychobiological conditions (e.g., perceptions, motivations, and salient features of the environment) that determine one's behavior at a specific moment within a particular place. Lewin referred to the nonsalient (nonperceived) features of the sociophysical environment as the "foreign hull" of the lifespace—those contextual circumstances located beyond the boundaries of the lifespace that, according to Lewin, are more amenable to sociological and biophysical studies than to psychological research.

Prior to the Internet's emergence as a powerful and pervasive force in society, the perceptual salience and behavioral influence of environmental conditions were generally correlated with their geographic proximity and immediacy to the individual. With the advent of the Internet and Web, however, individuals' opportunities to experience distant places and events are now much less bounded by spatial and temporal constraints. Whereas non-Internet forms of communication (e.g., reading a book, watching TV, talking with others on the telephone, or corresponding with them by surface or air mail) can bring geographically distant people and places psychologically closer to the individual, the Internet differs from these other media in some important respects. First, electronic mail and the Web make it possible for an individual to communicate simultaneously and interactively with scores, and even hundreds, of other persons—for example, through "instant messaging" among acquaintances that find themselves online at the same time. By contrast, TV programs are experienced more passively than interactively, and telephone conversations are usually restricted to dyads (or to slightly larger groups participating in "conference calls").

In addition to affording simultaneous contact with a large number of other people, Internet-based communications often combine textual, graphic, and auditory modalities (e.g., real-time video images of the people one is communicating with as well as dynamic views of their physical surroundings). Printed media are quite capable of depicting faraway people and places through photographs, drawings, and text, but they do not provide real-time interactive views of distant people and events; nor can they deliver nearly instantaneous, multimodal communications as exemplified by electronic mailings that contain document, voice, and video attachments. The Internet and Web also afford serendipitous encounters with large numbers of strangers in cyberspace and opportunities to explore hundreds and even thousands of communication channels (or Web sites) within relatively short intervals of time.

The capacity of the Internet to make remote places and events psychologically salient to those who use this new technology has important psychological consequences across the lifespan. On the positive side, young children and adolescents with regular access to the Web are likely to be exposed to diverse cultural influences and vast stores of information, thereby broadening their understanding of the world and strengthening their sense of connection with remote people and places. Similarly, working adults can use the Internet to expand their personal skills and knowledge so that they are better equipped to perform effectively in their jobs. And older adults can now use the Internet to maintain a proactive orientation toward other people and places, strengthen their ties to the outside world, and counter feelings of loneliness and isolation even as their physical mobility becomes more constrained with the passage of time (Lawton, 1999; Rook, 1984; SeniorsCan Internet Program, 2001; SeniorNet, 2001). Also, online communication networks can be used to reinforce social support and a sense of community among the members of place-based organizations, neighborhoods, and towns (Blanchard & Horan, 1998; Blumenstyk, 1997; Horan, 2000).

At the same time, however, the Internet can exert a profoundly negative, albeit indirect, influence on the development and well-being of individuals and

groups who are least likely to use it. Several demographic studies have shown that low levels of education and income make it much less likely for individuals to own computers and to have access to the Internet (Garces, 2000; NTIA, 2000). Moreover, certain regions of the world lack the requisite infrastructure (e.g., telephone lines and digital communications technologies) for residents to participate in the Internet and Web. Castells (1998) has referred to these regions as the *Fourth World*—a series of "black holes of informational capitalism" that have been cut off from the flow of information in the global economy. In light of these demographic trends, it is important to address the psychological and developmental consequences of the Internet and Web for those individuals who find themselves on the wrong side of the Digital Divide because of low socioeconomic status and/or electronic isolation. For younger individuals, developmental deficits among those living in poverty may become more severe as the Internet widens the rift between information-rich and information-poor segments of the world's population. At the same time, Internet-deprived older adults may find themselves caught in a spiral of increasing poverty caused by their restricted access to job opportunities that require training in information technology (cf. Freeman & Aspray, 1999). If these developmental deficits among individuals who lack access to information technology are not redressed, they are likely to provoke increasing conflict and destabilization among the developed and underdeveloped countries of the world (cf. Castells, 1998).

Even among more affluent members of society who have ready access to the Internet and Web, increased use of digital communications technologies can be a source of negative behavioral, developmental, and health outcomes. For instance, parents' frequent use of home-based computers may interfere with developmental processes by constraining opportunities for parent-child interaction, thereby promoting an ambiance of nonresponsiveness in family environments (Stokols, 1999; Wachs & Gruen, 1982). Also, the Internet and Web have created new opportunities for engaging in criminal activities online such as "cyber stalking," child sexual abuse, identity theft, and financial fraud and for promoting racism and hate crimes (Hayes & Boucher, 1997; Mannix, 2000). And, aside from these criminal abuses, individuals' growing use of digital communications technologies has been linked in some studies to higher levels of self-reported loneliness, reduced social contact with family members and friends, and experiences of chronic distraction, overload, and stress resulting from a surfeit of electronic communications (cf. Kraut et al., 1998; Milgram, 1970; Nie & Erbring, 2000). Considering these potentially negative consequences of society's growing reliance on digital communications, an important challenge for future theory development and research is to specify the contextual circumstances under which people's use of the Internet and Web has the most positive and least detrimental effects on psychological, behavioral, and health outcomes.

The theories, methods, and findings from environment behavior studies offer a valuable but relatively untapped perspective from which to approach the theoretical questions and research challenges outlined above. Earlier research on the psychological and social consequences of the Internet have focused primarily on intrapersonal and interpersonal processes and outcomes while giving less attention to the ways in which the Internet is transforming people's day-to-day transactions with their place-based physical and social milieus (Gackenbach, 1998; Kiesler & Kraut, 1999; McKenna & Bargh, 2000; Turkle, 1995). In the remaining portions of the chapter, we examine these issues from the perspective of environmental and ecological psychology to better understand how society's growing reliance on digital communications has altered and will continue to transform people's encounters with their sociophysical surroundings (Barker, 1968; Bechtel, 1997; Bell, Fisher, Baum, & Greene, 1990; Michelson, 1970; Proshansky et al., 1976).

THE CHANGING ECOLOGY OF HUMAN-ENVIRONMENT RELATIONS IN THE INTERNET ERA: ENVIRONMENTAL PSYCHOLOGY AS A FOUNDATION FOR THEORY DEVELOPMENT AND RESEARCH

Environmental psychology emerged as an organized area of interdisciplinary scientific inquiry during the late 1960s and early seventies (cf. Bronfenbrenner, 1977; Craik, 1973; Ittelson et al., 1974; Moos, 1976). The emergence and rapid expansion of this field was attributable in part to growing societal concerns about environmental pollution, adverse global environmental

changes, and the behavioral consequences of overcrowding (Carson, 1962; Ehrlich, 1968; Kates & Wohlwill, 1966). At the same time, concerted efforts by many researchers to address conceptual gaps in psychological science (especially those concerning the behavioral and health impacts of the large-scale environment) further contributed to the burgeoning growth of environmental psychology and social ecology. The historical evolution and substantive concerns of environmental psychology are well covered in other chapters of this volume, so we provide only a brief and general overview of these developments.

By the late 1970s, the field of environmental psychology consisted of multiple scientific paradigms (Craik, 1977), each organized around a particular facet of human-environment transaction (e.g., environmental cognition, spatial behavior, environmental stress, ecological psychology, environmental attitudes and assessment, experimental analyses of environmentally protective behavior). Some of these research areas emphasized people's active efforts to interpret and restructure their surroundings (e.g., environmental cognition and spatial behavior), whereas others reflected a more reactive stance toward the environment (e.g., environmental assessment, health effects of urban stressors). In an effort to integrate these distinct research paradigms and explain how individuals use different modes of relating to their environments in a sequential, organized fashion, environmental psychologists drew heavily on the principles of ecology and open systems theory (cf. Stokols, 1977).

Ecological theories were first developed by biologists working during the late 1800s (Clements, 1905; Darwin, 1859/1964; Warming, 1909) and later elaborated by psychologists and sociologists in their analyses of human response to urban environments (Alihan, 1938; Hawley, 1950; Park, Burgess, & McKenzie, 1925). Ecological psychologists, for example, conceptualized behavior settings as systemically organized, place-based units of people-environment transaction (Barker & Schoggen, 1973; Wicker, 1979). Other theorists focused on the "ecology of human development" and documented the ways in which individuals' multiple life settings (e.g., residential, day care, work environments, public spaces), spanning micro-, meso-, and macrolevels, jointly influence their psychosocial development over the life course (Bronfenbrenner, 1979; Friedman & Wachs, 1999).

Central to ecological analyses of environment and behavior are certain basic assumptions and principles derived from open systems theory (Emery, 1969; Katz & Kahn, 1966; von Bertalanffy, 1950). A core assumption of systems theory is that people strive to achieve equilibrium or homeostasis with their physical and social milieus (Altman, 1975; Barker, 1968; Emery & Trist, 1972; Moos, 1976). Some theorists referred to this state of balance as person environment (PE) "congruence" or "fit" (Michelson, 1970; Wicker, 1972). They also noted that when levels of PE fit are perceived by an individual to be inadequate, that person is more likely to experience symptoms of emotional and physiological stress than when conditions of fit are viewed as more favorable (Michelson, 1985).

Another principle of ecological systems theory suggests that people's relationships with their surroundings are goal directed and reflect reciprocal phases of influence between individuals and their environments. For example, Stokols (1978) proposed that the multiple paradigms of environmental psychology correspond to different facets or phases of *human-environment optimization,* a dynamic and sequential process by which individuals strive to achieve "optimal environments"—those that maximize the fulfillment of their needs and the accomplishment of their goals and plans. In many situations, people are forced by situational constraints to accept undesirable environmental conditions, or at best to "satisfice" (Simon, 1957)— that is, achieve less than optimal improvements in their surroundings. Stokols notes: "Although environmental optimization is never realized in its ideal form, the concept is heuristically useful in emphasizing the goal-directed and cyclical nature of human-environment transactions and in suggesting certain processes by which these transactions occur" (p. 258). These fundamental processes of person environment transaction include the *interpretive, evaluative, operative,* and *responsive* modes of dealing with one's surroundings.

The assumptions of systems theory and the research foci of environmental and ecological psychology provide a useful starting point for considering the transformative impacts of the Internet and Web on the quality of people's lives and the patterning of their routine activities and projects. The cumulative evidence from several programs of environment behavior research suggests that humans strive (1) to establish and maintain meaningful psychological and social connections with the material world, reflected in their strong emotional attachments to particular objects and places; and (2) to optimize the degree of fit between their personal and collective needs for identity, affiliation, social support, emotional and physical security, and environmental legibility, on the one hand, and conditions present in the physical and social environment that, ideally, facilitate the fulfillment of those needs, on the other. Moreover, (3) individuals are most likely to experience psychological, social, and physiological stress when levels of person environment fit are perceived to be low (e.g., conditions of prolonged stimulation overload; infringements on one's privacy in residential, work, or institutional settings; lack of access to aesthetic surroundings and natural environments). The evidence supporting these propositions is consistently strong across several paradigms of environment behavior research. The field of environmental and ecological psychology thus provides a useful backdrop for developing a conceptual analysis and programmatic agenda for future research on the ways in which the Internet and Web are transforming the quality and structure of people-environment transactions. These issues are addressed below.

A CONCEPTUAL FRAMEWORK AND AGENDA FOR FUTURE RESEARCH

A conceptual framework for future research on the environmental psychology of the Internet is outlined in Table 41.1, adapted from (Stokols, 1978). As in the earlier version of this table, four basic modes of person environment transaction are shown along with key paradigms of environment behavior representing each mode. Under the active-cognitive or *interpretive* mode, for example, the paradigms of environmental cognition and personality and the environment are listed. Within the lower right cell, denoting the reactive-cognitive or *evaluative* mode, research on environmental attitudes and people's evaluative assessments of particular places are included. In the upper right cell of the table, representing the active-behavioral or *operative* mode, research on how people use the spatial environment to regulate privacy and other aspects of interpersonal relations (e.g., processes of personal space regulation, territoriality) and on their environmentally-protective behavior (e.g., processes of resource conservation, recycling) are listed. Finally, in the lower right cell, depicting the reactive-behavioral or *responsive* mode, research on people's reactions to

Table 41.1
Influence of the Internet on Four Modes of Human-Environment Transaction:
Questions for Theory Development and Research

Form of Transaction

	Cognitive*	Behavioral
	Interpretive Mode	*Operative Mode*
Active	Environmental Cognition	Human Spatial Behavior
	Will frequent exposure to computer-simulated environments on the Web reduce individuals' sense of environmental coherence and legibility?	Is spatial proximity being replaced by electronic connectivity as a requisite for social contact and friendship formation?
	Personality and Environment	Environmentally Protective Behavior
	Do certain dispositions (e.g., sensation seeking) enable individuals to retain a stronger sense of environmental coherence following exposure to multiple simulated environments on the Web?	Can future efforts to promote environmental conservation be made more effective through the use of informative Web sites that convey futuristic scenarios of environmental degradation?
	Evaluative Mode	*Responsive Mode*
	Environmental Attitudes	Environmental Stress
Reactive	Do short-term encounters with virtual places on the Web lead to incomplete or biased appraisals of those environments?	How will individuals' exposure to increasing digital communications affect their susceptibility to chronic stress and related health problems?
	Environmental Assessment	Ecological Psychology
	Will greater access to simulated views of remote places weaken people's attachments to their proximal environments and relationships?	How might the potential conflicts between virtual behavior settings and the real environments from which they are accessed be minimized or avoided?

Phase of Transaction

Source: Adapted from Stokols, 1978.

* In this framework, the term *cognitive* refers to both informational and affective processes.

environmental stressors (e.g., high density, noise, traffic congestion) and to conditions of under- and overstaffing in their everyday behavior settings (the ecological psychology paradigm), are shown.

The conceptual framework presented in Table 41.1 extends Stokols's (1978) representation of research paradigms in environmental psychology by incorporating a series of questions about changes in the nature of people-environment relations that may be occurring due to the rapid growth of the Internet and Web. These questions offer a useful starting point for future theory development and research on the environmental psychology of the Internet. In the following sections of the paper,

we consider new directions for Internet-related research as they pertain to each of the four basic modes of people-environment transaction described earlier.

INFLUENCE OF THE INTERNET ON PEOPLE'S INTERPRETATION OF THEIR SURROUNDINGS

Research on environmental cognition examines the ways in which individuals develop mental representations of their sociophysical environments (Lynch, 1960; Milgram & Jodelet, 1976). For example, studies of cognitive mapping processes in humans have examined prominent physical features and social meanings of urban environments that promote high levels of *imageability*, or the capacity of a place to evoke strong and memorable mental images. Another core construct in this research area is environmental *legibility*, or the extent to which the layout and organization of places are perceived to be coherent and understandable by occupants.

The rapid growth of the Internet and Web poses several new questions for future research on environmental cognition. First, access to the Internet offers individuals unprecedented opportunities for visiting digitally simulated environments via their computers—for example, art museums, concert halls, and cultural centers—many of which are located in faraway places. This enables computer users to acquire detailed previews and greater knowledge about unfamiliar places before they actually visit them. At the same time, however, greater opportunities to encounter places virtually through computer-based digital photos and video simulations might hasten the pace but reduce the coherence of people's environmental experiences. Earlier studies suggest that humans have an intrinsic need to experience their physical and social environments kinesthetically—that is, through direct encounters with places that are associated with multiple tactile, olfactory, visual, and auditory cues (Hall, 1966). As the proportion of individuals' environmental experiences shifts from direct, kinesthetic encounters with places toward increasingly simulated and fragmented views of those settings, how will their sense of coherence and legibility be affected? Several lines of research suggest that humans strive to maintain a strong sense of environmental coherence (Antonovsky, 1981; Kaplan & Kaplan, 1989). Extrapolating from these studies, it seems plausible that individuals' exposure to an increasingly rapid and diverse array of simulated environments on the Internet may place considerable strain on their capacity to achieve a coherent understanding of their surroundings.

Research within the personality paradigm of environmental psychology (Craik, 1976; Little, 1987) further suggests that individuals may vary widely in their preferences for exposure to multiple, digitally simulated environments on the Internet, and their capacities to cultivate and retain a sense of coherence in the face of rapid computer-mediated experiences of diverse places. For example, individuals scoring high on the Sensation-Seeking Scale (Zuckerman, 1979) may prefer higher levels of exposure to multiple simulated environments on the Web and

experience less mental fatigue and loss of perceived environmental coherence than those who score low on the sensation-seeking dimension (Smith, Johnson, & Sarason, 1978).

Several other questions concerning environmental cognition and legibility are raised by the advent of the Internet and Web. For instance, do the graphic designs and visual qualities of some Web sites evoke stronger images and memories than others, thereby prompting visitors to return more frequently to those sites? Also, do computer-simulated previews of unfamiliar places enable individuals to acquire more legible mental maps and a stronger sense of coherence once they actually visit those places than would be possible without the benefit of these digital previews? In this regard, prior studies suggest that the psychological and health benefits of virtual visits to unfamiliar places may be especially evident among frail elderly persons who must relocate from their private residence to an institutional care facility (Pastalan, 1983).

INFLUENCE OF THE INTERNET ON PEOPLE'S EVALUATIONS OF THEIR SURROUNDINGS

The environmental attitudes and environmental assessment paradigms are centrally concerned with the ways in which people evaluate their surroundings (Craik & Feimer, 1987). Whereas environmental attitudes reflect an individual's tendency to respond either positively or negatively to a particular place, environmental assessments can entail collective as well as individual judgments about previously or currently occupied environments. Also, many environmental assessment projects are undertaken to reveal people's preferences or concerns about future environments that they have not yet encountered (e.g., a design committee's review of site plans for a future neighborhood recreation center).

The fact that the Internet and Web afford computer users greater opportunities to visit multiple remote environments virtually rather than directly raises important questions about environmental evaluation processes. First, because computer-mediated encounters with places are often of short duration and emphasize highly selective visual information about those settings, the virtual visitor is deprived of the opportunity to experience the place in a more complete and sustained fashion. Do these ephemeral encounters with virtual places lead to incomplete (e.g., visually dominated) and biased appraisals of the actual places that are simulated on the Web? In some instances, digital simulation may make remote environments appear more attractive and desirable than they actually are. Consequently, greater opportunities to make virtual visits to a broad range of remote locations might artificially inflate a visitor's "comparison level for alternatives" (Thibaut & Kelley, 1959), thereby weakening his or her attachment to a presently occupied environment. Might this grass-is-always-greener phenomenon, piqued by frequent exposure to simulated environments on the Web, weaken people's affective ties to their immediate surroundings and prompt faulty decision-making about potential relocation opportunities? Or, more generally, contribute to a weakened "sense of place" and an erosion of "place identity" among community members (Meyrowitz, 1985; Proshansky et al., 1983)?

Another set of Internet-relevant questions pertains to the ways in which people experience aesthetic stimuli in their physical and social environments. The Internet and Web make it possible for people to view a painting or listen to a concert through computer-based video and audio simulations. However, the social contacts that occur when a person visits a local art museum or attends a musical performance in person are lost when she or he experiences those stimuli and events in digitized form (Stokols, in press). The face-to-face social context of individuals' aesthetic experiences not only enriches their appreciation of the focal stimuli but also may play an important role in fostering stronger social ties among community members for the betterment of each individual—associations sometimes referred to as "social capital" (Putnam, 1995). These Internet-related research issues concerning environmental evaluation processes take on even greater significance when viewed from the vantage point of prior studies highlighting individuals' needs for strong and stable ties to their everyday environments (cf. Firey, 1945; Fried, 1963; Rochberg-Halton & Csikszentmihalyi, 1981).

Influence of the Internet on Spatial Behavior and Environmental Protection Efforts

The operative mode of human-environment transaction encompasses the myriad ways in which people actively modify their physical and social surroundings. Building a home, decorating one's office, and participating in a neighborhood recycling program exemplify behaviors that directly alter the structure or quality of a particular environment. Two

paradigms of environmental psychology that emphasize individuals' behavioral modifications of their surroundings are *proxemics*—the study of how people use space in social situations (Altman, 1975; Sommer, 1969)—and analyses of environmentally protective (or destructive) behavior, including studies of energy conservation, waste recycling efforts, and the defacement of environments through littering and graffiti (Geller, Winett, & Everett, 1982; Oskamp, 2000).

Earlier studies of spatial behavior have examined how people regulate their interaction distances (or personal space) with others through both verbal and nonverbal behaviors and how they establish territorial boundaries within the context of specific place-based settings. For example, Altman's model of spatial behavior emphasizes the ways in which individuals adjust personal space and territorial boundaries to achieve desired levels of privacy with co-occupants of particular settings (Altman, 1975). To the extent that desired privacy levels are achieved, the individual is able to avoid stressful experiences such as social isolation at one extreme and perceived crowding at the other.

The central role of spatial and temporal proximity in interpersonal relationships is underscored by field studies documenting the strong influence of door-to-door proximity among neighbors on the development of local friendship networks and patterns of political and consumer behavior (Festinger et al., 1950). With the advent of the Internet and Web, however, the constraining influence of spatial and temporal proximity on informal social interaction, privacy regulation, and friendship formation has been diminished by the availability of electronic networks (e.g., e-mail listserves, Web-based chat rooms) that facilitate frequent communication among participants located in geographically distant areas. Thus, it appears that physical proximity is gradually being replaced, or at least supplemented, by electronic connectivity as a requirement for interpersonal contact and as a basis for managing privacy and communicating both personal and collective identities (Kiesler, 1997; Turkle, 1995).

Some researchers contend that people's diminishing reliance on place-based, face-to-face encounters with others and on geographically anchored centers of higher education, health care delivery, and political engagement eventually will weaken the social fabric of communities, resulting in greater loneliness and reduced social support

(Kiesler & Kraut, 1999; Meyrowitz, 1985; Noam, 1995). By contrast, others argue that individuals are effectively using their electronic networks to develop and maintain strong interpersonal and professional affiliations (Cole et al., 2000; Horan, 2000; Wellman, 1999). Rather than using spatial proximity as a basis for meeting others, individuals with regular access to the Internet are now establishing *virtual communities* for purposes of finding companions who share common professional, recreational, or health-related interests. According to (Blanchard & Horan, 1998), "virtual communities of interest" are comprised of geographically dispersed individuals who come together on the Internet to share information, ideas, and emotional support. "Place-based virtual communities," on the other hand, are established by participants working or residing in the same location to reinforce their face-to-face interactions. The Blacksburg Electronic Village (BEV) exemplifies a place-based virtual community that was established to enhance residents' sense of community and civic engagement in Blacksburg, Virginia (Cohill & Kavanaugh, 2000).

The rise of the Internet and Web also poses important questions for future studies of environmentally protective behavior. In the past, efforts to promote energy conservation and the recycling of waste products have relied heavily on community-based information campaigns and household-specific customer feedback and monetary incentive programs organized by local utility companies (Bator & Cialdini, 2000; Geller et al., 1982). However, future efforts to promote environmental conservation and reverse adverse global environmental changes are likely to be channeled through comprehensive, authoritative, and visually striking Web sites that convey futuristic scenarios of environmental degradation and offer visitors extensive information about ways to curb energy consumption, global warming, and ozone depletion and enhance biodiversity (International Council for Science, 2001; United States Environmental Protection Agency, 2001a, 2001b).

Impact of the Internet on Environmental Stress and Behavior Setting Processes

The responsive mode of human-environment transaction pertains to individuals' behavioral and physical responses to environmental conditions. Two research paradigms that reflect a strong emphasis on the responsive mode include studies of human response to environmental stressors, such as high density noise, traffic congestion, and uncomfortable climate (Evans, 1982; Glass & Singer, 1972; Milgram, 1970), and ecological psychology, which has documented the influence of organizational conditions such as under- and overstaffing in behavior settings on their participants (Barker, 1968; Bechtel, 1997; Schoggen, 1989; Wicker, 1979).

The term *stress* denotes an imbalance between the environmental demands confronted by an individual and his or her capacity to cope with those demands (Selye, 1956). The construct *psychological stress* refers to an imbalance between one's *perception of environmental demands* and her or his *perceived ability to cope* with those conditions (Lazarus, 1966). Residents of large cities, for example, are prone to experiencing "urban overload," a form of stress that occurs when the quantity and rate of environmental stimuli exceed an individual's ability to process and cope with them (Milgram, 1970).

Research on environmental stress offers a useful backdrop for considering the potential behavioral and health impacts of information overload resulting from a surfeit of digital communications. The *State of the Internet 2000* report, mentioned earlier, chronicles the dramatic growth of the online population worldwide during the 1990s (ITTA, 2000). The exponential rise in Internet use and digital communications also is reflected in a study conducted by America Online, Inc., which found that e-mail usage per AOL subscriber increased by 60% over the past year, while AOL's total e-mail usage increased 120% during the same period (Messaging Online, Inc., 2000). Moreover, a report released by the University of California, Berkeley, School of Information Management and Systems estimated that, although it has taken 300,000 years for humans to accumulate 12 "exabytes" (i.e., one billion gigabytes) of information, it will take only 2.5 more years to create the next 12 exabytes (Lyman & Varian, 2000).

These trends in Internet use and information production suggest that individuals' information-processing capacities will continue to be taxed in the coming years by their exposure to an onslaught of digital communications transmitted via desktop and laptop computers, hand-held digital devices, mobile cellular phones, and fax machines. Not only will the quantity of communications increase, but also the variety of settings and time periods in which individuals can be contacted digitally by friends, work associates, and strangers. Widespread use of the Internet and Web has promoted a syndrome of being "always online" among regular computer users who, in effect, remain "tethered" to multiple electronic devices—not only while occupying traditional work environments but also while in residential and recreational settings—except when they are sleeping or choose to go "offline" (Guzzetta, 2001).

Confronted by an ever expanding flow of information sent via multiple communication channels and received at several locations throughout the day, computer users' vulnerability to attentional overload and stress is likely to increase in the coming years. Prior studies indicate that chronic stress can undermine people's resistance to disease and behavioral functioning across diverse settings (Cohen, 1980; Cohen & Williamson, 1991). To meet the performance and health challenges posed by a proliferation of digital communications, individuals and groups must develop improved strategies for filtering, sorting, prioritizing, and storing information. Some of these coping strategies will be facilitated by technological advances (e.g., the message-filtering capabilities of advanced e-mail systems). But perhaps the most effective strategies for managing information overload will not be technological in nature but depend instead on the ability of individuals to spend portions of their time offline in *restorative environments* (Kaplan & Kaplan, 1989)—those that enable them to escape from their usual activity routines and afford ample opportunities to engage in spontaneous or nondirected attention—for example, in natural environments that are both beautiful and tranquil (Korpela & Hartig, 1996; Ulrich, 1983). Restorative settings are defined by their capacity to promote relaxation and alleviate stress.

Research in the area of ecological psychology suggests additional ways in which the structure of place-based behavior settings can either enhance or undermine individuals' ability to cope with an increasing deluge of computer-mediated information. The basic unit of analysis in ecological psychology is the *behavior setting,* a physical location in which the members of a particular group come together to perform a program of activities on a recurring basis (Barker, 1968). Examples of behavior settings include offices, homes, or the regularly scheduled practices of a basketball team that take place in a high school gymnasium.

In recent years, Barker's conceptualization of place-based behavior settings has been extended to account for people's growing participation in *virtual behavior settings*, or electronic sites on the Internet created through the shared interactions of members that develop a symbolic sense of space or place

through sustained computer-mediated communications among participants (Blanchard, 1997). Examples of virtual behavior settings include chat rooms and multiuser domains (MUDs) on the Web. An important topic for future research concerns the ways in which individuals' participation in virtual behavior settings either complements or conflicts with the behavioral program of the place-based environment (e.g., a home or workplace) in which their computer is located and from which they access multiple Web sites. Because people's experiences of virtual settings are essentially "nested" in physically situated host environments, a new type of mesosystem (i.e., linkage between two or more settings; Bronfenbrenner, 1979) has been posited: the *r-v mesosystem* unit comprised of a *r*eal (place-based) host environment and a *v*irtual behavior setting nested within it (Stokols, 1999).

In some cases, an individual's participation in a virtual setting conflicts with the norms and activities of the host setting—for example, when an office worker engages in recreational Web surfing on the job, thereby arousing the resentment of coworkers and supervisors. In other instances, the relationship between a virtual setting and the host environment is complementary—for instance, an educational environment where the instructor encourages students to visit course-related Web sites using computers located in the classroom for purposes of supplementing the material covered in the instructor's lectures. The potential conflicts that can occur between the behavioral programs of virtual settings and their host environments constitute an additional source of attentional overload and interpersonal stress during the Internet era. These considerations suggest that the design of future behavior settings and communities should be guided by the goal of optimizing rather than compromising the complementarity or fit between virtual and real settings—especially considering that individuals participate in both types of settings simultaneously.

SUMMARY AND CONCLUSIONS

This chapter examined the impacts of the Internet and Web on people's relationships with their physical and social environments. Several theoretical questions posed by the increasing prevalence of digital communications in society were considered. For instance, will individuals' participation in the Internet weaken their emotional attachments to proximal environments and relationships? To what extent will individuals' personal and collective identities become less dependent on their involvement with particular places (cf. Firey, 1945; Proshansky, 1978) and more closely associated with their electronic networks or virtual communities of interest (Blanchard & Horan, 1998; Wellman, in press)? How will individuals' simultaneous participation in real and virtual behavior settings influence their vulnerability to distraction and interpersonal conflict? And how will the expanding flow of digital communications affect individuals' susceptibility to chronic overload, psychological stress, and health problems?

These and related questions were considered from the perspectives of environmental and ecological psychology. Several theories, methods, and findings from multiple paradigms of environment behavior research provided a useful starting point for considering potential impacts of the Internet and Web on human-environment transactions. A conceptual framework and research agenda were proposed as the basis for establishing a new research domain, the *environmental psychology of the Internet*. Several topics for future investigation were discussed, including the influence of computer-mediated communications and social contacts on the strength of people's emotional ties to particular geographic locations, the role of personal dispositions in mediating the psychological and social consequences of individuals' participation in the Internet and Web, and the social and health impacts of individuals' simultaneous participation in noncomplementary real and virtual behavior settings.

The primary focus of this chapter was on theoretical rather than methodological issues. Yet, several methodological challenges remain to be addressed in future research, including (1) the combined use of multiple methodologies (e.g., time budget analyses, physical trace measures, retrospective interviews) to assess individuals' time allocation to both real and virtual settings; (2) development of criteria for assessing the perceived legibility, imageability, and aesthetic value of cyberenvironments on the Web; (3) creation of measures for gauging an individual's cumulative exposure to digital information and communications over a specified time interval and the effects of that exposure on his or her wellbeing; and (4) development of criteria for identifying complementary or conflicting relationships between the real and virtual settings comprising a person's meso- or exosystems. Taken together, these conceptual and methodological issues raise several provocative questions about the changing ecology of human-environment relations in the Age of the Internet and offer an exciting agenda for future research.

REFERENCES

Alihan, M. A. (1938). *Social ecology: A critical analysis.* New York: Cooper Square.

Altman, I. (1975). *The environment and social behavior.* Monterey, CA: Brooks/Cole.

Antonovsky, A. (1981). *Health, stress, and coping.* San Francisco: Jossey-Bass.

Barker, R. G. (1968). *Ecological psychology: Concepts and methods for studying the environment of human behavior.* Stanford, CA: Stanford University Press.

Barker, R. G., & Schoggen, P. (1973). *Qualities of community life.* San Francisco: Jossey-Bass.

Bator, R., & Cialdini, R. (2000). The application of persuasion theory to the development of effective proenvironmental public service announcements. *Journal of Social Issues, 56*(3), 527–541.

Bechtel, R. B. (1997). *Environment & behavior: An introduction.* Thousand Oaks, CA: Sage.

Bell, P. A., Fisher, J. D., Baum, A., & Greene, T. E. (Eds.). (1990). *Environmental psychology* (3rd ed.). New York: Holt, Rinehart and Winston.

Blanchard, A. (1997). Virtual behavior settings: An application of behavior setting theories to virtual communities. Claremont, CA: Center for Organizational and Behavioral Sciences, Claremont Graduate University.

Blanchard, A., & Horan, T. (1998). Virtual communities and social capital. *Social Science Computer Review, 16,* 293–307.

Blumenstyk, G. (1997, January 17). An experiment in "virtual community" takes shape in Blacksburg, VA: The "electronic village" shows the promise and some of the limitations of the idea. *Chronicle of Higher Education,* A24.

Bronfenbrenner, U. (1977). Toward an experimental ecology of human development. *American Psychologist, 32,* 513–530.

Bronfenbrenner, U. (1979). *The ecology of human development: Experiments by nature and design.* Cambridge, MA: Harvard University Press.

Carson, R. (1962). *Silent spring.* Boston, MA: Houghton Mifflin.

Castells, M. (1998). *End of millennium.* Malden, MA: Blackwell.

Clements, F. (1905). *Research methods in ecology.* Lincoln: University of Nebraska Press.

Cohen, S. (1980). Aftereffects of stress on human performance and social behavior: A review of research and theory. *Psychological Bulletin, 88,* 82–108.

Cohen, S., & Williamson, G. M. (1991). Stress and infectious disease in humans. *Psychological Bulletin, 109,* 5–24.

Cohill, A., & Kavanaugh, A. (2000). *Community networks: Lessons from Blacksburg, VA* (2nd ed.). Norwood, MA: Artech House.

Cole, J. I., Suman, M., Schramm, P., van Bel, D., Lunn, B., Maguire, P., Hanson, K., Singh, R., & Aquino, J. (2000). *The UCLA Internet Report: Surveying the Digital Future* [Online]. Los Angeles: Center for Communication Policy, University of California, Los Angeles. Available: www.ccp.ucla.edu. October 26, 2000

Cooper, C. (1974). The house as symbol of the self. In J. Lang, C. Burnette, W. Moleski, & D. Vachon (Eds.), *Designing for human behavior* (pp. 130–146). Stroudsburg, PA: Dowden, Hutchinson & Ross.

Craik, K. H. (1973). Environmental psychology. *Annual Review of Psychology, 24,* 403–422.

Craik, K. H. (1976). The personality research paradigm in environmental psychology. In S. Wapner, S. B. Cohen, & B. Kaplan (Eds.), *Experiencing the environment* (pp. 55–79). New York: Plenum Press.

Craik, K. H. (1977). Multiple scientific paradigms in environmental psychology, I. *International Journal of Psychology, 12,* 26–31.

Craik, K. H., & Feimer, N. (1987). Environmental assessment. In D. Stokols & I. Altman (Eds.), *Handbook of environmental psychology* (Vol. 2, pp. 891–918). New York: Wiley.

Darwin, C. (1964). *On the origin of species.* Cambridge, MA: Harvard University Press. (Original work published 1859)

Downs, R. M., & Stea, D. (Eds.). (1973). *Image and environment: Cognitive mapping and spatial behavior.* Chicago: Aldine.

Ehrlich, P. (1968). *The population bomb.* New York: Ballantine.

Emery, F. E. (Ed.). (1969). *Systems thinking.* London: Penguin Books.

Emery, F. E., & Trist, E. L. (1972). *Towards a social ecology: Contextual appreciation of the future in the present.* London: Plenum Press.

Evans, G. W. (Ed.). (1982). *Environmental stress.* Cambridge: Cambridge University Press.

Festinger, L., Schachter, S., & Back, K. (1950). *Social pressures in informal groups.* New York: Harper.

Firey, W. (1945). Sentiment and symbolism as ecological variables. *American Sociological Review, 10,* 140–148.

Freeman, P., & Aspray, W. (1999). *The supply of information technology workers available in the United States.* Washington, DC: Computing Research Association.

Fried, M. (1963). Grieving for a lost home. In L. Duhl (Ed.), *The urban condition* (pp. 151–156). New York: Basic Books.

Friedman, S. L., & Wachs, T. D. (Eds.). (1999). *Measuring environment across the lifespan: Emerging methods and concepts.* Washington, DC: American Psychological Association.

Gackenbach, J. (Ed.). (1998). *Psychology and the Internet: Intrapersonal, interpersonal, and transpersonal implications.* San Diego, CA: Academic Press.

Garces, R. F. (2000, April 14). *Experts propose policies to bridge California's Digital Divide, improve health* [Online]. The California Center for Health Improvement. Available: www.cchi.org/pdf/WrkHlth2.pdf

Geller, E. S., Winett, R. A., & Everett, P. B. (1982). *Preserving the environment: New strategies for behavior change.* New York: Pergamon Press.

Glass, D. C., & Singer, J. E. (1972). *Urban stress.* New York: Academic.

Guzzetta, J. D. (2001). *Transcending boundaries with advanced technology: A closer look at social, behavioral, and health implications of the non-traditional workplace environment.* Unpublished manuscript, Department of Urban and Regional Planning, University of California, Irvine.

Hall, E. T. (1966). *The hidden dimension.* Garden City, NY: Doubleday.

Hawley, A. (1950). *Human ecology: A theory of community structure.* New York: Ronald Press.

Hayes, B., & Boucher, G. (1997, November 11). Internet a molesters' tool, police warn. *Los Angeles Times,* pp. B-1, B-4.

Horan, T. A. (2000). *Digital places: Building our city of bits.* Washington, DC: Urban Land Institute.

International Council for Science. (2001, March 22). *Diversitas: The International Programme of Biodiversity Science* [Online]. Available: www.icsu.org/DIVERSITAS

International Technology and Trade Associates, Inc. (2000, October 29). *State of the Internet 2000* [Online]. Available: www.itta.com/internet2000.htm

International Telework Association & Council. (2001, March 26). *Telework America (TWA) 2000 Research results and executive summary* [Online]. Available at www.telecommute.org/twa2000/research_results_summary.shtml

Internet Software Consortium. (2001, March 29). *Internet domain survey, January 2001* [Online]. Available: www.isc.org/ds/WWW-200101/index.html

Ittelson, W. H., Proshansky, H. H., Rivlin, L. G., & Winkel, G. (1974). *An introduction to environmental psychology.* New York: Holt, Rinehart and Winston.

Kaplan, R., & Kaplan, S. (1989). *The experience of nature: A psychological perspective.* New York: Cambridge University Press.

Kates, R. W., & Wohlwill, J. F. (1966). Man's response to the physical environment. *Journal of Social Issues, 22,* 1–140.

Katz, D., & Kahn, R. L. (1966). *The social psychology of organizations.* New York: Wiley.

Kiesler, S. (Ed.). (1997). *Culture of the Internet.* Mahwah, NJ: Erlbaum.

Kiesler, S., & Kraut, R. (1999). Internet use and ties that bind. *American Psychologist, 54,* 783–784.

Kling, R., & Iacono, S. (1991). Making a "computer revolution." In C. Dunlop & R. Kling (Eds.), *Computerization and controversy: Value conflicts and social choices* (pp. 63–74). Boston: Academic Press.

Korpela, K., & Hartig, T. (1996). Restorative qualities of favorite places. *Journal of Environmental Psychology, 16,* 221–233.

Lawton, M. P. (1999). Environments for older people. In S. L. Friedman & T. D. Wachs (Eds.), *Measuring environment across the lifespan: Emerging methods and concepts* (pp. 91–124). Washington, DC: American Psychological Association.

Lazarus, R. (1966). *Psychological stress and the coping process.* New York: McGraw-Hill.

Lewin, K. (1936). *Principles of topological psychology.* New York: McGraw-Hill.

Little, B. (1987). Personality and the environment. In D. Stokols & I. Altman (Eds.), *Handbook of environmental psychology* (Vol. 1, pp. 205–244). New York: Wiley.

Lyman, P., & Varian, H. R. (2000, October 20). *How much information?* [Online]. Berkeley: School of Information Management and Systems, University of California, Berkeley. Available: www.sims.berkeley.edu/how-much-info

Lynch, K. (1960). *The image of the city.* Cambridge, MA: Massachusetts Institute of Technology Press.

Mannix, M. (2000, August 28). The Web's dark side. *U.S. News & World Report,* 36–45.

McKenna, K. Y. A., & Bargh, J. A. (2000). Plan 9 from cyberspace: The implications of the Internet for personality and social psychology. *Personality and Social Psychology Review, 4,* 57–75.

Messaging Online, Inc. (2000, October 29). *AOL per-user email figures climb 60 percent in 1999* [Online]. Available: www.messagingonline.net/mt/html/feature020400.html

Meyrowitz, J. (1985). *No sense of place: The impact of electronic media on social behavior.* New York: Oxford University Press.

Michelson, W. H. (1970). *Man and his urban environment: A sociological approach.* Reading, MA: Addison-Wesley.

Michelson, W. H. (1985). *From sun to sun: Daily obligations and community structure in the lives of employed women and their families.* Totowa, NJ: Rowman & Allenheld.

Milgram, S. (1970). The experience of living in cities. *Science, 167,* 1461–1468.

Milgram, S., & Jodelet, D. (1976). Psychological maps of Paris. In H. M. Proshansky, W. H. Ittelson, & L. G.

Rivlin (Eds.), *Environmental psychology* (2nd ed., pp. 104–124). New York: Holt, Rinehart and Winston.

Mitchell, W. J. (1995). *The city of bits: Space, place, and the infobahn.* Cambridge, MA: Massachusetts Institute of Technology Press.

Moos, R. H. (1976). *The human context: Environmental determinants of behavior.* New York: Wiley.

Nasar, J. L. (Ed.). (1988). *Environmental aesthetics: Theory, research, and applications.* Cambridge: Cambridge University Press.

National Telecommunications & Information Administration. (2000, March 26). *Americans in the information age falling through the net* [Online]. Available: www.ntia.doc.gov/ntiahome/digitaldivide

Negroponte, N. P. (1995). *Being digital.* New York: Vintage.

Nie, N. H., & Erbring, L. (2000, March 29). *Internet and society: A preliminary report* [Online]. Stanford Institute for the Quantitative Study of Society. Available: www.stanford.edu/group/siqss/Press_Release/Preliminary_Report.pdf

Noam, E. M. (1995). Electronics and the dim future of the university. *Science, 270,* 247–249.

Oskamp, S. (2000). Psychological contributions to achieving an ecologically sustainable future for humanity. *Journal of Social Issues, 56*(3), 373–390.

Park, R., Burgess, E., & McKenzie, R. D. (Eds.). (1925). *The city.* Chicago: University of Chicago Press.

Pastalan, L. A. (1983). Environmental displacement: A literature reflecting old person-environment transactions. In G. D. Rowles & R. J. Ohta (Eds.), *Aging and milieu: Environmental perspectives on growing old* (pp. 189–203). New York: Academic Press.

Proshansky, H. M. (1978). The city and self identity. *Environment and Behavior, 10,* 147–169.

Proshansky, H. M., Fabian, A. K., & Kaminoff, R. (1983). Place identity: Physical world socialization of the self. *Journal of Environmental Psychology, 3,* 57–83.

Proshansky, H. M., Ittelson, W. H., & Rivlin, L. G. (Eds.). (1976). *Environmental psychology: People and their physical settings* (2nd ed.). New York: Holt, Rinehart and Winston.

Putnam, P. D. (1995). Bowling alone: America's declining social capital. *Journal of Democracy, 6,* 65–78.

Rheingold, H. (1993). *The virtual community: Homesteading on the electronic frontier.* Reading, MA: Addison-Wesley.

Rochberg-Halton, E., & Csikszentmihalyi, M. (1981). *The meaning of things: Domestic symbols and the self.* New York: Cambridge University Press.

Rook, K. S. (1984). Promoting social bonding: Strategies for helping the lonely and socially isolated. *American Psychologist, 39,* 1389–1407.

Schoggen, P. (1989). *Behavior settings: A revision and extension of Roger G. Barker's Ecological Psychology.* Stanford, CA: Stanford University Press.

Schuler, D. (1996). *New community networks: Wired for change.* Reading, MA: Addison-Wesley.

Selye, H. (1956). *The stress of life.* New York: McGraw-Hill.

SeniorNet. (2001, April 2). *Bringing wisdom to the information age* [Online]. Available: www.seniornet.org

SeniorsCan Internet Program. (2001, April 2). *SeniorsCan* [Online]. Available: www.crm.mb.ca/index.html

Simon, H. A. (1957). *Models of man: Explorations in the Western Educational Tradition.* New York: Wiley.

Smith, R. E., Johnson, J. H., & Sarason, I. G. (1978). Life change, the sensation-seeking motive, and psychological distress. *Journal of Consulting and Clinical Psychology, 46,* 348–349.

Sommer, R. (1969). *Personal space: The behavioral basis of design.* Englewood Cliffs, NJ: Prentice-Hall.

Stokols, D. (Ed.). (1977). *Perspectives on environment and behavior: Theory, research, and applications.* New York: Plenum Press.

Stokols, D. (1978). Environmental psychology. In M. R. Rosenzweig & L. W. Porter (Eds.), *Annual review of psychology* (Vol. 29, pp. 253–295). Palo Alto, CA: Annual Reviews.

Stokols, D. (1995). The paradox of environmental psychology. *American Psychologist, 50,* 821–837.

Stokols, D. (1999). Human development in the age of the Internet: Conceptual and methodological horizons. In S. L. Friedman & T. D. Wachs (Eds.), *Measuring environment across the lifespan: Emerging methods and concepts* (pp. 327–356). Washington, DC: American Psychological Association.

Stokols, D. (in press). Environmental aesthetics and well-being: Implications for a digital world. In B. Cold (Ed.), *Aesthetics, well-being, and health.* Aldershot, England: Avebury.

Stokols, D., & Altman, I. (Eds.). (1987). *Handbook of environmental psychology* (Vols. 1–2). New York: Wiley.

Stokols, D., & Montero, M. (2001). *Impacts of the Internet Internet on people-environment transactions: A social ecological view.* Unpublished manuscript, Department of Urban and Regional Planning, University of California, Irvine, CA.

Thibaut, J. W., & Kelley, H. H. (1959). *The social psychology of groups.* New York: Wiley.

Turkle, S. (1995). *Life on the screen: Identity in the age of the Internet.* New York: Simon & Schuster.

Ulrich, R. S. (1983). Aesthetic and affective response to natural environment. In I. Altman & J. F. Wohlwill (Eds.), *Behavior in the natural environment: Human behavior and environment: Advances in theory and research* (Vol. 6. pp. 85–125). New York: Plenum Press.

United States Environmental Protection Agency. (2001a, March 22). *EPA's global warming site* [Online]. Available: www.epa.gov/globalwarming

United States Environmental Protection Agency. (2001b, March 22). *Ozone depletion* [Online]. Available: www.epa.gov/docs/ozone/index.html

von Bertalanffy, L. (1950). The theory of open systems in physics and biology. *Science, 3,* 23–29.

Wachs, T. D., & Gruen, G. (1982). *Early experience and human development.* New York: Plenum Press.

Warming, E. (1909). *Oecology of plants: An introduction to the study of plant communities.* Oxford, England: Clarendon Press.

Wellman, B. (Ed.). (1999). *Networks in the global village.* Boulder, CO: Westview Press.

Wellman, B. (in press). Physical place and cyberplace: The rise of personalized networking [29 Pages]. *International Journal of Urban and Regional Research* [Online serial], *25.* Available: www.chass.utoronto.ca/~wellman /publications

Wicker, A. W. (1972). Processes which mediate behavior-environment congruence. *Behavioral Science, 17,* 265–277.

Wicker, A. W. (1979). *An introduction to ecological psychology.* New York: Cambridge University Press.

Zuckerman, M. (1979). *Sensation seeking: Beyond the optimal level of arousal.* Hillsdale, NJ: Erlbaum.

CHAPTER 42

On to Mars!

ROBERT B. BECHTEL

WHEN I WAS LAST AT the Johnson Space Center, in Houston, Texas, to attend a consultant's meeting, I asked whether we were *really* going to Mars. I was definitely assured that we were, and when I asked when, the date 2024 was given. Later, when I talked with David Dinges who heads a team with the National Space Biomedical Research Institute (NSBRI), he suggested 2014. Others had their own dates. I began to see that the Mars expedition date was not a fixed entity. Daniel Goldin, Director of the U.S. National Aeronautics and Space Administration (NASA), set the date 2010 as the time when the decision will be made whether to go to Mars.

Most people are unaware that a number of teams are working on the Mars expedition to determine its feasibility. NSBRI alone has eight teams: (1) Bone Demineralization/Calcium Metabolism; (2) Cardiovascular Alterations; (3) Immunology, Infection, and Hematology; (4) Muscle Alterations and Atrophy; (5) Neurovestibular Adaptation; (6) Human Performance Factors, Sleep, and Chronobiology; (7) Radiation Effects; and (8) Technology Development Program. And, in addition, there are 41 projects scattered among these teams. There are also many teams in the Johnson Space Center like the Mars Exploration Study Team, the Habitability Design Center, the Design Reference Mission, the Integrated Performance Team, the TransHab study team, and many others. At various stages of their development these teams meet together, issue reports, and upgrade their missions.

The teams in NSBRI and the Johnson Space Center are also complemented by the Marshall Space Flight Center, Lewis Research Center, Ames Research Center, Kennedy Space Center, and Langley Research Center.

The goal of this chapter is to set down what we have learned from these teams and other sources that will be useful in deciding on the Mars expedition. Yet, this is a frustrating, almost futile task because it must be understood from the start that the Mars expedition is so different from anything done in space so far that much or even most of what we have learned may not apply at all. Why do I say something that seems so self-defeating? Because the Mars expedition is so much longer and more involved than any other expedition that it takes space flight to an entirely new level. What makes it so different are those two elements that are basic to any travel: distance and time. The Mars expedition will be much longer in time than any previous space flight by any person. The Russian Valery Polyakov holds the record for the length of time any human has been in space, 437 days. The Mars expedition will be somewhere around 972 days, a little more than twice as long, even though each leg of the journey may be shorter. The farthest any human space travel has reached is the 200,000 miles to the moon. Mars is more than 30 *million* miles away! The consequences of these time and distance variables are staggering. Talking from moon to Earth involved just a few seconds' lag. Talking from Mars may involve as much as 40 minutes' lag. This is not a conversation!

THE WINDOWS IN SPACE

Given the current technology of space travel, we are locked into finding a "window" in space when we can take advantage of the position of Mars to make it the shortest trip possible so we can send the biggest payload. It takes in the range of 200 to 225 tons of rocket to send an expedition to mars. The window appears every 26 months. In that time frame Mars moves to a place in its orbit so that a rocket launched within 2 weeks of the beginning of the window can make it there, spend a year, and return. The trip will take about 259 days to get there and about the same time to get back.

Yet the average reader may have seen figures that do not agree with this. For example, *National Geographic* (Long, 2001) published a mission scenario in its January 2001 issue that gives the above figures on page 12. But the Mars exploration team in their 1997 NASA publication, *Human Exploration of Mars*, gives a scenario of only 150 days to Mars, 619 days on the surface and 879 days total. Why is there such variation in time? It is because each window is different. All of the 26-month windows differ in some way. The period from 2007 to 2009 is considered a "worst-case mission opportunity," while the period after those dates improves. Thus the figures given by the exploration team are for a mission that begins February 1, 2014, and ends June 29, 2016, a much more favorable period. So the windows stretch and shrink at different times, making each possible trip a different calculation in time provided the payload remains relatively the same. Thus, the public is likely to see many scenarios of Mars expeditions that seem to be different in the times calculated depending on the particular years in which the windows are chosen.

The 26-month windows operate in a 15-year cycle so that every 15 years the same set of windows starts over again. 2009 is a worst case, but 2018 is a "best case." Thus, it is likely 2018 would be a good year for a mission. The logic of this is complicated by the exploratory team, which suggests no less than three expeditions (Drake, 1998) starting in 2009.

ON BEING WEIGHTLESS

Probably no other single factor is as troubling in space flight as weightlessness. Even for the brief periods that many astronauts use to train for it in the "vomit comet," a jet plane that brings about weightlessness for a few minutes as it climbs upward in a circle, a good many will feel queasy and vomit. More than half the persons who go into space and endure weightlessness become sick. Usually this passes after several days and the body adjusts.

There are also vestibular adjustments to be made. Many astronauts report feeling as if they are falling if they turn their heads too quickly. Linenger (2000, pp. 205–206) reported an almost uncontrollable panic when he tried his extravehicular activity (EVA) outside *Mir*. The problem seemed to be that he lost all the reference points close to his body once he got away from *Mir* and had the sensation of constantly falling at great speed, "faster than anything that I, who had gone supersonic a time or two, had ever experienced in my life." It was all he could do to keep from panicking and gradually took control by convincing himself it was okay to fall.

Immediately upon being weightless, however, certain bodily changes occur that are noticeable. The large muscles of the legs force the blood to the upper body and the face feels flushed and one gets "bird legs." The head has a constant "stuffed up" sensation.

But it is not these small things that are the really troubling part of weightlessness, but rather the loss of bone and muscle tone, cardiovascular losses, immune system losses, and loss of eye-hand coordination that cause real problems. The loss of muscle tone and bone tissue is so severe that the Russian cosmonauts in *Mir*, the Russian space station, had to be carried out of the landing vehicle and endure 2 or more weeks of rehab before normal activities could be resumed. Some take longer and some can do it in a few days, but there is a real question as to whether the density of bone ever returns to its former state. Thus the length of the travel is a major problem because the bone density seems to be lost at a rate above 1% per month. So severe is the bone loss that there is a danger of broken bones. In space this is a major disaster.

But it is the sheer discomfort of weightlessness while trying to do the everyday tasks of life that causes more immediate distress to space travelers: putting on clothes, taking them off, trying to move from one part of the cabin to another, eating almost anything, drinking any liquid, attempting to use a screwdriver without twisting your whole body. Moving around becomes a process of "swimming" through empty space by propelling yourself with a push.

Attempts have been made to alleviate the bone loss by regimens of exercise. Since a lack of gravity does not permit the ordinary task of jogging, a harness of bungee cords is rigged for the astronaut to push against while running on a treadmill. Since the harness does not provide nearly the same stress on the bones as gravity, the practice has questionable value. Some promising experiments with animals and birds have increased bone density by the use of vibrating platforms (Long, 2001). These experiments have yet to be done in a weightless environment with humans.

And then there are the weightless toilets (Pogue, 1991). Since there is no gravity, the toilets have to operate on a vacuum. This means having a vacuum seal between one's derriere and the seat. This is more than a little trouble. Urine and feces do not fall in a weightless environment; they are ejected from the body with some muscular force and will

Figure 42.1 Shuttle toilet.

continue on their path until interrupted. The advantage of a vacuum toilet is that it sucks the objectionable debris away. But when one sees the toilet seat for the shuttle (see Figure 42.1), it is obvious this is not the large appliance most of us are used to. One astronaut (who wants to remain anonymous) claims he is not a golfer and cannot "hit" the seat with that kind of accuracy. A vacuum cup is provided, as is seen in the illustration, to catch any wandering urine or fecal matter that escapes. The trouble is, when one rises up to use the cup, the vacuum seal is broken and more things may escape. Going to the toilet in space is a hardship that must be endured.

Other toilet aids are always available. The adult diaper is usually a subject astronauts like to avoid. And, of course, there are other strategies. As one aptly put it, "looking at stars, pissing in jars."

The elements which do not get sucked into the toilet end up on the circulation screen, which has to be regularly cleaned. As for showers . . . you don't. Linenger talks about how nice his fellow astronauts were when they met him on *Mir* and were still receptive—after he had gone 5 months without a shower. But there are large handiwipes as a substitute. This is not to say that there are no provisions for showers or specially made shower stalls that recycle water. The problem is whether the space and weight will permit such luxuries on a Mars trip.

KEEP 'EM BUSY

One of the lessons learned from studying isolated confined environments is to maximize the positive aspect of the stay by giving everyone a useful job to do and work them more than the usual number of hours (Bechtel & Ledbetter, 1976). Norman Thagard, the first U.S. astronaut on *Mir* said, "The most serious problem I ever felt like I suffered up there was boredom, which wasn't a serious problem, except I think you ought to avoid it." (Thagard, 1997, p. 46). Other astronauts talked about this as well. Thus, it is very important to provide useful tasks so that the space travelers feel their time is used well.

Shannon Lucid (1998) was occupied by experiments with quail eggs, dwarf wheat, and candle flames. Her Russian counterparts had to spend most of their time just keeping *Mir* running. She discovered that the number of abnormalities in the developing quail eggs was 4 times the number in a control group in normal gravity. The wheat produced seeds, sure enough, but they were all empty. The candle flames burned with a spherical shape, not the long flames we are used to seeing, and then they would turn blue and went out. Amazingly, wax droplets condensed around the candle flame after it went out—and stayed there. These findings illustrate why the weightless environment is such a useful laboratory and how it provides an endless variety of experiments that can be done nowhere on Earth. As Thagard says, "You don't want to go up there and work crossword puzzles, you want to go up there and do experiments and get results." (Thagard, 1997, p. 46).

THEM VERSUS US

The essence of the "them versus us" problem is the view of astronauts or cosmonauts on the scene in space versus the operators at control central, who, it is felt, do not often appreciate the handicaps and limitations of the immediate work environment.

In 1973, the relations between the mission control center and Skylab became so strained that the astronauts told Houston they were not going to talk with them for a day. Thus, the first rebellion against "them" took place. Thagard, Linenger, and many other astronauts talk about this and report about how the cosmonauts experience the same phenomenon. Thagard says (1997, p. 43), "I shouldn't have been asked to do things I hadn't seen before." The cosmonauts told Thagard, "do what you want to do and tell them what they want to hear."

Linenger (2000, p. 131) said, "mission control in Moscow became our enemy rather than our friend, our nemesis rather than our support structure . . . we had no confidence in them. Nor did we feel we could trust anything they told us." There seems to have been a general tendency to "blame the crew for anything that goes wrong." And on *Mir* something was always going wrong.

The Russians, however, had special circumstances that made *Mir* especially prone to the them-versus-us phenomenon. The private company that owned *Mir* was called Energia, and the cosmonauts were their employees. If they did well, they would get a bonus. But if they made mistakes, *they were fined.* Thus, the cosmonauts tried very carefully to minimize problems, feeling that Energia was just looking for an excuse to fine them.

It must also be said that *Apollo 13* was an example of how the them-versus-us problem was reversed. Anyone who has seen the popular movie on *Apollo 13* or the PBS film was impressed by how the ground crew worked round the clock to find practical solutions to the mechanical problems that threatened the lives of the astronauts, and the movie followed reality in this respect.

The Mars expedition may eliminate this problem with communication time lags up to 40 minutes, making it impossible to have meaningful interactions in emergencies and leaving the flight crew almost entirely on their own. The character of the Mars expedition will require an independence of the astronauts that has never been experienced before.

THE CULTURE FACTOR

It became evident on *Mir* that there were many problems that arose because of cultural differences. When a launch of the shuttle was postponed at Kennedy Space Center because of weather, the Russians could not understand how a launch could be postponed. The *Soyuz*, the Russian supply rocket, always takes off on time.

Language is always a problem. Apparently, Shannon Lucid did not pass her language exam to the satisfaction of the Russians. But she went on the mission anyway. When the cosmonauts went outside for extravehicular activity (EVA), they taped over the switches so she could not operate them. Was this because they just didn't trust her, because she was a woman, or because they didn't feel they could successfully communicate? Shannon Lucid never mentioned this incident in her published account.

But culture can also be a plus factor. Lucid mentions how sharing the different foods was a high point of the meals. She liked the Russian soups, they liked our mayonnaise. She also makes the point of how satisfying it was to share life stories with the Russians; to compare how a child of the Texas panhandle came to share a space vehicle with a Russian Air Force officer and a Russian engineer. All three of them had grown up with the fear of an atomic war between their countries.

An interesting fact of culture was reported by both Thagard and Linenger: The Russian commanders were very affable during training but became authoritarian once in space. This required a period of adjustment where the American astronauts followed the lead of their Russian colleague in dealing with the commander. This often required a "blowup," after which the authoritarian posture would soften. Since this was a difficulty that did not come up in training, it remains a problem how to deal with it by developing a training exercise.

Regardless of how much the culture factor is a problem, it will require an extension of the training time, and it does appear that the Mars mission will be an international undertaking.

THE SUN ALSO RADIATES

We live in a sheltered environment on Earth. The sun sends off solar flares that bombard the Earth with radiation but the rays are turned away by the Earth's magnetic field (the Van Allen Belt) and the atmosphere (Burch, 2001). Not so in space, but more so on Mars. While Mars has practically no magnetosphere, the three-eighths atmosphere does provide some protection. What must be considered is the radiation dose that the astronauts will encounter in such a long-term flight and on the longer exploration of the surface. So far the adventures into space have been very lucky not to have encountered the full blast of a solar storm. Current policy is that no astronaut should have more than 3% above the dose that would account for the normal amount of cancer in the population. So far, there is no projection of the Mars trip that would exceed that ratio.

Every astronaut experiences occasional streaks of light passing through the visual field. These are the so-called cosmic rays from deep space. They are "heavier" rays than those from the sun spots. Linenger (2000, p. 244) describes them: "Some nights while on *Mir* I would be awakened by bright flashes in my eyes, caused by heavy particles penetrating my closed lids and then striking and exciting the nerve endings in my retina." Linenger points out that the Van Allen magnetic belt around the Earth does offer some protection, even in space, because the orbit of *Mir* is not always above it. The radiation he describes occurs when the vessel flies outside the belt.

TO SLEEP BUT NOT PERCHANCE

Sleep disturbances are a common occurrence when diurnal rhythms are disturbed. *Mir* would circle the Earth every 90 minutes, producing a sunrise and sunset each time. The critical question is how much these disturbances affect the space traveler's ability to function in a safe manner. The NSBRI team (see their Web site at wysiwyg://11/http://www.nsbri.org/research/sleepdesc.html) claims that "typically astronauts lose two hours of sleep per day while in orbit." Compounded with the effects of weightlessness, this can produce disruptions in brain functions, decreased mental speed, impaired attention, poor memory, sleepiness, mood disturbance, and stress. Is this anything that a good nap wouldn't cure? Apparently not. Some possible remedies might include changing the work schedule. Sleeping as an activity involves strapping yourself in a sleeping bag that is attached to a wall so you don't wander around the cabin in the weightless environment. Pogue (1991) reported sleeping only 6 hours a night in Skylab. At present there seems to be no evident solution to this problem. Practically every astronaut and cosmonaut reported sleep deprivation.

SEX? NOT YET

When Valentin Tereshkova, the first woman in space, went on her mission the dates were carefully chosen to fit between her menstrual periods (Lothian, 1993). Thus, another problem was avoided for the moment. When Shannon Lucid had her stay on *Mir* extended, there was no problem because she was already past menopause. But women do go into space, and they will not stop menstruating on demand, so this is now dealt with on a regular basis. How does one accommodate a mixed sex crew? Since there is no gravity, the human egg does not properly drop down the fallopian tube and ectopic pregnancy (pregnancy in the tubes) can be fatal. Thus, pregnancy in space is to be avoided as a danger unless birth control is foolproof. It is very difficult to get anyone to talk about sex in space, as Barbara Gallagher (2000) discovered.

Perhaps one lesson can be learned from Shannon Lucid's experience on *Mir*. After putting together both her own published report (Lucid, 1998) and the comments of male astronauts like Thagard (1997) it is clear that she was able to tolerate, and even smooth over, differences that the males could not easily deal with. There seems to be a female element of tolerance that might be an added boost to the habitability of an isolated and confined environment. And the boost is not just for the irascible males. Females in isolated environments report being "appreciated" more because of their scarcity. Nevertheless, mixing the sexes does produce an added risk in the eyes of many males (Gallagher, 2000), and it is a topic on which there is virtually no data whatever.

HABITABILITY

How does one design and construct an environment that will support a team in space for 2 or 3 years? Everything has to be either carried along or sent ahead. The principle that drives the design is to be as economical as possible on weight, which means a structure that can be used to both carry the explorers to Mars and serve as their dwelling on the surface. The inevitable solution is to reuse the shell of the transit vehicle. And the only way to test the habitability of this vessel is to build one according to the specifications of these two requirements. Figures 42.2 and 42.3 show the structure made, according to the latest research, at the Johnson Space Center in Houston.

Figure 42.4 shows the 20 foot-high circular building that was used to simulate isolation in previous studies, with trials lasting up to 91 days. It will be recalled that the Biosphere 2 experiment lasted for 2 years but failed to sustain either oxygen or the proper food level (Bechtel, McCallum, & Poynter, 1997). So far, there has been no other simulation that has lasted that long a time. The Russians have used isolation simulations of similar periods, but these did not test the oxygen or food supply.

The primary goal of a space simulation has been to grow plants that will both supply the oxygen level required for human life and at the same time provide sufficient food. The dwarf wheat grown in space by Shannon Lucid previously has been made to produce its own seeds that are fertile in space (see Figure 42.5), and a variety of "salad" crops are being tried. But up to this point there is no simulation that

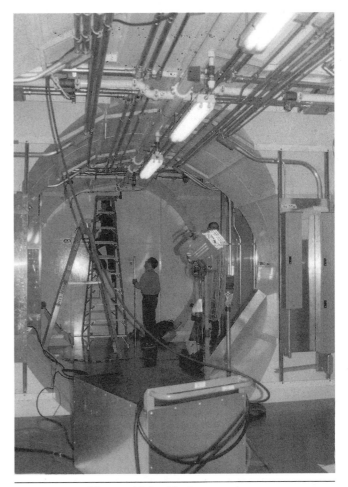

Figure 42.3 Shelter mockup.

has tested out a mix of plants that could sustain the voyage time required.

Of course, it is not necessary to put plants into space to test their response to lack of gravity. Carlson (2001) discovered that plants responded very slowly to gravity. It takes a full minute for plant hormones to respond to a change in gravity. This means that constantly rotating plants at the rate of under 1 minute will cause them to behave as if there were no gravity. Carlson describes such an apparatus and how it can be used for experiments in zero and various degrees of partial gravity.

The most necessary element, next to oxygen, is water. All the water that is needed must be taken along. Despite all the excitement about water that *was* on Mars, there can be no gamble taken on finding any water. That means every bit of water must be recycled. A recycling plant has already been built for urine (see Figure 42.6). The column contains large granules whose surfaces help to expose bacteria to

Figure 42.2 Shelter mockup.

Figure 42.4   Twenty-foot circular building.

the urine so it may be decomposed, purified, and recycled.

Perhaps not as critical as the food-oxygen-water problem is the question of psychological habitability. Yet when human conflicts arise, as they did in the Biosphere 2 simulation, one has to wonder whether the psychological issues are even more important. Three of the Biospherians were having therapy sessions by phone 18 months into the operation. Of course, this would be impossible with the time lags on a Mars mission. Psychological conflicts do not have to be serious before they can interfere with the alertness and objectivity required in the everyday operations of space flight. Therefore, the psychological habitability issue becomes one of major importance. Every attempt is made to design an environment that will foster the well-being of the astronaut team.

It is here that many of the lessons learned in *Mir* may be applied. The extreme conditions of *Mir* only serve to make some lessons more valuable. One thing that becomes clear is that the training *before* the mission is a valuable predictor of how well the team will function. The Russians have long used the training mission as a selection process and carefully observed the interactions of the trainees and considered these interactions as the best predictors of later performance. Unfortunately, the Russians do not

Figure 42.5   Dwarf wheat.

Figure 42.6 Urine recycling.

keep any systematic data that can be reported, only anecdotal comments.

The design team of architects at the Johnson Space Center are concerned with such things as the position of windows, the design of crew quarters, privacy, and a host of other issues on such a long and constrained flight. Each detail may seem trivial by itself, but the combination of comfort, privacy, and work environments may be extremely critical to the success of the mission. Many examples of human stress from the *Mir* records show periods when the cosmonauts would get extremely angry at Moscow, and the near fatal accidents on *Mir* contributed not a little to the stress. There was a serious fire that was then downplayed by the cosmonauts and then a collision with the supply ship, which was also downplayed. During these incidents such small things as the clutter in the environment became critical. It was necessary to close a hatch to prevent air from escaping and everyone dying of asphyxiation. Yet, the hatchway was so cluttered with cables that it could

not be closed and no one knew what was carried by the cables. Would they cut their own air supply or electricity by cutting them? This was a very stressful situation and the decision was made to cut the cables and close the hatchway regardless because, if they did not, they would be dead anyway.

The lesson to be learned from this incident, and several similar ones, is that clutter can be extremely dangerous. Yet, clutter was one of the most evident environmental factors on *Mir*. There were so many boxes, pieces of equipment, stray cables, and just plain junk that the U.S. astronauts were alarmed. In many cases the cosmonauts had to call Moscow to find out where things were that had been stowed away by previous cosmonauts. And in many of these cases this meant calling the former cosmonaut at his home.

It is obvious that such conditions could be far worse on a Mars mission. But the *Mir* lesson is to have a place for everything and especially a place to put disposables. It reminds one of a slogan adopted by the forest service: Every litter bit hurts. We get so used to gravity taking everything to the floor where we can sweep it up, it is hard to imagine designing for an environment where nothing can be left to drift in the air, not a Kleenex, not the droplets from a sneeze, not the tiny hairs from a shave, the sweat globules from exercise, pencils, pieces of paper, any of the bric-a-brac we take for granted in our gravitated world. Everything must have a place and all the habits that shed matter must be relearned and retrained.

Yet even in this weightless world some of the habits of gravity will not be given up. People still want to sit down at a table to eat. Sitting is itself a new experience in space. It is more accurate to say "tying oneself down." This is because even though there may be a chair, it will not be itself sitting but may have to be rescued from the ceiling. Gathering at a table, then, can be a very different experience from what is expected on Earth.

Of course, gathering at a table on Mars will be more like the world we know. But this also raises the question of how the table relates to the rest of the environment. Strictly speaking, a rocket vessel is strongest when it has a seamless surface. Any interruption of this seamless surface creates a weakened vessel. Airliners will crack at the windows and would be much stronger if there were none of these violations of what should be a seamless tube. Nevertheless, the need for a connection to the outer world is imperative. A compromise has been made to provide a single window next to the table.

All of the astronauts and cosmonauts speak about being able to look out a window at the Earth and stars. Taking pictures through a window is one of the most enjoyable tasks. Thus, a visual connection to the outer world is a necessity for a habitable environment.

WHAT IS RECREATION?

One of the most interesting observations that can be made about space travel so far is that it often seems as though meaningful work will often be chosen over what would ordinarily be seen as recreation. It is not as though recreation is ignored. Each astronaut is given a "package" of movies, tapes, extra food, and memorabilia to lighten the load of separation from the Earth environment. But in a significant number of cases the astronauts and cosmonauts will choose to perform extra work on experiments or maintenance over a chance to watch movies or listen to music. Some insight on this may be provided by the theory of *flow* (Csikszentmihalyi, 1990). Csikszentmihalyi sees any person as experiencing flow by doing something that the person can do well, that provides a meaningful product to others, and that allows the person to lose a sense of time and self. This is very close to why some of the American astronauts claim they choose running experiments rather than recreational pursuits. While it may at first seem that this is similar to the "keep 'em busy" phenomenon mentioned earlier, it really relates more to why some will choose meaningful work above what seems to the average person to be more enjoyable. The astronauts and cosmonauts express it as a "that's what we're there for" choice. Csikszentmihalyi claims this is happiness. I'm not sure the astronauts would go that far, but it is beyond just work or fun.

THE ROBONAUTS

All during the history of space travel the question of human versus robot viability has been raised. Isn't it much more reasonable to send automated vehicles without humans to do the work of space exploration and thus save the risk to human life? While seasoned space travelers may accept the risk to human life, is it really worthwhile? Some point to the *Apollo 13* accident as an example of how a

mission can be saved by having humans aboard. Others point out that, if there had been no humans aboard, it would not have been necessary to go to all the trouble.

Certainly there have been failures of robot missions. The recent Mars failures are as good an example as any. Tens of millions of dollars are lost when such a simple thing as converting to centimeters and grams is overlooked. But it must always be considered that no human life was lost. Halyard (1996), a visionary of space travel, foresees androids that are capable of human thought as a great assistance to humans. And, of course, robots would be more than capable of the long distances of interstellar travel.

At the present time, however, all the planning seems to be focused on having a human crew make the trip to Mars.

SUMMARY

At present it does appear as though the Mars expedition will be in the favorable time slot of 2016 to 2018 provided the decision to go is made in 2010 as currently planned. It also appears likely that there will be more than one trip, although only one may be occupied by a human crew. This is because it does not appear likely a base can be set up that can be sustained only on the oxygen, water, and food contained in one rocket. Thus, there will probably be two or more rockets preceding the manned flight to carry the wherewithal needed to sustain an exploratory expedition to the surface.

The astronauts will probably be composed of both males and females and have an international representation. The exact number remains uncertain, but three seems to be a minimum and six seems to be an optimal number according to current thought.

With present technology it is likely the rocket shell will also serve as the dwelling on Mars unless some presently untried technology proves out like the inflatable building (Drake, 1998). Training for the expedition will likely begin 2 years before the flight and will involve language learning for both sides. It is unlikely that three nations will be represented, but it is possible if one astronaut is very conversant already in a second language. It is imperative that one member of the crew will be a medical doctor; another will more than likely be a geologist.

But all this remains in the realm of speculation more than 9 years before the decision to go can be made. Many things can change before then, not the least of which is budgets.

REFERENCES

Bechtel, R., & Ledbetter, C. (1976). *The temporary environment.* Hanover, NH: Cold Regions Research and Engineering Laboratory.

Bechtel, R., McCallum, T., & Poynter, J. (1997). Environmental psychology and Biosphere 2. In S. Wapner, J. Demick, T. Yamamoto, & T. Takahashi (Eds.), *Handbook of Japan-United States environment-behavior research: Toward a transactional approach* (pp. 235–244). New York: Plenum Press.

Burch, J. (2001). The fury of space storms. *Scientific American, 284,* 86–94.

Carlson, S. (2001). Geotropism, one last time. *Scientific American, 284,* 78–79.

Csikszentmihalyi, M. (1990). *Flow: The psychology of optimal experience.* New York: Harper & Row.

Drake, B. (Ed.). (1998). *Reference mission version 3: Addendum to the human exploration of Mars: The reference mission of the NASA Mars exploration study team.* Houston, TX: National Aeronautics and Space Administration, Johnson Space Center.

Gallagher, B. (2000). No sex in space? *Scientific American, 282*(1), 22.

Halyard, R. (1996). *The quest for water planets: Interstellar colonization in the 21st century.* Show Low, AZ: American Eagle.

Linenger, J. (2000). *Off the planet.* New York: McGraw-Hill.

Long, M. (2001). Surviving in space. *National Geographic, 199,* 6–29.

Lothian, A. (1993). *Valentina Tereshkova, first woman in space.* Cambridge, MA: Pentland Press.

Lucid, S. (1998). Six months on *Mir. Scientific American, 278,* 46–55.

Pogue, W. (1991). *How do you go to the bathroom in space?* New York: Tom Doherty Associates.

Thagard, N. (1997, May 2). Lessons from MIR. Remarks made to the Committee on Space Biology and Medicine, Washington, DC.

Author Index

Aamodt, M. G., 431
Aarts, H., 89
Abdou, O., 452
Abel, T., 38, 40, 90, 543
Abey-Wickrama, I., 503
Abler, R., 253
Abramovitz, J., 76, 512
Abramson, P., 59
a'Brook, M. F., 503
Ackoff, R. L., 298
Acquino, A., 431
Adachi, K., 375
Adair, J., 193
Adams, D., 218, 225, 328
Adams, L., 652
Adams, M. M., 230
Adams, R. M., 652
Adelsberg, R., 384
Adeola, F. O., 245
Adkins, C. L., 505
Agrawal, A., 151
Agre, P. E., 653
Agrest, D., 348
Aguilar, M. A., 58
Ahern, K. D., 502, 503
Åhlund, O., 380, 383
Ahmed, P. K., 59
Ahrentzen, S., 348, 354, 356, 357, 358
Aiello, A., 39, 43, 45, 60, 259
Aiello, J. R., 402, 648, 651, 652
Aiken, L. S., 493
Aitken, C. K., 260, 547
Aitken, S. C., 219
Ajdukovic, D., 651
Ajzen, I., 39, 40, 58, 195, 256, 257, 545
Akagi, T., 375
Akande, A., 651
Akert, R. M., 525
Alard, L., 445, 451
Albas, C., 651, 652
Albas, D., 652
Albert, W. S., 249, 250
Albets, D. M., 431
Albrecht, J., 247
Albrecht, S. L., 163, 164, 166, 169
Aldwin, C. M., 490
Alexander, C. N., 483
Alexander, E., 192, 196
Alexander, R. A., 481
Alferink, L., 531
Alfi, P., 502
Alihan, M. A., 665

Ali Khan, S., 66
Alinsky, S., 599, 607
Al-Kodmany, K., 616, 623
Allen, A., 652
Allen, G., 430
Allen, J., 40, 543, 548
Allen, T., 281, 447
Allen, V. L., 4
Allende, J., 60
Alliger, G. M., 234
Allmendinger, P., 611
Allport, G., 173
Alt, M., 465
Alterman, R., 191, 197, 198
Altman, I., 29, 30, 35, 42, 47, 55, 98,
    104, 108, 110, 115, 116, 117, 195,
    196, 203, 204, 205, 206, 207, 210,
    211, 212, 213, 214, 215, 216, 217,
    219, 293, 347, 404, 422, 525, 541,
    573, 607, 609, 648, 661, 666, 669
Altman, L., 4
Altmann, D., 185
Amabile, T., 449, 454, 455
Amérigo, M., 56
Amering, M., 133, 134
Amoyal, R., 73
Ancoli-Israel, S., 385
Anders, K. T., 382, 384, 386
Andersen, P. A., 652
Anderson, C. A., 481, 483, 484, 487,
    488, 491
Anderson, D., 417, 483
Anderson, G. C., 180
Anderson, J. F., 301
Anderson, J. R., 309
Anderson, K. B., 481, 487, 488, 491
Anderson, L., 57
Anderson, M., 520
Anderson, R. E., 653
Andersson, G., 230
Andreae, J., 283
Andreoletti, C., 129, 130
Annerstedt, L., 378, 379, 380, 381,
    383, 386
Antes, J., 430
Anthony, K. H., 139, 140
Antonovsky, A., 668
Aoki, K., 431
Appels, A., 370
Appleton, J., 178, 649
Appleyard, D., 69, 286, 325, 417
Aptekar, L., 516

Apter, D., 7
Aquino, J., 662, 670
Aragall, F., 74
Aragonés, J. I., 56
Arce, C., 56
Archea, J., 275
Archer, D., 58
Arcury, T., 58
Ard, L., 309, 312
Ardener, S., 347
Ardrey, R., 29
Argyle, M., 648, 652
Argyris, C., 312, 313, 315, 613
Arkkelin, D., 56
Armendariz, L. I., 260, 264
Arnau, R. C., 180, 181, 182
Arndt, M., 471
Arnold, C., 521
Arnstein, S. R., 607, 617
Aronson, E., 58, 67, 329, 525, 535,
    536, 537, 546, 547
Arrow, K. J., 91
Arthur, W., 225
Asakawa, K., 233
Aschoff, J., 487
Ashburner, J., 174, 186
Asmus, C., 363, 488
Asp, J., 378
Aspray, W., 664
Atkinson, S. F., 69
Atlas, R., 420
Atran, S., 173
Audirac, I., 194
Auerhahn, K., 486
August, R. A., 119, 120, 123
Auliciems, A., 483
Austin, J., 269, 542
Axelrod, L. J., 552
Ayalon, H., 191
Ayalon, O., 141
Ayers, V., 301
Azmon, Y., 198

Baas, L., 64, 570, 571, 572
Baccolo, T. P., 502
Bachelard, G., 108, 141
Bachrach, K., 570
Back, K., 29, 661, 669
Bacon, F., 222
Bacow, L. S., 595, 600
Baddenes, D., 58
Baden, J., 40

Baenninger, M., 186
Baeyens, F., 180
Bafna, S., 275, 276, 279
Bagozzi, R. P., 40, 545
Bahi-Fleury, G., 58
Bailey, J. S., 526, 542
Baird, G., 308
Bairstow, A. -M., 435
Baker, A., 385
Baker, J. K., 69
Baker, W. E., 623
Balée, W., 151
Ballard, D., 60
Ballieux, R. E., 502
Balling, I., 471
Balling, J., 465, 471
Balogun, S. K., 651
Balsley, J. R., 69
Baltes, P. B., 3
Banister, D., 191
Bannister, D., 279
Barbarbault, R., 33
Barberà, S., 86
Bargh, J. A., 89, 665
Barker, F. W., 31, 32, 34
Barker, J., 117, 122, 123, 365, 369
Barker, R. G., 29, 30, 114, 115, 116,
    117, 118, 119, 120, 122, 123, 211,
    665, 666, 670, 671
Barlett, P., 150
Barnard, W. A., 652
Barnes, G. S., 417
Barnes, R., 336
Barnes, T., 67
Barnett, D., 366, 368
Barnett, E., 260
Barnett, G. A., 487
Barnston, A. G., 489
Baron, R. A., 483, 484, 488
Baron, R. M., 419, 423
Barrett, K. C., 547
Barth, F., 148
Barton, A., 561, 579
Barton, H., 400, 402
Barton, M., 259
Basbaum, A., 182
Bass, B. M., 481
Bat-Chava, Y., 501, 502, 503, 504
Bateson, G., 577
Bator, R., 670
Batty, M., 275, 276
Baum, A., 16, 56, 196, 326, 401, 402,
    403, 482, 525, 568, 569, 570, 571,
    648, 651, 665
Baum, L., 465
Bauman, Z., 59
Baumer, E., 486
Baxandall, M., 288
Bazerman, M. H., 87
Beach, H., 576
Beales, G., 282
Beatty, S. E., 329
Beatty, W. W., 184
Beauregard, R., 192

Beavon, D. J. K., 419
Bechtel, R., 16, 31, 36, 47, 56, 58, 75,
    115, 191, 260, 263, 264, 293, 301,
    370, 463, 609, 621, 651, 665, 670,
    678, 681
Beck, C. A., 601
Beck, E. M., 517
Beck, U., 565
Becker, F., 331, 446, 448, 449, 570,
    573
Becker, L. J., 329
Becker, M. H., 549
Becker, S., 570
Beebe-Center, J. G., 174
Beers, L., 57, 58, 551
Behnke, E. A., 97
Behrens, W., 33, 34, 57
Behringer, J., 614, 620, 623
Beidel, D. C., 137
Bela, D., 577
Belenky, M. F., 355
Belk, R., 543
Bell, A., 45
Bell, P. A., 16, 56, 363, 482, 488, 525,
    648, 651, 652, 665
Bell, R., 420
Bellamy, J. A., 74
Bellamy, L. J., 517
Bellelli, G., 378
Bellman, H. S., 599
Belloni, C., 623
Bellucci, C., 423
Belluck, P., 354
Bem, D. J., 535, 536, 537
Benedikt, M. L., 275
Benefield, A., 468, 469, 471, 477
Ben-Joseph, E., 279
Bennet, W., 225
Bennett, N., 283
Bennett, W., 225
Bennis, W., 455, 571
Ben-Rafael, E., 191
Benson, D. M., 378
Bentler, P. M., 257, 258, 259, 262, 267,
    269
Bentley, A. F., 203
Benusa, D., 471
Berdie, D. R., 301
Berenguer, J., 40, 58
Berg, L., 378
Bergen, S. D., 245
Berger, I., 245, 260, 551
Berger, P., 98, 565
Berglund, B., 501, 502, 506
Bergsma, H. M., 548
Bergsma, L. C., 548
Berkeley, E. P., 347
Berkes, F., 151
Berkowitz, L., 488
Berlin, B., 151
Berman, S., 566, 567
Bernard, Y., 56
Bernecker, C., 451

Bernfeld, D., 607
Bernstein, B., 281
Bernstein, I. H., 263
Bernstein, J., 430, 431
Berntson, G. G., 173, 174
Berrenberg, J. L., 551
Bertini, G., 11
Bessa, J., 66
Beven, C. E., 260, 550
Bevis, C., 419
Bhatt, M., 618
Bianchetti, A., 378, 383
Bible, D. S., 416
Biederman, P., 455
Biel, A., 35, 40, 41, 42, 43, 44, 46, 88,
    89, 90
Bierbawer, G., 59
Biersack, A., 150
Bigwood, C., 359
Bih, H., 206
Billig, M., 45
Bilodeau, S. W., 519
Binney, S. E., 245
Birch, E., 347
Birney, R., 467
Bishop, T., 471
Bistrup, M. L., 397
Bitgood, S., 462, 463, 464, 465, 466,
    467, 468, 469, 470, 471, 473, 474,
    475, 477
Bixler, R. D., 364
Black, J. S., 40, 543
Black, M. E., 388
Blades, M., 251, 430
Blair, M. L., 519
Blakely, E. J., 415, 416
Blakely, E. Q., 531
Blalock, H. M., Jr., 301
Blamey, R., 36, 40, 41
Blanchard, A., 123, 664, 670, 671, 672
Blanchard, K., 64
Bland, S. H., 515
Blankenship, V. E., 488
Bleck, D. S., 143
Blitt, J., 155
Block, J., 370
Blocker, T. J., 571
Blowers, A., 73
Bluck, S., 174
Blumberg, L., 507
Blumenstyk, G., 664
Blumenthal, R., 430
Boffelli, S., 378
Bogard, W., 560
Bolin, R., 516, 560
Bollnow, O., 108
Bolt, R. A., 654
Bolton, P. A., 516
Bonaiuto, M., 30, 31, 35, 38, 39, 43,
    45, 46, 47, 60, 218, 259
Bond, A., 69
Bond, L. A., 355
Bonet, M. R., 74
Bonett, D. G., 259

Bonnes, M., 29, 30, 31, 32, 33, 35, 37, 38, 39, 43, 45, 46, 47, 56, 60, 218, 259, 609
Bontempo, D., 179
Booher, D. E., 608, 610, 611, 613, 619, 620
Böök, A., 67, 286
Boon, M., 329
Boons, F., 64
Booth, C., 347, 357, 614, 615, 621, 622, 623
Boram, R., 465
Bord, R. J., 330
Bordass, B., 306, 309
Bordass, W., 309, 314
Borden, I., 348
Bordo, S., 358
Borkan, B., 519
Bornstein, G., 88
Borun, M., 465, 470, 475
Boster, J. S., 148
Boucher, G., 664
Bovy, P. H. L., 249
Bowen, B. D., 301
Bower, G. H., 548
Bowlby, J., 131
Bowlby, S. R., 352
Bowler, R., 569
Bowman, C. G., 351
Boxall, P. C., 38
Boyanowsky, E. O., 493
Boyce, P., 451
Boyce, T. E., 527, 529, 530, 532
Boyd, J., 468
Boyden, S., 33
Boyer, E. L., 356
Boys, J., 351
Bradburn, N., 234
Bradbury, J. A., 158
Bradley, M. M., 181, 183
Bradney, N., 239
Brady, M. A., 155
Bragg, E. A., 38
Braidotti, R., 358
Brainard, G., 451
Branch, K. M., 158
Brandon, G., 542
Brandstätter, H., 235, 239, 489
Bråne, G., 381
Brantingham, P. J., 419
Brantingham, P. L., 419
Brantner, J. P., 483, 484
Bratt, C., 259, 543
Bratton, W., 415
Brawley, E. C., 376, 382, 383, 386
Breakwell, G., 43, 47, 367
Brehm, J. W., 531
Breitbart, M. M., 355
Bremner, J. D., 131
Bresolin, B., 286
Bretherton, I., 131
Breu, J., 328
Brewer, J. K., 226
Brewer, M. B., 42, 43, 88

Brickman, P., 577
Brideau, L., 493
Bright, B., 618
Bright, C., 76
Brill, M., 293, 294, 309, 445, 448, 449, 451, 452
Briller, S., 387
Brinkman, H., 651
Brizzolara, M. S., 489
Broadbent, D., 452
Broady, M., 417
Brock, K., 452
Brodkin, I. A., 182
Brodsky, S. L., 651
Brody, D. J., 500
Brody, G. H., 657
Bromet, E., 513
Bromley, A., 309
Bronfenbrenner, H., 30
Bronfenbrenner, U., 3, 4, 130, 140, 192, 237, 595, 609, 665, 671
Bronzaft, A. L., 501, 502, 503, 504, 505, 506, 508
Brosschot, J. F., 502
Broste, S. K., 501
Brothers, K. J., 330
Brower, S., 74, 327, 414, 417, 422
Brown, B., 259, 421, 431, 455, 502, 581
Brown, B. B., 204, 205, 207, 208, 210, 211, 212, 214, 215, 216, 217, 218, 219, 422
Brown, B. W., 483, 484
Brown, C., 431, 500
Brown, D. C., 384
Brown, D. R., 222
Brown, G., 216, 218
Brown, J. D., 370
Brown, L., 57, 76, 430, 541
Brown, M. G., 281
Brown, P., 559, 560, 566, 570, 571, 572, 573, 577
Brown, R., 3, 41, 46
Brown, W., 462
Browne, M. W., 259
Brubçhn, M., 75
Bruderman, M., 88
Brulle, R. J., 164
Brunault, M. S., 652
Brundtland, G. H., 57
Bruner, J., 33
Brunson, L., 337
Brunswik, E., 30, 101
Bruschke, G. V., 542
Bryan, H., 69
Bryant, F. B., 262
Bryant, K. J., 286
Bryden, M. P., 184
Brydon-Miller, M. L., 467
Bryk, A. S., 237, 489, 492
Buchecker, M., 58
Buck, R., 178
Buckwalter, K. C., 378, 383
Budd, R., 134

Budescu, D., 88
Bullard, R., 572, 592
Bullinger, M., 174, 503
Burby, R. J., 516, 519
Burch, J., 680
Burdett, R., 277, 278
Burdge, R. J., 260, 542, 543
Burgess, E., 665
Burgess, J., 45, 649, 651
Burker, E., 379, 381, 383
Burkhardt, R. L., 542
Burn, S. M., 329, 530, 542
Burns, E., 423
Burns, L. E., 133
Burns, W., 576
Buron, L., 414
Burridge, R., 400, 402
Burrough, P. A., 252, 253
Burton, D., 572
Burton, E., 191
Burton, J. R., 207, 211
Burton, M. A., 38
Busby, P. L., 363
Buse, L., 236
Bushnell, M. C., 180
Busk, P. L., 230
Bustard, W., 284
Butcher, M., 464
Butler, D., 431
Butler, J., 358
Buttel, F. H., 161, 163, 165, 166, 169
Buttimer, A., 108
Button, K., 191
Buttram, B. A., 536
Byerts, T., 293, 294
Byrne, B. M., 257, 265

Cable, C., 563
Cable, S., 563
Cacioppo, J. T., 173, 174, 175, 176, 178
Cain, C., 387, 388
Caldwell, A. B., 173
Calef, W., 512
Caliandro, V., 279
Calip, T., 476
Calkins, M., 376, 379, 380, 381, 382, 384, 386, 387
Calthorpe, P., 207
Calvert, J., 493
Calvo, S., 577
Calvocoressi, L., 135
Camacho, D., 563
Camerer, C. F., 86
Cameron, D., 378
Campbell, A., 563, 566
Campbell, D., 308, 336
Campbell, H., 611, 620
Campbell, N. A., 547
Campbell, R., 469
Campbell, S., 383, 385, 451
Canals, R. M., 57, 72
Cano, I., 43
Canter, D., 29, 30, 31, 37, 108, 325

Canter, L. W., 69
Cantor, R., 152, 153
Cantrell, P. J., 651
Capdevila, I., 66
Caplan, M. E., 652
Caporael, L. R., 88
Caporaso, J., 516
Capozzi, L., 174
Carifio, M. S., 652
Carley, M. J., 69
Carlisle, R., 477
Carlsmith, J. M., 484, 536
Carlson, S., 681
Carneiro, R. L., 148
Carnes, S., 560
Carnevale, P. J. D., 87
Carp, F. M., 374
Carpenter, S., 598
Carpman, J. R., 309, 325, 330, 331, 427, 428, 429, 431, 433, 434, 438, 439
Carr, D., 64, 74, 97
Carr, W., 613
Carreon, D., 374, 375, 377, 388
Carrere, S., 174
Carrier, B., 180
Carrougher, G. J., 180
Carrus, G., 38, 39, 43, 46
Carson, R., 34, 665
Carter, B., 73
Casey, A., 465
Casey, C. F., 546
Casey, E. S., 106, 108
Casey, T., 107
Cassidy, T., 56
Castells, M., 31, 58, 59, 607, 608, 661, 664
Castrechini, A., 60
Castro, R. de, 56, 58, 74
Catalano, R., 395, 398
Catterall, A., 620
Cattermole-Tally, F., 173
Catton, W. R., Jr., 160, 161, 163, 166
Cavalini, P., 486
Cavenaugh, K. L., 483
Chadwick, E., 399
Chafetz, P. K., 378, 384
Chalfonte, B., 454
Chalmers, J., 517, 571, 578, 579
Chambers, R., 615, 622
Chammah, A. M., 86
Chandler, E. F., 38
Chapin, D., 16, 22, 24
Chappell, J. E., Jr., 493
Charleston, S., 431
Charney, D. S., 135
Charon, H., 374, 386
Chase, J., 39
Chaudhury, H., 376
Chavis, D. M., 39, 421
Chawla, A. P., 182
Chawla, L., 365, 366, 369, 619
Chea, W. E., 7, 8
Cheatwood, D., 482, 483

Chemers, M., 219, 573
Chen, S., 501
Chen, T., 501
Cheng, S., 548
Cheremisinoff, N. P., 67
Cheremisinoff, P. N., 67
Cherian, J., 223
Cherry, E., 304
Cherry, K., 195
Chiang, H., 501
Chir, B., 503
Chisholm, R. E., 608, 623
Cho, S. H., 487
Chodorow, N., 349
Choi, C., 180
Choi, J., 184
Choi, Y., 285
Choi, Y. H., 173
Choi, Y. K., 285, 430
Choriki, D., 16, 24
Chou, C.-P., 258, 259
Christenson, G. A., 134
Christianson, E. H., 58
Chu, J. A., 136
Church, R. B., 235
Churchman, A., 42, 191, 192, 193, 194, 195, 196, 197, 198, 218, 219, 347, 350, 609, 612, 615, 616, 618, 619, 632
Cialdini, R., 39, 44, 58, 89, 90, 525, 670
Cicchetti, D., 229, 368
Cicinelli, J. G., 249, 250
Cigler, B. A., 516
Cirio, A. M., 502
Clamon, C., 383
Clark, A., 186
Clark, D. M., 134
Clark, D. W., 652
Clark, E. F., 10
Clark, F. E., 69
Clarke, J. C., 134
Clarke, K. C., 244, 248, 249, 251, 252, 253
Clarke, R. V., 417, 418
Clarke, S. W., 535
Clason, C., 515
Clayton, S., 35, 41, 603
Clearwater, Y. A., 653
Cleary, T. A., 383
Cleeland, C. S., 180
Cleghorn, A., 471
Clements, F., 665
Clitheroe, C., 618
Clore, G. C., 548
Clore, G. L., 489
Coate, J., 654
Coates, D., 577
Cobb, J. B., 59, 60
Cobb-Walgren, C., 548
Cobern, M. K., 525, 526, 530, 531, 542
Cochran, C. D., 652
Cochran, W. G., 222
Cogan, D., 180

Cogan, R., 180
Cohen, D. S., 184
Cohen, I., 73
Cohen, J., 225, 258, 265
Cohen, L., 490, 570
Cohen, M., 467, 560
Cohen, P., 225, 258, 265
Cohen, R., 306, 309
Cohen, S., 196, 401, 450, 451, 452, 491, 505, 564, 583, 599, 663, 671
Cohen, U., 376, 379, 380, 382, 383, 385, 386, 388
Cohen-Mansfield, J., 381
Cohill, A., 670
Cohn, E., 481, 483, 484, 485, 486, 487, 490, 491, 492, 493, 577
Cohn, S., 335
Colarelli, C. J., 142
Colbern, T., 566
Colby, B. G., 61, 592, 594, 601
Colding, J., 151
Cole, J. I., 662, 670
Cole, M., 120
Cole-Harding, S., 185
Coleman, D., 348
Coles, M. G. H., 175
Coley, R. L., 337
Collazo, J., 9
Collett, D., 325
Collier, G. A., 151
Collier, J., Jr., 20
Collier, J. J., 301
Collins, B., 449, 451
Collins, D., 571
Collins, J., 430
Collins, S., 245
Colman, A. W., 86
Colombotos, M., 564
Colquhoun, A., 289
Colson, E., 150
Colvin, C. R., 370
Commander, C., 379, 381, 383
Cone, J. D., 260, 324, 525, 529, 531
Conigliaro, L., 652
Conklin, H., 151
Conn, M., 363, 365
Connell, C. M., 40, 257, 259, 260, 545
Connelly, S., 615, 616, 617
Connor, D. M., 607
Conroy, P., 468
Conti, G. J., 207
Continisio, M., 31, 39
Conway, D., 292
Conway, P., 348
Cook, D., 406
Cook, M., 134
Cook, R., 301, 327
Cook, S. W., 531, 551
Cook, T. D., 222, 224
Coons, D., 377, 379
Cooper, B., 384
Cooper, C., 573, 661
Cooper, H., 222, 224, 229
Cooper, S., 309

Cooper Marcus, C., 19, 141, 363, 371
Cope, J. G., 526, 530
Copenhaver, E., 560
Corbett, M. N., 330
Corcoran, W. T., 484, 485
Cordray, D. S., 222, 224, 229
Cormick, G., 599
Cornelius, R., 564
Cornell, E. H., 325, 431
Cornwell, T. B., 548
Corral, V., 58
Corraliza, J., 40, 56, 57, 58, 60
Corral-Verdugo, V., 259, 260, 264, 550
Corson, W., 60
Corvalan, C., 394
Cose, E., 326
Costanza, R., 35
Costanzo, M., 58, 67, 329
Cosyne, P., 483
Cota, A., 471
Cotham, F., 429
Cotterell, J. L., 367
Cotton, J. L., 483
Cotton, T., 464
Couch, S., 168, 560, 561, 562, 579
Couclelis, H., 245, 249
Coupland, N., 596
Cousins, S., 253
Coyer, B. W., 579
Cozad, R. L., 500
Craglia, M., 245
Craik, K. H., 28, 29, 69, 122, 661, 665, 668
Crane, N., 378
Cranz, G., 358
Crawford, M., 471
Creen, T., 563, 567, 570, 577
Cressler, D. L., 143
Crews, J. I., 542
Crombez, G., 180
Cromley, E. C., 353
Cronick, K., 633, 634
Cronin-Golumb, A., 383
Cropper, V. L., 208
Crosby, L. A., 550
Crouter, A. C., 192
Crowe, T. D., 418
Cruikshank, J., 598
Csikszentmihalyi, I., 233
Csikszentmihalyi, M., 233, 234, 235, 236, 237, 238, 239, 349, 454, 669, 684
Cudeck, R., 259
Cullerton, S., 652
Cullingworth, J. B., 191
Cunill, N., 630
Cunningham, M. R., 489
Cuny, F. C., 518
Curhan, J. R., 87
Curry, E. W., 575
Cuthbert, B. N., 181
Cuthbertson, B., 562, 579
Cutter, S., 75, 572

Cuttle, K., 449
Cyr, K. A., 486

Dabholkar, P. A., 40, 545
Dahlstrand, U., 89, 90
Dahms, W., 491
Daigle, V. L., 652
Daily, G. C., 162
Dallas, J., 504, 507
Dalmanian, J., 32
Damasio, A., 172
Dandekar, H., 347
Danemeyer, C., 471
Dangermond, J., 245
Danubio, M. E., 157
Danze, E., 348
Darby, S. J., 384
Dardel, E., 108
Darke, J., 347
Darley, J. M., 329, 541
Darwin, C., 649, 665
da Silva, J. A., 249
Davey, G. C. L., 134
Davidoff, L. J., 350
Davidoff, P., 607, 608, 610
Davidovitch-Marton, R., 73, 195, 198
Davidson, C., 153, 561
Davidson, L., 568, 569, 570
Davies, J. L., 483
Davis, D., 40
Davis, G., 293, 301, 316, 317, 326
Davis, J., 470
Davis, J. A., 265
Davis, J. H., 87
Davis, L. L., 651
Davis, M., 182
Dawes, R. M., 41, 42, 86, 88
Dawson, D., 451
Dawson, R., 651
Day, F. A., 572
Day, K., 349, 354, 358, 374, 375, 377, 379, 380, 382, 383, 385, 386, 388
Dean, J., 648, 652
Deane, F. P., 134
Deasy, C. M., 298
de Boer, J., 570
DeCarlo, T., 652
DeCharms, R., 567
Deci, E. L., 542, 544
de Cock, K. M., 406
De Cremer, D., 42
Dee, N., 69
Degen Kolb, H. J., 519
Deignan, E., 502, 503, 504
DeLepper, M. J., 253
Delgado, E., 542
DeLoughry, T. J., 653
De Maertelaer, V., 486
DeMeurs, N., 252
de Meyer, F., 483
Demick, J., 4, 6, 7, 9, 10, 11, 12, 30, 35, 36, 47, 129, 130, 219
DeNeve, K. M., 481, 487, 488, 491
Denney, J., 652

Dennis, E. E., 60
Denniston, D., 76
Denton, N., 414
Denton, S., 414
Denzin, N. K., 19
De Oliver, M., 260, 550
DeParle, J., 428
DePasquale, J. P., 527
de Rivera, J., 547
Derksen, L., 40, 168
Descola, P., 148
Desmarais, S., 57, 58, 551
Desmidt, E., 469
Despres, C., 191, 194, 612
d'Estrée, T. P., 591, 592, 594, 601
Desyllas, J., 281
Detweiler, J. H., 245
Deutsch, M., 103, 595
Devlin, A., 430, 431
Devrotes, A., 180
DeWalt, B., 150
DeWalt, K., 150
Dewey, J., 203, 512, 521
de Wied, M., 180, 181, 182
Dexter, E. G., 481
De Young, R., 40, 223, 259, 260, 531, 542, 544
Diagne, A., 545
Diamond, J., 465
Diamond, W. D., 542
DiBartolo, L., 483
di Castri, F., 31, 32, 34, 35
DiChiro, G., 571
Dickerson, C. A., 546, 547
Dickinson, J., 75, 384
Dickson, B. R., 542
Diekstra, R. F. W., 134
Dierking, L., 471
Diette, G., 180
Dietz, P., 259
Dietz, T., 36, 38, 40, 41, 46, 58, 90, 167, 259, 260, 543
Dijkstra, A., 327
Dimotta, S., 380
Dixler, E., 347
Dixon, J., 45
Dixon, R. A., 3
Dobbs, A., 450
Dockett, K., 422
Doctor, J. N., 180
Dodd, D. K., 224
Dodge, K. A., 368
Dodge, R. W., 487
Dogu, U., 430
Doherty, S., 251
Dohrenwend, B. P., 566
Dohrenwend, B. S., 566
Doig, W., 381
Doise, W., 33, 41
Dolan, S., 64
Donnelly, P., 216, 416, 420
Donnerstein, E., 504
Doob, L., 599
Doriot, P., 651

Dorr, N., 481, 487, 488, 491
Dosey, M., 648
Doty, K., 325
Douglas, M., 44, 45, 148, 152, 153
Dovey, K., 107, 108, 109
Dower, N., 38
Downs, M., 575
Downs, R. M., 325, 662
Doxa, M., 275, 276
Drabek, K., 573
Drabek, T. E., 512, 513, 517, 519
Drake, B., 677, 684
Dreblow, L., 471
Dreger, R. M., 38
Drobny, N. L., 69
Drucker, S. J., 347, 352
Druckman, D., 59, 580, 596
Dubitsky, S., 493
Duensing, S., 465
Duerk, D., 304, 336
Duff, D. F., 648
Duffy, F., 282, 289, 309, 317, 446, 449,
    451
Duggar, G. S., 519
Duke, K. M., 69
Duke, M. P., 651
Dukes, E. F., 590, 593, 594, 599, 600,
    601, 604, 605
Dumanoski, D., 566
Duncan, G. H., 180
Duncan, N., 350
Dunham, D. N., 179
Dunlap, R., 37, 38, 40, 58, 160, 161,
    162, 163, 164, 165, 166, 167, 168,
    259, 260, 262, 264, 545, 565
Dunn, L., 513
Dunn, S., 76
Durant, R. F., 591, 593, 598
Duranti, A., 3
Durham, W., 150
Durkheim, E., 489
Durning, L., 348
Duron, Y., 56
Dürrenberger, G., 614, 620, 623
Durrett, C., 353, 354
Durrheim, K., 45
Duthie, E. H., 378
Dworkin, J., 233
Dwyer, S. A. R., 387, 388
Dwyer, W. O., 39, 525, 526, 530, 531,
    542
Dyer, C., 575
Dynes, R. R., 512

Eals, M., 184
Eamer, R., 386
Eason, L., 465
Easterling, D., 576
Easterling, W. E., 56, 73
Eastwood, R., 489
Eaton, S. B., 651
Ebert, J., 483
Ebreo, A., 40, 75, 542, 543, 544, 545,
    547, 549, 550, 551

Eccleston, C., 180
Eck, J. E., 419
Eckberg, D. L., 571
Edelstein, M., 560, 561, 562, 563, 564,
    565, 566, 567, 569, 570, 571, 572,
    573, 574, 576, 577, 578, 579, 580
Edgerton, R., 152
Edney, J. J., 40, 85, 88, 369, 648
Edwards, D., 45
Edwards, T. C., 58, 551
Edwards, W., 86
Eelen, P., 180
Egenhofer, M. J., 246, 251
Ehrlich, P., 665
Eibisch, C., 105, 108
Eich, E., 182
Eisemon, T., 331
Eisenhardt, K. M., 91
Eiser, J. R., 46
Eisto, I., 46
Ekman, P., 548
Elden, M., 613
Elder, J. P., 536
Ellen, P. M., 548
Ellen, P. S., 545
Ellul, J., 653
Elmståhl, S., 380, 383
Elworth, J. T., 40
Embree, L., 97
Emery, F. E., 663, 666
Endreny, P., 566
Epstein, J., 652
Epstein, S., 367, 368
Erbring, L., 665
Ercolani, A., 39, 218, 259
Ergenzen, N., 286
Erikson, J. B., 536
Erikson, K., 560, 561
Erkip, F., 430, 651
Ernst, K., 483
Escobar, A., 620
Esteban, E., 500
Evans, G., 30, 174, 196, 282, 286, 325,
    367, 401, 450, 451, 452, 453, 488,
    491, 502, 503, 505, 506, 562, 564,
    583, 648, 649, 652, 670
Evans, J. C., 97
Evans, M. J., 152
Evans, R., 283
Everett, B. P., 85
Everett, P. B., 324, 330, 525, 527, 529,
    669, 670
Ewing, R., 191
Eyferth, K., 364, 367

Faber, D., 561
Faber Taylor, A., 337
Fabian, A., 29, 35, 58, 108, 368, 370,
    661, 669
Faggiani, D., 420
Fahringer, D. C., 69
Fairweather, G. W., 143
Falk, J., 465, 471
Falkemark, G., 91

Fals Borda, O., 639
Faludi, A., 610
Faraj, S., 654
Farbstein, J., 293, 308, 309, 317
Farina, A., 579
Farinaro, E., 515
Farrington, C., 654
Fatouros, D. A., 277
Fava, S., 350
Fay, T. H., 500, 502
Feaver, D. B., 430
Feeley, P. A., 260, 551
Feimer, N., 668
Fein, S., 492
Feinstein, S. S., 610, 611
Feiock, F. C., 550
Feldman, H. S., 483, 484, 486
Feldman, N., 464
Feldman, R., 619
Feldman, R. M., 355, 368
Feldman, R. S., 525
Fell, R., 385
Fellows, J., 325
Felson, M., 418, 420, 490
Fenster, T., 198, 349, 350, 356
Fenton, D. M., 549, 603
Ferguson, E., 10, 249
Ferguson, F., 571, 573
Ferman, B., 422
Fernsler, F., 451
Ferrand, J. L., 543, 548
Ferreira-Marques, J., 39
Ferris, W., 481
Festinger, L., 29, 90, 455, 536, 546,
    661, 669
Field, S., 486
Fields, H. L., 182
Figueredo, A. J., 259, 260
Finch, A. J., Jr., 516
Findlay, R. A., 346
Fine, M., 192
Finegan, J. E., 551
Finegan, J. K., 185
Finger, M., 58
Finke, G., 430
Finlay, T., 476
Finlayson, B., 260, 547
Finsterbusch, K., 69, 576
Fiorino, D., 577, 591, 593, 598
Fiorito, E., 177, 367
Firebaugh, G., 489
Firehock, K., 605
Firey, W., 669, 672
Fischer, C. S., 657
Fischer, K. W., 546, 547
Fischer-Kowalski, M., 161
Fischhoff, B., 37, 75, 147, 328, 566,
    578
Fish, R., 454, 654
Fishback, J. F., 531
Fishbein, M., 39, 40, 58, 195, 256,
    257, 545
Fisher, J. D., 16, 56, 482, 525, 648,
    651, 665

Fisher, M., 184
Fisher, R. A., 222
Fishman, D. B., 116, 120, 121, 122
Fiske, S. T., 594
Fitchen, J., 573
Fitzpatrick, C., 518
Fitzsimmons, S. J., 69
Fitzwater, E., 378, 379
Flagg, G., 311
Flanagan, M., 481, 487, 488, 491
Flavin, C., 57, 76
Fleischmann, R. L., 135
Fleiss, J. L., 224
Fleming, I., 568, 569, 570, 571
Fleming, R., 568
Flexer, B., 465
Flora, S. R., 528
Florin, P., 421
Floyd, H. H., 566
Floyd, M. F., 364
Flury, A., 250
Flynn, C. B., 517
Flynn, J., 564, 571, 576, 578, 579
Flynn, K., 652
Flynn, L. R., 549
Flyvbjerg, B., 611, 618
Focke, J. W., 303
Folke, C., 151
Foltz, W., 599
Ford, W., 468, 469
Fordyce, W. K., 651
Foreman, H., 431
Forester, J., 608, 617
Forrest, C., 141
Forrest, R., 418
Forskargruppen för det nya
   vardagslivet., 607
Fort, T. R., 531
Foster, D. H., 45
Foster, N., 287, 388
Fothergill, A., 515
Foulks, E., 568
Fowler, E. P., 421
Fowler, F., 416, 420, 422
Fowlkes, M., 560, 562, 563, 566, 571,
   574, 576, 577, 579
Fox, A., 326, 370, 414, 416
Fox, C. R., 86
Fox, K. A., 117, 122
Fox, M. B., 350
Foxall, G., 309
Frackowiak, R. S. J., 174, 186
Francis, J., 309
Francis, M., 608
Francis, R. S., 562, 576
Franck, K., 326, 348, 349, 350, 351,
   352, 355, 357, 358, 359, 414, 416
Frank, A., 251
Franklin-Casey, C., 40
Fransson, N., 36
Fredrickson, B. L., 548
Freedman, J. L., 326
Freeman, H., 406
Freeman, P., 664

Freese, L., 161
Freeze, A., 561, 566
Freire, P., 634, 636
French, D., 386
French, H., 76
French, S. P., 516, 519
Freudenberg, N., 563, 570, 571, 572,
   577, 583
Freudenburg, W., 59, 61, 69, 163, 166,
   167, 168, 563, 574, 576, 577, 578,
   583
Freundschuh, S. M., 251
Frey, J., 483, 484, 486, 487
Fridley, J. L., 245
Fried, M., 140, 573, 662, 669
Fried, Y., 451
Frieden, B., 191
Friedman, A., 306, 307, 308, 309, 348,
   462, 465
Friedman, J., 608
Friedman, S. L., 665
Friedman, Y., 607, 608
Friedsam, H. J., 515
Friend, J., 624
Friere, P., 599
Friesema, H. P., 516
Frieze, I. H., 565, 567
Frijda, N. H., 546
Frisancho, A. R., 482
Frisbie, D., 419
Frisoni, G. B., 378, 383
Frith, C. D., 174, 186
Fritz, C., 511
Froese, A. D., 224
Fromme, D. K., 652
Frondaroli, C., 651
Frost, R. O., 135
Frueh, B. C., 137
Frühwirth, M., 489
Fry, P. A., 249, 250
Fuchs, L. S., 651
Fuhrer, U., 40, 118, 120, 218, 219,
   367, 369, 370, 546
Fujii, S., 89
Fujita, N., 249, 251
Fukusima, S. S., 249
Fulcomer, M., 379, 380, 382, 383, 384,
   388
Fuller, C., 312
Fuller-Thomson, E., 400, 401
Fullerton, C., 511
Funahashi, K., 375
Furia, L. del, 69
Furness, T. A., III, 180
Fusari, A., 378
Fussler, C., 58, 59

Gabaldón, A. J., 630
Gabe, J., 400, 403
Gackenbach, J., 662, 665
Gadamer, H.-G., 106
Gaddy, J., 451
Gadian, D. G., 174, 186
Gaffen, D. J., 481

Gajewski, F., 423
Galaburda, A. M., 185
Gale, N. D., 249, 251
Galea, L. A. M., 184
Galegher, J., 454
Galinsky, E., 9
Gallagher, B., 680
Gallardo, B., 134
Gamba, R. J., 544
Gambert, S. R., 378
Ganiban, J., 368
Gans, H., 574
Ganter, M. A., 245
Gantz, B. S., 224
Garber, J., 368
Garces, R. F., 662, 664
García, S., 64
García-Mira, R., 56
Gardiner, H. N., 174
Gardiner, R. A., 421
Gardner, G., 56, 57, 58, 59, 76, 168,
   328, 526, 537
Gärling, T., 35, 36, 40, 42, 44, 46, 87,
   88, 89, 91, 92, 286, 367
Garofalo, J., 415
Garr, D. J., 347, 350
Garrett, M., 191
Garrison, C. Z., 516
Garrison, J. L., 516
Garrrett, W., 450
Gartrell, J., 40, 168
Garvill, J., 367
Gasparotti, A., 378
Gastil, R. D., 481
Gatchel, R., 568, 569
Gatens, M., 358
Gatersleben, B., 368
Gattoni, F. W. G., 503
Gaulin, S. J. C., 184, 649
Gauvain, M., 219
Geaghan, J. P., 551
Geen, R. G., 504
Geertz, C., 148, 566
Gehring, W. J., 175
Geiser, K., 563
Gelder, M. G., 134
Geller, E. S., 39, 64, 324, 330, 525, 526,
   527, 528, 529, 530, 531, 532, 533,
   534, 535, 536, 542, 543, 669, 670
Gendron, R. C., 551
Gergen, K. J., 4
Gerlach, K., 450
Gerow, J. R., 525
Gerrard, M., 578
Gerson, L. W., 486
Geschwind, N., 185
Gesell, G., 571, 578, 579
Getzells, J., 191
Gheza, A., 378
Ghisla, K. M., 383
Ghosh, S. K., 117
Giacomini, V., 31, 32
Gibbs, L. M., 560, 566, 568, 570, 571,
   576, 577

Gibbs, M., 564, 567, 569, 570, 571
Gibson, J., 30, 272, 276, 454
Gibson, T., 623
Giddens, A., 169, 565
Giesriel, M., 568
Gifford, D., 35
Gifford, R., 36, 56, 88, 191, 223, 328, 331, 332, 450, 451, 491, 493, 651, 652
Gilbert, D. T., 541
Gilbert, T., 195
Giles, H., 596
Giles, M. B., 548
Giles, M. S., 155
Gill, D., 560, 567, 568, 574, 575
Gill, J. D., 550
Gillett, R., 431
Gilligan, C., 357
Gillilan, S., 218, 328
Gillin, J. C., 383
Gillis, A., 400
Gillman, S., 233
Gilmore, G. C., 383
Gilroy, R., 347, 357, 614, 615, 621, 622
Ginat, J., 204, 210, 213, 214, 215, 217
Ginosar, O., 191, 218, 219
Ginsberg, L., 519
Ginsberg, Y., 195, 197
Ginzburg, H., 560, 576
Giorgi, A., 95
Giuliani, F., 58, 59, 635, 636
Giuliani, M. V., 56
Gladwing, T. N., 38
Glass, D., 452, 505, 564, 670
Glass, G. V., 222
Glasson, J., 69
Glavovic, B., 590, 594
Glazer, B. G., 213
Gleason, B., 195
Gleser, G., 513, 516, 560
Glynn, N. J., 180
Godaert, G. L. R., 502
Goethert, R., 608, 614, 615, 616, 617, 618, 623, 624
Goffman, E., 29, 100, 281, 559, 573, 579, 656
Goffman, I., 402
Goldberger, A. S., 258
Goldenhar, L. M., 40, 257, 259, 260, 545
Goldman, M., 652
Goldring, E., 560, 569
Goldsmith, E., 549
Goldsteen, R., 560, 576
Goldstein, A. P., 527
Goldstein, G., 516
Goldstein, K. M., 489
Goldwater, B. C., 179
Golledge, R., 246, 249, 250, 251, 286, 293, 427, 430
Goltsman, S., 74, 195
Gonzales, M. H., 329
González, M. H., 67
Gonzalez, R., 230

Gooch, G. F., 264
Good, C. D., 174, 186
Good, M., 180
Goodchild, M. F., 248, 252, 253
Goodchild, M. J., 244, 250
Goodman, K. J., 152
Goodman, N., 274
Goodman, W. K., 135
Goodwin, C., 3
Gordon, M. T., 349
Gordon, R. A., 482
Gornitsky, L. B., 19
Gorsuch, R. L., 258, 261
Götestam, K. G., 386
Gottdiener, M., 150
Gottfredson, S. D., 414, 417, 418
Gottfried, J., 465
Gould, K. A., 166
Grace, M., 513, 516, 560
Graham, D. T., 155
Graham, H., 284
Grajewski, T., 271, 278, 281
Gramling, R., 163, 166
Grankvist, G., 89
Grannis, P., 307, 336
Granovetter, M., 281
Grant, M. A., 309, 325, 330, 331, 427, 428, 429, 431, 433, 434, 438, 439
Grass, J. A., 180
Gratton, G., 175
Graumann, C. F., 97, 99, 101, 103, 104, 105, 107, 108, 109
Graumann, K., 35, 43, 45
Gray, J., 308
Gray, T. W., 542
Greaves, T., 152
Greed, C. H., 347
Green, B., 513, 560
Green, B. F., 229
Green, B. L., 513, 516, 560
Green, D. R., 253
Green, E. C., 152
Green, K. B., 505
Green, L., 417
Greenaway, S., 134
Greenberg, C. I., 651
Greenberg, S. W., 419
Green-Demers, I., 544
Greene, B. F., 527
Greene, D., 534, 536
Greene, J., 378, 421
Greene, L. S., 157
Greene, M. R., 517
Greene, T. C., 16, 56, 525, 648, 651
Greene, T. E., 482, 665
Greenstein, S. M., 180
Greenwald, A. G., 230, 370
Gregerson, J., 312
Gregory, W. L., 328
Griffin, R. J., 165
Griffin, S., 358
Griffitt, W., 488
Griggs, S., 465, 466, 467
Grimm, L. G., 258

Grimshaw, G. M., 185
Grindle, A. C., 542
Groat, L., 191, 356, 612
Grob, A., 259, 546
Groh, C. J., 388
Gross, R. C., 135
Grossman-Alexander, M., 174, 177
Grossnickle, W. F., 526, 530
Grosz, E., 358
Gruen, G., 505, 664
Guagnano, A., 90
Guagnano, G. A., 38, 40, 259, 543
Guàrdia, J., 58, 59
Guba, E., 639
Gubbins, S., 542
Guerrini, G. B., 378
Guglielmi, L., 378
Guha, R., 148
Gulliver, P. H., 596
Gump, P. V., 116
Gumpert, G., 347, 352
Gunn, J. D., 150
Gunnip, K., 469
Gunter, V., 559, 566
Gupta, M., 618
Gurevitch, J., 225
Gurwitsch, A., 98
Gustafsson, M., 35, 40, 44, 46, 88, 89, 91
Güth, W., 87
Guthrie, D., 230
Gutterman, E., 568
Guyer, J., 149
Guzzetta, J. D., 671
Gwiasda, V. E., 414
Gwyther, L. P., 378

Haas, J. E., 513
Habermas, J., 613, 620
Hacker, W., 120
Hackett, P., 309
Hackmann, A., 134
Haddock, C. K., 224
Hadley, M., 31, 32, 34
Haenlein, H., 618
Hagelin, J. S., 483
Haggard, L., 203, 206, 207, 211, 215
Hahn, H., 195
Haines, M., 502, 506
Haines-Young, R., 253
Hajinikolaou, E., 277
Hakkert, A. S., 327
Hale, W. D., 652
Hall, E., 29, 293, 647, 648, 653, 668
Hall, J. A., 229
Hall, M., 570
Hallman, W., 567, 571
Halmo, D. B., 152
Halpern, D., 404
Halweil, B., 76, 541
Halyard, R., 684
Hamamoto, W., 431
Hamberger, W., 468, 469
Hambrick-Dixon, P. J., 505

Hamdi, N., 608, 614, 615, 616, 617, 618, 623, 624
Hamid, P. N., 548
Hamilton, L., 562
Hamilton, W., 649
Hammond, K. R., 601
Hammond, M. M., 330
Hammond, P., 86
Hampson, E., 184, 185, 186
Hancocks, D., 476
Hanley, G., 431
Hanley, I. G., 382
Hannigan, J. A., 166
Hansen, D. A., 501
Hanshaw, B. B., 69
Hanson, J., 271, 272, 274, 276, 278, 280, 282, 283, 284, 285, 287
Hanson, K., 662, 670
Hanyu, K., 336
Harackiewicz, J. M., 219, 544
Harburg, E., 400
Harcourt, W., 620
Hardaker, G., 59
Hardcastle, D. M., 549
Harden, J., 369
Hardin, G., 85, 595, 596
Hardin, G. H., 552
Hardin, G. J., 33, 40, 41, 44
Hardin, R., 42
Hardin, S. B., 516
Hare, M., 152
Harison, D. A., 229
Harkins, D., 11
Harland, P., 546
Harloff, H. J., 105, 108
Harmon, W., 565
Harper, B. L., 152, 153
Harper, C. S., 85
Harper, D., 20
Harpster, L., 544
Harr, J., 560, 572
Harré, R., 100
Harries, K. D., 483, 485, 487
Harries-Jones, P., 157
Harrington, M. J., 58, 551
Harris, M., 135
Harris, P. B., 259
Harris, R. J., 230
Harris, S. G., 152, 153
Harrison, A. A., 651, 653
Harrison, C. M., 45
Harrison, L., 66, 67
Harrison, P. I., 517
Hart, R., 285, 348, 363, 364, 365
Hartig, T., 174, 182, 184, 218, 366, 367, 368, 369, 370, 407, 671
Hartley, J. A., 148
Hartman, H., 222, 224
Hartmann, D. P., 228
Hartney, C., 569
Hartsock, N., 349
Hartsough, D., 572
Harvey, B., 64
Harvey, D., 610

Harvey, L. O., Jr., 601
Harvey, O. J., 44
Hastie, R., 601
Hastorf, A., 579
Hatcher, J. W., 531
Hatcher, S. L., 567, 570
Hatfield, D. B., 542
Haughton, G., 191
Haugtvedt, C. P., 209, 546
Hawerott, M., 469
Hawkes, D., 289
Hawley, A., 665
Hawley, F. F., 481
Hayden, D., 347, 351, 353, 354, 355
Hayduk, L. A., 648
Hayes, A. F., 230
Hayes, B., 664
Hayes, C., 604
Hayes, S. C., 260, 324, 525, 529, 531
Haygood, L. V., 600
Hayward, J., 466
Hayward, U. G., 467
Hayword, G., 573
Head, J., 506
Headland, T., 152
Healey, P., 43, 608, 609, 610, 620
Heaney, D., 69
Hearnshaw, H. M., 255
Hearnshaw, H. W., 249
Heath, C., 654
Heath, T., 194
Heberlein, T., 168
Hebl, M. R., 174, 177
Heck, R. H., 256, 269
Hedges, L. V., 222, 224, 225, 226, 227, 228
Hediger, H., 648
Hedin, J., 285
Hedman, B., 622
Heerwagen, J., 158, 309, 310, 449
Heft, H., 363, 366, 369
Hegarty, M., 249
Hegarty, P., 283
Heidegger, M., 99, 106, 107, 108, 109, 355
Heider, F., 559, 567
Heidrick, G., 180
Heijnen, C. J., 502
Heiman, M., 577
Hein, G., 465
Heinemann, F., 96
Heinen, J. T., 551
Heins, J. A., 184
Heise, L., 404
Hektner, J. M., 233
Heller, K., 39
Heller, M., 248
Heller, N. B., 484, 487
Henderson, C., 348
Henderson, G., 408
Hendricks, C., 235
Hendrix, S., 430
Heninger, G. R., 135
Henley, N., 348

Henley, R., 651
Henry, A. L., 224
Hepner, G. F., 69
Herin, S., 384
Herman, J. F., 184
Hern, W. M., 653
Hernández, B., 58
Herrera, M., 550
Herridge, C. F., 503
Hershberger, R., 292, 293, 294, 296, 297, 301, 302, 304
Hershey, J., 543
Hertwich, E. G., 71
Herz, L., 383, 385
Hess, E. H., 178, 179
Hester, R., 141, 363
Hester, R. T., Jr., 608
Heth, C. D., 325, 431
Hewitt, J., 651
Hewitt, K., 511
Hiatt, L., 381, 382
Hickling, A., 624
Hidley, J. H., 527
Hilgartner, S., 578
Hill, C. L., 135
Hill, K., 466
Hill, M., 197
Hillary, R., 66
Hillier, B., 271, 272, 273, 274, 276, 277, 278, 279, 280, 282, 283, 284, 285, 287, 288, 289
Himelstein, P., 651
Hine, D., 450
Hine, D. V., 88
Hine, D. W., 36, 223, 328
Hine, E., 301
Hines, J., 36, 58, 223, 468, 469
Hiramatsu, K., 501, 502, 503, 504
Hirschel, J. D., 483
Hirschon, R., 350
Hirshi, K., 470
Hishikawa, Y., 383, 385
Hissam, C. P., 652
Hitchcock, J., 196
Hochschild, A. R., 234
Hockings, M., 73
Hodes, R. L., 180
Hodges, A., 40, 546
Hodgson, C. C., 381
Hodson, S. J., 527
Hoel, L. A., 491
Hofbauer, R. K., 180
Hoff, M., 476
Hoffman, A., 7, 10
Hoffman, H. A., 184
Hoffman, H. G., 180
Hoffman, M. S., 489
Hogarth, R. M., 85
Hoglund, J. D., 380
Hokkanem, T. J., 46
Holaday, B., 364
Holahan, C. H., 28
Holahan, C. J., 363

Holanda, F. de, 279
Holman, E. A., 136
Holmes, A., 500
Holmes, D., 378
Holmes, R. M., 651
Holmes, T. H., 140
Holmes, T. S., 140
Holzer, E., 36
Homel, R., 418
Homer-Dixon, T., 155
Honn, V. J., 387, 388
Hood, M., 463, 466, 475
Hood, W. R., 44
hooks, b., 355
Hooper, N. E., 651
Hope, T., 414
Hopper, J. R., 40, 329, 542, 543
Horan, T., 662, 664, 670, 672
Horelli, L., 351, 352, 353, 354, 355,
    356, 357, 358, 607, 608, 609, 613,
    614, 615, 616, 618, 619, 621, 622,
    623
Horgen, T. H., 307, 308, 310
Hori, H., 383, 385
Hormuth, S. E., 235, 237
Hornborg, A., 580
Hornik, J., 223
Horowitz, D., 598
Horowitz, H., 293
Horowitz, M. J., 648
Hosch, H. M., 651
Hovell, M. F., 536
Hovland, C., 536
Howard, G. S., 35, 36, 38, 525, 526,
    542
Howard, J. A., 40
Howard, R. B., 648, 649
Howarth, E., 489
Howland, E. W., 180
Hoyle, R. H., 257, 258, 259, 263, 269
Hozumi, S., 383, 385
Hrubovcak, J. C., 383
Hsieh, C., 416
Hsieh, P., 501
Hu, L. -T., 259
Huber, G. P., 313
Hudson, J., 512
Huebner, R. B., 548
Huebscher, R., 604
Huertas-Jourda, J., 97
Huffcutt, A., 225
Huffman, K. P., 526, 530
Huffman, K. T., 526, 530
Hughes, A. O., 483
Hughes, F., 348
Hughes, I., 134
Hulchanski, D., 400, 401
Hull, R. B., 543
Humbach, E., 378
Humphrey, C. R., 330
Humphreys, M. A., 482, 485
Hungerford, H., 36, 58, 223, 544
Hunn, E., 151
Hunsley, J., 550

Hunt, E., 184, 186
Hunter, A., 58
Hunter, C., 191
Hunter, J. E., 224, 225
Huntington, E., 102, 493
Hurin, S., 542
Hurlburt, R. T., 235
Husserl, E., 98
Hussian, R. A., 384
Hutchins, M., 475, 476
Hutchinson, S., 387
Huttcutt, A. I., 225
Hygge, S., 174, 503
Hypen, K., 452

Iacofano, D. S., 74
Iacono, S., 661
Ikeda, K., 517
Illich, I., 567
Inglehart, R., 38, 59
Inhelder, B., 275
Íñiguez, L., 58, 61, 73
Innes, J., 608, 610, 611, 613, 619, 620
Inoue, W., 11
Irwin, A., 578
Isaac, J., 213
Isaacs, N., 308
Isen, A. M., 182
Ishii, S., 11
Israel, T., 141
Ito, A., 501, 504
Ito, T. A., 178, 486
Ittelson, W., 28, 29, 30, 85, 98, 172,
    301, 401, 661, 665
Iwata, B. A., 527
Iwata, O., 544
Izard, C. E., 368

Jackman, P., 309
Jackson, J. M., 525, 526, 530, 531
Jacobs, H. E., 542
Jacobs, J., 215, 326, 421
Jacobs, M., 158, 400
Jacobs, S., 562, 564
Jacobs, W. J., 137
Jacobson, H., 59
Jacobson, L., 595
Jacobson, R. D., 431
Jalongo, M. R., 371
James, P., 58, 59
James, W., 233, 528
Jang, D. P., 173
Janis, I., 561
Janoff-Bulman, R., 565, 567
Janowsky, J. S., 185
Jansen, R. W. J., 484
Janz, N. K., 549
Jarmon, R. G., 483, 484, 486
Jaroff, L., 507
Jenks, M., 191
Jennings, J., 452
Jensen, F., 153, 561
Jess, P., 59
Jiménez, B., 58

Joanette, Y., 380
Job, R. F. S., 506
Jodelet, D., 58, 667
Johaneson, H., 469
Johansson, L.-O., 91
Johansson-Stenman, O., 91
Johnson, A. K., 74
Johnson, B. D., 383, 384, 387, 388
Johnson, J. H., 668
Johnson, L., 23
Johnson, N. B., 329
Johnsrude, I. S., 174, 186
Jones, A., 192, 195
Jones, D., 364, 366, 385
Jones, E., 579
Jones, E. E., 651
Jones, E. M., 75
Jones, F. N., 503
Jones, R. E., 38, 58, 164, 165, 259, 545
Jones, T., 574, 651
Jonker, J., 66
Jordan, E. H., 429
Jordan, N. L., 648
Jöreskog, K. G., 257, 258
Jørgensen, T., 66
Jorgenson, D. O., 488
Joroff, M. L., 307, 308, 310
Joseph, D., 500
Jossa, F., 515

Kaaja, M., 616, 619, 623
Kadleck, C., 420
Kahle, L. R., 329
Kahn, P., 562
Kahn, R. L., 117, 118, 666
Kahneman, D., 46, 86, 595
Kaiser, E. J., 516
Kaiser, F. G., 35, 40, 259, 367, 369,
    370, 543, 546, 551
Kales, E., 36, 40, 41
Kallai, J., 137
Kallgren, C. A., 39, 44, 89, 90
Kallus, R., 192
Kalof, L., 36, 38, 40, 58, 90, 259, 260,
    543
Kaloyanova, F., 400
Kals, E., 547
Kalsher, M. J., 530
Kameron, J., 564
Kaminoff, R., 58, 108, 325, 368, 370,
    661, 669
Kaminski, G., 117, 123, 124
Kaminstein, D., 572
Kane, H., 57, 76
Kant, I., 15
Kantola, S. J., 328, 545, 547
Kantrowitz, M., 308, 317
Kao, J., 443
Kaplan, B., 4, 6
Kaplan, K. J., 651
Kaplan, R., 46, 182, 206, 310, 367,
    431, 449, 467, 547, 668, 671
Kaplan, S., 46, 182, 367, 430, 431, 449,
    467, 547, 603, 649, 668, 671

Kapp, F. T., 560
Karlsson, I., 381
Karp, D. G., 543
Kartez, J., 516
Karuza, J., Jr., 577
Kasarda, J. D., 414
Kasl, S., 400
Kasof, J., 505
Kates, R. W., 665
Katschnig, H., 133, 134
Katz, D., 117, 118, 647, 666
Katz, E., 35, 38
Katz, N., 519
Katzev, R., 39, 530
Katzev, R. A., 530
Katzev, R. D., 530, 542
Kaufman, J. L., 192
Kaufman, S., 572, 577
Kaufman-Gilliland, C. M., 88
Kavanaugh, A., 670
Kaya, N., 651
Keable, E., 445, 451
Keating, K. M., 167
Keating, M., 60
Keaty, M., 431
Keeting, B., 561
Keller, S., 347
Kellert, S. R., 547, 649
Kellett, J., 403
Kelley, H., 44, 567, 669
Kellman, S. G., 413
Kelly, J. G., 4
Kelman, H., 599
Kemmis, S., 613
Kempton, W., 148, 550
Kennedy, J., 451, 465, 474
Kennett, P., 418
Kenny, D. A., 419, 423
Kenrick, D. T., 483, 525
Kerber, K. W., 653
Kernohan, D., 308
Kerr, J. H., 368
Kerr, N. L., 88
Kevan, S. M., 487
Key, I., 573
Key, W. H., 513, 519
Khakee, A., 619
Kibbee, E., 180
Kidder, L., 192, 577
Kidder, T., 443, 455
Kieffer, C., 639
Kiesler, S., 240, 653, 655, 662, 665, 669, 670
Kieszak, S. M., 500
Kihlgren, M., 381
Kilpatrick, F. P., 30
Kim, J., 261
Kim, S. H., 275, 276, 279, 590
Kim, S. I., 173
Kimball, L., 615, 623
Kimble, C. E., 216
Kimmel, M. J., 86
Kimura, D., 184, 185
Kincaid, D., 307

King, J. C., 119, 122
Kipnis, D., 173
Kirasic, K. C., 431
Kirby, K. M., 350
Kirchler, E., 239, 489
Kirkland, L. H., 66
Kirscht, J. P., 89, 549
Kitamura, R., 89
Kitchin, R. M., 184, 325
Klatzky, R. L., 249, 250, 251
Klauber, M., 385
Klausner, S. A., 170
Klaver, J., 66
Kleban, M., 379, 380, 382, 383, 384, 388
Klein, J., 409, 410
Klem, L., 265
Klenow, D. J., 516
Kliksberg, B., 630
Kline, L. M., 652
Kling, R., 661
Kluckhohn, C., 158
Knapel, C., 309
Knapp, D., 186
Knight, R. C., 282
Knowles, E. S., 648, 651
Knowlton, A. R., 121
Kobak, R. R., 368
Kobashi, K., 650
Kockelmans, J. J., 97, 105
Koepke, K. M., 378
Koffka, K., 5, 100
Kogewa, M., 651
Kohn, A., 531
Kohn, I., 326, 414, 416, 562
Kok, G., 329, 549
Kolb, D. A., 613
Kolbo, J., 568
Komanoff, C., 507
Komorita, S. S., 86, 88
Konakayama, A., 329
Konar, E., 293, 294, 309, 445, 448, 449, 451
Konkel, R. S., 158
Koons, B., 421
Koppelaar, L., 488, 651
Koran, J., 465, 471
Koran, M. L., 465
Korol, M., 516, 560
Korosec-Serfaty, P., 104
Korpela, K., 365, 366, 367, 368, 369, 370, 371, 609, 671
Koslowsky, M., 640
Koss, E., 383
Kosztolanyi, P., 137
Kottak, C., 149, 150
Kovach, C. R., 387, 388
Kovach, R. C., Jr., 431
Kramer, A. F., 184
Kramer, P., 489
Kramer, R. M., 43, 88
Kramer, T., 560
Krantz, D., 450, 451, 452
Krantz, P. J., 330

Krasner, L., 527
Kraus, N., 571, 578, 579
Krause, C., 562, 571
Krause, M. S., 135
Krause, T. R., 527
Kraut, R., 240, 454, 653, 654, 655, 665, 670
Krech, S., III, 150, 152
Kreps, G. A., 511
Kripke, D., 383, 385
Kristensen, H., 87
Kroeber, A. L., 158
Kroll-Smith, J. S., 168, 559, 560, 561, 562, 566, 579
Kromm, D., 382, 386
Kromm, Y. H. N., 382, 386
Kronsnick, J. A., 301
Kruks, S., 612, 613
Kruse, L., 35, 43, 45, 56, 59, 99, 101, 102, 103, 104, 108, 109
Kryter, K. D., 500, 502
Ku, J. H., 173
Kubat, A. S., 280
Kubey, R., 234, 238, 239
Kuch, K., 133
Kuethe, J. L., 651
Kuhn, T., 565
Kuipers, B., 430
Kukkonen, H., 608, 618, 619, 622
Kuller, R., 331, 450
Kumlin, R. R., 304
Kunreuther, H., 519, 576, 579
Kunzendorf, R. G., 652
Kuo, F., 337, 367, 431, 467
Kuperschmid, B. J., 388
Kuremyr, D., 381
Kurtz, E., 421
Kuse, A. R., 184, 186
Kuusela, V., 452
Kyttä, M., 369, 619

Lab, S. P., 415, 483
Lacey, M., 500
Ladd, F. C., 363
LaFrance, M., 653
Lahar, C., 430
Lahey, B. B., 525
Lahtela, K., 452
Laike, T., 450
Lalli, M., 58, 368
Lam, S., 546
LaMay, C., 60
Lambin, E., 149
Landau, B., 431
Landberg, H., 155
Lang, J. T., 3
Lang, L., 248
Lang, P. J., 178, 181
Langer, E. J., 326
Langer, K., 621
Langford, M., 19
Langworthy, R. H., 484, 487
Lankford, S., 466

Lansana, F. M., 549, 552
Larkin, P., 325
LaRoche, E., 483, 484, 486
Larrick, R. P., 492
Larson, J. H., 651, 652
Larson, R., 233, 234, 235, 236, 237, 238, 239
Laser, P. S., 488
Lash, S., 565
Lasswell, T., 298
Latkin, C. A., 121, 122
Latour, B., 150
Laue, J. H., 599
Laufer, R., 369
Launier, L. R., 219
Lauridsen, P. K., 531
Laurini, R., 246, 251
La Vigne, N., 418
Lavine, T., 5
Law, D. J., 184
Lawrence, R., 326, 395, 396, 398, 399, 401, 402, 407, 408, 409, 618, 619, 622
Lawton, C. A., 431
Lawton, M. P., 208, 374, 378, 379, 380, 382, 383, 384, 386, 388, 664
Lawton, P., 293, 294
Layman, M., 571, 578, 579
Lazarus, R., 219, 490, 546, 548, 670
Leahey, T. H., 233
Leaman, A., 287, 289, 306, 309, 314
Lease, G., 150
Leavitt, H., 450, 457
Leavitt, J., 353, 355, 357
LeBeau, J. L., 483, 484, 485, 487
Lebensfeld-Schwartz, P., 6
LeBlanc, W., 420
Lebow, A. S., 134
Leccese, M., 207
Lechtzin, N., 180
Leckliter, I. N., 531
Ledbetter, C., 678
Ledewitz, S., 380
Lee, D. R., 108, 347
Lee, S. J., 550
Lee, T., 31
Lee, Y.-J., 40, 260
Leeming, F. C., 39, 525, 526, 530, 531, 542
LeFevre, J., 235
Leff, E., 149
Legault, L. R., 550
Leger-Krall, S., 387
Legovini, A., 630
Lehman, D. R., 552
Lehman, G. R., 530
Lehman, J., 465
Lehman, S., 564
Lehnert, S., 105, 108
Leissner, P., 381
Leistritz, F. L., 69
Lennon, S. J., 651
Lenssen, N., 76

Leonard, A., 516, 560
Leonard, D., 651
Leonard-Barton, D., 544
Leopold, L. B., 69
Lepore, S. J., 282, 488, 502, 505, 652
Lepori, B., 359
Lepori, R. B., 355, 359
Lepper, M. R., 534, 536
Lerner, M. J., 567
Lerner, R. M., 3
Lesko, W., 450
L'Esperance, L., 350
Lester, M., 566
Leventhal, G., 542
Leverington, F., 73
Levesque, D. F., 489
Levi, L., 57
Levin, M., 613
Levine, A., 560, 562, 563, 566, 570, 571, 574, 576, 577, 578, 579
Levine, M., 431, 467
Levitt, L., 542
Levy, C., 623
Levy, S., 653
Levy-Leboyer, C., 39, 56
Lewin, K., 4, 5, 17, 30, 36, 100, 103, 104, 172, 208, 324, 564, 613, 648, 663
Lewis, A., 542
Lewis, B., 135
Lewis, C., 604
Lewis, G. J., 491
Lewis, S., 561
Leyson, J., 158
Li, S., 490
Lichtenstein, S., 75, 566, 578
Lieberg, M., 364
Liebow, E., 148, 150, 153, 155, 156, 158
Liebowitz, B., 374, 379, 380, 386
Light, R., 222, 224
Lightfoot, N., 180
Limb, M., 366
Lincoln, Y., 19, 639
Lind, E. A., 549, 603
Lindahl-Kiessling, K., 155
Lindberg, E., 286
Lindblom, C. E., 610
Lindburg, D., 476
Lindell, M., 517
Lindeman, D. A., 378
Lindesay, J., 378, 379, 386
Lindholm, G., 367
Lindsay, J. J., 549
Lindsay-Hartz, J., 547
Lindvall, T., 501, 502
Lindy, J., 516, 560
Lineberry, R., 516
Linenger, J., 677, 679, 680
Linkowski, P., 486
Linn, M., 465
Linn, N., 260, 542, 543, 549, 551
Linneweber, V., 73
Linschoten, J., 105

Lipman-Blumen, J., 450, 457
Lipscomb, D. M., 500
Lipscomb, J., 564
Lipsey, M. W., 229, 548
Little, B., 4, 29, 668
Little, P. E., 148
Little, R., 307
Litwak, H., 477
Litwak, J. M., 470
Livesey, N., 174
Livieratos, C., 277
Lloyd, K. E., 531
Lloyd, R. E., 249, 251
Llwellyn, L., 69
Lober, D. J., 550, 551
Lodwick, D., 565
Loehlin, J. C., 257, 259, 269
Loewy, B. Z., 542
Lofland, L., 357
London, W. B., 486
Long, M., 677, 678
Long, R., 451
Longley, P. A., 252
Lonigan, C. J., 516
Loomis, J. M., 249, 250, 251
Loomis, R., 462, 464, 466
Lopes, L. L., 595
López, R., 58
Lord, K. R., 548
Lorsch, H., 452
Losito, B. D., 177, 367
Lothian, A., 680
Loucks, D. P., 603
Loudon, I. S., 395
Louis, T. A., 222, 224
Love, S. Q., 531
Low, S. M., 108, 148, 149
Lowe, W., 651, 652
Lubart, T., 449
Lubchenco, J., 163
Lucas, S. B., 406
Luce, R. D., 86, 596
Lucero, R. J., 483, 484
Lucid, S., 678, 680
Luck, R., 618
Luckmann, T., 98, 99, 104, 565
Ludlow, A., 449
Ludwig, T. D., 542
Luff, P., 654
Lukashok, A. K., 363
Luke, D. A., 218, 219
Lundmark, V., 240, 653, 655
Lunn, B., 662, 670
Lustig, N., 630
Lutter, T., 470
Lutzenhiser, L., 167, 168
Luzar, E. J., 545
Lyketsos, C., 385
Lyman, P., 663, 670
Lynch, K., 272, 278, 286, 325, 363, 662, 667
Lynn, D., 452
Lynne, G. D., 40, 546
Lynott, J., 590, 594

Maas, M. L., 378, 383
Mabey, D., 406
MacEachren, A. M., 249
MacFarlane, S. W., 483
Machlis, G. E., 167
Mackenzie, T. B., 134
Mackewn, A., 184
MacKintosh, E., 350
MacMahon, K., 487
Macnaghten, P., 45, 46, 161, 169
MacPherson, D. K., 328
Madansky, M., 223
Madell, J. R., 500, 501
Mader, G. G., 519
Maes, M., 483
Magaziner, J., 378
Magnusson, D., 4
Maguire, D. J., 248, 252, 253
Maguire, E. A., 174, 186
Maguire, P., 662, 670
Maier, P. A., 420
Mainieri, T., 245, 260, 545, 551
Majka, T. J., 416, 420
Makela, E., 544
Maki, R. H., 180
Makofske, W., 561, 565, 566, 577
Maldonado-Lugo, R., 18
Malinak, J., 229
Malinowski, J. C., 363, 364, 365, 366
Malone, E., 150
Malone, T., 34, 59
Maloney, M. P., 37
Mandal, M. K., 652
Mandell, W., 122
Mandler, G., 546
Mang, M., 367
Mangione, T., 416, 420, 422
Manley, J. T., 386
Mann, S. H., 330
Mann, T., 336
Mann, V. A., 184
Mannetti, I., 31
Manning, F. E., 205
Manning, J., 466
Mannix, M., 664
Manstead, A. S. R., 39
Manzo, L. C., 58, 550
Maple, T., 476
Marans, R., 40, 260, 293, 301, 621
Marans, W. W., 263
Marascuilo, L. A., 230
Marble, D. F., 244, 252
March, L., 275
Marchand, N., 380
Marchon, I., 431
Marcia, J. E., 371
Marcus, C. C., 293, 294
Margai, F. L., 549
Margalef, R., 59
Margulis, S., 293, 294, 309, 445, 448, 449, 451
Mark, D. M., 246, 251
Mark, M. M., 489
Markland, R. B., 484, 487

Markowitz, H., 476
Markowitz, J., 568
Markus, H., 579
Markus, T., 272, 283, 288, 449
Marmar, C. R., 131, 136
Marmot, M., 397, 406, 408
Marples, D. R., 560, 579
Marris, P., 140
Marsden, J., 387
Marshall, R., 611, 620
Marshall-Baker, A., 384
Martin, A., 400
Martin, C., 150, 152
Martin, F., 486, 615, 622
Martin, J., 66, 385
Martin, M., 208, 332
Martin, W., 465
Martínez-Alier, J., 59, 60
Martínez-Torvisco, J., 58
Martorella, H., 38, 39, 43
Martsolf, S. W., 245
Martson, L., 500
Martzke, J. S., 178
Marutza, V. R., 263
Masaki, S., 184
Mascolo, M. F., 547
Maslow, A., 655
Maslow, K., 378
Mason, C., 464
Mason, R., 245
Mason, W., 385
Massey, C., 470
Massey, D., 414
Massey, O., 59
Masterson-Allen, S., 570
Matheau, A., 75
Mathes, E. A., 431
Matheson, C., 91
Matrix, S., 347, 348
Matt, G. E., 229, 230
Mattelart, A., 59
Matthews, G. A., 527
Matthews, H., 366
Matthews, M. H., 184, 364
Matthews, R. W., 488
Mattoon, A., 76
Mattsson, R., 331
Maxwell, L., 369, 506
Mayer, H., 512
Mayer, J. A., 536
Mayer, R., 384
Mayerl, M., 607
Mayerl, R., 607
Maynard, H., 143
Mayne, T. J., 130
Mayo, C., 653
Mayo, E., 29
Mazerolle, L. G., 423
Mazey, M. E., 108, 347
Maziarka, S., 400
Mazumdar, S., 448
Mazur, A., 165, 560, 566, 572
Mazure, C., 135
Mazzerolle, L. G., 420

McAllister, C. L., 379, 381
McBride, R., 430
McBurney, D. H., 649
McCalla, M. E., 420
McCallum, R. C., 269
McCallum, T., 681
McCamant, K., 353, 354
McCarthy, D., 505
McCarty, J. A., 543
McCaughey, B. G., 511
McCaul, K. D., 180
McClannahan, L. E., 330
McCleary, R., 516
McClellan, P. J., 138
McClelland, C. L., 88
McClelland, L., 531
McClintock, M., 235
McCloskey, M., 632
McColl, S., 450
McCollum, A. T., 140
McCord, C., 406
McCormick, K., 207
McCorquodale, D., 348
McCoy, J., 447, 448, 450, 453, 454, 455
McCracken, A. L., 378, 379
McCue, M., 180
McDonnell, R. A., 253
McDougle, C. J., 135
McDowell, L., 194, 351
McElroy, J. C., 651
McFarlane, B. L., 38
McGee, T., 563, 565, 570
McGinn, R., 502, 503
McGuire, R. H., 550
McGuire, T., 149
McIndoe, G., 308
McIntyre, P., 153, 561
McKay, C. P., 653
McKearnan, S., 598, 610, 618, 623
McKenna, K. Y. A., 665
McKenna, W. R., 97
McKenzie, R. D., 665
McKenzie-Mohr, D., 36, 39, 56, 57, 58, 67, 328, 532, 551
McKibben, B., 585
McLain-Kark, J., 384
McLellen, T., 568
McMahon, T. A., 260, 547
McManus, P., 463
McMichael, A., 394, 399, 402
McNaughton, B. L., 186
McQuaid, M., 347
McSween, T. E., 527
McWhorter, J., 531
Meadows, D. H., 33, 34, 57, 60
Meadows, D. L., 33, 34, 57, 60
Meagher, M. W., 180, 181, 182
Medley, C., 249
Medyckyj-Scott, D. J., 251, 255
Meecham, W. C., 503
Meehan, R. L., 519
Meeks, J. W., 421
Meertens, R. M., 42
Meffert, H., 75

Mehrabian, A., 652
Meidinger, E., 66
Meier, R. F., 165
Meira, M. E., 632
Meisels, M., 648
Melillo, J. M., 163
Melin, L., 386
Mellen, J., 475
Melton, A., 464, 467, 468, 469, 471, 473
Melzack, R., 182
Menard, S., 544
Meng, X.-L., 230
Menzies, R., 134
Merleau-Ponty, M., 98, 106, 107
Merry, S. E., 418
Mertig, A. G., 38, 58, 164, 165, 545
Mertz, C. K., 564, 576, 578
Messick, D. M., 41, 42, 43, 44, 46, 88, 90
Messner, S. F., 481
Metastasio, M., 43, 45
Metastasio, R., 45, 60
Metcalf, R. C., 174
Metzger, W., 95
Metzler, T. J., 136
Meyer-Arnold, E. A., 387, 388
Meyerowitz, J. J., 351
Meyrowitz, J., 669, 670
Michael, M., 45
Michael, R. P., 486
Michaelson, L., 611
Michels, K. M., 222
Michelson, W., 166, 263, 293, 301, 347, 349, 352, 357, 621, 661, 665, 666
Mickunas, A., 97
Mies, M., 108
Mikami, S., 517
Mikkelson, E., 560, 566, 577
Mikula, G., 41
Milbrath, L., 57, 60, 565, 570, 571, 576, 577
Miles, D., 301
Miles, M. A., 177, 367
Miles, R., 465
Mileti, D. S., 512, 513, 515, 517, 518, 520, 521
Milgram, S., 656, 665, 667, 670
Millar, S., 33
Miller, D., 542, 546, 547, 579
Miller, G. A., 116
Miller, J. G., 118
Miller, G. T., Jr., 57
Miller, M., 465
Miller, N., 486
Miller, P., 519, 560, 562, 563, 566, 571, 574, 576, 577, 579
Miller, R., 63, 560, 576, 577
Milroy, B. M., 355
Min, Y., 278
Minami, H., 11, 47, 219
Mineka, S., 134
Minkler, M., 632

Mintz, N., 655
Minuchin, S., 3
Mishima, H. R., 542
Mishima, K., 383, 385
Mitchell, C., 630
Mitchell, C. M., 379, 381, 383
Mitchell, C. R., 158
Mitchell, J., 76, 134
Mitchell, M. F., 483, 485
Mitchell, R., 164, 165, 400, 578
Mitchell, W. J., 663
Mitgang, L. D., 356
Mitrany, M., 196, 213
Miyata, Y., 651
Mobley, A. S., 548
Moeser, S. D., 430
Moffat, S. D., 185
Mohanty, J. N., 97
Mol, A. P. J., 169
Moleski, W., 293
Molotch, H., 566
Monaco, C., 378
Monahan, D. R., 431
Moneta, G. B., 233
Monson, N., 180
Montada, L., 36, 40, 41, 547
Montagne, M., 327
Montello, D. R., 249, 250, 251
Montero, M., 662
Mooney, H. A., 163
Mooney, P., 385
Moore, C., 599, 600
Moore, D. A., 87
Moore, G., 31, 285, 293, 365, 609, 616
Moore, H., 358, 515
Moore, J., 4, 8
Moore, K. D., 379, 381
Moore, R., 74, 363
Moore, S., 545
Moos, R. H., 490, 491, 665, 666
Morales, M., 74, 75
Moran, E. F., 150
Moreno, E., 56, 58, 60, 61, 62, 64, 68, 69, 70, 71, 75
Morgan, C., 544
Morgan, D. G., 379, 384
Morgenstern, O., 86
Morley, D., 347
Moro, J., 184
Morrin, K. A., 431
Morris, J., 406
Morrison, D. E., 164
Morrow, P. C., 651
Morstad, A. L., 185
Mortensen, B. K., 565
Moscovici, S., 33, 41, 58, 60
Moser, C., 347, 349, 350, 351, 353, 355, 356
Moser, G., 56, 58, 75
Mosher, C., 577
Mosley, J., 430
Mosteller, F., 222, 224
Moxen, J., 64, 66
Moxness, K., 452

Muchow, H., 102, 108
Muchow, M., 102, 108
Mueller, C., 261
Mugerauer, R., 106, 109
Mukherjee, N., 651
Mukopadhyay, T., 240, 653, 655
Mullen, B., 225
Mulligan, C. B., 234, 237
Munné, F., 61
Munyon, W. H., 309, 312
Murphy, M., 545
Murray, C., 417
Murray, H. A., 4
Myers, J. P., 566
Myers, R. A., 651
Myers, S., 387, 388
Myerson, G., 45

Nabhan, G. P., 152
Nadar, L., 596
Nadler, N., 500, 502, 503, 504
Nakasone, T., 501, 504
Namazi, K. H., 382, 383, 384, 387, 388
Napton, M. L., 572
Narayana, C., 223
Nasar, J. L., 336, 662
Nash, R. F., 35
Natanson, M., 107
Nazarea, V., 151
Nebes, R., 452
Negley, E. N., 386
Negroponte, N. P., 662, 663
Neisser, U., 4
Nelkin, D., 566
Nelson, G., 381
Nelson, J., 383
Nelson, M., 347
Nemiroff, L. S., 57, 58, 551
Nesdale, A. R., 545
Nesselroade, J. R., 3
Netten, A., 379, 380, 383
Netting, R. M., 148
Neuberg, S. L., 525
Neuman, K., 543
Neutra, R., 564
Newberry, B., 569
Newbrough, J. R., 39
Newburry, W. E., 38
Newby, H., 350
Newcomb, K., 33
Newcombe, N., 186, 431
Newell, P. B., 367, 368, 369, 370
Newhouse, N., 545
Newman, O., 326, 414, 416, 648
Newman, R. W., 482
Newsham, G., 450
Ng, C. F., 331
Ngo, L. H., 569
Nicell, P. L., 385
Nichols, U., 477
Nie, N. H., 665
Niebuhr, M. A., 301
Nielsen, J. Mc. C., 40

Nielson, J. M., 329, 542, 543
Nieme, P., 452
Nieuwdorp, G. H. E., 570, 571, 572, 577
Nigg, J. M., 517, 519, 562
Nijkamp, P., 191
Nishiyama, S., 11
Niskar, A. S., 500
Noack, P., 364, 367
Noam, E. M., 670
Nobili, G., 378
Noe, F. P., 58, 264, 543
Nonaka, I., 613
Norberg, A., 381
Norberg-Schulz, C., 107, 109
Norcross, J. C., 130
Norman, D., 31, 465, 474
Norris, F., 515
North, C., 569, 576
Northrup, J., 464
Norton, D. P., 310
Noschis, K., 609, 619
Nowicki, S., 651
Null, R., 195
Nunnally, J. C., 263
Nurminen, M., 394
Nutter, J. B., 419
Nyamwange, M., 544
Nyerges, T. L., 246, 251

O'Donnell, C. R., 208, 219
Oakey, R., 483
Obregon-Salido, F. J., 550
O'Brian, B., 430
O'Brien, M., 364, 366
O'Connor, J., 502, 503
O'Connor, M., 64
Odum, E. P., 31
Ogden, J., 476
Öhman, M., 46
Ohta, R. J., 384, 387
Okabe, A., 431
Okawa, M., 383, 385
O'Keeffe, M., 568, 569
Okuda, S. M., 58, 551
Oldeman, R. A. A., 34
Oldenburg, B., 549
Oldham, G., 451
O'Leary, E. S., 515
O'Leary, M., 329
O'Leary, R., 591, 593, 598
Olivegren, J., 608
Oliver-Smith, A., 148
Olkin, I., 224, 225, 226, 227, 228
Olmsted, J. E., 152
Olsen, H., 327
Olsen, M., 549, 565
Olsen, R., 431, 467
Olshansky, E., 184
Olson, G. W., 483, 484
Olson, J., 445, 451, 543
Olson, L., 218, 328, 414
Olson, M., 88
Olson, M., Jr., 40, 41, 42

Olson, R., 60
Olsson, T., 367
Omahe, K., 59
O'Meara, M., 76
Omori, Y., 651
O'Neal, E. C., 504, 652
O'Neill, B., 33
O'Neill, M., 325, 430
Opotow, S., 35, 41, 603
Oppenheimer, F., 465
Orbell, J., 88
Orcutt, J. D., 653
Orhun, D., 284
Orians, G., 449, 649
O'Riordan, T., 512
Ormandy, D., 400, 402
Orme-Johnson, D. W., 483
Ornstein, S. W., 309
Orr, D., 565
Ortiz, P., 630
Orwin, R. G., 229
Orwoll, E. S., 185
Oskamp, S., 36, 37, 39, 42, 56, 57, 58, 61, 63, 67, 75, 85, 245, 260, 481, 491, 525, 526, 527, 530, 542, 544, 545, 551, 669
Osmond, H., 324
Osterberg, A. E., 346
Ostroff, C., 229
Ostrom, E., 40, 59
O'Sullivan, D., 275, 276
Osvath, A., 137
Ottum, M., 561
Oulette, J., 451
Overton, W., 431
Oviatt, S. K., 185
Owens, P., 279, 364, 365, 614
Oxley, D., 104, 203, 205, 206, 207, 211, 215
Ozawa, C., 191
Oziemkowska, M., 122

Packard, R., 428, 429, 430
Pader, E. J., 355
Paigen, B., 576, 577
Painter, J., 543
Painter, S. L., 141, 142
Painter, T. S., 548
Palinkas, L. A., 575
Palmer, K., 155
Palmorani, A., 59
Pandey, J., 488
Pandora, K., 124
Papaleo, B., 502
Pape, K. D., 651
Pardini, A. U., 530
Park, R., 665
Parker, P. M., 481
Parker, R. N., 486
Parkinson, D., 513
Parkkila, S., 370
Parks, C. D., 88
Parmelee, P. P., 208
Parrott, W. G., 489

Parshall, S. A., 307
Parsons, K. C., 482, 486
Parsons, R., 174, 177, 179, 182, 184
Parsons, Y., 384, 386
Pascal, B., 172
Passchier, W. F., 500, 502, 503, 508
Passchier-Vermeer, W., 500, 502, 503, 508
Passerini, E., 520, 521
Passini, R., 380, 427, 430, 431
Pastalan, L. A., 668
Pasternak, B. S., 505
Pastides, H., 394
Pastor, S. K., 69, 578
Pat-Horenczyk, R., 385
Patterson, D., 180, 468, 469, 471, 473, 477
Patterson, M., 240, 648, 653, 655
Patterson, P., 566
Patton, M. Q., 601, 619
Paulesich, R., 67
Paulson, F. L., 491
Paulus, P., 196, 401, 402, 403, 488
Pawlik, K., 35, 36, 39, 236
Paxson, L., 349, 350, 352
Paykel, E. S., 140
Paz, D. H., 519
Pearlman, E., 430
Pearson, J., 67
Pearson, K., 222
Peart, R., 471
Pease, K., 417
Pease, W. S., 71
Peatross, D., 281
Pedersen, D. M., 651
Pedersen, P., 59
Peeters, D., 483
Peicott, J., 9
Peled, A., 141
Pellegrino, J., 184, 249, 250, 251, 381
Pelletier, L. G., 544, 550
Pelto, P., 150
Peña, W., 303, 307
Penn, A., 271, 275, 276, 277, 278, 279, 280, 281
Pennebaker, J. W., 488
Penner, B., 348
Peponis, J., 275, 276, 277, 278, 279, 280, 281, 282, 285, 430
Pepper, S. C., 203
Pereira, J., 515, 516
Perez, K., 387
Perez, M. E., 548
Perin, C., 573
Peris, M. E., 66
Perkins, D., 122, 216, 219, 421, 581
Perry, J. D., 486
Perry, R., 517
Perry, S., 180
Pershing, A., 431
Persinger, M. A., 489, 493
Perucci, F., 622
Perugini, M., 39, 259
Peter, T., 157

Peters, M. L., 502
Peterson, A., 481
Peterson, C., 567
Peterson, R., 347, 350
Peterson, T., 602
Petterson, J., 575
Pettigrew, T., 58
Pettus, A. M., 548
Petty, R. E., 178, 209, 546
Peuquet, T. J., 252
Pezdek, K., 286
Philip, D., 56
Phillips, C., 379, 381, 383
Phillips, K., 185
Piaget, J., 275
Pickles, J., 108
Picou, J. S., 560, 567, 568, 572, 574, 575
Picou, S. J., 575
Pierce, M., 468, 477
Piercy, M., 348
Pihlström, N., 364
Pillemer, D. B., 224
Pine, E., 654
Pinheiro, J., 58, 260, 264
Pirages, D., 565
Pistiner, A. H., 327
Pitkin, H., 616
Pitt, D., 37, 56
Plakke, B. L., 500
Platt, A., 76
Platt, J., 85
Platt, R. H., 512
Podd, J. V., 134
Podpadec, T. J., 46
Poe, D. B., 331
Pogrebin, L. C., 429
Pogue, W., 678, 680
Poku, N., 155
Pol, E., 35, 56, 57, 58, 59, 60, 61, 62, 67, 69, 70, 71, 73, 74, 75
Pollak, C. P., 503
Pollock, P. H., 572
Pollock, V. E., 486
Polt, J. M., 178, 179
Popkin, S. J., 414
Porfiriev, B. N., 511
Porter, B. E., 39, 525, 526, 530, 531, 542
Porter, W. L., 307, 308, 310
Posey, D. A., 151
Postel, S., 57, 76
Potapchuk, W., 600
Potter, J., 45
Powell, J. D., 578
Powell, K., 317
Poynter, J., 681
Prabhu, M., 337
Pravatiner, M. A., 420
Preiser, W. F. E., 293, 294, 295, 306, 307, 308, 309, 310, 331, 335, 619, 622
Preisser, J. S., 379, 381, 383
Presson, C. C., 249

Preston, D. A., 486
Price, L. H., 135
Price, M., 59, 383
Price, P., 569, 576
Price, R. H., 116, 117
Price, S. K., 653
Prince, S. H., 512
Proffitt, M., 387
Proshansky, H., 29, 35, 191, 368, 370, 401
Proshansky, H. H., 661, 665
Proshansky, H. M., 17, 28, 29, 47, 58, 85, 108, 301, 661, 665, 669, 672
Pruitt, C., 381
Pruitt, D. G., 86, 87, 590
Prussin, L., 348
Prybeck, T. R., 560, 569
Punch, M., 24
Punsola, A., 73
Putnam, L. L., 602, 603
Putnam, P. D., 669
Puy, A., 75
Pynoos, J., 384, 387

Quarantelli, E. L., 511, 512, 517
Quick, D. L., 476
Quinn, C., 650
Quintana, F., 59
Quirk, M., 10

Rabinowitz, H. Z., 306, 307, 308, 309, 310, 619, 622
Rabinowitz, V. C., 577
Rae, S., 385
Raffestin, C., 395, 396, 409
Raft, D., 180
Rafter, K., 327
Raggi, G., 378
Rahe, R. H., 140
Rahmani, M., 40, 546
Raifa, H., 86, 596
Rainforth, M. V., 483
Rainville, C., 380
Rainville, P., 180
Rajecki, R., 385, 388
Rampazi, M., 623
Rand, J., 469, 470, 474
Randers, J., 33, 34, 57, 60
Ranieri, P., 378
Ransberger, V. M., 484
Ranyard, R., 45
Raper, J. F., 252, 253
Rapoport, A., 29, 30, 31, 86, 87, 88, 196, 417, 448, 449, 455, 609
Rapoport, R., 38
Rapp, H., 123
Rappaport, J., 59, 218, 219, 632
Rappaport, R. A., 148
Rashid, M., 275, 276, 279
Rasmussen, S. A., 135
Rathunde, K., 233, 239
Ratiu, E., 58
Ratner, H. H., 366
Raudenbush, S. W., 237, 489, 492

Ravetz, A., 406
Raw, G. J., 309
Raymond, L. W., 502
Rayner, S., 150, 152, 153
Rea, M., 451
Read, S., 279
Reams, M. A., 551
Recchia, V., 75
Rechlin, L., 382
Recktenwald, W., 338
Redclift, M., 161, 163, 164, 167, 168
Redford, K. H., 152
Redondo, J. P., 6
Reed, D., 630
Reeves, J. L., 182, 384
Regnier, V., 385
Rehner, T., 568
Reich, M., 577, 579
Reichel, D. A., 531
Reicher, S., 45, 46
Reid, D., 568
Reifman, A. S., 492
Reiger, H., 67
Reim, B., 564
Reis, H. T., 234
Reiskin, E. D., 38
Reitsma, R., 604
Reizenstein, J. E., 307, 310, 332
Reko, H. K., 560, 574, 576
Relph, E., 30, 108
Remesar, A., 73, 75
Remland, M. S., 651
Rendell, J., 348
Rengert, G., 419
Renner, M., 76, 541
Reno, R. R., 39, 44, 89, 90
Repola, A., 46
Reppeto, R. C., 57
Reser, J. P., 219
Rheingold, H., 615, 623, 663
Rhind, D. W., 248, 252, 253
Rhudy, J. L., 180, 181, 182
Ribeiro, G. L., 150
Rich, R., 122, 421, 571
Rich, V., 560
Richards, J., 138
Richards, M. H., 235, 236, 238, 239
Richardson, K., 467
Ricoeur, P., 150
Ridley, S., 561
Rieradevall, J., 71
Riger, S., 194, 349
Riley, A. W., 531
Rimé, B., 488
Rind, B., 490
Rindskopf, D., 224
Rioux, S., 11
Ristvedt, S. L., 134
Ritondale, G., 378
Rittel, H. W. J., 593
Ritzdorf, M., 194, 351, 353, 356
Rivano-Fischer, M., 651
Rivlin, L., 18, 21, 22, 23, 28, 85, 301, 369, 401, 661, 665

Robbins, C., 307
Roberts, M., 351
Roberts, W., 651
Robertson, J., 561
Robins, L. N., 560, 569
Robinson, E., 464, 467, 470, 471, 472
Robinson, J., 234
Robinson, M. D., 180
Roca, M., 67
Rochberg-Halton, E., 349, 669
Rocheleau, D., 148
Rodin, M., 575
Rodriguez, V. C., 618
Roeder, S., 652
Roederer, J., 34, 59
Roehl, J., 420
Roenigk, D., 516
Roessler, G., 449
Rogers, E. M., 549
Rogers, G. O., 517
Rogge, M., 570, 572
Rogoff, B., 29, 30, 98, 110, 195, 203, 609
Rohe, W. R., 419
Rohles, F. H., Jr., 485
Roininen, J., 613, 619, 622
Rollag, M., 451
Roncek, D. W., 420
Ronis, D. L., 89
Roodman, D., 76
Rook, K. S., 664
Room, R., 486
Roosens, E., 142
Roosevelt, A., 148
Roper, J., 167
Rosa, E. A., 167, 168, 169
Rose, G., 347
Rosebrook, D., 568
Rosen, G., 399
Rosen, L. D., 653
Rosenbaum, D. P., 414, 422
Rosenberg, M. S., 225
Rosenfeld, S., 465
Rosenheck, T., 313
Rosenstock, I. M., 549
Rosenthal, R., 193, 224, 225, 229, 230, 491, 595
Rosner, T. T., 382, 384
Rosner, V., 348
Rosnow, R., 193, 224, 230
Ross, C., 279
Ross, E., 148, 483
Ross, H., 648
Ross, M. H., 601
Ross, R. J., 481
Ross, V., 383, 385
Rossano, M. J., 249
Rossi, J., 75
Rossi, P. H., 515, 516, 520
Roszak, T., 35, 38, 653
Rothblatt, D. N., 347, 350
Rothman, J., 601
Rothman, S. M., 352
Rothschild, J., 348

Rotstein, A., 157
Rotton, J., 481, 483, 484, 485, 486, 487, 489, 490, 491, 492, 493
Rouse, M. A., 565
Rovet, J. F., 185
Rowell, A., 542
Rowles, G., 141
Roys, M., 309
Ruback, R. B., 488, 651
Rubenson, D., 449
Rubin, C., 500, 516
Rubin, D. B., 225, 230
Rubin, G., 348
Rubin, J. Z., 590
Rubinstein, C., 481
Rubinstein, N. J., 131, 141
Rudd, J. R., 530
Rudel, T. K., 167
Rueda, S., 73, 75
Ruedi, K., 348
Ruff, C., 184
Ruggieri, V., 651
Ruggles, A. J., 249
Rule, B., 450
Runco, M., 449
Runnion, A., 531
Russell, D., 561
Russell, J., 196, 575
Russell, J. A., 30, 37, 336, 363
Russell, J. C., 575
Russell, M., 486
Rustin, M., 364, 366
Ryan, M., 76
Ryan, R. M., 542, 544
Ryan, W., 579
Rydin, Y., 45

Sabini, J., 489
Sabo, K., 613, 614, 619
Sabucedo, J. M., 56
Sachs, A., 76
Sacilotto, P. A., 651, 652
Sadan, E., 632
Saegert, S., 30, 35, 56, 213, 326, 348, 349, 351, 355, 357, 363
Sagalyn, L., 191
Sage, C., 167, 168
Sagi, P., 519
Sagie, A., 640
Sahlins, M., 149
Said, E., 150
St. John, M., 465
Sakuma, N., 184
Salkovskis, P. M., 134
Sally, D., 87
Salman, A., 180
Sampat, P., 76
Sampat, S., 76
Sampson, C. S., 599
Samuelson, C. D., 85, 90
Sánchez, E., 631, 638, 639, 641
Sand, L. K., 541, 548, 552
Sandercock, L., 194
Sanders, D. H., 143

Sanders, J. L., 489
Sanders, P., 451
Sandler, H., 652
Sanger, D. E., 500
Sanoff, H., 74, 293, 335, 431, 607, 608, 614, 618, 619, 621, 622, 624
Sansone, C., 219, 544
Santandreu, A., 631
Sarason, I. G., 668
Sarbin, T. R., 30
Sasanuma, S., 184
Satin, K., 564
Satlin, A., 383, 385
Savage, L. J., 86
Savino, B., 502, 503
Savitsky, J., 572
Sawhill, R., 500
Saxton, J., 380
Sayette, M. A., 130
Scandura, D. A., 384
Scarborough, J., 651
Scarr, S., 4
Schachter, S., 661, 669
Schaefer, A., 64
Schaeffer, M., 568
Schan, J., 36
Schapp, W., 106
Schein, E. H., 316
Schelling, T., 596
Scherer, K. R., 546
Scherl, L. M., 219
Scherlis, W., 240, 653, 655
Schiavo, R., 364, 365, 650
Schiele, B., 464
Schlossberg, R., 489
Schmidt, F. L., 224, 225
Schmidt, J., 16
Schmittberger, R., 87
Schmitz, S., 184, 186
Schnaiberg, A., 166, 167
Schneekloth, L., 194, 307, 308, 310, 356, 357, 611, 612, 613
Schneider, B., 233, 234, 235, 236, 237, 238, 239
Schneider, F., 450
Schoenfeld, A. C., 165
Schoggen, P., 115, 116, 122, 123, 665, 670
Scholten, H. J., 253
Schön, D., 307, 308, 310, 312, 313, 315, 613
Schoolmeesters, L. J., 180
Schorr, J., 560, 576
Schrage, M., 443
Schramm, P., 662, 670
Schramm, U., 307, 308, 309
Schroeder, A., 282, 652
Schroeder, K., 560
Schubert, F., 75
Schuett, M. A., 64, 74
Schuler, D., 653, 663
Schultz, P. W., 245, 542, 543, 545, 546, 551
Schumacher, D., 547

Schumacher, S., 464
Schumacher, T., 279
Schur, K., 501
Schütz, A., 98, 99, 104, 107
Schwab, J., 563
Schwartz, G. E., 4
Schwartz, H., 141
Schwartz, S. H., 38, 39, 40, 89, 90,
    256, 542, 543
Schwarz, N., 489
Schwarze, B., 87
Schwarzwald, J., 180
Schwela, D., 394
Schwepker, C. H., 548
Schwerin, D., 579
Scoones, I., 148, 150
Scott, A. L., 648
Scott, D., 260, 545
Scott, G., 381
Scott, M. M., 124
Scott, P., 431
Scott, R., 579
Scott, T. E., 249
Scotuzzi, A., 378
Screven, C., 462, 463, 464, 466, 469,
    470, 471, 473, 474
Seamon, D., 96, 97, 106, 107, 108,
    109, 215
Sebba, R., 364
Secchiaroli, G., 29, 30, 31, 35, 37, 47,
    56, 609
Seebohm, T. M., 97
Sefscik, A., 650
Seguin, C., 550
Seidel, A., 376
Seidl, C., 86
Seidman, E., 218, 219
Selam, J., 151
Seligman, C., 328, 329, 551
Seligman, M., 567
Selin, S. W., 64, 74
Seltzer, E., 191
Selye, H., 670
Semenik, R., 543
Sensales, G., 43, 45, 60
Serena, J. M., 67, 71
Serlin, R. C., 230
Serrato, M., 281, 447, 448
Serrell, B., 463, 472, 474
Servino, L., 378
Sexton, R. J., 329
Shachter, S., 29
Shadish, W. R., 224
Shafer, L., 465
Shannon, M. P., 516
Shaper, A., 406
Sharma, A., 618
Sharp, L., 615, 616, 617
Sharpe, D., 229
Sharpe, T., 614, 620
Shatkin, S. F., 483
Shats, M., 489, 491
Shaw, H., 507
Shaw, L. G., 570, 571, 576, 577

Sheaffer, J., 512
Shehayeb, D., 454
Shelley, T. L., 565
Shepherdson, D., 475
Sherif, C. W., 44
Sherif, M., 44
Sherman, M. F., 548
Sherman, N. C., 548
Sherry, D. F., 184, 186
Sherwood, D. L., 58, 551
Shettel, H., 464, 465, 466
Shettel-Neuber, J., 475
Shibley, R., 306, 307, 308, 310, 317,
    356, 611, 612, 613
Shimmin, S., 61
Shimoda, T. A., 259, 543
Shin, M. B., 173
Shipman, K., 542
Shippee, G., 328, 531
Shiva, V., 108
Shkilnyk, A., 563
Shoaf, K., 516
Shoesmith, J., 386
Sholl, M. J., 249
Shonholtz, R., 599
Shore, R. E., 505
Shorrock, L., 408
Shoultz, B., 142
Shpancer, N., 3
Shrader-Frechette, K. S., 577
Shrivastava, P., 560, 576
Shrum, L. J., 543
Shullaw, G., 383
Shumaker, S. A., 207
Shusterman, D., 564
Sieber, J. E., 15, 16, 20
Siegel, S., 142
Siero, F., 329
Siero, S., 329
Sigelman, C. K., 652
Siksna, A., 279
Silbereisen, R. K., 364, 367
Silverman, I., 184, 185
Silverman, M. A., 379, 381
Sime, J., 56, 61, 609
Simmel, G., 120
Simmons, D. A., 325, 330, 331, 431,
    439
Simmons, J., 550
Simon, D., 423
Simon, H. A., 666
Simons, G., 653, 655
Simons, R. F., 177, 367
Simpson, M. E., 486
Sims, W., 446
Sinclair, R. C., 489
Singer, E., 566
Singer, J., 452, 505, 564, 568, 571, 670
Singh, R., 662, 670
Sinha, S. P., 651
Sitarenios, G., 185
Sivek, D. J., 544
Siverman, I., 185
Skea, D., 378, 379, 386

Skinner, B. F., 527, 530, 531
Skogan, W. G., 415
Skorjanc, A. D., 652
Skorpamich, M. A., 286
Slater, P., 571
Sloan, D., 364, 366
Sloane, P. D., 378, 379, 381, 383, 387,
    388
Slop, M., 327
Slough, D., 464
Slovic, P., 37, 75, 147, 519, 560, 564,
    566, 571, 576, 578, 579
Smeltzer, L., 651
Smith, A., 452
Smith, B. J., 651
Smith, C., 286, 568
Smith, E., 560, 569, 576
Smith, F., 365, 369
Smith, G. T., 263, 269
Smith, H. G., 503
Smith, M., 117, 120, 194
Smith, R. E., 668
Smith, R. H., 180
Smith, S., 209, 400, 546
Smith-Sebasto, N. J., 548
Sneider, C., 465
Sneider, G., 465
Snodgrass, J., 196
Snook-Hill, M., 651
Snow, J. N., 651
Snow, R., 58, 264
Snyder, M., 41, 42, 43, 415, 416
Snyder-Hiatt, L. H., 380
So, F., 191
Sobel, D., 363, 369
Soderstrom, J., 560
Sohn, D., 228, 229
Soliman, H., 563
Solomon, S. D., 560, 569
Sommer, B., 364, 365
Sommer, R., 29, 31, 117, 122, 208,
    281, 293, 294, 324, 327, 330, 332,
    609, 647, 648, 651, 669
Sommers, P., 491
Sonnenfeld, D. A., 169
Sörbom, D., 257
Sorensen, J., 69, 517, 560
Soskin, M., 40
Soulé, M., 150
Southworth, M., 279
Spain, D., 347, 348, 355
Spangle, W. E., 519
Speck, B. W., 228
Spencer, C., 367, 430
Spencer, H., 649
Spiegelberg, H., 96, 97
Spinhoven, P., 134
Sprague, J., 347, 350, 354
Sprandel, G., 653
Spreckelmeyer, K., 293, 309
Sproull, L., 654
Srivastava, P., 652
Staats, H., 39, 40, 368, 546
Stadler, S. J., 483, 485, 487

Staffans, A., 620
Stall, S., 355
Stallings, R. A., 512
Stamps, A. E., 223, 226, 227, 228, 336
Standers, R., 489, 491
Standeven, M., 306, 309
Standing, L., 452
Stanley, L., 307
Stansell, C., 350
Stansfeld, S., 502, 506
Stanton-Hicks, M., 180
Staples, B., 205, 210, 214
Staples, S., 564
Stark, N., 550
Starke, L., 76
Stea, D., 325, 430, 612, 613, 618, 622, 662
Steadman, P., 275
Stedinger, J. R., 603
Steel, G. D., 174
Steele, C., 385
Steele, F., 446, 448, 449
Steinmayer, K. M., 22
Steinsapir, C., 583
Steketee, G., 135
Stenzel, J., 502, 507
Stephens, K. K., 652
Stephens, S., 576
Stephenson, J. S., III, 517
Steptoe, A., 370
Sterling, E., 451
Stern, E., 249
Stern, J. A., 179
Stern, P., 35, 36, 37, 38, 39, 40, 41, 42, 46, 47, 56, 57, 58, 59, 73, 85, 90, 165, 168, 259, 260, 328, 525, 526, 527, 537, 543, 551, 580, 603
Stern, R. M., 253
Stern, W., 647
Sternberg, R., 449
Sternlieb, J., 435
Stevenson, G., 400
Steward, J., 149
Stewart, N. J., 379, 384
Stimpson, C., 347
Stoffle, R., 152, 153, 561
Stoinski, T., 476
Stokes, E., 466
Stokols, D., 3, 4, 5, 6, 8, 28, 29, 30, 35, 37, 47, 55, 56, 123, 130, 136, 147, 149, 193, 196, 309, 363, 400, 403, 450, 451, 452, 525, 541, 607, 661, 662, 664, 665, 666, 667, 669, 671
Stoll, C., 653
Stone, J., 561
Stone, J. I., 488
Stone, J. V., 153
Stone, R., 563, 570, 571, 576
Stonich, S., 150
Strachan, P. A., 64, 66
Straf, M. L., 224
Strand, R. L., 501
Strathman, A., 549
Stratton, L. O., 648

Straus, E., 105
Strauss, A., 118, 213
Strayer, J., 651
Streff, F. M., 530
Stringer, E., 612
Stringer, P., 4, 8
Ströker, E., 102, 108
Strube, M. J., 228, 230, 651
Stuart, L. I., 69
Stueland, T., 501
Stump, C., 374, 375, 377, 388
Suárez, E., 58
Subotincic, N., 138
Sudman, S., 234
Sue, D., 3
Sue, S., 3
Suedfeld, P., 131, 174, 336
Suleiman, R., 87, 88
Suler, J., 655
Sull, K. K., 652
Sullivan, S. E., 229
Sullivan, W. C., 337, 367
Suman, M., 662, 670
Summit, J. E., 651
Sumner, N. R., 260, 550
Sundström, E., 196, 363, 443, 444, 448, 457
Sundström, P., 622
Sunn, K. M., 650
Sureda, V., 57, 72
Surrette, M. A., 431
Susskind, L., 598, 610, 618, 623
Svane, F., 614
Svane, O., 73
Svenson, O., 37, 147
Swan, J. H., 364
Swanson, D. C., 58, 551
Swanson, E. A., 378, 383
Sweaney, A. L., 207, 211
Sweep, F. C. G. J., 502
Swift, J., 475
Swinkels, L. M. J. W., 502
Swinson, R. P., 133
Syme, G. J., 260, 328, 545, 547, 549, 550, 603
Symes, M., 307
Szalai, A., 408
Szasz, A., 164, 561, 563, 572, 573, 577
Szigeti, F., 316, 317

Tacken, M., 486
Tacon, P., 368
Tagg, S. K., 325
Taira, K., 501, 504
Tajfel, H., 41, 43, 58, 88
Takahashi, L., 194
Takahashi, T., 3
Takala, M., 36
Takashi, K., 383, 385
Takeuchi, H., 613
Talbot, J., 431, 449, 467
Tames, S., 382, 384
Tangney, J. P., 546, 547
Tanucci, G., 31

Tarr, D., 481
Tassinary, L. G., 173, 174, 175, 176, 177, 178, 179
Tauscher, J., 503
Taylor, A., 325, 367
Taylor, B., 325, 450
Taylor, C., 100, 105, 516
Taylor, D. E., 164, 167
Taylor, H., 251, 430
Taylor, J. E., 134
Taylor, J. R., 550
Taylor, N., 69, 607, 608, 610, 611
Taylor, P. J., 165
Taylor, P. W., 35
Taylor, R., 121, 122, 414, 415, 416, 417, 418, 420, 421, 422, 423, 455
Taylor, S., 259, 367, 370, 465, 546, 594
Teague, G. B., 486
Tedesco, J. F., 652
Teeland, L., 398
Teklenburg, J. A. F., 274
Tellegen, A., 178
Tempest, W., 502
Tepper, I., 180
Teresi, J., 378
Terrazas, A., 186
Tesh, S., 156
Tesser, A., 367
Tetlow, K., 382, 383, 384, 385
Thagard, N., 678, 679, 680
Tharp, R. G., 208, 219, 532, 535
Thibaut, J., 44, 549, 669
Thibodeau, R., 546, 547
Thiel, P., 272
Thiessen, E. M., 603
Thøgersen, J., 39, 40, 41, 89, 551
Thomas, S. L., 256, 269
Thomas-Larmer, J., 610, 618, 623
Thomas-Slayter, B., 148
Thompson, C., 603
Thompson, D., 66, 402, 463, 475
Thompson, P., 483
Thompson, S., 38, 259
Thorne, B., 348
Thornton, S., 572, 577
Thorpe, G. L., 133
Thurber, C. A., 363, 364, 365, 366
Tienda, M., 414
Tiernan, C. P., 346
Tierney, S., 451
Tillery, E., 483, 484, 486
Timm, N. H., 230
Timmermans, H. J. P., 274
Tinbergen, N., 648
Tipper, D. G., 651
Tisdal, C., 466, 467
Titchner, J. L., 560
Tittler, B., 652
Tobiasen, J. M., 652
Todd, H. F., 596
Todd, P., 259, 546
Tognoli, J., 397, 402
Tolman, E. C., 30, 101
Tomao, E., 502

Tomei, F., 502
Tomera, A. N., 36, 58, 223
Toplyn, G., 452
Torgerson, D., 61, 69
Torre, S., 347
Torres, P., 73
Tosteson, H., 578
Toth, R., 561
Tout, A., 465
Townsend, P., 148, 152
Townsley, S., 381
Trabucchi, M., 378, 383
Tracy, A. P., 551
Traugott, M., 153, 561
Travers, A., 653
Trevisan, M., 515
Trist, E. L., 663, 666
Troster, A. I., 184
Troutwine, R., 652
Troy, P., 191
Trufan, S. J., 135
Trump, R., 568
Tsourou, C., 400, 402
Tsu, V. D., 490
Tuan, Y.-F., 45, 108
Tuan, Y. R., 131
Turk, A., 246, 251
Turkel, A., 465
Turkle, S., 665, 669
Turnbull, O., 484
Turner, A., 275, 276
Turner, J., 41, 43, 58, 88, 248, 542, 608
Turner, R. H., 519
Turner, S. M., 137
Turner-Henson, A., 364
Tuson, K. M., 550
Tuxill, J., 76
Tversky, A., 46, 86, 595
Tversky, B., 251, 430
Twigger-Ross, C., 47, 367
Twitchell, F. S., 542
Tyler, T., 41, 42, 43, 549, 603
Tymitz, B., 465
Tyson, G. A., 484
Tzamir, Y., 325

Ulbricht, C. A., 245
Ulrich, R., 140, 174, 177, 182, 183, 367, 449, 547, 649, 653, 671
Underhill, P., 309
Unipan, J., 260
Unnava, H. R., 548
Untch, E. M., 548
Unwin, D. J., 249
Updegraff, N., 561
Urbanczyk, S., 652
Urry, J., 161, 169
Ursano, R. J., 511
Uzzell, D., 58, 60, 75, 367, 431

Vaidya, J., 178
Valdero, T., 260
Valentine, J. H., 483
Valera, S., 58, 59, 75

Valley, K. L., 87
Valsiner, J., 3
van Andel, J., 364, 366
van Bel, D., 662, 670
van de Kragt, A. J., 88
van den Berg, J. H., 105
Vandenberg, S. G., 184, 186
van der Steen, J., 488
Van Dyck, R., 134
van Eijndhoven, J. C. M., 570, 571, 572, 577
Vanetti, E., 430
Van Gerwen, L. J., 134
Van Houten, R., 527
Van Houwelingen, J. H., 329
van Knippenberg, A., 89
van Koppen, P. J., 484
Van Lange, P. A. M., 41, 42, 44
Van Liere, K. D., 37, 38, 40, 58, 165, 259, 260, 262, 264, 545
Vanman, E. J., 179
van Peursen, C. A., 98
Van Raaij, W. F., 329
van Vliet, M., 502
van Vliet, W., 347
Van Vugt, M., 41, 42, 43, 46, 85
Varian, H. R., 663, 670
Vaughan, E., 328
Vaughan, L., 281
Vayda, A. P., 150
Veiel, L., 385
Veitch, J., 450, 451
Veitch, R., 56, 488
Vela, C., 59
Venkatesh, S. A., 414
Verbaten, M. N., 180, 181, 182
Verplanken, B., 89
Vespä, K., 351, 352, 353, 354, 355, 356, 357, 358, 608
Vidal, T., 56, 73, 75
Videbeck, R., 179
Vining, J., 40, 75, 260, 542, 543, 544, 545, 547, 549, 550, 551
Vinsel, A., 212
Vis, A. A., 327
Vischer, J., 308, 309, 311, 331, 618, 619
Vissing, Y., 562, 576
Vitousek, P. M., 163
Vittas, M. E., 572
Vivas, J., 61
Vlahov, D., 122
Vlek, C., 36, 39, 41, 42, 46
Volicer, L., 383, 385
Volk, D., 512
von Bertalanffy, L., 666
Von Bismarck, W. B., 542
von Borgstede, C., 90
von Eye, A., 3
von Neumann, J., 86
von Uexküll, J., 5, 99, 647
von Uexkull, T., 580
Voogd, H., 611, 615
Voyer, D., 184

Voyer, S., 184
Vrij, A., 488, 651
Vyner, H., 560, 566

Wachs, M., 191
Wachs, T., 3, 505, 664, 665
Wachter, K. W., 224
Wacquant, I., 630
Wade, B., 283
Wagner, L., 378
Waldman, A., 379, 380
Walker, C. A., 648
Walker, L., 549
Wall, P. D., 182
Wallace, A., 513
Wallace-Jones, J., 69
Wallbaum, A. B. C., 174
Waller, D., 186
Walmsley, D. J., 491
Walters, B. B., 150
Walther, T., 75
Waltman, J., 651
Waltz, W., 180
Wandersman, A., 122, 421, 562, 566, 567, 571, 576
Wang, L., 516
Wang, S., 400, 401
Wang, T., 39, 530, 542
Wangari, E., 148
Wanous, J. P., 229
Wapner, S., 4, 6, 7, 8, 9, 10, 11, 12, 30, 35, 36, 47, 130, 219
Ward, C., 608
Ward, J., 491
Ward, L. M., 30, 37, 363
Ward, M. P., 37
Ward, S., 431
Warming, E., 665
Warren, D. H., 249
Warren, D. M., 151
Warren, N., 180
Wasilchick, J., 419
Wates, N., 608, 614, 615, 616, 617, 618, 621, 622, 624
Wathern, P., 63, 67
Watson, B. G., 525
Watson, D., 178, 489, 532, 535
Watson, G. B., 85
Watson, J. D., 531
Watson, R., 545
Wear, T. D., 249
Wearing, A. J., 260, 547
Webber, M. W., 593
Weber, P., 76
Weber, R., 493
Weber, T., 184
Weber-Burdin, E., 515, 516, 520
Weenig, M. W. H., 549
Weg, E., 88
Wegenburg, A. F. van, 274
Weibel, R., 248
Weick, K. E., 118
Weidema, B., 71
Weidemann, S., 309, 445, 451

Weigel, J., 37
Weigel, R. G., 654
Weigel, R. H., 37
Weil, M. M., 653
Weiland, P. S., 591, 593, 598
Weinberg, A. S., 166
Weinrich, M. W., 516
Weinrich, S., 516
Weinstein, M. D., 58
Weinstein, N., 550, 564, 566
Weinstock, J. S., 355
Weir, C., 544
Weisberg, H. F., 301
Weisburd, D., 414, 417, 419, 422
Weisenberg, M., 180
Weisman, G. D., 121, 376, 379, 382, 383, 386
Weisman, J., 286, 427, 431
Weisman, L. K., 347, 348, 355
Weiss, C. H., 307, 317
Weiss, D. S., 136
Weiss, M. J., 481
Weiss, W., 536
Weissman, M., 134, 140
Weist, D., 516
Weitch, J. A., 223
Weitzer, W. H., 282
Wekerle, G., 347, 349, 350, 351, 354
Welch, P., 311
Wellman, B., 661, 662, 670, 672
Wellman, J. D., 543
Wells, A., 134
Wells, N. M., 367
Welte, J. W., 486
Welter, B., 351
Wendt, J. S., 46
Wener, R., 309, 325
Wenger, W. D., 179
Wenzel, M., 41
Werlen, B., 97, 107
Werner, C., 26, 30, 104, 203, 204, 205, 206, 207, 208, 210, 211, 214, 215, 216, 217, 218, 219, 259, 328, 542, 544
Werner, H., 5, 6
Werner, P., 381
Wescoat, J. L., 512
West, J. P., 550
West, S. G., 493
Westerberg, U., 491
Westfall, S. C., 651
Westlander, G., 124
Westphal, L. M., 619
Wetherell, W. D., 430
Whalen, S., 239
Whall, A. L., 388
Wheeler, F., 467
Wheeler, L., 234
Wheeler, M., 595, 600
Whipple, B., 180
White, B. J., 44
White, E. T., 306, 307, 308, 309, 310, 331, 619, 622
White, G. F., 419, 512, 513

Whitman, I., 69
Whittington, D., 516
Whitton, J. L., 489
Whitzman, C., 349, 354
Whyte, A., 31
Whyte, W., 208
Whyte, W. F., 613
Whyte, W. H., 279, 281, 301, 327
Wicker, A., 30, 39, 115, 117, 118, 119, 120, 122, 123, 210, 211, 219, 665, 666, 670
Widegren, O., 543
Wiemann, J. M., 596
Wiener, J. L., 548
Wiese, D., 178
Wieselquist, J., 387, 388
Wiesenfeld, E., 58, 59, 619, 632, 635, 636, 637
Wigglesworth, S., 348
Wilcox, D., 608, 614, 616
Wildavsky, A., 45, 148, 152, 153
Wiley, A., 337, 367
Wilke, H., 88, 91, 546
Wilkins, L., 560, 566
Wilkinson, C. R., 136
Wilkinson, J. R., 153
Wilkinson, R., 397, 406, 408
Willems, E., 234
Williams, J. R., 419
Williams, K., 191, 234
Williams, N., Jr., 519
Williams, P., 400, 403
Williamson, G. M., 671
Willits, F. K., 260, 545
Wilson, C. E., 500
Wilson, C. R., 481
Wilson, D. B., 229
Wilson, D. W., 504
Wilson, E., 347, 351, 352, 547, 649
Wilson, H. S., 387
Wilson, J. R., 185
Wilson, K., 208, 219
Wilson, R. B., 91
Wilson, T. D., 488, 525
Wilson, W. J., 414
Wilson-Doenges, G., 208, 415
Wiltzius, S. F., 378
Windley, P., 293, 294
Wineman, J., 275, 276, 279, 281, 285, 309, 336, 447, 448, 450
Winer, B. J., 222
Winett, R. A., 223, 324, 330, 525, 527, 529, 531, 669, 670
Winget, C., 516, 560
Winget, V., 560
Winkel, F. W., 651
Winkel, G., 30, 35, 349, 363, 467, 661, 665
Winkler, R. C., 223
Winter, D., 35, 36, 38, 56, 525
Wisner, B., 612, 613
Wit, A., 88
Witelson, S. F., 184
Withers, T., 180

Wittfogel, K. A., 148
Wohlford, S., 195
Wohlwill, J., 28, 46, 102, 108, 363, 366, 369, 374, 482, 562, 665
Wolf, C. P., 69
Wolf, E., 148
Wolf, F. M., 224
Wolf, R., 463, 465
Wolfe, A. K., 148
Wolfe, M., 16, 23, 24, 369
Wolfe, R., 234, 237
Wolfe, T., 414
Wolfenstein, M., 563, 567
Wolff, P. C., 69
Wölfing, S., 40, 367, 370, 546
Wollin, D. D., 327
Wong, C. Y., 327
Woodgate, G., 163, 164
Woodrow, P., 520
Woods, R., 347
Woodward, A., 353
Woolley, H., 367
Worchel, S., 652
Wormith, J. S., 652
Worsley, P., 608
Wright, H., 114, 115, 119, 122, 123, 431
Wright, J. D., 515, 516, 520
Wright, R., 486
Wrigley, R., 348
Wunsch, J., 602
Wyman, M., 363
Wynne, B., 151, 576

Xu, J., 271, 278, 279

Yamagishi, T., 90
Yamaguchi, H., 651
Yamamoto, T., 11, 47, 219, 501, 504
Yan, Y. Y., 483, 486
Yandle, T., 572
Yang, X.-L., 250
Yankou, D. J., 388
Yarmey, D., 234
Yarnold, P. R., 258, 262
Yates, J. F., 89
Yates, S. B., 651
Yatrakis, K., 347
Ycaza, C., 420
Yeandle, S., 347
Yearley, S., 165, 166
Yezer, A. M., 516
Yogev, A., 191
Youn, T. I. K., 583
Young, B. S., 519
Young, D., 363
Young, G., 398
Young, I. M., 348, 349, 355, 358, 359
Young, J., 59, 76, 493
Young, K. S., 653
Young, O., 59, 580

Zaidel, D., 327
Zajonc, A., 96

Zakay, D., 88
Zakzanis, K. K., 229
Zaner, A., 501, 506
Zaner, R. M., 97
Zani, B., 59
Zanna, M., 543
Zautra, A., 570
Zeisel, J., 31, 299, 308, 326, 332, 414, 621

Zelezny, L., 223, 542, 543
Zelson, M., 177, 367
Zieles, A., 431
Zigurs, I., 604
Zillmann, D., 488
Zimmerman, R., 572
Zimring, C., 282, 285, 306, 307, 308, 309, 310, 311, 312, 313, 336, 428, 430

Zorn, M., 325
Zube, E., 37, 56, 306, 307, 308, 309
Zube, W. H., 36
Zuboff, S., 456
Zuckerman, D., 652
Zuckerman, M., 668
Zumpe, D., 486
Zuzanek, J., 234, 238, 240

Subject Index

ABC contingency (activator/behavior/consequence), 528
Accessibility, 272, 354
Accountability *vs.* responsibility, 535–537
Action research (AR), 612–613
Actively caring model (Geller), 543
Adaptation:
  and agency, 149
  and toxic contamination, 561–563
Adolescents in school environment, 238–239
Advocate, planner as, 610
Affiliative-conflict model, 648
Agency, 91, 149–151
Agoraphobia, 131–134
AIDS prevention, 10–11, 121–122
Air quality:
  environmental conflict and, 591–592
  in workplace, 452
Ambient/environment (terminology), 580
Animal habitat design, 475–476
Anonymity, 21–22
Anorexia nervosa, 131–132
Anthropocentrism *vs.* biocentrism, 38
Anthropology. *See* Environmental anthropology
Applied behavioral analysis, 39, 525. *See also* Behavior(s)
Applied/experimental environmental psychology,
  323–324
Architectonic details (in workplace), 453, 454, 455
Architecture. *See also* Behavioral-based architectural
  programming; Postoccupancy evaluation (POE)
  environmental psychology and, 31
  phenomenology of, 109
  spatial structure and environmental behavior, 271–291
Articulate/diffuse developmental polarity, 7
Astronauts. *See* Mars expedition/astronauts
Attachment theory, 131
Attention fixation training (AFT), 137
Attitude change (conservation behavior and theory), 546
Audit. *See* Environmental audit (EA)

Behavior(s). *See also* Conservation behavior;
  Proenvironmental behavior, increasing
  assessing as dependent variable, 551
  changing environmental, 208–209
  environmentally relevant, 39–46
  field of environmental behavior studies, 192
  images/media and, 328
  impact of research on environmental, 335–346
  self-perception based on, 536–537
  setting, 116, 119, 121, 122, 123, 670–671
  single *vs.* categories of, 551
  specific environmental relevant, 39–46
  stages of (three), 532–533

Behavioral-based architectural programming, 292–305
  benefits and limitations of, 293–294
  diagnostic interviewing, 294–297
  diagnostic observation, 297–301
  general observation, 298
  history of, 292–293
  literature search and review, 294, 295
  methods, 294–303
  prospects for, 303–304
  questionnaires and surveys, 301–302, 303
  space inventory, 298, 299
  systematic observation, 300–301
  trace observation, 299–300
  walk-through observation, 298
  work sessions, 302–303
Behavioral constraint perspective (personal space), 648
Behavioral mapping, 278
Behavioral self-reports, validity of, 550–551
Beneficence, 15
Biocentrism *vs.* anthropocentrism, 38
Biogeographical construct, 101–102
Biological mechanisms of infectious diseases, and
  household population density, 404–405
Birthing rooms, 359
Blame-affixing adversarial model, 153
Body buffer zone (personal space), 648
Building(s):
  built space, social functions of, 271–272
  cognitive mapping and, 325
  layouts, 282
  patterns of movement and copresence in, 280–283
  strong *vs.* weak program, 280
  topology of social space and geometry of, 272–286
  two kinds of (constructing and cultivating), 355

Caregiving for the caregiver, 142
Caretaking, women's, 357–358
Categories:
  of behavior, 551
  environmental, 44–46
  of psychosocial/environmental problems, 133
Cause:
  formal, 214–217
  map, 118
  relations, 265–266
Cell phones and personal space concept, 654–655
Children:
  emotions, 363–364
  language development/cognition/learning (and noise),
    505–506
  place preferences, 363–373
    age and, 364–365

Children (Continued)
  environmental self-regulation, 367–368
  factors affecting, 366
  gender and, 364–365
  place identity/attachment, and restorative
    experiences, 369–371
  privacy, 369
  restoration, 366–367, 369–371
  territoriality and territorial range, 369
  theoretical generalizations on developmental shifts
    in, 365–366
  theoretical speculations, 368–371
  sexual abuse of, 136
  urban contexts for, 10
Christmas Street study, 206–208
City(ies). See also Urban planning and environmental
    psychology
  domesticating urban space, 354
  downtown plazas, 326–327
  hydraulic hypothesis, origins of city-state, 148
  identity of and identification with, 109–110
  neighborhood improvement, 327
  planning policy, 423
  planning theories, 610
  spatial cognition and traffic patterns, 325
  spatial configuration and movement in, 277–280
Classroom design, 327
Climate determinism, 101–102
Climate/weather, and crime, 481–498
  applications, 493
  archival data, 491–492
  field settings as naturalistic (and realistic)
    laboratories, 493
  future directions (discovering new relationships),
    491–493
  general affective aggression model (GAAM), 488
  handling data, 492–493
  humidity/wind/and other weather variables,
    485–486
  NAE model, 490
  negative affect models, 487–489, 490
  relationships between climate and crime, 481–487
  routine activity theory, 490
  seasonal differences, 486–487
  social contact and avoidance theories and, 489–491
  summary of research results, 483–484
  theory: explaining the relationships, 487–491
Clinical psychology, 9, 129–146
  agoraphobia, 133–134
  categories of psychosocial/environmental problems,
    133
  changes associated with psychiatric hospitalization
    (psychological context of person), 9
  child sexual abuse, 136
  Diagnostic and Statistical Manual of Mental Disorders,
    Fourth Edition, and physical environment,
    132–133
  dissociation, 131–132, 136
  environmental disasters, 136 (see also Disaster(s))
  and environmental psychology:
    clinical approaches in environmental psychology,
      140–143
    environmental approaches in clinical psychology,
      132–137

  examining life domains, 130
  examining overall life situations, 130
  examining settings, 130
  examining situations, 130
  fear of flying, 134
  hoarding behavior, 135
  housing problems, 133
  microsystem/mesosystems/exosystems/
    macrosystems, 130
  obsessive-compulsive disorder (OCD), 134–135
  panic disorder, 133–134
  PTSD, 135–136
  sexual abuse, 135–136
  specific phobia, 134
  terrorism, 136
  theoretical and conceptual frameworks, 129–132
  treatment, 137–138
  treatment settings, 138–140
Cognitive dissonance, 90
Cognitive-experiential self theory (CEST), 367–368
Cognitive/knowledge fix, 168
Cognitive mapping and GIS, 246
Cohousing, 353
Collaborative planning. See Participatory planning
Comfortable Interaction Distance Scale, 651
Comfort model and personal space, 648
Commons dilemma, 41–44, 596. See also Prisoner's
    dilemma game (PDG)
Communication, and environmental conflict, 596
Community household model, 355
Community participation, 629–643
  agricultural community example, 632–635
  Catuche project example, 635–637
  concept of, 631
  current status of research in, 638–639
  examples, 630, 632–638
  explanatory framework for continuity of, 639–641
  forms of, 631–637
  integrating environmental psychology and community
    social psychology, 637
  in Latin America in recent years, 630
  participatory planning strategies, 632
  propositions (eight), 639–641
  public hearing, 631–632
  stakeholder negotiation, 632
  Venezuelan natural disaster (December 1999) example,
    637–638
Company environmental department, 62
Competency states (four), 534
Computer-aided communications, and behavior setting,
    123
Computer-assisted negotiations, 603–604
Computer-supported communication. See Internet
Computer usage in research, 20–21
Confidentiality, 21–22
Confirmatory factor analysis (CFA), 256, 257, 262
Conflict:
  environmental (see Environmental conflict)
  full ecology perspective and, 33
  paradigm of, 42
  resolution (see Environmental conflict resolution)
Congenital adrenal hyperplasia (CAH), 185
Connections between private dwellings and public
    space, 352–354

Conscious competence/incompetence, 534
Conservation behavior, 259–260, 329, 330, 541–558. *See also* Proenvironmental behavior, increasing
    assessing behavior as dependent variable, 551
    attitude change, 546
    emerging theoretical/methodological perspectives on, 541–558
    energy savings and goal setting, 329
    health belief model, 549–550
    learning theory (operant conditioning; applied behavioral analysis), 542
    less frequently used approaches, 548–549
    levels of analysis, 552
    lifestyles, 544
    methodological approaches to conservation problems, 550–552
    model of actively caring (Geller), 543
    motivational, moral, and value theories, 542–544
    norm activation model, 542–543
    personality and individual differences, 548
    political action, 550
    procedural justice theories, 548–549
    recycling, and green design, 330
    recycling, and modeling, 329
    self-determination theory, 544
    self-regulation, 544
    single behaviors *vs.* categories of behaviors, 551
    social influence and diffusion models, 549
    structural model of proenvironmental behavior, 259–260
    theoretical approaches to conservation problems, 541–550
    theories of emotion and affect, 546–548
    theory of planned behavior (TPB), 545–546
    theory of reasoned action, 545
    validity of behavioral self-reports, 550–551
    value system (Schwartz), 543
Constancy hypothesis, 100
Constructivism, 5
Consultancy, environmental, 61–62
Contamination, 559–588, 592
    acute *vs.* chronic events, 560
    blame for, 576
    dialectic of double binds, 577–578
    enabling response, 570–573
    and environmental racism, 572
    government and post-contamination blame, 576–577
    grassroots involvement, 571–572
    inversion of environment, 574–576
    inversion of home, 573–574
    lifescape impacts, 565–567, 579
    lifestyle impacts, 563–565
    loss of health optimism, 566–567
    loss of personal control, 567–573
    natural *vs.* human caused disaster, 576
    regulatory systems for preventing, 578
    risk perception shadow, 561
    signal events, 560
    social distrust, 576–579
    stigma, 573, 579
    toxic shock and adaptation, 561–563
    toxic site regulation/remediation and waste disposal, 592

Context, 3–14
    moderators, 4
    reflections on, 3–5
    Stokols's treatment of, 4–5
Control, personal:
    environmental contamination and loss of, 567–573
    in workplace, 453–454
Convex spaces, 275, 276
Coping modes, 7–8
Crime:
    defensible space theory and, 326
    fighting, and cognitive mapping, 325
    Internet and, 664
    weather and (*see* Climate/weather, and crime)
Crime prevention through environmental design (CPTED), 413–426
    chain of reasoning to be analyzed, 413, 417–423
    definitions, 414–417
    documenting prevention rather than displacement, 415, 416–417
    establishing causality, 415–416
    example of influence, 414
Criminal justice researchers, 121
Crowding, 196, 325–326, 402–403, 648. *See also* Density
    alleviating, 325–326
    vs. population density, 196, 402–403
Culture:
    astronauts, and differences in, 679–680
    automobile driving and, 11
    cultural ecology, 148
    nature as agent of change, 150
    personal space and, 657
    risk modeling and, 152–155
    sociocultural context of person, 9
Cyber stalking, 664

Decision making:
    environmental conflict and, 595
    interdependence in citizen/political, 89–92
    maximizing impact of studies on, 339–345
Decision-oriented research, 341
Decision support system, 245
De-differentiated, 7–8
Defensible space theory, 326, 648
Dementia, design and, 331, 374–393
    bathing rooms, 387–388
    building configuration, 379–380
    care population, 378
    cluster, 381, 382
    dining room, 331
    household/group size, 378–379, 381
    kitchens and dining rooms, 385–386
    neighborhood, 381
    noninstitutional design, 380–382
    outdoor areas, 385
    pod, 381, 382
    relationship between research and design, 376–377
    resident rooms, 386–387
    safety, 384–385
    sensory stimulation and lighting, 383–384
    signage, 382–383
    state of research on, 374–376
    therapeutic impact of design, 377–388

Dementia, design and (Continued)
  toilets, 387–388
  unit, 381, 382
Density, 196, 277, 326–327, 401–402, 403. See also
    Crowding
  bonusing, 326–327
  vs. crowding, 196, 402–403
  internal/external, 403
Design:
  animal habitat, 475–476
  case studies (research influencing/changing design),
    439–440
  classroom, 327
  crime prevention through environmental (CPTED),
    413–426
  dementia and, 331, 374–393
  exhibitions, 467–474
  green, 330
  multiple sclerosis (MS) and, 332
  personal space and, 652–653
  psychology, 142
  recycling and, 330
  relationship between research and, 376–377
  social, 330–332
  socially significant descriptions of space and, 287–289
  therapeutic impact of, 377–388
  treatment settings, 138–140
  wayfinding elements, 431, 432
  zoos, 475–476
Determinism, climate, 101–102
Developmental history of place, 142
Developmental polarities, 6–7
Development vs. sustainability, 58
Diabetes onset (physical context of person research), 9
Diagnostic and Statistical Manual of Mental Disorders,
    Fourth Edition, and physical environment, 132–133
Dialectic of double binds, 577–578
Differentiated and hierarchically integrated, 8
Diffuse/articulate developmental polarity, 7
Digital Age and personal space, 653–656. See also
    Internet
Digital Divide, 664
Digital elevation models (DEMs), 248
Digital terrain models, 248
Dilemma, commons, 41–44, 596. See also Prisoner's
    dilemma game (PDG)
Directed attention fatigue (DAF), 182, 183
Disaster(s):
  age and, 516
  contemporary reconceptualization, 515
  deaths, injuries, and dollar losses, 515
  definition of, 511–512
  economic impacts, 516
  environmental, 136
  hazards adjustment paradigm, 514–515
  human caused vs. natural, 576
  impact of, 515–516
  mitigation of, 514
  natural, 131, 168, 219, 576
  preparedness/response, 156, 514, 518–520
  psychological impacts, 515–516
  race/ethnicity and, 516
  recovery/reconstruction, 514, 520–521
  research, history and future of, 511–524

  socioeconomic status and, 516
  warning systems, 516–518
Discrete/syncretic developmental polarity, 7
Discursive construction and use of environmental
    categories, 44–46
Dissociation, 131–132, 136
Distancing, and personal space, 648
Distributive (or fixed-sum) negotiations, 87
Divorce, and housing environment, 140–141
DO IT process, 529–533, 537
  defining (D), 529
  intervening (I), 530–532
    consequences for environmental protection, 530
    feedback techniques, 531–532
    rewards vs. penalties, 530–531
    types of reward contingencies, 531
  observing (O), 529–530
  testing (T), 532
Dominant Social Paradigm (DSP), 37–38
DO-RITE (behavioral changes), 324

Eating disorders, 137
Eco-analysis method, 141
Ecofeminism, 108
Eco-labels, and life cycle assessment (LCA), 69–71
Ecological psychology, 35, 114–126
  behavior setting, 116, 119, 121, 122, 123, 670–671
  cause map, 118
  "lived days" analysis, 122–123
  pragmatic psychology, 120–122
  prospective directions for, 120–123
  recent developments in, 117–120
  societal and disciplinary contexts in development of,
    114–117
Ecological revolution, 31–35
Ecological self, 37–38
Ecological systems theory, 665–666
Ecological world views, 37–38
Ecology:
  full/natural perspective, 32–36, 38
  industrial, 169
Economic globalization, 59
Ecosystem as unit of analysis, 31–32
Education, environmental (vs. environmental
    management), 60
Educational exhibition, 461
Educational remedies, 156
Edwards Aquifer conflict, 602–603
Emotion:
  children's place preferences and, 363–364
  communication and, 548
  motivation and, 546–548
  pain control and, 181
  structure of, 548
  theories of, 546–548
Energy savings. See Conservation behavior
Engineering, 31
Environment:
  functions of (three), 162
  inversion of, 574–576
  as living space, 162
  as mirror, 142
  as supply depot, 162
  as waste repository, 162

Environmental anthropology, 147–159
  agency, 149–151
  beyond-blame model, 153–155
  blame-affixing adversarial model, 153
  consent, 155
  dimensions of assessing model applications, 154
  equity, 155
  growth and scarcity, 155–156
  key themes, 149
  liability, 155
  risk and culture models, 152–155
  time, 155
  traditional ecological knowledge systems, 151–152
Environmental audit (EA), 65, 67, 68, 329–330
Environmental autobiography (tool), 141
Environmental awareness/concern, 36, 164–165
Environmental behavior (EB) social science research,
    impact of, 335–346
  changing places and policies, 338–339
  examples of high-impact research, 345
  kinds of impact possible, 336–339
  maximizing impact of: hypotheses (five) distinguishing
      high-impact *vs.* low-impact studies, 339–345
    designing the research, 342–344
    presenting the findings, 344–345
    selecting dependent variable, 341–342
    selecting funding source, 339
    selecting independent variable, 339–341
  reaching general public, 337
  reaching policy makers, 337–338
  reaching practitioners, 337–338
  views on, 335–336
Environmental cognition in everyday life, 325
Environmental commitment construct, 36
Environmental communication: discursive construction
    and use of environmental categories, 44–46
Environmental concern construct, 36
Environmental conflict, 589–606
  air quality, 591–592
  characteristics of, 592–594
  communication and, 596
  complexity of, 589, 592–593
  definition of terms, 590
  future directions for research/practice, 604–605
  government and, 593
  impact assessments, 595
  incentive structure, 595
  interjurisdictional nature of, 593
  landuse, 591
  psychological sources of, 594
  regulatory responsibility, 589–590
  related psychological research, 601–604
    computer-assisted negotiations, 603–604
    Edwards Aquifer conflict, 602–603
    environmental justice, 603
    Orme Dam conflict, 601–602
  risk assessment and, 593, 595
  sources of, 594–596
  structural sources of, 594
  toxic site regulation/remediation and waste disposal,
      592
  types of, 590–592
  value conflicts, 595, 604
  water supply damage, 589, 591
Environmental conflict resolution:
  administrative, 597–598
  facilitated dialogue, 600
  facilitation, 599, 600
  institutional, 596–598
  interactions, 598
  judicial, 597
  legislative, 598
  limitations, 598
  mediation, 599–600
  negotiated rule making, 600
  process and outcome goals, 601
  public, 598–601
Environmental Design Research Association (EDRA),
    292–293, 294, 335–336, 608
Environmental impact assessment (EIA), 65, 67–69
Environmental impact study (EIS), 67–69
Environmental intervention, 60–61
Environmentalism, 163–164
Environmental justice, 164, 167
Environmental management (EM), 55–84
  applied fields, 73–75
  company environmental department, 62
  consultancy, 61–62
  criticisms made of sustainable development, 60
  defining, 55–57, 61
  vs. development (emphasis), 58
  eco-labels, 69–71
  environmental audit (EA), 65, 67, 68
  vs. environmental education, 60
  environmental impact assessment (EIA), 65, 67–69
  environmental impact study (EIS), 67–69
  vs. environmental intervention, 60–61
  global concerns, 56, 59
  government agencies, 62–63
  ISO 14000, 64–66
  legal context as defining element of, 63–64
  life cycle assessments (LCA), 65, 69–71
  local agenda 21 (LA21), 65, 71, 72
  management systems, 64–66
  organizations (four types) of working within field of
      environmental protection, 61–62
  psychologist role, 60–63
  quality of life, 57
  revolution from the top, 59–60
  social cohesion and, 58–59
  Social Impact Detection/Barcelona (DIS/BCN), 69–70
  social impact study (SIS), 69
  solidarity (intragenerational and intergenerational),
      57
  sustainability as framework for, 57–60
  sustainability indicators, 73, 74
  sustainability as new positive social value, 58
  sustainability as point of convergence, 57–58
  technocratic paradigm and, 55
  tools of, 63–73
Environmental objects, three types of behavioral
    operations, 101
Environmental philosophy, 38
Environmental problems. *See also* Environmental conflict
  causes of, 166–167
  cognitive/knowledge fix, 168
  impacts of, 167–168
  intermediary behavioral fix (penalties/rewards), 168

Environmental problems. *See also* Environmental conflict
(*Continued*)
  societal awareness of, 163–166
  structural fix, 168
Environmental psychology: improvements through
    application of, 323–334
  cognitive mapping, and spatial cognition, and quality
    of life, 325
  commitment, 328–329
  crowding, alleviating, 325–326
  downtown plazas, 326–327
  green design, 330
  images, media, and environmentally responsible
    behavior, 328
  learning settings/classrooms, 327
  living spaces, 326
  problem prevention, 328
  social design, 330–332
Environmental psychophysiology, 172–190
  vs. cognitive psychophysiology, 173
  concomitants, 178–179
  definitions, 173
  environmental psychology research and, 179–186
  examples from embodied perspective, 179–186
  invariants, 179
  markers, 177–178
  outcomes, 176–177
  pain control, 180–184
  relationships in (five general), 174–176
  sexually dimorphic spatial abilities, 184–186
  vs. social psychophysiology, 173
  specificity/generality (two-dimensional taxonomy),
    176–179
Environmental racism, 164, 167
Environmental sociology, 160–171
  causes of environmental problems, 166–167
  current research emphases, 166–168
  current trends/controversies, 168–169
  foci of, 161–163
  impacts of environmental problems, 167–168
  institutionalization of, 163
  and the larger discipline, 160–161
  societal awareness of environmental problems,
    163–166
  solutions to environmental problems, 168
Epidemiological studies, and residential environment
    and health, 403–404
Equilibrium model (personal space), 648
Equity, and environmental sociology, 167
Ethic of care, 358
Ethic of justice, 358
Ethics in research, 15–27
  anonymity, 21–22
  assistants/employees, 24–25
  beneficence principle, 15
  computer usage, 20–21
  confidentiality, 21–22
  imperatives, 25–26
  implied promises, 23–24
  informed permission, 20, 22
  issues, 16–21
  justice principle, 16
  methods, 18–21
  norms, 16
  payment to respondents, 22–23

politics and personal orientations, 25
  principles (three), 15–16
  protocol handling, 24
  respect principle, 15–16
  selection of participants, 17–18
  terminating, 23
  topics, 17
  trust, 21
  volunteers, 18
  worthiness of study, 17
Evaluation implementation theory, 317
Evolutionary theories (personal space), 649
Exhibition design, 467–474. *See also* Visitor studies
  arrangement of objects/displays, 469
  attraction/distraction of open door, 469
  attraction of salient object, 468–469
  circulation/traffic flow, 468–469
  competition from other exhibit elements, 471
  complementary role of interpretive labels, 473
  conflicting messages, 474
  confronting/correcting misconceptions, 470
  contrast with setting background, 468
  ease of cognitive processing, 470
  educational messages, 473–474
  figure-ground contrast, 470
  handouts, 470
  hands-on flips, 471
  identifying high-interest content, 470
  increasing cognitive-emotional arousal, 470–471
  inertia, 469
  instructions on what to look for or what to do, 471
  labels, 469–470, 471, 473, 474
  lighting, 468
  limited capacity of attention and, 471–472
  line-of-sight placement, 468
  literary techniques, 474
  mental imagery, 470
  message clarification, 471
  minimizing distractions, 471
  minimizing perceived effort, 469–470
  motivating focused/sustained attention, 469–471
  novelty of surroundings, 471
  response facilitation, 474
  right-turn bias, 469
  selectivity, 468
  semantic complexity, 474
  sensory overload (density of labels/objects), 470
  size, 468
  sounds, 471
  stimulus salience (distinctiveness), 468
  syntactic complexity, 473–474
  3-D objects, 470–471
  writing style, 470
Existential phenomenology, 97–98
Experience, temporality/historicity of, 105–106
Experience sampling method (ESM), 233–243
  common approaches to, 234–237
  data management and analysis, 236–237
  defined, 233–234
  diaries, 234
  family relationships and patterns of communication,
    239
  importance of experience in psychological research,
    233
  recommendations for future use of, 239–240

research questions addressed by, 237–239
self-report, 235, 240–242
signaling device, schedule, and self-report, 234–236
validity/reliability, 237
working with participants, 236
Experiential space, 102
Experimental/applied environmental psychology, 323–324
Exposure therapy, 137

Facilitated dialogue, 600
Facilitation, 599, 600
Fear of flying, 134
Feedback effectiveness studies, 329
Feminist perspective. *See* Women and environment
Feminist planning research, 194–195
Field terminology, 656
Field theory, 100
Flexible/rigid developmental polarity, 7
Flight distance (personal space), 647
Flooding, 137
Flow of behavior change model, 534, 537
Focus theory of normative conduct, 39
Formal cause, 214–217
Framing, 604
Freedoms, 559
Full ecology perspective, 32–36, 38
Funding source selection, 339

Gender. *See also* Women and environment
equality, and health status, 404
importance (misplaced) given to, 358
lifespace and, 103
political ecology and, 148
vs. sex, 358
sexually dimorphic spatial abilities, 184–186
Gendered environment concept, 103, 105
General affective aggression model (GAAM), 488
General systems theory, 116, 117
Genotypes/phenotypes, 218, 284
Geocoding, 244
Geographic information science (GISc), 247, 249–251
Geographic information system (GIS), 244–255
applied/theoretical dimensions of, 246–247
choosing appropriate, 251–252
cognitive mapping and, 246
components of (four major), 244
data (spatializing/encoding/computerizing), 249, 251
definitions of, 244–245
digital terrain models, 248
overlay model/problem, 248, 249
purpose/functions of, 247–248
sources for information on, 252–253
speculation about future of, 252
theoretical, 246–247, 249–251
using, 249
visual landscape models, 248–249
Geography of women, 108
Germ theory, 398
Global environment concerns, 56, 167
Globalization:
anthropological twist on, 148–149
economic, 59
information, 59
population, 59

Global Positioning System (GPS), 250
Global values/ethics, 37–38
Global warming, 521
Goal setting, and commitment, 328–329
Goodness of fit, 256, 258–259, 266–267
Government:
dialectic of double binds, 577–578
environmental conflict and, 593
environmental management and, 62–63
post-contamination blame, 576–577
regulatory systems, 63–64, 578, 589–590
Grassroots involvement, 571
Greed-efficiency-fairness (GEF) hypothesis, 91
Green design, 330
Greenhouse effect, 408
Green psychology, 35
Group identity, 88
Growth and scarcity, 155–156

Habit(s), changing, 89–90
Habitat, human, 107
Handicapped, needs of, 354
Hazards, environmental, 328. *See also* Disaster(s)
Hazards adjustment paradigm, 514–515
Health:
anxiety, 566–567
belief model, 549–550
defined, 395–396
environmental psychophysiology and, 173
loss of optimism about (and contamination), 566–567
noise and, 502–503, 508
residential environment and, 394–412
risk assessment and lifestyle, and exposure pathways, 564
systems/services, 397–398
women's status in society and, 404
Hearing, 499–501
loud sound and loss of, 500–501
measuring loudness, 499
sound and, 499–500
Hermeneutical:
phase in phenomenology, 97
and phenomenological approach, 106–110
Historicity:
of human situatedness, 105
of lifespace, 103
Hoarding behavior, 135
Holistic/developmental/systems-oriented approach, 5–9
concept of person and of environment, 5
constructivism, 5
coping modes, 7–8
developmental assumptions, 6–9
developmental polarities, 6–7
holistic assumptions, 5–6
research examples, 9–11
spatiotemporal nature of experience, 6
structural and dynamic analyses, 5
Holistic/molar perspective, 30
Home(s). *See also* Housing
connections between private dwellings and public space, 352–354
environment, role of in family conflict, 140
inversion of, 573–574
office in, 456

Hospital(s):
  birthing rooms, 359
  changes associated with psychiatric hospitalization
    (psychological context of person), 9
  communication improvements in mental hospital
    buildings, 324
  courtyards, 331
  psychiatric wards, 401
  wayfinding, 437–438
Household:
  population density, 401, 404–405
  relationship to larger world, 354
Housing. See also Residential environment and health
  alternatives, 353–354
  cohousing, 353
  dwelling/home/building, 108–109
  environment, after divorce, 140–141
  problems, 133
  residential pride in, 326
Human-environment optimization, 666
Human exemptionalism paradigm (HEP), 38, 161, 260,
    265, 267
Human interdependence research paradigm, 85–94
  applications of, 89–92
  interdependence in citizen decision making, 89–90
  interdependence in political decision making,
    90–92
  prisoner's dilemma game (PDG), 42, 86–88, 596
Human service fields, and personal space, 657
Hydraulic hypothesis, 148

Impact assessments, 65, 67–69, 595
Implied covariance matrix, 258
Incentive structure, 595
Indigenous knowledge, 151
Indissoluble correlation, 98
Individual differences, 7–9
Individual distance (personal space), 647, 648
Individuation-Attachment Questionnaire, 651
Industrial ecology, 169
Industrial settings, factors contributing to long-term
    impact of behavior change interventions in, 527
Industry and post-contamination blame, 576
Information globalization, 59
Informed permission, 20, 22
Instructional intervention, 533
Integration:
  and choice, 277
  core, 277
  and movement, 277–281
  value of a space, 283
Integrative (or variable-sum) negotiations, 87
Intelligibility in spatial organization, 278
Intentionality, 98
Interactional space/distance, 656
Interactive computer-assisted negotiation support
    (ICANS) system, 603–604
Interdependence:
  in decision making (citizen/political), 89–92
  social psychology of, 41–44
Interfused/subordinated developmental polarity, 6–7
Intermediary behavioral fix (penalties/rewards), 168
International Standardization Organization (ISO), 63,
    64–66

Internet, 655–656, 661–675
  changing ecology of human-environment relations in
    era of, 665–666
  conceptual framework/agenda for future research,
    666–671
  dimensions/growth, and behavioral impacts of,
    662–663
  environmental psychology as foundation for theory
    development/research, 665–666
  influence of on four modes of human-environment
    transaction, 667–671
    environmental stress and behavior setting processes,
      670–671
    evaluation of surroundings, 668–669
    interpretation of surroundings, 667–668
    spatial behavior and environmental protection
      efforts, 669–670
  negative influences of, 664–665
  personal space and, 655–656
  theoretical questions concerning environment/
    behavior in age of, 663–665
Intersubjectivity dimension, 102
Intervention:
  environmental, 60–61
  in industrial settings, 527
  instructional, 533
  motivational, 533–534
  supportive, 533, 535
IPAT equation (environmental impact equals population
    times affluence times technology), 167
Isovist, 275

Justice:
  distributive, 41
  environmental, 603
  procedural, 41
  psychology of social, 41
  research principle of, 16

Knowledge:
  cognitive fix, 168
  indigenous, 151
  preknowledge and attitudes, 475
  systems (traditional ecological), 151–152

Labels:
  and built spaces, 283–285
  eco-labels, 69–71
  exhibition, 469–470, 471, 473, 474
Labile/stable developmental polarity, 7
Landscape:
  external (of daily life), 237
  internal, 238
  in phenomenological psychology, 105–106
Landuse (environmental conflict), 591
Layout plans, 274–275
  convex area, 275
  graphs, 276
Learning settings/classrooms, 327
Learning theory: operant conditioning (applied
    behavioral analysis), 542
Legal context as defining element of EM, 63–64
Legal/organizational remedies, 156
Legal uses (personal space), 653

Life cycle assessment (LCA), 65, 69–71
Lifescape impacts, 565–567, 579
Lifespace, 101–104
Lifestyle, 544, 563–565
Lifeworld, 97–99, 104–110
Lighting/illumination:
    dementia, and sensory stimulation and, 383–384
    exhibitions and, 468
    therapist's office, 140
    wayfinding design elements, 432
    in workplace, 450–451
"Lived days" analysis, 122–123
Living space, 162, 326
Local agenda 21 (LA21), 65, 71, 72
Local levels of agency, 150

Management. *See* Environmental management (EM)
Marketers, social, 328
Mars expedition/astronauts, 676–685
    cultural differences, 679–680
    favorable time slots, 677
    habitability, 681–684
    pregnancy in space, 680
    radiation, 680
    recreation, 684
    robot *vs.* humans, 684
    sex/gender, 680
    sleep disturbances, 681
    them *vs.* us problem, 679
    weightlessness, 677–678, 683
Mass media communication, 45–46
Meaning, focus on, 96–97
Media/images, and environmentally responsible
    behavior, 165, 328
Mediation, 599–600
Mental disorders and physical environment, 132–137, 282.
    See also Clinical psychology; Dementia, design
Mental hospital buildings, 324. *See also* Hospital(s)
Mental well-being, noise and, 503–504
Meta-analysis, 223–232
    basic steps in, 224
    choice of dependent variable, 224–225
    choice of sample size, 225
    choice of software, 225
    definition, 222
    examples of in environmental psychology, 226–228
    hypothetical examples of traditional and meta-analytic
        reviews, 223
    methods of, 224–225
    weaknesses of, 228–230
Miasma theory, 399
Microsystem/mesosystems/exosystems/macrosystems,
    130, 237
Model(s):
    measurement, 258
    null, 267
    restricted/inclusive, 266–267
    structural, 259–260
Modeling (learning from watching others), 329
Motivating pro-environment behavior:
    focus on positive consequences, 528–529
    lifestyles, 544
    model of actively caring, 543
    norm activation model, 542–543

self-determination theory, 544
    self-regulation, 544
    theories of conservation behavior, 542–544
    value system, 543
Motivational intervention, 533–534
Motivational prime theory of emotions, 182
Movement density and integration, 277–281
Moving/relocation, 140
Multiple regression (MR), 256, 258
Multiple sclerosis (MS), design challenges for, 332
Museums. *See also* Visitor studies
    definition, 461
    environmental psychology in, 461–480
    formal *vs.* informal education, 461–462
    spatial analysis and, 285

Natural agency, 150
Natural disasters, 131, 168, 219, 576. *See also*
    Contamination
Natural hazards, 168
    policies, 521–522
    research, 513
Natural psychology, 35
Nature as agent of cultural change, 150
Negative affect escape (NAE) model, 488, 490
Negative affect models, 487–489
Negotiated rule making, 600
New ecological paradigm (NEP), 161
New environmental paradigm (NEP) scale, 37–38, 165,
    260, 262, 263, 265, 267
New Urbanism, 207–208, 611
NIMBY (not in my backyard) effect, 75, 578
Noise, 451–452, 499–510, 564
    children's language development, cognition, and
        learning, 505–506
    health danger of, 508
    hearing loss and loud, 500–501
    measuring loudness, 499
    mental well-being and, 503–504
    physical health and, 502–503
    role of government and citizen in abatement efforts,
        508
    sleep disruption and, 503
    sound and hearing, 499–500
    stress and, 501–502, 564
    in workplace, 451–452
Nonequilibrium view of nature, 150
Nonnormed fit index (NNFI), 259
Nonterritorial offices, 457
Norm(s), 16, 89–90
    injunctive, 89
    personal, 90
    prescriptive, 90
    in research, 16
    social, 90
Norm-activation model/theory, 39, 40, 90, 542–543
Normed fit index (NFI), 259

Obsessive-compulsive disorder (OCD), 134–135
Office:
    cell, 446
    club, 447
    den, 446–447
    design, 138–140

Office *(Continued)*
  hive, 446
  therapist's *(see* Therapist's office)
  types, 446–447
Organizational learning, POE as, 312–317
Organizational settings, 282–283
Orme Dam conflict, 601–602
Orthogenetic principle, 7, 8
Overlay model, and GIS, 248, 249
Overload theory (personal space), 648

Pain control, 180–184
Panic disorder, 133–134
Parenthood, transition to (sociocultural context of
    person), 9
Participatory planning, 607–628, 632
  action research and, 612–613
  community control, 617
  conditions for selecting tools and methods,
    614–618
  consultation level of participation, 617
  context clarification, 615–616
  defining, 609–612, 620
  eligibility of participants, 616
  enabling tools, 614–615, 618, 620, 621–624
    diagnostic, 614, 621–622
    expressive, 614, 622
    organizational, 614, 623–624
    political, 614, 624
  environmental psychology and, 609
  framing methodological approach to, 608–614
  future research, 620–621
  impact of, 618–619
  levels of participation, 616–617
  literature on planning theories, 609–612
  methodological approach to, 612–614
  names/varieties of, 608
  partnership level of participation, 617
  power issues, 620
  problematic nature of, 607–608
  process phases, 616–617
  research on, 620–621
  selecting tools/methods, 618
  sources constructed from, 608–609
Path analysis (PA), 256, 257
Pathology. *See* Clinical psychology
Payment to respondents (in research), 22–23
Perception(s):
  environmental conflict and, 594–595
  psychology of, 30
Permanency planning, 142
Personal Guidance System (PGs), 250
Personality and individual differences (conservation
    behavior theory), 548
Personal space, 324, 647–660
  affiliative-conflict model, 648
  applications, 652–653
  approach distance, 651
  behavioral constraint perspective, 648
  body buffer zone, 648
  comfort model, 648
  defensible space, 648
  design uses, 652–653
  in digital age, 653–656

  distancing, 648
  equilibrium model, 648
  evolutionary theories, 649
  field studies, 650–651
  figure placement tests, 651
  flight distance, 647
  future directions, 656
  in human service fields, 657
  individual distance, 647, 648
  legal uses, 653
  measurement methods, 649–651
  overload theory, 648
  paper/pencil tests, 651
  physiological recording, 651
  popular culture and, 657
  precursors and related concepts, 647–648
  predictions of spatial behavior in functional
    framework, 650
  proxemics, 647
  research findings, 651–652
  retreat, 651
  search for theory of, 648–649
  simulations, 651
  spatial preference, 651
  stop distance, 651
  teaching uses, 653
  terminology, 656
  territory, 647–648
  utility of concept of, 648
Person-in-environment (unit of analysis), 30
Persuasion, direct, 535–536
Phenomenological approach to people-environment
    studies, 95–113
  constitutive phenomenology, 97
  convergence of developments, 97–104, 106
  dwelling/home/building, 108–109
  existential phenomenology, 97–98
  generation of space, 107
  and hermeneutical approach, 106–110
  human habitat, 107
  human sciences: approximations to conceptions of
    lived space, 99–101
  identity of and identification with cities, 109–110
  landscape, 105–106
  lifespace, 101–104
  lifeworld, 97–99, 104–110
  lived space, 108
  making place, 107
  people-environment studies, 96–97
  the sciences and, 107
  situatedness, 99, 106
  space *vs.* place, 108
  spatiality, space, and place, 107–108
  terminology, 95–97
  varieties/phases (four) in phenomenology, 97
  women's experience as sexed bodies, 359
Phenotypes/genotypes, 218
Phobia, 134
Physiological recording (personal space), 651
Physiology. *See* Environmental psychophysiology
Place, 30, 31, 107–108, 141, 338–339
  construct of, 30, 31
  making, 107
  personal identity and, 141

preference studies (*see* Children, place preferences)
space *vs.*, 108
Place-specific perspective, 31
Planning:
  city (*see* Urban planning and environmental
    psychology)
  collaborative (*see* Participatory planning)
  feminist, 194–195
  permanency, 142
Plazas, 327
Policy. *See also* Government
  changing, 338–339
  educational remedies, 156
  environmental, 156–157
  implications, healthy residential environments,
    407–409
  legal/organizational remedies, 156
  reaching makers of, 337–338
  role of government and citizen in noise abatement, 508
  structural remedies, 156
Political action theory and conservation behavior, 550
Political activity settings, 123
Political decision making, interdependence in, 90–92
Political dimension, environmental issues, 46–47
Political enabling tools, participatory planning, 614, 624
Political space, 123
Politics/personal orientations in research and practice,
  25
Population density *vs.* crowding, 402–403
Population globalization, 59
Porches, front, 207–208
Post-natural world, 559
Postoccupancy evaluation (POE), 306–319
  background, 307
  creating appropriate conditions for learning through,
    314–317
  defining, 307
  as diagnosis, 311
  evaluation implementation theory, 317
  fine-tuning, 310–311
  history, 308
  incentives/disincentives, 315
  for innovation testing, 311–312
  learning from, 310–317
  methods, 308–309
  models, 309–310
  as organizational learning, 312–317
  project-based, 310–312
  quality maintenance, 312
  scope, 308
  setting operation theory, 315
  for strategic decision support, 312
  terminology, 308
  theory and, 317
Posttraumatic stress disorder (PTSD), 135–136, 141,
  567–570, 575
  and loss of control, and contaminated community,
    567–570, 575
  and sexual abuse, 135–136
Power, 225, 620
Pragmatic psychology, 120–122
Predictors (independent variables), 257
Preparedness and response, 518–520
Prescriptive norm, 90

Prescriptive principles, 408
Principal-agent theory, 91
Prisoner's dilemma game (PDG), 42, 86–88, 596
  cooperation, 87
  defection, 87
  distributive (or fixed-sum) negotiations, 87
  group identity, 88
  integrative (or variable-sum) negotiations, 87
  provision threshold, 87
  ultimatum, 87
Problem structuring, in policy making, 156
Procedural justice theories, 548–549, 603
Process phases, 616–617
Proenvironmental behavior, increasing, 525–540. *See also*
  Conservation behavior
  ABC contingency (activator/behavior/consequence),
    528
  accountability *vs.* responsibility, 535–537
  behavior-based self-perception, 536–537
  challenge of, 537–538
  direct persuasion, 535–536
  DO IT process (general behavior analysis method) for
    solving behavioral dimensions of environmental
    sustainability, 529–533, 537
  external factors, 528
  factors contributing to long-term impact of behavior
    change interventions in industrial settings, 527
  flow of behavior change model, 534, 537
  focus on observable behavior, 527–528
  focus on positive consequences, 528–529
  intervention approaches (instructional/supportive/
    motivational), 533–535
  lack of environmental impact, behavioral community
    studies, 526–527
  principles (three basic), 527–529
  stages of behavior (three), 532–533
Protocol handling, 24. *See also* Ethics in research
Provision threshold, 87
Proxemics, 647
Psycho-environmental data: models of, 256–257
Psychological Distance Map, 651
Psychophysiology. *See* Environmental psychophysiology
Public, reaching general, 337

Quality of life:
  cognitive mapping/spatial cognition and, 325
  planning and, 193
Quotidian world, 107

Racism, environmental, 164, 167, 572
Radical environmental populism, 573
Recovery and reconstruction, 520–521
Recycling. *See* Conservation behavior
Reflexive reasoning, 595
Reflexivity in data gathering, 213–214
Regulations, environmental, 63–64, 578, 589–590
Rescue efforts and cognitive mapping, 325
Research. *See also* Ethics in research; Meta-analysis
  contextual *vs.* noncontextual, 4
  maximizing impact of, 339–345
Residential environment and health, 394–412. *See also*
  Health
  contributions of environmental psychology, 401–405
  contributions of epidemiological studies, 403–404

Residential environment and health (Continued)
   definitions and interpretations, 395–399
   ecological perspective, 398–399
   environment, 396–397
   health, 395–396
   historical review, 399–400
   integrating epidemiological, psychological, and
      sociological interpretations, 404–405
   methodological principles, 400–401
   principles of healthy residential environments and
      policy implications, 407–409
   prospects/future directions, 409–410
   recent developments and conditions in industrialized
      countries, 405–407
   supportive environments, 397
Rigid/flexible developmental polarity, 7
Risk:
   assessment of and environmental conflict, 593, 595
   beyond-blame model, 153–155
   blame-affixing adversarial model, 153
   consent dimension, 155
   dimensions of assessing model applications, 154
   environmental, 148
   equity dimension, 155
   liability dimension, 155
   models in environmental anthropology, 152–155
   time dimension, 155
Risk perception shadow, 561
Root mean square error of approximation (RMSEA), 259
Routine activity theory, 490

Scarcity, and growth, 155–156
Schizophrenia, 142–143
Science, and environmental problems, 165
Security-exploration, 142
Self, ecological, 37–38
Self-confirming images, 595
Self-determination theory, 544
Self-expression in workplace, 448, 455–456
Self-fulfilling prophecies, 595
Self-regulation:
   environmental/mental/social strategies, 368
   theory, and conservation behavior, 544
   view of place selection, 367
Setting operation theory, 315
Sexual abuse, 135–136
Sexually dimorphic spatial abilities, 184–186
Signage:
   dementia and design, 382–383
   wayfinding, 432, 434, 435, 436
Situatedness, 99
Sleep disruption, noise and, 503
Social construction of environmental problems, 165–166
Social design, 330–332
Social distrust, 576–579
Social identity theory, 43
Social Impact Detection/Barcelona (DIS/BCN), 69–70
Social impact study (SIS), 69
Social influence and diffusion models (conservation
      behavior), 549
Socially significant descriptions of space and design,
      287–289
Social marketers, 328
Social norms, 90

Social psychology of interdependence, 41–44
Social psychophysiology, 173
Social Readjustment Rating Scale, 140
Social science, impact of, 335–346
Societal awareness of environmental problems,
      163–166
Sociology. See Environmental sociology
Sociophysical unit of analysis, 30
Solidarity (intragenerational and intergenerational), 57
Sound (in workplace), 451–452
Space. See also Personal space
   accessibility measures, 272
   appropriation of, 104–105
   built (social functions of), 271–272
   defensible space, 326, 648
   generation of, 107
   generative function of, 272
   inventory, 298, 299
   lived, 99–101, 108
   outer (see Mars expedition/astronauts)
   vs. place, 108
   syntax, 279, 283, 286, 287
   translating two-dimensional spatial layout into graph,
      274
      connectivity, 274
      depth, 273
      integration, 273
      justified, 273
      nodes, 273, 274
      space syntax stated in terms of, 272–275
      syntactic accessibility, 273
      topological and numerical parameters, 273
Space-time systems, 244
Spatial abilities, sexually dimorphic, 184–186
Spatial behavior, influence of Internet on, 669–670
Spatial cognition and cognitive mapping and GIS, 246,
      247
Spatial data, encoding, 249, 251
Spatial organization in workplace, 445–458
Spatial-physical environment, emerging environmental
      psychology as psychology of, 28–31
Spatial structure of environment and behavior, 271–291
   descriptive theory (topology of social space and
      geometry of buildings), 272–286
   layouts and directly observable social behavior, 282
   layouts as codes, 283–285
   patterns of movement and copresence in buildings,
      280–283
   socially significant descriptions of space and design,
      287–289
   spatial configuration and movement in urban areas
      (recognizing regular patterns and formulating
      morphological principles), 277–280
   spatial exploration as cognitive problem and as social
      function, 285–286
   theoretical comments, 286–287
Spatiotemporal nature of experience, 6
Specimen record technique, 119
Stable/labile developmental polarity, 7
Staffing theory, 116
Statistical tools, classical, 258
Stigma, environmental, 573, 579
STIRPAT model (stochastic impacts by regression on
      population, affluence, and technology), 167

Stress:
    Internet and, 670–671
    loss of personal control and, 567–570
    noise and, 501–502
Structural equations modeling (SEM), 256–270
    causal relations, 265–266
    complex relationships, 257
    components of, 257–258
    confirmatory factor analysis, 257, 262
    data, matrix of correlations as input, 260–261
    direct/indirect effect, 257–258
    elements of, 258–259
    estimation, 258, 265–266
    factor analysis, 257
    factor construction, 261–263
    goodness of fit, 258–259, 266–267
    implied covariance matrix, 258
    measurement model, 258
    models of psycho-environmental data, 256–257
    model specification, 258
    multiple regression, 258
    program example, 267–268
    reliability/validity, 263–264
    restricted/inclusive models, 266–267
    structural models in environmental psychology/
        conservation behavior, 259–260
Subordinated/interfused developmental polarity, 6–7
Substance related disorders, 137–138
Supportive intervention, 533, 535
Sustainability:
    as framework for environmental management, 57–60
    indicators, 73, 74
Sustainable development:
    environmental anthropology and, 148
    environmental psychology of, 35–46
    full ecology perspective, 35–36
    United Nations mandate for, 34–35
SWOT analysis, 615
Syncretic/discrete developmental polarity, 7
Systematic desensitization, 137
Systematic phenomenology, 233
Systems (microsystem/mesosystems/exosystems/
    macrosystems), 130
Systems theory, 665

Teams in workplace environment, 448
Technocratic paradigm, 55
Telecommuting, 456–457
Terrain visualization, 248–249
Territoriality, 324
Territory (personal space), 647–648
Terrorism, 136
Theoretical environmental psychologists, 323–324
Theory of color, 96
Theory of environmental turbulence, 563, 570
Theory of interdependence, 44
Theory of natural movement, 271
Theory of planned behavior (TPB), 39–40, 545–546
Theory of reasoned action (TRA), 39, 256–257, 259, 545
Theory of staffing, 116, 123
Theory of virtual community, 271
Therapist's office, 138–140
    artwork, 140
    clocks, 139

    degree of visibility, 139
    entrances/exits, 139–140
    examples of how portrayed in films, 139
    furniture, 140
    image, 139
    issues important in design of, 139–140
    lighting, 140
    location, 139
    plants, 140
    privacy, 139
    proximity to rest room, 139
    views, 140
Threshold, 276
Toxic exposure. *See* Contamination
Traffic, vehicular, 279, 564
Transactionally oriented research, 203–221
    applying formal cause, 214–217
    aspects (four: people, psychological processes, physical
        settings, and time), 204, 210–213
    assumptions (three), 203
    multiple world views, 205–206
    project breadth, 211
    project scope, 217
    reflexive data gathering, 213–214
    research illustrations, 206–210
        changing environmental behaviors, 208–209
        Christmas Street in summer and at Christmas,
            206–208
        New Urbanism and front porches, 207–208
    steps (eight) in implementing, 210–217
    time/continuity/change intrinsic to phenomena,
        205
    transactional world view, 203–210, 218–219
Treatment settings, environmental psychology of,
    138–140. *See also* Clinical psychology
Trust, 21

Umwelt, 99, 100
Uncertainty (social/environmental/strategic), 87–89
Unconscious incompetence/competence, 534
United Nations mandate for sustainable development,
    34–35
Universal plan offices, 457
Urban planning and environmental psychology, 191–200.
    See also City(ies)
    attempts at bridging the two fields, 195
    common/different assumptions, 193–195
    differences in the two fields, 191–193
    examples, 195–197
    experience in application, 197–198
    implications, 198
Urb concept for measuring extent of community settings,
    116

Validity, 263–264
    concurrent, 263
    construct, 263
    content, 263
    convergent construct, 263
    discriminant construct, 264
    predictive, 263
Value-belief-norm (VBN) theory, 90
Value conflicts, 595, 604
Value system (Schwartz), 543

Variables, maximizing impact of research studies:
  selecting dependent variable, 341–342
  selecting independent variable, 339–341
Vehicular traffic, 279, 564
View (in workplace), 449, 453, 454, 455–456
Viewpoint, 98
Virtual behavior settings, 123, 671
Virtual communities, 271, 670
Virtual offices, 456
Visibility polygon, 275
Visitor studies, 462–465, 466–467, 474–476
  audience research, 466
  automatic recording, 463
  conceptual orientation, 467
  critique of measurement in museums, 464
  customer relations, 474
  eclecticism in, 464–465
  emerging field of, 462
  entrance and lobby, 466–467
  exhibit and program evaluation/development, 466
  focused observations, 463
  food service, 475
  gift shop, 475
  history of, 464–465
  leisure visitors, 463
  macroarchitecture, 475
  methodology of, 462–465
  nonvisitors, 463
  observational methods, 463
  orientation and circulation, 466
  quantitative *vs.* qualitative methodology, 463
  rest rooms, 474
  school groups, 463
  scope of, 465–466
  self-report methods, 463–464
  services/amenities, 474–475
  setting factors, 466
  target audiences, 462–463
  time sampling, 463
  tracking studies, 463
  visitor variables, 475
  wayfinding, 467
Visual access, 275
Visual landscape models, 248–249
Volunteers, 18

Warning systems, 516–518
Waste repository (function of environment), 162
Water supply damage, 589, 591
Wayfinding, 427–442, 467
  architectural and interior design differentiation, 431
  behavioral elements/obstacles, 431, 433
  case studies (research influencing/changing design), 439–440
  costs of disorientation, 427–428
  defining, 427
  design elements/obstacles, 431–432, 433–435
  environmental psychology's contributions to ease of, 438
  facility layout, 431
  guidelines, 438–439
  importance of ease of, 427–428
  landmarks, 431–432

  lighting, 432
  literature on, 429–431
  maps, 432
  medical center example, 437–438
  obstacles to ease of, 433–437
  operational elements/obstacles, 432–433, 435–437
  perspectives of users, staff, administrators, 428–429
  previsit information, 433
  signage, 432, 434, 435, 436
  staff training, 433, 436
  system and maintenance, 431–433
  terminology, 433, 436
  usefulness of broad view of, 437–438
  visitor studies, 467
Weather:
  vs. climate, 481
  crime and (*see* Climate/weather, and crime)
Women and environment, 347–362
  design alternatives that incorporate connections, 353
  geography of women, 108
  health and status in society, 404
  identifying gender differences and women's needs, 348–350
  making/maintaining environments, 354–356
  making the invisible visible and important, 356–359
  proposing alternatives: making connections, 352–354
  recognizing fictions, 350–352
  segmentations, 350–352
Work environments, 443–460
  air quality, 452
  ambient properties, 450–451, 453–456
  architectonic details, 448–449, 453, 454, 455
  cell, 446
  club, 447
  control, 453–454
  den, 446–447
  functional opportunity, 454–455
  hive, 446
  home offices, 456
  illumination, 450–451
  interactions of people and workplace, 452–456
  nonterritorial offices, 457
  nonverbal self-expression, 455–456
  office types, 446–447
  recent studies, 444–452
  resources, 449–450, 453, 454, 456
  self-expression/personalization, 448
  sound, 451–452
  spatial organization, 445–458
  status of empirical research, 444
  strategies of research, 444
  teams, 448
  telecommuting, 456–457
  thermal comfort, 450
  universal plan offices, 457
  view, 449, 453, 454, 455–456
  virtual offices, 456
Work narratives, 119–120
Worst-case thinking, 595

Zone system, 656
Zoo exhibit design, 475–476